P9-DDW-773

The Dictionary of

Canadian
Quotations
and Phrases

Revised and Enlarged Edition

The Dictionary of

Canadian Quotations and Phrases

Revised and Enlarged Edition

Robert M. Hamilton and Dorothy Shields

McClelland and Stewart

McClelland and Stewart Limited,
The Canadian Publishers,
25 Hollinger Road, Toronto, Ontario.
M4B 3G2

Canadian Cataloguing in Publication Data

Main entry under title:
The Dictionary of Canadian quotations and phrases

Includes index.
ISBN 0-7710-3846-1

1. Quotations, Canadian (English)° 2. Canada —
Quotations, maxims, etc. I. Hamilton, Robert M.,
1912-   II. Shields, Dorothy, 1922-

PN6081.D488 1978   C818'.02   C78-001615-7

Printed and bound in the United States of America

CONTENTS

PREFACE

This book contains quotations and phrases selected from predominantly Canadian sources but includes also those which originated with outside observers of the Canadian scene - British, American, French - from the beginnings of our history up to the present. The topics covered comprise those which are distinctly Canadian, such as the Canadian Pacific Railway, Sir John A. Macdonald, Separatism, and many others. A second main component is what Canadians themselves have said on such universal subjects as Ability, Clothes, Faces, Love, Patriotism, Youth, and hundreds of others.

Many of the quotations and phrases gathered together here have been used time and again by writers and speakers. Others may be unfamiliar but because of their turn of phrase, their wit, satire, or pithiness have been quoted by someone and therefore were judged appropriate for inclusion. Although this edition contains three times as many quotations as the first edition, we are keenly aware that such a compendium even though devoted to only one country can never be complete. If some readers are unable to find here the occasional quotation which they believe to be Canadian, perhaps it was excluded because we were unable to verify it. We tried wherever possible to trace a quotation to its origin and cited the source to enable the reader to search out the context if he so desires.

In his Introduction to the first edition of this book Bruce Hutchison wrote a paragraph which we think says a great deal more than we could ever express about our hopes and reasons for compiling this work and it is worth repeating. "The discerning reader, coming to this book with no knowledge of Canada, could form a pretty accurate picture of its history from the casual observations of its makers, large and small. All the great issues and causes on which the nation was founded and maintained are here, with the comments of the men who fought them. Conquest, rebellion, Confederation, war, peace, politics - all are suddenly illumined by their participants, speaking directly to us across the years. But something much more interesting, and perhaps in the end more important, emerges from these exhibits - they convey, as perhaps no other Canadian book has ever conveyed, the full texture and salty flavor of Canadian life."

In the notes appended to the quotations in each entry, book titles, periodicals, and newspapers are shown in italics. The year of publication, or in the case of a newspaper, the day, month, and year, is usually followed by the page number where the text appears. Where the source is a poem, the title of the poem is given in quotation marks followed by the year of original publication only. No paging is necessary in such cases. The treatment for shorter pieces of writing, such as essays, letters, editorials, speeches, is similar. The spelling given here follows the original. Words added for clarity have been placed in the conventional square brackets.

As in the first edition of this work by Robert M. Hamilton, published in 1952, the subjects are arranged alphabetically. For the statistically minded, there are almost 2,000 subject headings with more than 10,300 quotations and phrases. Cross references will be found in the subject list at the beginning of the volume.

We wish to acknowledge our gratitude to our colleagues at the library of the University of British Columbia for their assistance and forbearance. The University librarian, Basil Stuart-Stubbs, arranged for R.M. Hamilton to take a three months leave of absence to enable him to devote time more effectively to the final stages of selection of the material. Special thanks go to the staff members of the Special Collections Division and the Interlibrary Loan Division of the library. We also wish to record our gratitude to the staff of the Newspaper Room at the National Library in Ottawa and for the excellent facilities provided there for the use of microfilm, and to the reference staffs of the Library of Parliament and the University of Toronto libraries.

R.M.H.
D.S.

LIST OF SUBJECTS
WITH CROSS-REFERENCES

A

List of Subjects with Cross-references

C

E

F

List of Subjects with Cross-references

G

O

Q

S

ABBREVIATIONS

Periodical titles:

Amer. pol. sci. rev. — American political science review

B.C. hist. quart. — British Columbia historical quarterly

B.C. library quart. — British Columbia library quarterly

British American mag. — British American magazine

British med. jour. — British medical journal

Can. law jour. — Canada law journal

Can. ann. rev. — Canadian annual review

Can. antiq. and numismatic jour. — Canadian antiquarian and numismatic journal

Can. art — Canadian art

Can. author — Canadian author

Can. banker — Canadian banker

Can. bookman — Canadian bookman

Can. commentator — Canadian commentator

Can. criminal cases — Canadian criminal cases

Can. defence quart. — Canadian defence quarterly

Can. dimension — Canadian dimension

Can. forum — Canadian forum

Can. geog. jour. — Canadian geographical journal

Can. geographer — Canadian geographer

Can. Hist. Assoc. Proceedings — Canadian Historical Association Proceedings

Can. illus. news — Canadian illustrated news

Can. jour. econ. and pol. sci. — Canadian journal of economics and political science

Can. jour. of agricultural economics — Canadian journal of agricultural economics

Can. jour. of corrections — Canadian journal of corrections

Can. library jour. — Canadian library journal

Can. lit. — Canadian literature

Can. mag. — Canadian magazine

Can. Med. Assoc. jour. — Canadian Medical Association journal

Can. mercury — Canadian mercury

Can. monthly — Canadian monthly and national review

Can. public admin. — Canadian public administration

Can. reader — Canadian reader

Can. rev. of sociol. and anthrop. — Canadian review of sociology and anthropology

Can. tribune — Canadian tribune

Can. unionist — Canadian unionist

Commerce jour. — Commerce journal

Contemporary rev. — Contemporary review

Dalhousie rev. — Dalhousie review

Edinburgh rev. — Edinburgh review

Geographical jour. — Geographical journal

Globe mag. — Globe magazine

H. of C., Debates — House of Commons Debates

Inter-American quart. — Inter-American quarterly

International jour. — International journal

Johns Hopkins hosp. bull. — Johns
Hopkins hospital bulletin
Jour. of Amer. folklore — Journal of
American folklore
Jour. of Can. stud. — Journal of
Canadian studies
McClure's mag. — McClure's
magazine
Methodist mag. — Methodist
magazine
Montreal med. jour. — Montreal
medical journal
National rev. — National review
New world quart. — New world
quarterly
New York Times book rev. — New
York Times book review
Northern rev. — Northern review
Ontario hist. — Ontario history
Poetry mag. — Poetry magazine
Putnam's monthly mag. — Putnam's
monthly magazine
Queen's quart. — Queen's quarterly
Research rev. — Research review
Review of hist. pubs. — Review of
historical publications
Saskatchewan hist. — Saskatchewan
history
Saturday rev. — Saturday review
Tamarack rev. — Tamarack review

Univ. of Tor. quart. — University of
Toronto quarterly
University mag. — University
magazine
Waterloo rev. — Waterloo review
Weekend mag. — Weekend magazine
World rev. — World review

Other:

b. — born
c. — century
ca. — about
ch., chap.; Ch., Chap. — chapter
Champlain Soc. — Champlain Society
d. — died
ed. — editor; edition
No. — Number
Proc. — Proceedings
Pub. Arch. Can. — Public Archives of
Canada
rev. — revised
Roy. Comm. — Royal Commission
Roy. Soc. Can. — Royal Society of
Canada
Trans. — Transactions (where part of
title)
trans. — translated
Vol. — Volume

Aberhart, William

Never mind why.

> WILLIAM ABERHART, a favourite response to his questioning students, qu. in J.A. Irving, *Social credit movement in Alberta*, 1960, 16.

Bible Bill.

> WILLIAM ABERHART, Premier of Alberta, 1935-1943, radio religion preacher from Calgary's Palace Theatre, first on a Sunday in November 1925 as head of the Bible Institute.

Who is he, in yonder hall,
Calling to Albertans all?
Aberhart, 'tis he with glory
Sending forth a won'drous story.

> ALBERTA SOCIAL CREDIT PARTY, campaign song, 1935.

I am a perfect pattern of a pious
   prophet-premier,
I am popular with victims of
   intellectual anemia,
I've solved the pressing problem of the
   common commissariat,
And how to pinch and plunder the
   Provincial proletariat.

> J.J. ZUBICK, *The Rebel* (Calgary) June 25, 1937; qu. in W.H. Kesterton, *A history of journalism in Canada*, 1967, 229, referring to William Aberhart, premier of Alberta; a parody on Gilbert & Sullivan.

The divine right of Aberhart is the basis of the premier's philosophy. The cabinet is just Aberhart eight times. He just makes up his mind what to do and then calls in the boys and lets them know.

> JOHN HUGILL, Edmonton *Journal*, Sept. 23, 1937, 6.

Be enthusiastic, be ambitious, develop a distinct personality; have a hobby and "ride it hard".

> WILLIAM ABERHART, four maxims for successful living ascribed to him at Memorial Service, Crescent Heights High School, Calgary, May 27, 1943.

You either believed he was right and followed him wherever he led or you had nothing to do with him.

> ERNEST MANNING, premier of Alberta after Aberhart's death, 1943.

The most certifiable Canadian exemplar of charisma in the past century.

> ROGER GRAHAM, in J.S. Moir, ed., *Character and circumstance*, 1970, 35.

Aberhart offered them hope, and spell that in capital letters, when nobody else offered them sweet bugger all but the old promises.

> ANON., qu. in Barry Broadfoot, *Ten lost years 1929-1939*, 1973, 313.

Ability

You are as sharp as a needle.

> T.C. HALIBURTON, *Nature and human nature*, 1855, I, 245.

If you haven't it in your head you must have it in your heels.

> ANON., proverb, Riverport, N.S., 19th c.

People are always ready to admit a man's ability after he gets there.

> ROBERT C. (BOB) EDWARDS, Calgary *Eye Opener*, Jan. 27, 1912.

Some men talk modestly about their abilities when they should be apologizing for their privileged opportunities.

> PETER MCARTHUR, d. 1924, qu. in *The best of Peter McArthur*, 1967, 36.

Abortion

We recommend that the Criminal Code be amended to permit abortion by a qualified medical practitioner on the sole request of any woman who has been pregnant for 12 weeks or less.

> CANADA. ROYAL COMM. ON THE STATUS OF WOMEN, *Report*, 1970, Sect. 242, 286.

This uterus is not government property.

> ANON., slogan of women's liberation groups agitating for change in Canadian abortion law, 1970.

A woman should have control over her own body.

> CANADA. ROYAL COMM. ON THE STATUS OF WOMEN, *Report*, 1970, 285.

In this case I think that it should be essentially the women who would have the louder say in this because they are the ones who are carrying the fetus, they are the ones who are victimized by bad abortions, they are the ones who have to take the very frightening moral decisions of killing something which is living inside them.

> PIERRE E. TRUDEAU, to high school students Dartmouth, N.S., Oct. 29, 1971.

Absence

Of love's fair ministers thou art the
  chief.
To jaded souls, asleep beside their
  vows,
Thou givest hopes, keen joys and
  vague alarms;
Beneath thy touch the brown and
  yellow leaf
Turns to pink blossom, and the
  spring-bright boughs
Frame lovers running to each other's
  arms.

> ETHELWYN WETHERALD, "Absence", 1907.

She cannot say which task to choose or
  shun,
Absence picks up what presence has
  begun.

> ROBERT FINCH, "Absence", 1961.

Your absence has not taught me
how to be alone, it merely has
shown that when together we cast
a single shadow on this wall.

> DOUG FETHERLING, "Your absence has not taught me", 1971.

Abstinence

Since God created man upon the face of the earth there never was a more downright absurdity imposed upon and supported by any enlightened and civilized people, than that of absolute abstinence from all intoxicating liquors.

> REV. ROBERT MURRAY, *The Baptist missionary magazine*, Vol. II, Sept., 1835, 175.

Academics

Just as we measure the progress of democratic government by its freedom from the spoils system, so that faithful servants are not dispossessed whenever a new party comes into power, so we can measure the rank and stability of a university by the security given to a professor to pursue and expound his investigations without being compelled to justify himself to those who differ from him.

SIR ROBERT FALCONER, *Academic freedom*, 1922.

The more one sees of the academic mind, the more one feels how necessary it is that it should be supplemented or balanced by wide political outlook or experience, to save course of action which mean defeat in the end of the causes it is intended to support. Logic is a means to an end. The academic mind is apt to make, of logic, an end in itself.

W.L. MACKENZIE KING, *Diaries*, June 25, 1938; qu. by V. Hoar, comp., *The great depression*, 1969, 108.

So far as the Canadian academic migration is concerned, this means an awareness of the growth of a North American nationality in which the old loyalties are cherished, not for provincial exclusiveness but for the maintenance of the enduring verities which embody the ideals of human rights and freedom as expressed in the history and institutions of both Canada and the United States.

JAMES T. SHOTWELL, *Can. hist. rev.*, March, 1947, 42.

Like many other Canadians, however, I am disturbed at the apparent indifference of the experts to the disappearance of the old-fashioned concept of the "educated person" who chose to rest his reputation on his bearing and conversation, rather than on degrees and "research".

HILDA NEATBY, *So little for the mind*, 1953, vii.

We seem to be doing an admirable job of squandering the priceless human resources available to us. It can, in fact, be argued on the basis of the fragments of information at hand that we are utilizing to the full the talents of probably no more than one-third of our academically gifted young men and women.

R.W.B. JACKSON AND W.G. FLEMING, in C.T. Bissell, ed., *Canada's crisis in higher education*, 1957, 76.

And we watch come out in their twos
    and threes
The professors of the humanities,
Well-fed, half-drunk from their
    formal dinner,
Old phonies all, each a miserable
    sinner.
And I can't help smiling – are these,
    are these
The ones who are touted as "our
    enemies"?

RAYMOND SOUSTER, "On Hart House steps", 1958.

Each generation of prissy Anglo-Saxon academics in this country makes the same mistake, for the even tenor of their lives prevents them from understanding the tempestuous world in which the poet must have his being.

IRVING LAYTON, *The swinging flesh*, 1961, xi.

It seems unlikely, considering the polyglot nature of a modern university, that a Board elected directly from its faculty members would be more than a congress of hostile ambassadors from entrenched interests.

MURRAY S. DONNELLY, in G. Whalley, ed., *A place of liberty*, 1964, 146.

To remember that we are colleagues in the same system with our competitors is not easy. The threat from within is in fact this individualism, this unwillingness to organize.

KENNETH HARE, *Our university freedom in the Canadian context*, 1968, 22.

Canadian academics will soon become fit specimens for the anthropologists. We've been colonized one way by the British and now we're being colonized by the Americans. Perhaps the switch has made us aware of it.

JAMES A. STEELE, *Weekend mag.*, Mar. 22, 1969, 3.

Those who take part in the ceremony of Kissing the Backside of the Ph.D. Octopus do well not to invite scrutiny of their postures, and it is considered unprofessional as well as unconventional to look into the more general implications of philosophical methods. But the rest of us may still fix these ungainlinesses with our roving glance.

F.E. SPARSHOTT, *Looking for philosophy*, 1972, 134.

Acadia

Happy Acadia! though around thy
    shore
Is heard the stormy wind's terrific
    roar;
Though round thee Winter binds his
    icy chain,
And his rude tempests sweep along the
    plain,
Still Summer comes, and decorates thy
    land
With fruits and flowers from her
    luxuriant hand.

OLIVER GOLDSMITH, *The rising village*, 1825 (1834, 37).

In the Acadian land on the shores of
    the basin of Minas,
Distant, secluded, still, the little village
    of Grand Pré
Lay in the fruitful valley.

HENRY W. LONGFELLOW, *Evangeline*, 1847.

And where the Acadian village stood,
    its roofs o'ergrown with moss,
And the simple wooden chapel with its
    alter and its cross,
And where the forge of Basil sent its
    sparks toward the sky,
The lonely thistle blossomed, and the
    fireweed grew high.

A.W.H. EATON, "The re-settlement of Acadia", 1889.

Obstinate as an Acadian.

ANON., quoted as a "proverb" in, *Review of hist. pubs.*, 1900, 95.

In 1748, the Acadians considered themselves Acadian, the French considered them unreliable allies, and the English, unsatisfactory citizens.

NAOMI GRIFFITHS, *The Acadians: creation of a people*, 1973, 37.

Acceptance

I do not care, because
I see with bitter calm,
Life made me what I was,
Life makes me what I am.

ROBERT W. SERVICE, "The coco-fiend", 1921.

I am sceptical that the universe has any purpose; it seems to me it just *is*.

D.G. JONES, *Delta*, No. 3, Apr., 1958, 19.

Accountants

The C.A.'s calculating talents
For making loss and profit balance
Make him the perfect friend to bring
To your final reckoning.

> MAVOR MOORE, "The accountant", *And what do you do?*, 1960, 55.

Accusation

There was no evidence that she had not carried out, with equal success, other more difficult missions.

> JUSTICE W.F. SPENCE, Canada. Roy. Comm. of Inquiry into Matters Relating to one Gerda Munsinger, *Report*, 1966, 4.

Achievement

It is not under the immediate stress of a great emotion that a great work is produced; most often it is the result of the long, silent cogitation, when the mind sits in autumnal luxury thinking to itself.

> BLISS CARMAN, *The kinship of nature*, 1904, 67.

Superlative achievement comes more often from the man who broadens the basis of his own culture all through life without lessening the intensity of work in his chosen field.

> WILDER PENFIELD, address, Univ. of Melbourne Medical School, August, 1962.

Everything I did, I wish I had done better. I wasn't big enough, smart enough to do better.

> JOSEPH R. SMALLWOOD, press conference, St. John's, Nfld., Jan. 13, 1972, after announcing his resignation.

What you conceive and believe, you achieve.

> GERRY PATTERSON, advertising executive, personal motto, qu. in *Maclean's*, Apr. 1973, 92.

Acquiescence

There is only one thing worse than a guilty custom and that is a guilty acquiescence.

> EMILY MURPHY, ("Janey Canuck"), about 1925, qu. in B.H. Sanders, *Emily Murphy, crusader*, 1945, 192 and 212.

Acting

Three-quarters of acting is listening.

> KATE REID, *The Globe and Mail*, Nov. 25, 1967, 22.

Anybody can act. Most of us do nothing else.

> RICHARD J. NEEDHAM, *A friend in Needham*, 1969, 18.

Acting is not being emotional, but being able to express emotions.

> KATE REID, Toronto *Globe and Mail*, June 4, 1973, 8.

Action

The principle of life is movement, and stagnation is death. So that if a thing has no play, you may be sure it has no life.

> BLISS CARMAN, *The kinship of nature*, 1904, 244.

Gradually the calculated act must give way to the act of faith.

> PAUL-EMILE BORDUAS, *Refus global*, 1948, 7 (Trans.).

By walking I found out
Where I was going.

> IRVING LAYTON, "There were no signs", 1963.

The word betrays the act;
The act alone is pure.
The rest is literature:
Fishbait for fools and pedants.

> IRVING LAYTON, "Silence", 1963.

actions are the tamed
animals of my mind
they stalk the streets
in a mild manner
and are a disappointment
to my dreams.

> DON BAILEY, "Aquarius as a zoo story", 1971.

Activity

The Diety has endowed man with activity: He has placed him in circumstances, in which activity expended upon industrious pursuits acquires property; and property enables him to enjoy the comforts of life, and to be the friend of every good and benevolent design.

> THOMAS MCCULLOCH, *The letters of Mephibosheth Stepsure*, 1821, Letter 13.

Actors

Actors in Canada are a little too much of the Fly-by-night order, to hold a *high* social status.

> HORTON RHYS, *A theatrical trip*, 1861, 54.

When actors begin to think, it is time for a change. They are not fitted for it.

> STEPHEN LEACOCK, "The decline of the drama", 1921.

You can be a full-time garbage collector in Toronto and you'll be accepted as such. Nobody says, "If he were any good he'd be collecting garbage in New York!" Or you can be a successful doctor or lawyer or accountant. You're not expected to prove how good you are by moving away to practise medicine or law or accounting in Hollywood or London.

> LARRY MANN, in 1964, qu. in Alex Barris, *The Pierce-Arrow showroom is leaking*, 1969, 95.

I used to think that one thing led to another. You know, that you *build* a career. But Broadway, parts in Hollywood movies, things like that, they don't necessarily *lead* to anything any more.

> ERIC HOUSE, qu. in *Saturday night*, November, 1972, 21.

Actresses

There is no future for an actress in Canada. The Meccas are elsewhere.

> TOBY ROBINS, in *The Globe and Mail*, Sept. 14, 1968, 28.

Adaptation

Life is largely a process of adaptation to the circumstances in which we exist.

> HANS SELYE, *The stress of life*, 1956, vii.

Administration

Nothing is administratively impossible.

> C.D. HOWE, a favourite dictum, qu. in P. Newman, *Renegade in power*, 1963, 36.

Adolescents

There is a touch of the fascist in most adolescents; they admire the strong man who stands no nonsense; they have no objection to seeing the weak trampled underfoot; mercy in its more subtle forms is outside their understanding and has no meaning for them.

> ROBERTSON DAVIES, *Tempest-tost*, 1951, 63.

It is in the solving of adolescent conflicts that the outbursts arise.

WILLIAM E. BLATZ, *Human security*, 1966, 8.

Adoration

Where never mower's boot has trod
Nor sickle sheared the hours,
I'll plant you as my garden's god,
And twine you round with flowers.

JAY MACPHERSON, "Inland", 1957.

Adultery

Adultery is the same the world over; it's only the method of approach that varies.

SIR JAMES LOUGHEED, chairman of the Senate divorce committee, about 1920.

To the heart of woman forgiveness is, *naturally*, easier; also, for her, the injury to her self-esteem is less cruel. Those around her display pity and kindness. The husband, however, though he may suffer quite as much, receives no sympathy for the injury done to his family; the infidelity of his wife exposes him to ridicule.

QUEBEC. COMM. DES DROITS CIVILS DE LA FEMME, *Deuxième rapport*, Mar. 15, 1930, 41 (Trans.)

Adults

When you were a little girl you always thought that adults were infallible. Well, now you know that grown-ups are just very tall children and it has come as a bit of a shock.

JANET BONELLIE, "Why are the people staring?", in *Tamarack rev.* No. 48, 1968, 20.

Adults are children who have failed to find a substitute for the charm they lost.

IRVING LAYTON, "Some observations and aphorisms", *Tamarack rev.*, Spring, 1968, 6.

Adventures

"Having adventures comes natural to some people," said Anne serenely. "You just have a gift for them or you haven't".

L.M. MONTGOMERY, *Anne of Avonlea*, 1909, 209.

Adversity

It's easy to fight when everything's
        right,
    And you're mad with the thrill and
        the glory;
It's easy to cheer when victory's near,
    And wallow in fields that are gory.
It's a different song when everything's
        wrong,
    When you're feeling infernally
        mortal;
When it's ten against one, and hope
        there is none,
    Buck up, little soldiers, and chortle!

ROBERT W. SERVICE, "Carry on", 1916.

Advertising

One has to talk a great deal of nonsense if one wishes to get the attention of the public directed to a little sense; to sugarcoat the pill as it were, if it is intended to be swallowed.

J.J. PROCTER, *The philosopher in the clearing*, 1897, 160.

The best advertisement in the public eye is the show-ring award, and criticism.

JAMES BURNETT, *Farmer's advocate*, July 3, 1907.

Advertising may be described as the science of arresting the human intelligence long enough to get money from it.

> STEPHEN LEACOCK, "The perfect salesman", *The garden of folly*, 1924, 128.

There is a new marvel of science which is already playing an important part in the art of indirect advertising and which is destined to become a still larger factor in the future. It is radio broadcasting. There are certain necessary and proper limitations with respect to the employment of this agency and it is essential that broadcasting be surrounded with such safeguards as will prevent the air becoming what might be described as an atmospheric bill board.

> SIR HENRY THORNTON, address, Philadelphia, June 21, 1926, Advertising Clubs of the World.

The First Carload of Kotex to Cross Canada.

> ANON., banner on C.P.R. express car in yard at Vancouver, 1927.

The activating force which, harnessed to improvements in designing and manufacture, caused the old ways to be discarded and the new to become the rule, has been advertising.

> H.E. STEPHENSON and C. MCNAUGHT, *Story of advertising*, 1940.

We are indeed fighting for our lives. The pernicious influence of American advertising reflected especially in the periodical press and the powerful persistent impact of commercialism have been evident in all the ramifications of Canadian life.

> HAROLD A. INNIS, *The strategy of culture*, 1952, 19.

Hail to the huckster! Knight errant of our time!
Proudly he rides to war for the barons of soap,
Perpetually storming the castles of the home.

> F.R. SCOTT, "Social sonnets; II", 1954.

If I were a red-blooded Canadian and could think of a way of fighting off Madison Avenue and Hollywood without damaging the liberties of my countrymen, I would get about the work immediately.

> RICHARD ROVERE, U.S. writer, in *Maclean's*, Nov. 5, 1960, 38.

Give me the writing of a nation's advertising and propaganda, and I care not who governs its politics.

> HUGH MACLENNAN, *Maclean's*, Nov. 5, 1960, 59.

Only the advertisements preach the lie direct, this trumpery of the word, garbage of dreams.

> L.W. ELLIS, "Daily newspaper", 1964.

Ideally, advertising aims at the goal of a programmed harmony among all human impulses and aspirations and endeavours. Using handicraft methods, it stretches out toward the ultimate electronic goal of a collective consciousness.

> MARSHALL MCLUHAN, *Understanding media*, 1964, 227.

What is editorial content? The stuff you separate the ads with.

> ROY THOMSON, qu. in Russell Braddon, *Roy Thomson of Fleet Street*, 1965, 127.

It is within the power of advertising agencies to exert a profound influence on the life style of the Canadian people. The advertising they create, to a considerable extent sets the standards of taste and the levels of consumer demand for a nation.

> CFRB, Toronto, in Senate Special Committee on the Mass Media, *Report*, I, 1970, 245.

The measure of editorial acceptability becomes how does it fit, or will it interest the affluent. As a consequence, the mass media increasingly reflect the attitudes and deal with the concerns of the affluent. We don't have mass media, we have class media – media for the upper and middle classes.

> JERRY GOODIS, qu. in Senate, Special Committee on the Mass Media, *Report*, Vol. 1, 1970, 245.

There are some days when I really wish that I owned a chain of bawdy houses instead of being in advertising. But those days are diminishing. Now it's only maybe 20 out of 31 days a month.

> JERRY GOODIS, in *Maclean's*, Apr., 1972, 13.

Sometimes if the truth sounds like a lie [in advertising] you shouldn't tell it.

> GERALD PATTERSON, advertising executive, qu. in *Maclean's*, Apr., 1973, 92.

Advice

The difficulties were enhanced by an almost undue reliance of the Government on expert advice.

> HAROLD A. INNIS, *History of the* C.P.R., 1923, 91.

Advice is sought to confirm a position already taken.

> SIR WILLIAM OSLER, in Cushing: *Life of Osler*, 1926.

It wasn't so much what you said as when you said it. Last in line was a good place to be.

> ANON., confidant of L.B. Pearson on his readiness to accept advice during his term as Prime Minister, 1963-68.

Affection

There is a private spring to everyone's affection; if you can find that, and touch it, the door will fly open, tho' it was a miser's heart.

> T.C. HALIBURTON, *Sam Slick's wise saws*, 1853, I, 70.

Affirmation

"Affirm life," I said, "affirm
The triumphant grass that covers the worm;
And the flesh, the swinging flesh
That burns on its stick of bone."

> IRVING LAYTON, "Epigraph", 1961.

Last night I thought I would not wake again
but now with this June morning I run ragged to elude
The Great Iambic Pentameter
who is the Hound of Heaven in our stress
because I want to die
writing Haiku
or better,
long lines, clean and syllabic as knotted bamboo. Yes!

> PHYLLIS WEBB, "Poetics against the Angel of Death", 1962.

Affluence

The one thing I dread is affluence. I have a lovely office now, with pictures on the wall and a swivel chair, and I can't do anything.

> SIR FREDERICK BANTING, qu. by Lloyd Stevenson in *Sir Frederick Banting*,

1946, 289, remark to friend after moving to Banting Institute, Sept., 1930.

The last trump was blown
on the horn of plenty:
"Consume, consume"
echoed the mass-produced
populations, their own products.

> RENALD SHOOFLER, "What happened", 1966.

Affluence creates poverty.

> MARSHALL MCLUHAN, at American Booksellers Assoc. luncheon, Washington D.C., June 1969, qu. in Vancouver *Sun*, June 7, 1969, 31.

Affluence gives people a desire for personal freedoms. The well-educated and well-to-do have faith in their ability to run the show.

> MARTIN GOLDFARB, in *Maclean's*, Aug. 1970, 28 (Maclean's-Goldfarb rept.)

Age

And now we are aged and gray,
    Maggie,
The trials of life nearly done,
Let us sing of the days that are gone,
    Maggie,
When you and I were young.

> GEORGE W. JOHNSON, "When you and I were young, Maggie", in his *Maple leaves*, Hamilton, 1864.

I have come too soon into too young a country.

> OCTAVE CRÉMAZIE, letter to Abbé H.R. Casgrain Aug. 10, 1866, referring to Louis-Honoré Frechette (Trans.). Paraphrase of Alfred de Musset: "Je suis venu trop tard dans un pays trop vieux".

But four times twenty years gives
    Fate,
Divides, controls, bids consecrate −
    Twenty for growing, for laughter,
      and yearning,
    Twenty for loving, and mating, and
      learning,
    Twenty for making a name with the
      best,
    Twenty for wisdom, remembrance,
      and − rest.
He who would have Life's full estate,
Keeps thus his years inviolate.

> FREDERICK A. DIXON, "Four times twenty", 1884.

The work of the world has been done by men who had not reached *la crise de quarante ans*.

> SIR WILLIAM OSLER, "Importance of postgraduate study", in *Lancet*, 1900.

Pleasure's forsaken us, Love ceased to
    smile;
Youth has been funeralled; Age travels
    fast.
Sometimes we wonder: is it worth
    while?
There, we have gained to the summit
    at last.

> ROBERT SERVICE, "A song of success", 1912.

Our madcap youth is over,
Gone its unclouded skies,
And you and I, O Lover,
Grow old and staid and wise.

> NORAH M. HOLLAND, "A song of age", 1924.

We grow old by moments and not by years.

> BEVERLEY BAXTER, *Strange street*, 1935, 36.

You begin as "little man" and then "little boy", because a little man is littler than a little boy; then "sonny" and then "my boy" and after that "young man" and presently the interlocutor is younger than yourself and says, "say, Mister".

STEPHEN LEACOCK, "This business of growing old", 1940.

When a man drops out at the age of eighty, people can't say he's a quitter.

W.R. MOTHERWELL, in 1940, qu. in Grant MacEwan, *Fifty mighty men*, 1958, 135.

After seventy, one's reason tells one that the anticipation of many more years of life is not justifiable; one should count every year after one's seventieth as "velvet".

LEWELLYS F. BARKER, *Time and the physician*, 1942, 333.

I wish I could stick around a while to see how things turn out.

JOHN W. DAFOE, to a fellow writer on the *Free press*, Dec. 23, 1943 near the end of his career as editor, qu. in M. Donnelly, *Dafoe of the Free Press*, 1968, 201.

But we who were young together once Are growing old apart.

JOE WALLACE, "As we come to the second sleep", 1956.

Small satisfactions here and there explain the slightly greying hair; age is a cage and I go there, hands up, nudged by a fake revolver.

PHYLLIS WEBB, "Small satisfactions", 1962.

Sometimes very young children can look at the old, and a look passes between them, conspiratorial, sly and knowing. It's because neither are human to the middling ones.

MARGARET LAURENCE, *The stone angel*, 1964, 6.

You don't change when you grow old. You remain just the same. But everything else changes. Your home. Your friends. Your city. The things you are used to just disappear, one by one. And you are left alone.

GREGORY CLARK, 1965, qu. in J. Carroll, *The death of the Toronto Telegram*, 1971, 193.

I've reached an age where I can't use my youth as an excuse for my ignorance any more.

JANET BONELLIE, "Why are the people staring?" in *Tamarack rev.* No. 44, 1967, 17.

The charm of age,
My dear, is not to stage
A desperate rebellion
Against what must be,
But to be.

C.J. NEWMAN, "Instructing the old on growing old", 1967.

He is one of those people who look older than they are when they're young and younger than they are when they're old.

ALICE MUNRO, "Postcard", 1968.

We westerners realize that even if there is snow on the roof that does not imply that the fire has gone out in the furnace.

JOHN G. DIEFENBAKER, H. of C., *Debates*, Mar. 25, 1970, 5446.

I sorrow a little
that I'm only an aging person
onlooker
petrified behind glass.

> DOROTHY LIVESAY, "Where I usually sit",
> 1971.

Aggression

Life is the aggressor, not death. When life ceases aggressing, death takes over.

> IRVING LAYTON, "Aphs", *The whole bloody bird*, 1969, 99.

Aging

Aging can be regarded as a disease. Like any other disease, it is probably preventable or curable.

> DR. HANS SELYE, *Maclean's*, Aug. 15, 1959, 14.

People do not really age by living a number of years. I am convinced that we grow old only by deserting our ideals. We are, in fact, as old as our doubts and our despairs, but we are as young as our faith and our hope, especially faith and hope in our youth, which is, after all, the same as saying our faith and our hope in our country's future.

> GEORGES VANIER, Affiliation, Boy Scouts of Canada and Les Scouts Catholiques de Canada, Secteur Francais, Feb. 22, 1967.

Agitation

Henceforth, there must be no peace in the Province, no quarter for the plunderers. Agitate! *Agitate*!! AGITATE!!! Destroy the Revenue; denounce the oppressors. Everything is lawful when the fundamental liberties are in danger. "The guards die — they never surrender."

> EDMUND BAILEY O'CALLAGHAN, M.P.P., *The vindicator*, Apr. 21, 1837, 3, editorial.

I don't like agitation, even for a good object.

> T.C. HALIBURTON, speech in Glasgow, 1857.

Anybody can start a movement by beginning with himself.

> STEPHEN B. LEACOCK, "Great national problems", in *Winnowed wisdom*, 1926.

Crowds would see visions, and his thoughts, like birds
Burdened with messages, would find their homes.
Already in mind he saw the breasts of men
Opening to free the phoenix of their dreams.

> GEORGE WOODCOCK, "The agitator", 1947.

Well, Mutchmor, and where are you going to raise hell this time?

> LESLIE FROST,, Premier of Ontario, to J.R. Mutchmor, qu. in *Mutchmor, the memoirs of James Ralph Mutchmor*, 1965, 144.

Rock the boat, ladies and gentlemen. It's invigorating. But don't forget you can capsize the boat. We don't want to swim just because we've sunk.

> LESTER B. PEARSON, speech, Ottawa, Young Liberal Federation of Canada, Apr. 15, 1966.

Agreement

Isn't it queer that only sensible people agree with you.

> ROBERT C. (BOB) EDWARDS, Calgary *Eye Opener*, Oct. 5, 1912.

When you come, as you will, to places of authority and influence and you face the acute issues which may divide our country part from part, may I commend this principle of action to your best thought and interest —

compulsion is ruled out; we proceed by agreement, or for a time we rest content not to proceed at all.

> GEN. A.G.L. MCNAUGHTON, speech, Queen's University, Kingston, Oct. 21, 1944.

And as it happened we agreed
On many things, but on the need
Especially of mental strife
And of a whole new source of life.

> GEORGE JOHNSTON, "A saint", 1959.

Men are driven to revenge themselves on those who have denied them the two things they most want: agreement and praise.

> IRVING LAYTON, "Aphs", *The whole bloody bird*, 1969, 104.

He came, he saw, he concurred.

> CLYDE GILMOUR, "The Max Ferguson Show", CBC Radio, Feb. 11, 1972, attributed.

Agriculture

The clearest and most significant uniformity regarding Canadian agriculture for more than three hundred years has been its deliberate and consistent use as a basis for economic and political empire.

> VERNON C. FOWKE, *Canadian agricultural policy: the historical pattern*, 1946, 3.

One of the most significant features of the national policy has been a persistent disregard of the competitive inferiority of agriculture within the price system.

> VERNON C. FOWKE, *The national policy and the wheat economy*, 1957, 290.

Bareness equals barrenness equals infertility equals uselessness for agriculture.

> WREFORD WATSON, *Can. geographer*, Vol. 13, 1969, 16.

Air Age

The Air Age faces mankind with a sharp choice – the choice between Winged Peace or Winged Death. It's up to you.

> BILLY BISHOP, *Winged peace*, 1944, 175.

Airplanes

In travelling past the grandstand he took an apple from his pocket and threw it at the judge's box, striking the corner, which illustrates that the airplane might be destructively useful when employed for military purposes.

> VICTORIA *COLONIST*, May 31, 1911, 9, re flight by Charles F. Walsh.

Alberta

In token of the love which thou has shown
For this wide land of freedom, I have named
A province vast, and for its beauty famed,
By thy dear name to be hereafter known.

> MARQUIS OF LORNE, Governor-general, 1878-83, to his wife, H.R.H. Princess Louise Caroline Alberta, after a visit to the West.

Alberta or bust!

> ANON., sign on a caravan of American settlers who left Nebraska, May, 1900.

If we cannot feed, clothe and shelter the people of Alberta, tell me who else is going to do it?

> WILLIAM ABERHART, address, Canadian Club, Toronto, Sept. 13, 1935.

Here's to Alberta, the land of the free,
The land of the grasshopper, bot fly and bee.

> ANON., qu. in David P. Gagen, ed., *Prairie perspectives*, 1970, 7.

Alcoholism

The son of an alcoholic tends to become an alcoholic; the daughter tends to marry one.

> ANON., researcher, Medical Unit of the Alcoholism and Drug Research Foundation, Toronto; qu. in *Maclean's* Feb. 1969, 82.

Alcoholism is excessive, inappropriate drinking followed by harmful consequences, followed by excessive, inappropriate drinking.

> ALLAN CLEMENTS, Unemployment Insurance Comm., Pacific Region Employee Counselling Program, qu, Vancouver *Sun*, March 11, 1975, 6.

Allegiance

I have just taken the most shameful oath of my life. I have sworn allegiance to the Queen of England.

> DAVID OUELETTE, newly elected Social Credit member for Drummond-Arthabaska after being sworn in as an M.P., July, 1962.

Alone

Living alone is a life without mirrors.

> MERLE SHAIN, *Some men are more perfect than others*, 1973, 107.

Ambition

Our people don't want English capital nor English people here, – they have no ambition beyond their present possessions, & never want to go beyond the sound of their own Church bells.

> LOUIS-JOSEPH PAPINEAU, qu. by Stewart Derbishire in *Report to Lord Durham*, May 24, 1838 (*Can. hist. rev.*, Mar., 1937, 57).

Throw away, in the first place, all ambition beyond that of doing the day's work well.

> SIR WILLIAM OSLER, "The army surgeon", 1894.

I praise Thee for my will to strive.
I bless Thy goad of discontent.

> CHARLES G.D. ROBERTS, "The aim", 1903.

A man who would walk the heights must walk alone.

> ROBERTSON DAVIES, *A jig for the gypsy*, 1954, 51.

It's not where you are. It's where you're headed that matters.

> JOSEPH R. SMALLWOOD, *Time*, Feb. 14, 1972, 15.

American Revolution

The central fact of Canadian history: the rejection of the American revolution.

> NORTHROP FRYE, Roy. Soc. Can., *Studia varia*, 1957, 24. (presented June 11, 1956)

Americanism, Anti-

It is authors of silly books, editors of silly papers, and demagogues of silly parties that keep us apart.

> T.C. HALIBURTON, *Wise saws*, 1853, ch. 26.

That shot fired at Fort Sumter, on the 12th of April, 1861, had a message for the north as well as for the south . . . That shot fired at Fort Sumter was the signal gun of a new epoch for North America, which told the people of Canada, more plainly than human speech can express it, to sleep no more except on their arms.

> THOMAS D'A. MCGEE, speech in Legislative Assembly, 1861.

War will come some day between England and the United States and India can do us yeoman's service by sending an army of Sikhs, Ghoorkas and Belochees &c, &c, across the Pacific to San Francisco and holding that beautiful and immoral city with the surrounding California as security for Montreal and Canada.

SIR JOHN A. MACDONALD, letter to J.S. Maine, Calcutta, Apr. 9, 1867.

When we come to appreciate these conditions – the requirements of a separate national identity seeking to establish itself across a many-ribbed continental belt, seeking to maintain itself against internal divisions and against strong external affinities, and fearing the encroachments that come from the radiating influences, social and economic, of a neighbouring and vastly larger state – then we see that the image formed by Canadians of Americans is as natural a phenomenon as the rising sun.

R.M. MACIVER, in H.F. Angus, ed., *Canada and her great neighbour*, 1938, xxv.

While Americans are benevolently ignorant about Canada, most Canadians seem malevolently informed about the United States.

MERRILL DENISON, *Saturday review*, June 7, 1952, 25.

It would be hard to overestimate the amount of energy we have devoted to this cause. One can never tell what will be the next occasion on which we'll gird up our loins and save ourselves once again from the United States. One can only predict with confidence that the occasion will come.

FRANK H. UNDERHILL, *Queen's quart.*, Vol. 60, 1954, 471.

Canadians will suffer whenever we use anti-Americanism as a cloak for our own ignorance, whenever we use American institutions and policies as a scapegoat for our own sins of omission, whenever we blame American inventiveness and energy for what is really our own lack of vision. Again and again contempt for an articulate American patriotism goes hand in hand with a complete lack of faith in Canada.

WALTER E. SWAYZE, *Queen's quart.*, Vol. 64, 1957, 336.

W.L. Mackenzie King prepared the present condition of Canada, in which the country is so irradiated by the American presence that it sickens and threatens to dissolve in cancerous slime. Only those liberal intellectuals who are always compulsively eager to despair of their country could defend the statesmanship that produced such a result.

W.L. MORTON, *Can. hist. rev.*, 1964, 320.

America stresses the value of competition rather than co-operation, and thus contradicts most traditional moral, ethical and religious philosophies. It is a society based on the idea of inequality, a society that accepts inequality not only as inevitable but as a moral end which ought to be preserved. It is a society based on maximizing personal wealth which defies the pursuit of self interest.

JOHN WARNOCK, *Can. dimension*, Nov. -Dec., 1967, 11.

In a sense the creation of Canada is an anti-American act and there is no Canadian who is not in some way anti-American.

ROBERT FULFORD, *Crisis at the Victory Burlesk*, 1968, 187.

I can no longer convince myself that we have even a snowball's chance in hell of escaping ultimate ravishment at the hands of the Yankee succubus. And what really hurts is the belated recognition on my part that there never was much chance; that Canadians have become so fatally infected with a compulsive desire to be screwed, blued, and tatooed as minions of the U.S.A. that they not only do not wish to be saved – they are willing to fight against salvation will all the ferocity of cornered rats.

FARLEY MOWAT, "Letter to my son" in Al Purdy, ed., *The new Romans*, 1968, 1.

Let the country continue to be a land of un-American activities. Boil me no melting pots and dream me no dreams.

LARRY ZOLF, in Al Purdy, ed., *The new Romans*, 1968, 124.

Canada, today, seems to be "enjoying" – if that is the word – a "love-hate" relationship with the United States.

W. EARLE MCLAUGHLIN, H. of C. Standing Comm. on External Affairs and National Defence, *Proceedings*, No. 15, Feb. 25, 1970, 15.6.

There is really no anti-Americanism here as far as I can see. The American business manager can go to the golf club or anywhere else. Some people actually look up to the guy: they think he must know more because he's an American. It's a curious Canadian hangup.

MAX SALTSMAN, M.P., Waterloo-Cambridge, qu. in R.L. Perry, *Galt, U.S.A.*, 1971, 35.

Americanization

The people of that country [Canada] are first to be seduced from their allegiance, and converted into traitors, as preparatory to the making them good citizens.

JOHN RANDOLPH, U.S. Congress, Dec. 10, 1811, *Abridgment of the debates of Congress*, Vol. IV, 1857, 438.

We often say that we fear no invasion from the south, but the armies of the south have already crossed the border. American enterprise, American capital, is taking rapid possession of our mines and our water power, our oil areas and our timber limits.

SARA JEANETTE DUNCAN, *The imperialist*, 1904, 404.

The English-speaking Canadians protest that they will never become Americans – they are already Americans without knowing it!

SAMUEL E. MOFFETT, *The Americanization of Canada*, 1907, 119.

Never for a moment are you oppressed by the thought that Canada is becoming Americanized in the national sense.

H.S. GULLETT, an Australian traveller, in *United Empire*, II, No. 6, June 1911, 418.

Americans you already are by your language, your nasal accent, your common slang, your dress, your daily habits; by the Yankee literature with which your homes and clubs are flooded; by your yellow journals and their rantings; by your loud and intolerant patriotism; by your worship of gold, snobbery and titles.

HENRI BOURASSA, *The spectre of annexation and the real danger of national disruption*, 1912, 23.

Let any English-speaking Canadian sit down in his corner and divest himself of whatever is American in origin and impulse and culturally and intellectually he'll look like a half-skinned rabbit.

ARTHUR PHELPS, *These United States*, 1941.

They're forever trying to make me feel at home in my own club!

ANON., old time member of Calgary Women's Club, referring to fellow club members recently arrived from the United States, qu. in J. Barber, *Good fences make good neighbours*, 1958, 67.

The history of the relations of the two countries in recent years discloses a talent approaching genius on the part of some Canadians for making it look as though Canada is victimized by the Americans six days of the week.

JOSEPH BARBER, *Good fences make good neighbours*, 1958, 266.

Insistence that it is a real problem seems to me a piece of hypocrisy perpetuated by commercial greed aiming to exploit the Canadian inferiority complex under the guise of patriotism; and its main significance – in keeping with the irrationality from which it starts – is that it consistently supports policies well designed to bring about the very things it claims to dislike – American ownership of Canadian industry, and a second-rate Canadian economy.

HARRY JOHNSON, address to Canadian Club, Toronto, Nov. 5, 1962, qu. in P.V. Lyon, *Policy question*, 1963, 53.

If you put a hundred Americans in one room and a hundred Canadians in another and place before each group fundamental questions on which they should have views, I think you would find striking differences between the collective opinions of the two.

VINCENT MASSEY, address, Association of Canadian Clubs, Charlottetown, June 1, 1964.

Year by year, American influence becomes more pervasive in every phase of Canadian life. Reason tells us that it cannot be otherwise; instinct and tradition move us to resist, often to resent.

ARNOLD HEENEY, address, Oxford Univ. (Eng.), June 19, 1964.

We like you, but we are also worried about you. American cultural, economic, and political influences so pervade our way of life that we have begun to wonder if our relatively small nation can retain its independence in the face of the strong pressures generated by our giant neighbor.

BELAND H. HONDERICH, Toronto *Star*, address, International Press Institute, Quebec City, Mar. 12, 1965.

But of course America itself is becoming Americanized in this sense, and the uniformity imposed on New Delhi and Singapore, or on Toronto and Vancouver, is no greater than that imposed on New Orleans or Baltimore.

NORTHROP FRYE, in C.F. Klinck, ed., *Literary history of Canada*, 1965, 847.

When Canadians are offered, at a political price, preferred access to American lettuce I think we should say it's spinach, and to hell with it!

J.H. DALES, *Jour. of Can. stud.*, Aug., 1967, 39.

Sooner or later, commercial imperatives will bring about free movement of all goods back and forth across our long border; and when that occurs, or even before it does, it will become unmistakably clear that countries with economies so inextricably intertwined must also have free movement of the other vital factors of production – capital, services, labour. The result will inevitably be substantial economic integration, which will require for its full realization a progressively expanding area of common political decision.

GEORGE BALL, *Discipline of power*, 1968, 113.

To think of the U.S. is to think of ourselves – almost.

GEORGE P. GRANT, in Al Purdy, ed., *The new Romans*, 1968, 39.

We may be the first country that will provide the world with an answer to the anxious question that the whole West is putting to itself. Can one safeguard human values; can one avoid the anonymity of the new conformism, while still having full access to the civilization of today? In other words, will Canada be able to keep its own character while availing itself of all the advantages of American life?

NAIM KATTAN, in Al Purdy, ed., *The new Romans*, 1968, 140.

The U.S. exile in Canada is different politically, socially, culturally and individually from any other exile we could conceivably harbour, because of the immense effect of U.S. imperialism in Canada, because of his own conditioning before he comes here, and because of the attitude of resident U.S. citizens in Canada.

ROBIN MATHEWS, *Canadian dimension*, Feb.-Mar., 1970, 10.

Of all peoples on earth, Canadians are least able to understand the process of Americanization. America is total environment: it envelops us as a mist, penetrating every sphere of our cultural, political, economic, and social environment.

ABRAHAM ROTSTEIN, in I. Lumsden, ed., *Close the 49th parallel etc*, 1970, 210.

I think in terms of avoiding a situation where Canada is just completely owned, and has no voice, just a puppet like Poland or Czechoslovakia, a country then stripped of all its important leaders because there are no important decisions to be made here, stripped of all its scientists, technicians and so on which would undermine our cultural life.

JACK MCCLELLAND, qu. in R.L. Perry, *Galt, U.S.A.*, 1971, 115.

Under the benevolent supervision of C.D. Howe, the economic continentalist who was King's perfect associate, American ownership of Canadian industry grew apace. This whole trend is now probably irreversible.

DONALD G. CREIGHTON, *Towards the discovery of Canada*, 1972, 169.

I want to stress that I am not anti-American. I'm not even pro-Canadian because that would oblige me to condone that peculiar myopia that has become almost a national symbol here. But I care very much for this country. I care very much about our future. And I don't intend to be bullied, smothered or owned by any other country. There are other people who feel as I do. I call them Canadians.

JACK MCCLELLAND, *Toronto calendar magazine*, March, 1972.

You are a big country now, but you still tend to feel small and fragile. If the U.S. gets a cold, you get pneumonia.

HERMAN KAHN, press conference, Ottawa, Aug. 22, 1972.

Americans

You must learn the American language, if you want to understand the American people.

T.C. HALIBURTON, *Sam Slick*, 1838, 56.

The Yankees in the land abound
For Uncle Sam gets all around,
And with his push and grit and go
Is sure to make the country grow.

> E.F. MILLER, in *Grain growers guide*,
> Sept. 20, 1911, 28.

We like the Americans we know, but
we do not like the United States.

> ANON., quoted in *Canada and her great
> neighbor*, ed. H.F. Angus, 1938.

You know, I don't believe I ever in my
life even thought to think about Canada.

> ANON., American woman to Arthur
> Phelps, qu. in, *These United States*,
> 1941.

Those people in the United States.

> JOHN DIEFENBAKER, H. of C., *Debates*,
> Jan. 31, 1963, 3328, referring to the
> Kennedy administration.

The redeeming feature of Americans
is their capacity for self-criticism.
Since they are so good at self-criticism,
they do not need much help from
Canadians – we should be much
more usefully employed in criticizing
ourselves. Canadians, it seems to me,
are at least as open to criticism as
Americans in almost every respect,
and yet how seldom do we subject
ourselves to searching self-examina-
tion?

> DESMOND PACEY, in Al Purdy, ed., *The
> new Romans*, 1968, 158.

There are few forces more ruthless
than Americans doing good.

> JOHN W. HOLMES, in Dyck and Krosby,
> eds. *Empire and nations*, 1969, 79.

Quick! Can you name three
    Canadians?
Any three Canadians at all?

> JULIUS NOVICK, *The New York Times*,
> May 13, 1973, Sec. II, 3.

Americans in Canada

The American weapons are hard cash,
commercial skills, raw energy and the
printed and spoken word. Thus armed,
they are steadily digging up and eating Canada, with good-humoured re-
lish and total appetite. They are everywhere as thick as starlings – starlings
with scoop-shaped claws and crops to
match.

> NICHOLAS MONSARRAT, *Sunday tele-
> gram*, June 25, 1967; qu. in M. Wade,
> ed., *Regionalism in the Canadian com-
> munity 1867-1967*, 1969, 274.

The average American executive has
an obsession with activity. Everything
has to be kept moving to the point
where, very often, he will be going
around in circles just for the sake of
keeping moving, rather than going in
a straight line. Now the Canadian way
is moving at a slower pace – and this
sometimes exasperates the Americans.
But the Canadian will move in a
straight line while the American will
go in circles.

> GEOFFREY FELLOWS, management con-
> sultant, qu. in R.L. Perry, *Galt, U.S.A.*,
> 1971, 37.

Anger

Wild, like a man
in the skin of a bear that is
not yet killed.

> ANDREAS SCHROEDER, "Sands", 1969.

Trust no man until you have made
him angry.

> IRVING LAYTON, "Aphs", *The whole
> bloody bird*, 1969, 101.

There is sometimes even an ecstasy in
anger.

> JACK BIRNBAUM, M.D., *Cry anger, a cure
> for depression*, 1973; attributed.

Anglicans

Anglicanism was the focus of the lost cause which had to retreat from the new American nation to the Canadian bush.

A.R.M. LOWER, *Canadians in the making*, 1958, 137.

We of this so-English Church, with the rest of Canada, can in this Confederation Year confess our repeated failure to understand our French-speaking brothers.

REV. H.H. CLARK, address, General Synod of the Anglican Church of Canada, 23rd session, Ottawa, Aug. 22, 1967.

Anguish

But to have possessed a unique anguish has been some solace through the years.

MALCOLM LOWRY, "The days like smitten cymbals of brass", 1962.

Animals

Have the wild things no moral or legal rights? What right has man to inflict such long and fearful agony on a fellow-creature, simply because that creature does not speak his language?

ERNEST THOMPSON SETON, *Wild animals I have known*, 1900, 357.

Let's face it, man is an unnatural animal.

IRVING LAYTON, "Aphs", *The whole bloody bird*, 1969, 95.

Dignity and industry lend size to the muskrat.
His size is his own, and mete.
The whale may think his dignity is greater.

The muskrat would be able, if the thought struck him,
to prove his own title to this quality, sooner or later.

ALFRED BAILEY, "The muskrat and the whale", 1973.

Animosity

Father, you have no idea how I enjoy and cherish my animosities.

SIR CHARLES HIBBERT TUPPER, to his father on being chided for holding resentments against political opponents.

It is never a sound policy to harbour a grudge nor even to resent an injury, except when inspired by sheer malice.

SIR WILFRID LAURIER, letter to a western supporter, qu., Skelton, *Laurier*, 1921.

Annapolis (Fort) N.S.

Annapolis, Annapolis! Oh, yes, Annapolis must be defended; to be sure, Annapolis should be defended. Pray, where is Annapolis?

DUKE OF NEWCASTLE, Prime Minister, 1758; Horace Walpole, *George II*, 1822.

Annexation

Delenda est Canada!

WILLIAM SHIRLEY, Gov. of Massachusetts, to State Assembly, 1746; from "Delenda est Cartago" – Destroy Carthage – Cato the Censor, in Roman Senate, c. 174; qu. in F. Parkman, *A half century of conflict*, vol. 2, 1899, 169.

The Unanimous Voice of the Continent is Canada must be ours; Quebec must be taken.

JOHN ADAMS, 1776, after defeat of Montgomery at Quebec.

Canada, acceding to this confederation, and joining in the measures of the United States, shall be admitted into, and entitled to all the advantages of this Union: but no other colony shall be admitted into the same unless such admission be agreed to by nine states.

U.S., *Articles of confederation*, XI, Nov. 15, 1777.

In the mean time the acquisition *of Canada is not an object with us,* we must make valuable what we have already *acquired* and at the same time take such measures as *to weaken it as a British province.*

JAMES MONROE, letter to Thomas Jefferson from Trenton, N.J., Nov. 1, 1784.

The annexation of Canada this year as far as the neighborhood of Quebec, will be a mere matter of marching, and will give us experience for the attack of Halifax the next, and the final expulsion of England from the American continent.

THOMAS JEFFERSON, letter to Duane, Aug. 4, 1812.

Every man of sense, whether in the Cabinet or out of it, knows that Canada must at no distant period be merged in the American Republic.

EDINBURGH REV., 1825, 290.

Fifty-four-forty, or fight!

WILLIAM ALLEN, speech in U.S. Senate, 1844; leading to demand that Oregon be reoccupied by U.S. up to 54 degrees 40 seconds by force if necessary; U.S. Democratic Party slogan, 1844.

On Loyalty we cannot live,
One ounce of Bread it will not give,
Clear the way for Annexation,
Or we shall meet with starvation.

ANON., Annexation Ballad, 1849; qu. in R. Reid, *Canadian style*, 1973, 315.

No matter what the subject of complaint, or what the party complaining; whether it be alleged that the French are oppressing the British, or the British the French – that the Upper Canadian debt presses on Lower Canada, or Lower Canadian claims on Upper – whether merchants be bankrupt, stocks depreciated, roads bad, or seasons unfavourable – annexation is invoked as the remedy for all ills, imaginary or real.

LORD ELGIN, letter to Lord Grey, March 14, 1849.

I have no fear that the people of Upper Canada would ever desire to become the fag-end of the neighbouring republic.

GEORGE BROWN, Nov. 10, 1859, at Reform Convention, Toronto.

I should say that if a man had a great heart within him he would rather look forward to the day when, from that point of land which is habitable nearest to the Pole to the shores of the great Gulf, the whole of that vast continent might become one confederation of States.

JOHN BRIGHT, speech of 1861.

I do not believe it is our destiny to be engulfed into a Republican union, renovated and inflamed with the wine of victory, of which she now drinks so deeply – it seems to me that we have theatre enough under our feet to act another and a worthier part; we can hardly join the Americans on our own terms, and we never ought to join them on theirs.

T. D'A. MCGEE, speech. "American relations and Canadian duties", Quebec, May 10, 1862.

If the Maritime Provinces would join us, spontaneously, to-day – sterile as they may be in the soil under a sky of steel – still their hardy population, their harbours, fisheries, and seamen, they would greatly strengthen and improve our position, and aid us in our struggle for equality upon the ocean. If we would succeed upon the deep, we must either maintain our fisheries or absorb the provinces.

E.H. DERBY, *Report to revenue commissioners*, U.S., 1866.

When the experiment of the "dominion" shall have failed – as fail it must – a process of peaceful absorption will give Canada her proper place in the great North American Republic.

HORACE GREELEY, qu. in P.B. Waite, *Life and times of confederation*, 1962, 29; from New York *Tribune*, May 10, 1867.

I know that Nature designs that this whole continent, not merely these thirty-six States, but that this whole continent, shall be, sooner or later, within the magic circle of the American Union.

WILLIAM H. SEWARD, address in Boston, qu. in Montreal *Gazette*, June 27, 1867, 2.

For the admission of the states of Nova Scotia, New Brunswick, Canada East and Canada West and for the organization of the territories of Selkirk, Saskatchewan and Columbia.

U.S. CONGRESS, July 2, 1886, wording of a Bill, H.R. 754.

The British North American colonies would in time, and probably at no very distant time, unite themselves to the group of states, of which they were already by race, position, commercial ties, and the character of their institutions, a part. No one could stand by the side of the St. Lawrence and doubt

that in the end they would do this, but they would be left to do it of their own free will.

GOLDWIN SMITH, speech in England, 1866.

I can't help thinking that it would be a grand thing to see one Government rule from the Equator to the North Pole.

JOHN BRIGHT, to Sir Charles Tupper, 1867, in London; Tupper, *Recollections*, 1914, 61.

It seems to me impossible that we should long hold B.C. from its natural annexation.

C.B. ADDERLEY, Parliamentary Under-Secretary for Colonies, Minute Sept. 17, 1867 to Duke of Buckingham. (Col. Off. 60, Vol. 28).

The opening by us first of a North Pacific Railroad seals the destiny of British possessions west of the 91st. meridian. Annexation will be but a question of time.

U.S. SENATE, *Report on Pacific railroads*, Feb. 19, 1869, 1363.

Americans will not take any definite step; they feel that Canada must come into the Confederation, and will of herself. The American party in Canada is always at work.

RALPH W. EMERSON, remarks to William Allingham, Nov. 1872.

Mr. Smith has come into a peaceful community to do his best for the furtherance of a cause which means simply revolution.

TORONTO *GLOBE* , editorial Oct. 27, 1874 on Goldwin Smith.

In ten years this sleepy Canada will be ripe for annexation – the farmers in Manitoba, etc., will demand it themselves. Besides, the country is half-annexed already socially – hotels, newspapers, advertising, etc., all on the American pattern. And they may tug and resist as much as they like; the economic necessity of an infusion of Yankee blood will have its way and abolish this ridiculous boundary line – and when the time comes, John Bull will say "Yea and Amen" to it.

> FRIEDRICH ENGELS, letter to Victor Sorge, dated Montreal, Sept. 10, 1888.

Sharers in such a realm, heirs to such vast and varied privileges, Canadians are not for sale.

> W. GEORGE BEERS, of Montreal, speech in Syracuse, Nov. 1888.

Nobody who has studied the peculiar methods by which elections are won in Canada will deny the fact that five or six million dollars, judiciously expended . . . would secure the return to Parliament of a majority pledged to the annexation of Canada to the United States.

> NEW YORK WORLD , 1890.

I think political union with the States, though becoming our probable, is by no means our ideal, or as yet our inevitable future.

> EDWARD BLAKE, letter to Toronto Globe, Mar. 11, 1891. This remark inspired Grip, Mar. 28, 1891, to publish a cartoon showing Blake as the Sphinx with Sir John A. Macdonald kneeling in front asking, "Speak! Tell us! What do you think is our ideal or inevitable future, then?"

Let the fight come if it must; I don't care whether our sea coast cities are bombarded or not; we would take Canada.

> THEODORE ROOSEVELT, then Police Commissioner, New York City, later U.S. President, letter to Henry Cabot Lodge, Dec. 20, 1895.

The day of annexation to the United States is past. Our future lies elsewhere.

> STEPHEN B. LEACOCK, University mag., Feb. 1907, 140.

'Annexation', so much dreaded and denounced, what is it, I ask once more, but the reunion of two great sections of the English speaking people?

> GOLDWIN SMITH, Reminiscences, 1910, 418.

Enter upon and prosecute from time to time such negotiations with the British Government as he may deem expedient for the annexation of the Dominion of Canada to the United States of America.

> W.S. BENNET, Congressman from N.Y., in a resolution addressed to the President, Feb. 16, 1911.

We answer to a higher destiny.

> SIR WILFRID LAURIER, on annexation, qu., Willison's monthly, 1928, 1.

Do not encourage any enterprise looking to Canada's annexation of the United States. You are one of the most capable governing peoples of the world, but I entreat you, for your own sakes, to think twice before undertaking management of the territory which lies between the Great Lakes and the Rio Grande. No, let us go our own gaits along parallel roads, you helping us and we helping you.

> WARREN G. HARDING, Pres. U.S., speech in Vancouver, July 26, 1923.

If we allow ourselves to be obsessed by the danger of American cultural annexation, so that the thought preys on us day and night, we shall only become a slightly bigger Ulster.

FRANK H. UNDERHILL, *Can. forum*, XXXI, 1951-52, 102.

It is possible for a pessimist in 1962 to say that the press generally may be at least partly responsible for a general easing of public opinion to the point where absorption of Canada into the United States is in the foreseeable future.

ARNOLD EDINBOROUGH, in John A. Irving, ed., *Mass media in Canada*, 1962, 27.

The longest unmanned frontier in the world is an artificial one and I look forward to the day when it will disappear and Canadians will join fully in the American adventure. To say this in Canada is still to invite cat-calls and rotten eggs. We would lose our identity, they say, our independence. But Texas or Maine still have distinctive identities and we are even now economically dependent on the United States.

MORDECAI RICHLER, *Holiday*, Apr. 1964, 47.

What is resented in Canada about annexation to the United States is not annexation itself, but the feeling that Canada would disappear into a larger entity without having anything of any real distinctiveness to contribute to that entity: that, in short, if the United States did annex Canada it would notice nothing except an increase in natural resources.

NORTHROP FRYE, *The bush garden*, 1971, iv.

Answers

There is no center;
the centers
travel with us unseen
like our shadows
on a day when there is no sun.
We must move back:
there are many foregrounds.

MARGARET ATWOOD, "A place: fragments", 1966.

But when the child asks me
Because Why
or
Why Because
I can only say
Go outside and play.

RED LANE, "Margins IV", 1968.

Anxiety

As long as man is capable of anxiety he is capable of passing through it to a genuine human destiny.

NORTHROP FRYE, *The modern century*, 1967, 49.

Apartments

The apartment house, the greatest enemy of childhood ever contrived. The stork flies past it, the baby clutched under its wing, looking for a country cottage.

STEPHEN LEACOCK, "Women's level", 1945.

Apathy

By far the most dangerous foe we have to fight is *apathy* – indifference from whatever cause, not from a lack of knowledge, but from carelessness, from absorption in other pursuits, from a contempt bred of self-satisfaction.

SIR WILLIAM OSLER, address, "Unity, peace and concord", 1905.

Aphorisms

An aphorism should be like a burr: sting, stick, and leave a little soreness afterwards.

IRVING LAYTON, "Aphs", *The whole bloody bird*, 1969, 103.

Appeals

Do not appeal to Ceasar, you will lose
Time, money and liberty, perhaps
   your head;
Appeal to almost anything else instead.

ROY DANIELLS, "Acts 26:32", 1963.

Appearances

The higher the polish the more indurated you will find the substance.

T.C. HALIBURTON, *Sam Slick*, 1840, 210.

The Canadian women, while they retain the bloom and freshness of youth, are exceedingly pretty; but these charms soon fade, owing, perhaps, to the fierce extremes of their climate, or the withering effect of the dry, metallic air of stoves, and their going too early into company and being exposed, while yet children to the noxious influence of late hours, and the sudden change from heated rooms to the cold, bitter, bitter winter blast.

SUSANNA MOODIE, *Roughing it in the bush*, 1852, 221.

You are only what you are when no one is looking.

ROBERT C. (BOB) EDWARDS, Calgary *Eye Opener*, May 11, 1918.

I do not like my appearance anywhere – a little fat round man, no expression of a lofty character, a few glimpses here & there of the happier self.

W.L. MACKENZIE KING, *Diary*, July 22, 1927.

Appearance I both love and distrust and think of as an enchanting mistress, fertile in invention, endlessly playful. But it's Reality I'm wedded to – to Truth. And the truth about ourselves is very uncomplimentary, very unpleasant.

IRVING LAYTON, *The swinging flesh*, Foreword, 1961, ix.

We are all so anxious that people should not think us different.

MARGARET LAURENCE, "The rain child", 1962, in *The tomorrow-tamer*, 108.

Appeasement

What's The Cheering For?

WINNIPEG *FREE PRESS*, editorial on the day the Pact of Munich was signed, Sept. 30, 1938.

Canada's government was more appeasement-prone than England's in the 1930's, and Canadian statesmen as a whole made mid-western Americans look, by comparison, like internationalists.

ROBERT FULFORD, Toronto *Star*, Dec. 3, 1964, 43.

Appetite

Appetite is essentially insatiable, and where it operates as a criterion of both action and enjoyment (that is, everywhere in the Western world since the sixteenth century) it will infallibly discover congenial agencies (mechanical and political) of expression.

MARSHALL MCLUHAN, *Horizon* (London), Oct., 1947, 135.

Apples

The apple harvest time is here,
The tender harvest apple time:
A sheltering calm unknown at prime
Settles upon the brooding year.

BLISS CARMAN, "In apple time", 1888.

Art thou the topmost apple
    The gatherers could reach,
Reddening on the bough?
    Shall I not take thee?

BLISS CARMAN, *Sappho*, 1903.

I remember how the marketwomen of
Paris, wheeling barrows of apples of
doubtful origin, used to cry them as
"Canada! des vraies Canada!"

SAMUEL ELIOT MORISON, *The European
discovery of America*, 1971, 429.

Appreciation

A man should be able to appreciate a
good thing even when it happens to be
his own.

PETER MCARTHUR, *To be taken with salt*,
1903, 149.

April

As memory of pain, all past, is peace,
And joy, dream-tasted, hath the
    deepest cheer,
So art thou sweetest of all months that
    lease
The twelve short spaces of the flying
    year.

ARCHIBALD LAMPMAN, "April", 1884.

Winter's done, and April's in the skies,
Earth, look up with laughter in your
    eyes!

CHARLES G.D. ROBERTS, "An April adoration," 1896.

Lo, now comes the April pageant
And the Easter of the year.
Now the tulip lifts her chalice,
And the hyacinth his spear.

BLISS CARMAN, "On Ponus Ridge", 1909;
("Resurgam").

Once more in misted April
    The world is growing green.
Along the winding river
    The plumey willows lean.

BLISS CARMAN, "An April morning",
1916.

April is no month for burials.
Blood root and trilium break out of
    cover,
And crocuses stir blindly in their cells,
Hawthorns bloom whitely, laburnums
    shudder
Profusion from dim boughs – slight
    daffodils
Defy the pale predominance of colour.
April is rather a month for subtle
    spells.

LEO COX, "Rite of spring", 1933.

April Earth,
a spring bride,
with cherry petal confetti
to congratulate.

CAROL COATES CASSIDY, "Japanese
April", 1939.

Archaeology

I would rather talk about archaeology
to a ten-year-old boy than to an educated man.

WILLIAM J. WINTEMBERG, qu. in Nansi
Swayze, *Canadian portraits, Jenness,
Barbeau, Wintemberg, the man hunt-
ers*, 1960, 155.

Archery

Don't fail string
Shaft fly true
As bird flew
As shaft grew
As clear morning
As spring certain
No time more to sing
The singing was well done before.

> PETER SUCH, *Riverrun*, 1973, 56 (Nono-sabasut's archery song).

Arches

There was an arch of cheeses – an arch of salt – an arch of wheels, an arch of hardware, stoves, and pots and pans – an arch of sofas, chairs, and household furniture – an arch of ladders laden with firemen in their picturesque costumes – an arch of carriages – an arch of boats, a free trade arch, a protectionist arch – an arch of children, and last of all, an arch – no, not an arch, but rather a celestial rainbow – of lovely young ladies.

> LORD DUFFERIN, speech at Brockville, Ont., Sept., 1874, referring to the welcome arches that greeted him on his visits to the fall fairs of rural Ontario.

Architecture

The orders of architecture baffle all description: every one builds his cottage or house according to his fancy, and it is not a difficult thing, in passing through the country, to tell what nation the natives of the houses "hail from", if we are aware of any of the whims and conceits that characterize them.

> JOHN MACTAGGART, *Three years in Canada*, 1829, I, 308.

I believe it will take a thousand years to develop a national style in Canada, but I do see a light in the west over a grain elevator.

> ERIC ARTHUR, in Bertram Brooker, ed., *Yearbook of the arts in Canada: 1928-29*, 112.

O Architect, thrice happy man are
  you,
Who of all men can make his dreams
  come true!

> DONALD A. FRASER, "Realization", 1930.

I think we may properly recognize genuine romantic associations as one of the very real "delights" that architecture can offer us.

> ALAN GOWANS, *Looking at architecture in Canada*, 1958, 33.

International meaningless.

> HAROLD MERRILEES, Manager, Greater Vancouver Visitors and Convention Bureau, on the style of architecture of the new Edmonton Airport, qu. in Vancouver *Sun*, Jan. 29, 1964, 11.

Forget the differences; emphasize the common values all Western peoples hold. Create a great Western architecture and you will create a great Canadian architecture. Cultivate the great traditional values of the West and this historically improbable country will become a great nation.

> ALAN GOWANS, *Building Canada – an architectural history of Canadian life*, 1966, 179.

It is through outward forms that we can most obviously recognize a tradition in architecture; but we understand it only as we know its spirit.

> ALAN GOWANS, *Building Canada – an architectural history of Canadian life*, 1966, 15.

I'm not interested in repeating things. I'd become bored. The real fascination of architecture lies in the subject, in redefining the purpose of a building. If I can't push a building a little further forward than I have, then I'm not interested in doing it.

ARTHUR ERICKSON, qu. in *Time*, Feb. 14, 1972, 21.

Architecture is a backdrop for worthwhile human activity.

RAYMOND MORIYAMA, qu. in *Time*, July 9, 1973, 10.

Archives

Of all national assets, archives are the most precious; they are the gift of one generation to another and the extent of our care of them marks the extent of our civilization.

ARTHUR G. DOUGHTY, *The Canadian Archives and its activities*, 1924, 5.

The archives hold the strata of the
  vanished years
That shaped the minds of men.

M. EUGENIE PERRY, "The archives", 1955.

Arctic

The Land of Little Sticks.

ANON., the tree line between the dwindling northern forest and the tundra, in the Barrens.

This gloomy region, where the year is divided into one day and one night, lies entirely outside the stream of history.

W.W. READE, *Martyrdom of man*, III, 1872.

May you reap the profit of the few miles of land I have taken for Canada.

CAPT. JOSEPH E. BERNIER, address, Canadian Club, Ottawa, Oct. 16, 1909, speaking to Sir Wilfrid Laurier.

This Memorial is erected today to commemorate the taking possession for the Dominion of Canada of the whole Arctic Archipelago lying to the north of America from longitude 60 degrees west to 141 degrees west up to latitude 90 degrees north. Winter Harbour, Melville Island. C.G.S. *Arctic*, July 1st, 1909. J.E. Bernier, Commander.

CAPT. JOSEPH E. BERNIER, *Report*, Ottawa, 1910, 194.

Capt. Joseph Elzear Bernier, Canada's master seaman, who has done everything but bring the North Pole home on deck.

C.H.J. SNIDER, in *Can. hist. rev.*, 1928, 74.

The inaccessible Arctic has disappeared overnight.

H.A. INNIS, in *Can. hist. rev.*, 1935, 200.

The time has arrived when it is possible "to hobo" across the north-west passage and one of these days when cheap excursion rates are provided to the Canadian Arctic perhaps Canadians will become alert to its possibilities.

H.A. INNIS, in *Can. hist. rev.*, 1936, 198.

The whole history of the Canadian North can be divided into two periods — before and after the aeroplane.

H.L. KEENLEYSIDE, in *Can. geog. jour.*, 1949, 167.

Nowadays this country has become as remote as Wall Street. If a Canadian wishes to visit the Canadian Arctic, he has to get permission from Washington.

A.Y. JACKSON, *A painter's country*, 1958, 111.

It is still difficult to impress upon the public and industry at large that the most essential quality of the Arctic is not cold, or gold, or polar bears, but a central position in the world community.

MICHAEL MARSDEN, in R. St. J. Macdonald, ed., *The arctic frontier*, 1966, 26.

The Arctic has problems for life which extend considerably beyond ice, snow and cold water.

M.J. DUNBAR, *Ecological development in polar regions*, 1968, 5.

The arctic expresses the sum total of all wisdom:
Silence. Nothing but silence. The end of time.

WALTER BAUER, "Canada", 1968.

Canada regards herself as responsible to all mankind for the peculiar ecological balance that now exists so precariously in the water, ice and land areas of the Arctic archipelago. We do not doubt for a moment that the rest of the world would find us at fault, and hold us liable, should we fail to ensure adequate protection of that environment from pollution or artificial deterioration. Canada will not permit this to happen.

PIERRE E. TRUDEAU, H. of C., *Debates*, Oct. 24, 1969, 39.

Ardour

If you would know the secret of success with women, it is said in a word – *ardour*.

ARNOLD HAULTAIN, *Hints for lovers*, 1909, 123.

Argument

To bung up a man's eyes ain't the way to enlighten him.

THOMAS C. HALIBURTON, *Sam Slick's wise saws*, 1853, ch. 4.

We are weakest
When we are caught contending with our children!

CHARLES HEAVYSEGE, *Saul*, 1857. pt. 3.

These are good bunkum arguments.

SIR JOHN A. MACDONALD, letter to Sidney Smith, Dec. 6, 1857.

In order to carry on an argument you must descend to the other man's level.

PETER MCARTHUR, *To be taken with salt*, 1903, 151.

From argument men go to deeds if their heart's in what they say.

THOMAS H. RADDALL, "Blind MacNair" in *Tambour*, 1945, 383.

Never give 'em more than one barr'l to start with. But if they are foolish enough to ask for more, then give 'em the other barr'l right between the eyes.

J.W. DAFOE, qu. in, G.V. Ferguson: *John W. Dafoe*, 1948.

There are three sides to every argument. Yours. The other guy's. And the right side.

MORDECAI RICHLER, *Son of a smaller hero*, 1955, 163.

Men and women are supposed to argue, and one of the reasons why they get married is so they won't have to argue with strangers.

H. GORDON GREEN, *Professor go home*, 1967, 131.

We are hard on each other
and call it honesty,
choosing our jagged truths
with care and aiming them across
the neutral table.

> MARGARET ATWOOD, in *Power politics*,
> 1971, 24.

It is by argument and refutation that
philosophy lives.

> F.E. SPARSHOTT, *Looking for philosophy*,
> 1972, 120.

No one is more pitifully foolish than
the person who attempts to prove by
argument that the world is round.

> ALDEN NOWLAN, "Scratchings", 1974.

Aristocracy

We have no aristocracy but of virtue
and talent, which is the only true
aristocracy, and is the old and true
meaning of the term.

> THOMAS D'A. MCGEE, *Confederation de-
> bates*, Feb. 9, 1865, 146.

I believe in the true aristocracy of
energy, learning, ability, and integrity;
an aristocracy whose marks and titles
are found in the earnest efforts of a
man to do his duty and to excel in its
discharge; and whose distinctions are
such as a free people themselves confer by the expression of their confidence, by mandates to the great council of the country, by selection for high
offices of public trust, by the commission to regulate the affairs, to guide
the high destinies of the people among
whom they live. That is the aristocracy
and the only aristocracy which is suited to our day and country.

> EDWARD BLAKE, qu., Ross, *Patriotic reci-
> tations*, 1893, 183.

Armistice Day

Year after year we gather and shout
  commands in the Square,
Wait for the Governor-General, say a
  few words of prayer,
Lay our wreaths in order, mothers and
  big shots first,
In memory of those who have made it
  to the other side of the worst.

> GEORGE JOHNSTON, "Remembrance",
> 1966.

Army

Push on, brave York Volunteers!

> GENERAL ISAAC BROCK, incorrectly but
> frequently ascribed, before he fell at the
> Battle of Queenston Heights, Oct. 13,
> 1812; ref. to Third Regt. of York Militia.

The volunteers are all fine boys and
  full of lots of fun
But it's mighty little pay they get for
  carrying a gun;
The Government has grown so lean
  and the CPR so fat
Our extra pay we did not get —
You can bet your boots on that!

> ANON., song of troops on their way west
> to quell North West rebellion in 1885.

Without drill there can be no discipline; without discipline there can be
no cohesion; without cohesion, no success.

> COL. JAMES MASON, speech in Toronto,
> Dec. 28, 1900.

Stanfield's Unshrinkables.

> ANON., regimental nickname, 193rd
> Nova Scotia Highlanders whose Colonel
> was John Stanfield, M.P., in war of
> 1914-1918.

Recruiting in the province of Quebec has not been as productive as it should, and the primary reason is the attitude of the French Canadian clergy who, from the beginning, have discouraged recruiting under the pretext that France deserves to be punished. You yourself know this clerical mentality.

SIR WILFRID LAURIER, letter to Hon. Phillippe Roy, Paris, June 15, 1916. (Pub. Arch. Can.), (Trans.)

If anybody can do it, the Canadians can.

LORD BYNG, Sept. 25, 1918, on the fighting ability of the Canadian troops; in, Currie Papers: Currie vs. Wilson and Preston, page 1809; (Pub. Arch. Can.)

That development was due to the valour, the endurance and the achievement of the Canadian Army in France and Belgium which inspired our people with an impelling sense of nationhood never before experienced.

SIR ROBERT BORDEN, Letters to Limbo; Mar. 6, 1933, (1971, 6.)

Whenever the Germans found the Canadian Corps coming into the line, they prepared for the worst.

DAVID LLOYD-GEORGE, War memoirs, Vol. VI, 1936, 3367.

The violent, obedient ones
Guarding my family with guns.

GEORGE JOHNSTON, "War on the periphery", 1951.

Canada is an unmilitary community. Warlike her people have often been forced to be; military they have never been.

C.P. STACEY, Official history of the Canadian Army in the Second World War, Vol. 1, 1955, 3.

Army Command

No Canadian, American or other 'national' commander, unless possessing quite phenomenal qualities, is ever rated quite as high as an equivalent Britisher. It also means that, to a British Army Commander, such as Leese, the Canadian cohesiveness created by the existence of a Canadian higher formation, such as a Corps, is a distinctly troublesome factor.

GEN. H.D.G. CRERAR, Memorandum, General Officer Commanding-in-Chief First Canadian Army, July 2, 1944, Crerar files, Vol. 1.

Art

'The Discobolus is put here because he
    is vulgar,
He has neither vest nor pants with
    which to cover his limbs;
I, Sir, am a person of most respectable
    connections –
My brother-in-law is haberdasher to
    Mr. Spurgeon'.
O God! O Montreal!

SAMUEL BUTLER, "A psalm of Montreal", 1875, written after a visit to the Montreal Museum of Natural History where he found a plaster cast of the Discobolus hidden in a store-room.

Stowed away in Montreal lumber
    room
The Discobolus standeth and turneth
    his face to the wall,
Dusty, cobweb-covered, maimed and
    set at naught,
Beauty cryeth in an attic and no man
    regardeth:
O God! O Montreal!

SAMUEL BUTLER, "A psalm of Montreal", 1875.

The Canadians are beginning life afresh: I would that they could begin art afresh also.

J.E. HODGSON, British artist, when Canadian govt. invited him to comment on a Canadian art exhibition, London, Eng. 1886; qu. in J.B. McLeish, *September gale*, 1955, 39.

Half of art is knowing when to stop.

J.A. RADFORD, *Can. mag.*, Dec., 1893.

New Art, New Movements, and New
   Schools,
All maimed and blind and halt!
And all the fads of the New Fools
Who cannot earn their salt.

BLISS CARMAN, "Spring feeling", 1895.

Said Life to Art — "I love thee best
Not when I find in thee
My very face and form, expressed
With dull fidelity,

But when in thee my craving eyes
Behold continually
The mystery of my memories
And all I long to be.

CHARLES G.D. ROBERTS, "Life and art", 1901.

Art generalizes while science itemizes.

PETER MCARTHUR, *To be taken with salt*, 1903, 151.

Deadness is the first condition for art: the second is absence of soul, in the human and sentimental sense. With the statue its lines and masses are its soul, no restless inflammable ego is imagined for its interior: it has *no inside*: good art must have no inside: that is capital.

WYNDHAM LEWIS, *Tarr*, 1918, (1951, 328).

The truest art, that which necessity creates that beauty may live, civilization destroys.

ARTHUR LISMER, in *Can. bookman*, Oct., 1925, 160.

Our condition will not improve until we have been thoroughly shocked by the appearance in our midst of a work of art that is at once successful and obscene.

A.J.M. SMITH, *Can. forum*, Apr., 1928, 601.

To return to the term "Creative Art". This is the definition a child once gave it: "I think and then I draw a line round my think". Children grasp these things more quickly than we do. They are more creative than grown-ups. It has not been knocked out of them.

EMILY CARR, address, Women's Canadian Club, Victoria, Mar. 4, 1930.

A work of art
is a consistency
among incommensurables,
or it is that
which remains equal
to itself.

W.W. EUSTACE ROSS, "Art", 1930.

Tonight I give lecture to Art Students' League. I want a picture of a horse to show that animal is beautiful because every part made for function, without ornament. In Paris I would show woman, but in Toronto I show a horse.

ANON., French artist, qu. *Open house*, 1931, 93.

Great art consists of going beyond reality and not in evading it. One must be able to say, "That is how it is — and something more." Art lies in that "more".

HECTOR DE SAINT-DENYS-GARNEAU, *Journal*, Apr. 15, 1935, 1954 (Trans.)

But how shall I hear old music? This is
   an hour
Of new beginnings, concepts warring
   for power,

Decay of systems – the tissue of art is
   torn
With overtures of an era being born.

   F.R. SCOTT, "Overture", 1936.

Religion and art are almost the same
thing anyway. Just different ways of
taking a man out of himself, bringing
him to the emotional pitch that we call
ecstasy or rapture. They're both a
rejection of the material, common-
sense world for one that's illusory, yet
somehow more important. Now it's
always when a man turns away from
this common-sense world around him
that he begins to create, when he looks
into a void, and has to give it life and
form.

   SINCLAIR ROSS, *As for me and my house*,
   1941, 199.

A great art is fostered by artists and
audiences possessing in common a passionate and peculiar interest in the
kind of life that exists in the country
where they live.

   E.K. BROWN, *On Canadian poetry*, rev.
   ed., 1944, 17.

Art is the common denominator of
union between men more than race,
creed, history or personality. Art binds
us together more than any other
human activity in life.

   ARTHUR LISMER, qu. by Lawren Harris in
   Arthur Lismer: paintings 1913-1949,
   1950, 28.

While patterns are the main resource
of the painter and his primary object is
to stir us by their rhythmic elabora-
tion, this is by no means the whole
story; representation, his auxiliary or
supplementary resource, enables him
to accomplish this object much more

effectively and with greater precision
and sureness.

   REID MACCALLUM, *Imitation and design
   and other essays*, 1953, 33.

In acceptance of likeness we may on
the whole discern something like humility, a readiness to accept and abide
by the limitations of created nature,
both in ourselves and in objects. Its
rejection may very well manifest an
arrogant pretension to transcend these
limitations.

   REID MACCALLUM, *Imitation and design
   and other essays*, 1953, 53.

There is no manifesto here for the
times. There is no jury but time.

   J.W.G. MACDONALD, in *Painters Eleven*,
   catalogue of exhibition, Toronto, Feb.
   12, 1954, qu. in W. Withrow, *Contemporary Canadian painting*, 1972, 10.

Good art is the record of a good
   society,
A society without art has proved itself
   corrupt by absolute demonstration.
We must look to our ethics.

   LOUIS DUDEK, *Europe*, Poem 77, 1954.

Let us enjoy the emergence and the
promise of art in our land, arising
from the contemplation of our environment and of our people, and from
the wonder of living in Canada.

   ARTHUR LISMER, radio address, Feb. 22,
   1954.

Art is not something for ourselves to
hoard like a possession; it's a force
within a man; since we must have
books, let books be for knowledge, but
nature for experience.

   ARTHUR LISMER, qu. in John A.B. McLeish, *September gale*, 1955, 195.

The frontier view of the arts still prevails; they are regarded as light recreation, a brief diversion, a stimulus comparable to half a bottle of whiskey.

ROY DANIELLS, in J. Park, ed., *The culture of contemporary Canada*, 1957, 2.

For many years we had a country with little or no art, now it seems we are to have art without a country.

A.Y. JACKSON, *A painter's country*, 1958, 160, referring to modern Canadian non-objective art.

No word meaning "art" occurs in Aivilik, nor does "artist": there are only people. Nor is any distinction made between utilitarian and decorative objects.

EDMUND CARPENTER, *Eskimo*, 1959, ("Art").

Art to the Aivilik is an act, not an object; a ritual, not a possession.

EDMUND CARPENTER, *Eskimo*, 1959, ("Art").

Art lies in understanding some part of the dark forces and bringing them under the direction of reason.

ROBERTSON DAVIES, *A voice from the attic*, 1960, 111.

The Conference was a great success. Every meal was over-subscribed!

ANON., re Canadian Conference of the Arts, O'Keefe Centre, Toronto, May, 1961; qu. in *Can. lit.*, No. 9, 34.

Art, on the other hand, begins with the world we construct, not with the world we see. It starts with the imagination, and then works towards ordinary experience: that is, it tries to make itself as convincing and recognizable as it can.

NORTHROP FRYE, *The educated imagination* (1962) 1964, 22.

We accept political coercion, economic domination, Coca-Cola and predigested mass communication, while we resist exposure to the more humane and civilized arts from the U.S.A.

ARTHUR MCKAY, *Can. art*, Sept./Oct., 1964, 280.

For the first time in human history we have enough power, energy, and ability to program the entire human environment as a work of art.

MARSHALL MCLUHAN, *The structurist*, No. 6, 1966, 65.

The real basis for the opposition of artist and society is the fact that not merely communications media and public relations, but the whole structure of society itself, is an anti-art, an old and wornout creation that needs to be created anew.

NORTHROP FRYE, *The modern century*, 1967, 86.

Do not reach to touch it
nor labour to hear.
Return to your hand
the sense of the hand;
return to your ear
the sense of the ear.

P.K. PAGE, "Cry Ararat", 1967.

Man in Canadian art is rarely in command of his environment or even at home in it.

ELIZABETH KILBOURN, in *Tamarack rev.* No. 46, 1968, 125.

Ottawa doesn't know its arts from a hole in the ground.

ANON., qu. in *Can. ann. rev.*, 1968, 445.

The real basis and urge of the arts is divine discontent.

LAWREN HARRIS, qu. in Bess Harris, ed., *Lawren Harris*, 1969, 118.

the link between
the buried will and the upper
world of sun

> MARGARET ATWOOD, "For archeologists",
> 1970.

There are two kinds of art. Man art
and woman art. They are two different kinds of people, so the art comes
out differently.

> JOYCE WIELAND, qu. by Sandra Gwyn in
> Canada. Roy. Comm. on the Status of
> Women, *Studies*, "Women in the arts in
> Canada", 1971, 25.

Once objects are saved solely as Art,
you may be sure that for all practical
purposes they are dead, and you may
suspect that the civilization collecting
them for only that reason has begun to
die too.

> ALAN GOWANS, *The unchanging arts*,
> 1971, 31.

I think of Canada as female. All the
art I've been doing or will be doing is
about Canada.

> JOYCE WIELAND, interviewed in *Take
> one* (Montreal), Feb. 7, 1972, 24.

The simpler art is — the richer it is.

> JAMES REANEY, qu. in *Can. forum*, June
> 1972, 42.

Art should always be a mystery. It isn't
possible to totally explain any work of
art, anyways, since it is this mysterious
quality which makes art so beautiful.

> JOHN MEREDITH, qu. in W. Withrow,
> *Contemporary Canadian painting*,
> 1972, 146.

The middle class builds itself certain
cultural instruments with the money
of everyone and is using them for its
own profit and enjoyment. But some
of the shareholders have no access to
the benefits. Our aim is to democratize
the arts.

> GERARD PELLETIER, on his appointment
> as Secretary of State, 1968; qu. in *Ma-
> clean's* Dec. 1972, 84.

[Art is] that area of an artist's aspiration in which he fails.

> HAROLD TOWN, Toronto artist, qu. in
> *Maclean's*, Jan. 1975, BC 7.

Art is what people who are interested
in art refer to as art.

> ABRAHAM ROGATNICK, Director, Van-
> couver Art Gallery, qu. in *Maclean's*,
> Jan. 1975, BC 7.

Art is museums. Art is curators. Art is
committees. Art is product. Art is
wheeling and dealing. Art is manipulation. Art is status. Art is hierarchy.
Art is social climbing. Art is not done
by artists. Art is not thought. Art is not
personal expression. Art has nothing to
do with a person in silent communion
with his/her soul, psyche, need, wish,
dream, desire, hope, and all good
things.

> ALVIN BALKIND, Curator of contempo-
> rary art, U.B.C., qu. in *Maclean's*, Jan.
> 1975, BC 7.

Artists

Has Canada no poet to describe the
glories of his parent land — no painter
that can delineate her matchless scenery of land and wave? Are her children dumb and blind, that they leave
to strangers the task of singing her
praise?

> SUSANNA MOODIE, *Mark Hurdlestone*,
> 1853, Intro.

An artist has more than two eyes,
that's a fact.

> T.C. HALIBURTON, *Sam Slick's wise saws*,
> 1853, II, 18.

If the artist were ungodly,
Prurient of mind and heart,
I must think they argue oddly
Who make shrines before his art.

> BLISS CARMAN, "To Raphael", 1896.

If our artists and writers but realized the truth the triumphs of science have given them more glorious symbols. Art is the only enduring expression of science.

PETER MCARTHUR, *To be taken with salt*, 1903, 154.

If he asks for bread, he is offered a tombstone. I always suspect an artist who is successful before he is dead.

JOHN MURRAY GIBBON, *Pagan love*, 1922.

They squeeze and little themselves hoping to please or sell. I tell you it is better to be a street-sweeper or a char or a boarding-house keeper than lower your standard. These may spoil your temper but they need not dwarf your soul.

EMILY CARR, an address Mar. 4, 1930 to Victoria, B.C. Women's Canadian Club. (Separately pub. 1955).

In art one must judge a man by his best, never by his worst; by his highest reach, not by his lowest fall.

STEPHEN LEACOCK, *Charles Dickens*, 1934, 172.

What do they care for your books, will
    they ever read a chapter through or
    a verse without yawning,
Do you ever think they will stand
    before your painting and enjoy it
Without something lewd to suggest to
    the mind, or something they do not
    understand to be laughed at,
What do they care how you eat your
    heart out, how you kill yourself
    slowly or quickly, how you go mad.

RAYMOND SOUSTER, "The enemies", 1944.

If the world were not fundamentally God's world, it could not grow artists. The chaos could not blossom into poets for its final flowers.

JOHN MACNAUGHTON, *Essays*, 1946.

The artist is an agitator, a disturber of the peace – quick, impatient, positive, restless and disquieting. He is the creative spirit of life working in the soul of man.

NORMAN H. BETHUNE, qu. in Allan and Gordon, *The scalpel, the sword*, 1952, 157.

The function of the artist is to disturb. His duty is to arouse the sleepers, to shake the complacent pillars of the world. He reminds the world of its dark ancestry, shows the world its present and points the way to its new birth.

NORMAN H. BETHUNE, qu. in Allan and Gordon, *The scalpel, the sword*, 1952, 156.

There are only three sources of acquiring knowledge – nature, science, illumination – the artist skips the middle one.

ARTHUR LISMER, qu. in John A.B. McLeish, *September gale*, 1955, 195.

Time uses the man of action, but the artist uses time.

ROBERT WEAVER, in *Tamarack rev.* No. 4, 1957, 35.

My knowledge of my limitations is one of my chief defects as an artist.

ROBERTSON DAVIES, *A Masque of Mr. Punch*, 1963, Introd. xi.

What must concern the artist today, above all, is the organized nature of twentieth-century wickedness.

IRVING LAYTON, *Balls for a one-armed juggler*, 1963, xx.

I promise to run, not walk, to the nearest exit only when Italian artists, French artists, and the rest are told by their fellow countrymen that they must leave their native lands to develop themselves. Canada is immense and unknown; a hundred lifetimes would not be enough to bring me near to the bone of it.

HAROLD TOWN, *Enigmas*, 1964, [9].

It is true too that the artist must sleep, which is perhaps the main difference between him and God.

MALCOLM LOWRY, *Dark as the grave wherein my friend is laid*, 1968, 154.

For the craftsman, how is what. For the mystic, what is how. For the artist what and how are one.

WILLIAM MCELCHERAN, qu. in *Artscanada* Apr.–May, 1971, 71.

Québec libre, hell! Québec broke! Without my Ontario market I couldn't survive.

ANON., French-Canadian artist, qu. by William Withrow in *Contemporary Canadian painting*, 1972, 15.

Artists are great survivors.

WILLIAM WITHROW, *Contemporary Canadian painting*, 1972, 15.

Aspiration

So to address our spirits to the height,
And so attune them to the valiant
  whole,
That the great light be clearer for our
  light,
And the great soul the stronger for our
  soul.

ARCHIBALD LAMPMAN, "The largest life", *Atlantic monthly*, Mar., 1899.

Assassination

Never yet did the assassin's knife reach the core of a cause or the heart of a principle.

THOMAS D'ARCY MCGEE, speech in Montreal, on the death of Lincoln, 1865.

In Pierre Elliott Trudeau, Canada has at last produced a political leader worthy of assassination.

IRVING LAYTON, "Obs II", *The whole bloody bird*, 1969, 55.

Assault

In a moment the pirates were all around us, rolling their eyes, gnashing their teeth, and filing their nails.

STEPHEN B. LEACOCK, "Soaked in seaweed", 1911.

Associations

When men are prevented from discussing political matters openly, and seeking in a fair and legitimate manner the redress of what they regard as grievances, they will naturally resort to secret conclaves, and plots and conspiracies, and seek strength and redress in organizations which the law knows only to condemn.

TORONTO *GLOBE*, June 22, 1871.

Man is a social, gregarious, and clubable animal and there is no doubt that the present is eminently an era of associations.

SIR RICHARD CARTWRIGHT, speech at Seaforth, Ont., Oct. 27, 1886.

Women form, perhaps, where men are concerned, the single exception to the rule that in union there is strength. One woman often enough is irresistible; two (be the second her own mother) break the charm; an association of women is the feeblest of forces.

ARNOLD HAULTAIN, *Hints for lovers*, 1909, 41.

Any association, organization, society or corporation, whose professed purpose or one of whose purposes is to bring about any governmental, industrial or economic change within Canada by the use of force, violence or physical injury, to person or property, or by threats of such injury, or which teaches, advocates, advises, or defends the use of force, violence or terrorism or physical injury to person or property, in order to accomplish such change, shall be an unlawful association.

CANADA, *Criminal code*, section 98, in force 1919-1936.

Astrology

It is always possible to discover *something* lucky about everything; astrology is the Pollyanna of the occult sciences.

ROBERTSON DAVIES, *Samuel Marchbanks' almanack*, 1967, 143.

Atheism

How far devotion to the interests of the race and heroic or philanthropic action will be affected by the departure of theistic belief will be seen when the kingdom of atheism or agnosticism has fully come.

GOLDWIN SMITH, "Morality and theism" in *Guesses at the riddle of existence*, 1897, 242.

Atlantic Ocean

The Union of the Provinces restores us to the ocean, takes us back to the Atlantic, and launches us once more on the modern Mediterranean, the true central sea of the western world.

THOMAS D'A. MCGEE, speech at Cookshire, Que., Dec. 22, 1864.

Atomic Bombs

If you were near the explosion without adequate protection, you would be seriously affected by the immediate radiation in addition to being killed or injured by the blast or fire.

CANADA. EMERGENCY MEASURES ORGANIZATION, *Eleven steps to survival*, 1961, 8.

And there was silence till God spoke.
Two billion years
Before his monstrous mouth
Pronounced its sharp, atomic NO.

F.R. SCOTT, "Span", 1969.

Atomic Energy

If it were ever found possible to control at will the rate of disintegration of the radioelements, an enormous amount of energy could be obtained from a small quantity of matter.

ERNEST RUTHERFORD, Professor of physics, McGill University, *Radioactivity*, 1904, 338.

Okay, let's go.

C.D. HOWE, in 1942 re initiating Canada's nuclear program, qu. by C.J. Mackenzie in *Globe mag.*, Oct. 28, 1961, 19.

Atomic Missiles

Should the system begin to fire it will mean our efforts to preserve the peace and the safety of the world have failed.

PIERRE E. TRUDEAU, H. of C., *Debates*, Mar. 19, 1969, 6853.

Attack

Sometimes the best method of defending one's self is to attack, and in that case Canadian soldiers might be sent to Spain, and it is quite certain that they might legally be so despatched to the Iberian Peninsula.

SIR WILFRID LAURIER, interview, qu., in Toronto *Globe*, Oct. 4, 1899.

Attainment

We come indeed from Hell and climb to Heaven; the Golden Age stands at the never attainable end of history, not at man's origins. Every step forward is bound to be a compromise; right and wrong are inescapably mixed; the best we can hope for is to make right prevail more and more; to reduce wrong to a smaller and smaller fraction of the whole till it reaches the vanishing point. Europe regards the past; America the future. America is an ideal and as such has to be striven for; it has to be realized in partial victories.

FREDERICK PHILIP GROVE, *A search for America*, 1927, 436.

Attraction

Then and now and always, wide away
    and the length of a span,
I gather that I must gather, by
    impulse, election:
In me only is attraction,
It alone can attract me,
So am I myself, and none other,
Myself − a mystery! a mouthpiece!

GRACE BLACKBURN, "Chant of the women", 1926.

Audacity

Audacity is beloved of women; but it must be an audacity born of Sincerity and educated by Discretion.

ARNOLD HAULTAIN, *Hints for lovers*, 1909, 138.

Audacity is missing in Canada.

ROBERT FULFORD, London *Times*, Supp. on Canada, Nov. 30, 1959, xx.

But I say to you, they do not know
    where to look, and have not the eyes
    to see.
For audacity is all around us,
Boldness sits in the highest places,
We are riddled with insolence.

F.R. SCOTT, "Audacity", 1964.

Audiences

The lack of an audience? But even the lack of an audience is not the important thing. The important thing is that *you* have such an audience *in mind* when you speak. Whether it is really there does not matter. In case of need you can imagine it.

FREDERICK PHILIP GROVE, *In search of myself*, 1946, Prologue, 10.

Audio Visuals

We are back in acoustic space. We begin again to structure the primordial feelings and emotions from which 3000 years of literacy divorced us.

MARSHALL MCLUHAN, *Counterblast*, 1954.

Auditor General

Why give him more money to hire more people to find more mistakes?

CHARLES DRURY, President of the Treasury Board, Dec., 1969, re the Auditor General, qu. in *Maclean's*, July 1973, 63.

If parliament wants to condone his breaking the law and not do anything about it, that is fine − but the government is not stepping into this matter.

PIERRE E. TRUDEAU, H. of C. *Debates*, Mar. 8, 1972, 635.

The history of my 13 years in office has been the history of the buck that never stopped.

> MAXWELL HENDERSON, retired Auditor General of Canada, in *Maclean's*, July 1973, 26.

August

Fair the land lies, full of August,
  Meadow island, shingly bar,
Open barns and breezy twilight,
  Peace, and the mild evening star.

> BLISS CARMAN, "The ships of St. John", in *Can. mag.*, Dec. 1893, 148.

Now the goldenrod invades
Every clearing in the hills;
The dry glow of August fades,
And the lonely cricket shrills.

> BLISS CARMAN, "At the yellow of the leaf", 1903.

Authority

Wherever there is authority, there is a natural inclination to disobedience.

> T.C. HALIBURTON, *Sam Slick's wise saws*, 1853, I, 186.

For Canadians the principle of authority has been established prior to the principle of liberty.

> WILLIAM KILBOURN, *The elements combined*, 1960, 82.

We are afraid of authority; we live in a climate of magic, where under penalty of death we must infringe no taboo, we must respect all the formulae, all the conformisms.

> JEAN-PAUL DESBIENS, (Frère Untel), *Impertinences of Brother Anonymous*, 1962, 58.

The oldest problem of political philosophy, although it is not the only one, is to justify authority without destroying the independence of human beings in the process.

> PIERRE E. TRUDEAU, *Federalism and the French Canadians* 1968, xxii.

Authors

Some authors write for fame, some for money, some to propagate particular doctrines and opinions, some from spite, some at the instigation of their friends, and not a few at the instigation of the devil.

> WILLIAM DUNLOP, *Statistical sketches*, 1832, 1.

Compiler, rhymer, author, advocate,
Writer of disquisitions on the State.
Analyst, sketcher, and what not,
  besides
Accoucher-general to the labouring
  scribes.

> ALEXANDER C. STEWART, *The poetical review*, 1896, 8.

Get over the border as soon as you can; come to London or go to New York; shake the dust of Canada from your feet. Get out of a land that is willing to pay money for whiskey, but wants its literature free in the shape of Ayer's Almanac.

> ROBERT BARR, *Can. mag.*, Nov. 1899, 6.

Only a maker of books can appreciate the labours of others at their true value.

> SIR WILLIAM OSLER, address, "Books and men", 1901.

Fame, from a literary point of view, consists in having people know you have written a lot of stuff they haven't read.

> ROBERT C. (BOB) EDWARDS, *Summer annual*, 1920, 57.

O Canada, O Canada, Oh can
A day go by without new authors
   springing
To paint the native purple, and to plan
More ways to set the selfsame welkin
   ringing?

> F.R. SCOTT, "The Canadian Authors
> meet", *Can. forum*, Dec., 1935.

I have lived *for* poetry, but I have
lived *by* prose.

> CHARLES G.D. ROBERTS, d. 1943, favourite
> remark in his later years.

A great poet or author is a greater
resource to his country in time of war
than a battleship.

> ROBERT J.C. STEAD, in *Can. author*, Mar.,
> 1943, 6.

All the characters in this book are
fictitious, including the author.

> PAUL HIEBERT, Sarah Binks, 1947.

There is no Canadian writer of whom
we can say what we can say of the
world's major writers, that their readers can grow up inside their work
without ever being aware of a circumference.

> NORTHROP FRYE, in Carl F. Klinck, ed.
> *Literary history of Canada*, 1965, 821.

Canada has produced no author who is
a classic in the sense of possessing a
vision greater in kind than that of his
best readers.

> NORTHROP FRYE, in Carl F. Klinck, ed.,
> *Literary history of Canada*, 1965, 821.

Susanna Moodie has finally turned
herself inside out, and has become the
spirit of the land she once hated.

> MARGARET ATWOOD, *Journals of Susan-
> na Moodie*, 1970, 64.

Autobiography

Set even a realist to write autobiography and he instantly becomes an idealist.

> PETER MCARTHUR, d. 1924, qu. in *The
> best of Peter McArthur*, 1967, 254.

Though names I change from time to
   time
A stickler for correctness I'm.
To write God-honest truth I strive,
And here, to best of memory, I've.

> ROBERT SERVICE, *Ploughman of the
> moon* (autobiography) 1945, viii.

Automation

The dominating trend on our continent towards automation and conformism means that our lives are being
taken away from us. We are becoming
fossils in a land of plenty which is also
a moral vacuum.

> JEAN-C. FALARDEAU, *Roots and values in
> Canadian lives*, 1961, 14.

Persons grouped around a fire or can-
dle for warmth or light are less able to
pursue independent thoughts, or even
tasks, than people supplied with electric light. In the same way, the social
and educational patterns latent in automation are those of self-employment
and artistic autonomy.

> MARSHALL MCLUHAN, *Understanding
> media*, 1964, 359.

Automobiles

An automobile of the latest design
   Its use I will never disparage.
But for comfort and pleasure pray
    give me for mine
A McLaughlin reliable carriage.

> ROBERT MCLAUGHLIN, advertisement for
> McLaughlin Carriage Co., Oshawa,
> 1905, attributed.

When I think of the motor-car silent
and swift,
In the dark sky of transport, so long
overcast,
I see in my vision a limitless rift
That heralds the dawn of the best
things at last,
There is comfort and speed in the
automobile
That none can deny, and no one
gainsay;
Then I know that with me you will
readily feel
How thankful I am that I'm living
today.

PERCY H. PUNSHON, "The transition of
transportation", 1911.

Whiskey Sixes.

ANON., term applied to McLaughlin Six
Specials by the rum running fraternity
in Alberta, about 1920.

The man whose hands were on the
wheel
Could trace his kinship through her
steel,
Between his body warped and bent
In every bone and ligament,
And this "eight-cylinder"
stream-lined,
The finest model yet designed.

E.J. PRATT, "The man and the machine",
1932.

The trouble is that too often there is
forty horsepower under the bonnet
and one asspower at the wheel.

JOHN MACNAUGHTON, to D.D. Calvin,
qu., Queen's quart., 1933, 359.

The modern car is part of the Canadian way of life, with Canadians convinced that owning a motor vehicle is
a basic right.

CANADIAN AUTOMOBILE ASSOCIATION,
brief to the Federal Government, March
1954; qu. Maclean's Apr. 15, 1954, 6.

Once surrounded by his metal-and-
glass turret, every man became equal
to every other man, just as every
metal-and-glass turret, despite the efforts of their advertisers to the contrary, was approximately equal in
value and in efficiency to every other
metal-and-glass turret.

A.R.M. LOWER, Canadians in the making,
1958, 425.

I wasn't driving too fast, I was flying
too low.

PHILLIP A. GAGLARDI, B.C. Minister of
Highways, 1955-1968, paraphrase of remark to patrol officer when stopped for
speeding, qu. in P. Sherman, Bennett,
1966, 174.

The boys sport leather jackets and
levis,
but that's their underwear,
the car is their real clothing.

ALDEN NOWLAN, "Saturday night", 1961.

Women drive like men but get blamed
for it.

MRS. ETHEL MCLELLAN, Canadian Good
Roads Assoc. Convention, Quebec City,
Oct. 1-5, 1962, qu. in Liberty, "Cross
Canada", Dec., 1962.

Red Orange Green Arrows Side Streets
No Parking
A car with a headache, it looks like a
shark,
Glittering, really rather beautiful;
demonic engine
Humming to the children and the old
ladies − come here,
Under my wheels and I'll toss you.
Glittering
Hard merciless cars.

JAMES REANEY, "A message to Winnipeg" 1962.

Conservative prices, sociable credit,
liberal trade-ins with NDP (no down
payment).

ANON., car dealer's sign, Vancouver, qu.
in Liberty, Sept. 1962.

Desire nothing in this world but time to do your work, love, kisses, serious talk, laughter, great works of art, and a white Jaguar so you can get to these things more quickly.

JACK LUDWIG, *Confusions*, 1963, 275.

It's an unwritten rule that the biggest car maker (GM) sets the pace. We're not big enough to get into a price cutting tangle with them.

RON TODGHAM, Pres., Chrysler Canada, Interview, qu. in Toronto *Telegram*, Feb. 13, 1965, 16.

I turned the speedometer back to 5000
   miles changed the oil
polished the headlights to look at
   death
adjusted the rear-view mirror to look
   at life
gave it back its ownership card
and went away
puzzled by things

ALFRED PURDY, "My '48 Pontiac", 1968.

What's the average man's life but a succession of automobiles? When he dies, we should carve on his tombstone simply the makes and years.

RICHARD J. NEEDHAM, *A friend in Need-ham*, 1969, 8.

The cars are lined up, edging slowly
on the north lanes, the windshields
glitter, it is the city moving,
the drivers intent on getting out,
   getting
away from something
they carry always with them.

MARGARET ATWOOD, "The end of the world — weekend, near Toronto", 1970.

The automobile's appetite for roads and highways is gargantuan, and they have replaced rivers and railway tracks as the physical arbiters of our environment. It is said that each year a million acres of land in North America is covered with concrete or asphalt — mostly for new highways or parking lots.

ALAN EDMONDS, *Maclean's*, Sept., 1970, 8.

There will always be black limousines; it is only the people in the black limousines who change.

LIONEL TIGER AND ROBIN FOX, *The imperial animal*, 1971, 1.

Autonomy

We are not defending the autonomy of the provinces simply because it is a question of a principle, but rather because autonomy is to us the basic condition, not of our survival which is assumed from now on, but of our assertion as a people.

JEAN LESAGE, Federal-Provincial Conference, Ottawa, Nov. 26-29, 1963, "Opening statement by the Prime Minister of Quebec".

Canada had become an autonomous Dominion during the First World War; she reverted to the position of a dependent colony during the Second.

DONALD CREIGHTON, *Canada's first century*, 1970, 245.

Autumn

Autumn, like an old poet in a haze
Of golden visions, dreams away his
   days.

CHARLES SANGSTER, "The happy harvesters", 1860.

In this shrill moon the scouts of Winter
ran
From the ice-belted north, and
whistling shafts
Struck maple and struck sumach, and
a blaze
Ran swift from leaf to leaf, from
bough to bough,
Till round the forest flashed a belt of
flame.

ISABELLA VALANCY CRAWFORD, "Malcolm's Katie", 1884.

The cornfields all are brown, and
brown the meadows
With the blown leaves' wind-heaped
traceries,
And the brown thistle stems that cast
no shadows,
And bear no bloom for bees.

ARCHIBALD LAMPMAN, "In October",
1888.

Miles and miles of crimson glories,
Autumn's wondrous fires ablaze;
Miles of shoreland red and golden,
Drifting into dream and haze.

WILFRED CAMPBELL, "Lake Huron",
1889.

Along the line of smoky hills
The crimson forest stands,
And all the day the blue-jay calls
Throughout the autumn lands.

WILLIAM W. CAMPBELL, "Indian summer", 1889.

For weeks and weeks the autumn
world stood still,
Clothed in the shadow of a smoky
haze;
The fields were dead, the wind had
lost its will,
And all the lands were hushed by
wood and hill,
In those grey, withered days.

WILFRED CAMPBELL, "How one winter
came in the lake region," 1893.

Thus without grief the golden days go
by,
So soft we scarcely notice how they
wend,
And like a smile half-happy, or a sigh,
The summer passes to her quiet end.

ARCHIBALD LAMPMAN, "September",
Harper's mag., Sept., 1893.

There is something in the autumn
that is native to my blood –
Touch of manner, hint of mood;
And my heart is like a rhyme,
With the yellow and the purple and
the crimson keeping time.

BLISS CARMAN, "Vagabond song", 1894.

Clothed in splendour, beautifully sad
and silent,
Comes the autumn over the woods and
highlands,
Golden, rose-red, full of divine
remembrance
Full of foreboding.

ARCHIBALD LAMPMAN, "Sapphics", 1899.

The hound of the autumn wind is
slow,
He loves to bask in the heat and sleep.

PETER MCARTHUR, "An Indian wind
song", 1907.

Slowly the days grow colder, the long
nights fall;
Plows turn the stubble, fires are
tended, and apples
Mellow in cellars; and under the roots
of maples
Mice are burrowing. And the high
geese call.

CHARLES BRUCE, "Fall grass", 1951.

Autumn: the leaves? Of course they
fall.
The wind? The same dirge as last year.
In broad daylight the mist surrounds
Grips you like a friend's displeasure.

IRVING LAYTON, "The buffaloes", 1955.

Sumachs bleed early.

The gray corpse of winter
will lie long in this valley.

> RAYMOND SOUSTER, "Sumachs bleed
> early", 1961.

Autumn is the bite of a harvest apple.

> CHRISTINA PETROWSKY, "Autumn", 1967.

Aviation

The Silver Dart.

> ANON., name of first aeroplane to fly,
> Feb. 24, 1909, Baddeck, N.S. Owner-
> pilot was John A.D. McCurdy.

But give me the air! Always the air!
  The clean ways, and wings, wings,

To reach beyond accepted things,
And venture flights unendable!

> TOM MACINNES, "Aspiration", 1918.

Bush pilot.

> ANON., term popular in the 1920's for the
> men who flew transport airplanes into
> the North-West Territories.

Awakening

The cock was awake.
He was like
A brilliant cloud from which
His morning-crow came like a flash.

> WALTER BAUER, "Fragment of the cock-
> crow", 1968.

B

Babies

The Stork Derby.

> ANON., the competition in human fecundity resulting from the terms of the will of Charles Vance Millar, died Oct. 31, 1926, who bequeathed $500,000 to the Toronto woman who bore the most children during 10 years after his death. The claims of four women, each with nine children, were accepted, and two others received settlements.

Baby bonus.

> ANON., phrase invented by the Toronto *Telegram*, Jan. 29, 1944, qu. in Elisabeth Wallace, *The changing Canadian state* (thesis, Columbia Univ.) 1950, 309.

Babies for Export.

> HAROLD DINGMAN, title of article published in *New liberty*, Dec. 27, 1947 ref. to alleged black market in Alberta babies.

We all want to increase the population of this country and for that purpose if they are equally good people I don't believe that any immigrant, no matter where he comes from or how good he is, is as good as another Canadian baby, because the immigrant has to learn to be a Canadian and the baby is a Canadian to start with.

> J.W. PICKERSGILL, speech at Victoria, Apr. 12, 1955.

Diaper backward spells repaid. Think about it.

> MARSHALL MCLUHAN, at American Booksellers Assoc. luncheon, Washington D.C., June 1969, qu. in Vancouver *Sun*, June 7, 1969, 31.

Baldness

The old boy's head, for all his barber's care,
Shines daily more and more.
The only thing to stop his falling hair
Appears to be the floor.

> GEOFFREY B. RIDDEHOUGH, "Epigram at the end of fall", 1972.

Baldwin, Robert

The man of one idea.

> ROBERT BALDWIN, a scornful taunt used by opponents, about 1840, on his fight for Responsible Government.

I consider him of more importance to the connexion than three regiments.

> LORD ELGIN, on Robert Baldwin's loyalty to Britain, letter to Lord Grey, Jan. 28, 1850. In a letter June 28, 1851, Elgin refers to him as "The most Conservative public man in U. Canada."

Banff, Alta.

In creating Banff, God assumed the role of a farsighted parks superintendent and designed the area with a view to future tourism.

> EDWARD MCCOURT, *The road across Canada*, 1965, 170.

Bank of Canada

The Bank of Canada is not responsible to the Government.

DONALD FLEMING, H. of C., *Debates*, Dec. 2, 1960, 442.

We are facing serious economic difficulties in Canada, both in our domestic economy and in our trade and financial relations with other nations. The undersigned economists wish to express to you that we have lost confidence in the ability of the Bank of Canada under its present management to play its proper role in ameliorating and resolving these difficulties.

H.C. EASTMAN and STEFAN STYKOLT, letter, early Dec., 1960 to D.M. Fleming, Minister of Finance, signed by 29 economists.

Bankers

My child, you should Never say hard or unkind things about Bankers' Toadies. God made Bankers' Toadies, just as He made snakes, slugs, snails and other creepy-crawly, treacherous and poisonous things. NEVER therefore, abuse them – just exterminate them, and to prevent all evasion Demand the *Result* you want – $25.00 a month and a lower cost to live.

G.P. POWELL and J.L. UNWIN, *Bankers' Toadies'*, pamphlet, Edmonton, February (?), 1938.

Bankruptcy

Bankruptcy is when you put your money in your hip pocket and let your creditors take your coat.

ROBERT C. (BOB) EDWARDS, Calgary *Eye Opener;* attributed.

Banks, Harold C.

He is of the stuff of the Capones and the Hoffas of whom the dictators throughout history, from the earliest times to the totalitarians, Hitler and Stalin, are prototypes. He is a bully, cruel, dishonest, greedy, power-hungry, contemptuous of the law.

CANADA. ROYAL COMM. ON DISRUPTION OF SHIPPING ON THE GREAT LAKES, etc., *Report*, 1963, 249.

Banks and Banking

The most efficacious and the most immediate means which the Canadians have to protect themselves against the fury of their enemies, is to attack them in their dearest parts – their pockets – in their strongest entrenchments, the banks.

LOUIS JOSEPH PAPINEAU, in Montreal *Gazette*, Dec. 11, 1834.

Whoever may get the milk, the Barings and Glyns will have the cream, that is certain.

TORONTO *GLOBE*, Jan. 20, 1860.

We fear the Bank of Montreal has the Government in its power, and is disposed to play the tyrant.

HAMILTON *TIMES*, qu., TORONTO *GLOBE*, Oct. 30, 1867.

The tradition of Canadian banking is evolution and not revolution.

C.R. FAY, in *Can. hist. rev.*, 1923, 186.

Think of tomorrow
Divide your pay in two,
Take what you need to live,
Put the balance in safety.

ANON., bank pay envelope message, qu. in Canada, Roy. Comm. on Price Spreads, *Report*, 1935, 110.

Montreal finance went into the west with the Bank of Montreal and to-day the old warfare of the embattled frontiersman against "the banks" and sound money, which Mackenzie fought in Upper Canada a century ago, is being waged on the last frontier by Mr. Aberhart.

> A.R.M. LOWER, in *Can. hist. rev.*, 1938, 209.

The basic criticism of the bankers is rather that they neither understood nor were willing to learn the economic consequences of their own actions, and they consequently provided a great deal of ill-informed opposition to the subsequent formation of a central bank.

> R. CRAIG MCIVOR, *Canadian monetary, banking and fiscal development*, 1958, 130, referring to the Bank of Canada.

The minister will huff and puff but will never succeed in blowing any fresh winds of competition into an industry which, by its very nature, is a monopoly.

> COLIN CAMERON, H. of C., *Debates*, July 5, 1966, 7245.

Canada's first American bank.

> ANON., graffito on Bank of Montreal building in Vancouver, 1974; ref. to appointment of William D. Mulholland, U.S. citizen, as president Jan. 1, 1974; also, changing of its motto of "Canada's First Bank" to "The First Canadian Bank"; also, selection of U.S.–based PR firm to do its advertising in Canada.

Baseball

In the beginning was the word, & the word was "Play Ball".

> GEORGE BOWERING, "Baseball", 1967.

Bats

Every man has his favourite bird. Mine is the bat.

> ROBERT C. (BOB) EDWARDS, attributed by Stubbs, *Lawyers and layman*, 1939, 180; Edwards' *Summer annual*, 1920, 67: "The genial doctor's favourite hobby is ornithology; his favourite bird being the Bat".

He hangs from beam in winter upside down
But in the spring he right side up lets go
And flutters here and there zigzagly flown
Till up the chimney of the house quick-slow
He pendulum-spirals out in light low
Of sunset swinging out above the lawns.

> JAMES REANEY, "A suit of nettles: February", 1958.

Bay Street

I've been watching the development of Canadian opinion on the protection of secondary industry and on American investment in Canada for some years; and to anyone brought up in the great city of Toronto, like myself, but successful in escaping from that self-satisfied environment, it's very easy to see that what is at work is not so much the noble spirit of Canadian independence, as the small, smug mind and large, larcenous hands of Bay Street.

> HARRY G. JOHNSON, *The Canadian quandary*, 1963, 114.

Beards

Despite the varieties of beards and moustachios, never will you hear from your osculatrix the source of her knowledge of that variety.

> ARNOLD HAULTAIN, *Hints for lovers*, 1909, 233.

Beards

He lifted up the hem
  of her dress
but being intellectual
  and something of a painter
he quickly let it fall
again, saying
with an abruptness
  that dismayed her:
    I never did care
for Van Dycks!

IRVING LAYTON, "Sensibility", 1954.

Bears

It is not easy to free
myth from reality
or rear this fellow up
to lurch, lurch with them
in the tranced dancing of men

EARLE BIRNEY, "The bear on the Delhi road", 1962.

Beauty

Ask a Northern Indian what is beauty, and he will answer: a broad, flat face; small eyes, high cheek-bones, three or four broad black lines across each cheek; a low forehead, a large, broad chin; a clumsy hook nose, a tawny hide, and breasts hanging down to the belt.

SAMUEL HEARNE, *Journey from Prince of Wales Fort in Hudson's Bay*, 1795, 89.

Make thou my vision sane and clear,
That I may see what beauty clings
In common forms, and find the soul
Of unregarded things!

CHARLES G.D. ROBERTS, "Prologue", 1893.

Beauty

Man soon tires of mere beauty. In fact, man, the inconstant creature, soon tires of mere anything.

ARNOLD HAULTAIN, *Hints for lovers*, 1909, 150.

The medicine for heartache
That lurks in lovely things.

BLISS CARMAN, "Peony", 1916.

In mount or vale, throughout the
  changing year,
From all the by-ways of the world,
  I peer
Into the secret places where they
  wind
Almost beyond the utmost reach of
  mind,
And beauty, beauty everywhere I
  find.

ALBERT D. WATSON, "To worlds more wide", 1917.

Lord of the far horizons,
  Give us the eyes to see
Over the verge of sundown
  The beauty that is to be.

BLISS CARMAN, "Lord of the far horizons", 1925.

Beauty is always breaking on the reef
That shelters righteousness with calm
  content;
The stolid coast of commonplace
  belief
Is shaken as the recreant surge is blent
With patient granite. Crest on rebel
  crest
Goes blazing up that ancient keep
  secure;
Still the grey coast lifts its massive
  breast
That loveliness may struggle − to
  endure.

CHARLES BRUCE, "Surf", 1932.

Beauty was mother's porridge in a
bowl.
Milk, oatmeal, and molasses built my
soul.

> KENNETH LESLIE, "Beauty is something
> you can weigh in scales", 1934.

This is the beauty
of strength
broken by strength
and still strong.

> A.J.M. SMITH, "The lonely land". 1943.

There is no excellent beauty but hath a
strangeness in the proportions.

> HUGH MACLENNAN, *Two solitudes*, 1945,
> 322.

Look well, who love all lovely things,
The hour is, but the hour has wings.

> AUDREY A. BROWN, "All Fools' Day",
> 1948.

Beauty is ordered in nature
   as the wind and sea
shape each other for pleasure; as the
      just
know, who learn of happiness
   from the report of their own actions.

> LOUIS DUDEK, *Europe*, Poem 95, 1954.

Beauty, like male ballet dancers,
makes some men afraid.

> MORDECAI RICHLER, *Son of a smaller
> hero*, 1955, 142.

This veritable temporary truth, I
   mourn,
this beauty
      which is never seen
but only remembered –

> AL PURDY, "Vestigia", 1958.

Listen. If I have known beauty
let's say I came to it
asking

Oh?

> PHYLLIS WEBB, "Some final questions",
> in *Naked poems*, 1965.

What's lovely
is whatever makes the adrenalin run;
therefore I count terror and fear
   among
the greatest beauty. The greatest
beauty is to be alive, forgetting
   nothing,
although remembrance hurts
like a foolish act, is a foolish act.

> JOHN NEWLOVE, "The double-headed
> snake", 1968.

There is nothing wrong with one
thinking oneself beautiful as long as
one doesn't think that others aren't.

> STEPHANIE NYNYCH, *Like I see it*, 1972,
> 87.

Beaverbrook, Lord

The Beaver.

> ANON., a popular reference to Lord
> Beaverbrook, born William Maxwell
> Aitken in Newcastle, N.B., 1879.

I'll not give up my temper. I'll not give
up my passions. I've enjoyed them far
too much to put them away. I'll not
give up my prejudices, the very foundation of my strength and vigor.

> LORD BEAVERBROOK, on reaching age 70,
> 1949.

Positive, bee; comparative, Beaver;
superlative, Beaverbrook.

> ANON., a columnist in a Canadian paper,
> on Lord Beaverbrook's death June 9,
> 1964; qu. in *Time*, June 19, 1964, 55.

Beavers

For his crest, on a wreath argent sable,
a beaver proper.

> Royal letter, Newmarket, 1632, by
> which KING CHARLES I granted a coat of
> arms to Alexander, Viscount of Stirling,
> Lord Alexander of Canada; the first use
> of the beaver in Canadian heraldry.

The officials of Canada are looking not for the Western Sea, but for the sea of beaver.

> JEAN-FRÉDÉRIC-PHÉLYPEAUX MAUREPAS, about 1720 qu. in Joseph L. Rutledge, *Century of conflict*, 1956, 296.

Previous to the discovery of Canada (about 320 years ago) this Continent may be said to have been in the possession of two distinct races of Beings, Man and the Beaver.

> DAVID THOMPSON, *Narrative of his explorations in Western America, 1784-1812*, (Champlain Soc. 1916, 197).

To every small Lake, and all the Ponds they builded Dams, and enlarged and deepened them to the height of the dams. Even to grounds occasionally overflowed by heavy rains, they also made dams, and made them permanent Ponds, and as they heightened the dams increased the extent and added to the depth of the water. Thus all the low lands were in possession of the Beaver, and all the hollows of the higher grounds. Small streams were dammed across and Ponds formed; the dry lands with the dominions of Man contracted, everywhere he was hemmed in by water without the power of preventing it.

> DAVID THOMPSON, *Narrative of his explorations in Western America 1784-1812*, (Champlain Soc. 1916, 198).

We are now killing the Beaver without any labor, we are now rich, but shall soon be poor, for when the Beaver are destroyed we have nothing to depend on to purchase what we want for our families, strangers now overrun our country with their iron traps, and we, and they will soon be poor.

> ANON., an old Indian, qu. by David Thompson, *Narrative of his explorations in Western America, 1784-1812*, (Champlain Soc. 1916, 204).

The beaver is not a bad cognisance for a young country which is shaping itself out of the rough; for he is an enterprising pioneer of the wilderness; a clearer and improver of the ground; a clever feller of trees; an ingenious constructor of dams and utiliser of waters; and his aims are all laudably domestic; he is a comfortable, prudent, family animal, and must have a lodge and home of his own: he therefore builds for himself a spacious house and provides it with convenient surroundings; and at frequent intervals he sends from his abode an able-bodied detachment, to go and do elsewhere in the land as he himself has done.

> REV. HENRY SCADDING, *Can. monthly*, Vol. 9, 1876, 487.

If the pig had his rights, he would be our national emblem, instead of the beaver. What has the beaver done for us, anyway? The pig, on the other hand, sustained our fathers in their fight against the wilderness, and yet his name is a name of scorn.

> PETER MCARTHUR, *In pastures green*, 1915, 266.

I'm at last beginning to understand why the beaver is our national emblem. I thought, once it was due to the industriousness of what had been designated as merely an amplified rat. But I was wrong there. For outside its industry the beaver has one peculiar and distinguishing trait. That peculiarity stems from the conviction that its home isn't habitable until it has been well damned.

> ARTHUR STRINGER, address, Empire Club, Toronto, Apr. 14, 1949.

The symbol of Canada is the beaver, that industrious rodent whose destiny it was to furnish hats that warmed better brains than his own.

> ROY DANIELLS, in Julian Park, ed., *The culture of contemporary Canada*, 1957, 2.

Yet the beaver, in spite of his smile, is hardly adequate. He chops down trees, he builds dams, he prepares for the winter. But his destiny has been to be skinned by foreign interests.

> ROY DANIELLS, Roy. Soc. Can. *Trans.*, 1963, 246, on the beaver as a national symbol.

Beds

The clothes of a boarding house bed, though produced ever so far both ways, will not meet.

> STEPHEN B. LEACOCK, "Boarding house geometry", in *Literary lapses*, 1910.

A bed without a woman
is a thing of wood and springs, a pit
to roll in with the Devil.
        But let
her body touch its length and it
        becomes
a place of singing wonders, eager
        springboard
to heaven and higher.

> RAYMOND SOUSTER, "A bed without a woman", 1955.

Beer

An honest brew makes its own friends.

> JOHN MOLSON, Montreal, attributed, 1786; appears on the Molson's Brewery beer bottle label.

Sold honestly and in an open and aboveboard manner, temperance beer will just fill the bill nicely and keep the boys satisfied and contented.

> ROBERT C. (BOB) EDWARDS, Calgary *Eye opener*, July 8, 1916.

A plentiful supply of it can make an important contribution to the well-being of the nation.

> E.P. TAYLOR, 1941, press statement in reply to Prime Minister King's request that Canadians drink less, qu. in P. Newman, *Flame of power*, 1959, 237.

I've met the Queen. I've met the Princess Royal. I've met Sir Anthony Eden. But never once did I get a glass of Canadian beer.

> MICKEY O'ROURKE, V.C. of Vancouver, on his return from the V.C. centenary celebrations in London, 1956, age 81.

Bees

The swarthy bee is a buccaneer,
A burly velveted rover,
Who loves the booming wind in his ear
As he sails the seas of clover.

> BLISS CARMAN, "A more ancient mariner", 1890.

Bees, Quilting

The day is set, the ladies met,
    And at the frame are seated;
In order placed they work in haste,
    To get the quilt completed.
While fingers fly, their tongues they
        ply,
    And animate their labours,
By counting beaux, discussing clothes,
    Or talking of their neighbours.

> ANON., untitled, in Brockville *Recorder* June 1, 1930, 4.

Behaviour

Send me better men to deal with, and I will be a better man.

> SIR JOHN A. MACDONALD, to a farmer-elector, qu. by Cartwright, *Reminiscences*, 1912, 46.

Most people who are old enough to know better often wish they were young enough not to.

> ROBERT C. (BOB) EDWARDS, Calgary *Eye opener*, Apr. 30, 1912.

Any doctor or any person has the right to reject human behavior but he does not have the right to reject the human being.

> DR. LIONEL SOLURSH, qu. in *Globe and Mail*, Jan. 28, 1969, 11, regarding drug addicts.

When I go to the window and tap on it
he looks up at me, stops his barking
and moves away from my sight.
If God would throw beer cans at men
they'd behave better.

> RAYMOND FRASER, "The dog in the yard next door", 1969.

A truly immoral man, I suppose, is the one who advises people to behave as in fact they are behaving.

> RICHARD J. NEEDHAM, *A friend in Needham*, 1969, 17.

The things we say are
true; it is our crooked
aims, our choices
turn them criminal.

> MARGARET ATWOOD, *Power politics*, 1971, (untitled poem) 24.

Being

The female kind of ambition which concentrates on being rather than doing.

> HUGH MACLENNAN, *Each man's son*, 1951, 77.

The question is, what
was the question we could
never quite remember?
It had something to do
with the past, the future;
we say history, we say
the revolution, we say
what is beyond our being
that will hold in itself
childhood and death, work
and what we've loved.

> DAVID HELWIG, "Poem for the end of the revolution", 1972.

Belief

Seein' is believin'.

> T.C. HALIBURTON, *Sam Slick's wise saws*, 1853, I, 41.

For long ago, when the world was
    making,
    I walked through Eden with God
    for guide;
And since that time in my heart
    forever
    His calm and wisdom and peace
    abide.

> BLISS CARMAN, "Wanderer", 1892.

Lord of my heart's elation
Spirit of things unseen,
Be thou my aspiration
Consuming and serene!

> BLISS CARMAN, "Lord of my heart's elation", 1903.

But you came empty-handed, and
    your tongue
    Babbled strange tidings none could
    wholly trust.
And if we half-believed you, it was
    only
    Because we would, and not because
    we must.

> CHARLES G.D. ROBERTS, "To a certain mystic", 1934.

Personally I don't consider I started living until after I started believing.

> JACK MINER, d. 1944, in *Jack Miner, his life and religion*, 1969, lxi.

Whether you are really right or not doesn't matter; it's the belief that counts.

> ROBERTSON DAVIES, *Overlaid*, 1948, 23.

And though she did not holy believe
She'd lost the hellfire of her disbelief.

> ANNE WILKINSON, "Swimming lesson", 1955.

Nothing is absolute any longer. There is a choice of beliefs and a choice of truths to go with them. If you choose not to choose then there is no truth at all. There are only points of view . . .

> MORDECAI RICHLER, *Son of a smaller hero*, 1955, 99.

I believe there is more room inside than outside. And all the diversities which get absorbed can later work their way out into fantastic things, like hawk-training, IBM programming, mountain-climbing, or poetry.

> GWENDOLYN MACEWEN, "I believe", 1966.

The happy hungry man believes in food
The happy homeless man believes in a home
The happy unloved man believes in love
I wouldn't mind believing in something myself.

> GEORGE JONAS, *Happy hungry man*, 1970, 9.

Belonging

Nobody
belongs anywhere,
even the
Rocky Mountains
are still
moving.

> GEORGE BOWERING, *Rocky Mountain foot*, 1968, 125.

I belong here
in the world's country and
out
out, beyond
however far
the echoing rings run
in the Welshman's glorious air
to the end of
no end.

> ANNE MARRIOTT, "Countries", 1971.

Benefactors

The benefactor is hated to the same degree as his benefaction is valued and approved.

> IRVING LAYTON, "Aphs", *The whole bloody bird*, 1969, 101.

Bennett, Richard B.

R.B. Bennett is a tough guy who wants to be kissed.

> ROBERT C. (BOB) EDWARDS, attributed, qu. in G.R. Stevens, *History of the C.N.R.*, 1973, 347.

Such as I have I consecrate with myself to the service in which I am.

> R.B. BENNETT, referring to his fortune, on accepting the leadership of the Conservative Party, Oct. 12, 1927, Conservative Leadership Convention, Winnipeg.

Bennett's conduct to me since he got his leadership has been very bad. It could scarcely have been worse. He is a very small man and has oceans of trouble ahead. At present the fates are with him.

> ARTHUR MEIGHEN, letter to T.R. Meighen, Apr. 22, 1930.

I have nothing to say against Mr. Bennett, but I must say I don't like his friends.

> L.A. TACHEREAU, speech in Ste. Anne de Beaupré, July 20, 1930, on R.B. Bennett.

My government.

> RICHARD B. BENNETT, phrase sometimes used in his speeches; usually reserved for royalty.

Mr. Bennett did not impress me as having much imperial sentiment. To him these imperial problems were simply matters of business – an opportunity for seeing how much he could get out of others and how little he could give himself.

> VISCOUNT SNOWDEN, *Autobiography*, 1934, Vol. 2, 872.

I am 65 years old. When one reaches my time of life, ambitions dim, the love of power dies, the plaudits of the multitude can scarce be heard, its condemnation is just as meaningless. Therefore I speak without much thought of my place in the national scene after polling day. I want you to think without like or dislike of me. I will speak only as your interests require me to speak.

> RICHARD B. BENNETT, radio broadcast address, Sept. 6, 1935.

I'd send for the leader of the Opposition.

> W.L. MACKENZIE KING, qu. in B. Hutchison, *Mr. Prime Minister*, 1964, 240, in reply to question in the House of Commons on what would he do if confronted with a parade of nude Doukhobor women. Reference is to R.B. Bennett; after 1935.

There is a tide in the affairs of men which, taken at the Eddy, leads on to fortune.

> LEONARD BROCKINGTON, ref. to the death of Mrs. E.B. Eddy, widow of the Hull, Que., match manufacturer, in 1921 when Bennett inherited part ownership of the Eddy Match Co.

Bennett is clever, well-informed, has a remarkable memory and, when his own financial interests are involved, an able businessman. He is disgustingly conceited and feels he outweighs all other Canadians in importance. He is contemptuous of the intelligence and efforts of others – in every respect a lone wolf (except perhaps in the rutting season when, of course, no male associates are welcome).

> GEORGE BLACK, letter to R.J. Manion, Jan. 12, 1940 (Pub. Arch. Can.)

When he laughs, it is as though he were making a good-natured concession to the weaknesses of others.

> GRATTAN O'LEARY, on R.B. Bennett, qu. in *Maclean's*, Oct. 7, 1961, 65.

Bennett, W.A.C.

In the light of this person's record for reliability, we should have known better. We should have withheld publication until the report itself could be checked. We should have realized that this dignitary was not above doctoring the facts.

> *VANCOUVER SUN* , editorial, Aug. 20, 1959, 1, apology to H. Lee Briggs for

erroneous report on contents of a Royal Commission report on affairs of the B.C. Power Commission.

They see in me what Social Credit stands for — it gets things done.

> W.A.C. BENNETT, qu. in G. Clark, *Canada, the uneasy neighbour*, 1965, 260.

I believe in certain basic things. My fundamental thing is that the only excuse for people being in public life, the only excuse for government, is to do those things, on a constructive basis, that people cannot do for themselves.

> W.A.C. BENNETT, qu. in P. Sherman, *Bennett*, 1966, 179.

Lochinvar of the West.

> RAMSAY COOK, *Canada and the French-Canadian question*, 1966, 155.

I'm plugged in with God.

> W.A.C. BENNETT, Premier of B.C., qu. in Ottawa *Citizen* Sept. 5, 1969, 6.

Why doesn't he (Réal Caouette) go to British Columbia, where there is a Social Credit government, and make a speech about the bigot (W.A.C. Bennett) who runs that government?

> PIERRE ELLIOTT TRUDEAU, speech to Ontario Liberals Annual Convention, Ottawa, Feb. 12, 1972.

Bethune, Dr. Norman H.

Every Communist must learn this true communist spirit from Comrade Bethune.

> MAO TSE-TUNG, eulogy of Norman Bethune, December, 1939, qu. in R. Stewart, *Bethune*, 1973, 197.

A great humanitarian, to be a Canadian of national historical significance.

> CANADA. GOVERNMENT, Declaration; announcement by Hon. Mitchell Sharp, Canadian Trade Fair, Peking, Aug. 17, 1972.

Betrayal

And he will also remember
  In his gut
Times when his yea should have been
  yea
And it was yea but:
Perhaps his best friend hunted in the
  street
And his door shut.

> GEORGE JOHNSTON, "Love in high places", 1966.

Bible

We want the whole damned Bible, and nothing but the Bible.

> ANON., a Protestant school trustee at an Ontario board meeting. Reference is to the use for scripture readings in the schools of the expurgated "Ross Bible" (see this entry). Qu. in Toronto *Globe*, Feb. 8, 1886.

Ross Bible.

> ANON.; *Bible* from which passages had been expurgated lest they be offensive to Roman Catholics, used for scripture readings in Ontario schools. Named after George W. Ross, minister of education in the Mowat government, 1886-1890.

The Bible forms the lowest stratum in the teaching of literature. It should be taught so early and so thoroughly that it sinks straight to the bottom of the mind, where everything that comes along later can settle on it.

> NORTHROP FRYE, *The educated imagination* (1962) 1964, 110.

Bibliographies

Bibliographies are always a surprise to the uninitiated.

> F.W. HOWAY, in *Can. hist. rev.*, 1929, 79.

Biculturalism

A modus vivendi without cordiality.

ANDRE SIEGFRIED, *Canada*, 1937, 255.

Bicycle

No more remarkable development has been witnessed in our day than the rapid growth of the use of the bicycle. It has furnished a new means of locomotion, has solved for a great many people the old problem of rapid transit in the cities, and at the same time has given a new and healthy exercise, all at comparatively small cost.

MANITOBA FREE PRESS, Mar. 29, 1899, 4, editorial.

Bigotry

Two greater calamities have never befallen mankind than the transportation of the negro to this hemisphere and the dispersion of the Jews.

GOLDWIN SMITH, qu. by Malcolm Ross, in C.T. Bissell, ed., *Our living tradition*, Ser. 1, 1957, 45.

Bilingualism

The Divinity could be invoked as well in the English language as in the French.

SIR WILFRID LAURIER, H. of C., *Debates*, 1877, 94.

I have no accord with the desire expressed in some quarters that by any mode whatever there should be an attempt made to oppress the one language or to render it inferior to the other; I believe that would be impossible if it were tried, and it would be foolish and wicked if it were possible.

SIR JOHN A. MACDONALD, H. of C., *Debates*, Feb. 17, 1890, 745.

The French Canadian father who today does not have his son learn English does not do justice to his child, for he forces him to remain behind in the struggle for existence.

SIR WILFRID LAURIER, H. of C., *Debates*, Feb. 17, 1890.

My children, be well up in French, but not *too* well up in English!

LOUIS LAFLÈCHE, Bishop of Three Rivers, Que. (1870-98). (Trans.)

The preservation and simultaneous growth of two national languages and two different types of mental culture, far from being an obstacle to the progress of Canada, constitute its most powerful factor and our greatest national asset.

HENRI BOURASSA, *Independence or imperial partnership?*, 1916, 54.

The soul of Canada is a dual personality, and must remain only half revealed to those who know only one language.

FRANK OLIVER CALL, *Spell of French Canada*, 1926.

If one knows his neighbour's tongue, he possesses the key of his house.

ABBÉ ARTHUR MAHEUX, *What keeps us apart?* 1944.

Language of the day.

COLLÈGE MILITAIRE ROYAL, St. Jean, Que., refers to alternative use of French and English for all activities for 15 days each month, late 1950's.

Speak white.

ANON., anti-French phrase; heard from the audience in Vancouver, Apr. 1964 at public meeting of the Royal Comm. on Bilingualism and Biculturalism.

You can have a state with one language, you can have a state with two official languages, you can have a state with three or four. It is done in other places. The more you have, the more difficult it is, of course. We are trying with two. Let us make a success of two. We will think about the third or fourth later on.

PIERRE E. TRUDEAU, speech, Edmonton, June 4, 1968, qu. in B. Shaw, *The gospel according to St. Pierre*, 1969, 54.

To the average English Canadian, bilingualism means acquiring a second language; at the moment, to many French Canadians it means the likelihood of losing a first one.

RONALD SUTHERLAND, in *Can. lit.* No. 45, 1970, 21.

We all want the good things North America has to offer. But if we insist on the North American way of life, we cannot avoid the dominant North American way of speech.

DONALD G. CREIGHTON, *Towards the discovery of Canada*, 1972, 267.

Bill of Rights

The Canadian Bill of Rights is important, not so much because of the power which it transfers to the Courts to protect basic rights, but because of the influence which it will have on intelligent citizens.

D.A. SCHMEISER, *Civil liberties in Canada*, 1964, 53.

Biography

Biographies written by sons are, as a rule, only one degree less contemptible than those written by daughters.

ANON., in W.L. Grant and F. Hamilton, *Principal Grant*, 1904.

Just say I was born and that I am not dead yet.

A.M. KLEIN, qu. by Miriam Waddington, *Can. forum*, Oct.-Nov., 1972, in response to request for blurb for cover of his *Hitleriad*, 1944.

One must say that a biography only becomes interesting and alive when the biographer is a partisan.

F.H. UNDERHILL, in *Can. hist. rev.*, 1945, 69.

Biography is a distinct and special branch of historical writing. Of all branches it is perhaps most closely related to the art of the novel, and this in both a legitimate and illegitimate sense. In a biography, as in a novel, the phases of historical development, the conflict of historical forces, are seen, not in generalities and abstractions, but concretely, in terms of a central main character, a set of subordinate characters, and a series of particular situations.

DONALD G. CREIGHTON, *Can. hist. rev.*, Mar., 1948, 3.

The number of biographies of Canadians that are in any real sense definitive can be numbered on the fingers of one hand.

W. KAYE LAMB, Presidential address, Canadian Historical Association, Annual Meeting, Edmonton, June 4-7, 1958.

One reason many people find Canadian history dull is that most of the characters that appear in it are mere shadows; we tend as a consequence to know much more about treaties and constitutions than about the men who shaped and made them.

W. KAYE LAMB, Presidential address, Canadian Historical Association, Annual Meeting, Edmonton, June 4-7, 1958.

Biology

Note, please, the embryo.
    Unseeing
It survives into being.
Elan vital,
Thyroid, gonads *et al.,*
Preserve the unities.

    F.R. SCOTT, "Teleological", 1945.

Birches

The bees are busy in their murmurous
    search,
The birds are putting up their woven
    frames,
And all the twigs and branches of the
    birch
Are shooting into tiny emerald flames.

    ARCHIBALD LAMPMAN, "Nesting time",
    1900.

Birds

The red-bird pauses in his song,
    The face of man aye fearing,
And flashes like a flame along
    The border of the clearing.
The humming-bird above the flower
    Is like a halo bending.

    ALEXANDER MCLACHLAN, "Hall of shad-
    ows", 1874.

To-night the wind roars in from sea;
The crow clings to the straining tree;
Curlew and crane and bittern flee
The dykes of Tantramar.

    CHARLES G.D. ROBERTS, "The tide on
    Tantramar", 1893.

Shy bird of the silver arrows of song,
    That cleave our Northern air so
        clear,
Thy notes prolong, prolong,
    I listen, I hear:
"I — love — dear — Canada,
Canada, Canada."

    THEODORE H. RAND, "The white-throat",
    1900.

From streams no oar hath rippled
    And lakes that waft no sail,
From reaches vast and lonely
    That know no hunter's trail,
The clamour of their calling
    And the whistling of their flight
Fill all the day with marvel,
    And with mystery, the night.

    PETER MCARTHUR, "Birds of passage",
    1907.

Stop this yowl and go to your story and
enter the joy of birds. Wake the old
sail up, hoist it up into the sky on lark
songs. Lay the foundations strong and
flat and coarse on the croaks of the
crows and the jays and the rooks. Fill it
with thrush songs and blackbirds, and
when the day is petering out wrap the
great white owl's silent wings round it
and let the nightingale sing it to sleep.

    EMILY CARR, *Hundreds and thousands;
    journal,* Apr. 6, 1934.

Look for birds with your ears.

    WILLIAM E. SAUNDERS, letter to R.G.
    Dingman, Apr. 11, 1943.

I watched a bird tossed down the wind
that never fought or uttered cry,
surrendered to that boundless air,
caught up in that great mystery.

    RAYMOND SOUSTER, "I watched a bird",
    1954.

The stork questioned the swan whose
    moving song
Was more than usually sweet and long:
What's the good news? You'd think
    you were a lark!
I'm going to die, the swan answered
    the stork.

    ROBERT FINCH, "Aria senza da capo",
    1961.

All summer long
only
the whispers of swallows
the cooing of wood doves
now
in this dawning
the scream of the jay
        sharp as the north wind
        ragged as icicles.

> RONA MURRAY, "Picture", 1968.

Today at dawn
for an endless minute
I listened to a bird
fighting for its life
in the claws of a cat,
thinking: much the same way
death will take us all.

> RAYMOND SOUSTER, "Today at dawn",
> 1969.

Swiftly darting in the setting light,
The doomed sparrow feels the falcon's
    wings.
How beautiful are they both in flight.

> IRVING LAYTON, "Divine image", 1971.

Where do the birds sleep?
    in the trees
But how do they sleep?
    upright on branches,
    leaning against the trunks
How do they keep from falling?
    they sleep, and the wind
    cradles them.

> BRENDA FLEET, "Poem for Bill", 1971.

Does there beat in the breast of every
    bird
the same novelty and discovery,
as if he, the first bird, and only true
    bird,
breathed this life, found this leaf?

> LOUIS DUDEK, "At the round window",
> 1971.

A puff of feathers, crimsoned grey,
    Upon the garden-walk:
God careth for the sparrow, yea,
    And also for the hawk.

> GEOFFREY B. RIDDEHOUGH, "Benedicite,
> omnia opera", 1972.

Birth

Why was I born?
I do not know.
I ask my face a thousand times a
    day
and find no answer.

> STEPHEN LEACOCK, "Sorrows of a super-
> soul", *Nonsense novels*, 1911, 91.

Some mistakes
We make in childhood haunt us all life
    long.
Perhaps. But I suspect that we went
    wrong
Earlier, indeed, in being born.

> DARYL HINE, "Letter from British Co-
> lumbia", 1970.

At birth you are programmed for life.

> AGNES HIGGINS, Director, Montreal Diet
> Dispensary, qu. in *Weekend mag.*, Oct.
> 12, 1973, 2.

Birth Control

Mary mother, we believe
That without sin you did conceive,
Teach, we pray thee, us believing,
How to sin without conceiving.

> ANON., "Maiden's prayer", qu. by Hugh
> John Macdonald in letter to James
> Henry Coyne, Dec. 15, 1871. (Coyne
> papers, Univ. of W. Ont.)

"I know", she said, "that you're
    sincere,
I love you for it, dearie,
But dammit, Frank, let's try this year
Some practice with the theory".

> GEORGE BAIN, *I've been around and
> around and around*, 1964, 58.

It seems to me that the church is just a little hypocritical in maintaining that use of the Pill is such a heinous sin, while the deliberate withholding of the male semen from the female ovum precisely during that relatively short period when the ovum is receptive to it – one might say, yearning for it – is all right.

H.G. CLASSEN, *The time is never ripe*, 1972, 73.

Birthdays

Most adult birthdays, if they ever get beyond an attenuated ritual, are times of mild regret or mild relief; regret that another set of seasons has slipped so fruitlessly away, relief that it has slipped away without disaster.

GEORGE WOODCOCK, in *Can. lit.* No. 41, 1969, 5.

Bishop, Wm. (Billy)

Death came to Air Marshal Billy Bishop in the early morning. He died at that chill hour before the coming of the dawn – an hour when he must often have been making ready for his solitary flights.

JOHN BASSETT, Montreal *Gazette*, Sept. 12, 1956, 8.

Blackflies

And the black flies, the little black flies,
Always the black fly no matter where you go.
I'll die with the black fly a-pickin' my bones
In North Ontario, io, in North Ontario.

WADE HEMSWORTH, "The black fly song", 1949.

Blacks

Sometimes he'd like
to slip his blackness
on a white man and say,
walk around a little,
see how it feels.

RAYMOND SOUSTER, "Jazzman", 1967.

To be black and female, in a society which is both racist and sexist, is to be in the unique position of having nowhere to go but up.

ROSEMARY BROWN (B.C., M.L.A.), qu. in *Saturday night*, Jul./Aug., 1975, 31.

Blake, Edward

There are scores of earnest and able young men in Canada who would willingly range themselves under Mr. Blake's leadership, were it not that they are repelled by a manner as devoid of warmth as is a flake of December snow, and as devoid of magnetism as is a loaf of unleavened bread.

JOHN C. DENT, *The last forty years*, II, 1882, 480.

Blake will neither lead nor be led.

SIR WILFRID LAURIER, letter to J.D. Edgar, Nov. 11, 1891. (Pub. Arch. Ont.).

Of course I am more anxious to see you return to Canadian politics, but this country is too small for the full play of your abilities.

J.S. WILLISON, to Blake, June 14, 1892.

Mr. Blake, on the other hand, was constitutionally incapable of serving loyally under anybody.

SIR RICHARD CARTWRIGHT, *Reminiscences*, 1912, 134.

Disabled by tempermental defects, this man of whom giants might well be afraid let his soul be harried by insects and to the gnats gave victories which belonged to the gods.

> SIR JOHN S. WILLISON, *Reminiscences political and personal*, 1919, 69.

The kindliest of men to his intimates, he wore the sensitive man's mask of indifference to the public. Ill-health and a nervous temperament unfitted him for the drudgery and disappointments of politics. He was moody and nervous when things were not going well. Yet without any of the lesser arts, he cast a spell over every man in parliament. We felt in the presence of genius, and would have been proud to serve to the end, had he not drawn himself aloof.

> SIR WILFRID LAURIER, on Edward Blake, to O.D. Skelton, qu. in Skelton's *Laurier*, 1921, I, 223-4.

He felt he could go on beating Blake, every four or five years, until the end of the chapter.

> DONALD CREIGHTON, *John A. Macdonald, The old chieftain*, 1955, 471, referring to Macdonald.

Edward Blake was a failure in politics. He was the most tragic failure that has yet appeared in our Canadian public life.

> FRANK H. UNDERHILL, in C.T. Bissell, ed., *Our living tradition: seven Canadians*, 1957, 4.

Blake commanded the Commons because he knew so much; he bored the Commons because he said so much.

> PETER B. WAITE, *Canada 1874-1896*, 1971, 32.

Blessings

Blessings, like disasters, have a habit of coming in pairs.

> FREDERICK P. GROVE, *Fruits of the earth*, 1933, 34.

May your road rise with you;
May the wind blow always at your
  back;
May the good Lord hold you in the
  hollow of His hand.

> ANON., Cape Breton woman giving a Gaelic blessing (trans.) qu. in E. McCourt, *The road across Canada*, 1965, 40.

Bluebirds

Blue on the branch and blue in the
  sky,
And naught between but the breezes
  high,
And naught so blue by the breezes
  stirred
As the deep, deep blue of the Indigo
  bird.

> ETHELWYN WETHERALD, "The indigo bird", 1907.

Blue Jays

A jay to prove this silver silence true
Startles the marvel with a word of
  blue.

> ROBERT FINCH, "The marvel", 1948.

"Bluenose"

The wood of the vessel that will beat the *Bluenose* is still growing!

> ANGUS J. WALTERS, Skipper of *Bluenose*, launched Apr. 26, 1921, qu. in B. and P. Backman, *Bluenose*, 1965, 51.

Blushing

There is a divine and cosmic secret hidden beneath every blush.

> ARNOLD HAULTAIN, *Hints for lovers*, 1909, 211.

I'm ashamed I don't blush, except in
    company . . .
          my cheeks
burning as though Christ slapped
    them!

> ALDEN NOWLAN, "The wickedness of Peter Shannon", 1967.

Boarding Houses

A single room is that which has no parts and no magnitude.

> STEPHEN B. LEACOCK, "Boarding house geometry", in *Literary lapses*, 1914.

Boasting

At this time when our country's destiny, its very independent existence perhaps, is a matter of doubt and anxiety, it behooves us to be silent and do no boasting, but look seriously about us for the wisest thing to be said and done at each crisis.

> ARCHIBALD LAMPMAN, public lecture, Ottawa, Feb. 19, 1891.

Boating

Faintly as tolls the evening chime,
Our voices keep tune and our oars
    keep time.
Soon as the woods on shore look dim,
We'll sing at St. Anne's our parting
    hymn.
Row, brothers, row, the stream runs
    fast,
The Rapids are near, and the
    daylight's past.

> THOMAS MOORE, "Canadian boat song", 1804.

Bobolinks

Never dost thou dream of sadness –
All thy life a merry madness,
Never may thy spirits sink –
    Bobolink!   Bobolink!

> ALEXANDER MCLACHLAN, "Bobolink", 1874.

Bodies

Our parson looks after the souls of his flocks; but they have bodies too; and I do assure you, that, in these times, the most of people's bodies cost them more trouble than their souls.

> THOMAS MCCULLOCH, *Letters of Mephibosheth Stepsure*, 1821, Letter 6.

But the body alone could not satisfy
    need
When greatness and power of thought,
And sweetness of mind and heed for
    mankind
Were qualities still being sought.

> LOIS DARROCH, "The unattainable", 1942.

Here, where summer slips
Its sovereigns through my fingers
I put on my body and go forth
To seek my blood.

> ANNE WILKINSON, "The red and the green", 1955.

Fellow flesh affords a rampart,
And you've got along for comfort
All the world there ever shall be, was,
    and is.

> JAY MACPHERSON, in *The boatman*, 1957, 48.

Within my templed flesh
a god of pain presides
over love's slow murders
and hate's long suicides.

> FRED COGSWELL, "Within my templed flesh", 1959.

    May our
Bodies be a gift
Which we can give
Without excess of pride,
Which we receive
Without excess of greed.
And may our flesh
Be food for that
Deep emptiness
Which like a hunger
Troubles our brief lives.

> D.G. JONES, "In this present mood", 1961.

This woman's shaped for love, one
    thinks each breast
might have been grown to fit in a
    man's hand,
her mouth moulded by constant kisses,
    and
her legs devised by an evangelist.

> ALDEN NOWLAN, "This woman's shaped
> for love", 1961.

As the mist leaves no scar
On the dark green hill,
So my body leaves no scar
On you, nor ever will.

> LEONARD COHEN, "As the mist leaves no
> scar", 1961.

Nakedness is our shelter.
Bones are only temporal.
Yes, there will be splinters.
Yes, there will be cancers
to split this partial temple.

> PHYLLIS WEBB, "Bomb shelter", 1962.

you know I am a god
who needs to use your body
who needs to use your body
to sing about beauty
in a way no one
has ever sung before.

> LEONARD COHEN, "I met you", 1968.

Without the cage I cannot want
Or love or think or say;
Its barriers limn the forms of life
As sun-spokes shape the day.

> FRED COGSWELL, "The cage", 1968.

Your body is not a word,
it does not lie or
speak truth either.

It is only
here or not here.

> MARGARET ATWOOD, *Power politics*,
> 1971, 25.

Boer War, 1899-1902

It is stated that the Order-in-Council
providing for the enlistment and the
sending of our troops makes a special
reserve as to future action and prevents the present one to be considered
as precedent. The precedent, sir, is the
accomplished fact.

> HENRI BOURASSA, letter Oct. 18, 1899 to
> Laurier on breaking with him over his
> Boer War policy.

This war will not add an ounce of
glory to the English flag.

> HENRI BOURASSA, H. of C., *Debates*, June
> 7, 1900, 6907.

Bombing

When I see the falling bombs
Then I see defended homes.
Men above and men below
Die to save the good they know.

> F.R. SCOTT, "Conflict", 1945.

More roads are opened than are closed
    by bombs
And truth stands naked under the
    flashing charge.

> F.R. SCOTT, "Recovery", 1945.

I did it for kicks.

> YVES LABONTÉ, qu. in Pierre Berton, ed.,
> *Historic headlines*, 1967, 123, re Mont-
> real bombing, 1963.

Book Reviews

Reviewers gain reputation less by the justness of their criticism than by their own ability to write well and entertainingly, and though this may sometimes cause hardship to authors, it is inevitable. Reviewers themselves live and work under special strain. If they praise much they appear to be simple fellows, too readily pleased, for it is a widespread belief that a truly critical mind exists in a constant state of high-toned irascibility. But blame always looks well.

> ROBERTSON DAVIES, *A voice from the attic*, 1960, 28.

A book is criticized by the reviewer in direct proportion as the reviewer is criticized by the book: no man can find wisdom in print which is not already waiting for words within himself.

> ROBERTSON DAVIES, *Samuel Marchbanks' almanack*, 1967, 98.

Books

The world is before me – a library open to all – from which poverty of purse cannot exclude me – and in which the meanest and most paltry volume is sure to furnish something to amuse, if not to instruct and improve.

> JOSEPH HOWE, letter to George Johnson, Jan. 1824 (Pub. Arch. Can.).

You may stop a man's mouth by a crammin' a book down his throat, but you won't convince him.

> T.C. HALIBURTON, *Sam Slick*, 1836, ch. XXIV.

They showed how contradictions throng,
How by our weakness we are strong,
And how we're righted by the wrong.

> ALEXANDER MCLACHLAN, "Companions in solitude", 1874.

A Canadian book is sure, with the stigma of a colonial imprimatur upon it, not to circulate beyond the confines of the Dominion; and, therefore, when a Canadian writes a meritorious book like Todd's "Parliamentary Government", or Heavysege, "Jephthah's Daughter", he seeks a publisher abroad.

> JAMES DOUGLAS, JR., address to the Literary and Historical Soc. of Quebec, Mar. 3, 1875.

Pure Books on Avoided Subjects.

> ANON., phrase used in advertising "Self and Sex" series of books distributed in Canada by William Briggs, 1897.

The bald truth is that Canada has the money, but would rather spend it on whiskey than on books.

> ROBERT BARR, in *Can. mag.*, Nov., 1899, 5.

Divide your attention equally between men and books.

> SIR WILLIAM OSLER, "The student life", an address, 1905.

The classics are only primitive literature. They belong to the same class as primitive machinery and primitive medicine.

> STEPHEN B. LEACOCK, "Homer and humbug", *Century mag.*, Oct. 1913.

A good book has no ending.

> R.D. CUMMING, *Skookum Chuck fables*, 1915, 160.

A great book is a mine as well as a mint; it suggests and excites as much thought as it presents in finished form.

> GEORGE ILES, *Canadian stories*, 1918, 182.

Give me a book for use! If the margins are too wide, cut them down; if the covers are too clumsy, tear them off. If you buy a book as a work of art, put it in your cabinet and order a modern edition for reading.

SIR W. VAN HORNE, to a book collector, qu. in Vaughan: *Van Horne*, 1920, 374.

If Canada is in their bones and their hearts they will write Canadian books.

JOHN W. DAFOE, *Manitoba Free press*, Nov. 29, 1923; qu. in J. Aitchison, ed., *Political process in Canada*, 1963, 111.

I sat up most of the night reading and re-reading *Orion* in a state of the wildest excitement. It seemed to me a wonderful thing that such work could be done by a Canadian, by a young man, one of ourselves.

ARCHIBALD LAMPMAN, unpublished essay, extract in *Lyrics of earth* ed. by D.C. Scott, 1925. Intro., 8, ref. to C.G.D. Roberts' book *Orion*, pub. in 1880.

Books worth reading are inspired by the ruthless, intolerant and cynical impulses.

T.B. ROBERTON, in Winnipeg *Free press*, Feb. 4, 1929.

Whether these are sufficient in numbers or high enough in standard to constitute in themselves a literature is a matter of little importance; . . . their real value consists in that they interpret the Canadian spirit and that they express the Canadian point of view.

ERNEST JACKSON HATHAWAY, d. 1930, "How Canadian novelists are using Canadian opportunities" (unpub.), qu. in *Jour. of Can. stud.*, Aug., 1974, 4.

The trouble with Canada is not that Canadians don't buy books as well as the people of other countries – in terms of comparative population Canadians do buy books; the trouble is that there is not much sense of adventure in reading in our own people: they go for the books that have a big sale in other countries.

MORLEY CALLAGHAN, *Univ. of Tor. quart.*, Jan. 1938, 161.

To how many people in Canada are books the daily companions they ought to be? Shall we say five hundred? Or is that too flattering? I mean, of course, outside of educational institutions.

FREDERICK PHILIP GROVE, *Univ. of Tor. quart.*, July, 1938, 459.

We have a book-shelf reaching from Halifax to Victoria; and on it stands one single book, written by a Frenchman transient in Canada. That, in sober fact, is the situation; and to me it is appalling; for a book is a book only when it is read; otherwise it is a bundle of gathered sheets of soiled paper.

FREDERICK PHILIP GROVE, *Univ. of Tor. quart.*, July, 1938, 451, referring to Louis Hemon's *Maria Chapdelaine*.

This Book Belongs to Norman Bethune and His Friends.

NORMAN BETHUNE's bookplate in the 1930's; Ted Allan, S. Gordon, *The scalpel, the sword.* 1952.

It doesn't weigh enough.

ANON., book salesman, explaining why a certain book wouldn't sell in Canada, 1930's, qu. in Michael Joseph, *The adventure of publishing*, 1949, 131.

Any Canadian who turns up his nose at a Canadian book because it is a Canadian book, is a foule byrd.

LAWRENCE J. BURPEE, qu., *Can. author*, Mar., 1943, 6.

Canada is caught up in this modern crisis of liberalism as are all other national communities. But in this world-debate about the values of our civilization the Canadian voice is hardly heard. Who ever reads a Canadian book?

> FRANK H. UNDERHILL, Presidential address, Canadian Historical Assoc., Toronto, May, 1946.

I read American books with an American accent, and English books with an English accent, and Canadian books in the voice of a friend of mine who speaks the best Canadian I have heard.

> ROBERTSON DAVIES, *Table talk*, 1949, 181.

Since the fall of Quebec, much of English-speaking Canada has been populated – if somewhat thinly – by a highly literate people, drawn in part from the educated classes of the Old Country, yet in its two hundred years of existence it has produced few good books and not a single great one.

> E.A. MCCOURT, *Royal commission studies*, 1951, 74.

Canadians don't buy Canadian books. It's a proven fact. And if they won't, who will?

> ANON., frequently heard remark qu. by Thomas H. Raddall in *Dalhousie rev.*, Vol. 34, Summer, 1954, 144.

If the old scornful question were ever asked in our day, "Who reads an American book?" the answer would be shouted, "Canadians".

> MIRIAM CHAPIN, *Contemporary Canada*, 1959, 248.

The child has an enviable capacity to fall in love with a book. His response is total – intellect, emotion and spirit caught and held in one great involution.

> JOAN SELBY, in, *Can. lit.* No. 6, 1960, 32.

A generation of children raised without books would not be a lost generation but a dangerous generation. Children robbed of books can be children robbed of their birthright.

> JOHN B. MACDONALD, Patron, Young Canada Book Week, 1964, *Can. library jour., 3 July, 1964, 16.*

Ruined by a book! Such was my awful fate. Henry Miller had no effect on me; D.H. Lawrence left me cold; I yawned my way through Frank Harris's memoirs. But then I came across a copy of Eaton's catalogue; and, leafing idly through it, discovered photographs of men wearing full-length winter undergarments.

> RICHARD J. NEEDHAM, *Needham's inferno, 1966, 58.*

Who needed books – when all their plots and all their wisdoms might be had, for the looking, in a cloud-burst or a smile? Who needed books, when he had memory?

> ERNEST BUCKLER, *Ox bells and fireflies,* 1968, 195.

It interests me that Huck Finn – which is quite an interesting book – is regularly taught to Canadian students as a central experience of youth coming into experience in the new world. It's interesting, sure, but *Who has seen the wind,* by W.O. Mitchell, is much more relevant to Canadian students and is very rarely taught.

> ROBIN MATHEWS, *Weekend mag.*, Mar. 22, 1969, 3.

By its very nature, the school textbook industry is highly public. It even forms a part of the life of a nation. It is therefore hard to understand why a nation – and, to a still greater degree, its leaders – can allow such a valuable asset to slip into foreign hands.

BERNARD MORRIER, Montreal *La Presse*, Nov. 4, 1970, A4 (Trans.)

Yearly books, which appeared for the Christmas trade.

ROBERTSON DAVIES, *Feast of Stephen*, 1970, 38.

The interest in Canadian books has been expanding very rapidly for 15 years. The sales figures have been steadily climbing. We've known for 15 or 20 years that it's a lot easier to sell a Canadian book in Canada than an imported book. In fact, it has traditionally been easier to sell a lousy Canadian book than a good foreign book.

JACK MCCLELLAND, qu. in R.L. Perry, *Galt, U.S.A.*, 1971, 117.

Borden, Sir Robert

A well-meaning, but torpid person.

ROBERT C. (BOB) EDWARDS, Calgary *Eye opener*, Sept. 11, 1920, 1.

The Conservative party as such carries no indelible imprint from the man who for nearly a quarter of a century led it. He led it by going alongside. He was not a great partisan. He had no overwhelming and audacious bigotries.

AUGUSTUS BRIDLE ("DOMINO"), *Masques of Ottawa*, 1921, 30.

His stature rises as the perspective lengthens but it has some way to go yet before justice is done him. I had many a heart to heart talk with him down the years, and after each of them I was in the habit of saying to myself: "Either he's a Grit in disguise or I'm a Tory".

JOHN W. DAFOE, letter Sept. 16, 1943, qu., *Can. hist. rev.*, 1944, 104.

Happy indeed are they who, as the night of life approaches, find that the inner vision does not fade. Happier still are they who, as the shadows lengthen have full assurance that they bore with head unbowed a strong man's measure of the heat and burden, who are conscious that they enjoy the undimmed confidence of everyone who shared with them their struggles and anxieties, and who have just cause to hope that when all is over there will be heard from their fellow men the simple and sincere benediction: "He served his country well".

ARTHUR MEIGHEN, on Sir Robert Borden. H. of C., *Debates*, Aug. 5, 1960, 7594.

Boredom

We have found that boredom is a malady itself. To help relieve his boredom, man has invented games which purposely place him in dangerous and puzzling situations.

D.O. HEBB, Dept. of Psychology, McGill Univ., qu. in *Queen's quart.*, Vol. 66, 1959, 108.

Boredom is the source of independent effort.

WILLIAM E. BLATZ, *Human security*, 1966, xi.

The long days mate with
the nude on the calendar.
I have packed time like a suitcase
Now there is nothing left to do
but organize my boredom.

SUSAN MUSGRAVE, "January 6", 1970.

Bores

The eye of youth sometimes lightens;
the eye of the bore is glazed with the
film of stupidity. There are gloomy
bores, and agreeable bores, and eager
bores and stuffy bores, but once they
have set their course and determined
their character, they do not change.

ROBERTSON DAVIES, *Samuel Marchbanks' almanack*, 1967, 171.

Bosses

The average North American is too
good at thinking of himself as a boss,
to be able to hate bosses as a class.

B.K. SANDWELL, *Saturday night*, May 18,
1935, 1.

Boundaries

It scarcely requires a common geographical chart, to expose to universal
contempt the fallaceous boundaries
prescribed to Canada.

"PORTIUS", *Letter to the Earl of Shelburne*, 1783, 12.

The whole territory we were wran-
gling about was worth nothing.

LORD ASHBURTON, on his participation in
the Maine boundary dispute, 1843, qu.,
Greville, *Memoirs*, Pt. 2, I, 469.

What is a better boundary between
nations than a parallel of latitude, or
even a natural obstacle? – what really

keeps nations intact and apart? – a
principle. When I can hear our young
men say as proudly, "our Federation,"
or "our Country," or "our Kingdom,"
as the young men of other countries
do, speaking of their own, then I shall
have less apprehension for the result of
whatever trials the future may have in
store for us.

THOMAS D'A. MCGEE, *Confederation debates*, Feb. 9, 1865, 145.

Even if all the territory Mr. Mowat
asks for were awarded to Ontario,
there is not one stick of timber, one
acre of land, or one lump of lead, iron
or gold that does not belong to the
Dominion, or to the people who purchased from the Dominion Government.

SIR JOHN A. MACDONALD, speech in Toronto, May 30, 1882, on the Ontario
boundary dispute with Manitoba.

The deep humiliation which every
self-respecting and patriotic Canadian
feels at the result of the Alaskan
boundary arbitration lies not only in
the loss of territory, but in the conviction that our rights were surrendered
and are likely to be again surrendered
"on the altar of American friendship".

VANCOUVER *PROVINCE*, editorial, Oct.
21, 1903.

Canada is bounded on the north by
gold, on the west by the East, on the
east by history and on the south by
friends.

FRANCES SHELLEY WEES, "Geography lesson", 1937.

Culture is suspiciously examined at
every Customs office; barbarism
laughs at frontiers.

GILBERT NORWOOD, *Spoken in jest*,
1938, 69.

We have our undefended border with the United States, so celebrated in Canadian oratory, only because it is not a real boundary line at all: the real boundary line, one of the most heavily defended in the world, runs through the north of the country, separating a bourgeois sphere of control from a Marxist one.

> NORTHROP FRYE, *The modern century*, 1967, 18.

A fence is what exists between neighbours who are prepared to trade goods, ideas, and gossip, but who understand perfectly well where rights begin and end. To live and develop, Canada needs fences. No nation will exist for long in a world of closed frontiers.

> RAMSAY COOK, *Maple leaf forever*, 1971, 5.

Boundary, Canada — United States

And from the said lake [Mistassini], a line to run southward into 49 degrees north latitude . . . and that latitude to be the limit.

> HUDSON'S BAY CO., proposal made 1714, qu., in David Mills, *Rept. on boundaries of Ontario*, 173.

Medicine line.

> ANON., U.S. prairie Indian name for the Canadian border, especially on the escape of Sitting Bull and the Sioux into Canada in May, 1877.

I could tell you more, but that is all I have to tell you. If we told you more — why, you would not pay any attention to it. That is all I have to say. This part of the country does not belong to your people. You belong on the other side; this side belongs to us.

> CHIEF SITTING BULL, to General Terry (U.S.) at Fort Walsh, Oct. 17, 1877

negotiating the return of and pardon for Sioux Indians who had fled to Canada following the defeat of Custer.

The Dominion of Canada is not what it might have been if we had known what we now know at the time of the boundary negotiations with the United States; and there is no heavier charge, among all the heavy charges that may be brought against the British government in relation to the colonies, than that which arises from the ignorance and neglect that were shown . . .

> SIR CHARLES W. DILKE, *British Empire*, 1899, 35.

The fact is England cares nothing about the boundary but their fear of offending the Canadians is something inconceivable. That collection of bumptious provincials bullies them to any extent and they dare not say a word.

> HENRY CABOT LODGE, Alaskan Boundary Commission, letter to daughter July 28, 1903.

There may be a spectacle perhaps nobler yet than the spectacle of a united continent, a spectacle which would astound the world by its novelty and grandeur, the spectacle of two peoples living in amity side by side for a distance of 4,000 miles, a line which is hardly visible in many quarters, with not a cannon, with not a gun frowning across it, with not a fortress on either side, with no armament one against another, but living in harmony, in mutual confidence, and with no other rivalry than a generous emulation in commerce and the arts of peace.

> SIR WILFRID LAURIER, H. of C., *Debates*, Mar. 7, 1911.

There is just one thing in which you excel Canada, I admit, and that is with regard to your northern boundary, for, while you have the greatest nation under the sun as your northern boundary, we must admit we only have the north pole.

CHARLES HOPEWELL, to an American, Empire Club speech, Dec. 7, 1911.

Shake! cries a voice from the mountain
    Shake! shouts a voice from the mine;
Shake! Let the hands of brothers
    Meet over the Boundary Line.

CLIVE PHILLIPS-WOLLEY, "A Christmas greeting", 1917.

We are 'sitting pretty' here in Canada. East and west are the two oceans far away; we are backed up against the ice cap of the pole; our feet rest on the fender of the American border, warm with a hundred years of friendship.

STEPHEN LEACOCK, "I'll stay in Canada", 1936, in Klinck & Watters, *Canadian anthology*, 1957, 212.

Three thousand miles of border line
Two nations side by side.
Each strong in common brotherhood
And Anglo-Saxon pride.
Yet each the haven and the home
For all of foreign birth,
And each the final fusion point—
The melting pot of earth.

GUY BILSFORD, "A century of peace" in W.R. Bowlin, comp. *Book of historical poems*, 1939.

Where else in the world can you find another case like ours – three thousand miles of forts and not a single frontier?

ROBERT BENCHLEY, speech to Canadian-American luncheon, N.Y., qu., *Oxford pamphlets on world affairs*, Toronto, 1939, No. 1.

The "undefended frontier" was in reality defended by something stronger than bullets and bayonets, an aroused desire for self-sufficiency,

adroitly fostered by those who could profit by such self-sufficiency.

JOE P. SMITH, in *Can. hist. rev.*, 1940, 219.

Our frontier has long been immune from conflict, it is true, but it has suffered grievously from the effects of rhetoric. As a matter of fact, some of the realities have been obscured by the clouds of oratory which hang over this famous border. It has long been undefended, but realists have observed that the disparity of population has made armaments for one country futile and for the other superfluous.

VINCENT MASSEY, *On being Canadian*, 1948, 115.

4000 Miles of "Irritation".

MERRILL DENISON, title of editorial in *Saturday rev.*, June 7, 1952, 25, referring to Canadian-U.S. border.

The boundary of the 49th parallel, apparently anchored by contract, is really anchored and can be securely anchored only in the conscience of the American people and in the dumb will of the Canadian people to be themselves. No paper document and no military forces could sustain such an unlikely design; it is sustained by some 175,000,000 separate human beings in the unconscious course of their daily lives.

BRUCE HUTCHISON, *The struggle for the border*, 1955, 3.

The border between the United States and Canada – 3,986.8 miles without a single fort or gun to protect it – is the most friendly and least visible line of international power in the world. It is crossed daily by thousands of travellers who hardly notice it in their passage. It is washed by a Niagara of genial oratory and illuminated, or sometimes obscured, by a perpetual diplomatic dialogue. On both sides the border is taken as a fact of nature, almost as an act of God, which no man thinks of changing.

> BRUCE HUTCHISON, in Livingston T. Merchant, ed., *Neighbours taken for granted*, 1966, 3.

Bourassa, Henri

I regret your going. We need a man like you at Ottawa, though I should not want two.

> SIR WILFRID LAURIER, in Oct., 1899, on resignation of Bourassa over Laurier's Boer War policy, qu. in J. Schull, *Laurier*, 1965, 469.

So far, I have found no difficulty in practising O'Connell's maxim, that is, in taking my theology at Rome and my politics at home.

> HENRI BOURASSA, letter to Goldwin Smith, Apr. 3, 1902.

I take my theology from Rome but my politics from home.

> HENRI BOURASSA, letter to Goldwin Smith, Dec. 29, 1907.

I know that you boast that you have beaten Bourassa and put him out of business; but as a matter of fact he has conquered you. He may not command your allegiance but he controls your minds. You all think his thoughts, talk his language, echo his threats; and I should suspect that when Sir Wilfrid Laurier passes away – may that day be long distant – that you will accept him as your chief.

> JOHN W. DAFOE, letter to Thomas Coté, Apr. 6, 1916. (Pub.Arch.Can.)

When Henri Bourassa died at the end of August practically every constitutional point which he raised in the first fifty years of his life, and for the raising of which he was denounced as a traitor by a large part of the English-speaking Canada, had become established constitutional practice.

> B.K. SANDWELL, *Saturday night*, Sept. 20, 1952, 7.

Boxing

You know the secret of fighting? Don't get hit. I fought twenty years and I never would have lasted otherwise.

> JIMMY MCLARNIN, qu. in Toronto *Star*, Nov. 6, 1973, C1.

Boyhood

And in his mind
The sifting, timeless sunlight would not find
Memories of stylish Florence or of sacked Rome,
Rather the boyhood that he left at home;
Skating at Scarborough, summers at the Island,
These are the dreams that float beyond his hand.

> DOUGLAS LEPAN, "One of the regiment", 1953.

Boys

O Memory, take my hand today
And lead me thro' the darkened bridge
Washed by the wild Atlantic spray
And spanning many a wind-swept ridge
Of sorrow, grief, of love and joy,
Of youthful hopes and manly fears,
Oh, let me cross the bridge of years
And see myself again a boy!

> WILLIAM H. DRUMMOND, "Child thoughts", Oct., 1900.

The parent who could see his boy as he really is, would shake his head and say: "Willie is no good, I'll sell him."

> STEPHEN B. LEACOCK, "The lot of the schoolmaster", *Maclean's*, Sept., 1915.

Brother, little brother, your childhood
  is passing by,
And the dawn of a noble purpose I
  see in your thoughtful eye.
You have many a mile to travel and
  many a task to do;
Whistle a tune as you go, laddie,
  whistle a tune as you go.

LILIAN LEVERIDGE, "Over the hills of home," 1918.

If there is one thing which utterly destroys a boy's character, it is to be needed. Boys are unendurable unless they are wholly expendable.

ROBERTSON DAVIES, *Tempest-tost*, 1951, 246.

On the hot
cobbles hoppity
he makes a jig up
this moppet
come alive from chocolate
sudden with all
small boys'
joy
dancing under the sun

EARLE BIRNEY, "Bangkok boy", 1962.

Bragging

As often as not it is the consciousness of a lack, not of a possession, that prompts us to preach or to brag.

GEORGE ILES, *Canadian stories*, 1918, 173.

Brains

You can grow corn or potatoes, but you cannot grow brains. Brains come hard and they come high.

SIR WM. OSLER, Canadian Club, Toronto, Dec. 29, 1904.

As the pen is mightier than the sword so are brains mightier than the muscles.

ROBERT L. BORDEN, speech in Gananoque, Jan. 17, 1906.

Each of us has in his possession the most remarkable of galaxies – twelve billion nerve cells with their myriads of subconstellations in the compact universe of the human brain. It is this inner space of the mind which surely, of all our natural resources, offers the most exciting potentialities.

WILLIAM FEINDEL, *Memory, learning and language*, 1960, 11.

Bravery

The one predominating passion of the savage nature is bravery.

AGNES C. LAUT, *Pathfinders of the west*, 1904, 9.

I'm not leaving. I must stay.

PIERRE E. TRUDEAU, St. Jean Baptiste Day demonstration in Montreal, June 24, 1968, on the reviewing stand, after being subjected to violent action by demonstrators.

Bribery

The evil is in the low condition, or rather total absence of honour & dignity which make all classes, high & low, accessible to bribery of every description.

SIR WILFRID LAURIER, letter to Blake, July 10, 1882.

The foundation of party government is bribery, is it not? Men are party men for the spoils. They support the government for the time for the sake of the spoils. If a man "kicks" and gives an independent vote against the party he loses their patronage, does he not? Is not bribery the corner-stone of party government?

JUSTICE JOHN D. ARMOUR, in the conspiracy case, *Queen v. Bunting;* Toronto *Globe*, Dec. 5, 1884, 2.

We bribed them all, and generally acquired nearly everything in sight. We literally owned the Province. Public officials in Canada, so far as my experience goes, do not have that suspicious hesitancy in accepting money that characterizes some officials in this country. The Langevin crowd did not scruple to take all they could get.

OWEN E. MURPHY, interview pub. in *New York Times*, repub. in Toronto *Globe*, Nov. 23, 1891; Murphy was associated with Thomas McGreevy, a large railroad contractor in Quebec.

Upon my word I do not think there was much to be said in favour of the Canadians over the Turks when contracts, places, free tickets on railways, or even cash was in question.

SIR EDMUND HORNBY, *Autobiography*, 1928, 90.

Brides

"Who gives away this woman?" Then
  Whoever does is silly:
She's given herself to countless men,
  So why not now to Willy?

GEOFFREY B. RIDDEHOUGH, "Give away", 1972.

Bridges

Canada is a country of bridges, and the bridge is one of the most beautiful of human creations.

LORD TWEEDSMUIR, speech to Engineering Inst. of Canada, Montreal, June 15, 1937.

British

Four millions of Britons who are not free.

EDWARD BLAKE, speech at Aurora, Ont., Oct. 3, 1874; ref. to Canadians.

He is ready, if the occasion presents itself, to throw the whole English population in the St. Lawrence.

SIR WILFRID LAURIER, letter to Mme. Joseph Lavergne, Nov. 29, 1901, referring to her son, Armand.

Canada for the British.

ISAAC MOSES BARR, founder of the Barr colony, *Pamphlet No. 3*, 1903, sub-head.

We in Canada are trustees for the British race. We hold this land in allegiance, we hold it in development, for our brothers, who are the sons of those who won it for us.

F.B. CUMBERLAND, Empire Club speech, Toronto, 1904.

Till the Americans came to England the people were an honest, law-abiding race, respecting their superiors and despising those below them.

STEPHEN LEACOCK, *My discovery of England*, 1922, 59.

I want to make Canada all Canadian and ALL BRITISH!

JOHN G. DIEFENBAKER, speech at Macdowall, Sask., election campaign Sept., 1926.

British Columbia

Island versus Mainland.

ANON., a familiar phrase in the colonies of Vancouver Island and British Columbia before their union in 1866.

British Columbia, the land of golden opportunities.

GEORGE BROWN, *Confederation debates*, Feb. 8, 1865, 8.

True Loyalty's to Motherland
And not to Canada,
The love we bear is second-hand
To any step-mama.

JOSEPH D. PEMBERTON, ascribed, letter to *British colonist*, Victoria, 1870, qu. in R. Reid, *Canadian style*, 1973, 85.

Of all the conditions usually attached to a union of this colony with Canada, that of early establishment of railroad communication from sea to sea is the most important. If the railroad scheme is utopian, so is Confederation. The two must stand or fall together.

NEW WESTMINISTER *BRITISH COLUMBIAN*, Feb. 2, 1870.

No union between this Colony and Canada can permanently exist, unless it be to the material and pecuniary advantage of this Colony to remain in the union. The sum of the interests of the inhabitants is the interest of the Colony. The people of this Colony have, generally speaking, no love for Canada; they care, as a rule, little or nothing about the creation of another Empire, Kingdom, or Republic; they have but little sentimentality, and care little about the distinctions between the form of Government of Canada and the United States.

JOHN S. HELMCKEN, B.C., *Debates on Confederation*, Mar. 9, 1870, 13.

No union on account of love need be looked for. The only bond of union outside of force — and force the Dominion has not — will be the material advantage of the country and pecuniary benefit of the inhabitants. Love for Canada has to be acquired by the prosperity of the country, and from our children.

JOHN S. HELMCKEN, B.C., *Debates on Confederation*, Mar. 9, 1870, 13.

I would not object to a little revolution now and again in British Columbia, after Confederation, if we were treated unfairly; for I am one of those who believe that political hatreds attest the vitality of a State.

AMOR DE COSMOS, speech in Victoria, Mar. 10, 1870.

The Government of the Dominion undertake to secure the commencement simultaneously, within two years from the date of the Union, of the construction of a Railway from the Pacific towards the Rocky Mountains, and from such point as may be selected, east of the Rocky Mountains, towards the Pacific, to connect the seaboard of British Columbia with the railway system of Canada; and further, to secure the completion of such Railway within ten years from the date of the Union.

CANADA., *Terms of Union;* terms and conditions under which the Colony of British Columbia entered into union with the Dominion of Canada, at the Court at Windsor, May 16, 1871, item 11.

Splendor sine occasu, (Splendour without diminishment.)

BRITISH COLUMBIA, Motto on provincial coat-of-arms, 1871.

The West beyond the West.

ANON., 19th century term for B.C.

They won't secede, they know better.

EDWARD BLAKE, speech at Aurora, Ont., Oct. 3, 1874.

I think British Columbia a glorious province, a province which Canada should be proud to possess, and whose association with the Dominion she ought to regard as the crowning triumph of federation.

LORD DUFFERIN, speech in Victoria, Sept. 20, 1876.

Who undertook to fix upon this Dominion that incubus of British Columbia, that excrescence of British Columbia, that cancer, financially, of British Columbia, that was eating into out vitals and entailing a heavy financial burden upon the country for all time to come?

ARTHUR GILLMOR, (Charlotte, N.B.), H. of C., *Debates*, Apr. 4, 1879, 1015.

The spoilt child of Confederation.

TORONTO *GLOBE* , Feb. 26, 1884.

British Columbia was part British and part American; it would require the completion of the railway to make her part of the new dominion.

PIERRE BERTON, *The last spike*, 1971, 217, ca. 1885.

It is an empty land. To love the country here – mountains are worshipped, not loved – is like embracing a wraith.

RUPERT BROOKE, *Letters from America*, 1919, 153.

Japanese Columbia.

ANON., term popular in early 1920's, in B.C.

It is war now between the Oriental and the Euro-Canadian for possession of British Columbia: the prize region of the whole Pacific.

TOM MACINNES, *Oriental occupation of B.C.*, 1927, 7.

British Columbia is Canada's westernmost province and geographic centre of the British Empire.

S.F. TOLMIE, Premier of B.C., in C. Martin, Ed., *The book of Canada*, 1930, 253.

We are an empire in ourselves and our hills and valleys are stored with potential wealth which makes us one of the greatest assets of the Dominion.

T.D. PATTULLO, Premier of B.C., letter to R.B. Bennett, Dec. 18, 1933. (Prov. Arch. B.C.).

If I had known what it was like I wouldn't have been content with a mere visit. I'd have been born here.

STEPHEN LEACOCK, *My discovery of the west*, 1937, 173.

Yea, then I moved west to my hill's margin
and saw a soft middleclass swaddled in trees,
in unfrequented churches and fears not a few.

EARLE BIRNEY, "Trial of a city", 1952.

A British Columbian is a man who has a California-type house, a Montreal mortgage, an English car, and a Scottish dog. His wife, who comes from Regina or maybe it is Calgary, either has a cat whose forbears came from Persia, or she has a small bird from the tropics which she keeps in a cage allegedly imported from Eastern Canada, but more likely made in Japan.

BARRY MATHER, Vancouver *Sun* columnist, in R.E. Waters, ed., *British Columbia: a centennial anthology*, 1958, 482.

British Columbians like to think of their province as a large body of land entirely surrounded by envy.

ERIC NICOL, in *Maclean's*, May 10, 1958, 36.

The first almighty fact about British Columbia is mountains. They stand in rank upon rank, from the peaks and passes of the Rockies to where the Coast Range plunges its feet into the Pacific Ocean.

RODERICK HAIG-BROWN, "With its face to the west", in, *The face of Canada*, 1959, 179.

The provincialism of a British Columbian is no more than a part of his Canadianism and the well-worn political trick of trying to divide Ottawa from the rest of the country now rates nothing more than good natured laughter.

RODERICK HAIG-BROWN, *The living land,* 1961, 260.

I hate practically everything B.C. stands for. I hate the shoddy, uncaring development of natural resources, the Chamber of Commerce mentality that favours short-term material gain over all other considerations, the utter contempt for human values of every kind.

RODERICK HAIG-BROWN, speech to Canadian Author's Assoc., Victoria, B.C. June 21, 1965.

Life in British Columbia is so pleasant that it seems absurd to waste any part of it trying to improve on nature.

EDWARD MCCOURT, *The road across Canada,* 1965, 178.

From Vancouver to Ottawa was 3,000 miles, but from Ottawa to Vancouver it was 3,000,000 miles.

ANON., favourite saying of British Columbians, qu. in P. Sherman, *Bennett,* 1966, 138.

A lady-in-waiting with great expectations, British Columbia blushed and palpitated with each new thrust into its interior.

MARTIN ROBIN, *The rush for spoils; the company province, 1871-1933,* 1972, 40.

They have a God-given right to suffer more; they will suffer, suffer, suffer.

W.A.C. BENNETT, to Jes Odam, reporter June 5, 1973, meaning that the people of B.C. had not yet suffered enough for electing a socialist government in 1972 and defeating his Social Credit government.

Out here you get all the McDonald hamburger stands. Kamloops is the epitome of the plastic new towns. But there · are people alive who can remember big trees in Kitsilano.

GLENN LEWIS, qu. in *Maclean's,* June 1973, 30.

British Commonwealth of Nations

Nobody can imagine such an impossibility as a state of states or a cat of cats. The British Commonwealth of Nations is really nothing but a phrase − a very foolish phrase.

JOHN S. EWART, 1921, qu. in *Can. hist. rev.,* 1933, 140.

The unity of the British Commonwealth of Nations is at bottom a moral unity, and only in the exercise of a highly-refined political morality is there hope for its continuance.

ROBERT A. MCKAY, *Changes in legal structure of the Commonwealth,* 1931.

We are supposed to be associated with the British Commonwealth of Nations, although no such thing exists. We are alleged to be a part of a third British Empire, although there never was more than one, and we have ceased to be part of it.

JOHN S. EWART, in *Can. hist. rev.,* 1933, 123.

Canada is the true architect of the present British Commonwealth of Nations.

BRUCE HUTCHISON, Winnipeg *Free Press,* Nov. 23, 1943.

The British Commonwealth has within itself a spirit which is not exclusive but the opposite of exclusive. Therein lies its strength. That spirit expresses itself in co-operation. Therein lies the secret of its unity. Cooperation is capable of indefinite expansion. Therein lies the hope of its future.

> W.L. MACKENZIE KING, speech to British Parliament, May 11, 1944.

The Commonwealth is an organism, not an institution, and this fact gives promise not only of continued growth and vitality but of flexibility as well.

> PIERRE E. TRUDEAU, Commonwealth conference, Jan. 15, 1969, London, England.

British Empire

The sun never sets on it.

> T.C. HALIBURTON, *Sam Slick*, 1840, 273.

We hold a vaster empire than has been!

> SIR LEWIS MORRIS, "Song of Empire", written on occasion of Queen Victoria's jubilee, June 20, 1887; used as inscription on Canadian "All Red" postage stamp issued 1898 to commemorate adoption of Empire penny postage.

For myself I am a true Briton. I love the old land dearly. I am glad that I was born a British subject; a British subject I have lived for three score years and something more. I hope to live and die a British subject. I trust and hope that my children and my grand-children who have also been born British subjects will live their lives as British subjects, and as British subjects die.

> SIR OLIVER MOWAT, speech in Toronto, Feb, 18, 1891. (See: Sir John A. Macdonald, for a similar statement.)

The more I analyse the vital parts and the lusty members of this admirable political creation, with its nerves of steel and its rich blood, the more my admiration of England has grown. I was always glad enough to be a British subject, as most of my compatriots are,

but now I experience the full pride in my British citizenship.

> HENRI BOURASSA, H. of C., *Debates*, Mar. 12, 1901.

A galaxy of free nations.

> SIR WILFRID LAURIER, speech in London Guildhall, July 11, 1902.

The most pressing need of the Empire is a new aristocracy in which the highest place will be accorded to those who inherit the spirit of great men rather than to those who inherit their blood.

> PETER MCARTHUR, *To be taken with salt*, 1903, 148.

In the scrolls of the future it is already written that the centre of the Empire must shift — and where, if not to Canada?

> SARA JEANNETTE DUNCAN, *The imperialist*, 1904, 399.

It is an Empire not of force, or politics, but of mind, of literature, of ideas and tendencies, civil and social. As such it has no peer in history.

> GOLDWIN SMITH, address at dedication of Goldwin Smith Hall, Cornell Univ., June 19, 1906.

Dedicated to all who love their country and whose country is the British Empire.

> H.A. KENNEDY, *New Canada and new Canadians*, 1907, the dedication.

Quebec is the acknowledged cradle of Greater Britain. It rests with you whether it shall be regarded as its heart and soul. There is not a Briton in New Zealand, Australia, or South Africa whose high status in the world does not come to him in direct descent from Quebec.

> LORD GREY, letter to Sir Wilfrid Laurier, Mar. 2, 1908. (Pub.Arch.Can.)

The British Empire is a partnership of nations of equal status united in a partnership of consent.

JOHN W. DAFOE, speech, Imperial Press Conference, Aug. 6, 1920.

It is possible to hold that not Chamberlain but Laurier, not Milner but Smuts, not the British Cabinet but the members of the Imperial Conferences, have been the true leaders into our present greatness.

J.L. MORISON, *Can. hist. rev.*, 1921, 194.

It is in many ways the most wonderful experiment in political relations that has ever been attempted. It is absolutely unique, unparalleled, unprecedented, in its structure and relationship.

O.D. SKELTON, Canadian club, Ottawa, Jan. 21, 1922.

As it was in Canada that the death blow to the old British Empire was struck, so it was in Canada that the New British Empire had its birth.

W.R. RIDDELL, Empire Club Toronto speech, Apr. 25, 1929.

Six independent states are not an empire or a commonwealth. They are six kingdoms. And as they have the same King, their association is that of a Personal Union.

JOHN S. EWART, Ottawa *Citizen*, Jan. 3, 1930.

We are Canadians here and we don't want any peregrinating Imperialists to dictate our defence policies . . . We in Canada can take care of our policies, defence and others.

IAN MACKENZIE, Minister of National Defence, in answer to a statement by Viscount Elibank in Toronto, Aug. 19, 1936.

Canada is the most Puritanical part of the Empire and cherishes very much the Victorian standards in private life.

LORD TWEEDSMUIR, letter to Stanley Baldwin, Nov. 9, 1936.

British North America Act, 1867

We are laying the foundation of a great State − perhaps one which at a future day, may even overshadow this country. But, come what may, we shall rejoice that we have shown neither indifference to their wishes, nor jealousy of their aspirations, but that we honestly and sincerely, to the utmost of our power and knowledge, fostered their growth, recognizing in it the conditions of our own greatness.

LORD CARNARVON, House of Lords, *Debates*, Feb. 19, 1867, col. 576b, on 2nd. reading of B.N.A. bill.

To impart anything like liveliness to a discussion of the British North America Act requires the touch of Voltaire.

GOLDWIN SMITH, remark qu. in E. Wallace, *Goldwin Smith, Victorian liberal*, 1957, 231.

A Constitution like ours, complicated and delicate in its adjustments, requires for its interpretation that measure of learning, experience and practice which those who live under it, who work it, and who are practically engaged in its operation are all their lives acquiring. The British North America Act is a skeleton. The true form and proportions, the true spirit of our Constitution, can be made manifest only to the men of the soil.

EDWARD BLAKE, H. of C., *Debates*, Feb. 26, 1880, 253.

The object of the Act (the British North America Act) was neither to weld the provinces into one, nor to subordinate provincial governments to a central authority.

LORD WATSON, judgment, 1892, of the Privy Council.

Division of legislative authority is the principle of the British North America Act, and if the doctrine of necessarily incidental powers is to be extended to all cases in which inconvenience arises from such a division that is the end of the federal character of the Union.

JUSTICE LYMAN POOR DUFF, City of Montreal v. Montreal Street Railway, (1910) Supreme Court Reports, Vol. 43, 232.

The British North America Act, was made for the people of Canada and not the people of Canada for the British North America Act; and if the act does not conform to conditions as we find them in the country today, then we ought to amend it so as to bring it into conformity with existing conditions.

ABRAHAM A. HEAPS, H. of C., *Debates*, Feb. 6, 1928, 225.

The British North America Act planted in Canada a living tree capable of growth and expansion within its natural limits.

LORD SANKEY, *Appeal cases*, 1930, 136.

The Statute of Westminster of 1931 is the logical outcome of the British North America Act of 1867. It was Sir John A. Macdonald who conceived the whole design at a time when scarcely anybody, including his own colleagues, fully understood him; and his successors, Laurier, Borden and King, have merely put the increasingly less and less significant touches to a work which is now finished.

D.G. CREIGHTON, in *Can. hist. rev.*, 1945, 123.

I used to say to my classes in constitutional law, "We have a *rendez-vous* with the B.N.A. Act. It's going to come some day!"

F.R. SCOTT, address, Assn. of Can. Law Teachers and Can. Pol. Sc. Assn., Charlottetown, June 11, 1964.

The British North America Act is a Constitution for a "horse-and-buggy" age.

EUGENE FORSEY, paraphrase of a common statement, dismissed as one of the seven devils of our pseudo-history in "Our present discontents", speech, Acadia Univ., Oct. 19, 1967.

The British North America Act was designed by British overlords; from which it follows, of course, that we must now scrap it and give ourselves a homemade one.

EUGENE FORSEY, paraphrase of a common statement, dismissed as one of the seven devils of our pseudo-history in "Our present discontents", speech, Acadia Univ., Oct. 19, 1967.

Bringing the constitution home.

CANADA. CONSTITUTIONAL CONFERENCE. SECRETARIAT., "Process of Constitutional Review," Feb., 1971.

Brock, Sir Isaac

There was a bold commander, brave
    General Brock by name,
Took shipping at Niagara and down to
    York he came,
He says "My gallant heroes, if you'll
    come along with me,
We'll fight those proud Yankees in the
    West of Canaday!"

ANON., song, War of 1812, now entitled "Come all you bold Canadians".

Most of the people have lost all confidence – I however speak loud and look big.

SIR ISAAC BROCK, letter to Sir George Prevost, July 20, 1812, qu. by J.M. Hitsman, *The incredible war of 1812*, 1965, 62.

No tongue can blazen forth their fame –
The cheers that stir the sacred hill
Are but mere promptings of the will
That conquered them, that
   conquers still;
And generations yet shall thrill
At Brock's remembered name.

CHARLES SANGSTER, "Brock", Oct. 13, 1859.

Thank you, General Brock.

AMEX: THE AMERICAN EXPATRIATE IN CANADA, Vol. 2, No. 1, 1969, dedication.

Brothers

We who are left will slowly wither out
To tottering senescence and a drought
Of youthful dreams, though touch'd to
   wistfulness
By memories of old springtime and
   your face.

WATSON KIRKCONNELL, "In perpetuum frater", 1965.

Brown, George

After some five minutes' conversation in the *Globe* office with a hungry-looking, bald-headed individual in his shirt sleeves, and nails in mourning, I desired to see the Honourable Brown himself. Much to my surprise I found that he stood before me.

HORTON RHYS, *A theatrical trip for a wager*, 1861.

We acted together, dined at public places together, played euchre in crossing the Atlantic, and went into society in England together. And yet on the day after he resigned we resumed our old positions and ceased to speak.

SIR JOHN A. MACDONALD, after Brown's resignation from the Cabinet, Dec. 1865.

The great reason why I have been able to beat Brown is that I have been able to look a little ahead, while he could on no occasion forego the temptation of a temporary triumph.

SIR JOHN A. MACDONALD, letter to M.C. Cameron, Jan. 3, 1872.

I fancy that in his own home circle his presence has been a perpetual sunshine.

DANIEL WILSON, journal, Apr. 23, 1880.

His nature was a rushing mountain
   stream;
His faults but eddies which its
   swiftness bred.

JOHN W. BENGOUGH, on the death of George Brown, May 9, 1880, *Grip*, repr. *Grip's Comic Almanac*, 1881, p. 68.

Budget Speeches

Mr. Speaker, I should like to ask the Minister of Finance a question regarding the preparation of last night's budget speech. Can the minister assure us that he and his government official alone prepared the budget speech without the assistance of outside consultants or ghost writers from Toronto?

DOUGLAS M. FISHER, H. of C., *Debates*, June 14, 1963, 1169. Seriously damaged reputation or wisdom of Walter L. Gordon, Min. of Finance.

Budgets

The modern governmental budget is, and must be, the balance wheel of the economy. Its very size is such that if it were permitted to fluctuate up and down with the rest of the economy, instead of counter to the swings of economic activity, it would so exaggerate booms and depressions as to be disastrous.

DOUGLAS C. ABBOTT, speech, Nov., 1949.

The budget of the province is not big enough to meet all needs. We must therefore serve our friends first. If I had a loaf of bread that was too small to allow me to share it with both my friends and my enemies, I would share it exclusively with my friends.

MAURICE DUPLESSIS, in Quebec Legislature, debate on Roads Dept. estimates; qu. in P. Laporte, *The true face of Duplessis*, 1960, 53.

This is an ignorant budget prepared by ignorant people. Your victory party is premature. Just you wait till this hits the fan.

ANON., Dept. of Finance official, to E.J. Benson, at celebration on presentation of Liberal Party budget by Walter Gordon June 13, 1963.

The financial capitals of the world have just about had enough from Canada. Last Friday the initial reaction to the budget was one of bewilderment and dismay. Yesterday it was anger and scorn. Today, our friends of the western world fully realize that we don't want them or their money and that Canadians who deal with them in even modest amounts will suffer a 30% expropriation of the assets involved.

ERIC KIERANS, Pres., Montreal Stock Exchange, Brief June 18, 1963 to Minister of Finance, Walter Gordon, after presentation of his budget, re 30% securities tax proposal.

Buffalo

Thus it continues till you leave ye woods behind
And then you have beast of several kind
The one is a black a Buffillo great
Another is an outgrown Bear which is good meat

HENRY KELSEY, *Journal*, 1690.

Plains provisions.

ANON., Red River colony term for buffalo meat, early 19th. century.

The Running of the Buffalo.

ANON., phrase used for the summer hunt of the buffalo by the Hudson's Bay Co., 1820 to 1860.

Far as the eye could reach, these plains were covered with troops of buffalo; thousands and thousands were constantly in sight.

EARL OF SOUTHESK, *Saskatchewan and the Rocky Mountains: a diary and narrative of travel in 1859 and 1860*, 1860, 109.

The deep, rolling voice of the mighty multitude came grandly on the air like the booming of a distant ocean.

THE EARL OF SOUTHESK, *Saskatchewan and the Rocky Mountains*, 1860 (1875, 92).

In your own land you are, I know, a great chief. You have abundance of blankets, tea and salt, tobacco and rum. You have splendid guns and powder and shot, as much as you can desire. But there is one thing that you lack – you have no buffalo, and you come here to seek them. I am a great chief also. But the Great Spirit has not dealt with us alike. You he has endowed with various riches, while to me he has given the buffalo alone.

ANON., Cree Chief to Viscount Milton, in Milton and Cheadle, *The northwest passage by land*, 1865, 66-67.

And, lo! before us lay the tameless
   stock,
Slow wending to the northward like
   a cloud!
A multitude in motion, dark and
   dense –
Far as the eye could reach, and
   farther still,
In countless myriads stretched for
   many a league.

> CHARLES MAIR, *Tecumseh*, 1886.

One stride he took, and sank upon
   his knees,
Glared stern defiance where I stood
   revealed,
Then swayed to earth, and, with
   convulsive groan,
Turned heavily upon his side, and
   died.

> CHARLES MAIR, "The last bison", 1890.

Buildings

A Gothic pile, with the variety of
forms and outlines in which its charm
resides, or an Elizabethan manor-
house, with its many gables, must in
Canada be a mere snow-trap.

> GOLDWIN SMITH, *The Bystander*, Apr.,
> 1880, 178, referring to Parliament
> Buildings, Ottawa.

There were four buildings on this
corner [King and Simcoe Streets, To-
ronto] – Government House itself,
Upper Canada College, a church, and
a saloon (to use the venerable term); a
pale little joke of the time was that the
four buildings represented legislation,
education, salvation, and damnation.

> VINCENT MASSEY, *What's past is pro-*
> *logue*, 1963, 7, referring to 1890's.

Great buildings symbolize a people's
deeds and aspirations. It has been said

that, wherever a nation had a conscience and a mind, it recorded the
evidence of its being in the highest
products of this greatest of all arts.
Where no such monuments are to be
found, the mental and moral natures
of the people have not been above the
faculties of the beasts.

> JOHN SHAW, Mayor of Toronto, on open-
> ing of the City Hall, Sept. 18, 1899.

One day I hope to see Canadian cities
take as much pride in their theatres as
they do in their grain elevators.

> BARRY JACKSON, Birmingham Repertory
> Theatre, to theatre audience in Edmon-
> ton, November, 1929, qu. in Betty Lee,
> *Love and whiskey*, 1973, 79.

The knack of building houses which
have faces, as opposed to grimaces, is
retained by few builders.

> ROBERTSON DAVIES, *Tempest-tost*, 1951,
> 14.

See that the wreck of all things made
   with hands
Being fixed and certain, as all flesh is
   grass
   The grandiose design
Must marry the ragged matter, and of
   the vision
Nothing endure that does not gain
   through ruin
   The right, the wavering line.

> JOHN GLASSCO, "Gentleman's farm",
> 1958.

Every graveyard in Canada, if it could
speak, would say "amen" to the slab.
Well, that's what this building says for
Toronto. You've got a headmarker for
a grave and future generations will
look at it and say: "This marks the spot
where Toronto fell."

> FRANK LLOYD WRIGHT, qu. in Toronto
> *Star*, Sept. 29, 1958, 25, referring to
> Viljo Revell's plan for new City Hall.

Never have I seen so many ugly buildings create such an altogether beautiful city as Montreal.

VILJO REVELL, (Finnish designer of Toronto City Hall) in *Montrealer*, Sept. 1959, 50.

If I were asked by some stranger to North American culture to show him the most important religious building in Canada, I would take him to Toronto's Maple Leaf Gardens.

WILLIAM KILBOURN, *Religion in Canada*, 1968, 6.

It gives me great pleasure to declare this thing open – whatever it is.

PRINCE PHILIP, on opening Vancouver City Hall Annex, Oct. 29, 1969.

Habitat is in the tradition of spontaneous self-made environments, the beginnings of a contemporary vernacular.

MOSHE SAFDIE, *Beyond Habitat*, 1970, 118.

Burials

The flesh that I wore chanced ever to be
Less of my friend than my enemy.
So bury it deeply – strong foe, weak friend –
And bury it cheaply – and there it ends.

ISABELLA VALANCY CRAWFORD, "His clay", in Toronto *Evening telegram*, Oct. 22, 1884.

We buried her in Spring-time.
The sparrow in the air
wept that we should hide with earth the face of one so fair.

LEONARD COHEN, "Ballad", 1956.

Business

I know of no money-making business in Canada except the Law, Store Keeping, Tavern Keeping, and perhaps I may add horse dealing.

JOHN LANGTON, letter to his brother, Oct. 21, 1844.

Every successful enterprise requires three men – a dreamer, a businessman, and a son-of-a-bitch.

PETER MCARTHUR, a favorite epigram coined about 1904 after failure of his jointly-published *The Daily Paper* in England.

Dear Doctor: I have not received a reply to my former letter. Let me assure you that the machinery of the Union Trust Company requires oil. Please turn on the tap. We need the surplus of the I.O.F. Yours sincerely, George E. Foster.

GEORGE E. FOSTER, a private letter read by J.A. Macdonald, editor of the *Globe*, in a campaign address, North Toronto, Oct. 6, 1908.

Permit me to congratulate you on your prompt action in sending troops to Cape Breton. It is undoubtedly saving riot, bloodshed and much destruction of property, and as we have large interests in that section of the country, we have reason to be thankful.

SIR EDWARD CLOUSTON, letter to Laurier, July 15, 1909. (Pub. Arch. Can)

To hell with profits.

SIR JOSEPH FLAVELLE, 1917, wartime claim, qu. in C.L. Burton, *Sense of urgency*, 1952, 209.

We will now get all we can out of the people of Canada.

ANON., attributed to directors of Grand Trunk Railway, about 1922; qu., Vaughan, *Van Horne*, 207.

The history of Canada since Confederation – the outcome of a politico-commercial, or a commercio-political conspiracy, if consequences are any indication of motive – has been a history of heartless robbery of both the people of the Maritimes and of the Prairie Sections of Canada by the Big 'Vested' Interests – so called from the size of their owners' vests – of the politically and financially stronger Central Provinces.

E.A. PARTRIDGE, *A war on poverty*, [1925?] 77.

The depressing thing about Canada is not so much that the Holts and Gundys and Beauharnois gangs should succeed in collaring most of its natural resources as that most of our young men should be growing up with dreams of emulating these worthies or of becoming yes-men under them.

FRANK H. UNDERHILL, *Can. forum*, July, 1931, 370.

Most prudent people hesitate to do business with their relatives. When the necessity arrives, the results are seldom a stimulant of family affection. Each kinsman expects the other by reason of his kin to make kindly concessions.

WALTER FENTON, *Queen's quart.*, 1932, 716.

The patriotic way for the true French Canadian to live is to save and become a small proprietor. English methods are not ours. The French became great by small savings and small business.

ANON., Roman Catholic curé, qu. by E.C. Hughes, *French Canada in transition*, 1943, 151. (Trans.)

We make more money out of men than we ever make out of things.

W. GARFIELD WESTON, qu. in *Maclean's*, Aug. 15, 1948, 48.

A full and active business life can never be completely satisfying. The price is usually emotional and cultural atrophy.

D.H. MILLER-BARSTOW, *Beatty of the C.P.R.*, 1951, 10.

I think all of us recognize the fact that there are some things which it is more appropriate to have done by public authorities than by free enterprise. But I think we are all most happy when free enterprise does what is required to be done and public authorities do not have to intervene.

LOUIS ST. LAURENT, H. of C., *Debates*, May 4, 1953, 4764.

Highly individualistic, success-oriented persons, such as the Crestwood Heights family tends to produce, may be eminently suited to the business world but of limited usefulness beyond it.

JOHN R. SEELEY, et al., *Crestwood heights*, 1956, 222.

Man has always been alive to the itching in his palm. But only a few remarkable Canadians have evolved their acquisitive impulses into economic influence so immense that it grew beyond their control, like a forest fire that feeds on itself.

PETER C. NEWMAN, *Flame of power*, 1959, 11.

The multinational firm.

HOWE MARTYN, Professor, phrase coined in 1961, based on a similar phrase coined by an American in 1958.

Effective control lies in the hands of directors, paid officials and manipulators who should not, but frequently do, operate a company on the basis of "Who's to stop us!"

FRASER ROBERTSON, *Globe and Mail*, Nov. 20, 1961, 26.

The ineffective administration of the Combines Investigation Act is an aspect of the compromise between the power of the vote and the power of the dollar that is a feature of Canadian democracy.

> G. ROSENBLUTH and H.G. THORBURN, *Canadian anti-combines administration, 1952-1960*, 1963, 100.

Miniature replica effect.

> H. EDWARD ENGLISH, *Industrial structure in Canada's international competitive position*, 1964; ref. to the results of foreign branch plant development.

Modern business is a complex, fast-moving thing. The fit and educated survive. The remainder go into politics.

> HERB SURPLIS, business columnist, Calgary *Herald*, qu. in *Liberty*, Feb. 1964.

No one should ever have to do business through a board of directors; all those conflicting opinions are a waste of time. This means that an efficient businessman is obliged to buy up all the shares in his own business.

> ROY THOMSON, attributed by Russell Braddon in *Roy Thomson of Fleet Street*, 1965, 213.

If you look around Canada at the thousands of small plants, well, you know how many of them are subsidiaries. I would guess that half of them couldn't exist if they didn't have parents to provide the engineering to stay abreast of technology.

> HARRY WILKES, executive, qu. in R.L. Perry, *Galt, U.S.A.*, 1971, 62.

Contrary to what obtains in other countries, the relationship between government and business in Canada appears to be one of the mutual lack of trust and arms-lengthsmanship.

> JOHN H. MOORE, address, Canadian Corporate Management Co. Ltd., Annual meeting, Toronto, Apr. 7, 1971.

Branch plant industry.

> ANON., phrase commonly applied to Canadian industry. Sometimes stated as "branch plant economy".

Business Men

Doctors, auctioneers and bakers,
Dentists, diplomats and fakirs,
Clergymen and undertakers.

> E.J. PRATT, "The witches' brew", 1925.

I could write a beautiful and perfectly sincere epitaph upon the average Toronto business man, but to live with he is dull.

> W.L. GRANT, Principal of Upper Canada College, letter to Sir John Willison, Feb. 3, 1927. (Pub.Arch.Can.)

What do you think of the Fifty Big Shots who are exploiting the country?

> WILLIAM ABERHART, radio broadcast, May 24, 1935; based on Watt H. McCollum, *Who owns Canada*, 1934, 7, referring to Company Directors.

After more than a week in one spot, I grow stale. I get my best ideas away from the office.

> E.P. TAYLOR, qu. in P. Newman, *Flame of power*, 1959, 228.

Canadians seem to be happier than Americans. At least they're more contented and more balanced. They don't hemorrhage if an order is slow getting out and, after all, they argue, is one late order worth an ulcer?

> ANON., an American, qu. in *Maclean's* Apr. 20, 1963, 53.

So the businessman has replaced the warrior and the aristocrat.

> LOUIS DUDEK, *Delta*, May 1963, 9.

A businessman has to be a little like a turtle – develop a hard shell, but be a bit soft underneath; proceed with caution but, above all, stick your neck out once in a while.

> D.C. HOLGATE, Dominion Bridge official, speaking in Winnipeg; qu. in *Liberty*, Aug. 1963.

The thoughts of an executive
Are always consecutive.
His mighty brain
Gives him no pain.
His desk is kept neat
To rest his feet.
His loves are various
And secretarious.

> BRUCE HUTCHISON, *Western windows*, 1967, 75.

Buying and Selling

Buy from them that has *got* to sell, and *sell* to them that is *obliged* to buy; and cinch 'em all good and hard – that's all the secret there is to business.

> M. ALLERDALE GRAINGER, *Woodsmen of the West*, 1908, 87.

The buyer may still beware, but he no longer knows of what he must beware.

> CANADA. ROYAL COMM. ON PRICE SPREADS, *Report*, 1937, 234.

Cabinet

Give me better wood and I will make you a better cabinet.

> SIR JOHN A. MACDONALD, a reply sometimes made to criticisms of his choice of cabinet ministers.

A crowd of commonplaces.

> LADY ABERDEEN, *Journal*, Dec. 13, 1894, on the members of Sir John Thompson's cabinet.

We fought like blazes.

> JOSEPH I. TARTE, on ministers in Sir Wilfrid Laurier's government; Tarte was a minister, 1896-1902.

I never wanted to be in the Cabinet, but I would like to be the Minister of Defence for one year, and by that time there would be no need for that department.

> AGNES MACPHAIL, H. of C., *Debates*, Feb. 19, 1929, 273.

Please do not interrupt me, can you not see I am engaged in a Cabinet meeting.

> RICHARD B. BENNETT, frequently quoted apocryphal reply to Ottawa citizen who spoke to him while out walking.

The cabinet has, in fact, taken over the allotted role of the Senate as the protector of the rights of the provinces and it has done an incomparably better job.

> R. MACGREGOR DAWSON, *Government of Canada*, 1947, 212.

The Premier, when choosing his cabinet, can select a man of indifferent talent as a minister to meet local demands for representation, without the affairs of the department degenerating into chaos.

> HUGH G. THORBURN, *Politics in New Brunswick*, 1961, 159.

The most impressive array of brains and professional experts ever assembled in a Canadian cabinet.

> JOHN T. MCLEOD, Univ. of Toronto political science professor, qu. in Toronto *Star*, Apr. 22, 1963, referring to Lester B. Pearson's cabinet.

I hope there is no inclination in the Cabinet to say, "I didn't agree with the decision". If they do, they won't remain members of the cabinet long, not long at all.

> PIERRE E. TRUDEAU, press interview, Ottawa, Apr. 23, 1968.

Pearson's standing by his most important Minister would have impressed us all deeply, as we were impressed by his failure to do so.

> JUDY LAMARSH, *Memoirs of a bird in a gilded cage*, 1969, 65, referring to Walter Gordon, Minister of Finance.

I asked [Prime Minister Pearson] if it would not be a kindness to give Newman a chair on the grounds that it was most uncomfortable for him to have to crouch for several hours under the table while Cabinet meetings were in session. I was delighted to notice two ministers looking surreptitiously under the table to see if Peter was really there.

> WALTER GORDON, referring to Cabinet leaks cited by Peter Newman, qu. in D. Smith, *Gentle patriot*, 1973, 401.

Cabinet Ministers

No go.

> JOHN SANDFIELD MACDONALD, early in 1858, telegram to Sir John A. Macdonald on being offered a place, with two other reformers, in the cabinet.

If I had my way, they should all be highly respectable parties whom I could send to the penitentiary if I liked.

> SIR JOHN A. MACDONALD, to Sir Richard Cartwright, about 1870, qu., Cartwright, *Reminiscences*, 304.

It is the function of Ministers — we know it, and I do not quarrel with it — to say nothing that can be caught hold of, nothing in advance of the popular opinion of the day, to watch the current of that opinion, and when it has gathered strength, to crystallize it into Acts of Parliament. That is the function of a Liberal Minister. The function of a Tory Minister is to wait till he is absolutely forced to swallow his own opinions.

> EDWARD BLAKE, speech at Aurora, Ont., Oct. 3, 1874.

I have been represented as a Protestant minister; there was not one of the canvassers of the honourable gentlemen opposite that did not represent to the people that I was not a Minister of the Crown, but that I was a Protestant minister.

> SIR WILFRID LAURIER, H. of C., *Debates*, Feb. 11, 1878, on his personal defeat in Drummond-Arthabaska by-election.

The time has come, I think, when we must choose men for their qualifications rather than for their locality.

> SIR JOHN A. MACDONALD, letter to J.A. Chapleau, June 6, 1888.

I notice that a lot of commonplace men get into cabinets nowadays.

> FRANK B. CARVELL, retort to Martin Burrell, Minister of Agriculture, when he voiced his doubt that Carvell would ever become a minister, H. of C., *Debates*, 1916.

My dear Prime Minister, I believe that you misunderstood the nature of my request; high as my ambition can aspire, I do not expect to become a deputy minister; I merely want to be a minister.

> ANON., Liberal backbencher to W.L.M. King, qu. in M. Lamontagne, *Canadian public administration*, XI, 1968, 265.

Embarrass me with a large number of Quebec Conservative M.P.'s of cabinet calibre.

> JOHN DIEFENBAKER, speech at Montreal, Mar. 26, 1958, during election campaign.

There is an obligation not simply to observe the law but to act in a manner so scrupulous that it will bear the closest public scrutiny. It has been said that the elementary qualifications demanded of a minister are honesty and incorruptibility. But it is not enough to have those qualities. Our attitudes and conduct must be such as to reflect them.

> LESTER B. PEARSON, letter to Cabinet Ministers, Nov. 30, 1964. Known as "Pearson's Code of Ethics"

The unwritten, and unjust, parliamentary convention [is] that for a French-Canadian minister to reply in French to a question asked in English is a sign of weakness and uncertainty.

RICHARD J. GWYN, *The shape of scandal*, 1965, 62.

Pearson just let his ministers lie where the axes had felled them, and he harmed not only himself but his administration by doing so. He lost their affection but, more importantly, their respect and loyalty.

JUDY LAMARSH, *Memoirs of a bird in a gilded cage*, 1968, 92.

Calgary

Calgary is impossible. It has become so . . . so *nouveau*.

ANON., society matron from Edmonton, qu. in Joseph Barber, *Good fences make good neighbors*, 1958, 65.

The Greatest Outdoor Show On Earth.

CALGARY STAMPEDE; their current self-estimate of the show which began in 1912.

Calgary should be a warning and a representation to all Canada of the road ahead for a society that allows itself to be reduced to the prostitution of living largely as a resource extractor for another society. Canada as a whole has been suffocated by this reality throughout its history. In Calgary the process has reached its logical conclusion, with the death of the community.

JAMES LAXER, *The energy poker game*, 1970, 44.

Callaghan, Morley

The Canadian Morley Callaghan, at one time well known in the United States, is today perhaps the most unjustly neglected novelist in the English-speaking world.

EDMUND WILSON, *New Yorker*, Nov. 26, 1960, 224.

[I wonder whether] the primary reason for the current under-estimation of Morley Callaghan may not be simply a general incapacity – apparently shared by his compatriots – for believing that a writer whose work may be mentioned without absurdity in association with Chekhov's and Turgenev's can possibly be functioning in Toronto.

EDMUND WILSON, *New Yorker*, Nov. 26, 1960, 237.

Morley Callaghan is not only the first and most important of the modern short-story writers in Canada; he was also for many years almost the only writer of fiction in this country who gave continuing evidence that the spirit of contemporary literature could exist here.

ROBERT WEAVER, *Canadian short stories: second series*, 1968, vii.

I expect that one could produce a case for Callaghan's particular style incorporating that poise, prudence and detachment which are ingredients in the Canadian personality. But his literary heritage is American; his literary sense is American.

VICTOR HOAR, *Morley Callaghan*, 1969, 118.

Canada

Not less large than Canada.

RABELAIS, *Pantagruel*, 1548, Bk. iv, ch. 2; (N'estoit moins grand que de Canada).

You know that these two nations [France and England] are at war for a few acres of snow, and that they are spending for this fine war more than all Canada is worth.

> VOLTAIRE, *Candide*, 1759, ch. 23. (Trans.)

If I dared I would beg you on my knees to rid the government of France forever of Canada. If you lost it, you lose almost nothing. If you insist that it be returned, you will receive back only a perpetual cause of war and humiliation.

> VOLTAIRE, letter to the Marquis de Chauvelin, Oct. 3, 1760. (Trans.)

[Pitt] divided his propositions thus, either to retain all Canada, Cape Breton, and exclude the French from their fishing on Newfoundland, and give up Guadeloupe and Gorée, or retain Guadeloupe and Gorée with the exclusion of the French Fishery on Newfoundland, and give up some part of Canada, and confine ourselves to the Line of the Lakes . . . He did not talk of one of them as sine qua nons.

> DUKE OF NEWCASTLE, letter to Hardwicke, Dec. 3, 1760.

. . . His Most Christian Majesty cedes and guarantees to his Britannick Majesty, in full right, Canada . . .

> TREATY OF PARIS, Feb. 10, 1763.

Yes here are form'd the mouldings of a soul,
Too great for ease, too lofty for control.

> [CORNWALL BAYLEY], *Canada, a descript-poem*, 1806.

I wish the British Government would give you Canada at once. It is fit for nothing but to breed quarrels.

> ALEX. BARING (Lord Ashburton), to John Q. Adams, U.S. ambassador, London, 1816.

Canada must neither be lost nor given away!

> WILLIAM IV, at the time of the Maine boundary dispute, about 1836.

Feller Citizens, this country is goin' to the dogs hand over hand.

> T.C. HALIBURTON, *Sam Slick*, 1836, ch. XXXI.

Canada is a colony, not a *country;* it is not yet identified with the dearest affections and associations, rememberances, and hopes of its inhabitants: it is to them an adopted, not a real mother.

> ANNA B. JAMESON, *Winter studies and summer rambles*, 1838, vol. 1, 100.

Advancing quietly; old differences settling down, and being fast forgotten; public feeling and private enterprise alike in a sound and wholesome state; nothing of flush or fever in its system, but health and vigour throbbing in its steady pulse: it is full of hope and promise.

> CHARLES DICKENS, *American notes*, 1842.

And now the winter's over, it's
    homeward we are bound,
And in this cursed country we'll never
    more be found.
Go back to your wives and
    sweethearts, tell others not to go
To that God-forsaken country called
    Canaday-I-O.

> EPHRAIM BRALEY, Maine lumberjack (attrib.), "Canaday-I-O", 1850's.

Why should Canada, wild and unsettled as it is, impress one as an older country than the States, except that her institutions are old. All things seem to contend there with a certain rust of antiquity, such as forms on old armour and iron guns, the rust of convention and formalities. If the rust was not on the tinned roofs and spires, it was on the inhabitants.

HENRY DAVID THOREAU, *Journal,* Sept. 11, 1851.

Canadians! – as long as you remain true to yourselves and her, what foreign invader could ever dare to plant a hostile flag upon that rock-defended height, or set his foot upon a fortress rendered impregnable by the hand of Nature? United in friendship, loyalty and love, what wonders may you not achieve? to what an enormous altitude of wealth and importance may you not arrive?

SUSANNA MOODIE, *Roughing it in the bush,* 1852, Vol. 1, 19.

At that period my love for Canada was a feeling very nearly allied to that which the condemned criminal entertains for his cell – his only hope of escape being through the portals of the grave.

SUSANNA MOODIE, *Roughing it in the bush,* 1852, Vol. 1, 138.

Always the prairies, pastures, forests, vast cities, travellers, Kanada, the snows;
Always these compact lands tied at the hips with the belt stringing the huge oval lakes.

WALT WHITMAN, "Our old feuillage", 1855.

The nursing mother of half a continent.

TORONTO *GLOBE*, Dec. 10, 1861.

One vast confederation stretching from the frozen north in unbroken line to the glowing south, and from the wild billows of the Atlantic westward to the calmer waters of the Pacific main . . . one people, and one language, and one law, and one faith, and, over all that wide continent the home of freedom, and a refuge for the oppressed of every race and every clime.

JOHN BRIGHT, speech at Birmingham, Dec. 18, 1862.

British America is not one state. It is a rope of sand, made up of a number of petty provinces, and peopled with dissimilar and often antagonistic races.

SIR JOHN W. DAWSON, Annual University Lecture, McGill Univ., Nov. 27, 1863.

There is no galvanizing a corpse! Canada is dead – dead church, dead commerce, dead people. A poor, priest-ridden, politician-ridden, doctor-ridden, lawyer-ridden land. No energy, no enterprise, no snap.

TORONTO *LEADER*, Apr. 28, 1870.

Thank God, we have a country. It is not our poverty of land or sea, of wood or mine, that shall ever urge us to be traitors.

GEORGE M. GRANT, *Ocean to ocean,* 1873, 366.

The province, the sect, Orangeism, Fenianism, Freemasonry, Oddfellowship, are more to the ordinary Canadian than Canada.

GOLDWIN SMITH, *The political destiny of Canada,* 1878, 61.

Four nations welded into one
with long, historic past,
Have found, in these our western
wilds, one common life at last.
Through the young giant's mighty
limbs that stretch from sea to sea
There runs a throb of conscious life,
of waking energy;
From Nova Scotia's misty coast
to far Pacific shore,
She wakes, a band of scattered homes
and colonies no more,
But a young nation, with her life
full beating in her breast,
A noble future in her eyes,
the Britain of the West.

AGNES M. MACHAR, *(Fidelis),* "Dominion Day, 1879", in *Can. monthly,* III, 9.

O Child of nations, giant-limbed,
  Who stand'st among the nations
    now
Unheeded, unadorned, unhymned,
  With unanointed brow, –
How long the ignoble sloth, how long
  The trust in greatness not thine
    own?
Surely the lion's brood is strong
  To front the world alone!

> CHARLES G.D. ROBERTS, "Canada", January, 1885; ("O Child of nations.")

It is a goodly land; endowed with great recuperative powers and vast resources as yet almost undeveloped; inhabited by populations moral and religious, sober and industrious, virtuous and thrifty, capable and instructed – the decendants of a choice immigration, of men of mark and courage, energy and enterprise, in the breasts of whose children still should glow the sparks of those ancestral fires.

> EDWARD BLAKE, to the Members of the West Durham Reform Convention, Feb. 6, 1891.

God bless our mighty forest-land
Of mountain, lake and river,
Whose loyal sons, from strand to
    strand,
  Sing "Canada Forever".

> AGNES M. MACHAR, "A song for Canada", 1899.

Up Along.

> ANON., term for Canada used by fishermen of Newfoundland, about 1900.

Canada is essentially a country of the larger air, where men can still face the old primeval forces of Nature and be braced into vigour, and withal so beautiful that it can readily inspire that romantic patriotism which is one of the most priceless assets of a people.

> LORD TWEEDSMUIR, (anonymously) "Topics of the Day", *The Spectator*, July 6, 1901, 8.

The motherland for us, is all of Canada, that is to say a federation of distinct races and autonomous provinces. The nation which we wish to see develop, is the Canadian nation, composed of French Canadians and English Canadians, that is two elements separated by language and religion, and by the legal dispositions necessary for the conservation of their respective traditions, but united in an attachment of brotherhood, in a common attachment to a common motherland.

> HENRI BOURASSA, *Le Nationaliste*, Apr. 3, 1904, 2. (Trans.)

Canada for Canadians.

> Slogan used by the NATIONAL TRADES AND LABOUR CONGRESS OF CANADA, about 1904.

There never was a time in the history of Canada when there was a greater reason for optimism, nor a greater need for it. The development of the last few years has been magnificent; the development of the next few years depends on our having confidence. The country is rich, immigration is proceeding apace, the Government is doing its duty, and the rest lies with the people – the capitalists, bankers, the businessmen, and the other classes.

> *CANADIAN MAGAZINE*, Vol. 24, 1905, 487.

Canada has given and taken all along the line for nigh on three hundred years, and in some respects is the wisest, as she should be the happiest, of us all.

> RUDYARD KIPLING, *Letters to the family*, 1908, 8.

Sweet is the breath of the prairie,
  where peace and prosperity reign,
And joyous the song of the city, where
    all is expansion and gain.

> ROBERT STEAD, "The man of the house", 1908.

In 1908 Canada has become a star to which is directed the gaze of the whole civilized world. That is what we have done.

> SIR WILFRID LAURIER, speech, Sept. 30, 1908 at Cornwall, Ont., during federal election campaign.

O Canada! Dominion of the North,
How vast the path whereon thy sun
   rides forth!

> GRANT BALFOUR, "Canada", 1910.

God has made Canada one of those nations which cannot be conquered and cannot be destroyed, except by herself.

> NORMAN ANGELL, address, Canadian Club, Toronto, June 2, 1913.

Canada is a country without a soul.

> ANON., American friends qu. by Rupert Brooke, *Letters from America*, 1916, 49.

Canada is a live country, live, but not, like the States, kicking.

> RUPERT BROOKE, *Letters from America*, 1916, 83.

Of all the loveless, lifeless lands that writhe beneath the wrath of God, commend me to Canada!

> ALEISTER CROWLEY, about 1923, *Confessions*, 1970, 502.

This country is much more than a chain of wheat fields, and gold mines, and pulpwood forests; it is more even than the union of nine separate provinces: it is the expression of certain ideas.

> VINCENT MASSEY, Canadian club, Ottawa, Jan. 20, 1924.

Canada, the foremost of all British colonies, strong in the association of two peoples, distinguished in both war and peace, mighty producer of the fruits of the earth, mighty breeder of men, to be loved for the wonderful beauty of mountains, rivers, lakes and plains, as well as for all the pleasing delights of sun and snow.

> TERROT R. GLOVER, Public Orator at Cambridge University, England at conferring of honorary degree on W.L.M. King, Nov. 22, 1926. Trans. from the original Latin. (See H.G. Wood, *Glover*, 1953, 133.)

Land of the matchless march of lake
   and stream!
Land of the virile seasons!

> WILSON MACDONALD, "Ode on the Diamond Jubilee of Confederation", 1927.

We had a new country but old peoples; wealth collectively and in the future, but individual poverty; a store of tradition and a prevalent illiteracy – and so much to be done that we had little time to study how we should do it.

> RAYMOND KNISTER, Intro. to *Canadian short stories*, 1928, xii.

Her [Canada's] power, her hopes, her future guarantee the increasing fellowship of the Nordic races of the East and the West; in fact, no state, no country, no band of men can more truly be described as the linchpin of peace and world progress.

> WINSTON CHURCHILL, *Saturday evening post*, Feb. 15, 1930, 51; See: *Mackenzie King record*, I, 106, for another version.

At the beginning, in the middle, and at the end of any study of Canada, one must reiterate that Canada is American.

> ANDRE SIEGFRIED, *Canada*, 1937, 13.

I firmly believe that this glorious land should be first. But first in what? That's the question.

> MAURICE N. EISENDRATH, *The never failing stream*, 1939, 26.

Canada is a secondary and second-rate country without much depth of experience: everyone admits that – too freely, sometimes.

> A.R.M. LOWER, in *Can. hist. rev.*, 1941, 12.

No one knows my country, neither the stranger nor its own sons. My country is hidden in the dark and teeming brain of youth upon the eve of its manhood. My country has not found itself nor felt its power nor learned its true place. It is all visions and doubts and hopes and dreams. It is strength and weakness, despair and joy, and the wild confusions and restless strivings of a boy who has passed his manhood but is not yet a man.

> BRUCE HUTCHISON, *The unknown country*, 1942, 3.

I am the mirror of your picture
until you make me the marvel of your
    life.
Yes, I am one and none, pin and pine,
    snow and slow,
America's attic, an empty room,
a something possible, a chance, a
    dance
that is not danced. A cold kingdom.

> PATRICK ANDERSON, "Poem on Canada", 1945.

O county doubly split! One way
Tugged eastward; one to U.S.A.:
One way tugged deep toward silver
    Rome;
One way scotched stubborn here at
    home;
What panacea for your ills?
(Le Sacré Coeur de Crabtree Mills).

THEODORE SPENCER, (Professor of English, Harvard Univ.) "A Church seen in Canada", 1949.

Canada is my kind of country.

> DONALD GORDON, d. 1969; explaining his resistance to job opportunities abroad, qu. in P. Newman, *Flame of power*, 1959, 218.

Canada means, to us in Europe, just Toronto and Montreal. For the rest of the country we think of trappers, Eskimos, Mounted Police and hockey players.

> RENE F. SIMON, Swiss lawyer, qu. in *Liberty*, Sept., 1963.

Canada has available to her the best of everything – British politics, French culture, American technology. Unfortunately she settles for French politics, American culture and British technology.

> ANON., qu. in *Financial post*, May 2, 1964, 6; first used by radio station CBL, Toronto; claimed by J.R. Colombo as a poem titled "Oh Canada" (1965) in A. Purdy, ed. *The new Romans*, 1968, but with different wording. (See below.)

Canada is more important to the United States than any other single country.

> LIVINGSTON MERCHANT, *Atlantic monthly*, Nov., 1964, cover (special issue on Canada).

If Canada is an 'unknown country' this is, in an important measure, a matter of choice. It is a consequence of a widespread wish to avoid ridicule, emotional display, public quarrels, obvious discrimination, and injustice, and to cultivate instead a certain shrewd and indirect managing of social reciprocities.

KASPAR D. NAEGELE, in B.R. Blishen, et al., eds., *Canadian society*, 1964, 512.

I am not among those who believe that Canada was created by God. It became a nation because of the vain-glory of the English; because of the treachery of the French (who could have protected their colonists easily); because of the incompetence of the Americans (who were on the verge of capturing the country twice); and because of the enslavement and virtual extinction of the Hurons, Iroquois and Algonquins. No matter what we choose to say of it, Canada is a whole series of accidents. If it should expire in its present form the world would survive and so, almost certainly, would Canada's separate parts. I don't expect my children to suffer much if Quebec should withdraw from Canada or Canada withdraw from Quebec.

RALPH ALLEN, Toronto *Star*, May 19, 1965, 5.

With its wealth of human, linguistic, and cultural resources, *Canada* reflects the world in microcosm.

CANADA. ROY. COMM. ON BILINGUALISM AND BICULTURALISM, *Report*, 1967, Vol. 1, li.

Canada was the idealist's end of Empire – a people united in reconciliation, a colony emancipated, a wilderness civilized, the principles of parliamentary democracy transferred in triumphant vindication from an ancient capital to a new.

JAMES MORRIS, *Pax Britannica*, 1968, 324.

Canada could have enjoyed:
  English government,
    French culture,
      and American know-how.
Instead it ended up with:
  English know-how
    French government
      and American culture.

JOHN R. COLOMBO, in *The new Romans*, ed. by Al Purdy, 1968, 159.

Here you receive another kind of wisdom
Bitter and icy and not to everyone's taste.
This earth says:
I was here long before you and the likes of you came;
Unmolested I conversed with wind and rivers,
Don't forget that, my friend. –
The wind blows cold from Labrador:
I have a message for you from the ice age.

WALTER BAUER, "Canada", 1968. (Trans.)

a country nourished on self-doubt
where from the reverse image of detractors
an opposite nation is talked into existence
that doesn't resemble any other one
a cross-breed plant that survives the winter

AL PURDY, "A walk on Wellington Street", 1968.

Canada, a country without myths.
We need none. I sit by the fire
And let my native wit buzz,
Here in the cabin by the lake.

RALPH GUSTAFSON, "At Moraine Lake", 1969.

I have felt forest and prairie sky,
Mountain and rocky lake,
Hot and frozen space – and all of us.
A youthful stumbling country that is
    me.

CHRISTOPHER CHAPMAN, "Poem", 1969.

This two-cultured, multi-ghettoed,
plural community, this non-nation,
nay-saying no-place of an un-Eden,
this faceless unidentifiable blank on
the map, "this wind that lacks a flag",
this Canada of ours.

WILLIAM KILBOURN, *Canada: a guide to
the peaceable kingdom*, 1970, xi.

This impossible *anti*nation.

LESLIE ARMOUR, American-Canadian
professor of philosophy, University of
Waterloo, qu. in R.L. Perry, *Galt,
U.S.A.*, 1971, iii.

Canada is not so much a country as
magnificent raw material for a country.

ALDEN NOWLAN, in *Maclean's*, June,
1971, 16.

I have not seen
a land more
endearingly frightful
like a recurring nightmare
of embraces
How shall I tell the world;
here I have seen the old child
cradling a people.

M. LAKSHMI GILL, "The land", 1972.

Perhaps we are a country more feminine than we like to admit, because
the unifying, regenerative principle is
a passion with us.

DOROTHY LIVESAY, *Collected poems: the
two seasons*, 1972, v.

I'm talking about Canada as a state of
mind, as the space you inhabit not just
with your body but with your head.
It's that kind of space in which we find
ourselves lost.

MARGARET ATWOOD, *Survival*, 1972, 18.

Canada (Name)

Of the two wild men which we took in
our former voyage, it was told us, that
this was part of the Southerne coaste &
that there was an Island, on the Southerly parte of which is the way to goe
from Honguedo (where the year before we had taken them) to Canada,
and that two days journey from the
sayd Cape, and Island began the King-
dome of Saguenay, on the North shore
extending toward Canada.

JACQUES CARTIER, *Second voyage
1535-36*, (Aug. 12, 1535) *Hakluyt's voyages*, 1904, Vol. III, 214.

This bay [Chaleurs Bay] is the same
that is laid down on some maps as
Baye des Espagnols; and there is an old
tradition, that Spaniards entered it
before Cartier and that, seeing no
signs of any mines there, they had
several times repeated the words, *Aca
nada* – nothing there.

P.F.X. DE CHARLEVOIX, *History of New
France*, 1744 (Shea trans. vol. 1, 1900,
113).

One individual chooses Tuponia and
another Hochelaga, as a suitable name
for the new nationality. Now I would
ask any member of this House how he
would feel if he woke up some fine
morning and found himself, instead of
a Canadian, a Tuponian or a Hochela-
gander.

THOMAS D'A. MCGEE, *Confederation debates*, Feb. 9, 1865, 126; Tuponia is
from "The United Provinces of North
America".

Canada as Intermediary

So long as Canada remains a part of the British Empire, Canada's position, geographically, is such that she must be either a hostage or a link of union between Great Britain and the United States.

SIR RICHARD CARTWRIGHT, speech in Toronto, Aug. 29, 1911.

Canada is the linchpin of the English-speaking world. Canada, with those relations of friendly, affectionate intimacy with the United States on the one hand and with her unswerving fidelity to the British Commonwealth and the Motherland on the other, is the link which joins together these great branches of the human family, a link which, spanning the oceans, brings the continents into their true relation.

SIR WINSTON CHURCHILL, speech, Mansion House, London, England, Sept. 4, 1941, at luncheon in honour of W.L. Mackenzie King.

We all look to you as the link with America. That fraternal association must be kept up, and we look to you above all to keep the two together. Canada is the interpreter.

SIR WINSTON CHURCHILL, to W.L.M. King at a dinner at Chequers, England, May, 1944, qu. in B. Fraser, *The search for identity*, 1967, 79.

There seems to stand poised the "Spirit of Canada', a hinge between the Old World and the New: a priceless hinge of pure gold.

FIELD MARSHAL B.L. MONTGOMERY OF ALAMEIN, farewell broadcast to people of Canada after visit, Sept., 1946.

Canada is the vital link in the English-speaking world and joins across the Atlantic Ocean the vast American democracy of the United States with our famous old island and the fifty millions who keep the flag flying here.

SIR WINSTON CHURCHILL, speech, Guildhall, London, England, Nov. 19, 1951, welcoming Princess Elizabeth and the Duke of Edinburgh home from visit to Canada.

The frequently repeated claim that Canada serves as a bridge or an interpreter, while it may be justified on some special occasions, is more often a myth that is cherished for the sake of self-esteem.

EDGAR MCINNIS, in R.M. Clark, ed., *Canadian issues*, 1961, 100.

Canada Council

Our golden apple is divisible, but it cannot be endlessly divided if it is to provide any sustenance worth having.

CANADA COUNCIL, *Annual report, 1960-61*, 16.

For our soul there is something called the Canada Council which supports the arts, humanities, and sciences, and is relentlessly dedicated to the discovery and deification of mediocrity.

HAROLD TOWN, *Enigmas*, 1964, [1].

Received three canada council grants without wch all that ive bin abul to help do cud no way have happened got thru hope to get nothr one soon nd that th canada council b abul to work its way to eventual subsidy uv the working artist writr poet.

BILL BISSETT, *nobody owns th earth*, 1971, acknowledgment.

It's an angel for vested interests.

NATHAN COHEN, Toronto drama critic, qu. *Maclean's*, Dec., 1972, 82.

After 1967 the council threw away the chance to articulate new directions for itself, and for the arts. Instead, we started floundering around.

> DAVID SILCOX, former senior arts officer, qu. in *Maclean's*, Dec., 1972, 82.

Canadian-American Relations

Should any American soldier be so base and infamous as to injure any Canadian or Indian in his person or property, I do most earnestly enjoin you to bring him to such severe and exemplary punishment, as the enormity of the crime may require. Should it extend to death itself, it shall not be disproportioned to its guilt, at such a time and in such a cause.

> GEORGE WASHINGTON, letter from Cambridge, Mass., Sept. 14, 1775 to Col. Benedict Arnold.

To promote a disposition favourable to friendship and good neighbourhood.

> GREAT BRITAIN. TREATIES., *Treaty of amity, commerce and navigation between His Britannic Majesty and the United States of America*, signed at London, Nov. 19, 1794, 1796, 10.

The policy which the United States actually pursues is the infatuated one of rejecting and spurning vigorous and ever-growing Canada, while seeking to establish feeble states out of decaying Spanish provinces on the coast and islands of the Gulf of Mexico. I shall not live to see it, but the man is already born who will see the United States mourn over this stupendous folly.

> WILLIAM H. SEWARD, *Cruise to Labrador*, 1857.

God prevent a *War;* and with our own Bastards.

> JOSEPH PARKES, letter to Edward Ellice, Dec. 26, 1861. (Pub.Arch.Can.), referring to possible war with U.S. North.

The star-spangled banner is in fact a fine flag, and has waved to some purpose; but those who live near it, and not under it, fancy they hear too much of it.

> ANTHONY TROLLOPE, *North America*, 1862, 55-56.

The clover lifts its trefoil leaves to the evening dew, yet they draw their nourishment from a single stem. Thus distinct, and yet united, let us thrive and flourish.

> JOSEPH HOWE, speech in Detroit, Aug. 14, 1865.

Tramp! Tramp! Tramp! The new
  Dominion,
Now is knocking at the door,
So, goodbye, dear Uncle Sam,
As we do not care a clam
For your Greenbacks or your bunkum
  any more.

> ANON., "Song of the 'Dominion Boys' in British Columbia", about 1869.

Remember, Canada lives cheek by jowl with the United States.

> SIR RICHARD CARTWRIGHT, to Lord Carnarvon, Colonial Secretary, 1874-8.

We decline Cousin Jonathan's offer to run the farm on shares. We are able to get in our own harvest and attend to our own stock and catch our own fish and mind our own business. We will exchange work and lend things and be neighbourly, but we will not tolerate stray cattle in our meadow nor trespassers in our corn patch.

> J.S. WILLISON, Toronto *Globe*, July 2, 1888, 2.

Canada is like an apple on a tree just beyond our reach. We may strive to grasp it, but the bough recedes from our hold just in proportion to our effort to catch it. Let it alone and in due time it will fall into our hands.

> JAMES G. BLAINE, U.S. Secretary of State, 1889, qu. in W.E. Harris, *Canada's last chance*, 1970, 34.

I say that there is a deliberate conspiracy, by force, by fraud, or by both, to force Canada into the American Union.

> SIR JOHN A. MACDONALD, speech, Academy of Music, Toronto, Feb. 17, 1891.

I am a subject of the British Crown, but whenever I have to choose between the interests of England and Canada it is manifest to me that the interests of my country are identical with those of the United States of America.

> SIR WILFRID LAURIER, speech in Boston, Nov. 17, 1891.

I am a Chinese Wall protectionist. I don't mean merely in trade. I mean everything. I'd keep American ideas out of this country.

> SIR WILLIAM VAN HORNE, to a visiting U.S. senator, qu. in P. Newman, *Flame of power*, 1959, 93.

It is far more to Canada's advantage than ours to be on good terms with us. Lord Salisbury, in a private conversation the other day, compared her to a coquettish girl with two suitors, playing one off against the other. I should think a closer analogy would be to call her a married flirt, ready to betray John Bull on any occasion, but holding him responsible for all her follies.

> JOHN HAY, U.S. ambassador to London, letter to John W. Foster, Dec. 27, 1897.

The best and most effective way to maintain friendship with our American neighbours is to be absolutely independent of them.

> SIR WILFRID LAURIER, H. of C., *Debates*, July 30, 1903.

There will be no more pilgrimages to Washington. We are turning our hopes to the old motherland.

> SIR WILFRID LAURIER, attributed remark on the Fielding budget of Apr. 22, 1907.

It is her own soul that Canada risks today. Once that soul is pawned for any consideration, Canada must inevitably conform to the commercial, legal, financial, social and ethical standards which will be imposed upon her by the sheer, admitted weight of the United States.

> RUDYARD KIPLING, message cabled Sept. 7, 1911, to the Montreal *Star* prior to the general election, Sept. 21.

Canada is the greatest country under the Stars and Stripes.

> JAMES A. MACDONALD, Editor, Toronto *Globe*, speech in Massey Hall to Assoc. Clubs of America, 1914.

Historically, Canada is a by-product of the United States.

> ARCHIBALD MACMECHAN, *Can. hist. rev.*, 1920, 348.

The United States makes a rule today and we follow it tomorrow; or, to put it differently, they take the snuff and we do the sneezing.

> SAMUEL W. JACOBS, H. of C., *Debates*, Mar. 30, 1921, 1360.

A good friend says, sometimes, that the difference between Canada and the United States is that the United States are a great country, with a great people, who are not as great as they think they are; and Canada is a great country, inhabited by a great people who are much greater than they believe themselves to be.

BEECHAM TROTTER, *A horseman and the west*, 1925, 128.

Nobody knows better than the historian how much courage it still takes to tell the truth about American-Canadian relations, and how near the surface these antiquated but latent prejudices are still to be found.

CHESTER MARTIN, in *Can. hist. rev.*, 1937, 10.

Economically the story is one story and politically it is either less or more than two.

S. MORLEY SCOTT, in *Can. hist. rev.*, 1938, 378.

The history of much of North America might be termed the history of the rivalry of New York and Montreal.

A.R.M. LOWER, *North American assault on Can. forest*, 1938, 58.

Four-and-twenty Yankees,
All very dry,
Crossed the Yankee border
To get Canadian rye.
When the rye was open,
They began to sing,
"To hell with Calvin Coolidge,
God save the King."

ANON., qu. by Murry Hubbard, N.B. farmer in W. Stewart, *Maclean's*, Aug., 1969, 25.

The Siamese Twins of North America who cannot separate and live.

J.B. BREBNER, *North Atlantic triangle*, 1945, xi.

For Canada friendship with the United States is the first essential of existence and the first instinct of nature.

DONALD CREIGHTON, *Can. hist. rev.*, Vol. 26, 1945, 120.

Children of a common Mother. – Brethren dwelling together in peace and unity.

ANON., south and north inscriptions on Peace Arch at Douglas, B.C. – Blaine, Wash., on the border, erected 1946.

If I thought there was a danger of Canada being placed at the mercy of powerful financial interests in the United States, and if that were being done by my own party, I would get out and oppose them openly.

W.L. MACKENZIE KING, *The Mackenzie King record*, IV, 273; May 6, 1948, to L.B. Pearson.

The days of relatively easy and automatic political relations with our neighbour are, I think, over.

LESTER B. PEARSON, address to Empire and Canadian Clubs, Toronto, Apr. 10, 1951.

Whatever hope of continued autonomy Canada may have in the future must depend on her success in withstanding American influence and in assisting the development of a third bloc designed to withstand the pressure of the United States and Russia.

HAROLD A. INNIS, *Changing concepts of time*, 1952, 127.

We Canadians claim the special privilege, as a close neighbour and a candid friend, of grousing about our big, our overwhelming partner, and of complaining at some of the less attractive manifestations of her way of life. It makes our own junior status seem relatively superior and helps us forget some of our own problems and mistakes.

LESTER B. PEARSON, (Leader of His Majesty's Loyal Opposition), speech, English-Speaking Union of the United States, New York City, Nov. 23, 1953.

Ours is a sovereign nation
Bows to no foreign will
But whenever they cough in
    Washington
They spit on Parliament Hill.

J.S. WALLACE, "A sovereign nation", 1953.

There was a new phenomenon in Canadian life – not the old, silly, jealous anti-Americanism of the Loyalist tradition, but a country-wide dismay and distrust of American leadership and a troubled sense that our closest and most trusted friends had been attacked by a spiritual illness that left us baffled as to how we were to conduct our affairs with them.

B.S. KEIRSTEAD, Canada in world affairs, September 1951 to October 1953, 1956, 36.

Living with a giant isn't so bad, when it is a free and democratic country. Our big neighbour irritates us and ignores us, but it also stimulates us, and it is an endless source of free entertainment. Whatever else it may do, it doesn't frighten us.

G.M. CRAIG, letter, Globe and Mail, Mar. 15, 1954, 6.

Canadians, say our American friends, are too polite to argue. Let us be honest. We are not too polite; no one can be too polite. But we may be too lazy and too timid.

VINCENT MASSEY, address to Canadian Club, Montreal, Nov. 7, 1955.

It is bad to be a chore boy of the United States. It is equally bad to be a colonial chore boy running around shouting "ready, aye, ready".

LESTER B. PEARSON, Sec'y. of State for Ext. Affairs, H. of C., Debates, Nov. 27, 1956, 51, in defense of policy in Middle East crisis.

You know, it seems ridiculous. We both speak the same language. We think alike. We behave the same. Don't you think you would be better off as the 49th state?

DWIGHT D. EISENHOWER, U.S. Pres., about 1956, to Lionel Chevrier, in Washington, D.C., qu. L. Chevrier, St. Lawrence seaway, 1959, 60.

The cardinal thesis of the nationalist school was that, at all costs, Canada had to fight its way out from under the traditional influence of British imperialist and colonial rule; and that one of the best ways of doing it was to use the influence of the United States as a counter-balance against the pressure from Westminster.

GEORGE FERGUSON, Editor, Montreal Star, paper read to Can. Pol. Sci. Assoc. 1956.

We have gone through the revolution of 1940. In that year we passed from the British century of our history to the American century. We became dependent upon the United States for our security. We have, therefore, no choice but to follow American leadership. And our American century is going to be a much tougher experience for us than our British century was.

FRANK UNDERHILL, address, Michigan State Univ., Feb., 1957.

It must be the most one-sided love affair in international history.

TORONTO GLOBE AND MAIL, Apr. 11, 1957, 6, editorial.

Canada, a relatively weak country unable to defend itself from the giant, has always been the supreme test of American morality, a test visible to the entire world. A Canadian is bound to say that the test, despite certain lapses, has been magnificently met. No great power in the world's history has ever treated a small neighbour as well as the modern United States has treated Canada. Our survival is the proof of that treatment.

BRUCE HUTCHISON, *Harper's mag.*, May, 1958, 50.

I am not anti-American. But I am strongly pro-Canadian.

JOHN DIEFENBAKER, New York *Times*, July 13, 1958.

If ever a Canadian wants to go to a better place all he has to do is come down to this country. But if an American wants to go to a better place, he has to die first.

ANON., an American to J.R. Kidd, quoted in speech to National Assoc. of Public School Adult Educators, Buffalo, Nov. 5, 1959.

Canada is America's attic.

ROBERTSON DAVIES, qu. in *Letters in Canada*, 1960, 426; derived by him as stated in *A voice from the attic*, 1960, 3, from Patrick Anderson's poem, "Poem on Canada", "I am one and none, pin and pine, snow and slow, America's attic, an empty room".

Perhaps the most striking thing about Canada is that it is not part of the United States.

J. BARTLET BREBNER, *Canada*, 1960, ix.

If Canada wants the United States to do something, she must be able to prove that it is in the national interests of the United States to do it.

HUGH G.J. AITKEN, *American capital and Canadian resources*, 1961, 156.

Geography has made us neighbours. History has made us friends. Economics has made us partners. And necessity has made us allies. Those whom nature hath so joined together, let no man put asunder. What unites us is far greater than what divides us.

PRES. JOHN F. KENNEDY, address to Canadian House of Commons and Senate, Ottawa, May 17, 1961.

Despite this tremendous competition, Canada has survived, and by surviving deserves to survive.

W.L. MORTON, Winnipeg *Free press*, Oct. 23, 1961, 35.

The fact that we worship at the same supermarkets leads to unwarranted conclusions about the identity of our political lives.

JOHN W. HOLMES, *Foreign affairs*, 40, 1961, 108.

The United States is our friend whether we like it or not.

ROBERT THOMPSON, H. of C., *Debates*, Jan. 31, 1963, 3315.

Why do you think that the United States should treat Canada differently from Guatemala, when reason of state requires it and circumstances permit?

PIERRE ELLIOTT TRUDEAU, *Cité libre*, Apr., 1963, 10. (Trans.)

That's the way we Canadians feel about you Americans. You can decapitate us and you can dismember us, just so long as you don't interfere with us.

LESTER B. PEARSON, 1964, to U.S. Secy. of State, Dean Rusk, referring to *N.Y. Times* murder report, qu. by Peter C. Newman in *The new Romans*, 1968, 7.

It is in the abiding interest of both countries that, wherever possible, divergent views between the two governments should be expressed and if possible resolved in private, through diplomatic channels.

A.D.P. HEENEY and L. MERCHANT, *Canada and the U.S. Principles for partnership*, 1965, 49.

We in the United States, friendly and well disposed toward Canada, confident of our power yet conscious of our unsought burdens in the confusing, dangerous world in which we live, all too often tend to assume that Canadians are really just like Americans and should be counted on to react to nearly everything in the same fashion. Nor is it surprising that the general run of Canadians and Americans get on well together as individuals and that each complacently assumes that he "understands" his friend's country.

LIVINGSTON T. MERCHANT, *Neighbours taken for granted*, 1966, x.

Americans take Canada for granted, and Canadians are forever saying so. By this they mean that Americans assume Canada to be bestowed as a right and accept this bounty, as they do air, without thought or appreciation. Perhaps they do; and perhaps they should. For, if it were not taken as a bounty of nature, America might not grasp Canada at all for sheer difficulty in figuring out what Canada is.

DEAN ACHESON, in L.T. Merchant, ed., *Neighbours taken for granted*, 1966, 134.

Complete economic union with the United States would be a disaster for Canada. We would be swallowed up. The kind of industrial expansion we shall need in the next decade to provide jobs for a rapidly increasing labour force would not occur in Canada.

The expansion, or most of it, would be more likely to take place south of the border. In these circumstances, hundreds of thousands of young Canadians would be forced to seek employment in the United States.

WALTER GORDON, *A choice for Canada*, 1966, 92.

Whenever the United States moves to protect its own economic interests at the expense of Canada the general Canadian reaction is to recognize such moves as legitimate ones. By these strange Canadian standards, it is acceptable for an American to be nationalistic and it is deplorable for a Canadian to want his country to survive.

LARRATT HIGGINS, address to the Woodsworth Foundation, Nov. 12, 1966.

Most Canadians cannot talk about the U.S. outside the context of themselves as Canadians.

AL PURDY, *The new Romans*, 1968, ii.

As I see things, there is no guarantee that the privileged position presently enjoyed by Canadians as "most-favoured serfs" will last. The day is near when the Yankees will see no further need to pamper us – they'll own us outright.

FARLEY MOWAT, in Al Purdy, ed., *The new Romans*, 1968, 5.

Remember – a man who sells *himself* into slavery does not earn the gratitude of his master; instead he earns a deep contempt. We Canadians have well earned such contempt – and a wise slave knows that a contemptuous master is more to be feared, in the long run, than an angry one.

FARLEY MOWAT, in Al Purdy, ed., *The new Romans*, 1968, 5.

One is tempted to conclude, in fact, that there could not be a Canada without the United States – and may not be a Canada with one.

J.M.S. CARELESS, in Al Purdy, ed., *The new Romans*, 1968, 134.

Dependence is addictive and the dynamics of dependence are cumulative.

KARI LEVITT, *New world quart.*, IV, 2, 1968, 114.

America's strengths *as a state* are its gravest flaws; Canada's weaknesses *as a state* are its greatest virtues.

GEORGE WOODCOCK, in Al Purdy, ed., *The new Romans*, 1968, 76.

Living next to you is in some ways like sleeping with an elephant; no matter how friendly and even-tempered is the beast, if I may call it that, one is affected by every twitch and grunt. Even a friendly nuzzling can sometimes lead to frightening consequences.

PIERRE E. TRUDEAU, speech to National Press Club, Washington, Mar. 25, 1969.

Americans should never underestimate the constant pressure on Canada which the mere presence of the United States has produced. We are a different people from you. We are a different people partly because of you.

PIERRE E. TRUDEAU, address, National Press Club, Washington, Mar. 25, 1969.

Canada exists and will continue to exist by sufferance of the United States.

JOHN HOLMES, H. of C., Standing Committee on External Affairs and National Defence, *Minutes of proceedings and evidence*, No. 1, Nov. 6, 1969, 14.

O see Can a da
By the doom's early light
How so loudly we failed
At the twilight's first dawning
Whose blood stars blighted stripes
Through the perilous night
O'er the ramparts we watched
Came so endlessly screaming

And the rockets red glare
The bombs bursting in air
Give proof thru the night that
The death comes from there
O say
　　does that
Star-spangled
　　　　　banner
　　　　　　　now
Wave
O'er the land of the cree
The home of the brave

B.P. NICHOL, "Inquiry of ministry, question no. 468 by Mr. Saltsman, order of the day no. 16, Nov. 13, 1969 page viii".

The most striking feature of the Canada of the 1970's will be, in my view, a readiness on the part of Canadians to accept, and even welcome, the fact that their country is not quite "a nation like the others". There will be a recognition of the very special relationship with the United States and a greater willingness to seek ways to exploit this unique position rather than to worry and complain about it.

ROY A. MATTHEWS, *Foreign affairs*, Jan., 1969, 343.

It is very unlikely that there will be any significant change until the world-wide American empire begins to break up. And even then, Canada will be the last colony to be liberated.

JOHN W. WARNOCK, in I. Lumsden, ed., *Close the 49th parallel etc.*, 1970, 133.

History has made the United States the dearest enemy of Canadians, geography has made it also Canada's closest associate, and has produced a present-day relationship that oscillates between guarded friendliness and muted hostility.

GEORGE WOODCOCK, *Canada and the Canadians*, 1970, 25.

Canadians should constantly remember that in negotiating with the only nation that has repeatedly attacked us on our own soil and daily exerts the crudest kind of pressure on our government, the pistol is always on the table and alongside the brief. We had better have a little powder of our own handy and make sure that it is dry.

G. FRANKFURTER, *Baneful domination*, 1971, 196.

Few Canadians would deny that if there has been undue Canadian subservience it has not been imposed from outside but willingly accepted from within. And in strictly Canadian-American relations there has, on the whole, been an impressive history of consultation, co-operation and good will.

ANDREW BREWIN, in J.H. Redekop, ed., *The star-spangled beaver*, 1971, 99.

The American Dream still has its allure; its idealization of egalitarian prosperity shimmers eternally. But the American reality that has superseded it has caused us to murmur with the former President Diaz of Mexico: "So far from God, so near the United States".

PETER NEWMAN, *Saturday rev.*, Mar. 13, 1971, 17.

We are forever tied to the United States by reason of geography, history and circumstances, so let's not whine about it but rather make the most and the best of it in intelligent and practical ways.

NORMAN A.M. MACKENZIE, Ottawa *Citizen*, Apr. 8, 1971, 6.

My guess is that Canada will remain like the Japanese wife – one step behind. The cue will come from Washington.

RALPH NADER, address, Toronto, May 27, 1971, referring to new car safety standards.

In a secular sense we're not going to move away from the United States; we're going to be friends willy-nilly, and probably more willy than nilly.

PIERRE E. TRUDEAU, interview with James Reston, New York *Times*, Ottawa, Dec. 21, 1971.

This pressure by United States officials has become excessive; they not only badger us for information on new policies before they are publicly available, but seem to expect us to report probable decisions to them first for approval.

ANON., a senior government official, qu. in D.W. Carr, *Recovering Canada's nationhood*, 1971, 63.

We seem destined to lose our independence and eventually become part of the United States. Most Canadians do not want this. But our leaders seem quite unable to comprehend the implications of trends that, if not soon reversed, will lead inevitably to the break-up of our country.

WALTER GORDON, *Maclean's*, Sept., 1972, 38.

The process by which the Dominion became a branch-plant dependency and a military satellite of the American Republic began with the Ogdensburg Agreement of 1940; and since then Canada's subordination to American foreign policy and American capital has continued progressively with scarcely a serious interruption.

DONALD G. CREIGHTON, *Towards the discovery of Canada*, 1972, 169.

The international ideal is not the justification, but merely the excuse, for the continental empire dominated by the United States. Our first task is to expose this pious fraud and to free ourselves from its spurious moral compulsions.

DONALD G. CREIGHTON, *Towards, the discovery of Canada*, 1972, 279.

Canadian-British Relations

What shall we do with Canada?

HENRY VINCENT, title of pamphlet reprinted from Leeds (England) *Mercury*, 1838.

Ponder this well and make as I do the first question on every political dogma advanced no matter by whom, what will its effect be on the British Connexion.

WILLIAM HENRY DRAPER, letter to John Sandfield Macdonald, Mar. 25, 1841. (Pub.Arch.Can.)

Whenever the "British yoke" becomes burthensome to North America it will be broken like a pack-thread, and I would be one of the first to break it.

JOSEPH HOWE, letter to Lord Falkland, Apr. 9, 1846.

I trust that for ages, for ever, Canada may remain united with the mother country. But we are fast ceasing to be a dependency, and are assuming the position of an ally of Great Britain. England will be the centre, surrounded and sustained by an alliance not only with Canada, but Australia, and all her other possessions; and there will thus be formed an immense confederation of freemen, the greatest confederacy of civilized and intelligent men that has ever had an existence on the face of the globe.

SIR JOHN A. MACDONALD, speech, Legislative Assembly, Apr. 19, 1861.

It is very grievous to see half a continent slipping away from the grasp of England with scarcely an effort to hold it.

ALEXANDER T. GALT, letter to his wife, May 25, 1865, referring to the lack of sympathy of Gladstone and his friends toward the Canadian delegation promoting Canadian Confederation.

Instead of looking upon us as a merely dependent colony, England will have in us a friendly nation – a subordinate but still a powerful people – to stand by her in North America in peace or in war.

SIR JOHN A. MACDONALD, *Confederation debates*, 1865, 44.

I hope to live to see the day, and if I do not, that my son may be spared to see Canada the right arm of England – to see Canada a powerful auxiliary of the Empire – not, as now, a cause of anxiety and a source of danger.

SIR JOHN A. MACDONALD, H. of C., *Debates*, May 3, 1872, on the Washington Treaty.

Take up your freedom; your days of apprenticeship are over.

THE TIMES (London), editorial on Canada and the San Juan water arbitration award, Oct. 30, 1872; advice often summarized as "cut the painter"; see Tennyson quotation below.

And that true North, whereof we
    lately heard
A strain to shame us "keep you
    to yourselves;
So loyal is too costly! friends –
    your love
Is but a burthen; loose the bonds
    and go."
Is this the tone of empire? here
    the faith
That made us rulers?

LORD TENNYSON, epilogue to "Idylls of the King"; written Nov., 1872, after reading a "villainous" editorial in *The Times* on Canada, Oct. 30, 1872.

Those who dislike the colonial connection speak of it as a chain, but it is a golden chain, and I for one, am glad to wear the fetters.

SIR JOHN A. MACDONALD, H. of C., *Debates*, Mar. 30, 1875, 981.

I have listened a lot and I conclude that Canada is more British than Britain.

ALEXANDER MACKENZIE, letter to Lord Dufferin, June 25, 1875, during discussions with the Disraeli government in London. (Pub.Arch.Can.)

I believe . . . that everything that extends the liberties of Canadians, everything that accords to Canada and her statesmen greater breadth of view in the management of their own affairs, is more likely to conduce to the advancement of Imperial interests and greatness than any curbing policy that keeps us down to the grindstone.

ALEXANDER MACKENZIE, H. of C., *Debates*, Apr. 21, 1882.

Why should we waste money and men in this wretched business? England is not at war, but merely helping the Khedive to put down an insurrection, and now that Gordon is gone, the motive of aiding in the rescue of our countrymen is gone with him. Our men and money would therefore be sacrificed to get Gladstone and Co. out of the hole they have plunged themselves into by their own imbecility.

SIR JOHN A. MACDONALD, letter to Tupper, Mar. 12, 1885.

Colonies are destined to become nations, as it is the destiny of a child to become a man. No one, even on the other side will assume that this country, which will some day number a larger population than Great Britain is forever to remain in its present political relations with Great Britain. The time is coming when the present relations of Great Britain and Canada must either become closer or become severed altogether.

SIR WILFRID LAURIER, H. of C., *Debates*, 1888, I, 363.

For myself I am a true Briton. I love the old land very dearly. I am glad that I was born a British subject; a British subject I have lived for three-score years, and something more – I hope to live and die a British subject. I trust and hope that my children and my grand-children, who have also been born British subjects, will live their lives as British subjects and as British subjects die.

SIR OLIVER MOWAT, address, Toronto, Feb. 18, 1891.

The silken chain which binds the Dominion and the Mother-land together.

J. CASTELL HOPKINS, *Can. mag.*, Dec., 1893, 171.

A Nation spoke to a Nation,
  A Queen sent word to a Throne:
"Daughter am I in my mother's house,
  But mistress in my own.
The gates are mine to open,
  As the gates are mine to close,
And I set my house in order,"
  Said our Lady of the Snows.

RUDYARD KIPLING, "Our Lady of the Snows, 1897", London *Times*, Apr. 27, 1897.

If we were to be compelled to take part in all the wars of Great Britain, I have no hesitation in saying that . . . sharing the burden, we should also share the responsibility. Under that condition of things, which do not exist, we should have the right to say to Great Britain: If you want us to help you, call us to your councils.

SIR WILFRID LAURIER, H. of C., *Debates*, Mar. 13, 1900.

Imperialism means that the British Empire is one and that her interests are one, and that what makes the British Empire great makes Canada great; that if Britain falls Canada falls; that if Canada is hurt the Empire is hurt; that if you strike a blow at the Empire you strike Canada.

GEORGE W. ROSS, speech at Niagara, Aug., 1901.

Canada for the British and Why Not!

ISAAC M. BARR, *British settlements in North Western Canada*, 1902, "Acknowledgements".

It is the brightest gem in the Crown of the British Empire.

SIR WILFRID LAURIER, speech in London, Eng., July 1, 1902; originally appears as a reference to freedom in a poem by R. Heber, in *Pietas universitatis Oxoniensis*, 1761: "The brightest jewel in the British crown".

How can Canadians love the British Empire which they have not seen, when they do not love their own country which they have seen.

JOHN S. EWART, inaugural address, Canadian Club of Winnipeg, 1904, *Report*, 1904-1906, 17.

I am one who believes in Canada first and the Empire next.

W.F. MCLEAN, H. of C., *Debates*, Feb. 11, 1907. (See also, Political Phrases: "Canada first".)

I stand in the first place for the British Empire against the world, and within the British Empire I stand first for Canada.

SIR ROBERT BORDEN, a frequent declaration, 1905-12; also July 25, 1930, in support of R.B. Bennett, "The British Empire first and, within the British Empire, Canada first".

There is no ignorance of Canada now in the United Kingdom. I wish there were a little greater knowledge of the British Empire in Canada.

LORD NORTHCLIFFE, address, Canadian Club, Toronto, Oct. 23, 1908.

Natural growth is better than revolution; partnership between Canada and Great Britain is in the interests of both; the political tie between Canada and Great Britain leads to the working of educative influences between the two countries; it will lead to Canada's bearing her share of Britain's burdens.

GEORGE M. WRONG, *Can. nationalism and the Imperial tie*, 1909.

England will never fire a shot in our defence against the United States.

HENRI BOURASSA, speech, Monument National, Montreal, Jan. 20, 1910. (Trans.).

Great Britain presided but the Dominions met her on equal terms.

SIR ROBERT BORDEN, referring to the first meeting of the Imperial War Cabinet, Mar., 1917.

Fifteen years of saying no.

JOHN W. DAFOE, *Laurier: a study in Canadian politics*, 1922, 64, re: Laurier's resistance to pressures for close involvement in Empire affairs.

Let there be no dispute as to where I stand. When Britain's message came, then Canada should have said: "Ready, aye ready; we stand by you." I hope the time has not gone by when that declaration can yet be made. If that declaration is made, then I will be at the back of the government.

> ARTHUR MEIGHEN, address, Toronto Business Men's Conservative Club, Sept. 22, 1922, after the "Chanak affair"; see speech by Laurier, H. of C., *Debates*, Spec. session, Aug. 19, 1914, 10, for earlier and similar use of the phrase "Ready, aye ready".

I am for the British Empire next to Canada, the only difference being that some gentlemen are for the United States before Canada. I am for the British Empire after Canada.

> RICHARD B. BENNETT, H. of C., *Debates*, May 6, 1930.

Canadian Broadcasting Commission

The CBC has never learned how to let an individual make a career of his own talent.

> ANDREW ALLAN, *Globe and Mail*, Jan. 16, 1971, 25.

Canadian-French Relations

It seems to me that, and I take it for granted as true, that if France wants to improve relations with Canada as they have said they did, the first rule of the game would be not to try and interpret our internal law, our constitutional law, but to ask the federal government, which speaks for Canada in its foreign relations, as to what that law is.

> PIERRE E. TRUDEAU, to the Press, Ottawa, Oct. 15, 1969.

Canadian Legion

In this stale Valhalla,
One re-lives the battle of the bottles,
And the wound he caught in action
With a harlot at Versailles.

> JOHN OWER, "Edmonton Legion", 1967.

Canadian National Railway

The efficiency of the System emphatically demands the maintenance of it in its integrity. The policy of the Conservative party toward this great undertaking will be, reduced to briefest words, "amalgamation, never; competition, ever!"

> RICHARD B. BENNETT, speech in Montreal, June 26, 1930, on the Canadian National Railway.

CN

> ALAN FLEMING, logo introduced by CNR in 1960.

Canadian Pacific Railway

They do not consider that they can hold the country without it.

> J.S. HELMCKEN, *Diary*, June 8, 1870, qu. in *B.C. hist. quart.* IV (2), Apr., 1940, 120, referring to a committe of the Privy Council.

With the construction of the railway the country will be populated by Englishmen; without it by Americans.

> TORONTO *GLOBE*, Mar. 23, 1870.

I am confident that a bushel of wheat will never go to England over an all-rail route from Saskatchewan to the seaboard.

> EDWARD BLAKE, speech at Aurora, Ont., Oct. 3, 1874.

Two streaks of rust across the wilderness.

> EDWARD BLAKE, attributed reference to the future of the Canadian Pacific.

Until this grand work is completed, our Dominion is little more than a "geographical expression".

> SIR JOHN A. MACDONALD, letter to Sir Stafford Northcote, May 1, 1878.

We have as much interest in British Columbia as in Australia, and no more. The railway once finished, we become one great united country with a large interprovincial trade and a common interest.

> SIR JOHN A. MACDONALD, letter to Sir Stafford Northcote, May 1, 1878

I shall not be present; I am an old man, but I shall perchance look down from the realms above upon a multitude of younger men – a prosperous, populous, and thriving generation – a nation of Canadians, who will see the completion of the road.

> SIR JOHN A. MACDONALD, speech at Hochelaga depot on return from Europe after negotiating for completion of the Railway, Sept. 27, 1880.

It will never pay for its axle-grease.

> EDWARD BLAKE; attributed. Also attributed to Sir Richard Cartwright, George W. Ross, and the Liberal Party leaders, all of whom were in opposition to Tupper's proposals to help finance the Railway, especially during the years 1880-81. Ross (*Getting into Parliament*, 1913, 118) uses the phrase as a summation of his attitude.

If I have no other bequest to leave to my children after me, the proudest legacy I would desire to leave was the record that I was able to take an active part in the promotion of this great measure by which, I believe, Canada will receive an impetus that will make it a great and powerful country at no distant date.

> SIR CHARLES TUPPER, H. of C., *Debates*, 1880-81, 74.

The Canadian Pacific Railway will run, if it is ever finished, through a country frost-bound for seven or eight months in the year, and will connect with the eastern part of the Dominion a province which embraces about as forbidding a country as any on the face of the earth.

> HENRY LABOUCHÈRE, "The Canadian Dominion bubble", *Truth*, Sept. 1, 1881.

The history of the world offers no such evidence of push as the work of this year has done. Sherman's march to the sea was nothing to it. When the road is completed there will be nothing in history to compare with it.

> R.B. CONKEY, qu. in Winnipeg *Sun*, Aug. 30, 1882.

Like a vision I could see it driving my poor Indians before it, and spreading out behind it the farms, the towns and cities you see today. No one who has not lived in the west since the Old-Times can realize what is due to that road – that C.P.R. It was Magic – like the mirage on the prairies, changing the face of the whole country.

> FATHER ALBERT LACOMBE, qu. in Katherine Hughes, *Father Lacombe: the black-robe voyageur*, 1920, 273.

Well, boys, he'll do it. Stay over till tomorrow. The day the Canadian Pacific busts, the Conservative party busts the day after.

> JOHN HENRY POPE, Winter, 1883, to Van Horne and other C.P.R. officials, after persuading Sir John A. Macdonald to extend another loan to the company.

Have no means paying wages, pay car can't be sent out. Unless you send immediate relief, we must stop.

> SIR WILLIAM VAN HORNE, telegram to Donald Smith, Spring, 1884.

Stand fast, Craigellachie.

> GEORGE STEPHEN, President of the C.P.R. Syndicate, complete text of cable, sent from London to Donald Smith in Montreal, Oct., 1884 announcing victory in obtaining financing for completion of C.P.R.; war cry of the Clan Grant, named after a rock in the Spey Valley, Scotland.

In 1871, the project of constructing the Pacific was a sublime audacity.

> J.A. CHAPLEAU, H. of C., *Debates*, 1885, 2566.

The last spike will be just as good an iron one as there is between Montreal and Vancouver, and anyone who wants to see it driven will have to pay full fare.

> SIR WILLIAM VAN HORNE, qu. in Walter Vaughan, *The life and work of Sir William Van Horne*, 1920, 131.

The last spike.

> On Nov. 7, 1885, the driving of the last spike at Craigellachie, B.C., by Donald A. Smith, marked the completion of the construction of the C.P.R. to the Pacific Ocean.

All I can say is that the work has been done well in every way.

> SIR WILLIAM VAN HORNE, speech at last spike ceremony at Craigellachie, B.C. marking completion of the C.P.R., Nov. 7, 1885.

Here was driven the last spike completing the Canadian Pacific Railway from ocean to ocean, November 7, 1885.

> ANON., Inscription on cairn at Craigellachie, B.C.

For some of us are bums, for whom
    work has no charms,
And some of us are farmers, a-working
    for our farms,
But all are jolly fellows, who come
    from near and far,
To work up in the Rockies on the
    C.P.R.

> MORLEY ROBERTS, song of the construction men, qu. in his *The western avernus*, 1887, 57.

It is the Tory Government on wheels.

> TORONTO *GLOBE*, Mar. 2, 1891, 4.

To have built that road would have made a Canadian out of the German Emperor.

> SIR WILLIAM VAN HORNE, after renouncing his American citizenship, qu. in Peter Newman, *Flame of power*, 1959, 92.

As long as I live and continue in the ministry, never will a damned American company have control of the Pacific. I will resign my place as minister rather than consent to it.

> SIR GEORGE-ÉTIENNE CARTIER, qu. in Beckles Willson, *Lord Strathcona, the story of his life*, 1902, 183.

"How High We Live," said the Duke to the Prince, "on the Canadian Pacific Railway".

> ANON., advertising slogan adopted by Wm. Van Horne, 1890.

Wise Men of the East Go West by the C.P.R.

SIR WILLIAM VAN HORNE, advertising slogan, adopted about 1890.

Since we can't export the scenery, we shall have to import the tourists.

SIR WILLIAM VAN HORNE, about 1895.

Cutting a melon.

ANON., term used about 1898 to signify a supposed financial "deal" whenever the C.P.R. applied for an increase in its capital stock.

Sample of Ordinary Everyday C.P.R. Wreck.

ROBERT C. (BOB) EDWARDS, Calgary *Eye Opener*, May 5, 1906, caption under photographic reproduction of a bad train wreck (not C.P.R.). Used at a time when the C.P.R. had banned the *Eye Opener* from its trains, this and other captions and photographs were effective in having the ban lifted.

Come to Alberta and go into partnership with the Canadian Pacific.

C.P.R., slogan in the West, about 1908.

No Crop, no Payment!

C.P.R., slogan in the West, about 1908.

The Great Colonizer.

ANON., a reference to the Railway in recognition of its efforts in western land settlement.

The most stupendous contract ever made under responsible government in the history of the world.

W.T.R. PRESTON, referring to the awarding by Macdonald of the contract to build the C.P.R. to George Stephen's syndicate, 1880.

No single work of any man in any part of the world at any period of the world's history has so obviously and directly contributed to the making of a nation as the transcontinental railway in Canada.

C.P. LUCAS, *Greater Rome and greater Britain*, 1912, 119.

Be it understood the C.P.R., Clifford Sifton and the Almighty comprise the Trinity of Canada, ranking in importance in the order named.

ROBERT C. (BOB) EDWARDS, Calgary *Eye Opener;* attributed.

The Canadian Pacific Railway was given a bit of a line here and a bit of a line there and almost as much land as it wanted, and the laughter was still going on when the last spike was driven between east and west.

RUDYARD KIPLING, *Letters of travel (1892-1913)*, 1920, 28.

Where are the coolies in your poem,
    Ned?
Where are the thousands from China
    who swung
    Their picks with bare hands at forty
    below?

F.R. SCOTT, "All the spikes but the last", 1957, on E.J. Pratt's poem, *Towards the last spike*, 1952.

The C.P.R. was immortalized by Hollywood in 1949 when Twentieth Century-Fox made *Canadian Pacific,* a film purportedly about the building of the railway.

PIERRE BERTON, *The last spike*, 1971, 423.

Canadian Press

That's the trouble with the Canadian Press. It's one of those faceless corporations with no soul to save and no ass to kick.

J.R. BURNETT, Editor, Charlottetown *Guardian*, about 1937 at C.P. 50th. anniv. dinner; qu. G. Purcell, Toronto, Apr., 1967.

Canadian Shield

Hidden in wonder and snow, or
   sudden with summer,
This land stares at the sun in a huge
   silence
Endlessly repeating something we
   cannot hear.

F.R. SCOTT, "Laurentian Shield", 1954.

The Shield! The Canadian Shield! Come, Muse of rockbound nationalists, for whom our stammering typing engine waits smiling with teeth of alphabets. You who inflate the eloquence of Northern laureates, come, let us celebrate the real estate. Sing, learned dame – as so often before – not of men, not of poor flesh and blood, but of rocks, stones, mud, bogs, fens, muskegs, permafrost, tundra!

KILDARE DOBBS, *The great fur opera; annals of the H.B.C.*, 1970, 36.

Canadianism

Little Canadians.

ANON., from "Little Englanders"; a term used early 20th century to describe nationalists.

We have decided that our own Supreme Court was not good enough for the people of Canada; we have never had enough national spirit to provide ourselves with a distinctive national Flag; we have people in Canada objecting to standing up when "O Canada" is sung; we have trifled with the question of nationality and citizenship until the young Canadian is never quite sure whether he is a Canadian or a Hottentot because he had a Hottentot grandmother; we have put enthusiasm into every national day but our own; we have those who spoke up for Canada denounced as traitors.

JOHN W. DAFOE, *Manitoba Free press*, Sept. 17, 1925, editorial.

When it is possible, of course, what we do should have a Canadian character. We should be ourselves and the traveller, the tourist, the visitor from wherever he comes, will respect us the more if we are. No one looks his best in somebody else's clothes!

VINCENT MASSEY, address to Federal-Provincial Conference on Tourists and the Canadian Tourist Association, Oct. 23, 1957.

Possibly the only definition of Canadianism that some citizens might agree on is the wry observation that "a Canadian is someone who has turned down a chance to go and live in the United States."

BRIAN MOORE, *Canada*, 1963, 12.

for these were brave men and subtle
   women,
      spritely lovers
who could not love themselves and it is
hard that we have only
one life for mostly we cannot
   command the
      courage outright to exist

DENNIS LEE, "Civil elegies", No. 7, 1972.

Canada is the only country I know of in which, throughout my lifetime, to be pro-Canadian has been interpreted in terms of a negative attitude towards other countries.

NORMAN WARD, in J.H. Redekop, ed., *The star-spangled beaver*, 1973, 5.

Canadians

Both on account of the feudal system and the aristocratic government, a private man [is] not worth so much in Canada as in the United States; and, if your wealth in any measure consist in manliness, in originality and independence, you had better stay here.

HENRY THOREAU, *Excursion to Can.*, 1850, advice to Americans.

The Canadian people are more practical than imaginative. Romantic tales and poetry would meet with less favour in their eyes than a good political article from their newspapers.

SUSANNA MOODIE, *Mark Hurdlestone*, 1853, Intro.

North American Chinamen.

ANON., pre-Confederation, British Columbia term used to describe the "Canadians" who were unpopular because of their thriftiness.

As long as I live, as long as I have power to use in the service of my country, I shall repel the idea of changing the nature of its different elements. I want the marble to remain the marble; I want the granite to remain the granite; I want the oak to remain the oak; I want the sturdy Scotchman to remain the Scotchman; I want the brainy Englishman to remain the Englishman; I want the warm-hearted Irishman to remain the Irishman.

SIR WILFRID LAURIER, speech to Acadians, Arichat, N.S., Aug. 15, 1900. (Trans.)

We first saw light in Canada, the
　　land beloved of God;
We are the pulse of Canada, its
　　marrow and its blood;
And we, the men of Canada, can
　　face the world and brag

That we were born in Canada
　　beneath the English flag.

PAULINE JOHNSON, "Canadian born", 1903.

Our fathers came to win us
　　This land beyond recall —
And the same blood flows within us
　　Of Briton, Celt, or Gaul —
Keep alive each glowing ember
　　Of our sireland, but remember
Our country's Canadian
　　Whatever may befall.

WILLIAM H. DRUMMOND, "Canadian forever", 1905.

I move about in Canadian circles to some extent and I hear nothing but bad reports of all the men I look up to in Canadian life. They must be a very wicked set, but I must confess that Canadians speak as badly of the men in private life. Canada is a village street, many thousands of miles long.

LORD BEAVERBROOK, letter, July 4, 1917 to R.B. Bennett.

The habitant is the true Canadian for he has no other country.

RAMSAY TRAQUAIR, *Atlantic monthly*, 1923, 823.

The French-Canadian in a real sense is the truest Canadian. He has lived on the soil for three hundred years, and the family ties with another world have long been broken. To Canada alone does he feel attached, for England conquered him and France first deserted him and then travelled a political and spiritual road his clergy has taught him to abhor. He sees no hope coming from without; he knows he must build up his own resources.

F.R. SCOTT, *Canada today*, 1938, 72.

More appallingly, Canadians are at bottom not interested in their own country; I honestly believe they prefer to read about dukes and lords, or about the civil war in the United States. They are supposed to be born explorers; but they have not yet heard that the human heart and soul are perhaps the only corners in this universe where unexplored and undiscovered continents are still abounding. This lack of mental aliveness is fundamental. Canada is a non-conductor for any sort of intellectual current.

FREDERICK PHILIP GROVE, *Univ. of Tor. quart.*, July, 1938, 460.

My roots are in this soil,
Whatever good or bad, what vain
    hope or mighty triumph lies in you,
That good or bad, that destiny is
    in me.
Where you have failed, the fault is
    on my head.
Where you are ignorant or blind or
    cruel, I made you so.
In all your folly and your strength
    I share,
And all your beauty is my heritage.

GWEN PHARIS (RINGWOOD), "Oh Canada, my country", written 1940: qu., A.R.M. Lower, *Colony to nation*, 1946, 561.

I accept now with equanimity the question so constantly addressed to me, "Are you an American?" and merely return the accurate answer, "Yes, I am a Canadian".

LESTER B. PEARSON, "Canada and the United States", Jan. 31, 1941; *Words and occasions*, 1970, 25.

We Canadians are a worthy, thrifty people, perfectly safe and constituting no problem to the countries in control of our destinies: we are therefore uninteresting.

A.R.M. LOWER, in *Can. hist. rev.*, 1941, 8.

For we are young, my brothers, and full of doubt, and we have listened too long to timid men.

BRUCE HUTCHISON, *Unknown country*, 1942.

In every generation Canadians have had to rework the miracle of their political existence. Canada has been created because there has existed within the hearts of its people, a determination to build for themselves an enduring home. Canada is a supreme act of faith.

A.R.M. LOWER, *Colony to nation*, 1946, 561.

There are as many ways of being Canadian as there are of being French or British, and many more than there are of being American or Irish.

LISTER SINCLAIR, *Here and now*, June, 1949, 17.

The people of Trois Pistoles and the loggers of the Charlottes are too busy working and building to have time for self-analysis – and these and others like them comprise the great majority of the Canadian people.

LESLIE ROBERTS, *Canada: the golden hinge*, 1952, 10.

Historically, a Canadian is an American who rejects the revolution.

NORTHROP FRYE, *Univ. of Tor. quart.*, Vol. 22, No. 3, Apr., 1953.

We are inescapably, and almost from the first, the bifocal people. The people of the second thought. To remain a people at all we have had to think before we speak, even to think before we think. Our "characteristic prudence" is not the Scot in us, or the Puritan, or the "North Irish". It is this bi-focalism, this necessity for taking

second thought, for keeping one foot
on each bank of the Ottawa.

> MALCOLM ROSS, *Our sense of identity*,
> 1954, ix.

In the disordered lines of battle the
lineaments of a new creature, the
Canadian, neither British nor French,
had first appeared in America – a
young face yet, blurred in infancy,
indistinguishable to foreigners but
slowly setting into harder lines.

> BRUCE HUTCHISON, *The struggle for the
> border*, 1955, 257, referring to the War
> of 1812.

What matters in the long run is not
that we are Canadian, but that *because* we are Canadian we have an
unparalleled opportunity to contribute
something new and vital to a world
that needs and wants it and expects it
of us.

> MAVOR MOORE, *Univ. of Tor. quart.*,
> Oct., 1956, 16.

Deferring to beadle and censor;
not ashamed for this,
but given over to horseplay,
the making of money

> IRVING LAYTON, "From colony to na-
> tion", 1956.

The urban Canadian gets sick of books
about the wilds and the people who
inhabit them; the Western Canadian
has a notion that Eastern Canadians
are effete pseudo-Englishman; the
French Canadians consider themselves
the only genuine article; the New
Canadians sometimes betray a belief
that we had no art until they arrived.

> ROBERTSON DAVIES, *Publishers' weekly*,
> Oct. 15, 1956, 1867.

The Canadian whose father accepted
Canada as a spiritual dependency of
some external power is thinking of it
now solely as a nation in its own right.
Though the nation is diverse, confused, self-centred, a little dizzy and
smug from success at the moment, it is
essentially whole. It has become cog-
nate and organic. The Canadian
knows, better than his father knew,
that he belongs to it and no other.

> BRUCE HUTCHISON, *Canada: tomorrow's
> giant*, 1957, 5.

The Canadian is often a baffled man
because he feels different from his
British kindred and his American
neighbours, sharply refuses to be
lumped with either of them, yet cannot make plain this difference.

> J.B. PRIESTLY, in introduction to *The
> Bodley Head Leacock*, 1957.

From south to north, from coast to
        coast,
    Victorian or Acadian,
Whatever blood our veins may boast,
    We all are pure Canadian.

> V.B. RHODENIZER, "Theme song", 1958.

As a people we are still uninterested in
ideas, and as a consequence are too
imitative of stronger cultures, too respectful of the lords of opinion and of
style abroad. We are, as a result, often
derivative and commonplace.

> LORNE PIERCE, *A Canadian nation*,
> 1960, 36.

We should now give to ourselves, and
to others, the image of a people whose
ambition is not so much to reach the
moon, as to transcend our psychological space in order to reach the nations
around us, closer at hand, but also
better worth loving.

> JEAN-CHARLES FALARDEAU, *Roots and
> values in Canadian lives*, 1961, 62.

I believe it real and accurate to say that we can contribute a very great deal to the world *if Canada remains Canadian*. Culturally we can contribute, and politically we can contribute. If two centuries have produced such a nation as ours, now is not the time to give it up, for it was never really needed before now.

HUGH MACLENNAN, in *The price of being Canadian*, ed. D.L.B. Hamlin, 1961, 33.

Think Canadian. We're better than we think.

ANON., C.B.C. disc jockey on signing off program of Canadian records, 1964, qu. in A. Heisey, *The great Canadian stampede*, 1973, 20.

We are all learning to be Canadians, whether we have recently immigrated, whether we are the sons and daughters of immigrants, or whether our ancestors came to New France or were United Empire Loyalists. And we are all teaching one another.

MITCHELL SHARP, address, Canadian Club, Montreal, Nov. 23, 1964.

Our stodginess has made us a society of greater simplicity, formality, and perhaps even innocence than the people to the south.

GEORGE P. GRANT, *Lament for a nation*, 1965, 70.

Canadians are generally indistinguishable from the Americans, and the surest way of telling the two apart is to make the observation to a Canadian.

RICHARD STARNES, U.S. Scripps-Howard columnist, qu. in Gerald Clark, *Canada: the uneasy neighbour*, 1965, 4.

If Canadians can be drawn together by the passion of objectivity, by the ardour to remain disinterested, by the great and compelling urge to suspend all judgment other than the rational and mature, we shall automatically be a people unto ourselves, in a world mostly gone mad.

ERIC NICOL, *100 years of what?*, 1966, 45.

Canadians move slowly, but when they are aroused they move with remarkable speed. Someone suggested recently that our way of life is "puritanism touched by orgy". Our history is a record of stolidity broken by bold imaginativeness.

CLAUDE T. BISSELL, *The strength of the university*, 1968, 190; address given at Los Angeles, Jan., 1966.

French Canadians mistake the nearly silent and the usually flexible English-speaking attitude as an absence of conviction or determination.

KENNETH MCNAUGHT, in Peter Russell, ed., *Nationalism in Canada*, 1966, 70.

Imagine a Canadian Dream, which implied that everybody in the world ought to share it! Imagine a Committee on Un-Canadian Activities! You can't. Un-Canadianism is almost the very definition of *Canadianism*.

HUGH HOOD, in 1967, qu. in W. Kilbourn, *Canada, a guide to the peaceable kingdom*, 1970, 32.

Father
Ragueneau Lord Selkirk
and John A. – however
far into northness
you have walked –
when we call you
turn around please and
don't look so
surprised.

MIRIAM WADDINGTON, "Canadians", 1967.

I am a Quebecker. I am a French Canadian with all my heart. However, I am also deeply and irrevocably a Canadian. I am convinced that one does not prevent the other.

PIERRE E. TRUDEAU, speech, Montreal, Nov. 10, 1968. (Trans.)

Canadians are a good people – I can find nothing else to say against them.

IRVING LAYTON, "Aphs", *The whole bloody bird*, 1969, 98.

If the national mental illness of the United States is megalomania, that of Canada is paranoid schizophrenia.

MARGARET ATWOOD, *Journals of Susanna Moodie*, 1970, 62.

A Canadian is someone who drinks Brazilian coffee from an English tea-cup, and munches a French pastry while sitting on his Danish furniture, having just come home from an Italian movie in his German car. He picks up his Japanese pen and writes to his Member of Parliament to complain about the American takeover of the Canadian publishing business.

CAMPBELL HUGHES, Canadian Book Publishers Council, adapted; qu. *Time*, Mar. 1, 1971, 8; *Maclean's*, Apr., 1973, 81, etc.

There is no such thing as a model or ideal Canadian. What could be more absurd than the concept of an 'all-Canadian' boy or girl? A society which emphasizes uniformity is one which creates intolerance and hate. A society which eulogizes the average citizen is one which breeds mediocrity.

PIERRE E. TRUDEAU, speech, Ukranian-Canadian Congress, Winnipeg, Oct. 9, 1971.

I just am a Canadian. It is not a thing which you can escape from. It is like having blue eyes.

ROBERTSON DAVIES, in *Maclean's*, Sept., 1972, 42.

Canadians, Black

The Negro Canadian, while less clamorous for civil rights because less well-organized, less well-led, and given fewer provocations, may also have come to know himself as a Canadian first and as a Negro by chance.

ROBIN W. WINKS, *Dalhousie Rev.*, Winter, 1968-69, 453.

Canals

It would never be a paying investment till it was filled in, and a railway run on top of it.

SIR JOHN A. MACDONALD, qu. E.B. Biggar, *Anecdotal life*, 1891, 226, on Rideau Canal.

Cancer

Strange dying
that of the cancerous one
choking on his own
hysteric growth.

STEVE SMITH, "Strange dying, theirs", 1964.

Canoeing

Distance from hence by Judgement at
   ye lest
From ye house six hundred miles
   southwest
Through Rivers which run strong with
   falls
thirty three Carriages five lakes in all.

HENRY KELSEY, *Journal*, 1691, Introd. (Kelsey papers, Ottawa, 1929).

Now for a bracing up of stalwart
    shoulders,
  And now a load to lift;
An uphill tramp through tangled
    briars and boulders,
  The irksome weight to shift,
    And through it all, the far
incessant calling
    Of waters falling.

    PAULINE JOHNSON, "The portage", 1893.

What the camel is to desert tribes,
what the horse is to the Arab, what the
ship is to the colonizing Briton, what
all modern means of locomotion are to
the civilized world today, that, and
more than that, the canoe was to the
Indian who lived beside the innumerable waterways of Canada.

    WILLIAM WOOD, *All afloat*, 1921, 16.

Canada is a canoe route.

    A.R.M. LOWER, *Queen's quart.*, Vol. 66,
    1959, 204.

A Canadian is somebody who knows
how to make love in a canoe.

    PIERRE BERTON, attributed by D. Brown,
    in *Can. mag.*, Dec. 22, 1973, 3.

Cant

You have to cant a little with the
world, if you want even common civil
usage.

    THOMAS C. HALIBURTON, *Sam Slick's wise
    saws*, 1853, ch. 10.

Cape Breton

What, is Cape Breton an island? wonderful! My dear sir, you always bring
us good news. Egad! I'll go directly
and tell the King that Cape Breton is
an island.

    DUKE OF NEWCASTLE, British Prime Min-
    ister; attributed by Smollett, *Humphrey
    Clinker*, 1771.

My cup of pride would have been
filled to overflowing if I could have
uttered my first feeble cry on the
island of Cape Breton.

    LIONEL FORSYTH, d. 1957, a frequent
    remark to Eastern audiences in mock
    seriousness.

North America is a large island to the
west of the continent of Cape Breton.

    RAY SMITH, "Cape Breton" in *Tamarack
    rev.*, No. 43, 1967, 50.

Capital

Scarcity of capital and formidable obstacles to development and unity have
made us look on government enterprise as a practical device for meeting
special problems rather than the result
of an ideological deviation.

    W.A. MACKINTOSH, in H.G.J. Aitken et al.,
    *The American economic impact on
    Canada*, 1959, 68.

The problem and source of danger to
the future of Canada lie in the fact
that those who control the key sectors
of the economy have taken as their
premise that U.S. capital is and will be
dominant, that Canadian development
is necessarily subordinate to and dependent on ("integrated with") the
drive of U.S. groups for their own
profit.

    L.C. and F.W. PARK, *The anatomy of big
    business*, 1962, 51.

Capital has no nationality.

    ROBERT W. BONNER, address to the Em-
    pire Club, Toronto, Dec. 10, 1970.

Capital Punishment

Ninety percent of them die like cowards.

    ARTHUR B. ENGLISH, [Arthur Ellis,
    pseud., "official executioner"], qu. in A.
    O'Brien, *My friend, the hangman*,
    1970, 16, referring to those executed.

Capitalism

The capitalistic system has grown up and it is in use because, and only because, the experience of mankind has proven it to be the best way of doing what has to be done.

SIR CLIFFORD SIFTON, speech, about 1925, qu., Dafoe, *Sifton*, 510.

We believe that the social realization of the Kingdom of God is not compatible with the continuance of the capitalistic system, and we think the Church should now uncover fearlessly the anti-social and unchristian basis of that system and declare unremitting war upon it.

TORONTO CONFERENCE, UNITED CHURCH OF CANADA, *Resolutions*, 1933.

Only in times of peace can the wastes of capitalism be tolerated.

F.R. SCOTT, *Queen's quart.*, Summer, 1935, 217.

To those who object that capitalism is "rooted in human nature", we answer: Possibly, but so was cannibalism. We no longer eat each other. A civilization is within our reach in which we shall no longer exploit each other.

LEAGUE FOR SOCIAL RECONSTRUCTION, *Social planning for Canada*, comp. by Eugene Forsey, J. King Gordon, Leonard Marsh and others, 1935, 69.

The time is fast arriving when special privileges at the expense of the welfare of the community will be considered as a luxury which no civilized nation can afford.

LEAGUE FOR SOCIAL RECONSTRUCTION, *Social planning for Canada*, comp. by Eugene Forsey, J. King Gordon, Leonard Marsh and others, 1935, 39.

If property, profit, the reward of toil, the fundamental instinct of the human race to gain, to acquire, to have, to reach somewhere, is taken away, then I for one do not feel that we have anything worth fighting for.

ARTHUR MEIGHEN, speech in Toronto, Jan. 22, 1941.

The capitalist mentality, with its emphasis on private property and self-regulating markets, reduced both land and labour to "commodities", which could be bought and sold for profit. The grotesque and immoral enormity of this fundamental feature of capitalism can be seen if we remind ourselves that "land" is simply another name for nature, and that "labour" is only another name for man.

JACK MCLEOD, *Agenda 1970: proposals for a creative politics*, 1968, 46.

Capitulation

They've shot my flag to ribbons, but in rents
    It floats above the height;
Their ensign shall not crown my battlements
    While I can stand and fight.
I fling defiance at them as I cry,
    "Capitulate? Not I."

PAULINE JOHNSON, "And he said, 'Fight on'", 1913. Her last poem written shortly after doctors told her that her illness would be her final one.

Captives

I wish I had been born beside a river
Instead of this round pond
Where the geese white as pillows float in continual circles
And never get out.

JAMES REANEY, "The Upper Canadian", 1949.

Care

Life is a chart as well as a coast, and a little care will keep you clear of rocks, reefs, and sandbars.

> THOMAS C. HALIBURTON, *Sam Slick's wise saws*, 1853, ch. 17.

Consistent care is more important than maternal care.

> WILLIAM E. BLATZ, *Human security*, 1966, 9.

Careers

To most men, there should come a time for shifting harness, for lightening the load one way and adjusting it for greater effort in another. That is the time for the second career, time for the old dog to perform new tricks.

> WILDER PENFIELD, address, Canadian Club, Montreal, Dec., 1959.

Caribou

The Caribou is a travelsome beast, always in a hurry, going against the wind. When the wind is west, all travel west; when it veers, they veer.

> ERNEST THOMPSON SETON, *The Arctic prairies*, 1911.

Carleton, Lord

Tradition made Carleton divine; research makes him human. The portrait of this Irishman, as touched up by his English biographer, was almost an idol to Canadians. The picture was beautiful — that of a soldier, a political sage, and one might almost add, a saint all combined. It was made for worship, not for understanding. No such perfect man was ever born, not even in Ireland.

> A.L. BURT, in Can. Hist. Assoc., *Report*, 1935, 76.

Carr, Emily

I made myself into an envelope into which I could thrust my work deep, lick the flap, seal it from everybody.

> EMILY CARR, *Growing pains*, 1946, 187.

Old woman, of your three days'
        anatomy
Leviathan sickened and spewed you
        forth
In a great vomit on coasts of eternity.
Then, as for John of Patmos, the river
        of life
Burned for you an emerald and jasper
        smoke
And down the valley you looked and
        saw
All wilderness become transparent
        vapour,
A ghostly underneath a fleshly stroke,
And every bush an apocalypse of leaf.

> WILFRED WATSON, "Emily Carr", 1955.

Essentially she did not like people; nothing in them compelled her interest sufficiently to make her want to express their qualities, good or bad, in paint.

> EDYTHE HEMBROFF-SCHLEICHER, *M.E.*, *A portrayal of Emily Carr*, 1969, 44.

Cartier, Sir George E.

I am an Englishman speaking French.

> SIR GEORGE ETIENNE CARTIER, a saying of his later years. In 1858, Cartier was introduced to Queen Victoria and he told Her Majesty that a Lower Canadian was "An Englishman who speaks French"; in a speech in London, Mar. 10, 1869, he said "French Canadians as well as myself were Englishmen speaking French." (See Boyd, *Cartier*, 1914, 297.)

Cartier was as bold as a lion. He was just the man I wanted. But for him Confederation could not have been carried.

> SIR JOHN A. MACDONALD, Jan. 29, 1885, to his secretary Joseph Pope, after unveiling statue of Cartier in Ottawa.

Cartier, Jacques

In the sea-port of Saint Malo 'twas
  a smiling morn in May
When the Commodore Jacques
    Cartier
  to the westward sail'd away;
In the crowded old Cathedral all
  the town were on their knees
For the safe return of kinsmen from
  the undiscover'd seas;
And every autumn blast that swept
  o'er pinnacle and pier
Filled manly hearts with sorrow and
  gentle hearts with fear.

> THOMAS D'A. MCGEE, "Jacques Cartier",
> 1858.

Canada, like the country of Canaan,
was inhabited by a sinful race, and
God in his justice had sentenced them
to destruction. But, in his bounty, he
wished to give them the opportunity
of averting the terrible sentence that
loomed over their heads. Jacques Cartier therefore appeared in their midst
as if heaven-sent with his following of
pious priests, like Abraham among the
guilty Canaanites.

> LOUIS LAFLÈCHE, Bishop of Three Riv-
> ers, *Quelques considérations sur les
> rapports de la société civile avec la
> religion et la famille*, 1866, 54. (Trans.)

Cartoons

No cartoon of any vitality can be
made of a man whose outstanding
traits are his simple dignity.

> A.R.M. LOWER, in Can. Hist. Assoc., *Re-
> port*, 1940, 57.

Cartwright, Sir Richard

I, as a member of the Liberal-Conservative party owe him such a debt of
gratitude that if it shall be necessary to
retain his services in the party which
he does not lead, and which would not
have him for a leader, and which

barely tolerates him as a supporter –
if it be necessary in order to retain him
in that capacity, I, for one, will propose a subsidy to Parliament to keep
him there.

> SIR JOHN THOMPSON, on Sir Richard
> Cartwright, H. of C., *Debates*, June 28,
> 1892.

He above all others made in the same
mould, which, thank God, nature
broke when she cast him.

> SIR JOHN THOMPSON, on Sir Richard
> Cartwright, H. of C., *Debates*, June 28,
> 1892.

The Rupert of debate.

> ANON., *Sir Richard Cartwright*, so called
> because of his skill as a debater; Sir
> Wilfrid Laurier also called *Sir Louis
> Davies*, 'A Rupert of debate'.

The Nestor of Canadian Politics.

> ANON., *Sir Richard Cartwright* (d. 1912),
> a popular nickname; Toronto *Globe*,
> Dec. 11, 1902.

The Knight of the Rueful Countenance.

> ANON., *Sir Richard Cartwright*, Member
> of Parliament and Senator from 1863 to
> 1912.

Blue Ruin Dick.

> ANON., *Sir Richard Cartwright*, Member
> of Parliament and Senator from 1863 to
> 1912.

Carving

A sharp stone tool
to gouge a parallel pattern of lines
on both sides of the swan
holding it with his left hand
bearing down and transmitting
his body's weight
from brain to arm and right hand
and one of his thoughts
turns to ivory.

> AL PURDY, "Lament for the Dorsets",
> 1968.

Cats

Pure blood domestic, guaranteed,
Soft-mannered, musical in purr,

The ribbon had declared the breed,
Gentility was in the fur.

> E.J. PRATT, "The prize cat", 1937.

Women I love, and also cats,
With just this reservation that's
Basic: in no two-footed She
Can I condone felinity,
Save when, with loyalty and sense,
She spreads her claws in my defence.

> GEOFFREY B. RIDDEHOUGH, "The separatist", 1972.

Causes

Youth will have to learn that it is much more difficult to live for a cause than to die for it.

> DR. HANS SELYE, address, Canadian Club, Toronto, 1963, qu. in *Liberty*, "Cross Canada", June, 1963.

In those days, the vanquished
surrendered their swords like
    gentlemen,
the victors alone
surrendered their illusions.
The easiest thing to do for a Cause
is to die for it.

> ALDEN NOWLAN, "In those old wars", 1967.

Caution

The Canadian mind suffers as the mind of every country which is not a nationality must suffer, and caution takes the place of enterprise.

> WILLIAM H. RUSSELL, *Canada: its defences, conditions, and resources*, 1865, 98.

If we will only be natural, and stop going about in this eternal defensive fear of being ourselves, we shall discover that we are very like the Americans both in our good qualities and in our bad qualities.

> FRANK H. UNDERHILL, *Can. forum*, Vol. 31, 1951-52, 102.

The Canadian, located between two great communities, the English and the American, is provincial to both. He would, therefore, be in a superb position to develop habits of critical insight if the development of such habits were not paralyzed by colonial timidity or Scottish caution.

> MARSHALL MCLUHAN, *American mercury*, Vol. 74, Mar., 1952, 95.

Nobody ever did anything by pussy-footing.

> DONALD GORDON, qu. by Peter Newman, *Flame of power*, 1959, 202.

Canadians have had wariness ground into them for three hundred and fifty years.

> J.B. BREBNER, *Canada: a modern history*, 1960, 522.

There seems to be less optimism, less faith in the future, less willingness to risk capital or reputation. In contrast to America, Canada is a country of greater caution, reserve, and restraint.

> KASPAR NAEGELE, in B.R. Blishen, et al., eds., *Canadian society*, 1961, 27.

Individually, by contrast with the individual American, the Canadian seems older, more self-contained, more cautious, less expressive.

> KASPAR NAEGELE, in B.R. Blishen, et al., eds., *Canadian society*, 1964, 503.

Canadians are mildewed with caution.

> MARSHALL MCLUHAN, qu. in *Weekend mag.*, Mar. 18, 1967, 4.

One of Canada's greatest tragedies is that sober second thoughts so often prevail.

> RICHARD J. NEEDHAM, *A friend in Needham*, 1969, 44.

Cedar Trees

I heard the cedars speak as friend to
friend,
Bending easily to hear one another,
Brother with brother, who have lived
long together;
Only to life have the cedars learned to
attend.

> ROY DANIELLS, "Epithalamion in time of peace", 1949.

Cemeteries

This is the paradise of common things,
The scourged and trampled here
find peace to grow,
The frost to furrow and the wind to
sow,
The mighty sun to time their
blossomings;
And now they keep
A crown reflowering on the tombs of
kings,
Who earned their triumph and have
claimed their sleep.

> DUNCAN CAMPBELL SCOTT, "In the country churchyard", 1893.

Censorship

Let your readers here pause and marvel. And by and by, when their astonishment is surmounted, I may enlarge upon the works and untimely end of the great Censor, who soared beyond Parnassus, and died in a dung heap.

> THOMAS MCCULLOCH, *Stepsure letters*, 1960, 149, Letter 18, 1823.

Books, printed paper, drawings, paintings, prints, photographs or representations of any kind of a treasonable or seditious, or of an immoral or indecent character.

> CANADA. LAWS, STATUTES, etc., *Customs act*, 1859, (ch.17) and later, varies; long known as sec. 1201; Sched. C, Prohibited goods.

According to Mgr. Laflèche, in order to be a good Catholic, an M.P. should vote for a law he believed bad from a national or constitutional point of view, once a bishop found it to be good. That is the denial of all political freedom, the overturning of the basic principles of the constitution, it is a heresy as dangerous for the Church as for the State.

> LAURENT O. DAVID, *Le clergé canadien, sa mission, son oeuvre*, 1896, 89. (Trans.)

Censorship of any kind is morally unjustified and practically self-defeating.

> GEORGE WOODCOCK, "Areopagitica rewritten", in *Can. lit.*, No. 2, Autumn, 1959, 4.

Ceremony

Ceremony was invented by a wise man to keep fools at a distance.

> ROBERT C. (BOB) EDWARDS, Calgary *Eye Opener*, May 6, 1916.

Certainty

That's for damsure.

> MARGARET (MA) MURRAY, associated with *Bridge River – Lillooet news* (B.C.), 1933-1973, favourite saying.

Miss E. Cora Hind was rather terrifying. She was more positive about everything than most people are about anything.

> W.A. MCLEOD, qu. by Kennethe Haig, in M.Q. Innis, ed., *The clear spirit*, 1966, 120.

Champlain, Samuel de

The great discoverer came,
Finding another Indies than he
   guessed
To reward his daring quest,
And fill the wonder-volume of
   Romance,
The sailor of little Brouage, the
   founder of New France,
Sturdy, sagacious, plain:
Samuel de Champlain.

> BLISS CARMAN, "Champlain", 1909.

No other European colony in America is so much the lengthened shadow of one man as Canada is of the valiant, wise, and virtuous Samuel de Champlain, Xaintongeois (of Saintonge).

> SAMUEL ELIOT MORISON, *Samuel de Champlain: father of New France*, 1972, 227.

Chance

The great lesson of modern science is that nothing really "happens". There is no such thing as chance, for every act in your life has a causative force. Everything is pushed from behind.

> EMILY MURPHY, ("Janey Canuck"), qu. in B.H. Sanders, *Emily Murphy, crusader*, 1945, 1, chapt. heading.

Teach me to navigate the fjords of
   chance
Winding through my abyssal
   ignorance.

> MALCOLM LOWRY, "The Pilgrim", 1962.

Change

Changing one thing for another is not always reform.

> T.C. HALIBURTON, *Sam Slick*, 1840, 159.

Hands of chance and change have
   marred, or moulded, or broken,
Busy with spirit or flesh, all I most
   have adored.

> CHARLES G.D. ROBERTS, "Tantramar revisited", 1886.

Make me over in the morning
From the rag-bag of the world!

> BLISS CARMAN, "Spring song", 1894.

Changes for the better are often resented. Old boots were once new — and hated.

> GEORGE ILES, *Canadian stories*, 1918, 172.

Variability is the law of life.

> SIR WILLIAM OSLER; attributed.

The only person sure of himself is the man who wishes to leave things as they are, and he dreams of an impossibility.

> GEORGE M. WRONG, *Can. hist. rev.*, 1921, 315.

The political instinct of the race is practical rather than logical, and one observes an invariable tendency to avoid change until it is manifest.

> SIR ROBERT BORDEN, *Canada and the Commonwealth*, 1929, 86.

I shall not wonder more, then,
But I shall know.

> RAYMOND KNISTER, d. Aug., 1932. Last lines of his poem "Change", carved on his tombstone, Port Dover, Ontario.

A malady like a journey is killing us
    slowly.
On the long inconstant travels of the
    mind
Towards the paradise we are
    approaching daily
But never reach, on endless days in the
    sun
Walking the deserts of our insular land
Between the pectoral hills and salt
    lagoon,
We are haunted each evening by
    time's gorgon face.
The sickness of change is rotting our
    lives like ice.

> GEORGE WOODCOCK, "Waterloo bridge",
> 1947.

MAKE WAY FOR MAGIC! MAKE
    WAY FOR OBJECTIVE
    MYSTERY!
MAKE WAY FOR LOVE!
MAKE WAY FOR WHAT IS
    NEEDED!

> PAUL-EMILE BORDUAS, *Refus global*,
> 1948, 10. (Trans.)

I rest upon the shore of Changeless
    change,
The landscape and horizon of
    Eternity.

> DIANA SKALA, "By the sea", 1952.

The old's laid by, the new will not last
    long;
Error's the fruit of trial, and all that is
    is wrong.

> RAYMOND HULL, "All change", 1953.

Unselfishness recognizes change and
variety as delightful, Child, remember
that.

> EMILY CARR, qu. in Carol Pearson, *Emily
> Carr as I knew her*, 1954, 144.

The stone in my hand
Is my hand
And stamped with tracings of
A once greenblooded frond,
Is here, is gone, will come,
Was fire, and green, and water,
Will be wind.

> ANNE WILKINSON, "Poem in three parts",
> 1955.

Times have changed. Places have
changed. We must dance to the tune
of the stranger.

> ADELE WISEMAN, *The sacrifice*, 1956,
> (1972, 42).

Form has its flow
a Heraclitus-river with no river bank
we can play poise on now.

> MARGARET AVISON, "Intra-political",
> 1960.

every decision, word, thought, positive
    act,
causes the sum of the parts of a man's
    self to change,
and he betrays himself into the future
    day after uncertain day.

> AL PURDY, "Collecting the square root of
> minus one", 1961.

Social change, ripening to the point of
radical social transformation, is the
law of development of human society.

> LESLIE MORRIS, *Can. tribune*, Nov. 9,
> 1964, 5.

Much will have to change in Canada if
the country is to stay the same.

> ABRAHAM ROTSTEIN, *The prospect of
> change*, 1965, Intro., xvii.

All things change, and yet the heart remains.

> RONALD BATES, "All things change", 1968.

How strange these changes are, while
  we grow older,
Less capable of coping with the new.

> RONALD BATES, "All the sad changes", 1968.

Here you're in
there you're out
that's how the world goes
roundabout.

> PHYLLIS GOTLIEB, "Ordinary, moving", 1969.

Life is confrontation, and vigilance, and a fierce struggle against any threat of intrusion or death. We are unworthy of our ideal if we are not ready to defend, as we would life itself, the only roads to change that respect the human person.

> PIERRE E. TRUDEAU, to National Liberal Party Policy Convention, Ottawa, Nov. 20, 1970; qu. in D. Smith, *Bleeding hearts, bleeding country*, 1971, 86.

The first visible effect of freedom is change. A free man exercises his freedom by altering himself and – inevitably – his surroundings. It follows that no liberal can be other than receptive to change and highly positive and active in his response to it, for change is the very expression of freedom.

> PIERRE E. TRUDEAU, to the Liberal Party Policy Conference, Nov. 20, 1970, in his *Conversations with Canadians*, 1972, 86.

What I've learned is not to believe in magical leaders any more; that character and compassion are more important than ideology; and that even if it's absurd to think you can change things, it's even more absurd to think that it's foolish and unimportant to try.

> PETER C. NEWMAN, *Home country*, 1973, 22.

Chaos

Everywhere some small design
Erupts, and the profusion foals
Chaos on the mind.

> D.G. JONES, "Blue jay in Haliburton", 1961.

Character

Climate, locality and occupation, form or vary character, but man is the same sort of critter everywhere.

> T.C. HALIBURTON, *Nature and human nature*, 1855, II, 386.

As a rule, women are far better readers of character than are men.

> ARNOLD HAULTAIN, *Hints for lovers*, 1909, 51.

It's the bad that's in the best of us
Leaves the saint so like the rest of us!
It's the good in the darkest-curst of us
Redeems and saves the worst of us!
It's the muddle and hope and
  madness;
It's the tangle of good and badness;
It's the lunacy linked with sanity
Makes up, and mocks, humanity!

> ARTHUR STRINGER, "Humanity", 1920.

The real test of character is in surprise. It is the unforeseen crisis, the sudden calamity, the unexpected shock, when the man is off guard, which shows truly what he is.

> A. MACMECHAN Roy.Soc.Can., *Trans.*, 1926, II, 3.

What a man considers indecent is an important clue to his character.

> ROBERTSON DAVIES, *A voice from the attic*, 1960, 264.

Charity

Much is required of them to whom much is given.

> THOMAS C. HALIBURTON, *Sam Slick's wise saws*, 1853, ch. 3.

He clothed the needy, the hungry fed,
Pitied the erring, the faltering led,
Joyed with the joyous, wept with the
  sad,
Made the heart of the widow and
  orphan glad,
And never left for the lowliest one
An act of kindness and love
  undone . . .

> PAMELIA V. YULE, "Littlewit and Loftus", 1881.

How read you the Scriptures? What
    say they? These three with
    the world now abide,
  Hope, charity, faith, and the great-
    est is charity – blessed above
    all.
Our hands should be fruitful and
    open. The field for our giving
    is wide,
And blessing shall follow the gifts,
    though the power to give may
    be small.

> BARRY STRATON, "Charity", 1884.

Thou askest not to know the creed,
    The rank or name is naught to
    thee;
Where'er the human heart cries
    "Help!"
  Thy kingdom is, O Charity!

> MARY MORGAN, "Charity", 1887.

We rush in the keen pursuit of our various ambitions while want pleads at our elbow. It is not that we are hard or indifferent. We are busy. Always busy.

> JOHN J. KELSO, founder of the Children's Aid Society of Toronto, 1891, qu. in *Globe and Mail*, Dec. 29, 1973, 7.

The hardest lesson of all to learn is that the law of the higher life is only fulfilled by love, i.e. charity.

> SIR WILLIAM OSLER, "The master word in medicine", in *Montreal med. jour.*, 1903.

Charity is infinitely divisible. He who has a little can always give a little.

> PETER MCARTHUR, *To be taken with salt*, 1903, 156.

Pauperism exists only because of charity and would soon pass away if almsgiving ceased.

> J.J. KELSO, *Poorhouses and charity*, 1905, 11.

Remain the well-wrought deed in
    honour done,
The dole for Christ's dear sake, the
    words that fall
In kindliness upon some outcast one–
They seemed so little: now they are
    my All.

> JOHN MCCRAE, "Upon Watts' picture *Sic transit*", 1919.

Charity begins at home. It should also end there.

> IRVING LAYTON, "Aphs", *The whole bloody bird*, 1969, 102.

Chastity

Some modern cynics make assertion
That chastity's a sex-perversion.
Such a description should go far
To make it much more popular.

> GEOFFREY B. RIDDEHOUGH, "Ray of hope", 1972.

Cheating

We like to do our cheating before we sign on the dotted line.

> ROBERT C. (BOB) EDWARDS, attributed, qu. in G.R. Stevens, *History of the C.N.R.*, 1973, 227.

Cheese

We have seen thee queen of cheese
Lying quietly at your ease,
Gently fanned by evening breeze,
Thy fair form no flies dare seize.

> JAMES MCINTYRE, the Cheese Poet, "Ode on the mammoth cheese", 1884.

To prove the wealth that here
    abounds,
One cheese weighed eight thousand
    pounds,
    Had it been hung in air at noon
Folks would have thought it was the
    moon,
    It sailed with triumph o'er the seas,
'Twas hailed with welcome, queen of
    cheese.

> JAMES MCINTYRE, "Oxford cheese ode", 1889.

To us it is a glorious theme,
To sing of milk and curds and cream,
Were it collected it could float
On its bosom, small steam boat,
Cows numerous as swarm of bees,
Are milked in Oxford to make cheese.

> JAMES MCINTYRE, "Oxford cheese ode", 1889.

Then let the farmers justly prize
The cows for land they fertilize,
And let us all with songs and glees
Invoke success into the cheese.

> JAMES MCINTYRE, "Lines read at a dairy-men's supper", 1889.

Chickens

Cock of the walk, he took the choicest
    fodder,
and he was totem stud and constable
until his comb and spurs were frozen,
    bled,
and then the hens, quite calmly,
    picked him dead.

> ALDEN NOWLAN, "Hens", 1958.

Childbirth

Now double wing-beat
Breasting body
Till cloudways open
Heaven trembles:
    And blinding
    searing
        terrifying
            cry!

> DOROTHY LIVESAY, "Serenade for strings", 1941.

Childhood

All days thereafter are a dying off,
A wandering away
From home and the familiar. The
    years doff
Their innocence.
No other day is ever like that day.

> A.M. KLEIN, "Autobiography", 1943.

All these were the toys and pets
Of a childhood and a youth
A house where he was little
And afraid to swear
Because the Lord might hear
And send a bear.

> JAMES REANEY, "The school globe", 1946.

The very genius of childhood lies not in analysis, but in response.

> JOAN SELBY in, *Can. lit.* No. 6, 1960, 32.

Children

Now to this very day, when'er you see
A baby well contented, crying "Goo!"
Or crowing in this style, know that it is
Because he then remembers in great
    joy
How he in strife, all in the olden time,
Did overcome the Master, conqueror
Of all the world. For that, of creatures
    all,
Or beings which on earth have ever
    been
Since the beginning, Baby is alone
The never yielding and invincible.

GLOOSCAP, Micmac legend, N.S. and
Newfoundland; anglicized version.

If he has a family, so much the better,
as children are the best *stock* a farmer
can possess, the labour of a child seven
years old being considered worth his
maintenance and education.

WILLIAM DUNLOP, *Statistical sketches*,
1832, 6.

The Indians apparently have no idea
of correcting or restraining their children; personal chastisement is unheard
of. They say that before a child has
any understanding there is no use in
correcting it; and when old enough to
understand, no one has a right to
correct it.

ANNA B. JAMESON, *Winter studies*, 1837.

The simplicity, the fond, confiding
faith of childhood, is unknown in
Canada. There are no children here.

SUSANNA MOODIE, *Roughing it in the
bush*, 1852, Vol. 1, 139.

Boys are mothers' sons. It's only gals
who take after their father.

T.C. HALIBURTON, *Nature and human
nature*, 1855, I, 361.

Not in science, not in art,
Hides the balm for the poor heart:
We are bound, until made free
By the great humility!
Knowledge is the tree of woe.
All your fathers found it so:
All philosophy is vain —
Be a little child again.

ALEXANDER MCLACHLAN, "Fate", 1856.

Childhood alone is glad. With it time
    flees
In constant mimes and bright
    festivities.

CHARLES HEAVYSEGE, poem no. IV, in
Jephthah's daughter, 1865.

If education be not enforced the question arises whether the children are
not better cared for by spending a
portion at least of their time at work,
rather than wasting it on the public
streets.

CANADA. COMMISSIONERS APPOINTED TO
ENQUIRE INTO THE WORKING OF MILLS
AND FACTORIES . . . , *Report*, 1882, 3
(Sessional papers, No. 42).

A child that has a quick temper, just
blaze up and cool down, ain't never
likely to be sly or deceitful.

L.M. MONTGOMERY, *Anne of Green Gables*, 1908, 105.

Ah! Why have I lost the eyes of
childhood?

ADJUTOR RIVARD, *Chez nous*, 1914.
(Trans.)

They think more of the future of their
children than the past of their grand-
parents.

ARTHUR HAWKES, on Anglo-Canadians,
in *The birthright*, 1919, 88.

A woman never stops to consider how
very uninteresting her children would
be if they were some other woman's.

ROBERT C. (BOB) EDWARDS, Calgary *Eye
Opener*, Aug. 9, 1919.

Children are not a handicap to any woman. They open up a new world to their mother, the rainbow-hued world of childhood, with its delightful confidences and the unforgettable times when, all the world shut out, mother and child wander together through the world of story books.

> NELLIE MCCLUNG, *Maclean's*, Feb. 15, 1928, 75.

The Quints.

> ANON., a popular abbreviation of quintuplets as applied to the Dionne sisters, born at Callander, Ont., May 28, 1934.

The most important thing in the world today is the bringing up of children.

> C. BROCK CHISHOLM, speech in Washington, D.C., Oct. 23, 1945.

Two weeks here in the sun and air
Through the charity of our wealthy
    citizens
Will be a wonderful help to the little
    tots
When they return for a winter in the
    slums.

> F.R. SCOTT, "Social notes: Summer camp", 1945.

Are you Canada's child?
Do you wander her meadows, gather
    her bright flowers,
Do you walk her grey streets, follow
    her winding roads on your way
    to school?
Are you Canada's child?

> FRANCES SHELLEY WEES, "Canada's child", 1947.

But his children were all he had been able to give the world, and they were his only continuity.

> HUGH MACLENNAN, *Barometer rising*, 1951, 309.

Children wet with birth
Remember to their dying dust
The lost aquarium of Eden

> ANNE WILKINSON, "Swimming lesson", 1955.

Children have amazing powers of resilience.

> WILLIAM E. BLATZ, *Human security*, 1966, 9.

Sleep on my child,
still in your innocence,
may you have miracles.
Sleep in the shallow
bay of the motionless
sunlight and coracles.

> DAVID HELWIG, "Cradle song", 1967.

Our open hands encounter
the closing flower the early
hour and we run with the sun
fly against wind high-jump
the rainbows until we become
the enchanted land ourselves.

> MIRIAM WADDINGTON, "Runners", 1967.

Wherever I go
Whatever I do
there is one thing that is always
    happening
and that is me

> RED LANE, "Is happening it happens to", 1968.

Our children need to be treated as human beings — exquisite, complex and elegant in their diversity.

> LLOYD DENNIS, Ontario educator, qu. in *Maclean's*, Sept., 1969, 5.

My definition of a civilized country would be one that doesn't have, and doesn't need, a Children's Aid.

> RICHARD J. NEEDHAM, *A friend in Needham*, 1969, 6.

It is the function of the parents to eat the child. It is the function of the child to defend himself against being eaten.

RICHARD J. NEEDHAM, *A friend in Needham*, 1969, 21.

The day the child realizes that all adults are imperfect he becomes an adolescent; the day he forgives them, he becomes an adult; the day he forgives himself he becomes wise.

ALDEN NOWLAN, "Scratchings", 1971.

Soon I will be old and die, and my children will live as I have lived, and know what I have known, and wonder as I wondered.

RAYMOND FRASER, "Legacy", 1971.

There are no lobbyists for children.

MARY VAN STOLK, *The battered child in Canada*, 1972, preface, viii.

They were always unintended,
like beauty or like joy,
yet now they are my life
and time and place of being.

DAVID HELWIG, "The children", 1972.

Children's Rhymes

Awkum bawkum
Curious kawkum,
Ellikum bellikum bony bus.
If you'd a been where I'd a been,
You'd a been out.

(Ottawa, Ont.)

Eny, meny, hippery dic,
Delia, dolia, dominic,
Hoachy poachy, noma noachy,
Te, tan, tush,
Ugly, bugly, boo,
Out goes you.

(Thamesville, Ont.)

Inty, minty, figgity, feg;
El, del, domen, egg,
Urky, purky, stone and rock;
Ann, dan, tush.

(Carleton Place, Ont.)

Kaiser Bill went up the hill,
To see the boys in France.
Kaiser Bill came down the hill
With bullets in his pants.

(Recited during war of 1914-18.)

One-ery, two-ery, dickery-dee,
Alabo, crackabo, tender-lea;
Twin, twan, just began,
Twiddle, twaddle, twenty-one.
O-u-t spells out.

(Perth, Ont.)

One-zol, two-zol, zig-zol sam,
Bob-tail vinegar, tiddle-um-a-tan,
Harum scarum, virgum marum,
Tee, taw, tum.
O-u-t spells out.

(Toronto, Ont.)

Chinese

The Chinese ulcer is eating into the prosperity of the country and sooner or later must be cut out.

DAILY BRITISH COLONIST AND VICTORIA CHRONICLE, Aug. 11, 1878, in a plea for restricted Chinese immigration.

As a railway navvy, the Chinaman has no superior.

J.A. CHAPLEAU, *Report of Royal Commission on Chinese Immigration*, 1885, cxxx.

I know that he is a Member of Parliament, and I know that he is the President of the Young Conservative Association, but he is over in Paris as, I presume, the head of this organization that is mentioned. Is he paid? Are their expenses paid by the Dominion Government? And just whom does he represent, and what right has this Chinaman to make these statements in Paris on behalf of the Canadian people?

> SEN. J.W. DEB. FARRIS, Senate, *Debates*, July 10, 1958, 306, referring to Douglas Jung.

Christianity

The diffusion of Christianity is the most important subject that can engage the attention of men.

> EGERTON RYERSON, "A review of a sermon; preached by the Honourable and Reverend John Strachan, D.D. at York, Upper Canada, third of July, 1825, on the death of the late Lord Bishop of Quebec", *The Colonial advocate*, May 11, 1826.

A Christianity whose message has historically been one of personal salvation is face to face with what is very clearly, not just a personal, but a mass or collective problem, and for this it finds its resources inadequate.

> UNITED CHURCH OF CANADA. FIFTH GENERAL COUNCIL, *Record of proceedings*, 1932, 287.

Often in darkness underfoot I feel
The immemorial stones that pave the
    Way.

> ROY DANIELLS, "The road", 1963.

A violent revolution – violent in the psychological and social rather than the physical sense – is needed to save Christianity.

> PIERRE BERTON, *The comfortable pew*, 1965, 129.

To this pass has Christianity come:
There is no God, and Jesus is his son

> IRVING LAYTON, "Crisis theology", *Collected poems*, 1971, 405.

Christmas

Bright shines the sun across the drifts,
And bright upon my Christmas gifts;
    They brought Him incense, myrrh,
        and gold,
    Our little Lord who lived of old.

> MARJORIE PICKTHALL, "A little child's song of Christmas", 1913.

Give each new day its own good cheer
    All other days apart,
And every day throughout the year
    Keep Christmas in your heart.

> ALBERT D. WATSON, "Christmas", 1914.

Glory to God, this wondrous môrn,
On earth the Saviour Christ is born.

> BLISS CARMAN, "Bethlehem", Dec., 1928.

A child who believes in Santa Claus, who really and literally believes, because his daddy told him so, that Santa comes down all the chimneys in the world on the same night has had his thinking ability permanently impaired if not destroyed.

> G. BROCK CHISHOLM, speech, Ottawa, Nov. 5, 1945.

Beneath the mistletoe to trade a kiss,
And quaff a cup of eggnog Christmas
    day –
If you can take out time enough for
    this,
Drop in and see us when you pass this
    way.

> LIONEL FORSYTH, d. 1957, invitation to friends for Christmas.

Church

The habits and opinions of the people of Canada were, in the main, averse from the absolute predominance of any single church.

> LORD STANLEY, letter to Bagot, Oct. 8, 1841.

I am an outside pillar of the Church.

> JOHN SANDFIELD MACDONALD, first Premier of Ontario, about 1870.

We early freed ourselves from the incubus of a State Church.

> EDWARD BLAKE, speech at Aurora, Ont., Oct. 3, 1874.

It always depresses me to go to church. In those prayers and terrible hymns of our service we are in the presence of all the suffering in the world since the beginning of time. We have entered the temple of sorrow and are prostrate at the feet of the very God of Affliction.

> ARCHIBALD LAMPMAN, letter to Edward William Thomson, Nov. 2, 1897.

The outcome of it all was a vague general impression that Montreal consists of banks and churches. The people of this city spend much of their time in laying up their riches in this world or the next.

> RUPERT BROOKE, Letters from America, 1916, 51.

More people would go to church if it weren't exactly the proper thing to do.

> ROBERT C. (BOB) EDWARDS, Calgary Eye Opener, Mar. 9, 1918.

Denominationalism in Canada is still a stately tree, but the heart is dust.

> SALEM G. BLAND, The new Christianity, 1920, 136.

The two sides of the Church's responsibility are not in conflict; the causes of evil, of human maladjustment, may lie in the economic structure as well as in personal character, and Christianity can only be made complete by the rectifying of both.

> UNITED CHURCH OF CANADA. FIFTH GENERAL COUNCIL, Record of proceedings, 1932, 289.

Not endowments, property, support of the clergy, and a share in the government of a province or of its municipalities are the essential points in an establishment, after all, but rather beliefs, doctrine, discipline, forms of worship and of orders.

> A.H. YOUNG, in Can. hist. rev., 1932, 351.

The bootleggers have gone, the movies have gone, credit is gone, social life is gone, but thank God the Church remains.

> ANON., layman, on the Prairies in the 1930's, letter to Home Mission Board Secretary, United Church, qu. in J.I. MacKay, The world in Canada, 1938, 109.

Neither the Protestant churches nor the Jewish synagogues, to one or other of which the majority of Crestwood residents "belong", preach a fundamental cleavage between the way of the world and the way of the spirit.

> JOHN R. SEELEY, et al., Crestwood heights, 1956, 337.

The church is gone,
The street is paved,
The Home Bank thrives
Where Jesus Saved.

> IRVING LAYTON, "On my way to school", 1959.

The uncomfortable pew.

> PIERRE BERTON, The comfortable pew, 1965.

Trying to gain the whole world, the Church loses its own soul.

> GORDON A. CLARK, letter, *United Church observer*, May 15, 1966, 6.

Across Roblin Lake, two shores away,
they are sheathing the church spire
with new metal. Someone hangs in the
    sky
over there from a piece of rope,
hammering and fitting God's
    belly-scratcher.

> ALFRED PURDY, "Wilderness gothic", 1968.

Circumstances

Circumstances alter cases.

> T.C. HALIBURTON, *The old judge*, 1849, ch. 15.

Some weak, luckless wretches ever
    seem
Flying before the hounds of
    circumstance,
Adown the windy gullies of this life.

> CHARLES HEAVYSEGE, *Saul*, 1857.

Truly, circumstances alter cases; but circumstances do not change principles.

> EGERTON RYERSON, *Story of my life*, 1883.

When schemes are laid in advance, it is surprising how often the circumstances fit in with them.

> SIR WILLIAM OSLER, "Internal medicine as a vocation", 1897, in *Aequanimitas*.

We are no more victims of circumstances than circumstance is the shadow of ourselves.

> BLISS CARMAN, *The kinship of nature*, 1904, 83.

Cities and Towns

It must not be forgotten that the Syndicate has a say in the existence of almost every town or prospective town in the North-West. Individuals rarely have an opportunity of starting a town without their consent and co-operation.

> TORONTO *GLOBE*, Jan. 19, 1882, with reference to the C.P.R. Syndicate.

The beat, the thunder and the hiss
Cease not, and change not, night nor
    day.
And moving at unheard commands,
The abysses and vast fires between,
Flit figures that with clanking hands
Obey a hideous routine;
They are not flesh, they are not bone,
They see not with the human eye,
And from their iron lips is blown
A dreadful and monotonous cry.

> ARCHIBALD LAMPMAN, "The city of the end of things", 1900.

City life is like a spider's web – pull one thread and you pull every thread.

> JAMES S. WOODSWORTH, *My neighbour*, 1911, 26.

You can't think how sick one's heart gets for something *old*. For weeks I have not seen or touched a town as old as myself. Horrible! Horrible!

> RUPERT BROOKE, Letter to Edward Marsh from Calgary, Aug. 16, 1913, age 26.

Not so much the city beautiful as the city healthy that we wanted for Canada.

> CHARLES HODGETTS, Commission of Conservation, 6th Ann. meeting, Ottawa, Jan. 19-20, 1915, *Report*, 270.

Peasants who *will not* understand that increase of imports and volume of trade and numbers of millionaires are the measure of a city's greatness.

RUPERT BROOKE, *Letters from America*, 1916, 54, referring to Prov. of Quebec.

Are these things
designed for men?
Or men for these?
Or are men things?

W.W. EUSTACE ROSS, "The city enforces", 1930.

They're poor, tumbledown, shabby little towns, but they persist. Even the dry years yield a little wheat; even the little means livelihood for some. I know a town where once it rained all June, and that fall the grain lay in piles outside full granaries. It's an old town now, shabby and decrepit like the others, but it too persists. It knows only two years: the year it rained all June, and next year.

SINCLAIR ROSS, *As for me and my house*, 1941, 171.

We used to say the loneliness and the mystery were somewhere on the rims, a distant suburb; we were wrong. They are here. Here in the centre.

PATRICK ANDERSON, "Montreal mountain", 1945.

Why did cities hate, thwart, damage me so?

EMILY CARR, *Growing pains*, 1946, 291.

It is a fabled city that I seek;
It stands in Space's vapours and Time's haze.

A.M. KLEIN, *The second scroll*, "Gloss Aleph", 1951.

Treason or true, the Office of the Future
finds this city-pretty now a misfate
in its planes. Like every think of booty,
sir, it's copulated to destriction;
its lifeliness decreases and must ever
pass into nothingmist. Your town's dimnition
is, I fear, both inevoidable and everdue.

EARLE BIRNEY, "Trial of a city", 1952, 4; on Vancouver.

Down in pale alerooms democrats dawdled,
mazed dark in movies or dreamed on the corners
while wardheelers rode to polls to wangle taxes,
to money-change the Council and amend Magna Charta,
and fat lawyers grappled in long lovers' clinches.

EARLE BIRNEY, "Trial of a city", 1952, 39.

The metropolis today is a classroom; the ads are its teachers. The classroom is an obsolete detention home, a feudal dungeon.

MARSHALL MCLUHAN, *Counterblast*, 1954.

The metropolis is obsolete. Ask the Army.

MARSHALL MCLUHAN, *Counterblast*, 1954.

No Canadian product in the next generation will be more important than Canadian cities.

STEWART BATES, Central Mortgage & Housing, at School of Social Work, Univ. of Toronto, "Round table on man and industry", 1956, qu. in G. Vickers, *The undirected society*, 1959, 147.

Eastend was once a happy town where
  harmony and love
Was busting out at all the seams, and
  in the trees above,
The doves of peace were nesting, there
  were no signs of strife,
For each man loved his neighbour
  (and sometimes his neighbour's
  wife!).

    W.G. (BILLY) BOCK, "The civil war", 1958.

Those I hold dear are all the denizens
Whose unretraceable goings merge
  with mine
To weave the unmistakable design
That proves a city is its citizens.

    ROBERT FINCH, "Cities", 1961.

The ultimate purpose of a city is to be
discovered in a quality of heart and
mind.

    HUMPHREY CARVER, *Cities in the sub-
    urbs*, 1962, 51.

New York is Big but This is Biggar,
The Friendly Town.

    ANON., sign at entrance to Biggar, Sask.,
    1962.

Whether the people of Toronto and
Montreal like it or not and whether the
other parts of the country like it or not,
those two great cities cannot escape
their responsibility for the quality of
Canadian life. The whole country is
influenced for better or worse by the
standards they set.

    MITCHELL SHARP, Minister of Trade and
    Commerce, 1963-66; qu. *Maclean's,*
    Aug., 1969, 72.

Herein lies the true value of the past,
of a people's or a city's history: not in
mere age, the mere passage of the
years, but in the just pride it gives and
in the challenge it flings to us to be
worthy of our sires.

    A.R.M. LOWER, *Queen's quart.*, Vol. 72,
    Winter 1965/66, 664.

Ha, at last Old Crow will have airport
so the plane will just land on the stripe.
Old Crow has street light and some
house got light and now we will have
airport and next is highway to Old
Crow be good for people.

    EDITH JOSIE, *Here are the news*, 1966,
    129.

Will cities creep like moss
over these boulders stained by time
set in unpopulated space?

    ELIZABETH BREWSTER, "Train journey",
    1972.

Cities and Towns — Nicknames

Armstrong, B.C. – The Celery City

Bassano, Alta. – Best in the West by a
Dam Site.

Brandon, Man. – The Wheat City. –
Gateway to the North. – Vires acquirit
eundo – (motto: She acquires strength
in her progress.)

Brantford, Ont. – The Telephone City.
(Alexander G. Bell invented the telephone here, 1874) – Industria et perse-
verentia. (motto)

Brockville, Ont. – The City of the
Thousand Islands. – You are a Stranger
in Brockville Only Once.

Calgary, Alta. – The City of the Foothills.

Carlyle, Sask. – Where they Grow
WHEAT. (1910)

Charlottetown, P.E.I. – The Cradle of
Confederation. (From the conference
held in 1864 by delegates of the Maritime Provinces to discuss union, and at
which delegates from the Canadas attended.)

Chatham, Ont. – The Maple City. –
Canada's Southland City. – Greges,
agricultura et commercium – (motto:
Herds, crops and commerce.)

Cornwall, Ont. – The Factory Town.
– The Friendly City.

Dundas, Ont. — The Valley Town.

Edmonton, Alta. — The Crossroads of the World. — The Friendly City. — The Gateway to the North. — The Oil Centre of Canada. — Industry, Energy, Enterprise. (motto)

Fort Erie, Ont. — The Gateway to Canada.

Fort William, Ont. — The Golden Gateway From the Great West. — The Twin Cities. (With Port Arthur.) — A posse ad esse. (motto: From possibility to actuality.)

Fredericton, N.B. — The Celestial City. — Fredericopolis silvae filia nobilis. (motto)

Galt, Ont. — The Manchester of Canada.

Galt, Ont. — Galt, U.S.A. (From R.L. Perry's book, pub. 1972; Galt in 1973 became part of the new city of Cambridge).

Granby, Que. — The Princess of the Eastern Townships.

Guelph, Ont. — The Royal City. (Guelph was the name of the reigning family at time of founding by John Galt, 1827; incorporated, 1877.) — The Main Street of Ontario. — Fides, Fidelitas, Progressio. (motto)

Halifax, N.S. — The Gateway to the Dominion. (See also: HALIFAX, N.S.)

Hamilton, Ont. — The Ambitious City. (From R.J. MacGeorge, *Count or Counterfeit*, 1858: "the ambitious and stirring little city".) — The Birmingham of Canada. (Pamphlet title, pub. 1893.)

Ingersoll, Ont. — The Cheese Town of Canada.

Kamloops, B.C. — The Hub of the Interior.

Kelowna, B.C. — The Orchard City.

Kingston, Ont. — The Limestone City. — The Derry of Canada. (About 1860, when the Orangemen were predomi-

nant.) — Pro Rege, Grege, Lege. (motto: For the King, for the Community and for the Law.) (See also: KINGSTON, ONT.)

Kitchener, Ont. — The Industrial City.

Leamington, Ont. — The Sun Parlour of Canada. (Coat of arms.) — The Sunshine Town.

Lethbridge, Alta. — The City of Opportunity. — The Windy City. — Ad Occasionis Januan. (motto: The gateway to opportunity.)

London, Ont. — The Forest City.

Madawaska, N.B. — The Kingdom of Madawaska. (ANON., described by Miriam Chapon in *Atlantic Canada* 1956, 91, as "a mythical domain composed of hunks of Quebec, New Brunswick and Maine centred on the town of Madawaska"). (See also: MADAWASKA, N.B.)

Medicine Hat, Alta. — The Chicago of Western Canada. — The Gas City of Canada. — The Hat. — The Hub of the West. — The Place Where the Weather Comes From. (After the establishment of the weather station, 1910.) — The town that was born lucky. (Kipling, 1907.) — Enterprise. (motto)

Mitchell, Ont. — The Town Worth Living In.

Moncton, N.B. — The Bend. (Before 1855.) — The Hub of the Maritimes. — Resurgo. — (motto: We/They rise again.)

Montreal, Que. — The Metropolis — Concordia Salus. (motto)

Moose Jaw, Sask. — The Friendly City. (1908) — The Band City.

Nanaimo, B.C. — The Gateway to Vancouver Island. — The Hub of Vancouver Island.

Nelson, B.C. — The Queen City of the Kootenays.

New Westminster, B.C. — The Royal City. (Incorporated 1860). — The City of Stumps.

Niagara Falls, Ont. – The Honeymoon Centre of the World. – The Power City of the World.

North Battleford, Sask. – The Rising Star of Northern Saskatchewan. (1911)

North Bay, Ont. – The Gateway City.

North Sydney, N.S. – The Bar Town. (From a harbour sand bar.) – Goathill. (From Chapel Hill, a goat pasture.)

North Vancouver, B.C. – The Ambitious City. – The City of Homes and Industry. – Industry, Progress. (motto)

Oliver, B.C. – The Cantaloupe City.

Oshawa, Ont. – The Motor City of Canada. – Nulli Secundus. (motto)

Ottawa, Ont. – The Washington of the North. (Laurier, 1893) – Advance. (motto, 1844) (See also: OTTAWA, ONT.)

Owen Sound, Ont. – The Scenic City. – Arbor Virga Fuit.–(motto: The tree was once a sapling.)

Peterborough, Ont. – The Electric City. (The first to have incandescent street lighting.) – The Lift Lock City. – Nature Provides, Industry Develops. (motto)

Port Arthur, Ont. – The Gateway to the West. – The Twin Cities. (With Fort William)

Portage La Prairie, Man. – The Hub of Central Manitoba. – The Plains City. – The Prairie Gateway City.

Preston, Ont. – The Hub of Waterloo County.

Prince Albert, Sask. – The Capital of Saskatchewan's Top Two-Thirds. Gateway to the North. – The Pivot of the Saskatchewan Northland. – Esse quam videri. (motto)

Quebec, Que. – The Ancient Capital – The Gibraltar of America – Gift of God, I will develop you well (motto, from Champlain's ship *Don de Dieu*). (see also: QUEBEC CITY)

Regina, Sask. – Pile of Bones. (Official name; see Lt. Gov. Dewdney, Can. *Sess. paper 25B,* June 30, 1882, so-called from the accumulated bones of the buffalo; name changed to Regina by Princess Louise in autumn, 1882.) – The Queen City of the Plains. – Floreat Regina. (motto) (See also: REGINA, SASK.)

Saint Boniface, Man. – The Cathedral City. – The Holy City. (From Whittier, "Red River voyageur".) – The Industrial Section of Greater Winnipeg. – Salus a cruce. (motto) (See also: SAINT BONIFACE, MAN.)

St. Catharines, Ont. – The Garden City of Canada. – Industry and Liberality. (motto) – St. Catharines, city of the host of flowers. (From Lampman, "Niagara landscape", 1900.)

Saint John, N.B. – The Loyalist City. (From the 3,000 U.E. Loyalists who landed May 18, 1783; city incorporated May 18, 1785.) – O fortunati quorum jam moenia surgunt. (motto from Virgil: O fortunate are the people whose walls are even now arising.)

St. Mary's, Ont. – The Stone City.

Sarnia, Ont. – Canada's Chemical Centre.

Saskatoon, Sask. – The Hub City – The Hub City of the Hard Wheat Belt. (1908) – Saskatchewan's City of Opportunity. (slogan) – "We thought of Minnetonka for a name, but found some Saskatoon berries and that settled it". (John N. Lake, Temperance Colonization Co., on the founding, Aug. 20, 1882.)

Shawinigan Falls, Que. – The City of Light. (La Ville Lumière.) – Age quod agis. (motto: Do well what you do.)

Sherbrooke, Que. – The Queen City of the Eastern Townships. – Onward. (motto)

Stratford, Ont. – The Classic City. – Industry, Enterprise. (motto)

Sudbury, Ont. — The Hub of the North. — Industry, Enterprise, Integrity. (motto)

Sydney, N.S. — Down Where the East Begins. — The Pittsburgh of Canada. — The Steel City.

Thorold, Ont. — The Town of Seven Locks. (From the Welland Canal.) — Where the Steamships Climb the Mountain.

Toronto, Ont. — The Athens of the Dominion — The Belfast of America. — The Choral Capital of North America. — The City of Churches. (1890) — Hog Town. — The Queen City — Toronto the Good. (1890; from campaigning of Women's Temperance Union.) — Tory Toronto — Industry, Intelligence, Integrity. (motto adopted 1835 by William Lyon Mackenzie, the first mayor.) (See also: TORONTO, ONT.)

Trail, B.C. — The Smoky City.

Truro, N.S. — The Hub of Nova Scotia.

Vancouver, B.C. — Canada's Golden Gate. (1912) From Stumps to Skyscrapers. (1936) — Gas Town. (From Captain John "Gassy Jack" Deighton, builder of a hotel on Burrard Inlet, 1867.) — The Gateway to the Orient. (1906) — The Lion-Guarded City. (1925) — Queen of the Coast. (From E. Pauline Johnson, "A toast".) — The Sunset City. — The Terminal City. — By land and sea we prosper. (motto) (See also: VANCOUVER, B.C.)

Verdun, Que. — The Bedroom of Montreal. — The Pay as You Go City. (from its excellent financial state.)

Vernon, B.C. — The Hub of the North Okanagan.

Victoria, B.C. — The City of Gardens. — Semper Liber. (motto: Always free.)

Wallaceburg, Ont. — The Glass Town.

Waterloo, Ont. — The Hartford of Canada. — Stability. (motto)

Westmount, Que. — The Holy City.

Weston, Ont. — The Hub of York County. — Equal Justice to All. (motto)

Windsor, Ont. — The Automotive Capital of the British Empire. — The Most Southerly City in Canada. — The Sun Parlour of Canada. — Per mare per terras. (motto)

Winnipeg, Man. — The Chicago of the Canadian West. (1880) — The Gateway City. — The Gateway of the Canadian West. (1912) — The Peg. — Commerce, Prudence, Industry, (motto) (See also: WINNIPEG, MAN.)

Yorkton, Sask. — The Parkland's Trading Centre.

Citizens

With perfect citizens any Government is good.

STEPHEN LEACOCK, *"The Unsolved Riddle of Social Justice"*, 1920, 113.

We are full Canadian citizens, but we are much more than Canadian citizens — we are citizens of the whole Empire.

NEWTON W. ROWELL, Burwash lecture, Toronto, 1922.

Only members of the great races which have formed since its beginning as a country the population of Canada, and the other Aryan members of the population who will agree to identify themselves with the mother races, can be Canadian citizens.

CANADIAN NATIONALIST PARTY (Fascist), "Program and Regulations", 1938.

And the consenting citizens of a minor and docile colony are cogs in a useful tool, though in no way necessary and scarcely criminal at all and their leaders are honourable men, as for example Paul Martin.

DENNIS LEE, "Civil elegies", No. 5, 1972.

Citizenship

All we have to do is, each for himself, to keep down dissensions which can only weaken, impoverish and keep back the country; each for himself do all he can to increase its wealth, its strength and its reputation; each for himself – you and you, gentlemen, all of us – to welcome every talent, to hail every invention, to cherish every gem of art, to foster every gleam of authorship, to honour every acquirement and every gift, to lift ourselves to the level of our destinies, to rise above all low limitations and narrow circumscriptions, to cultivate that true catholicity of spirit which embraces all creeds, all classes and all races, in order to make of our boundless province, so rich in known and unknown resources, a great new Northern nation.

THOMAS D'A. MCGEE, speech in Quebec City, 1862.

As we are now, the words, "I am a Canadian" derive their force from the fact that they are equivalent to saying, "I am a British subject".

TORONTO *GLOBE* , 1865, qu., *Can. hist. rev.*, 1929, 127.

I am a Nova Scotian by birth and a Canadian by act of Parliament.

ALFRED JONES, M.P. for Halifax, 1888.

We hear much these days of education for citizenship, but the only real and effective education for citizenship lies in its actual practice.

FRED LANDON, Can. Hist. Assoc., *Report*, 1937, 86.

I, _____ , swear that I will be faithful and bear true allegiance to Her Majesty Queen Elizabeth the Second, her Heirs and Successors, according to law, and that I will faithfully observe the laws of Canada and fulfil my duties as a Canadian citizen. So help me God.

CANADA. *The Oath of Allegiance*, administered at citizenship ceremony; Dept. of Sec'y. of State, *How to become a Canadian citizen* (pamphlet), 1970.

I was taking lessons in a subject everyone has to master eventually, the art of being a citizen of the country in which you live.

ROBERT FULFORD, Editorial, *Saturday night*, Oct., 1970, 12.

My hands tremble
As I sign my naturalization papers
Making me a Canadian citizen
And Canada my final resting place.

TAKEO NAKANO, "My hands", 1971. (Trans.)

If taking out Canadian nationality were not a likelihood, I would not have taken the first step of accepting this job.

WILLIAM MULHOLLAND, U.S. citizen, interviewed on becoming President of the Bank of Montreal, effective Jan. 1, 1974, qu. in *Can. forum*, Jan., 1975, 4.

Civil Liberties

To maintain, defend, and extend fundamental human rights and civil liberties traditional in our society.

CANADIAN CIVIL LIBERTIES ASSOCIATION, founded 1965, aim.

Civil Service

The price of a commission in the government service is the free exercise of a glib tongue, deftness in canvassing, unscrupulousness in everything.

CANADIAN MONTHLY , Nov., 1876, 443.

The Civil Service of the country, though not the animating spirit, is the living mechanism through which the body politic moves and breathes and has its being. Upon it depends the rapid and economical conduct of every branch of your affairs; and there is nothing about which a nation should be so particular as to secure in such a service independence, zeal, patriotism and integrity.

LORD DUFFERIN, speech to Agricultural and Arts Association, Toronto, Sept. 24, 1878.

The permanent conviction had forced itself on the party members that there was not room for the entire male population of the country in the civil service.

J.E. COLLINS, *Canada under admin. of Lorne*, 1884, 211.

When they get a man into the Civil Service, their first duty is to crush him flat, and if he is a fool of a poet, or dares to think of any nonsense of that kind, draw him through a knot or a gimlet hole a few times, pile on the agony of toil, toil until his nerves are flattened out, all the rebound knocked out of him, and then – superannuate him on what he can squeeze out of them through friends or enemies.

CHARLES SANGSTER, letter to W.D. Lighthall, Nov. 15, 1888.

If you have any ambition; if you expect to make any headway in the world; if you place any value on your initiative, then, for Heaven's sake, steer clear of the Civil Service. If you want to become part of a machine by which you move along, without exercising your initiative, then the Civil Service is the proper place for you.

DONALD SUTHERLAND, H. of C., *Debates*, May 10, 1918, 1740.

The iniquitous examination system and the whole vertical system of promotions is the central core from which a stream of mediocrity seeps into our whole federal administration.

W.L. GRANT, in *Univ. of Tor. quart.*, 1934, 438.

He was educated at Lévis College, studied law for a time, then went into business, and finally took refuge in the Civil Service.

ENCYCLOPEDIA OF CANADA, 1935, 11, 35.

It is sometimes said that our national economic and financial affairs are somehow settled at a long table with W.C. Clark, Deputy Minister of Finance, at one end and Graham Towers, Governor of the Bank of Canada, at the other.

AUSTIN F. CROSS, *Public affairs*, Autumn, 1951, 19.

I can assure you that it is much more difficult to be an acknowledged authority on fiscal and monetary policy, foreign affairs, full employment, trade and like matters in the Civil Service community of Ottawa than it is here in the business community of Toronto.

MITCHELL SHARP, Ottawa *Journal*, Dec. 13, 1958, 7, on becoming vice-president of Brazilian Traction after leaving post of Deputy Minister, Dept. of Trade and Commerce.

The job security at Ottawa makes the Teamsters Union look like the Boy Scout movement.

THOMAS F. TYSON, Paperwork and Systems Management Project, Royal Comm. on Govt. Organization (Glassco), at a meeting, Hamilton, 1963, qu. in *Liberty*, "Cross Canada", Sept., 1963.

The public service is no place for the intellectual. The intellectual cannot do it justice. The environment is alien. Particularly the environment in which foreign policy is made.

JAMES EAYRS, *Right and wrong in foreign policy*, 1966, 53.

No Ottawa bastard was going to tell me ten thousand Eskimos were bastards.

> JUDGE JACK SISSONS, on a court argument by Dept. of Northern Affairs that Eskimo marriage was invalid, qu. in his *Judge of the far north*, 1968, 136.

The thing I like best about Gordon Robertson is that when I come in first thing in the morning he presents me with a series of answers to questions I didn't even know had been raised.

> PIERRE E. TRUDEAU, on the Clerk of the Privy Council, about 1970, qu. in *Maclean's*, Jan., 1973, 23.

Of all the growth industries in Canada, nothing matches the Ottawa bureaucracy.

> DOUGLAS FISHER, qu. by A. Fotheringham, Vancouver *Sun*, Apr. 14, 1975, 33, writing from Ottawa.

Civility

Civility is a cheap coin what is manufactured for nothing, and among folks in general goes further than dollars and cents.

> THOMAS C. HALIBURTON, *Sam Slick's wise saws*, 1853, ch. 9.

Civilization

Man has a kindship with each stone, each tree
Which only civilization drove him from:
If he returns, he'll find no loneliness.
Instead, a silence lifted from the heart
Which in a certain way, bears questioning.

> DOROTHY LIVESAY, "Hermit", about 1928.

I am profoundly distrustful of what is called civilization. Perhaps one has to have lived — as I have done; as I am

doing — on the frontier, or beyond the frontier, of a life that is reasonably secure in order to understand why I call the present civilization the consolidation of barbarism.

> FREDERICK PHILIP GROVE, *In search of myself*, 1946, 448.

Good God, if our civilization were to sober up for a couple of days, it'd die of remorse on the third.

> MALCOLM LOWRY, *Under the volcano*, 1947, 117.

It is perhaps a unique characteristic of civilization that each civilization believes in its uniqueness and its superiority to other civilizations. Indeed this may be the meaning of culture — i.e., something which we have that others have not. It is probably for this reason that writings on culture can be divided into those attempting to weaken other cultures and those attempting to strengthen their own.

> HAROLD A. INNIS, address, American Economic Assoc., Chicago, Dec. 30, 1950.

Each civilization has its own method of suicide.

> HAROLD A. INNIS, *The bias of communication*, 1951, 141.

The essence of man is his quality, not his quantity, and this is no place to stop halfway between ape and angel.

> N.J. BERRILL, *Man's emerging mind*, 1955, 237.

Civilization, creator of deathscapes, like a dull-witted fire of ugliness and ferocious stupidity.

> MALCOLM LOWRY, "The forest path to the spring", in *Hear us O Lord*, 1961, 276.

Classes

The upper-crust folks.

> T.C. HALIBURTON, *Sam Slick*, 1838, 53.

We have here no traditions and ancient venerable institutions; here, there are no aristocratic elements hallowed by time or bright deeds; here, every man is the first settler of the land, or removed from the first settler one or two generations at the furthest; here, we have no architectural monuments calling up old associations; here, we have none of those old popular legends and stories which in other countries have exercised a powerful share in the government; here, every man is the son of his own works.

THOMAS D'A. MCGEE, *Confederation debates*, Feb. 9, 1865, 146.

Power in politics is not found in Parliament but in the country, prior to the election. Politics only exist where there are classes, and any action taken by a class in defence of its interest is political action. Hence you cannot define any particular action as political, but any action used to control political power in order to utilize it for the benefit of that class — that is political action, and it matters not what method it takes.

JACK KAVANAGH, speech at Western Labour Conference, Calgary, Mar. 13, 1919.

Class organization is the only road along which civilization can travel to safety. I believe in that as I believe in God.

HENRY WISE WOOD, *Western independent*, Oct. 29, 1919.

The history of Canada is the record of the rise, development, and supremacy of class rule.

WILLIAM IRVINE, *The farmers in politics*, 1920, 198.

The root conflict of interest within our national society is not fundamentally sectional or geographical at all, i.e., it is not between the central provinces and the outlying provinces. It is a class conflict, between the small class which controls the sources of wealth and power and the other classes which are exploited by them.

F.H. UNDERHILL, *Can.jour.econ. and pol.sci.*, 1935, 402.

The appeal to the less fortunate to range themselves against the successful, is the easiest way to secure political victory in almost any country, but particularly so in Canada. Other class appeals carry elements of danger, but the first has been the major sin of politicians for several decades. It is an easy way to gain power, but some day the price has to be paid, and Canada's penalties do not seem to me far away.

ARTHUR MEIGHEN, letter to W.R. Givens, Feb. 12, 1938. (Pub.Arch.Can.)

French Canada has never shared the American creed of the classless society.

GUY ROCHER, in Rioux and Martin, *French Canadian society*, 1964, 341.

One of the most persistent images that Canadians have of their society is that it has no classes.

JOHN PORTER, *The vertical mosaic*, 1965, 3.

The promotion of dissensus on class issues is a way of mitigating dissensus on many non-class issues.

GAD HOROWITZ, *Jour. of Can. stud.*, 1, No. 3, Nov., 1966, 10.

Normally muffled in the national rhetoric, the reality of class conflict in Canadian society emerges from the study of aid to the civil power.

DESMOND MORTON, *Can. hist. rev.*, Vol. 60, 1970, 424.

Clay

This clay the same clay you can't walk

through when it gets wet won't stay down when it dries into dust.

GEORGE RYGA, *Ballad of a stone picker*, 1966, 7.

Clear Grits

Him! We don't want him, we only want men who are clear Grit.

DAVID CHRISTIE, to George Brown, late in 1849, when discussing the platform and members of the advanced Reformers. The term "Clear Grit" was soon afterward applied by the *Globe* to the new party, but it had been in use for years without reference to politics i.e. by T.C. Haliburton in *Sam Slick*, 1836.

All sand and no dirt, clear grit all the way through.

DAVID CHRISTIE, attributed, 1849. Also ascribed to Peter Perry, Malcolm Cameron, and William McDougall, all active in the formation of the Clear Grit party which took form at a convention at Markham, Ont., March, 1850.

A little miserable clique of office-seeking buncombe-talking cormorants who met in a certain lawyer's office in King Street, and announced their intention to form a new party on "Clear Grit" principles.

TORONTO *GLOBE*, Jan. 8, 1850.

"Clear grit" is pure sand without a particle of dirt in it.

ALEXANDER MACKENZIE, to C.H. McIntosh, Editor of the Strathroy *Despatch*, from a platform in an election campaign, West Middlesex, 1867.

Clericalism

Clericalism and democracy are mutually exclusive terms. For clericalism implies that the mass of ordinary people possess insufficient wisdom to direct their own destinies and need the guidance of superior persons who, of course, are the clerics. Thus it comes that every extension of democratic government is gall and wormwood to clericalism.

MANITOBA FREE PRESS, Feb. 21, 1916.

Climate

I no longer wonder the elegant arts are unknown here; the rigour of the climate suspends the very powers of the understanding.

FRANCES BROOKE, *The history of Emily Montague*, Vol. 1, 1769, 216.

I fear that I have not got much to say about Canada, not having seen much; what I got by going to Canada was a cold.

HENRY THOREAU, *Excursion to Canada*, 1850.

There can be but little doubt that the greater part of the vast region included under the name of British America is doomed to everlasting sterility on account of the severity of its climate.

LIPPINCOTT'S *GAZETTEER*, 1866.

Our bracing northern winters will preserve us from the effeminacy which naturally steals over the most vigorous races when long under the relaxing influence of tropical or even generally mild and genial skies.

TORONTO *GLOBE*, Mar. 31, 1869, 2.

The climate of Manitoba consists of seven months of Arctic winter and five months of cold weather.

NORTHERN PACIFIC RAILWAY CO., *Settler's guide to the North-west*, N.Y., 1882. Refuted in Can., Dept. of Agric., *Canadian Northwest; climate and productions; a misrepresentation exposed*, Ottawa, 1883.

The climate is most trying to tramps.

GEORGE M. GRANT, address to Canadian Club, New York, 1887.

A country of dry frost in winter, and of fruitful heat in summer, with numerous delightful climates in between — this is the rising nation, Canada.

WILFRED CAMPBELL, *Canada*, 1907, 1.

The stimulation of the climate may lead the Westerner to overmuch action and to make large drafts upon his future with confidence, but what he has done is so wonderful that he has reason in venturing upon wide horizons.

> SIR R. FALCONER, speech, *The quality of Canadian life*, 1917.

Canada is not a country for the cold of heart or for the cold of feet.

> PIERRE E. TRUDEAU, address, National Newspaper Awards Dinner, Toronto, Apr. 8, 1972.

Closure

Heaven is my witness that I would rather stand here today, defeated and in opposition by that appeal to the people than stand over there in office by the power of the gag.

> SIR WILFRID LAURIER, H. of C., *Debates*, Apr. 9, 1913, 7437.

If we want to get away with it, who is there to stop us?

> C.D. HOWE, qu. by E. Davie Fulton in H. of C., *Debates*, 1956, Vol. 5, 4757 (on closure).

The House was told, "Provide at once
This great financial prop,
This loan of almost all the cost,
With eighty million top."

A member said "I really think . . . "
The guillotine went "Chop".

> GEORGE BAIN, *I've been around and around* . . . 1964, 39, referring to pipeline debate, House of Commons, May-June, 1956.

Clothes

Good sense is as much marked by the style of a person's dress, as by their conversation.

> CATHERINE PARR TRAILL, *The Canadian settler's guide*, 1855, 22.

So sneer not at words, for experience
     taught me
That sensitive worth is so easily
     hurt;
And honour in patches this parable
     brought me:
The meanest of men often wear the
     best shirt.

> J.R. RAMSAY, "Win-on-ah", 1869.

Ladies are to wear low-necked dresses, without Court trains, and gentlemen are to be in full dress. Ladies, whose health will not admit of their wearing low-necked dresses may, on forwarding to the A.D.C. in waiting, a medical certificate to that effect, wear square cut dresses.

> E.G.P. LITTLETON, Military Secretary to Lord Lorne, Gov. Gen., Montreal, 1878, proclamation on vice-regal drawing-room.

Clothes and courage have so much to do with each other.

> SARA JEANNETTE DUNCAN, *An American girl in London*, 1891, 25.

Let him wear brand-new garments
     still,
Who has a threadbare soul, I say.

> BLISS CARMAN, "The mendicants", 1894.

What of all the colours shall I bring
     you for your fairing,
Fit to lay your fingers on, fine enough
     for you?
Yellow for the ripened rye, white for
     ladies' wearing,

Red for briar-roses, or the skies own
 blue?

> MARJORIE PICKTHALL, "The green
> month", 1913.

If a girl has a pretty face, no man on
earth can tell you what kind of clothes
she has on.

> ROBERT C. (BOB) EDWARDS, Calgary *Eye
> Opener*, Oct. 5, 1918.

Girls wore silk stockings, silk underwear, silk dresses; and nothing destroys
modesty and sexual morality in a girl
more quickly than the consciousness
that suddenly she wears attractive *des-
sous*.

> FREDERICK PHILLIP GROVE, *Fruits of the
> earth*, 1933, 279.

I knew him well. He was a vest
A gleam of shirt, a round of collar.
Felt hat, suit coat, pants neatly
 pressed.
None cared if he were dunce or
 scholar.
He was of shoes with shining lace,
Fur overcoat with each November.
There may, perhaps, have been a face –
His clothes are all that I remember.

> ALAN CREIGHTON, "Mr. Clothes", 1939.

When a man doesn't notice a woman's
clothes, he notices her.

> FREDERICK P. GROVE, *The master of the
> mill*, 1944, 74.

I attired myself suitably in Canadian
National Costume, consisting of a cowboy hat, a Red River flannel shirt, a
Quebec doeskin wamus, Bay Street
trousers (made of imported cloth and
beautifully creased) and St. Catherine's street shoes (patent leathers with
buttoned cloth tops); under this I wore
a hair shirt (to represent the Canadian
Puritan Conscience) and a pair of
underpants which have been sitting
for thirty years and are due for retirement (to represent the Civil Service);
in addition I wore a tartan cummer-
bund (to represent the Maritimes,

sometimes referred to as "the soft
underbelly of Canada") and a string of
ice-cubes around the brim of my hat
(to represent the immense promise of
our Northland).

> ROBERTSON DAVIES, *Table talk*, 1949,
> 165.

This business of good grooming can be
carried too far. For real attraction, a
girl's clothes should have that lived-in
look.

> ROBERTSON DAVIES, *Leaven of malice*,
> 1954, 160.

Who can tell what clothes may suffer
doomed to be hollow, to be thin,
unable to speak except by the gestures
of those who inhabit them.

> MARGARET ATWOOD, "Closet", 1968.

Clouds

On such a day the shrunken stream
 Spends its last water and runs dry;
Clouds like far turrets in a dream
 Stand baseless in the burning sky.

> ARCHIBALD LAMPMAN, "At the ferry",
> 1893.

In steady fleets serene and white,
The happy clouds go on.

> ARCHIBALD LAMPMAN, "April in the
> hills", 1896.

O follow the silken hollow shapes
of the clouds that go gliding the empty
rooms of the sky, around and above
the browning pulp of the peeled world
and the men and the metalled ants
 that multiply on the dead core.

> EARLE BIRNEY, "Images in place of log-
> ging", 1952.

Clubs

A club is a place where a gentleman
can get drunk respectably.

> PETER MCARTHUR, *To be taken with salt*,
> 1903, 154.

There is a crafty network of organizations of business men called Canadian Clubs. They catch people who look interesting, assemble their members during the mid-day lunch-hour, and, tying the victim to a steak, bid him discourse on anything that he thinks he knows.

RUDYARD KIPLING, *Letters to the family*, 1907, 13.

Membership in the 'right' clubs and associations, even though he may rarely appear there, is considered useful, if not essential, to validate the male career.

J.R. SEELEY et al., *Crestwood heights*, 1956, 295.

Clumsy

Misbegotten
born clumsy
bursting feet first
then topsy turvy
falling downstairs
the fear of
joy of
falling.

DOROTHY LIVESAY, "Ballad of me", 1967.

Coal

The Coal Trade – Dirty work makes clean money, our stomachs need never be empty while the bowels of the earth are full.

N.S. PHILANTHROPIC SOC., toast, Nov. 1, 1836.

"Then look at the beeowells of the airth; only think of the coal; and it's no use a-talkin', that's the only coal to supply us that we can rely on. Why, there ain't nothin' like it. It extends all the way from Bay of Fundy right out to Pictou through the Province, and then under all the Island of Cape Breton; and some o' them seams are

the biggest, the thickest, and deepest ever yet discovered since the world began. Beautiful coal it is too."

T.C. HALIBURTON, *The clockmaker*, 1838.

Canada is a country with coal-fields at both ends and the railways in between.

ANON., about 1900.

Cobalt, Ontario

For we'll sing a little song of Cobalt,
If you don't live there it's your fault.
Oh, you Cobalt where the wintry
    breezes blow,
Where all the silver comes from,
And where you live a life and then
    some,
Oh, you Cobalt, you're the best old
    town I know.

L.F. STEENMAN, "The Cobalt song", 1910.

Coca-Cola

Canada, alas, is forgetting that it is its pioneers who built this country and made it what it was; now it wants to be like everyone else and have autocamps instead of trees and Coca-Cola stands instead of human beings.

MALCOLM LOWRY, letter to Stuart Lowry, Fall, 1950. (*Selected letters*, 218).

At the start of proceedings
A portfolio of documents
On the cover of which appeared
In gold letters
            not
A Mari Usque Ad Mare
            not
E Pluribus Unum
            not
Dieu et Mon Droit
            but
COURTESY OF COCA-COLA
    LIMITED.

F.R. SCOTT, "National identity", 1963.

Four thousand saints surround me.
My soul is utterly taken by the man
Selling cokes from a red refrigerator
On the roof of Milan Cathedral.

RALPH GUSTAFSON, "On the top of Milan
Cathedral", 1966.

An area already fully CocaColonized,
to use the term of modern economists,
which means nothing more than being
conditioned to American-type goods
and desires. The fat pay-packets of the
American-owned companies assisted
willing Galtonians to advance from
CocaColonization towards Americanization.

ROBERT L. PERRY, *Galt, U.S.A.*, 1971, 6.

Coffins

Closed Caskets: disturbing. Although
there are many instances when he
would prefer a closed casket to long
hours spent at restoration, the funeral
director is evermindful of warnings of
the trade press that they result in the
sale of lower-priced goods.

ROBERT FORREST, *Death here is thy
sting*, 1967, 49.

Coincidence

Coincidence seems to me to be what a
Japanese friend of mine used to call "a
series of combination of events" which
meet at a certain point of time or
perhaps place. It is not as uncommon
as people think, and the older I grew
the more I believed in the fantastic
likelihood — whether relevant or irrelevant — of coincidence.

ETHEL WILSON, *Swamp angel*, 1954, 131.

Cold

Thou barren waste; unprofitable
    strand,
Where hemlocks brood on
    unproductive land,
Whose frozen air on one bleak winter's
    night
Can metamorphose *dark brown hares
    to white.*

STANDISH O'GRADY, "The emigrant",
1842.

With the thermometer at 30° below
zero and the wind behind him, a man
walking on Main Street, Winnipeg,
knows which side of him is which.

STEPHEN LEACOCK, *My discovery of the
west*, 1937, 39.

One night when the stars are
    exploding like nails
comes Zero himself with his needle,
an icicle full of the cold cocaine
but as tall as the glittering steeple
that pins us down in the town.

PATRICK ANDERSON, "Song of intense
cold", 1953.

It walked through your heart, it dissolved your kidney, it flashed down
your marrow and made an icicle of
your coccyx.

WYNDHAM LEWIS, *Self condemned*,
1954, 185.

Collections

The best thing a boy can do is to begin
to collect. Let him collect something
— I don't care what it is — and you
will find he begins to notice, and from
noticing he begins to classify and arrange. Interest develops, and wherever
he goes there is nothing connected
with his collection about which he is
not interested. The real education for
a boy is simply a matter of impressions.

SIR WILLIAM VAN HORNE, to S. Macnaughtan, *My Canadian memories*, 1920, 101.

Collective Security

Automatic commitments to the application of force is not a practical policy.

W.L. MACKENZIE KING, speech, League of Nations Assembly, Sept. 29, 1936.

I am an ardent advocate of collective security, but I wish I knew with whom to 'collect'.

J.H. BLACKMORE, H. of C., *Debates*, 1938, 1938.

The Government and people of Canada are anxious to know what armed forces, in common with other Members of the United Nations, Canada should maintain as our share of the burden of putting world force behind world law.

LOUIS ST. LAURENT, United Nations, General Assembly, Oct. 29, 1946.

Colonialism

The French, therefore, contented themselves with sending a colony to Canada, a cold, uncomfortable, uninviting region, from which nothing but furs and fish were to be had, and where the new inhabitants could only pass a laborious and necessitous life, in perpetual regret of the deliciousness and plenty of their native country.

SAMUEL JOHNSON, "The political state of Great Britain", 1756.

I do not believe that any nation has now attained, and I doubt whether any nation ever will attain, such a point of morality, as to be able to govern other nations for the benefit of the governed.

GOLDWIN SMITH, "The last Republicans of Rome", in *Lectures and essays*, 1881.

The chief fault of Canadians, politically, is their diffidence and their timidity. Imperialism has taught them their insufficiency, and big, robust and strong as they are, they reflect their education. Our mean colonialism is part of our fibre.

JOHN S. EWART, *Kingdom papers*, 1911, I, 54.

It is hardly too much to say that in some quarters there is a surviving colonialism which cannot forget that the British connection once involved colonial subordination, and would willingly demonstrate independence of Britain by avowing dependence upon the United States.

R.G. TROTTER, in *Inter-American quart.*, Jan., 1940.

The colonial is an incomplete person. He must look to others for his guidance, and far away for his criterion of value. He copies the parental style instead of incorporating what is best in something of his own. He undervalues his own contribution and overvalues what others can do for him. Old greatness is more to him than new truth.

FRANK R. SCOTT, *Preview*, Nov., 1942, 5.

The imperial and regional are both inherently anti-poetic, yet they go hand-in-hand, and together they make up what I call the colonial in Canadian life.

NORTHROP FRYE, in *Can. forum*, 1943, 208; repr. in his *Bush garden*, 1971, 133.

Our colonialism in relation to the United States is unavowed, but it is deep. The praise of a couple of New York reviewers will outweigh the unanimous enthusiasm of Canadian journals from coast to coast. There is every reason to suppose that as Canadian feeling becomes more and more friendly towards the United States, as it has done during the past quarter century, our cultural dependence on the Americans will grow.

> E.K. BROWN, *On Canadian poetry,* 1944, 19.

For more than a hundred years this country struggled, for the most part bloodlessly, to cease being a British colony. Now many of its inhabitants are afraid that their country will spend the next hundred years struggling, also bloodlessly, to avoid becoming a colony of the United States.

> *MACLEAN'S*, editorial, June 15, 1951.

Canada moved from colony to nation to colony.

> HAROLD INNIS, *Essays in Canadian economic history,* 1956, 405, referring to U.S. capital investment.

It is sadly ironic that in a world torn asunder by countries who are demanding and winning their independence, our free, independent and highly developed country should be haunted by the spectre of a colonial or semi-colonial future.

> WALTER L. GORDON, qu. by Kari Levitt, *Silent surrender,* 1970, 2.

Colonies

These wretched colonies will all be independent too in a few years and are a millstone round our necks.

> BENJAMIN DISRAELI, letter to Lord Malmesbury, Aug. 13, 1852, respecting Newfoundland fisheries.

I am no more against Colonies than I am against the solar system. I am against dependencies, when nations are fit to be independent.

> GOLDWIN SMITH, *The Empire,* 1863, 123.

Great Britain must presently reach the condition of shaking hands with her colonies instead of expecting them to touch their hats to her.

> PETER MCARTHUR, *To be taken with salt,* 1903, 158.

This colonial status is a worn-out bygone thing. The sense and feeling of it has become harmful to us. It limits the ideas, and circumscribes the patriotism of our people. It impairs the mental vigour and narrows the outlook of those who are reared and educated in our midst.

> STEPHEN LEACOCK, *University mag.,* 1907, 133.

Colours

The things that are unobtrusive and differentiated by shadings only – grey in grey above all – like our northern woods, like our sparrows, our wolves – they hold a more compelling attraction than orgies of colour and screams of sound. So I came home to the North.

> FREDERICK P. GROVE, *Over prairie trails,* 1922, 90.

I sometimes wonder if the Canadian liking for bright colours isn't the outcome of that prolonged session of white during the winter months.

> LADY BYNG, *Up the stream of time,* 1946, 11.

My favourite colour. Gold!

> ROY THOMSON, attributed remark to Princess Margaret, qu. in R. Braddon, *Roy Thomson of Fleet Street,* 1965, 242.

No color is as full of unfulfilled promises as black.

> GÉRALD ROBITAILLE, *Images,* 1969, 19.

Columbia River

We may dam the Columbia River, but we will not sell our birthright for a mess of wattage.

BARRY MATHER, M.P., New Westminster, opposing export of hydro power from B.C. to the U.S., qu. in *Liberty*, Feb., 1963.

The Americans know what the benefits are worth, and so do the Canadian critics. A billion dollars is a modest estimate. It will cost Canada about $100 million to give the Columbia away.

LARRATT HIGGINS, in I. Lumsden, ed., *Close the 49th parallel etc*, 1970, 236.

Canadian taxpayers, it has become clear, will be paying close to $200 million dollars for the privilege of turning control of the continent's fourth largest river over to the United States.

RICHARD C. BOCKING, *Canada's water – for sale?*, 1972, 92.

Columnists

The Dervish Khan, the Screamer of Qu'Appelle.

R.K. KERNIGHAN, pseudonym of the columnist, Winnipeg *Sun*, 1882.

The occupational disease of people in my line of work is infallibility, complicated by loquacity and carbonic acid gas in the blood.

ROBERTSON DAVIES, *Diary of Samuel Marchbanks*, 1947, 37.

Commerce

Depend upon it, our commercial embarrassments are our real difficulty. Political discontent properly so-called, there is none.

LORD ELGIN, dispatch, Winter, 1848; qu. in Walrond, ed., *Letters of Elgin*, 70.

We all traded whisky. Well, the Hudson's Bay Company traded rum up to the year 1860. I have seen as maney indans Drunk at Edmonton and Rocky Mountain House as ever i seen aney where else and when they got drunk we have put them to bed and treated them a good deal better than some of our civilized Bartenders.

W.S. GLADESTONE, employee of the Hudson's Bay Company, to Katherine Hughes, Aug. 11, 1910, in Gladestone File, Alberta Provincial Library.

Sooner or later, commercial imperatives will bring about free movement of all goods back and forth across our long border; and when that occurs, or even before it does, it will become unmistakably clear that countries with economies so inextricably intertwined must also have free movement of the other vital factors of production – capital, services and labour.

GEORGE W. BALL, *Discipline of power*, 1968, 113.

Committees

Those we know resemble inevitably
the shape of a committee meeting
varnished about the circumference
with the usual chairs,
and cloudy at the core
with the jargon of cigarette smoke.
The windows stick.

VIOLET ANDERSON, "Collectivist world", 1957.

Common Sense

Of all the seventeen senses, I like common sense about as well as any of 'em, arter all.

T.C. HALIBURTON, *Sam Slick*, 1840, 218.

He will not set the St. Lawrence on fire but he is a shrewd common sense man, and understands human nature, as his unlimited influence in the District of Quebec shows.

SIR JOHN A. MACDONALD, on Francis X. Lemieux, letter to J. Langton, Feb. 6, 1855.

Communication

Now, if you want to please the great mass of mankind you must talk platitudes: when you can't do that, the next best thing to do is to talk nonsense.

J.J. PROCTER, *The philosopher in the clearing*, 1897, 176.

Make us the half-way house of the empire.

GEORGE M. GRANT, letter to Sir Wilfrid Laurier, Feb. 25, 1899, referring to the Pacific cable project.

The ability to develop a system of government in which the bias of communication can be checked and an appraisal of the significance of space and time can be reached remains a problem of empire and of the Western world.

HAROLD A. INNIS, "Paper and the printing press", in *Empire and communication*, 1950; 1972 ed., last line.

Sir, it is not *you* who is not speaking to me! It is *I* who is not speaking to you!

JOHN V. CLYNE, Judge of the B.C. Supreme Court 1950-57, to Justice C.H. O'Halloran, B.C. Appeal Court; qu. Vancouver *Sun*, Nov. 18, 1972, 37.

Perfection of the *means* of communication has meant instantaneity.

MARSHALL MCLUHAN, "Culture without literacy", *Explorations*, Dec., 1953, 118.

Truth is given through oral tradition, mysticism, intuition, all cognition, not simply by observation and measurement of physical phenomena. To them, the ocularly visible apparition is not nearly as important as the purely auditory one.

EDMUND CARPENTER, *Eskimo*, 1959, ("Acoustic space").

It may be claimed — claimed without much challenge — that the communications of a nation are as vital to its life as its defences, and should receive at least as great a measure of national protection.

CANADA. ROY. COMM. ON PUBLICATIONS, *Report*, 1961, 4.

Exposed unceasingly to a vast network of communications which reaches to every corner of our land; American words, images and print — the good, the bad, and the indifferent — batter unrelenting at our eyes and ears.

CANADA. ROY. COMM. ON PUBLICATIONS, *Report*, 1961, 5.

As a nation, Canada represents the triumph of communications over geography.

NEIL COMPTON, in M. Oliver, ed., *Social purpose for Canada*, 1961, 70.

The medium is the message.

MARSHALL MCLUHAN, *Understanding media*, 1964.

The triumph of communication is the death of communication: where communication forms a total environment, there is nothing to be communicated.

NORTHROP FRYE, *The modern century*, 1967, 38.

The wind blows cold from Labrador:
I have a message for you from the ice age,
But I shall not decode it for you.

WALTER BAUER, "Canada", 1968.

The language of what belongs to man as man has long since been disintegrated.

GEORGE P. GRANT, *Technology and empire*, 1969, 140.

The standard we choose to employ is pretty straight-forward: *how successful is that newspaper, or broadcasting station, in preparing its audience for social change?*

SENATE. SPECIAL SENATE COMMITTEE ON MASS MEDIA, *Report*, Vol. 1, 1970, 84.

I thought of myself as one of those guys who write political slogans on walls. A signpainter, a shouting signpainter.

PAUL CHAMBERLAND, qu. by M. Reid, *The shouting signpainters*, 1972, 64.

It's not surprising that communication between human beings is so difficult, considering that so much of what each of us feels most deeply can't help but seem the merest trivia to almost everyone else.

ALDEN NOWLAN, *Various persons named Kevin O'Brien*, 1973, 32.

Communism

Communism, as a movement, is a mistake: but there is a communism which is deeply seated in the heart of every good man, and which makes him feel that the hardest of all labour is idleness in a world of toil, and that the bitterest of all bread is that which is eaten by the sweat of another man's brow.

GOLDWIN SMITH, "The labour movement", speech delivered before Mechanics' Institute of Montreal, 1872; *Ontario workman*, Jan. 2, 1973, 1.

The good still moveth towards the
    good:
  The ill still moveth towards the ill:
  But who affirmeth that we will
Not form a nobler brotherhood

When communists, fanatics, those
    Who howl their *"vives"* to
      Freedom's name
  And yet betray her unto shame,
Are dead and coffined with her foes.

GEORGE F. CAMERON, "In after days", 1887.

We did not come to the working class from communism. We came to communism from the working class. And we did not come to urge strikes by virtue of membership in the Communist Party. We became Communists because we participated in strikes.

TIM BUCK, address to the jury, Nov. 12, 1931, trial of 8 leaders of the Communist Party of Canada.

The evidence proves that the Communist Party of Canada is a member of the Communist International of Russia and that instead of determining its own policies, purposes, teachings and aims, it adopted and adopts those of the Communist International, and, therefore, whatever are the policies, purposes, teachings and aims of the Communist International are also automatically those of the Communist Party of Canada.

SIR WILLIAM MULOCK, 1931, Ontario Appeal Court judgment on conviction of Tim Buck.

If the Communists wouldn't organize demonstrations, it wouldn't be necessary for the police to break them up.

JIMMY SIMPSON, Mayor of Toronto, about 1934, qu. in T. McEwan, *He wrote for us*, 1951, 62.

They won't come to us, so I say, let us go to them. I hereby move that we go to Ottawa, to discuss work and wages with the federal cabinet.

> ANON., seconded by Arthur (Slim) Evans, at a meeting of the Relief Camp Workers Union, Vancouver, May 29, 1935; the beginning of the "On to Ottawa" march.

Mackenzie-Papineau Battalion.

> ANON., fighting unit made up of Canadians and Americans, Summer, 1937, part of the XVth International Brigade in the Spanish Civil War.

The Padlock Law.

> ANON., a popular name for the Quebec act of 1937, aimed at curbing Communist activities.

Communism is the most subtle of all evils, because its appeal is made in the name of freedom, and it marches under the banners of Freedom. Its appeal is to the masses, whom it promises to deliver from their chains. It speaks in the name of enlarged opportunity and increased security. It is, in reality, none of these. The immediate purpose of Communism is the complete control of the individual in the name of the state. Its ultimate aim is world domination. Beneath its mask are concealed the secret police, slave labour, and the concentration camp.

> W.L. MACKENZIE KING, speech at National Liberal Convention, Ottawa, 1948.

Our foreign policy today must, therefore, I suggest, be based on a recognition of the fact that totalitarian communist aggression endangers the freedom and peace of every democratic country, including Canada.

> LOUIS ST. LAURENT, H. of C., *Debates*, Apr. 29, 1948, 3449.

After all, the taint of Communism sticks even when the Communists are right, and for that reason, so the argument runs, when the Communists are in the right it is better to be wrong than to be on their side. With this kind of thinking we are damned.

> B.S. KEIRSTEAD, *Canada in world affairs September 1951 to October 1953*, 1956, 78.

Suppose Herbert Norman *had been* a Communist.

> RALPH ALLEN, *Maclean's*, May 11, 1957, 8; Herbert Norman, ambassador to Egypt, committed suicide in Cairo, Apr. 4, 1957 after being named as a communist by the U.S. Senate Sub-committee on Internal Security.

You stand like sober Marxists, nose to rump.
Your tails beat flies from each other's heads.

> IRVING LAYTON, *Swinging flesh*, 1961, 184.

Better red than dead.

> DONALD FLEMING, Toronto, June 15, 1962, quoting Lester Pearson. What Pearson actually said on C.B.C.-T.V., May 19, 1960 was that he would prefer to "live under Kruschev rather than die, and do what I could to throw Mr. Kruschev and his ilk out of power".

We live in an inter-dependent world and ultimately our relations with the communist world are governed by the general state of East-West relations and particularly by the climate and the relations between the United States and the Soviet Union. Because of these facts it is neither possible nor desirable that our relations with the communist world should be at wide variance with those of our closest friends and allies. Yet within these limits there are possibilities open to us which serve our interests and the interests of our allies.

PAUL MARTIN, Minister for External Affairs, speech, Toronto, Aug. 24, 1963.

It is not communism that should frighten us. It is the people who are starving in the world. That is what should make us ashamed.

PIERRE E. TRUDEAU, speech, Quebec City, June 15, 1968. (Trans.)

Communist idealism: giving people the benefit of the clout.

IRVING LAYTON, "Aphs", *The whole bloody bird*, 1969, 81.

Oh, 50 years ago, I thought I'd see something. Now, maybe, another 50 years.

JOHN BOYCHUCK, one of the founders of Communist Party of Canada, qu. in *Canadian magazine*, Jan. 22, 1972, 25.

If it's good enough for Moscow, it's good enough for me.

TIM BUCK, remark to Joseph Salsberg, qu. P. Sykes, Toronto *Star*, Nov. 20, 1972.

Compassion

As men and women become brutalized by the terrible events of this century, pride, not pity, becomes the stimulus for compassionate behaviour.

IRVING LAYTON, "Aphs", *The whole bloody bird*, 1969, 80.

Compatibility

Somewhere shots ring out every night,
laws stop up the breath of freedom,
injustice is done in the name of justice,
every morning executions, eyes
 breaking in the gloom.
And yet we awake every morning,
we two, in perfect harmony.

WALTER BAUER, *And yet*, 1968. (Trans. by Beissel).

Competition

The whole growth of economic organization, the subsequent development of the millionaire, and the final effort to avoid the ruinous waste of independent competition, are simply stages in the economic triumph of man over nature.

ADAM SHORTT, *Can. mag.*, Vol. 13, 1899, 496.

The biggest things are always the easiest to do because there is no competition.

SIR WILLIAM VAN HORNE, to S. Macnaughtan, *My Canadian memories*, 1920, 109.

Rivalry and struggle under equitable laws are the glory of living.

ARTHUR MEIGHEN, *Unrevised and unrepented*, 1949, 443.

It cannot be accepted as our law that only those conspiracies are illegal that completely eliminate or virtually eliminate all competition. To say that the prevention or lessening of competition must be carried to the point where there remains no competition, or virtually none, is tantamount to considering the words "prevent" or "lessen" as synonymous with "extinguish".

JUDGE HARRY BATSHAW, R. v. Abitibi Power and Paper Co. Ltd., et al. (1961), 131 *Can. crim. cases*, 251.

Complacency

But I'm still complacent
about my moral indignation;
just thinking about it
puts me on the side of the angels
who don't live in this town.

AL PURDY, "Hazelton, B.C.", 1962.

Complaints

The average man has more than one kick coming — to him.

> ROBERT C. (BOB) EDWARDS, Calgary *Eye Opener*, Dec. 15, 1917.

Compromise

Before looking for a middle way, let us try to discover who is right or wrong.

> HENRI BOURASSA, Oct. 12, 1899, qu. by Anne Bourassa in A. Bergevin et al., *Henri Bourassa*, 1966, xxv. (Trans.)

No one knows better than I do that the simple course in politics is not to compromise anything, but unfortunately it is not the road to practical progress.

> CLIFFORD SIFTON, letter to a resident of Brandon, Man., 1905; qu. in Dafoe, *Clifford Sifton*, 290.

Politics, after all, is the science of compromise.

> ROBERT C. (BOB) EDWARDS, Calgary *Eye Opener*, Feb. 5, 1921.

To compromise, no doubt, is to corrupt — to corrupt the simplicity of principle, the clarity of policy — but if so, then all politics corrupt and federal politics, the politics of the vast sectional and communal aggregations, especially so. To this conclusion all purists, all doctrinaires, and all Progressives, must ultimately come or abstain from power.

> W.L. MORTON, *The Progressive party*, 1950, 292.

We are, after all, politicians, not philosophers, and while we may look for the best of all possible worlds, we may have to take second-best. Compromise is possible if it looks in the right direction.

> PIERRE E. TRUDEAU, Commonwealth Conference, London, Eng., Jan. 10, 1969; qu. in *The best of Trudeau*, 1972, 45.

The Canadian genius for compromise.

> NORTHROP FRYE, *The bush garden*, 1971, 219.

Compulsion

We pay for our pleasure with pain;
But the dog will return to his vomit,
the hog to his wallow again.

> ROBERT SERVICE, "The black sheep", 1907.

Computers

No units of measurement yet devised are adequate for the computation of the power wielded by a beautiful woman.

> ARNOLD HAULTAIN, *Hints for lovers*, 1909, 174.

Fantasy is commonplace,
actuality the dream.

> DON W. THOMSON, "Cybernetics", 1961.

The more the data banks record about each one of us, the less we exist.

> MARSHALL MCLUHAN, *From cliché to archetype*, 1970, 13.

There's an old adage around computer companies. It's this: every forecast is wrong. That has to be true, otherwise I'd be out at the racetrack with a computer making money on sure things.

> DON CROFT, computer expert, qu. in *Maclean's*, Nov., 1970, 39.

Sharon, you are
one of the reasons
we needn't be
afraid of computers.

> ALDEN NOWLAN, "Sharon, Sharon", 1971.

If I could meet the guy who runs the programme, I'd tell him to throw Buzz out and buy himself a better computer – a computer with a conscience and a better sense of judgement.

> MARIA, a Compudate (Notre Dame de Grace, Que.) participant, 1972, qu. in A. Waller, *Data for a candlelight dinner*, 1973, 132. (Buzz is the popular name for the computer.)

Conciliation

His thought itself centred around the word *conciliation*. He recognized the social tensions developing in industrial Canada. To vanquish the dread spectre of social conflict, feared alike by both employees and employers, he proclaimed this blessed word to the Dominion.

> H.S. FERNS AND B. OSTRY, *The age of Mackenzie King*, 1955, 51, referring to King.

Conduct of Life

Support what is right, oppose what is wrong; what you think, speak; try to satisfy yourself, and not others; and if you are not popular, you will at least be respected; popularity lasts but a day, respect will descend as a heritage to your children.

> T.C. HALIBURTON, *Sam Slick*, 1838, 35.

By work you get money, by talk you get knowledge.

> T.C. HALIBURTON, *Sam Slick's wise saws*, 1853, I, 270.

Give and take, live and let live, that's the word.

> T.C. HALIBURTON, *Sam Slick's wise saws*, 1853, ch. 27.

There is no strength where there is no strain; seamanship is not learned in calm weather, and born of the vicissitudes and struggles of life are the wisdom, the dignity, and the consolations.

> JOSEPH HOWE, address, Ottawa Y. M.C.A., Feb. 27, 1872.

An open hand, an easy shoe,
And a hope to make the day go
    through.

> BLISS CARMAN, "Joys of the road", 1894.

A simple love, and a simple trust,
And a simple duty done,
Are truer torches to light to death
Than a whole world's victories won.

> WILFRED CAMPBELL, "Afterglow", 1899.

Not to be conquered by these
    headlong days,
But to stand free; to keep the mind at
    brood
On life's deep meaning, nature's
    altitude
Of loveliness, and time's mysterious
    ways;
At every thought and deed to clear the
    haze
Out of our eyes, considering only this
What man, what life, what love, what
    beauty is,
This is to live, and win the final
    praise . . .

> ARCHIBALD LAMPMAN, "Outlook", *Living age*, Mar. 14, 1903.

You may learn to consume your own smoke . . . Learn to accept in silence the minor aggravations, cultivate the gift of taciturnity and consume your own smoke with an extra draught of hard work, so that those about you may not be annoyed with the dust and soot of your complaints. More than any other the practitioner of medicine may illustrate the second great lesson, that we are here not to get all we can out of life for ourselves, but to try to

make the lives of others happier
. . . And the third lesson you may
learn is the hardest of all – that the
law of the higher life is only fulfilled
by love, i.e., charity.

> SIR WILLIAM OSLER, "The masterword in
> medicine", address at Univ. of Toronto,
> 1903.

As for you who stand on the threshold
of life, with a long horizon open before
you for a long career of usefulness to
your native land, if you will permit
me, after a long life, I shall remind
you that already many problems rise
before you. Let me tell you that for
the solution of these problems you
have a safe guide, an unfailing light, if
you remember that faith is better than
doubt and love is better than hate.
Banish doubt and fear from your life.
Let your souls be ever open to the
promptings of faith and the gentle
influence of brotherly love. Be adamant against the haughty, be gentle
and kind to the weak. Let your aim
and purpose, in good or ill, in victory
or defeat, be so to live, so to strive, so
to serve, as to do your part to raise
ever higher the standard of life and of
living.

> SIR WILFRID LAURIER, speech to Ontario
> Liberal Club convention, London, Oct.
> 11, 1916.

There's very little honey
    These days for any man:
Take it where you find it!
    Taste it while you can!

> TOM MACINNES, "Now then", 1918.

Oh, I eat all I can; I drink all I can; I
smoke all I can; and I don't give a
damn for anything.

> SIR WILLIAM VAN HORNE, qu. in Vaug-
> han, *Van Horne*, 1920, 272.

Behold a marvel! – He that stays
At the utmost fringes of his days,
He only a centre hath always.

> WARWICK CHIPMAN, "Immortality",
> 1930.

Seek out the new; reform the stubborn
    past;
Select and build; discard the
    emblazoned shell.
Expand the narrow concept; shape the
    last;
Men's boasts belittle and their dreams
    compel.
Our warfare's not against, but for
    mankind;
Our falling ramparts, barriers of the
    mind.

> F.R. SCOTT, "War", 1945.

My equilibrium, and equilibrium is
all, precarious . . .

> MALCOLM LOWRY, *Under the volcano*,
> 1947, 39.

There is no safety in the middle of the
road in any real testing time of men or
parties, peoples or faiths.

> CHARLOTTE WHITTON, address to found-
> ing convention of New Democratic
> Party, Ottawa, July 31, 1961.

Scorn Swift Success, Stay Solo, so when
    Soon
Comes Coward Call to Count the
    Crowding Cost
Outreach Old Orbits, Open Out your
    Own.

> F.R. SCOTT, "Signature", in *Signature*,
> 1964, 56.

Don't drop out, drop in. Don't cop out,
compete. Don't exit, excel.

> PIERRE ELLIOTT TRUDEAU, speech in
> Montreal, Oct. 19, 1969, advice to
> French Canadians.

Keep bees and
grow asparagus,
   watch the tides
   and listen to the
   wind instead of
the politicians
   make up your own
   stories and believe
   them if you want to
   live the good life.

MIRIAM WADDINGTON, "Advice to the young", 1972.

Do what you have to do – with everything you've got. You don't have to win each round, but if you've played hard – even if it's just a game of bridge or tennis – if you haven't been casual, haven't fooled around, you will have gone far in the pursuit of happiness. Which is the ultimate reason for living, isn't it?

J.V. CLYNE, in *Maclean's*, June, 1973, 41.

Confederation

A general union of all the Provinces might in my opinion be so modified as to regenerate British North America but a partial union appears to me pregnant with evil.

JOHN STRACHAN, Letterbook, Mar. 10, 1839, Ontario Archives.

We desire free trade among all the Provinces, under our national flag, with one coin, one measure, one tariff, one Post Office. We feel that the courts, the press, the educational institutions of North America, would be elevated by union; that intercommunication by railroads, telegraphs and steamboats would be promoted; and that, if such a combination of interests were achieved wisely and with proper guards, the foundations of a great nation, in friendly connection with the mother country, would be laid on an indestructible basis.

JOSEPH HOWE, letter to George Moffatt, May 8, 1849.

Resolved: – That whether protection or reciprocity shall be conceded or withheld, it is essential to the welfare of this colony, and its future good government, that a Constitution should be framed in unison with the wishes of the people, and suited to the growing importance and intelligence of the country, and that such Constitution should embrace a union of the British North American Provinces on mutually advantageous terms, with the concession from the Mother Country of enlarged powers of self-government.

BRITISH AMERICAN LEAGUE, *Proc.*, Nov. 3, 1849.

Resolved, that the union of confederation of the British Provinces on just principles, while calculated to perpetuate their connection with the parent State, will promote their advancement and prosperity, increase their strength and influence, and elevate their position.

JAMES W. JOHNSTONE, Conservative leader of the Opposition, resolution passed in N.S. Legislature, 1854.

See what an empire is here, surely the best in climate, soil, mineral, and other productions in the world, and peopled by such a race, as no other country under heaven can produce. No, Sir, here are the bundle of sticks; all they want is to be united.

THOMAS C. HALIBURTON, *Nature and human nature*, 1855.

There are few persons to whose minds this scheme has not presented itself in some shape or other.

SIR EDMUND HEAD, letter to Henry Labouchère, Jan. 26, 1856. [Pub. Rec. Off., C.O. 42/603]

That a general confederation of the Provinces of New Brunswick, Nova Scotia, Newfoundland and Prince Edward Island with Canada and the Western Territories, is most desirable, and calculated to promote their several and united interests, by preserving to each Province the uncontrolled management of its peculiar institutions, and of those internal affairs, respecting which differences of opinion might arise with other members of the Confederation, while it will increase that identity of feeling which pervades in possessions of the British Crown in North America.

> SIR ALEXANDER T. GALT, resolution moved in House of Assembly, Toronto, July 7, 1858.

That in view of the rapid development of the population and resources of Western Canada, irreconcilable difficulties present themselves to the maintenance of that equality which formed the basis of the Union of Upper and Lower Canada, and require this House to consider the means whereby the progress which has so happily characterized this province may not be arrested through the occurrence of sectional jealousies and dissensions. It is therefore the opinion of this House that the Union of Upper with Lower Canada should be changed from a Legislative to a Federative Union by the subdivision of the province into two more divisions, each governing itself in local and sectional matters, with a general legislature and government for subjects of national and common interest . . .

> SIR ALEXANDER T. GALT, resolution moved in House of Assembly, July 7, 1858 (*Votes and proc.*, 513).

Call upon them to tell you the details of their scheme, to show its working, to define the powers which they are willing to confer upon the central government; and at once you will discover that no two agree.

> GEORGE SHEPPARD, speech, Nov. 10, 1859, at meeting of the Liberal Convention of Upper Canada, Toronto, referring to the advocates of confederation.

Is this federation proposed as a step towards nationality? If so, I am with you. Federation implies nationality. For colonial purposes only it would be a needless incumbrance.

> GEORGE SHEPPARD, at convention of Upper Canada Reformers, Toronto, Nov., 1859.

I do place the question on the grounds of nationality. I do hope there is not one Canadian in this assembly who does not look forward with high hope to the day when these northern countries shall stand out among the nations of the world as one great Confederation . . . Who does not feel that to us rightfully belong the right and the duty of carrying the blessings of civilization throughout these boundless regions, and making our own country the highway of traffic to the Pacific?

> GEORGE BROWN, speech to Reform Convention, Toronto, Nov., 1859.

The only feasible scheme which represents itself to my mind as a remedy for the evils complained of, is a confederation of all the provinces. In speaking of a confederation, I must not be understood as alluding to it in the sense of the one on the other side of the line, for that has not been successful.

> SIR JOHN A. MACDONALD, speech in the Legislature, Apr. 19, 1861.

The union of all British America is not a question of gain with us; it is one of political *prestige* and nationality.

TORONTO *GLOBE* , Nov. 25, 1863, 2.

Any scheme that is to utilize the Maritime Provinces as make-weights for balancing the machinery of a new, untried, and more than doubtful expediency adapted to the exigencies of Canadian necessities is not likely, we fear, to find favour in any of the Lower Provinces.

JONATHAN MCCULLY, Halifax *Morning chronicle*, Aug. 4, 1864, 2.

Let the dog return to his vomit rather than Canada to division. In conclusion, I am pleased to think the day is rapidly approaching when the Provinces will be united, with one flag above our heads, one thought in all our bosoms, with one Sovereign and one constitution.

JOSEPH HOWE, speech in Halifax to leaders of Confederation from the Canadas, Aug. 13, 1864.

Who will oppose – who are now opposed to our union? Only those who have a vested interest in their own insignificance.

THOMAS D'A. MCGEE, "Prospects of the Union", remarks at Halifax, Aug. 14, 1864.

This question has now assumed a position that demands and commands the attention of all the colonies of British America. There may be obstructions, local prejudices may arise, disputes may occur, local jealousies may intervene, but it matters not – the wheel is now revolving and we are only the fly on the wheel; we cannot delay it – the union of the colonies of British America under the Sovereign is a fixed fact.

SIR JOHN A. MACDONALD, speech in Halifax, Sept. 12, 1864. The phrase "a fixed fact" was also used by S.L. Tilley in a letter to Francis Shanly, Dec. 20, 1864.

The main problems of government have been solved for us. The problem of a federal union has been worked out – a failure. The problem of a Legislative union has been worked out – a success.

S.E. DAWSON, Quebec *Morning chronicle*, Oct. 17, 1864, editorial.

Never was there such an opportunity as now for the birth of a nation.

S.E. DAWSON, Quebec *Morning chronicle*, Oct. 17, 1864, editorial.

All right!!! Constitution adopted – a most creditable document – a complete reform of all the abuses and injustices we have complained of!! Is it not wonderful? French Canadianism entirely extinguished!

GEORGE BROWN, letter, Oct. 27, 1864 to his wife. (Pub.Arch.Can.)

Shall we yield our independence –
    Fling our dearest rights away?
Shall we link our fate with a bankrupt
    State,
    And our native land betray?

ANON., "New Year's address to the friends and patrons of the Yarmouth *Tribune*", Jan. 1, 1865.

The Botheration Scheme.

JOSEPH HOWE, anti-Confederation letters, in Halifax *Morning chronicle*, Jan. 11 – Mar. 2, 1865, based on William Garvie's *Letters on confederation, botheration and political transmogrification*, (Halifax, 1865).

Although we have nominally a Legislative Union in Canada – although we sit in one Parliament, supposed constitutionally to represent the people without regard to sections or localities, yet we know, as a matter of fact, that since the union in 1841, we have had a Federal Union; that in matters affecting Upper Canada solely, members from that section claimed and generally exercised the right of exclusive legislation, while members from Lower Canada legislated in matters affecting only their own section. We have had a Federal Union in fact, though a Legislative Union in name.

SIR JOHN A. MACDONALD, *Confederation debates*, Feb. 6, 1865, 30.

The matter resolved itself into this, either we must obtain British North American Confederation or be absorbed in an American Confederation.

SIR GEORGE-ÉTIENNE CARTIER, *Confederation debates*, Feb. 7, 1865, 55.

Some entertained the opinion that it was unnecessary to have British North American confederation to prevent absorption into the vortex of American Confederation. Such parties were mistaken.

SIR GEORGE-ÉTIENNE CARTIER, *Confederation debates*, Feb. 7, 1865, 55.

We are in the rapids and must go on.

THOMAS D'A. MCGEE, *Confederation debates*, Feb. 8, 1865, 134.

Let us look at it in the light of a few months back – in the light of the evils and injustice to which it applies a remedy – in the light of the years of discord and strife we have spent in seeking for that remedy – in the light with which the people of Canada would regard this measure were it to be lost, and all the evils of past years to be brought back upon us again.

GEORGE BROWN, *Confederation debates*, Feb. 8, 1865, 115.

Events stronger than advocacy, events stronger than men, have come in at last like the fire behind the invisible writing to bring out the truth of these writings and to impress them upon the mind of every thoughtful man who has considered the position and probable future of these provinces.

THOMAS D'A. MCGEE, *Confederation debates*, Feb. 9, 1865, 127, on the previous advocates of federation.

I pronounced in favour of a Confederation of the two Provinces of Upper and Lower Canada as the best means of protecting the varied interests of the two sections. But the Confederation I advocated was a real Confederation, giving the largest powers to the local governments, and merely a delegated authority to the general Government.

ANTOINE-AIMÉ DORION, Leader of the Opposition, *Confederation debates*, Feb. 16, 1865, 250.

If this harness of the Confederation of the country is to be put on, we cannot but expect that it will chafe here and chafe there; but time will give relief and provide the remedy, as it has done in other circumstances before.

ALEXANDER CAMPBELL, *Confederation debates*, Feb. 17, 1865, 298.

I propose the adoption of the rainbow as our emblem. By the endless variety of its tints the rainbow will give an excellent idea of the diversity of races, religions, sentiments and interests of the different parts of the Confederation. By its slender and elongated form, the rainbow would afford a perfect representation of the geographical configuration of Confederation. By its lack of consistence – an image without substance – the rainbow would represent aptly the solidity of our Confederation. An emblem we must have, for every great empire has one; let us adopt the rainbow.

> HENRI G. JOLY, *Confederation debates* 1865, Feb. 20, 354.

Little Boy: "Father, what country do we live in?" Father: "My dear son, you have no country, for Mr. Tilley has sold us all to the Canadians for eighty cents a head."

> ANDREW R. WETMORE, New Brunswick election, Mar., 1865, imaginary dialogue between himself and his son told in his anti-Confederation speeches.

A plank of safety.

> MSGR. L.F. LAFLÈCHE, in letter to Boucher de Niverville, Mar. 2, 1865, qu. in J.W. Grant, *The church in the Canadian era*, 1972, 29. (Trans.)

Let us trust that this machinery, however faulty it may be, will yet under Providence open up for this country a happy career; while at the same time the House must not forget that it will for ever remove the great and crying evils and dissensions which have existed in Canada for the last ten years, and which have threatened to plunge the country into the most disastrous and lamentable state of discord and confusion.

> ALEXANDER T. GALT, *Confederation debates*, 1865, 71.

Messrs Tupper, Archibald and McCully, when the deed is done, may escape to Canada and stifle, as Arnold did, the reproofs of conscience amidst the excitements of a wider sphere and of more lucrative employment. But what is to become of the poor dupes who have been their accomplices in this dark transaction? Nineteen-twentieths of them will live and die at home, and all their lives must behold the averted faces of their indignant countrymen; and creep at last to dishonoured graves in the bosom of the province they have

betrayed, to poison the worms that consume them beneath the soil to which they were untrue.

> JOSEPH HOWE, "The Botheration papers", No. 9, 1865.

Prince Edward Island will have to come in, for if she does not we will have to tow her into the St. Lawrence.

> THOMAS D'ARCY MCGEE, 1865; attributed.

How they capered with the
    Parlez-vous
Till they kicked the buttons off their
    shoes,
Where'er they turned, on every hand,
They met the Wizard with his wand,
He sparkled in the ruby wine,
He glittered in the dresses fine,
He gleamed 'neath tresses all divine
Of ladies fair, 'tis no surmise,
He fairly dazzled in their eyes.
Yet there amid these scenes they laid
The cornerstone of what, they said,
Would make of us a mighty nation,
And christened it, "Confederation".

> ABRAHAM LINCOLN JR. (Pseud.), (Aspiring President of Confederation), "An abridged history of confederation", Sackville, (N.B.), *Borderer*, Mar. 17, 1865.

We are sold for the price of a sheepskin.

> JOSEPH HOWE, speeches in Nova Scotia, 1866. In the *Novascotian*, Aug. 13, 1866, he wrote that a visit of Tupper and Archibald to Ottawa to arrange a license system for American fishermen was really to sell the Nova Scotians for eighty cents a head, the per capita amount of the grant to Nova Scotia on entering Confederation. T.C. Haliburton, *Old judge*, 1849, ("Sheepskins and politics") uses the phrase, "Are you going to sell your country for a sheepskin?"

The days of isolation and dwarf-hood are past; henceforth we are a united people, and the greatness of each goes to swell the greatness of the whole.

HALIFAX *BRITISH COLONIST*, editorial, July 2, 1867.

In addressing for the first time the Parliamentary Representatives of the Dominion of Canada, I desire to give expression to my own deep feeling of gratification that it has been my high privilege to occupy an official position which has made it my duty to assist at every step taken in the creation of this great Confederation.

I congratulate you on the Legislative sanction which has been given by the Imperial Parliament, to the Act of Union, under the provisions of which we are now assembled, and which has laid the foundation of a new Nationality that I trust and believe will, ere long, extend its bounds from the Atlantic to the Pacific Ocean.

LORD MONCK, Governor General, Speech from the Throne, Senate, H. of C., *Debates*, Nov. 7, 1867, 5.

Born freemen, freemen we will die,
Part of a glorious nation;
Then let each loyal subject cry
"Confound Confederation!"

"FRED", "Anti Lyrics No. I", 1867, qu. in Halifax *Morning chronicle*, Dec. 24, 1867, 2.

If the Imperial Government should refuse our prayer, we shall then have to appeal to another nation to come to our aid.

MARTIN WILKINS, Attorney-General, N.S. House of Assembly, 1867, in an anti-Confederation speech.

We need above everything else the healing influence of time.

THOMAS D'A. MCGEE, speech in House of Commons, Apr. 5, 1868; on agitation in Nova Scotia for repeal of Confederation.

We will compel them to come in and accept this union, we will compel them by our fairness, our kindness, our love, to be one with us, in this common and this great national work.

THOMAS D'A. MCGEE, speech, House of Commons, Apr. 5, 1868; on agitation in Nova Scotia for repeal of Confederation.

No union on account of love need be looked for. The only bond of union outside of force — and force the Dominion has not — will be the material advantage of the country and pecuniary benefit of the inhabitants.

JOHN S. HELMCKEN, B.C., *Debates on confederation*, Mar. 9, 1870, 13.

Today British Columbia and Canada join hands and hearts across the Rocky Mountains.

VICTORIA *DAILY BRITISH COLONIST*, 20 July, 1871.

Confederation is only yet in the gristle, and it will require five years more before it hardens into bone.

SIR JOHN A. MACDONALD, letter to Sir John Rose, Mar. 5, 1872.

The immediate causes of Canadian Confederation were clearly enough the deadlock in the Canadian Parliament.

GOLDWIN SMITH, *Can. monthly*, Aug., 1872, 172; also, "The Father of Confederation was Deadlock", *The Bystander*, Apr., 1883, 86; also, "Whoever may claim to the parentage of Confederation — and upon this momentous question there has been much controversy — its real parent was Deadlock", *Canada and the Canadian question*, 1891, 143.

Awake, my country, the hour is great
with change!

> CHARLES G.D. ROBERTS, "Ode for the
> Canadian Confederacy", 1880.

The Provinces party to the bargain
were at the time of the compact
independent nations in the sense that
they enjoyed self-government subject
to the Imperial veto upon their legislation, to the Imperial appointment of
the Governor-General, and to the
Queen's command of the forces. The
Dominion was the creation of these
Provinces; or, in other words, was
created by the British Parliament at
the request of the Provinces. The
Dominion being non-existent at the
time the bargain was made, was plainly not a party to the bargain. It cannot
then, be a party to the revision of the
bargain.

> TORONTO *GLOBE* , Mar. 9, 1888.

The only means of maintaining Confederation is to recognize that, within
its sphere assigned to it by the constitution, each province is as independent of control by the federal Parliament as the latter is from control by
the provincial legislatures.

> SIR WILFRID LAURIER, in 1889, qu. in
> W.R. Lederman, *Courts and the Cana-
> dian constitution*, 1964, 49.

A great opportunity was lost in 1867
when the Dominion was formed out of
the several provinces. This remarkable
event in the history of the British
Empire, passed almost without notice.

> SIR JOHN A. MACDONALD, letter to Lord
> Knutsford, July 18, 1889.

Confederation is a compromise in itself, and without Confederation what
is Canada, where is it, or where would
it be?

> JAMES EDGAR, H. of C., *Debates*, Feb. 20,
> 1890, 900.

I have devoted my career to the
realization of an idea. I have taken the
work of Confederation where I found
it when I entered political life, and
determined to give to it my life, and
nothing will deter me from continuing
to the end in my task to preserve at all
price our civil liberty.

> SIR WILFRID LAURIER, speech before Club
> National, Montreal, Dec. 30, 1896.
> (Trans.)

Confederation is a compact, made
originally by four provinces but adhered to by all the nine provinces who
have entered it, and I submit to the
judgment of this house and to the best
consideration of its members, that this
compact should not be lightly altered.

> SIR WILFRID LAURIER, H. of C., *Debates*,
> 1907.

What has Confederation done for
Canada? What has Confederation not
done for Canada?

> EARL GREY, address, Canadian Club,
> Ottawa, Apr. 21, 1909.

Cartier required the support of the
Roman Catholic hierarchy of Quebec
to hold his personal position. Without
the support of the hierarchy confederation could not have been accomplished.

> SIR JOHN WILLISON, in *Federation of
> Canada 1867-1917*, 1917, 46.

I believe in the Canadian Confederation.

> SIR LOMER GOUIN, speech in Legislative
> Assembly, Quebec, Jan. 23, 1918.

To give to the central government,
which is drawn from the majority race
and the majority religion, the authority to interfere in the jurisdiction assigned to the provinces, is to destroy the
legislative independence of the provinces and make of it a snare and a
mockery.

SIR WILFRID LAURIER, letter to L.M. Gouin, July 18, 1918. (Trans.)

When McGee became its preaching friar from Sarnia to Halifax it was changed into a gospel rich in personal values and shot through with faith in personal redemption.

W.P.M. KENNEDY, in *Can. hist. rev.*, 1925, 167.

In the hearts and minds of the
    delegates who assembled
in this room on Sept. 1, 1864
was born the Dominion of Canada.

Providence being their guide
They builded better than they
    knew.

P.E.I. LEGISLATIVE CHAMBER. Inscription on plaque erected 1917, unveiled July, 1927, in Charlottetown; the quoted lines are from Milton, *Paradise lost*, book xii, and Emerson, "The problem" (adapted).

Confederation, indeed, was less the result of popular demand than the achievement of a few men of wide vision, impelled to their task by the political difficulties and the economic necessities of the provinces, spurred on by fears of foreign aggression, and helped in the hour of need by no inconsiderable support from Britain.

R.G. TROTTER, *Cambridge hist. Brit. Emp.; Canada*, 1930, 462.

Confederation itself, it will now be conceded, was almost a miracle.

CHESTER MARTIN, in *Can. hist. rev.*, 1937, 1.

Lacking materials out of which to reconstruct the story, or to discover how the scheme had come to be, historians have, almost to our own day, complacently accepted the stork theory of confederation.

W.M. WHITELAW, in *Can. hist. rev.*, 1938, 126.

Federation in 1867 became the instrument for westward expansion. It was the political expedient for bringing the West under the control of the St. Lawrence Valley.

R.G. RIDDELL, in *Can. hist. rev.*, 1940, 270.

Confederation was brought about to increase the wealth of Central Canada, and until that original purpose is altered, and the concentration of wealth and population by national policy in Central Canada ceases, Confederation must remain an instrument of injustice.

W.L. MORTON, *Univ. of Tor. quart.*, XV, 1946, 232.

Confederation was the constitutional instrument designed to permit Canada, the province, to re-establish an agricultural frontier to which it would have an exclusive *entrée*.

V.C. FOWKE, *Canadian agricultural policy*, 1946, 140.

It was the greatest blessing from God, next to life itself, ever conferred upon the people of Newfoundland.

JOSEPH SMALLWOOD, Premier of Newfoundland, to Peter C. Newman, qu. in *Maclean's*, Sept. 24, 1960, 2.

True confederation would be a psychological catastrophe for the French-Canadians.

MARCEL CHAPUT, *Why I am a separatist*, 1962, 46.

Confederation, the graveyard of minorities!

MARCEL CHAPUT, *Why I am a separatist*, 1962, 73.

Will a dynamic, progressive society place Quebec on the same footing as the rest of Canada? Then, and only then, shall we find out whether Confederation was really a hoax.

> FERNAND OUELLET, *Liberté*, IV, Mar. 21, 1962, 112. (Trans.)

Confederation may not have been technically a treaty or a compact between states, but it was an understanding or a settlement between the two founding races of Canada made on the basis of an acceptable and equal partnership.

> LESTER B. PEARSON, H. of C., *Debates*, Dec. 17, 1962, 2723.

It is wrong to say that Confederation has been a total failure for French Canadians; the truth is rather that they have never really tried to make a success of it. In Quebec we tended to fall back upon a sterile, negative, provincial autonomy; in Ottawa our frequent abstentions encouraged paternalistic centralism.

> PIERRE E. TRUDEAU, *Federalism and the French Canadians*, 1968, 31 (orig. pub. anon., 1965).

Confederation has been like a mail-order bra: intended to contain and uplift, it has instead drawn attention to the cleavage.

> ERIC NICOL, *100 years of what?*, 1966, 42.

Is this the end of Canada?

> MONTREAL *SEPT-JOURS*, No. 14, Dec. 17, 1966; title of an issue devoted to problems of Confederation. (Trans.)

For those who built this land
  With courage and endurance,
We laud and bless thy name;
  Be thou their sons' assurance;
Proud of the days of yore,
  From sea to sea we stand
For freedom's heritage
  In Canada our land.

> R.B.Y. SCOTT, winning Centennial hymn in contest conducted by the Canadian Council of Churches, 1967.

Confederation was a "pact".

> EUGENE FORSEY, paraphrase of a common statement, dismissed as one of the seven devils of our pseudo-history in "Our present discontents", speech, Acadia Univ., Oct. 19, 1967.

Confederation has been a political union of several provinces, not a cultural compact between the two ethnic communities, English and French.

> DONALD CREIGHTON, *Canada's first century*, 1970, 353.

Confederation Centennial 1967

Canada is going through a mental depression at present which is having a worse effect upon us than the economic depression of the 1930's. As we approach the centenary of Confederation we are numbed by the realization that we seem to have lost whatever inspiring or unifying sense we may once have had of a common national purpose.

> FRANK H. UNDERHILL, Toronto *Star*, Oct. 8, 1966, 7.

O God our Heavenly Father
We lift our hearts to Thee.
In thankfulness and gladness
We sing from sea to sea;
For Thou hast richly blessed us
With countless gifts of love,
And always Thou hast showered us
With mercies from above.

REV. KENNETH MOYER, centennial hymn chosen by the Canadian Interfaith Conference, qu. in *Globe and Mail*, Dec. 3, 1966, 48.

CA-NA-DA – We love Thee –
(One little two little three little
Canadians)
CA-NA-DA – Proud and Free –
(Now we are Twenty Million)
North, South, East, West,
(Four little five little six little
Provinces)
There'll be Happy Times,
(Now we are ten and the Territories
Sea to Sea)
Church Bells will Ring, Ring Ring –
(Un petit deux petits trois Canadiens)
It's the Hundredth Anniversary of
Confederation,
(Maintenant nous sommes Vingt
Millions)
Everybody Sing. Together.

BOBBY GIMBY, "Canada: A Centennial song", 1966.

For Centennial Year, send President Johnson a gift: an American tourist's ear in a matchbox. Even better, don't bother with the postage.

RAY SMITH, *Tamarack rev.*, Autumn, 1967, 53.

Confederation, Fathers of

Among the Ministers I made many friends – John (usually called Jack) Macdonald, Sir Francis Hincks, Sir William [sic] M'Nab, Cartier, Brown a journalist, and several others. All able men with unlimited powers of consuming champagne.

SIR EDMUND HORNBY, (1854), *Autobiography*, 1928, 64.

The Fathers of Confederation.

ANON., popular term applied to the 33 delegates at the Quebec conference, Oct., 1864.

Theirs was the vision, theirs the faith
far-seeing,
And theirs the force that forged our
unity,
That called a nation into instant being
And stretched its boundaries from
sea to sea.

CHARLES G.D. ROBERTS, "These three score years", read at New Brunswick celebration of Canada's Diamond Jubilee, Fredericton, July 1, 1927.

If Macdonald is entitled to be called the Father of Confederation it would appear that Alexander Hamilton has some claim to be designated as its grandfather.

W.B. MUNRO, *Amer. influences on Can. govt.*, 1929, 20.

Statesmen they were by every fair test; but they were politicians too – politicians resourceful and not too scrupulous.

J.W. DAFOE, in *Can. hist. rev.*, 1932, 52.

[Thomas] Dalton has been called the godfather of Confederation, as he was one of the first Colonial writers to urge a federation of the provinces.

R. CARD, in *Can. hist. rev.*, 1935, 177.

The intentions of the Fathers of Confederation . . . have in fact been largely frustrated by judicial decision, especially those of Lord Haldane, who might very suitably be termed the Step-father of Confederation.

E. FORSEY, *Can. journ. econ. and pol. sci.*, 1936, 596.

The only living father of Confederation.

ANON., term used in 1950's in reference to Premier Joseph Smallwood of Newfoundland, which joined Canada Apr. 1, 1949.

Confidence

Confidence reposed in a third party is always hazardous, and generally betrayed.

SUSANNA MOODIE, *Geoffrey Moncton*, 1855, 183.

If the Prime Minister ever again says Canadians lack confidence, I'll give him a kick in the pants.

CONN SMYTHE, television interview, May 3, 1967, after Toronto Maple Leafs won the Stanley Cup.

You can show other people your scratches, but not your wounds.

RICHARD J. NEEDHAM, *A friend in Needham*, 1969, 10.

Conflict

There is no conflict that love or bullets Could not resolve in time.

GEORGE JONAS, "Peace", 1962.

Conformity

The diffused fear in which we live sterilizes everything we do. If we write, all our propositions must be justifiable before potential inquisitors; if we act, all our acts must be measured by the traditional standards, i.e., they must be repetitions. So, we choose the safest path: Say nothing, think nothing.

JEAN-PAUL DESBIENS, *Les insolences du Frère Untel*, 1960, 67. (Trans.)

I want to be a non-conformist, like everybody else.

ANON., Vancouver teen-ager, quoted by Mamie Moloney, Vancouver *Sun* columnist qu. in *Liberty*, Aug., 1962.

Confusion

I am confused, therefore I am.

JACK LUDWIG, *Confusions*, 1963, 33.

Conquest

Perhaps the most durable conquest is the incomplete one.

ARNOLD HAULTAIN, *Hints for lovers*, 1909, 134.

The Conquest, 1759

Happy Laurentia, to thy farthest
    shore,
    Lavish of life, a chosen band she
    led;
And to those royal towers her standard
    bore,
    Whence fell Oppression, Gallic
    tyrant, fled.

W.H. REYNALL, in *Pietas universitatis Oxoniensis* . . . . 1761.

Some are for keeping Canada, some Guadaloupe. Who will tell me which I shall be hanged for not keeping.

WILLIAM PITT, attributed, qu. in H. Neatby, *Quebec, the revolutionary age, 1760-1791*, 1966, 7.

The peace is made, My Very Dear Brothers, for the well-being of humanity.

MONSEIGNOR J.F. PERREAULT, of Three Rivers, *Mandement*, May 26, 1763. (Trans.)

He who has conquered by force has only half vanquished his enemy.

FRANÇOIS-XAVIER GARNEAU, about 1826, to the English clerks in the office of Archibald Campbell, a Quebec notary.

Half the continent had changed hands at the scratch of a pen.

> FRANCIS PARKMAN, *Montcalm and Wolfe*, 1884, Vol. II, 376, on Vaudreuil's capitulation of Montreal, Sept., 1760.

The statement that has been made so often that this is a conquered country is *à propos de rien*. Whether it was conquered or ceded, we have a constitution now under which all British subjects are in a position of absolute equality having equal rights of every kind – of language, of religion, of property and of person. There is no paramount race in this country; we are all British subjects, and those who are not English are none the less British subjects on that account.

> SIR JOHN A. MACDONALD, H. of C., *Debates*, Feb. 17, 1890, 745.

A happier calamity never befell a people than the conquest of Canada by the British arms.

> FRANCIS PARKMAN; attributed.

The lilies withered where the Lion trod.

> OLIVER WENDELL HOLMES, "Francis Parkman", Nov., 1893.

The wound of 1760 has never closed completely.

> ABBÉ LIONEL GROULX, *La France d'outre-mer*, 1922, 30. (Trans.)

The catastrophe of 1760.

> ABBÉ LIONEL GROULX, *Notre maître, le passé*, 1944, 162. (Trans.)

The conquest of 1760 was the cause of a social disintegration.

> PHILIPPE GARIGUE, *L'option politique du Canada Français*, 1963, 9. (Trans.)

The Conquest dominates English-Canadian nationalism, just as it does French-Canadian nationalism, giving the former a sense of belonging to the winning side, the latter a yearning for lost glories. The Conquest, then, is the burden of Canadian history.

> RAMSAY COOK, *Canada and the French-Canadian question*, 1966, 146.

Conscience

Conscience is that within us that tells us when our neighbours are going wrong.

> PETER MCARTHUR, d. 1924, qu. in *The best of Peter McArthur*, 1967, 231.

Your conscience is what your mother told you before you were six years old.

> BROCK CHISHOLM, qu. *Maclean's* Jan. 15, 1946, 9.

Conscience: self-esteem with a halo.

> IRVING LAYTON, "Aphs", *The whole bloody bird*, 1969, 79.

Consciousness

Cosmic consciousness, then, is a higher form of consciousness than that possessed by the ordinary man.

> RICHARD M. BUCKE, *Cosmic consciousness*, 1901, 1.

I like to think that subconscious Canada is even more important than conscious Canada and that there is growing up swiftly in this country, under the surface, the sense of a great future and of a great separate destiny – as Canada.

> JOHN GRIERSON, qu. in F. Hardy, ed., *Grierson on documentary*, 1946, 247.

Conscription, Military

The volunteers themselves found how ineffective the voluntary system was, and how unfairly it worked. While they were not only undergoing the hardships and dangers of campaigning, but were also suffering financial loss, their stay-at-home fellow-countrymen, whom they were defending, were making money and were at ease in Zion.

ANON., 1870, in *Can. hist. rev.*, 1923, 101.

We have never ceased to say that a tax-of-blood is the logical and inevitable consequence of the principles and acts imposed by the two parties who have in turn ruled this country. The germ of Conscription was contained in the volunteer expedition to South Africa.

HENRI BOURASSA, in *Le Devoir*, May 29, 1917. (Trans.)

We will resist Conscription and we will not have Conscription, not because we are cowards, but because we have received from God and the King the mission of making of this country a prosperous land and not one of exile and misery.

HENRI BOURASSA, speech in Montreal, June 7, 1917. (Trans.)

We need conscription, not only of bodies but of wealth, to strike the blow at war-lordism. The new democracy is coming, paid for in blood, when men shall come more directly into their own.

JOSEPH ATKINSON, Toronto *Daily star*, address at Newcastle, Ont., Aug., 1917.

The basic principle of the State is compulsion. This is fundamental in its entire organization. It runs through every system of law, both civil and criminal, through practically all the conventions of society; without it law, order, system and organization could not exist.

SIR JAMES LOUGHEED, Senate, *Debates*, Aug. 3, 1917, on Conscription.

The racial chasm which is now opening at our feet may perhaps not be overcome for many generations.

SIR WILFRID LAURIER, letter to A.B. Aylesworth, Oct. 16, 1917. (Pub. Arch. Can.)

Parliament, according to my belief, has no mandate to vote conscription. I do not myself believe that I am held to conform to the said law, and I have no intention of so doing, and I ask the population not to conform, knowing full well what I am doing presently and to what I expose myself. If the government wants a mandate for conscription, let it come before the people, without this time fooling them.

CAMILLIEN HOUDE, Mayor of Montreal, referring to National Registration. Statement at press conference, Montreal, Aug. 2, 1940, qu. by R.B. Hanson in H. of C., *Debates*, Aug. 3, 1940, 2402.

Conscript wealth as well as men.

CANADIAN COMMONWEALTH FEDERATION, Campaign slogan, Jan.-Feb., 1942; see *Saturday night*, Mar. 7, 1942, 26.

If we have to conscript wealth to win the war we will. But people of common sense do not advocate that until the last gasp.

ARTHUR MEIGHEN, election speech while running for membership in H. of C. by-election in York South, 1942.

Are you in favour of releasing the Government from any obligation arising out of any past commitments restricting the methods of raising men for military service?

> CANADA. GOVERNMENT, question put to Canadian electorate in plebiscite, Apr. 27, 1942.

If, in reference to the very difficult question of service overseas, anyone can conceive of a policy which is better calculated to serve the national interest, than the one the government has formulated, and which is clearly and concisely expressed in the words: "Not necessarily conscription, but conscription if necessary," I shall be first to advocate its acceptance.

> W.L. MACKENZIE KING, H. of C., *Debates*, July 7, 1942, 4011; probably adapted from editorial, Toronto *Star*, June 11, 1942.

Conservation

The father of the conservation movement on the continent.

> MINNEAPOLIS *JOURNAL*, 1906, qu. in *Jack Miner, his life and religion*, (1969) xlv, ref. to Jack Miner.

The best and the most highly economic development and exploitation in the interests of the people can only take place by having regard to the principles of conservation.

> SIR CLIFFORD SIFTON, inaugural address, Commission of Conservation, Ottawa, Jan. 18, 1910.

If we go on as we are, we will destroy in the next century everything that the poets have been singing about for the past two thousand years.

> FRED BODSWORTH, qu. in Royal Bank of Canada, *Monthly letter*, June, 1967.

The challenge of wilderness travel in Canada is two-edged: the personal challenge to *explore,* and the public challenge to *preserve* – while yet we are able.

> ERIC W. MORSE, *Wilderness Canada*, ed. by Borden Spears, 1970, 55.

Conservatism

It is well known, sir, that while I have always been a member of what is called the Conservative party, I could never have been called a Tory, although there is no man who more respects what is called old-fogey Toryism than I do, so long as it is based upon principle.

> SIR JOHN A. MACDONALD, speech in St. Thomas, 1860.

The Conservative, who defends his country's old institutions, may do much good, as he also may do much evil, if he be obstinate in maintaining abuses, which have become intolerable.

> SIR WILFRID LAURIER, speech to Club Canadien, Quebec, June 26, 1877. (Trans.)

Conservatism and old fogeyism are totally different things; the motto of the one is, "Prove all things, and hold fast that which is good," and of the other, "Prove nothing but hold fast that which is old".

> SIR WILLIAM OSLER, "Importance of postgraduate study", in *Lancet*, July 14, 1900, 75.

The very word conservative means that we conserve all that is good; that we reject all that is bad, and we must use our intelligence, our intellect, our training for the purpose of determining what we shall reject and what we shall conserve and retain.

R.B. BENNETT, paper read at First Annual Liberal-Conservative Summer School, Pickering College, Newmarket, Ont., 1933.

I believe that the essential characteristic which identifies the Conservative is his belief that there is and must be an underlying moral and spiritual content to all political philosophy and action if it is to have lasting value.

E. DAVIE FULTON, address, Young Progressive Conservatives, Toronto, Mar. 19, 1960.

As Canadians we attempted a ridiculous task in trying to build a conservative nation in the age of progress, on a continent we share with the most dynamic nation on earth. The current of modern history was against us.

GEORGE P. GRANT, *Lament for a nation*, 1965, 68.

To express conservatism in Canada means *de facto* to justify the continuing rule of the business man and the right of the greedy to turn all activities into sources of personal gain. The conservative idea of law has often been in the mouths of the capitalists, but seldom in their actions.

GEORGE P. GRANT, *Philosophy in the mass age*, 1966, 109.

Conservative Party

Never did we see such an assemblage of long-visaged Tories. They appeared as if they were following the hearse of conservatism to the grave.

BATHURST *COURIER* , Feb. 5, 1836, on the departure of Sir John Colborne from Toronto.

There would be a new house and new people to choose from, and our aim should be to enlarge the bounds of our party so as to embrace every person desirous of being counted as a "progressive Conservative", and who will join in a series of measures to put an end to the corruption which has ruined the present Government and debauched all its followers.

SIR JOHN A. MACDONALD, letter to Capt. James McGill Strachan, Feb. 9, 1854. (Pub.Arch.Can.)

The party nowhere – damned, everlastingly damned.

SIR JOHN A. MACDONALD, 1854, qu. in letter by A. Campbell, Pub. Arch. of Can., *Macdonald papers*, Mar. 8, 1855.

So pray do become true blue at once: it is a good standing colour and bears washing.

SIR JOHN A. MACDONALD, to Sir Alexander T. Galt, letter, Nov. 2, 1857.

The heart of the average Tory is deceitful above all thengs and desperately wecked.

ALEXANDER MACKENZIE, Prime Minister, speech at Clinton, Ont., July 5, 1878. (Contemporary reflection of Scottish burr.)

A fully circumcized Conservative.

SIR WILLIAM VAN HORNE, qu. by Sir John A. Macdonald letter to H.H. Smith, Mar. 3, 1884, referring to the employment of conservatives on the C.P.R.

We say no matter what your antecedents are, whether you are an old Tory, a Baldwin Reformer, or whatever you were in the past, if you honestly and conscientiously agree with us and our policy for the country in the future, we stretch out to you the right hand of fellowship and greet you as a Liberal-Conservative or a Conservative-Liberal.

SIR JOHN A. MACDONALD, qu., *Willison's monthly*, 1927, 84, about 1885.

If there is one thing to which the Conservative party has been true in the past; if there is one thing to which I hope it will be true in the future, it is the unity of the races in Canada.

ROBERT L. BORDEN, speech in Ottawa, Mar. 1, 1901.

In Quebec the Conservative Party is a pretty lively corpse.

J.G.H. BERGERON, speech in Toronto, Dec. 14, 1905.

Failing principles the Conservatives fell back on personalities.

STEPHEN LEACOCK, *National rev.*, Jan., 1909.

Looking again to the future, and bringing up the past only to shed its light, let me say: There will be more danger on the side of the party itself than on the side of the leader you will choose. Even here at this Convention the supreme consideration is not: who shall be the leader of the party? The supreme consideration is: what manner of party shall he have to lead?

ARTHUR MEIGHEN, speech at Winnipeg Conservative Convention, Oct. 10, 1927.

For a long time the Conservatives had a corner on superiority and, for a long time, a corner on patriotism. I mean one's devotion to one's country was always an open question, unless one is a Conservative and an Anglican. If you are a Conservative, a Methodist and an Orangeman, you can get by.

AGNES MACPHAIL, speech to Canadian Club, Toronto, Mar. 4, 1935.

The Conservative Party must stand for all that its name implies. The word "Conservative" suggests stability and security at a time when the whole world longs for stability and security. The word implies sound business methods as opposed to radical experiments. In a world gone mad the word "Conservative" offers hope of common sense and orderly progress. It is a word which carries into the realm of practical politics the Biblical injunction "prove all things; hold fast that which is good".

GEORGE DREW, speech in Toronto, Apr. 17, 1940.

Well, I nearly got my fingers burned.

SIDNEY E. SMITH, on his last minute withdrawal as a candidate for leadership at the Conservative Party Convention, Winnipeg, Dec., 1942.

The P.C. Member says time spent wooing support in Quebec is wasted.

FINANCIAL POST, Aug. 27, 1954, editorial. Erroneous interpretation of Gordon Churchill's conclusion that to win a federal election the Conservatives must increase support in Ontario to balance Liberal support in Que. See also Hugh McLennan, *Maclean's*, Dec., 1964, 55, "When Gordon Churchill followed this up with his now-famous boast that his party had proved it possible to form a government without depending on Quebec for a single seat, the lid blew off in La Belle Province and the separatist movement was born"; and John D. Harbron, *Queen's quarterly*, Autumn, 1962, 354, "Churchill had said the party could win without Quebec".

Tonight we've kicked it off. We've lit the flame. Now we've got to wrap it up real big and send that li'l ole' Liberal Party packin'!

JOEL ALDRED, at start of election campaign, Massey Hall, Toronto, Apr. 25, 1957.

The electorate was persuaded by sheer repetition that Conservative leadership was inherently deficient and that Conservative governments could do little but harm, Liberal governments nothing but good.

> J.M. BECK, *Government of Nova Scotia*, 1957, 164, referring to Nova Scotia.

I vote with the Tories but dine with the Grits.

> GRATTAN O'LEARY, qu. in *Maclean's*, June 7, 1958, 65.

The Conservative Party's problems were, as always, insurmountable, its policies insufferable, and its prospects invisible.

> PETER NEWMAN, *Renegade in power*, 1963, 48, termed "a hoary epithet".

The Conservative Party is building on the ruins of the future.

> ANON., a Dominican Friar, to a member of E.A. Goodman's staff, Conservative Centennial Convention, Montmorency Conference, Courville, Que., Aug. 7-10, 1967.

Conservatives

Good conservatives reluctantly backing into the twentieth century.

> FRANK H. UNDERHILL, "Critically speaking", C.B.C. broadcast, Oct. 31, 1954, referring to Hilda Neatby and Donald Creighton.

The only protection a Conservative enjoyed in the province of Saskatchewan was under the provisions of the game laws.

> JOHN G. DIEFENBAKER, H. of C., *Debates*, Apr. 29, 1966, 4542, referring to 1950's.

Consistency

The man who is consistent must be out of touch with reality. There is no consistency in the course of events — in history, in the weather, or in the mental attitude of one's fellow men.

> LORD BEAVERBROOK, qu. by Alan Wood, *The true history of Lord Beaverbrook*, 1965, 157.

(Pattern I deny
and that
is part of a pattern).

> GEORGE BOWERING, "Circus maximus", 1966.

Consistency is the most important quality in guiding a child. Sincere affection can compensate for inevitable lapses in operation, but "love" without consistency is a dangerous indulgence.

> WILLIAM E. BLATZ, *Human security*, 1966, 7.

No Canadian is more inconsistent than he who follows one party consistently.

> ANON., qu. in James M. Beck, *Pendulum of power*, 1968, 100.

Constitution

That it is desirable to give the Canadians a constitution in every respect like the constitution of Great Britain, I will not say, but I earnestly hope that they will enjoy as much of our laws and as much of our constitution as may be beneficial for that country, and safe for this.

> LORD NORTH, H. of C. (London), *Debates*, 1774, 248, ed. by Cavendish.

This province is singularly blessed, not with a mutilated Constitution, but with a Constitution which has stood the test of experience, and is the very image and transcript of that of Great Britain.

> JOHN GRAVES SIMCOE, Lieut.-Gov., at close of first Upper Canada legislature session, Oct. 15, 1792.

The Constitution, the *whole* Constitution, and *nothing but* the Constitution.

> JOSEPH HOWE, *Novascotian*, Jan. 3, 1828, motto on masthead.

Preserve the balance of the constitution for your life.

> T.C. HALIBURTON, *Sam Slick*, 1838, 58.

We want not only the Constitution, but as regards the administration of our local affairs, the whole Constitution and nothing but the Constitution.

> ROBERT BALDWIN, speech to Reform Association, Mar. 25, 1844; the motto of the Brockville *Gazette* (1828-32) was, "The Constitution, the whole Constitution, and nothing but the Constitution".

Not one hair's breadth farther do we go, or desire to go: but not with one hair's breadth short of that will we ever be satisfied.

> ROBERT BALDWIN, reference to the English constitution, on objects of the Reform Association, founded, Toronto, 1844.

In framing the constitution care should be taken to avoid the mistakes and weaknesses of the United States system, the primary error of which was the reservation to the different states of all powers not delegated to the general government. We must reverse this process by establishing a strong central government to which shall belong all powers not specially conferred on the provinces. Canada, in my opinion, is better off as she stands than she would be as a member of a con-

federacy composed of five sovereign states, which would be the result if the powers of the local governments were not defined. A strong central government is indispensable to the success of the experiment we are trying.

> SIR JOHN A. MACDONALD, speech at Quebec Conference, Oct. 11, 1864.

The primary error at the formation of their constitution was that each state reserved to itself all sovereign rights, save the small portion delegated. We must reverse this process by strengthening the General Government and conferring on the Provincial bodies only such powers as may be required for local purposes.

> SIR JOHN A. MACDONALD, B.N.A. Discussions in Conference, Quebec, Oct. 15, 1864; J. Pope, *Confederation*, 1895, 54, referring to U.S. Constitution.

If the Delegates will survive the lavish hospitality of this great country, they will have good constitutions – perhaps better than the one they are manufacturing for the Confederation.

> EDWARD WHELAN, Charlottetown *Examiner*, Oct. 17, 1864, reporting on the Quebec Conference.

The ink was scarcely dry upon our Constitution when we began to think constitutionally. We began to think federally.

> G.W. ROSS, Empire Club, Toronto, speech, May 12, 1905.

The Canadian Confederation, as I have shown, is the result of a contract between the two races, French and English in Canada, treating on an equal footing and recognizing equal rights and reciprocal obligations. The Canadian Confederation will last only to the extent that the equality of rights will be recognized as the basis of public law in Canada, from Halifax to Vancouver.

HENRI BOURASSA, *La langue française et l'avenir de notre race*, 1913, 15. (Trans.)

Canada stands practically alone in modern, self-governing, democratic countries in her inability to change her constitution in accordance with what may be the development of political thought.

SIR CLIFFORD SIFTON, in *Can. hist. rev.*, 1922, 9.

Whenever Mr. King is out of power the constitution is in danger.

ARTHUR MEIGHEN, federal election campaign, July, 1926.

I often think what a difference it would have made if I had accepted the brief from the federal government in place of that of the provincial government. I'm in no doubt I'd have won it; and that might have altered the whole subsequent constitutional evolution of authority in the Dominion. Now I am sorry that I wasn't on the other side.

LORD HALDANE, to Gen. A.G.L. McNaughton in 1927, qu. in John Swettenham, *McNaughton*, 1968, Vol. 1, 232.

The most serious specific threat to any orderly kind of future for Canada lies in the nature of our Constitution. The "property and civil rights" clause of section 92 of the British North America Act will make short work of our war-time measures and will very quickly reduce us to the bedlam of provincialism again. Can any sane person believe that ten competing authorities, mostly parochial, will give us anything but anarchy leading perhaps to revolution?

A.R.M. LOWER, *War and reconstruction*, 1942, vi.

Preposterous as it may seem, no one knows where the constitution begins or ends.

H. MCD. CLOKIE, in *Can. jour. econ. and pol. sci.*, 1942, 1.

The only condition needed to modify the constitution, either at once or gradually, is the existence of dynamic forces capable of winning public opinion to their side.

GILLES MERCURE, *Le Devoir*, Nov. 17, 1956, 13. (Trans.)

I do not think that the dead hand of the past should be allowed to stay the onward march of progress. Human rights are sacred but constitutions are not.

T.C. DOUGLAS, *Globe and Mail*, Apr. 13, 1966, 7.

In Saskatchewan, if we had a hundred problems, the constitution would be the one hundred and first.

ROSS THATCHER, speech at Toronto, Confederation of Tomorrow Conference, Nov., 1967.

Associate state.

ANON., a concept based on representation by nation instead of by population to give Quebec complete political equality, supported by various leaders, 1967.

If we open the constitution, it will be a can of worms.

PIERRE E. TRUDEAU, news conference, Toronto, June 23, 1971, quoting remark he made in mid 1960's.

I'm a One Canada man and I've always been a One Canada man. I say the same thing from coast to coast. When I put my foot on the dog's tail in Halifax, it barks right in Vancouver.

RÉAL CAOUETTE, qu. in Toronto *Star*, Oct. 7, 1971, 4.

The Victoria Charter.

ANON., Constitutional proposals of June, 1971 on political and language rights, etc. resulting from a conference in Victoria, B.C.

Constitution, British

You know my enthusiasm respecting the constitution of England. Every encomium I ever read in its favour is short of my idea of its perfection: . . . of all modes of government I pronounce it to be the best.

CHIEF JUSTICE WM. SMITH, letter to B. Watson, Oct. 24, 1788 (Pub. Arch.)

So much for the wisdom of giving a British Constitution to men who can neither read nor write, and who are mulish enough to refuse and kick at those who ought to lead.

LORD DALHOUSIE, letter, May 5, 1822.

As I advance in years I appreciate the more the wisdom of that British Constitution under which I was born and brought up, and under which I have grown old, which has given to the various portions of the Empire their separate free governments.

SIR WILFRID LAURIER, address at Tercentenary Celebration, Quebec, 1908.

It is a strange mystical sort of thing, this British Constitution that we love. It is partly unwritten; it is partly written. It finds its beginnings in the lore of the past; it comes into being in the form of custom and tradition; it is founded upon the common law. It is made up of precedents, of magna chartas, of petitions and bills of rights; it is to be found partly in statutes, and partly in the usages and practices of Parliament. It represents the highest achievement of British genius at its best.

W.L. MACKENZIE KING, speech, Ottawa, July 23, 1926.

Consumers

If everyone would but *consume*
I'll *bet* there'd be a business boom.

D.M. ROBINSON, "Happiness preferred", 1938.

If Canadians are determined to emulate the Americans as consumers, then Canadians will have to pay the inevitable price, which has come to be equally conspicuous environmental deterioration, and the gradual, but certain erosion of collective and individual choice.

JOHN A. LIVINGSTON, *Ontario naturalist*, Dec., 1970, 10.

Contact

We've created a society in which, if you touch another person, you apologize.

RICHARD J. NEEDHAM, *A friend in Needham*, 1969, 41.

Contentment

In nature one is content with enough; in civilization one is never content.

BLISS CARMAN, *The kinship of nature*, 1903, 167.

Contentment consists largely in not wanting something that is out of your reach.

ROBERT C. (BOB) EDWARDS, Calgary *Eye Opener*, Feb. 11, 1913.

True contentment comes from within. It dominates circumstance. It is resignation wedded to philosophy; a Christian quality seldom attained except by the old.

ROBERT SERVICE, *Ballads of a Bohemian*, 1921, 140.

Content is something men pursue
When all the time it follows you –
Till breathlessly you stand apart
And find it steeping in your heart.

> AL PURDY, "Blind", 1944.

On such a wet and blustery night as
this
May each man have his flame and
house and food,
From pain his freedom now, as Mercy
is,
And in his natural thought to count his
good.

> RALPH GUSTAFSON, "On such a wet and
> blustery night", 1960.

Continentalism

We are ourselves an American people
geographically and commercially,
though we retain our British connection; our situation is continental, and
our politics, in the large and best sense,
must needs be continental.

> THOMAS D'A. MCGEE, speech in London,
> Ont., Sept. 26, 1861.

I should say that, if a man had a great
heart within him, he would rather look
forward to the day when, from that
point of land which is habitable nearest to the Pole, to the shores of the
Great Gulf, the whole of that vast
continent might become one great
confederation of States.

> JOHN BRIGHT, speech, Rochdale, Eng.,
> Dec. 4, 1861.

I see one vast confederation stretching
from the frozen North in unbroken
line to the glowing South, and from
the wild billows of the Atlantic westward to the calmer waters of the
Pacific main, – and I see one people,
and one language, and one law, and
one faith, and, over all that wide
continent, the home of freedom, and a
refuge for the oppressed of every race
and of every clime.

> JOHN BRIGHT, speech, Birmingham,
> Eng., Dec. 18, 1862.

The Liberals are the continental, their
opponents the anti-continental party.

> GOLDWIN SMITH, in *The Bystander*,
> May, 1890.

The continent is an economic whole,
to run a Customs line athwart it and
try to sever its members from each
other is to wage a desperate war
against nature. Each several Province
of the Dominion is by nature wedded
to a commercial partner on the south,
though a perverse policy struggles to
divorce them.

> GOLDWIN SMITH, *Canada and the Cana-
> dian question*, 1891, 284.

We must decide whether the spirit of
Canadianism or of Continentalism
shall prevail on the northern half of
this continent. To-day Canada is the
mistress of her destiny. She commands
both the Atlantic and the Pacific; she
holds the highway of the world.

> ROBERT L. BORDEN, election message to
> the people of Canada, issued at St. John,
> N.B., Sept. 20, 1911, re: reciprocity
> agreement.

If I were to offer, not a definition, but
a working description of an alert Canadian citizen just now, I could say he
is one (man or woman) increasingly
aware of being North American in the
continental sense without being American in the national sense.

> ARTHUR L. PHELPS, speech at Univ. of
> New Brunswick, Feb. 18, 1947, *Com-
> munity and culture*, 10.

I felt sure that the long objective of the
Americans was to control this Continent. They would want to get Canada
under their aegis.

> W.L. MACKENZIE KING, *The Mackenzie
> King record*, IV, 269; to Hume Wrong,
> Mar. 30, 1948.

Continentalism, for good or ill, is triumphant.

> ROBIN W. WINKS, *Canada and the United States: the Civil War years*, 1960, 380.

Every prospect for further economic development open to Canada appears to carry with it, as an inescapable consequence, increasing integration in a continental economy in which the United States must be the dominant partner.

> HUGH G.J. AITKEN, *American capital and Canadian resources*, 1961, 15.

For Canada cosmopolitanism and internationalism mean, in fact, continentalism. Opening our frontiers to the world means in practise opening them to the United States. A policy of cultural laissez-faire means, *not* that we subject ourselves to a wide variety of ideas emanating from a host of different sources bearing in upon us with equal intensity. Inevitably, owing to the sheer size and weight and proximity of the American cultural establishment, it means that we are subjected to one set of ideas emanating from one source.

> ALLAN SMITH, "An open letter on nationalism and the universities in Canada", no date, distributed privately, qu. in I. Lumsden, ed. *Close the 49th parallel, etc.*, 1970, 176.

Continentalism had divorced Canadians from their history, crippled their creative capacity, and left them without the power to fashion a new future for themselves.

> DONALD G. CREIGHTON, *Canada's first century, 1867-1967*, 1970, 355.

The new dominance of ethnic values in Canadian domestic politics and the resulting outbreak of cultural conflict had destroyed national unity at the moment when it was desperately needed. The review of the Canadian constitution, begun in confusion and irresolution, with conflicting purposes and no common goal in sight, was likely to end in futility; and the failure of this unavailing effort was certain to bring continentalism one long stage forward towards its final triumph.

> DONALD G. CREIGHTON, *Canada's first century, 1867-1967*, 1970, 356.

Contrariness

Your treason is my reason,
Your poison is my raisin.

> ROBERT FINCH, "The five", 1946.

Convention

What are orthodox methods? They're rules adopted by old-established outfits to prevent young new outfits from making money. Well, I couldn't afford to be orthodox when I was young: I had to make money! Now, of course, it's different, I can afford to follow the rules. Now I've made a lot of money and I'm hell-bent on convention!

> ROY THOMSON, about 1949, qu. in Russell Braddon, *Roy Thomson of Fleet Street*, 1965, 154.

Conventions, like clichés, have a way of surviving their own usefulness. They are then excused or defended as the idioms of living. For everyone, foreign by birth or by nature, convention is a mark of fluency. That is why, for any woman, marriage is the idiom of life.

> JANE RULE, *The desert of the heart*, 1964, 7.

Conversation

Conversation is more than half the time a refuge from thought or a blind to conceal it.

> T.C. HALIBURTON, *Sam Slick's wise saws*, 1853, I, 161.

The commonest and cheapest of all pleasures is conversation. It is the greatest past-time of life.

> EMILY MURPHY, "Janey Canuck's Motto", Edmonton *Bulletin*, 1920's, qu. in B.H. Sanders, *Emily Murphy*, 1945, 326.

There are two things in ordinary conversation which ordinary people dislike — information and wit.

> STEPHEN LEACOCK, "Are witty women attractive to men", *Last leaves*, 1945, 3.

Conversation has more vitality, more fun and more drama than writing. What I say is being used as a probe and it's not a package. I'm probing around without making special pronouncements. Most people say things as the result of thinking, but I use it to probe.

> MARSHALL MCLUHAN, qu. in *Weekend mag.*, Mar. 18, 1967, 4.

Make love, make money, make war; but please, please, don't ever make conversation.

> RICHARD J. NEEDHAM, *A friend in Needham*, 1969, 14.

Converts

It is easier to make an infidel than a convert.

> T.C. HALIBURTON, *Nature and human nature*, 1855, II, 145.

Conviction

Let me say to you that you should never let your religious convictions be affected by the acts of men. Your convictions are immortal. Their foundation is eternal. Let your convictions be always calm, serene, and superior to the inevitable trials of life. Show to the world that Catholicism is compatible with the exercise of liberty in its highest sense; show that the Catholics of this country will render to God what is God's, to Caesar what is Caesar's.

> SIR WILFRID LAURIER, speech to Young Liberals, Montreal, Dec. 1896, qu. by Mason Wade in C.T. Bissell, ed., *Our living tradition*, Ser. 1, 1957, 101.

One must be most careful in drawing an inference in a criminal case. It must not be a mere guess or suspicion. A man is not to be convicted on a guess, however shrewd that guess may be. It must be an inference which the mind naturally and logically draws from the proven facts.

> JUSTICE JACK SISSONS, R. v. Kyd (1957) 23 *Western weekly reports*, 648.

Cooking

I feel a recipe is only a theme, which an intelligent cook can play each time with a variation.

> JEHANE BENOIT, *Encyclopédie de la cuisine Canadienne*, 1963, 12. (Trans.)

One thing we did prove conclusively: there *is* a Canadian cuisine, and it is unique in all the world.

> SALLY HENRY and others, *Laura Secord Canadian cook book*, (Canadian Home Economics Assoc.) 1966, intro.

Cooperation

Co-operation is not a one-way street.

> MAURICE DUPLESSIS, favourite phrase used in speeches as Premier of Quebec, 1936-39, 1944-59.

C.C.F.

No C.C.F. Government will rest content until it has eradicated capitalism and put into operation the full program of socialized planning which will lead to the establishment in Canada of the Co-operative Commonwealth.

> CO-OPERATIVE COMMONWEALTH FEDERATION, *Regina Manifesto*, 1933. This clause was eliminated at C.C.F. National Convention, Winnipeg, 1956.

One is constrained to marvel at the confidence of those who undertake the regeneration of society by act of Parliament.

> ALL-CANADIAN CONGRESS OF LABOUR, *Can. unionist*, Vol. VII, No. 3, Aug., 1933, 36.

We aim to replace the present capitalist system, with its inherent injustice and inhumanity, by a social order from which the domination and exploitation of one class by another will be eliminated, in which economic planning will supersede unregulated private enterprise and competition, and in which genuine democratic self-government, based upon economic equality will be possible.

> CO-OPERATIVE COMMONWEALTH FEDERATION, *Regina Manifesto*, 1933.

Again and again we have stated that we have no connection whatever with the Communist party.

> JAMES S. WOODSWORTH, H. of C., *Debates*, Feb. 5, 1934, 265.

The political arm of labour in Canada.

> CANADIAN CONGRESS OF LABOUR, term used to describe the C.C.F. at annual convention, 1943.

For most of its history the role of the C.C.F. has been that of a voice crying in the wilderness, a conscience informing, animating, goading old parties into some overdue reforms.

> ANDREW BREWIN, *Can. forum*, Oct., 1943, 150.

If we are to retain the democratic control of our elected representatives we must apply ourselves to the task of setting up the kind of machinery that will allow every C.C.F. member the opportunity and the responsibility of having some part in formulating government policy.

> T.C. DOUGLAS, C.C.F. Convention, *Minutes*, 1950.

Co-operatives

There are still moments at meetings of Canadian agriculturalists when one feels that co-operation is a veneer; when the women are in the room the apprehension vanishes.

> C.R. FAY, *Co-op. at home and abroad*, 1924.

True co-operation is wrung out of the bitter need of the weak.

> H. MICHELL, in *Can. jour. econ. and pol. sci.*, 1937, 410.

For co-operatives, as for all organizations involved in community education and development, the task is unending. Having once begun it, we can never be done with it.

> A.F. LAIDLAW, in James A. Draper, ed., *Citizen participation: Canada*, 1971, 328.

Corporations

It is no part of a newspaper's function to defend a corporation: it is always able to defend itself.

SIR CLIFFORD SIFTON, frequently said to John W. Dafoe, about 1900.

It has been difficult not to be impressed by the fact that the corporate form of business not only gives freedom from legal liability, but also facilitates the evasion of moral responsibility for inequitable and uneconomic practices.

CANADA. ROY. COMM. ON PRICE SPREADS, *Report*, 1934.

The large corporation dominating its field, and aided by some sort of government regulation or support, runs straight through the heart of Canadian history.

WILLIAM KILBOURN, *The elements combined*, 1960, 82.

Corporations and not doctrinaire socialism are the wave of the future.

GEORGE P. GRANT, *Lament for a nation*, 1965, 92.

New Brunswick is the outstanding example of conglomerate ownership.

SENATE. SPECIAL COMMITTEE ON MASS MEDIA. *Report*, Vol. 1, 1970, 70.

Multi-national corporations are a phenomenon of the contemporary economy; they are here to stay and it is necessary to adjust to this fact. A country like Canada cannot be first in everything if it is not to endanger its standard of living. It has to make a choice.

GERARD FILION, President, Canadian Manufacturers' Association, qu. in *Industrial Canada*, June, 1971, 13.

Corporate welfare bums.

DAVID LEWIS, New Democratic Party leader, phrase used at various times during federal election campaign, Sept., 1972 in reference to "many major Canadian companies".

Corporatism

Corporate arrangements are a thousand times preferable to cartels or to direct State control over the economy. Corporative rules are adopted openly, with the consent of a majority of the interested parties, under the supervision of both public authorities and of groups responsible for protecting the consumers.

MAXIMILIEN CARON, *L'organisation corporative au service de la démocratie*, 1942, 24. (Trans.)

Corruption

Down with Rolph and Malcolm Cameron. We can stand anything else − we can stand Toryism, we can stand Sir Allan McNab and John A. Macdonald, but we cannot stand Rolph. Corrupt may be Sir Allan McNab and steeped to the chin in Toryism, and John A. Macdonald may be following in his footsteps, a budding Tory at least − they are not bad fellows, however, for Tories − but put down Rolph and Cameron.

TORONTO *GLOBE* , during election 1851; Rolph and Cameron were Clear Grits.

They have Walpoles in the ministry, not Pitts; the government is steeped to the very lips in infamy; they are tainted with corruption, collectively and individually, both in their public and private characters. All honour has gone from them, and all loyalty even to one another; and the only bond by which they are held together now is the bond of common plunder.

> SIR JOHN A. MACDONALD, speech on address from the throne, Legis. Assembly, 1854; origin of the phrase, "steeped to the lips in corruption".

Corruption pervades every tissue of our society.

> SIR WILFRID LAURIER, letter to Blake, Dec. 7, 1881.

Another mistake which our leaders make is this – they seem to think the people are pure. It is a great mistake; they are as corrupt as the government that represents them at Ottawa. Until the Reformers can score one against Sir John by superior low cunning, they will be beaten at the elections.

> "CONSTANT READER", in the Toronto Globe, May, 1882.

The name of Peter McGonigle will ever stand high on the roll of eminent confiscators.

> ROBERT C. (BOB) EDWARDS, Calgary Eye Opener, Oct. 6, 1906.

I shall allow no man to make an attack on me or my character without retorting. I shall discuss the character of Honourable members opposite whether they be Ministers or private members and their connection with wine, women and graft.

> GEORGE W. FOWLER, H. of C., Debates, Feb. 19, 1907, in answer to remarks by Duncan Ross, M.P.; this led subsequently to the resignation of a cabinet minister.

Men, as a rule, do not and cannot rise above the level of their general environment; and under our form of party government, if one side becomes corrupt, more especially if after proof of its corruption it is successful for a time, it is pretty certain to corrupt a great many of the other side also, or at any rate to lower the whole tone of public life.

> SIR RICHARD CARTWRIGHT, Reminiscences, 1912, 199.

Whether I paid Members of Parliament or government officials, and I'm not saying which, certainly it was somebody powerful enough to push the Immigration Department around.

> ONOFRIO MINAUDO, Sicilian Mafia member, later deported, to Mack Lang, Toronto Telegram, 1964; qu. in G. Donaldson, Fifteen men, 1969, 227.

Inventive, ingenious, incompetent and corrupt, Morgan, and Morgan alone, drove Atlantic forward to catastrophe and, like all the well-known swindlers of history, he did so with a fatalistic and cynical disregard of those principles of fair and honest dealing which have been generally accepted and adhered to for generations in both the civilized and savage world.

> JUSTICE S.H.S. HUGHES, Ontario. Royal commission appointed to inquire into the failure of Atlantic Acceptance Corporation Ltd., Report, 1969, Vol. 3, 1519. Reference is to C. Powell Morgan.

The thing which amazes me is that I know perfectly well, as a historian, that there is corruption in any government – there's always corruption. It's bad when it's more than fifteen percent.

> MICHEL BRUNET, interview with R. Cook, in The craft of history, 1973, 74.

Cosmetics

Blue is the colour of your true love's
   hair
And green her eyes are lidded,
And red her lips beyond compare,
And all her toe-nails – ibid.

> PAUL HIEBERT, Willows revisited, 1967, 66; "Dolling up", by Wraitha Dovecote, associate of Sarah Binks.

Cosmopolitan

For I am of that forlorn hope
  That is the only hope of man, –
From corner stone to curve and cope
  I am a cosmopolitan!

> GEORGE F. CAMERON, "Proem", 1873.

Costs

We are like the child of some stock-
broker who can enjoy the fruits of his
father's endeavours by living the
swinging life, but likes to exclude from
his mind where the money comes
from.

> GEORGE P. GRANT, *Lament for a nation,*
> 1970, Introd., ix.

Coughing

"God", he said when he could speak
again, "I'm going to fetch up the
callouses off the soles of my feet in one
of those spells".

> ROBERTSON DAVIES, *Leaven of malice,*
> 1954, 210.

Coup D'Etat

The *coup d'état* is an attempt to
change the government by a sudden
sharp attack against the actual machinery of administration. Under the proper conditions, a comparatively small
number of determined men can capture the state at low cost.

> D.J. GOODSPEED, *The conspirators,* 1962,
> ix.

Courage

A brave man is sometimes a
  desperado.
A bully is always a coward.

> T.C. HALIBURTON, *Sam Slick's wise saws,*
> 1853, I, 105.

Be hooted and hissed by the mob,
  From pillar to post be driven,
Be sneered at by every snob:
  Of such is the kingdom of heaven.

> ALEXANDER MCLACHLAN, "Cowardice",
> 1900.

Strong for the red rage of battle;
  sane, for I harry them sore;
Send me men girt for the combat,
  men who are grit to the core.

> ROBERT SERVICE, "The law of the Yu-
> kon", 1907.

If there were no cowards there would
be no bullies.

> GEORGE ILES, *Canadian stories,* 1918,
> 170.

Courage, cleanliness, charity:
  Hold by these to the end of the
    tether,
For only these may lead us free:
  We who are all in the mud together.

> TOM MACINNES, "Ballade of virtues",
> 1918.

There are times when it requires more
courage to stand still than to go forward.

> JOHN OLIVER, when Premier of B.C.,
> 1918-27.

We who have trod the borderlands of
  death,
Where courage high walks hand in
  hand with fear,
Shall we not hearken what the Spirit
  saith:
'All ye were brothers there, be
  brothers here'?

> CANON FREDERICK G. SCOTT, "The un-
> broken line", 1922.

Courage is something you have only
when you're young. It's a part of good
health and good looks and the feeling
that no evil ever can touch you.

> THOMAS H. RADDALL, "The golden age",
> in *A muster of arms,* 1954, 22.

When the world comes up to you snarling and threatening, stand your ground and spit in its face. It will then apologize, draw back, and meekly ask if there's anything it can do to help you.

RICHARD J. NEEDHAM, *A friend in Needham*, 1969, 7.

To live with courage is a virtue, whatever one may think of the dominant assumptions of the age.

GEORGE P. GRANT, in Eli Mandel, ed., *Contexts of Canadian criticism*, 1971, 121.

Courts

I never allow a point of law to be raised. This is a court of justice, not a court of law.

GEORGE T. DENISON, Toronto Police Magistrate, qu. in J.F. Fraser, *Canada as it is*, 1905, 51.

In the Court-house one learns sad things, terrible things that may not be written down on paper, and that many would fear to read. One feels that nothing can ever thrive again which is good or pure.

EMILY MURPHY "Janey Canuck", Police Magistrate in Edmonton, qu. in B.H. Sanders, *Emily Murphy, crusader*, 1945, 149.

The whole effect of the Court is devoted to *changing the child's mind*. Restraint must come from within.

JUDGE HELEN GREGORY MACGILL, late 1920's, qu. in E.G.M. MacGill, *My mother, the judge*, 1955, 207.

Ninety-five per cent of the people are guilty as charged. Those cases that are thrown out are thrown out mostly on evidentiary gaps in the Crown's case.

ANON., a prosecutor, qu. in B.A. Grosman, *The prosecutor*, 1969, 63.

Courtship

It gives to women's curiosity a curious pleasure to compare the methods of men's proposals.

ARNOLD HAULTAIN, *Hints for lovers*, 1909, 115.

A man imagines he wins by strenuous assault. The woman knows the victory was due to surrender.

ARNOLD HAULTAIN, *Hints for lovers*, 1909, 125.

By what men are won, most women seem thoroughly to comprehend. By what women are won, few men know. Perhaps, No woman knows by what she herself is won.

ARNOLD HAULTAIN, *Hints for lovers*, 1909, 132.

Cows

And the ladies dress in silk
From the proceeds of the milk,
But those who buy their butter,
How dear it is, they mutter.

JAMES MCINTYRE, "Oxford cheese makers song", 1884.

When potatoes were in blossom,
    When the new hay filled the mows,
Sweet the paths we trod together,
    Bringing home the cows.

CHARLES G.D. ROBERTS, "Bringing home the cows", 1893.

Their bodies glisten sharply red,
With shaggy brow and curving horn,
Large waggling ear, grass-bending head.
With dainty hoof and solemn lurch
They munch along their quiet search.

ALAN CREIGHTON, "Pastoral", 1936.

Nothing improves the value of a cow so much as to cross it with a C.N.R. locomotive.

> DONALD GORDON, paraphrase of remark to Canadian Club luncheon, qu. in P. Newman, *Flame of power*, 1959, 205.

Hast milk to spare, o cow, then let
The lacteal bounty flow for me,
And give in unrestricted jet
The vitamins from A to G.

> PAUL HIEBERT, "Hast milk to spare", 1967.

Cows are together so much they must be nearly
all lesbians fondling each other's dugs by moonlight.

> AL PURDY, "The winemaker's beat-étude", 1968.

Cradles

O God, do Thou bless the houses where the cradle is held in honour! Bless those hearths where many a birth comes to cheer the ancient cradle and bring it perpetual youth! Bless the family who hold in reverence the virtues of former days, to the glory of our Church and of our country!

> ADJUTOR RIVARD, *Chez nous*, 1914, 21. (Trans.)

Craigellachie, B.C.

I wasn't there, I was too busy.

> SIR HERBERT HOLT, explaining his absence from "last spike" ceremony, Nov. 7, 1885.

Creativity

It cannot be denied that a vast and disproportionate amount of material coming from a single alien source may stifle rather than stimulate our own creative effort; and, passively accepted without any standard of comparison, this may weaken critical faculties.

> CANADA. ROYAL COMM. ON NATIONAL DEVELOPMENT IN THE ARTS, LETTERS AND SCIENCES, *Report*, 1951, 18.

this made-ness out of self-madness
thrown across their bones to keep them warm

> PHYLLIS WEBB, "Making", 1962.

Passionate human love, the scenes of nature,
agony of bringing into life
child or thought or shaped colour –
these triumph over our lives' horror.

> R.G. EVERSON, "Credo", 1963.

that the full belly means only
further hungers, that we cannot now return
to younger appetites, that we can no longer
eat the bright-ancestral food,
that we alone must set out table single-handed,
that we alone must account for the grease of our spoons.

> GWENDOLYN MACEWEN, "Strange breakfasts", 1963.

We espouse this freedom of expression because of a conviction, supported by experience, that individual creativity, whether in the arts or in the humanities or in science or in technology, constitutes our social capital; in art, it gives measure to our culture.

> JUSTICE BORA LASKIN, *Can. crim. cases*, 1966, 305.

There's words enough, paint and brushes enough, and thoughts enough. The whole difficulty seems to be getting the thoughts clear enough, making them stand still long enough to be fitted with words and paint. They are so elusive, like wild birds singing above your head, twittering close beside you, chortling in front of you, but gone the moment you put out a hand.

> EMILY CARR, *Hundreds and thousands*, 1966, 264.

A good workman removes his scaffolding.

> ANON., qu. by J.A. Boudreau in *Can.hist. rev.*, Vol. 48, 1967, 373.

I touch you, I am created in you
somewhere as a complex
filament of light

> MARGARET ATWOOD, "I was reading a scientific article", 1968.

Creative life is a dynamic bridge between opposites.

> LAWREN HARRIS, in Bess Harris and R.G.P. Colgrove, eds., *Lawren Harris*, 1969, 4.

A sane people whom the gods visit, not very often, with moments of creative madness.

> GEORGE WOODCOCK, *Canada and the Canadians*, 1970, 96.

Credit

Credit should be used to exploit success; not to reinforce failure.

> W.A. JENKINS, Chairman, Nova Scotia Land Settlement Board, commenting on loans to farmers, qu. in *Liberty*, Nov., 1962.

My fortune is as large as my credit rating, and my credit rating is limitless.

> ROY THOMSON, qu. in Russell Braddon, *Roy Thomson of Fleet Street*, 1965, 138.

Credit Cards

Money is a poor man's credit card.

> MARSHALL MCLUHAN, to Peter C. Newman, qu. in *Maclean's*, June, 1971, 42.

Credos

I am not interested in politics. I am here in Ottawa as Prime Minister today and I may be gone tomorrow. I don't care. Life has given me about everything a man can desire. I am sixty-one, old enough to sit back and enjoy what I have but what I have I owe in a considerable degree to Canada and if I can do anything for Canada, that is what I want to do.

> RICHARD B. BENNETT, in Oct., 1931, qu. in C. Ondaatje, *Prime Ministers of Canada 1867-1967*, 1967, 122.

Moved by un unshakable faith in God, a profound love for Canada, ardent sentiments of patriotism and nationalism, a complete loyalty and devotion toward our Gracious Sovereign who forms the recognized principle of active authority, a complete respect for the British North America Act, for the maintenance of order, for national prosperity, for national unity, for national honour, for the progress and happiness of a greater Canada, I pledge solemnly and explicitly to serve my Party.

> CANADIAN NATIONALIST PARTY (Fascist), Pledge recited at meetings, 1930's.

The shadows of evening lengthen about me, but morning is in my heart. I have lived from the forties of one century to the thirties of the next. I have had varied fields of labour, and full contact with men and things, and I have warmed both hands before the fire of life. The rich spoils of memory are mine. Mine, too, are the precious things of today — books, flowers, pictures, Nature and sports . . . The best thing of all is friends. The best of life is always farther on . . .

> SIR WILLIAM MULOCK, on retiring as Chief Justice of Ontario on his 93rd birthday, Jan. 19, 1936.

It is the seas I have not sailed
That beat against my breast,
It is the heights I have not scaled
That will not let me rest,
It is the paths I have not gone
That tempt my restless feet,
It is the flowers I have not known
That are forever sweet,
It is the lips I have not kissed
That lure my soul astray,
It is the voice my soul has missed
That calls me night and day.

LIONEL FORSYTH, qu in P. Newman,
Flame of power, 1959, 136.

Fortune came and fortune fled; but,
believe in my sincerity when I say that
this is no reason for sympathy. It is
only the lot of all of us, at least of all
who strive – the joy of the upward
struggle, the successes, disappointments and defeats. Perhaps it has been
my fate to have had more than the
average on both sides of the account,
but I promise you there is going to be
nothing of bitterness carried forward
after the page is turned.

ARTHUR MEIGHEN, address, Conservative
Convention, Winnipeg, Dec. 9, 1942.

I believe in Canada, with pride in her
    past, belief
in her present and faith in her future.
    I believe in the quality of Canadian
    life, and in the
character of Canadian institutions.
    I believe in the Commonwealth of
    Nations within
whose bounds we have found freedom,
    and outside which
our national life would lose its
    independent being.
    I believe in our abiding friendship
    with our nearest
neighbours; an honest friendship
    without either the
subservience or the mimicry which
    must impair true partnership.
    I believe that Canada is one, and

that if our minds
dwell on those things which its parts
    have in common,
we can find the unity of the whole.
    I believe that with sound work, the
    spirit of a team,
and an awareness of ourselves, we can
    look forward to
achievements beyond our imagining.

VINCENT MASSEY, *On being Canadian*,
1948, 184-5.

Life, if you have a bent for it, is a
beautiful thing. It consists, I do believe, of having a sense of urgency.

C.L. BURTON, *A sense of urgency*, 1952,
25.

There are two principles on which I
stake my life. "He who will try to save
his life will lose it"; and "All things are
possible to them that truly love."
Within this exciting paradox of belief I
walk happily.

DR. MARION HILLIARD, *A woman doctor
looks at love and life*, 1957, 13.

The world is my country
The human race is my race
The spirit of man is my God
The future of man is my heaven.

F.R. SCOTT, "Creed", 1964.

Essence? analyse the metal
    constituents:
nickel-steel, imposed form – but I
    keep thinking
of mineral molecules before and after
    they got there,
the lyric rubble mind that holds and
    joins –
Mind that gets bloody tired! – you,
    too, reader
need shock after shock – for myself
    continuous discovery
else in the midst of somnolence: defeat
    after defeat.

AL PURDY, "Mind process re a faucet",
1966.

I can never receive a gift.
I work for my pay, exist for my
   statistics,
Love for my love and might die for
   my life.
I resent being understood.
I dislike.

> GEORGE JONAS, "I dislike", 1967.

I had done it by hard work and long hours, by making it evident that I was available for whatever was to be done; by welcoming every opportunity for new and more responsible duties; and by accumulating all the experience possible in all the varied aspects of my profession.

> LESTER B. PEARSON, *Mike*, Vol. 1, 1972, 282.

Credulity

This is yet the childhood of the world, and a supine credulity is still the most charming characteristic of man.

> SIR WILLIAM OSLER, address, "Recent advances in medicine", Baltimore, Feb. 22, 1891.

Crime

The crimes and passions of most men are alike, with only this difference, that some have greater art of concealing them.

> SUSANNA MOODIE, *Geoffrey Moncton*, 1855, 101.

Inadequate Penalties put a premium on crime.

> J.W. BENGOUGH, *The prohibition Aesop*, about 1896, 17.

He had broken the law. How he had come to do so, it passed his imagination to recall. Crime always seems impossible in retrospect.

> STEPHEN LEACOCK, "The hostelry of Mr. Smith", *Sunshine sketches of a little town*, 1912, 12.

Steal a loaf of bread, and you can get two years of nineteenth-century prison life; cut a couple of children down in a brakeless car while driving drunk without a license, and you might get two weeks in the "local", with time off for good behaviour.

> HAROLD TOWN, *Enigmas*, 1964 [2].

It was almost a beautiful thing, what she did.

> GARY LANE, hairdresser, on his friend, Kathleen Ann Spiller's stealing of $492,000 from the Royal Bank in Penticton, B.C., 1968, qu. in *Maclean's*, Feb., 1969, 77.

The alarmed discussion of swiftly rising crime rates is simply not warranted by those few increases which are the exception rather than the rule. It would be more appropriate to refer to sharply rising rates of parking tickets, although this would not coincide with popular notions of a crime wave.

> LYNN MCDONALD, *Can. rev. of sociol. and anthrop.*, Vol. 6, 1969, 223.

Crises

In unforseen crises man alone has the perfect intelligence; man alone is lord of himself; man alone knows what to do, and what to say.

> J.J. PROCTER, *The philosopher in the clearing*, 1897, 55.

All that we have seen and heard has led us to the conviction that Canada is in the most critical period of its history since Confederation. We believe that there is a crisis, in the sense that Canada has come to a time when decisions must be taken and developments must occur leading either to its break-up, or to a new set of conditions for its future existence.

> CANADA. ROY. COMM. ON BILINGUALISM AND BICULTURALISM, *Prelim. report*, 1965, 133.

A crisis has never been avoided by silence. A confrontation is always the only way to bring an issue to a head.

JOHN TURNER, speech, Montreal Reform Club, Oct. 16, 1967.

Criticism

Not only the bitterest words, but the most direct and pointed personalities are justifiable in the exposure of public crime.

ROBERT GOURLAY, *Statistical account of Upper Canada*, 1822, ccxxxlv.

As regards Canadian literary criticism, it is woefully lacking in scholarship, poise and judicial discrimination. All our goslings are swans.

THOMAS O'HAGAN, *Can. bookman*, June, 1927, 169.

True feeling is critical as well as honest thought.

JOHN MACNAUGHTON, *Essays*, 1946.

A public that tries to do without criticism, and asserts that it knows what it wants or likes, brutalizes the arts and loses its cultural memory.

NORTHROP FRYE, *Anatomy of criticism*, 1957, Intro.

Art for art's sake is a retreat from criticism which ends in an impoverishment of civilized life itself. The only way to forestall the work of criticism is through censorship, which has the same relation to criticism that lynching has to justice.

NORTHROP FRYE, *Anatomy of criticism*, 1957, Intro.

Criticism can talk, and all the arts are dumb.

NORTHROP FRYE, *Anatomy of criticism*, 1957, 4.

Criticism is to art what history is to action and philosophy to wisdom.

NORTHROP FRYE, *Anatomy of criticism*, 1957, 12.

Literal understanding occupies the same place in criticism that observation, the direct exposure of the mind to nature, has in the scientific method.

NORTHROP FRYE, *Anatomy of criticism*, 1957, 77.

Criticism becomes more sensible when it realizes that it has nothing to do with rejection, only with recognition.

NORTHROP FRYE, *Anatomy of criticism*, 1957.

I think that any kind of literary criticism that purports to be more than an honest expression of what a particular reader feels about a particular book is a sham.

ALDEN NOWLAN, *Fiddlehead*, Spring, 1960, 42.

Informed public criticism of any government policy, especially one of some complexity, is highly desirable, but it is important to note the source of criticism.

H.E. ENGLISH, in T.N. Brewis et al., *Canadian economic policy*, 1961, 45.

There is no simple correspondence between an objective record of political, social, and economic events, on the one hand, and on the other, a criticism of the arts, whose creation and appreciation are suffused with subjectivity.

ROY DANIELLS, in C.F. Klinck, ed., *Literary history of Canada*, 1965, 193.

Parody is also criticism.

GEORGE WOODCOCK, "The selective poet" (Turning new leaves), in *Can. forum*, Aug., 1966, 115.

Nothing is a criticism that is not a comment on something *qua* performance, and anything whatever is a performance in so far as it is a potential object of criticism, and is taken as a performance in so far as it is criticized or taken to be subject to criticism.

F.E. SPARSHOTT, *The concept of criticism*, 1967, 42.

Painful self-criticism as opposed to defensive self-depreciation has never been a very important feature of Canadian life.

DONALD CAMERON, *Faces of Leacock*, 1967, 173.

The only criticism that is worth anything is the kind that tells the writer something he didn't know about his own work.

ALDEN NOWLAN, letter to Anne Greer, 1967, qu. in *Fiddlehead*, Aug., 1969, 22.

The better poets of every age seem all the same size to contemporaries: it takes many years before the comparative standards become clear and contemporary critics may as well accept the myopia which their near-sighted perspective forces on them.

NORTHROP FRYE, *The bush garden*, 1971, 126.

Like poetry criticism may tell lies and yet provide us with the only memory we can have and which, if we are to survive, we must possess.

ELI MANDEL, *Contexts of Canadian criticism*, 1971, 25.

There is an instinctive unwillingness on the part of critics and readers in established cultures to yield a place in the sun to artists on the periphery, or to admit that they really can meet the competition.

HUGH MACLENNAN, speech, University of British Columbia, Mar. 3, 1973.

His criticism was an unconscious reflection of imperialist attitudes to Canadians in general, a hostility towards whatever is stubbornly different in our culture, and a contempt for what cannot be evaluated in American terms.

EARLE BIRNEY, on an American critic, "Epilogue", in B. Nesbitt ed., *Earle Birney*, 1974, 209.

Critics

Bow down, ye scribes, before the
    mighty *Week,*
Malicious vendor of the base critique,
Lean Egotist, that claims the right
    divine
To whip the slavish scribblers into line.

ALEXANDER C. STEWART, *The poetical review*, 1896, 20; Goldwin Smith was editor of *The Week.*

The critic who discovers a flaw in Canadian literature is considered very clever; but the critic who discovers genius in our poetry or prose is immediately taunted with nationalistic prejudice.

WILSON MACDONALD, in *Open house*, ed. by W.A. Deacon and W. Reeves, 1931, 147.

The Critic, Sir, the Critic is to blame
Who with insulting clemency misuses
One rule for home, and one for
    foreign, muses.

I.A. MACKAY, "And spoil the child", 1931.

The Canadian critic, when he emerges, will have a wider task to embrace; he will have to be something of a psychologist, something of a sociologist, something of a philosopher, something of a mythologist, besides having a developed consciousness of formal values and an imagination that is both creative and receptive.

GEORGE WOODCOCK, *Dalhousie rev.*, Autumn, 1955, 222.

The beauty of being a critic
is that one can write as if one were
　　infallible
and be forever wrong.
For if one makes a howling error
of judgment such as casting talent
aside, or throwing obloquy
on genius, or praising an ass
one can forget, later, like one's readers
and praise what one called a bore
as infallibly as before.

　　LOUIS DUDEK, "A cornet for critics",
　　1958.

Conservative critics seem to have a
nostalgia for Paradise, a hope of returning to the innocence of Eden,
unbiting the bite and hanging the
apple once again on the bough of the
Tree of Knowledge. They would have
us unlearn all that has been learned,
forget Cézanne, Braque and Picasso,
the Bauhaus, Freud and Jung, chemistry, photography, electronics and nuclear physics.

　　ROBERT AYRE, in Malcolm Ross, ed., The
　　arts in Canada, 1958, 17.

The critic is the public's friend.
From lofty summits we descend
To answer the eternal question:
Is it Art or Indigestion?

　　MAVOR MOORE, "The critic", And what
　　do you do?, 1960, 15.

The conscientious Canadian critic is
one who subscribes to The New York
Times so that he knows at first hand
what his opinion should be.

　　ERIC NICOL, A scar is born, 1968, 85.

The outstanding quality of the average
Canadian reviewer might be described
as failure of nerve. When confronted
with the spanking new literature of his
own country he tends to be timorous,
hesitant or evasive; or, at the opposite
extreme, he becomes truculent, contemptuous or vitriolic.

　　PHYLLIS GROSSKURTH, in Can. lit., No.
　　46, 1970, 56.

Crowds

Give me a meeting or assembly of
men, whether it be small or large, and
in that meeting I will find passions and
prejudices, noble in themselves, but
which can be easily excited into dangerous passions and prejudices.

　　SIR WILFRID LAURIER, H. of C., Debates,
　　Feb. 17, 1890.

The Crown

If it (the Crown) has to carry on the
government in unison with a representative body, it must consent to
carry it on by means of those in whom
that representative body has confidence.

　　LORD DURHAM, Report, 1839; ed. Lucas,
　　1912, Vol. II, 278.

Disguise it how you may, the idea that
underlies this plan is this, and nothing
else – that we are to create here a
something – kingdom, vice-royalty or
principality – something that will
soon stand in the same position towards the British Crown that Scotland
and Ireland stood in before they were
legislatively united with England; a
something having no other tie to the
Empire than the one tie of fealty to
the British Crown.

　　CHRISTOPHER DUNKIN, Confederation
　　debates, 1865, 527.

It must be remembered the sovereign
holds a two-fold position; that the
sovereign is not only the first branch of
the legislature, and as such has a right
to inquire into such matters, but is also
the head of the executive and is the
executive. The crown governs the
country; the crown chooses its own

ministers, and this house has no control, and the Senate has no control over the crown in this respect, except in deciding whether they have confidence in the ministers chosen.

> SIR JOHN A. MACDONALD, H. of C., *Debates*, Nov. 3, 1873.

The proper basis of the British Empire was that it was to be composed of a galaxy of nations under the British Crown.

> SIR WILFRID LAURIER, H. of C., *Debates*, Dec. 2, 1907, 42.

The Crown is the supreme executive in the United Kingdom and in all the Dominions, but it acts on the advice of different Ministries with different constitutional units; and under Resolution IX of the Imperial War Conference, 1917, the organization of the Empire is to be based upon equality of nationhood.

> SIR ROBERT BORDEN, Memorandum circulated on behalf of the Dominion Prime Ministers, at the Paris peace conference, Mar. 12, 1919.

When the remaining steps have been completed, the relations of the Six Kingdoms to one another will be that of a Personal Union. There will be no longer one dominant state and five subordinate states. All will be equal. And our people must learn what that means. They must become familiar with the idea of a divisible King, a King with several crowns, a King with several sets of advisers to whom he pays equal deference and by whom he is separately guided – possibly in conflicting directions.

> JOHN S. EWART, *Independence papers*, 1930, Vol. 11, 337.

The authority of the Government is not delegated by the House of Commons; the authority of the Government is received from the Crown.

> JAMES L. ILSLEY, H. of C., *Debates*, Nov. 12, 1945, 2020.

In Quebec the Crown evokes polite dissent or revolutionary anger without dampening creativity in music, art or literature. But in English Canada the Crown has had a crippling effect, contributing to a state of psychic confusion that is termed an "identity crisis" in an individual.

> JOHN CONWAY, in H.L. Dyck and H.P. Krosby, eds., *Essays in honour of Frederic H. Soward*, 1969, 15.

Crows

What subtle alchemy dissolved the
   night
And out of sheer invisibility
Extracted all its essence, setting free
One jet of ebon in expansive flight?

> ALBERT D. WATSON, "The crow", 1921.

Jet crows cawing and cawing above,
Crows in the sky:
Is it a song they shout –
Or a warning cry?

> DOROTHY LIVESAY, "City wife", 1932.

One for sorrow,
Two for mirth,
The third a wedding
And fourth a birth.

> ANON., "Crows", an old New Brunswick superstition, qu. in Lena Newman, *An historical almanac of Canada*, 1967.

one crow for sorrow
two crows for joy
three crows for a girl
four crows for a boy
five crows for silver
six crows for gold
seven crows a secret that can never be
   told

> ANON., a Saskatchewan woman, qu. by Colleen Thibaudeau in *Alphabet*, #16, Sept., 1969, 68.

Cruelty

The cruelty of nature is part of a constructive pattern, whereas that of society is purely destructive and arbitrary.

DESMOND PACEY, *Ten Canadian poets*, 1958, 307.

Culture

The cold narrow minds, the confined ideas, the by-gone prejudices of the society are hardly conceivable, books there are none, nor music, and as to pictures! – the Lord deliver us from such! The people do not know what a picture is.

ANNA JAMESON, on society in Toronto, 1837.

I'm sick of refinement, I'm weary of
     art,
I hate all refinement that withers the
     heart;
Away with your dandies your
     creatures of steam,
With nothing but buttons where hearts
     should have been.

ALEXANDER MCLACHLAN, "I long not for riches", 1856.

To Canadian literature I have given more time and labour than it deserves. Canadians are mainly barbarians and consist, ninety-nine out of one hundred, of backs and stomachs. To expect our polished boors to enjoy art in any of its developments is too much.

CHARLES MAIR, letter, July 1, 1891 to Col. Denison, qu. in Norman Shrive, *Charles Mair: Literary nationalist*, 1965, 214.

Culture seems a kind of craze in Canada. What they mean by it is perhaps hazy even to themselves; but they undoubtedly have a yearning for something which is not specie [sic].

JAMES MAVOR, "Hasty judgments", in his private log, Sept. 1, 1892.

Culture is the consciousness of truth expressed in conduct. Good form appears to be the accumulated weariness of centuries expressed in a general air of boredom.

PETER MCARTHUR, *To be taken with salt*, 1903, 149.

With the Greek, let us measure our contribution to civilization in what we give to the humanities. With the Hebrew, let us believe that God continues to work through the centuries and that He may work for continents as well as men. With the founder of our faith, let us believe that all life is sacred and all human life but the reflected image of the Divine.

W.L. MACKENZIE KING, speech, "Culture and religion", 1914.

The only positive test of any work of art is the favour of the cultured man.

WILLIAM ARTHUR DEACON, *Poteen*, 1926, 120.

To be truly and productively cultivated three things are necessary, and three only. The first is to appropriate all the heritage of the past (or at least as much of it as can be compassed); the second is to see the present as it really is, unobscured by prejudice and wishful thinking; the third is frankly to speak forth one's findings in one's own idiom – which may be national or continental or even imperial, but which in our present state of development is most likely to be sectional.

A.S.P. WOODHOUSE, in *Univ. of Tor. quart.*, Apr., 1941, 350.

This is their culture, this – their
     master passion
Of giving shelter and of sharing bread,
Of answering rocket signals in the
     fashion
Of losing life to save it . . .

E.J. PRATT, "Newfoundland seamen", 1943.

A Canadian culture of English and French inspiration will never reach the level which we desire for it, as long as appropriate measures have not been taken against the invasion of the Canadian Press by one of the most hateful forms of written production from the United States, as long as thousands of pages *made in the United States* are reproduced without alteration by English language newspapers or translated for French language readers, as long as *pulp magazines, comics* and small works of the same nature are imported and distributed without restriction as they are presently in Canada.

LA SOCIÉTÉ DES ECRIVAINS CANADIENS, *Memorandum*, to Roy. Comm. on Nat. Dev. of Arts, Letters and Sciences in Can., Oct. 20, 1949, 8.

Culture is that part of education which enriches the mind and refines the taste. It is the development of the intelligence through the arts, letters and sciences.

CANADA. ROY. COMM. ON NATIONAL DEV. IN THE ARTS, LETTERS AND SCIENCES, 1949-1951, *Report*, 1951, 7.

We benefit from vast importations of what might be familiarly called the American cultural output. We import newspapers, periodicals, books, maps and endless educational equipment. We also import artistic talent, either personally in the travelling artist or company, or on the screen, in recordings and over the air. Every Sunday, tens of thousands tacitly acknowledge their cultural indebtedness as they turn off the radio at the close of the Sunday symphony from New York and settle down to the latest American Book of the Month.

CANADA. ROY. COMM. ON NAT. DEV. IN THE ARTS, LETTERS AND SCIENCES, *Report*, 1951, 14.

Culture is concerned with the capacity of the individual to appraise problems in terms of space and time and with enabling him to take the proper steps at the right time.

H.A. INNIS, *The bias of communication*, 1951, 85.

Culture then means human improvement. It is something essentially humanistic. It proposes to make men, not French Canadians. There is no opposition here but only a distinction of priorities: to make men out of French Canadians and not French Canadians out of men.

HECTOR DE ST. DENYS GARNEAU, *Journal*, 1954, 206. (Trans.)

There is the fostering of specifically Canadian aspects of North American culture and the fostering of the double culture of Canada in the sense of making the two great cultural groups far more conscious of what each other stands for and what each group has to give and to receive.

DENIS BROGAN, in G.P. Gilmour, ed., *Canada's tomorrow*, 1954, 277.

Why does a country like Canada, so late upon the international scene, feel that it must rapidly acquire the trappings of older countries — music of its own, pictures of its own, books of its own — why does it fuss and stew, and storm the heavens with its outcries when it does not have them?

ROBERTSON DAVIES, *Leaven of malice*, 1954, 197.

A large number and a wide variety of Canadians are becoming more and more conscious that in many important respects Canada is a very dull place to live in; that economic opportunities are immense but, having made enough money to live comfortably, there is comparatively little in Canada to nourish the spirit.

TYRONE GUTHRIE, *Twice have the trumpets sounded*, 1954, 154.

Culturally, Canada must be both French and English if it is not to be American.

MASON WADE, in J. Park, ed., *Culture of contemporary Canada*, 1957, 394.

Morose scrutiny of Canadian culture has in recent years become a national amusement almost on the scale of professional hockey.

ROBERT FULFORD, *Tamarack rev.*, Spring, 1958, 68.

Our elite culture may sometimes show real signs of a distinctive Canadian individuality, but our mass culture becomes ever more indistinguishable from that of our neighbours.

FRANK H. UNDERHILL, *Queen's quart.*, Autumn, 1959, 369.

If our culture is to be further enriched, it must be given the means of expression in creative forms in appropriate surroundings.

LESLIE M. FROST, open letter, *Globe and Mail magazine*, Oct. 1, 1960, 11, on opening of O'Keefe Centre in Toronto.

What would happen in Canada if full sovereignty were invoked and the southern border were sealed tight against American mass culture – if the airways were jammed, if all our comic books were embargoed, if only the purest and most uplifting of American cultural commodities were allowed entry? Native industries would take over, obviously. Cut off from American junk, Canada would have to produce her own.

RICHARD H. ROVERE, American reporter, in *Maclean's*, Nov. 5, 1960, 36.

Cancult is not hard to spot but it's impossible to kill. It is a Canadian cultural process by which literature and art are demoted to the status of a crutch for Canadian nationalism. It is a process which makes culture into an artificial historical event, a part of an unending quest for Canadian identity.

ROBERT FULFORD, Toronto *Daily star*, Jan. 19, 1961, repr. in *Can. reader*, Mar., 1961, 7.

Cancult.

ROBERT FULFORD, Toronto *Daily Star*, Jan. 19, 1961. "A Canadian cultural process by which literature and art are demoted to the status of a crutch for Canadian nationalism".

We have moved from an era when business was our culture to one in which culture is our business. What has been until recently the business of the university is now becoming the business of the business world itself.

MARSHALL MCLUHAN, qu. by Claude Bissell in *Queen's quart.*, Vol. 68, Spring, 1961, 3.

The baffled state with which the Canadian youth confronts his cultural heritage.

NORTHROP FRYE, in G. Stanley and G. Sylvestre, eds., *Canadian universities today*, 1961, 30.

Canada has preserved and confirmed the essentials of the greatest of civilizations in the grimmest of environments. It is an accomplishment worthy of a better end than absorption in another and an alien society, however friendly and however strong in its own ideals.

W.L. MORTON, *The Canadian identity*, 1961, 114.

Can culture be considered from a nationalist point of view? I don't think so. Culture is something essentially human in its aims – it is essentially humanist. To 'form' French-Canadians, that is to say to make them conscious of themselves as such, is perhaps a popular notion, but it lacks all sense. It's even against sense and against nature.

HECTOR DE SAINT-DENYS GARNEAU, *The Journal of Saint-Denys Garneau*, translated by John Glassco, 1962, 103.

That underarm perspiration odour of impotent old men.

IRVING LAYTON, *The laughing rooster*, 1964, Preface, 23.

In both new attire and new buildings, our unified sensibility cavorts amidst a wide range of awareness of materials and colours which makes ours one of the greatest ages of music, poetry, painting and architecture alike.

MARSHALL MCLUHAN, qu. in *Weekend mag.*, Mar. 18, 1967, 6.

Branch-plant economies have branch-plant cultures. The O'Keefe Centre symbolizes Canada.

GEORGE P. GRANT, *Lament for a nation*, 1965, 41.

Modern civilization makes all local cultures anachronistic. Where modern science has achieved its mastery, there is no place for local cultures.

GEORGE P. GRANT, *Lament for a nation*, 1965, 54.

I don't think a culture is safeguarded or maintained. I don't think you can lock it behind walls. I don't think you can preserve it. It must live on its own power.

ANON., Saskatoon school teacher, qu. in Canada. Royal Comm. on Bilingualism and Biculturalism, *Preliminary report*, 1965, 63.

The 19th Century helped us make business into a culture. The 20th Century turns culture into business and all cultural matters are enormously profitable.

MARSHALL MCLUHAN, qu. in *Weekend mag.*, Mar. 18, 1967, 6.

If I were still a practising as distinct from an advisory Canadian, I would be much more concerned about maintaining the cultural integrity of the broadcasting system and with making sure Canada has an active, independent theatre, book-publishing industry, newspapers, magazines and schools of poets and painters. I wouldn't worry for a moment about the differences between Canadian or American corporations.

JOHN KENNETH GALBRAITH, interview with Robert McKeown, *Weekend mag.*, Mar. 25, 1967, 30.

No heritage is worth preserving unless it can survive the sun, the mixed marriage, or the foreign periodical. Culture cannot be legislated or budgeted or protected with tariffs. Like potatoes.

MORDECAI RICHLER, in Al Purdy, ed., *The new Romans*, 1968, 14.

The people of my acquaintance who show contempt for Canadian things are, invariably, Canadians.

CHARLES LYNCH, Ottawa *Citizen*, Jan. 21, 1968, qu. in Mathews & Steele, *The struggle for Canadian universities*, 1969, 48.

As cultures converge through science and technology, cultural differentiation, in the sense in which we have usually meant it, will end. In fact, we may have reached the point where culture has become a myth, in the sense of a belief in a non-existent world which might become a reality. The more culture becomes a myth, the less can it become a working concept of social science.

JOHN PORTER, *Can. rev. of sociol. and anthrop.*, Vol. 6, No. 2, 1969, 118.

A policy of cultural laissez-faire means, *not* that we subject ourselves to a wide variety of ideas emanating from a host of different sources bearing in upon us with equal intensity. Inevitably, owing to the sheer size and weight and proximity of the American cultural establishment, it means that we are subjected to one set of ideas emanating from one source.

PROF. ALLAN C.L. SMITH of Univ. of B.C., "An open letter on nationalism and the universities in Canada", unpub., qu. in I. Lumsden, *Close the 49th parallel*, 1970, 176.

Although branch-plant industry, branch-plant trade unions, branch-plant culture and branch-plant universities are undermining traditional Canadian values, yet these values persist.

KARI LEVITT, *Silent surrender*, 1970, 144.

A cultural vision that grows out of the rock, whether the rock is the Laurentian Shield or the globe itself.

DOUGLAS JONES, *Butterfly on rock*, 1970, 11.

Curling

Then soop, soop, soop! soop, soop,
     soop!
And draw the creepin stane a wee;
The ice may thaw, the day may snaw,
     But aye we're merry round the tee.

ANON., Ontario Curling Club, *Annual*, 1876, 109.

Oh! cheerful frost, we'd welcome thee, –
Each curler's voice shouts loud with
     glee.
We'd gladly gather round the tee
     And ne'er gang hame;
We'd play as long as we could see,
     Grand roarin' game!

"W. Toronto", in Ontario Curling Club, *Annual*, 1877, 106.

For on the rink distinctions sink,
     An' caste aside is laid;
Whate'er ye be, the stane and tee
     Will test what stuff ye're made.

ALEXANDER MCLACHLAN, "Curling song", 1900.

Currie, Gen. Sir Arthur

Currie retrieves Haig's reputation from the Passchendaele mud.

JOHN SWETTENHAM, *To seize the victory*, 1965, 164, Chapter heading, referring to the victory at Passchendaele, Nov., 1917, of Currie and the 1st and 2nd Canadian Divisions.

General Currie has been relieved of his command for inefficiency exhibited in the last battle (Passchendaele) and excessive loss of life.

ANON., spurious report attributed to Frank Oliver during Liberal campaign and repeated by Sir Wilfrid Laurier in a political speech, Dec. 5, 1917.

Custom

From getting accustomed to anything
– no matter how sacred – to growing indifferent, is, alas! not a very
difficult transition; truly, custom is an
enemy as dangerous to reverence as it
is to love.

FRANCIS W. GREY, *The curé of St. Philippe*, 1899, ch. 5.

The morality of convention cannot be
overvalued. It is based on consideration for others, and that is the beginning of morality. There is a religion in
ritual itself, and ritual is not monarchical, it is human and everlasting.

GILBERT PARKER, *Tarboe*, 1927.

Customs

The toll-takers and revenue officers on
the bridge showed the usual apathy of
their genus. Had the King of Oude
appeared with all his court on ele-
phants, they would have merely been
puzzled how to assess the animals.

W.H. RUSSELL, *Canada: its defences, condition, and resources*, 1865, 31, referring to the bridge at Niagara Falls.

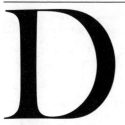

Dafoe, John W.

When, if ever, I am a candidate for Parliament, I shall first give up the editorship of the Free Press; and, as upon the whole I think I would sooner be the editor of the Free Press than Prime Minister of Canada, I don't think I am likely to be a candidate in any constituency for some time to come.

> JOHN W. DAFOE, letter to J.H. Metcalfe, July 27, 1926.

Well, he was no good around the place.

> CAL DAFOE, on being asked why his brother John W. Dafoe went into journalism, qu. in R.L. McDougall, ed., *Our living tradition: 4th series*, 1962, 93.

A Western Liberal nationalist.

> RAMSAY COOK, *The politics of John W. Dafoe and the Free Press*, 1963, ix.

Dairying

Fair Canada is our Theme,
Land of rich cheese, milk and cream.

> JAMES MCINTYRE, theme on title page of *Poems*, 1889.

Daisies

Over the shoulders and slopes of the dune
I saw the white daisies go down to the sea,
A host in the sunshine, an army in June,
The people God sends us to set our heart free.

The bobolinks rallied them up from the dell,
The orioles rallied them out of the wood;
And all of their singing was, 'Earth, it is well!'
And all of their dancing was, 'Life, thou art good!'

> BLISS CARMAN, "Daisies", 1894.

Dalhousie University

Dalhousie College was an idea prematurely born into an alien and unfriendly world, deserted by its parents, betrayed by its guardians, and throughout its minority abused by its friends and enemies alike.

> D.C. HARVEY, *Intro. hist. of Dalhousie Univ.*, 1938.

Dance

It may be made a question whether nations, like individuals, have not their 'Ruling Passion'. If so, I shall not hesitate to pronounce the ruling passion of Canada to be a passion for dancing, but English and Canadian dancing are two distinct things. The natives appear to consider it rather in the light of an exercise conducive to health, than as a sportive amusement. Probably also the severity of the climate renders some such diversion useful as contributing to relax the too great rigidity.

> ANON., *Canadian letters, 1791 and '93*; qu., *Can. antiq. and numismatic jour.*, 3rd. ser. ix.

Fiddling and dancing, and serving the devil.

> T.C. HALIBURTON, *Nature and human nature*, 1855, I, 215.

Going to dances, in a series of different but equally ravishing ball-room dresses, was apparently one of the principal functions of their existence.

> DONALD G. CREIGHTON, *The road to Confederation: The emergence of Canada, 1863-1867*, 1964, 159, referring to French-Canadian ladies of the 1860's.

The Cabinet Ministers – the leading ones especially – are the most inveterate dancers I have ever seen; they do not seem to miss a dance during the live-long night. They are cunning fellows; and there's no doubt it is all done for a political purpose; they know that if they can dance themselves into the affections of the wives and daughters of the country, the men will certainly become an easy conquest.

> EDWARD WHELAN, letter, Quebec, Oct. 21, 1864 in Charlottetown *Examiner*, Oct. 31, 1864, 2, reporting on Inter-Colonial Union Conference.

Why should not these poor people dance? It is their only amusement and sober beyond words in comparison to a Scottish reel.

> LORD MINTO, in John Buchan, *Lord Minto, a memoir*, 1924, 176-7, referring to suppression of Indian's traditional dancing by Commissioner for Native Affairs.

They dance best who dance with desire
Who lifting feet of fire from fire
Weave before they lie down
A red carpet for the sun.

> IRVING LAYTON, untitled epigraph in *Red carpet for the sun*, 1959.

In the dancer's inviolate maze
Time neither triumphs nor stays.

> DARYL HINE, qu. in Canada Council, *Report*, 1961/2, 12.

The dancer alone in his dance
utters the terrible sound of his limbs.

> ELI MANDEL, "Crusoe", 1967.

The authentic dance
is the wobbly stance
of the living man

> LIONEL KEARNS, "Poetic", 1967.

I'm short for a dancer, five-foot-three. I'm about the shortest dancer in the company. I'm told I appear taller on stage and that's a compliment to me. If you have presence, you seem taller.

> VERONICA TENNANT, qu. in Toronto *Telegram*, Apr. 17, 1971, "Toronto Week", p. 6.

And yet
from where I usually sit
my feet slide and skate
my arms gesticulate . . .
I stay in love with movement
hug hug
the dancers
this world's youngest
most daring dancers.

> DOROTHY LIVESAY, "Where I usually sit", 1971.

we are two
not one
the dance
is one

> F.R. SCOTT, "Dancing", 1973.

A nation's character and soul is typified by its dances.

> BORIS VOLKOFF, favourite saying, qu. in *Globe and Mail*, Mar. 12, 1974, 15.

Danger

There is something terribly exciting in beholding a fellow-creature in imminent peril, without having the power to help him.

SUSANNA MOODIE, *Roughing it in the bush*, 1852, 37.

In periods of great danger we act with remarkable vigor and stupidity.

JOHN GRAY, in *Tamarack rev.* No. 3, 1957, 44.

Dates

December 11, 1931, the coming into force of the Statutes of Westminster, – "the most important date in Canadian history."

JOHN S. EWART, address to University Club, Ottawa, Sept. 21, 1932.

The more it is studied the clearer it becomes that 1870 was one of the critical years in Canadian history.

M.H. LONG, in *Can.hist.rev.*, 1936, 453.

1864, "the year of destiny" for Canada.

CHESTER MARTIN, in *Can.hist.rev.*, 1937, 8.

Daughters

Her body bears, inside the changing flesh,
rivers of collected suns,
jungles of force, coloured birds
and laziness.

MICHAEL ONDAATJE, "Lovely the country of peacocks", 1967.

Davin, Nicholas Flood

The Bald Eagle of the Plains.

ANON., *Nicholas Flood Davin*, M.P. for Assiniboia, 1887-1900.

Dawson, Yukon

Dawson looks like a stout man who has grown very thin and yet wears the cloths made for him in his adipose days. Although it has been difficult for Dawson to accommodate itself to straightened circumstances, the adaptation has been effected heroically. The boom has gone, but business remains.

T.A. RICKARD, *Through the Yukon and Alaska*, 1909, 184.

Day

Lovely the day, when life is robed in splendour
Walking the ways of God and strong with wine:
But the pale eve is wonderful and tender,
And night is more divine.

MARJORIE PICKTHALL, *The drift of pinions*, 1913.

The day is done, done, done. The day is done.

DUNCAN CAMPBELL SCOTT, "The end of the day", 1935.

The Dead

If we did not as brothers live.
Let us here as brothers lie.

ANON., Inscription over entrance to graveyard at La Ronge, Sask.

I have been thinking a good deal of how pleased your mother and father, and mine, would have been to see us both at the head of the Liberal party in our respective spheres of action. They were all great friends, as you know, and I can well imagine what their rejoicing would have been had they been spared to the present time. Personally, I feel quite confident that, though they may be concealed from our view, we are not hidden from theirs.

W.L. MACKENZIE KING, letter to T.D. Patullo, Nov. 4, 1933. (Pub.Arch.B.C.)

He lived in the world, and it is a good world to live in
It is a good world to die from, and he died.

F.E. SPARSHOTT, "Ghandi", 1958.

Underneath this grassy mound
Sleeps one who for a while
Walked by our side on common
    ground
A country mile.

A.J.M. SMITH, "In the churchyard at South Durham, Quebec", 1967.

I feel good about the dead;
they remind me
that all this loneliness will end.

JOHN F. DONNELLY, "Solace", 1967.

Deafness

My last four years in the House at Ottawa were purgatory to me. To sit there like a dummy when perhaps something I knew all about was being discussed – to know absolutely nothing of what was being said and then to read next day in Hansard speeches that I could have torn to tatters if I could have heard a word of them – kept me raging in impotent anger.

ALLAN AYLESWORTH, letter to Sir Wilfrid Laurier, Oct. 19, 1917. (Pub.Arch.Can.)

Death

Let the dead be, we don't often inherit their talents or their money; and if we did, why should we be answerable for their follies?

T.C. HALIBURTON, Sam Slick's wise saws, 1853, II, 140.

Arrived this day at the canyon at 10 a.m. and drowned running the canoe down. God bless my poor wife.

J. CARPENTER, of Toronto, an Overlander going to the Cariboo, B.C., entry in his diary, Sept. 30, 1862, before losing his life in the rapids of the Grand Canyon, Fraser River.

As for me, I'm time-weary,
    I await my release.
Give to others the struggle,
    Grant me but the peace;
And what peace like the peace
    Which Death offers the brave?
What rest like the rest
    Which we find in the grave?

NICHOLAS F. DAVIN, "An epic of the dawn", 1884.

Every day in which I have neglected to prepare myself to die, was a day of mental alienation.

LOUIS RIEL, interview shortly before his death, qu. in Regina Leader, Nov. 19, 1885, 4.

Death always carries with it an incredible sense of pain; but the one thing sad in death is that which is involved in the word separation – separation from all we love in life.

SIR WILFRID LAURIER, H. of C., Debates, June 8, 1891.

They who should see me in that
    hour would ask
What spirit, or what fire, could ever
    have been
    Within that yellow and discoloured
    mask;
For there seems life in lead, or in a
    stone,
But in a soul's deserted dwelling none.

ARCHIBALD LAMPMAN, "Death", July, 1891.

The hands were wrinkled; the face was cold; the body was wet; the man was drowned and dead.

GILBERT PARKER, *Pierre and his people*, 1892.

I shall leave the world, – political, social and theological, in a considerable ferment, and I hardly know whether to rejoice that I shall be out of the fray or grieve that I shall miss the fun.

GOLDWIN SMITH, letter to Andrew White, Dec. 7, 1894.

The wind of death that softly blows
    The last warm petal from the rose,
The last dry leaf from off the tree,
    To-night has come to breathe on
    me.

The wind of death, that silently
    Enshroudeth friend and enemy.

ETHELWYN WETHERALD, "The wind of death", 1896.

So often have I met death face to face
His eyes now wear the welcome of a
    friend's.

FREDERICK G. SCOTT, "Dion", 1899.

For you, as once of old you came, at
    last
Would surely come, and with
    unfaltering faith
Lead me beyond the dominance of
    death.

FRANCIS SHERMAN, "The house of night", 1899.

Infinite compassion is in thee
    unsealed;
In thee, all griefs are lost, all wounds
    are healed,
And death is silent, dreamless ecstasy.

WILLIAM E. MARSHALL, "To sleep", 1907.

Master, I've filled my contract,
    wrought in Thy many lands;
Not by my sins wilt Thou judge me,
    but by the work of my hands.
Master, I've done Thy bidding, and
    the light is low in the west,
And the long, long shift is
    over . . . Master, I've earned it –
    Rest.

ROBERT SERVICE, "Song of the wage-slave", 1907.

For what is it to die,
Be it a man, or tree, or any other
    thing,
So that in death is service, and the
    world
Be thrust one hair's-breadth nearer to
    the dawn.

BERNARD F. TROTTER, "The log-boom", 1912.

Death, you know, to the clergy, is a different thing from what it is to us.

STEPHEN LEACOCK, "The Rev. Mr. Drone", *Sunshine sketches of a little town*, 1912, 99.

So, stand by your glasses steady,
This is a world of lies.
Here's a toast to the dead already;
Hurrah for the next man who dies.

ANON., 60 Squadron, R.C.A.F., favourite World War I toast to the tune of the "Lost Chord", qu. in W.A. Bishop, *Courage of the early morning*, 1965, 109.

The Department of Militia and Defence deeply regrets to inform you . . .

CANADA. DEPT. OF MILITIA AND DEFENCE, opening words of the official telegram sent to next of kin of those killed or wounded in action, World War, 1914-18.

Too dear for death to dim, or life cast down.

MARJORIE PICKTHALL, "Vale", 1916.

Call no man happy till he dies.

> SIR WILLIAM OSLER, *Diary*, Aug. 31, 1917, on the death of his son killed in action.

We must all in the graveyard lie:
   This is the last of certainties:
Strange horizons some descry,
   That to the masses are fantasies:
   But take your choice of theories
To meet an end so villainous,
   In this at least each one agrees:
This World of ours goes ruinous.

> TOM MACINNES, "Ballade of woeful certainties", 1918.

Out of the winds' and the waves' riot,
   Out of the loud foam,
He has put in to a great quiet
   And a still home.

> MARJORIE PICKTHALL, "Ebb tide", 1923.

Outside of Life, including life,
   I watch the world go by
And smile to think that, after all,
   I must come back to die.

> PETER MCARTHUR, d. 1924, qu. in *The best of Peter McArthur*, 1967, xxii.

Without a hail at parting
Or any colors shown,
My friend has gone aboard her
For the Isles of the Unknown.

> BLISS CARMAN, "Passing strange", 1929.

I don't want to trickle out. I want to pour till the pail is empty, the last bit going out in a gush, not drops.

> EMILY CARR, *Hundreds and thousands: the journals*, Sept. 23, 1936.

This is the sheath, the sword drawn;
   These are the lips, the word spoken;
This is Calvary toward dawn;
   And this is the third day token –
The opened tomb and the Lord gone:
   Something Whole that was broken.

> A.J.M. SMITH, "Beside one dead", 1938.

Give me my stick. I'm going out to No Man's Land. I'll face it.

> STEPHEN LEACOCK, "This business of growing old", 1940.

Happy is youth who shatters soul and
   body
on the heroic gates of death,
freedom is his,
the prerogative of victory.

> LLOYD HAINES, "Agonistes", 1942.

The longer I live the more impressed I am with the difficulties of getting out of this world.

> JOHN W. DAFOE, to Grant Dexter, qu. in *Dafoe of the Winnipeg Free press 1901-1944*, 1944, 22.

I'd sooner be frightened to death than bored to death.

> P.K. PAGE, "The woman", 1947.

Death loves a shining mark.

> PAUL HIEBERT, *Sarah Binks*, 1947, 180.

We are devil-worshippers, we Canadians, half in love with easeful Death. We flog ourselves endlessly, as a kind of spiritual purification.

> ROBERTSON DAVIES, *Tempest-tost*, 1951, 332.

He never did a permanent thing
Except in meeting death.

> LESLIE MELLICHAMP, "Jake", 1952.

My grandmother on her bed
Struggles for breath;
Though she still sips at life
She would swallow death.

> RAYMOND SOUSTER, "My grandmother", 1954.

Death's the friend who never falters,
The only one who never alters.

> ARTHUR S. BOURINOT, "Everything on Earth must die", 1955.

Beauty buds from mire
And I, a singer in season, observe
Death is a name for beauty not in use.

> IRVING LAYTON, "Composition in late
> spring", 1956.

I am a bird cage
A cage of bone
With a bird

The bird in my cage of bone
Is death building his nest.

> HECTOR DE SAINT-DENYS-GARNEAU, "Bird
> cage", 1956. (Trans.)

Death turned me first, will twirl me
  last
And throw me down beneath the grass
And strip me of this stuff, this dress
I am, although its form be lost.

> ANNE WILKINSON, "Variations on a
> theme, V", 1957.

This is the sorrow — all things sublime
Must fall to ordinary death, while time
With neat dispatch and no heroics
  writes
An epitaph for wholeness and restores
Our partial sight.

> MIRIAM WADDINGTON, "Ordinary
> death", 1957.

If a man must die he has a right to die
in peace, as he would prefer to do if
asked. Positive action to take a life is
not permitted. But the negative decisions that ease and shorten suffering
have always been ours to make.

> WILDER PENFIELD, address, Medical
> Convocation, Queen's Univ., May, 1957.

Who comes?
It is the hound of death approaching?
Away!
Or I will harness you to my team.

> ANON., Eskimo poem; trans. by Edward
> Carpenter in *Anerca*, 1959.

There is nothing to say.
What a waste of breath they said
What a waste of breath
Speaking about death they said
Speaking about death.

> A.J.M. SMITH, "Speaking about death",
> 1959.

Lilac was the colour of my brother's
  dying
for lilacs blossomed in his last week's
  lying,
blossomed, ran riot down the
  summer's garden,
while life in him shrivelled and death
  gave no pardon.

> RAYMOND SOUSTER, "Lilac was the
> colour", 1961.

If death can fly, just for the love of
  flying,
What might not life do, for the love of
  dying?

> MALCOLM LOWRY, "For the love of dy-
> ing", 1962.

There is no death in all the land,
I heard my voice cry;
And I brought my hand down on the
  butterfly
And felt the rock move beneath my
  hand.

> IRVING LAYTON, "Butterfly on rock",
> 1963.

It wasn't important, he was English.

> ANON., a French Canadian on the death
> of a watchman killed by a bomb alleg-
> edly set by the F.L.Q. in Montreal,
> 1963; qu. by Leon Dion, *Can. forum*,
> Aug., 1963, 106. (Trans.)

a whisper stops at death's frontier
— 8 diatonic degrees above or below
the octave cannot penetrate those
  borders
not ballistae or hydrogen locksmiths
can sesame open those gates nor one
soft decibel of human music slip thru.

> ALFRED PURDY, "A very light sort of blue
> faded from washing", 1965.

Oh, a man's got to die of something!

> ADAM SHORTT, frequent remark, qu. in A.R.M. Lower, *My first seventy-five years*, 1967, 135.

I look towards the door. I cannot see round the door. I am not overmuch concerned with what is on the other side of the door.

> A.R.M. LOWER, *My first seventy-five years*, 1967, 377.

At whatever age, I hope to die young.

> JEAN LEMOYNE, qu. in *Time*, Sept. 13, 1968, 19.

now the last
blood-burst
of his joy-pain
is past
he leaves no stain
on time's cold rose.

> FRED COGSWELL, "The man-worm", 1968.

Not so much by age, but the deliberate hardening of mind turns us toward the grave.

> DOUGLAS FLAHERTY, "Ponce de Leon", 1969.

"Look!" I cried. "Look at my face!
Doesn't anybody know me"?

Then a hood covered my head.
"Don't make it harder for us", the
    hangman whispered.

> ALDEN NOWLAN, "The execution", 1969.

How can I die alone.
Where will I be then who am now
    alone,
what groans so pathetically
in this room where I am alone?

> GEORGE BOWERING, "You too", 1969.

But don't die
stay with me in the same world

or I'm lost and desolate
for here the light and dark
that touches you touches me
that you are here at all
delays my own death
an instant longer

> AL PURDY, "Idiot's song", 1970.

The trouble is there is too
Much death for compassion.

> RALPH GUSTAFSON, *Theme and variations for sounding brass*, 1972, Coda.

I fear continually that the premature
    night
Will hunt me down darkly one noon,
That time will betray me and I'll fall
And with lips attuned to earth
I shall drink as though I had never
    known
The pit of isolation.

> WACLAW IWANIUK, "I fear continually that the premature night", qu. in National Film Board, *Canada*, 1973, [90].

I am my own my entire responsibility
And when in the course of time and
    the fullness
of my years detumescently empty
I go down eventually
into the valley of the shadow of death
I expect to make my own travel
    arrangements

> AL PURDY, "The Pope's 1968 encyclical", 1973.

I doubt that death is real. One always runs the risk of a resurrection.

> ANDRÉ LAURENDEAU, in *André Laurendeau: witness for Quebec*, 1973, 290.

Debate

I know not with what weapon the Honourable Member will attack me, except it be with the jawbone of an ass.

> JAMES SIMMS, Attorney-Gen., Nfld. House of Assembly, about 1833, refer-

ring to John Kent, qu. in D.W. Prowse, *A history of Newfoundland*, 1895, 430.

Whenever there was a hair to split the hon. member never failed to have his razor and his cork-block at hand.

> THOMAS D'ARCY MCGEE, Canada. Legis. Assembly, Quebec, *Debates*, reported in Quebec *Morning chronicle*, Apr. 1, 1862.

One great secret of successful debate: when you have a man under your hammer never be tempted into doubtful ground and give him a chance to diverge. How often I witnessed men in the House who had a case, and who really had their opponents cornered doddle off into other ground and give the enemy a chance to change the subject and come out not too badly worsted.

> ARTHUR MEIGHEN, letter to T.R. Meighen, Feb. 9, 1943.

This is degenerating into a debate.

> JACK W. PICKERSGILL, H. of C., *Debates*, Aug. 10, 1956, 7352.

Debt

Debt hangs about the neck of an honest man like a millstone; and, in this country, it requires no ordinary uprightness and activity, to prevent him from sinking under the load. Running into debt, and long credits, have been the destruction of both property and religion among us.

> THOMAS MCCULLOCH, *The letters of Mephibosheth Stepsure*, 1821, Letter 9.

But of all evils, to borrow money is perhaps the worst. If of a friend, he ceases to be one the moment you feel that you are bound to him by the heavy clog of obligation. If, of a usurer, the interest, in this country, soon doubles the original sum and you owe an increasing debt, which in time swallows up all you possess.

> SUSANNA MOODIE, *Roughing it in the bush*, 1852, 80.

Ledger influence.

> ANON., a phrase common in Halifax, about 1867. The votes of people who were deeply in debt to Halifax merchants were easily influenced by the threat of legal proceedings, known as "ledger influence"; later came to mean much the same as "pull".

The debtor is more protected by law here than anywhere else in Canada. Alberta is a debtor's paradise.

> ADAM KIBSEY, Edmonton Credit Granters' Assoc., interview, qu. in Vancouver *Sun*, Sept. 9, 1964, 23.

Debt, National

No kind of government whatsoever, be it oriental despotism or moderate western monarchy can prevent the state treasury from increasing its debt, following the increase of population and national interests.

> SIR GEORGE-ÉTIENNE CARTIER, Quebec, Legislative Assembly, Apr. 4, 1859. (Trans.)

Canada joined the large collection of countries that keep pushing ahead of them a heavy National Debt; all the best countries have unredeemable national debts.

> A.R.M. LOWER, *Colony to nation*, 1946, 468.

Decay

It was not that things decay, that the works of man are ephemeral, he believed he saw deeper than that. The things themselves were decay. The works themselves were corruption, the monuments were *made* of worms.

> LEONARD COHEN, *The favourite game*, 1963, 131.

Deceit

The things we say are
true; it is our crooked
aims, our choices
turn them criminal.

> MARGARET ATWOOD, *Power politics*,
> 1971, 24.

Decisions

Sometimes we can
  pick up nothing, start nothing;
poise lost, stance lost,
      neither in the wind nor out of it
we must wait, on choppy seas,
    till the wind turn,
    till the moon come round,
and wind and tide, again, draw on.

> D.G. JONES, "The time of the fictitious
> 'I'", 1957.

One thing you can't blame the present
government for is not making decisions. They made decisions to make
decisions, decisions to change decisions
and decisions to cancel decisions. The
plains around Parliament Hill are
strewn with decisions.

> W.S. LLOYD, Premier of Sask., on Federal
> Finance Minister Walter Gordon's
> budget, June 13, 1963.

Political decisions are decisions which
are of importance to the community,
decisions on public matters. And it is a
fact that the most important of these
decisions are not made by our political
élite but by other élites which are *not*
accountable to the community.

> GAD HOROWITZ, *Jour. of Can. stud.*,
> Nov., 1966, 3.

I make most decisions with my heart;
my head simply looks after the administrative details.

> RICHARD J. NEEDHAM, *A friend in Need-
> ham*, 1969, 10.

Deeds and Doing

Pretty is as pretty does.

> THOMAS C. HALIBURTON, *Sam Slick's wise
> saws*, 1853, ch. 6.

As far as I can judge, not much good
can be done without disturbing something or somebody.

> EDWARD BLAKE, speech at Aurora, Ont.,
> Oct. 3, 1874.

For Law immutable hath one decree,
No deed of good, no deed of ill can
    die;
All must ascend unto my loom and be
Woven for man in lasting tapestry,
Each soul his own.

> ISABELLA VALANCY CRAWFORD, "The
> King's garments", 1905.

Highest thought is ever told in deeds.

> PETER MCARTHUR, *The prodigal*,
> 1907, 22.

If all the kind deeds never done
    Should blossom into flower,
The earth would be a paradise
    This very hour.

> ALBERT D. WATSON, "This very hour",
> 1913.

A man can always find time to do a
thing if he has the inclination.

> ROBERT C. (BOB) EDWARDS, *Summer an-
> nual*, 1920, 35.

It rather occurs to me that it's the
commonplace people who *do* things.

> STEPHEN B. LEACOCK, "The drama as I
> see it: II", *Harpers*, Mar., 1923, 439.

It may be those who do most, dream
most.

> STEPHEN LEACOCK, "How not to write
> more poetry", in *How to write*, 1944,
> 179.

Nobody ever did anything by pussy-footing.

> DONALD GORDON, qu. in P. Newman, *Flame of power*, 1959, 202.

If Americans 'fix', and Britons 'cope', Canadians, it has been suggested, 'adapt'.

> VINCENT MASSEY, *Confederation on the march*, 1965, 90.

Do not try to do extraordinary things but do ordinary things with intensity.

> EMILY CARR, *Hundreds and thousands*, 1966, 32.

Defeat

I am hurt but I am not slain
I'll lay me down and bleed a while
Then I'll rise and fight again.

> ANON., "Sir Andrew Barton", traditional ballad, incorrectly quoted by T.C. Douglas on his defeat, election night, June 18, 1962. Similar use made by John Diefenbaker, Nov. 16, 1966.

One of the worst stings of defeat is the sympathy that goes with it.

> ROBERT C. (BOB) EDWARDS, Calgary *Eye Opener*, June 8, 1912.

The world defeats only him who has already been defeated in his heart.

> FREDERICK P. GROVE, *Fruits of the earth*, 1933, 165.

Defence

I have no reply to make to your general other than from the mouths of my cannon and muskets. He must learn that it is not in this fashion that one summons a man such as I. Let him do the best he can on his side as I will do on mine.

> FRONTENAC, Oct. 17, 1690, rejoinder to Major Savage, rep. of Admiral Phips from New England who demanded the surrender of the Colony; qu. by W.J.

Eccles in *Canada under Louis XIV 1663-1701*, 1964, 181.

And His Royal Highness agrees, that all other armed vessels, on these lakes shall be forthwith dismantled, and that no other vessels of war shall be there built or armed.

> SIR CHARLES BAGOT, "Exchange of notes between H.M. Minister at Washington and the U.S. Sec'y. of State concerning the naval force to be maintained on the Great Lakes, Washington, 28-29 April, 1817" (The Rush-Bagot agreement).

The reciprocal duties of subject and Sovereign are not attenuated by distance, but, on the contrary, are often enhanced, since they are cherished against the relaxing influence of such distance. Those who talk, therefore, of it being unreasonable to expect the Empire to defend Canada, forget that Canada *is* the Empire in North America.

> THOMAS D'A. MCGEE, speech in House of Assembly, Mar. 27, 1862; his conclusion was, "The lion must bear the lion's share".

Canadian vigilance must sleep no more except upon its arms. We have burst into a new era – the halcyon has fled to other climes and latitudes – the storm and peril are daily visible in our horizon.

> THOMAS D'A. MCGEE, speech in House of Assembly, Quebec, Mar. 27, 1862.

What men love best they defend best; what they truly believe in, for that they will bravely die.

> THOMAS D'ARCY MCGEE, "A plea for a British American nationality", in *British American mag.*, Aug., 1863.

You have sent your young men to guard your frontier. You want a principle to guard your young men, and thus truly defend your frontier.

> THOMAS D'A. MCGEE, in Legislative Assembly, Feb. 9, 1865.

We were and are willing to spend our last men and our last shilling for our mother country.

> SIR ALEXANDER T. GALT, speech in Cornwall, Mar. 2, 1866.

Soft my babes, let music charm you;
"Quebec Scheme's" a blessed thing;
Not a Fenian will dare to harm you,
When under Canada's wing.

> ANON., "Lullaby", addressed to Nova Scotians in Liverpool (N.S.) *Transcript*, Mar. 15, 1867, qu. in *Dalhousie rev.*, 1970/71, 73.

This country cannot be surrounded by the United States — we are gone if we allow it — we should be in their hand when they choose to shut it. We must have our back to the North.

> SIR ALEXANDER T. GALT, speech at Lennoxville, Que., May 22, 1867.

Strong arms shall guard our cherished
    homes
When darkest danger lowers,
And with our life-blood we'll defend
        This Canada of ours,
        Fair Canada,
        Dear Canada,
    This Canada of ours.

> JAMES D. EDGAR, "This Canada of ours", 1870.

Canada is ready to join the mother country in her offensive and defensive league, to sacrifice her last man and her last shilling in defence of the Empire and the flag of England.

> SIR JOHN A. MACDONALD, speech in London, Eng., Jan. 4, 1886.

Much of its property is not worth stealing; but all the more will it hold on with grim tenacity to all that is worth anything.

> GEORGE M. GRANT, on Canada, speech to Canadian Club, New York, 1887.

We put our trust in Providence — but kept our powder dry.

> JOHN MCDOUGALL, Methodist missionary and Indian commissioner, *Saddle, sled and snowshoe*, 1896, 131.

There are here neither masters nor valets; there are neither conquerors nor conquered ones; there are two partners whose partnership was entered into upon fair and well-defined lines. We do not ask that our English-speaking fellow-countrymen should help us to draw closer to France; but, on the other hand, they have no right to take advantage of their overwhelming majority to infringe on the treaty of alliance, and induce us to assume, however freely and spontaneously, additional burdens in defence of Great Britain.

> HENRI BOURASSA, lecture, Montreal, Oct. 20, 1901. (Trans.)

The secret of Imperial defence is Imperial dispersion.

> T. ARNOLD HAULTAIN, in *The monthly rev.*, June, 1903.

The Governor in Council may place the Militia, or any part thereof, on active service anywhere in Canada, and also beyond Canada, for the defence thereof, at any time when it appears advisable so to do by reason of emergency.

> CANADA. LAWS, STATUTES, etc.,. *Militia Act*, 1904, C. 23, Sect. 70.

Jack Frost effactually and gratuitously guards us on three thousand miles of our northern coast, and in this he does us a distinct service, greatly relieving national expenditure and contributing much to our sense of security.

F.A. WIGHTMAN, *Our Canadian heritage*, 1905, 280.

The first duty of a free citizen is to be prepared to defend his country.

DONALD A. SMITH (Lord Strathcona), letter to Sir Frederick Borden, 1907, on contributing $250,000 for the encouragement of military training.

We are loyal to the British Crown and will defend the Empire in Canada with the last drop of our blood, but we are free and independent and no one – not Laurier or even His Majesty – has the right to ask us to go beyond our shores.

HENRI BOURASSA, speech at Ste. Rose, Sept. 6, 1911. (Trans.)

I would like you to remember that those who are or who become responsible for that Empire defence must, in the very nature of things, have some share in that policy which shapes the issues of peace and of war. I would like you to understand that Canada does not propose to be an 'adjunct' even of the British Empire, but, as has been well and eloquently expressed, to be a greater part in a greater whole.

SIR ROBERT BORDEN, speech at Royal Colonial Inst., London, Eng., July 10, 1912.

As far as fighting goes, I prefer to do mine here, and if I have to shed my blood I prefer to shed it here where I know it will be for freedom.

F.J. DIXON, speech in Winnipeg, May 27, 1917.

The main objective of the United States force would undoubtedly be Montreal and on to Ottawa. The next important objective of the United States would be the occupation of the Ontario Peninsula, including the cities of Hamilton and Toronto. The other objectives at which the American Land Forces would be moved against would be Quebec, Winnipeg, the Island of Vancouver and South Western British Columbia, i.e., the area including Vancouver and New Westminster.

COL. J. SUTHERLAND BROWN, *Defence Scheme No. 1*, Apr. 12, 1921, Ch. II. (Army Records)

Firm stands the red flag battle-blown,
And we shall guard our own,
Our Canada,
From snow to sea,
One hope, one home, one shining
   destiny!

MARJORIE PICKTHALL, "Star of the north", 1926.

I believe that if war must come again, Great Britain is our first line of defence, yours and ours – perhaps our only external line.

ARTHUR MEIGHEN, speech in Cleveland, Nov. 13, 1937.

Let us not be stampeded; let us do our duty by this little nation of 10,000,000 and trust in God.

RAOUL DANDURAND, Senate, *Debates*, 1937, 16, on defence against German militarism.

The Dominion of Canada is part of the sisterhood of the British Empire. I give to you assurance that the people of the United States will not stand idly by if domination of Canadian soil is threatened by any other Empire. We can assure each other that this hemisphere, at least, shall remain a strong citadel wherein civilization can flourish unimpaired.

FRANKLIN D. ROOSEVELT, speech in Kingston, Ont., Aug. 18, 1938.

We, too, have our obligations as a good friendly neighbour, and one of them is to see that, at our instance, our country is made as immune from attack or possible invasion as we can reasonably be expected to make it, and that should the occasion ever arise, enemy forces would not be able to pursue their way, either by land, sea, or air to the United States, across Canadian territory.

W.L. MACKENZIE KING, speech at Woodbridge, Ont., Aug. 21, 1938.

In strength together we will stand,
Defending our beloved land,
   This Canada of ours;
And never shall it cease to be
A nation where all men are free
In harmony from sea to sea,
   This Canada of ours.

PERCY J. PHILIP, "This Canada of ours", 1945.

If we as a nation are concerned with the problems of defence, what, we may ask ourselves, are we defending? We are defending civilization, our share of it, our contribution to it. The things with which our enquiry deals are the elements which give civilization its character and its meaning. It would be paradoxical to defend something which we are unwilling to strengthen and enrich, and which we even allow to decline.

CANADA. ROY. COMM. ON NATIONAL DEV. IN THE ARTS, LETTERS AND SCIENCES, 1949-1951, *Report*, 1951, 274.

Our military defences must be made secure; but our cultural defences equally demand attention; the two cannot be separated.

CANADA. ROY. COMM. ON NATIONAL DEVELOPMENT IN THE ARTS, etc., *Report*, 1951, 275.

DEW — Distant Early Warning.

ANON., acronym, electronic network constructed by the United States across the north of Canada, completed 1957.

NORAD — North American Air Defense Command.

ANON., acronym, established in 1957.

Canada is physically joined to the United States just like the Siamese twins. If one of the twins gets hurt the other one suffers. It is just as impossible to separate the defence of Canada from that of the United States as it would be to separate the Siamese twins and expect them to survive.

CHARLES FOULKES, "Canadian defence policy in a nuclear age", *Behind the headlines*, XXI, May, 1961, 10.

It is a safe prediction that at the end of this century, Canada will occupy the north half of the North American continent and the United States will occupy the south half. This geographical fact has a vitally important strategic consequence. It means that the United States is bound to defend Canada from external aggression almost regardless of whether or not Canadians wish to be defended. We may call this the involuntary American guarantee.

R.J. SUTHERLAND, *International jour.*, XVII, Summer, 1962, 202.

The Canadian government has not as yet proposed any arrangement sufficiently practical to contribute effectively to North American defence.

U.S. DEPT. OF STATE, news release of Jan. 30, 1963, in reply to John Diefenbaker's statement on Canadian defence.

It is, for the foreseeable future, impossible to conceive of any significant external threat to Canada which is not also a threat to North America as a whole. It is equally inconceivable that, in resisting clear and unequivocal aggression against Canadian territory, Canada could not rely on the active support of the United States.

CANADA. DEPT. OF NATIONAL DEFENCE, *White paper on defence*, Ottawa, Mar., 1964, 13.

Our military commitments should, perhaps, be a little bit more North American, not for reasons of isolationism, but because this is where the next world war will take place.

PIERRE E. TRUDEAU, speech, Edmonton, June 4, 1968, qu. in B. Shaw, *The gospel according to St. Pierre*, 1969, 127.

Today the Canadian government accepts a far greater dictation of defence policy from Washington than it was ever willing to accept from London.

JOHN W. WARNOCK, *Alliances and illusions*, 1969, 48.

Never believe a minister of National Defence because (a) he may change his mind, (b) he may not know what he's talking about, or (c) he may be lying.

DALTON CAMP, in Lewis Hertzman, *Alliances and illusions*, 1969, xviii.

Our eventual forces will be highly mobile and will be the best-equipped and best-trained forces of their kind in the world.

PIERRE E. TRUDEAU, *A defence policy for Canada*, press statement, Apr. 3, 1969.

Our fear is not that the U.S. Army will destroy Toronto a second time, but that Toronto will be programmed out of existence by a Texas computer. And it would be more a sell-out than a take-over.

JOHN HOLMES, in J.H. Redekop, ed., *The star-spangled beaver*, 1971, 93.

Definition

Once more I ask for definition; this is one of my fads.

JOHN S. EWART, 1904, speech to Canadian Club, Toronto.

Our Canadian preference, in spite of the clearness of our physical climate, is for living constantly in an atmosphere of mental haze. We never make issues clear to ourselves. We never define our differences so that they can be understood clearly or reconciled.

FRANK H. UNDERHILL, *Can. forum*, Sept., 1944, editorial, 126.

Delinquents

The basic condition of so-called delinquents is "boredom". Violence is often the result of, rather than the cause for, the anti-social behaviour.

WILLIAM E. BLATZ, *Human security*, 1966, 6.

Delusions

The danger of delusions of grandeur is, on the whole, to be feared less than the danger of paralyzing abnegation.

JOHN HOLMES, *The better part of valour*, 1970, 27.

Demands

There are among us some narrow-minded men who cry: "No compromise; all or nothing." What an aberration! When a minority affirms that it will concede nothing, that it demands everything or will accept nothing less than everything, he is blind three times over who does not see that the inevitable result will be: nothing.

SIR WILFRID LAURIER, letter to L.M. Gouin, July 18, 1918. (Trans.)

Democracy

The Democracy which shall make government the organ of public reason, and not of popular passion or of demagogism which trades upon it, is yet in the womb of the future.

GOLDWIN SMITH, *Schism in the Anglo-Saxon race*, 1887, 17.

That form of civic life
Which liberty and government by the sage
Secures, nowhere in that round world is seen.
Democracy puts apes in power, and howls
Hosannas praising not humility
Divine an ass bestriding, but the ass Himself.

NICHOLAS FLOOD DAVIN, "Eos: an epic of the dawn", 1889.

If democracy is right, women should have it. If it isn't, men shouldn't.

MAY CLENDENAN, in *Grain growers' guide*, Feb., 1915; qu. in C.L. Cleverdon, *The woman suffrage movement in Canada*, 1950, 79, ref. to the vote.

I hold it to be true that you cannot make a real democracy out of ignorant people. The preliminary to making a democracy, if the word is to mean anything, is that your people shall be educated.

G.M. WRONG, address, Canadian Club, Ottawa, Dec. 8, 1916.

Democracy is rarely beautiful in its working, for the many still refuse to be refined, restrained and artistic.

G.M. WRONG, R.S.C., *Trans.*, 1917, Sec. II, 63.

The Kingdom of Heaven and perfect democracy are synonymous terms.

HENRY WISE WOOD, *Grain growers' guide*, Dec. 11, 1918, 35.

Democracy may be simply defined as the people in action.

HENRY WISE WOOD, *Grain growers' guide*, July 2, 1919, 7.

Democracy is the consensus of opinion of the majority of the people crystallized into law.

J.J. MORRISON, *Farmers' sun*, July 31, 1919, 3.

No form of government makes greater demands upon the intelligence and sacrificial service of its citizens than does democracy.

H.A. CODY, Canadian Club, Ottawa, Dec. 15, 1919.

As democracy grows, liberty disappears.

SIR ANDREW MACPHAIL, *Dalhousie rev.*, July, 1924, 176.

In Canada, democracy has been even more of a condition and less of a theory than it has been in the United States.

A.R.M. LOWER, in Can. Hist. Assoc., *Report*, 1930, 67.

Democracy has made half truths and even lies its coins in controversy. It has given the demogogue a field for his own profit and we may wonder if it has a balance of truth in its favour.

GEORGE M. WRONG, in *Can. hist. rev.*, 1933, 7.

If any one ever had any doubt as to the existence of a Divine Provider, the operation of democratic institutions is sufficient to dispel that doubt, as nothing short of Divine Power could hold together such elements of chaos.

CHARLES J. DOHERTY, (d. 1931) qu., *Standard dict. Can. biog.*, 1934, 154.

I believe in the British system of democracy, and would submit to almost anything before surrendering those liberties which we as British subjects enjoy, but if anyone tells me that fidelity to party and fidelity to country are always compatible, or that the wisdom of mere numbers is the wisdom of heaven, then I tell him that he loves applause far more than he loves truth.

ARTHUR MEIGHEN, speech, Royal York Hotel, Toronto, Jan. 16, 1939.

Democracy is a great institution, but on account of the men thrown up sometimes, its institutions are very often in a perilous position.

ALEX. J. MCPHAIL, *Diary*, 1940, 88.

There is no greater farce than to talk of democracy. To begin with, it is a lie; it has never existed in any great country.

HENRI BOURASSA, in *Le Devoir*, Feb. 11, 1943. (Trans.)

If the democratic ideal of the supreme importance of individual personality is clearly understood and firmly held by the bulk of the people and if enough persons with an informed intelligence participate actively in democratic politics, the needed controls can probably be devised and the required caution is likely to be exercised.

J.A. CORRY, *Democratic government and politics*, 1951, 649.

However democracy may be defined, we feel its true meaning deep inside us even when we cannot express it.

LESTER B. PEARSON, *Democracy in world politics*, 1955, viii.

The public's will is no guarantee of a strong democracy. If there are enough weak, dependent, faithful, obedient, immature, irresponsible, superstitious or hating people, or people who want to be followers, in a population a 'Strong Man' will be what they want, until they get one, and then they cannot get rid of him.

G. BROCK CHISHOLM, interview, Vancouver *Sun*, Oct. 1, 1956, 23.

The 'average man' is not mature enough to function satisfactorily in a democracy. How could he be when we have not been teaching independent thinking and personal integrity in our educational system?

G. BROCK CHISHOLM, interview, Vancouver *Sun*, Oct. 1, 1956, 23.

A fundamental condition of representative democracy is a clear allocation of responsibilities.

PIERRE E. TRUDEAU, *Cité libre*, Feb., 1957, 9. (Trans.)

Historically, French Canadians have not really believed in democracy for themselves; and English Canadians have not really wanted it for others.

> PIERRE E. TRUDEAU, *Can. journ. econ. and pol. sci.*, Vol. 24, No. 3, Aug., 1958, 297.

If I were to quote all the material proving that French Canadians fundamentally do not believe in democracy, and that on the whole neither the pulpit, nor the Legislative Assembly, nor the radio, nor the press is doing much to instil such a belief, I would 'exhaust time and encroach upon eternity'. In 1958, French Canadians must begin to learn democracy from scratch.

> PIERRE E. TRUDEAU, *Can. journ. econ. and pol. sci.*, Vol. 24, Aug., 1958, 304.

There is some consolation in the reflection that so far no *coup d'état* has ever overthrown a vigilant, practicing democracy.

> D.J. GOODSPEED, *The conspirators*, 1962, 238.

True direct democracy is that the elected must govern, and must not be governed by the electors. Unless the elected govern, you have a dictatorship. If the electors govern, you have anarchy.

> W.A.C. BENNETT, qu. in P. Sherman, *Bennett*, 1966, ix.

Above all, it is our determined wish to make government more accessible to people, to give our citizens a sense of participation in the affairs of government, and full control over their representatives.

> PIERRE E. TRUDEAU, *The just society*, election pamphlet, May, 1968.

Demography

quick march one-two one-two
threeandahalf die every two seconds
ten are born every three seconds
twohundred ejaculations per minute
    on target
to say nothing of the intercepted ones
over sixthousand burials per hour
ebb and tide of semen and sand
on the bluff shores of time.

> HENRY BEISSEL, "New wings for Icarus", Part 2, 1966.

Demonstration

I will do this and that, and break
    The backbone of their large conceit,
    And loose the sandals from their
        feet,
And show 'tis holy ground they shake.

> GEORGE F. CAMERON, "In after days", 1887.

Dentists

If it hurts, don't pay me.

> T. GLENDON MOODY, Vancouver dentist, qu. in *Can. mag.*, Dec. 2, 1972, 24; re: newspaper ad, Vancouver, 1915, promoting "oralthesia".

When I realized — with certainty and no equivocation — that a toothache caused me more agony than all the wretchedness and misery of Africa and Asia, I resolved to give up worrying my head about man's destiny and to see my dentist more often.

> IRVING LAYTON, "Aphs", *The whole bloody bird*, 1969, 74.

Dependence

Woman's dependence upon man is his chief source of strength.

> ARNOLD HAULTAIN, *Hints for lovers*, 1909, 180.

Depression (1930-37)

Land of Bull and Baling-Wire.

> ANON., phrase describing Canada during the Depression, referring to boastful talk and "making-do".

The Dirty Thirties.

> ANON., term describing the depression years of the 1930's, so called in reference to dust storms and drought on the prairies.

The present interruption in the normal trading relationships of the world is not going to persist. There are a sufficient number of reasonably favourable factors in the Canadian situation, so that the resumption of the expansion of Canada cannot be long delayed.

> SIR HERBERT HOLT, Pres., Royal Bank, Jan. 8, 1931.

Emergency measures, however, are of only temporary value, for the present depression is a sign of the mortal sickness of the whole capitalist system, and this sickness cannot be cured by the application of salves. These leave untouched the cancer which is eating at the heart of our society, namely, the economic system in which our natural resources and our principal means of production and distribution are owned, controlled and operated for the private profit of a small proportion of our population.

> CO-OPERATIVE COMMONWEALTH FEDERATION, "Regina Manifesto", July, 1933, drafted by Frank H. Underhill.

The untold misery of the slump has made sustained objective study extremely difficult and has led economists on all sides to desert the subject and flee to politics. The results are disastrous.

> HAROLD A. INNIS, *Saturday night*, Oct. 28, 1933, 7.

Depth

We seek depth.
The surface is not enough.
Depth of experience, feeling.
To dive beneath the surface.
The surface is not enough.
Depth. Into depth.
We make depth, the deep.

> W.W.E. ROSS, "Depth", 1935.

Desertion

There is nothing which brings home to the heart with such force the iron discipline of war as the execution of men who desert from the front line.

> CANON FREDERICK G. SCOTT, *The Great War as I saw it*, 1934, 210.

Deserts

My dear, if we all got what we deserved, some of us might be in a bad way.

> SIR JOHN A. MACDONALD, to his wife, qu. by Sir Joseph Pope in his (memoirs) *Public servant*, 1960, 156.

Desire

O foolish ones, put by your care!
Where wants are many, joys are few.

> BLISS CARMAN, "The mendicants", 1884.

Come where the urge of desire
    availeth,
And no fear follows the children of
    men;
For a handful of dust is the only
    heirloom
The morrow bequeaths to its morrow
    again.

> BLISS CARMAN, "Wanderer", 1893.

O wild, dark flower of woman,
   Deep rose of my desire,
An eastern wizard made you
   Of earth and stars and fire.

CHARLES G.D. ROBERTS, "The rose of my desire", 1903.

Starving, savage, I aspire
   To the red meat of all the world;
I am the Tiger of Desire!

TOM MACINNES, "The tiger of desire", 1918.

Despair

But matters are never so bad but that they may be worse.

SUSANNA MOODIE, *Roughing it in the bush*, 1852, 129.

Upward, around, and downward I
   explore,
E'en to the frontiers of the ebon air;
But cannot, though I strive, discover
   more
   Than what seems one huge cavern
   of despair.

CHARLES HEAVYSEGE, "The stars", 1865.

I curse him, and he leers; I kick him,
   and he whines;
But he never leaves the stone at my
   door.
Peep of day or set of sun, his
   croaking's never done
Of the Red Wolf of Despair at my
   door.

BLISS CARMAN, "The red wolf", 1893.

There is no hope for such as I on earth,
   nor yet in
Heaven
Unloved I live, unloved I die, unpitied,
   unforgiven.

ROBERT SERVICE, "The harpy", 1907.

Our house is dead.
We shall build it again
But our home is gone.
And the world burns on.

MALCOLM LOWRY in *Can. lit.* No. 8, 1961, 20.

Let judges secretly despair of justice: their verdicts will be more acute. Let generals secretly despair of triumph: killing will be defamed. Let priests secretly despair of faith: their compassion will be true.

LEONARD COHEN, "Lines from my grandfather's journal", 1961.

Destination

By walking I found out
where I was going

IRVING LAYTON, "There were no signs", 1963.

And the feeling is constant
I have
the feeling of nearing now
a destination

RED LANE, "Margins XIII", 1968.

Destiny

Society contains not the whole of man. Human societies die; man never dies. Man has a higher destiny than that of states.

EGERTON RYERSON, lecture, "The social advancement of Canada", Niagara, Oct. 13, 1849.

Every radiant winged To-morrow
   hidden in the distant years,
Has its poise of joy and sorrow, has its
   freight of hopes and fears.
Every hour upon the dial, every
   sand-grain dropped by Time,
Quickens man, by useful trial, for his
   march to the Sublime.

CHARLES SANGSTER, "A poet's love", 1856.

The political destiny of our own country seems to be involved in utter uncertainty and impenetrable obscurity.

> EGERTON RYERSON, letter to Sophie Ryerson, May 28, 1865.

It is not our poverty of land or sea, of wood or mine, that shall ever urge us to be traitors. But the destiny of a country does not depend on its natural resources. It depends on the character of its people.

> GEORGE M. GRANT, *From ocean to ocean*, 1873.

There is no such thing as free will; destiny rules.

> CHARLES MAIR, "Memoires and reminiscences", in Toronto *Star weekly*, Nov. 14, 1925.

Canadian destiny is an evolution in progress. It has not been defined. It cannot yet be defined.

> W.L. MORTON, *The Canadian identity*, 1961, 83.

A Canadian is someone who knows he is going somewhere, but isn't sure where.

> W.L. MORTON, qu. in Gerald Clark, *Canada: the uneasy neighbour*, 1965, 54.

In my helplessness and loneliness, I listened to an old word, a word learned in school but up to then devoid of meaning and sonorously dull. This word came suddenly to life and rose up, echoing in the air which reverberated to the buzz of helicopters and the wail of sirens – the word 'Destiny'.

> JACQUES FERRON, Montreal *Le Devoir*, Nov. 14, 1970, Lit. Supp., xi. (Trans.)

When Canadians borrowed American conceptions of manifest destiny, they were inclined to make more of the divine character of British institutions than of the divine election of the Canadian people.

> J.W. GRANT, *The church in the Canadian era*, 1972, 29.

Destruction

A madhouse is designed for the insane, a hospital for wounds that will
    re-open;
a war is architecture for aggression,
and Christ's stigmata body-minted
    token.
What are we whole or beautiful or
    good for
but to be absolutely broken?

> PHYLLIS WEBB, "Breaking", 1962.

Details

A thousand details crowd upon my mind that would be productive of the most salutary consequences.

> JOHN GRAVES SIMCOE, letter to Hon. Henry Dundas, Nov. 16, 1796. (Public Record Office).

Devil

The devil is passing out of fashion.

> STEPHEN LEACOCK, "The devil and the deep sea", in *Essays and literary studies*, 1916, 41.

DEW Line

For most of the post-war period Canada has harboured the DEW line (Distant Early Warning), a radar network designed to warn the United States of a bomber attack from beyond its shores. Now that this network has become obsolete and been abandoned, Canada's role may be reversed. She now stands as a DEW line for the rest of the world, revealing in high defintion what may be expected from the global penetration of the American corporation.

> ABRAHAM ROTSTEIN, *The round table,* July, 1968, 260.

Diamonds

As false as a diamond from Canada.

> ANON., a popular French saying, after 1542, when Jacques Cartier returned from Canada with quartz which he thought was precious until it was tested. (Trans.)

Dictionaries

After all, there is no such literature as a Dictionary.

> SIR WILLIAM OSLER, letter to students, Jefferson Med. Coll., 1914, qu. in Cushing, *Osler,* 238.

Why don't you buy a good Oxford dictionary, it is good for weak spells.

> SAMUEL W. JACOBS, advice to his daughter who was having difficulty with her spelling, qu. in B. Figler, *Sam Jacobs Member of Parliament,* 1959, 1970, 255.

Diefenbaker, John G.

If that . . . is elected leader of the Conservative party, I'll go back to Ireland.

> GRATTAN O'LEARY, in 1956, attributed, qu. by John Saywell in *Can. ann. rev.,* 1963, 4.

I will make mistakes, but I hope it will be said of me as was said of another in public service, when I give up the highest honour that you can confer on any man, he was not always right, sometimes he was on the wrong side but never on the side of wrong.

> JOHN G. DIEFENBAKER, Conservative Leadership Convention, Dec. 10, 1956.

I do not like his publicity. It stresses the importance of the man and puts the Party in the background. Few men can be bigger than their political party. And when it so happens that they are, the party suffers when they go.

> MAURICE DUPLESSIS, interview with Pierre Sévigny, mid-April, 1957. qu. in Sévigny, *This game of politics,* 1965, 60.

Diefenbay-ker, Diefenbay-ker,
Diefenbay-ker, Yeah!
He will lead us
On to victory,
On Election day.
John's the man
Who'll get 'em swingin'
Swinging back our way.
It's Diefenbay-ker, Diefenbay-ker,
Diefenbay-ker, YEAH!

> ALLISTER GROSART, ditty composed to emphasize correct pronunciation of "Diefenbaker", election campaign, 1957.

I could not have called him a S.O.B. I did not know he was one – at that time.

> JOHN F. KENNEDY, attributed, referring to his alleged penciled notation on an official paper during visit to Ottawa, May 16-18, 1961; for another version see Hugh Sidey, *John F. Kennedy, President,* 1964, 382: "That's untrue. I'm not that stupid. I've been around long enough to know better than to do that. And besides, at that time I didn't know him so well."

Everyone is against me except the people.

> JOHN G. DIEFENBAKER, his theme in 1963 general election; see also below.

I've been derided. I've been condemned. It seems everyone is against me but the people.

JOHN G. DIEFENBAKER, election speech statement, Port Hope, Ontario, Mar. 8, 1963.

Yes, they are against me. There are great forces against me, great interests against me, both national and international. They are against me. Everyone is against me but the people.

JOHN G. DIEFENBAKER, frequent ending to campaign speeches, election of Apr. 8, 1963.

I ask myself, is a thing right, and if it is right I do it.

JOHN G. DIEFENBAKER, at a meeting in Brantford, Ont. near end of 1963 election campaign.

It is scarcely an exaggeration to say that fewer tears were shed over the fall of Canadian Prime Minister John Diefenbaker than over the upset of any major Commonwealth political figure since Oliver Cromwell.

ROBERT ESTABROOK, Washington *Post*, report from London, Apr. 1963, qu. in P. Newman, *Renegade in power*, 1963, 382.

The right instincts were in him, but throughout his stormy stewardship, they languished in the cupboard of his soul. He gave the people a leadership cult without leadership.

PETER C. NEWMAN, *Renegade in power*, 1963, xi.

It was typical of the man from Prince Albert that his strongest political testament in these final days of power was not the defence of some principle, but a quarrel with the projection of his image.

PETER C. NEWMAN, *Renegade in power*, 1963, 248.

A platitudinous bore.

JOHN F. KENNEDY, reported assessment of John G. Diefenbaker, qu. by J.K. Nesbitt, Vancouver *Sun*, Jan. 9, 1964, 6.

John George Diefenbaker became Prime Minister in the fullness of time and the vagary of the democratic system but he was never equipped for the office and made of it, considering his opportunities, the most notable failure in its history.

BRUCE HUTCHISON, *Mr. Prime Minister*, 1964, 314.

His inability to govern is linked with the inability of the country to be sovereign.

GEORGE P. GRANT, *Lament for a nation*, 1965, 4.

"Fight on, my men", said Richard Barton,
"I am wounded but I am not yet slain.
I'll lay me down and rest a while
And then I'll rise and fight".

ANON., "Sir Andrew Barton", traditional ballad, incorrectly quoted by John Diefenbaker, National Conservative Convention, Nov. 16, 1966. "Fight on, my men", said Sir Andrew Barton, "I am wounded but I am not yet slain. I'll but lie down and bleed awhile And then I'll rise and fight again". (See also T.C. Douglas under DEFEAT.)

The besetting disease of Canadian public life for almost a decade had been Diefenbakerism: the belief that promises were policies, that rhetoric was action, and that the electorate believed in Santa Claus.

RAMSAY COOK, *The maple leaf forever*, 1971, 27.

In Diefenbaker's passion is incorporated all the grievances of his audience; he absorbs their indignation and, at the end, after they have laughed with him, cheered him, felt their nerve-ends respond to his voice, they find that he has repossessed their hopes, and they believe in him as they have not believed in anyone for a long, long time.

> DALTON CAMP, *Gentlemen, players and politicians*, 1971, 334.

When I appeared, they [the jurors] concluded there must be something of injustice in the case. I represented to them what a defence counsel should be.

> JOHN G. DIEFENBAKER, *One Canada; memoirs*, Vol. 1, 1975, 110.

Differences

Pro and con have single stem
Half a truth dividing them.

> F.R. SCOTT, "Conflict", in *Poetry mag.*, April, 1941.

Difficulties

Keep in mind, though, this eternal truth: Difficulties do not crush men, they make them.

> ARTHUR MEIGHEN, speech at St. Mary's, Ont., Sept. 13, 1942.

Dignity

We want national dignity. But dignity isn't something you can simply reclaim. Dignity isn't a constitution locked up in an English safe.

> JEAN-PAUL DESBIENS, *For pity's sake*, 1965, 126.

Dignity and industry lend size to the muskrat.
His size is his own, and mete.
The whale may think his dignity is greater.
The muskrat would be able, if the thought struck him,
to prove his own title to this quality, sooner or later.

> A.G. BAILEY, "The muskrat and the whale", 1973.

Diplomacy

Britain has lost more by the pens of her state officials than she has won by the sword.

> TORONTO *GLOBE*, Mar. 26, 1858.

I am greatly disappointed at the course taken by the British Commissioners. They seem to have only one thing in their minds – that is, to go to England with a Treaty in their pockets, – no matter at what cost to Canada.

> SIR JOHN A. MACDONALD, letter to Tupper, Apr. 1, 1871, on Washington Treaty negotiations.

I told them frankly we were all but ruined from first to last by English diplomacy and treaty making and we would have no more of it at any price.

> ALEXANDER MACKENZIE, letter to Alexander Galt, July 15, 1875, referring to discussions with the Disraeli government in London. (Pub.Arch.Can.)

The history of the diplomatic service of England, as far as Canada is concerned, has been a history of error, blunder, wrong, and concession.

> EDWARD BLAKE, H. of C., *Debates*, 1882, 1074.

All that Canada owes to Great Britain is a great deal of Christian forgiveness.

> SIR RICHARD CARTWRIGHT, attributed; see his speech, H. of C., *Debates*, Mar. 14, 1888, p.156: "I do not think for my part, that we are under any deep debt of gratitude to English statesmen, that we owe them much, unless, perchance, it may be the duty, as Christian men, to forgive them for the atrocious blunders which marked every treaty, or transaction, or negotiation that they have ever had with the United States where the interests of Canada were concerned".

British diplomacy has cost Canada dear.

> CHARLES W. DILKE, *Problems of Greater Britain*, 1890, 64.

We have suffered on the Atlantic, we have suffered on the Pacific, we have suffered on the Lakes, we have suffered wherever there has been a question to be discussed between British diplomats and foreign diplomats.

> SIR WILFRID LAURIER, speech in Toronto, Sept. 26, 1907.

The qualifications for a successful diplomat in Washington are, in order of importance, (1) a good head for liquor and (2) a capacity for producing, orally and on paper, polite guff at a moment's notice.

> HUME WRONG, letter to Mrs. G.M. Wrong, July, 1927.

We've got to bring this thing to a head. I will take sight unseen any resolution which the Canadian delegate will propose.

> FIORELLO H. LAGUARDIA, in U.N. Social and Humanitarian Affairs Comm., Lake Success, N.Y., 1946.

I wait until that bastard takes his position, then take the opposite.

> MAURICE POPE, Paris Peace Conference, Summer, 1946, referring to head of Australian delegation, Herbert Evatt. Qu. in Arnold Heeney, *The things that are Caesar's*, 1972, 87.

Canada's role was not that of Sir Galahad to save the whole world unless we were in a position to do it.

> W.L. MACKENZIE KING, *The Mackenzie King record*, IV, 135; said at cabinet meeting, Dec. 18, 1947.

I am afraid most of External Affairs have become imbued with the attention they have received from the Americans and the place the Americans have allowed them to take in the foreground of international affairs.

> W.L. MACKENZIE KING, Mar. 30, 1948, *The Mackenzie King record*, Vol. 4, 1970, 270.

The members of our Department of External Affairs still seem to be getting their intellectual clothes tailored for them in the west end of London.

> FRANK H. UNDERHILL, *25 years of Canadian foreign policy*, C.B.C., 1953, 10.

Diplomacy is largely the art of making an indiscretion sound like a platitude and politics that of making a platitude sound like a pronouncement.

> LESTER B. PEARSON, speech on receiving honorary degree, New School for Social Research, New York, June 9, 1959.

The time has come to drop the idea that Canada's role in world affairs is to be an 'honest broker' between the nations. We must decide instead that our role is to determine the right stand to take on problems, keeping in mind the Canadian background and, above all, using Canadian common sense. In effect, the time has come to take an independent approach.

> HOWARD GREEN, H. of C., *Debates*, Feb. 10, 1960, 930.

We told the Soviet ambassador to take back his note and do with it what he would like. I don't want any misinterpretation of that remark. That was diplomacy in action.

JOHN DIEFENBAKER, election meeting, Toronto, June 14, 1962, re Soviet protest against installation of nuclear weapons on Canadian soil.

Americans don't even know we're a sovereign country here. They think we're a Guatemala or something.

ALVIN HAMILTON, press conference, Mar. 6, 1963.

Canadian diplomacy, like any youngster, is still wondering how it will finally look.

MARCEL CADIEUX, *The Canadian diplomat: an essay in definition*, 1963, 100.

It is not, repeat, not at all necessary that the Canadians either agree or disagree. What is important is that the Canadian transmit the message and be willing to do that and report back accurately what is said.

HENRY CABOT LODGE, U.S. ambassador to Saigon, diplomatic message to Dean Rusk, U.S., on Blair Seaborn, Canada's member of the Int'l Control Comm., Vietnam, May 25, 1964.

Diplomacy is letting someone else have your way.

LESTER B. PEARSON, qu. by Peter Newman, Vancouver *Sun*, Mar. 18, 1965, 31.

Canadian authorities must have confidence that the practice of quiet diplomacy is not only neighbourly and convenient to the United States but that it is in fact more effective than the alternative of raising a row and being unpleasant in public.

A.D.P. HEENEY and L. MERCHANT, *Canada and the U.S. Principles for partnership*, 1965, 33.

The foreign service officer is a naysayer in statecraft, the abominable no-man of diplomacy. His mission in life is to preserve the *status quo* from those who propose to alter it. Where the new idea or the fresh approach cannot be banished, his impulse is to denature them.

JAMES EAYRS, *Fate and will in foreign policy*, 1967, 50.

They call themselves the quiet Canadians, but I like to call them, with as much pejorative intent as I can muster, the 'smooth Canadians', as in the whiskey advertisements. The world of the smooth Canadians, and the methods they commend, are the world and methods of traditional, old-fashioned, secret diplomacy — swaddled in green baize, bundled in red tape, shrouded by the Official Secrets Act.

JAMES EAYRS, *Can. forum*, June, 1967, 56.

All bureaucracy's conservative, but the conservatism of diplomatic bureaucracy is in a class by itself. The normal reaction of a foreign office to some new foreign policy idea or some fresh foreign policy approach is to want to make it go away. The ethos of diplomacy is an ethos of suspicion — suspicion tempered by scepticism, snow tempered by ice.

JAMES EAYRS, *Fate and will in foreign policy*, 1967, 50.

I think the whole concept of diplomacy today . . . is a little bit outmoded. I believe much of it goes back to the early days of the telegraph, when you needed a dispatch to know what was happening in country A, whereas now you can read it in a good newspaper.

PIERRE E. TRUDEAU, qu. in *Maclean's*, Dec., 1969, 35, from a TV interview early in 1969.

To act the part of the quiet Canadian, you've got to keep quiet all the time. But if you keep quiet all the time, you won't be heard, and your case will go by default.

JAMES EAYRS, in W. Kilbourn ed., *Guide to the peaceable kingdom*, 1970, 216.

A great lather has been worked up in Canada over the merits of "quiet diplomacy". Diplomacy is by nature quiet and cannot very well be anything else.

JOHN W. HOLMES, *Better part of valour*, 1970, 51.

. . . Doesn't the service of quiet diplomacy require dirty hands?

DENNIS LEE, "Civil elegies", No. 5, 1972.

In my experience of Canadian-American negotiations which stretches over thirty years, Canadian delegations have, in most cases, been outmanoeuvred by those on the U.S. side of the table.

ARNOLD HEENEY, *The things that are Caesar's*, 1972, 201.

Disabilities

Men who have worked a lifetime to earn a living and provide for their families and have generously paid their way through society suddenly become suspect once they have been injured.

SENATE. SPECIAL SENATE COMMITTEE ON POVERTY, *Proceedings*, evidence of the Welfare and Workmen's Compensation Committee, Just Society, Mar. 12, 1970, 28:8.

Disappointment

Do not the keener disappointments of life flow from attainment rather than from failure?

W.H. BLAKE, *Brown waters*, 1915, 25.

Being alive you will be disappointed
By disappointing your nature
Or being disappointed by it;
Whether you're finally awarded or avoided
Whether you're looking for caresses or for kicks.

GEORGE JONAS, qu. in *Can. lit.*, No. 48, 1971, 41.

Disarmament

There *was* a valid distinction between an offensive and a defensive weapon: if you were in front of it, it was offensive; if you were behind it, it was defensive.

LESTER B. PEARSON, *Mike*, Vol. 1, 1972, 91, referring to discussions at World Disarmament Conference, Geneva, 1932-34.

Those of us who believed, and still believe, that disarmament is necessary to make the world safer did not realize the tenacity with which national leaders – men of *realpolitik* – would cling to the grisly symbols of power, would fear to move from the precarious national security given by the possession of great armaments.

E.L.M. BURNS, *A seat at the table: the struggle for disarmament*, 1972, 203.

Disaster

Disaster precedes reform.

PETER MCARTHUR, a favourite expression.

Disaster is my way of life. I'm the kind of man that when he has his back to the wall, the wall collapses.

RICHARD J. NEEDHAM, *A friend in Needham*, 1969, 8.

Discards

It is a long road that has no ashcans.

> JOHN G. DIEFENBAKER, H. of C., *Debates*, Feb. 19, 1968, on the Liberal Party's minority defeat on a money bill.

Discipline

We hear a great deal nowadays of something that is called "moral persuasion" but in my opinion a good spanking and no nagging afterwards is a much better thing.

> L.M. MONTGOMERY, *Rilla of Ingleside*, 1912, Ch. 16.

Discipline is the Foundation of Character and the Safeguard of Liberty.

> SIR WILLIAM VAN HORNE, Boy Scout motto suggested to Sir Sam Hughes; qu., Vaughan, *Van Horne*, 1920, 357.

Now, discipline is the method of making difficult things a habit; it is the way of exacting in a crisis the performance planned in sober calm.

> T. MORRIS LONGSTRETH, *The silent force*, 1927, 12.

I have never been able to accept any discipline except that which I impose upon myself – and there was a time when I used to impose it often. For, in the art of living, as in that of loving, or of governing – it is all the same. I found it unacceptable that others should claim to know better than I what was good for me.

> PIERRE E. TRUDEAU, *Federalism and the French-Canadians*, 1968, XXI.

Discontent

Many of the ills of life are unavoidable; and wherever this is the case, a discontented mind bears the calamity, and has the grumbling into the bargain.

> THOMAS MCCULLOCH, *The letters of Mephibosheth Stepsure*, 1821, Letter 11.

A new and thriving country like this, teeming with discontent and vain regret, amidst abundance, impresses upon me very strongly the truth that the least things in our daily course of life take often the deepest root.

> JOHN HENRY LEFROY, letter from Toronto to his mother, Nov. 20, 1844.

Praise be to glorious Discontent.
The questing soul's own counterpart;
Unsatisfied, insatiate,
Mother of creative art.

> JOAN RICHARDSON, "In praise of discontent", 1962.

Discovery

Discovery begins by finding the discoverer.

> GEORGE ILES, *Canadian stories*, 1918, 169.

Each day discovery delights me,
　My child's quick thought, old music
　　newly heard;
The friend emerging from the
　　stranger lights me
　Along the ever-branching lanes of
　　human search.

> EARLE BIRNEY, "Trial of a city", 1952, 46.

In the sense that Columbus discovered America, Canadians seem to be eternally engaged in the discovery of Canada.

> J.D. FERGUSON, *Monetary times annual review*, 1954, qu. by Hon. Gaspard Fauteux, address, Empire Club, Toronto, Apr. 8, 1954.

Discrimination

It is hereby recognized and declared that in Canada there have existed and shall continue to exist without discrimination by reason of race, national origin, colour, religion or sex . . .

> CANADA. LAWS, STATUTES etc., *Canadian Bill of Rights*, Aug. 10, 1960. Recognition and declaration of rights and freedoms.

Discussion

At no time was there any danger that some transfiguring flood of sweetness and light would undermine vigorous discussion or destroy those resources of prejudice and conviction which make for fruitful conflict.

> GEORGE WHALLEY, *Writing in Canada*, 1956, ix.

One has apparently to choose between a competent discussion of trivialities and a series of emotional outbursts about what matters.

> FRANCIS SPARSHOTT, *Looking for philosophy*, 1972, 92.

Disease

Hardware disease.

> ANON., term coined to describe condition of starving prairie cattle which ate door knobs, pieces of iron, etc., 1930's.

The apparent cause of illness is often an infection, an intoxication, nervous exhaustion, or merely old age, but actually a breakdown of hormonal adaptation mechanism appears to be the most common ultimate cause of death in man.

> HANS SELYE, *Maclean's*, Dec. 1, 1951.

Is it not that all people have, in life itself, a disease from which they will not recover?

> MARTIN ROHER, *Days of living*, 1959, 38.

I contract a severe case of funereal disease everytime I go to Ottawa. The cure for FD is simple enough – wine, women and song. But Canadians haven't discovered it; and the whole purpose of their political, educational, and ecclesiastical institutions is to make sure they never do.

> RICHARD NEEDHAM, *Needham's inferno*, 1966, 88.

Biggest disease – being unwanted.

> *CANADIAN REGISTER*, Oct. 30, 1971.

Disloyalty

And they accuse us, gentlemen, of disloyalty! And to whom, do you think? To Sir Charles Metcalfe! Is Sir Charles Metcalfe the embodiment of the British Constitution? Is the British Constitution liable to be carried off by a cancer?

> LEWIS T. DRUMMOND, Montreal politician, speech to his constituents, about 1844. Metcalfe was Governor-General, 1843-45, and died of cancer, 1846.

Dismissals

I'd a made him make tracks.

> THOMAS C. HALIBURTON, *Sam Slick*, 1836.

Dissent

To agree, to disagree, to harness diversity, to respect dissent: perhaps this is the real essence of Canada.

> ROBERT L. PERRY, *Galt, U.S.A.*, 1971, 106.

Distance

You can't drive a team of horses with reins 4,000 miles long. By the time you give the signal, you've missed the turn.

> GORDON CAMERON, Commissioner of the Yukon, qu. in *Canada month*, July, 1967, 16.

Disunity

I expected to find a contest between a government and a people: I found two nations warring in the bosom of a single state: I found a struggle not of principles but of races: and I perceived that it would be idle to attempt any amelioration of laws or institutions, until we could first succeed in terminating the deadly animosity that now separates the inhabitants of Lower Canada into hostile divisions of French and English.

> LORD DURHAM, *Report*, 1839, (Luccs, ed., 1912, II, 16.)

It is scarcely possible to conceive descendants of any of the great European nations more unlike each other in character and temperament, more totally separated from each other by language, laws, and modes of life, or placed in circumstances more calculated to produce mutual misunderstanding, jealousy and hatred.

> LORD DURHAM, *Report*, 1839, ed. Lucas, Vol. 2, 1912, 27.

We have two races, two languages, two systems of religious belief, two sets of laws, two systems of everything.

> GEORGE BROWN, Canada. Legis. Assembly, June 22, 1864.

If ever, in time to come, we should have the misfortune to become divided – as foreigners have sought before – that will be the signal for all the disasters which we have until now so happily avoided. But let us hope that the lessons of the past will guide us in the future!

> LOUIS RIEL, to the Nation of the Northwest, Apr., 1870.

English and French, we climb by a double flight of stairs toward the destinies reserved for us on this continent, without knowing each other, without meeting each other, and without even seeing each other, except on the landing of politics.

> PIERRE J-O. CHAUVEAU, *L'instruction publique au Canada*, 1876, 335. (Trans.)

Let us stop our fratricidal battles!

> HONORÉ MERCIER (Premier of Quebec), appeal of 1885 to the French Canadians. (Trans.)

There is no use in attempting manifest impossibilities, and no impossibility apparently can be more manifest than that of fusing or even harmonizing a French and Papal and a British and Protestant community.

> GOLDWIN SMITH, *The Bystander*, Dec., 1889, 7.

We have come to a period in the history of this young country where premature dissolution seems to be at hand. What will be the outcome? How long can the present fabric last? Can it last at all?

> SIR WILFRID LAURIER, letter to Edward Blake, 1891.

The Canadian nation will attain its ultimate destiny, indeed it will exist, only on the condition of being biethnic and bilingual, and by remaining faithful to the concept of the Fathers of Confederation: the free and voluntary association of two peoples, enjoying equal rights in all matters.

> HENRI BOURASSA, *La conscription*, 1917, 20. (Trans.)

Among most Canadians there is little eagerness to explore the varieties of Canadian life, little awareness how much variety exists, or what a peril that variety is, in time of crisis, to national unity.

E.K. BROWN, *On Canadian poetry*, rev. ed., 1944, 24.

Two nationalisms opposing one another in the bosom of the same state.

MICHEL BRUNET, *Canadians et Canadiens*, 1954, 123. (Trans.) (Paraphrase of Lord Durham.)

Canada by contrast is a good case of a plural society because it is so exactly the converse of the ideal-typical nation state. The two major populations are distinguished by almost everything but race: language, religion, territory, and culture. As a consequence, constitutional adjustments have been made to accommodate government to reality, and political adjustments are continuously made to strengthen the agencies of accommodation.

LEONARD BROOM, New York Academy of Sciences, *Annals*, Jan., 1960, 881.

The enemy is inside the camp; the split is inside ourselves; and each accuses the other of the disease he knows he himself suffers from.

GEORGE WHALLEY, *Queen's quart.* Vol. 68, Summer, 1961, 238.

With two colonial beginnings, two languages, two main religions, Canada is really two countries, held together by three nation-saving bywords – conservatism, caution, and compromise – bequeathed to us by Britain.

WILLIAM TOYE, *A book of Canada*, 1962, 18.

The two cultures vegetate side by side; they grow poorer on a diet of French and English imitations and American buffoonery because they have not yet discovered the richness of their own thinking. We are a people without understanding, without communication, without love. And this voluntary misunderstanding can be summed up in one question: "When are we going to have the courage to accept one another?"

SOLANGE CHAPUT ROLLAND, *Dear enemies*, 1963, 6.

Canada is a reality whose very existence is only possible by the coexistence of two antagonisms.

PAUL CHAMBERLAND, *Parti pris*, Summer, 1964, 66. (Trans.)

Three possibilities have always existed for the 'English' and 'French' in Canada: assimilation of the French – an unspoken article of faith even today among many of the English, separation of the two groups into independent nations, and partnership. Up to the present the choice has been for partnership but the terms of union have never been agreed upon finally by both parties. The nation has always been in a state of civilized civil war.

PETER DESBARATS, *The state of Quebec*, 1965, xiv.

Thus concentrating on themselves, and on what we may call their own self-conquest, they view the rest of Canada as a single entity – "les Anglais" – the non-self, The expression "two nations" still rings in our ears, it was so often heard in our Quebec meetings.

CANADA. ROY. COMM. ON BILINGUALISM AND BICULTURALISM, *Preliminary report*, 1965, 48.

It should be clear enough that a tendency to identify stronger social ties outside the national borders than within could become extremely significant in situations of either individual or collective cross-pressure.

JOHN C. JOHNSTONE, *Young people's images of Canadian society*, Studies of the Roy. Comm. on Bilingualism and Biculturalism, No. 2, 1969, 34.

If Canada is more than ever before threatened with schism, we believe we must look for the cause very largely in the manner in which today's citizens have learned the history of their country.

MARCEL TRUDEL and GENEVIEVE JAIN, *Canadian history textbooks: a comparative study*, Studies of the Roy. Comm. on Bilingualism and Biculturalism, No. 5, 1970, 133.

Pierre Laporte did not die for *national unity* as many circles in Ottawa would have it; *he died because of national disunity.*

SOLANGE CHAPUT ROLLAND, *The second conquest, Reflections II*, 1970, 182, referring to kidnapping and murder of Pierre Laporte by the F.L.Q., Oct., 1970.

Divers

Upon the ecstatic diving board the
   diver,
poised for parabolas, lets go
lets go his manshape to become a bird.
Is bird, and topsy-turvy
the pool floats overhead, and the white
   tiles snow
their crazy hexagons. Is dolphin. Then
is plant with lilies bursting from his
   heels.

A.M. KLEIN, "Lone bather", 1948.

Diversity

The society of allegiance admits of a diversity the society of compact does not, and one of the blessings of Canadian life is that there is no Canadian way of life, much less two, but a unity under the Crown admitting of a thousand diversities.

W.L. MORTON, Presidential address, Canadian Historical Association, Annual Meeting, Kingston, Ont., June 11, 1960.

Our Canada is no longer made of two founding races, or should I say floundering races, but through immigration is made up of numerous races, and our real problem is to blend them into one Canada, not two or more.

ANON., Calgary man, qu. in Roy. Comm. on Bilingualism and Biculturalism, *Prelim. report*, 1965, 46.

Divinity

Mankind is in the grasp of divine currents too strong to be resisted.

SALEM BLAND, *The new Christianity*, 1920, 100.

Divorce

If you still want marriage to mean anything at all, you must open the door of divorce equally wide.

FREDERICK P. GROVE, A *search for America*, 1927, 92.

Is there any provision for the children?

JAMES S. WOODSWORTH, M.P., 1921-1942. Question asked on each divorce bill sent through House of Commons, qu. by Blair Fraser in *Maclean's Canada*, 1960, 12.

A divorce is like an amputation, you survive but there's less of you.

MARGARET ATWOOD, *Surfacing*, 1972, 42.

After you're divorced, you're still stuck with yourself.

> MERLE SHAIN, *Some men are more perfect than others*, 1973, 104.

Doctors

It's my theory that more folks die of the doctor than the disease.

> THOMAS C. HALIBURTON, *Sam Slick's wise saws*, 1853, ch. 11.

May the hospitalities of the Penitentiary be extended to all "Herb Doctors", "Indian Physicians" and "German and Reform Practicioners of medicine".

> REV. R.J. MACGEORGE, in Streetsville *Weekly review*, Apr. 22, 1854.

The practice of medicine is an art, not a trade; a calling, not a business; a calling in which your heart will be exercised equally with your head.

> SIR WILLIAM OSLER; attributed.

As little as possible and as much as necessary.

> DR. THOMAS S. CULLEN, a favourite answer to patients who asked what he planned to do in surgical operations.

Miracle-man.

> DR. MAHLON W. LOCKE, died 1942, Williamsburg (Ont.) doctor known for his success in treating patients with arthritis and foot ailments; also referred to as "Hoof-doctor".

To me he is the personification of drama. One man fighting barehanded against a score of creeping diseases. One man breaking canes and crutches! One man upon whom rests the last hope of an army of crippled people.

> REX BEACH, *Cosmopolitan*, Aug., 1932, on Dr. Mahlon W. Locke, Williamsburg, Ont., d. 1942.

We should be like monks going about in sandals and bare garments. Our purpose is to guard and resurrect the human body. It should be as holy as our purpose.

> NORMAN BETHUNE, to his wife, Frances, qu. in Allan and Gordon, *The scalpel, the sword*, 1952, 71.

If there are men who respond to the appeal of the church sufficiently to abandon all their worldly possessions and take up the frugal life of a monastery, then there will be doctors ready to set aside private gain in order to become priests in the service of the people's health. We'll go into the slums, into the districts where the need is greatest.

> NORMAN BETHUNE, to his wife, Frances, ca. 1935, qu. in Allan & Gordon, *The scalpel, the sword*, 1952, 75.

In the United States a Canadian doctor has a position of special prestige. I have been told — I need hardly say by a Scot — that you occupy in the States very much the position that a Scotchman does in England.

> LORD TWEEDSMUIR, speech, conf., Ontario Medical Assoc., London, May 27, 1936.

Our single aim must always be
The maintenance of normalcy:
So that the human commonwealth
May die off in the best of health.

> MAVOR MOORE, "The doctor", *And what do you do?*, 1960, 11.

The professional, in whatever line, must always be subject, in the final analysis, to the laity, or democracy cannot function.

> TORONTO *GLOBE AND MAIL*, July 11, 1962, 6, editorial, re: Saskatchewan medicare dispute.

Dogs

Every dog has his day in this world.

> T.C. HALIBURTON, *The attaché*, 2nd ser., 1844, vol. II, 26.

A good dog is so much a nobler beast than an indifferent man that one sometimes gladly exchanges the society of one for that of the other.

> SIR WILLIAM BUTLER, *Wild north land*, 1873, 25.

Je suis un chien qui ronge lo
En le rongeant je prends mon repos
Un temps viendra qui n'est pas venu
Que je morderay qui maura mordu.
  (I am a dog that gnaws his bone,
  I couch and gnaw it all alone,
  The time will come, which is not
    yet,
  When I'll bite him by whom I'm
    bit.)

> ANON., inscription in stone set over doorway of a house at the end of Buade St., near Mountain Hill, Quebec City, once occupied by Nicolas Philibert, merchant, killed in a quarrel by Le Gardeur de Repentigny, 1748. The translation is by William Kirby, the author of *The golden dog*, 1877, a novel based on the above.

Newfoundland dogs are good to save children from drowning, but you must have a pond of water handy and a child, or else there will be no profit in boarding a Newfoundland.

> H.W. SHAW (Josh Billings), lecture at San Francisco, 1885.

"I am Death, I only offer
  Peace – the long day done,
Follow me into darkness."
  "Welcome! Friend, lead on;

Only spare my dog, let something
  Grieve when I am gone!"

> CHARLES P. MULVANY, in *Canadian birthday book*, 1887, 28.

It is commonly said at some of the posts that to drive successfully these native dogs the driver must be able to swear in English, French, and Indian. But as there are no words in the Indian language in which to swear the native words used are only those of reproach or entreaty.

> EGERTON RYERSON YOUNG, *Stories from Indian wigwams and northern campfires*, 1893, 127.

You may depend upon it, a four-legged creature, unlike a two-legged one, has a reason for everything he does.

> MARSHALL SAUNDERS, *Beautiful Joe*, 1894, (1920, 118).

Never trust a man whose dog has gone back on him.

> ROBERT C. (BOB) EDWARDS, Calgary *Eye Opener*, Feb. 19, 1910.

Every dog wonders why the other dog was born.

> R.D. CUMMING, *Skookum Chuck fables*, 1915, 158.

Mr. Murple's got a dog that's long
And underslung and sort of pointed
  wrong:
When daylight fades and evening
  lights come out
He takes him round the neighbour
  lawns about
The which he does in drops and by
  degrees
Leaving his hoarded fluid only where
Three-legged ceremonious hairy care
Has been before and made a solemn
  sign.

GEORGE JOHNSTON, "Noctambule", 1959.

Dollard Des Ormeaux, Adam

Beside the dark Utawa's stream two
  hundred years ago,
A wondrous feat of arms was wrought,
  which all the world should know;
'Tis hard to read with tearless eyes that
  record of the past
It stirs the blood and fires the soul as
  with a clarion's blast.
What though no blazoned cenotaph,
  no sculptured columns tell
Where the stern heroes of my song, in
  death triumphant, fell;
What though beside the foaming flood
  untombed their ashes lie —
All earth becomes the monument of
  men who nobly die.

GEORGE MURRAY, "How Canada was saved", 1874, a ballad on the fight between Dollard des Ormeaux and the Indians on the Ottawa River, in 1660.

If Dollard were alive today, we can be sure that he would take up his role as leader of the elite and remind it of its solemn duty. No longer would he hear, as long ago on the bastions of Pointe-a-Callieres, the confused appeal of a race still to be born, but the anxious, trembling voice of a people dispersed in all parts of the continent and conscious of the old barbarous coalition closing upon it once again.

ABBE LIONEL GROULX, address, Montreal, Jan. 31, 1919, "If Dollard were alive today". (Trans.)

Arise, Dollard, and live on your granite pedestal. Summon us, with your virile charm, with a hero's accents. We lift toward you our hands quivering like palm leaves, ardent with ambition to serve. Together we shall work for the reconstruction of our family's house. And should you command it, O Dollard, O powerful leader, we are ready to follow you to the supreme holocaust for the defence of our French tongue and our Catholic faith.

ABBÉ LIONEL GROULX, address, Monument National, Montreal, Jan. 31, 1919. (Trans.)

Dominion

He shall have dominion also from sea to sea, and from the river unto the ends of the earth.

PSALMS, 72nd., verse 8. Sir Leonard Tilley is credited with using this verse in 1867 as the source of the official word dominion in designation of the Canadian Confederation; see, a letter by his son, L.P.D. Tilley to G.S. Holmstead, June 28, 1917 in the Public Archives, Ottawa. Origin of the legend on the Canadian Coat of Arms: *A mari usque ad mare.* — From sea to sea.

And His Dominion shall be from sea even to sea, from the river even to the ends of the earth.

ZECHARIAH, ch. 9, verse 10; sometimes cited as the source for the word dominion, and for the Canadian motto. (See entry, above.)

By another Act the Dominion of Canada is to be extended, modelled, and governed . . .

U.S. CONTINENTAL CONGRESS, *Journals*, 1774. (1904 ed., 87-88)

His Majesty's Dominion in British North America.

SIR EDMUND HEAD, 1858, qu., Can. Hist. Assoc., *Report*, 1929, 14; an early instance of the use of the word dominion.

On reading the above [letter] over I see that it will convey the impression that the change of title from Kingdom to Dominion was caused by the Duke of Buckingham. This is not so. It was made at the instance of Lord Derby, then [1867] foreign minister, who feared the first name would wound the sensibilities of the Yankees.

> SIR JOHN A. MACDONALD, letter from Rivière-du-Loup to Lord Knutsford, July 18, 1889.

[Dominions are] autonomous Communities within the British Empire, equal in status, in no way subordinate one to another in any aspect of their domestic or external affairs, though united by a common allegiance to the Crown, and freely associated as members of the British Commonwealth of Nations.

> IMPERIAL CONFERENCE, London, 1926. *Summary of proceedings*, 1926, 12.

We are called a dominion, although we have become a kingdom. We are said to be a confederation, although we are a federation.

> JOHN S. EWART, *Can. hist. rev.*, 1933, 123.

Dominion Day

With the first dawn of this gladsome mid-summer morn, we hail the birthday of a new nationality. A united British America, with its four millions of people, takes its place this day among the nations of the world.

> TORONTO *GLOBE* , July 1, 1867.

Monday, 1st Dominion Day!! This first day of July, in the year of our Lord 1867, is the Birth Day of the Dominion of Canada. Nova Scotia has entered to-day into a new state of things, having now entered into a partnership, forever, with New Brunswick and the Canadas. The booming of the cannon early this morning announced the Birth of the New Dominion and the ringing of the Church Bells proclaimed the gladness.

> ADOLPHUS GAETZ, *Diary*, July 1, 1867. (Pub.Arch.Can.)

Well, it's the day when people celebrate retaining their national identity by travelling to the U.S.A. to do their shopping.

> PETER PERUGINI, Vancouver restaurateur, qu. in *Liberty*, Sept., 1963.

Doomed

When the doomed are most eloquent
in their sinking,
It seems that then we are least strong
to save,
And pray that his prove no titanic
case.

> MALCOLM LOWRY, "The doomed in their sinking", 1962.

Doubts

With light and with darkness
We're compassed about;
The clearer our vision,
The darker our doubt.
The knot of our destiny
Will not undo;
The bars of our prison
We cannot get through.

> ALEXANDER MCLACHLAN, "A dream", 1856.

Doubt not, nor dread the greatness of thy fate.

> CHARLES G.D. ROBERTS, "Ode for the Canadian Confederacy", 1880.

Doubt is the beginning, not the end, of wisdom.

> GEORGE ILES, *Canadian stories*, 1918, 167.

Doubts are inseparable from life.

> JOHN MACNAUGHTON, *Essays*, 1946.

Douglas, Sir James

The Father of British Columbia.

> SIR JAMES DOUGLAS, founder of Fort Victoria, 1843, later governor of Vancouver Island, and of British Columbia.

Sir James Douglas, K.C.B.
1803-1877
'Father Of British Columbia'

> Inscription on tablet in the lobby of the Legislative Chamber, Victoria, B.C.

Doukhobors

The Minister recommends that under the power vested in your Excellency in Council by the above provision, the Doukhobors, settling permanently in Canada, be exempted unconditionally from service in the Militia upon the production in each case of a certificate of membership from the proper authorities of their community.

> CANADA. PRIVY COUNCIL, *Order in Council*, Dec. 6, 1898; H. of C., *Debates*, June 13, 1944, 3955.

Oh, it was awful the first time we took our clothes off, with all those people looking. Something just made us do it.

> ANON., member of Sons of Freedom sect, late 1920's, qu. in H. Hawthorn, ed., *The Doukhobors of British Columbia*, 1955, 167.

On the basis of our principles and religious convictions in the faith of Jesus Christ, we consider ourselves to be citizens of the whole universe; Christ is the King of all Kings, therefore we are his citizens. We categorically proclaim that we cannot be automatically citizens of this or any other country.

> JOHN J. VERIGIN, Doukhobor leader, 1947, qu. in G. Woodcock, *The Doukhobors*, 1968, 344.

'If somebody ask what you are doing, well tell them that we are burning our own. And then we will ask them: What have you done; half Europe has been burned?'

> MICHAEL VERIGIN, Doukhobor leader, transcript of trial evidence, Nelson, B.C. June 14, 1950, testimony of Paul Terasoff.

Jam the jails.

> SONS OF FREEDOM SECT, slogan used in civil disobedience demonstrations in B.C., 1960's.

If the Doukhobors take off their clothes, members of the negotiating team could do the same. Then they could all find a sunny spot and have a conference.

> DR. CHARLES FRANTZ, U.S. anthropologist, addressing Univ. of Alberta students, qu. in *Liberty*, Mar., 1963.

I probably have seen more of my female constituents in the nude than any other Member.

> HERBERT W. (BERT) HERRIDGE, M.P. for Kootenay West (B.C.) 1945-1968, qu. in *Weekend mag.*, Sept. 17, 1965, 13.

The Solution. There can be only one answer. That is to break the chain. The only way the chain can be broken is by removing the new links – the children.

> SIMMA HOLT, *Terror in the name of God*, 1965, epilogue, 288.

Draft Dodgers, American

I don't feel any stranger moving to Toronto than if I had moved to Kansas City – only freer.

> ANON., qu. by Donald Duncan in *Ramparts*, Apr., 1967, 30.

Drama

Though swift be the action and final
    the conflict,
The drama is silent.

E.J. PRATT, "Silences", 1937.

I preach the importance of the play.

NATHAN COHEN, qu. in *Maclean's*, June
8, 1957, 72.

The drama may be called that part of
theatrical art which lends itself most
readily to intellectual discussion; what
is left is theatre.

ROBERTSON DAVIES, *A voice from the
attic*, 1960, 158.

We've had theatre of cruelty (the
rebirth of tragedy – the imitation of
our death-wish); we've had theatre of
absurd (the rebirth of comedy – the
imitation of our bitter laughter); we've
had the theatre of detachment (the
rebirth of the miracle play – Mother
Courage drags her cross). The one
thing we never imitate enough is just
– games, play – imitation itself.
The instinct to just "have fun" – to
make a pattern simply because like a
whooping crane we can't help doing a
spring dance with our bodies. Look at
kids playing hopscotch.

JAMES REANEY, *Listen to the wind*, programme note, 1st performance, London,
Ont., July 26, 1966.

Dreamers

What we need is dreamers who will
stop and listen into themselves instead
of mirroring the insane scrambling
which goes on about us; who will go
into the wilderness to discover new
continents, not in any unexplored or
undiscovered ocean, but in the human
heart and soul. I have a haunting
suspicion that that is the only corner
left in this world where undiscovered
continents are still abounding. Let us

find worlds within the world to which
we have not yet reacted.

FREDERICK PHILIP GROVE, *It needs to be
said*, 1929, 114.

Dreams

Dreams are one of the greatest mysteries in the unsolved problem of life.

SUSANNA MOODIE, *Geoffrey Moncton*,
1855, 68.

They lingered on the middle heights
    Betwixt the brown earth and the
        heaven;
They whispered, "We are not the
        night's,
    But pallid children of the even".

WILFRED CAMPBELL, "The dreamers",
1889.

You are playing on the shores of life
and so am I. You are beginning to
think and dream, and so am I. We are
only children till we begin to make our
dreams our life. So I am one with you,
for only now do I step from dreams to
action.

SIR GILBERT PARKER, *When Valmond
came to Pontiac*, 1897, 21.

If no man dreams, there will be nothing for the workers to fulfil.

L.M. MONTGOMERY, *Rilla of Ingleside*,
1921, ch. 23.

A people of men who place practical
things above all others become
wealthy; but a people of dreamers
must become great.

FREDERICK P. GROVE, *A search for America*, 1927, 75.

Aye, child by wistful child they turned
Where dull the yellow street-lamps
  burned,
And for a breath they caught the
  gleam,
And for a moment dreamed the
  dream.

ARTHUR STRINGER, "The children's
theatre", 1929.

Dreams have a way of realizing their
potential growth. The best thing a
man can say of himself is that he has
grown with the growth of his dreams.

FREDERICK P. GROVE, *Fruits of the earth*,
1933, 139.

They taught me how to patch and
  darn,
And sew a thin fine seam;
But what if I should have to mend
A broken dream?

EILEEN CAMERON HENRY, "Untaught",
1938.

Dreams are an
inconvenient reminder
of something that is being
overlooked in
the straight-line
rationalistic view
of things.

W.W. EUSTACE ROSS, untitled poem, dated
1945, qu. in *Can. lit.*, No. 39, 1969, 58.

Watch out when we start to dream,
our dreams come true. Watch us, we
always win.

JOSEPH R. SMALLWOOD, Legis. Assemb.,
Newfoundland, Feb. 15, 1950, qu. in R.
Gwyn, *Smallwood*, 1968, 146.

Man's trouble isn't what he does nor
doesn't do, it's what he dreams.

HUGH MACLENNAN, *Each man's son*,
1951, 56.

But the dream, the dream, where did
  it begin?
In jewels, in stars, in powdery snow
Or sin?

MIRIAM WADDINGTON, "Night in October", 1955.

My life has not allowed me much time
for study. What a man does not learn
in the books he makes up for in his
dreams.

ADELE WISEMAN, *The sacrifice*, 1956
(1972, 32).

We are all children when we dream.

ALDEN NOWLAN, "The genealogy of
morals", 1962.

My dreams are clotted, flow like flags
  across my skies;
I have strange dreams and cannot tell
  where dreaming ends.

K.V. HERTZ, "A dream of his dead mother", 1963.

The people alive in dreams are real.

R.G. EVERSON, "Immortal in dreams",
1966.

I am not wishful in this dream of
immersion.

P.K. PAGE, "Element", 1967.

Once I built a house of cards and
It was five storeys high
but one day it collapsed,
And all my dreams expired.

RENDEL KULPAS, "Perspectives", 1968.

Whose dream is this, I would like to
  know:
is this a manufactured
hallucination, a cynical fiction, a lure
for export only?

MARGARET ATWOOD, "At the tourist centre in Boston", 1968.

It is only in dreams
When we are alone
That the terror behind life
Rises from the depths

> ELIZABETH BREWSTER, "Reality as escape", 1969.

The American dream is alive and well and living off Canada.

> BILL HOWELL, in *Maclean's*, Sept., 1971, 72.

Dress

The Frenchmen, who consider things in their true light, complain very much that a great number of the ladies in Canada have gotten into the pernicious custom of taking too much care of their dress, and squandering all their fortune and more upon it.

> PETER KALM, 1749, *Travels*, 1937, II, 525.

It is the prime duty of a woman of this terrestrial world to look well. Neatness is the asepsis of clothes.

> SIR WILLIAM OSLER, Commencement address to nurses, Johns Hopkins Univ., May 7, 1913.

At a Jewish event like this, the gowns are luxurious but somehow slightly vulgar. At the Bal des Petits Souliers, the gowns are not as expensive but there is much more natural elegance and greater chic. The St. Andrew's Ball is the tattiest of them all. At the St. George's Ball, the dresses look like leftovers from the thirties and forties. The St. Patrick's Ball, of course, doesn't mean anything.

> ANON., a fashion authority, qu. in Peter Desbarats, *State of Quebec*, 1965, 29, on Montreal balls.

The crafty Canadian always wants his neighbours to think that he has less money than he really has. He underdresses, for the possession of more than two suits might suggest affluence and a desire to seem glorious in the eyes of men. His wife probably has a fur coat, but she wears it to do the shopping, and to sweep off the stoop, so that it is really just a hardwearing overall, and not a token of wealth.

> ROBERTSON DAVIES, *Samuel Marchbanks' almanack*, 1967, 172.

Drew, George

George, you know the trouble with you is you don't read any poetry.

> GRATTAN O'LEARY, to George Drew, qu. in *Maclean's*, June 7, 1958, 66.

Drinking

The love of Rum is their first inducement to industry; they undergo every hardship and fatigue to procure a Skinfull of this delicious beverage, and when a Nation becomes addicted to drinking, it affords a strong presumption that they will soon become excellent hunters.

> DUNCAN MCGILLIVRAY, *Journal: North West Company on the Saskatchewan, 1794-5*, (1929 ed., 47).

Of all people in the world, I think the Canadians, when drunk, are the most disagreeable; for excessive drinking generally causes them to quarrel and fight, among themselves. Indeed, I had rather have fifty drunken Indians in the fort, than five drunken Canadians.

> DANIEL W. HARMON, *Journal*, Dec. 25, 1802 (Ed. by W. Kaye Lamb, 1957).

He drank like a fish.

> THOMAS C. HALIBURTON, *The old judge*, 1849.

We have an old sayin', "Only what I drink is mine".

> THOMAS C. HALIBURTON, *Sam Slick's wise saws*, 1853, ch. 23.

Here's a ho, boy!

> ANON., a drinking term popular in the West, 19th. century; in the early days the commonest form of cup was a buffalo horn; the signal to attack in the great buffalo hunts was the cry of "Ho!"

Drinking is the curse of Canada.

> SUSANNA MOODIE, *Life in the clearings*, 1853, 67.

A pledge I make, no wine to take;
Nor brandy red, that turns the head,
Not Whisky hot, that makes the sot;
Nor fiery rum, that ruins home,
Nor will I sin, by drinking gin;
Hard cider too, will never do;
No lager beer, my heart to cheer;
Nor sparkling ale, my face to pale.
To quench my thirst I'll always bring,
Cold water from the well or spring;
So here I pledge perpetual hate,
To all that can intoxicate.

> A.W. CHASE, *Dr. Chase's recipes*, 1868.

Whisky is the devil. If it was not for whisky I would not have shot McGee. I was as drunk as the devil when I did it.

> PATRICK JAMES WHELAN, assassin of Thomas D'Arcy McGee, qu. in Pierre Berton, *Historic headlines*, 1967, 18, attributed while in jail, 1868.

Pass the tea and let us drink
To the guardians of our land.
You can bet your life it's not our fault
That whisky's contraband!

> ANON., described as an old police song, N.W.M.P., Alberta, 1870's.

The average Victorian's sense of bliss apparently consists of the largest possible number of drinks in the shortest possible time, varied with cigars and billiards ad lib.

> R. BYRON JOHNSON, *Very far west indeed*, 1872, 45.

The Curse of Canada.

> GRIP, Feb. 28, 1874, cartoon on whiskey, by J.W. Bengough; from Susanna Moodie (1853), *see above*.

What is the cause of almost all larcenies? – drink! Of assaults? – drink! Fights, furious driving, interference with police? Drink, drink, drink!

> F.W. FENTON, Chief of Police, Montreal, 1874, qu. in P.B. Waite, *Canada, 1874-1896*, 1971, 3.

A little too much is just enough.

> GRIP'S COMIC ALMANAC, 1883, 38.

For though within this bright
    seductive place
My dollars go not far,
I never more shall see them face to
    face,
When they have crossed the bar.

> BLISS CARMAN, "Crossing the bar", 1895.

Banish-the-Bar.

> ANON., slogan adopted by the temperance movement, ca. 1905. qu. by James H. Gray, *Booze*, 1972, 70, as "the slogan that won the west".

When one is driven to drink he usually has to walk back.

> ROBERT C. (BOB) EDWARDS, Calgary *Eye Opener*, Aug. 4, 1906.

The ability to take a drink and let it alone takes constant practice.

> ROBERT C. (BOB) EDWARDS, Calgary *Eye Opener*, Feb. 19, 1910.

We write upon the drink question with almost pontifical authority.

> ROBERT C. (BOB) EDWARDS, Calgary *Eye Opener;* attributed.

D'ye ken Sam Hughes, he's the foe of booze,
He's the real champeen, of the dry canteen,
For the camp is dead, and we're sent to bed,
So we won't have a head in the morning.

> ANON., song of the Militia, after teetotaler Sam Hughes became Minister of Militia, 1911.

Gallons of trouble can come out of a pint flask.

> ROBERT C. (BOB) EDWARDS, Calgary *Eye Opener,* May 22, 1915.

I wish somehow that we could prohibit the use of alcohol and merely drink beer and whiskey and gin as we used to.

> STEPHEN LEACOCK, "This strenuous age", *Frenzied fiction,* 1917, 162.

Four and twenty Yankees, feeling very dry
Went across the border to get a drink of rye.
When the rye was opened, the Yanks began to sing,
"God bless America, but God save the King!"

ANON., American prohibition song; qu. the Duke of Windsor's *A king's story,* 1951; variant qu. in B. Riddell, *Regional disparity,* 1972, 5.

Three water-witches of the East,
Under the stimulus of rum,
Decided that the hour had come
To hold a Saturnalian feast,
In course of which they hoped to find
For their black art, once and for all,

The true effect of alcohol
Upon the cold, aquatic mind.

> E.J. PRATT, *The witches' brew,* 1925, 9.

Their lordships think that the decision in *Russell* v. *the Queen* can only be supported today . . . on the assumption of the Board [the Privy Council], apparently made at the time of deciding the case of *Russell* v. *the Queen,* that the evil of intemperance at that time amounted in Canada to one so great and so general that at least for the period [1882] it was a menace to the national life of Canada so serious and pressing that the National Parliament was called on to intervene to protect the nation from disaster. An epidemic of pestilence might conceivably have been regarded as analogous.

> LORD HALDANE, *Appeal cases,* 1925, 412.

This is how I drink too, as if I were taking an eternal sacrament.

> MALCOLM LOWRY, *Under the volcano,* 1947, 40.

Ontario's such a respectable place;
Drinking's no crime, but it's still a disgrace,
So hide us away behind curtain and screen
While we stealthily go through the motions obscene
In a manner genteel, correctly genteel,
Secret and stuffy, but always genteel.

> L.A. MACKAY, "Frankie went down to the corner", 1948.

One cannot but wonder if the French might not have held Canada if they had only been willing to drink water — certainly they could have held out longer.

> E.P. HAMILTON, *The French and Indian wars,* 1962, 99.

The effect of alcohol on different races is as remarkable as it is invariable. An Englishman becomes haughty; a Swede sad; an Irishman sentimental; a Russian fraternal; a German melodious. A Scotchman always becomes militant.

> JOHN KENNETH GALBRAITH, *The Scotch*, 1964, 119.

The Boy Scouts would never believe that I drink to let out the joy inside me. They'd say it's a lie. Maybe so, but it's a beautiful lie.

> DAVID HELWIG, "The streets of summer", 1969.

Indians also know, from long experience, that excessive drinking annoys white people. It gets them upset. They pay attention to a drunk Indian; a sober Indian they never see. Drinking is an excellent way for the Indian to get Canada's attention.

> HEATHER ROBERTSON, *Reservations are for Indians*, 1970, 273.

Increased availability of liquor leads inexorably to increased consumption and increased abuse.

> JAMES H. GRAY, *Booze*, 1972, 220.

A drunkard likes to be drunk. An alcoholic can't stand to be sober.

> ALDEN NOWLAN, "Scratchings", 1974.

Drought

The crop has failed again, the wind and sun
Dried out the stubble first, then one by one
The strips of summerfallow, seered with heat,
Crunched, like old fallen leaves, our lovely wheat.
The garden is a dreary, blighted waste,
The very air is gritty to my taste.

> EDNA JAQUES, "A farmer's wife" (In the drought area), [1934].

Drug Stores

I swivel on my axle and survey
The latex tintex kotex cutex land.
Soft kingdoms sell for dimes, Life Pic Look Click
Inflate the male with conquest girly grand.

> F.R. SCOTT, "Saturday sundae", 1945.

Drugs

To be indifferent to the growth of such an evil in Canada would be inconsistent with those principles of morality which ought to govern the conduct of a Christian nation.

> W.L. MACKENZIE KING, *Report on the need for the suppression of the opium traffic in Canada*, Queen's Printer, 1908, 13.

Let's put some pot in every chicken.

> ANON., political slogan rejected by Pierre E. Trudeau when campaigning for the leadership of the Liberal Party, 1968.

Pot, speed, LSD – phooey! I'm hooked on human beings, they're my drug – the great world and all the people in it.

> RICHARD J. NEEDHAM, *A friend in Needham*, 1969, 23.

A chemophilic society is one in which an abundance of intoxicating drugs is available to a large number of people who are receptive to their easy use. We live in such a society today even though our full potential for drug dependence has certainly not yet been realized.

> ANDREW I. MALCOLM, *The case against the drugged mind*, 1973, 3.

Drunk

The witness said, "Well, he may have been intoxicated, but he most certainly was not Yukon drunk".

> JACK SISSONS, qu. in J. Kettle and Dean Walker, *Verdict!*, 1968, 267.

Drunkards

Paradise for them is to get drunk.

> MONTCALM, *Journal des campagnes*, Aug. 29, 1757, on the Indians. (Trans.)

Look here, McGee, this government can't afford two drunkards, and you've got to stop.

> SIR JOHN A. MACDONALD to Thomas D'Arcy McGee, qu. in E.B. Biggar, *Anecdotal life of Sir John Macdonald*, 1891, 193.

Annabelle has yellow teeth
And solid rubber underneath,
Golden polish on her toes
And pink and purple underclothes.
Nothing effervesces quite
As Annabelle when she is tight.

> GEORGE JOHNSTON, "Annabelle", 1959.

I affirm that the agonies of the drunkard find a very close parallel in the agonies of the mystic who has abused his powers.

> MALCOLM LOWRY, "Preface to a novel", *Can. lit.* No. 9, 1961, 28.

Ducks

We have roamed the marshes, keen
    with expectation,
    Lain at eve in ambush, where the
    ducks are wont to fly;
Felt the feverish fervour, the thrilling,
    full pulsation,
    As the flocks came whirring from
    the rosy western sky.

> BARRY STRATON, "Evening on the marshes", 1884.

On a sudden seven ducks
With a splashy rustle rise,
Stretching out their seven necks,
One before, and two behind,
And the others all arow,
And as steady as the wind
With a swivelling whistle go.

> ARCHIBALD LAMPMAN, "Morning on the Lièvre", 1888.

Duels

I have no great fancy for being shot at whenever public officers, whose abilities I may happen to contrast with their emoluments, think fit to consider political arguments and general illustrations insolent and offensive.

> JOSEPH HOWE, letter to John Spry Morris, Apr. 24, 1840.

Dullness

We have often been told of our necessary dullness because we had no Revolutionary War, no French Revolution, no War Between the States.

> MILTON WILSON, in *Tamarack rev.*, No. 9, 1958, 91.

Dumb

I have come where there is nothing
    more to know,
Nothing to say.

> F.E. SPARSHOTT, "By the canal", 1958.

Dunlop, William "Tiger"

He is a verb in the active voice and the imperative mood, difficult to decline and impossible to conjugate.

> JOHN WILSON, *Blackwoods*, Vol. 32, Aug., 1832, 239.

Duplessis, Maurice

The only portable dictatorship in the democratic world.

> T.D. BOUCHARD, Quebec Liberal leader, referring to Quebec government of Maurice Duplessis, Oct., 1936.

I'll give Premier Duplessis and his policies a blanket endorsement.

> MITCHELL HEPBURN, about 1936, qu. in Neil McKenty, *Mitch Hepburn*, 1967, 152.

A vote against Maurice Duplessis or any of his candidates will be a vote for participation assimilation and centralization.

> MAURICE DUPLESSIS, Quebec election campaign, Trois-Rivières, Oct. 3, 1939. Use of the word "participation" was widely considered as a criticism of the federal Liberal government's declaration of war, Sept. 10, 1939.

The Union Nationale Party, it's me!

> MAURICE DUPLESSIS, frequently attributed, 1940's. (Trans.)

Mr. Duplessis has a portable government. He carries it in his brief case wherever he goes.

> GEORGES LAPALME, Leader, Quebec Liberal Party, 1950, qu. in P. Laporte, *The true face of Duplessis*, 1960, 24.

I know that certain sums of money have been contributed to the University's coffers over the past few years without this being made public, with the matter remaining unknown except to the Rector and his immediate Counsellors, and I know that we owe all this to the graciousness, the generosity and the great amiability, I was going to say and I will say, the sincere friendship that M. Duplessis has shown the Rector of Laval University.

> MGR. FERDINAND VANDRY, Rector of Laval Univ., speech at inauguration of the School of Commerce, qu. in *Cité libre*, June-July, 1952, 64. (Trans.)

One of Canada's greatest sons.

> JOHN BASSETT, qu. in *Globe and Mail*, Feb. 13, 1958, 36.

I have no family. My only responsibility is the welfare of Quebec. I belong to the province.

> MAURICE DUPLESSIS, qu. in Pierre Laporte, *The true face of Duplessis*, 1960, 33.

Durham, Lord

I would fain hope I have not lived altogether in vain. Whatever the Tories may say, the Canadians will one day do justice to my memory.

> LORD DURHAM, on his death-bed at Cowes, July, 1840.

Canada has been the death of him.

> JOHN STUART MILL, in 1840, qu. in J.C. Dent, *The last forty years*, 1881, Vol. 1, 12.

A believer in freedom who ruled with absolute authority.

> J.M.S. CARELESS, *Canada: a story of challenge*, 1953, 192.

The best historian of Canada.

> MICHEL BRUNET, *Queen's quart.*, Vol. LXIII, No. 3, Autumn, 1956, 430.

His Byronic moods, his imperious yet gracious manner, the carelessly baroque magnificence of his style of life soon became almost legendary in the Canadas. He had once confided to Creevey that he could 'jog along' on forty thousand pounds a year. He was known privately as 'King Jog'; but his political sobriquet was 'Radical Jack'.

> DONALD G. CREIGHTON, *The story of Canada*, 1959, 127.

Durham's Report, 1839

Nothing can be better than the statesmanlike tone and the temper of this masterly document; and it would be impossible to rate too highly the influence it is likely to exercise.

THE EXAMINER, (London, Eng.), Feb. 10, 1839.

The Report will be a most valuable textbook for Colonial Reforms in time to come – it has sapped the very foundation of our wretched Colonial system.

THE SPECTATOR (London), Feb. 16, 1839.

It is a farrago of false statements and false principles . . . the most fatal legacy that could have been bequeathed to our American colonies.

QUARTERLY REVIEW (Edinburgh), Mar., 1839, 505.

Lord Durham's plan is *English,* and directly tends to raise a nation of equal and prosperous freemen: the plan of his opponents is *Russian,* and directly tends to produce a few arrogant, insufferable nobles, and a multitude of wretched, insulted slaves.

KINGSTON UPPER CANADA HERALD , May, 1839.

French Canada of 1839 deliberately set itself to falsify Lord Durham's prophecy and who will say that it has not succeeded?

CHESTER MARTIN, in *Can.hist.rev.,* 1939, 184.

The work he accomplished was greater than the man.

LORD TWEEDSMUIR, in *Can.hist.rev.,* 1939, 117.

Duty

The greatest heroine in life is she who knowing her duty, resolves not only to do it, but to do it to the best of her abilities, with heart and mind bent upon the work.

CATHERINE PARR TRAILL, *The Canadian settler's guide,* 1855, 16.

I ask for no prouder monument, and for no other memorial when I die and go hence, than the testimony here offered, that I have done my duty.

SIR JAMES DOUGLAS, Apr. 8, 1864, in reply to deputation of well wishers prior to his leaving post of Governor of British Columbia.

However anxious I may be to be gracious and civil, I don't care a damn for any one when a matter of duty is involved.

LORD DUFFERIN, letter to Lord Kimberley, 1873.

No fidget and no reformer, just
A calm observer of ought and must.

BLISS CARMAN, "Joys of the road", 1894.

This bent, this work, this duty – for thereby
God numbers thee, and marks thee for His own:
Careless of hurt, or threat, or praise, or pelf,
Find it and follow it, this, and this alone!

ARCHIBALD LAMPMAN, "Salvation", 1900.

If he has to, he will not,
  He will if he mustn't;
He does if he shouldn't
  And should if he doesn't.

ALBERT D. WATSON, "Who is it?", 1908.

"Have you ever noticed," asked Anne reflectively, "that when people say it is their duty to tell you a certain thing you may prepare for something disagreeable? Why is it that they never seem to think it a duty to tell you the pleasant things they hear about you?"

L.M. MONTGOMERY, *Anne of Avonlea*, 1909, 68.

I've had a bellyful of duty, I've got something in me that wants more than duty and work.

ROBERTSON DAVIES, *Overlaid*, 1948, 18.

Eagles

Tecumseh watched the eagles
In summer o'er the plain,
And learned their cry, "If freedom
    die,
Ye will have lived in vain!"

> BLISS CARMAN, "Tecumseh and the ea-
> gles", 1918.

Earth

Nowadays the mess is everywhere
And getting worse. Earth after all
Is a battlefield.

> DARYL HINE, "The survivors", 1968.

jeez i wish i were lying face down on
    my chest and belly
breathin' easy on th soft grass earth
    rolling ovr th hills,
endlessly days turning into gold,
    seasons cycle
weaving into th forever needle thru
    frost, snow and
bright yellow bounty in warming days
    in th fire

> BILL BISSETT, "Far away from th radar
> wolves but all there", 1971.

Eating

More people are killed by over-eating
and drinking than by the sword.

> SIR WILLIAM OSLER, Oslerisms (Bean),
> 1905.

All I can say, to make myself perfectly
clear, is that eating puff-ball is like

standing in a familiar place and looking in a strange direction.

> GREGORY CLARK, Greg's choice, 1961, 60.

Ecology

Canadian action is an assertion of the
importance of the environment, of the
sanctity of life on this planet, of the
need for the recognition of a principle
of clean seas, which is in all respects as
vital a principle for the world of today
and tomorrow as was the principle of
free seas for the world of yesterday.

> PIERRE E. TRUDEAU, speech, Annual
> Meeting, Canadian Press, Toronto, Apr.
> 15, 1970.

Part of our heritage is our wilderness . . . We cannot wait for a disaster to prompt us to act. We need law
now to protect coastal states from the
excesses of shipping states. We now
know that spring is not automatic. We
now know that the responsibility is
ours to restore and maintain the health
of the biosphere.

> PIERRE E. TRUDEAU, speech, Annual
> Meeting, Canadian Press, Toronto, Apr.
> 15, 1970.

Economics

Hewers of wood and drawers of water.

> BIBLE; a phrase frequently used to de-
> scribe the Canadian economy during
> 19th. century; first used by William
> Lyon Mackenzie, speech at Streetsville,
> Ont., 1836.

Nature laid the foundation, Adam Smith and his successors built the columns, and, I believe, it has been given to me to place the keystone in the arch of Political Economy.

> WILLIAM ALEXANDER THOMSON, *An essay on production*, 1863, 46; qu. in *Jour. of Can. stud.*, May, 1969, 44.

The time has come, gentlemen, when the people of this Dominion have to declare whether Canada is for the Canadians, or whether it is to be a pasture for cows to be sent to England. It is for the electors to say whether every appliance of civilization shall be manufactured within her bounds for our own use, or whether we shall remain hewers of wood and drawers of water to the United States.

> SIR JOHN A. MACDONALD, campaign speech, qu. in Toronto *Mail*, Aug. 28, 1878.

Do'st thou not know, deluded one,
  That Adam Smith has clearly
      proved,
That 'tis self-interest alone
  By which the wheels of life are
      moved?

> T. PHILLIPS THOMPSON, "The political economist and the tramp", 1887.

Political causes alone seldom produce serious discontent, unless they affect injuriously the economic condition of the people.

> SIR WILFRID LAURIER, H. of C., *Debates*, Apr. 5, 1888, 556.

I challenge any man to prove, or even assert with any degree of authority or knowledge, that any banking institution, any wholesale house, or any department store, no matter how large, ever added one new dollar to the wealth of the realm; but the farmer who tills the soil and sells one bushel of wheat or grows a bullock for the

market adds to the wealth of the nation.

> SIR RODMOND ROBLIN, speech, Manitoba Grain Growers' Convention, Winnipeg, 1906.

The dominance of eastern Canada over western Canada seems likely to persist. Western Canada has paid for the development of Canadian nationality, and it would appear that it must continue to pay. The acquisitiveness of eastern Canada shows little sign of abatement.

> HAROLD A. INNIS, *A history of the Canadian Pacific Railway*, 1923, 294.

The economist can, of course, give us the facts. That is his job. He is a good cartographer, but a bad pilot. There were plenty of crises in the nineteenth century, when cold-blooded economic fact would have been the end of us if there had not been some vision to interpret it.

> VINCENT MASSEY, Canadian Club, Ottawa, Jan. 20, 1924.

As a nation I believe we are today wealthier than ever before in our history, yet, paradoxical as it may seem in this year 1932, the more bread we have, the more breadlines there are; the more shoes we produce, the more shoeless there are; the more clothes we manufacture, the more people there are without clothes; the more homes we build, the more there are looking for shelter; the more wealth we produce, the greater is the poverty.

> ABRAHAM A. HEAPS, H. of C., *Debates*, Nov. 21, 1932, 1409.

Democracy will defeat the economist at every turn at its own game.

> HAROLD A. INNIS, paper read at Liberal-Conservative Summer School, Newmarket, Ont., Sept., 1933.

The dole is a condemnation of our economic system. If we cannot abolish the dole, we should abolish the system.

R.B. BENNETT, radio address, Jan. 2, 1935.

All these new-fangled doctrines, when you examine them closely, have nothing inside them but some withered fallacy or some loose and livid lunacy.

ARTHUR MEIGHEN, speech to McGill Graduates' Society, Montreal, 1935.

Tory times are hard times.

ANON., Liberal Party adherents' claim, since 1930's.

With our own property, with our own work, with our own savings we build our economic servitude.

ABBÉ LIONEL GROULX, address, Montreal Junior Chamber of Commerce, Feb. 12, 1936. (Trans.)

If an economist becomes certain of the solution of any problem, he can be equally certain that his solution is wrong.

H.A. INNIS, qu., *Dalhousie rev.*, 1936, 226.

Mr. King never quite got it into his head during his economic studies at Toronto and Harvard that our civilization is dominated by carnivorous animals.

FRANK H. UNDERHILL, *Can. forum*, XXIV, Sept., 1944, 125.

Newfoundland must develop or perish.

JOSEPH R. SMALLWOOD, Aug. 2, 1949, qu. in R. Gwyn, *Smallwood*, 1972, 138.

"Please, please," I entreated, "look at my problem.
I and my brothers, regardless of race, are afflicted.
Our welfare hangs on remote policies, distant decisions,
Planning of trade, guaranteed prices, high employment –
Can provincial fractions deal with this complex whole?
Surely such questions are now supra-national!"

F.R. SCOTT, "Some Privy Counsel", 1950.

I don't think that free enterprise requires that governments do nothing about economic conditions. Governments can – and I believe governments should – pursue fiscal and commercial policies which will encourage and stimulate enterprise and wise government policies can do a lot to maintain the right kind of economic climate.

LOUIS ST. LAURENT, Annual Convention, Canadian Lumbermen's Association, Montreal, Feb. 9, 1953.

If we are economically dependent on the United States, can we remain politically independent? That is the question which will have to be decided by the present generation.

GORDON CHURCHILL, interview, Montreal *Star*, Nov. 19, 1957.

Each phase of expansion in Canada has been a tactical move designed to forestall, counteract, or restrain the northward extension of American economic and political influence. Primary responsibility for maintaining and strengthening this policy of defensive expansionism has fallen on the state.

HUGH G.J. AITKEN, *The state and economic growth*, 1959, 114.

While most of the world's great countries have established long-term programs of development and economic planning, Canada still sticks to its sacrosanct economic liberalism.

> RENÉ LÉVESQUE, qu. in *Canada month*, Dec., 1962, 23.

What really matters in Canada is a standard of private living and a standard of public services.

> JOSEPH R. SMALLWOOD, Ontario. Confederation of Tomorrow Conference, Nov. 27-30, 1967, *Proceedings*, 80.

Differences in both the levels of economic and social well-being and in economic opportunity among the various regions and provinces of Canada are large, and have persisted with only modest change for over forty years.

> ECONOMIC COUNCIL OF CANADA, *Fifth annual review*, 1968, 141.

Masters in our own house we must be, but our house is all of Canada.

> PIERRE E. TRUDEAU, Liberal Leadership Convention, Ottawa, Apr. 5, 1968.

It is more important to get bread on all tables first, before we spend all our money making sure that everyone can discuss our economic problems – in two languages.

> SAINT JOHN (N.B.) *TELEGRAPH-JOURNAL*, editorial, Dec. 17, 1968, 4.

So long as Canadian economic activity is dominated by the corporate elite, and so long as workers' rights are confined within their present limits, corporate requirements for profit will continue to take precedence over human needs.

> MELVILLE WATKINS and other N.D.P. dissident members, "The Waffle Resolution 133", submitted to the N.D.P. Convention, Winnipeg, Oct. 28-31, 1969.

A recession is when your neighbour has to tighten his belt. A depression is when you have to tighten your own belt. And a panic is when you have no belt to tighten and your pants fall down.

> T.C. DOUGLAS, qu. in *T.C. Douglas, a biographical essay*, 1971, unp., issued by the N.D.P.

We're happy as long as we enjoy the economic advantages of North American life, but when it comes to attitudes, culture and foreign policy, we flee to something non-American which we call Canadian. The question is: Can we continue to be within the economic empire of the United States and still maintain our difference? The differences are probably being eroded away without our realizing it. We want the best of both worlds.

> GERHARD FISCHER, history teacher, qu. in R.L. Perry, *Galt, U.S.A.*, 1971, 105.

The only way to get away from the influence of the American economy would be to float our half of the continent off somewhere else.

> JOHN KENNETH GALBRAITH, qu. by R.M. MacIntosh, address, Empire Club, Toronto, Feb. 3, 1972.

Economists

Our economists have played the humble self-imposed role of minor technicians, never questioning the major purposes of the capitalist system in which they found themselves . . . happy in their unambitious way as the intellectual garage-mechanics of Canadian capitalism.

> F.H. UNDERHILL, in *Can. jour. econ. and pol. sci.*, 1933, 404.

Economy

However much the Canadian taxpayer may favour a policy of strict economy in the abstract, he likes nothing so little as its application.

SIR JOSEPH POPE, *Memoirs of Macdonald*, 1894, II, 141.

I claim that we have come to a period in the history of our country when we must decide once and for all which shall prevail – profits or human welfare.

JAMES S. WOODSWORTH, H. of C., *Debates*, Mar. 14, 1922.

The way it was jokingly put in Ottawa at the time was that an investigation of the Canadian economy was, in Mr. Howe's view, an investigation of C.D. Howe; and he saw no need for that.

TOM KENT, Winnipeg *Free Press*, Apr. 21, 1958, 21, re announcement of Roy. Comm. on Canada's Economic Prospects, Apr., 1955.

If it should turn out that there is not the necessary combination of resources in sufficient quantities to permit a substantial rise in living standards in the Atlantic region, generous assistance should be given to those people who might wish to move to other parts of Canada where there may be greater opportunities.

CANADA. ROY. COMM. ON CANADA'S ECONOMIC PROSPECTS, *Preliminary report*, 1956, 99.

Canadian economic policy has historically been dominated by the ambition to create a country rival in power to the United States, and so to prove that the Americans were wrong to revolt from colonial rule in 1776. The ambition to outgrow the United States is a futile one: in spite of the boasting about Canada's faster growth in the postwar period, it is a fact that the growth was insufficient to raise the ratio of the Canadian to the American population to what it was in 1860.

HARRY G. JOHNSON, *Canada in a changing world economy*, 1962, 62.

The most decisive implication of the Canadian economy for the Canadian polity springs from the fact that there *is* a Canadian economy, a single, distinct, recognizable, working, Canadian body economic.

EUGENE FORSEY, speech, Ontario Secondary School Teachers' Federation, Toronto, Apr. 24, 1962.

Get the economy moving again.

LESTER B. PEARSON, Prime Minister, pledge made after Liberal victory, Apr. 8, 1963.

This still leaves, as I see it, a veto with the president of the United States with regard to the expansion of Canada's economy, which is something that is not in keeping with the sovereignty of this nation.

JOHN DIEFENBAKER, H. of C., *Debates*, July 22, 1963, 2438 re tax on U.S. purchases of Canadian securities.

It is very odd that, enjoying one of the highest standards of living in the world, Canadians in all walks of life should nevertheless believe that their economy is a frail, hothouse creation, whose very survival depends on the constant vigilance of a government gardener well provided with props and plant food. Who but historians could have created this chasm between reality and belief?

JOHN H. DALES, *The protective tariff in Canada's development*, 1966, 153.

We can do the things that are necessary to regain control of our economy and thus maintain our independence. Or we can acquiesce in becoming a colonial dependency of the United States, with no future except the hope of eventual absorption.

> WALTER GORDON, *A choice for Canada*, 1966, 124.

Every Canadian should pray every morning and evening that the U.S. economy will continue to prosper.

> MITCHELL SHARP, speech in Toronto, Nov. 6, 1971, qu. in R. Reid, *Canadian style*, 1973, 344.

Editors

We hope that Canadian editors will endeavour to do their best to encourage native talent. They should also pay for it.

> VARSITY, (Toronto), Jan. 23, 1886, edit.

Editors invariably get their own books published!

> AL PURDY, *Queen's quart.*, Vol. 76, 1969, 710.

Edmonton, Alta.

Edmonton is as big as Chicago, but it isn't all built up yet.

> ANON., early 20th. cent.; answer to an American visitor who asked the size of the city.

Education

Although the Canadian Peasants are far from being a stupid race, they are at present an ignorant people, from want of instruction – not a man in five hundred can read; perhaps it has been the policy of the clergy to keep them in the dark, as it is a favourite tenet with the Roman Catholic priests that ignorance is the mother of devotion.

> HUGH FINLAY, letter to Evan Nepean, Under-Secretary of State, Home Dept., London, 1784.

The attention paid to education in the United States is the grand secret of their power and the most indissoluble bond of their union.

> WILLIAM LYON MACKENZIE, in *Colonial advocate*, Jan. 22, 1829.

As Intelligence is power, such is an unavoidable opinion in the breasts of those who think that the human race ought to consist of two classes – one that of the *oppressors*, another that of the *oppressed*. But, if Education be to communicate the art of happiness; and if Intelligence consists of knowledge and sagacity; the question whether the people should be Educated, is the same with the question whether they should be happy or miserable.

> WILLIAM LYON MACKENZIE, *Catechism of education*, 1830, 24.

For a long time there have been complaints that the education given in our seminaries does not fully correspond to the needs of the century, that it is too much turned towards the study of ancient languages and old theories.

> LE CANADIEN, (Montreal), Jan. 8, 1836. (Trans.)

The true purpose of education is to cherish and unfold the seed of immortality already sown within us; to develop, to their fullest extent, the capacities of every kind with which the God who made us has endowed us.

> ANNA JAMESON, *Winter studies and summer rambles*, 1838.

One must be doctor, priest, notary, or lawyer. Outside of these four professions it seems there is no salvation for the young educated French Canadian. If by chance one of us had an invincible distaste for all four; if it was too painful for him to save souls, mutilate bodies, or lose fortunes, there remained only one course for him to take if he were rich, and two if he were poor; to do nothing at all in the first case, to exile himself or to starve to death in the second.

> PIERRE CHAUVEAU, *Charles Guérin,* 1843, 2. (Trans.)

By education, I mean not the mere acquisition of certain arts, or of certain branches of knowledge, but that instruction and discipline which qualify and dispose the subjects of it for their appropriate duties and appointments in life, as Christians, as persons in business, and also as members of the civil community in which they live.

> EGERTON RYERSON, *Report on system of instruction for Upper Canada,* 1847.

Be assured that no system of popular education will flourish in a country which does violence to the religious sentiments and feelings of the Churches of that country.

> EGERTON RYERSON, letter to Robt. Baldwin, July 14, 1849.

I am in favour of national school education free from sectarian teaching, and available without charge to every child in the province.

> GEORGE BROWN, election address, Haldimand election, 1850.

The want of education and moral training is the only *real* barrier that exists between the different classes of men. Nature, reason, and Christianity recognize no other.

> SUSANNA MOODIE, *Life in the clearings,* 1853, 75.

Let our School system be destroyed, and what remains to us of hope for the country?

> TORONTO *GLOBE*, Apr. 2, 1853, 159.

National education. – Common school, grammar school, and collegiate free from sectarianism and open to all on equal terms. Earnest war will be waged with the separate school system, which has unfortunately obtained a footing.

> TORONTO *GLOBE*, Oct. 1, 1853, statement of policy.

The best of colleges – a farmer's fireside.

> JOSEPH HOWE, on his own education; qu., in G.M. Grant, *Joseph Howe*, 1906, 33.

Catholic electors who do not use their electoral power in behalf of separate schools are guilty of the mortal sin; likewise persons who do not make the sacrifice necessary to secure such schools or send their children to mixed schools.

> ANDRÉ DE CHARBONNEL, Bishop of Toronto, pastoral letter, 1856.

To be true education it must involve both discipline and culture. Discipline alone gives strength, but would involve hardness and narrowness; culture alone might give elegance, but would tend to effeminacy. Discipline is masculine; culture is feminine; and as it is not good for man to be alone, let discipline be always wedded to culture.

> JAMES DE MILLE, address, Dalhousie College, Oct., 1878.

The education which we receive in all our colleges is in the hands of the priests. Very good men they are indeed, but prejudiced, biased, & except upon those branches of knowledge of which they have made a specialty, very ignorant. Very ignorant, especially are they of modern history. The books they have read, all the sources of information to which they have access, are the continental ultramontane books & press. They have there imbibed a horror of the very name of liberalism, which permeates the whole of their teaching.

> SIR WILFRID LAURIER, letter to Edward Blake, July 10, 1882. (Ont. Arch.)

What, after all, is education but a subtle, slowly-affected change, due to the actions of the externals − of the written record of the great minds of all ages, of the beautiful and harmonious surroundings of nature and art, and of the lives, good or ill, of our fellows? − these alone educate us, these alone mould the growing mind.

> SIR WILLIAM OSLER, "The leaven of science", in *Univ.* [of Penn.] *med. mag.*, 1894.

Influence, power, the future belong to those who are trained, who are best armed for the struggles of commerce, of industry and practical science. Nothing must be destroyed: but our system of education must be modified so that in all activities, in all careers, the French Canadian may not be on an inferior footing.

> SENATOR L.O. DAVID, *Le clergé canadien, sa mission, son oeuvre*, 1896, 107. (Trans.)

The truth is that education is the fruit of temperament, not success the fruit of education.

> LORD BEAVERBROOK, *Success*, 1921, chap. 5.

Education imposed from without may be a hindrance rather than a help.

> LORD BEAVERBROOK, *Success*, 1921, chap. 5.

Higher education in America flourished chiefly as a qualification for entrance into a moneymaking profession, and not as a thing in itself.

> STEPHEN LEACOCK, *My discovery of England*, 1922, 96.

When you educate a woman late in life, it always sort of upsets her.

> FRED JACOB, "Man's world", in his: *One-third of a bill*, 1925, 84.

The critical test of the value of our educational systems is the attitude of adults to their own mental growth.

> R.C. WALLACE, *A liberal education*, 1932.

I am without that education which standardizes my thoughts with those 10,000,000 others; I am not of the "caste", so my ideas flow and I think freely.

> GREY OWL (Archie Belaney), private notebook, 1930's, qu. in *Ontario hist.*, Vol. 63, 1971, 172.

One may obtain information from a good encyclopaedia, but the toughness of mind which enables a person to sift out random theories, empty shibboleths, dashing paradoxes, and imposing sophistries may only be gained from hard schooling.

> SIDNEY E. SMITH, inaugural Presidential address, Univ. of Manitoba, Oct. 12, 1934.

Medieval education was supposed to fit people to die. Any school-boy of today can still feel the effect of it.

> STEPHEN LEACOCK, "Education eating up life", *Too much college*, 1939.

But, in the wider sense, what I want to advocate is not to make education shorter, but to make it much longer – indeed to make it last as long as life itself.

STEPHEN LEACOCK, *Too much college*, 1939, vii.

Primary and secondary education has been an escape mechanism by which the bright and vigorous few from among the masses got away from the lowly classes in which they were born to join the elite of the nation. Education was the trap door that enabled them to go into the so-called professions. And thus education has been an instrument that has created classes in a supposedly classless society.

FATHER M.M. COADY, *The social significance of the co-operative movement*, 1945, 6.

Education should be coterminous with human life.

FATHER M.M. COADY, 1949, qu. in J.R. Kidd, ed., *Learning and society*, 1963, 142.

The educated like my work, and the uneducated like it. As for the half-educated – well, we can only pray for them in Canada, as elsewhere.

ROBERTSON DAVIES, *Fortune, my foe*, 1949, 95.

Education is the progressive development of the individual in all his faculties, physical and intellectual, aesthetic and moral.

CANADA. ROY. COMM. ON NATIONAL DEV. IN THE ARTS, LETTERS AND SCIENCES, 1949-51, *Report*, 1951, 6.

If the Federal Government is to renounce its right to associate itself with other social groups, public and private, in the general education of Canadian citizens, it denies its intellectual and moral purpose, the complete conception of the common good is lost, and Canada as such becomes a materialistic society.

CANADA. ROY. COMM. ON NATIONAL DEV. IN THE ARTS, LETTERS AND SCIENCES, *Report*, 1951, 8.

The present preoccupations with body building and character moulding are useless and may even be dangerous so long as we neglect and starve the mind.

HILDA NEATBY, *So little for the mind*, 1953, 335.

Assuming that we were born on giants' shoulders, we resist the suggestion that we must climb there by a hard and humbling process. We resist even more strenuously the idea that quiet and receptive contemplation, a reverence for the unknown and perhaps the unknowable, are as essential in learning as "planned activities". We assume that with money and know-how everything desirable can be achieved by short-cuts and accelerated programmes. We do not respect knowledge; we exploit it.

HILDA NEATBY, *A temperate dispute*, 1954, 97.

Canadian educationalists are alert to the needs of Canadian schools in psychological matters and while they may not go overboard in the philosophy of experimentalism, they will continue to keep their ears to the ground for every advance it may be possible for them to make within the limits of their competence and resources.

H.L. STEIN, in J. Katz, ed., *Canadian education today*, 1956, 51.

One would feel more confident as to the future if more of our educational experts had ideals and objectives that were fundamentally human. Job security and well-adjusted mediocrity in a mass population are not good enough. An evaluation of pupils not on a basis of mental competence but on a basis of dossiers of observed attitudes (school, street and home) savours of the police state as well as arrogating to the prying teacher the functions of home, church, community and Almighty God.

WATSON KIRKCONNELL, in J. Katz, ed., *Canadian education today*, 1956, 209.

It's misleading to suppose there's any basic difference between education and entertainment.

MARSHALL MCLUHAN, *Explorations*, Mar., 1957, 26.

The man who has ceased to learn ought not to be allowed to wander around loose in these dangerous days.

FATHER M.M. COADY, qu. in J.R. Kidd, *How adults learn*, 1959, 303.

The pursuit of learning is really the pursuit of fine living.

J. ROBY KIDD, address, Annual convention, Junior Leagues of America, Victoria, B.C., May 18, 1959.

All education is bad which is not self-education.

ROBERTSON DAVIES, *A voice from the attic*, 1960, 26.

Our age has robbed millions of the simplicity of ignorance, and has so far failed to lift them to simplicity of wisdom.

ROBERTSON DAVIES, *A voice from the attic*, 1960, 54.

Of what use is a University education to a young man unless he comes under the influence of instructors who can astonish him?

ROBERTSON DAVIES, *A voice from the attic*, 1960, 155.

In the dusty looking glass of grammar, Number, the young see the shape of their brain.

JAMES REANEY, *Twelve letters to a small town*, 1962, 10.

If French Canada is going to continue to insist that matters of education are exclusively the business of the provinces, then it will indeed be arguing that the rules are more important than the game.

GWETHALYN GRAHAM, letter to Solange Chaput Rolland, in *Dear enemies*, 1963, 108.

Log College.

ANON., quoted in William H. Elgee, *The social teachings of the Canadian churches*, 1964, 57.

Theoretically an industrial system sorts and sifts masses of people according to their interests and talents into the multifarious range of tasks which have to be performed. Social development based on industry means constantly emerging possibilities for which new skills are required. The richness of its educational system will determine an industrial society's chances of growth and survival.

JOHN PORTER, *The vertical mosaic*, 1965, 166.

Those who are reared in a milieu indifferent to education are not likely to acquire a high evaluation of it.

JOHN PORTER, *The vertical mosaic*, 1965, 172.

The inequalities that exist in the social class system arise in part from the inadequacy of educational institutions . . . Thus as the corporate system becomes even more firmly established the inequalities that arise because of parental position can be overcome only through a more open educational system.

> JOHN PORTER, *The vertical mosaic*, 1965, 293.

While education has made an important contribution to the growth of real income and productivity in Canada over the past half century, the even greater contribution of education to growth in the United States indicates that education has apparently been a factor tending to widen rather than narrow differences in income and productivity between the two countries over this period.

> ECONOMIC COUNCIL OF CANADA, *Second annual review*, 1965, 93.

At the heart of modern liberal education lies the desire to homogenize the world. Today's natural and social sciences were consciously produced as instruments to this end.

> GEORGE P. GRANT, *Lament for a nation*, 1965, 79.

One of our major functions in Canada is paying for the education of future American citizens.

> A.R.M. LOWER, *Can. hist. rev.*, Vol. 47, 1966, 160.

The history of education is essentially the history of mankind.

> MARGARET GILLETT, A *history of education: thought and practice*, 1966, 1.

It has been said that philosophy of education exists in Canada but that there is no Canadian philosophy of education.

> MARGARET GILLETT, A *history of education: thought and practice*, 1966, 405.

Education can and should make one more sensitive and compassionate – and also tough-minded. These are not warring opposites; these are attributes to be achieved in some large harmony.

> J. ROBY KIDD, in Can. Mental Health Assoc., *Probings*, 1968, 50.

Our children are growing up in a world where there are thousands of atom bombs, where our lakes and rivers are polluted, where the rich get richer and the poor get poorer, where there is a massive population explosion, and we're not saying anything about it in our courses.

> CHARLES BIGELOW, qu. in Toronto *Star*, Nov. 12, 1968, 6.

Seminars wilt under the assault of clichés, but come to life under the needle.

> GERALD S. GRAHAM, in M. Wade, ed., *Regionalism in the Canadian community 1867-1967*, 1969, 273.

To assert that people will learn because they are happy is to fly in the face of common knowledge, as every honest adult will admit when he recalls his youth.

> JAMES DALY, qu. in *Maclean's*, Sept., 1970, 30.

When you educate a man, you educate an individual; but when you educate a woman, you educate a family. And that's what I'm going to do.

> AGNES KRIPPS, former B.C. Social Credit M.L.A., qu. in Vancouver *Sun*, Mar. 17, 1973, 9.

Education, Continuing

Individuals learn throughout their lives, not merely at the beginning.

CANADIAN ASSOCIATION FOR ADULT EDUCATION, *A white paper on the education of adults in Canada*, 1966, 1.

The more effective the existing formal educational system becomes, the more acute the needs for a well-developed system of Continuing Education.

CANADIAN ASSOCIATION FOR ADULT EDUCATION, *A white paper on the education of adults in Canada*, 1966, 1.

Efficiency

One trouble with being efficient is that it makes everybody hate you so.

ROBERT C. (BOB) EDWARDS, Calgary *Eye Opener*, Mar. 18, 1916.

Effort

Not in perfection dwells the subtler
    power
  To pierce our mean content, but
    rather works
  Through incompletion, and the
    need that irks,
Not in the flower, but effort toward
    the flower.

CHARLES G.D. ROBERTS, "The cow pasture", 1893.

Persistence is the master of this life;
The master of these little lives of ours;
To the end − effort − even beyond
    the end.

DUNCAN CAMPBELL SCOTT, "Memory of Edmund Morris", 1916.

Everybody *does* everything and there is a surfeit of all things and everyone wants to flap out from the flagpole at the tiptop and nobody wants to climb the stairs and, step by step, get used to the higher air.

EMILY CARR, *Hundreds and thousands*, 1966, 114.

Eggs

If I prevent these eggs from being
    addled
You must not sneer; this egg may
    hatch a heart
That will not close itself against a
    golden dart.

JAMES REANEY, "Suit of nettles: March", 1958.

Thirty million eggs is not a lot of eggs.

ROBERT HARRISON, Financial Consultant, Canadian Egg Marketing Agency, Sept. 1974 on mass of eggs rotting in storage.

Egotism

It is impossible for any human creature to live for himself alone.

SUSANNA MOODIE, *Roughing it in the bush*, 1852, Vol. 2, 12.

The great secret of success is intense faith in oneself.

TORONTO *GLOBE*, May 23, 1865.

The cult of commercialized Christianity, in Ontario at least, has been placed on the basis of an exact science. The three great exponents of that cult are John Wesley Allison, Joseph Wesley Flavelle, and Newton Wesley Rowell. Ego is their god, autos their creed and moi-même their practice.

CHARLES MURPHY, H. of C., *Debates*, Mar. 19, 1918, 39.

The minute a man is convinced that he is interesting, he isn't.

STEPHEN B. LEACOCK, *Humour, its theory and technique*, 1935, 101.

He loved himself too much. As a child
was god.
Thunder stemmed from his whims,
flowers were his path.

> P.K. PAGE, "Paranoid", 1954.

Nothing
will ever unseat this superb
imperturbable rider.

> IRVING LAYTON, "Oil slick on the Rivi-
> era", 1967.

Election Campaigns

This is a fact which we all agree
Come election time in this country
Promise the electorate something for
free
Bribe him with his own money.
Oh, bribe him with his own moneeee.

> DUNCAN MACPHERSON, cartoon in Toron-
> to *Star*, in his: Toronto *Daily Star
> cartoons, 1959-62*, 1962, 1.

Election Funds

The fight goes bravely on . . . We
have expended our strength in aiding
outlying counties and helping our city
candidates. But a big push has to be
made on Saturday and Monday for the
East and West divisions . . . We
therefore make our grand stand on
Saturday. There are but half a dozen
people that can come down hand-
somely, and we have done all we
possibly can do, and we have to ask a
few outsiders to aid us. Will you be
one?

> GEORGE BROWN, letter to a Toronto
> banker, Senator John Simpson, Aug. 15,
> 1872; the "big push" letter.

Immediate, private. I must have another ten thousand — will be the last
time of calling. Do not fail me; answer
to-day.

SIR JOHN A. MACDONALD, Aug. 26, 1872,
telegram to J.J.C. Abbott, legal adviser
to Sir Hugh Allan who had been granted
a charter for construction of the Canadian Pacific Railway.

This evil is the bane of democracy; it is
the nightmare of every man in public
life who is anxious to give service to
the State.

> CLIFFORD SIFTON, in *New era*, 1917.

Gratefulness is always regarded as an
important factor in dealing with democratic governments.

> JOHN AIRD, JR., President of Beauharnois
> Corporation in H. of C., Special Comm.
> appointed to investigate Beauharnois
> Power Project, *Fourth report*, 1931, 823;
> cited in H. of C., *Debates*, 1931, 4260.

Election Slogans

1836. Hurrah for Sir Francis Head
and British Connection.

> FAMILY COMPACT, rallying-cry in Toron-
> to, election of 1836.

1856. Support the Governor.

> CONSERVATIVE PARTY, cry, New Bruns-
> wick election, July, 1856; refers to Lieu-
> tenant-Governor H.T. Manners-Sutton,
> who had dissolved the Assembly against
> advice of his council on the question of
> prohibition of liquor.

1857. Mowat and the Queen, or Morrison and the Pope.

> LIBERAL PARTY OF ONTARIO, provincial
> by-election, South Ontario, December,
> 1857; ref. to Oliver Mowat and J.C.
> Morrison.

1857. No Popery!

> LIBERAL PARTY, slogan used in opposition
> to Sir John A. Macdonald, election of
> 1857.

1857. Non-sectarian Schools.

> GEORGE BROWN, general election, 1857.

1861. No Looking to Washington!

CONSERVATIVE PARTY, slogan, election of July, 1861.

1867. Union and Progress.

CONSERVATIVE PARTY, slogan in 1867.

1868. Howe and Better Terms.

CONSERVATIVE PARTY, slogan in Hants, N.S., by-election, 1868, which Joseph Howe contested successfully after he entered the cabinet of Sir John A. Macdonald.

1875. By a Party, With a Party, but for the Country.

CONSERVATIVE PARTY, 1875; used by Sir John A. Macdonald, speech in Montreal, Nov. 24, 1875. (See also, "1883. With the Party, By the Party, For the Country").

**1882. The traitor's hand is at thy throat,
Ontario! Ontario!
Then kill the tyrant with thy vote,
Ontario! Ontario!**

LIBERAL PARTY, first lines of a song written by James W. Bengough for the June, 1882 election, sung to the tune of 'Maryland, my Maryland'; Edward Blake, leader, said the song would cost him Quebec as it referred to French-Canadians.

1882. Vote in favour of prosperity.

CONSERVATIVE PARTY, slogan used in the federal election, 1882.

1883. With the Party, By the Party, For the Country.

CONSERVATIVE PARTY, Ontario provincial election, 1883; see also, "1875. By a Party, With a Party, but for the Country".

1886. Millions for Corruption, but not a Cent for Nova Scotia!

LIBERAL PARTY, Nova Scotia, anti-Confederation slogan in repeal election, 1886.

1890. Mowat must go.

CONSERVATIVE PARTY OF ONTARIO, provincial election, 1890.

1891. A British subject I was born, a British subject I will die!

CONSERVATIVE PARTY, election 1891, from a statement by Sir John A. Macdonald. (See: MACDONALD, Sir JOHN A.)

1891. The Old Man, the Old Flag, and the Old Policy.

CONSERVATIVE PARTY, campaign motto, election, 1891, coined by L.P. Kribbs, news editor, Toronto *Empire*; also varied, as, "The Old Man, the Old Flag, the Old Party", and, "The Old Flag, the Old Policy, the Old Leader"; a reference to Sir John A. Macdonald.

1893. Reform the Senate!

LIBERAL PARTY, slogan, 1893.

1893. One Man, one Vote.

LIBERAL PARTY, slogan, Convention of 1893.

1894. It's Time for a Change.

CONSERVATIVE PARTY, slogan, Ontario, directed against the Mowat and Hardy governments, 1894 and after; also, Conservative Party slogan, Nova Scotia, June, 1925.

1896. The land for the settler and not for the speculator.

LIBERAL PARTY, slogan in the West, election of 1896.

1900. Shall Tarte rule?

CONSERVATIVE PARTY, query, Ontario, general election, 1900.

1902. Build Up Ontario.

GEORGE W. ROSS, slogan announced by him for Ontario Liberal party of 1902, at Toronto, Nov. 11, 1901.

1904. Canada First; Always Canada!

SIR WILFRID LAURIER's motto, election of 1904; also, "Canada first, Canada last and Canada always".

1904. Laurier and the Larger Canada.

LIBERAL PARTY, slogan, election of 1904.

1904. Let Laurier finish his work.

LIBERAL PARTY, election slogan, also used 1908.

1908. Work! Work! Work! Work! Let Laurier finish his work. Talk! Talk! Talk! Talk! Let Borden keep on with his talk.

LIBERAL PARTY, campaign song, chorus, 1908.

1911. Canada for Us, not for U.S.

CONSERVATIVE PARTY, slogan, election, 1911.

1911. Let Well Enough Alone.

CONSERVATIVE PARTY, cry, election of 1911, on Reciprocity, from a letter by Sir William Van Horne Mar. 8, 1911, pub. in the press.

1911. Empire or Continent, Which?

CONSERVATIVE PARTY, election of 1911.

1911. Follow my white plume!

LIBERAL PARTY, election of 1911. Sir Wilfrid Laurier, on returning from England, spoke in Montreal, July 11, 1911, – "Henry of Navarre at the battle of Ivry said, 'Follow my white plume, and you will find it always in the forefront of honour'. Like Henry IV, I say to you young men, 'Follow my white plume' – the white hairs of sixty-nine years – and you will, I believe I can say it without boasting, find it always in the forefront of honour".

1911. Laurier Prosperity.

LIBERAL PARTY, phrase, election of 1911.

1911. Let the farmer have his chance!

LIBERAL PARTY, Quebec, election of 1911.

1911. Let the People Decide.

CONSERVATIVE PARTY, slogan in attack on Reciprocity, election of 1911.

1911. No Truck nor Trade with the Yankees!

CONSERVATIVE PARTY, anti-Reciprocity slogan, 1911; attributed to Sir George Foster.

1911. Vote against National Suicide.

CONSERVATIVE PARTY, election of 1911; an anti-Reciprocity slogan.

1911. A Vote for Borden is a Vote for Bourassa.

LIBERAL PARTY, slogan in Ontario, election of 1911; in Quebec, the Party slogan was "A Vote for Bourassa is a Vote for Borden", used first by Sir Wilfrid Laurier, speech in St. Eustache, Aug. 22.

1911. A Vote for Borden is a Vote for King and Flag and Country.

CONSERVATIVE PARTY, election of 1911.

1911. No Navy made in London; – no Reciprocity made in Washington.

CHARLES H. CAHAN, Conservative Party slogan, coined in speech at Monument National, Montreal, Sept. 8, 1911. (Trans.)

1917. Don't Turn the Liberty Loan over to Quebec to Spend.

CONSERVATIVE PARTY, slogan, election of 1917.

1917. A Vote for Laurier is a Vote for the Kaiser.

CONSERVATIVE and UNIONIST PARTY, election of 1917.

1921. Canada needs Meighen.

CONSERVATIVE PARTY, slogan used in election campaign, Dec., 1921.

1921. Meighen Will Lead Us Through.

CONSERVATIVE PARTY, general election, 1921.

1925. Vote the Boys Home.

CONSERVATIVE PARTY OF NOVA SCOTIA, election, June, 1925.

1925. It's Time for a Change.

CONSERVATIVE PARTY, slogan, Ontario, directed against the Mowat and Hardy governments, 1894 and after; also, Conservative Party slogan, Nova Scotia, June, 1925.

1926. Don't be Robbed of the Robb Budget.

LIBERAL PARTY, slogan, election of 1926.

1926. Let Robb bring in the Next Budget.

LIBERAL PARTY, slogan, election of 1926.

1926. Ourselves Alone.

LIBERAL PARTY, slogan local to Nova Scotia and New Brunswick, election, 1926.

1926. Put King Back and Keep Prosperity.

LIBERAL PARTY, election of 1926.

1930. Let Uncle Sam go his own Way; our Way is with John Bull.

LIBERAL PARTY, tariff slogan, election of 1930.

1930. Canada First, then the Empire.

R.B. BENNETT, tariff policy as described in election of 1930.

1933. Why change? We are the only group with depression experience.

SIMON FRASER TOLMIE, Premier of B.C., 1928-1933, B.C. election campaign, Nov., 1933.

1933. Work and Wages.

B.C. LIBERAL PARTY, slogan in the election campaign, 1933.

1935. It's King or Chaos!

LIBERAL PARTY, campaign of 1935.

1948. Tucker or Tyranny.

LIBERAL PARTY, slogan, Saskatchewan election, 1948; ref. to Walter Adam Tucker.

1952. Carry On, Hugh John.

CONSERVATIVE PARTY, New Brunswick, under Hugh John Flemming, elections, Sept. 22, 1952, also in 1956 and 1960.

1957. Carry On John.

CONSERVATIVE PARTY, slogan adopted in support of John Diefenbaker, election, 1957.

1957. Follow John [Diefenbaker].

FRANK BERNARD, a slogan coined in 1957 by a Vancouver hotelman and which referred originally to John Taylor, Conservative candidate in Vancouver Burrard. Later adopted by Conservatives in support of Diefenbaker.

1957. It's time for a Diefenbaker Government.

CONSERVATIVE PARTY, slogan used in federal election campaign, June, 1957.

1957. Peace, Progress and Pearson.

LIBERAL PARTY, slogan of supporters of Lester Pearson, election campaign, 1957.

1957. Pearson the Peacemaker.

LIBERAL PARTY, slogan of supporters of Lester Pearson, election campaign, 1957.

1958. Roads to Resources.

JOHN G. DIEFENBAKER, slogan used during election campaign, Mar., 1958.

1960. So Long, Hugh John.

LIBERAL PARTY, New Brunswick, campaign in June, 1960, against Hugh John Flemming.

1960. Social Credit versus Socialism.

ANON., British Columbia election campaign, Sept., 1960.

1962. What have you got to lose?

> SOCIAL CREDIT PARTY (Créditiste), slogan in Quebec, federal election, 1962. (Trans.)

1962. Vote Social Credit, you have nothing to lose.

> RÉAL CAOUETTE, slogan used in 1962 federal election campaign.

1963. Better Pensions for All.

> LIBERAL PARTY, election pamphlet headline, federal election, Apr., 1963.

1965. He cared enough to come.

> JOHN DIEFENBAKER, or his supporters, as a theme of the Diefenbaker campaign, general election, Oct., 1965: orig. used in the U.S. by Nelson Rockefeller in the Oregon primary, 1964.

1968. Trudeau and One Canada.

> LIBERAL PARTY, slogan, election, Spring, 1968.

1971. New Deal for the People.

> N.D.P., Saskatchewan election campaign, June, 1971.

1971. Had Enough? Vote Liberal.

> LIBERAL PARTY OF ONTARIO, election campaign, Oct., 1971, referring to 28 years of Conservative rule.

1972. The Land is Strong.

> LIBERAL PARTY, federal campaign, Oct., 1972, originated by George Elliott, advertising executive.

Elections

The more broken heads & bloody noses there is the more election like.

> DAVID W. SMYTH, 1792, in *John Askin papers*, ed. M. Quaife, 1928, I, 427.

Nothin' improves a man's manners like an election.

> T.C. HALIBURTON, *Sam Slick*, 1836, ch. XV.

Elmes is wood
And Steele is good.
Both are tough,
And that's enough.

> ANON., election ditty in support of "Elmes Steele, the backwoodsman's friend", candidate from Simcoe County in 1841 election.

Elections sometimes attended with disastrous circumstances, a blow results in a cut or wound received from an opponent, and is proportionably severe and serious as the depth and length are deep and wide; for the purpose of healing those wounds and all others, such as scalds, cuts, sores, has Redding's Russia Salve been prepared.

> HALIFAX *ACADIAN RECORDER*, advertisement, July 25, 1857.

If you buy a man to stay at home, you can always tell whether he has kept his bargain or not.

> EDWARD BLAKE, speech at Aurora, Ont., Oct. 3, 1874.

If I could only go to the country I would sweep the Grits into the sea.

> SIR JOHN A. MACDONALD, to his friends, 1877-8; qu., Biggar, *Anecdotal life*, 167.

It is not for me, mes enfants, to tell you for which party you should vote, but I would have you remember that the place on high [pointing to the heavens] is *bleu*, while the other [pointing downward] is *rouge*.

> ANON., a French-Canadian priest to his congregation during a by-election in Quebec, ca.1878. Popular names for the Conservatives and Liberals were *bleus* and *rouges*, respectively. Wording and dates vary; see, Langelier, *Souvenirs politiques*, 1909, 135; *Can. mag.*, XVI, 28; Skelton, *Day of Laurier*, 47; Conservative conv., *Proc.*, 1938, 235-6.

John A., the Sachem, speaks:
. . . "It must be granted
That our friends are badly scattered,
And the chances are against us
In Ontario at present
As the country is divided.
Therefore let us re-distribute
What constituencies are doubtful
So as to enhance our prospects;
Hive the Grits where they already
Are too strong to be defeated;
Strengthen up our weaker quarters
With detachments from these
    strongholds;
Surely this is true to nature
In a mighty Tory chieftain!"

> TORONTO *GLOBE* , June 3, 1882.

I know an old lady in Toronto who solemnly assured me that her Conservative cow gave two quarts of milk more each day than it had done before the elections.

> SIR JOHN A. MACDONALD, speech in Ottawa; attributed.

An election is like a horse-race in that you can tell more about it the next day.

> SIR JOHN A. MACDONALD, qu. in Pope: *Memoirs of Sir J.A. Macdonald*, II, 202; said before the election of 1882.

The great mass of the electors are ignorant & a great majority of them never read, & remain as much in the dark as to what is going on in this country as if they were residing in Europe.

> SIR WILFRID LAURIER, letter to Edward Blake, July 10, 1882.

Ontario! Ontario!
You've knocked the Grits to
    Blazes O!
And so has Manitobio
Along with Nova Scotio.

> WINNIPEG *MANITOBAN*, after March election, 1887; qu. in *Queen's quart.*, Winter, 1962, 657.

I will build dams, wherever possible, adjacent to every farmer who aids me in this election.

I will give contracts on dams, bridges and trails to those only who support me and will stipulate that all laboring men who vote for me shall be employed on those works.

If those in favor of French language and Separate Schools exert themselves in my behalf, I will introduce legislation in sympathy with their views.

I am in favor of all things for my supporters and everything for myself.

> GEORGE F. GUERNSEY, election campaign statement, Fort Qu'Appelle, Sask., Oct., 1894.

Elections are not won by prayers alone.

> JOSEPH I. TARTE, statement, 1896.

I do not know, but Mr. Gibbons told us that the friends of Mr. Hyman having fought two elections and won fairly and having been deprived of the seat by unfair and fraudulent methods, came to the conclusion that they would fight the enemy with the devil's fire.

> SIR WILFRID LAURIER, H. of C., *Debates*, Nov. 23, 1906, 38.

Wolves, it is said, hunt in packs; the lion hunts alone. The way of the lion was the way of Sir John Macdonald. To-day the lion is dead, and all the furious howlings of the wolves do not carry one-tenth of the weight of the roar of the lion.

> SIR WILFRID LAURIER, speech at Strathroy, Sept. 19, 1908, on Sir Robert Borden's campaigning with a phalanx of provincial premiers.

Well, Sir, at this moment, I have only to say that history teaches us that defeats there are which are more honourable than victories. The gentlemen on the other side of this House are welcome to all the comfort they can get out of the Drummond-Arthabaska election.

SIR WILFRID LAURIER, H. of C., *Debates*, Nov. 21, 1910, 54.

I only know that it was a huge election and that on it turned issues of the most tremendous importance, such as whether or not Mariposa should become part of the United States, and whether the flag that had waved over the school house at Tecumseh Township for ten centuries should be trampled under the hoof of an alien invader, and whether Britons should be slaves, and whether Canadians should be Britons.

STEPHEN B. LEACOCK, "The great election in Missinaba County", *Sunshine sketches of a little town*, 1912, 213.

As one crosses the roaring forties of one's years, one's notion of real excitement is a good general election.

ROBERT C. (BOB) EDWARDS, qu. in J.W.G. MacEwan, *Poking into politics*, 1966, 90.

I have only one letter of recommendation and that is from His Holiness, the Pope. I have it here in my hand. I did not hear my opponent read one from His Holiness.

JEAN-FRANCOIS POULIOT, Liberal candidate, election campaign claim in Temsicouta, Quebec, 1924; later, he said, "The people of the riding really voted for His Holiness but it was Jean Francois Pouliot who came to Ottawa". See: G. Aiken, *Backbencher*, 1974, 15.

With every change of government in Canada we are made into a nation over again.

SIR JOHN WILLISON (d. 1927), attributed as said at the close of his life.

The election of 1896 must remain the classic example of a logical and inevitable end being reached by illogical and almost inexplicable popular processes.

JOHN W. DAFOE, *Clifford Sifton in relation to his times*, 1931, 92.

People who have the interest of their country at heart should unite to abolish a system which at election time drags so many of our leading citizens down to the level of gangsters.

R.H. MURRAY, address, Rotary Club, Kentville, N.S., Sept. 26, 1933.

It is a period described in North America as one when politicians go around shooting from the hip. It therefore behooves outsiders, even though friendly to all parties involved, to avoid not only participating in the shooting but keeping out of the line of fire.

LESTER B. PEARSON, Sec'y. of State for Ext. Affairs, advice to Canadians visiting British Isles during election, report of May 17, 1955.

Look here, my good man, when the election comes why don't you just go away and vote for the party you support. In fact, why don't you just go away.

C.D. HOWE, to a questioner after a meeting, general election, 1957, in Morris, Man.

When your party organizes a meeting, you'll have the platform, and we'll ask the questions.

C.D. HOWE, election campaign, 1957, Morris, Man., to Bruce Mackenzie, chairman of local Liberal Party Association.

We've lost everything. We've even won our own seat.

> MRS. LESTER B. PEARSON, to her husband, Mar. 31, 1958, on his winning Algoma East riding, general election.

Mainstreeting.

> JOHN G. DIEFENBAKER and associates, general election, Feb.-Mar. 1958; on his walking through downtown shopping centres, especially in Prince Albert, meeting and chatting with friends.

Gratifying? They're stupefying!

> JOHN G. DIEFENBAKER, in Toronto to a press reporter on the results of the election, Mar. 31, 1958, when he won 209 seats.

They ran a nearly perfect campaign. The only thing they did wrong was lose.

> WARREN ARMSTRONG, campaign manager for Donald Fleming, Conservative candidate, Toronto Eglinton, federal election, June, 1962, referring to the Liberals, qu. in Brian Land, *Eglinton*, 1965, 141.

When we were boys we used to stand on the corner and watch the girls go by. Some girls had IT and some didn't. Now, we could tell just like *that* which ones had IT and which ones didn't. And that's how you pick candidates — they've got to have IT.

> GEORGE HEES, speech, Ottawa West Conservative Association, election campaign, June, 1962, qu. in P. Newman, *Renegade in power*, 1963, 158.

I'm not going to go through this again if I can avoid it.

> LESTER B. PEARSON, *Mike, the memoirs*, Vol. 3, 1975, 197, ref. to election of 1963.

I'm an accountant in these things. The Toronto area has more seats than Saskatchewan, and we can win them.

> WALTER GORDON, voicing Liberal Party attitude towards the West, election campaign, 1965.

The country let us down.

> LESTER B. PEARSON, verdict on the adverse vote received by the Liberal Party, Nov. 8, 1965.

Election campaigns which feature policy are for parties with unpopular leaders; parties with popular leaders do not have to campaign on reckless, irresponsible promises. Besides, as everyone knew, people do not understand politics, but they do know who they like.

> DALTON CAMP, *Gentlemen, players and politicians*, 1970, 282.

It must have been something I did.

> ROSS THATCHER, Premier of Saskatchewan on the defeat of his party at the polls, June 23, 1971.

Politicians always create their own reality; during campaigns they create their own unreality.

> STEPHEN CLARKSON, *City lib., parties and reform*, 1972, 150.

I see a campaign as a bath of fire in which you're purified, and settle all the piddling little questions of whether this little thing was right or wrong. What's your over-all judgment? Is it yes or no?

> PIERRE E. TRUDEAU, Sept. 2, 1972, qu. in W. Stewart, *Divide and con*, 1973, 27.

Speak soft, take time,
The land is strong,
With slow and careful love
We learn the way to grow,
We learn the way to go.

> LIBERAL PARTY, "The land is strong", campaign song, federal election, Oct., 1972.

The only important poll is that taken by the electorate on election day.

> ROBERT STANFIELD, general election campaign, Oct., 1972.

Electoral Ridings

Sure it's a good idea. And as soon as we're in opposition, we'll demand it.

ROSS THATCHER, Premier of Sask., qu. in Vancouver *Sun*, July 6, 1971, 4, referring to the request to have the provincial ridings redrawn by an independent commission.

Electric Power

What think you, little river Thames, of our . . . great Ottawa that flings its foam eight hundred miles? What does it mean when science has moved us a little further yet, and the wheels of the world's work turn with electric force? What sort of asset do you think then our melting snow and the roaring river-flood of our Canadian spring shall be to us? What say you, little puffing steam-fed industry of England, to the industry of Coming Canada?

STEPHEN LEACOCK, Empire Club speech, Toronto, Mar. 19, 1907.

If the United States can utilize the electrical energy from the Canadian side immediately or in the near future, it will absorb nearly all of Canada's share before we have developed sufficiently to form a market for it.

SIR CLIFFORD SIFTON, qu. in A.V. White, *Memorandum respecting exportation of electricity,* Commission of Conservation, Ottawa, 1914. Reference is to the Niagara Falls power project.

Elites

The governmental elites at both federal and provincial levels play a crucial independent role.

RICHARD SIMEON, *Federal-provincial diplomacy: the making of recent policy in Canada,* 1972, 307.

Emasculation

God sour the milk of the knacking
    wench
with razor and twine she comes
to stanchion our blond and bucking
    bull,
pluck out his lovely plumbs.

ALDEN NOWLAN, "God sour the milk of the knacking wench", 1970.

Emergencies

"Emergency, emergency," I cried,
    "give us emergency,
This shall be the doctrine of our
    salvation.
Are we not surrounded by
    emergencies?
The rent of a house, the cost of food,
    pensions and health, the
    unemployed,
These are lasting emergencies, tragic
    for me."

F.R. SCOTT, "Some Privy Counsel", 1950.

Emigrants

In one sense and that no secondary one, all men have been emigrants or sons of emigrants since the first sad pair departed out of Eden.

THOMAS D'A. MCGEE, speech, House of Assembly, Quebec, May 10, 1862.

Here and there, by the trees
    half-hidden,
    We catch a glimpse of some
        pleasant home;
And the thought springs up to the lips
    unbidden,
    "O why should Canada's children
        roam?"

EDWARD H. DEWART, "Summer rambles", 1869.

Canada is a good country to *be* from. It has a gentler, slower pace – it lends perspective.

> PAUL ANKA, qu. in *Canadian magazine*, Jan. 22, 1972, 7.

Emigration

Emigration to the United States is the fear of the hour. It is indeed going on to an extent truly alarming and astonishing.

> WILLIAM RYERSON, letter to E. Ryerson, Apr. 22, 1838, qu., E. Ryerson, *Story of my life*, 1883, 184.

Emigrate ye Canadians! If England will not treat you with decency, shake the dust from your feet, cross the border and build up a home where tyranny does not dare show its head.

> CINCINNATI *NEWS*, quoted in Cobourg *Plain speaker*, July 28, 1838.

An exodus to the United States is going on from all the Provinces.

> GOLDWIN SMITH, *The Bystander*, May, 1880, 234. The term "The Exodus" was popularly applied to the movement of Canadian people to the U.S.; see, Laurier's speech, H. of C., *Debates*, Apr. 5, 1881, for another example.

They will do better away.

> ANON., a common remark in Prince Edward Island, about 1882, by parents referring to their children who had gone to the United States.

Canada's story begins in Lamentations and ends in Exodus.

> ANON., a popular witticism of the 1880's.

There is scarcely a farm house in the older provinces where there is not an empty chair for the boy in the States.

> TORONTO *MAIL*, 1887, qu. in D.G. Creighton, *Dominion of the north*, 1944, 354.

The Americans may say with truth that if they do not annex Canada, they are annexing the Canadians. They are annexing the very flower of the Canadian population, and in the way most costly to the country from which it is drawn, since the men whom that country has been at the expense of breeding leave it just as they arrive at manhood and begin to produce.

> GOLDWIN SMITH, *Canada and the Canadian question*, 1891, 233.

It was computed, after careful examination, that by 1896 at least every third able-bodied man in Canada between the ages of twenty and forty had emigrated to the United States.

> SIR RICHARD CARTWRIGHT, *Reminiscences*, 1912, 239.

Canada is being drained of her native-born to satisfy the demands of the United States. It is only a question of a very short time, unless diplomatic representations are made to the United States, before every native-born Canadian will be walking the streets of Chicago, Detroit, Boston or other American city, and we may see a specimen in our museum stuffed and properly mounted to show what a native-born Canadian was once like.

> SAMUEL W. JACOBS, H. of C., *Debates*, Apr. 23, 1925, 2363.

Pioneering young Canadians must have found that the inertia of their entrenched elders had drained Canadian life of colour, zest, adventure and the stimulation which comes from free-ranging experimentation in ideas, in material enterprises, and in the arts.

It must have been because they could not feel in Canada the sense of sharing in something more than the defence of things as they are that they left their country seeking "lots more of something else".

JOHN B. BREBNER, *Scholarship for Canada*, 1945, 8.

In the television production centre of Los Angeles these days there is a new minority group known as "snowbacks". In excess of 600,000 Canadians live and work in Los Angeles. They've left an impression.

BRIAN BRENN and HAROLD WALTERS, *Weekend mag.*, Aug. 14, 1971, 14.

Emotions

There are things in the heart too deep if not for tears most certainly for words.

RALPH CONNOR, *The major*, 1917, 186.

He had never been an easy man to love. There seemed to be a diamond in him in place of a heart.

HUGH MACLENNAN, *Each man's son*, 1951, 26.

Follow your heart, and you perish.

MARGARET LAURENCE, "The drummer of all the world", ca.1956, in *The tomorrow-tamer*, 11.

Employees

In a hierarchy every employee tends to rise to his level of incompetence.

LAURENCE J. PETER and RAYMOND HULL, *The Peter principle*, 1969, 25, frequently cited as "The Peter principle".

In time, every post tends to be occupied by an employee who is incompetent to carry out its duties.

LAURENCE J. PETER and RAYMOND HULL, *The Peter principle*, 1969, 27, known as "Peter's Corollary" (see also above).

Emptiness

How long before the emptiness will
  go, or will it always
Go on aching and crying and killing
  here in the darkness.

RAYMOND SOUSTER, "Ersatz", 1968.

End

Well, everything must have an end.
I have had my day
I have come home
I see things as they are.

JOHN GLASSCO, "The death of Don Quixote", 1964.

Endurance

During the height of the cold the thought occurred to me – Why am I enduring this? For pleasure – was the only reply, and the idea seemed so absurd that I laughed myself warm. Then as circulation returned, I remembered that I was taking a lesson in that most valuable of human studies – the art of Endurance; an art the poor learn perforce, and the rich do well to teach themselves.

EARL OF SOUTHESK, *Saskatchewan and the Rocky Mountains, Diary*, Nov. 3, 1859.

Enemies

Grant me, God, that in the battle,
  For a moment we may meet;
Let mine be the sword to send him
  Staggering to thy judgment seat.

ALEXANDER MCLACHLAN, "Hamilton's address", 1856.

Here lies the man I could have wished
  for friend!
How shall I atone for injuring him of
  old?

> CHARLES HEAVYSEGE, *Saul*, 1857.

I have outlived all my enemies. I have
therefore no apologies to make, nor
forgiveness to crave.

> EDWARD JOHN BARKER, d. 1884, founder
> of the *British whig*, Kingston, qu. by
> J.A. Edmison in *Historic Kingston*, No.
> 9, Nov., 1960, 54.

It is a good thing to find out what your
Enemy wants you to do and then do
the Opposite.

> J.W. BENGOUGH, *The prohibition Aesop*,
> about 1896, 23.

The question before Canada, is not
what she thinks or pays, but what an
enemy may think it necessary to make
her pay. If she continues wealthy and
remains weak she will surely be attacked under one pretext or another.

> RUDYARD KIPLING, *Letters to the family*,
> 1908, 70.

Take up our quarrel with the foe
To you from failing hands we throw
  The torch: be yours to hold it high.
  If ye break faith with us who die,
We shall not sleep, though poppies
    grow
In Flanders' fields.

> JOHN MCCRAE, "In Flanders' Fields",
> ("We shall not sleep"), *Punch*, Dec. 8,
> 1915, 468.

There is no earthly hope for a man
who is too lazy to acquire enemies.

> ROBERT C. (BOB) EDWARDS, Calgary *Eye
> Opener*, June 15, 1918.

A man always remembers his enemies,
but he sometimes forgets his friends.

> ROBERT C. (BOB) EDWARDS, in his *Annual*,
> 1922, 80.

Next a worthy friend, honour a worthy
foe.

> SIR RICHARD CARTWRIGHT, qu., *Standard
> dictionary Canadian biography*, 1934,
> 103.

There are enemy in front of us, behind
us and on our flanks, there is only one
safe place — that is on the objective.

> PAUL TRIQUET, Captain, Royal 22e Régi-
> ment, Dec. 14, 1943 at Casa Berardi,
> Italian campaign; see G.C. Machum,
> *Canada's V.C.'s.*, 1956.

I'd like to have you for an enemy.
  You think I do not mean that? But I
    do!
We ought to love our enemies, you see,
  So let me start, auspiciously, with
    you.

> GEOFFREY B. RIDDEHOUGH, "Starting in
> low gear", 1972.

Energy

Canada and the United States are
moving in the direction of a new and
significant policy for the development
of energy resources, particularly water
power, on a continental scale. Recent
technological advances which have
made the border increasingly irrelevant have brought about in both countries a willingness to consider an en-
couraging degree of integration.

> WESTERN CANADIAN-AMERICAN ASSEM-
> BLY, meeting, Aug., 1964, Harrison Hot
> Springs, B.C., *Report*, 1964, 4.

So many times in Confederation and
the history of Canada, the West, and
Alberta in particular, we have been
the ones seeking — we haven't been
the ones holding the cards, if you like.
We now do hold the cards in terms of
energy.

> PETER LOUGHEED, Premier of Alberta,
> qu. in *Globe and Mail*, Jan. 20, 1973, 1.

If you're not part of the solution, you're part of the problem.

CANADA. DEPT. OF ENERGY, MINES AND RESOURCES, slogan used Feb., 1976 on TV in its energy conservation campaign.

Engineering

200 miles of engineering impossibilities.

ANON., qu. in Walter Vaughan, *The life and work of Sir William Van Horne,* 1920, 108-109. Reference is to the Canadian Shield east of Fort William.

England

England would be better off without Canada; it keeps her in a prepared state for war at a great expense and constant irritation.

NAPOLEON I, in *Diary of P. Malcolm at St. Helena,* Jan. 11, 1817.

Your triumphant election on the 16th and ejection from the Assembly on the 17th must hasten the crisis which is fast approaching in the affairs of the Canadas, and which will terminate in independence and freedom from the baneful domination of the mother country and the tyrannical conduct of a small and despicable faction in the colony.

JOSEPH HUME, letter to W.L. Mackenzie, Mar. 29, 1834; ("The baneful domination" letter.)

I have been possessed . . . with the idea that it is possible to maintain on this soil of North America, and in the face of Republican America, British connection and British institutions, if you give the latter freely and trustingly. Faith, when it is sincere, is always catching.

LORD ELGIN, letter to Cumming Bruce, 1852.

If a day were ever to come when England was in danger, let the bugle sound, let the fires be lighted on the hills, and in all parts of the colonies, though we might not be able to do much, whatever we can do shall be done by the colonies to help her.

SIR WILFRID LAURIER, speech, Imperial Institute, London, Eng., June 18, 1897.

England, England, England,
    Girdled by ocean and skies,
And a power of a world and the heart
    of a race,
    And a hope that never dies.

WILFRED CAMPBELL, "England", 1899.

If you ask me as a French-Canadian why I am deeply attached to Great Britain, it is because I find in her institutions and under her flag all the protection I need. It is because she has been in the world the nurse of liberty. She has understood better than any other nation the art of government.

RODOLPHE LEMIEUX, speech in Toronto, Mar., 1905.

All we owe England is Christian forgiveness. Proportionally, Canada has done more for the War than England itself.

L.N. RICARD, speech in Montreal, May 24, 1917, during conscription crisis.

O mighty Soul of England, rise in
    splendour,
Out of the wrack and turmoil of the
    night,
And as of old, compassionate and
    tender,
Uphold the cause of justice and of
    right.

FREDERICK G. SCOTT, "To England", May, 1926.

They little know of "empire" who only "England" know.

> W.P.M. KENNEDY, in *Can. hist. rev.*, 1935, 311. (Cf. Kipling: "What should they know of England who only England know?").

She is part of you, heart of you –
England, England –
Will you answer the trumpet-call of God.

> AUDREY ALEXANDRA BROWN, "The pilgrims", 1937.

This, this is Britain, bulwark of our
    breed,
    Our one sure shield against the
        hordes of hate.
Smite her, and we are smitten; wound
    her, we bleed,
    Yet firm she stands and fears no
        thrust of fate.

> CHARLES G.D. ROBERTS, "Canada speaks of Britain", 1940.

English Language

Avoid awc-cent! Avoid awc-cent!

> BISHOP JOHN STRACHAN's advice to the students of Trinity College, which he founded in 1851.

Speak English if you wish but for God's sake speak it badly.

> LOUIS-FRANÇOIS-RICHER LAFLÈCHE, Bishop of Trois-Rivières, 1870-1898, qu. in T.D. Bouchard, *Memoirs*, 1960, Vol. 3, 132, and 143. (Trans.)

I myself talk Ontario English; I don't admire it, but it's all I can do; anything is better than affectation.

> STEPHEN B. LEACOCK, *How to write*, 1943, 121.

We do write with less and less self-consciousness in the Canadian dialect of English, which seems roughly to be the result of applying British syntax to an American vocabulary.

> LISTER SINCLAIR, *Here and now*, June, 1949, 16.

Canadians have a very distinct variety of English, far more different from that spoken in Britain than is the English spoken by Australians; yet Canadians – so imperceptibly, so constantly has the process operated – 'just get on with the job'; having this very different English, they therefore do not feel the need to have it at all.

> ERIC PARTRIDGE, *British and American English*, 1951, 64.

We hire twenty outstanding graduates each year at Ford [Motor Company of Canada] and find they cannot make a simple report in basic English.

> WILLIAM BOURKE, of the Ford Motor Co. of Canada, speech to Ontario Secondary School Headmasters' Assoc., McMaster Univ., 1963.

Englishmen

Bishop Taché has been here and has left for the Red River . . . He is strongly opposed to the idea of an Imperial Commission, believing, as indeed, we all do, that to send out an overwashed Englishman, utterly ignorant of the country and full of crochets, as all Englishmen are, would be a mistake.

> SIR JOHN A. MACDONALD, letter to Sir John Rose, Feb. 23, 1870.

Is there a man who can forget that, when the constitutional voice was useless, when our representations and our remonstrances remained for years and years unanswered, and when the peasants of St. Denis took up arms and faced the veterans of Waterloo, their commander was not a Canadian, but an Englishman named Wolfred Nelson? And, three days afterwards, when these same peasants were swept with the leaden hail at St. Charles, can it be forgotten that the man who again led them was an Englishman named Thomas S. Brown?

> SIR WILFRID LAURIER, speech in Quebec, 1877.

While the Frenchman wants you to have his opinions, the Englishman wants you to have opinions of your own.

> SIR WILFRID LAURIER, speech in Montreal, May 19, 1884. (Trans.)

The Englishman respects your opinions; but he never thinks of your feelings.

> SIR WILFRID LAURIER, speech in Montreal, May 19, 1884. (Trans.)

I owe it to the cause of truth to declare that the hostility towards us which we have been given to understand exists in the mother-country has never existed, at least not to the degree that has been pictured. The English people are free enough to have no fear of the comparative freedom of the colonies. The English government has never wanted to rule slaves. Who speaks of the English people, and of every class of population connected with them, speaks of independence and constitutional liberty.

> THOMAS J.J. LORANGER, speech, June 27, 1884.

An Englishman's social standing seems to depend on the number of people he can afford to despise.

> PETER MCARTHUR, To be taken with salt, 1903, 157.

The average Englishman has so deep a reverence for antiquity that he would rather be wrong than be recent.

> PETER MCARTHUR, To be taken with salt, 1903, 157.

Lord Dundonald, in his position, is charged with the organization of the Militia, but he must take counsel here when organizing a regiment. He is a foreigner – no – [Some hon. members. "No, no."] I had withdrawn the expression before Hon. gentlemen interrupted. He is not a foreigner, but he is a stranger.

> SIR WILFRID LAURIER, H. of C., Debates, June 10, 1904, 4620, on the dismissal of Lord Dundonald, General Officer Commanding, Canadian Militia.

He's a son of dear old England, he's a hero, he's a brick;
He's the kind you may annihilate but you can never lick.

> ROBERT J.C. STEAD, "The son of Marquis Noddle", 1917.

The Anglo-Saxon has never had too many friends.

> A.R.M. LOWER, in Can. hist. rev., 1931, 59.

It was all very simple; we had to choose between the English of Boston and the English of London. The English of London were farther away and we hated them less.

> HENRI BOURASSA, heard by Hilda Neatby, qu. in Can. Hist. Assoc., Report, 1956, 74, re French-Canadian preference after the Conquest, 1759.

You take yer av'rage Anglishman he'll allus do it the hard way, like standin' up in a hammock. Mind you they're a pretty friggid bunch anyways, havin' not bin in central heat since the Roamins was in their gloamin' 'bout 55 B.B.C.

> DON HARRON, Charlie Farquharson's histry of Canada, 1972, 27.

Enterprise

Zeal and enterprise, directed by a knowledge of our subject, are more rare and efficient commodities than the mere possession of capital; because they will carry capital and all other things with them.

THOMAS C. KEEFER, *The philosophy of railroads*, 1850, 6.

Had the men who undertook any great enterprise since time began realized half the obstacles and discouragements they would meet, they would never have started, but fortunately they didn't – and don't.

SIR WILLIAM VAN HORNE, a favorite maxim; qu., in Skelton, *Sir A.T. Galt*, 1920, 560.

Environment

We are moulded, we say, by the conditions and surroundings in which we live; but we too often forget that the environment is largely what we make it.

BLISS CARMAN, *The kinship of nature*, 1904, 83.

Canada, with its empty spaces, its largely unknown lakes and rivers and islands, its division of language, its dependence on immense railways to hold it physically together, has had this peculiar problem of an obliterated environment throughout most of its history.

NORTHROP FRYE, *The bush garden*, 1971, Preface, iii.

Envy

Each of us has achieved, or possesses, what is in the eyes of someone else the unattained crown of his life.

GILBERT NORWOOD, *Spoken in jest*, 1938, 122.

Envy, not death, is the great leveller.

IRVING LAYTON, "Aphs", *The whole bloody bird*, 1969, 94.

Equality

To grant an ordinary man equality is to make him your superior.

PETER MCARTHUR, *To be taken with salt*, 1903, 146.

When they speak of equality, English Canadians mean equality of individual civil rights, that is, of persons considered individually, while when we French Canadians speak of equality we do not mean civil rights at all, we mean collective national rights, we mean the rights of the French Canadian nation to develop in accordance with its own characteristics.

ANON., lawyer in Quebec, in Canada, Roy. Comm. on Bilingualism and Biculturalism, *Prelim. report*, 1965, 99. (Trans.)

Errors

It is a hierarchy of laws liberally illustrated by facts, which so ingeniously rule and are subject to one another, stay and uphold one another, that admiration is compelled for the sagacity of the great organizer, who, with unparalleled power of systemization, constructed so imposing an edifice of fallacy.

SIR WILLIAM OSLER, *Evolution of medicine*, 1913, on Ibn Sina's (Avicenna's) *Canon* of medical knowledge.

Knowing things that are not so is the worst kind of ignorance.

ROBERT C. (BOB) EDWARDS, Calgary *Eye Opener*, Nov. 3, 1917.

Error held in truth has much the effect of truth. In politics and religion this fact upsets many confident predictions.

> GEORGE ILES, *Canadian stories*, 1918, 177.

Escape

If a bear comes after you, Sam, you must be up and doin' or it's a gone goose with you.

> THOMAS C. HALIBURTON, *Sam Slick in England*, 1843, ch. 18.

And so we work; we play; we fret;
we scurry, hurry, worry — to forget.

> MALCOLM WRATHELL, "The Escapists", 1956.

And, when I close my eyes I see a ship
At anchor in the water of a bay.
I cling to that imaginary shape
Capable of taking me away
    To I do not know what ports.
    Perhaps tomorrow it departs,
Anonymous, invulnerable, free.

> DARYL HINE, "Don Juan in Amsterdam", 1960.

Beyond the manly and autumnal
arcades of calendared knowing
swings the implicit instant.
Clusters and cones of
light, leaf-shelved,
topple dimension down.

> MARGARET AVISON, "Chestnut tree, three storeys up", 1962.

I'm going out to flood the rink.

> LUCIEN RIVARD, attributed, to prison guards in Bordeaux Jail, Montreal, Mar. 2, 1965, prior to his escape. (Trans.)

War is hell, to be sure, but men have yet to come up with a better means of escaping from their jobs, their mothers, and their wives.

> RICHARD J. NEEDHAM, *A friend in Needham*, 1969, 18.

Eskimos

The Eskimo has developed individual equality farther than we, he is less selfish, more helpful to his fellows, kinder to his wife, gentler to his child, more reticent about the faults of his neighbour than any but the rarest and best of our race.

> VILHJALMUR STEFANSSON, in *Harper's monthly mag.*, Oct., 1908.

I first took possession of Baffin Land for Canada in the presence of several Eskimo, and after firing nineteen shots I instructed an Eskimo to fire the twentieth, telling him that he was now a Canadian.

> JOSEPH E. BERNIER (Captain), address to Empire Club, Toronto, Oct. 7, 1926.

We should not regard the Eskimos as foreigners but as friends. They are your fellow citizens. Their future is bound up in our future. If Canada is but a thin southern strip across which plies a shuttle railway we shall have no remarkable future.

> VILHJALMUR STEFANSSON, in Toronto *Star*, Apr. 14, 1933.

Inviolate their law of brotherhood;
Their ancient covenant, the common
    good.

> KATHRYN MUNRO, "Innuit", 1956.

They are adapting themselves, too, to our money economy, and learning to work for a daily wage.

> DIAMOND JENNESS, *The people of the twilight*, 1959, 250.

I am always afraid that "guilty" is said because the accused Eskimo thinks that this is what you wish him to say and he is anxious to please. I have repeatedly urged that pleas of "guilty" should not ordinarily be accepted from Eskimos.

JUSTICE JACK SISSONS, R. vs. Koonungnak (1963) 45, *Western weekly reports*, 298.

Cynics have said that it would be cheaper for the government to house Canada's total Eskimo population in the swank Chateau Laurier Hotel in Ottawa than it is to maintain the present Eskimo welfare services in the Arctic.

BRIAN MOORE, *Canada*, 1963, 107.

Proportionately, there are many more good Eskimo artists than there are white artists in North America or Europe.

GEORGE SWINTON, *Eskimo sculpture*, 1965, 12.

Must we advise them about our way of life in a voice so strong and sure that we fail to hear the words of wisdom they may have for us?

JAMES HOUSTON, in Earle Toppings, ed., *Canada*, 1967, 24.

Where are the Eskimo managers of Hudson's Bay posts? Where are the Eskimo police, the radio operators, the nurses? I'll tell you where they are. They are down at the welfare office drawing relief.

DUNCAN PRYDE, *Time*, May 2, 1969, 11.

I know I have had an unusual life, being born in a skin tent and living to hear on the radio that two men have landed on the moon.

MARY PITSEOLAK, Cape Dorset artist, in her *Pictures out of my life*, 1971, 80.

Essays

Nobody but invalids and retired clergymen read essays any more.

GREGORY CLARK, *Which we did*, 1936, Preface.

Establishment

I have little hope that the various establishments – political, financial, military, educational – will be able to accept the implications of the revolution. I think that they will try to set up some phony concessions and will be swept aside by sheer force of numbers.

JOHN RICH, in T. Lloyd, ed., *Agenda 1970*, 1968, 44, referring to the "emotional revolution" of the 1960's.

It's our aim to turn the IS-tablishment into the WAS-tablishment.

RANDY PROVO, U.B.C. activist, letter to *Ubyssey*, Apr. 1, 1968.

Eternity

Yet, patience – there shall come
Many great voices from life's outer sea,
Hours of strange triumph, and when few men heed,
Murmurs and glimpses of eternity.

ARCHIBALD LAMPMAN, "Outlook", 1888.

Eternity is in the heart,
Infinity is in the mind.

CHRISTINE L. HENDERSON, "Unrest", 1961.

Ethics

Ethics are merely a form of collective bargaining at the professional level.

JOHN C. PARKIN, address in Regina, to Sask. Symposium on Architecture, Oct. 21, 1961.

How much would we not benefit from rediscovering the sense of harmony and the noble prescriptions of such systems of ethics as those of Confucius, Achoke, or Buddha which, more than many Western ethical systems, have insisted on the demands of human dignity!

> JEAN-C. FALARDEAU, *Roots and values in Canadian lives*, 1961, 61.

Any new ethic, if it's to work, will have to find ways of reconciling growth with commitment, change with loyalty, and freedom with alienation, because a world in which new loyalties constantly replace old ones will make neurotics of us all.

> MERLE SHAIN, *Some men are more perfect than others*, 1973, 85.

Ethnic Groups

Our fellow-countrymen are not only those in whose veins runs the blood of France. They are all those, whatever their race or whatever their language, whom the fortune of war, the chances of fate, or their own choice have brought among us, and who acknowledge the sovereignty of the British Crown.

> SIR WILFRID LAURIER, speech at Quebec City, June 24, 1889. (Trans.)

We have altogether too many St. George, St. Andrew, St. Patrick and St. Jean Baptiste societies in this country for the national good.

> WILFRED CAMPBELL, in 1892, qu. by C.F. Klinck in *Wilfred Campbell*, 1942, 154.

History not only makes the bond with the past; it makes it also among the sons of the same race. It is history, more than blood, I venture to say, which generates ethnic feeling and makes it vigorous.

> ABBÉ LIONEL GROULX, *L'Almanach de la langue française*, 1924, 51. (Trans.)

You will be better Canadians for being Ukrainians.

> LORD TWEEDSMUIR, to a group of Ukrainians, in 1936, qu. in Peter Russell, ed., *Nationalism in Canada*, 1966, 84.

To what ethnic or cultural group did you or your ancestor (on the male side) belong on coming to this continent?

> CANADA. CENSUS, 1961, Population, Ethnic Groups By Age Group. *Bulletin* 1. 3-2, question.

It is common practice in Canada to restrict the term 'ethnic' to groups which are neither British nor French. Ethnicity, then, appears as a strange, possibly distasteful phenomenon: 'ethnic' seems to be given a sense something like 'foreigner'.

> CANADA. ROY. COMM. ON BILINGUALISM AND BICULTURALISM, *Report*, 1967, Book I, xxiv.

I resent that they think that because the chairman is an immigrant boy from Slovakia and the president is a Polack, we are third-class citizens.

> STEPHEN B. ROMAN, statement to press after Trudeau blocked sale of Denison Mines (uranium) to U.S., Mar. 2, 1970.

Other Canadians.

> ANON., phrase used to describe Canadians who are neither English nor French, qu. in Davis and Krauter, *The other Canadians*, 1971, 4.

Etiquette

Etiquette is a beneficient invention that enables a naturally disagreeable person to live with another without coming to blows.

> PETER MCARTHUR, *To be taken with salt*, 1903, 148.

Europe

It was European policy, European statesmanship, European ambition, that drenched this world with blood.

> N.W. ROWELL, League of Nations, Assembly, *Records* (first), 1920, 328.

Evening

And with one foot on the water,
    And one upon the shore,
The Angel of Shadow gives warning
    That day shall be no more.

> JOHN G. WHITTIER, "Red River voyageur", 1854.

When one strange night the sun like
    blood went down,
Flooding the heavens in a ruddy hue;
Red grew the lake, the sere fields
    parched and brown,
Red grew the marshes where the
    creeks stole down,
But never a wind-breath blew.

> WILFRED CAMPBELL, "How one winter came in the lake region", 1893.

The pensive afterthoughts of sundown
    sink
Over the patient acres given to peace;
The homely cries and farmstead noises
    cease,
And the worn day relaxes, link by link.

> CHARLES G.D. ROBERTS, "Where the cattle come to drink", 1896.

Evening
an old friend,
winds the sun,
pockets it
and departs.

> AVI BOXER, "Sunset", 1971.

Evil

All philosophy and all religions teach us this one solemn truth, that in this life the evil surpasses the good.

> JAMES DE MILLE, *A strange manuscript*, 1888, Ch. 26.

Evil is a basis for unity, not something to be fled from and rejected.

> JAMES REANEY, in R.L. McDougall ed., *Our living tradition*, 1959, 281.

Fret not thyself because of evil-doers.
Good advice but very hard to take.
Too many bastards always on the
    make;
Too many heiresses with crafty
    wooers;

> ROY DANIELLS, "Psalm 37", 1963.

Evolution

Evolution is an immense discovery, the most momentous ever made . . . Still, we are what we are, not apes but men.

> GOLDWIN SMITH, *In quest of light*, 1906, 14.

Human nature with its abysses and its mountains, its concentration camps and its cities celestial, its sadisms and altruisms, followed a long road before the eyes of the ape looked into the face of Christ.

> E.J. PRATT, Introduction to "Dunkirk", 1941. (Unpublished Mss.).

The soldiers merge and move with all
    of us
toward whatever mystery
bemused that fatal pliant fish
who first forgot the sea.

> EARLE BIRNEY, "Young veterans", 1945.

Exaggeration

The soul is not happy in exactitude, but loves the overbrimming measure.

> BLISS CARMAN, *The friendship of art*, 1904, 299.

I have always found that the only kind of statement worth making is an overstatement. A half-truth, like half a brick, is always more forcible as an argument than a whole one. It carries further.

> STEPHEN B. LEACOCK, *The garden of folly*, 1924.

Once your soul is dirty, then what difference is the shade of black?

> BRIAN MOORE, *The luck of Ginger Coffey*, 1960, 125.

this is a blowhard age
what will happen when our
    superlatives
shrink to fact?

> MALCOLM MILLER, "To be muttered", 1962.

Excellence

This country has some kind of an ingrown hatred of excellence. The way to being ignored in this country is to seek and crave and love excellence.

> MORLEY CALLAGHAN, interviewed by Donald Cameron, Nov. 16, 1971, in *Conversations with Canadian novelists*, 1973, Part 2, 30.

The real friend of the artist in this country is the guy who believes in *excellence*, seeks for it, fights for it, defends it, and tries to produce it.

> MORLEY CALLAGHAN, interviewed by D. Cameron, Nov. 16, 1971, in *Conversations with Canadian novelists*, 1973, Part 2, 31.

All you should say is, I know it's excellent, and the world will discover it *is* excellent. They'll discover it's Canadian, because they'll ask where it came from.

> MORLEY CALLAGHAN, interviewed by D. Cameron, Nov. 16, 1971, in *Conversations with Canadian novelists*, 1973, Part 2, 32.

Executions

May my execution and the execution of my gallows companions be of use to you. May they show you what you can expect from the English government. I have only a few hours to live, but I wanted to divide this precious time between my religious duties and my obligations to my fellow countrymen. It is for their sake that I am dying as an infamous murderer on the scaffold; for their sake I have given up my wholly dependant wife and children and for their sake I die crying: 'Long live Liberty! Long live Independence!'

> FRANÇOIS-MARIE THOMAS CHEVALIER DE LORIMIER, *Testament politique*, Feb. 14, 1839, 11 p.m., Prison de Montréal. (Trans.)

Execution is the ultimate injustice, the ultimate degradation of man.

> COLIN MACDOUGALL, *Execution*, 1958, 102.

Executives

One of the secrets of being an executive is never do anything that you can get someone to do for you.

> COL. ERIC PHILLIPS, qu. in his obit., *The Globe and Mail*, Dec. 28, 1964, 8.

I feel that Canadian executives want the American influence. They want it — until they're trapped.

> ANON., executive's wife, qu. in R.L. Perry, *Galt, U.S.A.*, 1971, 36.

Existence

I am confused, therefore I am.

> JACK LUDWIG, "Confusions", 1960.

Everything exists without a purpose.

> IRVING LAYTON, "Aphs", *The whole bloody bird*, 1969, 83.

Expatriates

We hear the voice of Canada, the voice of our own past, which says to us that we have left part of ourselves in Canada, and that we must some day return if we wish to be whole again. The other voice is often more powerful. It accuses Canada of betrayal. It says that she has betrayed the very inmost nature of our selves by denying us the spiritual resources of a homeland, a *patria*.

> BRIAN STOCK, *Atlantic*, Nov., 1964, 113.

Expenditures

No man is rich whose expenditure exceeds his means; and no man is poor, whose incomings exceeds his outgoings.

> T.C. HALIBURTON, *Nature and human nature*, 1855, II, 266.

Experience

I guess I warn't born yesterday.

> T.C. HALIBURTON, *Sam Slick*, 1836, ch. XV; also, "I have some wrinkles on my horn, for I warn't born yesterday", *Sam Slick's wise saws*, 1853, ch. 7.

They know by experience, and not by books; and experience is everything; it's hearin', and seein', and tryin'; and arter that, a feller must be a born fool if he don't know.

> T.C. HALIBURTON, *Sam Slick*, 1836, ch. XXXII.

The value of experience is not in seeing much, but in seeing wisely.

> SIR WILLIAM OSLER, "The army surgeon", 1905.

Almost every experience is good for a woman that doesn't kill her.

> EMILY MURPHY "Janey Canuck", a favourite statement, qu. in B.H. Sanders, *Emily Murphy, crusader*, 1945, 292.

The characteristics of innocence are happiness and curiosity; the characteristics of experience are knowledge and, most often, regret.

> ALAN BROWN, *Tamarack rev.*, No. 1, Autumn, 1956, 61.

Maidens are timorous
shy of experiment,
but with experience
appetent, ardent.

> GEORGE WHALLEY, "Admonishment", 1958.

All experience educates, and our social personality forms underneath our vanishing experiences like layers of chalk under a rain of dying protozoans.

> NORTHROP FRYE, in G. Stanley and G. Sylvestre, eds., *Canadian universities today*, 1961, 31.

In previous societies, age and experience were valued. Today, it would be only a slight exaggeration to say that the opposite happens. Youth has become a precious asset in a world where experience and age appear as handicaps which stabilize the individual and bring him to a standstill.

> MARCEL RIOUX, lecture, Mar. 11, 1965, Université de Montreal. (Trans.).

Most of today's problems are not solved by experience. The further we advance into the modern age, the less important experience will become. It's much more important to have the necessary adaptability with which to face and solve new problems.

> PIERRE E. TRUDEAU, press conference, Ottawa, Feb. 16, 1968.

But there are no objects outside of ourselves.
We learn our lessons wrinkle by wrinkle,
Humbly planting behind us now and then
The milestone of a missing tooth.

> GEORGE JONAS, "To an ex-girlfriend", 1969.

Explanation

Never deny; never explain.
That's my guiding rule of life.

> ROBERTSON DAVIES, Leaven of malice, 1954, 293.

Exploration

Had I done it alone by canoe, I might have boasted a little.

> SGT. F.S. FARRAR, R.C.M.P., third mate aboard the St. Roch, first ship to circumnavigate North America, ending May 29, 1960; qu. in N. and W. Kelly, The Royal Can. Mounted Police, 1973, 221.

when you see the land naked, look again
(burn your maps, that is not what I mean),

I mean the moment when it seems most plain
is the moment when you must begin again.

> GWENDOLYN MACEWEN, "The discovery", 1969.

Expo '67

Man and His World.

> EXPO '67, central unifying theme.

Man the Explorer
Man the Creator
Man the Producer
Man and the Community

> EXPO '67, areas of fair grounds exemplifying the main theme.

I came to the fair a nationalist, full of pride in Canada, I left it a humanist, full of hope for man.

> PETER NEWMAN, Toronto Daily star, Apr. 28, 1967.

External Affairs, Dept. of

Most of its postings are expendable. Much of its work is redundant. Many of its officials are unnecessary. The name is 'External', not 'Eternal'.

> JAMES G. EAYRS, Sept., 1969. Reprinted in his Diplomacy and its discontents, 1971, 8.

External Relations

Canada is just at the stage when she cannot walk alone, and yet resents being led.

> LORD STANLEY, letter to Lord Salisbury, Oct. 11, 1891. (Salisbury papers, Oxford Univ.)

In the course of the present war we have seen Canada emerge from nationhood into a position generally recognized as that of a world power.

W.L. MACKENZIE KING, H. of C., *Debates*, July 1, 1943, 4226.

It is high time that Canada had a government which will not knife Canada's best friends in the back.

HOWARD GREEN, H. of C., *Debates*, Nov. 27, 1956, 51, referring to Canada's stand on Suez crisis.

Extinction

The dinosaur didn't know it was extinct either. Dinosaurs never had it so good, as just before they vanished.

MARSHALL MCLUHAN, in *Weekend mag.*, Mar. 18, 1967, (No. 11), 4.

Eyes

I put my clothes on as quick as a wink.

THOMAS C. HALIBURTON, *Sam Slick's wise saws*, 1853, ch. 7.

For the sake of two
Sad eyes and true,
And the old, old love
   So long ago.

BLISS CARMAN, "Why", 1893.

Are a woman's eyes extra-ordinarily bright? *cherchez l'homme:* only a man (or champagne) brightens a woman's eyes.

ARNOLD HAULTAIN, *Hints for lovers*, 1909, 185.

Human eyes have but a certain store of tears. It is not difficult to weep them all away.

ARNOLD HAULTAIN, *Hints for lovers*, 1909, 283.

Tireless eye, so taut and long,
Touching flowers and flames with ease,
All your wires vibrate with song
When it is the heart that sees.

F.R. SCOTT, "Vision", 1964.

The impress of my eyes seeking a way in.

HEATHER SPEARS, "The Danish portraits", 1967.

Faces

Then all your face grew light, and
  seemed
  To hold the shadow of the sun;
The evening faltered, and I deemed
  That time was ripe, and years had
    done
  Their wheeling underneath the sun.

> BLISS CARMAN, "Low tide on Grand Pré",
> 1889.

I love the face of every man
Whose thought is swift and sweet.

> ARCHIBALD LAMPMAN, "Amor vitae",
> 1899.

A man's features are often a clue to his
character; a woman's rarely.

> ARNOLD HAULTAIN, *Hints for lovers*,
> 1909, 45.

From the dark pane
  As I draw near,
I see the silent, the invisible face
  Disappear.

> MARY QUAYLE INNIS, "Haunted", 1939.

You may look disagreeable and repel-
lent but that's because you can't help it
with that face of yours. Try to let
people realize that it is just your face;
that behind it you are all right.

> STEPHEN LEACOCK, "Casting out animos-
> ity", *Last leaves*, 1945, 89.

Factories

They had guards on the gates and
they'd let us out for the night.

> ANON., steel plant worker to *Globe and
> Mail* reporter, qu. in J. Kettle, *Foot-
> notes on the future*, 1970, 187.

Facts

Facts are stranger than fiction.

> T.C. HALIBURTON, *Sam Slick's wise saws*,
> 1853, I, 5.

I often wish that I could rid the world
of the tyranny of facts. What are facts
but compromises? A fact merely
marks the point where we have agreed
to let investigation cease. Investigate
further and your fact disappears.

> BLISS CARMAN, *Atlantic monthly*, May,
> 1906.

Some men spoil a good story by sticking to the facts.

> ROBERT C. (BOB) EDWARDS, Calgary *Eye
> Opener*, Jan. 25, 1919.

Facts never collide; in their long
procession there is always harmony
from the first movement to the last.

> ARTHUR MEIGHEN, Senate, *Debates*, Apr.
> 28, 1932, 296.

There are always two sides to a story
– he has his and I have mine, and
the facts lie between.

> MICHEL FOURNIER, N.B., Legis. Assem.,
> *Synoptic report of proceedings*, Mar.
> 24, 1953, 250.

Facts must be correct; theories must be fruitful. A "Fact", if incorrect, is useless – it is not a fact – but an incorrect theory may be even more useful than a correct one if it is more fruitful in leading the way to new facts.

HANS SELYE, *From dream to discovery*, 1964, 280.

Failure

You can't get blood out of a stone, you know.

THOMAS C. HALIBURTON, *Sam Slick's wise saws*, 1853, ch. 4.

We walk in blindness and dark night
Through half our earthly way;
Our clouds of weaknesses obscure
The glory of the day.

CHARLES SANGSTER, "My prayer", 1860.

And, through the gathering gloom, the silent rage
Of years undone came from the sea of death
To meet me there – and Time was lost to me
With all its wealth of opportunity.

WILLIAM E. MARSHALL, "Failure", 1894.

And each forgets, as he strips and runs,
With a brilliant, fitful pace,
It's the steady, quiet, plodding ones
Who win in the lifelong race.
And each forgets that his youth has fled,
Forgets that his prime is past,
Till he stands one day, with a hope that's dead
In the glare of the truth at last.

ROBERT SERVICE, "The men that don't fit in", 1907.

Having failed, disappear.

ARNOLD HAULTAIN, *Hints for lovers*, 1909, 140.

The man who never tried has no sympathy for the one who tried and failed.

ROBERT C. (BOB) EDWARDS, *Summer annual*, 1920, 27.

Much have we tried, and little done;
Much have we dreamed, and little won;
And back into the Gloom we lapse,
Confronted by the old Perhaps.

ARTHUR STRINGER, "The age end", 1929.

There is no search when nothing is left to seek,
Nothing to find when what was found is lost,
Nothing to lose when what is lost was all.

ROBERT FINCH, "Over", 1943.

Forgive us, who have not
Been whole or rich as fruit;
Who, through the eyes' lock enter
A point beyond the centre
To find our balance shot . . .
Our blueprint was at fault.

P.K. PAGE, "Forgive us, who have not been whole", 1947.

I like the lower towns, the place across the tracks, the poorer streets not far from the river. They represent failure, and for me failure here has a strong appeal.

NORMAN LEVINE, *Canada made me*, 1958, 41.

Failure teaches a man nothing except compassion for the failure of others.

KILDARE DOBBS, *Running to paradise*, 1962, 98.

I would say to the Prime Minister in the most kindly way possible that he must not let failure go to his head.

LESTER B. PEARSON, election campaign Mar., 1963, ref. to Diefenbaker.

The loneliest places of earth are not those where man has never set foot, but those from which he has withdrawn defeated.

> EDWARD MCCOURT, *The road across Canada*, 1965, 182.

Failure, after all, is the sugar of life: the more lumps you take, the sweeter you are.

> ERIC NICOL, *A scar is born*, 1968, Prologue.

I always see myself as one of life's rejects.

> BRIAN MOORE, in *Tamarack rev.* No. 46, 1968, 13.

I'm tired of building jigsaw puzzles. I keep losing pieces of the sky.

> SUSAN MUSGRAVE, "Exposure", 1970.

Fairs

'Twas not to buy or sell they came,
From far and near, the blind and lame,
The grave, the merry and the gay
Upon that old eventful day.
They all assembled, wild and free,
To have a ranting, roaring spree.

> W.P. LETT, untitled, written on the occasion of Bytown's (Ottawa) first fair, July, 1829.

Faith

Faith wanting, all his works fell short.

> CHARLES HEAVYSEGE, *Saul*, 1857.

To those who ever march with faith unbent,
Preserving in its fervid prime
A single purpose clear and plain,
Ready, although the twentieth time
To strike and fall, and strike again, –
Fate changes and the Gods relent.

> ARCHIBALD LAMPMAN, "Persistence", 1898.

Vaster than the world or life or death
my trust is
Based in the unseen and towering
far above;
Hold me, O Law, that deeper lies than
Justice,
Guide me, O Light, that stronger
burns than Love.

> DUNCAN CAMPBELL SCOTT, "Spring on Mattagami", 1906.

Nothing in life is more wonderful than faith – the one great moving force which we can neither weigh in the balance nor test in the crucible . . . To each one of the religions, past or present, faith has been the Jacob's ladder.

> SIR WILLIAM OSLER, in *British med. jour.*, June 18, 1910.

Who builds, but sits not on his throne,
Lest the king come, to him alone
The immortal Kingdoms shall be
known.

> WARWICK CHIPMAN, "Immortality", 1930.

Where knowledge is denied, faith comes in.

> FREDERICK P. GROVE, *Fruits of the earth*, 1933, 178.

Dear, you must know it is nothing to
me –
Faith is outmoded;
All those illusions I once held so fine
Have long been exploded.

> WINNIFRED A. HILLIER, "Frivolity", 1941.

Only the child-like dare
To walk by faith,
Only the simple-hearted
Take the Almighty at His word.

> MARY ELIZABETH COLMAN, "Hunger", 1942.

Fearfully the mind's hands dig
In the débris of thought, for the lovely
    body of faith.

> F.R. SCOTT, "Recovery", 1945.

And I who in my own faith once had
    faith like this,
but have not now, am crippled more
    than they.

> A.M. KLEIN, "The cripples", 1948.

If we on this continent have largely
lost the capacity to be near to God, we
have perhaps gained the capacity to be
near to Jesus.

> HUGH MACLENNAN, *Cross country*, 1949,
> 146.

For most people any faith is better
than no faith.

> BRIAN MOORE, in *Tamarack rev.* No. 46,
> 1968, 20.

Faith is needed today, not to move
mountains but to restrain people from
destroying one another out of self-
hatred and self-disgust.

> IRVING LAYTON, "Aphs", *The whole
> bloody bird*, 1969, 91.

It has to be re-appraised in a ruthless
world, where nothing is taken for
granted, nothing is assumed, nothing is
given, where everything has to be
examined, and everything has to be
established and the only risks to be
taken are the calculated ones.

> STANLEY B. FROST, *Standing and under-
> standing*, 1969, 17.

Falling

At Split Rock Falls I first saw my
    death
In a sudden slip the space of a breath;
My windmill body met the crazy
    shock
Of uncounted centuries of stubborn
    rock.

> RAYMOND SOUSTER, "At Split Rock
> Falls", 1958.

Fame

Madame, allow me to tell you that I
sometimes aspire to fame quite as
eagerly as many men . . . Women in
France during the late war went forth
at the head of the peasants to repel the
enemy. The women of Canada would
be no whit less eager to manifest their
zeal for the King should the occasion
arise.

> MADELEINE DE VERCHÈRES, letter to the
> Comtesse Maurepas, Oct. 19, 1699.
> (Trans.)

Fame I will have, but it must be alone.

> THOMAS SIMPSON, letter from Fort Garry,
> 1840.

I dreamed a dream when the woods
        were green,
And my April heart made an April
        scene,
    In the far, far distant land,
That even I might something do
That should keep my memory for the
        true,
    And my name from the spoiler's
        hand.

> THOMAS D'ARCY MCGEE, "A fragment",
> 1869.

To have done this is to have lived,
        though fame
Remember us with no familiar name.

> ARCHIBALD LAMPMAN, "The largest life",
> *Atlantic monthly*, Mar., 1899.

There are many kinds of fame, but the
best of all fame is the lustre and
distinction whose immediate results
mean the amelioration of the suffering
of mankind.

> ARTHUR MEIGHEN, speech in Ottawa,
> Feb. 13, 1923, on Dr. Banting.

It is strange how the memory of a man may float to posterity on what he would have himself regarded as the most trifling of his works.

> SIR WILLIAM OSLER, in Cushing: *Life of Osler*, 1926.

The moral is, if you wish to be famous, write a book about yourself, and be sure to leave everybody else out of the story.

> A.S. MORTON, *Under Western skies*, 1937.

Fame, the adrenalin: to be talked about;
to be a verb; to be introduced as *The*.

> ABRAHAM KLEIN, "Portrait of the poet as landscape", 1948.

Fame like a drunkard consumes the
  house of the soul
Exposing that you have worked for
  only this –
Ah, that I had never suffered this
  treacherous kiss
And had been left in darkness forever
  to founder and fail.

> MALCOLM LOWRY, "After publication of *Under the Volcano*", 1962.

It is one of the pleasant ironies of history, and cause of hope for all of us, that it is possible for a man to achieve great reputation and even enduring fame by doing something just a little worse than anyone else.

> EDWARD MCCOURT, *The road across Canada*, 1965, 179.

Families

My family lives at Alderville, but I live everywhere.

> JOHN SUNDAY, a Mississauga Indian, died Dec. 14, 1875, qu. in John Maclean, *Canadian savage folk*, 1896, 409.

Family trees are apt to be questionable about the roots.

> SIR WILLIAM VAN HORNE, to Lady Nicholson, 1909.

What is good enough for 'company' is not too good for your family, be it courtesy or the silver tea-pot.

> EMILY MURPHY, "Janey Canuck's Motto", Edmonton *Bulletin*, 1920's, qu. in B.H. Sanders, *Canadian portraits*, 1958, 130.

There is only one thing that is worse than to be left without your parents. And that is to be left without your children.

> ADELE WISEMAN, *The sacrifice*, 1956 (1972, 88).

My pleasures, how discreet they are!
A little booze, a little car,
Two little children and a wife
Living a small suburban life.

> GEORGE JOHNSTON, "War on the periphery", 1959.

It is in the basic emotional transactions within every Canadian family that the final success or failure of a viable Canadianism will be decided.

> CHARLES HANLY, in P. Russell, ed., *Nationalism in Canada*, 1966, 318.

We have to get rid of the conjugal family unit.

> BONNIE KREPS, womens' liberationist, qu. in *Maclean's*, Aug., 1969, 32.

The first half of our lives is ruined by our parents, and the second half by our children.

> RICHARD J. NEEDHAM, *A friend in Needham*, 1969, 24.

If in England the family is a mansion you live in, and if in America it's a skin you shed, then in Canada it's a trap in which you're caught.

> MARGARET ATWOOD, *Survival*, 1972, 131.

Family Allowances

This measure proceeds on the assumption that children are an asset to the state and that, in considering the resources of the state, human resources are of much more importance than material resources.

W.L. MACKENZIE KING, H. of C., *Debates*, 1944, V, 5331-2.

The Father of Family Allowance.

ANON., reference to Joseph R. Smallwood after 1949, term frequently stated to federal Liberals visiting Newfoundland.

Family Compact

The whole of the revenues of Upper Canada are in reality at their mercy; – they are Paymaster, Receivers, Auditors, King, Lords and Commons!

WILLIAM LYON MACKENZIE, *Sketches of Canada and the United States*, 1833, 409.

This family compact surround the Lieutenant-Governor, and mould him, like wax, to their will; they fill every office with their relatives, dependants and partisans; by them justices of the peace and officers of the militia are made and unmade.

WILLIAM LYON MACKENZIE, *Sketches of Canada and the United States*, 1833, 409.

The *family compact* of Upper Canada is composed of those members of its society who, either by their abilities and character, have been honoured by the confidence of the executive government, or who by their industry and intelligence have amassed wealth.

SIR FRANCIS B. HEAD, *Narrative*, 1839, 464.

Farmers

Let this be held the farmer's creed:
For stock seek out the choicest breed
In peace and plenty let them feed;
Your hands sow with the best of seed
Let it not dung nor dressing want
And then provisions won't be scant.

WEST RIVER (N.S.) FARMING SOC., motto, 1817.

Make a farmer of him, and you will have the satisfaction of seeing him an honest, an independent, and a respectable member of society; more honest than traders, more independent than professional men, and more respectable than either.

T.C. HALIBURTON, *Sam Slick*, 1836, ch. XXVI.

Each man seems to desire to dig the same piece of ground, and no more, that his father dug before him, & to dig it with the same spade; for an improvement in the instruments of cultivation or in the mode of culture would almost be regarded as an insult to the memory of the dead.

STEWART DERBISHIRE, *Report to Lord Durham*, May 24, 1838 (*Can.hist.rev.*, Mar., 1937, 57).

Attachment to the soil is the secret of the future greatness of the French-Canadian people. We hear a great deal of nationality, but I tell you that the race which will triumph in the future will be that which has held the soil.

SIR GEORGE-ETIENNE CARTIER, speech at Rimouski, Aug. 7, 1870. (Trans.)

His only joy since when a boy
  Has been to plod and moil,
Until his very soul itself
  Has grown into the soil.

ALEXANDER MCLACHLAN, "Neighbor John", 1874.

Manurin', ploughin', drainin', seedin',
All farmin's to be done by readin'!
O Lord! O Lord! it makes me mad,
When every striplin' of a lad,
And every edicated ass,
Who scarce knows growin' wheat from
    grass,
Must teach the likes o' me to farm,
Wi' Latin names as long's my arm;
Them criters teach the likes o' me?
Who farmed ere they could reach my
    knee,
Ain't it presumption? — Gee Buck
    Gee!

> ALEXANDER MCLACHLAN, "Old Canada",
> 1874.

I do not hesitate to state that farm work is the normal state of man here below, and that to which is called the mass of humankind.

> MGR. L.F. LAFLÈCHE, speech at Oka,
> Que., Aug. 9, 1895, (Trans.)

Bring me one of your students who has taken a degree and gone back to the farm and I shall be proud to be allowed to shake his hand.

> GOLDWIN SMITH (d. 1910), to his secre-
> tary, T.A. Haultain.

City people envy the farmer — but not to such an extent that they take advantage of the continuous opportunities to be one.

> ROBERT C. (BOB) EDWARDS, Calgary *Eye
> Opener*, Aug. 12, 1912.

Back to the land.

> ANON., a standard remedy for economic
> crisis advocated by the Roman Catholic
> church in Quebec, about 1912.

Oh, Lord, give us a good harvest, and a bloody war in Europe.

> ANON., Canadian pioneer's prayer qu. in
> A.R.M. Lower, *Canada, nation and
> neighbour*, 1952, 186.

The Farmers' Parliament.

> ANON., term in common use about 1915
> for annual conventions of the Saskat-
> chewan Grain Growers' Association at
> which political problems were debated.

To farm was an occupation easily parsed — subjunctive mood, past tense, passive voice! The farmer was third person, singular!

> HERBERT JOSEPH (HOPKINS) MOORHOUSE,
> *Deep furrows*, 1918, 40.

He is — and justly so — a confirmed and chronic kicker. He has got the habit and so much enjoys the sensation of being ill-used that he will often invent and imagine injuries which do not exist.

> ROBERT C. (BOB) EDWARDS, Calgary *Eye
> Opener*, Jan. 25, 1919, 1.

Then come our friends, good and true
With good of all the world in view;
The die is cast, it's up to you
    Organize! O organize!

> ANON., song of Alberta farmers, about
> 1920.

The farmers of the prairie lands are
    massing in their might,
Exulting in a Principle, a Cause for
    which they fight;
The sacred cause of Justice, the
    establishment of right,
And Equal Rights to all.

> ANON., "The day of right", a song of the
> Prairie farmers, about 1920.

Everything a farmer does is done in his spare time.

> SIR ANDREW MACPHAIL, address, Empire
> Club of Canada, Toronto, Mar. 4, 1920.

Yus farmers want to keep your boys at home. Don't let them go up to the city; keep them on the farm, — the temptations is more pure.

> ANON., a Senator, speech at Pakenham,
> Ont., election campaign of 1921.

Farmers are the only men who will remedy farm conditions.

> ALEXANDER J. MCPHAIL, in 1931, qu. in Grant MacEwan, *Fifty mighty men*, 1958, 194.

He was the first true "colonist", the "Abraham of the colony".

> R.M. SAUNDERS, in *Can.hist.rev.*, 1935, 394, on Louis Hébert.

The farmer is king, oh, the farmer is
    king,
And except for his wife and daughter,
Who boss him around, he runs the
    thing,
Come drought, come hell or high
    water.

> PAUL HIEBERT, "The farmer is king", in *Sarah Binks*, 1947, xi.

The peasant was always a suburban parasite. The farmer no longer exists; today he is a "city" man.

> MARSHALL MCLUHAN, *Counterblast*, 1954 [15] (pamphlet).

Whatever he is, *the* French Canadian is not a farmer, leave alone a peasant.

> W.E. HAVILAND, *Can. jour. of agricultural economics*, V, No. 2, 1957, 77.

But the heart accepts it all, this honest
    air
Lapped in green valleys where
    accidents will happen!
Where the bull, the buzz-saw and the
    balky mare
Are the chosen fingers of God for a
    farmer's sins,
Like the axe for his woods, and his
    calves and chicks and children
Destined for slaughter in the course of
    things.

> JOHN GLASSCO, "The rural mail", 1958.

Farming

Let us go back to our farming for this must be our goal. That is the first mine for which we must search, and it is of better worth than the treasures of Atahualpa.

> MARC LESCARBOT, *History of New France*, 1606, ed. Grant, 1907, II, 317.

No man who can become wealthy by hard work, will ever submit to the drudgery of farming.

> THOMAS MCCULLOCH, *The letters of Mephibosheth Stepsure*, 1821, Letter 3.

When the Spring comes, and the fields are dry enough to be sowed, they all have to be plowed, cause fall rains wash the lands too much for fall ploughin. Well the ploughs have to be mended and sharpened, cause what's the use of doin that afore its wanted. Well the wheat gets in too late, and then comes rust, but whose fault is that? Why the climate to be sure, for Nova Scotia aint a bread country.

> T.C. HALIBURTON, *Sam Slick*, 1836, 172.

Up, be stirring, be alive!
Get upon a farm and thrive!
He's a king upon a throne
Who has acres of his own!

> ALEXANDER MCLACHLAN, "Acres of your own", 1874.

The most magnificent expanse of virgin soil that remains unsubdued on the face of the earth.

> A. SUTHERLAND, *Summer in prairie land*, 1881.

None ever saw such crops as these,
So great the yield of oats and pease;
Fifty bushels to the acre
Makes us grateful to our maker.

> JAMES MCINTYRE, "Big crops of 1891".

One may put in a plow at Winnipeg and never touch anything but good soil all the way to Edmonton.

> ISAAC COWIE, *Western plains of Canada rediscovered*, 1903, 18.

Contented women, good chances for the education of the children, and a reasonably richly developed social life are in the long run of immensely more consequence than conveniences for growing crops. The place of the latter is to minister to the former. What shall it profit a country to be called, or to be, the Granary of the Empire if it lose the soul of happy rural life.

> CANADA. ROY. COMM. ON INDUSTRIAL TRAINING, *Report*, 1913, II, 1201.

Farming is one of the finest occupations in the world if taken in moderation.

> PETER MCARTHUR, *In pastures green*, 1915, 93.

Farms

The little lams are beautiful
There cotes are soft and nice
The little calves have ringworm
And the 2-year olds have lice!

> NELLIE MCCLUNG, *Sowing seeds in Danny*, 1908, 221, poem by a 12 year old.

There is a sweet nostalgic charm,
  About an old Ontario farm,
That pulls your heart strings all awry,
  A clean breath taking sweep of sky
And old grey barn built on a knoll.
  A young mare nuzzling at her foal.

> EDNA JAQUES, "Home relish", 1953.

Ours was a windy country and its crops
were never frivolous, malicious rocks
kicked at the plough and skinny cattle broke
ditch ice for mud to drink and pigs
were axed.

> ALDEN NOWLAN, "A poem to my mother", 1958.

The cities do not extend to each other,
the hamlets exist alone,
the suspicious basses of voices
of farmers mutter in the horse -
urined yards, the wives and the children
wait for the spring, summer, fall, the grass,
the quick, unlasting reprieve, gone
like that!

> JOHN NEWLOVE, "East from the mountains", 1965.

A country of quiescence and still distance
a lean land not fat
with inches of black soil on earth's round belly —
And where the farms are its as if a man stuck
both thumbs in the stony earth and pulled it apart to make room
enough between the trees
for a wife and maybe some cows and room for some
of the more easily kept illusions.

> AL PURDY, "The country north of Belleville", 1965.

Fashion

To plead fashion, is like following a multitude to do evil.

> CATHERINE PARR TRAILL, *The Canadian settler's guide*, 1855, 23.

Fashion is woman's sole law.

> ARNOLD HAULTAIN, *Hints for lovers*, 1909, 46.

Women are wearing the bosoms flatter, and their bottoms are carried higher and slightly to the right. They're still wearing dark circles under the eyes, as if they were dead but enjoying it.

> JOHN CROSBY, Toronto *Globe and Mail* columnist, reporting on Paris fashions, qu. in *Liberty*, Feb., 1963.

Since I got the classy suits and the sideburns, the success I've had with women this year over last has been phenomenal.

> DEREK SANDERSON, (hockey player), qu. in *Maclean's*, Jan., 1970, 13.

My idea of good fashion is that you wear it — it doesn't wear you.

> BETTY KENNEDY, qu. in *Can. mag.*, Nov. 11, 1972, 20.

Fate

To hunt and to be hunted makes
  existence;
For we are all chasers or the chased;
And some weak, luckless wretches ever
  seem
Flying before the hounds of
  circumstance . . .

> CHARLES HEAVYSEGE, *Saul*, 1857, pt.2.

Take things pleasantly & when fortune empties her chamberpot on your head — smile & say 'We are going to have a summer shower'.

> SIR JOHN A. MACDONALD, letter to T.C. Patteson, Jan. 18, 1878. (Pub. Arch. Can.)

Inexorably decreed
By the ancestral deed,
The puppets of our sires,
We work out blind desires,
And for our sons ordain
The blessing or the bain.

> CHARLES G.D. ROBERTS, "Origins", 1896.

Well, if that's our fate,
  I would rather go down with those I
    love
Than float among those I hate.

> TOM MACINNES, "Choice", 1918.

What must come would come; no use trying to fight; no use worrying. Too bad if anything happened; but if it did, it could not be helped.

> FREDERICK P. GROVE, *Fruits of the earth*, 1933, 115.

The cry of "Eenie, meenie, minie,
  moe",
By which children choose a loser in a
  game,
And by which Fate seems to choose
Which children shall be which:
One-eyed, wilful, hare-lipped, lame,
Poor, orphans, idiots, or rich.

> JAMES REANEY, "Dark lagoon", 1949.

Twaddle as we may about free will, some of us are bound to live in a context of farce, some in comedy, some in proletarian realism, some in melodrama, and a few — unhappy wretches — in tragedy.

> ROBERTSON DAVIES, *A voice from the attic*, 1960, 179.

And though they languished
for another land
underneath they clung
to their bitter lot
and blamed God.

> STEVE SMITH, "Wilderness", 1964.

I am bound
by a chain of events
each
forged in a foreign furnace
and molten moulded
hammered
on an anvil of fact
tempered
with circumstance.

> RED LANE, "Margins III", 1968.

The element follows you around.

> MALCOLM LOWRY, *October ferry to Gabriola*, 1970, 121.

Fathers

For thirty years he was my instructor, my playfellow, almost my daily companion. To him I owe my fondness for reading, my familiarity with the Bible, my knowledge of old colonial and American incidents and characteristics. He left me nothing but his example and the memory of his many virtues, for all that he ever earned was given to the poor. He was too good for this world; but the remembrance of his high principles, his cheerfulness, his child-like simplicity, and truly Christian character, is never absent from my mind.

> JOSEPH HOWE, on the death of his father, Dec. 27, 1835.

With a full knowledge of all that has passed, and all the consequences that have flowed from a day of weakness, I will say that an honester man does not breathe the air of heaven; that no son feels prouder of his father than I do to-day; and that I would have submitted to the obloquy and reproach of every act, not fifteen years, but fifty — ay, have gone down to the grave with the cold shade of the world upon me, rather than that one of his gray hairs should have been injured.

> GEORGE BROWN, speech in Legis. Assembly, 1858, on his father.

Your fathers are but silly fools,
  Old relics of a past age,
No wonder they can't comprehend,
  This go-ahead, this fast age.

> ALEXANDER MCLACHLAN, "Young Canada", 1861.

The name of Father, ever will it be
A name of music, true and sweet to
  me.
Behind the years, far back in
  childhood's day,
The name recalls my human trust and
  stay.

> GRANT BALFOUR, "Father", 1910.

And never more my father's voice
  Comes with insistent tone;
And I, alas! am all too free
  To tread my path alone.

> JAMES E. CALDWELL, "Peccavi", 1913.

My son, honor thy father and thy mother by improving upon their example.

> GEORGE ILES, *Canadian stories*, 1918, 182.

My father is gathered to his fathers,
  God rest his wraith!
And his son
Is a pauper in spirit, a beggar in piety,
Cut off without a penny's worth of
  faith.

> A.M. KLEIN, "Childe Harold's pilgrimage", 1940.

The sins of the fathers
are·cast on the sons.
Let them figure it out!

> WAYNE STEDINGH, "Pigalle", 1970.

my father and I are dying
at different speeds.

> MARVYNE JENOFF, "Undercurrent", 1972.

Fatness

Fat men are good natured because good natured men are usually fat.

> ROBERT C. (BOB) EDWARDS, Calgary *Eye Opener*, May 22, 1915.

Fatness in a woman is a sign of contentment and a contented wife indicates a satisfactory husband. What could be more gratifying to man than to be a satisfactory husband?

> REBA KINGSTON, *Living in clover*, 1965, 101.

Faults

Never exaggerate your faults; your friends will attend to that.

> ROBERT C. (BOB) EDWARDS, Calgary *Eye Opener*, Feb. 5, 1921.

Each of us has a flaw, and when two people love each other, each seems to expect the other to cure his flaw.

> HUGH MACLENNAN, *Each man's son*, 1951, 63.

Fear

Dream of that constable, his name is Fear, he'll be at your heels till you die.

> THOMAS C. HALIBURTON, *Sam Slick's wise saws*, 1853, ch. 4.

He (Riel) told me I was exposing myself too much. I replied that the enemy could not kill me. And I confess I was afraid of nothing.

> GABRIEL DUMONT, *Account of the North West rebellion, 1885*, Dec., 1888, qu. in *Can. hist. rev.*, Vol. 30, 1949, 267.

We build our little life by hour, by day;
God wakes — and winks a million years away;
He will have patience though ten thousand years
Have brought us still no further than our fears.

> ANNIE C. DALTON, "Flame and adventure", 1924.

Fear is a permanent curse in a democratic world.

> G.M. WRONG, in *Can.hist.rev.*, 1933, 8.

There are three enemies to a lost man — cold, hunger, and, last and most terrible, fear. Don't get scared, and all will be well.

> ERNEST THOMPSON SETON, *Trail of an artist-naturalist*, 1940, 360.

Telling it in plain words
Makes me see how I feared the wrong thing.

> MARGARET AVISON, "The Agnes Cleves papers", 1960.

It appears
that our fears
are well placed,
are well based.

> W.W. EUSTACE ROSS, untitled poem, pub. in *Can. lit.*, 1969, No. 39, 43.

Throughout history, rulers have put the fear of death into people. Canada's rulers have done better, by putting the fear of life into them.

> RICHARD J. NEEDHAM, *A friend in Needham*, 1969, 43.

Fear of deafness has stopped my ears.
Fear of blindness has sewn up my eyes.
Fear of nakedness has stripped me bare.
Fear of the desert has made me abjure drink.
Yet even now, bad joke for a black morning,
fear of silence has not stilled my tongue.

> ALDEN NOWLAN, "Five days in hospital", 1969.

in fear everything
lives, impermanence
makes the edges of things burn brighter.

> MARGARET ATWOOD, "Highest altitude", 1970.

Anxious
of course I'm anxious
afraid
of course I'm afraid
I don't know what about
I don't know what of
but I'm afraid
and I feel it's
right to be.

MIRIAM WADDINGTON, "Anxious", 1972.

Federalism

Federal government appears to me to be the only possible one in Canada because of our differences of race and creed, and also because of the variety and multiplicity of local needs in our immense territory.

SIR LOMER GOUIN, in *Quebec and Confederation*, ed. by Savard, 1918, 124.

There can be no federalism without the autonomy of the state's constituent parts, and no sovereignty of the various governments without fiscal and financial autonomy.

QUEBEC. ROY. COMM. OF INQUIRY ON CONSTITUTIONAL PROBLEMS, *Report*, Vol. III:2, 1956, 294.

Federalism is the most distinctive achievement of Canadian democracy.

ALEXANDER BRADY, *Democracy in the Dominions*, 1958, 65.

Canadian federalism is an experiment of major proportions; it could become a brilliant prototype for the moulding of tomorrow's civilization.

PIERRE E. TRUDEAU, *Cité libre*, Apr., 1962, 16. (Trans.)

Canada is a collection of ten provinces with strong governments loosely connected by fear.

DAVE BROADFOOT, television comedian, paraphrased by G. Clark in *Canada: the uneasy neighbour*, 1965, 47.

Co-operative federalism.

ANON., a concept of gradual decentralisation usually related to Quebec Province, about 1966.

Only a central authority that has the power to determine the general direction and content of the entire country's economic, fiscal, labour and social policies can create that national harmony which is absolutely essential to the peace and well-being of each of the Provinces as well as of *all individual Canadians*.

ANDREW BRICHANT, *Option Canada*, 1968, 43.

How any patriotic Canadian, how any Canadian who loves Canada can advocate anything that would make the Parliament of Canada impotent and the Government of Canada powerless; how any patriotic Canadian could want that for the sake of making his own or any other province strong at the expense of Ottawa is something that baffles me! I do not understand it! And I do not believe the people of Canada want it − in any province!

JOSEPH SMALLWOOD, Federal-Provincial Conference on the Constitution, Ottawa, Feb. 5-7, 1968.

To jeopardize the capacity of the federal government to act for Canada, in the name of protecting linguistic and provincial rights, when what is essential could be accomplished through constitutional guarantees and the institutions of federalism, would be to serve Canadians badly. Furthermore, the division of powers between orders of government should be guided by principles of functionalism, and not by ethnic considerations.

CANADA. GOVT. *Federalism for the future; a statement of policy*, Constitutional Conference, Ottawa, Feb. 5-7, 1968, 36.

Anything that tends in the direction at all of reducing Ottawa's importance, reducing Ottawa's authority, reducing Ottawa's strength, strikes a blow at us. We are weaker when Ottawa is weaker.

JOSEPH R. SMALLWOOD, Constitutional Conference, First meeting, Ottawa, Feb. 5-7, 1968, *Proceedings*, 1968, 189.

Canadian federalism owes its originality to the fact that its components are of two different kinds. The first are territorial or political, that is, states or provinces, which now number ten. The second are sociological, that is, two nations, societies or cultural communities united by history, one of which has had its roots implanted in Canadian soil for over three and a half centuries.

CANADA. CONSTITUTIONAL CONFERENCE. CONTINUING COMM. OF OFFICIALS, *Submission of the Quebec delegation*, July 24, 1968, 6.

It is a constant hazard of democracy that the loudest and most determined group is most often that which holds the most extreme and reactionary views. We shall certainly hear from those we do not understand or who are afraid of change. What we need is to rally the vast majority of reasonable and moderate Canadians, of both languages and all parties, who believe in improved and more equitable federalism.

PIERRE E. TRUDEAU, speech, University of Moncton, May 18, 1969.

Feeling

Feeling is the power that drives art. There doesn't seem to be a more understandable word for it, though there are others that give something of the idea; aesthetic emotion, quickening, bringing to life. Or call it love: not love of man or woman or home or country or any material thing, but love without an object — intransitive love.

DAVID MILNE, "Feeling in painting", in *Here and now*, May, 1948, 57.

Fellatio

When you kneel below me
and in both your hands
hold my manhood like a sceptre,

When you wrap your tongue
about the amber jewel
and urge my blessing

I understood those Roman girls
who danced around a shaft of stone
and kissed it till the stone was warm.

LEONARD COHEN, "Celebration", 1961.

Females

A woman always interprets abstract disparagement of her sex personally.

ARNOLD HAULTAIN, *Hints for lovers*, 1909, 44.

Though the female always runs away, she never runs so fast that she couldn't run faster; and it makes no difference whether the female has wings or fins, flippers or feet, it is all the same — the female always does the courting.

ARTHUR HEMING, *The drama of the forests*, 1921, 271.

Femaleness, as any doctor will tell you, is savage.

DR. MARION HILLIARD, *A woman doctor looks at love and life*, 1957, 87.

Feminists

Perhaps we are a country more feminine than we like to admit, because the unifying, regenerative principle is a passion with us. We make a synthesis of these two seasons, innocence and experience.

DOROTHY LIVESAY, *Collected poems*, 1972, Foreword.

All feminists may not be socialists, but all socialists must be feminists.

> ROSEMARY BROWN (B.C., M.L.A.),, qu. in *Saturday night*, Jul./Aug., 1975, 31.

Fences

Since that time I have had much experience of both beasts and fences; and I have always found that good fences make good friends and safe crops.

> THOMAS MCCULLOCH, letters of Mephibosheth Stepsure, Letter 9, *Acadian recorder*, Mar. 9, 1822, 2.

It's no use to make fences unless the land is cultivated.

> T.C. HALIBURTON, *Sam Slick*, 1836, ch. XVI.

Old fences drift vaguely among the
     trees
  a pile of moss-covered stones
gathered for some ghost purpose
has lost meaning under the
     meaningless sky.

> AL PURDY, "The country north of Belleville", 1967.

Fenians

In Toronto one extreme is made auxiliary to the other; Orangeism has been made the pretext of Fenianism, and Fenianism is doing its best to justify and magnify Orangeism.

> THOMAS D'A. MCGEE, 1858, *Irish position*, 1866, 15.

Weed out and cast off those rotten members, who, without a single governmental grievance to complain of in Canada, would yet weaken and divide us in these days of danger and anxiety.

> THOMAS D'A. MCGEE, speech at Montreal, 1865.

We are a Fenian brotherhood, skilled
     in the arts of war,
And we're going to fight for Ireland,
     the land that we adore;
Many battles have we won, along with
     the boys in blue,
And we'll go to capture Canada, for
     we've nothing else to do!

> ANON., Fenian battle song, 1866.

Shout! Shout! Shout! ye loyal Britons!
Cheer up, let the rebels come,
For beneath the Union Jack
We will drive the Fenians back,
And we'll fight for our beloved
     Canadian home.

> THOMAS WILSON, marble-cutter, of Brampton, Ont., 1866; sung to the tune of "Tramp, tramp, tramp, the boys are marching".

The Fenian snake is scotched but not killed . . . it may revive at any moment.

> SIR ALEXANDER T. GALT, speech on the Budget, June 26, 1866.

The Fenians would indeed have proved the invaluable, though involuntary benefactors of Canada, if the only experience derived from their foolish proceedings had been the proofs of warm attachment exhibited by Canadians universally for the land of their birth or adoption.

> PATRICK MACDOUGALL, *Report on militia*, 1866, in *Sessional papers*, 2, No. 4.

Fiction

There are stranger things in reality than can be found in romances.

> THOMAS C. HALIBURTON, *Sam Slick's wise saws*, 1853, ch. 6.

Fidelity

This is the circle we must trace
Not spiralled outward, but a space
Returning to its starting place.

Centre of all we mourn and bless,
Centre of calm beyond excess,
Who cares for caring, has caress.

F.R. SCOTT, "Caring", 1954.

The dream of romantic love is taken
more seriously in North America than
it is anywhere else in the world, which
is why we believe in fidelity and why
we believe in infidelity as well.

MERLE SHAIN, *Some men are more perfect than others*, 1973, 78.

Fighting

My orders are to fight.
    Then if I bleed, or fail,
Or strongly win, what matters it?
    God only doth prevail.

The servant craveth nought
    Except to serve with might.
I was not told to win or lose, −
    My orders are to fight.

ETHELWYN WETHERALD, "My orders",
1907.

There are people who say we will not
fight for England; will you then fight
for France? I speak to you of French
origin; if I were young like you and
had the same health that I enjoy today,
I. would join those brave Canadians
fighting today for the liberation of
French territory. I would not have it
said that the French Canadians do less
for the liberation of France than the
citizens of British origin. For my part I
want to fight for England and also for
France. To those who do not want to
fight either for England or for France
I say: Will you fight for yourselves?

SIR WILFRID LAURIER, speech, Maison-
neuve, Que., Sept. 21, 1916.

And when they interlocked, that night−
Cetacean and cephalopod −
No titan with Olympian god
Had ever waged a fiercer fight.

E.J. PRATT, *Titans*, 1926, 14.

We're so much alike that we can't
discuss. We can only fight.

STEPHEN LEACOCK, "Rebuilding the cities", Roy. Architectural Inst. of Canada,
Journal, Dec., 1942, 229.

Whenever I don't know whether to
fight or not − I always fight!

EMILY MURPHY, favourite expression, qu.
in Bryne H. Sanders, *Emily Murphy −
crusader*, 1945, 121.

Films

To make with a brush on canvas is a
simple and direct delight. To make
with a film should be the same.

NORMAN MCLAREN, about 1944, qu. by
Germaine Warkentin, *Tamarack rev.*
No. 5, 1957, 48.

Finality

Nothing finally is final −
every love is a rain
opening the bud to fire
asking and receiving its own Easter.

PHYLLIS WEBB, "Flux", 1962.

Finance

The Lord in silence works
Towards mysterious ends
The same omniscience lurks
In dividends.

A.M. KLEIN, "The diary of Abraham
Segal, poet", in *Can. forum*, May, 1932,
297.

Let me repeat what I said in Parliament in protesting against the surrender to a private institution of the

state's control over the nation's currency and credit: "Once a nation parts with the control of its currency and credit; it matters not who makes the nation's laws."

W.L. MACKENZIE KING, election speech at Saskatoon, Sept. 20, 1935.

Our whole war effort, both militarily and economic, at home as well as overseas, depends upon finance.

W.L. MACKENZIE KING, radio broadcast, Oct. 31, 1939.

Monetary nationalism is a reflection of the role of the state in the expansion of industrialism and the means by which the state is compelled to rely increasingly on expanded public debt to avoid increasingly its effects.

HAROLD A. INNIS, *Essays in Canadian economic history*, 1956, 271.

Political scientists fail to see the eroding effect that the 'power of the purse' will have on Canadian democracy if the present construction continues to prevail, and in particular what chaos will result if provincial governments borrow federal logic and begin using their own 'power of the purse' to meddle in federal affairs.

PIERRE E. TRUDEAU, in M. Oliver, ed., *Social purpose for Canada*, 1961, 382 ff.

The private sector of our economy is too weak to provide us with the 'rocket-launchers' that can blast us off the ramp of our debilitating poverty. Our principal "capitalist" for the moment — and for as far into the future as we can see — must therefore be the State. It must be more than a participant in the economic development and emancipation of Quebec; it must be a creative agent.

RENÉ LÉVESQUE, *Le Devoir*, July 5, 1963. (Trans.)

Where your treasury is, there your heart is also.

W.A.C. BENNETT, qu. in P. Sherman, *Bennett*, 1966, xi, re loan of one hundred million dollars to province of Quebec, Sept., 1964.

We tend not to make any distinction between investment that comes from central Canada, the United States or other foreign countries, regarding it all, somehow, as "foreign".

ATLANTIC PROVINCES ECONOMIC COUNCIL, *Brief*, qu. in R. Reid, *Canadian style*, 1973, 105, from Toronto *Star*, June 14, 1972.

An economist without sensitivity for national feelings might quite accurately look at the statistics and decide that Canada was merely an adjunct to the United States financial and industrial world.

STANLEY R. TUPPER and DOUGLAS L. BAILEY, *Canada and the United States: the second hundred years*, 1967, 100.

The story of the growth of American capital in Canada has yet to be fully told. Contrary to its proponents, its effect has not been to expand Canadian independence but to set in motion the·forces of national disintegration. It has choked off Canadian entrepreneurship and technological growth, bought off Canadian capital, and virtually destroyed Canada's once vigorous capitalist class.

C.W. GONICK, in I. Lumsden, ed., *Close the 49th parallel etc.*, 1970, 59.

Finance (Private)

Stand fast, Craigellachie!

See: C.P.R., 1884.

I have never been afraid to borrow.

E.P. TAYLOR, qu. in P. Newman, *Flame of power*, 1959, 241.

Financiers

There are poor worms most anxious to
  take shares
In every one of this great man's
  affairs.
So shed no tear at his forced
  liquidation:
It simply means a new incorporation.

> F.R. SCOTT, "Epitaphs: Financier", 1957.

Fines

I'd sooner be shot than fined.

> DAN HARRINGTON, last words after a gun
> battle while resisting arrest for whisky
> peddling, Hawk Lake, Ont. railway
> camp; Winnipeg *Times*, Aug. 14, 1880.

Fingers

My fingers are my light and eyes —
With them I read and find my way.
I write with them and sew and knit
They move, examine and create.

> SARA HAZEN, "My fingers", 1954.

Fish

Some years ago a friend of mine was
teaching his little boy the Lord's
Prayer, and the little fellow said: 'Our
Father which art in Heaven, halibut
be Thy name.'

> T.D. PATTULLO, Premier of B.C., address
> to Canadian Club, Ottawa, Jan. 12,
> 1924; see also A.J. Cross, *Cross roads*,
> 1936, 79, as a reference to Prince Rup-
> ert, B.C.

now to appear
surprised, aghast,
out of its element
into the day; —
out of the cold
and shining lake
the fish dripping
sparkling water.

> W.W. EUSTACE ROSS, "Fish", 1928.

What on earth did you ever do with
that fish?

> ANON., question frequently asked by
> Saskatchewan recipients of salt cod sup-
> plied by Red Cross to the needy, early
> 1930's.

Fisheries

The Newfoundland fisheries are more
valuable than all the mines of Peru.

> LORD BACON, about 1608, attributed;
> also: "Greater than the gold mines of
> Golgonda, there is none so rich".

. . . Some place far abroad
Where sailors gang to fish for cod.

> ROBERT BURNS, "The twa dogs", 1786,
> re: Newfoundland.

A Fishery, in my opinion, is that
branch of commerce which not only
requires every attention and encouragement but will not admit of the
smallest impediment or obstacle; and I
deprecate, as fatal to the interests of
the trade, which I have deeply at
heart, the establishment in any way of
Courts of Judicature, which may introduce the glorious uncertainty of the
law, and make room for troublesome
and litigious men to get a footing
among the inhabitants.

> JOHN JEFFERY, in Gt. Brit. *Rept. from
> the Committee on the state of trade to
> Newfoundland* [1793], 13.

The Fisheries — Banks which always
discount — the wealth we draw from
them need never be repaid.

> N.S. PHILANTHROPIC SOC., Toast, Nov. 1,
> 1836.

The fisheries are our trump card.

> SIR JOHN YOUNG (later Lord Lisgar),
> letter, Oct. 27., 1870, to Earl Kimberley,
> Colonial Secretary, prior to signing of
> Treaty of Washington. (Pub.Arch.Can.)

Well, here go the fisheries.

> SIR JOHN A. MACDONALD, May 8, 1871, to Hamilton Fish when signing the Treaty of Washington.

Fishocracy.

> P. TOQUE, *Newfoundland as it was*, 1878, 86. Term used to describe well-to-do merchants opposed to self-government for Newfoundland.

The Fisherman who would sell Bait to a Frenchman would steal the pennies off his dead mother's eyes.

> ANON., a political placard, Newfoundland, at the time of the passage of the Bait Act, 1886.

Fishermen

I'se the b'y that builds the boat,
And I'se the b'y that sails her!
I'se the b'y that catches the fish
And takes 'em home to Lizer.

> ANON., "I'se the b'y that builds the boat", Newfoundland song.

Fishing admiral.

> ANON., a term for the first skipper of a fishing boat to arrive in any Newfoundland harbour for the fishing season. (See Prowse, *History of Newfoundland*, 1895, 92).

In his ordinary blue flushing jacket and trousers, economically besmeared with pitch, tar, and fish slime, his head adorned with an old sealskin cap, robbed from an Indian, or bartered for a glass of rum and a stick of tobacco. The sacred temple of law and equity was a fish store, the judicial seat an inverted butter firkin. Justice might be won by the presentation of a few New England apples or a flowing bowl of calabogus, a favourite drink of the admirals composed of rum, molasses, and spruce beer.

> D.W. PROWSE, *History of Newfoundland*, 1895, 226, re: the "Fishing Admirals".

Oh, this is the place where the
    fishermen gather
With oilskins, boots and capeanns
    battered down;
All sizes of figures with squid-lines and
    jiggers
They congregate here on the
    squid-jiggin' ground.

> A.R. SCAMMELL, "Squid jigging-ground", a Newfoundland song.

here where heads of Hebridean mould
toss in crusted dories, hard fingers
sift dour living from the amber fins
that fleck these longdrowned Banks

> EARLE BIRNEY, "Maritime faces", 1952.

Down through history, ever since there were fishermen in Newfoundland, they have been crucified. That crucifixion was not always the crucifixion of cruelty. Today I accuse the fish merchants of Water Street, not of showing cruelty to the fishermen. I would almost prefer they did that. I accuse them of showing stupidity, of ignorance, of laziness, of which the fishermen are the victims.

> JOSEPH R. SMALLWOOD, speech in Newfoundland, Apr., 1954, qu. by R. Gwyn, *Smallwood*, 1968, 130.

Fishing

These waters plenty fish afford,
    The perch, and pike, and cat;
And there the spotted salmon swims,
    And sturgeon stored with fat.

> *THE METHODIST MAGAZINE*, 1828, 74.

Lurked in their watery lairs the trout,
But, silver and scarlet, I lured them
    out.
Wary were they, but warier still
My cunning wrist and my cast of skill.

> CHARLES G.D. ROBERTS, "The trout brook", 1893.

Never can tell when the bass is
   a-coming,
  Never can tell when he's going to
   bite;
First thing you know your reel will be
   humming,
  Strike him quickly and hold him
   tight.

WILLIAM H. ELLIS, *Wayside weeds*, 1914.

All the big fish in the sea were lost at
the gunnel.

ANON., Newfoundland saying; qu. Devine, *Folklore of Newfoundland*, 1937.

The weather for catching fish is that
weather, and no other, in which fish
are caught.

W.H. BLAKE, *Brown waters*, 1915, 29.

The science of fishing can be had from
books; the art is learned by the catching and the losing of fish.

W.H. BLAKE, *Brown waters*, 1915.

My fish this year have cost me only
fifty dollars a pound.

WEIR MITCHELL, quoted in J.M. Clarke,
L'Ile Percée, 1923.

When the East Wind blows the fish
  won't bite;
South Wind they bite least;
West Wind blows the bait right into
  their mouth;
North Wind they bite best.

JOE LAVALLY, Algonquin Park Indian
guide, d. 1947.

Your fishing line would be hanging
slack from the alder pole into the
pondlike stillwater. And then suddenly
the surge of a trout would stretch your
line taut and all at once your heart
would seem to spread out like a fan
and you would know exactly what
*trout*ness was, And *brook*ness. And
*leaf*ness. And, yes, *world*ness and *life*-
ness itself. You would move right out
– and gloriously – into everything
around you.

ERNEST BUCKLER, *Ox bells and fireflies*,
1968, 52.

The wolves say to the dogs what the
madman of me says to the citizen. I
need to go fishing until I need to
return.

J. MICHAEL YATES, *The Great Bear Lake
meditations*, 1970, (Long light, meditation 1).

Flag

All those subordinate matters which
foster a sentiment on union should be
studiously attended to – their flag
should be a modification of that of
England – the Union Jack with a difference of some kind.

SIR EDMUND HEAD, memo. on gov't. to
Lord Grey, 1851, qu., Can. Hist. Assoc.,
Report, 1928, 25.

I hope that the people of the United
States and Great Britain will always
remain true to those great principles
on which their institutions are founded, and that their flags may wave
together in beauty and harmony in
many a distant land, the one bearing
on it that emblem of the might of the
Creator, the starry heavens, which
express His infinite power, and the
other emblazoned with the emblem of
God's greatest work, the redemption
of man.

ALEXANDER MACKENZIE, Prime Minister,
speech in Saint John, N.B., 1876.

The Dutch may have their Holland,
  the Spaniard have his Spain,
The Yankee to the south of us must
  south of us remain;
For not a man dare lift a hand against
  the men who brag
That they were born in Canada
  beneath the British flag.

> PAULINE JOHNSON, "Canadian born",
> 1912.

It is only as those things which people
themselves represent and stand for are
known and respected, not only to their
friends but to themselves, that the
emblems and flag of a nation can be
held in the regard and esteem that
they should be. In other words it is not
a flag that makes a nation; it is a
nation that makes a flag.

> R.N. THOMPSON, H. of C., *Debates*, Sept.
> 10, 1964, 7821.

I believe we should have a national
flag that stands for Canada, that flies
as a symbol of Canada alone, that
neither dishonors nor betrays the past
but looks to the future; a flag that will
say one word and that word is "Canada".

> LESTER B. PEARSON, H. of C., *Debates*,
> Dec. 11, 1964, 11038.

This is the flag for the future, but it
does not dishonour the past. I hope
that Canada can go forward as a
united, strong and progressive country,
with this flag as its emblem.

> LESTER B. PEARSON, H. of C., *Debates*,
> Dec. 14, 1964, 11136.

The use of foreign flags by the general
public in Canada is a practice that
should be discouraged.

> GEORGE F.G. STANLEY, *The story of Ca-
> nada's flag*, 1965, 84.

Gules on a Canadian pale argent a
maple leaf of the first.

> HERALDS' COLLEGE. Heraldic description
> of Canadian flag, officially adopted
> Feb. 15, 1965.

Each time that the average citizen
looks at the new flag, he unconsciously
says to himself "That's me!"

> A.R.M. LOWER, *Queen's quart.*, Vol. 74,
> Summer, 1967, 237.

Flattery

Almost anybody will take any amount
of it.

> SIR JOHN A. MACDONALD, to Sir Joseph
> Pope, his secretary, about 1880.

Next to sympathy, flattery is perhaps
woman's most effective weapon.

> ARNOLD HAULTAIN, *Hints for lovers*,
> 1909, 195.

Candid words cannot compete with
candied words.

> R.J. MANION, *Life is an adventure*,
> 1936, 57.

Fleming, Sir Sandford

The Father of Standard Time.

> SIR SANDFORD FLEMING, who first ad-
> vocated a universal method of reckon-
> ing time, 1879.

Flies

Mosquitoes on the wet ground and
sand-flies in the dry, bull-dogs in the
sunshine, bugs in the oakwoods, ants
everywhere – it is maddening.

> EARL OF SOUTHESK, *Saskatchewan and
> the Rocky Mountains: Diary*, June 21,
> 1859.

Flight

Our hearts respond, our souls respond,
  The very we of us
Takes off, as one might say, beyond,
  But then comes back, alas!

> GEORGE JOHNSTON, "The dufuflu bird",
> 1959.

Floods

Each succeeding Springtime, the betting is almost even that the whole concern, Fort, town and inhabitants will form a stately procession on the watery road to Winnipeg.

> FORT MACLEOD GAZETTE, Nov. 14, 1882.

Chuck another sandbag on,
On the dike that's wide and long,
All we need is volunteers
And sandbags, sandbags, sandbags!

> EDDIE PALESHNUIK and EDDIE WERRUN,
> parody on "Music, Music, Music" composed at time of Winnipeg flood, May,
> 1950.

It was a miracle of guts and hard work. The miracle of one hundred thousand multiplied by ten. A million fingers in the dikes.

> WILLIAM HURST, City Engineer, Winnipeg, referring to saving Winnipeg from disaster during flood, May, 1950, qu. in F. Rasky, Great Canadian disasters, 1961, 187.

Flowers

You ask me for seeds and bulbs of the flowers of this country. We have those for our garden brought from France, there being none here that are very rare or very beautiful. Everything is savage here, the flowers as well as the men.

> MARIE DE L'INCARNATION, letter, Aug. 12,
> 1653 to a French Sister. (Trans.)

Green against the draggled drift,
Faint and frail and first,
Buy my northern bloodroot
And I'll know where you were
  nursed!
Robin down the logging road whistles,
  "Come to me!"
Spring has found the maple-grove, the
  sap is running free,
All the winds of Canada call the
  ploughing-rain.
Take the flower and turn the hour,
  and kiss your love again!

> RUDYARD KIPLING, "The flowers", 1895.

She has a deep hid virtue
No other flower hath.
When summer comes rejoicing
A-down my garden path,
In opulence of colour,
In robe of satin sheen,
She casts o'er all the hours
Her sorcery serene.

> BLISS CARMAN, "Peony", 1916.

We are the roadside flowers,
Straying from garden grounds,
Lovers of idle hours,
Breakers of ordered bounds.

> BLISS CARMAN, "Roadside flowers", 1916.

Surely no nobler theme the poet
  chants
Than the soft science of the blooming
  plants.

> STEPHEN LEACOCK, verses written in
> 1909, in College days, 1923, 57.

Today I am a god,
for I have made a universe with
  flowers.

> CAROL COATES CASSIDY, "Flower arrangement", 1939.

That one collects by the silver of
   moonlit meadows
The corollas that were closed by the
   coolness of evening
She makes of them a well-rounded
   bouquet
A soft heaviness cool on the mouth
And hurries to offer it to the master.

> HECTOR DE SAINT-DENYS-GARNEAU, "A
> dead man asks for a drink". (Trans. by
> F.R. Scott, 1962).

All across Canada we were struck by
the smallness of the flowers.

> V.S. PRITCHETT, in *Holiday*, Apr., 1964,
> 54.

orange & scarlet
poppies
riots & roots & heads of flame
poppies between my thighs.

> LUELLA BOOTH, "New York poem: IV",
> 1965.

Who would have guessed that when at
   last they go
The mind discovers their remembered
   snow
Still sheds the light of a white
   cyclamen?

> ROBERT FINCH, "The cyclamen", 1966.

and when a flower shot
out of my unclenched teeth
you left me nothing but
a tongue to say it with.

> DOROTHY LIVESAY, "The notations of
> love", 1967.

fabric —
textured zinnias; asters
the colours of chintz: thick
pot-shaped marigolds, the
sunflowers brilliant as
imitations.

> MARGARET ATWOOD, "Two gardens",
> 1970.

But once it's pointed out
you'll look for it always,
even in places
where you know it can't possibly be.

> RAYMOND SOUSTER, "Queen Anne's
> lace", 1972.

To be concerned with flowers is to be
in touch with dimensions of beauty
and wonder that often escapes us in a
hurried and harried life.

> PIERRE E. TRUDEAU, qu. in Vancouver
> *Province*, Sept. 15, 1973, 11.

Yet we chose careful messengers that
   hour,
Pinks, gladioli, roses — her own
   choice,
To place a moment by her other bed.
This was her making, these the words
   she said,
And she shall hear once more their
   happy voice
As she dies back to earth like any
   flower.

> F.R. SCOTT, "To Joan", 1973.

Blue flowers have appeared
along the edge of the lawn in front of
   my house,
blue flowers of which I know only
that they are beautiful and don't grow
   wild
in northeastern North America, and
   were never planted
by me.

> ALDEN NOWLAN, "Question period",
> 1974.

Flying

You see, the Crow owns the Air, and
will not let the Jay use it but on these
Terms: the Jay must pay Rent or he
can not fly nor sit on a Rock, so you
see the Fix he is in. Poor Jay! Yes, he is
Poor, but the Crow is Fat.

> J.W. BENGOUGH, "Lesson IV", *The up-to-
> date primer*, 1896, 8.

Others will follow the path we have
   taken,
Urged by our daring, our dreams and
   our dangers
Winging their way through the
   leagues of the air.

A.H. LAMBDEN, "Tragedy on the barrier",
1941.

Oh! I have slipped the surly bonds of
   earth
And danced the skies on
   laughter-silvered wings;
Sunward I've climbed, and joined the
   tumbling mirth
Of sun-split clouds − .

JOHN G. MAGEE, American citizen, killed
on active service with the R.C.A.F. Dec.
11, 1941, "High flight" written in September, 1941.

The plane, our planet,
Travels on roads that are not seen or
   laid
But sound in instruments on pilots'
   ears,
While underneath,
The sure wings
Are the everlasting arms of science.

F.R. SCOTT, "Trans Canada", 1945.

Pulled from our ruts by the
   made-to-order gale
We sprang upward into a wider
   prairie
And dropped Regina below like a pile
   of bones.

F.R. SCOTT, "Trans Canada", 1945.

Yet for a space we held in our
   morning's hand
the welling and wildness of Canada,
   the fling of a nation
We who have ridden the wings of our
   people's cunning
and lived in a star at peace among
   stars
return to our ferment of earth with a
   memory of sky.

EARLE BIRNEY, "North star west", 1952.

This is our talent, to have grown
Upright in posture, false-erect,
A landed gentry, circumspect,
Tied to a horizontal soil
The floor and ceiling of the soul;
Striving, with cold and fishy care
To make an ocean of the air.

F.R. SCOTT, "Lakeshore", 1954.

Me too! I would like to fly
Somewhere else beneath the sky,
Happy though my choice may be
Empty tree for empty tree.

GEORGE JOHNSTON, "Flight", 1959.

My room is floored with pity, my walls
   are shored with grief,
My roof is wide to Heaven, my door
   invites the thief;
Why am I not then airborne? They
   mock me, night and day,
The clock and the blundering diesel
   and the wee jets far away.

GEORGE JOHNSTON, "This way down",
1959.

The spread of silver wing
   Gathers us into long lanes of space.
We peer through panes of glass.

F.R. SCOTT, "Flying to Fort Smith", 1964.

Folklore

The folklore of industrial man.

MARSHALL MCLUHAN, *The mechanical
bride*, 1951, subtitle of the book; referring to the impact of advertising, journalism, movies and comic books on the
North American public.

Folly

We are all dying, like Wilde, beyond
   our means,
Dying, as sheep, for our folly rather
   than sins.

GEORGE WOODCOCK, "Waterloo bridge",
1967.

Food

When a Canadian has his belly full of fat meat he can be contented anywhere.

DANIEL WILLIAMS HARMON, *Journal*, Mar. 7, 1804. (Ed. by W. Kaye Lamb, 1957).

Talk not to us of intellectual raptures; the mouth and stomach are the doors by which enter true delight. Mutton chops, potatoes, bread, butter, milk, rice pudding, tea, and sugar: contrast dried horse-flesh and water, or martens, or nothing at all, with these luxuries.

DR. W.B. CHEADLE, *The North-west passage by land* (with Viscount Milton), 1865, 323, on arrival at Fort Kamloops, B.C., Aug. 29, 1863.

Frankly, I don't give a dam
For taste of things too long denied!
Very sick and tired I am
Of this our mutton that once was
    lamb!

TOM MACINNES, "Villanelle of mutton", 1918.

There was birch rine, tar twine, cherry wine and turpentine,
Jowls and cavalances, ginger beer and tea,
Pigs' feet, cats' meat, dumplings boiled in a sheet,
Dandelion and crackies' teeth at the Kelligrews Soiree.

ANON., "The Kelligrews soiree", Newfoundland song.

All flesh is grass (and clover we allow)
All good things that we eat the soil
    does give,
So must we nurture soil, and grass and
    cow
And tend them with great care that we
    can live.

ANGUS MEADOWBROOK, (pseud.?) in Ontario. Dept. of Planning, *Nith Valley conservation report*, 1951, 1.

If a man goes without food for one day, he will lie. If he goes without food for two days, he will steal. If he goes without food for four days, he will riot and kill. The food business is the most essential in the world, and the largest.

NATHAN STEINBERG, one of five brothers, owners of supermarket chain, qu. in Peter Newman, *Flame of power*, 1959, 180.

My enemies were certain I was
    starving,
It must have given them a fearful
    shock
Through the binoculars to see me
    carving
A roast of beef up on the barren rock.

ROY DANIELLS, "Psalm 23", 1963.

Anybody's going to eat me
he's going to know
he's had a meal.

PAT LOWTHER, "Baby you tell me", 1968.

Since people die, let us eat the dead. Now we have lost the taste for ordinary game.

IKTUKUSUK, a Baffin Island Eskimo, qu. in Ray Price, *The howling arctic*, 1970, 199.

Canadian agriculture is to be diverted from milk and grain for hungry people to meat products for affluent Americans.

NATIONAL FARMERS UNION, July, 1970, qu. by H.E. Bronson in G. Teeple, ed., *Capitalism and the national quest*, 1972, 131.

Eating is a sensual experience and our traditional mépris of sensuality is apparent in the many Canadians who refuse to think, talk about, or even notice food.

SONDRA GOTLIEB, *The gourmet's Canada*, 1972, qu. in *Canadian reader*, Vol. 13, No. 8, 4.

There was no way out but to eat human flesh and this I did.

> MARTEN HARTWELL, survivor of an airplane crash in the Northwest Territories; news conference, Edmonton, Feb. 27, 1973.

Fools

A fool exalted to dignity is merely a fool more conspicuous.

> THOMAS MCCULLOCH, *The letters of Mephibosheth Stepsure*, 1821, Letter 13.

You were always a fool, and always will be to the end of the chapter.

> THOMAS C. HALIBURTON, *Sam Slick in England*, 1843, ch. 2.

Rank folly is a weed that is often found in the tall rank grass of fashion.

> T.C. HALIBURTON, *Sam Slick's wise saws*, 1853, I, 128.

The vanity of fools is the wisdom of the wise.

> T.C. HALIBURTON, *Sam Slick's wise saws*, 1853, II, 121.

What this country wants more than anything else is a fool-killer.

> SIR W. VAN HORNE, 1891; qu. in Vaughan, *Van Horne*, 1920, 205.

I think you are the damndest – I was going to say the damndest fool I have ever known, but I can't say that because I have known two or three others who completed their record by dying in their foolishness, while your record is still incomplete and there is a faint chance that you may yet make a turn and end under suspicion of having had some sense.

> SIR W. VAN HORNE, letter to W.F. Luxton, founder of the *Man. Free press*, 1895; qu., Vaughan, *Van Horne*, 1920, 245.

There is hope for the man who can occasionally make a spontaneous and irrevocable ass of himself.

> PETER MCARTHUR, *To be taken with salt*, 1903, 153.

What place can there be for a minstrel
   now
Against these ghastly times
For one who would sing to a light
   guitar
His picaroonish rhymes
While the pain & filth of war, and the
   waste
Go on, and we lack for bread?
Oh the Dark Fool is loose in the world –
And the Fool of Joy is dead!

> TOM MACINNES, prologue to *The fool of joy*, 1918.

People always laugh at the fool things you try to do until they discover you are making money out of them.

> ROBERT C. (BOB) EDWARDS, Calgary *Eye Opener*, May 31, 1919.

The fool takes things as they come, but the wise guy lets a good many of them pass on.

> ROBERT C. (BOB) EDWARDS, *Summer annual*, 1920, 74.

A fool is a man who is not addicted to your own brand of folly.

> ROBERT C. (BOB) EDWARDS, Calgary *Eye Opener*; attributed.

I say you live in a world of unreality, and I believe that whether you call it a vision or what, I've stepped into reality, and I'm presenting reality in the disguise of a mask, the fool which is assumed, and I am an actor on the stage.

> JOACHIM FOIKIS ("The Town Fool"), in *The Ubyssey*, Mar. 29, 1968.

Football

O wild kaleidoscopic panorama of
jaculatory arms and legs.
The twisting, twining, turning,
tussling, throwing, thrusting,
throttling, tugging, thumping, the
tightening thews.
The tearing of tangled trousers, the jut
of giant calves protuberant.
The wriggleness, the wormlike, snaky
movement and life of it.

ANON., "The football match", in Lighthall, *Songs of the great Dominion*,
1889, 209.

This is a night when you can feel unity
in Canada.

MAYOR PHILIP GIVENS of Toronto, speech
at Toronto Grey Cup Dinner, Nov. 26,
1965, qu. in R. Reid, *Canadian style*,
1973, 172.

Our objective is to prevent the CFL
from going to the United States and
the U.S. leagues from coming into
Canada. It's that simple. I don't think I
have to reconcile it. If you have the
WFL [World Football League], there
are bound to be detrimental effects.
We have the power. We will use the
power.

MARC LALONDE, Minister of National
Health and Welfare, news conference,
Feb. 21, 1974, prior to introducing a bill
in H. of C., Apr. 10, 1974, to ban U.S.
leagues; it passed 2nd reading then died
on the order paper when Parliament
dissolved, Apr. 23.

Footnotes

. . . a form of gout by which scholars debilitate the body of literature.

STEPHEN LEACOCK, *Humour and humanity*, 1937, 83.

Force

I could not argue in favour of either
independence or annexation. If ever
the time came that either had to be
seriously discussed I would argue it
only in one way, and that would be on
horseback with my sword.

GEORGE T. DENISON (Police magistrate of
Toronto), remarks at National Club dinner, 1880.

I do not believe in moral issues being
settled by physical force.

J.S. WOODSWORTH, speech in Winnipeg,
June 4, 1916.

Please don't believe
The use of force
Is how we change the social course;
The use of force
You surely know
Is how we keep the status quo.

JOHN K. ROOKE, "The use of force", *Can.
forum*, Feb., 1940, 350.

Foreign Aid

Fortunately Canadians do not usually
care very much whether they are liked
or not; they regard the expectation of
gratitude as a weakness. They only
hope that when the projects are completed they will be remembered with
mild approval, though they do not
really expect to be remembered at all.

MIRIAM CHAPIN, *Contemporary Canada*,
1959, 281.

In any unprejudiced examination Canada shows up, to its shame, as a
first-class international piker. By any
yardstick, Canada is not giving enough
money, enough technical assistance or
enough leadership.

STANLEY WESTALL, *Globe and Mail*, Feb.
18, 1963, 7.

Aid without trade is incongruous and self-defeating.

> MITCHELL SHARP, speech, World Trade Week luncheon, Los Angeles, May 21, 1964.

Altruism as foreign policy is a misnomer, even if sometimes the fruits of policy are incidentally beneficial to foreigners.

> KEITH SPICER, A Samaritan state?, 1966, 11.

Foreign Control

Like Czechoslovakia, we are true internationalists: we don't interfere in our own internal affairs.

> JAMES BACQUE, "Should Canada interfere in its own internal affairs", in A. Wainwright, ed., Notes for a native land, 1969, 34.

Foreign Policy

We could not be freer than we are now, for we have no foreign policy to complicate things and no army to provide.

> TORONTO GLOBE, 1874.

You rule yourselves as fully as any people in the world, while in your foreign affairs, your relations with other countries, whether peaceful or warlike, commercial or financial, or otherwise, you may have no more voice than the people of Japan.

> EDWARD BLAKE, speech at Aurora, Ont., Oct. 3, 1874.

Foreign policy is simply an extension of domestic policy.

> O.D. SKELTON, speech, Canadian Club, Ottawa, Jan. 21, 1922.

The attitude of the government is to do nothing itself and if possible to prevent anything occurring which will precipitate one additional factor into the all-important discussions which are now taking place in Europe.

> W.L. MACKENZIE KING, H. of C., Debates, Mar. 23, 1936, 1333.

One cannot help feeling that, although collective security represents a conviction in so far as the Canadians are concerned, it is only a conviction de luxe.

> ANDRÉ SIEGFRIED, Canada, 1937.

The foreign policy of this country is so obvious that it does not require much discussion.

> RICHARD B. BENNETT, H. of C., Debates, Feb. 9, 1937, 702.

It is far more important to keep driving down the middle of the international political fairways than it is to improve our golf scores.

> LESTER B. PEARSON, H. of C., Debates, July 15, 1960, 6359.

Canadian foreign policy is arrived at by ordinance. We are half a democracy: domestic policy represents the public will (so we are told); foreign policy represents a private wisdom.

> DALTON CAMP, in Lewis Hertzman et al., Alliances and illusions, 1969, xii.

With the St. Lawrence as turbid as it is today, it is blind to keep watch on the Rhine. What does it matter whether Canada remains in NATO, remains in NORAD, remains in the Commonwealth? What matters is that Canada remains. A decision to let Gaza or Laos or Cyprus stew in their own juice – the imperative of classic isolationism – can be justified if it means putting our house in order. Instead, Canada stews in its own juice.

> JAMES EAYRS, Saturday night, Apr., 1971, 13.

Foreign Relations

The Suez Canal is nothing to us, and we do not ask England to quarrel with France or Germany for our sakes.

SIR JOHN A. MACDONALD, letter to Sir Charles Tupper, in London, Mar. 12, 1885.

Not only are we free to manage our domestic concerns, but, practically, we possess the privilege of making our own treaties with foreign countries, and in our relations with the outside world, we enjoy the prestige by a consciousness of the fact that behind us towers the majesty of England.

SIR JOHN A. MACDONALD, "To the electors of Canada", Feb. 7, 1891.

What have we to do with the affairs of South Africa? What interests have we in the Transvaal? Why should we take the money and the blood of the taxpayers of this country to squander them in these far-away regions?

LA PATRIE (Montreal), Oct. 10, 1899.

Canadians are becoming weary of negotiating with Washington through London, and of the solemn and elaborate farces called arbitration which for one hundred and twenty years have been robbing Canada to enrich the United States.

DAILY MAIL (London, Eng.), despatch from its Toronto correspondent, Oct., 1903.

What did we care for the Boer or what did we care for a few aliens in that country? That was not the thought. Britain needed help, or if she didn't need help she would take it.

GEORGE W. ROSS, speech, Empire Club, Toronto, May 12, 1905.

In matters between Canada and other countries, Canada should arrange her own affairs.

W.L. MACKENZIE KING, H. of C., Debates, Apr. 21, 1921.

Our external relations are enveloped in what might be called a highly luminous but cloudy halo.

CLIFFORD SIFTON, in Can.hist.rev., 1922, 11.

We are fortunate both in our neighbours and in our lack of neighbours.

W.L. MACKENZIE KING, H. of C., Debates, June 18, 1936, 3868.

Canada is a sovereign nation and cannot have dictated to her, by Great Britain, the United States or any other, the attitude she is to adopt in world affairs.

LORD TWEEDSMUIR, speech in Montreal, Oct. 12, 1937.

We have a habit of continually worrying about the problems of other countries in order to keep from worrying about our own.

H.A. INNIS, in Conference on Canadian-American affairs, 1939, 133.

Whatever hope of continued autonomy Canada may have in the future must depend on her success in withstanding American influence and assisting in the development of a third bloc designed to withstand the pressure of the United States and Russia, but there is little evidence that Canada is capable of these herculean efforts and much that she will continue to be justly regarded as an instrument of the United States.

HAROLD A. INNIS, Commerce jour. Jan., 1949, 13.

We are beginning to realize our position in the world, and it is precarious. We lie between the greatest and grimmest of the Grim Great Powers.

LISTER SINCLAIR, "The Canadian idiom", *Here and now*, No. 4, June, 1949, 17.

It is a question of whether we shall allow Kruschev with intimidation and threats to push us back and back to a point where we have nothing but our past to look back on.

JOHN DIEFENBAKER, H. of C., *Debates*, Sept. 11, 1961, 8175, on Berlin crisis.

Using a dozen vague, circumlocutory sentences where six short words would do, he spun out the smooth skein of Canada's foreign relations into webs of verbiage that he himself could not possibly have unravelled.

PETER C. NEWMAN, *The distemper of our times*, 1968, 202, on Paul Martin, Minister of External Affairs 1963-68.

We must recognize that, in the long run, the overwhelming threat to Canada will not come from foreign investments, or foreign ideologies, or even – with good fortune – foreign nuclear weapons. It will come instead from the two thirds of the peoples of the world who are steadily falling farther and farther behind in their search for a decent standard of living. This is the meaning of the revolution of rising expectations.

PIERRE E. TRUDEAU, speech, Univ. of Alberta, Edmonton, May 13, 1968.

Our information abroad has long been stumbling through a stunning sort of chaos.

CANADA. TASK FORCE ON GOVERNMENT INFORMATION, *Report*, 1969, 33.

We do not have preferences; we deal only with the rich.

DANIEL CATMUR, Canadian University Service Overseas, in: Senate. Standing Comm. on Foreign Affairs, *Proceedings*, Apr. 27, 1971, 15:9, referring to Canada's economic involvement in the Pacific area.

Foreigners

It is meaningless to call anyone a foreigner in this country. We are all foreigners here.

JOHN MARLYN, *Under the ribs of death*, 1957 (1971, 24).

Foresight

I look a little ahead.

SIR JOHN A. MACDONALD, the reason given for his defeat of George Brown.

Forests

The thicknesse of the wood and greatness of Forrests doe hinder the Sunne from warming the ground.

SAMUEL PURCHAS, *Purchas his pilgrims*, (1606) 1905, XVIII, 275.

There is, sir, a solitary loneliness in the woods of America to which no language can do adequate justice. It seems a shutting out of the whole moral creation.

JOSHUA MARSDEN, *The Narrative of a mission, to Nova Scotia, New Brunswick, and the Somers Islands . . .* 1816, letter 6.

Dread swell of sound! loud as the gusts that lash
The matted forests of Ontario's shore
By wasteful steel unsmitten.

WILLIAM WORDSWORTH, "The River Duddon", sonnet XIII, 1820.

It seemed almost inconceivable, that human beings should be permanent inhabitants of this wilderness – that domesticities and affections should often brighten the gloom of such a solitude — and that those leading passions, which agitate the hearts of all men, should be elicited and brought into action amidst the appalling loneliness and depressing monotony of the boundless forest.

JOHN HOWISON, *Sketches of Upper Canada*, 1821, 185.

I canna ca' this forest hame
  It is nae hame to me:
Ilk tree is suthern to my heart,
  And unco' to my s'e.

ANON., "My hame", in Cobourg *Star*, Dec. 27, 1831.

What struck me most were the primeval woods and forests which covered the hills at Gaspé, and for miles and miles through the interior. One felt one saw what Adam and Eve first opened their eyes upon.

LORD DUFFERIN, letter to Lady Dartrey, July 24, 1872.

And in the distance, far apart,
As if to shame man's proudest art,
  Cathedral arches spread;
While yonder ancient elm has caught
A glory past the reach of thought
  Upon his hoary head.

ALEXANDER MCLACHLAN, "October", 1874.

Into the stilly woods I go,
Where the shades are deep and the
  wind-flowers blow,
And the hours are dreamy and lone
  and long,
And the power of silence is greater
  than song,
Into the stilly woods I go,
Where the leaves are cool and the
  wind-flowers blow.

WILFRED CAMPBELL, "A wood lyric", 1899.

By their fathers the forest was dreaded and hated, but the sons, with rifles in hand, trod its pathless stretches without fear, and with their broad-axes they took toll of the ancient foe.

RALPH CONNOR, *The man from Glengarry*, 1901, 15.

We, like the miner, fail to realize that we have reached our last west; that nature so prolific to this country in this respect has no more virgin fields to offer, and that the only means by which a supply can be maintained to meet the enormous demands of future years is by husbanding the resources of the territory which we are now exploiting.

ELIHU STEWART, Canadian Forestry Assoc., Ninth Annual Meeting, Montreal, Mar., 1908.

The wild witchery of the winter woods.

WILFRED CAMPBELL, "Under the wild witchery of the winter woods", 1922.

Save The Forests!

NEW BRUNSWICK GOVERNMENT, slogan, 1924.

Tree boles pillared the forest's roof, and streaked the unfathomable forest like gigantic rain streaks pouring; the surge of growth from the forest's floor boiled up to meet it.

EMILY CARR, *Growing pains*, 1946, 107.

This is the noisy silence of a tree
The rustle in the fern is the noise of
  fear
A twig is a nerve; it snaps the heart to
  pounding.

ANNE WILKINSON, "Theme and variation", 1951.

Build here a fire, and from the
  sweetened pines
Tap remedies and liquors, resinous
  wines;
Deep in the gleaned logged-over forest
  find
Ferns that timeless sleep, time out of
  mind.

> MIRIAM WADDINGTON, "In the moun-
> tains", 1958.

In Canada there is too much of everything. Too much rock, too much prairie, too much tundra, too much mountain, too much forest. Above all, too
much forest. Even the man who passionately believes that he shall never
see a poem as lovely as a tree will be
disposed to give poetry another try
after he has driven the Trans-Canada
Highway.

> EDWARD MCCOURT, *The road across
> Canada*, 1965, 110.

Forgetfulness

Forgetfulness is her protection. Sometimes I wondered, though, how much
could be truly forgotten and what
happened to it when it was entombed.

> MARGARET LAURENCE, "The rain child",
> 1962, in *The tomorrow-tamer*, 115.

The thing that's really important in
life, I've discovered, is to forget bad
impressions.

> CELIA FRANCA, qu. in Toronto *Star*, Apr.
> 6, 1968, 35.

Forgiveness

A man has to be as willing to forgive
himself, as to forgive other people.

> PETER MCARTHUR, (d.1924) a favourite
> saying.

Forgive me Lord, but not my enemies.

> ROY DANIELLS, "Psalm 57", 1963.

Form

Form may be of more account than
substance. A lens of ice will focus a
solar beam to a blaze.

> GEORGE ILES, *Canadian stories*, 1918,
> 167.

Desire first, then structure
Complete the balanced picture.
The thought requires the form.

> F.R. SCOTT, "Dialogue", 1945.

Poetry can only be made out of other
poems; novels out of other novels.
Literature shapes itself, and is not
shaped externally: the *forms* of literature can no more exist outside literature than the forms of sonata and
fugue and rondo can exist outside
music.

> NORTHROP FRYE, *Anatomy of criticism*,
> 1957, 97.

Documentary on one side and myth on
the other: Life & Art. In this form we
can put anything and the magnet we
have set up will arrange it for us.

> JAMES REANEY, *Alphabet*, No. 1, 1960,
> editorial.

Formalities

Forms are things.

> SIR JOHN A. MACDONALD, favourite saying
> qu. by Sir Joseph Pope in *Public serv-
> ant*, 1960, 42.

Fortune-telling

Fortune-telling has never been held in
high repute in the community; and it
is as hazardous when carried out under
the most respectable auspices as when
practised in a back street in a manner
liable to attract the attention of the
police.

> CANADA. ROY. COMM. ON CANADA'S ECO-
> NOMIC PROSPECTS, *Final report*, 1957, 1.

Foster, Sir George E.

He has but one principle, that of self-interest. He has only one desire, the desire to insult. He belongs to the school of lying, hypocrisy and cowardice.

> E.E. CINQ-MARS, in *La Presse*, May 26, 1906 (Trans.); H. of C., *Debates*, May 29, 1906, 4032; a reference to Sir George E. Foster.

France

There are two Frances, the radical France and the conservative France, the France of unbelievers and Catholic France, the France that blasphemes and the France that prays. The second France is our France.

> THOMAS CHAPAIS, *Discours et conférences*, 1897, 39. (Trans.)

France lives and France is free, and Canada is the nobler for her sacrifice to help free France to live.

> ARTHUR MEIGHEN, address at Thelus Military Cemetery, Vimy Ridge, at unveiling of Cross of Sacrifice, July 3, 1921.

Franchise

There is no inalienable right in any man to exercise the franchise.

> SIR JOHN A. MACDONALD, *Debates on Confederation*, 1865.

Democracy, as measured by the franchise, came to Canada almost by stealth, certainly not as an army with banners.

> W.L. MORTON, Can. Hist. Assoc., *Report*, 1943, 73.

Franklin, Sir John

Not here! the white North has thy
    bones; and thou
Heroic sailor soul,
Art passing on thine happier voyage
    now
Toward no earthly pole.

> LORD TENNYSON, inscription on monument to Sir John Franklin in Westminster Abbey, 1875.

Frankness

I'm frank, brutally frank. And even when I'm *not* frank, I *look* frank.

> ROY THOMSON, qu. in Russell Braddon, *Roy Thomson of Fleet Street*, 1965, 154.

Fraser Canyon, B.C.

I have been for a long period among the Rocky Mountains, but have never seen anything like this country. It is so wild that I cannot find words to describe our situation at times. We had to pass where no human being should venture; yet in those places there is a regular footpath impressed, or rather indented upon the very rocks by frequent traveling.

> SIMON FRASER, *Journal of a voyage from the Rocky mountains to the Pacific ocean, 1808*, mss. 29.

Fredericton, N.B.

The twentieth century has not yet discovered it. Time somehow has missed it altogether, until you might say that this is the last surviving Home Town of America, uncorrupted and innocent as your grandmother.

> BRUCE HUTCHISON, *The unknown country*, 1942, 223.

Free Speech

I believe you realize the value in the interests of true liberty of a free utterance before his fellow countrymen, of the distinctive opinions held by a public man.

EDWARD BLAKE, speech at Aurora, Ont., Oct. 3, 1874.

It is to our own convictions, right or wrong, that we must after all be true. To put forward opinions we do not hold, or ignore difficulties we cannot solve, or deny or conceal the tendencies and results of policies we undertake to propound, would be dishonest and unworthy.

EDWARD BLAKE, to the Members of the West Durham Reform Convention, Feb. 9, 1891.

Parliament itself could not abrogate this right of discussion and debate.

JUSTICE DOUGLAS ABBOTT, *Dominion Law Reports* (2d), 1957, Vol. 7, 371.

Free Trade

It is in vain to suppose that a free-trade system will be beneficial to a new and struggling colony which has nothing to export but raw materials. It is rather calculated to enrich an old commonwealth, whose people by their skill and labour make such raw materials valuable, and return them for consumption. The result of the system has been that the suppliers of the raw material at last become hewers of wood and drawers of water to the manufacturers.

ABRAHAM GESNER, *Industrial resources of Nova Scotia*, 1849.

[Alexander Mackenzie] thinks that Free Trade is the Bible, the catechism, the creed and the paternoster of the political belief of Canada.

SIR JOHN A. MACDONALD, H. of C., *Debates*, 1870, 1202.

There are national considerations that rise far higher than the mere accumulation of wealth, than the mere question of trade advantage; there is prestige, national status, national dominion – and no great nation has ever risen whose policy was free trade.

SIR JOHN A. MACDONALD, H. of C., *Debates*, Mar. 7, 1878, 855.

Our adversaries wish to present to you an issue as between the present tariff and absolute free trade. That is not the true issue. Free trade is, as I have repeatedly explained, for us impossible; and the issue is whether the present tariff is perfect, or defective and unjust.

EDWARD BLAKE, address to the electors of West Durham, May 23, 1882.

I invite the most ardent free trader in public life to present a plausible solution of this problem, and I contend that he is bound to do so before he talks of free trade as practicable in Canada . . . The thing is removed from the domain of practical politics.

EDWARD BLAKE, speech at Malvern, East York, Jan. 22, 1887.

Assuming that absolute free trade with the States, best described as commercial union, may and ought to come, I believe that it can and should come only as an incident, or at any rate as a well-understood precursor of political union, for which indeed, we should be able to make better terms before than after the surrender of our commercial independence.

EDWARD BLAKE, to the Members of the West Durham Reform Convention, Feb. 6, 1891.

I may say that on principle I am a very strong freetrader. I have been fed and educated on free trade doctrines, but doctrines do not always apply to facts.

CLIFFORD SIFTON, letter to J. Fleming, Mar. 13, 1897.

We had a Free Trade party once. The Liberal Party before the advent of the golden silence of office was a Free Trade party.

F.J. DIXON, *Grain growers' guide*, Sept. 9, 1915.

Freedom

We will enjoy here that which is the great test of constitutional freedom – we will have the rights of the minority respected.

SIR JOHN A. MACDONALD, *Confederation debates*, Feb. 6, 1865, 44.

I felt as one, who being awhile
    confined
  Sees drop to dust about him all his
    bars: –
The clay grows less, and, leaving it,
    the mind
  Dwells with the stars.

GEORGE F. CAMERON, "Standing on tip-toe", 1885.

True greatness is the struggle to be
  free,
And he who would be truly great must
  bear
A thorny heart for lovely Freedom's
  sake.

THOMAS B.P. STEWART, "Lines to my mother", 1887.

Free institutions will not make free natures, and small is the number of those who are by nature free. Most of us crave for a sheepfold and a shibboleth.

GOLDWIN SMITH, *The Bystander*, N.S., Jan., 1890, 109.

Who wooed the west to win the east,
And named the stars of North and
  South,
And felt the zest of Freedom's feast
Familiar in his mouth.

CHARLES G.D. ROBERTS, "Epitaph for a sailor buried ashore", 1893.

I scorn your empty creeds, and bend
  my knee
  To none of all the gods adored by
  men;
I worship nothing, that I may be free!
  'Mayhap,' said one; 'you kneel to
  freedom then.'

ARTHUR STRINGER, *Epigrams*, 1896.

Freedom breeds loyalty. Coercion always was the mother of rebellion.

SIR WILFRID LAURIER; attributed.

Canada is a nation. Canada is free, and freedom is its nationality. Although Canada acknowledges the suzerainty of a sovereign power I am here to say that independence can give us no more rights than we have at the present day.

SIR WILFRID LAURIER, speech, London, Eng., June 18, 1897.

It is our proud boast that Canada is the freest country in the world. It is our boast that in this country liberty of all kinds, civil and religious liberty, flourish to the highest degree.

SIR WILFRID LAURIER, address at Tercentenary Celebration, Quebec, 1908.

Praise for faith in freedom
Our fighting fathers' stay,
Born of dreams and daring,
Bred above dismay.

> BLISS CARMAN, "In the day of battle",
> 1916.

Crowd back the hills and give me
    room,
  Nor goad me with the sense of
    things;
Earth cramps me like a narrow tomb,
  Your sunlight is too dense for wings;
    Away with all horizon bars;
    Push back the mountains and the
      stars.

> ALBERT D. WATSON, "Soul-lifted", 1920.

Since you who walked in freedom
And the ways of reason fought on our
  front,
We foresee the plot is solvable, the
  duel worthy.

> EARLE BIRNEY, "For Steve", 1945.

To be indifferent to one's own fate and
to be absorbed in another's, to forget
the shrinking of the body of flesh and
nerves as completely as if that body
were already in the grave and as if the
ghost that had driven and been driven
by it were already free of it — this
was to know freedom.

> PHILIP CHILD, Day of wrath, 1945, 252.

The real division in the world today is
not between socialism and capitalism,
it is between freedom and totalitarian-
ism.

> FRANK H. UNDERHILL, Can. forum, Aug.,
> 1947, 110.

By all the past we know our freedom is
renewable each moment.

> EARLE BIRNEY, "Trial of a city", 1952.

God had been created by man out of
necessity. No God, no ethic: no ethic

— freedom. Freedom was too much
for man.

> MORDECAI RICHLER, Son of a smaller
> hero, 1955, 72.

All elements of our tradition — the
secularist and the theist, the liberal
and the existentialist, the capitalist and
the socialist — claim freedom as particularly their own, and their interpretation of the word as the "true"
meaning.

> GEORGE P. GRANT, Queen's quart., Vol.
> 62, 1955, 515.

No more behind forbidden walls
A secret blossom blows
Its sacred incense hidden from
The proletarian nose.
All walls are down, or open wide,
And everything that grows
Is there to seek and there to share
And those who love her well may wear
All Hungary as a rose.

> JOE WALLACE, "Hungary", 1956.

Freedom wears a crown.

> JOHN C. FARTHING, from the title of his
> book pub. 1957.

Freedom is not a gift but something
that must be won. The only freedom is
that which has been torn from authority.

> GÉRARD FILION, qu. by Pierre E. Tru-
> deau, Can.jour.econ. and pol.sci., Vol.
> 24, Aug., 1958, 304. (Trans.)

I am a Canadian, a free Canadian,
free to speak without fear, free to
worship God in my own way, free to
stand for what I think right, free to
oppose what I believe wrong, free to
choose those who shall govern my
country. This heritage of freedom I
pledge to uphold for myself and for all
mankind.

> JOHN G. DIEFENBAKER, H. of C., Debates,
> July 1, 1960, 5649.

There is no absolute press freedom, there is no absolute freedom; there is no absolute freedom for speech, and for heaven's sake I hope we will hear the end of this, whatever else we do.

GRATTAN O'LEARY, Chairman, Royal Commission on Publications, *Proceedings*, 1960/61, on argument that taxing U.S. publications would violate freedom of speech, qu. in Ottawa *Journal*, Feb. 15, 1961, 4.

Freedom has nothing to do with lack of training; it can only be the product of training. You're not free to move unless you've learned to walk, and not free to play the piano unless you practice. Nobody is capable of free speech unless he knows how to use language, and such knowledge is not a gift: it has to be learned and worked at.

NORTHROP FRYE, *The educated imagination*, (1962) 1964, 148.

We are imprisoned in freedom. Most men would like to be freed from their freedom, so long as they could retain it nominally.

JEAN-PAUL DESBIENS, *For pity's sake*, 1965, 88.

On the political front, accepted opinions are not only inhibiting to the mind, they contain the very source of error. When a political ideology is universally accepted by the élite, when the people who "define situations" embrace and venerate it, this means that it is high time free men were fighting it. For political freedom finds its essential strength in a sense of balance and proportion. As soon as one tendency becomes too strong, it constitutes a menace.

PIERRE E. TRUDEAU, *Federalism and the French Canadians*, 1968, Foreword, xxi.

He stood, a point
on a sheet of green paper
proclaiming himself the centre,

with no walls, no borders
anywhere; the sky no height
above him, totally un-
enclosed
and shouted:

Let me out!

MARGARET ATWOOD, "Progressive insanities of a pioneer", 1968.

Only the tiniest fraction of mankind wants freedom. All the rest want someone to tell them they are free.

IRVING LAYTON, "Some observations and aphorisms", *Tamarack rev.*, Spring, 1968, 6.

There is a new loneliness in the modern world – the *solitude of speed*. We pass by each other on the throughways of our new freedoms.

STEPHEN VIZINCZEY, *The rules of chaos*, 1969, 202.

Perhaps an obsession with freedom is the persistent (thank God) dance of the young.

MARGARET LAURENCE, "Ten years' sentences", in *Can. lit.*, Summer, 1969, 14.

Freedom and justice do not depend on the goodness of the people up top, but on the courage of the people down below.

RICHARD J. NEEDHAM, *A friend in Needham*, 1969, 39.

No country can remain free unless its people are permeated with joyous disrespect for most of the laws and for all of the authorities.

RICHARD J. NEEDHAM, *A friend in Needham*, 1969, 38.

Men are entitled to as much freedom as they can get — no more and no less.

> IRVING LAYTON, "Aphs", *The whole bloody bird*, 1969, 84.

Freelancing

The trouble with freelancing is that if you take an extra half-hour over lunch, you think you are starving to death.

> JOCK CARROLL, qu. in *Can. lit.* No. 33, 1967, 51.

French Canadians

Nothing will satisfy the licentious fanaticks trading here, but the expulsion of the Canadians who are perhaps the bravest and the best race upon the Globe, a race, who could they be indulged with a few of the priviledges which the law of England deny to Roman Catholics at home, would soon get the better of every national antipathy to the conquerors and become the most faithful and most useful set of men in the American empire.

> GOV. JAMES MURRAY, letter to Lords of Trade, Oct. 29, 1764.

I glory in having been accused of warmth and firmness in my protecting the King's Canadian Subjects and doing the utmost in my Power to gain to my Royal Master the affection of that Brave, hardy people.

> GOV. JAMES MURRAY, letter to Lord Shelburne, Aug. 20, 1766.

I think there is nothing to fear from them, while we are in a state of prosperity, and nothing to hope for when in distress.

> SIR GUY CARLETON, letter to Lord Germain, Sept. 28, 1776.

The inhabitants, generally, are far from adventurous; they cling with pertinacity to the spot which gave them birth, and cultivate, with contentedness, the little piece of land which, in the division of the family property, has fallen to their share.

> PIERRE DE SALES LATERRIERE, *Political and historical account of Lower Canada*, 1830, 120.

Originally subjects of France,
Now subjects of Britain,
Which of the two countries do we
  prefer?
But have we not, I ask you, still more
  powerful bonds?
Before all let us prefer our own
  country:
Before all let us be Canadians!

> GEORGES-ÉTIENNE CARTIER, "Avant tout je suis Canadien", 1834. (Trans. by Aileen Garland.)

There can hardly be conceived a nationality more destitute of all that can invigorate and elevate a people, than that which is exhibited by the descendents of the French in Lower Canada, owing to their retaining their peculiar language and manners. They are a people with no history, and no literature.

> LORD DURHAM, *Report*, 1839, ed. Lucas, 1912, 294.

If we would make them civilised and free men, we must put them on an equality with the rest of the population, and we must have them speak the language and be partakers of those institutions, which are the language and institutions of every free man in North America.

> CHARLES BULLER, Gt. Brit., *Hansard*, 3rd. ser., 1839, Vol. 48, 1202.

The French Canadians if rightly managed are the natural instrument, by which the Government could keep in check the democratic and American tendencies of Upper Canada.

> CHARLES BULLER, letter to Sir Robert Peel, Sept. 9, 1841.

If ever this country should cease one day to be British, the last gun fired in defence of British sovereignty in America will be that of a French Canadian.

> ETIENNE-PASCAL TACHÉ, speech on militia, Legislative Assembly, Montreal, Apr. 24, 1846; varies. See: *La Minerve*, 27 avril, 1846, 2: "Si jamais ce pays cesse un jour d'être britannique, le dernier coup de canon tiré pour le maintien de la puissance anglaise en Amérique le sera par un bras Canadien".

May French Canadians remain faithful to themselves, may they be wise and perseverant, may they steadily refuse to be seduced by the glitter of social and political innovations! They lack the strength to succeed in such a calling. It is the task of the large nations to put new theories to the test.

> FRANÇOIS-XAVIER GARNEAU, *Histoire du Canada*, (1852), 4th. ed., 1882, Vol. 3, 396. (Trans.)

No man in his senses can suppose that this country can for a century to come be governed by a totally unfrenchified Govt. If a Lower Canadian Britisher desires to conquer, he must "stoop to conquer". He must make friends with the French; without sacrificing the status of his race or lineage, he must respect their nationality. Treat them as a nation and they will act as a free people generally do – generously. Call them a faction, and they become factious.

> SIR JOHN A. MACDONALD, letter to Brown Chamberlin, Jan. 21, 1856.

The only remedies are immigration and copulation and these will work wonders.

> SIR JOHN A. MACDONALD, letter to Brown Chamberlin, Jan. 21, 1856, his solution to the English minority situation in Lower Canada.

Here we sit to-day seeking amicably to find a remedy for constitutional evils and injustice complained of – by the vanquished? No, sir, – but complained of by the conquerors! Here sit the representatives of the British population claiming justice – only justice; and here sit the representatives of the French population, discussing in the French tongue whether we shall have it.

> GEORGE BROWN, *Confederation debates*, Feb. 8, 1865, 85.

For my part, I am not afraid of the French Canadian majority in the future Local Government doing injustice, except accidentally; not because I am of the same religion as themselves; for origin and language are barriers stronger to divide men in this world than is religion to unite them.

> THOMAS D'A. MCGEE, *Confederation debates*, Feb. 9, 1865, 143.

Our fathers' blood, shed for their faith, has become our most glorious and legitimate title of ownership to this land. Once its first inhabitants, who were to become our brothers, had disappeared, Providence put us in its rightful possession as legitimately as ever a people have been able to claim a country as their own.

> LOUIS LAFLÈCHE, Bishop of Three Rivers, *Quelques considerations sur les rapports de la société civile avec la religion et la famille*, 1866. (Trans.)

French Canada is a relic of the historical past preserved in isolation, as Siberian mammoths are preserved in ice.

GOLDWIN SMITH, *Political destiny of Canada*, 1878, 10.

We are French Canadians, but our country is not confined to the territory overshadowed by the citadel of Quebec; our country is Canada, it is the whole of what is covered by the British flag on the American continent, the fertile lands bordered by the Bay of Fundy, the Valley of the St. Lawrence, the region of the great lakes, the prairies of the West, the Rocky Mountains, the lands washed by the famous ocean where breezes are said to be as sweet as the breezes of the Mediterranean.

SIR WILFRID LAURIER, speech at Quebec City, June 24, 1889. (Trans.)

In Barrie, last election, I pointed out, in a few simple words, that the great danger which overshadowed Canada was the French national cry, this bastard nationality, not a nationality which will take us in as we will take them in, but a nationality which begins and ends with the French race — which begins and ends with those who profess the Roman Catholic faith, and which now threatens the dismemberment of Canada.

D'ALTON MCCARTHY, speech at Stayner, Ont., July 12, 1889.

I stand here as an example, a warning to any man raising his voice in Parliament in opposition to the French-Canadian influences at Ottawa.

D'ALTON MCCARTHY, speech at Picton, Ont. Dec. 28, 1894.

We are loyal to the great nation which gave us life. We are faithful to the great nation which gave us liberty.

SIR WILFRID LAURIER, speech in Paris, 1897, reported July 5, 1897.

Tell me what attitude should the French Canadians take in the Confederation? They must isolate themselves, as a separate body, or march at the head of the Confederation. It is necessary that we choose between English Imperialism and American Imperialism. I see no other alternative.

SIR WILFRID LAURIER, letter to Henri Bourassa, Nov. 2, 1899. (Pub. Arch. Can.).

The French genius is not the same as the Anglo-Saxon genius. We are French, you are English. Would you permit me to add that we are Canadians to the fullest extent of the word while, on many occasions, you are more British than Canadians. If there is any trouble in future, the trouble will come out of that difference.

ISRAEL TARTE, letter to Sir John Willison, Nov. 28, 1900. (Pub.Arch.Can.)

Your people are a power in the dominion. In the Empire they would be a nullity. In the chapter of political accidents they have become for the present the sheet-anchor of Canadian self-government.

GOLDWIN SMITH, letter to Henri Bourassa, Sept. 7, 1900.

We are not only a civilized race, we are the pioneers of civilization; we are not only a religious people, we are the messengers of the religious idea; we are not only submissive sons of the Church, we are, we ought to be, numbered among its zealots, its defenders, and its apostles.

MONSEIGNEUR LOUIS-ADOLPH PÂQUET, address, Quebec City, Ste. Jean-Baptiste Day, June 24, 1902. (Trans.)

To wish to obtain the esteem, the confidence, and the goodwill of our English fellow citizens in sacrificing our incontestable rights, in consenting ourselves to the rupture of the national compact which guarantees these rights and in accepting thefts, infringements, and insults in the same manner as we welcome fair dealing, is to doom ourselves in advance to scorn and slavery.

HENRI BOURASSA, speech, Monument National, Montreal, Apr. 17, 1905. (Trans.)

If Britain is ever in danger – nay, I will not say that – if Britain is ever on trial, I, a Canadian of French origin, will be the first to go to the people and call upon them to assist with all our might.

SIR WILFRID LAURIER, speech in Cobalt, Ont., Sept. 18, 1912.

French by descent and affection, we are British by allegiance and conviction.

RODOLPHE LEMIEUX, Canadian Club speech, Toronto, 1914.

Three hundred years ago we came, and we have remained. They who led us hither might return among us without knowing shame or sorrow, for if it be true that we have little learned, most surely nothing is forgot. We bore overseas our prayers and our songs; they are ever the same. We carried in our bosoms the hearts of the men of our fatherland brave and merry, easily moved to pity as to laughter, of all human hearts the most human; nor have they changed.

LOUIS HÉMON, *Maria Chapdelaine*, 1916, 259. (Trans.)

Strangers have surrounded us whom it is our pleasure to call foreigners; they have taken into their hands most of the rule, they have gathered to themselves much of the wealth.

LOUIS HÉMON, *Maria Chapdelaine*, 1916, 259, trans. by W.H. Blake, 1921. (See next quotation.)

Round about us strangers have come, whom we are wont to call barbarians; they have seized almost all the power; they have acquired almost all the money.

LOUIS HÉMON, *Maria Chapdelaine*, 1916, 212, trans. by Sir Andrew MacPhail, 1921. (See above, and following.)

Strangers have surrounded us, barbarians they seem to us, they have taken almost all the power, they have taken almost all the money, but in the land of Quebec nothing has changed. Nothing shall change for we are here to bear witness. This is the only clear idea we have of ourselves and our destinies, to persist, to keep our identity. And we have kept our identity; perhaps centuries in the future the world will turn to us and say: These people come from a race that does not know how to die.

LOUIS HÉMON, *Maria Chapdelaine*, (1916) qu. in W. Bovey, *French-Canadians today*, 1938, 113. (See above.)

Canada is to-day British because French Canadians refused to have it something else.

W.H. MOORE, *The clash*, 1918, 278.

It is one of the paradoxes of history that, had Canada been more completely anglicized in 1776, it would probably to-day be a part of the United States.

GEORGE M. WRONG, *Can. hist. rev.*, 1922, 72.

I have often said that the great problem for French Canadians is that there are no French Canadians.

ABBÉ LIONEL GROULX, letter to Pierre Chaloult, editor of *La Nation*, Que., Feb. 22, 1936. (Trans.)

The disturbing factor to the French Canadians is not the British Crown but British policy.

W. BOVEY, *French Canadians*, 1938.

French Canadians like to be ruled.

ESDRAS MINVILLE, *L'Avenir de nôtre bourgeoisie*, 1939, 34. (Trans.)

French-Canadians were always inclined to rely too heavily on politics as a means of exercising influence. They talked too much while the English kept their mouths shut and acted.

HUGH MACLENNAN, *Two solitudes*, 1945, 17.

Vanquished and conquered, separated from their metropolitan power, deprived of a business class, poor and isolated, ignorant, reduced to a minority in a country that their ancestors had founded, colonized by an absentee capitalism, the French Canadians have an absolute need for the vigilant intervention of the provincial state.

MICHEL BRUNET, *Le présence anglaise et les Canadiens*, 1958, 145. (Trans.)

Second-class citizens.

ANON., term used by French Canadian civil servants to describe their status in Ottawa, 1960's.

To sum up, the Anglo-Canadians have been strong by virtue only of our weakness.

PIERRE E. TRUDEAU, *Cité libre*, Apr., 1962, 10. (Trans.)

All the time and energy we have spent proclaiming our rights, invoking our spiritual mission, broadcasting our virtues, bemoaning our mishaps, denouncing our enemies, and declaring our independence – none of it has made one worker any more skilful, one civil servant any more competent, one businessman any richer, one doctor any more progressive, one bishop any more learned or one politician any less of an ignoramus.

PIERRE E. TRUDEAU, *Cité libre*, Apr., 1962, 10. (Trans.)

The whole French Canadian society is foundering. Our merchants show off their English company names, the billboards along our roads are all in English. We are a servile race; our loins were broken two hundred years ago and it shows.

JEAN-PAUL DESBIENS, *The impertinences of Brother Anonymous*, (Frère Untel), 1962, 30.

Even if there are many valiant defenders of the French cause outside Quebec, *we must unfortunately face the fact that Canada's French minorities have ceased working for the French side. They are now working for the English side.*

MARCEL CHAPUT, *Why I am a separatist*, 1962, 73.

Whether they choose to live in a true federation or whether they choose independence, they must rethink their entire society, at every level.

FERNAND OUELLETTE, *Liberté,* Mar. -Apr., 1964, 110. (Trans.)

Now, all of a sudden, the French Canadians expect someone to hand them everything on a platter. They claim that they have been depressed and held down. I would like to know – by whom? They've had every democratic right that every Canadian had.

> ANON., pres. of large corporation, qu. in P. Desbarats, *State of Quebec*, 1965, 50.

The keystone of a Canadian nation is the French fact.

> GEORGE P. GRANT, *Lament for a nation*, 1965, 20.

I am a son of a lumberjack and son of a farmer; a son of a day-labourer, son of a poor man, a son of the public-school system. I am all that. I have lived through all our troubles and have caught all our neuroses. I don't deny anything; I don't regret anything; I don't damn anything.

> JEAN-PAUL DESBIENS (Frère Untel), *For pity's sake*, 1965, 107. (Trans.)

After the original Indians and Eskimos, they were the first Canadians.

> LESTER B. PEARSON, "Good neighborhood", *Foreign affairs*, XLIII, No. 2, Jan., 1965, 253.

From the active, aggressive, commercial society of the eighteenth century, proud, independent and not a little arrogant, French Canada became the rural, suspicious, withdrawn, peasant society of the nineteenth century, dependent for its strength upon its renewed religious faith.

> GEORGE F.G. STANLEY, *New France: the last phase, 1744-1760*, 1968, 274.

From a constitutional point of view, the Quebec Legislature has no authority to speak on behalf of 'French Canada'.

> PIERRE E. TRUDEAU, *Federalism and the French Canadians*, 1968, 3.

I think French-Canadians have been betrayed by their élite for 100 years.

> PIERRE E. TRUDEAU, T.V. program, "Under attack", Feb. 13, 1968.

What is so endearing about the young French Canadians revolting against their tradition is that they sometimes write as if Voltaire's *Candide* had come off the press last week instead of two hundred years ago.

> GEORGE P. GRANT, *Technology and empire*, 1969, 67.

The whole task, I think, the whole problem consists in freeing the human spirit – not in freeing French-Canadians.

> HECTOR DE SAINT-DENYS-GARNEAU, in M. Richler, ed., *Canadian writing today*, 1970, 90.

In Quebec there is no "black problem". The liberation struggle launched by the American blacks nevertheless arouses growing interest among the French-Canadian population, for the workers of Quebec are aware of their condition as niggers, exploited men, second-class citizens.

> PIERRE VALLIÈRES, *White niggers of America*, 1971, 21.

French Canadians – Destiny

Our language, our institutions, and our laws.

> *LE CANADIEN* (Montréal), motto, 1806. (Trans.)

Whatever may happen, whatever government shall be established over them, they can see no hope for their nationality . . .

> LORD DURHAM, *Report*, 1839, ed. Lucas, 1912, 291.

I have little doubt that the French, when once placed, by the legitimate course of events and the working of natural causes, in a minority, would abandon their vain hopes of nationality.

> LORD DURHAM, *Report*, 1839, ed. Lucas, II, 307.

It is a shameful ambition for us French-Canadian Catholics to try to form a separate nationality to the detriment of the Protestants, Jews, etc., who also have the same rights to form a distinct nationality. We were not placed here by virtue of a preconceived idea, but by the force of circumstances, or rather, destiny. God did not want the New World to be made up of tribes divided one from the other and doomed to eternal weakness by living eternally separated.

GONZALVE DOUTRE, lecture, Institut Canadien, Montreal, Dec. 1, 1864. (Trans.)

For me, the safety of the French race lies not in isolation, but in competition. Give our children the best possible education, put them on an equal basis with those of the other race, and give them the legitimate pride they will have in such a competition. There is safety. There is autonomy.

SIR WILFRID LAURIER, letter to C. Angers, Dec. 9, 1896. (Pub. Arch. Can.)

Our race will survive, grow and prosper in the measure it remains peasant and rustic.

HENRI BOURASSA, Patriotisme, nationalisme, impérialisme, 1923, 56. (Trans.)

If the Great Powers stubbornly insist on clinging to the old concept of nationalism – which is out-dated now – peoples who have not found nationalism a happy experience may be the only ones who can give the world the fresh solution that it needs. I suspect that the coming people in the Americas may be the French Canadians.

ARNOLD TOYNBEE, World review, Mar., 1949, 12.

What we practice here is purity through sterilization, orthodoxy through silence, security through dull repetition. We imagine there is only one way to go straight, and that is never to set out; one way never to make mistakes and that is never to experiment; one way not to get lost and that is to stay asleep. We have invented a sure way to fight caterpillars – to cut down the trees.

JEAN-PAUL DESBIENS (Frère Untel), The impertinences of Brother Anonymous, 1962, 49.

I say to you, French Canadians, that we will build tomorrow's civilization together.

ANDRÉ MALRAUX, Minister of State for Cultural Affairs of France, paraphrase of frequently stated remark during State visit to Montreal, Oct., 1963; "Whatever the past, we shall build together the civilization of the Atlantic, the only completely free civilization in the world" (Trans.), address, opening of Exposition française de Montréal, Oct. 11, 1963, qu. in Le Devoir, Oct. 12, 1963, 1.

We French Canadians of the Province of Quebec have undeniable rights, but in addition to those rights which we claim, we also have duties to fulfil toward ourselves and toward others. It is not in anarchy that we will succeed, but in mutual trust and understanding.

RÉAL CAOUETTE, H. of C., Debates, Oct. 14, 1964, 9025.

I want to keep my French heritage, but it is just as important for me to keep my English chattels and to go to the limit of my American gift of invention. I need all that to make the total man.

JEAN LE MOYNE, Convergence (1960), 1966, 98.

The only way for French Canadians to ensure their stake in Canada's future is to participate in Ottawa.

> PIERRE E. TRUDEAU, speech, St. Hyacinthe, Que., June 24, 1968.

French Canadians – Survival

The French fact (le fait français).

> ANON., phrase used to designate the French "personality" of Quebec.

Barring Catastrophe shocking to think of, this Colony must to the end of Time, be peopled by the Canadian Race.

> SIR GUY CARLETON, in despatch to Lord Shelburne, Nov. 25, 1767.

You were born and have not ceased to be, French.

> COMTE D'ESTAING, Commander of the French fleet, proclamation to the French Canadians, Oct., 1778, qu. in H. Neatby, *Quebec: the revolutionary age 1760-1791*, 1966, 174. (Trans.)

We shall be the France of America afore long – the grand nation – the great empire. It's our distiny – every thing foretells it.

> T.C. HALIBURTON, *Sam Slick*, 1838, 153.

French Canadians are a separate people in America, a people of a distinct and vivacious national character, a new and healthy people whose origins are entirely warlike, with its language, its religion, its laws, its customs, a nation more densely populated than any other of the new world; which could be conquered but not dissolved by force to be absorbed into the milieu of the Anglo American race. Time alone could bring about that result; but not legislation, nor the sword.

> ALEXIS DE TOCQUEVILLE, letter to Henry Reeve, Clerk of the Privy Council of Great Britain, from Compiègne, Jan. 3,

1838 (Trans)., in *Can. hist. rev.*, Dec., 1938, 394.

If the French Canadians are to be ruled to their satisfaction, and who could desire to rule them otherwise? every attempt to metamorphose them systematically into English must be abandoned, and the attainment of that object, whether to be accomplished or not, must be left to time and the natural effect of the expected increase and predominance . . . of the English over the French Population. The desired result cannot be produced by measures which rouse an indignant spirit against it.

> SIR CHARLES METCALFE, despatch to Lord Stanley, Apr. 29, 1843. (Pub.Arch.Can.)

You may perhaps *Americanise*, but, depend upon it, by methods of this description, you will never *Anglicise* the French inhabitants of the Province. Let them feel on the other hand that their religion, their habits, their prepossessions, their prejudices if you will, are more considered and respected here than in other portions of this vast continent which is being overrun by the most reckless, self-sufficient and dictatorial section of the Anglo Saxon race, and who will venture to say that the last hand which waves the British flag on American ground may not be that of a French Canadian?

> LORD ELGIN, dispatch to Lord Grey, May 4, 1848.

With equality of numbers, and of sectional representation, the two nationalities cannot fall foul of each other; but with Confederation, as we shall be in a great minority in the General Parliament, which has all the important powers in relation to legislation, we shall have to carry on a constant contest for the defence and preservation of our political rights and of our liberty.

JOSEPH F. PERRAULT, *Confederation debates*, Mar. 3, 1865, 599.

French Canadians truly make up a nation; the valley of the St. Lawrence is their fatherland.

LOUIS LAFLÈCHE, Bishop of Three Rivers, *Quelques considérations sur les rapports de la société civile avec la religion et la famille*, 1866. (Trans.)

The French will always be French.

SIR JOHN A. MACDONALD, qu. by Lord Lorne to Macdonald, letter Apr. 10, 1884. (Pub. Arch. Can.)

We have a right to our national existence as a race apart, and woe to any man who will try to deprive us of it.

HONORÉ MERCIER, speech at Lac St. Jean, Que., qu. in J.O. Pelland, *Biographie, discours, conférences, de l'Hon. Honoré Mercier*, 1890, 689. (Trans.)

With courage, with perseverance, with union, with effort, and above all with a constant devotion to our religion and our language, the future must be ours. Sooner or later, marching on together, we shall arrive at the position of a great nation. The logical conclusion of my work can only be this — One day we shall be Catholic France in America.

N.H.E. FAUCHER DE SAINT-MAURICE, *La question du jour*, 1890. (Trans.)

Men, women, and children, it is for you to choose; you can remain slaves under colonial status, or become independent and free, among other peoples who with their all-powerful voices, invite you to the banquet of nations.

HONORÉ MERCIER, address, Montreal, Apr. 4, 1893. (Trans.)

God planted in the heart of every French-Canadian patriot "a flower of hope". It is the aspiration to establish, on the banks of the St. Lawrence, a New France whose mission will be to continue in this American land the work of Christian civilization that old France carried out with such glory during the long centuries.

JULES-PAUL TARDIVEL, *Pour la patrie*, 1895, 7. (Trans.)

It is not necessary that we possess industry and money. We will no longer be French Canadians but Americans almost like the others. Our mission is to possess the earth and spread ideas. To cling to the soil, to raise large families, to maintain the hearths of intellectual and spiritual life, that must be our role in America.

JULES-PAUL TARDIVEL, in 1902, qu. in R. Rumilly, *Histoire de la province de Québec*, 1943, Vol. 10, 83. (Trans.)

Our mission is less to manage capital than to stimulate ideas; it consists less in lighting the fires of factories than in maintaining and radiating afar the hearthlight of religion and thought.

MGR. LOUIS-ADOLPH PÂQUET, "Sermon sur la vocation de la race française en Amérique", Quebec City, June 23, 1902. (Trans.)

Our own brand of nationalism is French-Canadian nationalism. We have been working for the last twenty-three years toward the development of a French-Canadian national feeling: what we want to see flourish is French-Canadian patriotism; our people are the French-Canadian people; we will not say that our homeland is limited to the Province of Quebec, but it is French Canada; the nation we wish to see founded at the time appointed by Providence is the French-Canadian nation.

JULES-PAUL TARDIVEL, *La vérité*, Apr. 1, 1904, 5. (Trans.)

Our special task, as French Canadians, is to maintain in America the endeavour of Christian France. It is to defend against all comers, perhaps even against France herself, our religious and national heritage. This heritage does not belong to us alone. It belongs to all Catholic America.

HENRI BOURASSA, speech, Montreal, Monument National, Nov. 20, 1918. (Trans.)

The French Canada of tomorrow, an original creation, will be flesh of your flesh, the flower of your spirit. It will gush forth, resplendent with youth and beauty, from the breath of you young French Canadians, from your sociology as sons of Christ.

ABBÉ LIONEL GROULX, address, Montreal, Nov. 29, 1943, "Why we are divided". (Trans.)

It would indeed seem that God has allowed our people to grow in this corner of the country, despite past persecutions, so that it might become the purifying element of the whole Canadian nation.

ALFRED CHARPENTIER, Ma conversion au syndicalisme catholique, 1946, 134. (Trans.)

Whatever the future of mankind in North America, I feel pretty confident that these French-speaking Canadians, at any rate, will be there at the end of the story.

ARNOLD TOYNBEE, Civilization on trial, 1948, 161.

French Canada is completely consumed by the fear that it will disappear, that it will be assimilated by Anglo-American voracity.

SOLANGE CHAPUT ROLLAND, Dear enemies, 1963, 23.

The French Canadians' long search for a fatherland is ended.

MICHEL BRUNET, in Peter Russell, ed., Nationalism in Canada, 1966, 60.

The most crucial problem that confronts Quebec is not political, economic or educational, but one concerning family size. If births continue to decline in Quebec, neither independence, nor wealth, nor immigration can assure the survival of the French Canadian people. The Quebec government must be asked without delay for a birth-rate policy, and more broadly a family policy.

COUNCIL ON FRENCH LIFE IN AMERICA, Vie française, Mar.-Apr., 1967, 230; qu. in C.L. Boydell, ed., Critical issues in Canadian society, 1971, 6. (Trans.)

I was in Quebec City recently, a marvellous, wonderful place. I saw some models of French sculpture, but my motel was as American as you can imagine; the food was completely American. The only difference was the language, for Lord's sake, plus a few intellectuals who make poetry and stuff. Hell, that's not French culture. They're as far away from France as the rest of the Canadians are from England. I mean, how in hell can they be independent? It's all nonsense.

GUNNAR MYRDAL, qu. by P. Newman, Home country, 1973, 51.

French Language

So long as there are French mothers the language will not die.

SIR WILFRID LAURIER, H. of C., Debates, Mar. 16, 1886, 180.

It isn't arrogance, it's just timidity that prevents us from learning French. Besides, French Canadians won't let us practise. They're always breaking into English as we stutter our way through the language barrier.

> ANON., (paraphrase), popular English Canadian reaction.

In Europe no man's education is complete until he knows French. This is because the French language, for 300 years and more, has been the language of arts and letters. It will always remain with me the language of art and literature, but it has not the same force, the same elasticity, as English. If I were your age I would not leave school until I could speak and write French.

> SIR WILFRID LAURIER, speech at McMaster University, Dec. 17, 1913.

The preservation of its language is absolutely necessary to the preservation of the race, of its genius, its character and its temperament.

> HENRI BOURASSA, La langue française et l'avenir de notre race, 1913, 4. (Trans.)

The enemies of the French language or French civilization in Canada are not the Boches on the shores of the Spree, but the English-Canadian anglicizers, the Orange intriguers, or Irish priests.

> HENRI BOURASSA, about Apr., 1915, qu. in R. Rumilly, Henri Bourassa, 1953, 530. (Trans.)

To say that the French language is a national language in Canada, and to contend in the same breath that it is a foreign language in the Canadian provinces is utter nonsense.

> ERNEST LAPOINTE, H. of C., Debates, May 10, 1916, 3681.

There are certain spells during certain evenings — cognac is best for a starter — when my English slips from me like the shucked skin of a snake, and I converse only in the elegant French tongue. But what French! O God, O Montreal, what French!

> DOROTHY PARKER, "The grandmother of the aunt of the gardener", New Yorker, July 25, 1931.

Joual, this absence of language, is a symptom of our non-existence as French Canadians. No one can ever study language enough, for it is the home of all meanings. Our inability to assert ourselves, our refusal to accept the future, our obsession with the past, are all reflected in joual, our real language.

> JEAN-PAUL DESBIENS (Frère Untel), The impertinences of Brother Anonymous, 1962, 28.

Papa, j'ai eu seventy-five en français.

> RENÉ PRÉFONTAINE, Exec. Dir. of the Manitoba School Trustees Assoc., quoting his grade four son, qu. in T. Creery, French for the French, 1963, 11.

The most intolerant people to our point of view are our own compatriots who have lost their language. They want to feel they have "arrived" by speaking English.

> RENÉ PRÉFONTAINE, Winnipeg, qu. by T. Creery, French for the French, 1963, 12.

My native tongue is not French, it is franglais. Learning French was almost like learning a foreign language.

> FERNAND OUELLETTE, Liberté, Mar. -Apr., 1964, 91. (Trans.).

The Canadian community must invest, for the defence and better appreciation of the French language, as much time, energy, and money as are required to prevent the country from breaking up.

PIERRE E. TRUDEAU, *Federalism and the French Canadians*, 1968, 32.

That in all classes of grade one of primary school under the jurisdiction of the school board of St. Léonard-de-Port-Maurice, as of September 1968, the language of instruction be French.

ST. LÉONARD (QUE.) SCHOOL BOARD, regulation adopted June 27, 1968. (Trans.)

The French language has survived in North America for one reason only: because Canada has survived. The Fathers of Confederation reached a settlement which gave the French language the best chance it will ever have on this continent. And if we try to improve on that settlement, we do so at our peril.

DONALD G. CREIGHTON, *Towards the discovery of Canada*, 1972, 270.

French is the official language of the Province of Quebec.

QUEBEC. LAWS, STATUTES etc. Bill No. 22, "Official Languages Act", title I:1, 1974.

Fresh Air

Canadians hate air.

FRANCES MONCK, *My Canadian leaves*, 1891, 29.

The purity of the air of Newfoundland is without doubt due to the fact that the people of the outports never open their windows.

J.G. MILLAIS, *Newfoundland and its untrodden ways*, 1907.

Friends

Chimo.

ANON., Eskimo greeting (Chee'mo) meaning "I am your friend". Also, a drinking toast.

An intemperate advocate is more dangerous than an open foe.

T.C. HALIBURTON, *Sam Slick*, 1836, chap. XXIV.

Dear friend, I know this world is kin,
    And all of hate is but a breath,
We all are friends, made perfect in
    Our near relationship by death.

GEORGE F. CAMERON, "Death", 1887.

Nay, never once to feel we are alone,
While the great human heart around
    us lies:
To make the smile on other lips our
    own,
To live upon the light in others' eyes.

ARCHIBALD LAMPMAN, "The largest life", 1900.

No one who has a friend can be altogether at war with the world.

NELLIE L. MCCLUNG, *Sowing seeds in Danny*, 1908, 283.

A woman will tell a man friend what she will not tell a lover. Few lovers will understand this, fewer still will believe it.

ARNOLD HAULTAIN, *Hints for lovers*, 1909, 193.

If women were comprehensible to men, men and women would be friends, not lovers.

ARNOLD HAULTAIN, *Hints for lovers*, 1909, 29.

It is well that there is no one without a fault for he would not have a friend in the world.

ROBERT C. (BOB) EDWARDS, Calgary *Eye Opener*, Dec. 11, 1915.

I bow not down to any book,
No written page holds me in awe;
For when on one friend's face I look
I read the Prophets and the Law!

ROBERT NORWOOD, "After the order of Melchisedec", 1917.

Whether at sea or whether on shore,
  Or at the job or over the wine,
Whether on two legs, whether on four—
  All good fellows are friends of mine!

TOM MACINNES, "Ballade of friends", 1918.

A friend who knows your secret holds a mortgage on your peace of mind.

ROBERT C. (BOB) EDWARDS, Calgary *Eye Opener*, Dec. 25, 1920.

I have some friends, some honest
    friends,
And honest friends are few;
My pipe of briar, my open fire,
A book that's not too new.

ROBERT W. SERVICE, "I have some friends", 1921.

The difference between a friend and an acquaintance is that a friend helps where an acquaintance merely advises.

ROBERT C. (BOB) EDWARDS, Calgary *Eye Opener*, Aug. 20, 1921.

In all my wending
I've seen no sight
So full of friending
As you, eyebright!

GEORGE HERBERT CLARKE, "Eyebright", 1930.

Friend o' mine in the year oncoming
I wish you a little time for play
And an hour to dream in the eerie
    gloaming
After the clamorous day.

L.M. MONTGOMERY, "Friend o' mine", in *Good housekeeping*, Jan., 1936.

After all, I made some dough,
By and by I made some more;
Anywhere I like to go
Friends, my goodness, friends galore!

GEORGE JOHNSTON, "Smilers", 1959.

I'm not down-hearted. It's my friends who need cheering up.

GUY FAVREAU, after his resignation as Minister of Justice, June 29, 1965, qu. in R. Gwyn, *The shape of scandal*, 1965, 231.

An individual has only one or two friends in a lifetime.

WILLIAM E. BLATZ, *Human security*, 1966, xi.

Our enemies toughen us up by attacking us; it is our friends who gently sap away our strength.

RICHARD J. NEEDHAM, *A friend in Needham*, 1969, 50.

When you are down you will find
those who were once your friends
but they will be changed and
    dangerous.

MARGARET ATWOOD, "Procedures for underground", 1970, in book of same title, 1970, 24.

Friendship

I am persuaded nearly as good friends as civilized People & Savages generally are for that friendship seldom goes farther than *their* fondness for our property & *our* eagerness to obtain their Furs.

DANIEL WILLIAMS HARMON, *Journal*, Mar. 20, 1802 (Ed. by W. Kaye Lamb, 1957).

Grant me the quiet charm which
    friendship gives,
Which lives unchanged, and cheers
    me while it lives.

JOHN R. NEWELL, "Friendship", 1881.

A little axle grease will make the Red River Cart go a long way and so will friendship, if applied wisely.

ARCHBISHOP ALEXANDRE-ANTONIN TACHÉ, 1880's qu. in Dan Kennedy, *Recollections of an Assiniboine Chief*, 1972, 55.

Playing the Jesus game
I don't smile at strangers
because that might frighten them
into summoning the police.

ALDEN NOWLAN, "Playing the Jesus game", 1969.

Male bonding among primates is defined here as a particular relationship between two or more males such that they react differently to members of their bonding unit as compared to individuals outside of it.

LIONEL TIGER, *Men in groups*, 1969, 19.

Frogs

Breathers of wisdom won without a
quest,
Quaint uncouth dreamers, voices high
and strange
Flutists of lands where beauty hath no
change,
And wintry grief is a forgotten guest;
Sweet murmurers of everlasting rest.

ARCHIBALD LAMPMAN, "The frogs", 1888.

And loud and clear the prairie lark,
deep hid
In those vast fragrant meadows, sang;
the creek
Sent thousand-voiced upon the sultry
air
The bull-frog's weary canticle.

NICHOLAS FLOOD DAVIN, "Eos: an epic of the dawn", 1889.

For the unrest of passion here is peace,
And eve's cool drench for midday
soil and taint.
To tired ears how sweetly brings
release
This limpid babble from life's
unstilled complaint.

CHARLES G.D. ROBERTS, "Frogs", 1893.

Nobody but a Canadian can really appreciate frogs. As a musical instrument they do not exist in other countries, and it is as a musical instrument that they are of value in the expression of beauty in Canada.

B.K. SANDWELL, speech, Canadian Club, Ottawa, Mar. 13, 1920.

Quaint and low, like some remote
bassoon,
Across the marsh there came a
muffled croon,
And all alone one melancholy frog,
Squat on the butt of a sunken log,
Solemnly did serenade the Moon:—
In tone so low and quaint — like the
quaint bassoon.

TOM MACINNES, "The moonlit wheat", 1923.

Frontenac, Count

Many surpassed him in cruelty, none equalled him in capacity and vigor.

FRANCIS PARKMAN, *Count Frontenac and New France*, 1877, 458.

Frontiers

The story of the frontier like a saga
Sang through the cells and cloisters of
the nation.

E.J. PRATT, *Brébeuf and his brethren*, 1940.

The line which marks off the frontier and the farmstead, the wilderness from the baseland; the hinterland from the metropolis, runs through every Canadian psyche.

W.L. MORTON, *Canadian identity*, 1961, 93.

A moving frontier is essential to the vitality of a burgeoning nation. It tends to draw to it the boldest and most independent spirits in the country and they in turn, stimulated and tempered by its challenge, become a regenerating force. Canada, by its geography, was being denied this kind of transfusion.

PIERRE BERTON, *The national dream*, 1970, 19.

Fruit

A cent a pound, or on the ground.

ANON., slogan of Okanagan apple growers, early 1930's.

Frustration

But I lie alone in the shadowed grass, fond only, incapable of love or truth, caught in all I have done, afraid and unable to escape, formulating one more ruinous way to safety.

JOHN NEWLOVE, "By the church wall", 1965.

Fulfilment

Fulfilment is pursuit, not attainment.

MARTIN ROHER, *Days of living*, 1959, 143.

It's in the fight, in the striving, in the mountains unclimbed that fulfilment lies.

MERLE SHAIN, *Some men are more perfect than others*, 1973, 56.

Funerals

Bury me early in the morning, that only my friends may take the trouble to get up in time to follow me to the grave.

SIR MATTHEW BAILLIE BEGBIE, a few days before his death at Victoria on June 11, 1894.

Give us the flowers now and you need not bring any to our funeral.

ROBERT C. (BOB) EDWARDS, Calgary *Eye Opener*, Jan. 28, 1905.

Nothing is to me more odious than the pageantry of death.

GOLDWIN SMITH, *Reminiscences*, 1910, 46.

All now is over,
The dream is done,
Fasten the cover,
Shut out the sun.
Farewell to lover,
To rival, to friend,
To sorrow, to splendour,
To earth's weird wonder,
For this is the end.

WILFRED CAMPBELL, "Requiem", 1918.

Sorry I can't attend the funeral but I heartily approve of the event.

J.B. "JIM" MCLACHLAN, on death of Samuel Gompers, 1924, paraphrased as above by William (Bill) Bennett, Socialist journalist, on death of R.B. Bennett, 1947, qu. in Tom McEwan, *He wrote for us*, 1951, 62.

Easily to the old
  Opens the hard ground;
But when youth grows cold,
  And red lips have no sound,
Bitterly does the earth
  Open to receive
And bitterly do the grasses
  In the churchyard grieve.

WILSON MACDONALD, "Exit", 1926.

Flowers: a necessary evil. Arranging them, tending them, and disposing of them after the funeral requires considerable work, but they are considered to be an integral part of the "memory picture", and grumbling is done privately.

> ROBERT FORREST, *Death here is thy sting*, 1967, 49.

Memorial Societies: disgust. Few funeral men have had occasion to deal with a memorial society, but their opinions have been preformulated by the trade press, which terms memorial society members "burial beatniks".

> ROBERT FORREST, *Death here is thy sting*, 1967, 49.

If not one mourner feels at all
Bound to attend my funeral,
No one will have to hear, at least,
Eulogies of the dear deceased.
I'd hate to think, when dead, good
   Lord,
I'd cause the living to be bored.

> GEOFFREY B. RIDDEHOUGH, "In a cynical moment", 1972.

Fur Trade

The most obvious Benefit acquired by the Cessions made to your Majesty is the Fur & Skin Trade of all the Indians in North America.

> THE LORDS OF TRADE, to the King, June 8, 1763.

Fortitude in distress.

> BEAVER CLUB, Montreal, motto; founded 1775 by the partners of the North West Company.

While the trade is confined to a single company that Company is bound by every motive which self interest can supply to preserve the savages from wars, drunkenness, idleness or whatever else would divert them from the chase, and lessen the quantity of skins annually received at the different posts.

> DUNCAN MCGILLIVRAY, attributed, *Some account of the trade carried on by the North West Company*, 1809. (Pub. Arch.Can., *Report*, 1928, 63).

Philanthropy is not the object of our visits to these Northern Indians.

> GEORGE SIMPSON, of the Hudson's Bay Co., 1821, *Journal, Athabasca dept.*, ed. by Rich, 1938.

Colonization and the fur trade could not exist together.

> SIR GEORGE CARTIER and WILLIAM MCDOUGALL, communication on acquiring the property of the Hudson's Bay Company, addressed to Sir F. Rogers, London, Feb. 8, 1869.

It is no mere accident that the present Dominion coincides roughly with the fur-trading areas of northern North America.

> HAROLD A. INNIS, *The fur trade in Canada*, 1930, 396.

Furs

It makes little difference; Canada is useful only to provide me with furs.

> MADAME DE POMPADOUR, 1759, on being told of the fall of Quebec.

O the animals we have flayed
To clothe ourselves I poke among,
The rotting carcasses in a shallow pit.
I am looking for one that saved me.

> STUART MACKINNON, "On the way to the vivarium", 1969.

Futility

We shall not be futilitarians, however great the frustrations.

JOHN DIEFENBAKER, H. of C., June 13, 1958, on introducing Prime Minister Macmillan, of the U.K. to Parliament.

Future

The events that the future reserves for this country are of the highest importance. Canada is the country of our ancestors; it is our homeland, as it must be the adopted homeland of the different peoples who come from various parts of the globe in order to exploit its vast forests and find a permanent site for their homes and their interests. Like us, they must desire above all the happiness and prosperity of Canada. Such is the inheritance that they must strive to hand on to their descendants in this young and hospitable land. Like us, their children will have to be, above all, CANADIANS.

LOUIS-HIPPOLYTE LAFONTAINE, electoral manifesto, Aug., 1840. (Trans.)

They [Canadians] are naturally a fine people, and possess capabilities and talents, which, when improved by cultivation, will render them second to no people in the world; and that period is not far distant.

SUSANNA MOODIE, *Roughing it in the bush*, 1852, 223.

Things can't and won't remain long as they are.

THOMAS C. HALIBURTON, *Nature and human nature*, 1855, ch.19.

Deep, infinite deeps before us,
    Ruin riding in the wind,
Cloudy curtains hanging o'er us,
    And eternities behind.

ALEXANDER MCLACHLAN, "A dream", 1856.

Our Northern rising nationality has an example field before it — a brilliant future in the distance.

ALEXANDER MORRIS, *Hudson's Bay*, 1858.

To these objections, I answer, that though theoretical to-day, our future will be practical tomorrow; that I do not, and never did, place myself in the position of a preacher of loyalty; that I preach rather security, I preach precaution, I preach self-preservation.

THOMAS D'A. MCGEE, "The future of Canada", a lecture delivered in St. Lawrence Hall, Toronto, Nov. 26, 1863.

It may be doubted whether the inhabitants of the Dominion themselves are as yet fully awake to the magnificent destiny in store for them, or have altogether realised the promise of their young and hardy nationality. Like a virgin goddess in a primaeval world, Canada still walks in unconscious beauty among her golden woods and by the margin of her trackless streams, catching but broken glances of her radiant majesty as mirrored on their surface, and scarcely recks as yet of the glories awaiting her in the Olympus of nations.

LORD DUFFERIN, speech in Belfast, June 11, 1872, after appointment as Governor-General.

In a world apart, secluded from all extraneous influences, nestling at the feet of her majestic Mother, Canada dreams her dream, and forebodes her destiny — a dream of ever-broadening harvests, multiplying towns and villages, and expanding pastures, of constitutional self-government, and a confederated Empire; of page after page of honourable history, added as her contribution to the annals of the Mother Country and to the glories of the British race.

LORD DUFFERIN, speech in City Hall, Winnipeg, Sept. 29, 1877.

Of one thing you may be sure, that the country you call Canada and which your sons and your children's children shall be proud to call by that name, will be a land of power among the nations.

MARQUIS OF LORNE, speech in Winnipeg, 1881.

Be Canadians and the future is yours.

LOUIS FRÉCHETTE, qu., *Canadian leaves*, 1887, 131.

O Falterer, let thy past convince
  Thy future, – all the growth, the
    gain,
The fame since Cartier knew thee,
    since
  Thy shores beheld Champlain.

CHARLES G.D. ROBERTS, "Canada", 1887.

I hope that when another century has been added to the age of Canada it may still be Canada, and that its second century shall like its first be celebrated by Canadians, unabsorbed, – numerous, prosperous, powerful, and at peace. For myself, I should prefer to die in that hope than to die President of the United States.

SIR OLIVER MOWAT, speech at Niagara-on-the-Lake, July 16, 1892.

The flood of tide is upon us that leads on to fortune; if we let it pass it may never recur again. If we let it pass, the voyage of our national life, bright as it is today, will be bound in shallows.

SIR WILFRID LAURIER, H. of C., *Debates*, July 30, 1903, 7659.

We cannot look into the future; we cannot foresee the destiny of Canada;

but, sir, on this we rest well assured: that Canada has not been led through the perils and difficulties of its chequered career, that six million people have not been placed in command of the northern half of this continent with all its vast resources, that we shall occupy an ignoble and insignificant position amongst the nations of the earth.

CLIFFORD SIFTON, July, 1904, at Winnipeg Exhibition.

Thus stands the question of the future of Canada. Find for us something other than mere colonial stagnation, something sounder than independence, nobler than annexation, greater in purpose than a Little Canada. Find us a way.

STEPHEN B. LEACOCK, *University mag.*, Feb., 1907, 141.

Canada should define her own citizenship, Canada should make her own treaties, Canada, eventually, should select her own chief magistrate, be he king or president. I have no hesitation in laying this down as my belief in regard to Canada's future and her connection with the Empire.

W.F. MACLEAN, H. of C., *Debates*, Feb. 11, 1907, 2888.

I have in my veins all the sweet unrest
  of the wild places,
And if you toss me aside I will come
  hither again on the morrow;
For I am a force that you cannot deny;
I am an offering that you finally must
  accept
For I am the herald of new things in a
  new land.

WILSON MACDONALD, "Out of the wilderness", 1926.

What seek we to repair this piteous
time?
Our answer lies within us, and our
star;
We have to-morrow what to-day we
are.

> WARWICK CHIPMAN, "The millennium",
> 1930.

It would be well to bear in mind that
the present of today was the future of
yesterday and that it is what it is
because of the human actions, the
human decisions from yesterday.
Therefore the future will be what we
make it.

> JOHN W. DAFOE, speech, Toronto, Empire
> Club, Jan. 30, 1936.

One thing I will not do, and cannot be
persuaded to do, is to say what Canada
will do in regard to a situation that
may arise at some future time and
under circumstances of which we now
know nothing.

> W.L. MACKENZIE KING, speech in Toronto,
> Aug. 8, 1939.

It is with joy that we take the entire
responsibility of tomorrow.

> PAUL-ÉMILE BORDUAS, Refus global,
> 1948, 10. (Trans.).

The world is full of people whose
notion of a satisfactory future is, in
fact, a return to an idealized past.

> ROBERTSON DAVIES, A voice from the
> attic, 1960, 351.

The decisive point is that Canada's
youth is in reality an advantage rather
than a handicap. Her future is almost
certain to be greater than her past, and
this is the basis for the perpetual
hopefulness which pervades her literature and her literary criticism.

> DESMOND PACEY, intro., Creative writing
> in Canada, 1961, 6.

Modern man had a future up to about
the year 1900, from which time he
rapidly began losing it.

> A.R.M. LOWER, Queen's quart., Vol. 68,
> 1961/62, 542.

It will, I pledge you, be a time to
excite the daring, to test the strong and
to give new promise to the timid. It
will be indeed a time of direction and
decision, where our efforts are sustained, our purpose clear and our faith
high.

> LESTER B. PEARSON, radio and TV ad-
> dress, Apr. 23, 1963.

Corporations and not doctrinaire socialism are the wave of the future.

> GEORGE P. GRANT, Lament for a nation,
> 1965, 92.

The compelling need for the future is
not for national societies in a world
community — desirable though such a
social system would be today — but
rather for a world society fit for a
global village.

> MELVILLE H. WATKINS, in Peter Russell,
> ed., Nationalism in Canada, 1966, 301.

The pride, the grand poem
of our land, of the earth itself,
will come.

> JOHN NEWLOVE, "The pride", 1969.

Tomorrow is a dream
that rarely, if ever, comes true.
So drink the rum that makes the
dreams
that make tomorrow now.

> SANDRA KILBER, "Flight", 1969.

It is perhaps not too fanciful to imagine a future world in which the nation-state system will be transcended, for many purposes, by a totally new organization of affairs where countervailing powers are exercised by great international corporations and international labour unions, with – and this of course is the question – the public interest being assured through controls maintained by some sort of international regulatory agency.

ROY MATTHEWS, *Behind the headlines*, May, 1970, 15.

I have long considered it one of God's greatest mercies that the future is hidden from us. If it were not, life would surely be unbearable.

EUGENE FORSEY, in S. Clarkson, ed., *Visions 2020*, 1970, 94.

The future is beyond knowing, but the present is beyond belief.

WILLIAM IRWIN THOMPSON, *At the edge of history*, 1971, 163.

Canadians by and large tend to think of Canada as a land of immense potential. Not just as a big land, which it unquestionably is. Or a privileged land as many others enviously regard us. But as a land of limitless promise. A land perhaps, on the threshold of greatness.

PIERRE E. TRUDEAU, speech, Toronto & District Liberal Assoc., Mar. 3, 1971.

The test ahead of us is not a test of our social apparatus, but of ourselves.

BRUCE HUTCHISON, in *Maclean's*, Sept., 1972, 27.

We must march forward into the future – we have no place else to go.

JOHN V. CLYNE, speech in Toronto to a group of executives, qu. by Stuart Keate, Vancouver *Sun*, Nov. 8, 1972, 37.

The past is gone; the present is full of confusion; and the future scares hell out of me.

DAVID LEWIS STEIN, *Toronto life*, Sept., 1972, 57.

is there a rhythm drumming from
    vision?
shall we tower into art or ashes?

it is our dreams will decide
& we are their Shapers

EARLE BIRNEY, "The shapers: Vancouver", 1973.

Galt, Alexander T.

He will be far more dexterous in his treatment of figures, – far more clever in humbugging the House; but as to economy he is incapable of it. He has not the courage of a mouse, nor has he the sense of right and desire for the people's good necessary to induce him to apply the pruning knife to the expenses of the country.

> TORONTO *GLOBE*, Aug. 9, 1858, 2, referring to Galt's appointment as Inspector General.

He is finally dead as a Canadian politician. The correspondence between Cartier and himself, in which he comes squarely out for independence, has rung his death-knell, and I shall take precious good care to keep him where he is. He has seduced Cartwright away, and I have found out how it was managed. Cartwright and he formed at the Club last session a sort of mutual admiration society, and they agreed that they were the two men fit to govern Canada.

> SIR JOHN A. MACDONALD, letter to Sir John Rose, Feb. 23, 1870, on Sir Alexander T. Galt.

Games

Games are nature's most beautiful creation. All animals play games, and the truly Messianic vision of the brotherhood of creatures must be based on the idea of the game.

> LEONARD COHEN, *Beautiful losers*, 1966, 29.

Gardens

Canada gardens.

> ANON., a term adopted about 1845 in English counties, Kent, Yorkshire, Gloucestershire, etc., to describe small unfenced allotments provided for the poor; usually shortened to "The Canada".

To God in His glory. We two nations dedicate this garden and pledge ourselves that as long as men shall live, we will not take up arms against one another.

> ANON., inscription on cairn in International Peace Garden, on land donated by Manitoba and North Dakota 35 miles north of Rugby, N.D., the geographical centre of the continent.

The Marchbanks Weed Sanctuary.

> ROBERTSON DAVIES, term used by fictitious character, Samuel Marchbanks, in Peterborough *Examiner*, 1940's.

In goodly faith we plant the seed,
To-morrow morn we reap the weed.

> PAUL HIEBERT, *Sarah Binks*, "My garden", 1947, 12.

Do you like this garden that is yours? See to it that your children do not destroy it!

> MALCOLM LOWRY, *Under the volcano*, 1947, 128 and last page. (Trans.)

I have a garden closed away
And shadowed from the light of day
Where Love hangs bound on every
tree
And I alone go free.

> JAY MACPHERSON, "The garden of the
> sexes", 1957.

One day I grew taller than the tallest
plants in the garden.
The world looked in
and my eyes said yes.
And then after I had said good-bye,
something told me
I had been in the garden.

> STEVE SMITH, "The garden", 1964.

This is the garden of the world, and
grows nothing but weeds.

> HAROLD TOWN, *Enigmas*, 1964, [1].

Though lost in the ignorant traffic, still
I would rejoice.
There is some hidden wisdom in all
gardens.

> LOUIS DUDEK, "Flowers on windows",
> 1971.

Garrison Mentality

A garrison is a closely knit and belea-
guered society, and its moral and
social values are unquestionable. In a
perilous enterprise one does not discuss
causes or motives; one is either a
fighter or a deserter.

> NORTHROP FRYE in C.F. Klinck, ed.,
> *Literary history of Canada*, 1965, 830.

Gas

It is now inevitable that gas is to be the
light of the future – at least for some
time to come.

> MANITOBA *FREE PRESS*, Sept. 7, 1881.

Geese

Under the gold and green of the
auroras
Wild geese drove wedges through the
zodiac.

> E.J. PRATT, "Brébeuf and his brethren",
> 1941.

Genealogy

I have been too busy all my life to cast
a thought so far back as my grandfather.

> SIR W. VAN HORNE; attributed.

MY NAME IS PETER VAN
   ALSTINE
MY NAME IS MICHAEL GRASS
MY NAME IS OWEN ROBLIN
MY NAME IS GILBERT PURDY

> AL PURDY, "In search of Owen Roblin",
> 1974 [38].

Generosity

And there are times when the one who
      needs
   hates the one who supplies the need.
Those who give us too much take
      away
   everything that we possess.

> ALDEN NOWLAN, "Without her I would
> die", 1964.

Genius

Those who expect to see "A new
Athens rising near the pole", will find
themselves extremely disappointed.
Genius will never mount high, where
the faculties of the mind are benumbed half the year.

> FRANCES BROOKE, *The history of Emily
> Montague*, 1769; Ottawa, 1931, 88; In
> Quebec City.

It is wonderful what a personal interest the average man takes in discussions as to what constitutes genius.

> PETER MCARTHUR, *To be taken with salt*, 1903, 155.

The simplicity of genius is achieved only by much searching and a strenuous discipline.

> LORD TWEEDSMUIR, "Return to masterpieces", speech, Convocation Hall, Univ. of Toronto, Nov. 24, 1937.

O do not compromise with doubt
Or cage with dust a living thing;
Let your own inborn genius out,
Give your imprisoned power wing!

> HELENA COLEMAN, "Brother to stars", 1938.

I'm a genius, I'm a genius.
What more can I desire?
I toot upon my little flute
And twang upon my lyre.

> PAUL HIEBERT, *Sarah Binks*, "The genius", 1947, 33.

Genius contrives
to stir the heart
of every age.

> MARIEL JENKINS, "An exhibition of modern art", 1953.

I think it would be better to aim for a well-adjusted slob than a totally unadjusted genius.

> DR. ERIK E. LEYLAND, to Parent Teachers group, Vancouver, Oct. 26, 1963.

Literary greatness is genius in search of character.

> IRVING LAYTON, "Aphs", *The whole bloody bird*, 1969, 81.

Gentlemen

One who is never rude by mistake.

> ROBERT C. (BOB) EDWARDS, attributed, by M. Napier in E. Stafford, ed., *Flamboyant Canadians*, 1964, 193.

What do these enemies of the human race look like? Do they wear on their foreheads a sign so that they may be told, shunned and condemned as criminals? No. On the contrary, they are the respectable ones. They are honoured. They call themselves and are called gentlemen.

> NORMAN BETHUNE, qu. in Allen & Gordon, *The scalpel, the sword*, 1952, 315.

Geography

Canada is long and narrow; in fact, all frontier. The rapid extension of settlement up the Ottawa, and on each side of it, would give breadth and substance to the country.

> SIR EDMUND HEAD, *Confidential memo.*, undated, i.e. July, 1857.

A geography merely political has little significance, especially when close communications by water and rail and a community of language, ideas and interests suggest, and even constrain unity of plan and harmony of action.

> JAMES W. TAYLOR to Thomas D'Arcy McGee, June 25, 1862, Taylor Papers, Minnesota Historical Society.

Geographically we are bound up beyond the power of extinction.

> THOMAS D'A. MCGEE, speech in St. John, N.B., 1863.

In geographical form it [Canada] would resemble an eel. Its length would be everything, its breadth nothing.

> J.B.E. DORION, *Confederation debates*, Mar. 9, 1865, 863.

You cannot legislate against geography.

> SIR WILFRID LAURIER, speech at Somerset, Que., Aug. 2, 1887. (Trans.)

Geography and treaties have united to make [Canada's] unification difficult.

> GEORGE M. GRANT, address, Canadian Club, New York, 1887.

Those who are not of it bear this testimony, that once Canada was to them a mere geographical expression; now they know it not only as a great Colony of the crown, but all, save in name, a nation.

> G. MERCER ADAM, *Sir John Macdonald*, 1891, xvii; the phrase "a mere geographical expression" was used by Laurier, speech at Joliette, Aug. 17, 1911; taken from Metternich, before 1852, ref. to Italy.

Canada is a country of enormous distances.

> SIR JOHN WILLISON, *Railway question in Canada* (pam.), 1897; also, "A country of such magnificent distances", E.B. Osborn, *Greater Canada*, 1900, 105.

The Barrens.

> ANON., a common name for the Arctic regions and the northern part of the Canadian Shield.

Did you fight geography to make a Confederation? Then fight geography to keep a Confederation.

> GEORGE E. FOSTER, speech in North Toronto, Apr. 17, 1911.

In Canada man is making a nation in defiance of geographical conditions.

> W.L. GRANT, in *Geographical jour.*, Oct., 1911.

That the present Canada is not a natural geographical unit is an undeniable fact.

> OSCAR D. SKELTON, *The railway builders*, 1916, 28.

In the beginning was geography.

> W. STEWART WALLACE, in *Can. hist. rev.*, 1920, 139.

Geographically, Canada is a part of the North American continent. Is she, for war purposes, to regard herself as part of Europe? Is she to renounce all hope of future peace?

> JOHN S. EWART, *The independence papers*, II, 1930, 250.

The present Dominion emerged not in spite of geography but because of it.

> HAROLD A. INNIS, *The fur trade in Canada*, 1930, 397.

If some countries have too much history, we have too much geography.

> W.L. MACKENZIE KING, H. of C., *Debates*, June 18, 1936, 3868.

The extension of the American empire, the decline of its natural resources, and the emergence of metropolitan areas, supported capitalist expansion in Canada and reinforced the trend to regionalism. The pull to the north and south has tended to become stronger in contrast to the pull east and west.

> HAROLD A. INNIS, paper read before economics section, British Assoc. for the Advancement of Science, Nottingham, Eng., Sept. 11, 1937.

The real reason for Canada's tardy growth is to be found partly in her spiritual dependence on Great Britain, which has often paralyzed her energies, but to a far greater extent in her geographical proximity to the United States.

> JOHN MACCORMAC, *Canada; America's problem*, 1940, 200.

Rose on the map, with flakes as lakes of blue;
Fretted with rivers and provincial boundaries;
Straight at the base and jagged at the top –

The east-west dream mocks the north-south fact.

GUY GLOVER, "Canadian poem", 1947.

Even yet the landscape tends to overshadow the people.

DESMOND PACEY, *Creative writing in Canada*, 1952, 191.

Space enters the bloodstream. As you breathe it in, it is absorbed into a heightened awareness of sheer distance, the senses are dilated and seem to move in another element. This is an immense country.

CANADA. ROY. COMM. ON CANADA'S ECONOMIC PROSPECTS, *Final report*, 1957, 5.

The physical difficulties and complexities of this land have deeply affected our national character and history. They have made great virtues out of some of the sterner qualities − frugality and caution, discipline and endurance. Geography, perhaps even more than the influence of the churches, has made us puritans.

VINCENT MASSEY, address, Duke of Edinburgh's Second Commonwealth Study Conference, Univ. of Montreal, May 15, 1962.

The cruel, inhuman, negative splendour of his geographical space has made the French Canadian fundamentally different. By his land he is different. There is not the slightest doubt, for example, that at a certain level, hidden deep within himself, the French Canadian is a better interpreter of Chekhov's plays than of Racine's.

JEAN ETHIER-BLAIS, qu. by André Laurendeau in *Le magazine Maclean*, Feb., 1966, 44. (Trans.)

Mid-Canada Development Corridor.

RICHARD ROHMER, *Mid-Canada development corridor*, 1967, from the title of a report prepared for R. Rohmer by a planning firm, Acres Research and Planning Ltd.; ref. to the mid-Canada strip, east-west.

The size and emptiness of the land are two facts that are ever present in Canadian minds. Men are few and the solitudes are vast.

GEORGE WOODCOCK, *Canada and the Canadians*, 1970, 24.

Geology

In my youth, geology was nervously striving to accomodate itself to Genesis. Now it is Genesis that is striving to accomodate itself to geology.

GOLDWIN SMITH, *Lines of religious inquiry*, address, Toronto, 1904, 5.

Germans

Der Kaiser auf der Vaterland
Und Gott on high, all dings gommand,
Ve two, ach, don'd you understandt?
Meinself − und Gott . . .
Gott pulls mit me and I mit him −
Meinself − und Gott.

ALEXANDER MACGREGOR ROSE [GORDON], "Kaiser & Co.", written for the Montreal *Daily herald*, Oct., 1897.

Gerrymandering

Ontario, Ontario,
May surely claim her rights to know,
But now her foe's enslaving hand,
Has Gerrymandered all the land.

J.W. BENGOUGH, "Ontario, Ontario", May, 1882, written during election campaign.

Ghosts

As to ghosts or spirits they appear totally banished from Canada. This is too matter-of-fact country for such supernaturals to visit. Here there are no historical associations, no legendary tales of those that came before us. Fancy would starve for lack of marvellous food to keep her alive in the backwoods. We have neither fay nor fairy, ghost nor bogle, satyr nor wood-nymph; our very forests disdain to shelter dryad or hamadryad.

> CATHERINE PARR TRAILL, letter, May 9, 1833; *The backwoods of Canada*, 1839, 153.

Ghosts! There are no ghosts in Canada. The country is too new for ghosts. No Canadian is afearded of ghosts.

> SUSANNA MOODIE, *Roughing it in the bush*, 1852, Vol. 2, 13.

Canada is no place for ghosts. The country is too new for such gentry. We have no fine, old, ruined castles, crumbling monastic walls, or ivy-clad churches – no shelter here but the wild, wild wood.

> MAJOR SAMUEL STRICKLAND, *Twenty-seven years in Canada West*, 1853, Vol. 2, 184.

For I saw by the sickly moonlight,
    As I followed, bending low,
That the walking of the stranger
    Left no footmarks on the snow.

> CHARLES DAWSON SHANLEY, "The walker of the snow", in W.D. Lighthall, *Songs of the great Dominion*, 1889, 183.

Behold, behold the invulnerable ghosts
Of all past greatnesses about thee
    stand.

> MARJORIE PICKTHALL, "Canada to England", 1914.

A European can find nothing to satisfy the hunger of his heart. The air is too thin to breathe. He requires haunted woods, and the friendly presence of ghosts . . . For it is possible, at a pinch to do without gods. But one misses the dead.

> RUPERT BROOKE, *Letters from America*, 1916, 154-6.

The ghosts that walk our Canadian lanes crowd in on us from every nook of place and time. Our sense of time becomes multi-dimensional. Our sense of place, enlarged first by our own largeness, by the endless open horizon of our land, shatters all horizons.

> MALCOLM ROSS, *Our sense of identity*, 1954, xi.

It's only by our lack of ghosts we're haunted.

> EARLE BIRNEY, "Can.Lit.", 1962.

This western country is crammed
with the ghosts
of indians, haunting
the coastal stones and shores.

> JOHN NEWLOVE, "The pride", 1965.

Not only brave but prudent, and not
    only prudent but wise.
Go to sleep ghosts, we say, and wave
    our wise good-byes.

> GEORGE JOHNSTON, "Remembrance", 1966.

Gifts

I never look a gift horse in the eye.

> JOHN G. DIEFENBAKER, used during his campaign, general election, October, 1965.

Girls

It would be wise to suggest that girls destined for this country ought to be entirely free from any natural blemish or anything physically repulsive; that they should be healthy and strong for work in the country or at least have some skill at handwork.

> JEAN TALON, letter to Jean-Baptiste Colbert, Nov. 10, 1670 (Trans.), qu. in F. Parkman, *The old regime*, Vol. 2, 1915, 231.

Rich gals and handsome gals are seldom good for nothin' else but their cash or their looks.

> T.C. HALIBURTON, *The attaché*, 2nd. ser., 1844, 63.

Canadian girls are so pretty it is a relief to see a plain one now and then.

> MARK TWAIN, notebook written on a trip to Montreal, Nov., 1881.

How in the end, and to what man's desire
Shall all this yield, whose lips shall these lips meet?
One thing I know: if he be great and pure,
This love, this fire, this beauty shall endure;
Triumph and hope shall lead him by the palm:
But if not this, some differing thing he be,
That dream shall break in terror; he shall see
The whirlwind ripen, where he sowed the calm.

> ARCHIBALD LAMPMAN, "A forecast", 1888.

There's a girl at Calabogie, an' another at the Soo
An' with sparkin' and colloguin', I've been foolish with the two.

> WILLIAM H. DRUMMOND, "Marriage", 1908.

The littlest girl is a little woman. No boy knows this – and precious few grown-up men.

> ARNOLD HAULTAIN, *Hints for lovers*, 1909, 6.

In the short years between sixteen and twenty a girl's love will undergo rapid and startling developments.

> ARNOLD HAULTAIN, *Hints for lovers*, 1909, 9.

Don't think either that they are all dying to get married; because they are not. I don't say they wouldn't take an errant knight, or a buccaneer or a Hungarian refugee, but for the ordinary marriages of ordinary people they feel nothing but a pitying disdain. So it is that each one of them in due time marries an enchanted prince and goes to live in one of the little enchanted houses in the lower part of the town.

> STEPHEN LEACOCK, "The fore-ordained attachment of Zena Pepperleich and Peter Pupkin", *Sunshine sketches of a little town*, 1912, 169.

Mademoiselle from Armentieres, parley-voo?

> INGRAM (GITZ) RICE (d.1947), 5th Battery, Royal Canadian Artillery, 1915, song written to entertain the troops at a show in Armentieres, France.

I honour the girls who choose instead
The ancient duties, day by day,
As wives and mothers and makers of bread:
Good women give themselves away.

> TOM MACINNES, "Ballade of good women", 1918.

Last night in a land of triangles,
I lay in a cubicle, where
A girl in pyjamas and bangles
Slept with her hands in my hair.

> TOM MACINNES, "Zalinka", 1923.

Any girl, before she is married, is a kind of unexploded bomb.

> ROBERTSON DAVIES, *Tempest-tost*, 1951, 87.

"I'm not that kind of a girl", they explain to me. This is outrageous nonsense. Except for a statistical handful who have abnormally low metabolisms, everybody is that kind of a girl.

> DR. MARION HILLIARD, *A woman doctor looks at love and life*, 1957, 87.

Out of the sea I took you, laid my
    mouth
against your mouth and fed you with
    my breath
Sea lark, imaginary girl
who now insists on being real.

ALDEN NOWLAN, "Biography", 1961.

You are your breast's shape, the full
    length of your limbs,
You are your smile, your nailpolish,
    your dress,
Later I'll know you more. Still later
I'll know you even less.

GEORGE JONAS, "Eight lines for a script
girl", 1962.

Giving

The "giving" instinct of the average
French Canadian has been dulled by
generations of automatic contribution
to the bottomless collection plate of
the Roman Catholic Church.

PETER DESBARATS, The state of Quebec,
1965, 34.

Glaciers

the veins of bald glaciers blackened
white pulses of waterfalls
beat in the bare rockflesh

EARLE BIRNEY, "Biography", 1949.

The Globe, Toronto

When we commence with a man we
never let him go until we finish him.

ANON., quoted by Egerton Ryerson, letter in The Leader, July 12, 1863.

No journal ever did more to poison the
heart of society; the most virulent of
party organs, the most scandalous of
society papers would not have
wrought practically so much harm.

GOLDWIN SMITH, The Bystander, Jan.,
1883.

A literary despotism which struck
without mercy.

GOLDWIN SMITH, The Bystander, January, 1883.

Oh, I'm a Globe reporter.

MEL HAMMOND, in Toronto, 1906, when
asked at a Torrey-Alexander revivalist
meeting if he had made his peace with
God.

There were probably many thousand
voters in Ontario, especially among
the Scotch settlers (who always formed
the backbone of the Liberal party in
that province), who hardly read anything except their Globe and their
Bible, and whose whole political creed
was practically dictated to them by the
former.

SIR RICHARD CARTWRIGHT, Reminiscences, 1912, 9.

Glory

He doesn't know you can't catch the
glory on a hook and hold onto it. That
when you fish for the glory you catch
the darkness too. That if you hook
twice the glory you hook twice the
fear.

SHEILA WATSON, The double hook,
1959, 55.

Goals

A single goal satisfies most women; No
single goal ever yet satisfied the restless spirit of man.

ARNOLD HAULTAIN, Hints for lovers,
1909, 135.

God

A knowledge of God is the foundation
of all wisdom.

T.C. HALIBURTON, Sam Slick, 1840, 258.

We worship the spirit that walks
  unseen
Through our land of ice and snow:
We know not His face, we know not
  His place,
But His presence and power we know.

> THOMAS D'A. MCGEE, "The Arctic Indian's faith", 1858.

Let me see
Some portion of the truths that tend
By slow gradations up to Thee.

> CHARLES SANGSTER, "Mystery", 1860.

Yes, if you're a tramp in tatters,
  While the blue sky bends above,
You've got nearly all that matters,
  You've got God, and God is Love.

> ROBERT W. SERVICE, "Comfort", 1907.

The great world's heart is aching,
  aching fiercely in the night,
And God alone can heal it, and God
  alone give light;
And the men to bear that message, and
  to speak the living word,
Are you and I, my brothers, and the
  millions that have heard.

> FREDERICK G. SCOTT, "Our duty", 1909.

I took a day to search for God,
And found Him not. But as I trod
By rocky ledge, through woods
  untamed,
Just where one scarlet lily flamed,
I saw His footprint in the sod.

> BLISS CARMAN, "Vestigia", Harper's
> mag., 1921.

Between ourselves I must confess
Tho I may talk somewhat of God
Yet I have found no God, unless —
God is a state of consciousness.

> TOM MACINNES, "Unless", 1923.

The Spirit of God works through the
human mind in accordance with psychological laws, not otherwise.

> FREDERICK H. DUVERNET, Out of a
> scribe's treasure, 1927.

God judges us by what we would
  become,
  By the direction, not the distance
  gained;
Of all our shortcomings He knows the
  sum,
  Where we have failed, and what we
  have attained.

> H. ISABEL GRAHAM, Saint Ignace, 1935.

Wouldn't it be an awful sell for a lot of
us — all the artists and jokers, and
strivers-after-better-things — if God
turned out to be the Prime Mover of
capitalist respectability?

> ROBERTSON DAVIES, Leaven of malice,
> 1954, 158.

Each man creates God in his own
image.

> MORDECAI RICHLER, Son of a smaller
> hero, 1955, 44 and 232.

I study all day and pray all night.
My God, send me a sign of Thy
  coming
Or let me die.

> JAY MACPHERSON, "Ordinary people in
> the last days", 1957.

I worship God on my toes.

> F.H. VARLEY, qu. in Maclean's, Nov. 7,
> 1959, 64, in response to suggestion of
> Chester Massey that he kneel in prayer.

I looked up
to curse . . .
but then I saw
the reflection in God's eye.
Through his kaleidoscope
all turns are just as
beautiful.

> STEVE SMITH, "God's kaleidoscope",
> 1964.

The line we drew, you crossed,
and cross out, wholly forget,
at the faintest stirring of what
you know is love, is One
whose name has been, and is
and will be, the
I AM.

> MARGARET AVISON, "The word", 1966.

The universe has grown quite out of
my comprehension, and I can find no
comfortable deities at my fireside.

> A.R.M. LOWER, *My first seventy-five
> years*, 1967, 306.

– but the feeling I have
for something like this
replaces God

> ALFRED PURDY, "Arctic rhododendrons",
> 1967.

God has died and taken Man and Life
with Him.

> IRVING LAYTON, "Aphs", *The whole
> bloody bird*, 1969, 103.

What are the gods of this world but
organization, planning, efficiency, regimentation, discipline, and order?

> FRANK DAVEY, *Can. lit.*, No. 43, 1970,
> 57.

I met God yesterday.
He sat on a sort of throne
We were both slightly embarrassed.
"I have no answers for you," he said
finally.
I was relieved but tried not to show it.
I had no questions.

> GEORGE JONAS, *Happy hungry man*,
> 1970, 24.

I don't know what your relations to
God are, but mine are rather good. I
can talk to Him in a familiar tone and
He hasn't objected so far.

> PIERRE ELLIOTT TRUDEAU, reply to ques-
> tioner, Wingham, Ont., Oct. 18, 1972.

Gold

The Argonauts.

> ANON., a name given to the first miners
> in the Cariboo gold fields, 1850's.

The Fifty-eighters.

> ANON., a British Columbia term for
> prospectors in the Cariboo district, from
> the year of the discovery of gold, 1858.

Wherever there's a Father of Rivers
there's a mother of placers.

> ANON., B.C. coast miners, late 19th.
> century; the Indian name for the Fraser
> was, "Father of Rivers".

I wanted the gold, and I sought it;
  I scrabbled and mucked like a slave.
Was it famine or scurvy – I fought it;
  I hurled my youth into a grave.
I wanted the gold and I got it –
  Came out with a fortune last fall,–
Yet somehow life's not what I thought
    it,
  And somehow the gold isn't all.

> ROBERT W. SERVICE, "The spell of the
> Yukon", 1907.

Gold Rushes

Never, perhaps, was there so large an
immigration in so short a space of time
into so small a place.

> ALFRED WADDINGTON, *Fraser mines vin-
> dicated*, 1858, 16.

Golf

Golf is the favourite game in Scotland.
It is played everywhere. It is too slow a
game, however, for Canada. We
would go to sleep over it.

> JOHN B. MACLEAN, in 1891, qu. in Floyd
> S. Chalmers, *A gentleman of the press*,
> 1969, 62.

Golf may be played on Sunday, not being a game within the view of the law, but being a form of moral effort.

> STEPHEN LEACOCK, "Why I refuse to play golf", in *Other fancies*, 1923.

Golfers

And you see at a glance
among sportsmen they are the
  metaphysicians,
intent, untalkative, pursuing Unity.
(What finally gets you is their chastity)
And that no theory of pessimism is
  complete which altogether ignores
  them.

> IRVING LAYTON, "Golfers", 1955.

Good and Evil

Said the voice of Evil to the ear of
  Good,
  "Clasp thou my strong right hand,
Nor shall our clasp be known or
  understood
By any in the land".

> ISABELLA VALANCY CRAWFORD, "Gisli, the chieftain", 1905.

When the powers of good are present in the heart, and can find no outlet in action, they turn to evil.

> NELLIE L. MCCLUNG, *Sowing seeds in Danny*, 1908, 227.

A good man who goes wrong is just a bad man who has been found out.

> ROBERT C. (BOB) EDWARDS, Calgary *Eye Opener*, Sept. 22, 1917.

Say if you choose there is naught but
  good:
  Harden your heart and soften your
  brain:
Say wrong is right misunderstood:
  Close your eyes to filth and pain:
  Swear all is right and all is sane,
And all correct from days primeval:

And then – well, then what will
  you gain?
No man knoweth the end of evil.

> TOM MACINNES, "Ballade of evil", 1918.

Mine is the commonplace acceptance of good or evil.

> ALFRED PURDY, "O recruiting sergeants!", 1962.

An obsession with a nice scent
unknown among nature's great laws:
yet what men call good and evil
is but nail polish on their claws.

> IRVING LAYTON, "Nail polish", *Collected poems*, 1971, 540.

Good Taste

Good taste is the expression of a colossal incompetence. It is the "putting on" of the genteel audience as a mask or net by which to capture ambient snob appeal.

> MARSHALL MCLUHAN, *Through the vanishing point*, 1968, 213.

Goodness

There is no such thing as one's own good. Goodness is mutual, is communal; is only gained by giving and receiving.

> ARNOLD HAULTAIN, *Hints for lovers*, 1909, 309.

Good's the only warmth against a
  world
That freezes spring out of the years
  with lies.

> MALCOLM LOWRY, "In the shed", 1962.

It is as dangerous to overestimate the goodness of people as to underestimate their stupidity.

> IRVING LAYTON, "Aphs", *The whole bloody bird*, 1969, 83.

Gordon, Walter

The Toronto taxidermist who fills Mr. Pearson with flossy ideas.

JOHN G. DIEFENBAKER, ref. to Walter Gordon, election campaign, 1962.

Gossip

There was a young woman of Flores,
Who gave gossips material for stories.
    They said, "Only think
    Of that minx, and her mink,
And her men, and her motors, and
        mores!"

GEOFFREY B. RIDDEHOUGH, *Dance to the anthill*, 1972, 77.

Gourlay, Robert Fleming

There came to Oxford Robert
    Gourlay,
In his old age his health was poorly;
He was a relic of the past,
In his dotage sinking fast;
Yet he was erect and tall
Like noble ruined castle wall.
In early times they did him impeach
For demanding right of speech,
Now Oxford he wished to represent
In Canadian parliament,
But him the riding did not honour,
But elected Doctor Connor.

JAMES MACINTYRE, "Robert Fleming Gourlay"; Gourlay unsuccessfully contested Oxford Co. for the Ontario Legislative Assembly, 1860.

Government

It has been the cant of time immemorial to make mystery of the art of government. The folly of the million, and the cunning of the few in power, have equally strengthened the reigning belief; but it is false, deceitful and ruinous.

ROBERT GOURLAY, *Statistical account of Upper Canada*, 1822, II, 390.

The representative system is become the desire of all civilized nations, because it promises to nations a powerful lever to extirpate abuses; because it affords a popular efficacious action which penetrates into all parts of administration, and influences, in a salutary manner, all its agents, from the Sovereign to the lowest officer, recalling them continually to their destination, which is the peace and welfare of nations.

LOUIS JOSEPH PAPINEAU, speech, Montreal West election, Aug. 11, 1827. (Trans.).

The hour approaches in which the electors of Upper Canada are to decide whether a few factious and aspiring men shall yet a little longer mar the happiness of its inhabitants, or whether an honest and intelligent House of Assembly composed of our most deserving inhabitants will go hand in hand with the King and his excellent ministers in perfecting our political institutions and bestowing on us that free government which, although it is not happiness, is, when wisely employed, a sure means of procuring all the prosperity mankind can reasonably look for.

WILLIAM LYON MACKENZIE, address to the Reformers of Upper Canada, Toronto, Sept., 1834.

Government is founded on the authority, and is instituted for the benefit, of a people; when, therefore, any government long and systematically ceases to answer the great ends of its foundation the people have a natural right given them by the Creator to seek after and establish such institutions as will yield the greatest quantity of happiness to the greatest number.

TORONTO REFORMERS, Declaration of Aug., 1837.

Government, both in theory and practice, resides with the people.

> T.C. HALIBURTON, *Sam Slick*, 1838, 52.

Not government merely, but society itself seems to be almost dissolved; the vessel of the State is not in great danger only, as I had been previously led to suppose, but looks like a complete wreck.

> LORD DURHAM, letter to Glenelg, Aug. 9, 1838.

The government of the country *must* be carried on. It *ought* to be carried on with vigour. If that can be done in no other way than by mutual concessions and a coalition of parties, they become necessary. And those who, under such circumstances assume the arduous duties of becoming parties to them, so far from deserving the opprobrium that is too frequently and often too successfully heaped upon them, have, in my opinion, the strongest claims upon public sympathy and support.

> ROBERT BALDWIN, letter to Francis Hincks, Sept. 22, 1854.

Self-government would be utterly annihilated if the views of the Imperial Government were to be preferred to those of the people of Canada. It is therefore the duty of the present government distinctly to affirm the right of the Canadian Legislature to adjust the taxation of the people in the way they deem best, even if it should unfortunately happen to meet the disapproval of the Imperial ministry. Her Majesty cannot be advised to disallow such acts, unless her advisers are prepared to assume the administration of the affairs of the colony, irrespective of the views of its inhabitants.

> SIR ALEXANDER T. GALT, dispatch, Canada. *Sessional papers*, 1860. No. 38.

If coalition between two parties means that for the sake of emolument or position they sacrifice principle, then coalition government ought not to receive the confidence of the people. But if it means the junction of a number of men, who, forgetting old quarrels which have been wiped out, and who instead of raking up the ashes after the fire of dissension had burned away, finally extinguished it, and refused to prolong discord – then I say that coalition is the act of true patriots.

> SIR JOHN A. MACDONALD, speech, 1861; qu. E.B. Biggar, *Anecdotal life*, 1891, 180.

Happily, political institutions kill as seldom as they cure.

> GOLDWIN SMITH, *Lectures on modern history*, 1861, 20.

Retrenchment is the immediate duty, the duty of the day and the hour, – but the government must lead as well as save, it must march as well as fortify, it must originate plans for the future, as well as correct the errors of the past.

> THOMAS D'ARCY MCGEE, speech in Ottawa, Oct. 14, 1862.

In Canada you are reminded of the government every day. It parades itself before you. It is not content to be the servant, but will be the master; and every day it goes out to the Plains of Abraham or to the Champ de Mars and exhibits itself and its tools.

> HENRY DAVID THOREAU, *A Yankee in Canada*, 1866, (1961, 106).

Peace, order and good government.

> BRITISH NORTH AMERICA ACT, 1867, sect. 91; also, Unemployment Relief Act, 1934, sect. 2.

Whereas, it is admitted by all men, as a fundamental principle, that the public authority commands the obedience and respect of its subjects. It is also admitted that a people, when it has no Government, is free to adopt one form of Government in preference to another to give or to refuse allegiance to that which is proposed.

> PROVISIONAL GOVERNMENT OF THE NORTHWEST, Proclamation, Dec. 8, 1869, signed by John Bruce and Louis Riel.

For the honour of the country, no government should exist which has a shadow of suspicion resting upon it, and for that reason I cannot give it my support.

> DONALD A. SMITH (Lord Strathcona) H. of C., *Debates*, Nov. 5, 1873, on the "Pacific Scandal".

Canada is a hard country to govern.

> SIR JOHN A. MACDONALD, a favourite saying. Also used by Laurier, see his letter to John Willison, March 7, 1905, "This is a difficult country to govern".

The only conceivable basis for government in the New World is the national will; and the political problem of the New World is how to build a strong, stable, enlightened and impartial government on that foundation.

> GOLDWIN SMITH, *Political destiny of Canada*, 1878, 57.

We will govern our own country, we will put on the taxes ourselves. If we choose to misgovern ourselves we will do so, and we do not desire England, Ireland or Scotland to tell us we are fools.

> SIR JOHN A. MACDONALD, speech, Toronto, Nov. 3, 1881.

To govern is to have the courage, at a given moment, to risk power to save a principle.

> HENRI BOURASSA, Oct. 13, 1899 to Sir Wilfrid Laurier, qu. in J. Schull, *Laurier*, 1965, 384.

A people for high dreamings meant,
But damned by too much government.

> WILFRED CAMPBELL, in Campbell and Martin, *Canada*, 1907, 45.

Is not our whole system of government built upon the principle that all political power is vested in the people at large?

> *MANITOBA FREE PRESS*, June 18, 1914, 13.

A Government upon the defensive is a Government in distress.

> SIR JOHN WILLISON, *Reminiscences*, 1919, 31.

The people of Canada get better government than they deserve.

> SIR JOHN WILLISON, *Reminiscences*, 1919, 279.

Group government.

> ANON., a term used to describe the form of government advocated by Henry Wise Wood, especially in his speech at Crossfield, Oct. 21, 1919.

It is the small matters of individual and local interest that determine the fate of governments.

> J.D. MACLEAN, to H. McCutcheon, Apr. 20, 1920. Pub.Arch.B.C., Prov. Sec'y. Letterbook outward.

It is not the business of the Government to maintain the people – it is the business of the people to maintain the Government.

> JOHN OLIVER, Premier of British Columbia, 1918-27.

Policies which do not command a reasonable measure of support in each of the provinces are obviously not national and can only be enforced at the country's peril.

> J.W. DAFOE, 1927, in Cecil B. Hurst, *Great Britain and the Dominions*, 1928, 178.

It is commonplace that Canada has been the laboratory of the British Empire; a place where theories of government have had their first practical test; where, upon the breakdown of theories, other policies have been suggested and applied.

> JOHN W. DAFOE, 1927 in, Cecil B. Hurst, *Great Britain and the Dominions*, 1928, 178.

One-man Government.

> W.L. MACKENZIE KING, H. of C., *Debates*, Mar. 16, 1931, a reference to R.B. Bennett, Prime Minister.

The story of government in Newfoundland is one of the grossest cases of maladministration that can be produced since the Middle Ages and, if the politicians responsible for it had existed in those days, they would have received very short shrift.

> P.J.H. HANNON, Great Britain, H. of C., *Debates*, Vol. 284, Dec. 12, 1933, 280.

In our day any citizen who tried to follow intelligently all the public affairs and the public elections of his township, his county, his municipality, his school board and his sanitary district, his Province and his Dominion his Empire and his League of Nations, would have no time for anything else.

> STEPHEN LEACOCK, Presidential address, Can.Pol.Sci.Assoc., 1934.

Under a Liberal regime the Prime Minister states the foreign policy and the Cabinet Ministers state the policy for internal affairs without consultation with any of the members.

> J.A. GLEN, later Speaker of the H. of C., 1940-1945, letter to J.W. Dafoe, Oct. 9, 1936. (Pub.Arch.Can.)

Governments begin to die as soon as they gain power, and finally the popular will is accomplished when a government is defeated – it being only incidental that the opposing party is placed in the seats of the mighty.

> R.J. MANION, *Life is an adventure*, 1936, 266.

It is not easy to govern a country, part of whose people are more British than the king and part more Catholic than the pope.

> A.R.M. LOWER, *Colony to nation*, 1946, 417.

The government is becoming yearly more assertive and its activities more widespread; it has long since ceased to regard as its sole or even its chief function the enunciation of general rules of conduct and the assigning of punishments for their breach, and it is quite prepared to direct and drive people into righteousness; it has taken the position that it will not only punish deviations from its rules, but it will endeavour in many areas of social life to prevent such deviations taking place on any significant scale.

> R.M. DAWSON, *The government of Canada*, 1947, 314.

There are only two kinds of government – the scarcely tolerable and the absolutely unbearable.

> JOHN W. DAFOE, qu. in George V. Ferguson, *John W. Dafoe*, 1948, 59.

Government is an art, not a science, and an adventure, not a planned itinerary; and the humanities have been its oldest masters and surest guides.

> DONALD CREIGHTON, *Queen's quart.*, Vol. 61, Winter, 1954-55, 426.

Where else could I get as big a job?

> C.D. HOWE, to Walter Gordon when asked what he liked about his experience in politics, qu. in Denis Smith, *Gentle patriot*, 1973, 30.

I am one of those who believe that this Party has a sacred trust, a trust in accordance with the traditions of Macdonald. It has an appointment today with destiny, to plan and build for a greater Canada . . . one Canada, with equality of opportunity for every citizen and equality for every province from the Atlantic to the Pacific.

> JOHN G. DIEFENBAKER, opening speech, 1957 election campaign, Toronto, Apr. 25.

As long as I am in power no person is going to suffer because of the inaction of the Government.

> JOHN G. DIEFENBAKER, election campaign, Mar., 1958, Windsor, Ont.

Federal and provincial governments were not thought of as competing units, almost sworn enemies, but as complementary institutions all engaged in their allotted tasks for the benefit of the whole people of Canada.

> FRANK R. SCOTT, address, Roy. Soc. of Canada, June, 1961.

Not life, liberty and happiness, but peace, order and good government are what the national government of Canada guarantees. Under these, it is assumed, life, liberty and happiness may be achieved, but by each according to his taste. For the society of allegiance admits of a diversity the society of compact does not, and one of the blessings of Canadian life is that there is no Canadian way of life, much less two, but a unity under the Crown admitting of a thousand diversities.

> W.L. MORTON, *The Canadian identity*, 1961, 111.

The farmers, whose views on government were a mixture of idealism and ignorance, destroyed the party system and in effect the foundation on which cabinet government rests.

> M.S. DONNELLY, *The government of Manitoba*, 1963, 97.

The majority of French Canadians tend to look upon government, not as an agency whose power and authority stems from the people, not in the sense of 'our government', but as a force external to, and above the people, which makes laws they must obey and levies taxes they must pay.

> HERBERT F. QUINN, *The Union Nationale*, 1963, 18.

The dispute between levels of government in Canada is essentially connected with the power politics of the various groups of people involved and has very little to do with the welfare of the individual citizens of the country.

> MARC LALONDE, in P-A. Crépeau and C.B. Macpherson, eds., *The future of Canadian federalism*, 1965, 83.

Sometimes the government listens too much to experts and not enough to practical ideas.

> W.A.C. BENNETT, qu. in P. Sherman, *Bennett*, 1966, 67.

The tumultuous events of the past four days have pointed up in an unexpectedly dramatic way what has always been a major flaw in the makeup of the Liberal party: that it consists of a group of politicians who have little faith or interest in Parliament and prefer to transact the nation's business in the serene sanctity of the cabinet chamber and the ministerial office.

> PETER NEWMAN, Toronto *Star*, Feb. 22, 1968, 1, on the Government's defeat in the House of Commons by a minority Opposition.

There's nobody to tell me how the country should be run. I tell them.

> PIERRE E. TRUDEAU, on TV, June, 1968, qu. by Pauline Jewett in *Maclean's*, Sept., 1968, 8.

Canadian governments from the beginning have been governments of merchants.

> VERNON C. FOWKE, in Norman Ward, ed., *Politics in Saskatchewan*, 1968, 208.

When Washington sneezes, London, Tokyo, Bonn and Paris catch cold, and Ottawa – especially if a Liberal Government is in office – comes down with the flu.

> ANON., this variant qu. by Hugh Keenleyside in J.H. Redekop, *Star-spangled beaver*, 1971, 7.

At the heart of all governments there is chaos.

> A.R.M. LOWER, qu. in *Queen's quart.*, Vol. 80, 1973, 617.

[The goals of government] should be to realize maximum human dignity, maximum human welfare, maximum environmental quality, and minimum violence in human relationships.

> PIERRE E. TRUDEAU, to a Parliamentary dinner in Australia, qu. in *Maclean's*, Apr., 1972, 7.

Government Departments

A department of delay, a department of circumlocution, a department in which people could not get business done, a department which tired men to death who undertook to get any business transacted with it.

> SIR CLIFFORD SIFTON, H. of C., *Debates*, 1906, 4270, referring to the Department of the Interior.

There was correspondence between the local office and the Land Board in Winnipeg; from the Land Board to the Head Office here; correspondence backwards and forwards and forwards and backwards until the men dealing with the matter would lose track of it altogether.

> SIR CLIFFORD SIFTON, H. of C., *Debates*, 1906, 4270.

Government House

A miserable little house.

> GEORGE BROWN, on Rideau Hall, letter to Sir John A. Macdonald, Aug. 15, 1864.

Government House is a high-class inn at a busy cross-roads.

> ANON., qu. in Janet Adam Smith, *John Buchan*, 1965, 430.

Government, Responsible

You must place the Government in advance of public opinion. You must give those in whom the people have some confidence an interest in preserving the *system* of your Government, and maintaining the connection with the Mother Country, and then you will hear no more of grievances because real ones will be redressed, imaginary ones will be forgotten.

> ROBERT BALDWIN, letter to Lord Durham, Aug. 23, 1838.

If the Canadians are to be deprived of representative government, it would be better to do it in a straightforward way, than to attempt to establish a permanent system of government on the basis of what all mankind would regard as mere electoral frauds. It is not in North America that men can be cheated by an unreal semblance of representative government, or persuaded that they are out-voted, when, in fact, they are disfranchised.

> LORD DURHAM, *Report*, 1839. (Ed. Lucas, 1912, II, 299.

One event after another has occurred, calculated to impair confidence in the excellence of what by courtesy has been called Responsible Government.

> GEORGE SHEPPARD, in Toronto *Globe*, 1859, qu., *Can. hist. rev.*, 1935, 246.

Responsible government developed in reaction rather than in response to the true democratic spirit of the Canadian people.

> S.D. CLARK, *Movements of political protest in Canada, 1640-1840*, 1959, 4.

Governor-General

He may flutter and struggle in the net as some well-meaning Governors have done but he must at last resign himself to his fate; and like a snared bird be content with the narrow limits assigned him by his keepers.

> JOSEPH HOWE, letter to Lord John Russell, Sept. 18, 1839.

The Lord of the Bed-chamber sat in
    his shirt
(And D — dy the pliant was there),
And his feelings appeared to be very
    much hurt,
    And his brow overclouded with
    care.

> JOSEPH HOWE, "Lord of the Bed-chamber", (first verse), in *Nova Scotian*, May 20, 1845, on Lord Falkland, Governor.

If that system be continued, some colonist will, by and by, or I am much mistaken, hire a black fellow to horsewhip a Lieutenant-Governor.

> JOSEPH HOWE, speech in N.S. Assembly, Feb. 20, 1846; a reference to Lord Falkland who denounced Howe's friends, including the Speaker, to the Colonial Office in a dispatch later made public.

A Governor-General should be something more than a drill-sergeant, or a schoolmaster.

> TORONTO *GLOBE*, Oct. 13, 1860.

I would rather be the proprietor of the *Globe* newspaper for a few years than be governor-general of Canada, much less a trumpery little province.

> GEORGE BROWN, letter to his family, May 13, 1864.

One doesn't know what can induce a man to accept the post of Governor-General unless he should be a misanthrope or have hosts of relations at home whom he is anxious to make distant.

> GEORGE MACLEAN ROSE, *The great country, or impressions of America*, 1868, 286.

My only guiding star in the conduct and maintenance of my official relations with your public men is the Parliament of Canada — in fact, I suppose I am the only person in the Dominion whose faith in the wisdom and in the infallibility of Parliament is never shaken.

> LORD DUFFERIN, speech in Halifax, Aug. 8, 1873.

You may depend upon my doing my very best both to weld this Dominion into an Imperium solid enough to defy all attraction from its powerful neighbour across the Line, and to perpetuate its innate loyalty to the Mother Country.

LORD DUFFERIN, letter to the Earl of Carnarvon, Apr. 25, 1874.

I cannot describe to you the feeling of loneliness without peace, and of dull oppression which weighs upon the spirits of a person in my position.

LORD DUFFERIN, letter to the Earl of Carnarvon, Apr. 25, 1874.

[The Governor-General is like] the humble functionary we see superintending the working of some complicated mass of chain-driven machinery. This personage merely walks about with a little tin vessel of oil in his hand and he pours in a drop here and a drop there, as occasion or the creaking of a joint may require, while his utmost vigilance is directed to no higher aim than the preservation of his wheels and cogs from the intrusion of dust, grits, or other foreign bodies.

LORD DUFFERIN, speech at National Club, Toronto, Jan. 12, 1877.

I admit the responsibility of the Ministers for every utterance made by the Governor-General respecting public affairs, or which has any bearing on public affairs.

ALEXANDER MACKENZIE, H. of C., Debates, Mar. 1, 1877, 375.

If you come officially, tell the Governor-General to go to Hell. If you come unofficially you can go there yourself.

SIR JOHN A. MACDONALD, to secretaries trying to rouse him from a drunken stupor in order to greet the new Governor-General, the Marquis of Lorne, Halifax, November, 1878.

The King who reigns and does not govern is represented by a Governor-General who does the same, and the Governor-General solemnly delegates his impotence to a puppet Lieutenant-Governor in each province. Religious Canada prays each Sunday that they may govern well, on the understanding that heaven will never be so unconstitutional as to answer her prayer.

GOLDWIN SMITH, Canada and the Canadian question, 1891, 147.

The Earl [of Aberdeen] himself was a sensible and inoffensive man, but his wife was the most aggressive busybody who ever presided over Rideau Hall.

SATURDAY NIGHT, Toronto, Oct. 4, 1898.

We had far rather that he should speak his mind than that he should waste our time − and his own − in telling us how exceedingly green our grass is, and how much better we are than other people he has ever had the good fortune to meet.

TORONTO STAR, May 2, 1905.

Governors-General are not supposed to be of any real use to the country, but Canada has a right to expect that they will control themselves sufficiently to avoid injuring the land from which they draw a fat salary.

WINNIPEG TRIBUNE, Aug. 28, 1905, 4.

For nearly five years I have endeavoured in my public utterances to call the attention of the people to the importance of keeping before them high national and Imperial ideals. For nearly five years I have, quite conscious of my constitutional limitations, walked the tight-rope of platitudinous generalities and I am not aware of having made any serious slip.

LORD GREY, speech to Canadian Club, Winnipeg, Oct. 13, 1909.

I hope that my colleagues and I shall not be found wanting in respect or indeed in admiration for the wide military experience of Your Royal Highness and the high position which you hold as a Field-Marshal in His Majesty's Forces. It would appear to us that the matters under consideration do not call so much for the exercise of military skill or the application of military experience as the consideration of international law and the exercise of the common-place quality of common sense.

SIR ROBERT BORDEN, letter to Duke of Connaught, Gov.-Gen., Aug. 4, 1916.

The Governor-General of today is little more than a convenient peg on which to hang our system of government.

R. MACGREGOR DAWSON, *Principle of official independence*, 1922, 218.

The Governor-General of a Dominion is the representative of the Crown, holding in all essential respects the same position in relation to the administration of public affairs in the Dominion as is held by His Majesty the King in Great Britain.

IMPERIAL CONFERENCE, London, 1926. *Summary of proceedings*, 1926, 14.

We don't want any more Mintos. We don't want any more Greys. We certainly don't want any more Byngs. I sometimes wonder if we want any more of 'em at all, but we really do.

JOHN W. DAFOE, to George V. Ferguson, Mar. 21, 1927.

Man, according to Aristotle, is a political animal, but there is an exception in the case of a Governor-General. His views on public policy can only be the views of his Ministers. If he touches on the subject he must confine himself to

what may be called Governor-Generalities.

LORD TWEEDSMUIR, address, Canadian-American Conference, Kingston, Ont., June 17, 1937.

Nice chap, Massey, but makes one feel a bit of a savage.

LORD TWEEDSMUIR, comment on Vincent Massey, attributed by Thomas Franck, Vancouver *Sun*, July 11, 1964, 3; see also R. Braddon, *Roy Thomson of Fleet Street*, 1965, 139.

I would not like to think that a Canadian, alone of the Queen's subjects, would not be considered fit to represent her in Canada.

LOUIS ST. LAURENT, on appointing Vincent Massey Governor-General, Jan. 25, 1952, qu. in B. Hutchison, *Mr. Prime Minister*, 1964, 298.

Locomobility is an important quality for a Governor-General.

LORD TWEEDSMUIR, qu. by Vincent Massey, Annual Dinner of the Canadian Press, Toronto, Apr. 18, 1956.

Each year they give me their
　　combined advice
On plans to implement – or put on
　　ice.
Their views I give you, seated on the
　　Throne,
Reading the pages in a level tone.
Under their orders I can have no
　　choice,
The country hears me as His Master's
　　Voice,
Transmitting policies that are not
　　mine;
I'm just an old Trans-Canada Pipe
　　Line!

VINCENT MASSEY, address at Press Gallery dinner, Ottawa, Apr. 28, 1956.

I've travelled on my broad itinerary
A mari usque several times *ad mare.*
(There were, alas, imposed upon the
　　mileage,
The photographs; we might call them
　　the smileage.)

> VINCENT MASSEY, address at Press Gallery dinner, Ottawa, Apr. 28, 1956.

God save our gracious
　　Governor-General
Even though his appointment is just
　　protemoral
God save him just the same.

> PAUL HIEBERT, *Willows revisited*, 1967,
> 14; suggested anthem by John Swivel
> and Osiris Jones-Jones, associates of
> Sarah Binks.

My sole responsibility now is to see
that the government which you choose
from time to time, or rather the Prime
Minister, takes up the reins of office
and provides you with the government
you deserve. From then on I do constitutionally and as inconspicuously as
possible, whatever the Prime Minister
tells me to do.

> GOV.-GEN. ROLAND MICHENER, qu. in G.
> Frankfurter, *Baneful domination*, 1971,
> 295.

Grace Before Meals

We are thankful for these and all the
good things of life. We recognize that
they are a part of our common heritage and come to us through the
efforts of our brothers and sisters the
world over. What we desire for ourselves we wish for all. To this end may
we take our share in the world's work
and the world's struggles.

> J.S. WOODSWORTH, grace before meat, in
> *The first story of the Labor Church*,
> 1920.

Lord grant us capacity,
Longevity, elasticity,
Avoiding obesity.

> E.J. PRATT, grace used in his home. qu. by
> Earle Birney in *Our living tradition*,
> Ser. 3 & 4, 1959, 147.

Graft

Graft is still graft even if you call it a
commission.

> ROBERT C. (BOB) EDWARDS, Calgary *Eye
> Opener;* attributed.

The Bible says you should not muzzle
the ox which is threshing your corn. I
am sorry I cannot help you.

> ALEXANDER C. RUTHERFORD, Premier of
> Alberta, to Martin Nordegg in 1909, qu.
> in his *The possibilities of Canada are
> truly great*, 1971, 116, indicating that
> he did not wish to deter a high government official from becoming involved
> in a mining venture.

Grain Elevators

Up from the low-roofed dockyard
　　warehouses
it rises blind and babylonian
like something out of legend.

> A.M. KLEIN, "Grain elevator", 1948.

A box: cement hugeness, and
　　rightangles –
merely the sight of it leaning in my
　　eyes
mixes up continents and makes a
　　montage
of inconsequent time and
　　uncontiguous space.

> A.M. KLEIN, "Grain elevator", 1948.

Grand Trunk Pacific Railway

We cannot wait, because time does not
wait; we cannot wait because, in these
days of wonderful development, time
lost is doubly lost; we cannot wait,
because at this moment there is a
transformation going on in the condi-

tions of our national life which it would be folly to ignore and a crime to overlook.

SIR WILFRID LAURIER, H. of C., *Debates*, July 30, 1903, 7659, on the building of the Grand Trunk Pacific Railway.

[The Grand Trunk Pacific will] roll back the map of Canada and add depth to the country.

SIR WILFRID LAURIER, 1904; attributed.

For our own benefit, usefulness and dignity Canadians should be masters of their own country, and should have their all-Canadian route.

SIR WILFRID LAURIER, speech in Quebec, Oct. 5, 1904, on the Grand Trunk Pacific project.

That mad route, unknown, unsurveyed and uninhabited, through the North country, over granite ranges, from Winnipeg to Quebec.

MONTREAL *STAR*, Jan. 23, 1904, on the Grand Trunk Pacific project.

Grand Trunk Railway

The Grand Trunk Railway governs Canada at the present moment. Its power is paramount. The Ministry are mere puppets in its hands and dance whatever tune the Company pipes.

TORONTO *GLOBE*, Apr. 22, 1857.

The management of this railway is an organized mess — I will not say, a sink of iniquity.

EDWARD WATKIN, letter to his wife, Sept. 6, 1861.

What would Montreal be without the Grand Trunk? It has assured for us the commerce of the West.

SIR GEORGE-ETIENNE CARTIER, speech at a banquet given in his honour, Montreal, 1866.

While it is true, Mr. Speaker, that the Grand Trunk Railway stock was watered to the point of saturation, does my hon. friend from Shelburne and Queen's think that because it was thus watered to the point of saturation it should be entirely in the hands of Baptists?

SAMUEL W. JACOBS, H. of C., *Debates*, June 1, 1920, 3028, referring to remark of Wm. S. Fielding that the stock was mainly in the hands of Jews in London.

Grasshoppers

In looking toward the sun the sight resembled a heavy snowstorm of large flakes, passing through the air with great rapidity. They were upon the ground piled one upon the other so that we crushed thousands with every revolution of the carriage wheels.

JAMES TROW, *A trip to Manitoba*, 1875, 49.

The grasshoppers spin into mine ear
A small innumerable sound.

ARCHIBALD LAMPMAN, "Heat", 1889.

Gratitude

I don't wear gratitude
well. Or hats.

MARGARET ATWOOD, "Letters, towards and away", 1966.

Graveyards

We'll bury old Guibord
In the consecrated ground . . .
Guibord's coffin weighs exactly forty tons.

ANON., Montreal ditty, (Trans.) Joseph Guibord was under excommunication when he died 1869, and was not buried until 1875, because of opposition from the Church.

This is the paradise of common things,
  The scourged and trampled here
    find peace to grow,
  The frost to furrow and the wind to
    sow,
The mighty sun to time their
  blossomings;
  And now they keep
A crown reflowering on the tombs of
  kings,
  Who earned their triumph and have
  claimed their sleep.

  DUNCAN CAMPBELL SCOTT, "In the country churchyard", 1893.

Unaltering rest their perfect being
  cloaks –
A thing too vast to hear or feel or see–
Children of Silence and Eternity,
They know no season but the end of
  time.

  ARCHIBALD LAMPMAN, "In Beechwood cemetery", 1900.

Just think! some night the stars will
  gleam
Upon a cold grey stone,
And trace a name with silver beam,
And lo! 'twill be your own.

  ROBERT SERVICE, "Just think", 1912.

Cometh the night. The wind falls low,
  The trees swing slowly to and fro;
  Around the church the headstones
    grey
  Cluster like children strayed away
But found again and folded so.

  JOHN MCCRAE, "The night cometh", 1913.

Long years ago they went to take their
  rest
Beneath the spreading trees on yonder
  hill –
The field they cleared for use at God's
  behest,
And where the quiet tenants of his will
Are undisturbed of any joy or ill.

  WILLIAM E. MARSHALL, "Brookfield", 1914.

Stony fields and lonely roads,
  Meagre hamlets, very lean,
And most prosperous graveyards
  Lying all between.

  KATHERINE HALE, "Northern graveyards", 1923.

Now am I anchored; and forever now
Must here I tarry. For a woman gave
A child to me; and to the ground I
  bow;
My roots are growing down into a
  grave.

  FREDERICK PHILIP GROVE, "The dirge", written on the death of his daughter, 1927, qu. in *Dalhousie rev.*, Vol. 43, 1963, 239.

Motion and rest, love and hate, heaven
  and hell
Here cease their Punch-and-Judy
  show: all is well.
There is no pain in the graveyard or
  the voice
Whispering to the tombstones:
  "Rejoice, rejoice".

  IRVING LAYTON, "The graveyard", 1968.

Gravity

The gravest Beast is the Ass;
  the gravest Bird is the Owl,
The gravest Fish is the Oyster;
  the gravest Man is the Fool.

  GRIP; an independent journal of humour and caricature, founded by Phillips Thompson, May 24, 1873, its motto.

Greatness

He's great who's happy anywhere.

  CHARLES HEAVYSEGE, qu., *Canadian birthday book,* 1887, 100.

Being great is apparently a very pleasant pastime.

> PETER MCARTHUR, *To be taken with salt*, 1903, 148.

We shall not be great simply because we have a productive soil and natural resources; we shall be great only if we have our quota of great engineers, great authors, great orators, great sculptors and painters, great statesmen and great journalists.

> W.F. OSBORNE, Canadian Club, Montreal, Jan. 27, 1919.

To have greatly tried and to have failed; to have greatly wished and to be denied; to have greatly longed for purity and to be sullied; to have greatly craved for life and to receive death: all that is the common lot of greatness upon earth.

> FREDERICK PHILIP GROVE, *It needs to be said*, 1929, 87.

People do not become great by deliberately pursuing the unique rather than the universal.

> JOHN W. HOLMES, in D.L.B. Hamlin, ed., *Diplomacy in evolution*, 1961, 40.

Diplomat, democrat, economist, social philosopher, major prophet, John Kenneth Galbraith is one of the great men of our age. Certainly, he and Marshall McLuhan are the two greatest modern Canadians that the United States has produced.

> ANTHONY BURGESS, *Saturday rev.*, Apr. 20, 1968, 34.

Greed

It is the times that have changed, not the man. He is there still, just as greedy and rapacious as ever, but no greedier: and we have just the same social need of his greed as a motive power in industry as we ever had, and indeed a worse need than before.

> STEPHEN LEACOCK, *My discovery of England*, 1922, 163.

Greed is an affliction of the soul.

> MARGARET LAURENCE, "The pure diamond man", 1963, in *The tomorrow tamer*, 194.

Grief

One half the world lives by the grief
The other half endure;
And fine professions fatten on
The crimes they cannot cure.

> J.R. (i.e. ANDREW JOHN) RAMSAY, "One hundred years from now", 1886.

Idle to grieve, the light is on the
  highway,
There are mountain meadows to
  achieve,
Beyond in the pass the airy heights are
  my way,
Idle to grieve, glad heart, idle to
  grieve.

> DUNCAN CAMPBELL SCOTT, "Idle to grieve", 1921.

If you have lain in the night
And felt the old tears run
In their channels worn in the heart,
Pity me, Mary.

> MARJORIE PICKTHALL, *The woodcarver's wife*, 1922, 57.

The mind grown numb
How can the soul support
A grief so vast as this? Each dream is
  dead,
And not one hope remains as last
  resort.

> CLARA MAE BERNHARDT, "The seven last words", 1942.

Carry your grief alone,
No other wants it,
Each man has his own,
A fool flaunts it.

> ROBERT FINCH, "Alone", 1946.

What was it on the midnight cried
In the lapsed garden of green solitude?
A strangled sob of grief escaping
The bronze-green throat of the bird of
   pride.

   DOUGLAS LE PAN, "The peacock", 1953.

Daily, I flagellate myself for sins
   undone.
The simplest act of living sours
in this infant grief.

   GLEN SIEBRASSE, "Pupil", 1965.

Do not salt the stew with tears
Nor bake a bitter cherry pie
Grief will not stitch the tearing years
Nor anger arch our falling sky.

   JEAN BOUDIN, "Kitchen song", 1967.

The world's ill-handled sorrows
   intervene
And all the ornaments of clouds and
   trees
And water-broken sun denounce their
   joy
Roccoco to the grief.

   RALPH GUSTAFSON, "Gothic fugue",
   1972.

Gross National Product

The trouble, in a word, is that the
17th-century stone mason could help
Wren build a cathedral in honor of
God, but no assembly-line worker sup-
poses, in his wildest imaginings, that
he helps General Motors build an
automobile in honor of the GNP.

   BRUCE HUTCHISON, Globe and Mail,
   Nov. 25, 1970.

Why do western governments continue to worship at the temple of Gross
National Product? Isn't it time we paid
heed to resource exhaustion, to environmental deterioration, to the social
costs of over-crowding, to the extent of
solid waste disposal? Shouldn't we, in
short, be replacing our reliance on
GNP with a more revealing figure –

a new statistic which might be called
Net Human Benefit?

   PIERRE E. TRUDEAU, address, Liberal
   Party of Vancouver, May 1, 1971.

Index of net human benefit.

   PIERRE E. TRUDEAU, suggested as replacement for GNP as more accurate measure of society's standard of living, 1971
   (Can. ann. rev., 1971, 318). See above.

Group of Seven

The artists invite adverse criticism.
Indifference is the greatest evil they
have to contend with. But they would
ask you – do you read books that
contain only what you already know?
If not, they argue, you should hardly
want to see pictures that show you
what you can already see for yourselves.

   GROUP OF SEVEN, catalogue of the
   group's first exhibition, Toronto, 1920.

Oh, God, what have I seen? Where
have I been? Something has spoken to
the very soul of me, wonderful,
mighty, not of this world. Chords way
down in my being have been touched.
Dumb notes have struck chords of
wonderful tone. Something has called
out of somewhere. Something in me is
trying to answer.

   EMILY CARR, Journals, Nov. 17, 1927;
   Hundreds and thousands, 1966, 6; after
   seeing the Group's paintings in Toronto.

Groups

It is indisputable that some form of
group affiliation lying between the
extremes of the mass and the individual is a prerequisite for mutual health.

   JOHN PORTER, Vertical mosaic, 1965, 73.

Growth

The law of our youth is growth, the law of our growth is progress.

> EGERTON RYERSON, *Speeches and addresses*, 1865, 173.

Not with vain noise
  The great work grows,
Nor with foolish voice,
  But in repose, —
Not in the rush
But in the hush.

> CHARLES G.D. ROBERTS, "A song of growth", 1893.

To grow may mean to outgrow, to be charged with inconstancy as infertile ground is left for pastures new.

> GEORGE ILES, *Canadian stories*, 1918, 177.

All God's word is but one word 'grow'.

> PETER MCARTHUR, "The priest of Amon-Ra", (unpublished), qu. in W.A. Deacon, *Peter McArthur*, 1923, 122.

Things growing out of the ground are part of the unconsidered miracle in which we live.

> ARCHIBALD MACMECHAN, *The book of Ultima Thule*, 1927, 297.

I think that one's art is a growth inside one. I do not think one can explain growth. It is silent and subtle. One does not keep digging up a plant to see how it grew. Who could explain its blossom?

> EMILY CARR, *Hundreds and thousands*, 1966, 268.

For that was the way the world went,
for that was the way it had to be,
To grow, and in growing lose you
  utterly

> GWENDOLYN MACEWEN, "The return", 1969.

I wish I could grow backwards! I wish I could grow young again.

> GWENDOLYN MACEWEN, "The day of the twelve princes", 1970.

Guaranteed Wage

In the council's view, granted dynamic employment policies for job creation and manpower upgrading, the first line of defence against lack of income or insufficient income should be some kind of guaranteed income, as of right, for all Canadians.

> CANADIAN WELFARE COUNCIL, policy statement, Jan. 28, 1969.

Guests

Learn now
The imperturbable smile
That welcomes the guest.

> MYRTLE REYNOLDS ADAMS, "The last guest", 1958.

Guilt

And when his shoes began to hurt
Because his feet were becoming
  hooves
He did not let on to anyone
For fear they would shoot him for a
  monster.

> JAMES REANEY, "Antichrist as a child", 1949.

The chances of an innocent person being found guilty are as slim as human skill, effort, and conscience can make them. In the process of protecting the innocent, the courts do often turn loose the guilty, for the desire to be just overrides even the need to implement the law. And if the system cannot be perfect then that, surely, is where it should fail.

JOHN KETTLE and DEAN WALKER, *Verdict!*, 1968, [291].

Gulls

a gold-beaked gull
stared back at me
with implacable eyes
and his white wings made
a Saint Andrew's cross
against the October sky.

FRED COGSWELL, "The Bottle Dungeon: Saint Andrew's, Scotland", 1968.

Hair

I'm a musician too, I have a degree.
You can buy a wig.

> GERALD LEVEY, Vancouver magistrate, to
> Franklin Hamilton, guitarist, on order-
> ing him to have his hair cut, Dec., 1966.

The longhairs are not just beatniks;
they're deadbeats, and if growing their
hair long is going to be the prevailing
fashion (which, of course, it won't), we
will be seeing more and more of them
all the time in Magistrate's Courts.
There is just no future for them outside the beneficent confines of the
excellent penitentiaries and reformato-
ries that are ready and willing to
receive them. They will get a haircut
there, all right, and very fast.

> ONTARIO MAGISTRATE'S QUARTERLY , edi-
> torial, Vol. IV, No. 3, July, 1967, 2.

Silly it was of me, Doreen,
   To have such fantasies, of course,
And think your hair had ever been
   Nibbled by some short-sighted
      horse.
Still, can't you make it, in some way,
Look just a little less like hay?

> GEOFFREY B. RIDDEHOUGH, "On a
> chewy-haired blonde", 1972.

Her hair, right to the present day,
   Retains its golden hue.
It hasn't shown a trace of grey
   Since 1962.

> GEOFFREY B. RIDDEHOUGH, "Goldilocks",
> 1972.

Haliburton, T.C.

He believed in pretty nearly everything that has been abolished or is now
in process of demolition.

> C.W. JEFFERYS, qu. by Lorne Pierce in
> Sam Slick in pictures, 1956, xi.

Halifax, N.S.

This Harbour is of great extent,
And nature has, herself, formed there
A splendid Basin, and around about
Green fir-trees, which afford the eye
A pleasant prospect; at its edge
A Building used for drying Cod.

> SIEUR DE DIÈREVILLE, Relation of the
> voyage to Port Royal in Acadia or New
> France, Champlain Society, 1933, 74.
> (Trans.) Refers to visit to site of Halifax,
> 1699.

Hell or Halifax.

> ANON., the alternative destination of the
> United Empire Loyalists on their expul-
> sion from New England, about 1783.

That which made Amsterdam ought to
make Halifax.

> T.C. HALIBURTON, Sam Slick's wise saws,
> 1853, I, 161.

Into the mist my guardian prows put
   forth,
Behind the mist my virgin ramparts
   lie,
The warden of the Honour of the
   North,
Sleepless and veiled am I!

> RUDYARD KIPLING, "The song of the
> cities − Halifax", 1896.

Dear, dingy, old Halifax.

> CHARLES DUDLEY WARNER, qu., *Can. mag.*, 1899, 289.

Halifax sits on her hills by the sea
   In the might of her pride, –
Invincible, terrible, beautiful, she
   With a sword at her side.

> E. PAULINE JOHNSON, "Guard of the Eastern gate", 1903.

Eastern Canadian port.

> ANON., wartime designation used for security reasons.

This harbour is the reason for the town's existence; it is all that matters in Halifax, for the place periodically sleeps between great wars.

> HUGH MACLENNAN, *Barometer rising,* 1951, 7.

When they founded the town in 1749 His Majesty's Board of Trade and Plantations decided to name it in honour of their president, George Dunk. He happened to be Earl of Halifax and they chose the title rather than the family name. Haligonians are duly grateful.

> THOMAS H. RADDALL, in *Century, 1867-1967*, "The Canadian saga", 1967, 30.

Hallowe'en

This is the night of dark powers.
All the old pagan savagery, glossed by
   a few callow centuries of
   civilization, reappears.

> TRUE DAVIDSON, "Hallowe'en", 1939.

Hamilton, Ontario

Hamilton is curiously inhabited. There are more Englishmen there without any apparent occupation, and living upon apparently nothing, than in any other town in Canada.

> HORTON RHYS, *A theatrical trip for a wager*, 1861, 73.

Hands

Isn't it fortunate we don't have to put our souls into what our hands may be doing?

> L.M. MONTGOMERY, *Anne of Avonlea*, 1909, 181.

What moved me, was the way your
   hand
Lay cool in mine, not withering;
As bird still breathes, and stream runs
   clear –
So your hand; your dead hand, my
   dear.

> DOROTHY LIVESAY, "Lament", 1953.

To think by day is half my job,
To size up each approaching hand
And fit it with a surface bland;
I turn as smoothly as I can
To hand of wife and child and man.

> JAMES REANEY, "A suit of nettles: March", 1958.

Whenever I see a hand sticking out of a sleeve, I shake it.

> GEORGE HEES, qu. by P. Newman, *Renegade in power*, 1963, 152, re: political credo as President of the Progressive Conservative Assoc.

The hand has no point of view.

> MARSHALL MCLUHAN, *Through the vanishing point*, 1968, 35.

Hanging

The Americans come up here and admire us for the way we hang criminals. They sit in our club and say, "You certainly do hang them, don't you!" My! they'd like to hang a few! The day may be coming when they will. Meantime we like to hang people to make the Americans sit up.

> STEPHEN LEACOCK, "I'll stay in Canada", 1931, in *Funny pieces*, 1936, 288.

I saw the gallows lifted high
And in the cruel rope
The twisted law and sin of man
Strangled the Saviour's hope.

> J.E.H. MACDONALD, "Gallows and cross", 1933.

Will it hurt? Will I still be conscious when my neck breaks? You do die instantaneously, don't you?

> JOSEPH ALBERT GUAY, first convicted in-flight airplane bomber, Sept. 9, 1949, qu. by Roger Lemelin, in Leslie F. Hannon, ed., *Maclean's Canada*, 1960, 225. (Trans.).

How does it get done when it does get done?
Somehow the wait must come to the event:
Does the clock bring it on?

There is a man to bring it on
And for the moment he is you and me,
Here we meet, under the hanging tree.

> GEORGE JOHNSTON, "Under the tree", 1966.

Hanging makes us one
I am a hangman, you a hanging judge
Meet under the hanging tree
For the hard work that is waiting to be done
And the hanging tree broods over you and me . . .

> GEORGE JOHNSTON, "Under the tree", 1966.

Hangman

I consider it the most sacred calling any man could have, since I am entrusted with carrying out the highest sentence our courts can pass.

> ARTHUR B. ENGLISH, [Arthur Ellis, pseud., "official executioner"] qu. in A. O'Brien, *My friend, the hangman*, 1970, 15.

Happiness

In Canada, the most enlightened, patriotic, and humane inhabitants make extraordinary efforts to render the people dissatisfied with those simple enjoyments which still content it.

> ALEXIS DE TOCQUEVILLE, *Democracy in America*, Vol. 2, 1838, 134.

Happiness is rather a negative than a positive term in this world, and consists more in the absence of some things than in the presence of others.

> THOMAS C. HALIBURTON, *The old judge*, 1849, ch. 5.

Happiness lies in the absorption in some vocation which satisfies the soul.

> SIR WILLIAM OSLER, *Doctor and nurse*, 1891.

Therefore is joy more than sorrow, foreseeing
The lust of the mind and the lure of the eye
And the pride of the hand have their hour of triumph,
But the dream of the heart will endure by and by.

> BLISS CARMAN, "Wanderer", 1893.

And I, too, standing idly there,
With muffled hands in the chill air,
Felt the warm glow about my feet,
And shuddering betwixt cold and heat,
Drew my thoughts closer, like a cloak,
While something in my blood awoke,
A nameless and unnatural cheer,
A pleasure secret and austere.

> ARCHIBALD LAMPMAN, "In November",
> 1895.

And all around me the thin light,
So sere, so melancholy bright,
Fell like the half-reflected gleam
Or shadow of some former dream;
A moment's golden reverie
Poured out on every plant and tree
A semblance of weird joy, or less,
A sort of spectral happiness.

> ARCHIBALD LAMPMAN, "In November",
> 1895.

Because the tardy gods grew kind,
Unrest and care were cast behind;
I took a day, and found the world
Was fashioned to my mind.

> CHARLES G.D. ROBERTS, "The quest of the
> arbutus", 1896.

Joy in one's work, pleasure in one's
emotions, and satisfaction in one's
thoughts, go to make up the sum of
happiness.

> BLISS CARMAN, *The kinship of nature*,
> 1903, 27.

If all our scientific improvements, our
intensive organization, our mechanical
triumphs, all the devices which make
for increased production and simplifi-
cation of production – if all these
things do not help the worker to
greater happiness and to a better and
healthier life, what is the use of them?

> R.B. BENNETT, radio address, Jan. 4, 1935.

In Alberta, broadly speaking, happiness means credit.

> A.F. MCGOUN, *Can. journ. econ. and pol.
> sci.*, 1936, 513.

Try to buy happiness, by the quart or
by the yard, and you never find it.
Motion it away from you while you
turn to Duty and you will find it
waiting beside your chair. So with
Good Will on Earth. Cannons frighten
it. Treaties fetter it. *The Spirit brings
it.*

> STEPHEN LEACOCK, "To every child", in
> *Last leaves*, 1945, 107.

Your happiness is
water for the sun to dry.

> FRED COGSWELL, "In the morning cold",
> 1964.

Just remember, baby, there's more to
life than happiness.

> ANON., qu. by Frank Shuster, Toronto
> *Star*, Dec. 30, 1965.

There's a definite limit to how much
of our own happiness and good fortune we can ask others to bear.

> IRVING LAYTON, "Aphs", *The whole
> bloody bird*, 1969, 101.

Money doesn't bring happiness; success and fame don't bring happiness;
marriage doesn't bring happiness;
even love doesn't bring happiness.
Only happiness brings happiness.

> RICHARD J. NEEDHAM, *A friend in Need-
> ham*, 1969, 15.

There's a happiness that comes only to
those who have given up the idea of
happiness.

> RICHARD J. NEEDHAM, *A friend in Need-
> ham*, 1969, 17.

Harvest

The Land had put his ruddy gauntlet
on,
Of Harvest gold to dash in Famine's
face.

> ISABELLA VALANCY CRAWFORD, "Mal-
> colm's Katie", 1884.

It was like that on the farm. You always have to put the harvest first.

SINCLAIR ROSS, "Cornet at night", 1968.

Haste

Our day has almost made it seem true that to live without madness, one must live without haste.

BLISS CARMAN, *The kinship of nature*, 1904, 237.

Hate

Love and hatred are great sharpeners of the memory. It is as hard to forget an enemy as a friend.

SUSANNA MOODIE, *Geoffrey Moncton*, 1855, 323.

From love of you such strength did flow,
I was a god to drink of it;
And now, by God, I hate you so
It makes me weak to think of it.

L.A. MACKAY, "The ill-tempered lover", 1938.

Hate knows no firmer ground than gratitude.

A.M. KLEIN, *Hitleriad*, 1944.

I don't know if hate's the armour of love; which side he joined, or if he joined: but when he learned to hate those dreams ended –

MILTON ACORN, "In memory of Tommy, an orphan, etc.", 1962.

I shall rejoice when you are cold, dead clay;
Nor shall my hate be cheated by the dust
That fills your eyeless bones or cools your lust
With passionate embrace of quick decay.

IRVING LAYTON, "Release", 1964.

Hats

Not another one! You must give out dozens of these things.

PRINCE PHILIP on being presented with a white cowboy hat, Calgary, Oct. 23, 1969.

Hawks

I watched the grey hawk wheel and drop,
Sole shadow on the shining world.

ARCHIBALD LAMPMAN, "After rain", 1895.

Hay

How many perfumes come and go, but they
Are half-forgotten in the dew-wet day;
On mountain, mere, on hillside sand or sod,
There is no smell this side the fields of God
Like new-mown hay.

ROBERT K. KERNIGHAN, "Perfume of the sods", 1925.

Headaches

She walked forever antlered with migraines
her pain forever putting forth new shoots
until her strange unlovely head became
a kind of candelabra – delicate –
where all her tears were perilously hung
and caught the light as waves that catch the sun.

P.K. PAGE, "Portrait of Marina", 1954.

Health

If pigs or cattle in any province of this Dominion become sick, our Department of Agriculture would send expert after expert and spend Federal money freely in order to find out the cause and cure of that illness, but when we have human suffering, we are told it is not a federal question. I should like to know how long a human being has not been considered an equally valuable asset as a cow or a pig.

> ABRAHAM A. HEAPS, H. of C., *Debates*, Mar. 31, 1930, 1126.

In our highly geared, modern industrial society there is no such thing as private health – all health is public.

> NORMAN BETHUNE, speech, Montreal Medico-Chirurgical Soc., 1936, qu. in Allen & Gordon, *The scalpel, the sword*, 1952, 95.

The flush toilet cheats the land and pollutes the rivers.

> MIRIAM CHAPIN, *Contemporary Canada*, 1959, 234.

I am dangerously well.

> MAURICE DUPLESSIS, favourite reply to those inquiring after his health, qu. in P. Laporte, *The true face of Duplessis*, 1960, 25.

Plenty of salads, plenty of Scotch, and plenty of sex – if you can.

> DR. JAMES KEY, Assoc. Prof. of surgery at Univ. of Toronto, explaining the three-S rule to prevent heart disease and hardening of the arteries, qu. in *Liberty*, July, 1963.

One might ask whether our longer life today, beset as it is with chronic illness and exposed to such insidious risks as radiation and carcinogenic matter, is really healthier than the shorter life span of former generations which may have ended more abruptly as a result of some acute infectious disease.

> CANADA. ROY. COMM. ON HEALTH SERVICES, *Report*, Vol. 1, 1964, 225.

Heart

The mechanism of the human heart, when you thoroughly understand it, is, like all the other works of nature, very beautiful, very wonderful, but very simple. When it does not work well, the fault is not in the machinery, but in the management.

> T.C. HALIBURTON, *Nature and human nature*, 1855, I, 88.

Open, O heart, and let me view
The secrets of thy den;
Myself unto myself now show
With introspective ken.
Expose thyself, thou covered nest
Of passions and be seen;
Stir up thy brood, that in unrest
Are ever piping keen.
Ah! what a motley multitude,
Magnanimous and mean.

> CHARLES HEAVYSEGE, poem No. VII in *Jephthah's daughter*, 1865.

In my heart are many chambers,
    through which I wander free;
Some are furnished, some are empty,
    some are sombre, some are light;
Some are open to all comers, and of
    some I keep the key,
And I enter in the stillness of the night.

> JOHN READE, "In my heart", 1870.

Do not squander heartbeats in cardiac disease – live within your income.

> SIR WILLIAM OSLER, *Oslerisms* (Bean), 1905.

God made a heart of gold, of gold,
    Shining and sweet and true;
Gave it a home of fairest mold,
    Blest it, and called it – You.

> ROBERT W. SERVICE, "Sunshine", 1912.

The human heart is a foolish thing –
Plenty of rhyme but little of reason.

> LLOYD ROBERTS, "The human heart", 1937.

Hard hearts and soft heads generally go together.

> JOHN MACNAUGHTON, *Essays*, 1946.

Most hearts of any quality are broken on two or three occasions in a lifetime. They mend, of course, and are often stronger than before, but something of the essence of life is lost at every break.

> ROBERTSON DAVIES, *Leaven of malice*, 1954, 254.

Heat

I do wish I could gist slip off my flesh and sit in my bones for a space, to cool myself.

> T.C. HALIBURTON, *Sam Slick*, 1838, 86.

In the sloped shadow of my hat
   I lean at rest, and drain the heat;
Nay more, I think some blessed power
   Hath brought me wandering idly
     here:
In the full furnace of this hour
   My thoughts grow keen and clear.

> ARCHIBALD LAMPMAN, "Heat", 1888.

Heaven

As a rule man dies as he had lived, uninfluenced by the thought of a future life.

> SIR WILLIAM OSLER, *Science and immortality*, 1904.

To be a place of complete happiness heaven must be a place where we will be allowed to do the things we think ourselves fitted to do on earth.

> PETER MCARTHUR, d. 1924, qu. in *The best of Peter McArthur*, 1967, 124.

I believe in heaven and hell — on earth.

> RABBI ABRAHAM L. FEINBERG, *Storm the gates of Jericho*, 1964, 291.

Hecklers

If you don't stop that I'll kick you right in the ass.

> PIERRE E. TRUDEAU, Regina, July 17, 1969, to a boy throwing grain at him, qu. in *The best of Trudeau*, 1972, 16.

Hees, George

Nothing but Heesteria.

> ANON., Liberal cabinet ministers term for Hees' speeches, early 1950's.

I just happen to have brought my music with me.

> GEORGE HEES, referring to his ready answers to Opposition queries, House of Commons, late 1950's.

Y.C.D.B.S.O.Y.A.

> GEORGE HEES, letters on his tie clip, which stand for "You Can't Do Business Sitting On Your Ass," used to greet visitors while Minister of Trade and Commerce, 1961-63.

Hell

Hell isn't Indian.

> ORVIS DIABO, Caughnawaga Reserve Indian, qu. by Joseph Mitchell in the *New Yorker*, Sept. 17, 1949, 52.

Now when I am 85 years of age, they are now telling me that I will soon find Hell too small also.

> LORD BEAVERBROOK, 85th birthday dinner speech, London, Eng., May 25, 1964.

Help

All aid short of help.

> HAROLD WILSON, qu. by Blair Fraser in *The listener*, Mar. 26, 1953, 497, off-the-record remark which appeared in Canadian newspapers, referring to Canadian attitude.

The trouble with helping people is that they always expect something in return.

RICHARD J. NEEDHAM, *A friend in Needham*, 1969, 50.

You will walk wrapped in an invisible cloak. Few will seek your help
with love, none without fear.

MARGARET ATWOOD, "Procedures for underground", 1970, in book of same title, 1970, 25.

Henry, George

I feel sorry for Honest George. All he has is about a million or so that he made out of Acme Dairy. If any of you farmers water your milk you go to jail. But if you water your stock you get to be Premier of Ontario.

MITCHELL HEPBURN, speech at Windsor, Ont., during Ontario election campaign, June, 1934.

Hepburn, Mitchell

I swing well to the left where even some Liberals will not follow me.

MITCHELL HEPBURN, speech, Ontario by-election campaign, York West, May, 1932.

He is not fit to be premier of a pub.

GEORGE C. MCCULLAGH, letter to Eddie Wooliver, Aug. 28, 1937 (McCullagh papers), qu. in *Can.hist.rev.*, Vol. 47, 1966, 208.

If anyone sees him talking to himself, he will be able to conclude that the Ontario Cabinet is having a meeting.

ANON., qu. in Lindsay *Daily warder*, Apr. 17, 1937. Reference is to Hepburn assuming cabinet portfolios of Labour, Public Welfare, and Municipal Affairs in addition to that of Prime Minister and Provincial Secretary, on resignation of David Croll.

I will never be satisfied until King's political heels go through the wringer.

MITCHELL F. HEPBURN to Earl Rowe, Apr. 26, 1937, qu. in Neil McKenty, *Mitch Hepburn*, 1967, 120.

The afternoon paper made mention of the fact that Hepburn's bronchitis has developed into bronchial pneumonia. If this is so, it probably means the end of his earthly life. I don't often wish that a man should pass away but I believe it would be the most fortunate thing that could happen at this time.

W.L. MACKENZIE KING, *Diary*, June 15, 1940.

Heritage

I want to keep my French heritage, but it is just as important for me to keep my English chattels and to go to the limit of my American gift of invention. I need all that to make the total man.

JEAN LE MOYNE, *Convergence*, 1966, 98.

As much as any place in the world
I claim this snake-fence village
of A-berg as part of myself.

AL PURDY, *In search of Owen Roblin*, 1974 [52].

Heroes

It is natural for us to sigh for Washingtons and Franklins of our own and for endless anniversaries, to remind us of the deeds and the glories of our ancestors.

JOSEPH HOWE, speech at his trial for criminal libel, Mar. 2, 1835.

In the mighty field of thought
There are battles to be fought,
Revolutions to be wrought;
    Up, and be a hero!

ALEXANDER MCLACHLAN, "Up, and be a hero", 1874.

None dreameth tonight in his bed
That ruin was near and the heroes
That met it and stemmed it are dead.

ARCHIBALD LAMPMAN, "At the Long Sault", 1898.

Unscathed they stand, immutable,
    sublime,
    Great-souled, beyond the barriers of
    gloom,
In solemn light, above the wrecks of
    time,
    They rise triumphant, challenging
    the tomb.

ALBERT D. WATSON, "Myth", 1917.

Men may fail to be heroes to their valets but they are more successful with their biographers.

JOHN W. DAFOE, *Laurier*, 1922, 14.

The story of a nation's heroes is the fountain from which it draws the wine of its later life. There is no inspiration that quickens the ambition of youth, stimulates public service and deepens love of country like the memory of great men who have gone.

ARTHUR MEIGHEN, speech on Thomas D'Arcy McGee, Ottawa, Apr. 13, 1925.

The culture-heroes of Canada are practical men, builders and technicians, political or otherwise; and it is astounding how much success they have had in keeping this country united and growing.

J.M.S. CARELESS, Canadian Historical Association, *Report*, 1954, 17.

There is no story so fantastic that I cannot imagine myself the hero. And there's no story so evil that I cannot imagine myself the villain.

LEONARD COHEN, qu. in *Maclean's*, June, 1972, 6.

I say that we cannot make a hero of Papineau. He died in his bed. All heroes should die young, and not in bed.

MICHEL BRUNET, interview with R. Cook, in *The craft of history*, 1973, 70.

Men with the heads of eagles
No longer interest me
Or pig-men or those who can fly
With the aid of wax and
    feathers . . .

MARGARET ATWOOD, *You are happy*, 1974, 47.

Heroines

[Canadian] heroines have internalized the values of their culture to such an extent that they have become their own prisons.

MARGARET ATWOOD, *Survival*, 1972, 209.

Heroism

Heroism is not a memory of the past. It is the virtue by which a nation can preserve its identity and fulfill its destiny.

DONALD G. CREIGHTON, "Heroic beginnings", broadcast Feb. 21, 1973.

Herons

Smoke-blue he is, and grey
As embers of yesterday.
Still he is, as death;
Like stone, or shadow of stone.
Without a pulse or breath,
Motionless and alone
There in the lily stems:
But his eyes are alive like gems.

THEODORE G. ROBERTS, "The blue heron", 1926.

High Commissioner to London

It is rather hard on the Court of St. James but it is a great relief to the Province of Ontario.

AGNES MACPHAIL, H. of C., *Debates*, Mar. 26, 1931, on the appointment of Howard Ferguson as High Commissioner to London.

Highways

Sorry for the inconvenience.

P.A. GAGLARDI, B.C. Highways Minister, 1955-1968. Sign identified with highway repair or reconstruction.

Hincks, Francis

A clever little man, a typical sharp-eyed child of that unpleasantly prolific marriage between railways and responsible government, Hincks had gone about the business of furthering his own personal interests with the direct uncomplicated ingenuity of a precocious infant.

DONALD G. CREIGHTON, *John A. Macdonald – the young politician*, 1952, 198.

Historians

The historians of Canada (with the conspicuous exception of Garneau) have been literary balloonists. Ascending to a high altitude, they have observed what was on the surface, whilst the character of the Canadian people and its changes in different stages of growth, from the present settlements of the eighteenth century to the confederate nation of today – all this has not yet been written. The people of Canada have been left out of Canadian histories.

GEORGE SANDFIELD MACDONALD, in Celtic Soc., Montreal, *Transactions*, 1884-7, 131.

The Laurentian School.

ANON., term used in 1940's to denote historians who stressed the theme of national unity as against sectionalism; their "symbol" the St. Lawrence River.

Every historian must have a point of view; but it will be valuable to his readers precisely to the extent to which it escapes from the parochial and transitory. If it is based upon some general view of man and society, if it is built up in accordance with the rules of independent craftsmanship, if it is shaped by a strict theory of art, then it may be an inextinguishable source of illumination and delight.

DONALD G. CREIGHTON, *Can.hist.rev.*, Vol. 29, 1948, 6.

I don't know how true this is historically, but there is far too much accurate Canadian history now, and far too little accurate Canadian vision.

NORTHROP FRYE, in *Univ. of Tor. quart.*, Vol. 22, 1953, 272.

For the French-Canadian historians, history is an instrument in the service of the survival of the French-Canadian community and culture.

C.B. MACPHERSON, in Julian Park, ed., *The culture of contemporary Canada*, 1957, 183.

You may as well realize that you have no chance of achieving standing as an historian. You are a Canadian. If you were an American, people here in Canada would read your books and you would be acknowledged.

ANON., qu. in Joseph Barber, *Good fences make good neighbors*, 1958, 90.

As I try to sum myself up, the dreadful thought recurs to me that my endowments, such as they are, are very well equated to the occupation into which they have called me, that of *historian;* second-rate endowments married to second-rate calling? Most of my colleagues would be indignant at the calling of historian described as second-rate. The historian, they would say, is scholar — scientific scholar — indeed, a teller of tales (true tales, they would add), instructor of citizens, imaginative reconstructor of the past, literary man dealing in words and wedded to the art of writing. What more can you ask? Just one thing, I would answer: the creative gift! The gift that makes words take flight!

> A.R.M. LOWER, *My first seventy-five years*, 1967, 376.

I think that an historian's chief interest is in character and in circumstance. His concern is to discover the hopes, fears, anticipations and intentions of the individuals and nations he is writing about. His task is to reproduce as best he can the circumstances, problems and situations faced by another person in another time. He seeks insight and understanding that cannot be gained through application of sociological rules and general explanations.

> DONALD G. CREIGHTON, interview, qu. in Univ. of Toronto *Graduate*, June, 1968, 39.

History has dominated, if it has not overwhelmed, the social sciences; and economists, sociologists, and political scientists have taken their places alongside historians in a vast co-operative effort to explain to their fellow Canadians how they have come to be what, and where, they are.

> DONALD G. CREIGHTON, *Towards the discovery of Canada*, 1972, 50.

History

History, without moral philosophy, is a mere string of facts; and moral philosophy, without history, is apt to become a dream.

> GOLDWIN SMITH, *Rational religion*, 1861, 20.

I do not know. There are many facts in the history of this country, of which I am not aware, and a great many statements of facts in regard to history, I find controverted so often, that I am not able to state a positive opinion in regard to them.

> SIR JOHN THOMPSON, H. of C., *Debates*, Apr. 25, 1890.

History is but a record of the systematic, institutional plunder of the people by a shrewd and selfish few.

> ROBERT C. (BOB) EDWARDS, Calgary *Eye Opener*, Mar. 18, 1916, 4.

If it's all the same to history, it need not repeat itself any more.

> ROBERT C. (BOB) EDWARDS, Calgary *Eye Opener*, May 31, 1919.

To despise forgotten theories because they no longer hold good, and refuse on that account to look backward, is in the end to forget that man's highest ambition is to make progress possible, to make the truth of today into the error of yesterday — in short, to make history.

> GEORGE SIDNEY BRETT, *History of psychology*, Vol. 2, 1921, 6.

History does not preserve the past in a sterilized or mummified state. It preserves and transmits life; it may be a multiplier of forces.

> ABBÉ LIONEL-ADOLPHE GROULX, *Notre maître, le passé*, 1924, 16. (Trans.)

It is history which reveals the plan according to which the past develops. From the collective acts of our ancestors, from their resolutions, from their attitudes in daily work as in their gravest hours, develops a special body of thought, a long and perpetual intention which is tradition. History seizes this thought, it disseminates it to the bottom of everyone's soul, it creates the light and the force which orders the numerous activities of a people.

> ABBÉ LIONEL GROULX, *Notre maître, le passé*, 1924, 17. (Trans.)

Much Canadian history can only be read aright with one eye on the history of the United States.

> R.G. TROTTER, in *Can.hist.rev.* 1924, 213.

I did not realize that the old grave that stood among the brambles at the foot of our farm was *history*.

> STEPHEN B. LEACOCK, Can. Hist. Assoc., *Report*, 1925, 33.

The study of history is the playground of patriotism.

> G.M. WRONG, in *Can.hist.rev.*, 1927, 60.

I like history because my reading of it is accompanied by the comforting certainty that all the people I meet in its pages are dead.

> CECIL F. LLOYD, *Sunlight and shadow*, 1928.

History is capricious in its awards of fame. It fixes on dramatic incident and ignores the quiet service that may count for much more.

> G.M. WRONG, in *Can.hist.rev.*, 1932, 53.

Canada's history is as dull as ditchwater and her politics is full of it.

> MAURICE HUTTON, qu., *Can.hist.rev.*, 1935, 336.

History is the vast and complex tale of the working of the spirit of man.

> G.M. WRONG, *Can.hist.rev.*, 1936, 3.

In truth there is nothing in history like the problem of today.

> R.H. COATS, in *Can. jour. econ. and pol. sci.*, 1938, 152.

For me there is no greater subject than history. How a man can study it and not be forced to become a philosopher, I cannot tell. Questions the most profound and the most searching are forever being asked. History is poetry and art. It deals with the greatest story known to man — the whole story of his existence from the beginning of time down to the present. History is knowledge.

> GEORGE E. WILSON, Presidential address, Canadian Historical Assoc., Montreal, June 6-8, 1951.

There are two miracles in Canadian history. The first is the survival of French Canada, and the second is the survival of Canada.

> F.R. SCOTT, *L'Esprit*, Aug.-Sept., 1952, 178.

The time has come for history, in French Canada, to give up the chair of rhetoric.

> MARCEL TRUDEL, qu. in Michel Brunet, *Canadians et Canadiens*, 1954, 44. (Trans.)

History will continue to be made in Canada whether it is written or not. "Events stronger than advocacy, events stronger than men" will continue to challenge the Canadian character.

> CHESTER MARTIN, *Foundations of Canadian nationhood*, 1955, 515.

Men have need of history because, without it, the past threatens to overwhelm them.

> GUY FREGAULT, *La guerre de la conquête*, 1955, 459. (Trans.)

There are our several characters from early Canadian history at hand, and in search of an author. There is a world now scattered in the archives and the dust, waiting for whoever wants to try putting it together again.

> WILLIAM KILBOURN, *The firebrand*, 1956, xv.

Through the centuries, the forces moving towards totality on the one hand and towards limitation on the other have been roughly in balance with a tendency first to one side and then to the other.

> R.A. PRESTON, et al., *Men in arms*, 1956,16.

History has no rubbish heap.

> LOUIS BLAKE DUFF, qu. in *Saskatchewan hist.*, 1957, Vol. X, No. 3, 99.

We are not simply so many bipeds living within a given habitat which colours and determines all else in our lives. Man is a being who lives in time as well as in space; and the life of a people is rooted in time as well as environed by geography.

> JOHN FARTHING, *Freedom wears a crown*, 1957, 14, referring to Canadians.

We don't need to make our history interesting. It *is* interesting.

> VINCENT MASSEY, address at Fort Langley, B.C., Nov. 19, 1958.

Economic history consists of the story of what man does to his environment, whereas social history has to do with what his environment does to man.

> A.R.M. LOWER, *Canadians in the making*, 1958, xv.

There is nothing more dangerous than history used as a defence, or history used for preaching; history used as a tool is no longer history.

> MARCEL TRUDEL, *Cahiers de l'Academie Canadienne-Française*, 6, 1961, 119. (Trans.).

History is a needle
for putting men asleep
anointed with the poison
of all they want to keep

> LEONARD COHEN, "On hearing a name long unspoken", 1964.

A land so bleak and bare
a single plume of smoke
is a scroll of history

> F.R. SCOTT, "Mackenzie river", 1964.

It is about time that Canada entered history.

> CHARLES DE GAULLE, attributed, in Gerald Clark, *Canada: the uneasy neighbour*, 1965, 41.

History is much like ancestor-worship in religion and performs much of the same psychological and sociological functions.

> JOHN PORTER, *Vertical mosaic*, 1965, 495.

History! they shouted. Give us back our History! The English have stolen our History!

> LEONARD COHEN, *Beautiful losers*, 1966, 118, regarding French Canadians.

Canadians have always thought of their history as epic, and with good reason, though one should not lose one's sense of proportion, for it is an epic on a very small scale and made up of day-to-day events.

> JEAN LE MOYNE, *Convergence*, 1966, 62.

The reason Canadian history has never caught on, like sex, for instance, is that it has been hard up for royal mistresses and has suffered from domination by common sense, compromise and a callous favouring of the facts over the juicy bits.

ERIC NICOL, *An uninhibited history of Canada*, 1968, [31].

He did not wish to use history,
To teach it, to persuade with it, to
   moralize on it,
To win academic honours with it
Or to get his living by it
But only to watch the procession, the
   long procession
Leading to Belsen and Hiroshima.

ELIZABETH BREWSTER, "Lemuel Murray: contemplative", 1969.

I turn back, search
for the actual, collect lost
bones, burnt logs
of campfires, pieces of fur.

MARGARET ATWOOD, "Comic books versus Canadian history", 1971.

history is reality
dressed for the occasion;
it is the Messiah we all pray for
and reject

IRVING LAYTON, "For some of my student militants", *Collected poems*, 1971, 580.

Nothing is more likely to stunt the intellect than a knowledge of history unaccompanied by a sense of history.

ALDEN NOWLAN, "Scratchings", 1971.

History must be defended against attempts to abuse it in the cause of change; we should constantly be on our guard against theories which either dismiss the past or give it a drastically new interpretation.

DONALD G. CREIGHTON, *Towards the discovery of Canada*, 1972, 83.

How much history can you have in a hundred years?

BRUCE COCKBURN, qu. in *Saturday night*, June, 1972, 22.

Hitchhiking

I think sometimes that one of these days I'll just say to hell with all this, doing shows and making records, to hell with all this money, and I'll hit the road again, hitchhiking. Maybe I'll call up my buddy Steve, and ask him to go with me. Right across Canada and back.

STOMPIN' TOM CONNORS, qu. in *Maclean's*, Aug., 1972, 46.

Hobbies

It is our hobbies that keep us young.

ROBERTSON DAVIES, *Tempest-tost*, 1951, 85.

Hockey

This game appears to be a most fascinating one and the men get wildly excited about it. But there can be no doubt as to its roughness, and if the players get over keen & lose their tempers as they are too apt to do, the possession of the stick & the close proximity to one another gives the occasion for many a nasty hit. Tonight one man was playing with his nose badly broken & the game had twice to be stopped, once because a man got hit in the mouth & the other time because one of the captains was knocked down unconscious & had to be carried out.

LADY ABERDEEN, *Journal*, Jan. 20, 1894.

My stars! and this is hockey.
Hockey's the king of sports.
This is the thing to come to when
    you're
feeling out of sorts.

W.M. MACKERACHER, "The parson at the hockey match", 1908.

Great day for hockey, Livingstone was always arguing. Without him we can get down to the business of making money.

TOMMY GORMAN, referring to the exclusion of Eddie Livingstone and his Toronto team from the newly formed National Hockey League, Nov. 22, 1917.

Hockey night in Canada.

FOSTER HEWITT, Apr. 3, 1933, broadcasting a hockey game on radio from Toronto.

He shoots! He scores!

FOSTER HEWITT, Apr. 3, 1933, broadcasting a hockey game on radio from Toronto.

It is perhaps fitting that this fastest of all games has become almost as much of a national symbol as the maple leaf or the beaver. Most young Canadians, in fact, are born with skates on their feet rather than with silver spoons in their mouths.

LESTER B. PEARSON, London (Eng.), *The Times* (Canada number), May 15, 1939, xxxi.

If you can't beat them in the alley, you can't beat them on the ice.

CONN SMYTHE, owner of Toronto Maple Leafs hockey club, 1940's, qu. in *Maclean's*, Jan. 1, 1952, 13.

We don't own the Canadiens, really. The public of Montreal, in fact the entire Province of Quebec, owns the Canadiens. This club is more than a professional sports organization. It is an institution — a way of life.

HARTLAND MOLSON, in 1957, qu. in Stan Fischler, *The flying Frenchmen*, 1971, 9.

Nothing relaxes the boys like a good fight.

FRANCIS "KING" CLANCY, qu. by T. Frayne and P. Gzowski, *Great Canadian sports stories*, 1965, 118.

Canada has never had a major civil war. After hockey, Canadians would probably have found it dull.

JIM BROSNAN, American baseball star, in 1963, qu. in J. Batten, *Champions: great figures in Canadian sport*, 1971, 4.

And how do the players feel about it
this combination of ballet and
    murder?
For years a Canadian specific
to salve the anguish of inferiority
by being good at something the
    Americans aren't.

AL PURDY, "Hockey players", 1965.

In spite of what they'll say in the commissions on culture and the proliferating expositions and festivals and aids-in-grant to anybody who knows anybody else, the only true Canadian invention is a game called hockey.

RALPH ALLEN, Toronto *Star*, May 3, 1965, 4.

There is in hockey something that in a more pretentious nation would be called a mystique — and this has always been part of me.

SCOTT YOUNG, *The Leafs I knew*, 1966, 204.

Who ever knows, five months later, who won the Stanley Cup?

> ALVIN GEDDES, qu. in James H. Gray, *Men against the desert*, 1967, 66.

Fighting on the ice is a safety valve. Stop it and players would no doubt develop more subtle forms of viciousness.

> CLARENCE CAMPBELL, Pres., National Hockey League, qu. in *Maclean's*, Mar., 1969, 72.

coal-shovels clear a hockey rink for
  boys
to play war, mothers watch anxiously:
King Arthur's court, with Eaton's
  catalogue
for breastplate, a hockey stick for
  lance –

> ALFRED PURDY, "The time of your life", 1969.

Canadian professional hockey is proud and touchy. Canada is the birthplace of this tremendous game. You invented it and you always want to be the best. Prove it, then, in honest battle.

> ANATOLY TARASOV, coach, Russian hockey teams, in *Can. mag.*, Apr. 19, 1969, 3.

The NHL has never been a Canadian organization.

> CLARENCE CAMPBELL, Toronto *Telegram*, Sept. 9, 1969, 8.

Once you are alone with a goaler, size doesn't matter. A hard, low shot fired by a small player can be just as dangerous as one by a big fellow.

> HENRI ("POCKET") RICHARD, in A. O'Brien, *Young hockey champions*, 1969, 80.

Basically, hockey is one phase of the entertainment world. It's a business.

> CLARENCE CAMPBELL, in 1969, qu. in *Saturday night*, Jan., 1971, 18.

I don't even like to think about money *and* hockey. I played just as hard when I only got a ten-dollar bill once a week.

> BOBBY ORR, qu. in *In search of Canada*, 1971, 194.

The NHL ship is so tightly organized that even the robber barons of old couldn't have devised a more monopolistic feudal setup.

> NICK AUF DER MAUR, *Last post*, Apr. -May, 1971, 12.

When I scored that final goal, I finally realized what democracy was all about.

> PAUL HENDERSON, Team Canada, on scoring series winning goal in Moscow, Sept. 28, 1972.

This was more emotional than winning the Stanley Cup. A Stanley Cup's for your team and your city, but beating Russia is for your country.

> PHIL ESPOSITO, Team Canada, qu. in *Globe and Mail*, Oct. 2, 1972, S1.

Hockey captures the essence of the Canadian experience in the New World. In a land so inescapably and inhospitably cold, hockey is the dance of life, an affirmation that despite the deathly chill of winter we are alive.

> BRUCE KIDD, *The death of hockey*, 1972, 4.

Some nights you just go. You can't stop. The rhythm gets to you, or the speed. You're moving, man, moving, and that's all.

> ERIC NESTERENKO, hockey player, qu. in B. Kidd and J. Macfarlane, *The death of hockey*, 1972, 6.

Hockey is very important to Canada in a sense above and beyond politics. It has a psychological effect on the nation more important than many of the lofty political ideals we pretend to believe in.

BRUCE HUTCHISON, qu. in B. Kidd and J. Macfarlane, *The death of hockey*, 1972, 15.

You're standing on the greatest country in the world right here.

MICKEY REDMOND, Team Canada, qu. in *Globe and Mail*, Oct. 2, 1972, S1, re Canada.

I say the best Canadian poet is Phil Esposito, and that is not completely a joke . . . I would like to read a Canadian poet who connects in his own self image the tenderness of a mother and the aggressiveness of Phil Esposito.

YEVGENY YEVTUSHENKO, qu. in *Globe and Mail*, Dec. 6, 1973, 14.

Holidays

The Twenty-fourth of May
  Is the Queen's birthday;
If they don't give us a holiday
  We'll all run away.

ANON., popular jingle for Queen Victoria's birthday, associated with Empire Day in Canada, which originated with Clementina Fessenden, Hamilton, Ont., 1896. The two holidays were merged in Canada in 1904 three years after the death of the Queen.

One can always tell when one is getting old and serious by the way that holidays seem to interfere with one's work.

ROBERT C. (BOB) EDWARDS, Calgary *Eye Opener*, Dec. 20, 1913.

The Twenty-fourth comes just as the Canadian summer, when the weather is behaving normally, is beginning to bloom. It is the first public holiday which can be spent outdoors with comfort if the sun is shining, excepting a rare Good Friday. When the day is fine all the pent-up longing of old and young for open-air enjoyment is released, and the woods, the fields, the playgrounds and the highways beckon.

TORONTO *GLOBE*, May 24, 1924, 4, editorial, referring to Queen Victoria's birthday.

Home

If you want to know how to valy home, you should go abroad for a while among strangers.

T.C. HALIBURTON, *Sam Slick*, 1838, 126; *valy* means value.

The lank Canadian eager trims his
  fire,
And all around their simpering stoves
  retire.

STANDISH O'GRADY, *The emigrant*, 1841.

The Crown of the House is Godliness.
The Beauty of the House is Order.
The Glory of the House is Hospitality.
The Blessing of the House is
  Contentment.

ANON., inscription over the fireplace of a Lower Canada home, qu. in Lena Newman, *An historical almanac of Canada*, 1967.

Far from the perilous folds that are my home.

MARJORIE PICKTHALL, "Père Lalemont", 1905.

Hurled back, defeated, like a child I
    sought
The loving shelter of my native fields,
Where Fancy still her magic sceptre
    wields,
And still the miracles of youth are
    wrought.

    PETER MCARTHUR, "Earthborn", 1907.

O near lights, and far lights,
    And every light a home!
And how they gladden, sadden us
    Who late and early roam!

    ARTHUR STRINGER, "Night travel", 1907.

The home has passed, or at least is
passing out of existence. In place of it
is the 'apartment' – an incomplete
thing, a mere part of something,
where children are an intrusion, where
hospitality is done through a caterer,
and where Christmas is only the twen-
ty-fifth of December.

    STEPHEN LEACOCK, "The woman ques-
    tion", 1915.

Laddie, little laddie, come with me
    over the hills,
Where blossom the white May lilies,
    and the dogwood and daffodils;
For the Spirit of Spring is calling to
    our spirits that love to roam
Over the hills of home, laddie, over
    the hills of home.

    LILIAN LEVERIDGE, "Over the hills of
    home", 1918.

In the second floor area (the most
closely guarded, where outsiders are
concerned), the cleansing of the body
and the renewing of life in sleep or
sexual intercourse takes place.

    JOHN R. SEELEY, et al., *Crestwood
    heights*, 1956, 54.

A man should build himself a house
    and put himself inside
And fill it full of furniture, and get
    himself a bride
To fill it full of cooking smells and
    pickle smells and wit
And all in pleasure breed it full and
    make a nest of it.

    GEORGE JOHNSTON, "Domestic", 1959.

I am homesick I
am packing up
I am going home
but now I don't
know anymore
where home is.

    MIRIAM WADDINGTON, "My travels",
    1966.

I want to go home, but I can't, because
this is home.

    MARGARET LAURENCE, *The fire-dwellers*,
    1969, 250, said by housewife Stacey
    Cameron.

Homeless

Canadian displaced persons.

    ANON., term used to describe migrant
    prairie farm families, 1930's.

Homes

So a house is not the same for a
woman. She is not someone who walks
into the house, to make use of it, and
will walk out again. She *is* the house;
there is no separation possible.

    ALICE MUNRO, qu. in *Globe and Mail*,
    Aug. 15, 1972, 6.

Some women are buried in coffins, but
the majority are buried in bungalows.

    RICHARD J. NEEDHAM, *Globe and Mail*,
    Apr. 28, 1972, 6.

Homesteads

There are homesteads in the older countries of the world which no money would purchase; but where is the Canadian who will not sell out if only he gets his price?

> LONDON (ONT.) *EVENING ADVERTISER*, Sept. 6, 1865, editorial.

The homesteader was the only man who could start with nothing, lose money all his life, and die rich.

> GEORGE SHEPHERD, *West of yesterday*, 1965, 26.

Homosexuality

Homosexuality, like fellatio and cunnilinctus, is a matter of taste and custom.

> IRVING LAYTON, "Aphs", *The whole bloody bird*, 1969, 95.

Honesty

I believe it is in politics as in other matters, honesty is the best policy.

> T.C. HALIBURTON, *Sam Slick*, 1838, 119.

I am getting too old to form part of the school of 'chiselers', that is a bad school; I stick to the old rule, honesty is the best policy in the long run.

> SIR L.H. LAFONTAINE, letter to R. Baldwin, 1851.

The predominance of the principles of honour, honesty & morality in our government, legislation & business transactions of public men is now the only advantage we have over our American neighbours, & if these go, all is gone.

> EGERTON RYERSON, letter to his daughter, Sophie, Sept. 20, 1873.

I wonder, Carling, if God ever made a man as honest as you look.

> SIR JOHN A. MACDONALD, to Sir John Carling ("Honest John") in Council; Carling was a minister in Macdonald's cabinet, 1882–1891.

If honesty is exiled from the farm, where will it find a home?

> GOLDWIN SMITH, *Weekly sun*, Oct. 3, 1906.

Don't place too much confidence in a man who boasts of being as honest as the day is long. Wait until you meet him at night.

> ROBERT C. (BOB) EDWARDS, in Calgary *Eye Opener*; attributed.

You have got to be straight if you want to make friends with men of less intellectual training than your own.

> M. ALLERDALE GRAINGER, *Woodsmen of the West*, 1908, 27.

Ontario does not think I am a great man. It does not think I am honest. And honest I must be.

> SIR JAMES PLINY WHITNEY, Premier of Ont., after 1908 election, qu. in Sir John Willison, *Reminiscences political and personal*, 1919, 330.

Look boys, there's nothing up my sleeves but my elbows.

> LIONEL FORSYTH, at a tension-charged union-management meeting, DOSCO, Sydney, N.S., 1950.

A man who plays it straight will always have trouble with women. Women aren't accustomed to honest men; they don't know how to deal with them. Furthermore, an honest man forces a woman to be honest with him; women aren't accustomed to this, either.

> RICHARD J. NEEDHAM, *A friend in Needham*, 1969, 35.

We are hard on each other
and call it honesty.

the things we say are
true; it is our crooked
aims, our choices
turn them criminal

> MARGARET ATWOOD, *Power politics*,
> 1972, 24.

Hope

Canada is the land of hope; here
everything is new; everything going
forward.

> CATHERINE PARR TRAILL, letter, Sept. 20,
> 1834, in *The backwoods of Canada*.

Hope is a pleasant acquaintance, but
an unsafe friend.

> T.C. HALIBURTON, *Sam Slick's wise saws*,
> 1853, I, 281.

The houses hope builds are castles in
the air.

> THOMAS C. HALIBURTON, *Sam Slick's wise
> saws*, 1853, ch. 13.

So came the Autumn's ruddy prime,
And all my hopes, which had no
    morrow,
Like sea-weed cast upon the beach,
Like drift-wood barely out of reach
Of waves that were attuned to sorrow,
Lay lifeless on the strand of time.

> GEORGE MARTIN, in *Canadian birthday
> book*, 1887, 302.

Hope is faith holding out its hands in
the dark.

> GEORGE ILES, *Canadian stories*, 1918,
> 167.

Persecution's cruel mouth
Shows a twisted love of truth.
Deeper than the rack and rope
Lies the double human hope.

> F.R. SCOTT, "Conflict", 1945.

The world is getting
dark but I carry
icons I remember
the summer
I will never forget
the light.

> MIRIAM WADDINGTON, "Icons", 1969.

Horizons

It was a pleasant outlook for anyone
who loves the long view that the
prairie gives, where only the horizon
obstructs the vision.

> NELLIE MCCLUNG, *The second chance*,
> 1910, 206.

Horses

For, be we either man or hoss,
    We've all some inborn sin;
And what is Christianity
    But just a breakin' in?
Now, I gives all my hosses, sir,
    A Christian edication;
And nar a one but has some sense
    Of moral obligation.

> ALEXANDER MCLACHLAN, "Old hoss",
> 1874.

The Kentucky of Canada.

> ANON., ref. to P.E.I., so-called because of
> its harness racing.

Bronco dams they ran by on the
    ranges of the prairies
Heard the chicken drumming in the
    scented saskatoon,
Saw the jewelled humming-birds, the
    flocks of pale canaries
Heard the coyotes dirging to the
    ruddy Northern moon;
Woolly foals, leggy foals, foals that
    romped and wrestled.
Rolled in beds of golden-rod and
    charged to mimic fights
Saw the frosty Bear wink out and
    comfortably nestled

Close beside the vixen dams beneath
the wizard Lights.

C. GARSTIN, "Canadian remounts", in
Punch, Feb. 9, 1916.

Lucky, lucky white horse, lucky, lucky
lee!
Lucky, lucky white horse, bring luck
to me.

ANON., western Ontario rhyme; qu. *Jour.
of Amer. folklore*, 1938, 61.

Lord Ronald said nothing; he flung
himself from the room, flung himself
upon his horse and rode madly off in
all directions.

STEPHEN B. LEACOCK, "Gertrude the gov-
erness", in *Nonsense novels*, 1911.

Montcalm's black horse walked his
dying master slowly back into the city
through the St. Louis gate.

DONALD G. CREIGHTON, *The story of
Canada*, 1959, 78.

The breeding of race horses, a species
of mammal of unparalleled stupidity
and uselessness, is subsidized by public
funds in Ontario more generously than
research into muscular dystrophy.

HAROLD TOWN, *Enigmas*, 1964, [2].

Somewhere in God's own space,
There must be some sweet-pastured
place
Where creeks sing on and tall trees
grow,
Some Paradise where horses go;
For by the love that guides my pen
I know great horses live again.

STANLEY HARRISON, untitled; qu. in E.
McCourt, *Saskatchewan*, 1968, 102.

Hospitals

Now down I am, bed-bound, by my
will
Weighed, held level, lower than I
wended,
To ascend the vacant boundaries of
the bed,
The bleak ward strange and now oh
not friend.

HEATHER SPEARS, "Now above noise",
1958.

House of Commons

A spirit of awe and timidity hangs
over the House. I have addressed thousands of people without increasing my
heart action one beat; yet when I get
up in the House to ask the Minister of
Health one simple question, I am
afraid my heart will go out of my
mouth. If you are picking a candidate,
pick a strong one, who is able to go up
against that wall of steel.

AGNES MACPHAIL, in 1922, qu. in D.
French and M. Stewart, *Ask no quarter*,
1959, 74.

House of Temptation.

AGNES MACPHAIL, name given to House
of Commons, ca. 1923.

In the other Chamber I had been
addicted too much to the practice of
addressing myself to the question instead of to the public . . . the palm
of victory finally went to those who
addressed themselves to the public
instead of to the issue.

ARTHUR MEIGHEN, Senate, *Debates*, Feb.
8, 1932, 11.

I was not here during the whole of last
week, having been confined to my
house through illness, and I am a little
surprised to find that some person in
my stead voted for me. I wish to say
that the voice was not the voice of

Jacob although the hands were the hands of Esau.

SAMUEL W. JACOBS, H. of C., *Debates*, Mar. 15, 1937, 1758.

On the part of the government – and I think this is very important – it must be remembered that this is a house of minorities.

ROBERT THOMPSON, Social Credit Leader, H. of C., *Debates*, Oct. 2, 1962, 120.

I have always been a House of Commons man.

JOHN G. DIEFENBAKER, H. of C., *Debates*, June 4, 1964, 3920.

Since those days we have gone through not one but two elections. I think the time has now come when we should settle down and take an objective look at the basis of our operations, get on with the work before us and try to make this house of minorities function effectively, remembering particularly that two wrongs do not make a right.

ROBERT THOMPSON, Leader, Social Credit Party, H. of C., *Debates*, Feb. 1, 1966, 524.

The events of the week have made even the most cynical members of the House of Commons aware that their power to influence events is oozing away. Like courtiers involved in ceremonial rituals whose meaning has been lost, they grope through a curtain of words, searching dimly for some purpose to their fury.

PETER C. NEWMAN on the Gerda Munsinger charges in H. of C., in Vancouver *Sun*, Mar. 22, 1966, 4.

In theory the Commons can do anything; in practice, it can do little.

JOHN N. TURNER, *Politics of purpose*, 1968, 16.

Houses

A small house well filled is better than an empty palace.

THOMAS C. HALIBURTON, *Sam Slick's wise saws*, 1853, ch. 1.

We live in a rickety house
In a dirty dismal street,
Where the naked hide from day
And thieves and drunkards meet.

ALEXANDER MCLACHLAN, "We live in a rickety house", 1861.

Here, from my vantage-ground, I can
see the scattering houses,
Stained with time, set warm in
orchards, meadows, and wheat,
Dotting the broad bright slopes
outspread to southward and
eastward,
Wind-swept all day long, blown by the
south-east wind.

CHARLES G.D. ROBERTS, "Tantramar revisited", 1886.

John Tomkins lived in a house of logs,
On the second concession of Deer;
The front was logs, all straight and
sound –
The gable was logs, all tight and round
–
The roof was logs, so firmly bound –
And the floor was logs, all down to the
ground –
The warmest house in Deer.

WILLIAM W. SMITH, "The second concession of Deer", 1888.

One night I burned the house I loved,
It lit a perfect ring
In which I saw some weeds and stone
Beyond – not anything.

LEONARD COHEN, "One night I burned the house I loved", 1960.

Housewives

Every woman who works, and domesticity *is* work, has a right to ask for decent working conditions, and if she cannot get them, leave any man, husband or no, and work for herself until he can provide them.

MARION CRAN, *Women in Canada*, 1910, 110.

Empty hands are the curse and menace of modern women.

ARTHUR STRINGER, *Christina and I*, 1929.

Caught in the open door by sound
    unheard,
a woman will hesitate, mop in hand,
listening for possible mourning dove.
Then, unmindful of little yellow bird,
Turn to till the carpets of her land,
pressure of practical down-driving
    love.

VIOLET ANDERSON, "Warblers in willows", 1957.

The housewife who remains at home is just as much a producer of goods and services as the paid worker, and in our view she should also have the opportunity to provide for a more financially secure future.

CANADA. ROY. COMM. ON THE STATUS OF WOMEN, *Report*, 1970, 38.

Housing

Oh, much I wish that I were able
    To build a house like Cartwright's
    stable,
For it doth cause me great remorse
    To be worse lodged than
    Cartwright's horse.

DR. JAMES SAMPSON, Mayor of Kingston, 1839-40, and 1844, on the stables of J.S. Cartwright.

Housing has been studied and committee-ed to death.

TORONTO *GLOBE AND MAIL*, Dec. 13, 1967, 6, editorial.

Our housing policy can be summarized in three words: Pierre Elliott Trudeau.

PAUL MARTIN, address to Liberal Party workers, May, 1968; qu. in *Maclean's*, Oct., 1969, 13.

All Canadians have the right to be adequately housed whether they can afford it or not.

CANADIAN WELFARE COUNCIL. Canadian Conference on Housing, Toronto, Oct. 20-23, 1968, *The right to housing*, papers and proceedings, ed. by Michael Wheeler, 1969, 331.

Every Canadian should be entitled to clean, warm shelter as a matter of basic human right.

CANADA. FEDERAL TASK FORCE ON HOUSING AND URBAN DEVELOPMENT, *Report*, 1969, 22.

Howe, C.D.

Minister of Everything.

ANON., nickname used in early 1940's.

Who would stop us? Don't take yourself too seriously. If we wanted to get away with it who would stop us?

C.D. HOWE, H. of C., *Debates*, May 21, 1951, 3253.

That's not public enterprise; that's *my* enterprise.

C.D. HOWE, to opposition M.P. who suggested establishment of Trans-Canada Air Lines was a step toward socialism, qu. in P. Newman, *Renegade in power*, 1963, 36.

If we have overstepped our powers, I make no apology for having done so.

C.D. HOWE, H. of C., *Debates*, Apr. 21, 1953, 4197.

That would mean coming back to Parliament in three years, and I've more to do than spend my time amusing Parliament.

> C.D. HOWE, attributed, on revision of Defence Production Act, 1955, extending "extraordinary powers" given him in wartime; qu. in P. Newman, *Renegade in power*, 1963, 37; *Reporter* (N.Y.), July 11, 1957, 22.

We were too old. *I* was too old. I didn't have the patience any more that it takes to deal with Parliament. You know, over a year ago I went to the Prime Minister [St. Laurent] and suggested that he and I ought to retire. He wouldn't hear of it — I guess he'd decided he was going to live forever, and everything was to go on as it was going. So he said nonsense, we must both stay. So we did — and look what happened.

> C.D. HOWE to Blair Fraser, Dec., 1957, qu. in B. Fraser, *The search for identity*, 1967, 151, referring to Liberal defeat, election, June 10, 1957.

I never wanted to be the most popular man in Parliament. I always tried to give people what they were entitled to and no more.

> C.D. HOWE, qu. in *Globe and Mail*, Dec. 28, 1957, 8.

Howe, Joseph

I wish to live and die a British subject, but not a Briton only in the name.

> JOSEPH HOWE, speech in N.S. Legislature, Feb. 11, 1837.

The Tribune of Nova Scotia.

> ANON., a popular reference to Howe, 19th Century.

The Tribune of the People.

> ANON., a reference to *Joseph Howe*, a popular nickname in the 19th century.

That pestilent fellow, Howe.

> SIR JOHN A. MACDONALD, letter, Oct., 1867: 'Nova Scotia . . . has declared as far as she can against Confederation, but she will be powerless for harm, although that pestilent fellow, Howe, may endeavour to give us some trouble in England.'

The Old Man Eloquent.

> TORONTO *GLOBE*, Mar. 2, 1872, a reference to Howe in his later years.

There were more seminal ideas in that man's head than in any other man's with whose history I am familiar.

> SIR JOHN A. MACDONALD, to George Johnson, 1886.

Hudson Bay

Hudson's Bay is certainly a country that Sinbad the Sailor never saw, as he makes no mention of Musketoes.

> DAVID THOMPSON, *Narrative of his explorations in Western America, 1784-1812* (Champlain Soc. 1916, 29).

His name is written on the deep, the
    rivers as they run
Will bear it timeward o'er the world,
    telling what he has done.

> THOMAS D'A. MCGEE, "The death of Hudson", 1858.

Open the Bay! Who are they that say
    "No"?
Who locks the portals? Nature? She
    resigned
Her icy reign, her stubborn frost and
    snow,
Her sovereign sway and sceptre, long
    ago,
    To sturdy manhood and the master,
    Mind!

> CHARLES MAIR, "Open the Bay!", 1901.

Canada must control Hudson's Bay absolutely; it is the front and central door; and a knocker must be put on it.

> W.F. MACLEAN, speech to Canadian Club, Toronto, Feb. 24, 1904.

We claim Hudson Bay as Canadian territory.

> L.P. BRODEUR, Minister of Marine and Fisheries, H. of C., *Debates*, July 3, 1906, 6856.

Hudson Bay will become the Mediterranean of the North.

> LORD GREY, Governor-General, Nov., 1910.

On To The Bay!

> ON-TO-THE-BAY ASSOCIATION, formed in Winnipeg in 1924 to press for completion of the Hudson Bay Railway; motto.

Hudson's Bay Co.

The Governor and Company of Adventurers of England trading into Hudson's Bay.

> HUDSON'S BAY CO., charter of Incorporation, granted by Charles II, signed May 2, 1670.

The Company have for eighty years slept at the edge of a frozen sea; they have shown no curiosity to penetrate farther themselves, and have exerted all their art and power to crush that spirit in others.

> JOSEPH ROBSON, *An account of six years residence in Hudson's Bay*, 1752, 6.

Pro Pelle Cutem.

> HUDSON'S BAY COMPANY's motto, from the coat-of-arms – "The skin for the fur", [i.e. the beaver fur]; in more recent days, "Skin for skin".

Here Before Christ.

> ANON., northern hunters' saying, early 19th century, based on the Company's initials.

The Company.

> ANON., expression used in the West and North-West from early 19th. century.

Connubial alliances are the best security we can have of the goodwill of the Natives, I have therefore commended the Gentlemen to form connections with the principle Families immediately on their arrival, which is no difficult matter as the offer of their Wives & Daughters is the first token of their Friendship & hospitality.

> SIR GEORGE SIMPSON, *Report*, May 18, 1821, to governors of the Hudson's Bay Company from Fort Wedderburn.

Within their dominions every man's life, family, and goods, are safe. Order and ready obedience everywhere prevail.

> DAVID THOMPSON, qu. in J.J. Bigsby, *The shoe and canoe*, 1850, 274.

There can be no question that the injurious and demoralizing sway of that company over a region of four millions of square miles, will, ere long, be brought to an end, and that the destinies of this immense country will be united with our own. It is unpardonable that civilization should be excluded from half a continent, on at best but a doubtful right of ownership, for the benefit of two hundred and thirty-two shareholders.

> TORONTO *GLOBE*, 1852.

What? Sequester our very tap-root? Take away the fertile lands where our buffaloes feed? Let in all kinds of people to squat and settle and frighten away the fur-bearing animals they don't kill and hunt? Impossible! Destruction – extinction – of our time-honoured industry. If these gentlemen are so patriotic, why don't they buy us out?

> H.H. BERENS, Governor of Hudson's Bay Co., to the Duke of Newcastle, 1863; qu. Watkin, *Canada and U.S.*, 1887, 120.

The Hudson's Bay Company is one of the most hidebound concerns in existence.

SIR W. VAN HORNE, letter to W. Whyte, 1891; qu. in Vaughan, *Van Horne*, 1920, 196.

The Hudson's Bay Company never amounted to a damn until the North West Company joined it.

ANON., qu., Pinkerton, *Gentlemen adventurers*, 1931, 113.

It is the H.B.C. custom to ignore you when you become poor.

NULIGAK, *I, Nuligak*, 1966, 174. (Trans. by Maurice Metayer).

Human Nature

Who in their sole mind would fear the animals and the beastly gods It is human nature I abhor.

GWENDOLYN MACEWEN, "Magic animals: 4", 1972.

Humanities

A romantic age stands in need of science, a scientific and utilitarian age stands in need of the humanities.

GOLDWIN SMITH, *The Week*, Apr. 28, 1893.

Where the humanities are still taught, they seem to be losing their traditional character. It seems to us that the classics have been largely taken over by the philologist, that history is becoming a branch of sociology, that philosophy is under the shadow of psychology, that the study of English literature is losing its power to encourage good writing and wise reading. This is the true plight of the humanities; it is not so much that they have been deserted as that they have lost their way.

CANADA. ROY. COMM. ON NATIONAL DEVELOPMENT IN THE ARTS, LETTERS, AND SCIENCES, *Report*, 1951, 138.

Humanity

Above all nations is humanity.

GOLDWIN SMITH, an aphorism, about 1870; carved on a bench at Cornell University, where Smith taught; also, "Over all nations is Humanity", by W.L. MACKENZIE KING, *Industry and humanity*, 1918.

Within the politician's ribs,
  within my own, the time-bombs
  tick.
O men be swift to be mankind
  or let the grizzly take.

EARLE BIRNEY, "Time-bomb", 1945.

Sufficient psychological and sociological knowledge for the reconstruction of humanity already exists. Our aim must be the discovery of methods of spreading and applying that knowledge.

JOHN A. IRVING, *Science and values*, 1952, 51.

I do not know what to make of
  inhumanity
Beyond sharing and understanding it,
Inflicting it and having it inflicted
  upon me
Every day usually before noon.

GEORGE JONAS, "Conclusion", 1962.

We all know what the social sciences can do for humanism: suffocate it with prescriptive waffle.

PAUL WEST, "Canadian attitudes", *Can. lit.*, No. 16, 1963, 23.

The trouble other people have being German I have being human.

MARGARET ATWOOD, *Surfacing*, 1972, 130.

Humbug

It cannot be denied that in dealings with the public just a little touch of humbug is immensely effective, but it is not necessary.

SIR WILLIAM OSLER, *Internal medicine as a vocation*, 1897.

The greatest men of the past were all Masters of Humbug, and so are the greatest men to-day.

SIR W. VAN HORNE, letter, 1909, qu. in Vaughan, *Van Horne*, 1920, 357.

I assure you that there never was such humbug as this proposal.

JAMES H. THOMAS, Secretary of State for Dominion Affairs, on trade proposals of R.B. Bennett, Gt. Brit., H. of C., *Debates*, Nov. 27, 1930, 1550.

Humility

The last great lesson is humility before the unsolved problems of the Universe.

SIR WILLIAM OSLER, intro., *Life of Pasteur*, 1911, by Vallery-Radot.

If I were English, Canada
Should love me like the deuce,
But I was born in Canada
So what the hell's the use.

WILSON MACDONALD, "Song of a bloody Canuck", 1931.

First, and most obvious, is our national humility. We are a people bounded on one side by the northern lights and on the other, by an inferiority complex just as vivid, a people distracted by the mossy grandeur of the old world from which we came and by the power, wealth and fury of our American neighbours. We are the last people to realize, and the first to deny, the material achievements of the Canadian nation which all the rest of the world has already grasped and envied.

Self-depreciation is our great national habit.

BRUCE HUTCHISON, in Malcolm Ross, ed., *Our sense of identity*, 1954, 42.

God made this country to teach man humility.

ALDEN NOWLAN, "The glass roses", 1968.

Humour

There's many a true word said in jest.

THOMAS C. HALIBURTON, *Sam Slick's wise saws*, 1853, ch. 24.

To deny a woman's sense of humour is the last form of social insult.

STEPHEN LEACOCK, "Movies and motors, men and women", in *Further foolishness*, 1916, 170.

It has long been my custom in preparing an article of a humorous nature to go down to the cellar and mix up a half a gallon of myosis with a pint of hyperbole. If I want to give the article a decidedly literary character, I find it well to put in about half a pint of paresis. The whole thing is amazingly simple.

STEPHEN LEACOCK, "Humour as I see it", 1916, in *Further foolishness*, 1916, 294.

The world's humour, in its best and greatest sense, is perhaps the highest product of our civilization.

STEPHEN LEACOCK, "Humour as I see it", 1916, in *Further foolishness*, 1916, 311.

A man will freely confess that he has no ear for music, or no taste for fiction, or no interest in religion. But I have yet to see the man who announces that he has no sense of humour.

STEPHEN LEACOCK, *My discovery of England*, 1922, 223.

Humour in its highest meaning and its furthest reach does not depend on verbal incongruities, or on tricks of sight and hearing. It finds its basis in the incongruity of life itself, the contrast between the fretting cares and the petty sorrows of the day and the long mystery of the to-morrow. Here laughter and tears become one, and humour becomes the contemplation and interpretation of our life.

> STEPHEN LEACOCK, *Humour: its theory and technique*, 1935, 17.

The social scientist and especially the student of political economy is compelled to make his peace with satire or humour. The callous vulgarity which characterizes the humour of the medical profession is paralleled by cynicism in the social sciences.

> H.A. INNIS, *Can. journ. econ. and pol. sci.*, Vol. 10, May, 1944, 221.

A sense of humour — a real one — is a rarity and can be utter hell. Because it's immoral, you know, in the real sense of the word: I mean, it makes its own laws; and it possesses the person who has it like a demon. Fools talk about it as though it were the same thing as a sense of balance, but believe me, it's not. It's a sense of anarchy, and a sense of chaos. Thank God it's rare.

> ROBERTSON DAVIES, *A mixture of frailties*, 1958, 244.

What little I know of humor suggests that it is not something which a man possesses, but rather something which possesses him; it is constantly in operation, it has a dark as well as a light aspect, and its function is by no means that of keeping its possessor in fits of chuckles.

> ROBERTSON DAVIES, *A voice from the attic*, 1960, 202.

A great sense of humour can only exist in company with other elements of greatness.

> ROBERTSON DAVIES, *A voice from the attic*, 1960, 216.

Genial humour is fairly rare in literature; it is much more elusive than satiric wit.

> W.H. MAGEE, "Stephen Leacock", in *Can. lit.* No. 39, 1969, 37.

God has His own sense of humour. He gave grapes for making wine not to Quebec, but to Ontario.

> RICHARD J. NEEDHAM, *A friend in Needham*, 1969, 20.

Hunger

I know it is hard to be hungry and be a Christian.

> MORLEY CALLAGHAN, *Such is my beloved*, 1934, 41.

And starving can be overdone,
Though pain and grief that poets sing,
And frustrate life, may best be won,
From days that lack all nourishing.

> PAUL HIEBERT, "Starving can be overdone", 1967.

Hunting

Let us be much with nature: not as they
That labour without seeing, that employ
Her unloved forces, blindly without joy,
Nor those whose hands and crude delights obey
The old brute passion to hunt down and slay.

> ARCHIBALD LAMPMAN, "On the companionship with nature", 1900.

It is a strange anomaly that man, the greatest killer in the universe, and almost the only one that kills for sport when there is no need — he is the one who deplores and condemns killing by any other agency than himself. Hunting is a good thing: good for man, and not bad for the game; except for those individuals that are overtaken by the slayer.

WILLIAM E. SAUNDERS, in *W.E. Saunders — naturalist*, 1949, 29.

Beast of the Sea,
Come and offer yourself in the dear
early morning!
Beast of the Plain!
Come and offer yourself in the dear
early morning!

ANON., Eskimo poem, in Edmund Carpenter, ed., *Anerca*, 1959.

Though in any hunt I'm with the
quarry
it was no mouse's agony that I
felt when I heard the rush of a hawk's
wings
fall without warning from the harvest
sky.

ALDEN NOWLAN, "A night hawk fell with a sound like a shudder", 1961.

This is the weather when hunters
Wait in the marshes till shadows
Shake in the reeds, and then leap
With their guns into action. Happy,
they grieve
The dead birds, and everywhere
round them
The universe bleeds into darkness.

D.G. JONES, "Mr. Wilson, the world", 1968.

My friend is hunting to the left of me
somewhere
in the fog.

RED LANE, "Margins XIX", 1968.

They squeeze their triggers madly
And blast the does to bits,
And part of them is shattered
Each time a bullet hits.

FRED COGSWELL, "The huntsman", 1971.

The frustrations resulting from the repression of the full expression of the hunting syndrome lie behind most of the anger and alienation that have characterized socio-economic revolt.

L. TIGER and R. FOX, *The imperial animal*, 1971, 128.

Hurt

And if I hurt my knee
my good leg shows my poor leg
what to do

and if I hurt my arm
my good arm rubs my poor arm
into place

and if I hurt an eye
my good eye sees beyond the other's
range
and pulls it onward upward
into space.

DOROTHY LIVESAY, "Look to the end", 1971.

Husbands

That is a happy marriage in which a woman's husband is also her confidant.

ARNOLD HAULTAIN, *Hints for lovers*, 1909, 263.

Mother says a good husband should always bore his wife.

FRED JACOB, "The clever one", in his *One-third of a bill*, 1925, 36.

Good husbands make problems, too. A man who is gentle and affectionate with his wife will be gentle and affectionate with other women. Other women know this; so does his wife.

> RICHARD J. NEEDHAM, *A friend in Needham*, 1969, 3.

Actresses don't have husbands, they have attendants.

> MARGARET ANGLIN, qu. by Harding Lemay in *Inside, looking out*, 1971, 190.

A husband suspects one other man; a wife, all other women.

> RICHARD J. NEEDHAM, *Globe and Mail*, Apr. 30, 1971, 6.

Hutterites

The Brethren of the Hutterites Society settling permanently in Canada shall be exempted unconditionally from service in the Militia, upon the production in each case of a certificate of membership from the proper authorities.

> CANADA. LAWS, STATUTES, etc., Order-in-Council 1676, Aug. 12, 1899; rescinded, Order-in Council 768, Apr. 8, 1919.

Hypocrisy

There is an hypocrisy in vice as well as religion.

> T.C. HALIBURTON, *Sam Slick's wise saws*, 1853, II, 283.

Today we know too much. Having become democratic by ideology, we are divided into groups which eye each other like dull strangers at a dull party, polite in public and nasty when each others' backs are turned.

> HUGH MACLENNAN, "An orange from Portugal", in his *Cross country*, 1949, 25.

Do not dress in rags for me
I know you are not poor
Don't love me so fiercely
When you know you are not sure.
It is your world beloved
It is your flesh I wear.

> LEONARD COHEN, "I stepped into an avalanche", 1966.

Hypocrisy is the vaseline that lubricates social intercourse.

> IRVING LAYTON, "Aphs", *The whole bloody bird*, 1969, 102.

Hypocrites

Definition of a hypocrite: one who is too kind to be wholly honest and too honest to be wholly kind.

> ALDEN NOWLAN, "Scratchings", 1971.

Ice Worms

There's a husky, dusky maiden in the
arctic
In her igloo, she's waitin' there in vain,
Oh, I guess I'll put my mukluks on and
ask her,
If she'll wed me when the ice-worms
nest again.

> ANON., (n.d., sometimes attributed to
> Robert Service as the originator of a
> song which has been transformed).

Icebergs

Within the sunlight, vast, immaculate!
Beyond all reach of earth in majesty,
It passed on Southwards slowly to its
fate —
To be drawn down by the inveterate
sea,
Without one chastening fire made to
start
From alters built around its polar
heart.

> E.J. PRATT, "The sea-cathedral", 1932.

And out there in the starlight, with no
trace
Upon it of its deed but the last wave
From the *Titanic* fretting at its base,
Silent, composed, ringed by its icy
broods,
The gray shape with the palaeolithic
face
Was still the master of the longitudes.

> E.J. PRATT, *"The Titanic"*, 1935.

Dropped from its sloping womb
a huge cliff of blue
it roars its birth into an ocean
of slow death
returning
its giant pride
to deep water
to recycle silently
its self-destructive art.

> F.R. SCOTT, "Iceberg", 1973.

Idealists

An idealist is someone who has convinced himself other people are less
nasty than he is. A cynic in the
making.

> IRVING LAYTON, "Some observations and
> aphorisms", in *Tamarack rev.* No. 47,
> 1968, 6.

Ideals

O! pathless world of seeming!
O! pathless world of mine whose deep
ideal
Is more my own than ever was the
real.

> PAULINE JOHNSON, "Shadow river",
> 1895.

To have striven, to have made an
effort, to have been true to certain
ideals — this alone is worth the struggle. Now and again in a generation
one or two snatch something from dull
oblivion.

> SIR WILLIAM OSLER, address, "Study of
> the fevers of the South", Atlanta, May 6,
> 1896.

We want to be a nation but we cannot be a nation unless we fairly put before the people ideals which will appeal to all men whatever their religion or their race.

SIR WILFRID LAURIER, speech in Orillia, Oct. 19, 1904.

Let our purpose be ideal and our action be practical.

SIR WILFRID LAURIER; attributed.

Your people appear to believe that there exists in this country a large body of good men and women who if called together without the detested arts of politics will bring down from heaven happiness in flowing robes of pure white.

ARTHUR HAWKES, letter to T.A. Crerar, Sept. 5, 1925. (Pub. Arch. Man.)

It's a fine thing to have your head in the air, but it's always best to have your feet on the ground.

JOHN OLIVER, speech at Liberal convention, Vancouver, Mar. 11, 1927.

Somebody once told me that if I aimed at the sky I might at least hit a tree. If I wanted to hit a tree I'd shoot straight at it.

JOHN OLIVER, Premier of B.C., 1918-27.

Starving for fragrance on the lilied
    hills,
  Hungry for colour in a bower of
    rose,
Grieving for beauty amid daffodils,
  Man – the enigma – goes.

WILSON MACDONALD, "Enigma", 1931.

We must have social ideals as distinguished from what we have called the individual right.

R.B. BENNETT, speech to Montreal Board of Trade, Jan. 26, 1935.

Our bitterest wine is always drained from crushed ideals.

ARTHUR STRINGER, *The devastator*, 1944, 116.

The sheep call themselves idealists, and the wolves call themselves realists.

HUGH MACLENNAN, *Two solitudes*, 1945, 267.

Unending pursuit of an abstract ideal makes an impersonal world.

TREVOR LLOYD, in Howard Adelman and D. Lee, ed., *The university game*, 1968, 111.

Ideas

A feller with one idea grows rich, while he who calls him a fool dies poor.

T.C. HALIBURTON, *Sam Slick's wise saws*, 1853, I, 314.

The poor man of one idea is always in danger of being laughed at by people who have none.

ROBERT C. (BOB) EDWARDS, Calgary *Eye Opener*, June 6, 1902.

An idea, you know, is to some people a rare and valuable asset.

RALPH CONNOR, *The prospector*, 1904, 19.

New ideas are born in stables and brought up in jails. Whenever a new cause is struggling its way to recognition its adherents frequently have to die for it.

J.B. MCLACHLAN, qu. in *The maritime labour herald*, Nov. 17, 1923, 1.

Ideas are born; they develop; they are transformed; but they never die.

SIR ANDREW MACPHAIL, *Dalhousie rev.*, 1925, 22.

The Canadian public is ignorant, cowardly, and snobbish; it is mortally afraid of ideas and considers the discussion of first principles as a betrayal of bad manners.

> FREDERICK PHILIP GROVE, *Univ. of Tor. quart.*, July, 1938, 459.

This seeming incapacity for ideas, or rather this habit of carrying on our communal affairs at a level at which ideas never quite emerge into an articulate life of their own has surely impoverished Canadian politics.

> FRANK H. UNDERHILL, Presidential address to Can. Hist. Assoc. annual meeting, 1946.

An idea, when the time is right, is the greatest force in the world. Everything gives way to the overpowering force of an idea.

> W.A.C. BENNETT, favourite saying, qu. in P. Sherman, *Bennett*, 1966, 205.

Ideas that lie fallow, given opportune circumstances, eventually germinate.

> WILLIAM E. BLATZ, *Human security*, 1966, 9.

Explore the situation. Statements are expendable. Don't keep on looking in the rearview mirror and defending the status quo which is outmoded the moment it happened.

> MARSHALL MCLUHAN, qu. in *Weekend mag.*, Mar. 18, 1967, 4.

You grow up eating Kellogg's Corn Flakes and driving Chevrolet cars, and you know all the good things in your life come from somewhere else. So you think the place to go for *ideas* is where the corn flakes came from.

> LESLIE ARMOUR, Univ. of Waterloo, in R.L. Perry ed., *Galt, U.S.A.*, 1971, 10.

Identity

Unless we intend to be mere hewers of wood and drawers of water until the end, we should in right earnest set about strengthening the foundations of our identity.

> WILLIAM A. FOSTER, *Canada first; or our new nationality*, Toronto, 1871, 30.

Our national soul has not grown beyond infancy.

> MARIUS BARBEAU, address, Canadian Club, Toronto, Jan. 10, 1928.

What, to the members of other nations, does Canada stand for? So far, very little. Does that mean that our unrivalled sea-shores, our proud mountains, and our boundless prairies, unique on earth, have not tinged man's attitude to life and the world, or to God, whatever you care to call it? Does it mean that our broad slice of the universe as it was settled has not engendered a new human reaction to the outside world? I do not believe it.

> FREDERICK PHILIP GROVE, *It needs to be said*, 1929, 20.

We are not of these woods, we are not
   of these woods,
our roots are in autumn, and store for
   no spring.

> EARLE BIRNEY, "Hands", 1939.

You are so busy proving to the English that you are not Yankees, and proving to the Yankees that you are not English, you have no time to be yourselves at all.

> ANON., Australian professor of International Law to Judith Robinson, qu. in *Foreign affairs*, Oct., 1943, 70.

Our well-known Canadian laconicism is not always concealed wisdom, but a kind of dumbness, a frustration, a between-ness. We are continually on the verge of something but we don't quite get there. We haven't discovered what we are or where we're going and therefore we haven't much to say.

CHESTER DUNCAN, University of Manitoba, in talk to Winnipeg Poetry Society, Dec., 1947.

The surest way to the hearts of a Canadian audience is to inform them that their souls are to be identified with rock, rapids, wilderness, and virgin (but exploitable) forest. This pathological craving for identification with the subhuman may be illustrated in every department of Canadian culture.

HUGH KENNER, in M. Ross, ed., *Our sense of identity*, 1954, 203.

Something moves as it has never moved before in this land, moves dumbly in the deepest runnels of a collective mind, yet by sure direction toward a known goal. Sometimes by thought, more often by intuition, the Canadian people make the final discovery. They are discovering themselves.

BRUCE HUTCHISON, *Canada, tomorrow's giant*, 1957, preface.

If all of us
Who need roots
Start digging
At the same time
There just aren't
Going to be enough spades
To go around.

RAYMOND SOUSTER, "The need for roots", 1958.

The worth of life not being necessarily noise

we kept unusual silence, and then cried out
one word which has never yet been said —

ALFRED PURDY, "On Canadian identity", 1962.

This story of the loss and regaining of identity is, I think, the framework of all literature.

NORTHROP FRYE, *The educated imagination* (1962) 1964, 55.

The need for a special function in the world may reflect a pretentious nationalism, or it may reflect the need of a country, particularly a country uncertain of its identity, to feel responsible, to fulfill a mission, limited though this may be.

JOHN W. HOLMES, *Foreign affairs*, Vol. 41, No. 4, July, 1963, 663.

So far as national identity is concerned, I have no doubts at all that a Canadian is an animal recognizably distinct from an American, not just in the way he pronounces "out" or "about" or "twenty" but also in his attitudes and general character. My confidence on this score is the result of having observed Canadians in different international contexts, and listened to people of other nationalities discussing Canadian character and behaviour.

HARRY G. JOHNSON, *The Canadian quandary*, 1963, 12.

Searchers for a Canadian identity have failed to realize that you can only have an identification with something you can see or recognize. You need, if nothing else, an image in a mirror. No other country cares enough about us to give us back an image of ourselves that we can even resent.

GERMAINE WARKENTIN, "An image in a mirror", *Alphabet* No. 8, 1964.

If we are eventually to satisfy our-selves that we have at last achieved a Canadian identity, it will be only when we are satisfied that we have arrived at a better American way of life than the Americans have.

FRANK H. UNDERHILL, *The image of Confederation*, 1964, 69.

As a people, we appear uncertain about where we are going, how we are going and whether we are going sepa-rately or together. We are also worried about being absorbed en route by a big bold neighbour. We are suffering from a kind of national schizophrenia.

LESTER B. PEARSON, speech, Canadian Club, Vancouver, Sept. 17, 1964.

Canada nourished and raised me, edu-cated me, and threw me out into the world. She gave me everything – health, money, erudition – but she failed to give me the one thing essen-tial: a sense of identity, without which everything else is useless.

BRIAN STOCK, *Atlantic monthly*, Nov., 1964, 114.

And all power in its recalcitrance to that still uncoordinated, unblended and indigestible Canada that is ob-structing assimilation not only abroad but within itself! The problem we all have to face is the defence of individu-al identity against the centralized offi-cial domination that can so easily become a faceless despotism.

EDMUND WILSON, *O Canada; an Ameri-can's notes on Canadian culture*, 1965, 245.

With each passing month Canadians own less and less of their natural resources, their industry, their power to create and propagate ideas. With each passing month the task of main-taining a grip upon the essential germ of Canadian being, upon the Canadian

sense of place, becomes more and more difficult.

R.D. MATHEWS, in *Commonwealth litera-ture: unity and diversity in a common culture*, 1965, 166.

Give me back my fingerprints
My fingertips are raw
If I don't get my fingerprints
I have to call the Law.

LEONARD COHEN, "Give me back my fingertips", 1966.

Untraditional, North American, Jew-ish, Russian, and rootless in all four.

MIRIAM WADDINGTON, "Fortunes", 1966.

For multiple identity confuses
  anyway,
there must be a single total
all water-torrents of god-stuff.

AL PURDY, "Mind process re a faucet", 1966.

One of the derivations proposed for the word Canada is a Portuguese phrase meaning "nobody here". The etymology of the word Utopia is very similar, and perhaps the real Canada is an ideal with nobody in it. The Cana-da to which we really do owe loyalty is the Canada that we have failed to create.

NORTHROP FRYE, *The modern century*, 1967, 122.

Perhaps instead of constantly deplor-ing our lack of identity, we should attempt to understand and explain the regional, ethnic and class identities that we do have. It might just be that it is in these limited identities that 'Ca-nadianism' is found; and that except for our over-heated nationalist intel-lectuals, Canadians find this situation quite satisfactory.

RAMSAY COOK, *International Jour.*, Vol. 22, 1967, 663.

There are few things I find more irritating about my own country than this so-called "search for an identity", an identity which I've never doubted having in the first place.

AL PURDY, *The new Romans*, 1968, Intro., iii.

Contemporary man is a nomad, without ancestors, without posterity and without a country. Despite the consoling fiction of nationality, we are all displaced persons.

KILDARE DOBBS, *Reading the time*, 1968, x.

the knowledge of
our origins, and where
we are in truth,
whose land this is
and is to be.

JOHN NEWLOVE, "The pride", 1968.

What is so embarrassing is that while we are determined to defend our culture against any comer, nobody is sure what our culture is, how it differs from the British or American, or come to think of it, if we even have one. Once we were content with a modest but coy definition. We were neither British nor American, but something else. Something nice, very nice. The continued quest for that "something very nice" has created one of the few original Canadian enterprises, the What-Is-Our-Identity business, and a spiteful subsidiary, anti-Americanism.

MORDECAI RICHLER, in Al Purdy, ed., *The new Romans*, 1968, 12.

Has Canada got an identity – this everlasting, frustrating, humiliating question! It is like asking a person to state his reasons for being alive, the assumption being that if he cannot explain *why* he is alive, he must be presumed dead.

HUGH MACLENNAN, in G.F.G. Stanley, ed., *Canadian identity*, 1969, 23.

It is the only country in the world that knows how to live without an identity. You can be a French Canadian or an English Canadian, but you cannot be a "Canadian".

MARSHALL MCLUHAN, in 1969, qu. in Duncan Macpherson, *Macpherson's Canada*, 1969, 1.

A closer study of Canadian literature reveals both positive and negative characteristics; more especially it reveals not only the anxiety which results from the lack of any clearly defined identity, but also, and sometimes simultaneously, a confidence that such an identity exists and is to be realized.

D.G. JONES, *Butterfly on rock*, 1970, 14.

Is there some mysterious force in our character which drives us relentlessly in this introspective quest for our identity? Or is it just that in our assemblage along the United States border we have turned away from that great mass of Canada lying to the north, and in so doing set up a tension between our minds and our hearts? If this be the case, how unnecessary is our uncertainty. For if there is a distinctive Canadian characteristic, surely it is an awareness of space – a dynamism of spirit prompted by our sense of the frontier.

PIERRE E. TRUDEAU, annual meeting, Canadian Press, Toronto, Apr. 15, 1970.

Canadians have also had to deal with other forces beyond their control; economic forces, cultural forces, and perhaps most of all the thoughtless expansionism of our neighbour to the south. But out of these unique circumstances has been forged a special Canadian character, a Canadian tradition, a Canadian way-of-life – in fact a Canadian identity.

JOHN C. PARKIN, *Globe and Mail,* May 3, 1971, 7.

The battle for our cultural identity will be won or lost not in university libraries but in local drug stores and dirty book shops.

JOHN MUGGERIDGE, *Saturday night,* 86, No. 5 (May, 1971), 30.

Canadian identity will not be undermined by multi-culturalism. Indeed, we believe that cultural pluralism is the very essence of Canadian identity. Every ethnic group has the right to preserve and develop its own culture and values within the Canadian context.

CANADA. GOVERNMENT. *Response to report of the Roy. Comm. on bilingualism and biculturalism,* H. of C., *Debates,* Oct. 8, 1971, 8580.

I come from a country
of slow and diffident words
of broken rhythms
of unsaid feelings.

Next time I am born
I intend to come
from a different country.

ELIZABETH BREWSTER, "Gold man", 1971.

The famous Canadian problem of identity may seem a rationalized, self-pitying or made-up problem to those who have never had to meet it, or have never understood that it was there to be met. But it is with human beings as with birds: the creative instinct has a great deal to do with the assertion of territorial rights.

NORTHROP FRYE, *The bush garden,* 1971, Preface, i.

It seems to me that Canadian sensibility has been profoundly disturbed, not so much by our famous problem of identity, important as that is, as by a series of paradoxes in what confronts that identity. It is less perplexed by the question "Who am I?" than by some such riddle as "Where is here?"

NORTHROP FRYE, *The bush garden,* 1971, 220.

We went directly from being bastard Englishmen to being bastard Americans.

PETER NEWMAN, *Saturday rev.,* Mar. 13, 1971, 17.

It's just *Canadian.* Diverse. Complex. Fractionalized. Pleuralistic. *E pleuribus multi.* To agree to disagree, to harness diversity, to respect dissent: perhaps this is the real essence of Canada.

ROBERT L. PERRY, *Galt, U.S.A.,* 1971, 106.

You refuse to own
yourself, you permit
others to do it for you:
you become slowly more public,
in a year there will be nothing left
of you but a megaphone.

MARGARET ATWOOD, *Power politics,* 1971, 30.

The Americans are in the process of taking over Canada, not because they are conquerors, but because Canadians are so ready to surrender. It's that terrible ingrained uncertainty in us, the absence of knowing who we are and why we are here, which is gradually depriving us of nationhood.

PETER NEWMAN, in Thomas A. Hockin, *The Canadian condominium*, 1972, 169.

The contribution of education to a distinctive Canadian consciousness is largely accidental.

ALBERT TUCKER, Principal, Glendon College, qu. in Toronto *Star*, Sept. 13, 1972, 8.

Idleness

When the troubles of life arise out of idleness, a return to industry is usually the last shift.

THOMAS MCCULLOCH, *The letters of Mephibosheth Stepsure*, 1821, Letter 1.

True idleness consists in doing nothing, with the grace and mastery of an accomplishment; this is an art.

BLISS CARMAN, *The kinship of nature*, 1904, 59.

Let me lie among the daisies, with my
   stomach to the sky,
Making poses in the roses, in the
   middle of July,
Let me nestle in the nettles, let me
   there absorb the dew
On a pair of flannel breeches with the
   stitches worked in blue.

STEPHEN LEACOCK, "Idleness: a song for the long vacation", 1923.

Ignorance

Why are we born so ignorant! Why can we not learn the secrets of life, of destiny, of affinity, as we learn from books, other matters, which compared to these, have scarcely any relation to our happiness!

SIR WILFRID LAURIER, letter to Mme. Joseph Lavergne, Aug. 2, 1891.

Most ignorant are we of what we are most assured.

GEORGE M. GRANT, in *Can. mag.*, Oct., 1900, 492.

The greater the ignorance the greater the dogmatism.

SIR WILLIAM OSLER, *Montreal med. jour.*, 1902, 684.

Ignorance may find a truth on its doorstep that erudition vainly seeks in the stars.

GEORGE ILES, *Canadian stories*, 1918, 168.

There are some men who get more satisfaction out of their ignorance than most learned men get out of their knowledge.

PETER MCARTHUR, 1924, qu. in *The best of Peter McArthur*, 1967, 150.

The trouble with little people is that if we are not familiar with their particular form of ignorance, they think we know nothing.

PETER MCARTHUR, 1924, qu. in *The best of Peter McArthur*, 1967, 6.

Illusions

Illusion makes the better part of life.
Happy self-conjurors, deceived, we
   win
Delight and ruled by fancy live in
   dreams.

NICHOLAS F. DAVIN, "An epic of the dawn", 1884.

and maybe some cows and
room for some
of the more easily kept illusions

> ALFRED PURDY, "The country north of
> Belleville", 1965.

When I was nineteen I had no illusion
or had the illusion I had none.

> ELIZABETH BREWSTER, "Festival of reli-
> gion and the arts", 1972.

The only thing to do is to remember
that illusions are as necessary to politics as they are to all of us in our
individual lives; and, to search for
those rare moments of truth when the
veils slip away and the naked animal
shouts profanity.

> PETER DESBARATS, Vancouver *Sun*, Mar.
> 10, 1972, 4.

Imagination

It is perfectly true, and a truth always
to be borne in mind by statesmen,
that, in politics as in other departments
of life, the imagination has its claims
as well as the reason, and that while
the one is convinced the other requires
to be impressed.

> GOLDWIN SMITH, in *Can. monthly*, 1879,
> 211.

Imagination is the great gift of the
gods. Given it, one does not need to
look afar for subjects. There is romance in every face.

> ROBERT SERVICE, *Ballads of a Bohemian*,
> 1921, 96.

The truth is, imagination, in itself, has
no place in the equipment of a permanent writer. Imagination invents, it
does not create.

> SIR ANDREW MACPHAIL, Roy. Soc. Can.,
> *Proceedings*, 1939, 131.

Nobody stuffs the world in at your
eyes.
The optic heart must venture: a
jail-break
And re-creation.

> MARGARET AVISON, "Snow", 1960.

In ordinary life we fall into a private
and separate subconscious every night,
where we reshape the world according
to a private and separate imagination.

> NORTHROP FRYE, *The educated imagi-
> nation*, (CBC Massey Lectures, 1962)
> 1964, 103.

The fundamental job of the imagination in ordinary life, then, is to produce, out of the society we have to live
in, a vision of the society we want to
live in.

> NORTHROP FRYE, *The educated imagi-
> nation*, (1962) 1964, 140.

A failure of imagination has far wider
significance than most of those acts
which we usually refer to as sins.

> GWETHALYN GRAHAM, letter to Solange
> Chaput Rolland, in *Dear enemies*, 1963,
> 108.

It is because the unintelligent have no
imagination and the vast majority of
my clients are unintelligent.

> ARTHUR ELLIS, Canada's official execu-
> tioner, qu. in A. O'Brien, *Daredevils of
> Niagara*, 1964, 5, on why condemned go
> to their executions casually.

Very young children have no imagination. They have images. They are
realists and credulous. The apparent
imaginative powers lie in the adult
interpretation of their mistakes in
dealing with their world – inner and
outer.

> WILLIAM E. BLATZ, *Human security*,
> 1966, 5.

I believe there is more room inside than outside. And all the diversities which get absorbed can later work their way out into fantastic things, like hawk-training, IBM programming, mountain-climbing, or poetry.

GWENDOLYN MACEWEN, *A breakfast for barbarians*, 1966, Intro.

Real society, the total body of what humanity has done and can do, is revealed to us only by the arts and sciences; nothing but the imagination can apprehend that reality as a whole, and nothing but literature, in a culture as verbal as ours, can train the imagination to fight for the sanity and the dignity of man.

NORTHROP FRYE, *The stubborn structure: essays on criticism and society*, 1970, 105.

Immaturity

This is the case of the high-school land,
deadset in adolescence,
loud treble laughs and sudden fists,
bright chucks, the gangling presence.
This boy is wonderful at sports
and physically quite healthy;
he's taken to church on Sunday still
and keeps his prurience stealthy.

EARLE BIRNEY, "Canada: case history", 1945.

Immigrants

How great the ardor which their souls inspired,
who, leaving far behind their native plain,
Have sought a home beyond the western main;
And braved the terrors of the stormy seas,
In search of wealth, of freedom, and of ease.

OLIVER GOLDSMITH, (Canadian), "The rising village", 1825.

Dear, most justly dear to every land beneath the sun are the children born in her bosom, and nursed upon her breast; but when the man of another country, wherever born, speaking whatever speech, holding whatever creed, seeks out a country to serve and honour and cleave to, in weal or in woe,– when he heaves up the anchor of his heart from its old moorings, and lays at the feet of the mistress of his choice, his New country, all the hopes of his ripe manhood, he establishes by such devotion a claim to consideration, not second even to that of the children of the soil.

THOMAS D'ARCY MCGEE, speech in Quebec, May 10, 1862.

Sifton's pets.

ANON., reference to European immigrants brought to Canada through efforts of Clifford Sifton, when Minister of Interior, 1896 to 1905.

The scum of Europe.

ANON., term sometimes used to describe immigrants, 1900 to 1905.

New Canadians.

HOWARD A. KENNEDY, from his book, *New Canada and the new Canadians*, 1907.

In my new-made, day-old cities I apply them to the test,
Where they mix and clash and scramble with the Spirit of the West;
With the lust of gain before them, and the lust of sin within,
Where a few go down the deeper, but the many rise and win;
Where the sons of men are equal in the eyes of other men,
And the man who falls defeated rises up to fight again,
I mix 'em, mix 'em, mix 'em, in the turmoil of the town,

As I turn 'em out Canadians – all but
the yellow and brown.

ROBERT STEAD, "The mixer", 1908.

If there is such a country as Canada-
Ukraine, we do not know of it. Hyphens should be left at the port of
embarkation to be applied for when
the immigrant returns for good to the
land of his fathers.

JOHN W. DAFOE, 1913, qu. in M. Donnelly, *Dafoe of the Free press*, 1968, 73.

When I speak of quality I have in
mind, I think, something that is quite
different from what is in the mind of
the average writer or speaker upon the
question of immigration. I think a
stalwart peasant in a sheep-skin coat,
born on the soil, whose forefathers
have been farmers for ten generations,
with a stout wife and a half-dozen
children, is good quality.

CLIFFORD SIFTON, speech to Toronto
Board of Trade, Mar., 1922; *Maclean's*,
Apr. 1, 1922, 16. Sifton made similar
statements when he was Minister of the
Interior, 1896-1905.

Dazzled by sun and drugged by space
they wait,
These homeless peoples, at our prairie
gate;
Dumb with the awe of these whom
fate has hurled,
Breathless, upon the threshold of a
world!

ISABEL ECCLESTONE MACKAY, "Calgary
station", 1922.

In the light of experience it would be
unrealistic to say that immigrants who
have spent the greater part of their life
in tropical or subtropical countries
become readily adapted to the Canadian mode of life which, to no small
extent, is determined by climatic conditions. It is a matter of record that
natives of such countries are more apt
to break down in health than immigrants from countries where the climate is more akin to that of Canada.

WALTER E. HARRIS, Minister of Citizenship and Immigration, letter written in
1952, read into H. of C., *Debates*, Apr.
24, 1953, 4352.

I believe that a country attracts the
kind of immigrants it deserves.

HUGH MACLENNAN, "The art of city-living", in *Thirty and three*, 1954, 130.

The refugee is the everyman of our
time.

HENRY KREISEL, *The betrayal*, 1964, 16.

We are all immigrants to this place
even if we were born here: the country
is too big for anyone to inhabit completely, and in the parts unknown to us
we move in fear, exiles and invaders.
This country is something that must be
chosen – it is so easy to leave – and
if we do choose it we are still choosing
a violent duality.

MARGARET ATWOOD, *Journals of Susanna Moodie*, 1970, 62.

The old immigrant gods must fade to
inconsequence at the frontier if a new
civilization is to mature. If they don't,
they bring in relatives and even new
acquaintances and keep their subjects
colonial forever, always with a sense
that this place may not be home or
perhaps, at any rate, not one worthwhile defending.

ROBERT HARLOW, *Scann*, 1972, 134.

Immigration

I am led to conceive it indispensibly
necessary to overwhelm and sink the
[French-] Canadian population by the
introduction of a greater number of
English protestants, and this I believe
to be practicable.

JONATHAN SEWELL, letter to Sir James
Craig, early 1810.

Let them once immigrate, the clog which fettered them is suddenly removed; they are free; and the dearest privilege of this freedom is to wreak upon their superiors the long-locked-up hatred of their hearts.

> SUSANNA MOODIE, *Roughing it in the bush*, Vol. 1, 1852, 214, on emigrants from England.

If these sketches should prove the means of deterring one family from sinking their property, and shipwrecking all their hopes, by going to reside in the backwoods of Canada, I shall consider myself amply repaid for revealing the secrets of the prison-house, and feel that I have not toiled and suffered in the wilderness in vain.

> SUSANNA MOODIE, *Roughing it in the bush*, 1852, 291.

Never in the world's history, were a purely agricultural population so suddenly and unpreparedly converted into mere town labourers.

> THOMAS D'ARCY MCGEE, *The Irish position in British and in Republican North America*, 1866, 7.

The best kind of emigration agent [is] the successful settler in the new district.

> THOMAS WHITE, H. of C., *Debates*, Mar. 4, 1884, 637.

Our gates are open to the oppressed of Europe; but when they come here they must forget their feuds, forswear their racial aspirations and become Canadians, not only in name but in fact.

> *MANITOBA FREE PRESS*, Aug. 10, 1914, 11, editorial.

Michael Angelo, although he built St. Peter's at Rome, could not enter this country, because we do not want architects or carpenters from Latin countries. If he came from Iceland and could build an icehouse, we could use him.

> SAMUEL W. JACOBS, H. of C., *Debates*, Mar. 1, 1927, 776.

None of the founders of the early Christian church could enter Canada under the present regulations of the department. There are in the case of Jesus of Nazareth – I am saying it with all respect – four orders in council which would prohibit him from coming in here. There would be first, the order relating to the non-agriculturist class. Carpenters are not permitted to enter this country coming from that district. And then he would not have a proper passport; he would not be travelling by a continuous journey; and he would have no relatives in this country.

> SAMUEL W. JACOBS, H. of C., *Debates*, Mar. 1, 1927, 776.

Good-bye God, I'm going to Canada.

> ANON., remark attributed to a little girl on crossing Can.-U.S. border, 1930's, later altered by Toronto Board of Trade to "Good! By God, I'm going to Canada!"

With regard to the selection of immigrants, much has been said about discrimination. I wish to make it quite clear that Canada is perfectly within her rights in selecting the persons whom we regard as desirable future citizens. It is not a "fundamental human right" of any alien to enter Canada. It is a privilege.

> W.L. MACKENZIE KING, H. of C., *Debates*, May 1, 1947, 2646.

Large-scale immigration from the Orient would change the fundamental composition of the Canadian population. Any considerable Oriental immigration would, moreover, be certain to give rise to social and economic problems of a character that might lead to serious difficulties in the field of international relations.

W.L. MACKENZIE KING, H. of C., *Debates*, May 1, 1947, 2646.

A national government dealing with immigration policy is like a ship buffeted by contrary winds. Labour blows one way and employers another; French Canadians puff up a powerful blast against the prevailing English-speaking majority; various nationality associations exert their pressures; and a chill draught of prejudice against foreigners comes from some of the old stock. In these gusty waters the government must steer a course. Sometimes it may choose to use its auxiliary motors and go against the wind.

DAVID C. CORBETT, *Canada's immigration policy: a critique*, 1957, 37.

We in Canada seem to face an unpleasant choice. Either we are illiberal in our policy of admission, or else we expose non-whites in Canada to illiberal treatment.

DAVID C. CORBETT, *Canada's immigration policy: a critique*, 1957, 195.

Interesting and important as the external migration streams may be, they are dwarfed in volume by the migration streams flowing *within* Canada. The Canadian population is in a perpetual state of flux from migration as people change residence from one locality to another.

LEROY O. STONE, *Migration in Canada*, Dominion Bureau of Statistics, 1961 Census Monograph, (Queen's Printer, 1969), 26.

It is unlikely that any other society has resembled a huge demographic railway station as much as has the non-French part of Canada. As well as a society receiving immigrants it has been one producing emigrants either naturally or by harbouring the "birds of passage" who have stopped over in Canada while making the move from Europe to the United States.

JOHN PORTER, *The vertical mosaic*, 1965, 33.

Canada has two charter groups, the French and the English, although they have been by no means of equal strength in economic decisions, and since Confederation they have had conflicting ideas about who should enter the country.

JOHN PORTER, *The vertical mosaic*, 1965, 60.

The dependence on external recruitment has created the illusion of adequacy. It has also permitted the continuity of class-bound education as exemplified by the classical college system in Quebec and the academic collegiate system in Ontario.

JOHN PORTER, *The vertical mosaic*, 1965, 166.

Immortality

The heavens will not unveil
    themselves,
  Yet mortal eyes may see
In mortal frames the budding flowers
  Of immortality.

ALEXANDER MCLACHLAN, "A dream", 1856.

I ask is there end of it − any?
  If any, when comes it anigh?
I could die not the one death but many
  To know and be sure I should
    die . . .

To know that somewhere in the
    distance

When Nature shall take back my
   breath,
I shall add up the sum of existence,
And find that its total is — death!

> GEORGE F. CAMERON, "All heart-sick",
> 1887.

Space, in the dim predestined hour,
Shall crumble like a ruined tower.
I only, with unfaltering eye
Shall watch the dreams of God go by.

> CHARLES G.D. ROBERTS, "The unsleep-
> ing", 1896.

The immortal spirit hath no bars
   To circumscribe its dwelling place;
My soul hath pastured with the stars
   Upon the meadow-lands of space.

> FREDERICK G. SCOTT, "Dawn", 1899.

There is a part of me that knows,
Beneath incertitude and fear,
I shall not perish when I pass
Beyond mortality's frontier.

> BLISS CARMAN, "Non omnis moriar",
> 1901.

Thus on, till the light of all being is
   rippling around us
   On paths we have trod:
Till the sun bursts aloft o'er the hills
   where the morning hath found us
   Entempled with God.

> ALBERT D. WATSON, "Woman", 1923.

I shall say, Lord, "Is it music, is it
   morning,
Song that is fresh as sunrise, light that
   sings?"
When on some hill there breaks the
   immortal warning
Of half-forgotten springs.

> MARJORIE PICKTHALL, "Resurgam",
> 1925.

And in that twilight world, whose
   floodless sea
Washes the margin of a silent land,
We shall not walk alone, but hand
   in hand,
And Love shall warm our immortality
With an eternal spring; since even
   death
Cannot dispart our souls, nor chill our
   mingled breath.

> AUDREY ALEXANDRA BROWN, "Lao-
> damia", 1931.

Some persons refuse to stay dead.
They are in continual resurrection.
Their flesh is indestructible
Their blood still courses through the
   veins of humanity.

> HELMER O. OLESON, "Indestructibles",
> 1952.

Imperialism

In the government you called civilized, the happiness of the people is
constantly sacrificed to the splendour
of empire.

> CHIEF JOSEPH BRANT, letter, 1803, tran-
> scribed by Thomas Eddy, qu. in W.L.
> Stone, *Life of Joseph Brant*, 1838, Vol.
> 2, 481.

One Flag, One Throne, One Empire.

> MARGARET POLSON MURRAY, Imperial
> Order Daughters of the Empire motto,
> founded Feb. 1, 1900.

I am an Imperialist because I will not
be a Colonial.

> STEPHEN B. LEACOCK, *University mag.*,
> Feb., 1907, 133.

There can be no lasting Imperialism
which conflicts with Canadian nationality.

> DR. MICHAEL CLARK, speech in Calgary,
> Sept. 11, 1913.

They talks of England's glory and
   a-'oldin' of our trade,
Of Empire and 'igh destiny until we're
   fair flim-flammed;
But if it's for the likes o' that, that
   bloody war is made,
Then wot I say is: Empire and 'igh
   destiny be damned.

> ROBERT W. SERVICE, "A song of the
> sandbags", 1916.

Canada had not only to achieve autonomy inside the British Empire but also
to maintain a separate existence on a
continent dominated by the United
States. She thus has to come to terms
with two imperialisms, real or potential.

> DONALD G. CREIGHTON, *Conservative
> concepts*, Vol. 2, Spring, 1960, 6.

Imperialism was a sentiment and an
outlook before it became a policy.

> CARL BERGER, *The sense of power; stud-
> ies in the ideas of Canadian imperial-
> ism, 1867-1914*, 1970, 12.

Importance

Many a feller looks fat, who is only
swelled.

> THOMAS C. HALIBURTON, *Sam Slick's wise
> saws*, 1853, ch. 24.

Improvement

No conscious effort towards betterment, whether individual or collective,
is ever lost. It is held on the lap of
time.

> R.C. WALLACE, *Queen's quart.*, Vol. 61,
> 1954/55, 495.

No improvement in the human situation can take place independently of
the human will to improve and that
confidence in automatic or impersonal
improvement is always misplaced.

> NORTHROP FRYE, *The modern century*,
> 1967, 41.

Inadequacy

I was never drunk enough, never poor
enough, never rich enough.

> LEONARD COHEN, *Beautiful losers*, 1966,
> 153.

Incest

brother and sister
conjunctive and
peaceable

> PHYLLIS WEBB, "Suite of lies", 1965.

Income Tax

The Government's new income taxes
will be accepted with the cheerful
equanimity deserved by all measures
well designed to win the war.

> MONTREAL *STAR* , July 26, 1917.

Incompatibility

It is over, the ceaseless search is over,
Souls may collide but not like bodies
   mate,
After collision they must separate,
Minds are not twins as Calais is to
   Dover.

> ROBERT FINCH, "Over", 1943.

Incompetence

Incompetence plus incompetence
equals incompetence.

> LAURENCE J. PETER and RAYMOND HULL,
> *The Peter principle*, 1969, 107.

Create the impression that you have
already reached your level of incompetence.

> LAURENCE J. PETER and RAYMOND HULL,
> *The Peter principle*, 1969, 144.

Indecision

In love, as in all things, indecision spells ruination.

ARNOLD HAULTAIN, *Hints for lovers*, 1909, 124.

Independence

We cannot be independent.

WILLIAM LYON MACKENZIE, speech to the Reformers, Sept., 1834.

If in the hidden decrees of that wisdom by which this world is ruled, it is written that these countries are not for ever to remain portions of the Empire, we owe it to our honour to take good care that, when they separate from us, they should not be the only countries on the American continent in which the Anglo-Saxon race shall be found unfit to govern itself.

LORD DURHAM, *Report*, 1839, 310.

I see in British North America a region grand enough for the seat of a great empire. I find its inhabitants vigorous, hardy, energetic . . . I find them jealous of the United States and of Great Britain, as they ought to be; and therefore when I look at their extent and resources, I know that they can neither be conquered by the former nor permanently held by the latter. They will be independent, as they are already self-maintaining.

WILLIAM H. SEWARD, *Cruise to Labrador*, 1857.

Rob me of all the joys of sense,
Curse me with all but impotence;
Fling me upon an ocean oar,
Cast me upon a savage shore;
Slay me: but own above my bier:
"The man now gone still held yet here,
The jewel, Independence".

THOMAS D'A. MCGEE, "Independence", 1858.

If independence were to take place immediately it would precipitate us into the United States, but while I hold this view, I believe that the day for independence will come, and unless we were prepared for it, unless our legislation be framed with that view, we will be found then in the same position as now, and being unprepared for a separate political existence, we will have no choice with regard to our future.

SIR ALEXANDER T. GALT, H. of C., *Debates*, Feb. 21, 1870, 143.

We no more advocate Independence than we advocate the Day of Judgment.

WILLIAM A. FOSTER, speech to Canadian National Association, Toronto, Feb., 1875; *Canada first*, 1890, 80.

Gentlemen, we want no independence in this country, except the independence that we have at this moment.

SIR JOHN A. MACDONALD, in *Report in honour of Macdonald*, 1885, 103.

First feel throughout the throbbing land
A nation's pulse, a nation's pride –
The independent life – then stand
Erect, unbound, at Britain's side!

CHARLES MAIR, "In memory of William A. Foster", (1888).

I hold out to my fellow-countrymen the idea of independence, but, whenever the day comes, it must come by the consent of both countries, and we shall continue to keep the good feeling and the good will of the motherland.

SIR WILFRID LAURIER, H. of C., *Debates*, 1892, 1142.

I cling to the hope that – sooner or later, and rather soon than late – there may be born into the world an independent Canadian Commonwealth; nerving itself to solve, after its own fashion, the many racial and religious, moral and political, economic and material problems which confront us; united by enduring links of kinship and sympathy, hope and admiration, with three of the leading nations of the world; advancing, more effectively than now, our own varied interests as well as the true welfare of the old land, the proud mother of free nations as well as free Parliaments.

EDWARD BLAKE, letter to Laurier, 1892.

The words – a colony, a nation – never before in the history of the world were these two words associated before; never before were they applied to the same community, implying as they do at once the independence and the power of a sovereign people.

SIR WILFRID LAURIER, speech in Liverpool, June 12, 1897.

I am being reluctantly forced to the conclusion that the worst foes of political independence are independents. They will not accept any opinion as honest unless it agrees with their own.

SIR JOHN WILLISON, letter to H.I. Strang, about 1908.

The *raison d'être* of my political role is to remain independent of power.

HENRI BOURASSA, on refusing a Cabinet post, Sept., 1911.

No man can be independent beyond the trust of his fellowmen in his capacity, judgment, and probity. Bullheadedness is not independence.

SIR WILLIAM VAN HORNE, letter to W.F. Luxton, Winnipeg; qu., Vaughan, *Van Horne*, 1920, 245.

Real independence is not the product of tariffs and treaties. It is a spiritual thing. No country has reached its full stature, which makes its goods at home, but not its faith and its philosophy.

CANADIAN FORUM , Oct., 1920, editorial.

We are on the very verge of independence.

W.S. FIELDING, H. of C., *Debates*, Apr. 21, 1921.

My opinion is that Canada should assume a position of practical independence and carry on her own foreign policy without reference to anybody else and that Great Britain should have absolute control of her own policy without any interference from Canada.

CLIFFORD SIFTON, letter to John Willison, June 30, 1921.

If ever there were a time when Canada should turn a deaf ear to the siren song of European diplomats, it is now. Canada ought to sail by, lashed like Ulysses to the nationalist mast, with her ears stuffed with taxes.

JOHN S. EWART, in Toronto *Star*, Mar. 22, 1923.

Lean on no one. Find your own centre and live in it, surrendering it to no person or thing.

EMILY MURPHY, "Janey Canuck's Motto", series of quotations published daily in Edmonton *Bulletin*, 1920's, qu. in B.H. Saunders, *Emily Murphy crusader*, 1945, 326.

I belong to no one; alas, I am my own.

DARYL HINE, *Delta*, No. 6, 1959, 17.

What Canada really fears is not the old America, but America in its new role of world power. It fears that America in seeking to maintain its world power will make demand after demand on Canada, each reasonable in itself, until the substance of independence is modified out of existence.

W.L. MORTON, *The Canadian identity*, 1961, 84.

Independence or death. The dignity of the people of Quebec demands independence. The independence of Quebec is only possible through social revolution. Social revolution means a "free Quebec". Students, workers, peasants form your secret groups against Anglo-American colonialism.

FRONT DE LIBERATION QUEBECOIS (F.L.Q.) *Manifesto*, 1963. (Trans.)

Some may think it is unnecessary to continue stressing the need for Canada to retain her independence. But considering the rate at which it is being lost, I believe we should keep on pointing out what is happening. Of far greater importance, we should take steps that will reverse the present trends.

WALTER GORDON, *A choice for Canada*, 1966, xviii.

I do say that Canadians should not take their independence for granted; they should not underestimate the great difficulties in the way of maintaining it.

WALTER L. GORDON, *A choice for Canada*, 1966, xix.

My premise is that Canadians wish their country to remain independent both economically and politically. Moreover, we want the benefits gained from developing our nation to be shared by Canadians — not handed over to enterprising people in other countries for a fraction of their potential value.

WALTER GORDON, *A choice for Canada*, 1966, xx.

The spirit of independence. That was what the Prairies meant to the native peoples of these western provinces: that was what the Prairies were to mean to the newcomers who settled the plains during the late nineteenth and early twentieth centuries.

G.F.G. STANLEY in D.P. Gagan, ed., *Prairie perspectives*, 1970, 9.

Indian Summer

This dreamy Indian-summer day
    Attunes the soul to tender sadness;
We love — but joy not in the ray:
    It is not summer's fervid gladness,
But a melancholy glory
    Hovering softly round decay,
Like swan that sings her own sad story
    Ere she floats in death away.

SUSANNA MOODIE, "Indian summer", 1864.

Saw wood in Indian Summer.

ANON., saying of pioneer Ontario farmers, 1800's.

Of all Earth's varied, lovely moods,
The loveliest is when she broods
Among her dreaming solitudes
On Indian Summer days.

HELENA COLEMAN, "Indian summer", 1906.

Indians

They come like foxes through the woods, which afford them concealment and serve them as an impregnable fortress. They attack like lions, and, as their surprises are made when they are least expected, they meet with no resistance. They take flight like birds, disappearing before they have really appeared.

JÉRÔME LALEMANT, *Relation; from the summer of the year 1659 to the summer of the year 1660 (Jesuit relations,* Thwaites ed., Vol. 45, 197).

For a long time it has been considered a very good practice to visit the savages in our settlements in order to accustom these people to live like us and become instructed in our religion. I perceive, Monseigneur, that just the opposite has taken place, for instead of becoming accustomed to our laws, I assure you that they have given us everything they have that is most wicked and have taken for themselves only that which is bad and vicious in us.

MARQUIS DE DENONVILLE, letter to the Minister, Nov. 13, 1685. (Pub.Arch. Can.) (Trans.)

And whereas it is just and reasonable, and essential to our Interest, and the security of our Colonies, that the several Nations or Tribes of Indians with whom We are connected, and who live under our Protection, should not be molested or disturbed in the Possession of such Parts of Our Dominions and Territories as, not having been ceded to or purchased by Us, are reserved to them or any of them, as their Hunting Grounds.

GREAT BRITAIN. *Royal Proclamation,* Court of St. James, Oct. 7, 1763.

Let the savages enjoy their Desarts in quiet.

THOMAS GAGE, 1772, qu., *Can. hist. rev.,* 1932, 154.

For the prairie Indians the love of rum is their first inducement to industry; they undergo every hardship and fatigue to procure a skinfull of this delicious beverage, and when a nation becomes addicted to drinking, it affords a strong presumption that they will soon become excellent hunters.

DUNCAN MCGILLIVRAY, *Journal,* 1794-5, ed., A.S. Morton, 1929, 47.

They have no idea of amassing wealth for themselves individually; and they wonder that persons can be found in any society so destitute of every generous sentiment, as to enrich themselves at the expense of others, and to live in ease and affluence regardless of the misery and wretchedness of members of the same community to which they themselves belong.

ISAAC WELD JR., *Travels through the States, and the provinces of Upper and Lower Canada,* 1799, 402.

I love you. I have smoked out of the same pipe with you. You are now my brother. I thank you for the presents that you have given me. They are the first that we have received. They correspond with every part of your conduct toward us. You have a charitable heart. From the moment we saw you the dark clouds that covered us disappeared. We see clearly now.

PEGUIS, Ojibway chief, Red River, Man., on presents of rum, tobacco and ammunition received from Colin Robertson, Hudson's Bay Company, about 1815, qu. in J.W.G. MacEwan, *Portraits from the plains,* 1971, 11.

DIED — At St. John's, Newfoundland, on the 6th of June last in the 29th year of her age, Shanawdithit, supposed to be the last of the Red Indians or Beothuks.

LONDON (Eng.) *TIMES,* Sept. 14, 1829.

The fate of the red inhabitants of America, the real proprietors of its soil, is, without any exception, the most sinful story recorded in the history of the human race.

SIR FRANCIS B. HEAD, *A narrative,* 1839, appendix A, 2.

Spanish civilisation crushed the Indian; English civilisation scorned and neglected him; French civilisation embraced and cherished him.

> FRANCIS PARKMAN, *France and England*, 1865, 44.

The Chippewa and Swampy Cree Tribes of Indians and all other Indians inhabiting the district hereinafter described and defined do hereby cede, release, surrender and yield up to Her Majesty the Queen and successors forever, all the lands included within the following limits . . .

> CANADA. Treaty No. 1, signed at Red River, Man., Aug. 3, 1871.

This wild man who first welcomed the newcomer is the only perfect socialist or communist in the world. He holds all things in common with his tribe — the land, the bison, the river, and the moose.

> WILLIAM F. BUTLER, *The great lone land*, 1873, 242.

Daughters of the land.

> ANON., name given to Indian girls who became the wives of French adventurers, voyageurs and travellers during the early settlement of the West.

What I offer you is to be while the water flows and the sun rises.

> ALEXANDER MORRIS, treaty negotiations with the Indians, North-West Angle, Lake of the Woods, Oct. 1, 1873. Variations of the phrase were used by the Indian chiefs, such as POUNDMAKER, Aug. 23, 1876, "as long as the sun shines and water runs".

. . . The Indians shall have the right to pursue their avocations of hunting and fishing throughout the tract surrendered . . . subject to such regulations as may from time to time be made by Her Government . . . and saving and except such tracts as may, from time to time, be required or taken up for settlement, mining, lumbering or other purposes by Her Government or by any of the subjects thereof duly authorized by the said Government.

> CANADA. Treaty No. 3, signed at Kenora, Ont., Oct. 3, 1873.

It is very humiliating to a British subject to witness the wholesale poisoning of a nation that ought to have protection.

> JOHN MCDOUGALL, on the liquor trade on the Prairies, letter to David Laird, Jan. 7, 1874. (Pub.Arch.Can.)

The memory of the Redman
How can it pass away,
While his names of music linger
On each mount and stream and bay;
While Musquodoboit's waters
Roll sparkling to the main,
While falls the laughing sunbeam
On Chegogin's fields of grain?

> RICHARD HUNTINGTON, Yarmouth, N.S., "Indian names of Acadia", about 1875.

I see the Queen's Councillors taking the Indian by the hand saying we are brothers, we will lift you up, we will teach you, if you will learn the cunning of the white man.

> GOVERNOR JAMES MCKAY, on the signing of the Treaty at Fort Pitt, Sept. 7, 1876, qu. in Morris, *Treaties of Canada with the Indians*, 1953, 231.

Once I was rich, plenty of money, but the Americans stole it all in the Black Hills. I have come to remain with the White Mother's children.

> CHIEF SITTING BULL, to Lieut.-Col. A.G. Irvine, Asst. Comm., N.W.M.P., June 2, 1877, after fleeing to Canada following battle of Little Big Horn.

I will be the first to sign: I will be the last to break the Treaty.

> CROWFOOT, Blackfoot chief, on signing Treaty No. 7 at Blackfoot Crossing, Alta., Oct. 20, 1877.

Once all this mighty continent was ours,
And the Great Spirit made it for our use.

> CHARLES MAIR, *Tecumseh*, 1886.

It was not the redcoats who had secured the peace, it was Christianity.

> HENRY B. STEINHAUR, Ojibway Methodist missionary, qu. in George Young, *Manitoba memories, leaves from my life in the prairie province, 1868-1884*, 1898, 171.

Gitche Manito, the mighty,
  Mitche Manito, the bad;
In the breast of every Redman,
In the dust of every dead man,
  There's a tiny heap of Gitche —
  And a mighty mound of Mitche —
There's the good and there's the bad.

> CY WARMAN, *Weiga of Temagami*, 1908, foreword.

Shapely, slender, debonaire,
From her coils of blue-black hair
To her dainty moccasins:
And I met her, for my sins,
Somewhere back of Ottawa
  Among the oldest hills.

> TOM MACINNES, "The rime of Jacques Valbean", 1908.

They but forgot we Indians owned the land
From ocean unto ocean; that they stand
Upon soil that centuries agone
Was our sole kingdom and our right alone.
They never think how they would feel today,
If some great nation came from far away,
Wresting their country from their hapless braves,
Giving what they gave us — but wars and graves.

> PAULINE JOHNSON, "A cry from an Indian wife", 1912.

Walk on, walk on, walk on, on the breath of our grandfathers.

> ANON., Gitskan and Carrier Indians saying, qu. in *'Ksan; breath of our grandfathers*, Ottawa, 1972, title-page.

To be a slave was the most degrading thing. People used to say: never be a slave. If you're going to be a slave, take your own life.

> REV. PETER KELLY, referring to Haida attitude to slavery, qu. in N. Newton, *Fire in the raven's nest*, 1973, 129.

Thar's good and bad in Injun,
  An' thar's good and bad in White;
But, somehow, they is allus wrong,
  An' we is allus right.

> JOHN E. LOGAN, "The Injun", 1915.

The Protestant Indian is an Indian while the Catholic Indian is a Catholic . . . Scratch any sort of Protestant Indian and below his skin lie all the aspirations of his natural religion.

> J.M. CLARKE, *L'Ile Percée*, 1923, 18.

We have not yet realized that the Indian and his culture were fundamental to the growth of Canadian institutions.

> HAROLD A. INNIS, *The fur trade in Canada*, 1930, 397.

Not all the Indians are under formal treaties but all have had their needs provided for and the Government has more than fulfilled the letter of its obligations.

> D.C. SCOTT, *The Administration of Indian affairs in Canada*, (prepared for Fourth Bi-Annual Conference of The Institute of Pacific Relations, Hangchow, Oct. 18-Nov. 3) 1931, 2.

What we want is a really impartial history of North America written from the Indians' point of view.

> E.R. ADAIR, *Can. hist. rev.*, 1932, 341.

Civilization, as it flows past their doors, seems to be entrapping them in a backwash that leaves only one issue, the absorption of a few families into the aggressive white race and the decline and extinction of the remainder.

> DIAMOND JENNESS, *The Indians of Canada*, 1932, 264.

Culturally they have already contributed everything that was valuable for our own civilization beyond what knowledge we may still glean from their histories concerning man's ceaseless struggle to control his environment.

> DIAMOND JENNESS, *The Indians of Canada*, 1932, 264.

Canada's Indian goal is to make Indians self-supporting and to Christianize them. She does not, officially, acknowledge that Indian heritage and Indian society have greatness in them.

> JOHN COLLIER, *Indians of the Americas*, 1947, 297.

This is a grassy ghetto, and no home.
And these are fauna in a museum
  kept.
The better hunters have prevailed.
  The game,
losing its blood, now makes these
  grounds its crypt.
The animals pale, the shine of the fur
  is lost,
bleached are their living bones. About
  them watch
as through a mist, the pious prosperous
  ghosts.

> A.M. KLEIN, "Indian reservation: Caughnawaga", 1948.

"Indian" means a person who pursuant to this Act is registered as an Indian or is entitled to be registered as an Indian.

> CANADA. LAWS, STATUTES, etc., *The Indian Act*, 1951, ch. 29, s. 2.

Parliament, for its part, contented itself with voting whatever amount of money seemed necessary to fulfill Canada's treaty obligations towards its aborigines and then promptly forgot them, because their number was small and exercised no influence at the ballot box.

> DIAMOND JENNESS, *Can. journ. econ. and pol. sci.*, XX, No. 1, 1954, 98.

If we in Canada can freely grant aid, comfort and recognition to underdeveloped and distressed people all over the world at public expense, we can well afford to have a careful and continuous regard to the fulfilment of the legitimate, and indeed, humble, aspirations of our native population.

> JAMES GLADSTONE, first Indian Senator, Senate, *Debates*, 1958, 518.

I think the Indian Canadian wishes to enlarge the world in which he lives beyond the buckskin curtain of his reserve.

> MORRIS C. SHUMIATCHER, *The beaver*, Autumn, 1959, 14.

They have good reason to be suspicious, for in the past there have been occasions when a friendly hand from the government turned out to have a knife in it.

> SENATOR JAMES GLADSTONE, first treaty Indian to be appointed to the Senate, *Globe magazine*, June 25, 1960, 19.

They've seen through us.

> JOHN MCGILP, Superior of Indian Agencies for Saskatchewan, qu. in *Maclean's*, July 6, 1963, 49.

We're People First, Not Just Indians.

> ANON., wording on a placard carried by a group of Indians from Hay Lake, Alta., in a march on the Legislative Buildings, Edmonton, Feb. 22, 1965. [Sic].

Canada's war on the Indians was not a shooting war, like the Americans'; it was a long war of attrition that is still being waged, and that inflicts new defeats on every generation. The weapon we use is indifference.

> KEN LEFOLII, *The Canadian look: a century of sights and styles*, 1965, 65.

We will wait no longer.

> ANON., slogan appearing on Indian poster Northern Ontario, late 1960.

I like to think that had I been in Grant's position I would have had the courage to do as he did.

> JUDGE JOHN PARKER, referring to William E. Grant, Indian Agent, Whitehorse, who re-directed money from food funds to much needed Indian housing, qu. in Whitehorse *Star*, June 24, 1965.

The position we strongly hold is that Indians are citizens plus; that in addition to the normal rights and duties of citizenship they also possess certain rights simply by virtue of being Indians.

> H.B. HAWTHORN, *A survey of the contemporary Indians of Canada*, Vol. 1, 1966, 396.

Many non-Indians believe that nothing better can be expected from the descendants of Canada's original people, and many Indians and Eskimo oblige by acting in a way that confirms this expectation.

> CANADA. DEPT. OF INDIAN AFFAIRS AND NORTHERN DEVELOPMENT, *Indians and the law*, 1967, 55.

My nation was ignored in your history text books.

> CHIEF DAN GEORGE, address, Vancouver, July 1, 1967.

The Indians of Canada bid you
  welcome.
Walk in our moccasins the trail of our
  past.
  Live with us in the here and now.
Talk with us by the fire of the days to
  come.

> ANON., theme: Canadian Indian Pavilion, Expo 67, Montreal, 1967.

Burial ground
for more than bones
an entire race
lies buried here.

> HUGH COOK, "Indian cemetery, Squamish, B.C.", 1968.

I think that all of us feel a sense of guilt, not so much toward the Indian as toward the fact that we haven't really addressed our minds to his problem.

> PIERRE E. TRUDEAU, to students in London, Ont., Jan. 12, 1969.

The unjust society.

> HAROLD CARDINAL, from the title of his book subtitled "the tragedy of Canada's Indians", pub. 1969; from "The just society" phrase associated with Pierre E. Trudeau, 1968.

Indians have aspirations, hopes and dreams, but becoming brown white men is not one of them.

> HAROLD CARDINAL, *The unjust society*, 1969, 3.

Our people look on with concern when the Canadian Government talks about "the two founding peoples" without giving recognition to the role played by the Indian even before the founding of a nation-state known as Canada.

> HAROLD CARDINAL, *The unjust society*, 1969, 13.

Uncle Tomahawks.

> HAROLD CARDINAL, *The unjust society*, 1969, 22, referring to those who apologize for being Indian.

It is inconceivable that one section of a society should have a treaty with another section of a society. They should become Canadians as have all other Canadians.

> PIERRE E. TRUDEAU, on Canadian Indians, speech, Liberal Party dinner, Vancouver, Aug. 11, 1969.

We are different than we used to be. The government has us in a little box, with a lid on it. Every now and then they open the lid and do something to us and close it again. We are a dying race. Not this generation but the next, will die.

> WILLIE DENECHOAN, medicine man, Hay Lake, Alta., qu. in Heather Robertson, *Reservations are for Indians*, 1970, i.

Citizens Plus.

> INDIAN CHIEFS OF ALBERTA, a brief prepared for presentation to Prime Minister Pierre Trudeau in June, 1970; also referred to as The Red Paper.

Mudlarks.

> ANON., name for some women of The Pas, Man. who "live on the streets" and to whom "home is jail"; 1970's.

Ottawa is trying to make Indians little brown white men.

> CHIEF ADAM SOLWAY, of Calgary, at Can. Fed. of Univ. Women, 18th triennial conf., York Univ., Toronto, Aug. 18, 1970, qu. in *Globe and Mail*, Aug. 19, 1970, 9.

Since our forbears first set foot on this continent, the white man has been taking from the Indian: his food, his source of livelihood, his traditional way of life. The only thing the white man has refused to accept is perhaps the most valuable thing he had to offer: his unique sense of values.

> JOE ROSENTHAL, *Indians, a sketching odyssey*, 1971, 76.

A strong argument exists for viewing Canadian people of Indian ancestry as a colonial people, who have been treated and in effect controlled by outside authorities over which they had no direct control.

> JIM HARDING, in J. Harp and J.R. Hofley, eds., *Poverty in Canada*, 1971, 243.

We're not fooling around. We've got the bull by the tail, and we're looking him straight in the eye.

> CHIEF DAVE COURCHENE, radio interview, CBC-TV news, Feb. 22, 1973.

Indignation

Let anger take me in its grasp; let hate, Hatred of evil prompt me, and dictate.

> A.M. KLEIN, *Hitleriad*, 1944, 5.

Individuality

I like to let every feller grind his own axe.

> THOMAS C. HALIBURTON, *Sam Slick's wise saws*, 1853, ch. XVI.

It is the uncontemporary spirit that is the genius of discovery and art and invention.

> BLISS CARMAN, *The friendship of art*, 1904, 56.

There is only one way in the world to be distinguished: Follow your instinct! Be yourself, and you'll be somebody. Be one more blind follower of the blind; and you will have the oblivion you desire.

> BLISS CARMAN, *The friendship of art*, 1904, 173.

Woman is a species of which every woman is a variety. And every man must make up his mind to this, that Every woman is a study in herself.

> ARNOLD HAULTAIN, *Hints for lovers*, 1909, 29.

Canada is a most horribly individualistic place, with no one thinking of anything except the amount of money that they can make, by any means, in the shortest time.

> RUPERT BROOKE, letter to his mother, Sept. 8, 1913.

The nation is the individual in the aggregate. Surround the individual with the proper conditions and most of the real problems, the social problems, will cease to exist. Before the individual is born, make such labour laws and establish such conditions as will ensure him a healthy mother.

> W.J. HANNA, address to Civic Improvement League of Canada, Ottawa, Jan. 20, 1916.

And while your body wears away,
  And all your thoughts disintegrate,
You weave new vestures every day,
  And dreams with dreams obliterate:
  For you the outer ways await
Because of your desire to be:
  But high or low, thro' every state,
You remain essentially.

> TOM MACINNES, "Ballade of the self concealed", 1918.

In Alberta, the recognition of the helplessness of the individual, in the face of the intimate economic interdependence of men and of areas, has prevented the survival of an extreme individualistic point of view.

> W.A. MACKINTOSH and others, *Economic problems of the prairie provinces*, 1935, 87.

As individuals
The men lost their identity; as groups,
As gangs, they massed, divided,
  subdivided
Like numerals only.

> E.J. PRATT, *Towards the last spike*, 1952, 28.

All of us is Everyman and this is intolerable unless each of us can also be I.

> HUGH MACLENNAN, *The watch that ends the night*, 1959, 367.

In the end, it is upon the quality of individuals that all group movements depend.

> ROBERTSON DAVIES, *A voice from the attic*, 1960, 352.

Genuine individuality, distinct from egotism, seeks for communication which, in turn, implies community.

> ELI MANDEL, in *Tamarack rev.* No. 29, 1963, 87.

In the present context of Canadian politics, it is necessary above all else to reaffirm the importance of the individual, without regard to ethnic, geographic or religious accidents. The cornerstone of the social and political order must be the attributes men hold in common, not those which differentiate them. An order of priorities in political and social matters that is founded upon the individual as an individual, is totally incompatible with an order of priorities based upon race, religion or nationality.

> PIERRE E. TRUDEAU and others, "An appeal for realism in politics", *Cité libre*, May, 1964, 11. (Trans.) (See also next quotation.)

In the present context of Canadian politics, it is necessary above all else to reaffirm the importance of the individual, without regard to ethnic, geographic or religious accidents. The cornerstone of the social and political order must be the attributes men hold in common, not those that differentiate them.

> COMMITTEE FOR POLITICAL REALISM, *Can. forum*, May, 1964, 29.

Unlike the American value system, which has always emphasized the idea of the equality of peoples within a new nation, the Canadian value system has stressed the social qualities that differentiate people rather than the human qualities that make them the same.

> JOHN PORTER, in J.M.S. Careless and R.C. Brown, eds., *The Canadians, 1867-1967*, 1967, 396.

In the art of living, as in that of loving, or of governing – it is all the same – I found it unacceptable that others should claim to know better than I what was good for me.

> PIERRE E. TRUDEAU, *Federalism and the French Canadians*, 1968, xxi.

The state must take great care not to infringe on the conscience of the individual. I believe that, in the last analysis, a human being in the privacy of his own mind has the exclusive authority to choose his own scale of values and to decide which forces take precedence over others. A good constitution is one that does not prejudge any of these questions, but leaves citizens free to orient their human destinies as they see fit.

> PIERRE E. TRUDEAU, *Federalism and the French Canadians*, 1968, 11.

Cultivating a persona has turned Earle Birney into a professional grand old man, Irving Layton into a professional wild man, Al Purdy into a professional hick and Margaret Atwood into a professional blushing violet. No, the trouble with becoming any kind of legend is that it's much too hard to maintain.

> JOHN GLASSCO, interview, qu., *Time*, Dec. 2, 1974, 17.

Industrialization

We can approve or disapprove of such movements, but no people can escape them; to dam them out is impossible.

> ERROL BOUCHETTE, Roy. Soc. of Canada, *Transactions*, 1901, Sec. I, 117 (trans.), referring to move towards industrialization.

In Quebec industrialization was a tide to be stemmed because it was seen as a threat to French national survival. The solution to the question of national survival became confused with the solution to the problems of industrialization. The solution was expressed in a clerical-national creed: those who had not left the village should remain there, and those who had left should return.

> JOHN PORTER, *The vertical mosaic*, 1965, 333.

Industry

Some of us get impressions, vivid impressions, which call for our industry. This industry leads to facility, and everything becomes easy.

> SIR WILLIAM VAN HORNE, qu. Peter Newman, *Flame of power*, 1959, 93.

When it is understood that instead of working and saving you may vote yourself the earnings and savings of other people, industry will lose some of its charm.

> GOLDWIN SMITH, *Canada and the Canadian question*, 1891, 33.

One captain of industry is worth a good many of the rank and file.

> WM. PETERSON, Canadian Club, Ottawa, speech, Jan. 7, 1911.

Production, production, and more production!

> SIR THOMAS WHITE, 1917; misquoted by the newly-formed Canadian Press to western, anti-protection newspapers as "Protection, protection, and more protection!"

Labor can do nothing without capital, capital nothing without labor, and neither labor or capital can do anything without the guiding genius of management; and management, however wise its genius may be, can do nothing without the privileges which the community affords.

> W.L. MACKENZIE KING, Canadian Club speech, Montreal, Mar. 17, 1919.

Industry exists for the sake of humanity, not humanity for the sake of industry.

> W.L. MACKENZIE KING, *Industry and humanity* 1918; also, speech on accepting leadership of Liberal Party, Aug., 1919, Ottawa.

Whatever comes of the phase through which we are now passing I am sure that the world will be richer in the belief that industry is not for the enrichment of a few but rather for the betterment of the many.

> W.L. MACKENZIE KING, speech in Edmonton, July, 1933.

Instead of the government taking over industry when the war broke out, industry took over the government.

> CLARIE GILLIS, C.C.F. M.P. for Cape Breton, qu. in *The people's history of Cape Breton*, 1971, 40 (pamphlet); from *Steelworker and miner*, Apr. 12, 1941.

I cannot believe that we will long accept the present stupid philosophy that to achieve idleness is the goal of life, but rather will hitch our wagon to a star such as that which this summer brought a few great artists from England to our little Stratford-upon-Avon.

> R.K. STRATFORD, Imperial Oil Ltd., in *Canada's Tomorrow; papers and discussion . . . Conference, Quebec City, November, 1953*, 1954, 89.

Inflation

Inflation makes misery unanimous; it is universal poverty.

> ARTHUR MEIGHEN, speech, Kiwanis Club, Vancouver, Oct. 21, 1943.

It is painfully clear that in the Canadian economy, no combination of domestic policies, however soundly conceived, can accomplish this result (i.e. prevent inflation) when inflation is a more or less world-wide phenomenon.

> R. CRAIG MCIVOR, *Canadian monetary, banking and fiscal development*, 1958, 251.

The federal government cannot by itself control inflation. What this government can do and is determined to do – with the support of parliament – is to keep its own finances in order, take action to steady the economy and give leadership to the other governments in Canada and to the country at large.

MITCHELL SHARP, H. of C., *Debates*, Nov. 30, 1967, 4909.

Inflation no longer exists.

PIERRE E. TRUDEAU, Dec. 22, 1970, qu. in *Maclean's*, Oct., 1973, 12.

Information

I sometimes wonder if we are helped by too full a knowledge of medical literature. I must frankly confess that, had I read all that was written on diabetes and known all of the conflicting views and theories I would probably never have tackled the problem.

SIR FREDERICK BANTING, address, Mar. 6, 1924, Chicago; qu. in L.G. Stevenson, *Sir Frederick Banting*, 1947, 300.

He also said pity was loss of power.
    Someone had to tell the people
what was happening; it's indecent to
    let
the death of the last god go by
    unnoticed.

IRVING LAYTON, "Me, the P.M. and the stars", 1955.

Energy and production now tend to fuse· with information and learning. Marketing and consumption tend to become one with learning, enlightenment, and the intake of information. This is all part of the electric *implosion* that now follows or succeeds the centuries of *explosion* and increasing specialism.

MARSHALL MCLUHAN, *Understanding media*, 1964, 350.

Ingenuity

I treat each new situation with spontaneous ingenuity.

DONALD GORDON, qu. by Peter Newman, *Flame of power*, 1959, 202.

Ingratitude

Ingratitude is the most common form of self-respect.

PETER MCARTHUR, d. 1924, qu. in *The best of Peter McArthur*, 1967, 67.

Initiative

Always it devolves upon the man to take the initiative; and Always it devolves upon the woman to give the man an opportunity to take the initiative. But again, Always the man must pretend that he takes no initiative; and Always the woman must pretend that she gives no opportunity.

ARNOLD HAULTAIN, *Hints for lovers*, 1909, 137.

Injustice

To protest against the injustice would be idle; philanthropy likes injustice.

GOLDWIN SMITH, *The Bystander*, Apr., 1883, 96.

Innis, Harold A.

He valued, above everything else, the truth of synthesis.

DONALD G. CREIGHTON, *Harold Adams Innis: portrait of a scholar*, 1957, 120.

He had come to believe firmly that Canada must remain between the iron curtain and the gold curtain and do what she could to sustain the European point of view. It was in her own interest, as well as in the interest of Western civilisation, for the Dominion

to hold fast to the position of autonomy which she claimed in theory.

> DONALD G. CREIGHTON, *Harold Adams
> Innis: portrait of a scholar*, 1957, 133.

Innocence

Innocence is not suspicious, but guilt is
always ready to turn informer.

> THOMAS C. HALIBURTON, *Sam Slick's wise
> saws*, 1853, ch. 15.

That freedom, present in all children
and known as innocence, has been
destroyed or crippled by local certainties, by gods of local moralities, of
local justice, of personal salvation, of
prejudice and hate and intolerance –
frequently masquerading as love –
gods of everything that would destroy
freedom to observe and to think and
would keep each generation under the
control of the old people, the elders,
the shamans, and the priests.

> G. BROCK CHISHOLM, speech in Washing-
> ton, D.C., Oct. 23, 1945.

He wondered if innocence was like a
two-edged sword without a handle,
and if you gripped it and used it, it cut
you so painfully you had to lash out
blindly, seeking vengeance on someone for the bleeding.

> MORLEY CALLAGHAN, *The many co-
> loured coat*, 1960, 313.

it is not unfortunately
quite enough to be innocent
it is not enough merely
not to offend –

> JOHN NEWLOVE, "Ride off any horizon",
> 1968.

with any luck we'll lose everything
and then we cum
blazing naked and obscene into the
flashing tempul.

> BILL BISSETT, "Without a conductor",
> 1971.

Insects

When grasshoppers are so plenty as to
make pastures poor, gobblers grow fat.

> THOMAS C. HALIBURTON, *Sam Slick's wise
> saws*, 1853, ch. 6.

The Praying-Mantis mounts the stair,
Her tiny arms upheld in prayer;
In chasuble and stole,
She stands to read my soul.

> ANNIE C. DALTON, "The praying-mantis",
> 1935.

The worm has grown no teeth, no
jaws, no spiked claws, no poison fang,
no armoured back, no speedy feet:
nothing. Yet how it has endured! Soft,
slow, blind, brainless, defenceless, it
crawls stupidly through the earth,
through time, through life; persisting
over change and race, from the far
past to the far future.

> THOMAS B. ROBERTON, *Newspaper pieces*,
> 1936, 47.

The insect world and the world of men
never really meet – they interweave
in space and make a mutual nuisance
of themselves, but not much more
than that. Insects are small but their
world is large and they outbreed us all
the time.

> N.J. BERRILL, "Perfume, starlight and
> melody", in *Sex and the nature of
> things*, 1953, 70.

Insight

Make thou my vision sane and clear
That I may see what beauty clings
In common forms, and find the soul
Of unregarded things!

> CHARLES G.D. ROBERTS, "Songs of the
> common day", Prologue, 1893.

Insolence

I was much struck at Prescott – and
indeed all through Canada, though

more in the upper than in the lower province – by the sturdy roughness, some would call it insolence, of those of the lower classes of the people with whom I was brought into contact.

ANTHONY TROLLOPE, *North America*, 1862, 71.

Insomnia

There was a time when sleep
Was wont to approach me with her soundless feet
And take me by surprise. I called her not,
And yet she'd come; but now I even woo her,
And court her by the cunning use of drugs,
But still she will not turn to me her steps;
Not even to approach, and, looking down,
Drop on these temples one oblivious tear.

CHARLES HEAVYSEGE, *Saul*, 1857.

Instinct

I have sometimes thought Instinct to be a word invented by the learned to cover their ignorance of the ways and doings of animals for their self preservation; it is a learned word and shuts up all the reasoning powers.

DAVID THOMPSON, *Narrative of his explorations in Western America, 1784-1812*, (Champlain Soc., 1916, 102).

Institutions

I am very conscious of what it means to have been born in Canada, and I can think of no privilege so great as to have founded any good or enduring thing in this country. I know the value of money, but I should rather have created one of the institutions of my country than to possess millions.

SIR EDMUND WALKER, speech on his 50th. anniversary with the Canadian Bank of Commerce, July 24, 1918.

Governments
churches
institutions
you have suddenly crumbled
become nothing in my eyes.

RAYMOND SOUSTER, "It is time", 1962.

All our institutions express the way in which one lot of men dedicated to certain ends impose their dominance over other men. Our society is above all the expression of the dominance that the large-scale capitalist exerts over all other persons.

GEORGE P. GRANT, *Philosophy in the mass age*, 1966, 4.

Instruction

My theory is, if anything amuses
Me, it may serve to instruct others.

DARYL HINE, "Letter from British Columbia", 1970.

Insurance

The best insurance against disease is health. Only God can give you insurance against illness.

MAURICE DUPLESSIS, qu. in P. Laporte, *The true face of Duplessis*, 1961, 85; also in *Univ. of Tor. quart.*, Apr., 1958, 357.

A man may buy protection from
Old age, misfortune and The Bomb,
But never from the plaguy zealot
Whose vocation is to sell it.

MAVOR MOORE, "The insurance salesman", *And what do you do?*, 1960, 9.

Insurrection

The state of apprehended insurrection in the province of Quebec.

PIERRE E. TRUDEAU, H. of C., *Debates*, Oct. 6, 1970, 193, on invoking the War Measures Act.

Intellect

We forget that the measure of the value of a nation to the world is neither the bushel nor the barrel, but mind; and that wheat and pork, though useful and necessary, are but dross in comparison with those intellectual products which alone are imperishable.

SIR WILLIAM OSLER, "Teacher and student", 1892, in *Aequanimitas*.

How utterly destitute of all light and charm are the intellectual conditions of our people and the institutions of our public life! How barren! How barbarous!

ARCHIBALD LAMPMAN, in *The Globe*, Feb. 27, 1892.

Intellectuals

He was so intellectual that he was, as he himself admitted, a complete egg-nostic.

STEPHEN LEACOCK, "The entanglement of Mr. Pupkin", *Sunshine sketches of a little town*, 1912, 160.

I cannot understand why it is that men with brains are so seldom successful.

FRED JACOB, "And they met again", in *One third of a bill*, 1925, 62.

The heart is willing, but the head is weak. Modernity and tradition alike demand that the contemporary artist who survives adolescence shall be an intellectual. Sensibility is no longer enough, intelligence is also required. Even in Canada.

A.J.M. SMITH, *Can. forum*, Apr., 1928, 601.

Intellectuals in large numbers will sink the raft of any party, and if allowed to write a program will kill it.

HAROLD A. INNIS, address, meeting of the Summer Session, Univ. of B.C., Vancouver, 1935.

There is no other country in the world where intellectuals suffer from such low repute as in Canada.

ANON., a book reviewer, qu. by Hilda Neatby in *Tamarack rev.* No. 1, 1956, 37.

Poets.

MAURICE DUPLESSIS, term used in a derogatory sense, qu. in P. Laporte, *The true face of Duplessis*, 1960, 28.

We are the encyclopedists,
Fingers on our own pulse
Self conscious and pseudo clever;
Wayfarers outside the blood,
And have forgotten what we are.

ALFRED W. PURDY, "Dimensions", 1960.

To pretend to be less intelligent than one is deceives nobody and begets dislike, for intelligence cannot be hidden; like a cough, it will out, stifle it how you may. No man has ever won commendation for standing at less than his full height, either physically, morally, or intellectually. If you are an intellectual, your best course is to relax and enjoy it.

ROBERTSON DAVIES, *A voice from the attic*, 1960, 36.

They say I'm a good administrator and in my own field a good scholar but I'm no intellectual. What the devil is an 'intellectual' anyway?

SIDNEY E. SMITH, qu. in E.A. Corbett, *Sidney Earle Smith*, 1961, 39.

Wherever we look, intellectuals are talking away their feelings of impotence, creating a substitute world of ideas and images, and initiating one another into one another's private mythologies.

PAUL WEST, in *Can. lit.* No. 16, 1963, 19.

May heaven protect us, then, from intellectuals in search of their Canadian identity and from philosophers of history in search of Canadian destiny.

LIONEL RUBINOFF, in A. Wainwright, ed., *Notes for a native land*, 1968, 48.

No, Canada has never been staid and grey, but a great many Canadian intellectuals have been colour blind.

ALDEN NOWLAN, in *Maclean's*, June, 1971, 40.

Intelligence

It is a good mind
that can embody
perfection with exactitude.

PHYLLIS WEBB, "Suite II", 1965.

Intelligence can be used for many things. It seems to me it should be used especially for living.

JEAN-PAUL DESBIENS, *For pity's sake*, 1965, 105.

The growth of the intelligence is largely due to an inherited factor.

WILLIAM E. BLATZ, *Human security*, 1966, 8.

Intentions

What they have forgotten they have
forgotten.
What they meant to do instead of fall
is not in earth or time recoverable –
the fossils of intention, the shapes of
rot.

ALFRED PURDY, "Pause", 1962.

Good intentions, however, are no substitute for realism in pursuing a course of political action.

PIERRE E. TRUDEAU, in his ed. of *The asbestos strike*, 1974, 27.

Intercolonial Railway

No Intercolonial, no Transit.

DUKE OF NEWCASTLE, letter to E.W. Watkin, May 6, 1863: "I added words [to the despatches to British Columbia and Canada] which (without dictation) will be understood as implying 'No Intercolonial, no Transit.'"

Mr. Tilley, will you stop your puffing
and blowing
And tell us which way the railway is
going?

FREDERICTON *HEADQUARTERS*, Feb. 1, 1865, on the Intercolonial Railway.

International Joint Boards

[International joint boards] are, in large measure, a sham; they are places where Canadians meet Americans so the Americans can tell us what they intend to do and we can say, Yessir.

WALTER STEWART in *Maclean's*, Dec., 1971, 62.

Interviews

It is well known in this country that I am never interviewed.

SIR WILFRID LAURIER, cable to Lord Strathcona, London, on English press report of Dec. 22, 1909, in which he was reported as expressing himself to a newspaperman as being favourable to the British Liberal cause.

Intolerance

Intolerance is want of sense;
   Judge people by their deeds;
For Mammon's tools make wise men
      fools
   By playing on their creeds.

> ALEXANDER MCLACHLAN, "The spirits of
> the press", 1900.

What I inveigh against is a cursed spirit of intolerance, conceived in distrust and bred in ignorance, that makes the mental attitude perenially antagonistic, even bitterly antagonistic to everything foreign, that subordinates everywhere the race to the nation, forgetting the higher claims of human brotherhood.

> SIR WILLIAM OSLER, "Chauvinism in
> medicine", *Montreal med. jour.*, 1902,
> 688.

Sing deeds neglected, desecrations
   done
Not on the lovely body of the world
But on man's building heart, his
   shaping soul.
Mourn, with me, the intolerant, hater
   of sun:
Child's mind maimed before he learns
   to run.

> DOROTHY LIVESAY, "Of mourners", 1947.

Invaders

I will dine in Quebec on Christmas day or in Hell.

> RICHARD MONTGOMERY, attributed, *Journal of the most remarkable occurrences in Quebec since Arnold appear'd before the town on the 14th November, 1775*, in Quebec Lit. & Hist. Soc., *Historical documents*, 7th Ser., 1905, 101.

Push on, brave boys, Quebec is ours!

> RICHARD MONTGOMERY, Dec. 31, 1775, qu. in John Codman II, *Arnold's expedition to Quebec*, 1903, 238, just before his death when attacking Quebec City.

Invasion

Let but the rash intruder dare
   To touch our darling strand,
      The martial fires
      That thrilled our sires
Would flame throughout the land.

> CHARLES SANGSTER, "Song of Canada",
> 1860.

Beware the northerner, the barbarian, who comes in as a thief and, undaunted, sleeps with his boots in the bed of the princess, whose name is Culture!

> MARIUS BARBEAU, *Can. hist. rev.*, 1932,
> 417.

Invective

A man of cupidity, stupidity and malignant self esteem.

> JOSEPH R. SMALLWOOD, referring to errant colleague, qu. in R. Gwyn, *Smallwood*, 1972, 355.

Mangez de la merde!

> PIERRE E. TRUDEAU, Feb. 3, 1971 on Parliament Hill, to employees of the G. Lapalme Inc. trucking firm of Montreal formerly under contract to the Post Office. The Prime Minister was in his automobile when confronted by about 370 Lapalme drivers who booed and insulted him, according to Frank Diterlizzi, leader of the drivers. See Ottawa *Citizen*, Feb. 3, 1971, 1.

Fuddle-duddle.

> PIERRE E. TRUDEAU, House of Commons *Debates*, Feb. 16, 1971, see page 3423. A euphemism, not actually said in the House, but substituted later outside the House by the Prime Minister when interviewed by reporters. Two Progressive Conservative members, Lincoln Alexander and John Lundrigan claimed Trudeau had mouthed the obscenity "F- - - off" in the House. See *Globe and Mail*, Feb. 17, 1971, 2 and 6.

Invention

I follow the principle that it is unnecessary to invent, except in a minor way. Much more effective is to dig, dig, and keep on digging, around the general subject matter previously decided on.

ARTHUR HAILEY, *Close-up on writing for television*, 1960, 11.

The era of great men is over for ever. Man has been shrunk by his inventions.

IRVING LAYTON, "Aphs", *The whole bloody bird*, 1969, 96.

Investment

I want some of Mr. Manning's stock.

ANON., ascribed to supporters of E.C. Manning by Edmonton broker describing response to offer of Govt. of Alberta Gas stock, Mar., 1957, qu. in J. Barber, *Good fences make good neighbours*, 1958, 145.

Investment, American

We often say that we fear no invasion from the south, but the armies of the south have already crossed the border. American enterprise, American capital, is taking rapid possession of our mines and our water-power, our oil areas and our timber limits.

SARA JEANETTE DUNCAN, *The imperialist*, 1904, 404.

Canadian nationalism was systematically encouraged and exploited by American capital. Canada moved from colony to nation to colony.

HAROLD A. INNIS, *Changing concepts of time*, 1952, 121.

Americans like to invest in Canada because it is a calm, sensible nation.

MIRIAM CHAPIN, *Contemporary Canada*, 1959, 175.

Over the years 1957 to 1965 American direct investment companies in Canada obtained 73% of their funds from retained earnings and depreciation, and a further 12% from other Canadian sources. Only 15% of funds came from the United States.

KARI LEVITT, *New world quart. 4*, No. 2, 1968, 131.

Hail! fructifying effluence,
whose every flood is our good fortune,
depositing the silt of safe investment
wherein we grow our crop of shares,
irrigating the plain
of the world's second highest
standard of living, wherefrom we
    glean
our simple harvest
of hi-fi and freezer, Jag and yacht.

ERIC NICOL, "Dat ol' man river", 1968.

If there is one thing that worries Canadians more than economic domination, it is that someone, sometime, will try to do something about it.

GEORGE BAIN, *Globe and Mail*, Nov. 4, 1969, 6.

"Empire" is as American as cherry pie. As the imperial perimeter contracts – in Southeast Asia, in Latin America, even in Western Europe – the hard-driving entrepreneurs who have made this country what it is today are opening up a new empire in their own backyard. Canada is serving as a decompression chamber for a new generation of American imperialists during their transition to another level and venue of domination.

JAMES EAYRS, speech, 12th Annual Seminar on Canadian-United States Relations, Columbia University, New York, Nov. 17, 1970.

The people who say foreign investment is the lifeblood of Canada are living in the 18th century. They must believe in bloodletting, and it's our blood flowing south of the border that they're talking about.

> EDWIN A. GOODMAN, Committee for an Independent Canada, qu. in R.L. Perry, *Galt, U.S.A.*, 1971, 13.

Canada is being bought out with its own money.

> ANON., popular statement on operation of foreign finance in Canada, qu. in Thomas A. Hockin, *The Canadian condominium*, 1972, 120.

Investment, Foreign

A non-resident takeover confers great benefits on the Canadian economy.

> ERIC KIERANS, letter, June 18, 1963, to Walter Gordon, qu. by Gordon in H. of C., *Debates*, June 19, 1963, 1321.

Mr. Gordon has drawn the plans for Castle Canada, and waits for our endorsement to go ahead. All through time there have been those who have erected bastions to secure and protect what they have gained. Europe is studded with these curiosities of the past. But history has never been made by those who erected bastions and sheltered behind them. Rather it has been made by adventurers who scorned protection in order to explore and open up new territories. Canada was founded and developed by such adventurers.

> PATRICK MCGEER, B.C., MLA, qu. in *Canadian annual review*, 1966, 37, re: Walter Gordon's "agenda for independence".

Canadians ask themselves whether they have become free of Britain's colonial influence only to fall under the spell of the United States' economic imperialism.

> WALTER L. GORDON, *A choice for Canada*, 1966, x.

I, for one, still do not know with whom we are dealing. I, for one, do not know whose money it is, what country it comes from, what is the nature of the money and when I say that, I don't know if it is public subscription or private money. I don't know if it is government money of some foreign government and I don't know whether it's money coming out of Swiss banks owned by people we know nothing of, and I think it's fair that if the government knows we ought to know.

> SAUL CHERNIACK, Manitoba, Legis. Assembly, *Debates*, Jan. 19, 1967, 294.

British investors had put their money mainly into Canadian railway, industrial, and government bonds; and Canadians had used these funds to promote independent Canadian enterprises. American entrepreneurs, in sharp contrast, had concentrated on direct investment, and had thus already acquired ownership of control of a large number of Canadian businesses. The Canadians owed debts to the British; to the Americans they had conceded an ever-increasing equity in Canada.

> DONALD G. CREIGHTON, *Canada's first century, 1867-1967*, 1970, 181.

The honeymoon is over, and the realization is dawning that the heavy intake of direct investment and the consequent loss of economic control has restricted Canada's freedom of action in a highly competitive world economy.

> KARI LEVITT, *Silent surrender: the multi-national corporation in Canada*, 1970, 118.

Foreign direct investment can act as a transmission belt for the entry of foreign laws into Canada. It can bring cultural influences which may or may not be desirable. Foreign direct investment could also create difficulties in the formation of both domestic and foreign policy for Canada's image abroad.

> CANADA. PRIVY COUNCIL, *Foreign direct investment in Canada*, (The Gray report), 1972, 43.

Irishmen

They are always in love or in liquor, or else in a row; they are the merriest shavers I ever seed.

> T.C. HALIBURTON, *Sam Slick*, 1836, ch. XVI.

We are here living not on the banks of the Boyne, but on the St. Lawrence. We are new men in a new country. Our affairs are with the Imperial Government and the American Republic, not with James II or William III.

> THOMAS D'ARCY MCGEE, Montreal *New era*, July 21, 1857.

Where'er I turned, some emblem still
    Roused consciousness upon my
      track;
Some hill was like an Irish hill,
    Some wild bird's whistle called me
      back;
A sea-bound ship bore off my peace,
    Between its white, cold wings of
      woe;
Oh, if I had but wings like these,
    Where my peace went I, too, would
      go.

> THOMAS D'A. MCGEE, "Home-sick stanzas", 1858.

We Irishmen, Protestant and Catholic, born and bred in a land of religious controversy, should never forget that we now live and act in a land of the fullest religious and civil liberty. All we have to do is, each for himself, to keep down dissensions which can only weaken, impoverish and keep back the country.

> THOMAS D'A. MCGEE, speech in Quebec, May 10, 1862.

Far from their own beloved isle
Those Irish exiles sleep;
And dream not of historic past,
Nor o'er its memories weep;
Down where the blue St. Lawrence
    tide
Sweeps onward, wave on wave,
They lie – old Ireland's exiled dead,
In cross-crowned lonely grave.

> THOMAS O'HAGAN, "Days of sorrow – Grosse Isle", Aug. 15, 1909.

Irony

We are too young a people apparently for our writers to indulge in irony.

> F.H. UNDERHILL, in *Can.hist.rev.*, 1945, 69.

Our natural mode is therefore not compromise but "irony" – the inescapable response to the presence and pressures of *opposites in tension*. Irony is the key to our identity.

> MALCOLM ROSS, *Our sense of identity*, 1954, x.

Irrelevance

Its chief defect was that it was irrelevant to our circumstances, alien to our tradition, and useless for our fundamental purposes.

> DONALD G. CREIGHTON, Presidential address, Canadian Historical Association, Annual Meeting, Ottawa, June 12-15, 1957.

Islands

I am convinced that had the ancients who dreamed of the Blessed Isles lying far to the west – and in some instances spent their lives searching for them – ever reached Victoria and the islands of the gulf they would have been content to search no farther.

> EDWARD MCCOURT, *The road across Canada*, 1965, 195.

Isolation

Never did the "Empress Island" appear so magnificently grand, – she stood by herself, and there was a peculiar splendour in the loneliness of her glory.

ROBERT COONEY, *Compendious history of New Brunswick*, 1832, Intro., re: Great Britain.

In these troublesome days when the great Mother Empire stands splendidly isolated in Europe.

SIR GEORGE E. FOSTER, H. of C., *Debates*, Jan. 16, 1896; London *Times* reported a speech of Joseph Chamberlain, Jan. 22, under heading, "Splendid isolation"

Whether splendidly isolated or dangerously isolated, I will not now debate; but for my part, I think spendidly isolated, because this isolation of England comes from her superiority.

SIR WILFRID LAURIER, H. of C., *Debates*, Feb. 5, 1896, 1215.

Canada cannot be a hermit nation.

LORD JELLICOE, remark made 1910, and afterwards, re: naval armament.

May I be permitted to add that in this Association of Mutual Insurance against fire, the risks assumed by the different States are not equal? We live in a fire-proof house, far from inflammable materials. A vast ocean separates us from Europe.

RAOUL DANDURAND, speech, L. of N. Assembly, Oct. 2, 1924, in *Plenary records*, 222.

We do not believe that isolation from interest in world affairs is possible for Canada. No happening of any magnitude abroad is without its repercussions on our fortunes and our future.

W.L. MACKENZIE KING, H. of C., *Debates*, June 18, 1936, 3868, on Italo-Ethiopian conflict.

The Province of Canada bred many views, and the least of these was isolation.

G. DET. GLAZEBROOK, in Can.hist.assoc., *Report*, 1938, 104.

Canada makes isolation impossible for the United States.

JOHN MACCORMAC, *Canada, America's problem*, 1940, 1, re: World War II.

And more especially do we thank Thee, O Lord, for the Gut of Canso, Thine own body of water, which separates us from the wickedness that lieth on the other side thereof.

ANON., Presbyterian prayer, Cape Breton, qu. by A.R.M. Lower, *Canadians in the making*, 1958, 145.

I had never realized before how many people in Canada live nowhere.

ANON., (citizen of Toronto), qu. in R. Lucas, *Minetown, milltown, railtown*, 1971, 4, commenting on rural dwellers between Toronto and Ottawa.

each of us reflects
the despair of the separate
object.

MARGARET ATWOOD, "Part of a day", 1968.

Janitors

He is the same old willing horse
Who tends the furnace, sweeps the
    floors,
Puts out the garbage, rakes the
    ground,
And when you need him can't be
    found.

> MAVOR MOORE, "The janitor", *And what
> do you do?*, 1960, 57.

Japanese

Every little slit-eyed kid, every slit-
eyed woman and every slit-eyed man
would unfurl the flag of the Rising
Sun if the Japs invaded. Don't trust
any Jap. They're all for Japan and
none for the British Empire. There
isn't a good Jap – they're the worst
fiends in the world.

> BRIG. SUTHERLAND BROWN, to B.C. Con-
> servative Assn., Annual Convention,
> Vancouver, Jan. 10, 1942.

My hands tremble
As I sign my naturalization papers
Making me a Canadian citizen
And Canada my final resting-place

> TAKEO NAKANO, a *hokku* read before
> Emperor Hirohito, qu. in J.M. Minifie,
> *Open at the top*, 1964, 6.

Jealousy

The surest test of a dead love is that it
forgets how to be jealous.

> ARNOLD HAULTAIN, *Hints for lovers*,
> 1909, 108.

Jealousy, like modesty, and like virtue,
varies with every time and clime: what
is customary in Cairo would rouse
consternation in Kent, and what goes
in Vienna shocks New England.

> ARNOLD HAULTAIN, *Hints for lovers*,
> 1909, 221.

Jehovah's Witnesses

Is it love for God that moves Quebec
mobs to tear copies of God's Word, the
Bible, to shreds and burn them in
flames?

> JEHOVAH'S WITNESSES, "Quebec's burn-
> ing hate", Watch Tower Bible and Tract
> Society, 1946.

Jesuits

In Canada, not a cape was turned, nor
a mission founded, nor a river entered,
nor a settlement begun, but a Jesuit
led the way.

> GEORGE BANCROFT, *History of the U.S.*,
> 1834; elaborated in later eds., 1890, II,
> 138.

Jesus Christ

What a Friend we have in Jesus,
    All our sins and griefs to bear!
What a privilege to carry
    Everything to God in prayer!

> JOSEPH SCRIVEN, "What a Friend we
> have in Jesus", 1884.

How may we grasp again the hand
  that wrought
Such light, such fragrance, and such
  love,
O star! O rose! O Son of Man?

> E.J. PRATT, "Highway", 1932.

This Man of April walks again –
Such marvel does the time allow –
With laughter in His blessed bones,
And lilies on His brow.

> LEO KENNEDY, "Words for a resurrec-
> tion", 1936.

Not in these the source –
But in the sound of invisible trumpets
  blowing
Around two slabs of board,
  right-angled, hammered
By Roman nails and hung on a Jewish
  hill.

> E.J. PRATT, "Brebeuf and his brethren",
> 1940.

And You. Were You ever? Is this
picture the only You? It is here and
You are gone. It is You. No matter
what You are, it still is part of me.

> BRIAN MOORE, *The lonely passion of
> Judith Hearne*, 1955, last page.

No one
ran up
and shook
Christ's hand
The only others
with that kind
of inclination
Had theirs
nailed down
too.

> LIONEL KEARNS, "In-group", 1967.

Jews

And down these nineteen centuries
  anew
  Comes the hoarse-throated,
    brutalized refrain,
"Give us Barabbas, crucify the Jew!"
  Once more a man must bear a
    nation's stain.

> E. PAULINE JOHNSON, "Give us Barab-
> bas", written after Captain Alfred Drey-
> fus was exiled to Devil's Island, 1894.

In fact, if it were not for my Hebrew
persuasion I'd be prepared to go the
whole hog here and now.

> SAMUEL W. JACOBS, speech during tour of
> the West, July, 1915, qu. in B. Figler,
> *Sam Jacobs*, 1959 (1970), 34.

There is no mania quite so self-reveal-
ing as that of Jew-baiting.

> JOHN W. DAFOE, Winnipeg *Free press*,
> Apr. 1, 1933.

But one man, yet he had transformed
a continent of loneliness into a very
home.

> JACOB I. SEGAL, on the death of Han-
> naniah Meir Caiserman, Montreal, Dec.
> 24, 1950, qu. in B. Figler, *H.M. Caiser-
> man*, 1962, 313.

When young the Christians told me
how we pinned Jesus
like a lovely butterfly against the
  wood,
and I wept beside paintings of Calvary
at velvet wounds
and delicate twisted feet.

> LEONARD COHEN, "For Wilf and his
> house", 1956.

Yet cheer up Ezekiel and you
    Jeremiah who were once cast into a
    pit;
I shall not leave you here incensed,
    uneasy among alien Catholic saints
but shall bring you from time to time
    my hot Hebrew heart
as passionate as your own, and stand
with you here awhile in aching
    confraternity.

> IRVING LAYTON, "On seeing the sta-
> tuettes of Ezekiel and Jeremiah in the
> church of Notre Dame", 1956.

Who wants a Jew? This is our life, to
hammer on doors.

> ADELE WISEMAN, *The sacrifice*, 1956
> (1972, 70).

It's hard to be a gentleman – a Jew, I
mean – it's hard to be. Period.

> MORDECAI RICHLER, *The apprenticeship
> of Duddy Kravitz*, 1959, Pt. 4, chap. 1.

In their songs, Jews like to laugh and
cry at the same time and to combine
the religious tradition – transmitted
in Hebrew – with the secular experience, which is always expressed in the
intimate and vernacular Yiddish.

> MIRIAM WADDINGTON, in *Tamarack rev.*,
> No. 45, 1967, 80.

To be a Jew and a Canadian is to
emerge from the ghetto twice, for
self-conscious Canadians, like some
touchy Jews, tend to contemplate the
world through a wrong-ended telescope.

> MORDECAI RICHLER, *Hunting tigers
> under glass*, 1968, 8.

Jokes

Your jokes hit, and hit pretty hard, too.
They make a man think as well as
laugh.

> THOMAS C. HALIBURTON, *The attaché*,
> 1844.

One of the blessings of being a humorist is that all your mistakes pass off as
jokes.

> PETER MCARTHUR, *To be taken with salt*,
> 1903, 150.

Old jokes are easier than new ones,
and there is a mental ease in repetition
which avoids the pain of a new idea.

> STEPHEN LEACOCK, *Humour: its theory
> and technique*, 1935, 228.

Children, having decided that a joke is
funny, go on repeating it, laughing
more loudly each time, until they
collapse in hysteria. The mental age of
a man might be guaged by observing
how often he can laugh at the same
joke.

> ROBERTSON DAVIES, *Samuel March-
> banks' almanack*, 1967, 115.

Jokes are grievances.

> MARSHALL MCLUHAN, at American Book-
> sellers Assoc. luncheon, Washington
> D.C., June, 1969, qu. in Vancouver *Sun*,
> June 7, 1969, 31.

Journalism

It is perfectly true that the works of a
journalist are ephemeral: they go into
the nether world of old files and are
forgotten. But does not the same fate
befall a good many books? Look at the
back stacks of any great library. What
a necropolis of the immortals is there.

> GOLDWIN SMITH, speech to the Canadian
> Press Assoc., June 3, 1881.

You see, America is a country of
inventors; and the greatest of the inventors are the newspaper men.

> ALEXANDER GRAHAM BELL, address, Em-
> pire Club, Toronto, Nov. 1, 1917.

The journalist may be a powerful and effective reformer; he is seldom a sober and prudent statesman. A wise journalist will not go to parliament. A wise statesman will keep out of journalism.

SIR JOHN WILLISON, in *Federation of Canada*, 1917, 53.

A journalist is hardly an authority upon anything – unless perhaps upon the appraisal of the drift of public opinion.

JOHN W. DAFOE, Convocation address, Univ. of Manitoba, Winnipeg, May 17, 1923.

Journalism, that fleeting imitation of literature which gives its devotees successes of the minute at the cost of foregoing more enduring satisfactions.

JOHN W. DAFOE, *Manitoba Free press*, Apr. 7, 1924, 7.

People won't accept my style of news. I use slang, cuss words, sex. Some of my acquaintances are garbage men, harlots, newsboys, waitresses. I get drunk. I exaggerate. I don't believe in goodness.

GORDON SINCLAIR, in 1944, in *Will the real Gordon Sinclair please stand up*, 1966, 184.

A journalist is not something which just happens. Like poets, they are born. They are marked by a kind of altruistic nosiness.

ROBERTSON DAVIES, *Leaven of malice*, 1954, 157.

There are rivals in the foreign correspondents of newspapers whose dispatches can be as full, shrewd, and useful as any diplomat's. Sometimes they are based on an even greater knowledge and broader experience of the country – and its people – about which they are both writing.

LESTER B. PEARSON, *Diplomacy in the nuclear age*, 1959, 16.

At its best, journalism is concerned with the processing of existing knowledge; scholarship always seeks to add

to the store. The success of journalism will in the end be measured quantitatively, if not in terms of circulation figures, then in terms of satisfaction of the readers. Scholarship will be evaluated qualitatively, and by other scholars. Journalism will always seek to create its own kind of impact; academic writing is not concerned with impact, at least not with impact for its own sake. Journalism is frequently aimed at the emotions of its readers; true scholarship distrusts mere emotionalism.

MARSH JEANNERET, in E. Harman, ed., *The university as publisher*, 1961, 6.

The journalist is, without a doubt, the most interrupted man in the world.

JEAN LE MOYNE, *Convergence*, 1966, 127.

The only journalism course I feel qualified to give consists of five words, "Travel, suffer, love, read, write."

RICHARD J. NEEDHAM, *A friend in Needham*, 1969, 13.

Only journalists can make journalism work.

W. ARTHUR IRWIN, qu. in Senate. Special Comm. on Mass Media, *Report*, Vol. 1, 1970, 10.

Steamfitters, plumbers *et al*, have taken a more professional approach to their trade than journalists have; they at least insist on minimum standards of training.

SENATE. SPECIAL COMM. ON MASS MEDIA, *Report*, Vol. 1, 1970, 123.

I do not hold with the myth of the impartial observer; you cannot watch government as closely as I have over the past eight years and remain a detached outsider unless you are a political eunuch, and no eunuch is a trustworthy guide to the ultimate mysteries.

WALTER STEWART, *Shrug: Trudeau in power*, 1971, 6.

Judges

Why does a Judge's charge have more influence than an Attorney's speech? Because he belongs to *no side*.

> T.C. HALIBURTON, letter to Joseph Howe, Nov. 15, 1835.

The Justice, he feels very big,
    And boasts what the law can secure,
But has two different laws in his wig,
    Which he keeps for the rich and the poor.

> ALEXANDER MCLACHLAN, The emigrant, 1861.

It is not sufficient that the Bench should be pure, but it must also be above suspicion.

> SIR WILFRID LAURIER, H. of C., *Debates*, Feb. 6, 1884, 135.

True enough, I am, I believe, fully competent to discharge my judicial duties, but the time will surely come and cannot be far distant when I shall no longer be competent and may not have the discernment to be aware of my incapacity. I might then be tempted to continue in office when I could no longer perform its duties with satisfaction to the public.

> J.W. RITCHIE, Equity Judge, N.S., on his retirement, qu., *Can. law jour.*, 1912, 600.

I have myself heard a very able judge, afterwards chief justice of Ontario, on a prisoner being acquitted of the charge of stealing a cap, tell him to go and not steal any more caps.

> W.R. RIDDELL, *Can.hist.rev.*, 1924, 373.

Ignorance of the Law is no excuse, and yet some Judges continue to get by.

> ANON., *Willison's monthly*, June, 1926, 13.

Who should know better than he
Just how many years in prison
Will reform a slum-product,
Or whether ten or twenty strokes of the lash
Will put an end to assaults on young girls?

> F.R. SCOTT, "Justice", 1932.

Some of the Sections of this Bill go further than we have ever gone. They make a judge out of a man who is not a lawyer.

> R.B. BENNETT, H. of C., *Debates*, 1937, 2426, on Combines Investigation Act.

Judges are all political heelers or they would not be judges.

> AGNES MACPHAIL, speech in Kenora, Ont., June 22, 1943.

A woman with a family can keep court better than a man, in that she has performed such work for years in the management of her family. In training her boys and girls, she has had to do with false pretences, assault, incitement to breach of peace, cruelty to animals, cheating at play, loitering, obstruction to justice, misappropriation, false evidence, trespass, forcible entry, idle and disorderly persons, and many other offences of an anti-social character.

> ANON., friend of Emily Murphy's qu. in B.H. Sanders, *Emily Murphy – crusader*, 1945, 134.

There would seem to be little purpose in taking elaborate care to separate the judge from politics and to render him quite independent of the executive, and then placing him in a position as a Royal Commissioner where his impartiality may be attacked and his findings – no matter how correct and judicial they may be – are liable to be interpreted as favouring one political party at the expense of the other.

> R. MACGREGOR DAWSON, *The government of Canada*, 1947, 487.

It's far better to be a doddery old man than a doddery old magistrate.

> OSCAR ORR, Vancouver Magistrate on retiring 5 years before the required age of 75, qu. in *Liberty*, Nov., 1962.

Arrogance is the occupational hazard of the Bench.

> JAMES HENRY MACGILL, qu. in E.M.G. MacGill, *My mother, the judge*, 1955, 237.

He is kind as we would want to be
    kind
    Knows more than we know,
And he has consented to be our judge
    After a stern life as befits our justice,
    A sentimental life as befits our
        justice
A steady voice of a life whose tones
    speak
The steady words of our law to the
    hanging tree.

> GEORGE JOHNSTON, "Under the tree", 1966.

I believe the bench, like the navy, should be a silent service.

> JOHN R. CARTWRIGHT, qu. in *Globe and Mail*, Aug. 16, 1967, 3, on announcement of his appointment as Chief Justice of Canada.

People think I'm too tough on Indians. There's a law for the rich and one for the poor on liquor cases; if a guy can't pay his fine, he's got to go to jail.

> NEIL MCPHEE, Magistrate, The Pas, Man., qu. in Heather Robertson, *Reservations are for Indians*, 1970, 156.

I am sick of randy young lawyers who have sought to vent their ideological tumescence on me as a political prostitute.

> JUDGE LES BEWLEY, speech to National Conference on the Law, Ottawa, Feb. 2, 1972.

Judgment

I am disposed to judge of measures more than men.

> DONALD A. SMITH (Lord Strathcona), election speech,Sept.,1878, Selkirk, Man.

What we in Canada have always feared most is to be our own judges.

> HUGH MACLENNAN, in W. Kilbourn, ed., *Canada: a guide to the peaceable kingdom*, 1970, 13.

July

This is July of the bountiful heat,
Month of wild roses, and berries, and
    wheat.

> ALBERT D. WATSON, "July", 1917.

June

Behold, now, where the pageant of
    high June
Halts in the glowing noon!
The trailing shadows rest on plain and
    hill;
The bannered hosts are still,
While over forest crown and mountain
    head
The azure tent is spread.

> BLISS CARMAN, "The tent of noon", 1915.

In June and gentle oven
Summer kingdoms simmer
As they come
And flower and leaf and love
Release
Their sweetest juice.

> ANNE WILKINSON, "In June and gentle oven", 1955.

This June that takes the city to her
    breast
Is my year's dower;
As lovers rushed with sap relax their
    thighs
At bursting excellence of fire in flower
So am I burst by sun, and sired my
    seasons rest.

> ANNE WILKINSON, "March, April, June", 1968.

Justice

I will not say that Justice is more chaste and disinterested here than in France; but, at least, if she is sold, she is sold cheaper. We do not pass through the clutches of advocates, the talons of attorneys, and the claws of clerks. These vermin do not infest Canada yet. Everybody pleads his own case.

> BARON DE LA HONTAN, *Voyages*, 1705, Letter III, Quebec, May 15, 1684. (Trans.)

The great secret is speedy justice.

> T.C. HALIBURTON, *Sam Slick*, 1838, 108.

I shall send up your case for a new trial — by your Maker.

> JUDGE MATTHEW BAILLIE BEGBIE, to an undefended prisoner who stated he did not have a fair trial; before condemning him to death; 1870's, qu. in S. Banwell, *Frontier judge*, 1938, 28.

Justice is the same on the banks of the Saskatchewan or the Qu'Appelle as on the banks of the Red River or the Assiniboine.

> EDWARD BLAKE, H. of C., *Debates*, July 6 1885, 3076, on the rebellion in the West; paraphrased and embellished by Sir Wilfrid Laurier the next day, H. of C., *Debates*, 3119.

I am not here to dispense justice, I am here to dispose of this case according to law. Whether this is or is not justice is a question for the legislature to determine.

> SIR THOMAS W. TAYLOR, Chief Justice of Manitoba, 1887-99, a retort to a lawyer.

If I really thought you were guilty, I would give you ten years.

> JUDGE CHARLES B. ROULEAU (d.1910), Edmonton, on sentencing a Chinese to two years for an offence.

There is one thing you have forgotten in your deliberations and that is justice to women. I hope that at your future meetings you will give more attention to the cause of women. That is all I have to say.

> OLIVIA SMITH, English suffragette, in Ontario legislature, Mar. 19, 1910.

Be ours a nation evermore
    That no oppression blights,
Where justice rules from shore to
        shore,
    From Lakes to Northern Lights.

> ALBERT D. WATSON, "Hymn for Canada", 1913.

Chivalry is a poor substitute for justice, if one cannot have both. Chivalry is something like the icing on cake, sweet but not nourishing.

> NELLIE MCCLUNG, *In times like these*, 1915, 54.

'Tis easy enough to be merciful,
But to be just is an excellence
Beyond all flight of sentiment!

> TOM MACINNES, "Justice", 1918.

To bring justice to every man's door in this vast territory would mean flying twenty to thirty thousand miles a year over land as bleak and often more barren than the scene passing below.

> JACK H. SISSONS, *Judge of the far north: memoirs*, 1968, 58, en route to Yellow-knife, Oct. 15, 1955.

The Just Society.

> PIERRE E. TRUDEAU, see POLITICAL PHRASES.

The free university protecting the free minds within it is not in competition with the claims of justice, but an indispensable ally in the refining of justice in a complex society. The *status quo* must be kept under constant review.

> J.A. CORRY, Convocation address, St. Francis Xavier University, Antigonish, N.S., May 16, 1968.

The only passion which should move us at this moment is a passion for justice. Through justice, we shall defend our values, our order and our laws. Through justice, we shall rid ourselves of perversion and terrorism. Through justice, we shall recover our peace and our liberty.

> PIERRE E. TRUDEAU, radio and T.V. address, Oct. 18, 1970.

Justice to me is a warm spirit, born of tolerance and wisdom, present everywhere, ready to serve the highest purposes of rational man. To seek to create the just society must be amongst the highest of those human purposes. Because we are mortal and imperfect, it is a task we will never finish; no government or society ever will. But from our honest and ceaseless effort, we will draw strength and inspiration, we will discover new and better values, we will achieve an unprecedented level of human consciousness. On the never-ending road to perfect justice we will, in other words, succeed in creating the most humane and compassionate society possible.

> PIERRE E. TRUDEAU, speech, National Conference on the Law, Ottawa, Feb. 1, 1972.

Justification

The end does not
justify the means, there is no end.
The means are not justified or
unjustified, they exist.

> JOHN NEWLOVE, "The end justifies the means", 1968.

Juveniles

All who engage in Juvenile Court work realize that Yesterday's neglected child is Today's juvenile delinquent and Tomorrow's criminal.

> JUDGE HELEN GREGORY MACGILL, Vancouver, ca. 1943, qu. in E.M.G. MacGill, *My mother, the judge*, 1955, 237.

If I were an MP, I'd try to pass a bill decreeing that every time a boy or girl were sent to jail, one of their parents would have to go with them. I've a shrewd suspicion juvenile delinquency would be wiped out in five years.

> MRS. SPELL SHIPWARD, a Hamilton, Ont. tourist questioned in Ottawa's Parliament buildings, qu. in *Liberty*, Feb., 1963.

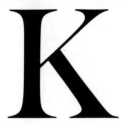

Killing

Man alone among the larger predators kills when there is no need, kills for the love of killing.

> JOHN STEVENS, introd. to F. Bodsworth *Last of the curlews*, 1963, vii.

The same government which sends you to jail for killing people also sends you to jail for refusing to kill people.

> RICHARD J. NEEDHAM, *A friend in Needham*, 1969, 22.

King, William Lyon Mackenzie

I could see a Divine Providence guiding me most lovingly. This will determine my course largely thro' life. I am determined to make it the beginning of an honourable career. I intend to go on now ever upward if God so wills.

> W.L. MACKENZIE KING, *Diary*, July 12, 1897.

Mackenzie King is doing excellent work and I believe that he has quite a political future before him.

> SIR WILFRID LAURIER, letter to Lord Minto, Apr. 13, 1909.

Somehow I believe God has a great work for me in this Dominion, maybe at some time to be its Prime Minister.

> W.L. MACKENZIE KING, *Diary*, Oct. 31, 1911.

I need a wife – God will send the right woman to me to share my life and to work out a realization of the high purpose in view.

> W.L. MACKENZIE KING, *Diary*, Aug. 7, 1919.

I was too heavy of heart and soul to appreciate the tumult of applause, my thoughts were of my dear mother & father & little Bell all of whom I felt to be very close to me, of grandfather & Sir Wilfrid also. I have sought nothing, it has come, it has come from God. The dear loved ones know and are about, they are alive and with me in this great everlasting Now and Here. It is to His work I am called, and to it I dedicate my life.

> W.L. MACKENZIE KING, *Diary*, Aug. 9, 1919 on his election to leadership of the Liberal Party.

Hark the herald angels sing
William Lyon Mackenzie King.

> ANON., campaign song, North York election, 1921, qu. in *Can. forum*, Apr., 1974, 27.

I feel I am being guided from above, that dear Mother & Father & Bell & Max the whole family in Heaven are guiding and directing me.

> W.L. MACKENZIE KING, *Diary*, Nov. 8, 1925.

He was a young man of military age, single, hale and hearty in body and mind and could well carry a rifle. But he skipped to the United States and stayed out of the country. And those men who stood by and did what they considered their duty are called renegades from the Liberal party.

HUGH GUTHRIE, speech, Brantford, Ont., election campaign, Oct., 1925, qu. in W.E. Elliott, *Politics is funny*, 1952, 13.

I had no idea who he was. They don't tell us, you know. All I knew was, a gentleman would be coming for a sitting at 10:30 in the morning. He just came in and sat down without saying anything.

HELEN HUGHES, Glasgow medium, early 1930's, qu. by Blair Fraser, *Maclean's*, Dec. 15, 1951, 60.

I have been thinking a good deal of how pleased your mother and father, and mine, would have been to see us both at the head of the Liberal party in our respective spheres of action. They were all great friends, as you know, and I can well imagine what their rejoicing would have been had they been spared to the present time. Personally, I feel quite confident that, though they may be concealed from our view, we are not hidden from theirs.

W.L. MACKENZIE KING, letter to T.D. Pattullo, Nov. 4, 1933. (Prov. Arch. B.C.).

I can tell you in my heart I am pretty radical.

W.L. MACKENZIE KING, speech in Vancouver, Sept. 28, 1935.

Government, when the nation quivered on the knife edge of war, had moved from the East Block to King's bedroom in the country.

BRUCE HUTCHISON, *The incredible Canadian*, 1953, 237, referring to King's control of the government and the nation, Sept., 1938.

Mr. King is a great man by almost any definition. You may not like him, and many do not, wasting their entire lives in hatred of him. But you cannot deny him.

BRUCE HUTCHISON, *The unknown country*, 1942, 96.

I am proud to believe there is no separation between those who are nearest and dearest to us, and I believe in the survival of the human personality. Thus I know that if I have had any success in life it has been due to my father and mother.

W.L. MACKENZIE KING, speech 25th. anniversary, leadership of the Liberal Party, Ottawa, Aug. 7, 1944.

Mr. King is obviously the most complete personification of this national Canadian characteristic who has ever appeared in our public life. He is the typical Canadian, the essential Canadian, the ideal Canadian, the Canadian as he exists in the mind of God.

FRANK H. UNDERHILL, *Can. forum*, Sept., 1944, 126, also Aug., 1948, 98, ref. to Canadian preference for leaving issues unresolved.

Mr. King never quite got it into his head during his economic studies at Toronto and Harvard that our civilization is dominated by carnivorous animals.

FRANK H. UNDERHILL, *Can. forum*, Sept., 1944, 125.

If ever a man in this world was guided from beginning to close in shaping the whole course of a session, I am that person. It has been the clearest evidence to me of guidance from Beyond that anyone could possibly have. What had seemed impossible, God has made not only possible but actually joyous and triumphant. Now it may come to be the same with the election itself.

W.L. MACKENZIE KING, *Diary*, Apr. 13, 1945.

He is said to be a man whose mind is strictly empiric, untroubled by feelings of inconsistency, representing the quintessence of the popular view of the moment, a judgment surely borne out by his political conduct. He is the ordinary man writ large.

A.R.M. LOWER, in *Can. hist. rev.*, 1946, 238.

The majority of the Canadian people have instinctively recognized that Mr. King is the leader who divides us least, and they have voted accordingly.

FRANK H. UNDERHILL, *Can. forum*, Vol. 28, Aug., 1948, 97.

His statesmanship has been a more subtly accurate, a more flexibly adjustable Gallup poll of Canadian public opinion than statisticians will ever be able to devise. He has been the representative Canadian, the typical Canadian, the essential Canadian, the ideal Canadian, the Canadian as he exists in the mind of God.

FRANK H. UNDERHILL, *Can. forum*, Aug., 1948, 98.

He succeeded with hardly a mistake for twenty-five years in giving expression, by way of that curious cloudy rhetoric of his, to what lay in the Canadian sub-conscious mind.

FRANK H. UNDERHILL, *Can. forum*, Sept., 1950, 122.

Was his basic constitutional creed really parliamentary democracy or plebiscitary democracy with a thin parliamentary veneer?

EUGENE A. FORSEY, *Can. journ. econ. and pol. sci.*, Vol. 17, 1951, 459.

The paramount egotist of his time.

BRUCE HUTCHISON, *The incredible Canadian*, 1953, 4.

The mystery of William Lyon Mackenzie King is not the mystery of a man. It is the mystery of a people. We do not understand King because we do not understand ourselves.

BRUCE HUTCHISON, *The incredible Canadian*, 1953, 1.

Mackenzie King was chiefly concerned to avoid committing himself to anything.

L.S. AMERY, *My political life*, II, 1953, 273.

He united a grey colourlessness of style, a grey ambiguity of thought, and a grey neutrality of action. He became an acknowledged expert in the difficult business of qualifying, toning down, smoothing out, and explaining away.

DONALD G. CREIGHTON, in *Canada's tomorrow*, C.P. Gilmour, ed., 1954, 228.

Mackenzie King, who was Prime Minister of Canada for twenty years, had crystal balls all over his office, indulged steadily in the fanciest kind of "spiritual" hocus-pocus, and never moved an inch without consulting an astrologer.

JOHN GUNTHER, *Inside Africa*, 1955, 798. (See also *Collier's magazine*, May 28, 1954)

Time had always been on his side. Time was on Canada's side. He had tried to maintain the nation's unity, to preserve its identity, to guard the infinite possibilities of its future.

DONALD G. CREIGHTON, *Dominion of the north*, 1957, 564.

He seemed to be in the centre
Because he had no centre,
No vision
To pierce the smoke-screen of his politics.

FRANK R. SCOTT, "W.L.M.K.", 1957.

How shall we speak of Canada,
Mackenzie King dead?
The Mother's boy in the lonely room
With his dog, his medium and his ruins?
He blunted us.

FRANK R. SCOTT, "W.L.M.K.", 1957.

He skillfully avoided what was wrong
Without saying what was right,
And never let his on the one hand
Know what his on the other hand was doing.

FRANK R. SCOTT, "W.L.M.K.", 1957.

Truly he will be remembered
Wherever men honour ingenuity,
Ambiguity, inactivity, and political longevity.

FRANK R. SCOTT, "W.L.M.K.", 1957.

We had no shape
Because he never took sides,
And no sides
Because he never allowed them to take shape.

FRANK R. SCOTT, "W.L.M.K.", 1957.

He used God just the same as he used everyone else.

ROBERT H. COATS, after reading R. Mac-Gregor Dawson's *William Lyon Mackenzie King*, Vol. 1, Feb., 1958, to Sen. N. Lambert.

An ordinary yet curiously unusual man, courteous but friendless, unobtrusive but dominating, with odd dark complexities beneath his correctly commonplace exterior, he had made himself appear a political necessity without ever acquiring much respect or inspiring any great affection.

DONALD G. CREIGHTON, *The story of Canada*, 1959, 259.

King's accomplishments were not the work of a knave and a fool. To contend otherwise is to indict us all. And it is to him, and not to his fallen foes, that we must turn to learn something about what it takes to rule Canada.

G. GERALD HARROP, *Queen's quart.*, Vol. 71, Spring, 1964, 1.

An issue exists for me by intuition or not at all. I either see it at once or it means nothing to me. I decide my policy right away. I may spend much time planning how to defend it but I know from the start what I want to do and how to do it.

W.L. MACKENZIE KING to Bruce Hutchison, qu. in his *Mr. Prime Minister*, 1964, 204.

I can deal best with men if I don't see too much of them.

W.L. MACKENZIE KING, to Bruce Hutchison, qu. in his *Mr. Prime Minister*, 1964, 215.

I found Kingsmere immensely comforting. For it assures us that the ultra-conventional little horse-trader who in our more despondent moments we equate with the national character was at times – perhaps during certain phases of the moon – a nonconformist beyond the wildest imaginings of the most nihilistic, pot-smoking, pad-dweller among us. If Kingsmere, through Mackenzie King, reflects a facet of national character, there is hope for us yet.

EDWARD MCCOURT, *The road across Canada*, 1965, 101.

Mackenzie King was a small, round man, a sphere of politics on whom the mantle of greatness slipped off. His ability to accommodate himself to every situation, without actually moving, won him the confidence of the Canadian people without affecting their disrespect.

ERIC NICOL, *100 years of what?*, 1966, 34.

I simply can't stand the worm at close quarter — bad breath, a fetid, unhealthy, sinister atmosphere, like living close to some filthy object. But get off a piece and he looks better and better.

ANON., a Liberal, qu. in *Can.hist.rev.*, Vol. 48, 1967, 278.

To an extraordinary degree, Mr. King regarded me as part of the furniture.

J.W. PICKERSGILL, qu. in P. Newman, *Distemper of our times*, 1968, 235.

An earnest, puritanical, sanctimonious young man, at once intensely self-centred and ostentatiously public-spirited, King was moved by the two driving ambitions, which he always contrived to reconcile, of serving suffering humanity and advancing his own career.

DONALD G. CREIGHTON, *Canada's first century, 1867-1967*, 1970, 162.

His verbal currency was invariably tendered in the highest denominations; but in practical politics he always dealt in very small change. He dignified ordinary and commonplace actions with sanctimonious moralizing; he loved to justify doubtful conduct by unimpeachable moral principles; he extolled the free and independent judgment of the people, and, in fact, relied on the calculated manoeuvres of partisanship. He made both big words and small deeds serve his turn. There was at once more in him than met the eye, and a great deal less than filled the ear.

DONALD G. CREIGHTON, *Canada's first century, 1867-1967*, 1970, 174.

Mr. King was not accustomed to make a clear distinction between his own interest, the party interest, and the national interest.

ESCOTT REID, in N. Penlington, ed. *On Canada*, 1971, 75.

William Lyon Mackenzie King
Sat in the middle & played with string
And he loved his mother like anything —
William Lyon Mackenzie King.

DENNIS LEE, "William Lyon Mackenzie King", 1974.

Kingfishers

The king-bird rushes up and out,
He screams and whirls and screams again.

DUNCAN CAMPBELL SCOTT, "The voice and the dusk", 1926.

Kingston, Ont.

Indeed, it may be said of Kingston, that one half of it appears to be burnt down, and the other half not to be built up.

CHARLES DICKENS, *American notes*, 1842.

Ah, it looks very well from the water.

EDWARD VII, remark to Sir Richard Cartwright. In 1860 he toured Canada (as Prince of Wales), and was kept aboard ship in Kingston harbour as a result of a difficulty arising out of his refusal to march under an arch erected by Orangemen.

Kisses

And when you bind your hair, and
    when
  You lie within your silken nest,
This kiss will visit you again,
    You will not rest, my love, you will
      not rest.

DUNCAN CAMPBELL SCOTT, "At the lat-
tice", 1893.

His lips, soft blossoms in the shade,
That kissed her silver lips – hers cool
As lilies on his inmost pool.

ISABELLA VALANCY CRAWFORD, "The lily
bed", 1905.

Strange – strange – that from the
momentary contact of lip with lip, an
infinitesimal surface of epithelial tissue, there can be called up from the
deeps of the soul emotions strange as
deep; emotions vague and thrilling;
emotions to which to give utterance
those lips are themselves powerless.

ARNOLD HAULTAIN, Hints for lovers,
1909, 230.

I like anything that's full of life and
full of enthusiasm. I think it's great.
Kissing, I guess, is an expression of that
for some people, and I find it rather
sweet. It has nothing to do with kissing
in the real sense, which I loathe to do
in public.

PIERRE E. TRUDEAU, interview in Can.
mag., qu. in B. Shaw, The gospel according to St. Pierre, 1969, 145.

Kitchens

I like a kitchen big enough
  To hold a rocking chair,
With windows looking to the sun,
  And flowers blooming there,
I like big cupboards by the wall,
  That hold a lot of things,
The cups hung up on little hooks;
  A yellow bird that sings.

EDNA JAQUES, "Farm homes", 1939, 1st
verse. (The words of this poem were cast
in a bronze plaque 45 feet high for the
San Francisco Exposition, 1939.)

Klondike

TO WHOM IT MAY CONCERN
I do, this day, locate and claim, by
right of discovery, five hundred feet,
running upstream from this notice.
Located this 17th day of August, 1896.

G.W. CARMACK, first claim in the Klondike, Rabbit (later Bonanza) Creek.

Out of the North there rang a cry of
  Gold!
And all the spacious regions of the
  West,
From rugged Caribou to where the
  crest
Of Mexican Sierras mark the old
Franciscan frontiers, caught the regal
  sound,
And echoed and re-echoed it, till
  round
The eager World the rumor of it
  rolled.

TOM MACINNES, "Lonesome bar", 1908.

It is doubtful if, in rapidity, size and
intensity, the Klondike gold rush has
ever been equalled in the whole range
of economic expansion.

HAROLD A. INNIS, Settlement and the
forest and mining frontiers, 1936, 183.

The great stampede, with all its
searchings and its yearnings, with all
its bitter surprises, its thorny impedi-
ments, and its unexpected fulfillments,
was, in a way, a rough approximation
to life itself.

PIERRE BERTON, Klondike, 1958, 435.

Knowledge

A longing still haunts us,
    Wherever we go,
And knowledge increases
    The draft of our woe;
And all that we cling to
    Is fleeting as breath,
And life is the valley
    And shadow of death.

> ALEXANDER MCLACHLAN, "A dream",
> 1856.

Knowledge is ever fatal, for Romance
Can only live in shades of ignorance.

> CHARLES HEAVYSEGE, poem No. V, in
> *Jephthah's daughter*, 1865.

Faith, science, doubt profound,
Searching for ampler knowledge from
    afar,
By turns have soared to question every
    star,
Have probed the earth to tell us
    whence we are,
And whither bound.

> DANIEL WILSON, *Canadian birthday
> book*, 1887, 90.

The knowledge of most men is just
enough to make them aggressively
ignorant.

> PETER MCARTHUR, *To be taken with salt*,
> 1903, 155.

To few it has been given to see things
as they are, to know that no opinion is
altogether right, no purpose altogether
laudable, and no calamity altogether
deplorable.

> STEPHEN LEACOCK, "A rehabilitation of
> Charles II", in *University mag.*, 1906,
> 268.

A man can never know too much.
Perhaps a woman can.

> ARNOLD HAULTAIN, *Hints for lovers*,
> 1909, 177.

It's awfully hard for a woman to
pretend not to know the things she
ought not to know.

> ROBERT C. (BOB) EDWARDS, Calgary *Eye
> Opener*, Sept. 7, 1912.

The quest for righteousness is Oriental,
the quest for knowledge Occidental.

> SIR WILLIAM OSLER, speech, Jewish Hist.
> Soc., London, Apr. 27, 1914.

Nearly all the knowledge in the world
has been acquired at the expense of
somebody's burnt fingers.

> ROBERT C. (BOB) EDWARDS, Calgary *Eye
> Opener*, Feb. 2, 1918.

It is no coincidence that in Hebrew the
word *Yadoa* is the word for knowing
and for the physical consummation of
love.

> KARL STERN, *The pillar of fire*, 1951, 3.

As the Flaming Sword receded
Eve walked a little ahead.
"If we keep on using this knowledge
I think we'll be back," she said.

> FRANK R. SCOTT, "Eden", 1954.

To know what we see or feel involves
stating it, at least to ourselves.

> MARGARET AVISON, "Poetry chronicle",
> in *Tamarack rev.*, Autumn, 1956, 80.

All knowledge is useful only if it is
used. How it is used is another matter.
Unused knowledge does not lie fallow
like a field "resting"; it just disappears.

> WILLIAM E. BLATZ, *Human security*,
> 1966, 7.

Labour

Labour is the true source of wealth.

> WILLIAM LYON MACKENZIE, *The Constitution*, May 24, 1837.

To the honest sons of labour Canada is, indeed, an El Dorado – a land flowing with milk and honey; for they soon obtain that independence which the poor gentleman struggles in vain to realize by his own labour in the woods.

> SUSANNA MOODIE, *Life in the clearings*, 1853, Intro. xii.

Ten hours a day of labour
In a closely lighted room
Machinery was her music
Gas her sweet perfume

> ANON., "A factory girl", from the *Ontario workman*, 1870-74, qu. in C. Lipton, *Trade union movement of Canada*, 1967, 54.

I ought to have a special interest in this subject because I am a working man myself. I know that I work more than nine hours every day myself, and then I think I am a practical mechanic. If you look at the Confederation Act, in the framing of which I had some hand, you will admit that I am a pretty good joiner; and as for cabinet making, I have as much experience as Jacques & Hay themselves.

> SIR JOHN A. MACDONALD, address to crowd of workingmen, July 11, 1872, Music Hall, Toronto.

The Annual Pilgrimage.

> ANON., term used to describe traditional annual meeting between trade union representatives and the Prime Minister, first took place in 1873.

I love this land of forest grand!
 The land where labour's free;
Let others roam away from home,
 Be this the land for me!
Where no one moils and strains and
 toils,
 That snobs may thrive the faster;
And all are free as men should be,
 And Jack's as good's his master!

> ALEXANDER MCLACHLAN, "Young Canada, or, Jack's as good as his master", 1874.

Our aristocracy of toil
 Have made us what you see,
The nobles of the forge and soil,
 With ne'er a pedigree!

> ALEXANDER MCLACHLAN, "Young Canada, or, Jack's as good as his master", 1874.

The working class of this Dominion will never be properly represented in Parliament or receive justice in the legislation of this country until they are represented by men of their own class and opinions.

> CANADIAN LABOUR CONGRESS, resolution passed at meetings, Dec. 26-28, 1883 in Toronto.

Labor Reform despised and sneered at by the college-bred peddlers of platitudes, and the horde of intellectual weaklings and parasites who prostitute their brains to the support of existing wrongs – will yet regenerate the world's literature and supply the mainspring and the motive for a newer and grander literary development in Canada as well as elsewhere.

ANON., (Enjolras), in *Palladium of labor*, Nov. 6, 1886, 1.

When the elections came round other subjects interfered – the man was a Catholic or a Protestant, or an infidel or a pagan – and the labour vote was knocked out of line.

ALFRED JURY, at Trades and Labour Congress, Annual Convention, Montreal, Sept. 5, 1889.

And toil hath fear for neighbour,
　Where singing lips are dumb,
And life is one long labour,
　Till death or freedom come.

ARCHIBALD LAMPMAN, "The city", 1899.

No English need apply.

ANON., early 1900's; used by Western farmers in advertisements for hired help; see B. Stewart, *The land of the maple leaf,* 1908, also *Willison's monthly,* Vol. 1, 1925, 125.

No Orientals need apply.

ANON., a notice outside many B.C. pulp-mills and other factories, 20th. cent.

There is only one class on the plains, and that is the working class. Here and there you meet a gentleman of leisure, but he is called a tramp.

HOWARD A. KENNEDY, *New Canada,* 1907.

Such a land is good for an energetic man. It is also not so bad for the loafer.

RUDYARD KIPLING, *Letters to the family,* 1907, 61.

The only difference between jail and a job is that here I am separated from my wife and family. Under capitalism all the workers are in jail all the time. And lots of them haven't got the security of shelter and food that is offered in a penitentiary.

J.B. MCLACHLAN, qu. in *The maritime labour herald,* Nov. 17, 1923, 1.

You may have a titled aristocracy and a moneyed aristocracy, but there is only one true aristocracy in any community, in my opinion, and that is the aristocracy of labour.

ABRAHAM A. HEAPS, H. of C., *Debates,* Feb. 14, 1929, 104.

I propose that any government of which I am the head will at the first session of Parliament initiate whatever action is necessary to that end [to protect the agriculturist and the worker, the manufacturer and the consumer], or perish in the attempt.

R.B. BENNETT, election speech, Winnipeg, June 9, 1930; usually quoted as "I will end unemployment or perish in the attempt".

We bear the burden home to bed
The furnace glows within our hearts:
Our bodies hammered through the
　　night
Are welded into bitter bread.

DOROTHY LIVESAY, "Day and night", 1935.

I will not tolerate the sit-down strike in this Province of ours. In the first place, it is nothing but illegal trespass. In the second place, it is against law and order.

MITCHELL HEPBURN, Premier of Ontario, qu. in *Globe and Mail,* Monday, Mar. 8, 1937, 1.

The curse of labour is past.
We have thrown the packs from our
  shoulders,
wiped the sweat from our brows, yet
multiplied the work which is not of
  our hands.

> E.J. PRATT, "A prayer-medley", 1937.

From those condemned to labour
For profit of another
We take our new endeavour.

> FRANK R. SCOTT, "Dedication", in *Poetry
> mag.*, Apr., 1941.

Under the dark industrial sky
we wonder why we have to die
who living, were valued at a wage
that starved our youth and murdered
  age?

> JAMES WREFORD, "Kirkland Lake", 1942.

Workers have the right to organize
and the right not to organize. Labour
has the right to organize, but not to
disorganize.

> MAURICE DUPLESSIS, election campaign
> preceding Quebec election, July 28,
> 1948.

The seed of our toil watered with the
sweat of our brows, has now ripened
into the fruits of our labours.

> LIONEL FORSYTH, (d.1957) addressing a
> group of DOSCO employees.

Labour leaders rarely share in the
informal aspects of the confraternity
of power. They do not, as we have
seen, have the range of honorific roles
that the corporate elite does. Nor does
the power of labour leaders extend
beyond their institutional roles. They
do not have the power, for example, to
exploit non-economic areas of social
life and harness them to the commercial principle as the corporate elite has
with the world of sport.

> JOHN PORTER, *The vertical mosaic*, 1965,
> 539.

The capitalists are people who want
only and live only for profits. The
Quebec workers live only for their
debts. The workers therefore want to
appropriate for themselves the wealth
they create so as to belong at last to
themselves.

> CORPORATION DES ENSEIGNANTS DU QUE-
> BEC, policy statement, qu. in *Globe and
> Mail*, Apr. 3, 1971, 8. (Trans.)

Every benefit possessed by the labour
force was conceived through the unions and not through management.
The employer has lost the advantage
of having given these benefits. He has
had to have them extracted from him.

> SENATOR ED LAWSON, Canadian Director
> of the Teamster's Union, qu. in *Ma-
> clean's*, Aug., 1972, 51.

Labour Relations

People are inclined to judge a dispute
in terms of "right" and "wrong": the
fact is that generally neither side is
wholly right or wholly wrong.

> H. CARL GOLDENBERG, address, Empire
> Club of Canada, Toronto, Nov. 15,
> 1962.

Labour Strikes

We may destroy our happiness by
inoculating our industrial system with
the maladies of a distant country
[England] and an alien state of society.

> TORONTO *GLOBE*, Apr. 1, 1872, on
> strikes.

From the union's standpoint the scab
may be a mean man, but sometimes he
is an heroic one.

> SIR W. VAN HORNE, 1912; qu. in Vaughan,
> *Van Horne*, 1920, 37.

What we want.
The demands of strikers are 1. The right to collective bargaining 2. A living wage 3. Reinstatement of all strikers. What we do not want. 1. Revolution 2. Dictatorship 3. Disorder.

> *WESTERN LABOUR NEWS, Strike bulletin,* May 30, 1919, during Winnipeg General Strike.

Bloody Saturday.

> *WINNIPEG GENERAL STRIKE,* June 21, 1919, when 2 men died and injury and property damage were widespread.

Big Ten.

> ANON., leaders of Winnipeg General Strike who were brought to trial, 1919.

My place is marching with the workers rather than riding with General Motors.

> DAVID CROLL, letter of resignation from Hepburn cabinet, Apr. 14, 1937, at time of General Motors strike.

Strikes are a public declaration that the parties aren't mature, intelligent or reasonable enough to settle their problems any other way.

> SENATOR ED LAWSON, Canadian director of the Teamster's Union, qu. in *Maclean's,* Aug., 1972, 51.

Labour Unions

United to support, not combined to injure.

> TORONTO TYPOGRAPHICAL SOCIETY, motto adopted, 1844.

It is in obedience to foreign agitation carried on by paid agents who have nothing to lose as the result of their mischievous counsels that the printers of this city have succumbed.

> TORONTO *GLOBE* , Mar. 26, 1872.

Ought a free citizen who professes to have at heart Labour's enfranchisement and to devote himself to that work, to wear the muzzle of partyism on his mouth and put his conscience in the keeping of politicians who seek only to delude and befool the workingman – with his assistance if possible? No – a thousand times – No!

> ANON., ("Enjolras"), in *Palladium of labour,* Oct. 24, 1885, 1.

No one can become a member who is not sober, and, as a consequence, union men and women are temperate, industrious in their habits. The universal testimony of wage earners is that the money paid by them to support their societies is as good an investment as they ever made.

> CANADA. ROY. COMM. ON THE RELATIONS OF LABOUR AND CAPITAL IN CANADA, *Report,* 1889, 114.

Never in the history of Canada have labour unions shown so much activity; never have they been so well organized, and never has that organization made such determined, and in many cases unreasonable, efforts to secure for labour the domination of Canadian factories, and to wrest from the employer his inherent rights, to control the policy of his business and manage it as he thinks best.

> CANADIAN MANUFACTURERS' ASSOCIATION, in *Industrial Canada,* Oct., 1903, 129.

The Englishman is not welcomed by the employers, because he brings his trade unionism with him, and Englishmen are the leaders in all strikes. The workmen themselves don't welcome him, because their cry is: "Winnipeg for the Winnipeggers, Canada for the Canadians, and to Gehenna with the unspeakable Englishman".

> JOHN FOSTER FRASER, *Canada as it is,* 1909, 111.

Where the Fraser River flows, each
fellow worker knows,
They have bullied and oppressed us,
but still our Union grows.
And we're going to find a way, boys,
for shorter hours and better pay,
boys!
And we're going to win the day, boys;
where the River Fraser flows.

JOE HILL, "Where the Fraser River
flows", 1912, in support of striking
workers laying track for the Canadian
Northern Railroad in B.C.

The main defect of Canadian Labour
is the lack of ideas. The leading spirits
are quietists. There is little that is
aggressive in the movement. It has no
vivid life. Its leaders are not sufficiently alive to the danger of their situation.

H.J. LASKI, *The voice*, June 9, 1916, 4.

The international labour movement, in
view of its doctrinal sources, no more
guarantees order than does the revolutionary individualism from which it
flows; no more, indeed, than does
communism, towards which this
movement's ideas lead by a natural, so
to speak, progression.

ESDRAS MINVILLE, *La législation ouv-
rière et le régime social dans la province de Québec*, 1939, 20. (Trans. by
Ramsay Cook.)

Co-operation yes – Domination no!

PERCY R. BENGOUGH, President of Trades
and Labour Congress, Trades and Labour Congress, *Journal*, Mar., 1949, 13,
on the attempt by the American Federation of Labor to disenfranchise Canadian members.

The Canadian branches of international unions also run their own affairs, with one qualification: that
strikes usually require the consent of
the international office, which must
foot the bill, and naturally cannot
undertake to issue blank checks to its
Canadian locals. Practically all the rest

of the chatter about 'American control' is eyewash, spouting from pure
ignorance.

EUGENE FORSEY, address to Canadian
Political Science Association, Ottawa,
June 13, 1957.

How dare these outsiders come into
this decent Christian Province and by
such desperate, such terrible methods
try to seize control of our Province's
main industry.

JOSEPH R. SMALLWOOD, speech, Feb. 12,
1959, referring to the International
Woodworkers of America.

Canada is the only ostensibly independent country whose labour organizations are run by leaders outside it.

MIRIAM CHAPIN, *Contemporary Canada*,
1959, 186.

Canada is unique in that it inherited a
trade-union structure which was created to meet problems in another country with an economy markedly different and immensely larger and more
diversified than our own.

DONALD N. SECORD, National Sec'y-
Treas., Can. Brotherhood of Railway,
Transport and General Workers, speech,
London and District Labour Council,
Nov. 15, 1960.

A labour movement that is without
interest in political matters is a labour
movement that is evading one of the
most fundamental responsibilities.

CLAUDE JODOIN, address, New Democratic Party Founding Convention, Ottawa, July 31, 1961.

International union.

ANON., designation given to American
unions solely because of membership in
Canada.

But in no important industrial country of the world has it ever happened that the workers should organize in unions based in a foreign country. That had absolutely nothing to do with internationalism! Indeed, such a development was bound to bear within it the danger of the very antithesis of internationalism – imperialism – the domination of workers in one country by bodies located in another country.

> CHARLES LIPTON, *The trade union movement of Canada*, 1967, 138.

The first thing I'd do is nationalize all the American trade unions. Canadian unions must be independent. Let them cry how much they want.

> GUNNAR MYRDAL, qu. by P. Newman, *Home country*, 1973, 51.

From the beginning the CIO was insistent upon showing the flag in Canada – the American flag, that is.

> IRVING M. ABELLA, *Nationalism, communism, and Canadian labour*, 1973, 219.

If almost all the organizing for the CIO was done by Canadians; if almost all the money needed for this organization was provided by Canadians; and if almost all the leadership in the new unions was provided by Canadians; then who needed the CIO?

> IRVING M. ABELLA, *Nationalism, communism, and Canadian labour*, 1973, 217.

There's been a tendency in the labour movement here, as well as everywhere else, to look at things on a pork chop basis, to go for the pay packet and ignore the political implications, the real nature of a worker's relationship to his job.

> HOMER STEVENS, Pres. of United Fishermen and Allied Workers Union, B.C., in *Maclean's*, June, 1973, 86.

Pelletier, Marchand and I express our solidarity with our asbestos comrades. Although we are unable to intervene, we hope a solution to your demands can be found.

> PIERRE ELLIOTT TRUDEAU, telegram about Mar. 28, 1975 to asbestos workers in Quebec on strike against Asbestos Corp.

The public can go to hell.

> JOE DAVIDSON, Pres., Canadian Union of Postal Workers, qu. in Vancouver *Sun*, July 17, 1975, 5.

Labrador

Many have sailed towards the North, on the coasts of the Baccalaos and Labrador; but as in those regions there was no appearance of riches, there is no more account of them than of others who went to Paria.

> ANTONIO DE HERRERA, in 1506, *Descripción de las Indias Ocidentales*, Decad. I, Lib. vi., 1726, 169. (Trans.)

Along the whole of the north shore I did not see one cart-load of earth and yet I landed in many places. Except at Blanc Sablon there is nothing but moss and short, stunted shrub. In fine I am rather inclined to believe that this is the land God gave to Cain.

> JACQUES CARTIER, *Voyage to Canada*, (1534), (Trans.); descriptive of the St. Lawrence Gulf and Labrador; *cf.*, Genesis, IV, 12.

Lacrosse

Lacrosse – our national field game.

> GEORGE W. BEERS, heading over letter in Montreal *Daily news*, Apr., 1867, later printed separately and distributed; earliest use of the phrase; see his *Lacrosse*, 1869, 58.

Father of Lacrosse.

> ANON., term applied to George W. Beers of Montreal who framed a set of rules for the game, 1860's.

Lake Erie

Lake Erie is weary
Of washing the dreary
Crowds of the cities
That line her shores.

> JAMES REANEY, "Lake Erie", 1949.

Lake Huron

How I long for Huron's shore:
How I long for Huron's beaches,
Where the wind-swept, shining
reaches
Wind in mists and are no more.

> WILFRED CAMPBELL, "By Huron's shore", 1889.

Lake Superior

Lake Superior is all the same stuff as what towns pay taxes for, but it engulfs and wrecks and drives ashore, like a fully accredited ocean — a hideous thing to find in the heart of a continent.

> RUDYARD KIPLING, *Letters to the family*, 1908, 28.

I am Lake Superior
Cold and grey.
I have no superior;
All other lakes
Haven't got what it takes;
All are inferior.

> JAMES REANEY, "Lake Superior", 1949.

Lakes

The great inland seas of Canada.

> JOHN MACTAGGART, *Three years in Canada*, 1829, II, 322.

Out in a world of death, far to the
northward lying,
Under the sun and the moon, under
the dusk and the day;
Under the glimmer of stars and the
purple of sunsets dying,
Wan and waste and white, stretch
the great lakes away.

> WILFRED CAMPBELL, "The winter lakes",
> 1889.

Red in the mists of the morning
Angry, coloured with fire,
Beats the great lake in its beauty,
Rocks the wild lake in its ire.

> WILFRED CAMPBELL, "Down in the island
> camp", 1889.

Domed with the azure of heaven,
Floored with a pavement of pearl,
Clothed all about with a brightness
Soft as the eyes of a girl,

Girt with a magical girdle,
Rimmed with a vapour of rest —
These are the inland waters,
These are the lakes of the west.

> WILFRED CAMPBELL, "The lakes of the
> west", 1889.

Reform ye scribblers, leave your mists
and frogs,
Lakes, loons, and *Injuns* and Acadian
bogs —
And hang the eternal paddle up to
dry;
Canoes, good sooth; when Pegasus can
fly,
To read our bards the world might
well mistake
Our wide Dominion for an endless
lake,
Dotted with isles where birch
expressly grows
The raw material for bark canoes.

> ALEXANDER C. STEWART, *The poetical
> review*, 1896, 24.

It sleeps among the thousand hills
  Where no man ever trod,
And only Nature's music fills
  The silences of God.

FREDERICK G. SCOTT, "The unnamed
lake", 1897.

The last weird lakelet foul with weedy
  growths
And slimy viscid things the spirit
  loathes,
Skin of vile water over viler mud
Where the paddle stirred unutterable
  stenches
And the canoes seemed heavy with
  fear.

DUNCAN CAMPBELL SCOTT, "The height
of land", 1916.

The plain fact is that the Canadian
will not summer anywhere except beside a lake. It does not matter much
how large the lake is, nor how clean,
nor what sort of odours emanate from
it. A lake is a lake.

B.K. SANDWELL, *The privacity agent*,
1928, 103.

The iron rocks
slope sharply down
into the gleaming water,
and there is a shining
to northern water
reflecting the sky
on a keen cool morning.

W.W. EUSTACE ROSS, "Rocky Bay", 1930.

The lake has drawn a counterpane of
  glass
On her rock limbs up to her island
  pillows
And under netting woven by the
  swallows
Sleeps in a dream and is a
  dream . . .

ROBERT FINCH, "The smile", 1946.

How different it is here upon the
  water!
Where every wave, rising, is a mirror
in whose imagined depths we see
  ourselves,
part desire, part reflection, and part
  flesh.

DARYL HINE, "Proust", 1954.

The lake is sharp along the shore
Trimming the bevelled edge of land
To level curves; the fretted sand
Goes slanting down through liquid air
Till stones below shift here and there
Floating upon their broken sky
All netted by the prism wave
And rippled where the currents are.

FRANK R. SCOTT, "Lakeshore", 1954.

Land

It is a grand country for the rich
speculator who can afford to lay out a
large sum in purchasing land in eligible situations; for if he have any
judgment he will make a hundred per
cent as interest for his money after
waiting a few years.

CATHERINE PARR TRAILL, Letter IX, Apr.
18, 1833; *The backwoods of Canada*,
1839, 140.

In the North American Colonies
. . . the function of authority most
full of good or evil consequences has
been the disposal of the public land.

LORD DURHAM, *Report*, 1839, Lucas ed.,
Vol. 2, 1912, 206.

For my part I do not see why God
should hold land and not pay taxes.

T. WIGGINS, letter to William Lyon Mackenzie, May 24, 1851, referring to clergy reserves.

Plaintiff, you go and divide the land into two parts and you, defendant, then take your choice.

> SIR MATTHEW BAILLIE BEGBIE, decision in a trial involving division of property between two brothers, at Kamloops, B.C., about 1860.

The Plain and Wood Cree Tribes of Indians, and all other Indians inhabiting the district hereinafter described and defined, do hereby cede, release, surrender and yield up to the Government of the Dominion of Canada for Her Majesty the Queen and Her successors forever, all their rights, titles and privileges, whatsoever to the lands included in the following limits.

> CANADA., Treaty No. 6, Forts Carleton and Pitt, signed Aug., 1878.

Fairly fit for settlement.

> CANADIAN PACIFIC SYNDICATE, from a clause in their contract with the government which provided for a land subsidy policy; *Canada, Statutes*, 44 Vict., Cap. I, 1881.

God Made Land Man Must Use Not For Spec.

> J.W. BENGOUGH, "Lesson XXIX", *The up-to-date primer*, 1896, 33.

Certainly it cannot be too often repeated, that the most solid basis for a nation is the possession of the land; that the question of "repatriation," that is of the return to the agricultural districts of the province of Quebec, remains the order of the day. Lay hold of the land, as far as circumstances will permit.

> EDMOND DE NEVERS, *L'avenir du peuple canadien-français*, 1896, 439. (Trans.)

Thank God, we are once more on British soil!

> WINSTON CHURCHILL, at Windsor Station, Montreal, Dec. 23, 1900, on descending from the train from Boston.

In so far as every tract of land in the whole Northwest which was considered to be fairly fit for settlement is concerned, it was covered with reservations of some kind in favor of railway companies.

> SIR CLIFFORD SIFTON, H. of C., *Debates*, May 31, 1906, 4314.

The people must get back on the land, must! must! must!

> PETER MCARTHUR, *In pastures green*, 1915, pref., x.

God knows there's plenty of earth for all of us!
Then why must we sweat for it, deny for it,
Pray for it, cry for it,
Kill, maim and lie for it,
Struggle and suffer and die for it —
We who are gentle and sane?

> LLOYD ROBERTS, "If I must", 1916.

The Landless Man to the Manless Land.

> ROBERT FORKE, attributed slogan when Minister of Immigration and Colonization, 1926-29.

Land is in the blood of all French-Canadians.

> HUGH MACLENNAN, *Two solitudes*, 1945, 332.

If the Canadian people are to find their soul, they must seek for it not in the English language or the French, but in the little ports of the Atlantic provinces, in the flaming autumn maples of the St. Lawrence valley, in the portages and lakes of the Canadian Shield, in the sunsets and relentless cold of the prairies, in the foothill, mountain and sea of the West and in the unconquerable vastness of the North. From the land, Canada, must come the soul of Canada.

> A.R.M. LOWER, *Colony to nation*, 1946, 560.

All we knew was that, however "young" the country might be, the landscape seemed old and violent and sad.

> PATRICK ANDERSON, *Search me*, 1957, 145.

A man without land is nothing.

> MORDECAI RICHLER, *The apprenticeship of Duddy Kravitz*, 1959; 1974 ed., p. 65 has "A man without land is nobody".

This land is your land, this land is my land,
From Bonavista to Vancouver Island,
From the Arctic islands to the Great Lakes waters;
This land was made for you and me.

> WOODY GUTHRIE, American singer, from his American version originally sung in 1956; adapted by Martin Bochner.

American land grab.

> Phrase describing the purchase of property in Canada by Americans, 1960's and 1970's.

We are still governed by the land, because we can see no way of governing it.

> ROBERT FULFORD, in Roloff Beny, *To everything there is a season*, 1967, 251.

This land is far more important than we are. To know it is to be young and ancient all at once.

> HUGH MACLENNAN, *The colour of Canada*, 1967, 17.

More than ever before, we have arrived at a point where we recognize, not only that the land is ours, but that we are the land's.

> D.G. JONES, *Butterfly on rock*, 1970, 3; paraphrase of Robert Frost, "The land was ours before we were the land's".

When the White Man came, we had the land and they had the Bibles; now they have the land and we have the Bibles.

> CHIEF DAN GEORGE, qu. in G. Walsh, *Indians in transition*, 1971, 51.

Landladies

A landlady can be reduced to her lowest terms by a series of propositions.

> STEPHEN B. LEACOCK, "Boarding house geometry", in *Literary lapses*, 1910.

Landlords

Land Lord Stays Still On Top Can't Down Him.

> J.W. BENGOUGH, "Lesson LXIII", *The up-to-date primer*, 1896, 67.

Landscape

O landscape lovely, looped
With loping hills wind-hoven
Galloping through cloud –
Landfall of love.

> DOROTHY LIVESAY, "Nocturne", 1955.

The most characteristic Canadian thing is the Canadian landscape.

> PAUL WEST, *Can. lit.* No. 13, 1962, 14.

Yet still I journey to this naked country to seek a form which dances in the sand.
This is my chosen landscape.

> GWENDOLYN MACEWEN, "Finally left in the landscape", 1966.

Languages

How can a man reach these people if he doesn't speak their language? To work through an interpreter is like hacking one's way through a forest with a feather.

> REV. JAMES EVANS, in 1838, qu. in N. Shipley, *The James Evans story*, 1966, 16, referring to the Cree Indians.

A considerable time must, of course, elapse before the change of a language can spread over a whole people; and justice and policy alike require, that while the people continue to use the French language, their Government should take no such means to force the English language upon them as would, in fact, deprive the great mass of the community of the protection of the laws.

LORD DURHAM, *Report*, 1839, ed. Lucas, Vol. 2, 1912, 296.

His Excellency reads French, and speaks it with the pure Parisian accent. He also reads Greek, Latin and Italian, and has made considerable progress in the study of hieroglyphics.

WILLIAM LEGGO, *Administration of Lord Dufferin*, 1878, 68.

I would rather have a man know less Latin and more Horse.

JAMES ROBERTSON, D.D., superintendent of Presbyterian missions in the northwest, late 1800's.

Let us deal with the dual languages in the North-West. In the Local House let us deal with the teaching of French in the schools. When these two matters are settled we will have accomplished something, and we may be able to do something better in the future.

D'ALTON MCCARTHY, speech at Stayner, Ont., July 12, 1889.

I have no accord with the desire expressed in some quarters that by any mode whatever there should be an attempt made to oppress the one language or to render it inferior to the other; I believe that it would be impossible if it were tried, and it would be foolish and wicked if it were possible.

SIR JOHN A. MACDONALD, H. of C., *Debates*, Feb. 17, 1890, 745.

What language is spoken in the Dominion of Canada? Canadian.

JAMES D. GILLIS, *Canadian grammar*, (Halifax), 1925, 3.

I can see no reason why we in Canada, when we have developed a style of our own, should not describe ourselves as using an English vocabulary, but a Canadian language.

B.K. SANDWELL, Canadian Club, Ottawa, Mar. 13, 1920.

Wherever there is a difference between the French text and the English text of a statute, the French text shall prevail.

QUEBEC (PROV.), LAWS & STATUTES, 1937, Chapt. 13, Sect. 1, 20 May, 1937.

Already I speak the both languages, English and Ukrainian.

ANON., a New Canadian, 1940's.

The infinitive is the language of quotations and generalisations.

LISTER S. SINCLAIR, *A play on words*, (Radio Drama, C.B.C., Nov. 12, 1944).

In Canada we have enough to do keeping up with two spoken languages without trying to invent slang, so we just go right ahead and use English for literature, Scotch for sermons, and American for conversations.

STEPHEN B. LEACOCK, *How to write*, 1944, 108.

It is a matter of distinct pride for us French Canadians that although we can speak English flawlessly, we do not do so. We give it enough of a French flavor so you will know we are French Canadians.

ANON., qu. by Harlan Hatcher, Canada-U.S. Conference on Mutual Relations, Washington, Feb. 7-8, 1955, *Report*, 1955, 40.

Two or three languages present no greater problem to the child than a single language.

WILDER PENFIELD, address, Women's Canadian Club, Montreal, Nov., 1958.

Expressions such as 'Speak White!', 'Stupid French Canadians', and others of the same ilk are common. In Quebec itself, thousands of people who can speak nothing but English are unashamed to exhibit this in public. The colonizers see us as inferior beings, and have no compunction about letting us know that they do.

FLQ (Front de Liberation du Québec), Manifesto, Apr. 16, 1963. (Trans.)

Today, the English language has unquestioned dominance in the Western Provinces, in Southern Ontario and in the Atlantic Region. Both languages are in more-or-less common use within a "Bilingual Belt" along the Quebec border but the interior of that province is solidly French-speaking.

RICHARD J. JOY, Languages in conflict, 1967, intro.

It was agreed, in 1867 that French "was to be recognized and applied in all federal fields on the same footing as" English.

EUGENE FORSEY, paraphrase of a common statement, dismissed as one of the seven devils of our pseudo-history in "Our present discontents", speech, Acadia Univ., Oct. 19, 1967.

I didn't know at first that there were two languages in Canada. I just thought that there was one way to speak to my father and another to speak to my mother.

LOUIS ST. LAURENT, attributed; see Dale Thomson, Louis St. Laurent: Canadian, 1967, 27, and B. Hutchison, Mr. Prime Minister, 1964, 288.

It is one of my secret hopes for Prime Ministers of the future that Canada will some day – perhaps in time for the bicentennial of Confederation, and through the desire of the people and the governments of the provinces – become a truly bilingual country from coast to coast – not by the compulsion of decree, but by the compulsion of desire.

LESTER B. PEARSON, address, National Centennial Conference, Quebec City, Apr. 24, 1967.

In terms of *realpolitik*, French and English are equal in Canada because each of these linguistic groups has the power to break the country.

PIERRE E. TRUDEAU, Federalism and the French Canadians, 1968, 31.

The English and French languages are the official languages of Canada for all purposes of the Parliament and Government of Canada, and possess and enjoy equality of status and equal rights and privileges as to their use in all the institutions of the Parliament and Government of Canada.

CANADA. LAWS, STATUTES, etc., Official languages act, 1968-69, c.54 s.2.

The brain of a man or woman that is made bilingual or multilingual early in life becomes a superior instrument.

WILDER PENFIELD, Second thoughts, 1970, 31.

Larks

The shore-lark soars to his topmost
   flight,
Sings at the height where the morning
   springs,
What though his voice be lost in the
   light,
The light comes dropping from his
   wings.

DUNCAN CAMPBELL SCOTT, "Ecstasy", 1926.

Go out and hear the lark. The time is at dawn.

WILLIAM E. SAUNDERS, in London *Free press*, 1939.

LaSalle, Sieur De

True Wizard of the Wild! whose art,
An eye of power, a knightly heart,
A patient purpose silence-nurst,
A high, enduring, saintly trust —
Are mighty spells — we honor these,
Columbus of the inland seas!

THOMAS D'A. MCGEE, "The launch of the *Griffin*", 1858; a reference to LaSalle.

He contained in his own complex and painful nature the chief springs of his triumphs, his failures, and his death.

FRANCIS PARKMAN, *[LaSalle]* – *Discovery of the great West*, 1869, 430, on LaSalle.

A tower of adamant, against whose impregnable front hardship and danger, the rage of man and of the elements, the southern sun, the northern blast, fatigue, famine, and disease, delay, disappointment, and deferred hopes emptied their quivers in vain.

FRANCIS PARKMAN, *LaSalle and the discovery of the great West*, 1869, (11th ed., 1879, 432).

Lateness

Ah! the clock is always slow;
It is later than you think;
Sadly later than you think;
Far, far later than you think.

ROBERT W. SERVICE, "It is later than you think", 1921.

Laughter

When a man laughs he's nearer to letting his money go.

RALPH CONNOR, *The prospector*, 1904, 79.

Bubbling spontaneously from the artless heart of child or man, without egotism and full of feeling, laughter is the music of life.

SIR WILLIAM OSLER, *Can. med. assoc. jour.*, Feb., 1912, 152.

The public will pay more for laughing than for any other privilege.

ROBERT C. (BOB) EDWARDS, Calgary *Eye Opener*, May 11, 1918, 3.

You may laugh through the whole of a farce,
You may laugh through the whole of a play,
But you never can laugh through the hole of your a—
For a man isn't built that way.

ROBERT C. (BOB) EDWARDS, attributed; qu. in E. Stafford, ed., *Flamboyant Canadians*, 1964, 196.

With age, laughter sinks deeper
Into the heart than youth permits.

DORIS HEDGES, "Tempo", 1967.

Laurier, Sir Wilfrid

I pledge my honour that I will give the whole of my life to the cause of conciliation, harmony and concord among the different elements of this country of ours.

SIR WILFRID LAURIER, valedictory speech to Undergraduate Society, McGill Faculty of Law, May 4, 1864.

That's Wilfrid Laurier from Quebec. He came up here ten years ago with a great reputation. He was a great orator, he had charm, he had everything. He was the main promise among Quebec Liberals. But since then all the promise has been proved to be without any basis. He has been a complete disappointment. He has no future. Why, just look at him now. He does nothing nowadays, but sit here in the Library, day after day, reading books!

ANON., member of press gallery to J.W. Dafoe during tour of Library of Parliament, 1884.

Silver-Tongued Laurier.

P.D. ROSS, despatch to the Montreal *Star*, Mar. 17, 1886, after hearing Laurier's speech in House of Commons on Riel's execution.

Nice chap, that. If I were twenty years younger, he'd be my colleague.

SIR JOHN A. MACDONALD, to Sir Joseph Pope, May, 1891.

Laurier will look after you should you need a friend when I am gone.

SIR JOHN A. MACDONALD, remark to Sir Joseph Pope, qu. in Pope, *Public servant*, 1960, 66.

Not Sir Wilfrid: plain Mr. Laurier; I am a democrat to the hilt.

SIR WILFRID LAURIER, in 1895 at Renfrew, Ont. when he was incorrectly addressed as Sir Wilfrid by a heckler; he was knighted two years later.

So long as I have a seat in this House, so long as I occupy the position I do now, whenever it shall become my duty to take a stand on any question whatever, that stand I will take not upon grounds of Roman Catholicism, not upon grounds of Protestantism, but upon grounds which can appeal to the conscience of all men, irrespective of their particular faith, upon grounds which can be occupied by all men who love justice, freedom and toleration.

SIR WILFRID LAURIER, H. of C., *Debates*, Mar. 3, 1896, 2759.

As far as Sir Wilfrid Laurier is concerned, you can say that he is too English for me with his programme of Imperial federation.

SIR CHARLES TUPPER, in *La Presse*, Montreal, Aug. 20, 1900. (Trans.)

That dam' dancing-master who had bitched the whole show.

DR. S. JAMESON, (of "Jameson Raid" fame) to Rudyard Kipling, qu. in his, *Something of myself*, 1937, 196; about 1902.

I would rather do business with a cad who knows his own mind.

JOSEPH CHAMBERLAIN, to Lady Minto (1904), qu. by J. Buchan, *Lord Minto*, 205.

My object is to consolidate Confederation, and to bring our people long estranged from each other, gradually to become a nation. This is the supreme issue. Everything else is subordinate to that idea.

SIR WILFRID LAURIER, letter to W.D. Gregory, Nov. 11, 1904. (Pub.Arch. Can.)

Not many years now remain to me. The snows of winter have taken the place of spring; but, however I may shew the ravages of time my heart still remains young, and I feel that I have as much strength as ever for the service of my country.

SIR WILFRID LAURIER, speech in Sorel, Sept. 6, 1908. (Trans.)

No other Canadian statesman has done so much to estrange the two great branches of the Canadian family.

OLIVAR ASSELIN, A *Quebec view of Canadian nationalism*, 1909, 34.

I do not pretend to be an Imperialist. Neither do I pretend to be an anti-Imperialist. I am a Canadian first, last and all the time. I am a British subject by birth, by tradition, by conviction — by the conviction that under British institutions my native land has found a measure of security and freedom it could not have found under any other regime.

SIR WILFRID LAURIER, H. of C., *Debates*, Feb. 3, 1910, 2959.

I am branded in Quebec as a traitor to the French, and in Ontario as a traitor to the English. In Quebec I am branded as a Jingo, and in Ontario as a Separatist. In Quebec I am attacked as an Imperialist, and in Ontario as an anti-Imperialist. I am neither. I am a Canadian.

SIR WILFRID LAURIER, speech in St. John, Que., 1911.

I am a Canadian. Canada has been the inspiration of my life. I have had before me as a pillar of fire by night and a pillar of cloud by day a policy of true Canadianism, of moderation, of conciliation.

SIR WILFRID LAURIER, speech in St. John, Que., 1911.

The Plumed Knight.

ANON., a nickname used after 1911; see 1911 − ELECTION SLOGANS ("Follow my white plume.")

What can one expect from the Liberal party while he is its leader? Charm of manner is not enough. If he kept his own hands clean he allowed his ministers and followers to plunder at will.

SIR JOHN WILLISON, letter to G.M. Wrong, Oct. 24, 1913, Univ. of Toronto Library, G.M. Wrong Papers.

If you please, paint me as a ruler of men.

SIR WILFRID LAURIER, attributed, 1916, as statement to Charles Huot who painted his portrait as one of a group in the Assembly chamber, Quebec.

It has been my lot to run the whole gamut of prejudices in Canada. In 1897 I was excommunicated by the Roman priests and in 1917 by Protestant parsons.

SIR WILFRID LAURIER, letter to W.D. Gregory, Dec. 27, 1917. (Pub. Arch. Can.)

I am a politician.

SIR WILFRID LAURIER, a saying of his later years.

Do you think we can trust the bastards with the old man's body?

CHARLES MURPHY, remark to a Press Gallery correspondent, on the funeral arrangements made for the burial of Laurier who died Feb. 17, 1919, referring especially to the former Liberals who joined Borden's Union Government in 1917.

The best man I have ever known. His instinctive honour, his kindliness and forgetfulness of self, that shining out of nobility and distinction of character which men call magnetism, made every man who entered his presence a better man for it.

ANON., a Canadian follower, on his death, qu. in O.D. Skelton, Life and letters of Wilfrid Laurier, 1922, II, 558.

A man who had affinities with Macchiavelli as well as with Sir Galahad.

JOHN W. DAFOE, Laurier, 1922.

He was, above all others, the nemesis of the Imperialists.

A.G. DEWEY, in Can.hist.rev., 1927, 284.

The farmers began whetting their axes for him on the rough edges of long-delayed hopes.

L.E. ELLIS, Reciprocity, 1911, 1939, 20.

He was never any good at figures, other than those of speech.

PAUL BILKEY, Persons, papers and things, 1940, 89.

There never was a man – not in my lifetime – from whom we could learn so much of the art of leadership as from Sir Wilfrid Laurier. One of the lamentations that I still indulge in is that I did not learn more from him.

> ARTHUR MEIGHEN, at his Testimonial Dinner, Canadian Club, Toronto, Dec. 3, 1957.

A black king.

> RENÉ LÉVESQUE, qu. in George Grant, *Lament for a nation*, 1965, 77.

Law and Lawyers

When you administer the law, your skins must be seven skins thick. Then the magic darts of your enemies will not penetrate, even if they prod you with their points.

> DAGANOWIDA, ca. 1570, Iroquois prophet and statesman who, with Hiawatha, formed the Confederacy of Five Tribes.

Resort shall be had to the laws of Canada and not to the laws of England.

> QUEBEC ACT, draft of Aug. 18, 1774, printed in Quebec *Gazette*.

A more sickening task cannot well be undertaken, than a perusal of the two vast volumes of "Laws of Prince Edward Island", numbering 1719 pages: the great curse of the Island has been a plethora of laws and lawyers, the little village or capital, Charlottetown, having for its share a legal confederacy aptly designated "the forty thieves".

> LIEUT. COL. B.W.A. SLEIGH, *Pine forests and hacmatack clearings*, 1853, 171.

It is of the very last importance that the administration of the affairs of the country should be according to law.

> SIR JOHN A. MACDONALD, speech in St. Catharines, 1860.

I never knew there was so much law in the world as I find in Canada.

> JOHN ANDERSON, fugitive slave from Missouri, on being discharged from a charge of murder, by Court of Common Pleas of Upper Canada, Feb. 18, 1861.

Boys, I am here to keep order and to administer the law. Those who don't want law and order can 'git', but those who stay with the camp, remember on what side of the line the camp is; for, boys, if there is shooting in Kootenay there will be hanging in Kootenay.

> JUDGE PETER O'REILLY, to American miners at Wild Horse Creek, B.C., 1864.

The preservation of law and order.

> ANON., a phrase identified with the R.C.M.P. since its early days; about 1875.

To legislate in advance of public opinion is merely to produce anarchy instead of maintaining law and order.

> ALEXANDER MACKENZIE, speech on prohibition bill, H. of C., *Debates*, Apr. 11, 1877, 1385.

Few, if any, laws could be made by Parliament for the peace, order and good government of Canada which did not in some incidental way affect property and civil rights; and it could not have been intended to exclude Parliament from the exercise of this general power whenever such incidental interference would result from it.

> SIR MONTAGUE SMITH, Decision, *Russell vs. the Queen*, Law Reports, Appeal Cases, 1882, 839.

The Statute books are exceedingly muddled. I seldom look into them.

> JUDGE MATTHEW B. BEGBIE, (d.1894), qu., *Canadian portraits*, 1940, 91.

The law is a hard, queer thing. I do not understand it.

> POUNDMAKER, statement to the court at his trial in Regina, Aug. 17, 1885.

I have had some experience, both in defending criminals and in prosecuting them; I have never shrunk in my calling, as a member of the Bar, from taking any man's case, no matter how desperate it might be, for the purpose of saying for him what he might lawfully say for himself; but I have sometimes spurned the fee of a blatant scoundrel who denounced everybody else in the world, and was himself the most truculent savage of them all.

> SIR JOHN THOMPSON, H. of C., *Debates*, June 28, 1892, 4370, on Sir Richard Cartwright.

Sergeant Fones has the fear o' God in his heart, and the law of the land across his saddle, and the newest breech-loading at that.

> SIR GILBERT PARKER, *Pierre and his people*, 1892, 6.

The law in Canada exists and is administered, not as a surprise, a joke, a favour, a bribe, or a Wrestling Turk exhibition, but as an integral part of the national character – no more to be forgotten or talked about than trousers.

> RUDYARD KIPLING, *Letters to the family*, 1908, 33.

Women are nearer the eternal laws than are men. Men govern themselves by the laws they themselves make. Women are lawless. Laws are for the temporal, the fleeting; for a given individual in a given society; for a particular race in a particular clime. Such laws are obeyed by women only under compulsion.

> ARNOLD HAULTAIN, *Hints for lovers*, 1909, 174.

If your honour please, I would not for a moment mutilate the majesty of the law nor contravene the avoirdupois of the testimony, but I would ask you to focalize your five senses on the proposition I am about to propound to you. In all criminal cases there are three essential elements – the *locus in quo*, the *modus operandi* and the *corpus delicti*. In this case I think I am safe in saying the *corpus delicti* and the *modus operandi* are all right, but there is an entire absence of the *locus in quo*. I therefore ask for dismissal of the case.

> ROBERT C. (BOB) EDWARDS, Calgary *Eye Opener*, qu. R. St.G. Stubbs, *Lawyers*, 186, 1939.

And they dwelt in sweet co-union,
    while the world looked on in awe,
For they lived and wrought by the law
    of Love, and not by the love of Law.

> ROBERT J.C. STEAD, "Mother and son", 1917.

I think that learned counsel is abusing the privilege of being stupid.

> SIR JAMES LOUGHEED, when chairman of Senate divorce committee, about 1920.

Half the population is trying to get liquor. Half is trying to prevent them. You'll never enforce any act with half the population against it.

> ROBERT C. (BOB) EDWARDS, speech in the Alberta Legislature, Apr. 16, 1921, attributed by M. Napier in E. Stafford ed., *Flamboyant Canadians*, 1964, 202.

Legislation is never needed to guide the man with vision. But it should protect that vast majority which is without it.

> FREDERICK P. GROVE, *A search for America*, 1927, 76.

I bind the Soul that fathered me;
I am the Law, and resolute
Against the growing of the Soul,
I hang, behead, electrocute.

J.E.H. MACDONALD, "The hanging", 1933.

The more you allow the courts to
clarify things the worse you make
them.

HENRI BOURASSA, in H. of C., 1935;
*Method of amending the B.N.A.
Act*, 10.

Never go to law for simple vengeance;
that's not what law is for. Redress, yes;
vengeance, no.

ROBERTSON DAVIES, *Leaven of malice*,
1954, 84.

Canadians are today perhaps more
aware of the differences in their attitudes toward the law than anything
else distinguishing them from Americans.

DENNIS HUME WRONG, *American and
Canadian viewpoints*, 1955, 38.

The lawyer is your friend because
He guides you through the maze of
   laws.
In fact we write them round about
So only we can make them out.

MAVOR MOORE, "The lawyer", *And what
do you do?*, 1960, 49.

I think a lawyer, before he studies law,
should study under a great actor as did
the great lawyers of France a century
ago.

ANTOINE RIVARD, qu. by Frank Hamilton, ed., *Maclean's Canada*, 1960, 108.

What you say may be in all them
books, all right, but it ain't the Law of
Killaloe.

ANON., Judge in Killaloe, Ont. to a
famous lawyer from Toronto; a favourite story of Ont. Premier Leslie Frost,
retired Nov., 1961.

The law should not be bent in the
interests of either policy or history,
and can be interpreted in the light of
neither.

G.P. BROWNE, *The judicial committee
and the British North America Act*,
1967, [v].

The successful intrusion of foreign law
constitutes a direct erosion of the sovereignty of the host country insofar as
the legal capacity of the latter to make
decisions is challenged or suspended.
Insofar as sudsidiaries become instruments of policy of the home country
rather than the host country, the capacity of the latter to effect decisions,
i.e. its political independence is directly reduced.

CANADA. TASK FORCE ON THE STRUCTURE
OF CANADIAN INDUSTRY, *Report*, 1968,
311.

The lawbreakers of today become the
lawmakers of tomorrow.

IRVING LAYTON, "Aphs", *The whole
bloody bird*, 1969, 85.

Since all the laws are written by men,
for men, I see no reason why women
should consider themselves bound by
them.

RICHARD J. NEEDHAM, *A friend in Needham*, 1969, 36.

The prospect for due process is not
outright abolition by the enemies of
our system, but gradual erosion by its
custodians.

CANADIAN CIVIL LIBERTIES EDUCATION
TRUST, *Due process safeguards*, Oct.,
1971, 48.

Laws and constitutions can prepare a soil in which mutual respect and trust can grow. Whether, in fact, they do grow depends on ourselves, whether French-speaking Canadians and English-speaking Canadians can become civilized enough to be friends despite their differences.

> J.A. CORRY, *The power of the law*, 1971, 62.

As a very young lawyer, from books
    that I read
    I thought justice and law were the
    same.
But I soon put that juvenile thought
    from my head
And I studied the rules of the game.

> SGT. JOE SWAN, Vancouver Police Force, "The one-percenters", in *Thin blue line*, Jan., 1975.

When my clients were caught, I
    fought hard to get bail
    Which was very important to me
For a man cannot steal when he's
    locked up in jail
And still pay an exorbitant fee.

> SGT. JOE SWAN, Vancouver Police Force, "The one-percenters", in *Thin blue line*, Jan., 1975.

Law Courts

Incorruptible and respected courts enforcing laws made by free men in Parliament assembled and dealing with specific matters, with specific sanctions to enforce their observance; these are the best guarantees of our rights and liberties. This is the tried and tested British way, and this is a better course to follow than the mere pious affirmation of general principles, to which some political societies are addicted.

> LESTER B. PEARSON, H. of C., *Debates*, July 4, 1960, 5661.

Laziness

Stick-in-the-mud.

> THOMAS C. HALIBURTON, *Sam Slick's wise saws*, 1853, 132.

Canada is not the land for the idle sensualist. He must forsake the error of his ways at once, or he will sink into ruin here as he would have done had he staid in the old country.

> CATHERINE PARR TRAILL, *The Canadian settler's guide*, 1855, 13.

We are all born lazy. Some of us get impressions, vivid impressions, which call for our industry; industry leads to facility, and everything becomes easy.

> SIR WILLIAM VAN HORNE, qu., S.B. Macnaughtan, *My Canadian memories*, 1920, 97.

You may do all you can for the other fellow, but it is a failure unless he, himself, is willing to get up in the morning.

> JACK MINER, d. 1944, in *Jack Miner, his life and religion*, 1969, 1vii.

Leacock, Stephen

Mr. Leacock is not a subtle wit. He must be taken in small doses and hardly bears reperusal. But a little of him in the right mood is very comforting.

> LONDON, *TIMES LITERARY SUPPLEMENT*, Nov. 10, 1910, 442.

I am a Liberal Conservative, or, if you will, a Conservative Liberal with a strong dash of sympathy with the Socialist idea, a friend of Labour, and a believer in Progressive Radicalism. I do not desire office but would take a seat in the Canadian Senate at five minutes' notice.

> STEPHEN LEACOCK, *The Hohenzollerns in America*, 1919, 232.

Leaders

The best chief is not the one who persuades most people to his point of view. It is rather the one in whose presence most find it easiest to arrive at truth.

> ANON., qu. by Dalton Camp from "The legend of the Long House people" in *The Canadian*, Nov. 12, 1966, 13.

I am not a leader of society. I am a follower of it. I follow it at a respectful distance, near enough to permit me to study its many interesting qualities, but far enough away to make it clear that I do not belong to it.

> B.K. SANDWELL, *The privacity agent*, 1928, 86.

Who will be the national leader? Who will prove to be a de Valera, a Mussolini, whose policies may be disputed — but who, over a ten-year span, psychologically made a new Ireland and a new Italy, just as Dollfuss and Salazar are building a new Austria and a new Portugal?

> ABBÉ LIONEL GROULX, *L'Action nationale*, Sept., 1934, 61. (Trans.)

A reconciler of irreconcilables.

> LEONARD S. KLINCK, at inauguration of Sidney E. Smith as President, Univ. of Manitoba, Oct. 12, 1934.

There is something about party politics which causes leaders of the same party frequently to regard each other with a much more hearty dislike and distrust than they feel towards most members of the opposition.

> FRANK H. UNDERHILL, in *Can.hist.rev.*, 1939, 392.

You certainly wouldn't turn to contemporary poets for guidance or leadership in the twentieth century world.

> NORTHROP FRYE, *The educated imagination*, (1962) 1964, 25.

Who takes the salute
has to tire his arches same as the troops
and straining crowds.

> R.G. EVERSON, "Got the sack", 1963.

When the organization fails, it is considered to be the failure of the leader. When its policy becomes incoherent, or when there is an absence of policy, the leader is blamed. When the party wants to protect this situation, it declaims its leader. This is also, of course, some kind of rough justice because in fact, while the party has not bestowed all its authority on the leader, the authority has been assumed.

> DALTON CAMP, address, Empire Club, Toronto, Oct. 20, 1966.

The world honours wise men but prefers to be governed by fools.

> RICHARD J. NEEDHAM, *A friend in Needham*, 1969, 43.

Leadership

If I am supported by their voice, I shall feel that I am right; if condemned, I am ready to retire into private life, and, perhaps, I am now fitted for little else.

> SIR ALLAN MACNAB, speech, House of Assembly, May 23, 1856, on his resignation from the prime ministership.

The politican does not choose the greater issue, but the one that will not split his party.

> J.W. BENGOUGH, *The prohibition Aesop*, about 1896, 33.

Is not excellence in the ranks almost as rare as excellence in command?

> GEORGE ILES, *Canadian stories*, 1918, 179.

Loyalty to the ballot box is not necessarily loyalty to the nation; it is not even loyalty to the multitude. Democracy has failed and fallen in many lands, and political captains in Canada must have courage to lead rather than servility to follow, if our institutions are going to survive.

ARTHUR MEIGHEN, speech, Royal York Hotel, Toronto, Jan. 16, 1939.

I think I know something of how many and conflicting are the voices that seek to influence your judgment and direct your decisions. I have always, therefore, been comforted in thought when I have read of your being at your mountain retreat at Berchtesgaden, knowing, as I do, how greatly the quiet and companionship of Nature helps to restore to the mind its largest and clearest vision.

W.L. MACKENZIE KING, letter to Adolf Hitler, Feb. 1, 1939.

This is a common feeling with many men that leadership consists in showing that one has power rather than in getting one's end by means that lead to agreement on the part of all. Only the latter to my mind is a true kind of leadership.

W.L. MACKENZIE KING, Diary, Apr. 3, 1945, qu. in J.W. Pickersgill, Mackenzie King record, Vol. 2, 1944-45, 1968, 349.

While the Liberal leadership is automatically equivalent to the premiership and therefore attracts men of the highest capabilities, the rival party can offer no such alluring prospects. An individual of moderate means may be persuaded to neglect his own affairs for a time in the slim hope of capitalizing upon a change in public opinion, but eventually he has no choice but to lay down the burden.

J. MURRAY BECK, The government of Nova Scotia, 1957, 163.

It is odd that I, who will probably win, want the job as little as anyone, while my opponent wants it more desperately than anyone.

LESTER B. PEARSON, on his election to the leadership of Liberal Party, Jan. 15, 1958, to a friend, qu. in Saturday night, Sept. 17, 1960, 12; (ref. to Paul Martin).

Mackenzie King genuinely believed and frequently said that the real secret of political leadership was more in what was prevented than what was accomplished.

J.W. PICKERSGILL, The Mackenzie King record, Vol. 1, 1960, 10.

If Canada is to remain in existence, the nation-building role must now be played by forces other than those of entrenched wealth – popular forces with democratic socialist leaders who know where they are going. English Canada needs a Lévesque.

GAD HOROWITZ, Canadian dimension, May, 1965, 15.

The talents required of federal leaders are no longer those of chieftaincy, but those of diplomacy.

GUY FAVREAU, in Gordon Hawkins, ed., Concepts of federalism, 1965, 48.

The function of democratic leadership, it seems to me, is to respect the past, convince the present and enlarge the future.

PETER C. NEWMAN, address, Empire Club, Toronto, Feb. 10, 1972.

League of Nations

I saw the brat born, and I am going to stay with it as long as it has a bit of life in its body.

JOHN W. DAFOE, speech, Empire Club, Toronto, Jan. 30, 1936.

You can't destroy that ideal. You can't bury it. You can't forget it. You may postpone it indefinitely or for generations but it will survive the tumult and the shouting. It will be there as long as there are stars in the Heavens, a beacon light to the generations.

JOHN W. DAFOE, speech, Empire Club, Toronto, Jan. 30, 1936.

These questions [Imperial relations, and defence], so politely retired to the wings, are now in the centre of the Canadian stage to which they returned the moment the League of Nations, with assurances of the most distinguished consideration, was ushered out into the darkness by Mr. Mackenzie King.

JOHN W. DAFOE, *Canadian-American affairs*, 1937, 225; reference to Mr. King's speech at Geneva, Sept. 29, 1936.

Learning

A man who is his own teacher is not complete. There must be implanted early the habits and discipline of learning. Even to think correctly must be taught. There is a logic in such things.

JOHN MARLYN, *Under the ribs of death*, 1957 (1971, 25).

Everyone has his own personal medium for learning. I find my learning in the field of illness. I, like every human on earth, learn through the act of dying.

MARTIN ROHER, *Days of living*, 1959, 5.

Human beings are condemned to learn by the suffering they inflict on one another.

IRVING LAYTON, "Aphs", *The whole bloody bird*, 1969, 81.

Leaves

A single leaf can block a mountainside; all Ararat be conjured by a leaf.

P.K. PAGE, "Cry Ararat", 1967.

Leaving

You worry that I will leave you.
I will not leave you,
Only strangers travel.
Owning everything,
I have nowhere to go.

LEONARD COHEN, "Owning everything", 1956.

Lectures

The part is numb
    On which I sit.
The rest of me
    Now envies it.

GEOFFREY B. RIDDEHOUGH, "After listening to a learned paper", 1972.

Legends

If modern Canada has no legend, then the opportunities for imagism are considerable.

PAUL WEST, in *Can. lit.* No. 13, 1962, 12.

When legends die,
Men may begin to create again; when institutions
Crumble, much spirit is set free.

C.J. NEWMAN, "On the death of an institution", 1967.

Legislators

Knowledge is not enough to make a man eligible. He might very well swallow the contents of twenty whole libraries, he shall not for all that, be more apt to become a legislator!

SIR GEORGE-ETIENNE CARTIER, Quebec, Legislative Assembly, May 27, 1853. (Trans.)

Legislatures

The Legislature [of Ontario] within its jurisdiction can do everything that is not naturally impossible, and is restrained by no rule human or divine. If it be that the plaintiffs acquired any rights, which I am far from finding, the Legislature had the power to take them away. The prohibition "Thou shalt not steal" has no legal force upon the sovereign body.

JUDGE W.F. RIDDELL, *Ontario law reports*, 18, 1909, 279.

Legs

Your tall French legs, my V for victory,
My sign and symphony, Eroica,
Uphold me in these days of my occupation
And stir my underground resistance.

FRANK R. SCOTT, "Will to win", 1954.

Leisure

As soon as we realize that leisure is as genuine and important an aspect of everyone's life as remunerative work, leisure becomes something that also demands discipline and responsibility.

NORTHROP FRYE, *The modern century*, 1967, 89.

Lemmings

The lemming is the god of the arctic – the helpless, maladjusted, nervous, frightened, persecuted deity, to which all life on the tundra must bow.

KATHERINE SCHERMAN, *Spring on an arctic island*, 1956, 86.

Lesbianism

back to the beginning born of woman
   & suckled & held
I always wanted to suckle a nipple
all the male nipples too small & the
   penis made me gag
that soft softness
riding my new freedom & feeling like
   a woman/lady child
inside & outside.

LIBBY OUGHTON, untitled, 1973, qu. in *Fiddlehead*, 101, 1974, 99.

Letters

Harry, my boy, never write a letter if you can help it, and never destroy one.

SIR JOHN A. MACDONALD, to Col. H.R. Smith, Dep. Sgt.-at-arms, H. of C., 1872-92; qu., *Correspondence*, ed. by Pope, xxiii.

The man who judges of a woman by her letters is a fool.

ARNOLD HAULTAIN, *Hints for lovers*, 1909, 52.

The Prime Minister with all due respect to him, is too fond of signing letters in the name of the people of Canada.

J.L. RALSTON, H. of C., *Debates*, Apr. 23, 1934, 2430, on R.B. Bennett.

Libel

Although prior to 1958 you had to prove the substance or the gist of every allegation, today that is not strictly true. If you prove the truth of one, which destroys reputation for all practical purposes, it is not injurious to the plaintiff to call him something else when he has really not much reputation left.

J.J. ROBINETTE, in Thompson Newspapers Ltd., Legal Seminar: *Libel, defamation, contempt of court, and the right of the people to be informed*, Toronto, Mar. 27, 1962, 4.

Liberal Party

The Grits.

ANON., a term derived from "Clear Grits" *(q.v.)* and applied after 1855 to the Brownites and Clear Grits, predecessors of the Liberal Party, and accepted by them to signify a modified version of original Clear Grit radicalism.

We are a free and happy people, and we are so owing to the liberal institutions by which we are governed, institutions which we owe to the exertions of our forefathers and the wisdom of the mother country. The policy of the Liberal party is to protect these institutions, to defend and extend them, and, under their sway, to develop the latent resources of our country. That is the policy of the Liberal party: it has no other.

SIR WILFRID LAURIER, speech, Club Canadien, Quebec City, June 26, 1877. (Trans.)

The Party of Purity.

LIBERAL PARTY, boast, about 1878.

See the faces of the Grits,
    Grizzly Grits,
What a woe-begone expression at
        present o'er them flits.
They are thinking, thinking deeply
How to run this country cheaply
And they wonder
How in thunder
    It is going to be done.
But the people − they who vote − of
        their twaddle take no note,
For they know the dismal, dreary,
        direful dole
    Of the Grits
Of the moribund, morose and
        melancholy Grits,
    Grits, Grits, Grits.
The greedy, grubby garrulous old
    Grits.

THE PEOPLE'S ALMANAC , supp. to Montreal *Gazette*, 1891.

The fault of the Liberal party was voluble virtue.

SIR JOHN WILLISON, *Reminiscences*, 1919, 36, referring to the government of 1874 to 1878.

An organized hypocrisy dedicated to getting and holding office.

JOHN W. DAFOE, letter to Clifford Sifton, June 21, 1919. (Pub. Arch. Can.)

The Liberal party will continue to stand as its illustrious leaders stood in the past, for unity, good will, and the open mind.

W.L. MACKENZIE KING, speech to Liberal supporters, Aug., 1919.

There never was a Farmers' Party while the Liberals were in power.

LIBERAL PARTY, *Group government compared with responsible government*, 1921.

Individual members of the Liberal party may have done what they should not have done, but the whole party is not thereby disgraced. The party is not disgraced, but it is in the valley of humiliation.

W.L. MACKENZIE KING, H. of C., *Debates*, July 30, 1931, 4387, after the Beauharnois Power inquiry.

It believes that personality is more sacred than property. In all its policies it has been guided by that principle, above everything else.

W.L. MACKENZIE KING, H. of C., *Debates*, Feb. 27, 1933, 2501.

Under a Liberal regime the Prime Minister states the foreign policy and the Cabinet Ministers state the policy for internal affairs without consultation with any of the Members.

J. ALLISON GLEN, (Speaker, H. of C., 1940-1945), letter to J.W. Dafoe, Oct. 9, 1936. (Pub.Arch.Can.)

If I cease to lead the party, I shall never cease to have the party's interest near to my heart.

> W.L. MACKENZIE KING, speech to Liberals on his possible retirement and the calling of a national convention to select his successor, Ottawa, Jan. 20, 1948.

Since I was sworn in as a Minister a couple of hours ago.

> LESTER B. PEARSON, Sept. 10, 1948, after accepting portfolio of External Affairs when asked when he had become a member of the Liberal Party.

Looks to me like you've been eating pretty well under a Liberal Government.

> C.D. HOWE, election campaign, June, 1957, at Carman, Man. when asked by a farmer why the Liberal government had reduced the price on oats by 5 cents a bushel. Howe patted the man on the stomach when he said it.

The Brass and the Grass.

> ANON., phrase used at Liberal party Convention, Ottawa, Jan. 14-16, 1958, ref. to party leaders and party rank and file.

In view of the desirability, at this time, of having a government pledged to implement Liberal policies; His Excellency's advisers should, in the opinion of this house, submit their resignation forthwith.

> LESTER B. PEARSON, H. of C., *Debates*, Jan. 20, 1958, 3520, motion put before House at first meeting after minority Conservative govt. assumed power.

Why didn't they do it then? Why didn't they do it when they were in power?

> JOHN DIEFENBAKER, speech, Feb. 12, 1958, Winnipeg, during election campaign, referring to Liberal platform.

The Liberals talk about a stable government, but we don't know how bad the stable is going to smell.

> TOMMY DOUGLAS, election campaign, general election, Oct., 1965; qu. in P. Newman, *Distemper of our times*, 1968, 369.

The real leader of the Liberal party in the winter and spring of 1963 was not Lester B. Pearson but John F. Kennedy.

> DONALD G. CREIGHTON, *Towards the discovery of Canada*, 1972, 170.

The Liberals in Saskatchewan are in Opposition, in Manitoba in hiding, in B.C. they're invisible and in Alberta they're a protected species.

> DAVID STEUART, Sask. Liberal leader, qu. in Vancouver *Sun*, Apr. 11, 1975, 36.

Liberalism

Our Holy Father, the Pope, and after him the Archbishop and bishops of this province, have declared that Catholic Liberalism is a thing to be regarded with the abhorrence with which one contemplates a pestilence; no Catholic is allowed to proclaim himself a moderate Liberal; consequently this moderate Liberal cannot be elected a representative by Catholics.

> IGNACE BOURGET, Roman Catholic bishop of Montreal, 1876, on Dr. Alfred Fortier, Liberal candidate, Chambly by-election. (Trans.)

For my part, as I have always said, I am a Liberal. I am one of these who think that everywhere, in human things, there are abuses to be reformed, new horizons to be opened up, and new forces to be developed.

> SIR WILFRID LAURIER, speech, Club Canadien, Quebec City, June 26, 1877. (Trans.)

The principle of Liberalism is inherent to the very essence of our nature, to that desire for happiness with which we are all born into the world, which pursues us throughout life and which is never completely gratified this side of the grave. Our souls are immortal, but our means are limited. We constantly gravitate towards an ideal which we never attain. We dream of good, but we never realize the best. We only reach the goal we have proposed to ourselves, to discover new horizons opening up, which we had not before even suspected. We rush on towards them and those horizons, explored in their turn, reveal to us others which lead us on ever further and further.

SIR WILFRID LAURIER, speech at Quebec City, June 26, 1877. (Trans.)

He who has not the privilege of being born a Liberal can never become one; and he who, not being born a Liberal, becomes one afterwards will fail in his Liberal principles and will become a traitor and a renegade.

SIR WILFRID LAURIER, speech at Club National, Montreal, May, 1884.

I am a Liberal of the old School, one of those who wish Government to mind its own business, who desire that at last man should have a chance of self-development, and who are no more inclined to submit to the tyranny of majorities calling themselves the State than to the tyranny of kings.

GOLDWIN SMITH, *Loyalty*, 1891, 4.

I am a Liberal of the English school. I believe in that school which has all along claimed that it is the privilege of all subjects, whether high or low, whether rich or poor, whether ecclesiastics or layman, to participate in the administration of public affairs, to discuss, to influence, to persuade, to convince, – but which has always de-

nied, even to the highest, the right to dictate to the lowest.

SIR WILFRID LAURIER, H. of C., *Debates*, Mar. 3, 1896, 2758.

I am a Liberal of the British school. I am a disciple of Burke, Fox, Bright, Gladstone, and of the other Little Englanders who made Great Britain and her possessions what they are, and I will not desert the ranks of their true followers because Mr. Chamberlain, or other renegade Radicals might choose in their megalomaniac ambition to call those great men blunderers.

HENRI BOURASSA, H. of C., *Debates*, Mar. 13, 1900, 1828.

It is never the purpose of Liberalism to obtain office – it is always the purpose of Liberalism to secure power. And power – to Liberalism – means only the opportunity to serve the people.

C. GORDONSMITH, in Montreal *Daily telegraph*, July 12, 1913.

Liberalism in North America, if it is to mean anything concrete, must mean an attack upon the domination of institutions and ideas by the business man.

FRANK H. UNDERHILL, address, Can. Hist. Assoc., Toronto, May, 1946.

For me, liberalism is the only philosophy for our time, because it does not try to conserve every tradition of the past; because it does not apply to new problems the old doctrinaire solutions; because it is prepared to experiment and take risks; and because it knows that the past is less important than the future.

PIERRE E. TRUDEAU, speech, Liberal Leadership Convention, Ottawa, Apr. 5, 1968.

Liberty

Independent thought, the salt without which all our liberties would lose their savour.

GOLDWIN SMITH, *The Empire*, 1863, v.

The spirit of liberty is not the result of culture. It may be found in the lowest man.

SIR WILFRID LAURIER, speech in Toronto, Dec. 10, 1886.

Without fair Liberty to make
The key-stone of the world's whole plan,
The arch we heap o'erhead will break,
And some fair morrow man will wake
To find beneath the ruins — man!

GEORGE F. CAMERON, "She is not mine", 1887.

Are we to be told that, because men are inimical to liberty, they shall not be given liberty? In our own doctrine and in our own view, liberty shines not only for the friends of liberty, but also for the enemies of liberty.

SIR WILFRID LAURIER, H. of C., *Debates*, Mar. 28, 1889, 903.

Out of a thousand years of suffering, bloodshed and contention, there has emerged in the last century the principle of common liberty. What is this liberty? It is the right of the men and women — not the men and women of the privileged classes only, but the men and women of all other classes — to live their lives, mentally, physically, morally, without interference to person or property.

CLIFFORD SIFTON, speech in Winnipeg, July 30, 1917.

The reason we enjoy our liberties now is because in the past they let people speak out. The people had brains enough to see what was foolish and what was false, and sense enough to reject what was false and hold to the truth, and I submit that should be the basis of our public policy in Canada today.

FRED J. DIXON, political reformer, address to the jury, at his trial for writing seditious libel arising out of the Winnipeg General Strike, Feb. 14, 1920.

We have all the liberty that is good for us, and some people think a good deal more.

JOSEPH POPE, letter to his son, Sept. 16, 1925.

Democracy implies liberty, something of which Canadians are so sure that they never mention it.

GEORGE M. WRONG, *Canadians*, 1938, 412.

If you want more liberty
try it the hard way,
if you have a mind
of your own
start with yourself,
there is no limit
to this thing.

TIBOR BARANYAI, "The relativity of freedom", 1962.

Be it Canada or Quebec, wherever the French-Canadian nation can find liberty it also will find its homeland.

DANIEL JOHNSON, *Égalité ou independance*, 1965, 123. (Trans.)

For a reason which amounts with me to a principle (and which is the first criterion I apply to all these phenomena of violence), the means already determine the end. If you wish to liberate a people, you must use means that put liberty to work.

FERNAND DION, Format 60, Radio-Canada, Oct. 20, 1970. (Trans.).

Librarians

What my fate is to be, I have no idea yet; but I look to be Librarian at Ottawa, a position that will greatly suit me . . . My pockets are full of flattering letters from the Cabinet since the last campaign.

MARTIN GRIFFIN, Editor, the *Mail*, letter to Sir John Thompson, July 21, 1882. (Pub.Arch.Can.#2977)

Librarians within the cloister
Are the pearls inside the oyster.

MAVOR MOORE, "The librarian", in *And what do you do?*, 1960, 53.

Libraries

We ought really to have – the Dominion of Canada really ought to have – a National Library.

SIR JOHN A. MACDONALD, H. of C., *Debates*, Apr. 16, 1883, 631.

Canada enjoys the dubious distinction of ranking with Siam and Abyssinia in at least one respect – none of the three possesses a national library.

LAWRENCE J. BURPEE, *University magazine*, Vol. 10, Feb., 1911, 152.

Money invested in a library gives much better returns than mining stock.

SIR WILLIAM OSLER; attributed.

Libraries are to this age, perhaps, what churches and cathedrals were to the Middle Ages.

B.K. SANDWELL, "The bibliothecary" in *The privacity agent*, 1928, 67.

I am but a common man of my period, I am what libraries and librarians have made me, with a little assistance from a professor of Greek and a few poets.

B.K. SANDWELL, "The bibliothecary", in *The privacity agent*, 1928, 71.

Professional librarians and many others are deeply concerned by the fact that Canadians are, as they put it, so intellectually undernourished that many of them now feel no hunger.

CANADA. ROY. COMM. ON NAT. DEV. IN THE ARTS, LETTERS AND SCIENCES, 1949-51, *Report*, 1951, 110.

If a list of North American universities were to be arranged in accordance with the number of volumes in their academic libraries, the best equipped Canadian universities would be distressingly far down in the roster.

CANADA. ROY. COMM. ON NAT. DEV. IN THE ARTS, LETTERS AND SCIENCES, *Report*, 1951, 139.

Tomes sag on the begrimed shelves locking in light.

MARGARET AVISON, "Prelude", 1959.

As a Canadian professor I am envious of the great libraries and other academic resources of the leading American universities such as Harvard, Yale, and California and at the same time patriotically contemptuous of the low standards of the weaker American universities and colleges. In this dual reaction of mixed envy and contempt, I am probably typical of Canadian academics; I hope I am typical also in my determination to do what I can to build up our own resources to the point where we shall not need to be defensive. The neglect of Canadian university libraries over the first hundred years of our history is nothing short of a national disgrace.

DESMOND PACEY, in Al Purdy, ed., *The new Romans*, 1968, 157.

Acquisitions, therefore, were usually gifts from the estates of people who had died, and our local auctioneer gave us any books that he could not sell; we kept what we wanted and sent the rest to the Grenfell Mission, on the principle that savages would read anything.

ROBERTSON DAVIES, *Fifth business*, 1970, 30.

We hear so much propaganda, an enormous amount of it from librarians, about the marvels of our library system. But nobody seems to face the fact that our library system *chokes* authors.

ROBERTSON DAVIES, qu. in editorial, *Books in Canada*, Vol. 2, No. 5, Nov., 1973.

Lice

And my true love,
She combs and combs,
The lice from off
My children's domes.

A.M. KLEIN, "Soirée of Velvel Kleinburger", (1935?).

Lies and Liars

To the first charge, Your Excellency I answer that it is a lie, to the second charge I say that it is a damned lie, and to the third charge that it is a damned infernal lie, and Your Excellency I have no more to say.

THOMAS TREMLETT, Chief Justice of Newfoundland, letter to the Governor, Oct., 1811.

It's all bunkum, you know.

THOMAS C. HALIBURTON, *Sam Slick's wise saws*, 1853, ch.2.

Canadians as a rule are far too tolerant of fraud and falsehood.

SIR RICHARD CARTWRIGHT, speech, Seaforth, Ont., Oct. 27, 1886.

"They say" is the biggest liar in Canada or any other country.

ROBERT C. (BOB) EDWARDS, Calgary *Eye Opener*, Aug. 22, 1903.

The three biggest liars in Alberta are: Robert Edwards, Gentleman; Hon. A.L. Sifton [Premier of Alberta]; Bob Edwards, Editor of *The Eye Opener*.

ROBERT C. (BOB) EDWARDS, Calgary *Eye Opener*; attributed.

A lie will travel a thousand miles while the truth is getting its boots on.

E.A. PARTRIDGE, Manitoba Grain Growers' Convention, Brandon, Aug. 8, 1905, qu. in R.D. Colquette, *The first fifty years*, 1957, 25.

Lie, lie for all you're worth; something will come of it.

OLIVAR ASSELIN, Preface, Oct. 12, 1910, to Jules Fournier, *Souvenirs de prison*. (Trans.)

Lo, something fair has risen like
A lily from the sod!
And the lie is now the truth of it,
Become the splendid truth of it –
Glory be to God!

TOM MACINNES, "White magic", 1918.

Truth can't beat your lies, but power can!

JAMES REANEY, *The killdeer*, 1962, Act. III.

If I tell a lie, it's only because I think I'm telling the truth.

PHILLIP A. GAGLARDI, in the B.C. Legislative Chamber, qu. in *Ubyssey*, Nov. 14, 1969, 2.

Life

The Great Sea has set me in motion
Set me adrift
And I move as a weed in the river
The arch of sky
And mightiness of storms
Encompasses me
And I am left
Trembling with joy.

ANON., Eskimo song, "Aii Aii", trans. by Tegoodligak, South Baffin Island.

We only know that we are here,
That life is brief and death is sure;
That it is noble to endure
And keep the eye of conscience clear.

GEORGE MARTIN, "W.H. Magee", 1887.

Cities might change and fall, and men might die,
Secure were we, content to dream with you
That change and pain are shadows faint and fleet,
And dreams are real, and life is only sweet.

ARCHIBALD LAMPMAN, "The frogs", 1888.

A little while and I will be gone from among you. Whither, I cannot tell. From nowhere we came; into nowhere we go. What is life? It is the flash of a firefly in the night. It is the breath of a buffalo in the winter time. It is as the little shadow that runs across the grass and loses itself in the sunset.

CROWFOOT, Blackfoot chief, shortly before his death Apr. 25, 1890.

The play is life; and this round earth
The narrow stage whereon
We act before an audience
Of actors dead and gone.

BLISS CARMAN, "In the wings", 1892.

Pillared dust and fleeing shadow
As the roadside wind goes by,
And the fourscore years that vanish
In the twinkling of an eye.

BLISS CARMAN, "Pulvis et umbra", 1893.

Blue, blue was the heaven above me,
And the earth green at my feet;
"O Life! O Life!" I kept saying,
And the very word seemed sweet.

ARCHIBALD LAMPMAN, "Life and nature", 1896.

Lovely humanities bloom among vanities,
Beamings of peace 'mid our tumult and strife;
Spiritualities close by realities,
Oh, who can read us the riddle of life?

ALEXANDER MCLACHLAN, "Life's contradictions", 1900.

Thy life is thine to make or mar,
To flicker feebly, or to soar, a star;
It lies with thee — the choice is thine, is thine.

ROBERT W. SERVICE, "Quatrains", 1907.

Unto my friends I give my thoughts,
Unto my God my soul,
Unto my foe I leave my love —
These are of life the whole.

ETHELWYN WETHERALD, "Legacies", 1907.

Fate has written a tragedy; its name is "The Human Heart",
The theatre is the House of Life,
Woman the mummer's part;
The Devil enters the prompter's box and the play is ready to start.

ROBERT W. SERVICE, "The harpy", 1907.

A little gain, a little pain,
A laugh, lest you may moan;
A little blame, a little fame,
A star-gleam on a stone.

ROBERT W. SERVICE, "Just think", 1912.

Living itself is life's completest treasure.

> PETER MCARTHUR, *In pastures green*, 1915, 331.

For life is as a leaf is, and like a flower it fails.

> MARJORIE PICKTHALL, "Song", 1916.

While some of us have more ups and downs in this world than others, we'll all be on the dead level sooner or later.

> ROBERT C. (BOB) EDWARDS, Calgary *Eye Opener*, Nov. 11, 1916.

The ring of spears, the winning of the fight,
The careless song, the cup, the love of friends,
The earth in spring – to live, to feel the light –
'Twas good the while it lasted: here it ends.

> JOHN MCCRAE, "Upon Watts' picture *Sic transit*", 1919.

I do not care, because
I see with bitter calm,
Life made me what I was,
Life makes me what I am.

> ROBERT W. SERVICE, "The coco-fiend", 1921.

Brief sweet laughter and tears,
A tumult of eddying strife,
Drift and the wreckage of years –
Life.

> NORAH M. HOLLAND, "Episodes", 1924.

Life has given me of its best –
Laughter and weeping, labour and rest,
Little of gold, but lots of fun;
Shall I then sigh that all is done?
No, not I; while the new road lies
All untrodden, before my eyes.

> NORAH M. HOLLAND, "Life", 1924.

Life is a killing experience.

> TOM MACINNES, *The teachings of the old boy*, 1927, 223.

The real value of your life can only be gauged by what it gives to the world. Life is redeemed by achievement. All its fun is in doing things.

> SIR WILFRED GRENFELL, *A Labrador logbook*, 1939, 63.

Come, flaunt the brief prerogative of life,
Dip your small civilized foot in this cold water
And ripple, for a moment, the smooth surface of time.

> FRANK R. SCOTT, "Surfaces", 1945.

Pulled down from all our life:
Of loving, talking, singing, sighing,
Of watching the weather through window panes,
Of howing, whating, whethering, whying;
Pulled down from all this
To a grave.

> JAMES REANEY, "The two kites", 1949.

Life, if you have the bent for it, is a beautiful thing. It consists, I do believe, in having a sense of urgency.

> C.L. BURTON, *A sense of urgency: memoirs of a Canadian merchant*, 1952, 25.

For all mankind is matted so within me
Despair can find no earthroom tall to grow;
My veins run warm however veers time's weather;
I breathe Perhaps and May and never No.
Under the cool geyser of the dogwood
Time lets me open books and live;
Under the glittering comment of the planets
Life asks, and I am made to give.

> EARLE BIRNEY, "Trial of a city", 1952, 43.

Everybody is trapped, more or less.
The best thing you can hope for is to
understand your trap and make terms
with it, tooth by tooth.

> ROBERTSON DAVIES, *Leaven of malice*,
> 1954, 219.

But the furies clear a path for me to
    the worm
who sang for an hour in the throat of a
    robin,
and misled by the cries of young boys
    I am again
a breathless swimmer in that cold
        green element.

> IRVING LAYTON, "The cold green ele-
> ment", 1955.

There are no easy signposts, only a
    lonely road
That each one travels with his
    suffering.

> MIRIAM WADDINGTON, "Interval", 1955.

To live. To breathe the crystal air
yet a while longer. To hold this shape
    and motion
and precarious mind unbroken. Not to
    die.
To live in the seed, to put forth a child.
To continue. To hold anxiously
to the crumbling earth, and swim
still in the sea of air and light.

> LOUIS DUDEK, "Meditations over a win-
> try city", 1956.

Life? Though man leap to Mars, he is
    lost in
this fury.

> EARLE BIRNEY, "Damnation of Vancouv-
> er", 1957.

So the final justification of the human
plight — the final vindication of God
himself, for that matter — is revealed
in a mystery of the feelings which
understand, in an instant of revelation,
that it is of no importance that God
appears indifferent to justice as men
understand it. He gave life. He gave it.

Life for a year, a month, a day or an
hour is still a gift.

> HUGH MACLENNAN, *The watch that ends
> the night*, 1959, 344.

Within my templed flesh
a god of pain presides
over love's slow murders
and hate's long suicides.

I curse him as I feel
his unrelenting sway —
but could a force less cruel
wring living out of clay?

> FRED COGSWELL, "Within my templed
> flesh", 1959.

In spring and fall, when serious young
    men
Comfort themselves that all that lives
    must die,
Tax and the teeming catalogue again
Come round, and give mortality the
    lie.

> GEORGE JOHNSTON, "Mail-order cata-
> logue", 1959.

Life can be thought of as water kept at
the right temperature in the right
atmosphere in the right light for a long
enough period of time.

> N.J. BERRILL, *You and the universe*,
> 1960, 145.

"Affirm life," I said, "affirm
The triumphant grass that covers the
    worm;
And the flesh, the swinging flesh
That burns on its stick of bone."

> IRVING LAYTON, "Epigraph", in *The
> swinging flesh*, 1961, xvii.

we must swim dark in phosphorous
    seas
with whales and rayfish and amoeba
with the spinning aqueous plethora
taste the faults salting down the tide
and in our nakedness
and in our peace abide.

> PHYLLIS WEBB, "Bomb shelter", 1962.

Improve the quality of Canadian life.

> ANON., phrase describing the ambitions of the Liberal government program, Apr., 1963.

The cost of living is seeing others die.

> RABBI ABRAHAM L. FEINBERG, *Storm the gates of Jericho*, 1964, 333.

Everyone gets gypped
sooner or later by death or disease or
what's inside them because the world
is that sort of place.

> ALFRED PURDY, "Mr. Greenhalgh's love poem", 1965.

I know
That life is earnest, time is tough,
But me, I'm not, I'm soft and slow.

> GEORGE JOHNSTON, "The bargain sale", 1966.

there are heroes in the seaweed
there are children in the morning,
they are leaning out for love
they will lean that way forever
while Suzanne she holds the mirror.

> LEONARD COHEN, "Suzanne takes you down", 1966.

Life is a horror movie, starring people you know.

> RICHARD J. NEEDHAM, *A friend in Needham*, 1969, 16.

The first half of our lives is ruined by our parents, and the second half by our children.

> RICHARD J. NEEDHAM, *A friend in Needham*, 1969, 24.

The important thing is not really the life of the senses, but the imprinting of ourselves on the evanescence of existence.

> GEORGE WOODCOCK, *Odysseus ever returning*, 1970, 107.

Nothing is written right of the granite hyphens
after the names and birthdates of my parents.
We always lived by making up as we went along.

> GREGORY M. COOK, "Chebogue cemetery", 1970, in *Fiddlehead*, May-July, 1970, 51.

There are rooms for rent in the outer planets
and neons blaze in Floral, Sask.
we live with death but it's life we die with
in the blossoming earth where springs the rose.

> AL PURDY, "Married man's song", 1970.

Life and Death

A marriage to-day,
    And a funeral to-morrow;
A short smile of joy,
    And a long sigh of sorrow.

> ALEXANDER MCLACHLAN, "The vision", 1856.

As you grow older, you realize that the only things which are a matter of life and death are life and death.

> RICHARD J. NEEDHAM, *A friend in Needham*, 1969, 24.

Light and Dark

Dark gives birth to Light; Light gives birth to
Dark. Dark loves Light; Light loves
Dark. They are children exploring each other's
bodies. If there is only one, there is none.

> SUNYATA MACLEAN, in *Poems to define the corona of silence*, 1970, 6.

Liquor

Fire water.

> ANON., term (trans.) used by Indians to describe brandy given them in exchange for furs; good liquor blazed up when poured on a fire, diluted liquor quenched it.

We have upwards of one hundred licensed houses and perhaps as many more which retail spirituous liquors without license; so that the business of one half of the town is to sell rum and the other half to drink it.

> ANON., resident of Halifax, N.S., 1760; qu., Sabine, *Report on the principle fisheries*, Washington, 1853, 62.

It would almost take a line of packet ships running between here and San Francisco to supply this Island with grog, so great a thirst prevails among its inhabitants.

> THE ROYAL EMIGRANT'S ALMANAC, (Mss. in B.C. Archives; ref. to Vancouver Island, 1853).

It will be long ere the poor,
  Will learn their grog to shun,
While it's raiment, food and fire,
  And religion all in one.

> ALEXANDER MCLACHLAN, "We live in a rickety house", 1861.

Chain Lightning, Tangle Foot, Death on Wires, Injin Killer.

> ANON., names given to bootleg whiskey peddled along the line of track laying of the C.P.R. in the 1880's.

A mixture of blue ruin, chain lightning, strychnine, the curse of God and old rye.

> R.K. KERNIGHAN, ("The Khan"), Winnipeg *Sun*, June 7, 1882, referring to the illegal liquor cached along the line of track laying for the C.P.R. in the Broadview area.

Whiskey drowns some troubles and floats a lot more.

> ROBERT C. (BOB) EDWARDS, Calgary *Eye Opener*, Apr. 3, 1915.

Booze has been a great eliminator.

> ROBERT C. (BOB) EDWARDS, Calgary *Eye Opener*, Apr. 3, 1915.

Squirrel Whiskey.

> ANON., name given to product of illicit stills which sprang up around McLeod, Alta., about 1923.

Listening

Listening
ear pressed against stone
it isn't quiet but silent
so that the sounds I hear
are not from outside me any longer
but gyrating dancing thoughts
or the small noise my body makes
in its act of living.

> AL PURDY, "Listening", 1967.

The most imperative need of our world is not for more and more speaking, subtler and subtler enunciations. It is for more, much more, *listening*. I am persuaded that listening is indicative of a much greater personal serenity of conviction than stormy and discourteous refusal to allow a divergent opinion to be expressed.

> ARTHUR GIBSON, *The faith of the atheist*, 1968, 16.

Literature

The translation of Homer into verse is the Polar Expedition of literature, always failing, yet still desperately renewed.

> GOLDWIN SMITH, *Cowper*, 1885, 91.

Write the truth, for that is what makes literature.

GEORGE M. WRONG, remark to the Canadian Authors Assoc., Toronto, Jan. 19, 1929.

Imaginative literature is not primarily concerned with facts; it is concerned with truth. It sees fact only within the web of life, coloured and made vital by what followed.

FREDERICK PHILIP GROVE, *A search for America*, author's note to the 4th ed., 1939.

The divided mind cannot produce the form of concentrated expression that has always been the harbinger of literary greatness; nor can the divided mind give itself wholly to the overwhelming enthusiasm for a concept or a cause that is necessary to the highest form of poetic communication.

W.P. WILGAR, *Dalhousie rev.* Oct., 1944, 271.

A great literature is the flowering of a great society, a vital and adequate society.

E.K. BROWN, *On Canadian poetry*, rev. ed., 1944, 27.

Literature is to the nation what memory coupled with intelligence is to the person.

DESMOND PACEY, ed., *Book of Canadian stories*, 1947, Intro. xii.

Literature is not a subject of study, but an object of study.

NORTHROP FRYE, *Anatomy of criticism*, 1957, 11.

Value-judgements are founded on the study of literature; the study of literature can never be founded on value-judgements.

NORTHROP FRYE, *Anatomy of criticism*, 1957, 20.

No country can have a sharply defined literature if it shares a language with other countries.

GEORGE WOODCOCK, *B.C. library quart.*, July, 1959, 19.

Literature doesn't evolve or improve or progress.

NORTHROP FRYE, *The educated imagination*, (1962) 1964, 24.

There is no direct address in literature: it isn't what you say but how it is said that's important there.

NORTHROP FRYE, *The educated imagination* (1962) 1964, 46.

Literature is a world that we try to build up and enter at the same time.

NORTHROP FRYE, *The educated imagination*, (1962) 1964, 73.

Literature is a human apocalypse, man's revelation to man, and criticism is not a body of adjudications, but the awareness of that revelation, the last judgment of mankind.

NORTHROP FRYE, *The educated imagination*, (1962) 1964, 105.

Literature is a coherent order of words.

NORTHROP FRYE, *The well-tempered critic*, 1963, 15.

butterflies of monarch myriad
with orange alphabets on their wings
are flying dictionaries.

GWENDOLYN MACEWEN, "Poem for G.W.", 1963.

(Sometimes I think life is much too serious for fooling around with mere literature.)

LOUIS DUDEK, *Delta*, May, 1963, 4.

The theory of literature is primarily concerned with detaching literature from experiential and practical uses of language.

> ELI MANDEL, in *Tamarack rev.* No. 29, 1963, 86.

To study literature is to experience Life at respectable second-hand.

> W.J. KEITH, "To study literature", 1964.

I think that history's closest association is with literature. I think a good historian ought to be substantially educated in English and French literature, particularly in novels in which the author views society in a wide scope and tries – sometimes in a series of volumes – to convey an impression of an entire age in the history of a nation.

> DONALD G. CREIGHTON, interview, qu. in Univ. of Toronto, *Graduate*, June 1968,

A country may have great corporations, but if it has no literature it is a country that has no soul. It is a shop keeper's society. The new nationalists, it seems to me, are concerned only with who is minding the store.

> MORLEY CALLAGHAN, speech on accepting the Royal Bank Award, June 15, 1970, in J. Metcalf, ed., *Sixteen by twelve*, 1970, 20.

One can learn more about people and society from creative literature than from scientific reports.

> RONALD SUTHERLAND, in *Can. lit.* No. 45, 1971, 20.

Literature, Canadian

A national literature is an essential element in the formation of national character. It is not merely the record of a country's mental progress; it is the expression of its intellectual life, the bond of national unity, and the guide of national energy.

> EDWARD H. DEWART, *Selections from Canadian poets*, 1864, ix.

Our colonial position, whatever may be its political advantages, is not favourable to the growth of an indigenous literature. Not only are our mental wants supplied by the brain of the Mother Country, under circumstances that utterly preclude competition; but the majority of persons of taste and education in Canada are emigrants from the Old Country, whose tenderest affections cling around the land they have left.

> EDWARD H. DEWART, *Selections from Canadian poets*, 1864, xiv.

Now, now more than at any other time ought the literary life of the New Dominion develop itself unitedly. It becomes every patriotic subject who claims allegiance to this our new northern nation to extend a fostering care to the native plant, to guard it tenderly, to support and assist it by the warmest countenance and encouragement.

> H.J. MORGAN, *Bibliotheca Canadiensis*, 1867, viii.

I believe the existence of a recognized literary class will by and by be felt as a state and social necessity.

> THOMAS D'A. MCGEE, "The mental outfit of the New Dominion", speech to Literary Club, Montreal, Nov. 4, 1867.

It must be admitted that Canada has not yet produced any works which show a marked originality of thought. Some humorous writings, a few good poems, one or two histories, some scientific and constitutional productions, are alone known to a small reading public outside of Canada. Striking originality can hardly be developed to any great extent in a dependency which naturally, and perhaps wisely in some cases, looks for all its traditions and habits of thought to a parent state. It is only with an older condition of society, when men have learned at last to think as well as to act for themselves, to originate rather than to reproduce, that there can be a national literature.

> JOHN G. BOURINOT, *Intellectual development of the Canadian people*, 1881, 116.

A national literature will inevitably come to us in good time.

> JOHN CHARLES DENT, *The last forty years*, II, 1881, 556.

Canada is ambitious of having a native literature; let her wait, and if she has the gift, it will come. She will one day awake and find herself famous in the world of letters.

> GOLDWIN SMITH, *The Bystander*, 1890, 291.

A good deal is being said about Canadian literature, and most of it takes the form of question and answer as to whether a Canadian literature exists. Of course it does not.

> ARCHIBALD LAMPMAN, "Two Canadian poets", speech, Ottawa, Feb. 19, 1891, in *Univ. of Tor. quart.*, XIII, July, 1944, 407.

To Canadian literature I have given more time and labor than it deserves.

> CHARLES MAIR, letter to Col. George T. Denison, July 1, 1891. (Pub. Arch. Can.)

Canada is a political expression. This must be borne in mind when we speak of Canadian literature.

> GOLDWIN SMITH, *Canada and the Canadian question*, 1891, 47.

You do not build a literature or an art out of stones and mortar, and you do not get it by paying dollars for it. You get it only because the nation which already has a national spirit and a national landscape and a national atmosphere and a set of national ideals cannot rest satisfied till it has expressed them for itself. And I hazard the conjecture, very humbly, that possibly at this moment you are still contented with ideals so very nearly like the English ones that you have not felt a very strong impulse to put things differently for yourselves. But you will.

> SIR HENRY NEWBOLT, address, Canadian Club, Ottawa, Feb. 27, 1923.

There will never be a Canadian literature until Canadians abandon the delusion that there ever can be such a thing as "Canadian" literature.

> SIR A. MACPHAIL, Roy.Soc.Can., *Proc.*, 1939, II, 127.

A more powerful obstacle at present to the growth of a great literature is the spirit of the frontier, or its afterglow.

> E.K. BROWN, *On Canadian poetry*, 1944, 20.

I have done more for Canadian literature than any living Canadian.

> MALCOLM LOWRY, letter to Stuart Lowry, Fall, 1950. (*Selected letters*, 222)

[Canada] whose literature I had had the childish dream of enriching with some well-chosen words.

> MALCOLM LOWRY, letter to George S. Albee, Mar. 17, 1957. (*Selected letters*, 398)

The invention of Canadian letters, as a distinct subject for academic study, has been a blessing only to those scholars who are paid to investigate it.

KILDARE DOBBS, *Tamarack rev.*, No. 8, 1958, 87.

The first qualification of the student of Canadian literature is a thick skin. He must be incapable of being bored.

KILDARE DOBBS, *Tamarack rev.*, No. 8, 1958, 87.

Our literature is not yet one of the world's great literatures, and may never be; but it is our own, and it has its modest successes as well as its dismal failures. Even in the failures, even in the Heavyseges and the Sangsters and the Mairs, there may be a legitimate Canadian interest. Our literary history may not be glorious, but it is ours and we should be aware of it – even if only to learn from our own mistakes.

DESMOND PACEY, *Creative writing in Canada*, 1961, 282.

In our literature, heroic action remains possible, but becomes so deeply tinged with futility that withdrawal becomes a more characteristic response than commitment. The representative images are those of denial and defeat rather than fulfillment and victory.

ROBERT L. MCDOUGALL, *Can. lit.*, No. 18, 1963, 11.

The literary, in Canada, is often only an incidental quality of writings which, like those of many of the early explorers, are as innocent of literary intention as a mating loon.

NORTHROP FRYE, in C.F. Klinck, ed., *Literary history of Canada*, 1965, 822.

Canadian literary themes have little social reference. Plots do not deal with the clash of social forces, social prog-

ress, social equality or the achieving of other social mobility.

JOHN PORTER, American Academy of Political and Social Science, *Annals*, Mar., 1967, Vol. 370, 53.

Complete immersion in the international style is a primary cultural requirement, especially for countries whose cultural traditions have been formed since 1867, like ours. Anything distinctive that develops within the Canadian environment can only grow out of participation in this style.

NORTHROP FRYE, *The modern century*, 1967, 57.

Literature is not only a mirror; it is also a map, a geography of the mind. Our literature is one such map, if we can learn to read it as *our* literature, as the product of who and where we have been. We need such a map desperately, we need to know about here, because here is where we live. For the members of a country or a culture, shared knowledge of their place, their here, is not a luxury but a necessity. Without that knowledge we will not survive.

MARGARET ATWOOD, *Survival*, 1972, 18.

Stick a pin in Canadian literature at random, and nine times out of ten you'll hit a victim.

MARGARET ATWOOD, *Survival*, 1972, 39.

It came as a shock to me to discover that my country's literature was not just British literature imported or American literature with something missing, that instead it had a distinct tradition and shape of its own.

MARGARET ATWOOD, *Survival*, 1972, 237.

People put down Canadian literature and ask us why there isn't a *Moby Dick*. The reason there isn't a *Moby Dick* is that if a Canadian did a *Moby Dick*, it would be done from the point of view of the whale. Nobody ever thought of that.

MARGARET ATWOOD, qu. in *Saturday night*, Nov., 1972, 24.

Living

He who lives dangerously lives well.

EDWARD MEADE, *Remember me*, 1946, 26.

Though all is available, nothing is taken
that is not pre-selected, hence the unsubstantial
is the practical, the theory all-important,
and the routines, sub-conscious theories
wall up the doorways slowly, one by one.

FRANK R. SCOTT, "I am employed", 1954.

Days of living are better than years of life.

MARTIN ROHER, *Days of living*, 1959, 132.

With the high cost of living as it is today, and the cost of dying as high, we find many people simply lingering in between.

MRS. VITAL BLANCHARD, B.C., presenting a brief to Royal Commission on Finance and Municipal Taxes, qu. in *Liberty*, "Cross Canada", Nov., 1963.

It's a man's duty to live as long as he can.

JOSEPH B. TYRRELL, qu. in Pierre Berton, *Great Canadians*, 1965, 114.

We live in an uncertain world, and we have to live uncertainly.

ERNEST HARRISON, *Let God go free*, 1965, 56.

Lobbying

When I see members of Parliament being lobbied, it's a sure sign to me that the lobby lost its fight in the civil service and the cabinet.

ANON., a lobbyist, qu. by Don McGillivray in Calgary *Herald*, Apr. 4, 1964, 5.

London, Ont.

I live normally in London, England. I am now in London, Ontario. The only difference I can find is that London, Ontario, is far friendlier than London, England.

RUPERT HARVEY, British adjudicator of the Dominion Drama Festival, 1934, qu. in Betty Lee, *Love and whisky*, 1973, 241.

Loneliness

There is fear
In the longing for loneliness
When gathered with friends,
And, longing to be alone.
Iyaiya-yaya!

ANON., Eskimo. "An old song of the sun and the moon and the fear of loneliness" (trans.), Bathurst Inlet.

When, looking round, the lonely settler sees
His home amid a wilderness of trees:
How sinks his heart in those deep solitudes,
Where not a voice upon his ear intrudes;

Where solemn silence all the waste
  pervades,
Heightening the horror of its gloomy
  shades.

    OLIVER GOLDSMITH, "The rising village",
    1825.

There is no other portion of the globe
in which travel is possible where loneliness can be said to live so thoroughly.

    WILLIAM F. BUTLER, *The great lone land*,
    1892, Preface, v.

So it is with us all; we have our friends
  Who keep the outer chambers, and
    guard well
Our common path; but there their
  service ends,
  For far within us lies an iron cell
Soundless and secret, where we laugh
  or moan
  Beyond all succour, terribly alone.

    ARCHIBALD LAMPMAN, "Loneliness",
    (1894) 1943.

It is only women who really know
loneliness.

    ARNOLD HAULTAIN, *Hints for lovers*,
    1909, 187.

I wonder will death be much lonelier
than life. Life's an awfully lonesome
affair. You can live close against other
people yet your lives never touch. You
come into the world alone and you go
out of the world alone yet it seems to
me you are more alone while living
than even going and coming.

    EMILY CARR, *Hundreds and thousands;
    journal*, July 16, 1933.

Who can know our loneliness, on the
immensity of prairie, in the dark forest
and on the windy sea rock? . . . We
flee to little towns for a moment of
fellowship and light and speech, we
flee into cities or log cabins, out of the
darkness and loneliness and the creeping silence.

    BRUCE HUTCHISON, *The unknown coun-
    try*, 1943, 3-4.

men are isled in ocean or in ice
and only joined by long endeavour to
  be joined.

    EARLE BIRNEY, "Pacific door", 1947.

Meanwhile, he
makes of his status as zero a rich
  garland,
a halo of his anonymity,
and lives alone, and in his secret shines
like phosphorus. At the bottom of the
  sea.

    A.M. KLEIN, "Portrait of the poet as a
    landscape", 1948.

Loneliness of men makes poets.
The great poem is a hymn to
  loneliness.
A crying out in the night with no ear
  bent to.

    RAYMOND SOUSTER, "In praise of loneli-
    ness", 1951.

    the trouble
is that each of us
lives in a separate world . . .

    ALDEN NOWLAN, "For Carol", 1967.

I crawl into my loneliness
But cannot find a place to hide.

    BERNICE LARSEN WEBB, "Fugitive", 1967.

Everyone is so
lonely in this
country that
it's necessary
to be fantastic —

    JOHN NEWLOVE, "Everyone", 1968.

There is no end
to our loving
and loving, no end
to our loneliness.

    GAIL FOX, "Origin of painting", 1969.

Perhaps the ultimate indignity is loneliness without privacy.

> ALDEN NOWLAN, "Scratchings", 1971.

Looking

Look! the child cries:
how can you stop looking?

> DOROTHY LIVESAY, "Perceptions", 1967.

Loons

Here beyond the silver reach in
  ringing wild persistence,
Reel remote the ululating laughter of
  the loons.

> DUNCAN CAMPBELL SCOTT, "Spring on
> Mattagami", 1906.

maybe even the northern loon
with his cry like a newborn ghost
of lakes and rivers and evergreen
  forests
hovering over the marshy distances
the voice behind the many faces of the
  north
which is the essence of Canada.

> AL PURDY, "Over the Pacific", 1968.

Losers

the world's enduring losers those
continual spendthrifts of their mortal
  selves.

> ALFRED PURDY, "To an attempted sui-
> cide", 1965.

Progressivist historians do not write
much about the losers of history, because belief in progress often implies
the base assumption that to lose is to
have failed to grasp the evolving truth.
Nevertheless, the losers existed and

they are well worth reading now that
we see what kind of society the winners have made.

> GEORGE P. GRANT, Technology and em-
> pire, 1969, 67.

Loss

Right can afford to lose.

> EMILY MURPHY, ("Janey Canuck"), qu. in
> B.H. Sanders, Emily Murphy, crusader,
> 1945, 249, chapter heading.

Lost

The windows of my room
  Are dark with bitter frost,
The stillness aches with doom
  Of something loved and lost.

> BLISS CARMAN, "A northern vigil", 1893.

Nothing is ever lost. It is only lost to
man's purpose.

> MARTIN ROHER, Days of living, 1959,
> 108.

With the maps lost, the voyages
Cancelled by legislation years ago,
This is become a territory without a
  name.

> MARGARET AVISON, "Not the sweet Cice-
> ly of Gerardes Herball", 1960.

I am lost,
nothing is to be said. I am plunged
into the black gap again.
It is not to be endured
easily, unthought of, never
to be dismissed with ease.

> JOHN NEWLOVE, "Nothing is to be said",
> 1965.

Lotteries

Chance, the essence of gambling, finds
its complete embodiment in the lot-

tery. The glory of a human being is reason, judgment, will power, and control over himself and his personal affairs. The lottery is the negation of all that. It is, in fact, the complete apotheosis of chance.

> SIR GEORGE E. FOSTER, Senate, *Debates*, June 17, 1931.

Love

She's like the swallow that flies so high,
She's like the river that never runs dry,
She's like the sunshine on the lee shore,
I love my love and love is no more.

> ANON., "She's like the swallow", Newfoundland ballad, no date.

"Love is swift as hawk or hind,
  Chamois-like in fleetness,
None are lost that love can find,"
  Sang the maid, with sweetness.

> CHARLES SANGSTER, "Lost and found", 1860.

O Love builds on the azure sea,
  And Love builds on the golden sand;
And Love builds on the rose-winged cloud,
  And sometimes Love builds on the land.

> ISABELLA VALANCY CRAWFORD, "Malcolm's Katie", 1884.

Love manifests itself in our bodies as instinctive craving, in our souls as devotion, and in our minds as pride.

> BLISS CARMAN, *The kinship of nature*, 1904, 214.

O Love! art thou a silver fish,
Shy of the line and shy of gaffing,
Which we do follow, fierce, yet laughing,
Casting at thee the light-winged wish?

> ISABELLA VALANCY CRAWFORD, "Said the canoe", 1905.

I have sought beauty through the dust of strife,
  I have sought meaning for the ancient ache,
And music in the grinding wheels of life;
  Long have I sought, and little found as yet
Beyond this truth: that Love alone can make
  Earth beautiful, and life without regret.

> ARTHUR STRINGER, "The final lesson", 1907.

Love dyes all things a cerulean hue. (What a pity it is not a fast colour!)

> ARNOLD HAULTAIN, *Hints for lovers*, 1909, 71.

Women detect the dawn of love while it is still midnight with man.

> ARNOLD HAULTAIN, *Hints for lovers*, 1909, 93.

A man dives headlong into love. A woman paddles into it. And the woman's hesitation at the brink of the stream exasperates the spluttering man.

> ARNOLD HAULTAIN, *Hints for lovers*, 1909, 114.

Love blinds the eyes of men, but opens the eyes of women.

> ARNOLD HAULTAIN, *Hints for lovers*, 1909, 190.

Oh, for a love like the air,
So infinite, soundless and broad
That every child of the earth may
share
The joy of the heart of God!

ALBERT D. WATSON, "The poet's prayer",
1913.

Too long has the whole process of lovemaking and marriage been wrapped in mystery.

NELLIE MCCLUNG, *In times like these,*
1915, 132.

It is easier to love in spite of faults than because of virtues.

ROBERT C. (BOB) EDWARDS, Calgary *Eye Opener*, Dec. 11, 1915.

Here we came when love was young.
Now that love is old,
Shall we leave the floor unswept
And the hearth acold?

BLISS CARMAN, "The homestead", 1916.

When a man is in love for the first time he thinks he invented it.

ROBERT C. (BOB) EDWARDS, Calgary *Eye Opener*, Nov. 24, 1917.

In the stars that gem the blue
Of the night,
In the storm and the dew,
There is light;
In the clouds that split with thunder,
In the soul athrill with wonder,
Over all and through and under,
There is Love and Light.

ALBERT D. WATSON, "To worlds more wide", 1917.

Love goes where it is sent.

ANON., proverb, Victoria Beach, N.S.

Love will ever find a way
To turn the darkest night to day:
Out of chaos and mischance,
And every wicked circumstance,
'Twill build itself a home again
Within the erring hearts of men;
But hell is made by its inhabitants.

TOM MACINNES, "Love", 1918.

He was good to his dog, he was good to
his cat,
And his love went out to his horse;
He loved the Lord and his Church, of
course,
For righteous was he in thought and
act;
And his neighbours knew, in addition
to that,
He loved his wife, as a matter of fact.

E.J. PRATT, "The history of John Jones",
1923.

Heart of my heart, O come with me
To walk the ways of Arcadie.

NORAH M. HOLLAND, "The awakening of
the lily", 1924.

One-sided love lasts best.

STEPHEN B. LEACOCK, in *Queen's quart.*,
1935, 79.

I don't love many, but when I do *I love hard.*

EMILY CARR, d. 1945, to Flora Hamilton
Burns, qu. in Mary Q. Innis, *The clear spirit*, 1966, 225.

Where the bog ends, there, where the
ground lips, lovely is love, not
lonely.
Land is love, round with it, where the
hand is;
wide with love, cleared scrubland,
grain on a coin.

P.K. PAGE, "Personal landscape", 1946.

So love, though measured breath by
  breath,
May seem like walking in a summer
  dream,
Visiting nowhere but pleasant places;
So love does often lead a filthy way to
  Death.

JAMES REANEY, "A fantasy and a moral",
1949.

Nay, but lacking love, all this living's
  lifeless,
love, too, of truth, and for our
  children's children,
joy in giving joy, and gaining love by
  loving,
lust of peace and fair thoughts, and
  loyalty to man.

EARLE BIRNEY, "Trial of a city",
1952, 40.

Short love is sweetest, and most love
curdles if you keep it.

ROBERTSON DAVIES, *A jig for the gypsy*,
1954, 29.

in the white, white, quivering
instability of love
we shake a world to order.

PHYLLIS WEBB, "The colour of light, IV",
1954.

Countries are of the mind
And when you moved upon my land
Your darkness ringed my light:
O landscape lovely, looped
With loping hills, wind-woven
Galloping through cloud −
Landfall of love.

DOROTHY LIVESAY, "Nocturne", 1955.

For love is not the getting, but the
  giving.
Love is in the loving, not the being
  loved.

MARGARET HARVEY WILTON, "Love is of
eternity", 1956.

As though I opened wide a furnace
  door
And hot flame seared my face:
I was surprised, that after breach of
  time
I could not love you less.

DOROTHY LIVESAY, "Time", 1957.

Look inward, love, and no more sea,
No death, no change, eternity
Lapped round us like a crystal wall
To island, and that island all.

JAY MACPHERSON, "The island", 1957.

We shut our eyes and turned once
  round
And were up borne by our down fall.
Such life was in us on the ground
That while we moved, earth ceased to
  roll,
And oceans lagged, and all the flames
Except our fire, and we were lost
In province that no settler names.

ANNE WILKINSON, "Variations on a
theme, III", 1957.

I forget whether I ever loved you
in the past − when you enter the
  room
your climate is the mood
of living, the hinge of now,
in time the present tense.

AL PURDY, "Where the moment is",
1958.

All that I love I kill, and keep
Encapsuled in a word.

F.E. SPARSHOTT, "Midas", 1960.

O Wolf of Love, whose green eyes
  gleam
Through darker thickets of my dream,
Though me you bit and slew beside
Sweet Chastity, my lamb of pride,
And flayed it of the woolly white
That hid the flesh of my delight,
I did not mind its death the least
But howled with you and joined the
  feast.

FRED COGSWELL, "Lycanthropy", 1960.

I recognize the vanity and scorn,
The fear, the greed, in short the mask
of love.

DARYL HINE, "A vision", 1960.

There is no flesh so perfect
As on my lady's bone,
And yet it seems so distant
When I am all alone.

LEONARD COHEN, "I long to hold some
lady", 1961.

Go by brooks, love,
Where fish stare,
Go by brooks,
I will pass there.

LEONARD COHEN, "Go by brooks", 1961.

This is the timeless news no page
awaits,
The right hand and the left hand do
no telling,
Love hides its struggle as it hides its
fruits.

ROBERT FINCH, "Ventures", 1961.

Love is surrender, concern, ecstasy.
Bamboozled out of their wits and
courage by the anti-life forces pressing
against them, Canadians have forgotten this; but the poets know that the
great theme is love.

IRVING LAYTON, Love where the nights
are long, 1962, Intro.

It is those whom we can hate that we
should love; it is those who really
threaten us that we are enjoined to
forgive; it is those who are dangerous
whom we are asked to negotiate with.

LESLIE DEWART, Christianity and revolution; the lesson of Cuba, 1963, 214.

It is no longer you or your voice
That torments me;
It's the blue butterflies looking for me
between the tall grasses
that grow from stilled desire and
disdain
as if they were my hands reaching for
your face.

IRVING LAYTON, "Blue and lovely, my
love", 1964.

Trying to make love with someone
who is as unskilled as you are seems to
me about as sensible as learning to
drive with a person who doesn't know
the first thing about cars either.

STEPHEN VIZINCZEY, In praise of older
women, 1965, 55.

The first love that I knew would last
I knew at last was first,
And it is in this manner
That the human race is cursed.

TOM EADIE, "Fall song", 1965.

        love
might set men free
yet hold them fast
in loyalty

DOROTHY LIVESAY, "The unquiet bed",
1967.

Your mouth upon my mouth
solves nothing but is good.
Light rises from the sea
and time spreads with the light.
Put your body to mine;
we are the world we caused.

ROBIN SKELTON, "Night poem, Vancouver Island", 1968.

In love-making as in war, there is no
substitute for victory.

IRVING LAYTON, "Some observations and
aphorisms" in Tamarack rev., No. 47,
1968, 6.

I'd rather
heave half a brick than say
I love you, though I do,
I'd rather
crawl in a hole than call you
darling, though you are.

> PHYLLIS GOTLIEB, "First person demonstrative", 1969.

There is a sadness known as love.
Its name is man. Its name is woman.
They have a house to hold them sad.

> JOYCE ODAM, "Halves", 1969.

Projecting current trends, the love machine would appear a natural development in the near future — not just the computerized datefinder, but a machine whereby ultimate orgasm is achieved by direct mechanical stimulation of the pleasure circuits of the brain.

> MARSHALL MCLUHAN, *Playboy*, Mar., 1969, 65.

We love in another's soul whatever of ourselves we can deposit in it; the greater the deposit, the greater the love.

> IRVING LAYTON, "Aphs", *The whole bloody bird*, 1969, 86.

Here's the whole matter in a little
   space
I love you to your hurt and my
   disgrace.

> FRANCIS SPARSHOTT, "Deep freeze", 1969.

A woman loves the man who tends her wounds almost as much as she loves the man who inflicts them on her.

> RICHARD J. NEEDHAM, *A friend in Needham*, 1969, 5.

The course of smooth love never did run true.

> RICHARD J. NEEDHAM, *A friend in Needham*, 1969, 47.

If you can explain why you love him, you don't.

> RICHARD J. NEEDHAM, *A friend in Needham*, 1969, 53.

To love is to listen;
and I am walking behind you in the
   wilderness,
you carrying the compass
and my trust.

> JOAN FINNIGAN, "Listen to me at Crowe Lake, my love", 1970.

I approach this love
like a biologist
pulling on my rubber
gloves & white labcoat

> MARGARET ATWOOD, "Their attitudes differ", 1971.

   You ask
like the wind, again and again and
wordlessly, for the one forbidden
   thing:

love without mirrors and not for
my reasons but your own.

> MARGARET ATWOOD, *Power politics*, 1972, 55.

Behind me in the mountain pass
   another man
stumbles among rocks and stars
he knows about me and I know about
   him
we plan to get together sometime
and have a word with you.

> AL PURDY, "8:50 a.m.", 1973.

Who is the moving
   or moved is no matter
but the birth of the possible
   song in the rafter

> EARLE BIRNEY, "Wind-chimes in a temple ruin", 1973.

Loving hasn't anything to do with who does what for whom, and when it has, it isn't love.

MERLE SHAIN, *Some men are more perfect than others*, 1973, 72.

Loving can cost a lot but not loving always costs more, and those who fear to love often find that want of love is an emptiness that robs the joy from life.

MERLE SHAIN, *Some men are more perfect than others*, 1973, 7.

If the inhabitants of
  the earth depended
for their survival on my
  keeping them always
    in mind, my world would be
empty — except for you.

ALDEN NOWLAN, "Tenth wedding anniversary", 1974.

Love Affairs

The number of affairs a man has after marriage is probably equal to the number he didn't have before it.

RICHARD J. NEEDHAM, *A friend in Needham*, 1969, 3.

Great love affairs are built on firm foundations which reach all the way down to the tightrope.

RICHARD J. NEEDHAM, *A friend in Needham*, 1969, 48.

Romantics and idealists might say that it is impossible for a happily married man to love anyone other than his wife, but all of us others know that this is simply not true; it is only the happily married man who can afford the chaos that love can bring into an ordered life, can take the excitement of the chaos and let the order eventually consume it.

ADRIENNE CLARKSON, *Hunger trace*, 1970, 166.

Lovelorn

What shall I do
Now my love is gone?
Toss on an empty
Bed alone?

PADRAIG O'BROIN, "Circle", 1963.

Lovers

That happy Parliament of two in which the Government for the time being finds no Opposition, and the budget estimates are all undisputed.

SARA JEANETTE DUNCAN, "Ottawa letter", *The Week*, May 10, 1888, 378.

Come to me
Not as a river willingly downward falls
To be lost in a wide ocean
But come to me
As flood-tide comes to shore-line
Filling empty bays
With a white stillness
Mating earth and sea.

FRANK R. SCOTT, "Union", 1945.

And where, in curve of meadow,
Lovers, touching, lie,
A church of grass stands up
And walls them, holy, in.

ANNE WILKINSON, "In June and gentle oven", 1955.

Then two in one the lovers lie
And peel the skin of summer
With their teeth
And suck its marrow from a kiss
So charged with grace
The tongue, all knowing
Holds the sap of June
Aloof from seasons, flowing.

ANNE WILKINSON, "In June and gentle oven", 1955.

My lover Peterson
He named me Goldenmouth
I changed him to a bird
And he migrated south

LEONARD COHEN, "Song", 1956.

What really makes me sick
is that everything goes on as it went
    before:
I'm still a sort of friend,
I'm still a sort of lover.

> LEONARD COHEN, "The cuckold's song",
> 1961.

Lovers here must meet on unsure
    ground
Like strangers in a circumspect hotel
Which, although luxurious and grand,
Trembles beneath their feet like earth
    in hell.

> DARYL HINE, "Don Juan in Amsterdam",
> 1965.

Early to bed, late to rise
makes lovers – us! – sprightly
    healthy & wise.

> SEYMOUR MAYNE, "Poor Seymour's alma-
> nac", 1966.

Lowry, Malcolm

Malcolm Lowry
Late of the Bowery
His prose was flowery
And often glowery
He lived, nightly, and drank daily,
And died playing the ukulele.

> MALCOLM LOWRY, "Epitaph", 1962.

Loyalty

All suspicion of disloyalty we cast
aside as the product of ignorance or
cupidity; we seek for nothing more
than British subjects are entitled to;
but we will be contented with nothing
less.

> JOSEPH HOWE, *Letters to Lord John
> Russell*, 1839.

No consideration of finance, no question of balance for or against them,
upon interchange of commodities, can
have any influence upon the loyalty of
the inhabitants of the British Provinces, or tend in the slightest degree to
alienate the affections of the people
from their country, their institutions,
their Government and their Queen.

> JOSEPH HOWE, speech in Detroit, July,
> 1865.

Loyalty to the Queen is a noble sentiment in which all true Liberals share,
but loyalty to the Queen does not
require a man to bow down to her
manservant, her maidservant, her ox
or her ass.

> ALEXANDER MACKENZIE, speech, with a
> bow at the last word in the direction of
> his political opponent, William Mac-
> dougall, at Lambton, election, 1867.

True Loyalty's to Motherland
And not to Canada,
The love we bear is second-hand
To any step-mama.

> JOSEPH D. PEMBERTON, letter to *British
> Colonist* (Victoria, B.C.), early 1870.

Shall we break the plight of youth
    And pledge us to an alien love?
No! we hold our faith and truth,
    Trusting to the God above.
Stand Canadians, firmly stand
Round the flag of Fatherland.

> JEAN TALON LESPERANCE, "Empire first",
> 1877, qu. in G.T. Denison, *Struggle for
> imperial unity*, 1909, 158; ref. to Brit-
> ain.

Shall not our love this rough, sweet
        land make sure,
    Her bound preserve inviolate,
        though we die?
    O strong hearts of the North,
    Let flame your loyalty forth,
    And put the craven and base to an
        open shame,
Till earth shall know the Child of
        Nations by her name!

> CHARLES G.D. ROBERTS, "An ode for the
> Canadian confederacy", 1880.

One loyal man is as good as ten rebels.

> SIR JOHN THOMPSON, speech in Owen Sound, Ont., Nov. 15, 1886.

O triune Kingdom of the brave,
  O sea-girt island of the free,
O Empire of the land and wave,
  Our hearts, our hands are all with
    thee!
Stand, Canadians, firmly stand,
Round the flag of Fatherland!

> JOHN (JEAN) LESPERANCE "Empire first", 1889 version.

Loyalty demands obedience.

> RALPH CONNOR, "Black rock", 1900, 134.

I think you will accept the proposition readily, that there was a time when there was no such thing as Canadian loyalty.

> GEORGE W. ROSS, speech, Empire Club, Toronto, 1905.

Loyalty, like affection, is a thing of the heart; it is not of the mouth or the pocket.

> SIR ANDREW MACPHAIL, *Essays in politics*, 1909, 34.

So far as I have been able to trace it this cry of loyalty appears to have taken its origin from certain hysterical women of the male sex, chiefly resident in Toronto.

> SIR RICHARD CARTWRIGHT, speech in Toronto, Aug. 29, 1911, on reciprocity issue.

Loyalty without intelligence may degrade a man to the level of a beast.

> PETER MCARTHUR, qu. by W.A. Deacon, *Peter McArthur*, 1923, 66.

A Canadian's first loyalty is not to the British Commonwealth of Nations but to Canada and Canada's king, and those who contest this, in my opinion, render a disservice to the Commonwealth.

> LORD TWEEDSMUIR, speech to Canadian Inst. Int'l. Affairs, Montreal, Oct. 12, 1937.

In Canada to be disloyal means to be disloyal to Great Britain. Such a crime as disloyalty to Canada scarcely exists.

> JOHN MACCORMAC, *Canada*, 1940, 127.

Luck

If your luck isn't what it should be write a "p" in front of it and try again.

> ROBERT C. (BOB) EDWARDS, Calgary *Eye Opener*, Jan. 13, 1912.

I am a great believer in luck, and I find the harder I work the more I have of it.

> STEPHEN B. LEACOCK; attributed.

It's better to be lucky than smart.

> JOHN BASSETT III, qu. in *Can. mag.*, June 2, 1973, 7.

Lumbering

Oh, when we get down to Quebec
    town,
  The girls they dance for joy.
Says one unto another one,
  'Here comes a shantyboy!'
One will treat us to a bottle,
  And another to a dram,
While the toast goes round the table
  For the jolly shanty-man.

> ANON., lumbermen's song, "O ye maidens of Ontario", early 19th cent.

O ye maidens of Ontario
  Give ear to what I write.
In driving down these rapid streams
  Where raftsmen take delight,
In driving down these rapid streams,
  As jolly raftsmen do,
While lowland loafing farmer boys
  Can stay at home with you.

> ANON., lumbermen's song, "O ye maid-
> ens of Ontario", early 19th cent.; su-
> perseded by "The maids of Simcoe".

Come all ye jolly shanty-boys, if ye
  want to hear a song,
Come sit ye down beside me, and I'll
  not detain you long,
'Tis of ten of our Canadian boys who
  volunteered to go,
To break the jam on Geary's rocks,
  with their foreman, Young Monroe.

> ANON., "The jam on Geary's rocks", song
> with *locale* on River Trent.

Talk not of old cathedral woods
  Their Gothic arches throwing,
John only sees in all those trees
  So many saw-logs growing.

> ALEXANDER MCLACHLAN, "Neighbor
> John", 1874.

The Main John.

> ANON., lumbermen's expression for
> woods bosses; originated in New Bruns-
> wick, from John B. Glasier (1809-1894),
> N.B. lumberman and Senator.

The ravenous sawmills in the pine
wilderness are not unlike the huge
dragons that used in popular legend to
lay waste the country; and like dragons, they die when their prey, the
lordly pines, are all devoured.

> WILLIAM H. WITHROW, *Our own country:
> Canada*, 1889, 127.

Lumberjacks

These are the men who live by killing
  trees—
their bones are ironwood, their
  muscles steel,
their faces whetstones and their hands
  conceal
claws hard as peavy hooks: anatomies
sectioned like the men in the Zodiac

> ALDEN NOWLAN, "These are the men
> who live by killing trees", 1961.

a happy lumberjack who lived on
  rotten whiskey,
and died of sin and Quaker oats age 90
  or so.

> AL PURDY, "Elegy for a grandfather",
> 1968.

Lung Cancer

Hobbling on canes my cancer-blasted
  friend
lights candles for our conversion,
as I light up another cigaret,
  and you light up another epigram,
and many ingenious sick cells
strangle his body and our souls.

> HARRY HOWITH, "Priorities", 1969.

Lust

the body blunt
needing the knife
the forked light-
ning of tongues.

> DOROTHY LIVESAY, "Four songs, III",
> 1967.

Luxuries

We can do without any article of
luxury we have never had; but when
once obtained, it is not in human
natur' to surrender it voluntarily.

> T.C. HALIBURTON, *Sam Slick*, 1836, chap.
> II.

Lynching

You lads are all tenderfeet, and have visions before you of taking part in a Neck-tie Social. There never has been a lynching in Canada, nor will there be as long as our force has the police duties to perform, so go away like sensible men, and remember that any attempt at lynching will be bad for those who try it!

COL. SAM STEELE, R.C.M.P., *Forty years in Canada*, 1915, 179; to a mob in Calgary, 1884.

McCullagh, George

We never met a man with such a personality. In his presence one felt he was being bombed with invisible rays, compelling one to listen to him, to agree with him, perhaps to fear him.

> J.V. MCAREE, *Globe and Mail*, Sept. 1, 1952, 6.

Macdonald, Sir John A.

John A. Macdonald is now the recognized leader, but he is anything but strong in reality.

> JOHN LANGTON, letter to his brother, Apr. 17, 1856.

Sir John A. Macdonald is about to retire to private life, a thoroughly used-up character.

> TORONTO *GLOBE* , Aug., 1858.

I know enough of the feeling of this meeting to know that you would rather have John A. drunk than George Brown sober.

> SIR JOHN A. MACDONALD, election speech, early in his career, after being attacked by the *Globe;* qu., E.B. Biggar, *Anecdotal life,* 1891, 194.

Ah, John A., John A., how I love you! How I wish I could trust you!

> ANON., Liberal member of the Legislature, 1863, to Sir John A. Macdonald; qu., Cartwright, *Reminiscences,* 1912, 47.

For twenty long years I have been dragging myself through the dreary waste of Colonial politics. I thought that there was no end, nothing worthy of ambition, but now I see something which is well worthy of all I have suffered in the cause of my little country.

> SIR JOHN A. MACDONALD, speech, Halifax, Sept. 12, 1864.

John A. Macdonald is always drunk now, I am sorry to say, and when some one went to his room the other night, they found him in his night shirt, with a railway rug thrown over him, practising Hamlet before a looking-glass.

> FRANCES MONCK, *Journal,* Oct. 20, 1864.

I am satisfied to confine myself to practical things – to the securing of such practical measures as the country really wants.

> SIR JOHN A. MACDONALD, *Confederation debates,* 1865, 1002.

Macdonald is a sharp fox. He is a very well informed man, ingratiating, clever and very popular. He is *the man* of the conference.

> HECTOR LANGEVIN, letter to Mgr. Jean Langevin, Mar. 1, 1867, referring to conference in London, Dec. 1866 to prepare final terms of union.

Sir John A. Macdonald, cabinet-maker.

> SIR JOHN A. MACDONALD, inscription in a visitor's book in Charlottetown, P.E.I.

His habit is to retire to bed, to exclude everybody, and to drink bottle after bottle of port.

> SIR STAFFORD NORTHCOTE, to Benjamin Disraeli, Apr. 28, 1870, qu. in Donald G. Creighton, *John A. Macdonald*, Vol. 2, 1955, 67.

Sir John is up!

> ANON., call heard when Sir John A. Macdonald rose to speak in Parliament on Nov. 3, 1873 during debate on the report of the Royal Commission on the financing of the construction of the C.P.R.

Mitchell, I am not very strong and I will require some little stimulant — I wish you would see that I have some gin and water sent to me from time to time.

> SIR JOHN A. MACDONALD, to Peter Mitchell in House of Commons, Nov. 3, 1873, stated in letter to A.F. Gault, Oct. 7, 1893; *Can. hist. rev.*, 1961, 216.

We have fought the battle of Confederation. We have fought the battle of unity. We have had party strife, setting Province against Province. And more than all, we have had, in the greatest Province, every prejudice and sectional feeling that could be arrayed against us. I throw myself on this House; I throw myself on this country; I throw myself on posterity, and I believe that, notwithstanding the many failings of my life, I shall have the voice of this country rallying round me. And, sir, if I am mistaken in that, I can confidently appeal to a higher court — to the court of my conscience and to the court of posterity.

> SIR JOHN A. MACDONALD, speech in defence of his railway policy, H. of C., *Debates*, Nov. 3, 1873.

Well! John A. beats the devil.

> LUTHER H. HOLTON, remark on Macdonald's restoration to office, election 1878.

Old Reynard.

> ANON., term used in reference to his artfulness and subtlety in politics.

You have a patience which I never saw equalled.

> ALEXANDER CAMPBELL, letter to Macdonald Oct. 19, 1881. (Pub. Arch. Can.)

Old To-morrow would be just the name for Sir John.

> COL. A.G. IRVINE, Commissioner N.W.M.P. late in 1881 to his adjutant, Supt. Cotton, and Ronald Prevost, in Ottawa; qu., E.B. Biggar, *Anecdotal life*, 1891, 320.

The Wizard of the North.

> ANON., a popular term.

A British subject I was born, and a British subject I hope to die.

> SIR JOHN A. MACDONALD, H. of C., *Debates*, 1882, 1078. Also, "As for myself, my course is clear. A British subject I was born — a British subject I will die", in, "To the electors of Canada", Feb. 7, 1891.

Of all the Dominion statesmen,
We ne'er expect to see,
One to compare in Canada
With Sir John A., K.C.B.

> CONSERVATIVE PARTY, song, election of June, 1882.

He cannot resist the solicitations of partisans, except perhaps in the case of judicial appointments, in regard to which his best sentiment is peculiarly romantic.

> GOLDWIN SMITH, letter to W.D. Le Sueur, June 2, 1882.

A rum 'un to look at, but a rare 'un to go!

> SIR JOHN A. MACDONALD, frequently repeated likening of himself to an old nag. Once, when riding to Markham Township Fair with Squire Millikan, he met an Irishman who had ridden over from Yonge Street on an old horse to see him. Sir John commented on the horse and the man said, "Faith, he's like yourself, Sir, a bit worse for wear." The reply was, "Yes, he's like myself, a rum 'un to look at, but a rare 'un to go." See also: *Grip's comic almanac*, 1883, 38; and, 1884, 11.

It is a happy association of ideas, and what a lamented friend of mine called the "eternal fitness of things", that a gentleman who in his life has done justice to so many John Collinses should at last find a John Collins to do justice to him.

> SIR RICHARD CARTWRIGHT, in House of Commons, on the publication of a biography of Macdonald by J.E. Collins, 1883; J. Willison, *Reminiscences*, 183.

When this man is gone, who will there be to take his place? What shepherd is there who knows the sheep or whose voice the sheep know? Who else could make Orangemen vote for Papists, and induce half the members for Ontario to help in levying on their own province the necessary blackmail for Quebec? Yet this is the work which will have to be done if a general break-up is to be averted.

> GOLDWIN SMITH, *The Week*, Feb. 28, 1884, 194.

The task of Sir John's political life has been to hold together a set of elements, national, religious, sectional and personal, as motley as the component patches of any 'crazy quilt', and actuated, each of them, by paramount regard for its own interest. This task he has so far accomplished by his consummate address, by his assiduous study of the weaker points of character, and where corruption was indispensable, by corruption. It is more than doubtful whether anybody could have done better than he has done. His aims, if they have not been the loftiest, have always been public, and in the midst of daily temptation he has kept his own heart above pelf. Indeed, if he had not, he could scarcely have played so successfully upon the egotism and cupidity of other men.

> GOLDWIN SMITH, *The Week*, Apr. 10, 1884.

You'll never die, John A.

> ANON., to Sir John A. Macdonald, when he spoke at a demonstration in his honour at Toronto, Dec. 17, 1884.

Seedy-looking old beggar, isn't he?

> ANON., remark made during speech by Sir John A. Macdonald at C.P.R. station, Winnipeg, July 13, 1886, qu. in Pope Papers, *Diary*, 18. (Pub. Arch. Can.)

I couldn't help thinking as I stood by that old man standing on the shores of the Pacific, with his grey hair blowing over his forehead, what a triumphal moment it must have been for him.

> JOSEPH POPE, of Sir John A. Macdonald addressing the crowd, C.P.R. station, Port Moody, B.C., July 24, 1886 on inauguration of transcontinental passenger service. Pope papers, *Diary*, 85. (Pub. Arch. Can.); varies in his *Public servant*, 1960, 56.

Time and I are a match for any two men.

> SIR JOHN A. MACDONALD, saying, qu. by P.B. Waite in Dyck and Krosby, eds., *Empire and nations*, 1969, 46.

The present government will last as long as Sir John Macdonald and when Sir John Macdonald disappears, after him the deluge.

> SIR WILFRID LAURIER, speech at Somerset, Que., Aug. 2, 1887. (Trans.)

I had no boyhood. From the age of fifteen I began to earn my own living.

SIR JOHN A. MACDONALD, to a friend, in his later years.

It is late, Bowell, good night.

SIR JOHN A. MACDONALD, to Mackenzie Bowell on leaving the House chamber for the last time, May 22, 1891.

Oh, that is no use, the machine is worn out.

SIR JOHN A. MACDONALD, in reply to the suggestion of Lord Stanley that he rest after suffering a slight stroke, qu. in letter of J.D. Edgar to his wife, June 14, 1891.

It may be said, without any exaggeration whatever, that the life of Sir John Macdonald, from the date he entered Parliament, is the history of Canada, for he was connected and associated with all the events, all the facts which brought Canada from the position Canada then occupied — the position of two small provinces, having nothing in common but a common allegiance, united by a bond of paper, and united by nothing else — to the present state of development which Canada has reached.

SIR WILFRID LAURIER, H. of C., *Debates*, June 8, 1891, 886.

Sir John Macdonald now belongs to the ages, and it can be said with certainty, that the career which has just been closed is one of the most remarkable careers of this century.

SIR WILFRID LAURIER, H. of C., *Debates*, June 8, 1891, 886.

Before the grave of him who, above all, was the father of Confederation, let not grief be barren grief.

SIR WILFRID LAURIER, H. of C., *Debates*, June 8, 1891, 887.

Death comes not with mere surcease of breath
To such as him. "The road to dusty death"
Not "all his yesterdays" have lighted. Nay,
Canada's "Old To-morrow" lives to-day
In unforgetting hearts, and nothing fears
The long to-morrow of the coming years.

PUNCH, June 20, 1891.

Had he been a much worse man he would have done Canada much less harm.

SIR RICHARD CARTWRIGHT, *Reminiscences*, 1912, 198.

I will say this for that old scoundrel John A. Macdonald, that if he once gave you his word, you could rely on it.

SIR RICHARD CARTWRIGHT, qu., Pope, *Day of Macdonald*, 1915, 118.

Only a Mohammed can come back to Mecca; only a Napoleon can return from Elba; only a Calvin can come back to Geneva; and only a Macdonald could come back to Ottawa after what occured in 1873 [the Pacific scandal].

B.H. STAUFFER, Empire Club, Toronto, speech, Feb. 18, 1915.

Opposition was but ever a spur to his valour.

HECTOR CHARLESWORTH, *Canadian scene*, 1927, 10.

To these mid-Victorian critics it seemed almost incredible that a man who enjoyed life so obviously, who was so frequently lacking in respectable earnestness, who seemed so ready to give up sober work and quiet repose for mere empty enjoyment, should have a really solid claim to be considered as a great national statesman.

DONALD G. CREIGHTON, *John A. Macdonald; the old chieftain*, 1955, 252.

Macdonald, John Sandfield

[My daughters] never stood in the presence of their father without fear, and never spoke a word to him in confidence in their lives.

MRS. JOHN SANDFIELD MACDONALD, qu. by George Brown, letter, Feb. 23, 1864, to his wife. (Pub.Arch.Can.)

The Axe-Grinder.

John Sandfield Macdonald, Premier of Ontario; Opposition's *sobriquet,* 1868, because of his political attitude of *quid pro quo.*

Petulance, bad temper, a garrulous, half-wandering, incoherent style of speech, a littleness and total want of dignity of bearing and expression; a readiness to blunder into a scrape, and a shabby, shuffling way of scrambling out of it; a reckless style of assertion, and a strange forgetfulness today of what may have been the utterances of yesterday.

TORONTO *GLOBE,* Dec. 21, 1870, 2, on J.S. Macdonald as head of govt. of Ontario.

McGee, Thomas D'Arcy

In the time of my boyhood I had a
  strange feeling,
That I was to die in the noon of my
  day;
Not quietly into the silent grave
  stealing,
But torn, like a blasted oak, sudden
  away.

GERALD GRIFFIN, (Irish poet) d. 1840, "The poet's prophecy", attributed to Thomas D'Arcy McGee by Lena Newman, *Historical almanac of Canada,* 1967; T.P. Slattery, *The assassination of Thomas D'Arcy McGee,* 1968, 433; but see Vancouver *Province,* Feb. 19, 1921, 27.

Ah, D'Arcy, D'Arcy! many doubt you,
And think we were as well without
  you –
That's why all loyal subjects flout you.

We seek not to be a new nation,
Nor do we yearn for annexation, –
Yet anything *but* Federation.

"FRED", [?] "Anti lyrics No. III", 1868, qu. in Halifax *Morning chronicle,* Jan. 10, 1868, 2.

Yea, we like children stood
When in his lofty mood
  He spoke of manly deeds which he
    might claim,
And made responses fit
While heavenly genius lit
  His melancholy eyes with lambent
    flame,
And saw the distant aureoles,
And felt the Future thunder in our
  souls.

CHARLES MAIR, "In memory of Thomas D'Arcy McGee", 1868.

Was it a wonder that a cry of agony rang throughout the land when murder, foul and most unnatural, drank the life-blood of Thomas D'Arcy McGee?

W.A. FOSTER, *Canada first, or, our new nationality,* 1871.

If ever a soldier who had fallen on the field of battle in the front rank of the fray had deserved well of his country, Thomas D'Arcy McGee had deserved well of Canada and her people.

SIR JOHN A. MACDONALD, H. of C., *Debates,* Apr. 7, 1886, 477.

D'Arcy McGee was, in truth, the Mazzini of Canadian national unity.

W. STEWART WALLACE, in *Can. hist. rev.,* 1920, 147.

McGill University

The Donaldas.

> ANON., nine Montreal girls whose education at McGill was financed by Donald A. Smith, 1884. They were the first women to attend McGill.

The distinction about old McGill is the men who are not there.

> STEPHEN B. LEACOCK, *My discovery of the West*, 1937, 138.

Machinery

Driving-rods, pistons,
rhythmical motion
pulleys and shafting
moving together;
drowsy, monotonous
in the warm atmosphere,
wheels whirring softly, –
subtle machinery.

> W.W. EUSTACE ROSS, "Machinery", 1930.

Human dignity? My motorcycle has more dignity than a man.

> J. MICHAEL YATES, favourite expression, qu. by George Amabile in *Dalhousie rev.*, Spring, 1973, 169.

Mackenzie, Alexander (Explorer)

I now mixed up some vermilion in melted grease, and inscribed, in large characters, on the South-East face of the rock on which we had slept last night, this brief memorial – 'Alexander Mackenzie from Canada by land, the twenty-second of July, one thousand seven hundred and ninety-three'.

> ALEXANDER MACKENZIE, *Voyages*, 1801, 349, inscription made on the shore of Dean Channel, Bella Coola River, B.C., celebrating the first crossing of the continent north of Mexico.

I have now resumed the character of a trader.

> ALEXANDER MACKENZIE, *Journal*, Aug. 24, 1793, Fort Chepewyan.

Mackenzie, Alex. (Prime Minister)

The fear has been gradually growing upon me, that my Prime Minister is not 'strong enough for the place'. He is honest, industrious, and sensible, but he has very little talent. He possesses neither 'initiative' nor 'ascendancy'.

> LORD DUFFERIN, letter to Lord Carnarvon, Apr. 16, 1874.

There was no gin and talk about MAC––––, no gin to his friends and talk for himself.

> GRIP, Apr. 3, 1880, "An intercepted letter".

Hurrah for Mackenzie the pride of the West!
Who has long fought the battle and conquered at last.
Long, long may he live his high office to hold,
For his sterling integrity has yet to be told.

> T.D., "The Hon. Alex. Mackenzie", Sarnia *Observer*, Jan. 26, 1892.

Consequences had to go to pieces before Alexander Mackenzie. God give us more such as he was, honest and true.

> S.H. BLAKE, speech at East York, after the funeral of Mackenzie, Apr. 1892.

Remember Mackenzie's mistakes!

> Admonition used among Liberals after 1896, referring to Mackenzie's submission to a wing of the party noted for its concern for principle and zeal.

We loved him for the enemies he had made.

SIR WILFRID LAURIER, speech in Massey Hall, Feb. 20, 1906.

If his strong point was having been a stone-mason, his weak point was being a stone-mason still.

GOLDWIN SMITH, *Reminiscences*, 1910, 436.

Like most active politicians, he was the last to know how he really rated with the public.

DALE C. THOMSON, *Alexander Mackenzie: clear grit*, 1960, 329.

Mackenzie, William Lyon

"Strike, the conflict is begun
Freemen! Soldiers! follow me;
Shout — the victory is won —
Canada and liberty!"

ANON., qu. by William Lyon Mackenzie in *Colonial advocate*, May 4, 1826, 7.

He is a little red-haired man about five feet nothing and extremely like a babboon but he is the O'Connell of Canada.

JOHN LANGTON, letter to his father, Apr. 25, 1834.

I am incapable of moderating the spirit of party — I am hot and fiery & age has not yet tempered as much as I could wish my political conduct & opinions.

W.L. MACKENZIE, letter to J. Neilson, Nov. 23, 1835; *Neilson papers*, VIII. (Pub. Arch. Can.)

My creed has been — social democracy — or equality of each man before society — and political democracy, or the equality of each man before the law.

W.L. MACKENZIE, in *Mackenzie's gaz.*, Dec. 23, 1840.

After what I have seen here, I frankly confess to you that, had I passed nine years in the United States before, instead of after, the outbreak, I am very sure I would have been the last man in America to be engaged in it.

WILLIAM LYON MACKENZIE, in Albany, N.Y., letter, Mar. 5, 1846 to his son, James, referring to the rebellion of 1837; qu. in C. Lindsey, *Life and times of Wm. Lyon Mackenzie*, Vol. 2, 1862, 290.

A singularly wild-looking little man with red hair, waspish and fractious in manner, one of that kind of people who would not sit down content under the government of an angel. He has evidently talent and energy; but he seems intent only in picking holes in other men's coats.

AMELIA MURRAY, Maid of Honour to Queen Victoria, after a visit to House of Assembly, Quebec, 1853, qu. in W. Kilbourn, *The firebrand*, 1956, 246.

The Little Rebel.

GEORGE BROWN, favourite term for Mackenzie, 1850's.

His mantle has fallen upon me, and it shall be taken up and worn. I never felt it could be done before. I see it now. With Miss . . . by my side I can stand out against all the world and stand I will. His voice, his words, shall be heard in Canada again and the cause he so nobly fought shall be carried on.

W.L. MACKENZIE KING, *Diary*, Feb. 26, 1898. Reference is to a nurse from Chicago who was unacceptable to his family.

A cowardly ruffian, who curiously enough bore not an Irish but a Scottish name.

SIR JOHN W. FORTESCUE, *History of the British army*, 1923, XI, 504.

He is the sort of character we most emphatically did not become.

> WILLIAM KILBOURN, *The firebrand*, 1956, xii.

Mackenzie was a crazy man,
He wore his wig askew.
He donned three bulky overcoats
In case the bullets flew.
Mackenzie talked of fighting
While the fight went down the drain.
But who will speak for Canada?
Mackenzie, come again.

> DENNIS LEE, "1838, 1970, 2020", 1970.

Mackenzie, Mann & Co. Ltd.

They should tell us, if they want to be absolutely fair: We have two money-bags at home, one belongs to the Canadian Northern Railway Company, the other to Messrs. Mackenzie, Mann and Company Ltd. We have taken all the money out of the money-bag belonging to the Canadian Northern Railway Company and we have placed it in the moneybag belonging to Mackenzie, Mann and Company Ltd. There is no more money in the first bag, it is all in the second; kindly fill up the first.

> G.H. BOIVIN, H. of C., *Debates*, May 14, 1914, 3719.

McLuhan, Marshall

McLuhan put his telescope to his ear;
What a lovely smell, he said, we have here.

> A.J.M. SMITH, "The taste of space", 1967.

Mr. McLuhan substitutes the printing press for Genesis, and the dissociation of sensibility for the Fall. In so doing he offers a fresh and coherent account of the state of the modern mind in terms of a congenial myth.

> FRANK KERMODE, in G.E. Stearn, ed., *McLuhan: hot and cool*, 1967, 180.

McLuhan reads books.

> ANON., qu. in *Queen's quart.*, 1971, 322.

McNaughton, Gen. A.G.L.

The Father of TCA.

> ANON., referring to Trans-Canada Airlines (since 1965, Air Canada) which began operation in 1937 along lines recommended by Gen. McNaughton.

If I am known for anything it is for the urgent insistence on using guns rather than the lives of our troops and for a proper co-ordination of all arms.

> GEN. A.G.L. MCNAUGHTON, press conference, Ottawa, Nov. 20, 1939.

Macphail, Agnes

God give us more women like Agnes Macphail;
When the miners were hungry, she never did fail.

> ANON., Nova Scotia ballad sung at Women's Social and Economic Conf., Calgary, about 1929, qu. in D. French and M. Stewart, *Ask no quarter*, 1959, 136.

Well, I told them the truth. They say the truth shall set you free. It's certainly set me free.

> AGNES MACPHAIL, after her defeat in federal election, 1940, qu. in M. Chapin, *Contemporary Canada*, 1959, 105.

I don't want to go down in history as a frustrated old maid.

> AGNES MACPHAIL, qu. in M. Stewart and D. French, *Ask no quarter*, 1959, 8.

Aggie is dead but lives on in the hearts of countless prison inmates who knew her and loved her. When the bell tolled for Aggie on February 13, 1954, it tolled for the inmates of every Canadian penitentiary.

> *TELESCOPE*, February, 1954, publication of the inmates of Kingston Penitentiary.

Madawaska, N.B.

Republic of Madawaska.

> JOHN BAKER, term used in proclamation of counterfeit republic, Aug. 10, 1827, during the Maine-New Brunswick border dispute. (See also Cities and Towns – Nicknames.)

Madness

The strength of the mad lies in the fear their madness inspires in the sane.

> ALDEN NOWLAN, "The foreigner", in *Miracle at Indian River*, 1968, 108.

Magazines

The Canadians read magazines, and pay for them. That is true; but it is also true that they want the best. Their standard is high, and unless the publisher can supply a publication which can compete with the important old world and United States serials, they will not have it, no matter how patriotic they may suppose themselves to be. Of course, the day is coming when Canada will have its great monthly and still greater quarterly, but the time is not yet ripe.

> GEORGE STEWART JR., address, Canadian Club of New York, 1887.

The publication and circulation of magazines by Canadians, for Canadians, telling about Canadians and what they are doing and what they have to sell, seems to us a basic and essential thread in the fabric of our national life.

> WALTER HARRIS, H. of C., *Debates*, Mar. 20, 1956, 2334.

Playboy, to cite one example, collects about as much money selling its magazine in Canada as do the seventeen largest English-language consumer magazines combined.

> CANADA. SPECIAL SENATE COMM. ON MASS MEDIA, *Report*, Vol. 1, 1970, 152.

Magic

God is alive. Magic is afoot. God is alive.
Magic is afoot. God is afoot. Magic is alive.
Magic never died.

> LEONARD COHEN, *Beautiful losers*, 1966, 157.

Majorities

There's no tyranny on airth equal to the tyranny of a majority.

> T.C. HALIBURTON, *Sam Slick*, 1838, 59.

It has been assumed as a principle that the direction of affairs should be in the hands of the two prevailing parties in each section of the Province, that the administration ought no more to govern Lower Canada by means of a majority obtained in Upper Canada, than it ought to govern the majority of Upper Canada by means of the aid that Lower Canada should give to it.

> R.E. CARON, letter to W.H. Draper, Sept. 18, 1845. (Pub.Arch.Can.)

Sandfield Macdonald didn't possess even a drinking majority; a man daren't go out to drink for fear the Ministry would be defeated before he got back.

> ANON., on the Legislative session of Feb. 19 to Mar. 21, 1864.

Given a Government with a big surplus, and a big majority and a weak Opposition, and you would debauch a committee of archangels.

> SIR JOHN A. MACDONALD, to Richard Cartwright, about 1869, qu. by Cartwright, *Reminiscences*, 1912, 305.

The voice of the majority is about as unreliable a thing as you can find anywhere, and it is generally wrong, until it becomes converted to the voice of the minority.

> J.J. PROCTER, *The philosopher in the clearing*, 1897, 126.

It is almost incomprehensible that the vital issues of death to nations, peace or war, bankruptcy or solvency, should be determined by the counting of heads and knowing as we do that the majority under modern conditions – happily the majority becoming smaller – are untrained and unskilled in dealing with the problems which they have to determine.

> RICHARD B. BENNETT, *Canadian problems*, 1933, 13.

If anyone tells me that fidelity to party and fidelity to country are always compatible, or that the wisdom of mere numbers is the wisdom of heaven, then I tell him that he loves applause far more than he loves truth.

> ARTHUR MEIGHEN, farewell tribute to R.B. Bennett, speech in Toronto, Jan. 16, 1939.

They must never demand of the majority that which the latter cannot give them.

> MICHEL BRUNET, *La présence anglaise et les Canadiens*, 1958, 292. (Trans.).

The principle of majority rule will work only in a society which is fairly homogeneous in composition; when the society is insufficiently homogeneous, majority rule becomes, or is resented as, an instrument of oppression.

> W.L. MORTON, *The Canadian identity*, 1961, 42.

Give us a comfortable majority.

> WALTER GORDON, plea to the electors, general election, Fall, 1965.

It seems to us to be no longer the traditional conflict between a majority and a minority. It is rather a conflict between two majorities: that which is a majority in all Canada, and that which is a majority in the entity of Quebec.

> CANADA. ROY. COMM. ON BILINGUALISM AND BICULTURALISM, *Preliminary report*, 1965, 135.

The majority is invariably vulgar.

> A.R.M. LOWER, *My first seventy-five years*, 1967, 26.

Male Chauvinism

I have found that women don't have that 'special little mechanism' that men have that enables them to get along with other people even if they don't like them.

> DONALD BAIRD, attributed, qu. in *Can. library jour.*, Oct., 1974, 423.

Malice

I say people will think ill of you no matter what you do. It's human nature.

> MAZO DE LA ROCHE, *The building of Jalna*, 1927 (1945, 180).

How the loonies hate each other
How they jeer & grunt & swear,
Their sullen faces happy
When another's wound they tear.

> IRVING LAYTON, "Dance, my little one", 1959.

Man

Man is a pipe that life doth smoke
As saunters it the earth about;
And when 'tis wearied of the joke,
Death comes and knocks the ashes out.

> CHARLES HEAVYSEGE, *Saul*, 1857, 45.

What is man, poor sinful man, or any
   of his race,
Without a greater power to keep him
   in his place?

   JAMES GAY, "What is man?", [1885].

Teach me the lesson that Mother Earth
   Teacheth her children each hour,
When she keeps in her deeps the basic
     root,
   And wears on her breast the flower.

And as the brute to the basic root
   In the infinite cosmic plan,
So in the plan of the infinite mind
   The flower of the brute is man.

   WILFRED CAMPBELL, "The lyre degenerate", 1905.

With good-will, and a touch of mirth,
   To clear and clean and plant and
     plan
The common levels of the Earth:—
   What more should God then ask of
     Man?

   TOM MACINNES, "Polity", 1918.

What is man but a little soul holding
up a corpse?

   MALCOLM LOWRY, *Under the volcano*,
   1947, 287.

The liberal society is that society in
which man is not merely a biological
organism, or a tool, or a hand, but
something in his own right, a being
with an unquestionable title to self-
respect and to dignity — as the theolo-
gians would put it, a child of God.

   ARTHUR R.M. LOWER, *This most famous
   stream*, 1954, 4.

I have not been unhappy for ten
   thousand years.
During the day I laugh and during the
   night I sleep.

   LEONARD COHEN, "I have not lingered in
   European monasteries", 1956.

The Lord that made Leviathan made
   thee
Not good, not great, not beautiful, not
   free,
Not whole in love, nor able to forget
The coming war, the battle still
   unmet.

   JAY MACPHERSON, "Leviathan", 1957.

Enough to know the human
As a mixed constitution
Imploring and fallible,
Choosing and despising ill.
Enough that we two can find
A laughter in the mind.

   IRVING LAYTON, "Parting", 1958.

Man is the unique creature, the rebel,
the thing of illimitable capacity for
creation or destruction, the one unpredictable being in a mechanistic cosmos, the truant of the universe.

   EARLE BIRNEY, "E.J. Pratt and his critics", in R.L. McDougall, ed., *Our living
   tradition*, 1959, 140.

To walk the earth
Is to be immersed,
Slung by the feet
In the universe.

   MARGARET AVISON, "Civility a bogey",
   1960.

Pray to yourself above all for men like
   me
that we do not quench
the man
in each of us.

   EARLE BIRNEY, "Letter to a Cuzco
   priest", 1962.

In China, a bullet has shattered my
   brain.
In Spain, the bayonets have pierced
   my side.

In America, I am crying for bread at
   my mother's knee.
I am rotting in Fascist prisons.
In Europe, I am driven by hunger and
   despair
   through the red shambles of another
   war.

> A.M. STEPHEN, "How are you?", 1963.

Since I no longer expect anything from
mankind except madness, meanness,
and mendacity; egotism, cowardice,
and self-delusion, I have stopped being
a misanthrope.

> IRVING LAYTON, "Some observations and
> aphorisms", *Tamarack rev.*, Spring,
> 1968, 5.

Management

Me, ruthless? Certainly not. But when
I'm right and management's consistently wrong, of course I get rid of
management.

> E.P. TAYLOR, about 1957, after forcing
> resignation of James Duncan, Pres. of
> Massey-Harris, qu. in P. Newman,
> *Flame of power*, 1959, 240.

1. What ought to be done.
2. How should it be done.
3. Who should do it.
4. Has it been done.

> JOSEPH E. ATKINSON, "Four things an
> executive should know", qu. in R. Hark-
> ness, *J.E. Atkinson of the Star*, 1963,
> 209.

The organization man is a political
celibate.

> WALLACE MCCUTCHEON, in I.A. Litvak,
> ed., *The nation keepers*, 1967, 150.

Manitoba

The voyageur smiles as he listens
   To the sound that grows apace;

Well he knows the vesper ringing
   Of the bells of St. Boniface.

The bells of the Roman mission,
   That call from their turrets twain,
To the boatman on the river,
   To the hunter on the plain.

> JOHN G. WHITTIER, "Red River voya-
> geur", 1860 written after reading Bond:
> *Minnesota, or, a trip to Selkirk Settle-
> ment*, 1854, 292.

Out and in the river is winding
   The links of its long red chain,
Through belts of dusky pine land
   And gusty leagues of plain.

> JOHN G. WHITTIER, "Red River voya-
> geur", 1860.

One thing is very apparent: unless the
English government shall promptly
respond to the manifest destiny of the
great interior of British America –
the basin of Lake Winnipeg – the
speedy Americanization of that fertile
belt is inevitable.

> J.W. TAYLOR, Amer. consul at Winnipeg,
> letter to Hon. S.P. Chase, dated St. Paul,
> July 17, 1861; in, U.S. Treas., *Rels.
> between U.S. and Brit. N.A.*, p. 26. (37
> Cong. 2d. Sess. House of Reps. Exec.
> doc. 146)

Manitoba was the key to the whole
territory, and when they had defined
its limits they had done a good work.

> SIR GEORGE-ETIENNE CARTIER, H. of C.,
> *Debates*, May 2, 1870, 1299, on the
> establishment of the Province.

The Prairie Province.

> J.C. HAMILTON, *The prairie province*,
> 1876; from the title of the book which
> gave the phrase general circulation;
> after 1905 it was extended to include
> Saskatchewan and Alberta, in "The
> Prairie Provinces".

From its geographical position, and its
peculiar characteristics, Manitoba may
be regarded as the keystone of that

mighty arch of sister provinces which spans the continent from the Atlantic to the Pacific. It was here that Canada, emerging from her woods and forests, first gazed upon her rolling prairies and unexplored North-West, and learned as by an unexpected revelation, that her historical territories of the Canadas, her eastern seaboards of New Brunswick, Labrador, and Nova Scotia, her Laurentian lakes and valleys, corn lands and pastures, though themselves more extensive than half-a-dozen European kingdoms, were but the vestibules and antechambers to that till then undreamed-of Dominion, whose illimitable dimensions alike confound the arithmetic of the surveyor and the verification of the explorer.

> LORD DUFFERIN, speech at City Hall, Winnipeg, Sept. 29, 1877.

The Manitoba Boom.

> ANON., a period of prosperity in the province, 1879 to 1883.

The Postage Stamp Province.

> ANON., a popular name given to the province after 1870 because of its original size and shape; speech of R.P. ROBLIN, Winnipeg, Mar. 7, 1907.

The Cinderella of Confederation.

> JOHN NORQUAY, in Manitoba budget speech, 1884.

Manitoba First!

> Motto, 1884, of MANITOBA FIRST PARTY, which contended that their interest lay solely in provincial advancement.

I know that through the grace of God I am the founder of Manitoba.

> LOUIS RIEL, *Queen versus Louis Riel*, 1886, 147.

Softly the shadows of prairie-land wheat
Ripple and riot adown to her feet;
Murmurs all Nature with joyous acclaim,
Fragrance of summer and shimmer of flame.

> EMILY MCMANUS, "Manitoba", 1913.

Some of Canada's provinces were acquired by adoption. On others the status was conferred after a rigorously supervised apprenticeship. Manitoba was simply conjured into being.

> F.A. MILLIGAN, Historical and Scientific Soc. of Man., *Transactions*, Ser. III, No. 5, 1950, 5.

My native province has always seemed to me an unusual and fascinating place, possessed both of a history of great interest and of a deep sense of history.

> W.L. MORTON, *Manitoba: a history*, 1957, vii.

Manitobans had been made, as Canadians had been made, of those who by endurance in loyalty to older values than prosperity, had learned to wrest a living from the prairie's brief summer and the harsh rocks and wild waters of the north.

> W.L. MORTON, *Manitoba: a history*, 1957, 473.

Manners

The manners and customs of the people were essentially Yankee, with less intelligence, civility and sobriety.

> PATRICK SHIRREFF, *A tour through North America, Canada and the United States*, 1835, 95.

This was my first lesson, that squeamishness and indelicacy are often found united; in short, that in manners, as in other things, extremes meet.

> T.C. HALIBURTON, *Sam Slick*, 1838, 175.

Vulgarity is always showy.

> T.C. HALIBURTON, *Nature and human nature*, 1855, I, 205.

Etiquette may perhaps be defined as some rule of social conduct. I have found that no such rule is necessary in Canada, for the self-respect of the people guarantees good manners.

> MARQUIS OF LORNE, address, Toronto, 1883, qu. in his *Memories of Canada and Scotland*, 1884, 347.

Manners and morals are never at a standstill. Either they rise or they decline. Like Empires.

> MAZO DE LA ROCHE, *The building of Jalna*, 1927 (1945, 272).

The first to go are the niceties,
The little minor conformities
That suddenly seem absurdities.

> F.R. SCOTT, "Degeneration", 1964.

Manner redeemeth everything:
   redeemeth
man, sets him among,
over, the other worms, puts
a crown on him, yes, the size of a
   mountain lake,
dazzling more dazzling!
   than a slice of sun

> IRVING LAYTON, "It's all in the manner", 1965.

Manufacturing

Let us beware how we allow the establishment of manufactures in Canada; she would become proud and mutinous like the English colonies. So long as France is a nursery to Canada, let not the Canadians be allowed to trade, but kept to their wandering, laborious life with the savages, and to their military exercises.

> MARQUIS DE MONTCALM, letter written before the fall of Quebec, 1759. (Trans.)

We are manufacturers not merely of articles of wood and stone, and iron and cotton and wool. We manufacture enthusiasms; we manufacture a feeling of pride in our country, a spirit of independence.

> CYRUS A. BIRGE, Pres. of Canadian Manufacturers' Assoc., *Industrial Canada*, Oct.,1903, 103.

If we make we are rich, if we do not make we inevitably become poor.

> GEORGE E. DRUMMOND, speech to Can. Manufacturers' Assoc., Montreal, July 21, 1904.

On Thursday I will beat them and on Friday I will continue to protect their just interests.

> SIR WILFRID LAURIER, on manufacturers, speech in Montreal, Sept. 19, 1911.

Made in Canada.

> ANON., slogan adopted by manufacturers after the Reciprocity election, 1911.

We were not prepared to admit that there was any article that could not at some point in Canada, and in time, be successfully manufactured.

> CANADIAN MANUFACTURERS' ASSOCIATION, Report of annual meeting, in *Industrial Canada*, 1912, 334.

Abuse of manufacturers was with him an instinct, a duty, a recreation and a profession.

> SIR JOHN WILLISON, on Sir Richard Cartwright, *Reminiscences*, 1919, 204-5.

Never again will there be any doubt that Canada can manufacture anything that can be manufactured elsewhere.

> C.D. HOWE, in 1943, qu. in L. Roberts *C.D., the life and times of Clarence Decatur Howe*, 1957, 120.

One might say with some degree of truth that Canada as a nation has been afflicted with a sort of branch plant syndrome, with much of our population being content to do just as they do in the States, except for doing it a little worse in quality, somewhat reduced in quantity, and considerably less sophisticated in style.

ROBERT D. BROWN, *Can. forum*, Dec., 1965, 198.

Maple Leaf

Resolved: that all Native Canadians joining in the procession, whether identified with the National Societies or not, should wear the maple leaf as the emblem of the land of their birth.

JAMES H. RICHARDSON, resolution adopted at a gathering of National Societies in St. Lawrence Hall, Toronto, Aug. 21, 1860 called together to arrange a welcome for the Prince of Wales (King Edward VII); regarded as the date of the adoption of the emblem for Canada.

In days of yore the hero, Wolfe,
    Britain's glory did maintain,
And planted firm Britannia's flag
    On Canada's fair domain,
Here may it wave, our boast, our
        pride,
    And, joined in love together,
The Thistle, Shamrock, Rose entwine,
    The Maple Leaf forever!
Chorus – The Maple Leaf, our
        emblem dear,
    The Maple Leaf forever!
God save our Queen, and heaven bless
    The Maple Leaf forever!

ALEXANDER MUIR, "The Maple Leaf forever", 1867.

Maple Trees

This tree – the maple – which grows in our valleys . . . at first young and beaten by the storm, pines away, painfully feeding itself from the earth, but it soon springs up, tall and strong, and faces the tempest and triumphs over the wind which cannot shake it any more. The maple is the king of our forest; it is the symbol of the Canadian people.

DENIS B. VIGER, speech, June 24, 1836, St. Jean-Baptiste Soc., Montreal. (Trans.)

Frosty nights and warm sun make the maple sap run.

ANON., saying of pioneer Ontario farmers.

Hail to the pride of the forest, hail
    To the maple tall and green,
It yields a treasure which never shall
        fail
    While leaves on its boughs are seen.
When the snows of winter are melting
        fast,
    And the sap begins to rise,
And the biting breath of the frozen
        blast
    Yields to the spring's soft sighs.

SUSANNA MOODIE, *Roughing it in the bush*, 1852.

All hail to the broad-leaved maple,
    With its fair and changeful dress!
A type of our youthful country
    In its pride and loveliness.

HENRY F. DARNELL, "The maple", 1864.

Outside, a yellow maple tree,
    Shifting upon the silvery blue
With tiny multitudinous sound,
    Rustled to let the sunlight through.

BLISS CARMAN, "The eavesdropper", 1893.

The scarlet of the maples can shake
    me like a cry,
Of bugles going by.

BLISS CARMAN, "A vagabond song", 1894.

Scarlet when the April vanguard
   Bugles up the laggard Spring,
Scarlet when the bannered Autumn
   Marches by unwavering.

BLISS CARMAN, "The grave-tree", 1898.

Above them are being planted the
maples of Canada, in the thought that
her sons will rest the better in the
shade of the trees they knew so well in
life.

ARTHUR MEIGHEN, speech at Vimy Ridge
army cemetery, July 3, 1921.

There is a story written no art can ever
   name,
And golden
As of olden
The fiery heralds run.
Across the fields of Canada we trace
   their path of flame.

A.M. STEPHEN, "Scarlet and gold – the
maples", 1923.

We have given to the maple a prominence which was due to the birch.

HAROLD A. INNIS, *The fur trade in Canada*, 1930, 397.

Sap is boiling,
Skies are clear,
Maple syrup
Time is here.

ARTHUR S. BOURINOT, "Sugar bush",
1951.

March

I, the invincible,
   March, the earth-shaker;
March, the sea-lifter;
   March, the sky-render.

ISABELLA VALANCY CRAWFORD, "March",
1884.

Maritimes

My mind has been strongly impressed
with the idea of uniting these Provinces with Canada, to the advantage of

both countries, and that by establishing the same laws, inducing a constant
intercourse and mutual interest, a
great country may yet be raised up in
America.

COL. ROBERT MORSE, "Report on Nova
Scotia 1784", in Douglas Brymner, *Report on Canadian archives, 1884*, 1885,
xxvii.

Your destiny and ours, is as inseparable as are the waters which pour into
the Bay of Chaleur, rising though they
do, on the one hand on the Canadian,
and on the other on the New Brunswick Highlands. Geographically we
are bound up beyond the power of
extinction.

THOMAS D'ARCY MCGEE, speech in St.
John, N.B., August, 1863.

We don't know each other. We have
no trade with each other. We have no
facilities, or resources, or incentives, to
mingle with each other. We are shut
off from each other by a wilderness,
geographically, commercially, politically and socially. We always cross the
United States to shake hands. Our
interests are not identical, but the very
opposite – they are antagonistic and
clashing.

HALIFAX *ACADIAN RECORDER*, July 27,
1866, on Confederation.

Herring-backs.

ANON., a popular name for Maritimers,
about 1875.

Come all you jolly lumbermen,
Whose better years have fled,
And I will sing of halcyon days
Before we had Confed;
When title to respect was writ
Upon each horny hand,
And the man who swung a broadaxe
Was a power in the land.

HEADLEY PARKER, "The days of Duffey
Gillis", 1899.

The age of wood, wind and water.

> CANADA. ROY. COMM. ON DOMINION-
> PROVINCIAL RELATIONS, *Report*, vol. 1,
> 1940, 22; the phrase refers to the "Gold-
> en Age" of the Maritime Provinces, the
> pre-Confederation era of prosperity
> based on fish and lumber exports, wood-
> en ship-building, and the carrying trade.

We give you ships and tides and men
Anchors a-weigh and wind-filled sail.
We give you back the sea again
In sailors' song and rousing tale;
And inland where the dark hills rise
Between you and the salt-thick foam
You hear the surf, the sea-gulls' cries
And eastward turn your hearts toward
  home.

> EILEEN CAMERON HENRY, "Harmony
> harbour", June, 1947.

The calamities of the Maritimes have
always been casually passed along as
acts of God, over which governments
have no responsibility; while apparently, from the official point of view
Divinity does not operate in other
sectors of Canada.

> J.J. HAYES DOONE, Senate, *Debates*, Mar.
> 26, 1952, 97.

With Confederation in 1867, they ex-
changed British domination for that of
central Canada and became a colony
of Ontario, cut off from their natural
markets in the United States, bound by
tariffs planned to build up Ontario's
manufacturers.

> MIRIAM CHAPIN, *Contemporary Canada*,
> 1959, 38.

Let's not forget that in some cases
Upper Canadians are the worst type of
foreigners.

> K.C. IRVING, of New Brunswick, July
> 1961, qu. in R. Hunt & R. Campbell,
> *K.C. Irving*, 1973, 28.

After dealing with four prime ministers of Canada for twenty-three years,
I am convinced that with the exception of a few brave souls, nobody in
Ottawa has the slightest belief in the
likelihood, or even the possibility, of
the four Atlantic Provinces ever being
much more than mere markets or
colonies for the rest of Canada. They
won't admit this; they'll deny it with
vehemence, sarcasm, wit, indignation,
and in a variety of other ways, for of
course they can't possibly admit it –
except in action.

> JOSEPH R. SMALLWOOD, *I chose Canada*,
> 1973, 483.

Markets

Canada is not one market but four,
widely separated from each other, and
each of them sparse in itself.

> GOLDWIN SMITH, *Canada and the Cana-
> dian question*, 1891, 284.

Today the tyrant rules not by club or
fist, but, disguised as a market re-
searcher he shepherds his flocks in the
way of utility and comfort.

> MARSHALL MCLUHAN, *The mechanical
> bride*, 1952, vi.

Marriage

Marriage changes states but not dispositions.

> THOMAS MCCULLOCH, *The letters of Me-
> phibosheth Stepsure*, 1821, Letter 10.

I cannot wonder at any nonsensical
affections I meet with in my own sex;
nor can I do otherwise than pity the
mistakes and deficiencies of those who
are sagely brought up with one end
and aim – to get married.

> ANNA B. JAMESON, *Sketches in Canada*,
> 1852, 88.

Matrimony likes contrasts; friendship seeks its own counterparts.

> T.C. HALIBURTON, *Sam Slick's wise saws*, 1853, II, 79.

Women, in a general way, don't look like the same critters when they are spliced, that they do before; matrimony, like sugar and water, has a natural affinity for, and tendency to acidity.

> T.C. HALIBURTON, *Nature and human nature*, 1855, II, 260.

One of our maxims should be — "Early marriages, and death to old bachelors".

> THOMAS D'ARCY MCGEE, speech in Quebec, May 10, 1862.

Whatever facilitates marriage prevents impurity, and whatever adds to the prosperity of the people facilitates marriage.

> GOLDWIN SMITH, *The Bystander*, Sept., 1880, 497.

Protestant marriage is legalized concubinage.

> JAMES VINCENT CLEARY, first Roman Catholic archbishop, Kingston, 1896.

So truly as a young man married is a young man marred, is a woman unmarried, in a certain sense, a woman undone.

> WILLIAM OSLER, "Nurse and patient", address, 1897, in *Aequanimitas;* from Shakespeare, "A young man married is a man that's marred".

If a girl could only marry the best man at her wedding there would be fewer matrimonial smash-ups.

> ROBERT C. (BOB) EDWARDS, Calgary *Eye Opener*, Aug. 4, 1906.

Most marriages are brought about by the following simple, yet fateful consideration: The man marries the woman he wants; the woman marries the man who wants her.

> ARNOLD HAULTAIN, *Hints for lovers*, 1909, 258.

Sentiment, not intellect, is the cementing material in marriage, and if man and wife cannot effuse a mutual sentiment, gradually they will grow apart.

> ARNOLD HAULTAIN, *Hints for lovers*, 1909, 262.

This year I must decide either to leave politics altogether or be the framer of future policies, and that decision seems to me to depend on the woman I marry. — Marry I must if I can, it is the right life for a man. I have delayed it already too long.

> W.L. MACKENZIE KING, *Diary*, Jan. 13, 1912.

The woman with the ideal husband very likely wishes she had some other kind.

> ROBERT C. (BOB) EDWARDS, Calgary *Eye Opener*, Dec. 6, 1913.

Oh why, do some of our best men marry such odd little sticks of pinhead women, with a brain similar in calibre to a second-rate butterfly, while the most intelligent, unselfish, and womanly women are left unmated? I am going to ask about this the first morning I am in heaven, if so be we are allowed to ask about the things which troubled us while on our mortal journey.

> NELLIE MCCLUNG, *In times like these*, 1915, 52.

The world has taunted women into marrying.

> NELLIE MCCLUNG, *In times like these*, 1915, 137.

I suggest that there is a splendid way out of the difficulty of marriage, and that is my way — stay out.

> AGNES MACPHAIL, H. of C., *Debates*, Feb. 26, 1925, 570.

Women become dangerous when they have no husbands to lie with them.

> NAUKATJIK, Eskimo, qu. in Knud Rasmussen, *Intellectual culture of the Inglulik Eskimos*, 1929, 301; *Report of the fifth Thule expedition 1921-24*, Vol. VII, No. 1.

Mating is like dinner-hour: the more fashionable you are the later it occurs.

> ARTHUR STRINGER, *Christina and I*, 1929.

Many a man in love with a dimple makes the mistake of marrying the whole girl.

> STEPHEN B. LEACOCK, qu. in Evan Esar, *Comic dictionary*, 1943, 129.

People who have never married have not really lived. People who have married and had no children have only half-lived. People who have one child only are a long way from the crown of human life.

> STEPHEN B. LEACOCK, "Woman's level", in *Last leaves*, 1945, 102.

God, what a lot we hear about unhappy marriages, and how little we hear about unhappy sons and daughters.

> ROBERTSON DAVIES, *Leaven of malice*, 1954, 256.

There's more to marriage than four bare legs in a blanket.

> ROBERTSON DAVIES, *A jig for the gypsy*, 1954, 28.

As a general thing, people marry most happily with their own kind. The trouble lies in the fact that people usually marry at an age where they do not really know what their own kind is.

> ROBERTSON DAVIES, *A voice from the attic*, 1960, 97.

Marriage for life, especially if decided on by the principals, is an exceedingly hazardous arrangement, as all experience shows. The line between love and lust is one that participants can neither draw for themselves nor on which they can accept counsel. And love is less than durable.

> JOHN KENNETH GALBRAITH, *The Scotch*, 1964, 28.

One of the outstanding features of this age is the number of intelligent women who do not marry. I have talked to hundreds of these fine, alert and very capable women in business, the professions, and the arts, and their reason was the same as mine: *the person* could not be subjected.

> AGNES MACPHAIL, qu. in Mary Q. Innis, *Clear spirit*, 1966, 195.

Almost every marital bed has three occupants – the man, the woman, and, wedged solidly between them, the marriage.

> RICHARD J. NEEDHAM, *A friend in Needham*, 1969, 2.

Recipe for a permanent marriage: stupidity; failing that, hypocrisy.

> IRVING LAYTON, "Aphs", *The whole bloody bird*, 1969, 92.

It is an odd fact that when a married couple fall out of love it is contempt for each other rather than sympathy which now becomes the dominant emotion.

> IRVING LAYTON, "Aphs", *The whole bloody bird*, 1969, 93.

Before marriage, people talk mainly about love; after marriage, they talk mainly about money.

> RICHARD J. NEEDHAM, *A friend in Needham*, 1969, 3.

We made love
on the floor of a broken
marriage, and everything
was Autumn and growing old.

> PEGGY FLETCHER, "Twin despair", 1971.

Five years married
and he has never once
wished he dared kill her, which means
they're happy enough.
But it isn't love.

> ALDEN NOWLAN, "The married man's poem", 1971.

Many marriages between two people
become marriages between one and a
half very quickly.

> MERLE SHAIN, *Some men are more perfect than others*, 1973, 74.

Marriage Proposals

Hannah, if thee will be the mother of
my children, I'll be the father of thine.

> JOSEPH GREEN, to Hannah Baker, Summerside, P.E.I., about 1830, qu. in L.C. Callbeck, *Cradle of confederation*, 1964, 144.

Either the wrong man proposes or the
right man proposes stupidly.

> ARNOLD HAULTAIN, *Hints for lovers*, 1909, 165.

Marxism

Until Christians understand and apply
the lessons of Marxism they cannot
enter the Kingdom of Heaven.

> EUGENE FORSEY, in *Towards the Christian revolution*, 1937.

Massey, Vincent

Fine chap, Vincent, but he does make
one feel a bit of a savage.

> LORD CRANBORNE, (Lord Privy Seal in Churchill's government) remark attributed in 1951.

Let the Old World, where rank's yet
vital,
Part those who have and have not title.
Toronto has no social classes –
Only the Masseys and the masses.

> B.K. SANDWELL, "On the appointment of Governor-General Vincent Massey, 1952", in F.R. Scott, ed., *The blasted pine*, 1957, 59.

Masterpieces

So I look not for masterpieces because
we have no more masters.

> GEORGE BOWERING, ed., *The story so far*, 1971, Preface.

Materialism

When all a man's gifts have been bent
on the realization of material and
realizable ends, the time is bound to
come, unless he fails, when he will
turn his spiritual powers against himself and scoff at his own achievements.

> FREDERICK P. GROVE, *Fruits of the earth*, 1933, 157.

The continued prevalence of a materialistic idealism keeps our national life
financially rich but culturally poor.

> ALAN CREIGHTON, in *Can. poetry mag.*, Apr., 1942, 5.

Owing to the facts of North American
civilization, Canadians who set store
by material development – and most
do – must inevitably be nationalists
of a qualified type.

> ALEXANDER BRADY, *Amer. pol. sci. rev.*, 47, Dec., 1953, 1030.

Banking and insurance have managed
to raise themselves almost to the level
of religions.

> ROBERTSON DAVIES, *Leaven of malice*, 1954, 157.

Materialism

Materialism is not scientific. Material-ism is a matter of faith. It is a kind of religion to which many cling in igno-rance, believing that the machine has already explained the spirit.

WILDER PENFIELD, address, Christ Church Cathedral, Montreal, May 25, 1958.

Maturity

We shall not by our reason or in our time reduce this expanding universe nor the intractable humans who occu-py so tiny a corner of it to tidy rational patterns. Behind the momentary cer-tainties lie the shifting uncertainties of tomorrow. The test of maturity is the ability to live with uncertainty and reckon with risk.

W.A. MACKINTOSH, address, Convocation, Royal Military College, late 1960's, qu. in *Queen's quart.*, Vol. 78, 1971, 119.

Maxims

Maxims are deductions ready drawn.

T.C. HALIBURTON, *Nature and human nature*, 1855, I, 120.

May

With throb of throstle and with throat of wren,
Full of soft cheepings comes the longed-for May;
With myriad murmuring life throughout each day,
It grows and greens in grove and field and glen.

J. ALMON RITCHIE, "May time", 1885.

Here's to the day when it is May
And care as light as a feather,
When your little shoes and my big boots
Go tramping over the heather.

BLISS CARMAN, "A toast", 1892.

Mayors

If I pull your chain, will you flush?

CHARLOTTE WHITTON, as Mayor of Otta-wa (1951-56), to the Lord Mayor of London, both wearing official robes and chains of office, in response to the Lord Mayor's question, "If I smell your rose will you blush?".

Me

I have trouble enough in keeping myself in line; I have no desire to try to keep others in line.

HENRI BOURASSA, H. of C., *Debates*, Feb. 19, 1900, 587.

Six foot three of indolence
Two hundred pounds of weed;
My better judgment voted me
Least likely to succeed.

AL PURDY, "Self-portrait", 1944.

I lay my cheek against cold stone
And feel my self returned to me
As soft my flesh and firm my bone
By it declare their quality.
I hear my distant blood drive still
Its obscure purpose with clear will.

JAY MACPHERSON, "Cold stone", 1957.

I love the slightly flattened sphere,
Its restless, wrinkled crust's my here,
Its slightly wobbling spin's my now
But not my why and not my how:
My why and how are me.

GEORGE JOHNSTON, "O earth, turn!", 1959.

I from my myness
must a you create
for your yourness
is inviolate.

FRED COGSWELL, "Lost dimension", 1960.

I really do like myself and could get along very nicely if I were the last man in the world. I may not have attained perfection, but I'm nearer to it than most people think.

NATHAN COHEN, Toronto *Daily star* entertainment critic, qu. in *Liberty*, Sept., 1963.

I am the victim of the Furies. On the rockbound coast of New Brunswick the waves break incessantly. Every now and then comes a particularly dangerous wave smashing viciously against the rock. It is called The Rage. That's me.

LORD BEAVERBROOK, qu. in *Time*, Sept. 6, 1963, 47.

I looked the sun straight in the eye,
He put on dark glasses.

F.R. SCOTT, "Eclipse", 1964.

The vision of the true face of our
  condition,
The man in the mirror who is always
  there.

JOHN GLASSCO, "A point of sky", 1964.

I am the desperate faithless one,
I am the unbeliever, the liar
always confessing, have faith in me!

Though inconstant as the wallowing
  sea,
I will not move from about your rock:
stay in this poem, stay with me!

JOHN NEWLOVE, "Stay in this room", 1965.

I know
That life is earnest, time is tough
But me, I'm not, I'm soft and slow.
Look I'm not asking half enough.
My prices are absurdly low.

GEORGE JOHNSTON, "The bargain sale", 1966.

Closed in this small tight room
there is a warm illimitable
thing inside me keeps me
alive and proud and sane.

MIRIAM WADDINGTON, "Second generation", 1966.

My cell is my naked self.
I am immune
from the mirrored vacuum
of human betrayal,
and in my presence
everything is the centre
of everything else.
My navel is the universe.
I do not serve time,
time serves me.
The turnkey cannot enter
my kingdom.

LEN GASPARINI, "Solitary confinement", 1967.

The woman I am
is not what you see
move over love
make room for me

DOROTHY LIVESAY, "The unquiet bed", 1967.

Wherever I go
whatever I do
there is one thing that is always
  happening
and that is me

RED LANE, "Is happening it happens to", 1968.

I am satisfied with my own short-comings letting myself happen.

AL PURDY, "The winemakers beatetude", 1968.

I stink therefore I am.

AUDREY THOMAS, *Mrs. Blood*, 1970, 11.

Before you begin to envy me
Remember only this:
My god's bidding is as remote from
  my nature
As your god's is from yours
And I find his commandments
As difficult to keep.

GEORGE JONAS, *Happy hungry man*, 1970, 34.

I have a little man running around inside me who is insatiable.

> JERRY GOODIS, advertising executive, qu. in *Maclean's*, Apr. 1972, 12.

The I you think you know
or seem to see in me
is but the I that I am forced to be
because both physically
and mentally
and socially
I am conditioned me.

> JACK SHADBOLT, *Minds I*, 1973, 5.

Meals

Breakfast, dinner, tea, or supper — whatever the name of the repast — it consisted much of the same materials, — tea, flour-cakes, and such meat as happened to be available.

> EARL OF SOUTHESK, *Saskatchewan and the Rocky Mountains; diary*, Dec. 3, 1859.

Any two meals at a boarding-house are together less than two square meals.

> STEPHEN B. LEACOCK, "Boarding house geometry", in *Literary lapses*, 1910.

A dinner party, to be successful, should have at least one interesting man who comes by himself.

> RICHARD J. NEEDHAM, *A friend in Needham*, 1969, 17.

Meaning

The question is, not what may be supposed to have been intended, but what has been said.

> LORD HALSBURY, Decision, Brophy vs. Atty.-Gen. of Manitoba, *Appeal cases*, Jan. 29, 1895, 216.

Words still manifestly force the understanding, throw everything in confusion and lead mankind into vain and innumerable controversies and fallacies.

> JOHN S. EWART, qu., in *Can. hist. rev.*, 1933, 137.

but what worries me is that you think
I mean something (no
the fact is that I am more enamoured
of the act of writing than of the act of
meaning (or being

> JOHN NEWLOVE, "Lynn Valley: depression", 1965.

Mechanization

Mechanization moreover implies more effective utilization of physical force. Machine guns are effective keys to the city.

> HAROLD A. INNIS, address, Sixth Annual Meeting, Canadian Political Science Assoc., Montreal, May 22, 1934.

The straightedge ruled out errors,
The tremors in the sensory nerves,
Pity and the wayward impulses,
The liberal imbecilities.

> E.J. PRATT, "Dunkirk", 1941, 2.

Media

The media are not toys; they should not be in the hands of Mother Goose and Peter Pan executives. They can be entrusted only to new artists, because they are art forms.

> MARSHALL MCLUHAN, *Counterblast*, 1954, [13] (pamphlet).

All the new media, including the press, are art forms which have the power of imposing, like poetry, their own assumptions. The new media are not ways of relating us to the old 'real' world; they are the real world and they reshape what remains of the old world at will.

MARSHALL MCLUHAN, *Counterblast*, 1954.

The medium is the message.

MARSHALL MCLUHAN, remark originally made in Vancouver, July 30, 1959, later used in several of his books, as text or titles.

In a culture like ours, long accustomed to splitting and dividing all things as a means of control, it is sometimes a bit of a shock to be reminded that in operational and practical fact, the medium is the message.

MARSHALL MCLUHAN, *Understanding media*, 1964, 7.

Our conventional response to all media, namely that it is how they are used that counts, is the numb stance of the technological idiot.

MARSHALL MCLUHAN, *Understanding media*, 1964, 18.

There is a basic principle that distinguishes a hot medium like radio from a cool one like the telephone or a hot medium like the movie from a cool one like TV. A hot medium is one that extends one single sense in "high definition". High definition is the state of being well filled with data.

MARSHALL MCLUHAN, *Understanding media*, 1964, 22.

Canada's mass media are operated as big business. Many of them, particulary in the large cities, are closely linked with corporate enterprise. Concentration of the control of the mass media is to be found in all industrialized and urbanized societies.

JOHN PORTER, *The vertical mosaic*, 1965, 462.

In this age of pervasive media, in a world of rapidly shrinking distances and in a human community of interdependence, politicians need not only be right, they must as well appear to be reasonable.

DALTON CAMP, *The Canadian*, Nov. 12, 1966.

All media work us over completely. They are so pervasive in their personal, political, economic, aesthetic, psychological, moral, ethical and social consequences that they leave no part of us untouched, unaffected, unaltered. The medium is the message. Any understanding of social and cultural change is impossible without a knowledge of the way media work as environments.

MARSHALL MCLUHAN, *The medium is the message*, 1967, 26.

Mass media are magnifiers of personality.

LOUIS DUDEK, "Poetry in English", 1969.

Newspapers are treacherous; they thrive on controversy and excitement. And when desperation, that is dearth of news, sets in they will manufacture excitement. Television is simply this process in caricature.

PETER WAITE, in J.S. Moir, ed., *Character and circumstance*, 1970, 231.

Medical Care

This is a democracy and in a democracy if a government is elected on a promise to cure arthritis by giving baths at Watrous, I would say it is the duty of that government if elected to say that you have to send arthritic patients to Watrous, whether or not it would do them any good.

PREMIER T.C. DOUGLAS, as Minister of Health, Sask. meeting Jan. 5, 1951, qu. in MacTaggart, *The first decade*, 1973, 131.

I made a pledge with myself long before I ever sat in this House in the years when I knew something about what it meant to get health service when you didn't have the money to pay for it. I made a pledge with myself that some day, if I ever had anything to do with it, people would be able to get health services, just as they are able to get educational services, as an inalienable right of being a citizen of a Christian country.

T.C. DOUGLAS, Premier, Saskatchewan, Legis. Assembly, *Debates*, Apr. 1, 1954, 59.

To our patients. This office will be closed after July 1st, 1962. We do not intend to carry on practice under the Saskatchewan Medical Care Insurance Act.

SASKATCHEWAN COLLEGE OF PHYSICIANS AND SURGEONS, text of sign supplied to all doctors, May, 1962.

Compulsory education requires compulsory financing (through taxes) and compulsory attendance at school. In contrast, a health programme requires only payment of taxes; there is no compulsion on anyone to accept or obtain services.

CANADA. ROY. COMM. ON HEALTH SERVICES, *Report*, I, 1964, 740.

No man can truthfully say he has freedom of choice if he is forced to participate in a compulsory state scheme for his medical services, whether he wishes to or not.

ERNEST MANNING, *National medicare*, [1965], 4, referring to Federal government's medicare proposal, qu. in *Queen's quart.*, 1968, 77.

A political fact of the 1970's in Ontario is that Government and Medicine are now a partnership.

A.B.R. LAWRENCE, Ont. Minister of Health, speech to the Ont. Med. Assoc., May, 1971, qu. in C.H. Shillington, *The road to medicare in Canada*, 1972, 188.

Medicine

The desire to take medicine is perhaps the greatest feature which distinguishes man from animals.

SIR WILLIAM OSLER, address, "Recent advances in medicine", Baltimore, Feb. 22, 1891.

Modern science has made to almost everyone of you the present of a few years.

SIR WILLIAM OSLER, *Montreal med. jour.*, 1895, 563.

The great republic of medicine knows and has known no national boundaries.

SIR WILLIAM OSLER, *Johns Hopkins hosp. bull.*, 1897, 161.

Gentlemen, I welcome the risk!

NORMAN BETHUNE, Saranac Lake, N.Y., 1927, hospitalized for tuberculosis, on insisting he be operated on for an experimental lung operation; qu. in Ted Allan and S. Gordon, *The scalpel, the sword*, 1952, 40.

Who put the benzedrine
In Mrs. Murphy's Ovaltine?

> LIONEL FORSYTH, arousing a somnolent
> audience at a Halifax luncheon, July,
> 1935, qu. in P. Newman, *Flame of
> power*, 1959, 135.

To summarize in a single sentence let
us say: Canadian neurology will possess French individualism and ingenuity, English fair play, and American
goodwill.

> DR. JEAN SIROIS, Quebec neurologist,
> Presidential address, Canadian Neuro-
> logical Soc., Quebec, June 7, 1956.

In all societies there have been individuals who claimed to be able to heal
their fellow man with their strange
practices; they used to be called sor-
cerers. Today they are known as doctors and their practices are known as
medicine.

> LOUIS-MARTIN TARD, *Si vous saisissez
> l'astuce*, 1968, 11. (Trans.)

Medicine Hat, Alta.

The only commonplace thing about
the spot was its name – Medicine
Hat, which struck me instantly as the
only name such a town could carry.

> RUDYARD KIPLING, *From tideway to
> tideway*, 1892.

You people in this district seem to
have all Hell for a basement.

> RUDYARD KIPLING, late 1907; qu. in
> Board of Trade, *Medicine Hat*, 1910,
> 39; ref. to abundant supply of natural
> gas.

Mediocrity

The danger of expressing democratic
equality in terms of a dull level of
mediocrity, the fatuous worship of the
common man not because he is a man
but because he is common, is too
familiar to need emphasizing.

> HILDA NEATBY, *So little for the mind*,
> 1953, 317.

Let us raise up a temple
To the cult of mediocrity,
Do nothing by halves
Which can be done by quarters.

> F.R. SCOTT, "W.L.M.K.", 1957.

If a mediocrity is someone who un-
thinkingly lives by rules made for him
by others, then this country can boldly
lay claim to being a paradise for
mediocrities.

> IRVING LAYTON, *Love where the nights
> are long*, 1962, 12.

Meetings

Always arrive at an important meeting
a few minutes late; then make an
entrance.

> W.A.C. BENNETT, political maxim, qu. in
> P. Sherman, *Bennett*, 1966, 62.

Meighen, Arthur

The gramaphone of Mackenzie and
Mann.

> R.B. BENNETT, H. of C., *Debates*, May 13,
> 1914, a reference to Meighen as the
> mouthpiece of the railway promoters.

It is too good to be true.

> W.L. MACKENZIE KING, *Diary*, July 8,
> 1920, referring to choice of Meighen as
> Prime Minister.

Our fight in the West was more *against* Meighen and his policies than *for* King.

> JOHN W. DAFOE, letter to Sir Clifford Sifton, Sept. 27, 1926. (Pub.Arch.Can.)

Meighen as a debater has, in my opinion, no equal in Canada, perhaps in the world – in English – but as a politician, an organizer, a leader, he is hopeless.

> GEORGE BLACK, letter to R.J. Manion, Jan. 12, 1940, personal and confidential. (Pub.Arch.Can.).

I felt tonight that public life in Canada had been cleansed, as though we had gone through a storm and got rid of something that was truly vile and bad, and which, had it been successful at this time, might have helped to destroy the effectiveness of our war effort. I felt most grateful to Providence for what Canada had been spared of division and strife.

> W.L. MACKENZIE KING, referring to the defeat of Meighen in federal by-election, York South, Feb. 9, 1942.

I never told a funny story in my life.

> ARTHUR MEIGHEN, to W.E. Elliott, qu. in his *Politics is funny*, 1952, 88.

Meighen had the gift of being admired by those who agreed with him.

> C.G. POWER, *A party politician: the memoirs of Chubby Power*, 1966, 73.

Memory

The glow of mind, the spirit's light,
  Which time or age can never take,
Will still shine on, undimmed and
    bright,
  And many a holy rapture wake.

> JOSEPH HOWE, "Tho' time may steal the roseate blush", 1827.

The memory of past favours is like a rainbow, bright, vivid, and beautiful; but it soon fades away. The memory of injuries is engraved on the heart, and remains for ever.

> T.C. HALIBURTON, *Sam Slick's wise saws*, 1853, I, 292.

Recollection
Will stick like smut upon one's
  memory.

> CHARLES HEAVYSEGE, *Saul*, 1857.

Summers and summers have come,
  and gone with the flight of the
    swallow;
Sunshine and thunder have been,
  storm, and winter, and frost;
Many and many a sorrow has all but
    died from remembrance.

> CHARLES G.D. ROBERTS, "The Tantramar revisited", 1887.

Here, as I sit – the sunlight on my
    face,
  And shadows of green leaves upon
    mine eyes –
My heart, a garden in a hidden place,
  Is full of folded buds of memories.

> ARCHIBALD LAMPMAN, "The child's music lesson", 1888.

And lonely memory searching through
  Found no such stars in the orbed
    past
As the first glad greeting 'twixt me
    and you,
  And the sad, mad meeting which
    was our last.

> NICHOLAS FLOOD DAVIN, "The Canadian year", 1889.

When you feel like doing a foolish thing remember that you have to live with your memory.

> ROBERT C. (BOB) EDWARDS, Calgary *Eye Opener*, Mar. 30, 1917.

Memory is cultivated and praised, but who will teach us to forget? A thousand remembrances of our folly and failure but lead us to expect more folly and failure.

GEORGE ILES, *Canadian stories*, 1918, 172.

Memory is one of the least reliable manifestations of the mind; it is the handmaid of will and desire.

J.W. DAFOE, in *Clifford Sifton*, 1931, 140.

The thought of you is like a glove
That I had hidden in a drawer:
But when I take it out again
It fits; as close as years before.

DOROTHY LIVESAY, "Time", 1932.

Speak through me, speak till I
    remember
Movement in the womb and green
    renewal
Sundrenched maples in September
And the sweep of time as a gull's wing
    slanting.

DOROTHY LIVESAY, "Speak through me", 1939.

The picture postcard and the mild watercolour and the savage oil painting, or even the hybrid camera, will not do. They render the land and sea static. The moving camera remains a moving attitude. Life keeps truly alive only in the memory and the imagination.

ETHEL WILSON, "On a Portuguese balcony", in *Tamarack rev.*, No. 1, 1956, 7.

They deadened her dither by dulling her memory.

WALLACE HAVELOCK ROBB, *Arrayed-in-wampum*, 1966, 14; qu. in "Letters in Canada", *Univ. of Tor. quart.*, No. 4, 1967, 445.

Surely, whether one man remembers a thing one way and the other another way, has nothing to do with veracity. It has to do with whether you have a good memory.

PIERRE E. TRUDEAU, qu. in Vancouver *Sun*, Mar. 20, 1976, 6.

Men

Here we are, all together
    Birds of a flock, but not of feather;
Lawyers, doctors, rogues and printers,
    A jolly lot of evil thinkers.

ROBERT MURDOCH, "A toast", 1890.

Linked to all his half-accomplished
    fellows,
Through unfrontiered provinces to
    roam —
Man is but the morning dream of
    nature,
Roused to some wild cadence weird
    and strange.

BLISS CARMAN, "Beyond the gamut", 1894.

From the seer with his snow-white
    crown
    Through every sort and condition
Of bipeds, all the way down
    To the pimp and the politician.

ARCHIBALD LAMPMAN, (d. 1899), an epigram, qu., in E.K. Brown, *On Canadian poetry*, 1943, 85.

Men will never disappoint us if we observe two rules: 1. To find out what they are; 2. To expect them to be just that.

GEORGE ILES, *Canadian stories*, 1918, 175.

Each one of them, in his fashion, was a good man. The trouble was that they *were* men, and being such, they were caught up in the strangling nets which man's plight cast over them: they could not always act the way their goodness wanted them to.

COLIN MCDOUGALL, *Execution*, 1958, 227.

Men are always out for what they can get.

ALICE MUNRO, "Postcard", 1968.

Beware of men who refer to other men as "boys".

RICHARD J. NEEDHAM, *A friend in Needham*, 1969, 34.

An attractive man is one you notice; a charming man is one who notices you.

RICHARD J. NEEDHAM, *A friend in Needham*, 1969, 35.

Men and Women

The moment a feller has a woman's secret he is that woman's master.

T.C. HALIBURTON, *The attaché*, 2nd. ser., 1844, 71.

Men are rarely intrepid in the presence of women; but women rarely stand in awe of men. Nothing differentiates the sexes more than this; but the psychological reason is difficult to discover.

ARNOLD HAULTAIN, *Hints for lovers*, 1909, 136.

A curious and latent hostility divides the sexes. It seems as if they could not approach each other without alarums and excursions. Always the presence of the one rouses anxiety in the breast of the other; they stand to arms; they resort to tactics; they manoeuvre.

ARNOLD HAULTAIN, *Hints for lovers*, 1909, 171.

Women know women. And Women know that women know men. And

Women know that men do not know women.

ARNOLD HAULTAIN, *Hints for lovers*, 1909, 206.

Men continually study women, and know nothing about them. Women never study men, and know all about them.

ROBERT C. (BOB) EDWARDS, Calgary *Eye Opener*, Oct. 15, 1910.

If a man understands one woman he should let it go at that.

ROBERT C. (BOB) EDWARDS, Calgary *Eye Opener*, Jan. 13, 1912.

Women know men better than they know themselves and better than men ever suspect.

SIR JOHN WILLISON, *Reminiscences*, 1919, 178.

To me the trying part is being a woman at all. I've come to the ultimate conclusion that I am a misfit of the worst kind. In spite of a superficial femininity – emotion with a foreknowledge of impermanence, a daring mind with only the tongue as an outlet, a greed for experience plus a slavery to convention – what the deuce are you to make of that? – as a woman? As a man, you could go ahead and stir things up *fine*.

MARJORIE PICKTHALL, letter, Dec. 27, 1919, qu. in Pierce, *Pickthall*, 104.

If only men could read women's thoughts they would take many more risks than they do.

ROBERT C. (BOB) EDWARDS, *Summer annual*, 1920, 36.

Man, in carving his future, usually finds a woman the mallet behind his chisel.

ARTHUR STRINGER, *The devastator*, 1944, 115.

It is surely a well-known fact
My dear,
That women are concave,
And men are convex?

JAMES REANEY, "The oracular portcullis", 1949.

Men who are attractive to most women are rarities, in this country, at any rate. I think that it is because a man, to be attractive, must be free to give his whole time to it, and the Canadian male is so hounded by taxes and the rigours of our climate that he is lucky to be alive, without being irresistible as well.

ROBERTSON DAVIES, *Table talk*, 1949, 71.

Take off this flesh, this hasty dress
Prepare my half-self for myself:
One unit, as a tree or stone
Woman in man, and man in womb.

DOROTHY LIVESAY, "On looking into Henry Moore", 1956.

The bitter truth about women is that their minds work precisely like those of men: the bitter truth about men is they are too vain to admit it.

ROBERTSON DAVIES, *Samuel Marchbanks' almanack*, 1967, 40.

As Goethe said, it is the Eternal Feminine that beckons us ever onward: he did not mention the Eternal Old Woman who holds us back.

ROBERTSON DAVIES, *Samuel Marchbanks' almanack*, 1967, 205.

Men and women suffer equally. The tragedy is not that they suffer, but that they suffer alone.

MARGARET LAURENCE, in Sinclair Ross, *The lamp at noon*, 1968, 11.

The difficulty is that women live in relationship to men, while men live in relationship to things.

RICHARD J. NEEDHAM, *A friend in Needham*, 1969, 30.

I have always considered it my duty to console widows for the fact their husbands are dead, married women for the fact their husbands are alive, and single women for the fact they have no husband at all.

RICHARD J. NEEDHAM, *A friend in Needham*, 1969, 4.

Every man on earth, I suppose, comes to the time when he's more interested in liquor than in women. But Canadian men seem to come to it rather early.

RICHARD J. NEEDHAM, *A friend in Needham*, 1969, 11.

Women don't necessarily want men to make love to them, but they want men to want to.

RICHARD J. NEEDHAM, *A friend in Needham*, 1969, 33.

Our society looks with astonishment, and stern disapproval, on any man who likes women as much as women like men.

RICHARD J. NEEDHAM, *A friend in Needham*, 1969, 36.

Every woman needs one man in her life who is strong and responsible. Given this security, she can proceed to do what she really wants to do – fall in love with men who are weak and irresponsible.

RICHARD J. NEEDHAM, *A friend in Needham*, 1969, 51.

Men and women are not equal; each is superior to the other.

ALDEN NOWLAN, "Scratchings", 1971.

She held
a child to her breast
and fed him
and
he became a man
She held
a man to her breast
and fed him
and
he became a child.

> M. LAKSHMI GILL, "Woman", 1972.

Behind every successful man stands a surprised woman.

> MARYON PEARSON, qu. by Lester B. Pearson, *Mike, the memoirs*, Vol. 1, 1972 (English ed., 1973, xii).

Menopause

Generations of panicky women have spawned enough untruths about the menopause to panic the next five generations.

> DR. MARION HILLIARD, *A woman doctor looks at love and life*, 1957, 153.

The change – if that's what you're determined to call it – begins at forty-five but, believe me, life begins at fifty.

> DR. MARION HILLIARD, *A woman doctor looks at love and life*, 1957, 162.

Mental Illness

If Canada had as many physically ill as there are mentally ill the government would declare a national emergency.

> DONALD SINCLAIR, Ont. Div., Canadian Mental Health Assoc., to a community services conference, Oct., 1963, qu. in *Royal Bank letter*, Jan., 1964, 4.

Merchants

Merchants are very useful, and we cannot do without them; but they live altogether by the labours of other people; and they usually live well.

> THOMAS MCCULLOCH, *The letters of Mephibosheth Stepsure*, 1821, Letter 9.

Whiskey jacks.

> ANON., traders at western forts who supplied liquor to the Indians in exchange for furs; about 1875.

The Water Street Millionaires.

> ANON., phrase applied to merchants in St. John's, Nfld. opposed to Confederation, during campaign, 1947-49.

Metaphors, Mixed

Where is the old mailed fist? Has it gone down the drain?

> A.P. MCPHILLIPS, H. of C., *Debates*, Jan. 6, 1958, 2922.

I am in sympathy with the resolution but what I say is this. Why go to work and foul our nest with a mess of pottage? We do not need it. We have got it now. Let us not take a chance.

> A.P. MCPHILLIPS, H. of C., *Debates*, Jan. 6, 1958, 2924.

Métis

They are generous, warm-hearted and brave and left to themselves, quiet and orderly. They are unhappily as unsteady as the wind in all their habits, fickle in their dispositions, credulous in their faith, and clannish in their affections.

> ALEXANDER ROSS, *The Red River settlement*, 1856, 242.

[The métis] are a harmless obsequious set of men and will, I believe, be very useful here when the country gets filled up.

> CHARLES MAIR, letter, Nov. 3, 1868, Toronto *Globe*, Dec. 14, 1868.

They will do anything but farm, will drive ore-trains four hundred miles to St. Cloud and back, – at the rate of 20 miles a day – go out on the buffalo hunt – fish – do anything but farm.

> CHARLES MAIR, letter, Nov. 27, Toronto *Globe*, Dec. 27, 1868.

The métis are a pack of cowards. They will not dare to shoot me.

> THOMAS SCOTT, to Louis Riel, Mar. 4, 1870, qu. by Paul Proulx, member of Riel's Council, in *Can. hist. rev.*, 1925, 231; executed that day.

I am the half-breed question.

> LOUIS RIEL, about 1884, in O.D. Skelton, *Life and letters of Sir Wilfrid Laurier*, 1921, Vol. 1, 296.

Do you suppose if the white settlers had the grievances the Half-breeds have, that they would not have made a disturbance? And in case they did, who is the man in Canada who would cry out against sending a commission to treat with them? These people are not rebels, they are but demanding justice.

> JAMES WALSH, qu. in Charles Mulvany, *History of the northwest rebellion of 1885*, 1885, 88.

Little enough was our learning,
  Small was our craft and skill,
But we saw the feet of the morning
  Go by – and our hearts were still.

> BLISS CARMAN, "Word from the moccasin trail", 1925.

Hell, everyone is getting to be Métis here.

> ANON., remark made in 1960's by white residents of the District of Mackenzie.

Metric Measurement

Mile, gallon and pound
root me in solid ground,
but metre, litre and gram!
Lhude sing goddamn!

> F.R. SCOTT, "Metric blues", 1973.

Middle Age

Middle age is at the door,
Hovering all too near,
Eyeing Youth with envy
And Old Age with fear.

> L.B. BIRDSALL, "Three ages", 1936.

Searching was half the world while
  searching lasted,
Finding was all the world created
  new,
Losing was hardest to believe come
  true,
But search, find, loss, not one of them
  is wasted

That shed this timeless moonlit week
  on week
In an uncumulative series. Frost
Could not quietlier gild and geld the
  fall.

> ROBERT FINCH, "Over", 1946.

Middle age has arrived when you have the choice of two temptations and you pick the one that gets you home earlier.

> JACK WASSERMAN, columnist, Vancouver *Sun*, qu. in *Liberty*, Mar., 1963.

Militia

The Men of Gore.

> ANON., the loyal forces under the command of Sir Allan MacNab during the rebellion of 1837 in Upper Canada; Gore was a district around Hamilton.

You must not take the militia seriously, for though it is useful for suppressing internal disturbances, it will not be required for the defence of the country, as the Monroe Doctrine protects us against enemy aggression.

SIR WILFRID LAURIER, 1902, to Lord Dundonald; *My army life*, 1926, 191.

Perhaps the most expensive and ineffective military system of any civilized community in the world.

COL. HAMILTON MERRITT, qu., *Can.hist. rev.*, 1923, 98.

Milk

Cow's milk is for calves.

DR. ALAN BROWN, qu. in *Maclean's*, Aug. 1, 1952, 34.

It moves direct from producer to consumer.
The cats can't get at it.
It doesn't have to be warmed up on a picnic.
It comes in such cute containers.

DR. ALAN BROWN, qu. in *Maclean's*, Aug. 1, 1952, 34, ref. to mothers' milk.

Million Dollars

I dare say my Honourable friend could cut a million dollars from this amount; but a million dollars from the War Appropriation Bill would not be a very important matter.

C.D. HOWE, H. of C., *Debates*, Nov. 19, 1945, 2251, usually contracted to "What's a million dollars?"

Millionaires

They're all millionaires in their minds.

ROBERT SERVICE, *The trail of '98*, 1910, 63, on the more than 200,000 travelers to the Klondike.

I mix a good deal with millionaires. I like them. I like their faces. I like the way they live. I like the things they eat. The more we mix together the better I like the things we mix.

STEPHEN B. LEACOCK, "How to make a million dollars", *Literary lapses*, 1910, 35.

He could make a gesture worthy of a millionaire and borrow the money to do it.

JOHN MARLYN, *Under the ribs of death*, 1957 (1971, 78).

Anyone can make a million.

MORTON SHULMAN, from the title of his book, *Anyone can make a million*, 1966.

How many millionaires do you know who aren't working for their second million? They're the ones working hardest. The people who don't want to work are those who are so poor they say "what's the use?" and give up.

RÉAL CAOUETTE, federal election campaign, Oct., 1972.

Mills

No more will the big wheel revolve
    with a clatter,
  No more the bolts turn with a
    turbulent clank,
As down the dim flume rush the
    wonderful water
  To burst forth in foam by the green
    covered bank.

ANDREW (J.R.) RAMSAY, "Atkinson's mill", 1880.

Mind

The human mind naturally adapts itself to the position it occupies. The most gigantic intellect may be dwarfed by being 'cabin'd, cribb'd, confined'. It requires a great country and great circumstances to develop great men.

SIR CHARLES TUPPER, "The political condition of British North America", a lecture in St. John, N.B., 1860.

No mind however dull can escape the brightness that comes from steady application.

SIR WILLIAM OSLER, address, "The way of life", Apr. 20, 1913.

It is good to have an open mind, but be sure it is not open at both ends.

ANON., a Toronto preacher, qu., *Willison's monthly*, Oct., 1925, 173.

His mind to him is tight as any park
where thoughts like raddled ducks are pulled
by lines unsensed on water ruled.

EARLE BIRNEY, "Introvert", 1944.

The mind continues free. This is a statement I have long considered. I have made every effort to disprove it, without success. The mind, I must conclude, is something more than a mechanism. It is, in a certain sense, above and beyond the brain, although it seems to depend upon brain action for its very existence. Yet it is free.

WILDER PENFIELD, address, Roy. Soc. of Canada, Ottawa, June 2, 1969.

Miner, Jack

At Kingsville on Lake Erie is a little patch of ground,
The stopping place for geese and swan when north or southward bound,
And every spring and autumn come thousands from the air
To visit with Jack Miner, who bids them welcome there.

EDGAR A. GUEST, "Jack Miner's fame", in *Jack Miner, his life and religion*, (1969) xliii.

Miners

They begin by being fair, but after a while cliques are formed, which run things to suit the men who are in them, or, what is just as bad, they turn the sessions into fun. Nobody can get justice from a miners' meeting when women are on one side.

JOSEPH LADUE, pioneer trader, interview recorded in 1896 by Lincoln Steffens, *McClure's mag.*, Sept., 1897, 964.

Mining

You'd maybe like to ken what pay
Miners get here for ilka day.
Jist twa pound sterling, sure as death
—
It should be four-atween us baith.
For gin ye count the cost o' livin'
There's naething left to gang and come on;
And should you bide the winter here
The shoppy-buddies'll grab your gear.
And little work ane finds to do
A' the lang dreary winter thro'.

JAMES ANDERSON, *Sawney's letters*, "Letter No. 1", 1864.

If the head of the rat is in Alaska and its tail in Montana, the body lies in British Columbia.

ANON., B.C. coast miners, about 1898, regarding gold fields.

Silver King.

ANON., re: Oliver Daunais, so-called because of his many ore discoveries in the Port Arthur region, early 1900's.

The richest half mile in the world.

ANON., a popular reference to Sir Harry Oakes' Lake Shore mine, Kirkland, Lake, Ontario.

Sure I've got
Warts on my fingers
Corns on my toes
Claims up in Porcupine
And a bad cold in my nose.
So, put on your snowshoes
And hit the trail with me
To P-o-r-c-u-p-i-n-e, — that's me.

> JOHN E. LECKIE, "The Porcupine song",
> 1910; for a variant, see MacDougall,
> *Two thousand miles of gold*, 1946, 136.

Come and see the vast natural wealth
    of this mine.
In the short space of ten years,
It has produced six American
    millionaires,
And two thousand pauperised
    Canadian families.

> F.R. SCOTT, "Natural resources", 1932.

A mine is the only thing that has its
obituary announced at the same time
as its birth notice.

> RÉNÉ LÉVESQUE, when Minister of Re-
> sources, Quebec, 1961-66, qu. in Scott &
> Astrid Young, *O'Brien*, 1967, 201.

To believe that colonization and mineral resource development go hand-in-
hand is to deny the facts of mineral
occurrence and depletion.

> W.K. BUCK AND J.F. HENDERSON, in V.W.
> Bladen, ed., *Canadian population and
> northern colonization*, 1962, 116.

Mining Promoters

You never can tell, my next visitor
might be Saint Joseph.

> GILBERT LABINE, rebuking his son who
> tried to weed out some of the grubstake-
> hungry prospectors who came to his
> office, after his discovery of radium in
> the Great Bear district on May 16, 1930.

Minorities

The rights of the minority must be
protected, and the rich are always
fewer in number than the poor.

> SIR JOHN A. MACDONALD, 1865, in Pope,
> *Confederation*, 1895, 58; a reference to
> the proposed Senate.

Number is going to make us weak, and
since under our constitutional system
number is power, we are going to find
ourselves at the mercy of those who do
not love us.

> ARCHBISHOP ALEXANDRE TACHÉ, letter to
> P. Aubert, July 17, 1872. (Trans.)

When you protect the minority in
Parliament, you are protecting the
interests of at all events a large number of people, whose interests have as
much right to be protected as those of
the majority.

> WILLIAM PUGSLEY, H. of C., *Debates*,
> 1913, 6375.

Usually minorities do not govern majorities. Except when the minority has
economic control over the area in
which it lives.

> MICHEL BRUNET, *Canadians et Canadi-
> ens*, 1954, 139. (Trans.)

Self-segregated minority.

> JEAN-CHARLES FALARDEAU, *Roots and
> values in Canadian lives*, 1961, 19,
> referring to the non-French of Quebec
> City.

The march of social progress is like a
long and straggling parade, with the
seers and prophets at its head and a
smug minority bringing up the rear.

> PIERRE BERTON, *The smug minority*,
> 1968, 157.

If I can speak as a member of one minority to another, Stick with it! Stick with it! With all your energies and abilities, play your full part in this society which you have helped to build and insist on your rights as members of it.

PIERRE E. TRUDEAU, speech, Feb. 8, 1970, to B'nai B'rith, Montreal.

No society can consent to have the decisions of its judicial and government institutions challenged or set aside by the blackmail of a minority, for that signifies the end of all social order.

JÉRÔME CHOQUETTE, Quebec Minister of Justice, press conference, Oct. 10, 1970.

Miracles

People who believe in miracles do not make much fuss when they actually encounter one.

ALICE MUNRO, "The dance of the happy shades" (short story), in vol. of the same title, 1968, 223.

Misfortunes

Misfortunes often put us wise to our own carelessness.

ROBERT C. (BOB) EDWARDS, Calgary *Eye Opener*, June 18, 1910.

Misses

A miss is as good as a mile.

THOMAS C. HALIBURTON, *Sam Slick's wise saws*, 1853, ch. 27; from earlier usage.

Missionaries

What an advantage Rome has, Protestants constantly send vulgar, underbred folk to supply their missions, Rome sends polished, highly-educated gentlemen.

EARL OF SOUTHESK, *Saskatchewan and the Rocky Mountains*, 1860, 167.

I am satisfied that the best civilizers are missionaries.

SIR JOHN A. MACDONALD, speech, 1861; qu., Biggar, *Anecdotal life*, 1891, 182.

It seems desired to make a marked distinction between Native & European Missionaries. But I hold that we are all of us now *Canadians* here & therefore none of us properly Europeans; nor can the Mission Agents properly be termed Natives though they may have mixture of Indian with European blood in their ancestry.

BISHOP W.C. BOMPAS, report to Church Missionary Society, Fort Vermilion, Alta., Nov. 18, 1878. (Pub.Arch.Can.).

When we in touch with heathens
   come,
We send them first a case of rum,
Next, to rebuke their native sin,
We send a missionary in.

STEPHEN LEACOCK, "The annexation of Natal", *College days*, 1923, 139.

Mistakes

There's many a mistake made on purpose.

THOMAS C. HALIBURTON, *Sam Slick's wise saws*, 1853, ch. 17.

If you think to run a rig on me, you have . . . barked up the wrong tree.

THOMAS C. HALIBURTON, *Human nature*, 1855, 124.

We have lots of time to make everything but mistakes.

HENRY WISE WOOD, d. 1941, qu. by Lew Hutchinson of Wheat Pool Board, Aug. 14, 1948, in William K. Rolph, *Henry Wise Wood of Alberta*, 1950, 6.

We have made mistakes, of course. Look at the Icelandic boats. An awful mistake. A blunder. It cost us a lot of money. And we have made other mistakes. I have made more than one mistake. The only man who makes no mistake is a man who does nothing, and that is a mistake. Therefore he makes one. I have made mistakes. They have been, perhaps, mistakes of the heart.

> JOSEPH R. SMALLWOOD, Legis. Assem., Newfoundland, March, 1951, qu. in R. Gwyn, *Smallwood*, 1968, 142.

When I make a boob, it's a beaut.

> GEORGE HEES, Trade Minister in Diefenbaker cabinet, qu. in Vancouver *Sun*, Sept. 15, 1961, 24.

Children make mistakes and the total eradication of these mistakes is impossible.

> WILLIAM E. BLATZ, *Human security*, 1966, 6.

The value of making mistakes is to learn which ones you enjoyed the most, so you can make them all over again.

> RICHARD J. NEEDHAM, *A friend in Needham*, 1969, 17.

I think for a moment that somewhere a mistake has been made. A simple one but one that affects us all. I wish there was someone who could tell me.

> DON BAILEY, *If you hum me a few bars I might remember the tune*, 1973, 154.

Mistresses

Mistresses tend to get a steady diet of whipped cream, but no meat and potatoes, and wives often get the reverse, when both would like a bit of each.

> MERLE SHAIN, *Some men are more perfect than others*, 1973, 36.

Mob

We have scorned the belief of our
    fathers
And cast their quiet aside;
To take the mob for our ruler
And the voice of the mob for our
    guide.

> BLISS CARMAN, "Twilight in Eden", 1925.

An aggregate of egos is a mob.

> NORTHROP FRYE, *The well-tempered critic*, 1963, 43.

Moderation

Moderation is the wisdom which never quite exhausts its reservoirs of power; which never permits depletion, and is, therefore, never exhausted.

> BLISS CARMAN, *The kinship of nature*, 1904, 285.

Nothing is more characteristic of Canadians than the inclination to be moderate.

> VINCENT MASSEY, *On being Canadian*, 1948, 30.

Pragmatism, moderation, the absence of ideological dogmatism are part of the Canadian's individuality, of his political style.

> PHILIPPE AUBERT DE LA RUE, *Canada incertain*, 1962, 127. (Trans.)

Our political and intellectual elites, true to the Canadian tradition, are moderately concerned about the impending demise of their country, and moderately determined to do something about it, on condition that whatever be done be moderately done. This moderation will be the death of us.

> GAD HOROWITZ, qu. in *Maclean's*, Feb., 1970, 2.

Modern Times

The world has drifted·far from its old anchorage and no man can with certainty prophesy what the outcome will be.

> SIR R. BORDEN, Nov. 11, 1918, in his diary, *Memoirs*, 1938.

Modernity is not a fad, it is the feeling for actuality.

> D.C. SCOTT, "Poetry and progress", 1922.

Modern life is conceived in the image of Victorian humanitarianism and the very people who scorn Victorian piety are those who are most vociferous when the social dividends which it entailed on its posterity cease to be paid to them.

> A.R.M. LOWER, *This most famous stream*, 1954, 127.

Who can forgive these times
That drive into cell, thread and bone
The anguish of breaking?

> MIRIAM WADDINGTON, "These times", 1955.

The mark of our time is its revulsion against imposed patterns.

> MARSHALL MCLUHAN, *Understanding media*, 1964, Intro. 5.

It is clear that modern man is a different creature, mentally, psychologically, and socially, from Biblical man, medieval man and, probably, Victorian man.

> PIERRE BERTON, *The comfortable pew*, 1965, 139.

I could not face the fact that we were living at the end of Western Christianity.

> GEORGE P. GRANT, *Technology and empire*, 1969, 44.

The evidence is there
but the mind cannot
bring itself
wholly to believe in
a dynasty of mad men.

> ALDEN NOWLAN, "Decline and fall", 1971.

The age of the Canadian rip-off.

> JACK MCCLELLAND, qu. by Clare MacCulloch in *Fiddlehead,* No. 100, 1974, 88.

Modesty

Modesty is brought forward and made way for. Assumption has the door shut in its face.

> T.C. HALIBURTON, *Sam Slick's wise saws,* 1853, II, 141.

Modesty is not one of the things taught in our public schools; on the contrary, girls at those schools learn to be boisterous, immodest, screaming, kicking creatures, such as was never seen even among pagans. Our public schools are destroyers of modesty, an abomination, and a disgrace.

> ARCHBISHOP JAMES V. CLEARY, Kingston *Daily news,* Nov. 16, 1887; qu. in C.E. Phillips, *Development of education in Canada,* 1957, 542.

I consider that modesty is the great national vice of Canada and the cultivation of a good healthy national conceit one of the highest duties of patriotism.

> JOHN LEWIS, in *Can. mag.,* Oct., 1900, 495.

Modesty is the most complex and the most varied of the emotions.

> ARNOLD HAULTAIN, *Hints for lovers,* 1909, 41.

If you drive modesty out of the world, you will go a long way toward driving out sexual morality also.

CHARLES F. PAUL, *Saturday night*, July 18, 1914, 1.

Canadians are happily still by temperament and training quite incapable of flaunting their nationality. Modesty and restraint are deeply ingrained Canadian characteristics.

R.H. HUBBARD, in J. Park, ed., *Culture of contemporary Canada*, 1957, 96.

If God had meant women to be modest, He'd have given them three hands.

RICHARD J. NEEDHAM, *A friend in Needham*, 1969, 36.

Monarchy

I, A: B: do promise and declare that I will maintain & defend to the utmost of my Power the Authority of the King in His Parliament as the Supreme Legislature of this Province.

GREAT BRITAIN. PRIVY COUNCIL, *Instructions to Lord Dorchester as Governor of Lower Canada*, Sept. 16, 1791. Oath required of settlers.

The Kingdom of Canada.

SIR JOHN BEVERLEY ROBINSON originated 1822; later adopted by Sir John A. Macdonald in first draft of British North America Act, 1867; mss. in Macdonald's handwriting in Public Archives.

In our Federation the monarchical principle would form the leading feature, while on the other side of the lines, judging by the past history and present condition of the country, the ruling power was the will of the mob, the rule of the populace.

SIR GEORGE-ÉTIENNE CARTIER, *Confederation debates*, 1865, 59.

The Executive Government and authority of and over Canada is hereby declared to continue and be vested in the Queen.

BRITISH NORTH AMERICA ACT, 1867, III, 9.

Our form of government is a representative monarchy.

SIR WILFRID LAURIER, speech in Quebec, June, 1877, before the Club Canadien. (Trans.)

America owes much to the imbecility of Louis XV and the ambitious vanity and personal dislikes of his mistress.

FRANCIS PARKMAN, *Montcalm and Wolfe*, 1884, Vol. 1, Intro., 3.

The perpetuation of monarchical forms, even though the life has long since gone out of them, doubtless tends to act as a curb to the fullest expression of democracy.

A.R.M. LOWER, in Can.Hist.Assoc., *Report*, 1930, 70.

Why should the Liberal party be in a position to decide who is to be King of the Canadian people?

J.S. WOODSWORTH, H. of C., *Debates*, Jan. 15, 1937, 14.

Surely if the King of the United Kingdom can be distinguished for legal purposes from the King of Canada, then the recognition of the King of the United Kingdom as King of Canada can wait until there is time to call parliament. If the selection of the King of Canada is of such minor importance, the question arises: why a King at all?

J.S. WOODSWORTH, H. of C., *Debates*, Jan. 15, 1937, 15.

[Americans were] astonished and even pained to find that Canadians preferred the shackles of monarchy.

JOHN MACCORMAC, *American and world mastery*, 1942, 253.

Now know ye that by and with the advice of Our Privy Council for Canada We do by this Our Royal Proclamation establish for Canada Our Royal Style and Titles as follows, namely, in the English language: Elizabeth the Second, by the Grace of God of the United Kingdom, Canada and Her other Realms and Territories Queen, Head of the Commonwealth, Defender of the Faith.

CANADA. PRIVY COUNCIL, "Proclamation of the Queen's title," May 28, 1953.

The moral core of Canadian nationhood is found in the fact that Canada is a monarchy and in the nature of monarchical allegiance. As America is united at bottom by the covenant, Canada is united at the top by allegiance. Because Canada is a nation founded on allegiance and not on compact, there is no process in becoming Canadian akin to conversion, there is no pressure for uniformity, there is no Canadian way of life.

W.L. MORTON, *The Canadian identity*, 1961, 85.

Nothing touched me quite so much as this comment in a Canadian newspaper: "He made the Crown Canadian." It was too generous a tribute; but that was what I had tried to do.

VINCENT MASSEY, *What's past is prologue*, 1963, 516.

Her Majesty is, for us, a symbol of a way of life which enabled us to grow by our own means and according to our own wishes.

RÉAL CAOUETTE, H. of C., *Debates*, Oct. 14, 1964, 9025.

In the present political context, it is useful to the legislative process. But whether this should be something permanent is a different question.

GUY FAVREAU, Minister of Justice, in reply to Conservative charges that the Liberals were planning to end the monarchy and make Canada a republic, Feb., 1965.

Tell me, are our people in Quebec still loyal?

PRINCE PHILIP, question asked of James Eayrs at a conference in Canada in 1967, qu. in Toronto *Star*, Feb. 14, 1972, 6.

If you're asking what I think about the monarchy, I will tell you quite frankly I couldn't care less.

PIERRE E. TRUDEAU, interview, CBC, "Twenty million questions", Mar. 16, 1967.

The monarchy was imposed on us, or, at best, we accepted it grudgingly, absent-mindedly, or because we dassn't do anything else.

EUGENE FORSEY, paraphrase of a common statement, dismissed as one of the seven devils of our pseudo-history in "Our present discontents", speech, Acadia Univ., Oct. 19, 1967.

If at any stage people feel that it has no further part to play then for goodness sake let's end the thing on amicable terms without having a row about it.

PRINCE PHILIP, press conference, Ottawa, Oct. 18, 1969.

It is completely a misconception to believe that the monarchy exists in the interests of the monarch. It exists solely in the interest of the people. We don't come here for our health. We can think of other ways of enjoying ourselves.

PRINCE PHILIP, press conference, Ottawa, Oct. 18, 1969.

There has been no change in policy, whatever it was, in regard to the relations between the Queen and the government.

> PIERRE E. TRUDEAU, H. of C., *Debates*, Apr. 29, 1970, 6409.

It is as Queen of Canada that I am here. Queen of Canada and of all Canadians, not just of one or two ancestral strains. I would like the Crown to be seen as a symbol of national sovereignty belonging to all. It is not only a link between Commonwealth nations, but between Canadian citizens of every national origin and ancestry.

> ELIZABETH II, address at State Dinner, Royal York Hotel, Toronto, June 26, 1973.

Money

Halifax currency.

> ANON., term used for the Spanish silver dollar rated at five shillings of about twenty cents each in Nova Scotia; in use 1750-1871.

Presents of money injure both the giver and receiver, and destroy the equilibrium of friendship, and diminish independence and self-respect.

> T.C. HALIBURTON, *Sam Slick*, 1838, 28.

The holey dollar.

> ANON., Prince Edward Island phrase for the Spanish dollar with a round hole cut in the centre; early 19th. century.

The York Shilling.

> ANON., the Spanish *real* in terms of the New York price of 12 1/2 cents used in Ontario, and thus distinguished from the Halifax shilling of about 20 cents; 1800-1850.

It is easier to make money than to save it; one is exertion, the other self-denial.

> T.C. HALIBURTON, *Sam Slick's wise saws*, 1853, II, 145.

The Cent Belt.

> ANON., a term common in British Columbia, middle 19th century, in reference to Ontario and Quebec; old residents of British Columbia prided themselves on using no sum less than a bit, or, twelve and a half cents. In 1861 newspapers were still sold for a bit, either a liberal fifteen cents, or a stingy ten cents.

'Tis money rules the world now,
    It's rank and education,
It's power and knowledge, sense and
        worth,
    And pious reputation.
Get cash, and 'gainst all human ills,
    You're armed and you're defended,
For in it even here on earth,
    All heaven is comprehended.

> ALEXANDER MCLACHLAN, "Young Canada", 1861.

A Blanket.

> ANON., originally a Hudson's Bay Co. note used in paying wages, during late 19th century; in the West, a term for a dollar bill.

A Shinplaster.

> ANON., paper currency of 25 cents introduced by Sir Francis Hincks, 1870, to drive out American silver.

Does thy soul to greed incline?
Dost thou treasure but for time?
Bolts and bars asunder fall;
Death shall rob thee of it all.
Hither thou canst nothing take:
Something *do*, for mercy's sake.

> ALEXANDER MCLACHLAN, *Can. birthday book*, 1887, 92.

A little of the needful.

> ANON., a popular phrase in New Brunswick; 19th century.

National Currency School.

> ANON., a small group, popularly called "The Rag Babies", precursors of modern Social Credit and the "funny money" people of the nineteenth century, comprising Thomas Galbraith and their House of Commons spokesman, William Wallace, and others, 1867-1900.

To us the money-getting art
  Is but the one thing real;
We seldom cherish in our heart
  A holy, high ideal.

> ALEXANDER MCLACHLAN, "Rein auld Adam in", 1900.

After all the easiest way to get money is to earn it.

> PETER MCARTHUR, *To be taken with salt*, 1903, 156.

Too many men salt away money in the brine of other people's tears.

> ROBERT C. (BOB) EDWARDS, Calgary *Eye Opener*, Mar. 30, 1917.

The size of a dollar depends entirely upon how many more you have.

> ROBERT C. (BOB) EDWARDS, *Summer annual*, 1920, 85.

There is no God but money, and Canada with its unparalleled natural resources is the most God-fearing country in the world.

> CARLETON W. STANLEY, *Hibbert jour.*, 1922, 280.

You've heard money talking? Did you understand the message?

> MARSHALL MCLUHAN, *The mechanical bride*, 1951, 138.

When you impose money on every situation, you destroy man's relations with one another. Everyone is then either employer or employee. Only obligations remain.

> NORMAN WILLIAMS, "The mountain", a play, 1956, in *Worlds apart*, 109.

Today, money speaks in much louder tones, and learning in much humbler, while both law and medicine have cut down their own status by leaning too far towards the cash.

> ARTHUR R.M. LOWER, *Canadians in the making*, 1958, 309.

Can-dollars.

> OSCAR ALTMAN, report to the U.S. Joint Econ. Comm.'s Sub-comm. on International Exchange and Payments, Jan., 1963, refers to U.S. dollars supplied to Europe by Canadian banks in New York City.

The love of money meant that as other passion receded, a man's life did not become less meaningful.

> JOHN KENNETH GALBRAITH, *The Scotch*, 1964, 28.

The love of money meant that a man's emotions were reliably engaged until the day he died.

> JOHN KENNETH GALBRAITH, *The Scotch*, 1964, 29.

Everybody wants to make money — but how many want it enough to work for it?

> ROY THOMSON, qu. in R. Braddon, *Roy Thomson of Fleet Street*, 1965, 585.

Funds, not sex, are at the root of human motivation.

> HUGH HOOD, *A game of touch*, 1970, 22.

Some of the young men walked
with a sway of the hip
as if they had conquered Montreal
  (which none of them knew)
or all the gold-mines of the north.
And like a messianic pronouncement
one word was heard again and again:
money.

> WALTER BAUER, "Emigrants", in *Imagine seeing you here*, ed. by R. Charlesworth, 1975, 93.

Monopoly

Crow Owns Air Jay Must Work Keep
Crow Fat

J.W. BENGOUGH, "Lesson IV", *The up-to-date primer*, 1896, 8.

Free enterprise does not, of course,
  mean silly competition,
And cutting prices is a sin for which
  there's no remission;
A "Gentleman's Agreement" is the
  best of all devices
To stabilize our dividends, our
  markets, and our prices;
For taking risks we've little love, we
  set our whole affection
On something like monopoly, with
  adequate protection.

JOHN D. KETCHUM, "Hymn to free enterprise", qu. in *The nation*, Mar. 18, 1944, 329.

Montcalm, Marquis De

I am extolled in order to foster Canadian prejudice.

MONTCALM, letter to his home in France, about 1758. (Trans.)

In truth the funeral of Montcalm was
the funeral of New France.

FRANCIS PARKMAN, *Montcalm and Wolfe*, 1884.

Montcalm and Wolfe! Wolfe and
  Montcalm!
Quebec, thy storied citadel
Attest in burning song and psalm
How here thy heroes fell!

CHARLES G.D. ROBERTS, "Canada", 1887.

Montreal

A little Babylon which has overwhelmed and intoxicated all the [Indian] nations with the wine of its prostitution.

ABBÉ FRANÇOIS BELMONT, (d.1732), *Histoire du Canada*. (Mss., trans.)

It is impossible to walk the streets of
Montreal on a Sunday or other holiday, when the shops are all closed,
without receiving the most gloomy
impressions. The whole city appears
one vast prison.

EDWARD ALLEN TALBOT, *Five years' residence in the Canadas*, Vol. 1, 1824, 66.

The heat, while we were in Montreal,
was intolerable – the filth intolerable
– the flies intolerable – the bugs intolerable – the people intolerable –
the jargon intolerable. I lifted up my
hands in thankfulness when I set foot
again in "these United States." The
only inn *existing* in Montreal was
burnt down three years ago, and
everything you ask for was burnt
down in it.

FANNY KEMBLE, letter Dec. 21, 1834, to
Charles Mathews, in his *Memoirs of
Charles Mathews*, 1838-39, Vol. 4, 321.

Neither driving nor walking can be
much enjoyed in the streets of Montreal.

JAMES SILK BUCKINGHAM, *Canada, Nova
Scotia, New Brunswick and other British provinces of North America*, 1843,
108.

The people, of whom there are but
two, the rich holding high estate, the
poor, holding nothing. There is nothing *middling* in Montreal. One of the
said two people, the high, are dissatisfied that they can't be higher; the
other, the low, are striving to be lower;
and it is probable that half a century
will see them attain their object.

CAPTAIN HORTON RHYS, *A theatrical trip
for a wager* . . . 1861, 52.

We are satisfied that Montreal must
make active exertions to maintain her
position as a business centre, or she
will be cut off by Toronto, which is
making vigorous and well-directed efforts to that end.

MONTREAL *GAZETTE*, Jan. 22, 1870.

This is the first time I was ever in a city where you couldn't throw a brick without breaking a church window.

MARK TWAIN, speech in Montreal, Dec. 5, 1881.

Reign on, majestic Ville-Marie!
Spread wide thine ample robes of
   state;
The heralds cry that thou art great,
And proud are thy young sons of thee.
Mistress of half a continent . . .

W.D. LIGHTHALL, "Montreal", 1889.

Montreal was the most dangerous city in the western world to be born in.

J.T. COPP, Canadian Historical Assoc., *Historical papers 1972*, 162, on health conditions, 1890's.

We get up in the morning and switch on one of Holt's lights, cook breakfast on Holt's gas, smoke one of Holt's cigarettes, read the morning news printed on Holt's paper, ride to work on one of Holt's streetcars, sit in an office heated by Holt's coal, then at night go to a film in one of Holt's theatres.

ANON., a Montrealer in the 1920's, qu. in Peter Newman, *Flame of power*, 1959, 23; ref. to Sir Herbert Holt.

The man who dares to offend the Montreal interests is the sort of man that the people are going to vote for today.

WILLIAM IRVINE, note to Arthur Meighen, Sept. 25, 1924. (Pub.Arch.Can.)

The older generation of wealthy Montrealer live comfortably and smugly on "The Mountain" alike in their devotion to their duty, to their tribal instincts, and to economic status as the measure of all things.

A.R.M. LOWER, in *Can.hist.rev.*, 1945, 327.

O city metropole, isle riverain!
Your ancient pavages and sainted
   routes
Traverse my spirit's conjured avenues!

A.M. KLEIN, "Montreal", 1948.

Grand port of navigations, multiple
The lexicons uncargo'd at your quays,
Sonnant though strange to me; but
   chiefest, I,
Auditor of your music, cherish the
Joined double-melodied vocabulaire
Where English vocable and roll
   Ecossic,
Mollified by the parle of French
Bilinguefact your air!

A.M. KLEIN, "Montreal", 1948.

If cities have gender, then Montreal, the second-largest French speaking city in the world, is masculine in every one of the innumerable ways in which a self-confident and self-satisfied man can display his maleness.

HUGH MACLENNAN, in *Thirty and three*, 1954, 64.

Montreal functions not because *Canadiens* and Canadians are brought up to admire each other's virtues, but because each group is trained from the cradle to think itself superior to the other, and at the same time to consider it thoroughly bad taste to interfere in the other's local affairs.

HUGH MACLENNAN, *Thirty and three*, 1954, 67.

Here in Montreal you can still understand what it means to stand on the edge of a new world.

JAMES MORRIS, Manchester *Guardian*, reprinted in Ottawa *Journal*, Nov. 2, 1960, 8.

City of eye shadow and athletic priests
French poodles and exquisite buttocks;
City of poets with enormous egos.
And the wild high courting yard of the
　　mountain.

> AL PURDY, "Towns", 1962.

Just as there are no Canadians, there
are no Montrealers. Ask a man who he
is and he names a race.

> LEONARD COHEN, *The favourite game*,
> 1963, Bk. 2, sec. 19.

Some say that no one ever leaves
Montreal, for that city, like Canada
itself, is designed to preserve the past,
a past that happened somewhere else.

> LEONARD COHEN, *The favourite game*,
> 1963, Bk. 2, sec. 19.

Moon

The moon like a paper lantern
Is lifted over the hill,
And below in the silent valley
Even the aspens are still.

> BLISS CARMAN, "The book of Pierrot",
> 1899.

June comes, and the moon comes
Out of the curving sea,
Like a frail golden bubble,
To hang in the lilac tree.

> BLISS CARMAN, "May and June", 1900.

The moon floated down
a river between two clouds
melted the stone banks and they
were gone.

> LOUIS DUDEK, "Night piece", 1946.

After the landing
on that torn landscape of the mind
and the first steps are taken
let a handful of moondust run thru my
　　hand
and escape back to itself
for these others
the ghosts of grief and loss
walking beyond the Sea of Serenity.

> AL PURDY, "Nine bean-rows on the
> moon", *Maclean's*, July, 1969, 8.

Their rockets changed nothing.
The moon is mysterious
still to those who have been alone with
　　her.

> ALDEN NOWLAN, "The moon landing",
> 1971.

Morality

In points of morals the average woman
is, even for business, too crooked.

> STEPHEN B. LEACOCK, "The woman ques-
> tion", *Maclean's*, Oct., 1915.

Canada is too moral.

> DOUGLAS BUSH, "Plea for Original Sin",
> *Can. forum*, Apr., 1922.

The basic issue behind today's problems is the struggle for moral authority.

> MARCUS LONG, "The issues behind to-
> day's problems", *Food for thought*,
> Nov., 1952, 16.

Incredibly, the moral structure of our
society is based on a complete reversal
of natural morality. Few societies have
gotten as far away from reality as ours
has.

> ALDEN A. NOWLAN, *Delta*, No. 9,
> 1959, 28.

Morality is nothing more nor less than
self-discipline.

> INSPECTOR HERBERT THURSTON, Toronto
> Police Morality Squad, qu. in *Ma-
> clean's*, Jan. 4, 1964, 14.

A morality which does not scorn joy and relates it to suffering may perhaps arise. Whether or how this will happen in our particular civilization cannot be determined. What can be determined however, within this present, is enough to enable us to at least try, with the very Word Himself, to take the cup and give thanks.

> GEORGE P. GRANT, *Philosophy in the mass age*, 1966, 111.

My whole position on morality versus criminality is that the criminal law should not be used to express the morality of any one group, religious or pressure groups, or others. The criminal law is not made to punish sin, it is meant to prevent or deter anti-social conduct. And this is a question not of religion; it is a question of public morality.

> PIERRE E. TRUDEAU, speech, Mount Royal Liberal Association, Montreal, Nov. 25, 1971.

Morals

They ate and drank and fought, it's
    true,
And when the zest was on they slew;
But yet their most tempestuous
    quarrels
Were never prejudiced by morals.

> E.J. PRATT, *The witches' brew*, 1925, 21.

Psychology and even to a certain extent the study of history all seem to lead to an endless relativity in faith and morals. There are no absolutes.

> REV. J.S. THOMSON, Moderator, address, Council, United Church of Canada, Ottawa, Sept. 17, 1958.

The state has no business in the bedrooms of the nation.

> PIERRE E. TRUDEAU, interview, Ottawa, Dec. 21, 1967, referring to revision of parts of the Criminal Code.

She's got the morals of a man.

> ANON., a co-ed student at Mount Allison Univ. on a fellow co-ed, qu. by Douglas How, *Weekend*, Oct. 2, 1971, 19.

Morning

Oh keep the world for ever at the
    dawn,
Ere yet the opals, cobweb-strung have
    dried;
Ere yet too bounteous gifts have
    marred the morn
Or fading stars have died.

> MARJORIE PICKTHALL, "Dawn", submitted to Toronto *Mail and empire*, 1900.

The waters ebb from the papered
    room, the air is filled with light;
Bacon smells and coffee smells begin
    the day's delight;
On to the public bus again and on to
    the big machine
Whose lop is a well-run kingdom,
    ruled by a decorous queen.

> GEORGE JOHNSTON, "The queen of lop", 1959.

morning spreads
its soft fat fingers
over our faces
pokes them
into our eyes
sur—
prising us awake
with soft punches

> bp NICHOL, "Sequence", 1970.

Mosaic

It is indeed a mosaic of vast dimensions and great breadth, essayed of the Prairies.

> VICTORIA HAYWARD, *Romantic Canada*, 1922, 187. The idea of a "mosaic" in ref. to Canada has been used by John M. Gibbon, *Canadian mosaic*, 1938; and John Porter, *The vertical mosaic*, 1965.

Mosquitoes

Neither are there any Snakes, Toads, Serpents, or any other venemous Wormes, that ever were knowne to hurt any man in that Countrey, but onely a very little nimble Fly, (the least of all other Flies) which is called a Muskeito; those flies seeme to have a great power and authority upon all loytering and idle people that come to the New-found-land: for they have this property, that when they finde any such lying lazily, or sleeping in the Woods, they will presently bee more nimble to seize on them, then any Sargeant will bee to arrest a man for debt.

> RICHARD WHITBOURNE, A discourse and discovery of New-found-land, 1622, [109].

Such an infinit abundance of bloud-thirsty Muskitoes, that we were more tormented with them than ever we were with the hot weather.

> THOMAS JAMES, The strange and danger-ous voyage; North-west passage, 1631.

Abundance of Musketers & at night coud not gett wood Enough for to make a smoke to Clear ym.

> HENRY KELSEY, Journal of a voyage, 1691, in the Kelsey papers, 1929, 26.

The mosquitoes are a terrible plague in this country. You may think that mosquitoes cannot hurt, but if you do you are mistaken, for they will swell your legs and hands so that some persons are both blind and lame for some days. They grow worse every year and they bite the English the worst.

> LUKE HARRISON, letter to William Harri-son, June 30, 1774 from Fort Cumber-land, N.S., qu. in H. Trueman, The Chignecto Isthmus, 1902, 214.

Darwin's theory of the survival of the fittest is, as applied to mosquitoes, a transparent fraud.

> ALEXANDER SUTHERLAND, A summer in prairie-land, 1881, 39.

Oh, pray, do not bother to close the windows. I think they are all in now.

> SIR JOHN THOMPSON, to Lady Minto when dining at Rideau Hall, 1893.

Motherhood

Motherhood is the goal of woman-hood.

> ARNOLD HAULTAIN, Hints for lovers, 1909, 35.

Brush from young women's eyes
Cloud of illusion —
She who in travail lies
She shall in travail rise.

> JESSIE L. BEATTIE, "Motherhood", 1940.

So up with test-tube babies
and harvest just prime seed
away away with womanhood
male sperm is all we need
and when we have dispensed with love
and passion and emotion
we'll all go back past embryos
to blobs of mental motion
aided and exceeded by
the robot and computer
which we'll develop out
to be more useful and much cuter.

> MARY YUILL, "A single parent turns off and on", qu. in M. Anderson, Mother was not a person, 1972, 158.

Mothers

Our children climb upon her knee
And lie upon her breast,
And ah! her mission seems to me
The highest and the best;
And so I say with pride untold,
And love beyond degree,
This woman with the heart of gold
She just keeps house for me.

JEAN BLEWETT, "She just keeps house for me", 1897.

Mothers, you have a right to see that no government be permitted to pass laws (in the Navy matter) destining for death those children whom you brought forth for the country.

HENRI BOURASSA, speech in Victoriaville, Sept. 17, 1911.

There will be a singing in your heart,
There will be a rapture in your eyes;
You will be a woman set apart,
You will be so wonderful and wise.
You will sleep, and when from dreams
  you start,
As of one that wakes in Paradise,
There will be a singing in your heart,
There will be a rapture in your eyes.

ROBERT W. SERVICE, "The mother", 1912.

The tender hands, the loving care
  That filled my childhood years;
The gentle songs at evening sung,
  That lulled away my fears;
The tolerance, her simple faith,
  Through life's impetuous reign;
Her silent watching helpfulness,
  Come back to me again.

JAMES C. SINGER, "Mother", 1929.

Our silent strength no help in this
  assault
We watched her time creep closer by
  the hour,
And every lengthened intake, each
  return,
Brought back some tender moment of
  her succour.
Each one of us was hers, and none his
  own.

F.R. SCOTT, "Bedside", 1945.

It is my opinion and I hope that you will agree with me, that there is no reason for burning incense to a woman simply because she has fulfilled the natural functions of her sex — because she has been no skulker of her maternal responsibility. This type of down-daunted mother is rapidly passing out, for we are coming to see that a mother who lets herself subside into a kind of burnt-sacrifice upon what is called the "family altar" is not really a good mother, nor a good citizen.

EMILY MURPHY, "Janey Canuck", qu. in B.H. Sanders, *Emily Murphy, crusader*, 1945, 264.

What is a man's mother but a gateway through which he enters the world, and which he leaves farther behind with every step?

ROBERTSON DAVIES, *At the gates of the righteous*, in *Eros at breakfast and other plays*, 1949, 121.

And I was born a boy for I bore a boy
And walked with him in the proud
And nervous satrapy of man —
Though who can hide the accent of a
  mother tongue?

ANNE WILKINSON, "I was born a boy . . . ", 1955.

When I saw my mother's head on the
  cold pillow,
Her white waterfalling hair in the
  cheeks' hollows,
I thought, quietly circling my grief, of
  how
She had loved God but cursed
  extravagantly his creatures.

IRVING LAYTON, "Keine Lazarovitch, 1870-1959", 1961.

Maternal dislike is more crippling than clubs.

JUNE CALLWOOD, in Canadian Mental Health Assn., *Probings*, 1968, 26.

A sweater is something you put on when mother feels cold.

ANON., qu. in Larry Solway, *The day I invented sex*, 1971, 8.

M adonna of my flesh
O varies and breasts
T ouch my mind and
H old my trembling fears.
E mbrace me,
R avaged woman, mother.

MARY SACHLA, qu. in M. Anderson, *Mother was not a person*, 1972, 124.

Motives

I don't care a rap *why* people do things in novels or real life. Working out motives is about as useful as a signboard on Niagara Falls.

SIR WILLIAM VAN HORNE, to a McGill English professor, qu. in P. Newman, *Flame of power*, 1959, 89.

Mountain Climbing

I said that he fell straight to the ice
　　where they found him,
And none but the sun and the
　　incurious clouds have lingered
Around the marks of that day on the
　　ledge of the Finger,
That day, the last of my youth, on the
　　last of our mountains.

EARLE BIRNEY, "David", 1942.

Mountains

I would not give the bleakest knoll on the bleakest hill of Scotland, for all these mountains in a heap!

CAPT. JOHN GORDON, commander, Royal Navy Pacific Squadron, 1844, on the B.C. mountains.

Sea of mountains.

VISCOUNT MILTON and W.B. CHEADLE, *North-west passage by land*, 1865, 366, has "Cariboo is a sea of mountains and pine-clad hills". The phrase "sea of

mountains" was used by Edward Blake in his speech at Aurora, Ont. Oct. 3, 1874 in "That inhospitable country, that sea of mountains" when referring to B.C. and the Rockies. Used also by the Victoria *British colonist*, 1871; and by George M. Grant, *From ocean to ocean*, 1873, 267 as a variant "seas of mountains".

Here, with the grand memorials of the great Creator surrounding me, I could spend the rest of my days content.

SIR JOHN A. MACDONALD, speech in Yale, B.C., July 22, 1886.

The common waters, the familiar
　　woods,
And the great hills' inviolate solitudes.

CHARLES G.D. ROBERTS, "Ave", 1892.

Cooling rill and sparkling fountain,
　　Purple peak and headland bold,
Precipice and snow-cloud mountain;
　　Lofty summits rising grandly into
　　　　regions clear and cold,
　　And innumerable rivers that
　　　　majestically rolled.

JAMES DE MILLE, "Behind the veil", 1893.

There's a land where the mountains
　　are nameless,
And the rivers all run God knows
　　where.

ROBERT W. SERVICE, "The spell of the Yukon", 1907.

The lonely sunsets flare forlorn
　　Down valleys dreadly desolate;
The lonely mountains soar in scorn
　　As still as death, as stern as fate.

ROBERT W. SERVICE, "The land that God forgot", 1907.

They saw the stars in heaven hung,
　　They heard the great Sea's birth,
They know the ancient pain that
　　　　wrung
　　The entrails of the Earth.

FREDERICK GEORGE SCOTT, "The storm", 1910.

I am homesick for the mountains —
My heroic mother hills —
And the longing that is on me
No solace ever stills.

> BLISS CARMAN, "The cry of the hill-
> born", 1912.

There is a mountain everyone must
climb,
Different for all yet it is the same.
We start to climb before we have a
name,
And nick the summit in our nick of
time.

> ROBERT FINCH, "The mountain", 1948.

The Colin Range was an amazing
place, a kind of cubists' paradise full of
geometric formations, all waiting for
the abstract painter.

> A.Y. JACKSON, *A painter's country*, 1958,
> 87.

Movies

The decent, the fair, win prizes; the
wicked
Their just deserts.
The prince weds Cinderella, and
virtue triumphs
Until it hurts.

> A.M. KLEIN, "Of psalmody in the tem-
> ple", 1938.

Photography and cinema have abolished realism as too easy; they substitute themselves for realism.

> MARSHALL MCLUHAN, *Counterblast*,
> 1954 (1969, 51).

Was he the director of this film of his
life? Was God? Was the devil? He was
an actor in it, but if God were the
director that was no reason why he
should not constantly appeal to Him to
change the ending.

> MALCOLM LOWRY, *Dark as the grave
> wherein my friend is laid*, 1968, 249.

The movies have always made their
money more or less dishonestly, usually by guessing what lies people want to
be told at a specific moment and then
telling them those lies.

> ROBERT FULFORD, *Marshall Delaney at
> the movies*, 1974, 135.

Mowat, Sir Oliver

You damned pup, I'll slap your chops
for you!

> SIR JOHN A. MACDONALD, to Sir Oliver
> Mowat, H. of Assembly, Apr. 19, 1861.

Mowat, that little tyrant.

> SIR JOHN A. MACDONALD, speech at York-
> ville, June 1, 1882, on Sir Oliver Mowat,
> Premier of Ontario.

Mud

A mixture of putty and bird-lime
would perhaps most nearly describe it.

> ALEX STAVELEY HILL, *From home to
> home, autumn wanderings in the
> north-west in the years 1881-1884*,
> 1885, 60, referring to Winnipeg.

The mud in our clearing is argillaceous, saponaceous, contumacious, and
anything but gracious.

> J.J. PROCTER, *The philosopher in the
> clearing*, 1897, 169.

Gumbo is the bane and the saviour of
Manitoba. It is a rich argillaceous
mould or loam formed by the lake
deposits and forest growth of ages, and
resting upon a clay sub-soil. Its dark
colour is due in part to the long
accumulation of the charred grasses
left by annual prairie fires and the
collection of decayed vegetable and
animal matter. But it is literally a
profusion of stored-up wealth.

> THOMAS WILBY, *A motor tour through
> Canada*, 1914, 157.

Munsinger, Gerda

I knew Pierre as a man. He knew me
as a woman. That's all there was to it.

GERDA MUNSINGER, Mar., 1966, qu. by
Peter Newman, *The distemper of our
times*, 1968, 406, referring to Pierre
Sevigny, when Assoc. Minister of Nat.
Defence, 1959-63.

There was a young lady from Munich
Whose bosom distended her tunic
Her main undertaking
Was cabinet making
In fashions bilingue et unique.

STEPHEN FORD, winner of limerick contest, *Maclean's*, May 14, 1966, 47.

Murder

This is a cold-blooded murder.

THOMAS SCOTT, to Rev. George Young,
just before his execution by Louis Riel's
court, Mar. 4, 1870.

The Muse

The Muse has thighs of moonlight and
    silver
her cunt is frozen gold
and that is why if any mortal woman
    need ask
my hands are always cold

ALFRED PURDY, "Side effect", 1970.

Museums

Like a sperm whale feeding on
    plankton
The City of Vancouver museum
At the corner of Hastings and Main
Opens its doors to the public.

WARREN STEVENSON, "East Hastings
Street", 1963.

Music

Voted that whereas: also the Organist
discovers a light mind in the several
tunes he plays, called Voluntaries to
the great offence of the Congregation,
and tending to disturb, rather than
promote true Devotion.

ST. PAUL'S CHURCH, Halifax, Church records, 1770, referring to Viere Warner;
qu. in *Dalhousie rev.*, Autumn, 1969,
379.

The exquisite powers of musical concert . . . are here almost unknown,
and except in two or three solitary
instances hardly attempted.

WILLIAM MOORSOM, *Letters from Nova
Scotia*, 1830, 97.

A squeak's heard in the orchestra,
    The leader draws across
The intestines of the agile cat
    The tail of the noble hoss.

GEORGE T. LANIGAN, (d.1886), "The ama-
teur Orlando".

And youth forgot its passion
    And age forgot its woe,
And life forgot that there was death
    Before such music's flow.

WILFRID CAMPBELL, "Orpheus", *Varsity
mag.*, 1886.

No logic can grasp thee!
Love can only clasp thee!
For wholly celestial thou art!
To guage thee by reason
Seems absolute treason,
All hail to thee, Queen of the heart!

ALEXANDER MCLACHLAN, "Music", 1900.

I spread a snare electric across the
    ether streams
To catch the dream enchantment with
    which the darkness teems;
Then down the ancient silence, like
    zephyrs through the wheat,
The truant tones come drifting
    melodious and sweet,
For all the heavens are freighted with
    inspiration-light;
The skies are raining music out of the
    lyric night.

ALBERT D. WATSON, "Lyric night", 1923.

"There is no art; there are only artists". A survey of music in Canada
offers such difficulties that one is
tempted to parody the above as follows: There is no Canadian music; but
there are musicians living in Canada,
and, to a lesser extent, Canadian musicians.

> LEO SMITH, in *Handbook of Canada*,
> 1924, 90, issued by the Local Comm. on
> the occasion of the meeting of the
> British Assoc. for the Advancement of
> Science, Toronto, Aug., 1924.

Our Prairies are Bach fugues. Our
Rockies are colossal symphonies. Our
rivers are melodies. Objectively, as
programme, we have everything that
makes great music as inevitable as
weather. But there is nobody with a
big enough imagination plus time and
experience, to write the music.

> AUGUSTUS BRIDLE, in B. Brooker, ed.,
> *Yearbook of the arts in Canada*,
> *1928/29*, 1929, 136.

The Sweetest Music This Side of Heav-
en.

> GUY LOMBARDO, theme of dance band,
> *Guy Lombardo and his Royal Canadi-
> ans*, active in U.S. and Canada since
> 1930.

I never hear a violin
But I remember you;
The melody of April rain
And sunlight breaking through.

> MARY F. EDWARDS, "Alone", 1942.

I have moved to music, wrapped
　　myself in song
　　As with a silver cloak, how bright,
　　how splendid!
Lovely was song: who knows but
　　lovelier yet
　　May be the silence after song is
　　ended?

> AUDREY ALEXANDRA BROWN, "The singer
> grows old", 1943.

The bright
Clear notes fly like sparks through the
air
And trace a flickering pattern of music
there.

> F.R. SCOTT, "Overture", 1945.

of the tapping heels and the tumbling
　　words
to a stillness of seas; his hands are birds
stirring within a cage of chords:
here is the music that no man ends.

> ROBIN SKELTON, "Man with a guitar",
> 1955.

Opera is a convention with a tradition
always attached to it. Part of the
tradition is the acceptance of the convention.

> BOYD NEEL, in Malcolm Ross, ed., *The
> arts in Canada*, 1958, 62.

Look for the *music* in the index of
almost any book of Canadian history
and you will find that the M's stop at
"Murray, James, Governor of Quebec!"

> HELMUT KALLMANN, *History of music in
> Canada: 1534-1914*, 1960, 27.

·you talked about sound, not
footstep sound, shiphorn, nightcry,
but
strings collecting, silver
and catgut, violas riding
the waves of May like soft ships,
yes

> GWENDOLYN MACEWEN, "Skulls and
> drums", 1963.

　　in the ear; the long
measure from the drums of our skulls
to the heart (and its particular tempo);
the music anchored there, gathered
in.

> GWENDOLYN MACEWEN, "Skulls and
> drums", 1963.

We have no Sibeliuses around. We have nobody identifiable with the soil in that way. We have no Canadian artists as Canadians.

> GLENN GOULD, qu. in *Holiday*, Apr., 1964, 154.

I'm standing here before you
I don't know what I bring
If you can hear the music
Why don't you help me sing.

> LEONARD COHEN, "I've seen some lonely history", 1966.

Look at a man. He always has to wear black evening clothes when he plays a concert. I am never happy wearing black on the platform. I feel it sometimes has a bad effect on the audience. I never wear red if I'm going to play the classics – Bach or Haydn. I do wear striking colours if I'm to play Dvorak or Bloch. I would never wear a pastel colour to play Strauss' "Don Quixote": I always wear pastels to perform Debussy and Fauré.

> ZARA NELSOVA, qu. in Toronto *Star*, Mar. 23, 1966.

the hand that does the drumming moves the world

> DOROTHY LIVESAY, "Zambia", 1967.

If a Frenchman has a fiddle, he doesn't need sleep.

> ANON., Quebec saying, qu. in Lena Newman, *Historical almanac of Canada*, 1967.

Music has ceased to be an occasion, requiring an excuse and a tuxedo and accorded, when encountered, an almost religious devotion; music has become a pervasive influence in our lives, and as our dependence upon it has increased, our reverence for it has in a certain sense declined.

> GLENN GOULD, qu. in Richard Kostelanetz, *Master minds*, 1967, 28.

Capture the ears of the young before Muzak and the school system get them!

> BARBARA PENTLAND, in *Musicanada*, July-Aug., 1969, 9.

Today all sounds belong to a continuous field of possibilities lying *within the comprehensive dominion of music.*

> R. MURRAY SCHAFER, *The new soundscape*, 1969, 2.

I maintain you can create a whole composition out of one note, by applying basic principles.

> HARRY SOMERS, address, Canadian Music Educators Association, Convention, Regina, Apr. 9-12, 1969.

I don't think too much about the words because the words are completely empty and any emotion can be poured into them. Almost all my songs can be sung any way. They can be sung as tough songs or as gentle songs or as contemplative songs or as courting songs.

> LEONARD COHEN, *Saturday night*, June, 1969, 26.

Language is sound as sense. Music is sound as sound.

> R. MURRAY SCHAFER, *When words sing*, 1970, 25.

What language do you listen to music in?

> GÉRARD PELLETIER, Sec'y. of State, reply to criticism that he arranged for French only commentary for a concert on Parliament Hill, July 1, 1972.

If you want to learn how to write fugues, write fugues.

> HEALEY WILLAN, qu. in *Can. forum*, Dec., 1972, 33.

Mystery

My Mary, there are no mysteries –
only wonders.

> REV. JAMES EVANS, in 1846, Wesleyan
> missionary to the Crees, qu. in N. Ship-
> ley, *The James Evans story*, 1966, 205.

Some mystery there must be –
Solution is not known.

> W.W. EUSTACE ROSS, "A death", 1934.

Mysticism

Sometimes you saw what others could
    not see.
    Sometimes you heard what no one
      else could hear: –
A light beyond the unfathomable
    dark,
    A voice that sounded only to your
      ear.

> CHARLES G.D. ROBERTS, "To a certain
> mystic", 1934.

Mythology

Is it true that the verbal structures of
psychology, anthropology, theology,
history, law and everything else built
out of words have been informed or
constructed by the same kind of myths
and metaphors that we find, in their
original hypothetical form, in literature?

> NORTHROP FRYE, *Anatomy of criticism*,
> 1957, 352.

The fundamental assumption of the
myth-making consciousness is the ascendancy of the creative human forms
over non-human ones. Of form over
chaos, of life over death. *Human creativity does not project an illusion, as
Marx would have it, but gives us the
power to see in Nature a human
shape.*

> RICHARD STINGLE, "To harpooneers", in
> *Alphabet*, 1960, no. 1,6.

In the solar cycle of the day, the
seasonal cycle of the year, and organic
cycle of human life, there is a single
pattern of significance, out of which
myth constructs a central narrative
around a figure who is partly the sun,
partly vegetative fertility and partly a
god or archetypal human being.

> NORTHROP FRYE, *Fables of identity*,
> 1963, 15.

As society develops, its mystical stories
become structural principles of story-
telling, its mythical concepts, sun gods
and the like, become habits of meta-
phorical thought. In a fully mature
literary tradition the writer enters into
a structure of traditional stories and
images.

> NORTHROP FRYE, in C. F. Klinck, ed.,
> *The literary history of Canada*, 1965,
> 836.

It is always a case of seeing through a
conventional pattern or faded myth to
something more immediate, vital or
violent, and the renewal of the old or
the creation of a new myth more
adequate to that immediate experience.

> D.G. JONES, qu. in G. Geddes, ed., *15
> Canadian poets*, 1970, 277.

It is not easy to free
myth from reality.

> EARLE BIRNEY, "The bear on the Delhi
> Road", 1973.

Names

Nicknames stick to people, and the most ridiculous are the most adhesive.

> T.C. HALIBURTON, *Sam Slick's wise saws*, 1853, II, 51.

There are few things a person resents more than to have his name misspelled.

> SIR JOHN A. MACDONALD, qu. by Sir Joseph Pope in *Public servant*, 1960, 42.

Gentlemen, where I come from, a black-hearted bastard is a term of endearment.

> DONALD GORDON, qu. by Peter Newman, *Flame of power*, 1959, 217.

You have no idea what it means, to come here and be addressed *by my first name*. I tell you, this is something that money can't buy.

> JOHN G. DIEFENBAKER, speech, Prince Albert, Sask., Apr., 1962; qu. in P. Newman, *Renegade in power*, 1963, 322.

I just heard Pickersgill laughing with Wigglesworth over the name Clutterbuck.

> ANON., qu. by Joe Smallwood, *I chose Canada*, 1973, 188; Jack Pickersgill asked U.S. Ambassador Wigglesworth how British High Commissioner Clutterbuck could live with a name like that.

Nation

To make a nation there must be a common life, common sentiments, common aims, and common hopes.

> GOLDWIN SMITH, *The Bystander*, Dec., 1889, 78.

Any attempt to call Canada a nation in the world sense, in the sense of international law or international negotiations, is simply an attempt to lift oneself by pulling at one's boot straps.

> W.S. FIELDING, H. of C., *Debates*, Sept. 11, 1919, 185.

Canada is a nation of the new world.

> W.L. MACKENZIE KING, speech in London, Eng., Sept. 4, 1941.

Most nations have been formed, not by people who desired intensely to live together, but rather by people who could not live apart.

> JEAN-CHARLES BONENFANT, Paper presented to Réunion Générale de l'Institut d'Histoire de l'Amérique française, Apr. 27, 1963. (Trans.)

A nation is a body of men who have done great things together in the past, and who hope to do great things together in the future.

> FRANK H. UNDERHILL, *Image of confederation*, 1964, 2.

In the psychological sense there is no Canadian nation as there is an American or French nation. There is a legal and geographical entity, but the nation does not exist. For there are no objects that all Canadians share as objects of national feeling.

> CHARLES HANLY, in P. Russell, ed., *Nationalism in Canada*, 1966, 312.

The nation is rapidly ceasing to be the real defining unit of society.

> NORTHROP FRYE, *The modern century*, 1967, 18.

Economic, military, and cultural interdependence is a *sine qua non* for states of the twentieth century, to the extent that none is really self-sufficient.

> PIERRE E. TRUDEAU, *Federalism and the French Canadians*, 1968, 169.

National Anthem

O Canada, our home and native land!
True patriot-love in all thy sons
  command.
With glowing hearts we see thee rise,
The true North strong and free,
And stand on guard, O Canada,
We stand on guard for thee.

> ROBERT STANLEY WEIR, "O Canada", 1908, verse I, varies, see below, 1974.

You may talk as you will about the intoning choirs of your European cathedrals, but the sound of "O Can-a-da", born across the waters of a silent lake at evening is good enough for those of us who know Mariposa.

> STEPHEN LEACOCK, "The marine excursions of the Knights of Pythias", *Sunshine sketches of a little town*, 1912, 83.

I think that it was just as they were singing like this: "O-Can-a-da", that word went round that the boat was sinking.

> STEPHEN B. LEACOCK, "The marine excursions of the Knights of Pythias", *Sunshine sketches of a little town*, 1912, 83.

Yes, we sing O Canada – but we sing it as a dirge, and not as a march.

> EMILY MURPHY, "Janey Canuck", a favourite comment, qu. in B.H. Sanders, *Emily Murphy crusader*, 1945, 294.

O Canada, our home, our ta de dah,
Our native land, Oh boom ta la la la.

> VICTORIA *COLONIST* , Oct., 1926, a parody on the many versions of words to the music of Calixa Lavallée; qu. in *Queen's quart.*, Vol. 69, 1962, 397.

Lincoln County Ontario Orangemen have labelled as subversive and unpatriotic the singing of "O Canada" in St. Catharines' schools.

> KINGSTON *WHIG-STANDARD* , Feb. 10, 1956.

O Canada! Our home and native land!
True patriot love in all thy sons
  command.
With glowing hearts we see thee rise,
The True North strong and free!
From far and wide, O Canada, we
  stand on guard for thee.
God keep our land glorious and free!
O Canada, we stand on guard for thee,
O Canada, we stand on guard for thee.

> ROBERT STANLEY WEIR, "O Canada", verse I, version in *Almanac of Canada*, 1974, "permission of Secretary of State".

National Colours

White and red.

> Designated for Canada by H.M. KING GEORGE V on Nov. 21, 1921, and contained in Coat of Arms.

National Emblems

The maple, again, is the emblem of the vitality and energy of a new country; vigorous and stately in its growth, changing its hues as the seasons change, equally at home in the forest, in the cultivated field, and stretching its green boughs over the dusty streets, it may well be received as a type of the progressive and versatile spirit of a new and growing country.

> SIR JOHN WILLIAM DAWSON, *Annual university lecture*, McGill Univ., Nov. 27, 1863, 2.

The beaver in his sagacity, his industry, his ingenuity, and his perseverance, is a most respectable animal; a much better emblem for an infant country than the rapacious eagle or even the lordly lion; but he is also a type of unvarying instincts and old-world traditions. He does not improve, and becomes extinct rather than change his ways.

> SIR JOHN WILLIAM DAWSON, *Annual university lecture*, McGill Univ., Nov. 27, 1863, 2.

Three maple leaves conjoined on one stem.

> Contained in Coat of Arms granted Canada by H.M. KING GEORGE V on Nov. 21, 1921.

National Heritage

A wise nation preserves its records, gathers up its muniments, decorates the tombs of its illustrious dead, repairs its great public structures, and fosters national pride and love of country, by perpetual reference to the sacrifices and glories of the past.

> JOSEPH HOWE, at the Howe family reunion, South Framingham, Mass., Aug. 31, 1871.

But that rare quality, that national
  dream,
  That lies behind this genius at its
    core,
  Which gave it vision, utterance;
    evermore,
It will be with us, as those stars that
  gleam,
  Eternal, hid behind the lights of
    day,
  A people's best, that may not pass
    away.

> WILFRED CAMPBELL, "Our heritage", 1905.

National Policy, 1878

I say what Canada wants is a national policy − a policy that shall be in the interest of Canada, apart from the principles of free-trade, apart from the principles of protection.

> SIR CHARLES TUPPER, H. of C., *Debates*, Feb. 25, 1876, 283.

That it be resolved that this House is of opinion that the welfare of Canada requires the adoption of a National Policy, which, by a judicious readjustment of the Tariff, will benefit and foster the Agricultural, the Mining, the Manufacturing and other interests of the Dominion; that such a policy will retain in Canada thousands of our fellow-countrymen now obliged to expatriate themselves in search of the employment denied them at home, will restore prosperity to our struggling industries, now so sadly depressed, will prevent Canada from being made a sacrifice market, will encourage and develop an active interprovincial trade, and moving (as it ought to do) in the direction of a reciprocity of Tariffs with our neighbours, so far as the varied interests of Canada may demand, will greatly tend to procure for this country, eventually, a reciprocity of Trade.

SIR JOHN A. MACDONALD, resolution moved in House of Commons, Mar. 12, 1878; *Journals*, 1878, 78; also, *Debates*, Mar. 7, 1878, 854.

The cradle of the National Policy.

ANON., a reference to the city of Hamilton, Ont., about 1878.

N.P.

ANON., term used, less for brevity than ridicule, by opponents of Sir John A. Macdonald's National Policy, after 1876; but also used by Macdonald in his correspondence.

The programme of the two Canadian annexationists is this: – First, N.P.; then distress; then commercial union; then more distress; then annexation, then the deluge.

TORONTO *GLOBE* , June 26, 1880, 6.

The New National Policy.

CANADIAN COUNCIL OF AGRICULTURE, new platform adopted Nov. 29, 1918, in opposition to the National Policy of 1878.

Macdonald's way of imposing the new tariff was simple: he just invited anyone who wanted a duty to come to Ottawa and ask for it.

A.R.M. LOWER, *Colony to nation*, 1946, 374.

Why can we not bring ourselves to say quite simply that the National Policy was a dismal failure?

JOHN H. DALES, *Queen's quart.*, Vol. LXXI, No. 3, 1964, 302.

It is high time that someone should write the history of Canada since Confederation as a triumph of the forces of economic and political development over the policies of Macdonald and his successors.

JOHN H. DALES, *Queen's quart.*, Vol. LXXI, 1964, 306.

National Policy (General)

There is grave danger in thinking of national policy in terms of popular slogans — in simplifying matters of infinite complexity. If important matters such as trade and investment are dealt with on a negative and emotional basis, serious damage will be done to our national welfare.

MERRIL W. MENZIES, letter to Dr. Glen Green, qu. in P. Newman, *Renegade in power*, 1963, 198.

Nationalism

The future of Canada, I believe, depends very largely on the cultivation of a national spirit.

EDWARD BLAKE, speech at Aurora, Ont., Oct. 3, 1874.

It is to the racial instinct that politicians appeal in order to blind us when they are forced to choose between duty and power. It is the same instinct that is addressed when one wishes to force the people to give their confidence to certain men among them even when they have betrayed the national interest or dishonoured the position that they occupy through corruption, debauchery, and malversation of all sorts. In a word, it is by speculating on this instinct that one seeks to draw from us a guilty indulgence for the renegades and gamblers of our race.

HENRI BOURASSA, *Revue canadienne*, Vol. 41, June, 1902, 435. (Trans.)

We Nationalists are not devotees of democracy.

HENRI BOURASSA, qu. by C. Murrow, *Henri Bourassa and French-Canadian nationalism*, 1968, 105.

Our own brand of nationalism is Canadian nationalism, based on the duality of the races and the special traditions this duality imposes. We are working toward the development of Canadian patriotism, which in our eyes is the best guarantee of the existence of two races and of the mutual respect they owe each other.

HENRI BOURASSA, *Le nationaliste*, Apr. 3, 1904, 2. (Trans.)

The nation we wish to see founded at the time appointed by Providence is the French-Canadian nation.

J.P. TARDIVAL, in *La verité*, June 1, 1904; qu. in R. Cook, *French-Canadian nationalism*, 1969, 147.

The general and superior interests of Canada must have priority over the more particular class or provincial interests; they must not be subordinated to a false imperial idea either. Now or never is the time to say: Canada to the Canadians and, in so saying, to yield neither to the Americans nor to the other parts of the Empire. Such is the true nationalist doctrine.

HENRI BOURASSA, *La convention douanière entre le Canada et les États-Unis, sa nature, sa conséquences, 1911* (pamphlet). (Trans.)

Canadian Nationalism is neither a party, a racial organization, nor a *separatist* movement. Its apparent weaknesses and real strength come largely from the fact that the leaders and the exponents of its principles have run all sorts of risks rather than let it become a mere political faction or the machine tool of existing parties.

HENRI BOURASSA, speech to Liberal Colonial Club, London, June 25, 1914.

A racial nationalism involves either isolation, or the supremacy of a dominant race in a mixed state . . . The wonder-worker is thus not race but liberty. Let us dismiss forever the superstition that there is any magic in race to hold people together and effect political unity. It is partnership in common liberties which unites people. The growth of the new nationalism in the British Empire is just a growth of liberty.

GEORGE WRONG, *Amer. hist. rev.*, 1916-17, 51.

There are too many nasty little self-centred nations in the world already; God forbid that Canada should add one to the number!

W.L. GRANT, in *Can.hist.rev.*, 1923, 80.

Nationalism provides the only sure basis for internationalism.

HAROLD A. INNIS, paper read at Liberal-Conservative Summer School, Newmarket, Ont., Sept., 1933.

The most substantial Canadian nationalism in times of peace has been economic nationalism.

J.B. BREBNER, Can. Hist. Assoc., *Report*, 1940, 8.

The nation must be something greater than the sum of its parts. If it is not so, it ceases to exist, it has lost the will to continue. By this elusive yet valid test, the Canadian people have created and are creating a nation.

GEORGE W. BROWN, in Can. Hist. Assoc., *Report*, 1944, 7.

The Canadian state cannot be devoted to absolute nationalism, the focus of a homogeneous popular will. The two nationalities and the four sections of Canada forbid it.

W.L. MORTON, *Univ. of Tor. quart.*, Vol. XV, No. 3, Apr., 1946, 234.

The wonder is that the tender plant of Canadian nationalism survived at all, for all little Canadian boys and girls have been subjected from the day on which they start school to an unending steeping in the liquid of "imperialism" and from the day they can read to an equally unending cultural (or anti-cultural) bombardment from the south.

> A.R.M. LOWER, *Canadians in the making*, 1958, 349.

Our nationalism is a defence mechanism. It is not a way of life.

> LORENZO PARÉ, qu. in M. Ross, ed., *The arts in Canada*, 1958, 128. (Trans.)

As a Canadian, I have been disturbed because nationalism in its recent form seems to me to appeal to, and to reinforce, the most undesirable features of the Canadian national character. In these I include not only the mean and underhanded anti-Americanism which serves many Canadians as an excuse for their failure to accomplish anything worthy of genuine national pride, but also what I think of, perhaps unfairly, as the small-town pettiness of outlook that is the shadow side of many Canadian virtues.

> HARRY G. JOHNSON, *International jour.*, Vol. 16, No. 3, 1961, 238.

Canadian nationalism as it has developed in recent years has been diverting Canada into a narrow and garbage-cluttered cul-de-sac.

> HARRY G. JOHNSON, *International jour.*, Vol. XVI, No. 3, Summer, 1961, 239; also, *The Canadian quandary*, 1963, 12.

Anglo-Canadian nationalism has never had much of an edge.

> PIERRE E. TRUDEAU, *Cité libre*, Apr., 1962, 9. (Trans.).

The exponents of the French-Canadian nationalist school, despite their generosity and their courage, are, for all practical purposes, going against progress.

> PIERRE E. TRUDEAU, *Cité libre*, Apr., 1962, 11. (Trans.)

Canadian nationalism? How old-fashioned can you get?

> E.P. TAYLOR, Toronto international financier, Winter, 1963, qu. in George P. Grant, *Lament for a nation*, 1965, 42.

We Canadians are in no danger of narrow nationalism; our peril is to be too little conscious of our own identity, too little given to understanding and preserving it.

> VINCENT MASSEY, *What's past is prologue*, 1963, 169.

In a world of rapid change and alienation, and nightmare not far beyond the horizon, nationalism can be a comforting thing.

> DOUGLAS LE PAN, in The American Assembly, *The U.S. and Canada*, 1964, 166.

The glue of nationalism will become as obsolete as the divine right of kings.

> PIERRE E. TRUDEAU, to joint meeting, Canadian Political Science Assoc. and Assoc. of Canadian Law Teachers, June 11, 1964, Charlottetown.

The greatest cost of chauvinism, here as elsewhere, is the inability to see one's own interests.

> A.E. SAFARIAN, in A. Rotstein ed., *The prospect of change*, 1965, 244.

Be it new and justified or retrograde and evil-natured, the spirit of nationalism is always a manifestation of the rankly primitive.

> JEAN LE MOYNE, *Convergence*, 1966, 59.

In the pseudo-sophistication of our adolescence, many Canadians would rather let the country fall apart than be accused of nationalism, a weakness not only malign but also corny. Some find pride in our having conceived the immaculate non-nation. A majority recognize with satisfaction, but without emotion, the blessings of a country which demands little of them – in service or in conformity.

JOHN HOLMES, in Peter Russell, ed., *Nationalism in Canada*, 1966, 205.

If we skip the state of nationalism we become not internationals (there are no such animals) but Americans. It is as simple as that.

A.R.M. LOWER, *My first seventy-five years*, 1967, 305.

Just as Canadian unity is based on diversity, so our nationalism must be international.

LESTER B. PEARSON, speech at Calgary, Mar. 29, 1967.

We are nationalists not in the sense that we want to keep Canada forever out of future mergers of nations, but in the sense that we want to keep Canada out of the *United States* in the foreseeable future. We are nationalists because we believe that something new can be created here – something different from what the Americans have created – and that something new might be a social democracy.

GAD HOROWITZ, *Can. dimension*, May-June, 1967, 9.

The point of Canadian nationalism is not to preserve a sovereign Canadian nation state for ever and ever no matter what, but to preserve it so long as the only unit capable of absorbing it is a larger and more terrible nationalism.

GAD HOROWITZ, *Can. forum*, May, 1968, 29.

What lies behind the small practical question of Canadian nationalism is the larger context of the fate of western civilisation. By that fate I mean not merely the relations of our massive empire to the rest of the world, but even more the kind of existence which is becoming universal in advanced technological societies. What is worth doing in the midst of this barren twilight is the incredibly difficult question.

GEORGE P. GRANT, *Technology and empire*, 1969, 78.

Fool
    you *are* home
      you were home
in the first place
      and
if you don't look out
      it's going to be
now this minute
    classic ESSO
      bloodlit SHELL
forever.

MIRIAM WADDINGTON, "Driving home", 1969.

For the past 150 years nationalism has been a retrograde idea. By an historic accident Canada has found itself approximately seventy-five years ahead of the rest of the world in the formation of a multinational state and I happen to believe that the hope of mankind lies in multinationalism.

PIERRE E. TRUDEAU, qu. in G. Donaldson, *Fifteen men*, 1969, 243; see also *Cité libre*, Apr., 1962.

Nationalism will end only when people are willing to admit their common inhumanity.

IRVING LAYTON, "Aphs", *The whole bloody bird*, 1969, 85.

Nationalism: a snarl wrapped up in a flag.

> IRVING LAYTON, "Aphs", *The whole bloody bird*, 1969, 79.

Nobody loves Canadian nationalism but the people.

> DENIS DUFFY, qu. in *Maclean's*, Feb., 1970, 2.

The consciousness of belonging to a nation, whether politically consecrated or merely yearned for, provides nationalists with a principle around which to organize the past, to criticize the present, and to construct the future.

> RAMSAY COOK, *The maple leaf forever*, 1971, 200.

Sure, "Keep it Canadian". But how? You know, who do we push around?

> PIERRE E. TRUDEAU, to the Press, June 29, 1971, after meeting with a delegation from the Committee for an Independent Canada.

Nationality

Oh, for a Canadian nationality which would ameliorate the unmitigated personal selfishness which pervades the land!

> TORONTO *GLOBE*, Oct. 20, 1847.

A New Nationality.

> THOMAS D'ARCY MCGEE, in *The new era*, in an article written in the Summer of 1857; the phrase reappeared in 1865 in parliament in the debate on Confederation.

I see in the not remote distance one great nationality bound, like the shield of Achilles, by the blue rim of ocean. I see it quartered into many communities, each disposing of its internal affairs, but all bound together by free institutions, free intercourse and free commerce. I see within the round of that shield the peaks of the western mountains and the crests of the eastern waves, the winding Assiniboine; the five-fold lakes, the St. Lawrence, the Ottawa, the Saguenay, the St. John and the basin of Minas.

> THOMAS D'ARCY MCGEE, speech, Legislative Assembly, May 2, 1860.

A Canadian nationality, not French-Canadian, nor British-Canadian, nor Irish-Canadian — patriotism rejects the prefix — is, in my opinion, what we should look forward to, — that is what we ought to labour for, that is what we ought to be prepared to defend to the death.

> THOMAS D'ARCY MCGEE, speech in Quebec, May 10, 1862.

We have a large class whose national feelings turn toward London, whose very heart is there; another large class whose sympathies centre here at Quebec, or in a sentimental way may have some reference to Paris; another large class whose memories are of the Emerald Isle, and yet another whose comparisons are rather with Washington; but have we any class of people who are attached, or whose feelings are going to be directed with any earnestness, to the City of Ottawa, the centre of the new nationality that is to be created?

> CHRISTOPHER DUNKIN, *Confederation debates*, Feb. 27, 1865, 51.

I would desire to see, Gentlemen, our new national character distinguished by a manly modesty as much as by mental independence; by the conscientious exercise of the critical faculties, as well as by the zeal of the inquirer.

> THOMAS D'ARCY MCGEE, address, "The mental outfit of the new Dominion", Montreal, Nov. 4, 1867.

I congratulate you on the legislative sanction which has been given by the Imperial Parliament to the Act of Union, under the provisions of which we are now assembled and which has laid the foundations of a new nationality that I trust and believe will, ere long, extend its bounds from the Atlantic to the Pacific Ocean.

> LORD MONCK, speech from the Throne, Nov. 7, 1867; presumably drafted by Sir John A. Macdonald.

It is impossible to foster a national spirit unless you have national interests to attend to.

> EDWARD BLAKE, speech at Aurora, Ont., Oct. 3, 1874.

The time will come when that national spirit which has been spoken of will be truly felt among us, when we shall realize that we are four millions of Britons who are not free.

> EDWARD BLAKE, speech at Aurora, Ont., Oct. 3, 1874.

The seed they sowed has sprung at last,
And grows and blossoms through the land.

> CHARLES MAIR, "In memory of William A. Foster", (1888); a reference to the "Canada First" movement.

Whatever pride of country a Canadian has, its object, for the most part, is outside Canada.

> ANON., qu. in Canada first, (W.A. Foster), 1890.

Soon, it may be, the desire for something more enduring which has always been manifest, will assert itself, and then Canada will have attained, to the full extent, national self-consciousness.

> ARTHUR G. DOUGHTY, Canada and its provinces, 1913, XI, 3.

I will readily admit anything that looks like national self-assertion; anything which advances Canada along the road to nationhood appeals to me.

> ERNEST LAPOINTE, H. of C., Debates, May 17, 1920, 2449.

Canadian national life can almost be said to take its rise in the negative will to resist absorption in the American Republic.

> DELBERT CLARK, in Canada and her great neighbor, ed., H.F. Angus, 1938, 243.

In our comfortable part of the world national maturity was to be measured in terms of a formal status intended actually to maintain a position of irresponsible dependency.

> R.G. TROTTER, in Can. hist. rev., June, 1945, 128.

If we want to stay a Nation, we must foot the bill.

> MACLEAN'S, editorial, Aug. 6, 1955, on U.S. building and manning the DEW line.

Nationality is of no consequence. In the things of the spirit there is no such barrier.

> JOHN MARLYN, Under the ribs of death, 1957, (1971, 24).

What is the price of being Canadian? The simplest answer is $10; this is what it costs an Italian or a German to be naturalized here. For the native-born, Canadian nationality is free of charge − a bargain surely.

> J.B. MCGEACHY, "The price of being Canadian", A touch of McGeachy, 1962, 71.

My passport is bilingual, though my heart is not.

> GILLES VIGNEAULT, qu. in *Time*, Jan. 24, 1972, 14.

NATO

The North Atlantic Community is today a real commonwealth of nations which share the same democratic and cultural traditions. If a movement towards its political and economic unification can be started this year, no one can forecast the extent of the unity which may exist five, ten, fifteen, or twenty years from now.

> ESCOTT REID, *International jour.*, Vol. 22, No. 3, 1967, 440.

I am afraid, in the situation we had reached, NATO had in reality determined all of our defence policy. We had no defence policy, so to speak, except that of NATO. And our defence policy had determined all of our foreign policy. And we had no foreign policy of any importance except that which flowed from NATO. And this is a false perspective for any country. It is a false perspective to have a military alliance determine your foreign policy. It should be your foreign policy which determines your military policy.

> PIERRE E. TRUDEAU, address to Alberta Liberal Assoc., Calgary, Apr. 12, 1969.

Natural Resources

'Rich by nature, poor by policy', might be written over Canada's door.

> GOLDWIN SMITH, *Canada and the Canadian question*, 1891, 24.

A people is never safe when it leaves the resources of its country unexploited. If it does not exploit them itself, others will come to exploit them for it, and thus give themselves a pretext for intervening in its affairs. Or yet again an industrial oligarchy will arise, which is not less to be feared.

> ERROL BOUCHETTE, Roy. Soc. Can., *Transactions*, 1901, Sec. I, 135. (Trans.)

The really remarkable thing about Canada is the incompetence of the Canadians. There they have been for 150 years in a country of exceptional richness, and look how little they've done with it.

> LORD ROBERT CECIL, letter to Hugh Cecil, Oct., 1905, Balfour Papers, Whittingehame, England.

To be the keeper of the country's conscience in regard to natural resources will always be found to be a thankless task, bringing to those who keep reminding us of our economic sins, more kicks than halfpence.

> CANADIAN MINING JOURNAL , editorial, Vol. 42, May 27, 1921, 418.

For my part, I would far sooner have waited a little longer, if possible, for the development of our national resources than see the people of Canada become, in the language of the Bible, hewers of wood and drawers of water to American capitalists.

> ABRAHAM A. HEAPS, H. of C., *Debates*, Feb. 20, 1928, 637.

Canada's vast untouched – and untouchable – resources.

> ANON., a witticism of the 1930's.

Our primitive era of national development by resource plundering is over; but our thinking is still unchanged.

> E. NEWTON-WHITE, *Hurt not the earth*, 1958, 185.

Even a very cursory examination reveals that present policies cannot possibly maximize the benefit to be derived from natural resources. They lead, on the contrary, to a startling amount of economic waste, and create problems of rural poverty and retarded technology.

> P.H. PEARSE, *Queen's quart.*, Vol. 73, 1966, 87.

If we're not going to use them, why not sell them for good hard cash?

> PIERRE E. TRUDEAU, TV program "Under attack", Carleton University, Feb. 24, 1970.

We should fill every Canadian's dream before we sell, and then charge the highest price they've ever seen.

> MEL WATKINS, rally at Queen's Park, Toronto, Sept. 12, 1970, on continental energy deal.

They gave away the forest,
They gave away the land,
They gave away the rivers,
They gave away the sand,

They gave away the silver,
They gave away the gold,
They tried to give away the air
But the air they couldn't hold.

> ANON., ascribed to F.R. Scott, poet; relative to the 1970's.

We have always been a subordinate people, a derivative people, because of our origin and our history as resource exporters. Our staple products have been the real chains of empire that have bound us first to Britain and now to the United States. It is through our resources that we have related most profoundly to mankind as a whole.

> JAMES LAXER, *The energy poker game*, 1970, 16.

The day is going to come when people are going to say, "Why were you so stupid? Why did you give it all away?"

> ERIC KIERANS, interview in Montreal, qu. in Toronto *Star*, Mar. 10, 1973, 15.

The country that is the source of the capital brought into Canada for the purpose of exploring for, finding, and extracting the natural resource, is the country to which that natural resource is taken for processing, manufacture, and consumption.

> RICHARD ROHMER, *The arctic imperative*, 1973, 12.

Naturalization

The expression "disability" means the disability of being an infant, lunatic, idiot, or married woman.

> CANADA. LAWS, STATUTES, *The naturalization act*, Rev. Stat. 1886, C.113, 2(a).

Nature

Natur' is natur' wherever you find it.

> T.C. HALIBURTON, *Sam Slick*, 1836, ch. XXI.

I sketch from nature and the draught
  is true.
Whate'er the picture, whether grave
  or gay,
Painful experience in a distant land
Made it my own.

> SUSANNA MOODIE, 1852, *Roughing it in the bush*, – title-page.

Not only in the cataract and the
  thunder
    Or in the deeps of man's uncharted
    soul,
But in the dew-star dwells alike the
  wonder,
    And in the whirling dust-mote the
    Control.

> CHARLES G.D. ROBERTS, "Immanence", 1896.

The greatest joy in nature is the absence of man.

> BLISS CARMAN, *The kinship of nature*, 1906, 166.

Have you seen God in His splendours, heard the text that nature renders?

> ROBERT W. SERVICE, "Call of the wild", 1907.

Something in my inmost thinking
  Tells me I am one with you,
For a subtle bond is linking
  Nature's offspring through and
    through.

> FREDERICK GEORGE SCOTT, "In the winter woods", 1910.

I love Nature more than Man.

> FREDERICK PHILIP GROVE, *Over prairie trails*, 1922, Preface, 14.

I am weak before the wind; before the
    sun
  I faint; I lose my strength;
I am utterly vanquished by a star;
  I go to my knees, at length,
Before the song of a bird; before
  The breath of spring or fall
I am lost; before these miracles
  I am nothing at all.

> A.M. KLEIN, "Out of the pulver and the polished lens", 1936.

The grace that is a tree
belongs to me;
the quietness of stone
I make my own;
from the strong hills I borrow
courage to face tomorrow.
My flesh itself is kin
to earth and all therein
and of my brother's heart
I am a part.

> JEAN WHITMAN, "Kinship", 1938.

The human mind has nothing but human and moral values to cling to if it is to preserve its integrity or even its sanity, yet the vast unconsciousness of nature in front of it seems an unanswerable denial of those values.

> NORTHROP FRYE, in C.F. Klinck, ed., *Literary history of Canada*, 1965, 830.

I don't care
how high the clouds are,
how white they curdle
in the whey of sky,
or if the sun
is kind to the flowers,
or why the wind
plays at storms in the trees.

The robin hiding
in the garden bushes
has a broken wing.

> RAYMOND SOUSTER, "Broken day", 1965.

Nature doesn't seem to care
whether we rise or fall,
live or perish,
love or hate,
murder or create.
Nature is neutral to all values.

> LOUIS DUDEK, "Nature", 1966.

The rational design that nature reflects is in the human mind only.

> NORTHROP FRYE, *The modern century*, 1967, 110.

Nature is just a lot of waste and cruelty, maybe not from Nature's point of view but from a human point of view. Cruelty is the law of Nature.

> ALICE MUNRO, *Lives of girls and women*, 1971, 87.

Navigation

No country under heaven is so completely adapted for internal navigation.

> WILLIAM DUNLOP, *Statistical sketches of Upper Canada*, 1832, 58.

To know the laws that govern the winds, and to know that you know them, will give you an easy mind on your voyage round the world; otherwise you may tremble at the appearance of every cloud.

> CAPTAIN JOSHUA SLOCUM, *Sailing alone around the world*, 1899, 146.

Navy

Laurier's tin-pot navy.

> Term used by opponents to Laurier's navy policy, 1909 and later; RODMOND P. ROBLIN, Premier of Manitoba, speech in Winnipeg, Oct. 26, 1909.

Governments cannot live forever, for governments are born to grow and die as well as men, and if I fall by the roadside not a murmur will pass my lips, but mark my words, whoever may take the reins of power will have to have a navy, as every nation with a seashore must have and has had in the past.

> SIR WILFRID LAURIER, letter to E.H. Lemay, Nov. 10, 1910. (Pub. Arch.Can.)

The people, who will be prepared for a Canadian navy when it will be necessary, do not wish to have a navy which is Canadian in time of peace and Imperial in time of war; that is to say, a navy which will be Canadian when it is to be paid for, in order to be Imperial when it is required for use.

> FREDERICK D. MONK, H. of C., *Debates*, 1910-11, col.612; quoting from a Liberal newspaper, *Arthabaska gazette*, Dec. 1, 1910.

Necessity

The country is a good country for those to whom it is adapted: but if people will not conform to the doctrine of necessity and expediency, they have no business in it.

> CATHERINE PARR TRAILL, *Backwoods of Canada*, 1836; (4th ed., 140).

Needs must when the Devil drives.

> THOMAS C. HALIBURTON, *Sam Slick's wise saws*, 1853, ch. 13.

Beware the casual need
By which the heart is bound;
Pluck out the quickening seed
That falls on stony ground.

> F.R. SCOTT, "Advice", 1945.

Negation

So be my never and long may nothing live,
Bless all distance and intensity
Which strain our kisses through a starry sieve,
And drowning you have also here drowned me.

> MIRIAM WADDINGTON, "You are my never", 1958.

Negotiators

He is the worst negotiator I ever saw in my life.

> SIR JOHN A. MACDONALD, letter to Sir John Rose, Feb. 13, 1873, on Sir Hugh Allen.

Neighbours

Someone is responsible. Every unjustly treated man, every defenceless woman, every neglected child has a neighbour somewhere. Am I that neighbour?

> JAMES S. WOODSWORTH, *My neighbour*, 1911, 20.

The greatest pleasure of country life is in having no neighbours. Why should I tolerate neighbours when I cannot tolerate myself?

> EMILY G. MURPHY, ("Janey Canuck"), *Open trails*, 1912, 116.

As a matter of fact your neighbours think just as disagreeable thoughts about you as you think about them.

ROBERT C. (BOB) EDWARDS, Calgary *Eye Opener*, Nov. 24, 1917.

"Qui dit voisins dit ennemis" as the nationalist French-Canadian penguin remarked to the English-Canadian penguin.

F.H. UNDERHILL, in *Saturday rev.*, (N.Y.), Oct. 24, 1959, 14 (trans: "Who says neighbours says enemies").

My neighbour doesn't want to be loved as much as he wants to be envied.

IRVING LAYTON, "Aphs", *The whole bloody bird"*, 1969, 88.

Neuroses

A psychotic is a man who thinks that two and two make 11 and will stake his life on it; a neurotic is a man who knows that two and two make four but can't stand it.

HUGH MACLENNAN, Conf. on "The price of being Canadian", organized by Inst. on Public Affairs and C.B.C., Toronto, Mar., 1961, qu. in *Financial post*, Mar. 4, 1961, 7.

Neutrality

But goats, like men, have never found Much standing room on neutral ground.

E.J. PRATT, "The fable of the goats", 1937.

The kind of neutrality I have in mind is that on which an independent, democratic, socialist society could find a place to stand. A neutrality that is committed, a neutrality that is constructive, a neutrality that is creative.

JAMES EAYRS, *Greenpeace and her enemies*, 1974, 346.

New Brunswick

The province of the Loyalists.

ANON., a popular term, 19th. century, referring to the United Empire Loyalists who settled the area.

In these uncertain times, the duty of New Brunswick is to draw, if possible, into closer relations with the loyal Provinces of Canada, though it may be for her interest to connect herself commercially with the United States. Duty and interest lead two different ways.

FREDERICTON *HEADQUARTERS*, Jan. 27, 1864.

Spem reduxit. (She [England] restored hope.)

NEW BRUNSWICK, official motto.

Sweet maiden of Passamaquoddy,
  Shall we seek for communion of
    souls
Where the deep Mississippi meanders,
  Or the distant Saskatchewan rolls?
Ah, no! in New Brunswick we'll find it –
  A sweetly sequestered nook –
Where the swift gliding
    Skoodoowabskooksis
  Unites with the Skoodoowabskook.

JAMES DE MILLE, "Sweet maiden of Quoddy", originally, "Lines to Florance Huntingdon, Maine", in *New Dominion and true humorist*, Saint John, Apr. 16, 1870, 171.

New Brunswick alone amid the faithless stood faithful.

ALEXANDER MACKENZIE, letter to Hon. James Young, Sept. 26, 1878, referring to New Brunswick remaining Liberal in the federal election, Sept., 1878.

Equal Opportunity program.

LOUIS ROBICHAUD, Premier of New Brunswick, program introduced in the Legislature, Nov. 16, 1965.

Evangeline's Revenge.

ANON., popular term for Louis Robichaud's Equal Opportunity program presented to the Legislature Nov. 16, 1965. Reference is to the alleged preference shown toward the French Canadian population of the province.

This is the only
country they know.
There are men here
who have never heard of Canada.

ALDEN NOWLAN, "Stoney ridge dance hall", 1969.

K.C. Irving *is* New Brunswick.

MICHAEL WARDELL, qu. in R. Hunt & R. Campbell, *K.C. Irving*, 1973, 30.

New Democratic Party

I'd rather waffle to the left than waffle to the right.

ED BROADBENT, at a public meeting, 1969, when accused of waffling on a question; later the word waffle was used to describe a dissident group in the party.

The Waffle manifesto.

N.D.P. "Resolution No. 133", submitted to the N.D.P. Convention, Winnipeg, Oct. 28-31, 1969 by N.D.P. Youth Federal Council and others. Has been popularly known as the Watkins' or "Waffle" Manifesto.

I often think that when people get into the polling booth, and they're just about to vote for us, the dead hand of their ghostly Liberal or Conservative grandfathers comes down and *takes* them.

DAVID LEWIS, election campaign speech, Oct., 1972, qu. in *Maclean's*, Jan., 1973, 56.

New France

In a word, people may live a very happy life here if they are virtuous, but not if they are lacking in this respect, for they are under too close a surveillance; thus I do not recommend to the unvirtuous that they come here, for they would be run out of the colony or at least forced to leave, as has happened to many.

PIERRE BOUCHER, *Histoire véritable et naturelle . . .* , 1664, Preface. (Trans.)

A colony precipitated since 1760 inside the smooth walls of fear.

PAUL-EMILE BORDUAS, *Refus global*, 1948, 1. (Trans.)

New Year

We stood on the bridge of the Ages —
    The current of Time upon earth.
The Old Year was sealing its record,
    The New Year had come to the
        birth.
In silence we stood by the ebb-tide
    And watched it melt into the sea —
A drop in that infinite ocean
    That has been and ever shall be.

MARY JANE LAWSON, "Midnight between the old year and the new", Dec. 31, 1882.

And so the old year has beautifully passed here in its faultlessly white snow robes, and the new has taken its place. What a wonderful record it has left in science, in research, in discoveries historical, and the light thrown thereby on the origin and progress of human development . . . The human unit and the composite of races and nations are seething with unrest, change, and re-formations. Upheaval first: what price results?

SIR GEORGE E. FOSTER, entry in his Diary, Jan. 1, 1930.

Upon the chaste scroll of the New
    Year,
I would inscribe for you
with bold and flowing strokes,
the Good Luck symbol,
and with full brush delineate,
the ideograph of Laughter.

> CAROL COATES CASSIDY, "Greeting",
> 1941.

Gentle and just pleasure
It is, being human, to have won from
    space
This unchill, habitable interior
Which mirrors quietly the light
Of the snow, and the new year.

> MARGARET AVISON, "New Year's poem",
> 1960.

We try to look cheerful, to smile,
as we go around the office shaking
    hands,
wishing one another Happy New
    Year:
but it's not that easy
with thirty-two hours
of loneliness, betrayal, loss
still left in the old one.

> RAYMOND SOUSTER, "It's not that easy",
> 1971.

Newfoundland

The Aire, in Newfound-Land is
    wholesome, good;
The Fire, as sweet as any made of
    wood;
The Waters, very rich, both salt and
    fresh;
The Earth more rich, you know it is no
    lesse.
Where all are good, Fire, Water,
    Earth, and Aire
What man made of these foure would
    not live there?

> ROBERT HAYMAN, *Quodlibets*, 1628, 31.

You say that you would live in
    Newfound-land,
Did not this one thing your conceit
    withstand;
You feare the *Winter's* cold, sharp,
    piercing ayre.
They love it best, that have once
    wintered there.
Winter is there, short, wholesome,
    constant, cleare,
Not thicke, unwholesome, shuffling, as
    'tis here.

> ROBERT HAYMAN, *Quodlibets*, 1628, 31.

Sweet Creatures, did you truely
    understand
The pleasant life you'd live in
    Newfound-land,
You would with *teares* desire to be
    brought thither:
I wish you, when you goe, faire wind,
    faire weather:
For if you with the passage can
    dispence,
When you are there, I know you'll ne'r
    come thence.

> ROBERT HAYMAN, *Quodlibets*, 1628, 31.

Quaerite prime regnum Dei.

> Provincial motto, on Arms granted by
> letters patent, Jan. 1, 1637; trans.: Seek
> ye first the kingdom of God.

The Ancient Colony.

> ANON., popular name for the Island.

Remember the day
When Carter and Shea
Crossed over the 'say',
To barter away
The rights of Terra Nova.

> ANON., anti-Confederation ditty, 1865;
> Carter and Shea were delegates to the
> Quebec Conference.

A short feast and a long famine.

> ANON., term used to describe the for-
> tunes of fishing. The catch was sold in
> the fall and food and drink were abun-
> dant but became scarce in the spring
> when the harbours were blocked by ice.

Hurrah for our own native isle,
Newfoundland
No stranger will hold one inch of her
strand
Her face turns to Britain, her back to
the Gulf
Come near at your peril, Canadian
wolf.

ANON., Newfoundland "Anti-Confeder-
ate song", 1869.

The people of Newfoundland shrink
from the idea of linking their destinies
with a Dominion in the future of
which they can at present see nothing
to inspire hope, but much to create
apprehension.

NEWFOUNDLAND, House of Assembly,
statement, 1870; qu. in Toronto *Weekly
globe*, Feb. 25, 1870.

We'll rant and we'll roar like true
Newfoundlanders,
We'll rant and we'll roar on deck and
below;
Until we see bottom inside the two
sunkers,
When straight through the Channel to
Toslow we'll go.

H.W. LEMESSURIER, "We'll rant and we'll
roar", also known as "The girls from
Toslow"; originally called "The Ryans
and the Pittmans", about 1880.

Black Monday.

ANON., Dec. 10, 1894, the first day of the
panic caused when the Commercial
Bank and the Union Bank closed their
doors.

A home entirely surrounded by hospitality.

ANON., Newfoundlanders' popular description of their land, often used in
answer to the phrase, "A piece of rock
entirely surrounded by fog".

I find that Newfoundland is said to be
celebrated for its codfish, its dogs, its
hogs, its fogs, and its bogs! That is a
very erroneous opinion, I assure you.

SIR WILLIAM WHITEWAY, speech in London, Eng., July 5, 1897.

When sun rays crown thy pine-clad
hills,
And Summer spreads her hand,
When silvern voices tune thy rills,
We love thee, smiling land . . .

As loved our fathers, so we love,
Where once they stood, we stand;
Their prayer we raise to Heaven
above,
God guard thee, Newfoundland.

SIR CAVENDISH BOYLE, Governor of Nfld.,
1901-04, "Ode to Newfoundland".

The Norway of the New World.

ANON., term used in government advertisements, 1915.

Politics in Newfoundland have never
been such as to inspire wholehearted
confidence in the ability of the people
to govern themselves wisely, but there
is general agreement that a process of
deterioration, which has now reached
almost unbelievable extremes, may be
said to have set in about a quarter of a
century ago.

GREAT BRITAIN. NEWFOUNDLAND ROYAL
COMMISSION, *Report*, 1933, 81.

I suppose we have here all the people
in Canada interested in having Newfoundland join Canada.

NORMAN ROBERTSON, qu. by R.A. MacK-
ay in *Dalhousie rev.*, Vol. 50, Summer,
1970, 230, referring to a meeting of five
people, Ottawa, Aug., 1946.

Confederation is good for the children.

JOSEPH R. SMALLWOOD, *The confederate*
(St. John's), May 31, 1948, qu. in P.
Neary, *The political economy of New-
foundland, 1929-1972*, 1973, 143.

You know, the one thing we don't have that we really need, is a martyr.

> JOSEPH R. SMALLWOOD, during confederation campaign, 1948, to Harold Horwood, qu. in M. Wade, ed., *Regionalism, 1867-1967*, 1969, 253.

Don't vote Confederation, and that's
  my prayer to you,
We own the house we live in, we own
  the schooner too;
But if you heed Joe Smallwood and his
  line of French patois,
You'll be always paying taxes to the
  men at Ottawa.

> RESPONSIBLE GOVERNMENT LEAGUE, anti-Confederation ballad, 1948.

The Happy Province.

> ANON., name popular with the inhabitants.

A new Province was born to Canada that day — God bless them both! But a Dominion was murdered.

> A.P. HERBERT, *Independent member*, 1950, 450, referring to Newfoundland's entry into Confederation, Apr. 1, 1949.

Those who lost the fight for freedom
  have the greater pride this day,
Though their country's independence
  lies the victim of the fray.
They have kept *their* faith
  untarnished, they have held *their*
  honour high,
They can face the course of history
  with a clear and steadfast eye;
They will have their day of sorrow,
  but will ever take the stand,
As the staunch and faithful servants of
  a well-loved Newfoundland.

> ALBERT PERLIN, qu. by R. Gwyn, *Smallwood*, 1968, 121; taken from *Daily news* (St. John's), Apr. 1, 1949.

Canada did not absorb Newfoundland. It would be historically and constitutionally as correct to say that Newfoundland absorbed Canada or took her over as that Canada absorbed Newfoundland. It was not the absorption of one country by another.

> JOSEPH R. SMALLWOOD, address, Nov. 19, 1959, Empire Club, Toronto.

This is *our* river, this is *our* waterfall, this is *our* land . . . We are developing it mainly, chiefly, principally for the benefit of Newfoundland. Newfoundland first. Quebec second. The rest of the world last.

> JOSEPH R. SMALLWOOD, Constitutional Conf., 2nd meeting, Ottawa, Feb. 10-12, 1969, *Proceedings*, 323.

Somewhere east of that line, north-south line in Quebec, or anywhere east of that in Quebec and in the four Atlantic Provinces — some little baby is going to be born tomorrow morning of whom you may say that a Court has condemned that Canadian baby to an inferior existence, food not so good, home not so good; schools not so good, hospitals not so good, roads not so good, municipal services not so good.

> JOSEPH R. SMALLWOOD, Constitutional Conf., 2nd meeting, Ottawa, Feb. 10-12, 1969, *Proceedings*, 323.

If I got elected six times without living there, I see no reason to live there now.

> JACK PICKERSGILL, to a reporter, Summer, 1972, on leaving public life; he represented Bonavista-Twillingate for 15 years in the House of Commons.

This poor bald rock.

> JOSEPH R. SMALLWOOD, qu. in R. Gwyn, *Smallwood*, 1972, xi.

We can be one of the great small nations of the earth.

JOSEPH R. SMALLWOOD, qu. in R. Gwyn, *Smallwood*, 1972, xii.

Why don't you learn to swim?

JEAN MARCHAND, Minister of Transport, H. of C., *Debates*, Sept. 18, 1973, 6670, during debate on transportation problems between the island and mainland, to opposition members from Newfoundland.

News

What, what, what,
What's the news from Swat?
 Sad news,
 Bad news,
Comes by the cable led
Through the Indian Ocean's bed,
Through the Persian Gulf, the Red
Sea and the Med-
Iterranean — he's dead;
The Akhoond is dead!

GEORGE T. LANIGAN, "A threnody", ("The Akhoond of Swat") after seeing the news, "The Akhoond of Swat is dead", in London newspapers, Jan. 22, 1878.

What I want to see in the *Montreal Star* is the sort of news, or item, or story or article which you would be tempted to read aloud to the person next to you if you saw it in a newspaper or book.

SIR HUGH GRAHAM, advice to John W. Dafoe June, 1883, qu. in Murray Donnelly, *Dafoe of the Free Press*, 1968, 12.

If you have anything to tell me of importance, for God's sake begin at the end.

SARA JEANETTE DUNCAN, *The imperialist*, 1904, 442.

We do not care what grief we bring
 your house
So long as it be news.

SARA JEAN MCKAY, "Newsflashes", 1938.

World news is Canadian news.

HARRY C. HINDMARSH, 1930's, frequent remark, qu. in Ross Harkness, *J.E. Atkinson of the Star*, 1963, 248.

I make the news, I don't read the news.

W.A.C. BENNETT, Premier of B.C., qu. in Vancouver *Sun*, Dec. 31, 1965, by Al Fotheringham.

So much Canadian news is carried in *Time* that it may be said confidently that no other journal provides as much information about Canada to as many readers throughout the world.

L.E. LAYBOURNE, Managing Director of *Time* (Canada), to Canada. Royal Comm. on publications, 1960; in its *Hearings*, Vol. 3, 19.

Here are the news.

EDITH JOSIE, Old Crow correspondent for Whitehorse *Star*, identifying phrase, also title of her book published in 1966.

Yesterday's news is tomorrow's history.

BLAIR FRASER, *The search for identity, Canada 1945-1967*, 1967, 1.

In a world where dynasties rise and fall at much the same rate as women's hemlines, the dynasty and the hemline look much alike in importance, and get much the same amount of featuring in the news.

NORTHROP FRYE, *The modern century*, 1967, 20.

Newspapers

How doth the little busy *Bee*
Abuse each shining hour,
Gathering scandal all the day,
For readers to devour.

> "JACQUES", pseud., newspaper writer, on the Hamilton *Bee*, a newspaper published 1812 to 1838.

We are paid for our labour in the satisfaction afforded our readers – the information diffused throughout the Province, and in the consciousness that in after times, these reports will convey to the generation that succeeds us, very valuable data from which to judge of the character and sentiment of the present age, and of the early habits and conditions of the country.

> JOSEPH HOWE, *Novascotian*, Apr. 24, 1834.

Our wood paying subscribers will please send us a few cords of wood at their earliest convenience.

> CORNWALL *OBSERVER*, Dec. 18, 1835.

The Editors of all the Great Liberal Organs are Roman Catholics, with an exception, and that one is an anythingarian.

> HALIFAX *MORNING POST*, 1847.

The Halifax Express.

> ANON., a system organized by six New York City newspapers whereby European news was received at Halifax, then relayed by "pony express" to Digby, by boat to St. John, N.B., then by telegraph to New York. First used Feb. 21, 1849, this marked the inception of the Associated Press.

The standard literature of Canada must be looked for in her newspapers.

> SUSANNA MOODIE, *Mark Hurdlestone*, 1853, I, xx.

The Canadian cannot get along without his newspaper any more than an American could without his tobacco.

> SUSANNA MOODIE, *Mark Hurdlestone*, 1853, I, xx.

It's a damned sharp curve, but I think we can take it.

> ROBERT SMILEY, Editor, Hamilton *Spectator*, telegram to Sir John A. Macdonald, 1854, on being asked to stop attacks on Robert Spence, Reformer, who was about to become a coalition colleague of Macdonald's.

Party leadership and the conducting of a great journal do not harmonize.

> GEORGE BROWN, letter to Luther H. Holton, May 13, 1867.

However and nevertheless sheets.

> ANON., phrase used to describe newspapers which tried to be politically independent, 1880's.

Politics and vituperation, temperance and vituperation, religion and vituperation; these three dietetic articles, the vituperative sauce invariably accompanying, form the exclusive journalistic pabulum of three-quarters of the people of Ontario.

> SARA JEANETTE DUNCAN, *The Week*, Sept. 30, 1886, 707.

Covers Prince Edward Island like the dew.

> *GUARDIAN*, Charlottetown, P.E.I. newspaper, established 1891, motto.

The *News* may be congratulated on having, under its new management, shown force enough to brave the second greatest of the three tyrannical powers which militate against independence – Party, Popular Passion, and Ads. Ads probably are the greatest of the three, but the next greatest is Popular Passion.

GOLDWIN SMITH, letter to John Willison, Jan. 20, 1903.

The press never killed a public man who deserved to live.

SIR JOHN WILLISON, *Reminiscences*, 1919, 66.

The editorial page of the daily newspaper is not as good as it was, because the editor has now to reach not only the educated but the uneducated, and adjusts his tone to their needs.

G.M. WRONG, *Can.hist.rev.*, 1921, 315.

The Misleader.

ANON., the Regina *Leader-post*, so called by many Saskatchewan farmers because of its opposition to the Wheat Pool in 1923.

I pay no attention whatever to the press.

W.L. MACKENZIE KING, to Lord Beaverbrook, qu., Hardy, *Mackenzie King of Canada*, 1949, 289.

Any journal whose opinions are made on the premises by its owners and officers, and the making of which is affected only by consideration of public interest so far as they make an appeal and by the interests of the property itself, is an independent journal.

J.W. DAFOE, in *Can.hist.rev.*, 1936, 62.

The newspaper whose support of a party is bought and paid for, directly or indirectly, out of party funds, is a propagandist sheet and not a public journal.

J.W. DAFOE, in *Can.hist.rev.*, 1936, 62.

The *Star* will print what I tell it to.

JOSEPH E. ATKINSON, owner of the *Star*, on Ontario Premier Hepburn's refusal to follow his dictates over the C.I.O., qu. by Neil McKenty in *Mitch Hepburn*, 1967, 139.

Pressure on newspapers comes, not from advertisers, but from readers who ask editors, as the Israelites asked Isaiah, to beguile them with pleasant errors. It is rarely that people criticize errors; it is only the truth that they ask us to retract.

GÉRARD FILION, Editor of *Le Devoir*, speech at a Chamber of Commerce meeting, Montreal, qu. by H. MacLennan, *Thirty and three*, 1954, 248.

The English papers in Quebec act like British administrators in an African colony . . . They keep a close check on the nigger-king but they wink at his whims. On occasion they permit him to chop off a few heads; it's part of the local folklore. But one thing would never occur to them: to expect the nigger-king to conform to the high moral and political standards of the British.

ANDRÉ LAURENDEAU, editorial, *Le Devoir*, July 4, 1958; ref. to Maurice Duplessis; gave rise to the nigger-king hypothesis in Quebec politics. (Trans.)

Passion. That's the thing. I don't care what you put in the paper so long as you say it with passion.

LORD BEAVERBROOK, advice to a new managing editor of *Daily express*, 1961, qu. in *Time*, Sept. 6, 1963, 48.

Do you have any newspapers for sale?

> ROY (LORD) THOMSON, frequently asked of newspaper owners; variable, 1960's.

I put it to you that our Canadian newspapers – those paragons who are doing all the shouting about Canadian identity these days – are in fact selling out on that very goal. For all their pretensions, they are actually – albeit partly unintentionally – the spotters for the barrage of American and British brainwashing that we have such cause to worry about right now. Through a sustained, substantial and significant pattern of coverage, they are managing to condition us daily to abandon our own real culture in favour of a blurred carbon of the two giants at our elbows.

> DONALD GORDON, *Saturday night*, Jan., 1964, 17.

To become a newspaperman you need the hide of a dinosaur, the stamina of a Chinese coolie, the wakefulness and persistence of a mosquito, the analytic powers of a detective and the digging capacity of a steam shovel.

> ROY GREENAWAY, *The news game*, 1966, 7.

There aren't many Canadian newspapers left for us to buy.

> LORD THOMSON, at Annual Meeting of Thomson Newspapers Ltd., Toronto, May 31, 1968.

Newspapers go to great pains to give honest, accurate accounts of the lies told by politicians.

> RICHARD J. NEEDHAM, *A friend in Needham*, 1969, 44.

Every reporter soon learns there are only a few newspapers where excellence is encouraged. If they are lucky or clever or restless, they will gravitate to those newspapers. If not, they will stay where they are, growing cynical about their work, learning to live with a kind of sour professional despair. Often you can see it in their faces. Most Canadian cityrooms are boneyards of broken dreams.

> SENATE. SPECIAL COMMITTEE ON MASS MEDIA, *Report*, 1970, Vol. 1, 65.

It is not the prestige of being owners and publishers of newspapers. It is not the earnest desire to lead, editorially, public thought toward progressive social reform and higher human purpose. The primary purpose is none of these. The primary purpose is to grasp power and more power.

> CHARLES MCELMAN, Senate, *Debates*, Mar. 10, 1971, 673.

Niagara Falls

The Niagara River near this place is only the eighth of a league wide, but it is very deep in places, and so rapid above the great falls that it hurries down all the animals which try to cross it, without a single one being able to withstand its current. They plunge down a height of more than five hundred feet, and its fall is composed of two sheets of water and a cascade, with an island sloping down. In the middle, these waters foam and boil in a fearful manner. They thunder continually, and when the wind blows in a southerly direction, the noise they make is heard for from more than fifteen leagues.

> FATHER LOUIS HENNEPIN, *Description de la Louisiane*, 1683, (1678). (Trans.)

I am metamorphosed; I am translated; I am an ass's head, a clod, a wooden spoon, a fat weed growing on Lethe's brink, a stock, a stone, a petrifaction. For have I not seen Niagara, the wonder of wonders, and felt – no words can tell *what* disappointment.

ANNA JAMESON, *Winter studies*, 1838, I, 83.

Niagara Spray racket.

ANON., the sale of white stones found around the base of Niagara Falls to gullible tourists as "congealed mist", 1830's.

Congealed mist.

ANON., fraudulent designation of white stones found around the base of Niagara Falls and sold to gullible tourists, ca. 1830.

My thoughts are strange, magnificent, and deep,
When I look down on thee; –
Oh, what a glorious place for washing sheep
Niagara would be!

ANON., in Susanna Moodie, *Life in the clearings*, 1853, 113.

When I first saw the falls I was disappointed in the outline. Every American bride is taken there, and the sight must be one of the earliest, if not the keenest, disappointments in American married life.

OSCAR WILDE, press interview, New York, 1882.

It's a terrible nightmare – I don't want to experience it again. I'd sooner be shot from a cannon.

ANNIE EDSON TAYLOR, first person to go over Niagara Falls in a barrel and survive, Oct. 24, 1901.

Here all the fury since the world was young
Is chanted on one tongue.

WILSON MACDONALD, "Niagara", 1926.

The principle of the thing seems much the same.

WINSTON CHURCHILL, Dec., 1941, on revisiting Niagara Falls after 40 years, qu. by Harold Macmillan in Canadian House of Commons, June 13, 1958.

Night

And Darkness, like a Fate, comes stealing down
In her black mantle, step by step, until
The trembling stars have dwindled down to one
Pale, solitary watcher.

CHARLES SANGSTER, "The Saint Lawrence and the Saguenay", 1856.

And when day passed and over heaven's height,
Thin with the many stars and cool with dew,
The fingers of the deep hours slowly drew
The wonder of the ever-healing night.

ARCHIBALD LAMPMAN, "The frogs", 1888.

Who are the mimes of the air
That wept on the woe of our flight,
That chanted a bitter despair
In the dark haunted heart of the night?

WILFRED CAMPBELL, "The last ride", 1889.

In the wide awe and wisdom of the night
I saw the round world rolling on its way,
Beyond significance of depth or height,
Beyond the interchange of dark and day.

CHARLES G.D. ROBERTS, "In the wide awe and wisdom of the night", 1893.

How deep the April night is in its
   noon,
The hopeful, solemn,
   many-murmured night!
The earth lies hushed with
   expectation; bright
Above the world's dark border burns
   the moon.

ARCHIBALD LAMPMAN, "April night",
1899.

When night-time comes, I'm always
glad I live in the country. We know
the real charm of night here as town
dwellers never do.

L.M. MONTGOMERY, *Rilla of Ingleside,*
1921, ch. 3.

Night, like a sacristan with silent step,
Passes to light the tapers of the stars.

BLISS CARMAN, "Winter", 1921.

Have you ever noticed how much
larger your troubles appear at night?

ROBERT C. (BOB) EDWARDS, Calgary *Eye
Opener*, Sept. 24, 1921.

I love the light, I'll have no traffic
With the nigger world of night.

ANNE WILKINSON, "The pressure of
night", 1955.

No

Fifteen years of saying 'no'.

JOHN W. DAFOE, *Laurier*, 1922, 64, on
Laurier's negative attitude to closer involvement in Empire affairs, 1897 to
1911.

There is in Canada, too, somewhere
seated on the throne of power, a man
who continuously says 'No' to life, not
only to his life but also to yours.

J.B. PRIESTLEY, *The listener*, June 7,
1956, 744.

We were born saying 'No'. Our ancestors, French and English, said 'No' to
the American Revolution in the 1770's
and 1780's. They said 'No' again to
democracy in 1837.

FRANK H. UNDERHILL, *The image of
Canada*, 1962, 11.

Normality

Christ i wudint know normal if i saw it
when

BILL BISSETT, *Nobody owns th earth*,
1971, title of poem.

Norman, Herbert

He was killed as surely as if somebody
had put a knife into his back.

ALISTAIR STEWART, H. of C., *Debates*,
Apr. 4, 1957, 3059, on the suicide of the
Canadian ambassador in Cairo as a
result of mention of his name by the
so-called U.S. Committee on Un-American Activities.

The North

But there is a Papal power there in
wakeful exercise, only less pestiferous
and godless than Paganism itself,
which must be enervated and annihilated, with all the inane supersti-
tions, and corruptions, and savagism of
every debased tribe of the frigid
North.

METHODIST CHURCH, *Missionary notices*,
Nov., 1854, on initiating the Methodist
entry into Hudson Bay Territory.

Together we Men of the North
. . . . will be able to teach the Yankees that we will be as our ancestors
always have been, the dominant race.

GEORGE T. DENISON, letter to Charles
Mair, Mar. 10, 1869.

Oh, we are the men of the Northern
  Zone;
  Shall a bit be placed in our mouth?
If ever a Northman lost his throne
  Did the conqueror come from the
    South?
  Nay, nay — and the answer blent
  In chorus is southward sent:
'Since when has a Southener's
  conquering steel
  Hewed out in the North a throne?
Since when has a Southener placed his
  heel
  On the men of the Northern zone?'

R.K. KERNIGHAN, "Men of the Northern
Zone", 1896.

This is the land of the rugged North;
  these wide,
Life-yielding fields, these inland
  oceans, these
Vast rivers moving seaward their wide
  floods,
Majestic music: these sky-bounded
  plains
And heaven-topping mountains; these
  iron shores,
Facing toward either ocean; fit home,
  alone,
For the indomitable and nobly strong.

WILLIAM WILFRED CAMPBELL, "To the
Canadian patriot", 1905.

Plumb-full of hush to the brim.

ROBERT W. SERVICE, "The spell of the
Yukon", 1907.

Why should the children of the North
  deny
The sanitary virtues of the sky?
Why should they fear the cold, or
  dread the snow,
When ruddier blood thro' their hot
  pulses flow?

WILLIAM HENRY TAYLOR, "Invocation",
1913.

It has been said that power, that
empire came from the north. Northern
people have always stood for courage
and unconquerability. They have the
muscle, the wholesomeness of life, the
strength of will.

DONALD A. SMITH, (Lord Strathcona), to
William Garson, qu., in B. Willson, *Life
of Strathcona*, 1915, 601.

If the average American or European
university graduate has ten ideas about
the North, nine of them are wrong.

VILHJALMUR STEFANSSON, *The northward course of empire*, 1922, 20.

I never have gone to the James Bay; I
never go to it; I never shall. But
somehow I'd feel lonely without it.

STEPHEN LEACOCK, "I'll stay in Canada",
1936, in Klinck & Watters, *Canadian
anthology*, 1957, 212.

In Canada the frontier which abounds
in poetry and latent hope is less the
West, as in the United States, than the
Northwest, or simply the North.

ANDRÉ SIEGFRIED, *Canada*, 1937, 28.

Now the North, which is common to
both East and West, is a natural bridge
to unite the two divisions. I look to the
North as one of the great unifying
factors in the future of the Dominion.

LORD TWEEDSMUIR, notes for Mackenzie
King's speeches in Britain, Summer,
1937.

Fear and suspicion engendered in Iran
can easily spread to Great Bear Lake
above the Arctic Circle in Canada and
bedevil economic developments there.
There is now no refuge in remoteness.

LESTER B. PEARSON, *Foreign affairs*, Vol.
24, July, 1946, 644.

What of this fabulous country
Now that we have it reduced to a few
   hot hours
And sun-burn on our backs?
On this south side the countless
   archipelagoes,
The slipway where titans sent
   splashing the last great glaciers;
And then up to the foot of the blue
   pole star
A wilderness.

DOUGLAS LE PAN, "Canoe-trip", 1948.

It has been said that Great Britain acquired her empire in a state of absence of mind. Apparently we have administered these vast territories of the north in an almost continuing state of absence of mind.

LOUIS ST. LAURENT, H. of C., *Debates*, Dec. 8, 1953, 698 on introducing a bill to establish the Dept. of Northern Affairs.

To hold in a verse as austere
As the spirit of prairie and river.
Lonely, unbuyable, dear,
The North, as a deed and for ever.

A.J.M. SMITH, "To hold in a poem", 1954.

To me, as to most northeners, the country is still an unknown quantity, as elusive as the wolf, howling just beyond the rim of the hills.

PIERRE BERTON, *The mysterious north*, 1956, 4.

I see a new Canada — a Canada of the north.

JOHN DIEFENBAKER, election campaign speech, Winnipeg, Feb. 12, 1958.

The northern character . . . has been fashioned in a spirit of cautious defensiveness as a means of preserving what might at any moment be snatched away.

CLAUDE BISSELL, qu. by Dave Godfrey, *Tamarack rev.*, Summer, 1963, 32.

The story of Canada's development of its North, then, can be summed up fairly accurately in one sentence: where there are profits, there are people.

BRIAN MOORE, *Canada*, 1963, 106.

The warders watch the sky watch
   them
the stricken hills eye both
A Mountie visits twice a year
And there is talk of growth.

EARLE BIRNEY, "Ellesmereland", 1965.

For those with eyes to see, the North is vitally and vividly alive. Long, long ago, men of other races out of another time recognized this truth and learned to call the northern regions "home".

FARLEY MOWAT, *Canada north*, 1967, 27.

This is not a Canada to call forth any man's love. But just north of it still lies a different kind of land — too barren ever to be thickly settled, too bleak to be popular like Blackpool or Miami. There is no reason to doubt that it will always be there, and so long as it is there Canada will not die.

BLAIR FRASER, *The search for identity*, 1967, 315.

The presence of a North in man is even more critical than the presence of men in the North.

JACK WARWICK, *The long journey*, 1968, 47.

A source of a flow of beneficent informing cosmic powers behind the bleakness and barrenness and austerity of much of the land.

LAWREN HARRIS, in Bess Harris and R.G.P. Colgrove, eds., *Lawren Harris*, 1969, 11.

(In the north
a woman can learn
to live with too much sadness.
Finding *anything* could be hard.)

SUSAN MUSGRAVE, "At Nootka Sound",
1970.

The north has a profoundly spiritual
effect upon man, somehow assuring
him of his importance at one time, and
convincing him of his insignificance at
another.

JIM LOTZ, *Northern realities*, 1970, 32.

Where I am is very cold and the ice
figures I collect for you never, somehow, survive the transport. And so
these small black tracks upon the page.
Where you are is too warm for me.
This message is a map which shows
my exact coordinates at this moment.
Follow it. Try to find me. I should like
to be here when you arrive, but in this
weather it is necessary to keep moving.

J. MICHAEL YATES, *The Great Bear Lake
meditations*, 1970, (Long dark, meditation 7).

Latter-day robber-barons, aided, abet-
ted and encouraged by prodigal politicians and obsequious bureaucrats, are
staging an unprecedented industrial
invasion – using 20th-century technology guided by 19th-century philosophy.

JAMES WOODFORD, *The violated vision*,
1972, Intro.

In the town of The Pas, Manitoba
It snows on the first of Octoba
From then, for six months,
It thaws only once
And never when I am quite soba.

ANON., qu. in *Maclean's*, Nov., 1973, 51.

North America

There is a North Americanism which
is Canadian and not 'American'.

MALCOLM ROSS, *Our sense of identity*,
1954, ix.

Northern Lights

I do not remember to have met with
any travellers into high Northern latitudes, who remarked their having
heard the Northern Lights make any
noise in the air as they vary their
colours or position; which may probably be owing to the want of perfect
silence at the time they made their
observations on those meteors. I can
positively affirm, that in still nights I
have frequently heard them make a
rustling and crackling noise, like the
waving of a large flag in a fresh gale
of wind.

SAMUEL HEARNE, *Journey from Prince
of Wales Fort in Hudson's Bay*, 1795,
224.

The sun has scarcely set behind the
dark, wavy outline of the western hills,
ere the Aurora Borealis mimics its
setting beams, and revels with wild
delight in the heavens, which it claims
as its own, now ascending with meteor
speed to the zenith, then dissolving
into a thousand rays of variegated
light, that vie with each other which
shall first reach the horizon; now flashing bright, brilliant and glowing, as
emanations of the sun, then slowly
retreating from view pale and silvery
white, like wandering moonbeams.

T.C. HALIBURTON, *Old judge*, 1849.

After nightfall there was a most beautiful aurora. Sometimes like a tent
with streams proceeding earthwards
and in every direction from a fixed
central point, sometimes like a very
grand arch stretching from east to
west through Arcturus, Vega, Cygnus

and the neighboring stars. Then it became a mass of glowing red, spreading over the eastern side of the heavens and gradually passing to the south.

EARL OF SOUTHESK, *Saskatchewan and the Rocky Mountains: A diary and narrative of travel in 1859 and 1860,* 1860, 183.

Here's to the Land of the rock and the
　　pine;
　　Here's to the Land of the raft and
　　the river!
Here's to the Land where the
　　sunbeams shine,
　　And the night is bright with the
　　North-lights' quiver!

WILLIAM W. SMITH, "Here's to the land", 1888.

In the north behold a flushing,
Then a deep and crimson blushing,
Followed by an airy rushing
　　Of the purple waves that rise!
As when armed host advances,
See a silver banner dances,
And a thousand golden lances
　　Shimmer in the Boreal skies!

J.K. FORAN, "Aurora Borealis", 1895.

There in the awe we crouched and
　　saw with our
　　wild, uplifted eyes
Charge and retire the hosts of fire in
　　the
　　battlefield of the skies.

ROBERT W. SERVICE, "Ballad of the Northern Lights", 1909.

Northwest Passage

Doubtles theare is a passadge.

WILLIAM BAFFIN, 1615, in *Voyages,* Hakluyt Society, 1881, 137, on the Northwest Passage.

There is a Northwest Passage to the intellectual world.

LAURENCE STERNE, *Tristram Shandy,* 1759-67, Book V, Chap. 42.

On every side of us are men who hunt perpetually for their personal Northwest Passage, too often sacrificing health, strength and life itself to the search; and who shall say they are not happier in their vain and hopeful quest than wiser, duller folk who sit at home, venturing nothing and, with sour laughs, deriding the seekers for that fabled thoroughfare − that panacea for all the afflictions of a humdrum world.

KENNETH ROBERTS, *Northwest passage,* 1937, Foreword.

North West Rebellion, 1885

This Northwest outbreak was a mere domestic trouble, and ought not to be elevated to the rank of a rebellion.

SIR JOHN A. MACDONALD, letter to Governor General Lansdowne, Aug. 28, 1885.

Had I been born on the banks of the Saskatchewan, I would myself have shouldered a musket to fight against the neglect of governments and the shameless greed of speculators.

SIR WILFRID LAURIER, speech, Champ de Mars, Montreal, Nov. 22, 1885; "the musket speech".

Before that time, when we were not enlightened, the word of the priest was the word of truth; but after that, when we get to be a little more enlightened, we saw that they could tell us lies.

GABRIEL DUMONT, at the Music Hall, Montreal, Apr. 24, 1888; *Le Pays,* July 10, 1915.

Many lives were lost during this unfortunate disturbance. On the other hand much good resulted. Disaffected halfbreeds and rebellious Indians were taught a salutary lesson; they learned something of the strength of British rule, and likewise experienced some-

thing of its clemency and righteousness.

> REV. JAMES WOODSWORTH, *Thirty years in the Canadian north-west*, 1917, 12.

Nor'Westers

The feudal state of Fort William is at
an end; its council chamber is silent
and deserted; its banquet-hall no longer echoes to the burst of loyalty, or the
'auld world' ditty; the lords of the
lakes and forests have passed away.

> WASHINGTON IRVING, *Astoria*, 1836, on the Nor'Westers, Chap.1.

Noses

I gaze, and as I gaze the wonder
grows, how one small face can carry so
much nose.

> ARTHUR H. GILLMOR, H. of C., 1879, to James Domville, another member; at-tributed.

Shame! It's more than a shame. 'Snout-
rage!

> J.R. CAMERON, Editor, Hamilton *Specta-tor*, on a Conservative newspaper's statement that it was a shame to discuss Sir John A. Macdonald's nose when his son Hugh John's qualifications for pub-lic office were under consideration, about 1900.

It's not for nothing that my nose is so
long.

> MAURICE DUPLESSIS, favourite expression, 1950's.

When you sniff the acoustics of your
nose are delightful.

> ALFRED PURDY, "Love song", 1970.

My nose is lonesome in the middle
of my face, but my nose is blessed
with patience.

> ALLEN SPERL, "Or is that music?", 1970.

Nostalgia

Whenever I passed .the house
At far, rare intervals
Memory stabbed,
The tree at the gate grieved.

> DOROTHY LIVESAY, "Neighbourhood", 1932.

Nothing

It is becoming gray now
The sun is gone
It is becoming dark now
The light of day gone
It is becoming neither night nor day
    now
And the darkness gone
It is becoming nothing nothing
    nothing
And everything gone.

> RAYMOND SOUSTER, "It is becoming gray now", 1949.

But still on the highest shelf of ever
washed by the curve of timeless
    returnings
lies the unreached unreachable
    nothing
whose winds wash down to the human
    shores

> EARLE BIRNEY, "November walk near False Creek mouth", 1961.

Nova Scotia

The very delicate meadows, with roses
white and red, and the very good fat
earth.

> SIR WILLIAM ALEXANDER, *Encourage-ment to colonies*, 1624.

Of all the vile countries that ever were
    known,
In the frigid or torrid or temperate
    zone,
From the accounts I have heard there
    is not such another;

It neither belongs to this world or the other.

> ANON., American Revolutionary song, 1770's.

Good God, what sums the nursing of that ill-throven, hardvisaged and ill-favored brat, Nova Scotia, has cost to this wittol nation.

> EDMUND BURKE, speech in Gt. Brit., H. of C., Feb. 11, 1780; *wittol* means cuckolded and submissive.

Nova Scarcity.

> ANON., term used by disaffected United Empire Loyalists, 1783, especially the literary group in Halifax.

Bluenose.

> ANON., the origin of this nickname is believed to be derived from the MacIntyre Blue potato, a long tuber with blueish eyes and "nose". As early as 1787 shipments of potatoes to Boston were invoiced as "blue noses". The Loyalist settlers in Annapolis and King's County applied the name to previous settlers. Much used by T.C. HALIBURTON, *Sam Slick*, 1836, and later books.

We profess to be *Colonial* and not merely *Nova Scotian* Patriots.

> COLONIAL PATRIOT, Pictou, N.S., July 22, 1829.

This is the infant hour, or, if you will, the childhood of our country; and it is, if not for you and me, at all events for the race among whom we live, and to whom our public declarations are addressed, to say what shall be her future progress; what resources shall be placed within her reach; what rules laid down for her guidance; what opinions and determinations indelibly impressed upon her mind.

> JOSEPH HOWE, speech, Halifax Mechanics' Inst., Nov. 5, 1834.

We are few in numbers; our country is but a narrow tract, surrounded by populous States; and we have no prospect of distinction — I had almost said of future safety — but from high mental and moral cultivation, infusing into every branch of industry such a degree of intellectual vigour as shall insure success, multiply population, and endow them with productive power.

> JOSEPH HOWE, speech, Halifax Mechanics' Institute, Nov. 5, 1834.

We bloom amid the snow.

> NOVA SCOTIA PHILANTHROPIC SOCIETY, motto, adopted 1834, and associated with the mayflower which was made the provincial floral emblem by statute, I Ed. VII, Cap. 10, 1936.

This place (that is, Nova Scotia) is as fertile as Illanoy or Ohio, as healthy as any part of the Globe, and right alongside of salt water; but the folks want three things, Industry, Enterprise, Economy.

> T.C. HALIBURTON, *Sam Slick*, 1836, ch. 33.

It will be our pride to make Nova Scotia a Normal School for the rest of the colonies showing them how representative institutions may be worked so as to secure international tranquility and advancement in subordination to the paramount interests and authority of the Crown.

> JOSEPH HOWE, letter to Charles Buller, Feb. 12, 1848.

To the Nova Scotian, the province is his native place, but North America is his country. The colony may become his home when the provinces become a nation. It will then have a name, the inhabitants will become a people, and the people have a country and a home.

Until that period it would seem as if they were merely comers and goers.

> T.C. HALIBURTON, *Old judge*, 1849, II, 228.

I am a clear lover of Old England, and to save her would blow Nova Scotia into the air.

> JOSEPH HOWE, letter to C.D. Hay, Nov. 12, 1866. (Pub. Arch. Can.)

Munit haec et altera vincit. (One defends and the other conquers.)

> NOVA SCOTIA., Motto on the provincial coat of arms.

Died! Last night at twelve o'clock, the free and enlightened Province of Nova Scotia. Deceased was the off-spring of old English stock, and promised to have proved an honour and a support to her parents in their declining years. Her death was occasioned by unnatural treatment received at the hands of some of her ungrateful sons.

> HALIFAX *MORNING CHRONICLE*, July 1, 1867.

When dawned the morn of '67,
   Fair and most prosperous was her state,
No happier country under Heaven,–
   Look at her now in '68!

> "FRED" [?], "Anti lyrics No. II", 1868, qu. in Halifax *Morning chronicle*, Jan. 3, 1868, 2.

If you are sulky, Nova Scotia,
We'll gladly let you float away
From out our Confederation;
You sicken us with silly agitation.
If any more our patience you do tax
We'll let you go to Halifax.

> JAMES MCINTYRE, "Nova Scotia: lines written when Nova Scotia was threatening to withdraw from Confederation" (1870's), published 1884.

Boys, brag of your country. When I am abroad, I brag of everything that Nova Scotia is, has, or can produce; and when they beat me at everything else, I turn round on them and say, 'How high does your tide rise?'

> JOSEPH HOWE, speech in Nova Scotia, qu., Grant, *Joseph Howe*, 1906, 2.

You don't need a big field to raise a big turnip.

> JOSEPH HOWE, on Nova Scotia, qu. in G.M. Grant, *Joseph Howe*, 1906, 37.

You have got us, and now you have got to keep us.

> JOSEPH HOWE, a remark made about 1869 to Cartwright and others.

The Mayflower Province.

> ANON., a popular term.

Restore our province as an independent, self-governing British dominion, make us once more free and independent in the matter of trade and commerce, competent to protect ourselves sanely and wisely from the products of Ontario and Quebec as well as other lands, then there would undoubtedly be a great revival in business and local manufacturing in this province. Instead of decreasing, as at present, our population would increase. In a comparatively short time, in my opinion, we would have a million people in Nova Scotia.

> H.W. CORNING, Member, in N.S. Legislature, Apr. 21, 1923, qu. in Halifax *Herald*, Apr. 23, 1923, 3.

A country's worth is not according to the number of square miles it possesses, but according to the square people it contains. Nova Scotia is very happy in this regard.

> E.N. RHODES, Premier of N.S., in C. Martin, ed., *The book of Canada*, 1930, 199.

From the sea-light of Yarmouth to the
    headlands of Bras d'Or,
From the swinging tides of Fundy to
    the wild Southern Shore,
The Gaspereau Valley, the dikes of
    Grand Pré,
Farms and mines and fishing fleets,
    river, lake and bay,
Lunenburg and Halifax and lovely
    Margaree,
Is all the Land of Acadie, the
    Sweetheart of the Sea.

> BLISS CARMAN, "Forever and forever",
> 1929.

New Nova Scotia.

> ANON., phrase used after Robert Stan-
> field came to power, 1956.

Nova Scotia contemplates its navel.

> MIRIAM CHAPIN, *Atlantic Canada*,
> 1956, 82.

North America is a large island to the
west of the continent of Cape Breton.

> RAY SMITH, *Tamarack rev.*, Autumn,
> 1967, 50.

Novelists

The first Canadian novelist.

> ANON., referring to Julia Catherine Hart
> (1796-1867) whose novel, *St. Ursula's
> convent, of the nun of Canada, con-
> taining scenes from real life*, was pub-
> lished by Hugh C. Thomson at Kings-
> ton, Ont., in 1824.

It makes me wild with rage to be
described as a "female novelist". You
never hear people referring to male
novels and gentlemen novelists. I'm a
novelist and I'm a woman.

> MARGARET LAURENCE, interview, *Satur-
> day night*, May, 1974, 20.

Novels

Professing Christians ought not to
countenance the production of novels.

> THE CHRISTIAN EXAMINER, 1840, qu. in
> William H. Elgee, *The social teachings
> of the Canadian churches*, 1964, 95.

Don't stick up your ears now, imagining that the great Canadian novel has
been written at last. Nothing of the
sort. It is merely a juvenilish story,
ostensibly for girls; [but] as I found the
Mss. rather interesting while reading it
over lately I am not without hope that
grown-ups may like it a little. Its title
is *Anne of Green Gables* and the
publishers seem to think it will succeed
as they want me to go right to work on
a sequel to it.

> L.M. MONTGOMERY, letter to Ephraim
> Weber, May 2, 1907. (Pub.Arch.Can.)

A novel should have a beginning and
an end and something of an infinitude
in between.

> FREDERICK PHILIP GROVE, "The novel",
> in *It needs to be said*, 1929, 127.

The best of novels are only scenarios,
to be completed by the reader's own
experience.

> ROBERTSON DAVIES, *A voice from the
> attic*, 1960, 13.

November

Far off the village lamps begin to
    gleam,
Fast drives the snow, and no man
    comes this way;
The hills grow wintery white, and
    bleak winds moan
About the naked uplands. I alone
Am neither sad, no shelterless, nor
    grey,

Wrapped round with thought, content
to watch and dream.

> ARCHIBALD LAMPMAN, "In November",
> 1888.

In November,
like last loving,
sun lays long lingering fingers
on the Winter's-verge of earth.

Sun finds strongholds summer never
    knew,
and so the heart can do.

> JOAN FINNIGAN, "In November", 1965.

Nuclear Warfare

I have lived since – as you have – in
a period of cold war, during which we
have ensured, by our achievements in
the science and technology of destruction, that a third act in this tragedy of
war will result in the peace of extinction.

> LESTER B. PEARSON, on accepting Nobel
> Prize, Oslo, Dec. 11, 1957.

Nuclear Weapons

If it had not been for the vision and
determination of Gilbert LaBine, we
wouldn't have had the bomb in time.

> WILLIAM L. LAURENCE, Science Editor,
> New York *Times,* qu. in P. Newman,
> *Flame of power,* 1959, 150.

[The Canadian Government] should
end at once its evasion of responsibility
by discharging the commitments it has
already accepted for Canada. It can

only do this by accepting nuclear
warheads.

> LESTER B. PEARSON, speech to York-Scar-
> borough Liberal Assoc., Jan. 12, 1963.

As they are deployed, they draw more
fire than those Jupiter missiles will.

> ROBERT S. MCNAMARA, U.S. Sec'y. of
> Defence, to sub-committee of House of
> Representatives Committee on Appro-
> priations, Feb. 13, 1963, referring to
> Bomarc missile bases in Canada. The
> Jupiter missiles were in Italy and Tur-
> key.

At the very least, they would cause the
Soviets to target missiles against them
and thereby increase their missile requirements or draw missiles on to
these Bomarc targets that would otherwise be available for other targets.

> ROBERT S. MCNAMARA, U.S. Sec'y. of
> Defence secret testimony to sub-com-
> mittee of House of Representatives
> Committee on Appropriations, Feb. 13,
> 1963, referring to Bomarc missile bases
> in Canada. The Bomarc had previously
> been acknowledged to be obsolete.

We don't intend to use Canada as a
dumping ground for nuclear warheads.

> JOHN G. DIEFENBAKER, speech, Win-
> nipeg, Mar. 4, 1963.

Happy days are here again. This is
what I have been saying all along. This
is a knock-out blow.

> JOHN DIEFENBAKER, to reporters, Toron-
> to, Mar. 29, 1963, referring to McNama-
> ra testimony to House of Representa-
> tives Committee. The fact that the Bo-
> marc missile had been declared obsolete
> he considered a "knock-out blow" to the
> Liberal party who advocated arming
> them with nuclear warheads.

The Pearson policy is to make Canada a decoy for intercontinental missiles.

> JOHN DIEFENBAKER, speech, Kingston, Ont., Mar. 29, 1963, referring to Liberal willingness to arm the Bomarc missile with nuclear warheads.

Never in our history has Canadian public opinion been so resolutely manipulated – by American politicians, American generals, the U.S. State Department, the American Embassy in Ottawa, *Newsweek* magazine and hosts of accommodating Canadians who jostled one another for room on the nuclear bandwagon.

> DALTON CAMP, in Lewis Hertzman, *Alliances and illusions*, 1969, xvii, referring to public acceptance of nuclear weaponry on Canadian soil, 1963.

The fact is that the argument for or against nuclear weapons for Canada is a political not a moral one.

> LESTER B. PEARSON, *Words and occasions*, 1970, 201.

Nudity

[I have agreed with nudity] since my mother bore me, when I was without dress, since that time.

> ANNIE KOFTINOFF, Doukhobor, at trial of Michael Verigin, June 14, 1950.

I think it's a marvellous thing. Not for myself, for Canada. For Canada!

> PAMELA ANNE GORDON, first Canadian "Playmate of the Month", *Playboy*, March, 1962.

Nuns

In pairs,
as if to illustrate their sisterhood,
the sisters pace the hospital garden
    walks.
In their robes black and white
    immaculate hoods
they are like birds,
the safe domestic fowl of the House of
    God.

> A.M. KLEIN, "For the sisters of the Hotel Dieu", 1948.

Nurses

It is a moot question which is the more fatally fascinating – the uniformed nurse or the weeded widow.

> ARNOLD HAULTAIN, *Hints for lovers*, 1909, 127.

O biblic birds,
who fluttered to me in my childhood
    illnesses
    – me little, afraid, ill, not of your
    race –
the cool wing for my fever, the
    hovering solace,
the sense of angels –
be thanked, O plumage of paradise, be
    praised.

> A.M. KLEIN, "For the sisters of the Hotel Dieu", 1948.

The essential warmth of the human spirit is indicated by the fact that nurses marry men, and gynecologists marry women.

> RICHARD J. NEEDHAM, *A friend in Needham*, 1969, 52.

Obedience

I don't ask for gratitude but I want obedience and do not think that I will demand it the less because we are under the English government. It is just and proper. Don't get a false notion of liberty; it doesn't justify insubordination.

> JEAN-OLIVER BRIAND, letter to Father Couturier, 1767 (Que. Archives of the Archbishopric). (Trans.)

Horse, or man, or dog aren't much good till they learn to obey.

> MARSHALL SAUNDERS, *Beautiful Joe*, 1893, (1920, 120).

Obituaries

Sir Herbert Holt is dead.

> Sept. 28, 1941; cheered when announced over loudspeaker at a baseball game in Delorimier Stadium, Montreal.

Obligations

Don't you know that there are some people in this world who resent nothing so much as the sense of an obligation which they can never repay? Campbell is one of those persons. He knows he can never requite me for what I have done for him in the past, and he hates me for it.

> SIR JOHN A. MACDONALD, qu. by Sir Joseph Pope in *Public servant*, 1960, 50, referring to Sir Alexander Campbell, 1880's.

We are either on God's side or evil's,
  We are either perjured or true —
And that, which we set out to do in the
  first place,
That must we do.

> WILFRED CAMPBELL, "Our dead", 1923.

Obscenity

A study of the vast untouched field of obscenity and blasphemy ranging from academic halls to the lumber and mining camps and the army would throw interesting light on the problem of realistic literature in Canada.

> H.A. INNIS, in *Can. hist. rev.*, 1944, 57.

Everyone commits an offence who makes, prints, publishes, distributes, circulates, or has in his possession for the purpose of publication, distribution or circulation any obscene written matter, picture, model, phonograph record or other thing whatsoever.

> CANADA. LAWS, STATUTES, ETC., 1953-54, *Criminal code*, C. 51, 150 (1).

For the purposes of this Act, any publication a dominant characteristic of which is the undue exploitation of sex, or of sex and any one of the following subjects, namely crime, horror, cruelty and violence, shall be deemed to be obscene.

> CANADA. LAWS, STATUTES, etc., *(Criminal Code)*, 1959, C.41, s.11.

In seeking a Canadian community standard based on the average appreciation of art, the Court, in my opinion, is not limited to a settled national consensus. The average in community attitudes is better struck according to the range of exposure that particular art or art forms have had in the localities of Canada where art is exhibited.

JUSTICE BORA LASKIN, *Canadian criminal cases*, 1966, 304.

Obsolescence

Obsolescence was a thing we had never heard about in those days. Things just wore out and were patched or repaired into new usefulness until they vanished.

HARRY BOYLE, *Homebrew and patches*, 1963, 4.

It's a long road that has no ashcans.

JOHN G. DIEFENBAKER, Feb., 1968, qu. in P. Nicholson, *Vision and indecision*, 1968, 371.

Ocean

The ocean, battering at my aloneness,
Creams into supplicating shapes, lifts
    arms,
And whispers with the grey
    knowledge of the dead:
Ours is the only true identity.

AL PURDY, "In mid-Atlantic", 1957.

October

On our Canadian climate I've little to
    say,
As I've lived in it many years and cold
    days,
This present month, October, without
    strife,
Is the beautifullest I ever saw in my
    life.

JAMES GAY, "On our climate", 1885.

And soon, too soon, around the
    cumbered eaves
Sly frosts shall take the creepers by
    surprise,
And through the wind-touched
    reddening woods shall rise
October with the rain of ruined leaves.

ARCHIBALD LAMPMAN, "September",
Harper's mag., Sept., 1893.

There is something in October sets the
    gypsy blood astir:
We must rise and follow her,
When from every hill of flame
She calls, and calls each vagabond by
    name.

BLISS CARMAN, "Vagabond song," 1894.

Ogopogo

Ogopogo.

ANON., the Okanagan Lake, B.C., serpent named by the Vancouver *Province*, Aug. 24, 1926, p. 7; from the chorus of a popular song: "I'm looking for the ogopogo, the funny little ogopogo. His mother was an earwig his father was a whale."

The Old

All the speeches, reports, documents, and theories about senior citizenship – and there are plenty of them – have not helped to dispel the conviction of a great number of senior citizens that they are the forgotten people of Canadian society.

MOSES MCKAY, Commissioner, Task Force on Senior Citizens of the Ontario Federation of Labour, *Target for senior citizens*, 1973, qu. in D.J. Baum, *The final plateau*, 1974, 48.

Old Age

Amidst the infirmities of age, it is a great comfort to old folks, that, whatever destruction time works in their memory, they never find it affecting their judgment.

THOMAS MCCULLOCH, *The letters of Mephibosheth Stepsure*, 1821, Letter 7.

Age in Canada is seldom honoured. You would imagine it almost a crime for anyone to grow old – with such slighting, cold indifference are the aged treated by the young and strong.

SUSANNA MOODIE, *Life in the clearings*, 1853, 373.

I heard the city time-bells call
   Far off in hollow towers,
And one by one with measured fall
   Count out the old dead hours.

I felt the march, the silent press
   Of time, and held my breath;
I saw the haggard dreadfulness
   Of dim old age and death.

ARCHIBALD LAMPMAN, "An impression", 1884.

Senility has its privileges.

EDWARD FARRER, comment on Chief Justice Lewis Wallbridge of Manitoba, 1884, on his denouncing in court statements which appeared in the Winnipeg *Times*.

Down the long road that dips into the valley,
The love-crowned visions of our youth have fled;
While like lost mariners we keep a tally
Of the sad years in desolation sped.

JAMES MCCARROLL, "The elm tree", 1889.

Ole Docteur Fiset of Saint Anicet,
   Sapré tonnerre! he was leev long tam!
I'm sure he's got ninety year or so,
Beat all on de Parish 'cept Pierre Courteau,
   An' day affer day he work all de sam'.

WILLIAM H. DRUMMOND, "Ole Docteur Fiset", 1898.

So long as my health continues as it is now, and that I can work, I am quite willing even as long as Methuselah, but at the first sign of weakening, let Providence, which has ever been kind to me, take me away. Nothing so sad as to survive one's self.

SIR WILFRID LAURIER, letter to John Willison, Nov. 8, 1901.

I am suffering from the incurable disease of over eighty years.

GOLDWIN SMITH, to friends, Niagara Falls, N.Y., 1903.

My second fixed idea is the uselessness of men over sixty years of age, and the incalculable effect it would be in commercial, political and in professional life if, as a matter of course, men stopped work at this age. In that charming novel *The fixed period*, Anthony Trollope discusses the practical advantages in modern life of a return to this ancient usage, and the plot hinges on the admirable scheme of a college into which men at sixty retired for a year of peaceful contemplation before a peaceful departure by chloroform. As it can be maintained that all the great advances have come from men under forty, so the history of the world shows that a very large proportion of the evils may be traced to the sexagenarians, nearly all the great mistakes politically and socially, all of the worst poems, most of the bad pictures, a majority of the bad novels and not a few of the bad sermons and speeches.

WILLIAM OSLER, farewell address at Johns Hopkins Univ., Feb. 22, 1905; gave rise to reports he advised chloroform after 60, denied in statement of Feb. 28.

Old age is the "Front Line" of life, moving into No Man's Land.

STEPHEN LEACOCK, "This business of growing old", 1940.

I feel age like an icicle down my back.

DYSON CARTER, *Night of flame*, 1943, 154.

Here's news for you and you're the last one told:
Slow down, my dear Cecelia. You are old.

L.A. MCKAY, "High time for Cecelia", 1946.

In the old of my age Life's basement
    bargain booth
Has marked me down from dollar tab
    to dime –
Tho' I insist conceitedly that I'm
No less of worth than what I was,
    forsooth.

TOM MACINNES, "In the old of my age", 1947.

I do not like that leader of yours. He called me an evil old man. I resent being called old.

JOSEPH E. ATKINSON, to Ontario Att'ny. Gen. W.H. Price after George E. Drew, Premier of Ontario, attacked Atkinson for an editorial in the *Star*, Mar. 21, 1947. Qu. in Ross Harkness, *J.E. Atkinson of the Star*, 1963, 345.

It is a sickening truth: old people fear living far more than they do dying.

DR. MARION HILLIARD, *A woman doctor looks at love and life*, 1957, 130.

Under the despoiled tree,
her park seat
soft with golden leaves,
the wrinkled
disconsolate woman
crimsons her lips.

A breeze
detaches the last
red leaf
and lays it
at her feet.

IRVING LAYTON, "Gift", 1964.

Growing older is the replacement of illusions by bladder trouble.

IRVING LAYTON, "Some observations and aphorisms", *Tamarack rev.*, Spring, 1968, 5.

There is no reason to think that just anything is good enough for the old people. They deserve the best you can do and they should get it.

ERNEST WINCH, to Frank Bergmann, carpenter who built houses for Winch's New Vista Society in B.C., begun 1948, qu. in *Maclean's*, Dec., 1973, 60.

The way we treat our old people amounts to saying: if you're so smart, how come you're not young?

WILLIAM ZIMMERMAN, Exec. Dir., Ottawa Social Planning Council, qu. in Vancouver *Sun*, Sept. 9, 1974, 4.

Olympic Games (Montreal, 1976)

You smell a rat and so do I. I share your suspicions.

PIERRE E. TRUDEAU, Apr. 13, 1972, re: Mayor Jean Drapeau's plans for financing the Montreal Olympics; qu. in *The best of Trudeau*, 1972, 98.

Our Olympic hopes are alive – in Texas.

JOHN CRAIG, in *Maclean's*, Nov, 1973, 112, referring to about 70 male track and field athletes enjoying U.S. sports scholarships.

The Olympics can no more have a deficit than a man can have a baby.

JEAN DRAPEAU, Mayor of Montreal, 1975, early in the discussion regarding financial difficulties related to buildings construction.

Ontario

The Earthly Paradise of Canada.

FATHER DE BRÉHANT DE GALINÉE, *Exploration of the Great Lakes, 1669-1670: Galinee's narrative,* Repr. in Ont. Hist. Soc., *Papers and records,* Vol. IV, 53. (Trans.)

For the purpose of Commerce, Union, and Power, I propose that the site of the Colony should be in that great Peninsula between the Lakes Huron, Erie and Ontario, a spot destined by nature sooner or later to govern that interior world.

JOHN GRAVES SIMCOE, letter to Sir Joseph Banks, Jan. 8, 1791.

It will be the very mockery of a province, 300 or 400 families scattered over a country some 400 miles in length, not having any towns and scarcely a village in the province.

A. LYMBURNER, speech, Mar. 16, 1791.

In Upper Canada
There is every joy and delight;
All requirements will prosper together.

We'll get berries and wine
And all else to our wish;
Nothing under the sun will fail us.

ANNE GILLIS, Glengarry, Ont., 1803. Gaelic song, trans., qu. in *Dalhousie rev.,* Summer, 1962, 197.

The Queen's Bush.

The area of the province between Toronto and Lake Huron, large tracts of which were colonized by the Canada Company, founded 1824; also called, "The Huron Tract".

If you lose Upper Canada, you will lose all your colonies, and if you lose them you may as well lose London.

DUKE OF WELLINGTON, to the Colonial Office, on the rebellion of 1837.

There are no mountains or seas, or differences of language to separate this Province from the United States, and this Province must be materially affected by the state of politics and of the popular mind in the neighbouring republic.

R.B. SULLIVAN, member Exec. Council of Upper Canada, report to Sir George Arthur, Lieut.-Gov., June 1, 1838.

Nothing, indeed, but industry and enterprise is needed to change the waste and solitary places of Upper Canada into a garden of Eden, which it is designed by the Supreme Architect to become.

MAJOR SAMUEL STRICKLAND, *Twenty-seven years in Canada West,* 1853, Vol. 1, 65.

The Western peninsula must not get control of the ship. It is occupied by Yankees and Covenanters – in fact, the most yeasty and unsafe of populations.

SIR J.A. MACDONALD, letter to Brown Chamberlin, June 21, 1856, in *Chamberlin papers.* (Pub.Arch.Can.)

Ontario is the milch cow for the other provinces.

ANON., a popular saying. The Toronto *Globe,* Nov. 4, 1879, refers to an earlier use; also, *The Week,* May 29, 1884, 402: "Ontario suspects that she is the milch-cow"; and, Mitchell Hepburn, speech in Toronto, Oct. 6, 1938; see also below, 1960.

Ut incepit fidelis sic permanet. (As loyal she began so shall she [ever] remain.)

ONTARIO, Motto on provincial coat-of-arms.

Ontario by herself might be a nation.
There is nothing at least in the nature
of things, however much there may be
in actual circumstances, to prevent
her.

> GOLDWIN SMITH, *The Bystander,* Dec.,
> 1889, 79.

The premier province of Canada.(1897)
The Banner Province.

> ANON., popular titles for the province.

Old Porcupine is a muskeg, Elk Lake a
    fire trap,
New Liskeard's just a country town,
    and Haileybury's just come back;
You can buy the whole of Latchford
    for a nickel or a dime —
But it's hobnail boots and a flannel
    shirt in Cobalt town for mine!

> L.F. STEENMAN, "The Cobalt song", 1910.

It is the province of Ontario which has
defeated us . . . It is becoming more
and more manifest to me that it was
not reciprocity that was turned down,
but a Catholic premier.

> SIR WILFRID LAURIER, letter, Oct. 5, 1911,
> qu. in O.D. Skelton, *Laurier,* II, 1921,
> 382.

There's going to be a new deal in this
province.

> MITCHELL HEPBURN, Ontario election
> campaign, May-June, 1934.

The Golden Horseshoe.

> ANON., name given to the area at the
> south western end of Lake Ontario,
> around Toronto.

Ontario is a state of mind, bounded on
the east by a foreign language, on the
north by wilderness, on the west by
the hungry prairies, and on the south
by another country.

> DOROTHY DUNCAN, *Here's to Canada,*
> 1941, 140.

Ontario, Ontario
There's no place like Ontario,
All Sons of Mitch-ell Hepburn know
There's no place like Ontario.

> ANON., sung by well-wishers of Hepburn
> at airport, New York, September, 1941.

I've had enough of this inert
Ontario, this eunuch sea
And pastured fenced nonentity.

> EARLE BIRNEY, "Eagle Island", 1941.

Nine Provinces, rich or poor as the
case may be, have joyously lapped up
the milk taken from the Ontario cow,
Now, the Ontario cow is running dry,
now, the nine Provinces have been
warned that they will have to do more,
produce more milk, for themselves.
Good; politicians will spend money
sensibly only if they themselves have
to collect it, in their own bailliwicks,
from their own constituents.

> TORONTO *GLOBE AND MAIL,* Oct. 28,
> 1960, 6, editorial.

A place to stand
A place to grow
Ontar-i-ar-i-ar-io.

> RICHARD MORRIS, song "Ontar-i-ar-i-
> ar-io", from the Ontario documentary
> film "A place to stand", 1967.

The more money that is made in
Ontario, the better for Newfoundland.
We joy in it! We take sheer delight! I
sit up and chuckle to myself over all
the money that is being made in
Ontario because equalization means
that the Government of Uncle Ottawa
collects it where it is made and passes
back to those provinces that have less.

> JOSEPH SMALLWOOD, Federal-Provincial
> Conference on the Constitution, Ottawa,
> Feb. 5-7, 1968.

It is almost bred in Ontarians to look at
Canada first, not Ontario. It's very
hard for these people to talk of On-

tario as distinct from Canada. Ontarians tend to talk in terms of Canada, not in terms of a provincial government.

> ANON., Ontario government official, qu. in Richard Simeon, *Federal-provincial diplomacy*, 1972, 207.

Ookpik

Ookpik.

> JEANNIE SNOWBALL, Eskimo at Fort Chimo, first sewed a sealskin copy of the Arctic owl, 1963, and it was promoted at the Philadelphia Trade Fair by Frank Hamilton and the federal Dept. of Trade and Commerce, November, 1963.

An Ookpik is nothing but hair.
If you shave him, he isn't there.

He's never locked in the zoo.
He lives in a warm igloo.

> DENNIS LEE, "Ookpik", 1974.

Opera

If an opera doesn't cost a lot, frankly it just isn't any good.

> HERMAN GEIGER-TOREL, Director of the Canadian Opera Company, qu. in *Weekend magazine*, Dec. 15, 1973, 38.

Opinion

A point of view can be a dangerous luxury when substituted for insight and understanding.

> MARSHALL MCLUHAN, *Gutenberg galaxy*, 1962, 216.

What do I care now what people say?
I cared too long.

> MARGARET LAURENCE, *The stone angel*, 1968, 6.

Though he labours to change your opinion, every man is secretly pleased that it is different from his own. It enables him to feel superior to you.

> IRVING LAYTON, "Aphs", *The whole bloody bird*, 1969, 97.

Opportunity

Opportunity comes to some men more frequently than to others but there are very few it does not visit at some time or other.

> LORD STRATHCONA, qu. in J.W. Pedley, *Strathcona*, 1915, 162.

The chief immediate direction of social effort should be towards the attempt to give to every human being in childhood adequate food, clothing, education, and an opportunity in life. This will prove to be the beginning of many things.

> STEPHEN B. LEACOCK, *Unsolved riddles of social justice*, 1920, 151.

Opposition

In Opposition all is virtue; in power all the reverse.

> NICHOLAS FLOOD DAVIN, "The fair Grit", a farce, Toronto, 1876.

The hope of the Opposition is in its leader.

> *CANADIAN MONTHLY*, July, 1877, 86, referring to Sir John A. Macdonald.

While we speak in England of "Her Majesty's Opposition", the Conservatives of Ontario have attempted to better the phrase, and style themselves "Her Majesty's Loyal Opposition."

> SIR CHARLES W. DILKE, *Problems of greater Britain*, 1890, 46.

Ever since it was formed it has been in the unfortunate position of having nothing to oppose. This has driven it to a candle-end and cheese-paring make-believe frame of mind that economy was a plank in its platform.

> REGINA *LEADER*, Apr. 10, 1902, 4, on the provincial Opposition.

Nothing, it would seem, could be more comical than a man paid by a Government for opposing its measures and striving to turn it out.

> GOLDWIN SMITH, in London *Spectator*, Dec. 2, 1905.

There are occasions when an opposition or a minority owes it to itself, on account of the strong views it holds upon some public measure, to oppose that measure with all the force at its command.

> SIR WILFRID LAURIER, H. of C., *Debates*, Apr. 9, 1913, 7433, when criticized for prolonged opposition to closure.

Canada emphasizes the professionalism of politics by making the Leader of the Opposition a paid officer of state.

> FELIX FRANKFURTER, U.S. Supreme Court Judge, *The public and its government*, 1930, 161.

We oppose, correct, and criticize. In doing so we cleanse and purify those in office. We are, in fact, the detergents of democracy.

> LESTER B. PEARSON, address, Annual Conference of American Newspaper Editors, Washington, Apr. 22, 1960.

The duty of the Opposition is to turn out the government.

> JOHN G. DIEFENBAKER, speech to the Ottawa Kiwanis Club, Mar. 13, 1964; also H. of C., *Debates*, Mar. 24, 1964, 3251, quoting Tierney.

The Leader of the Opposition claims that the Speech from the Throne rather surprised and disappointed him. He said it was a failure. The contrary would have surprised us. In my opinion, had the speech been dictated by the Holy Spirit himself to the Governor General, the Leader of the Opposition would have deemed necessary to present a motion of non-confidence to the House.

> PIERRE E. TRUDEAU, H. of C., *Debates*, Sept. 16, 1968, 63.

It is complete nonsense to have 29 ministers hanging around for 1-1/2 or two hours every day just in case some guy in the Opposition thinks up a question.

> PIERRE E. TRUDEAU, Halifax, Oct. 5, 1968; qu. in *The best of Trudeau*, 1972, 37.

If there's a good government you don't need an opposition.

> MAURICE DUPLESSIS, attributed, qu. in Claude Julien, *Canada: Europe's last chance*, 1968, 39.

If the Opposition accords so little respect to Parliament that it defines governing as evil, that getting on with the job is regarded as tyranny, then I am happy to be given the chance to join the issue.

> PIERRE E. TRUDEAU, H. of C., *Debates*, July 24, 1969, 11570.

That was your God-damned question.

> PIERRE E. TRUDEAU, H. of C., *Debates*, Feb. 28, 1972, 306, reply to Robert Stanfield, Leader of the Opposition, on a question relating to unemployment.

Oppression

People of Canada, We have been oppressed by the hand of a Transatlantic power, and unjustly and cruelly castigated with the rod of unrelenting mis-rule for a long series of years — so long, that the measure of Tyranny has filled to overflowing.

> ROBERT NELSON, "Commander in Chief of the Patriot Army", "Proclamation No. 2", Mar., 1838.

Optimism

"Oughtn't we to be prepared for the best too?" pleaded Anne. "It's just as likely to happen as the worse."

L.M. MONTGOMERY, *Anne of Avonlea*, 1909, 57.

Beware of an optimism founded on superficial judgements: otherwise you will dismiss Death as Nature's bounty toward the undertaking industry.

ROBERTSON DAVIES, *Samuel Marchbanks' almanack*, 1967, 17.

Orangemen

One School, One Flag, One Language.

ORANGE ASSOC. OF BRITISH AMERICA, founded, Brockville, Ont., 1830, by Ogle Robert Gowan, motto.

Derry's sons alike defy
Pope, traitor, or defender,
And peal to heaven their 'prentice cry,
Their patriot "No surrender."

OGLE R. GOWAN, a founder (1830) of the Orange Association of British America.

Here's a needle,
Here's a thread,
To sew a pig's tail
To an Orangeman's head.

ANON., Roman Catholic children's rhyme, Grey County, Ont., 19th century.

Teeter, totter,
Holy water,
Sprinkle the Catholics every one,
If that won't do,
We'll cut them in two,
And put them under the Protestants' drum.

ANON., children's rhyme, Grey and Brant Counties, Ont., 19th century; variant of Old Country rhyme.

Up the long ladder,
Down the short rope,
To hell with King Billy!
Three cheers for the Pope!

ANON., children's rhyme, Ontario, 19th century; the sentiments of the last two lines were frequently reversed.

They have dined him and wined him
in manner most royal,
Addressed and harangued him
to prove they are loyal;
They have bored him in parks,
and they've bored him in halls,
Danced him almost to death
in no end of balls.
They have bored him in colleges,
bored him in schools,
And convinced him that
Orange fanatics are fools.

R.J. DE CORDOVA, *The Prince's visit; tour of the Prince of Wales, 1860*, 1861.

Oratory

One sees them going up and coming down with rhythmic regularity, and suddenly they are lost in the polished phrases of a platitudinous peroration – the magician's handkerchief.

E.J. TARR, comparing the performance of W.L.M. King in debate with that of a juggler keeping several balls in the air at once: Isolationism, North Americanism, Imperialism, and Collectivism, qu. in *International affairs*, XVI, Sept.-Oct., 1937, 685-6.

He is an impressive if somewhat ponderous speaker, schooled in the art of uttering many words without being embarrassingly specific.

W.E. ELLIOTT, *Politics is funny*, 1952, 48, referring to Paul Martin.

I went out into a woodlot, day after day, and practiced speaking and pounding a pine stump with my clenched fists. I had discovered the power of words and gestures over people.

> WILLIAM ABERHART, qu. in John A. Irving, *The Social Credit movement in Alberta*, 1959, 12.

Orchards

Drilled battalions of apple-trees are drawn up on every southward facing slope.

> ARCHIBALD MACMECHAN, *The book of Ultima Thule*, 1927, 202.

Order

The primary and indispensable function of government is to ensure a firm framework of public order within which men can order their social life on the bases of habit, custom, and agreement.

> J.A. CORRY, *Democratic government and politics*, 1951, 6.

Lawyers and judges too often regard "order" as a shield for the protection of privilege through laws that have prevailed in another society and procedures that are incompatible with modern-day living.

> JUSTICE J.C. MCRUER, address, American Bar Assoc., Montreal, Aug. 8, 1966.

Order, like law, to be respected, must deserve respect. Disrespect for an order that does not deserve respect ought not to be condemned as degeneration, but commended as a healthy regeneration.

> JUSTICE J.C. MCRUER, address, American Bar Assoc., Montreal, Aug. 8, 1966.

Organization

It is not enough to have good principles; we must have organization also. Principles without organization may lose, but organization without principles may often win.

> SIR WILFRID LAURIER, speech at opening of Reform Club, Ottawa, June 19, 1893.

System, or as I shall term it, the virtue of method, is the harness without which only the horses of genius travel.

> SIR WILLIAM OSLER, *Teacher and student*, 1897.

In institutions the corroding effect of routine can be withstood only by maintaining high ideals of work; but these become the sounding brass and tinkling cymbals without corresponding sound practice.

> SIR WILLIAM OSLER, "Nurse and patient", 1897.

Today we are technicians, and the more progressive among us see no reason why love and hope should not be organized in a department of the government, planned by a politician and administered by trained specialists.

> HUGH MACLENNAN, "An orange from Portugal", in his *Cross country*, 1949, 25.

A democratic type of organization produced a far more socially conscious, responsible, and mature man than did the bureaucratic, competitive environment of industry.

> NORMAN ALCOCK, *The emperor's new clothes*, 1971, 24.

Advertising is my job, organization is my hobby.

> NORMAN ATKINS, advertising executive, qu. in J. Manthorpe, *The power and the Tories*, 1974, 3.

Organization of American States

I believe that all the free members of the organization of American states would be both heartened and strengthened by an increase in your hemispheric role. Your skills, your resources, your judicious perception at the council table – even when it differs from our views – are all needed throughout the inter-American community. Your country and mine are partners in North American affairs; can we not become partners in Inter-American affairs?

PRESIDENT JOHN F. KENNEDY, address to both Houses of Parliament, May 17, 1961.

Orgasm

I tear through the womb's room
       give birth
and yet   alone
      deep in the dark
earth
I am the one   wrestling
the element re-born.

DOROTHY LIVESAY, "The touching", 1967.

I drown
     in your identity
I am not I
    but root
       shell
          fire

DOROTHY LIVESAY, "The touching", 1967.

Orientals

Yes, we are all bad because we want a white British Columbia and not a place like Hawaii! Fifty years from now, unless something is done to stop it, all west of the Rockies will be yellow.

A.W. NEILL, H. of C., *Debates*, Feb. 19, 1942, 719.

To judge from the number of books on the subject, it is easy for us to achieve the spiritual grandeur of Orientals by adopting their postures or breathing. Oddly enough, no Orientals appear to believe that they can develop our scientific and government skill by posturing and breathing like *us*.

ROBERTSON DAVIES, *Samuel Marchbanks' almanack*, 1967, 160.

Originality

Men do not like originality; they are afraid and suspicious of it; and the only original that they will tolerate is original sin.

J.J. PROCTER, *The philosopher in the clearing*, 1897, 176.

At all costs men want to feel they are unique and original. We hate the man who expresses the same sentiments or maxims about life as we do.

IRVING LAYTON, "Aphs", *The whole bloody bird*, 1969, 101.

Orthodoxy

The heterodoxy of one age is the orthodoxy of the next.

GOLDWIN SMITH, in *Can. monthly*, 1879, Vol. 2, 241.

Imagination boggles at the vista of a Canadian Whitman or a Canadian Dos Passos. The prevailing literary standards demand a high degree of moral and social orthodoxy; and popular writers accept these standards without even . . . rueful complaint.

E.K. BROWN, "The problem of a Canadian poetry", *Masks of fiction*, 1961, 50.

Ospreys

The osprey disappears, dissolves,
As suddenly returns, his wing
Banked at another angle on the wind.
  And so all things
Deliquesce, arrange, and rearrange in
  field.

> D.G. JONES, "Mr. Wilson, The World",
> 1967.

Ottawa

As Bytown is not overrun with Americans it may probably turn out a moral, well-behaved town, and afford a lesson to its neighbours.

> JOHN MACTAGGART, *Three years in Canada*, 1829, II, 219.

If the Province of Canada is to remain one, it is essential that its Seat of Government should be fixed and recognized by all.

> SIR EDMUND HEAD, letter to Henry Labouchère, Mar. 28, 1857.

Ottawa is the only place which will be accepted by the majority of Upper and Lower Canada as a fair compromise. With the exception of Ottawa, every one of the cities proposed [as the capital site] is an object of jealousy to each of the others.

> SIR EDMUND HEAD, *Confidential memo.*, undated, i.e. July, 1857.

I am commanded by the Queen to inform you that in the judgment of Her Majesty the City of Ottawa combines more advantages than any other place in Canada for the permanent seat of the future Government of the Province, and is selected by Her Majesty accordingly.

> HENRY LABOUCHÈRE, letter to Sir Edmund Walker Head, Dec. 31, 1857.

The Westminster in the Wilderness.

> ANON., a derisive term used in Montreal, Toronto, and other cities, 1858, when Ottawa was chosen as capital.

Ottawa, as the capital of Canada, seems such a monstrous absurdity, that, like all who have penetrated to it, I can never treat its metropolitan future as anything more than a bad practical joke, in which no one ever saw any meaning, but which, now that the Prince has solemnly laid the foundation stone of "intended" Parliament buildings, is considered as having gone rather too far, and is awakening a feeling of almost indignation throughout Canada.

> N.A. WOODS, *The Prince of Wales in Canada and the United States*, 1861, 157.

Aye, but think of the attractions of Ottawa! They may be very great, but I think I may be pardoned if I prefer an old city beside the Thames. London is large enough for me, and you will no doubt prefer London with its magnificent proportions to Ottawa with its magnificent distances.

> JOSEPH HOWE, speech in Bridgetown, N.S., June 8, 1867.

I would not wish to say anything disparaging of the capital, but it is hard to say anything good of it. Ottawa is not a handsome city and does not appear destined to become one either.

> SIR WILFRID LAURIER, speech in Montreal, May 19, 1884. (Trans.)

A sub-arctic lumber-village converted by royal mandate into a political cockpit.

> GOLDWIN SMITH; attributed, by W. Buckingham in his *Mackenzie*, 1892, 129.

I keep a green spot in my heart for the city of Ottawa, and when the day comes, as it will come by and by, it shall be my pleasure and that of my colleagues, I am sure, to make the city of Ottawa as attractive as possibly could be; to make it the centre of the intellectual development of this country and above all the Washington of the North.

> SIR WILFRID LAURIER, address to the Reform Assoc. of Ottawa, June 19, 1893.

Ottawa means exile emphasized, accompanied with a feeling of helplessness. Happily, Ottawa does not mean Canada, nor does it represent Canada.

> LADY ABERDEEN, *Journal*, Jan. 30, 1895.

City of laws and saws.

> CHARLES G.D. ROBERTS, qu. in McL. Stewart, *First half century of Ottawa*, 1910, 7.

Grandeur is written on thy throne,
   Beauty encompasseth thy mien;
The glory of the North alone,
   Is thine, O Ottawa, my Queen.

Here as the years of promise roll
   Shall gather all a nation's pride.

> JAMES E. CALDWELL, "Ottawa", 1907.

There is very little intellectual atmosphere around the place, and one feels how much we have lost to the United States. We follow along and kid ourselves we are our own masters.

> HAROLD A. INNIS, letter to Gerald Graham, Dec., 1949, qu. in D.G. Creighton, *Harold Adams Innis*, 1957, 138.

Ottawa is the only city in North America that has an image of what it wants to become. It may be dull, but that's the true essence of the Canadian people.

> ANTHONY ADAMSON, Vice-chairman, National Capital Comm., in Ottawa, Dec. 3, 1959.

Ottawa is a cultural desert.

> JUDY LAMARSH, in *Weekend mag.*, Jan. 18, 1964, 3.

Ah, Mackenzie King
I think I understand you:
how easy to commune with the dead
in a city wholly divorced from reality.

> ALDEN NOWLAN, "The nation's capital", 1967.

The first thing you learn here
is that the country
bears the same relationship
to the government
that outer space
bears to the earth.

> ALDEN NOWLAN, "The nation's capital", 1967.

We have a very developed local industry, the industry of politics, and this city is flourishing with it. When I think of this industry which was established here a century ago or more by Queen Elizabeth – Queen Victoria – now you know where my heart is. I hope this gets out because it is certainly not creeping republicanism.

> PIERRE E. TRUDEAU, Ottawa, Feb. 20, 1970.

Ottawa River

Where the Ottawa pours its
   magnificent tide
Through forests primaeval,
   dark-waving and wide,
There's a scene which for grandeur
   has scarcely a peer, –
'Tis the wild roaring rush of the
   mighty Chaudiére.

> EVAN MACCOLL, "The Chaudiére", 1859.

O slave, whom many a cunning master
  drills
To lift, or carry, bind, or crush, or
  churn,
Whose damned and parcelled waters
  drive or turn
The saws and hammers of a hundred
  mills.

> ARCHIBALD LAMPMAN, "To the Ottawa
> river", 1900.

Outdoors

I fear no power a woman wields,
While I can have the woods and fields.

> ERNEST MCGAFFEY, (b.1861), "Song".

A white tent pitched by a glassy lake,
  Well under a shady tree,
Or by rippling rills from the grand old
  hills,
  Is the summer home for me.
I fear no blaze of the noontide rays,
  For the woodland glades are mine,
The fragrant air, and that perfume
  rare —
  The odour of forest pine.

> JAMES D. EDGAR, "Canadian camping
> song", 1893.

There is virtue in the open; there is
  healing out of doors;
The great Physician makes his rounds
  along the forest floors.

> BLISS CARMAN, "An open letter, Christ-
> mas, 1920", written while a patient at
> Lake Placid, N.Y.

Owls

The Snowy Owl, I've heard it said,
Lives on the entrails of the dead.
It loves to gorge on rotting bowel.
Which spoils it — as a table fowl.

> FARLEY MOWAT, "The snowy owl", 1967.

Ownership

Fat Man Rich Owns Things Which
State Should Hold.

> J.W. BENGOUGH, "Lesson XLIV", *The
> up-to-date primer*, 1896, 48.

Men are all alike. They *say* ours. But
they *mean* mine.

> MAZO DE LA ROCHE, *Delight*, 1926, (1961
> ed., 64).

Pride of ownership used to belong to
all men, but it's getting narrower.
Pride of possession today belongs to
the politicians. You find it. They take
it.

> SIR HARRY OAKES, qu. in Geoffrey Bocca,
> *The life and death of Sir Harry Oakes*,
> 1959, 75.

I own nothing and therefore I own
everything, with the added advantage
that I don't have to look after it.

> RICHARD J. NEEDHAM, *A friend in Need-
> ham*, 1969, 8.

Pacific Coast

We continued our journey, amused with the seals playing in the river; on the fifteenth, near noon, we arrived at Tongue Point, which at right angles stretches its steep rocky shores across the river for a full half a mile, and brought us to a full view of the Pacific Ocean, which to me was a great pleasure, but my men seemed disappointed.

> DAVID THOMPSON, *Journal*, July 14, 1811; *Narrative of his explorations in Western America, 1784-1812*, (Champlain Soc., 1916, 500).

Pacific Great Eastern Railway

1912 – We Started It; 1922 – Rusted; 1932 – Busted; 1942 – Disgusted; 1956 – We Made It!

> ANON., slogans celebrating the inaugural run of the P.G.E. from Vancouver to Prince George, B.C., Aug. 29, 1956.

Pacific Scandal

Draw on me for ten thousand dollars.

> SIR JOHN ABBOTT, legal advisor to the C.P.R., telegram in response to one from Sir John A. Macdonald of Aug. 26, 1872; a key factor in the Pacific Scandal of 1873.

These hands are clean!

> SIR JOHN A. MACDONALD, attributed by J.W. Bengough, in a cartoon in *Grip*, Aug. 16, 1873.

The Pacific Slander.

> SIR CHARLES TUPPER, phrase in reply to "The Pacific Scandal", 1873.

The Pacific Scandal shattered at one blow the fabric which Sir John Macdonald kept together by his skill in manipulation of individual interests, and the cohesive power of public plunder.

> TORONTO *GLOBE*, Jan. 22, 1874.

Pain

Stoicism is a dour retreat, for half the pleasure in pain is discussing it.

> MARTIN ROHER, *Days of living*, 1959, 116.

Painters

Some day they will know what I mean.

> TOM THOMSON, qu. in Blodwen Davies, *Tom Thomson*, 1935, 131.

Painting

The event happened in the year 1759, in a region of the world unknown to the Greeks and Romans, and at a period of time when no warriors who wore such a costume existed. The subject I have to represent is a great battle fought and won, and the same truth which gives law to the historian should rule the painter.

> BENJAMIN WEST, 1770, qu. in Oliver Warner, *With Wolfe to Quebec*, 1972, 215, referring to his portrayal of people in contemporary garb in his painting

"The death of Wolfe".

Now ve vill make a nize leetle vater-
colour. Ve vill put a round spot of red
in the centre, so. Zat is ze sun. Now ve
vill take some yellow, so, and some
purple, so, and before you know it, ve
haf a sky. Then ve put some trees on
this side and some odders on the odder
side, so. And then ve run a leetle
vaterfall down the meedle, so; and it is
finished. Now you have seen me make
a vater-colour. It is very simple. Make
one yourself.

> O.R. JACOBI, to students at Ontario Soc. of
> Artists, Toronto, about 1875.

Canadians won't bother to look at
anything small, and anything like
crisp, constructive drawing makes
them uneasy. But I have decided to do
what I know, without being influenced
by the opinion of a lot of farmers who
can hardly be trusted to go to bed
without attempting to blow out the
gas.

> WILLIAM CRUIKSHANK, letter to Edmund
> Morris, May, 1893, qu. in J. Russell
> Harper, Painting in Canada, 1966, 231.

Canada is frequently reviled as a
country naturally unsuitable for the
development of the art of painting.

> NEWTON MACTAVISH, Can. mag., Apr.,
> 1912, 544.

All their pictures look pretty much
alike, the net result being more like a
gargle or gob of porridge than a work
of art.

> H.F. GADSBY, Toronto Star, Dec. 12,
> 1913, 6, re: Group of Seven.

Hot Mush School.

> H.F. GADSBY,, in Toronto Star, Dec. 12,
> 1913, referring to young painters who
> later became the Group of Seven.

Something in the air moved us. The
artist just up and does something about
it without knowing what it was exactly
about. It was a genuinely Canadian
thing. The Group of Seven caught and
reflected the nationalism in the air.

> ARTHUR LISMER, Journal, on the origin of
> the Group of Seven, 1920.

Never buy a picture that you do not
fall in love with, or it will always be an
incubus and a source of dissatisfaction.
The purchase of a picture, like the
selection of wife, can hardly be done
by proxy.

> SIR W. VAN HORNE, qu. in Vaughan, Van
> Horne, 1920, 268.

I feel about my paintings exactly as if
they were my children. They are my
children, of my body, my mind, my
innermost being. When people call
them horrible and hideous I resent it
deeply – I can't help it.

> EMILY CARR, to Flora Hamilton Burns,
> 1924, qu. in Mary Q. Innis, The clear
> spirit, 1966, 230.

Next time I paint Indians I'm going
off on a tangent tear. There is something bigger than fact: the underlying
spirit, all it stands for, the mood, the
vastness, the wildness, the Western
breath of a go-to-the-devil-if-you-
don't-like-it, the eternal big spaceness
of it. Oh the West! I'm of it and I love
it.

> EMILY CARR, Hundreds and thousands,
> the journals, Nov. 14, 1927.

There is at the bottom of each artistic
conscience a love for the land of their
birth. It is said art knows no country
but belongs to the world. This may be
true of pictures, but great artists are no
more cosmopolitan than great writers,
and no immortal work has been done
which has not as one of its promptings
for its creation a feeling its creator had
of having roots in his native land and

being a product of its soil.

HOMER WATSON, d. 1936, undated Mss., qu. in J.R. Harper, *Painting in Canada*, 1966, 216.

What is the test of a picture? Not form or colour or design or technique. It is the intensity of experience and feeling, the existence of the thing *spiritually*.

EMILY CARR, *Hundreds and thousands; the journals*, Dec. 1, 1933.

A singing heart, I am convinced, and the mixing of joy and praise with the very paints, as well as the ideals and inspirations one receives, and the forgetting of oneself is the only way.

EMILY CARR, *Hundreds and thousands; the journals*, Feb. 18, 1934.

Movement is the essence of being. When a thing stands still and says, "Finished" then it dies. There isn't such a thing as completion in this world, for that would mean Stop! Painting is a striving to express life. If there is no movement in the painting, then it is dead paint.

EMILY CARR, *Hundreds and thousands; the journals*, May 3, 1934.

I think the most splendid thing would be to paint so simply that the common ordinary people would understand and see something of God in your expressing.

EMILY CARR, *Hundreds and thousands; the journals*, Sept. 8, 1934.

If the old school of painters had misinterpreted the spirit of the land, what of the poets and the politicians? Thoughts are insidious, elusive things. A regiment of critics may condemn a picture but they can do nothing about the vague longings and aspirations that the picture sets up in the heart of the individual — each man according to his own measure.

BLODWEN DAVIES, *Tom Thomson*, 1935, 99.

My name is written all over it.

JAMES W. MORRICE, on refusing to sign a painting; qu. in D.W. Buchanan, *James Wilson Morrice: a biography*, 1936, 41.

The danger in canvases is that of binding and crucifying the emotion, of pinning it there to die flattened on the surface. Instead one must let it move over the surface as the spirit of God moved over the face of the waters.

EMILY CARR, *Hundreds and thousands; the journals*, Sept. 14, 1937.

A man that can paint like that should wear a gold hat.

JOHN ARTHUR FRASER, as he stood before one of his own works, qu. in William Colgate, *Can. art*, 1943, 22.

The old way of seeing was inadequate to express this big country of ours, her depth, her height, her unbounded wideness, silences too strong to be broken — nor could ten million cameras, through their mechanical boxes, ever show real Canada. It had to be sensed, passed through live minds, sensed and loved.

EMILY CARR, *Growing pains*, 1946, 307.

Spring springs to winter winter; noon
    gulps night;
Follow me: spring to stumble; follow
    my leader
Off at the deep end here if feigning a
    header;
Façade, interior, highlight, lowlight,
    no light;
Skyscape, landscape, seascape,
    inchcape, escape;
Bath, bar, beef, ballet, ballet-beef,
    bar-bath;
Life, life's till, still life, still death, till
    death, death;
Full catalogue.

ROBERT FINCH, "Painter's progress", 1948.

Canada's reputation in the arts, both at home and abroad, is based mainly on her painting. All those who came before us recognized the importance of Canadian painting both as an art and as an expression of Canadianism.

CANADA. ROY. COMM. ON NATIONAL DEVELOPMENT IN THE ARTS, LETTERS, & SCIENCES, *Report*, 1951, 207.

Every damn pine tree in the country has been painted.

GRAHAM COUGHTRY, 1955, qu. by B. Hale, *Toronto painting*, 1972, 10.

The first artist who came to Canada noticed a kind of instinctive antagonism. He was a French portrait painter, who, making a drawing of an Indian in profile, was nearly scalped by the indignant sitter for making him only half a man. Criticism is more enlightened today, but not much.

A.Y. JACKSON, *A painter's country*, 1958, 116.

Some bad paintings I find very exciting, they do things that are so wrong they come close to being right. They are closer to being creative in their ineptitude than a lot of what I call factory-produced painting.

HAROLD TOWN, *Waterloo rev.*, No. 5, Summer, 1960, 13.

It [Collage] seems to me the one medium most suited to the age of conspicuous waste, and it's marvellous to think of the garbage of our age becoming the art of our time.

HAROLD TOWN, letter to Harriet Janis, Jan. 11, 1961, qu. in H. Janis and R. Blesh, *Collage*, 1962, 155.

Thomson's small oil sketches of the last years palpitate and throb. They are as direct in attack as a punch in the nose, and the sense of movement in them has the sweep and pull of a paddle entering water. Paint is thrust and smashed onto the board with axe-like swings; it seems almost a substitute for the coarse fare of the bush, making of the final picture a banquet for Thomson's Spartan senses.

HAROLD TOWN, in *Great Canadians, a century of achievement*, 1965, 110.

It's bad enough to have to live in this country without having pictures of it in your home.

ANON., an old lady to A.Y. Jackson, qu. in his *Introduction* to K.D. Pepper, *James Wilson Morrice*, 1966, x.

Only with the passage of time, only when thought has been clarified and evidence sifted and weighed, will we have a sure judgment of the esoteric painting of the present.

J. RUSSELL HARPER, *Painting in Canada, a history*, 1966, 414.

There is no finality, no final statement; everything remains to be re-created by every creative artist.

LAWREN HARRIS, qu. in Bess Harris, ed., *Lawren Harris*, 1969, 138.

On the other side
of the picture, the instant
is over, the shadow
of the tree has moved.

MARGARET ATWOOD, "Girl and horse, 1928", 1970.

If you really want to know what my paintings are about, you have to go inside them, get lost in them.

ARTHUR VILLENEUVE, qu. in *Weekend mag.*, Apr. 8, 1972, 20.

I see no difference whatever between the past and the present. The works of the past are neither closer nor farther removed. There has been no evolution: what has occurred should simply allow us to see better.

> JEAN-PAUL RIOPELLE, qu. in Pierre Schneider, *Riopelle*, 1972, 122. (Trans.)

When you are interested in life more than you are in painting, then your paintings can come to life.

> JACK CHAMBERS, qu. by W. Withrow, *Contemporary Can. painting*, 1972, 129.

Few Canadian nudes are energetic, pathetic or ecstatic.

> JERROLD MORRIS, *The nude in Canadian painting*, 1972, Intro., 4.

Palliser Triangle

The conquest of the desert in the Palliser Triangle in the 1930's is the greatest Canadian success story since the completion of the Canadian Pacific Railway.

> JAMES H. GRAY, *Men against the desert*, 1967, vii.

Parachutists

Missing the trees and tall buildings
  controlling wind and gravity
    with swinging skill
  and speaking no language
save the language of motion.
As they floated down
    we were all lifted
        up.

> F.R. SCOTT, "Open house, McGill", 1972.

Parades

The procession consisted of a band, about sixty men and boys carrying torches, a large number of which went out on the road, a carriage containing Sir John and Lady Macdonald, Mr. Beaty and Mr. McCormack, and an escort of rabble.

> TORONTO *GLOBE*, July 12, 1872, 4, describing procession following presentation of a jewel case to Lady Macdonald by the Trades Assembly.

Paradise

I remember as a child feeling that the Promised Land of our Bible at home lay just on the other side of a hogsback hill to the south of our farm.

> JAMES REANEY, in R.L. McDougall, ed., *Our living tradition*, 3d. ser, 1959, 271.

Parents

Only through the woman is the man bound to the family. And, since the family is ultimately dependent upon the man, the importance a woman attaches to the binding potency of her charms is as natural and legitimate as it is utilitarian and beneficial.

> ARNOLD HAULTAIN, *Hints for lovers*, 1909, 248.

The mentally defective are those who cannot make, or help to make, a home. We must make a happy and permanent home for them during their lives. The only Permanent Parent is the State.

> HELEN MACMURCHY, *The almosts*, 1920, 178.

Duty to parents is an obligation that some of us must recognize. However hellish parents may be, the duty is as real as the duty that exists in marriage.

ROBERTSON DAVIES, *Leaven of malice*, 1954, 256.

Parliament

This is a damned queer Parliament.

EDWARD RYAN, referring to first meeting of the P.E.I. Assembly, July 7, 1773, said to have been held at Cross Keys Tavern. Charlottetown. He was brought before the Bar of the House and discharged of his duties as Sergeant-at-arms and Door-Keeper.

Here I sincerely hope will be an end of Parliament in this Province.

LORD DALHOUSIE, letter, Nov. 22, 1827; qu., *Can. hist. rev.*, XII, 134.

The Bow-Wow Parliament.

ANON., the Newfoundland parliament, especially the first, 1833; from a caricature by John Doyle ("H.D.") in his, *Political sketches* – sketch no. 187, Mar. 30, 1832, in which a Newfoundland dog as Speaker puts the motion, "As many as are of that opinion say . . . Bow! Of the contrary . . . Wow! I think the Bows! have it".

The Bread-and-Butter Parliament.

ANON., the Upper Canada Assembly of 1836; Sir Francis Bond Head campaigned against the Reformers and warned the electors that their bread and butter depended on the way they voted.

Parliament is a grand inquest which has the ~ht to inquire into anything and everything.

SIR JOHN A. MACDONALD, speech, 1861, qu. in Biggar, *Anecdotal life*, 1891, 182.

As a Parliament they had a right to do what they pleased with their own.

SIR JOHN A. MACDONALD, in House of Commons, *Debates*, 1869: repr. 1972, II, 742, on increase of Nova Scotia subsidy without Imperial Act; from a statement of the Duke of Newcastle, that he had a right "to do what they liked with their own".

I could not have treated Parliament as a pregnant woman, and prolonged its existence for the sake of the lesser life attached to it.

LORD DUFFERIN, despatch to the Colonial Office, summer, 1873, on the question of proroguing after revelations made regarding the "Pacific Scandal".

The privileges of Parliament are the privileges of the People, and the rights of Parliament are the rights of the People.

EDWARD BLAKE, speech in London, Ont., Aug. 28, 1873.

The rules of the House are certainly the bulwark of freedom.

SIR WILFRID LAURIER, H. of C., *Debates*, 1913, 6383.

The rules of the House are made for the protection, not so much of the majority as of the minority. The majority can always protect itself.

RODOLPHE LEMIEUX, Speaker, H. of C., *Debates*, 1925, 2736.

The House of Commons is not a good legislative machine. The party turmoil, the harassing parliamentary and administrative duties of the Ministers, the attendance at caucuses and committees required of private members, the constant anxiety of all members to court the public and the press, all militate against good legislation.

R.A. MACKAY, *The unreformed Senate*, 1926, 108.

The public interest demands a dissolution of this House of Commons . . .
His Excellency having declined to accept my advice to grant a dissolution, to which I believe under British practice I was entitled, I immediately tendered my resignation.

W.L.MACKENZIE KING, H. of C., *Debates*, 1926, 5059.

To Ottawa from coast to coast
The chosen come to make the laws.
For weeks they talk about a lot
Of different things with scarce a pause:
The railway line to Hudson Bay,
Taxes and tariff, immigration,
The great St. Lawrence waterway,
And whether we are yet a nation.

ROBERT K. GORDON, "O for Ottawa", 1931.

The sovereignty of the people is delegated to Parliament, not to the executive, and when I say "Parliament" it means the authority as well as the majority in Parliament.

ERNEST LAPOINTE, in 1932, qu. by E. Davie Fulton, address, Empire Club, Toronto, Apr. 11, 1957.

Parliament will decide.

W.L. MACKENZIE KING, a declaration of policy, H. of C., *Debates*, Mar. 30, 1939, 2418.

Parliament has ceased to function.

M.J. COLDWELL, H. of C., *Debates*, June 1, 1956, 4552, referring to pipeline debate.

The people in the galleries have seen a farce tonight.

M.J. COLDWELL, H. of C., *Debates*, June 1, 1956, 4641, referring to pipeline debate.

Get on with your bloody motion.

JUDY LAMARSH, Secretary of State, in H. of C., Tuesday, Mar. 15, 1966, to Marcel Lambert, M.P. when he was presenting a motion of protest during the debate arising out of the first charge regarding association of Gerda Munsinger with former Conservative gov't. cabinet ministers; changed by Hansard reporters to read: "Make your motion".

If you are concerned more with style than with substance, and if you have a technocratic approach to problems why should you pay any attention to Parliament? Style is of no consequence here. The Prime Minister and his colleagues in Cabinet are not likely to persuade many members of the Oppostion. Style is important outside. It is important at the university, important in front of the camera. It is of no importance here.

DAVID LEWIS, H. of C., *Debates*, Mar. 5, 1970, 4424.

The perfect parliament would include delegates from the living, the unborn and the dead.

ALDEN NOWLAN, "Scratchings", 1974.

Parliament Buildings

Those buildings at Ottawa will be admirably suited for lunatic asylums, whenever the town is sufficiently prosperous to require them for that purpose.

N.A. WOODS, correspondent in The (London) *Times*, on the visit of the Prince of Wales to Ottawa, Sept. 1, 1860.

But the glory of Ottawa will be – and, indeed, already is – the set of public buildings which is now being erected on the rock which guards as it were the town from the river.

ANTHONY TROLLOPE, *North America*, 1862, 67.

The buildings were magnificent; style, extent, site, and workmanship all surprisingly fine . . . The buildings were just five hundred years in advance of the time; it would cost half the revenue of the province to light and heat and keep them clean. Such monstrous folly was never perpetrated before.

> GEORGE BROWN, on the Parliament Buildings; letter to Sir J.A. Macdonald, Aug. 15, 1864.

It contains acres of plaster and miles of cornice.

> JONATHAN MCCULLY, reference to the Parliament Buildings, in a speech made in Nova Scotia, 1866.

With the soft sun-touch of the
    yellowing hours
Made lovelier, I see with dreaming
    eyes,
Even as a dream out of a dream, arise
The bell-tongued city with its glorious
    towers.

> ARCHIBALD LAMPMAN, "The city", 1888.

Above her river, above her hill,
    Above her streets of brief renown,
In majesty austere and still
    Ottawa's gloried towers look down.

> WILFRED CAMPBELL, in Campbell and Martin, *Canada*, 1907, 95.

Fair, in the South, fair as a shrine that
    makes
The wonder of a dream, imperious
    towers
Pierce and possess the sky, guarding
    the halls
Where our young strength is welded
    strenuously.

> DUNCAN CAMPBELL SCOTT, "Ottawa before dawn", 1926.

Parliament, Members of

The law! the law! never mind the law
− turn him oot; turn him oot!

> JOHN STRACHAN, 1821, in Legislative Council, Toronto, on being informed that the law did not permit the Assembly to expel the reformer Barnabas Bidwell.

You are representatives of the people, and I put it to you, as you are greatly honoured, should you not greatly dare? You are sent to do your duty to your constituents, whether your acts always give satisfaction or not.

> JOSEPH HOWE, speech in N.S. Legislature, Mar. 22, 1841.

Brown promised, in terms that could
    not be withstood,
If we gave him a seat, it should be for
    our good,
Nor can we complain that he's altered
    his tone:
He sits for our good, but − he lies for
    his own.

> ALEXANDER MCDOUGALL, (of Nova Scotia), "On a member of the House of Assembly not remarkable for his veracity", *Bentley's miscellany*, , Feb. 1843, 160.

How many Canadian M.P.P.'s could obtain third class certificates from the most lenient of our educational examination boards?

> R.J. MACGEORGE, in Streetsville *Weekly rev.*, May 26, 1855.

A new member requires the experience of his first session in the house to teach him how to hang up his overcoat and hat and take his seat in a manner befitting a gentleman.

> SIR JOHN A. MACDONALD; attributed as a frequent statement.

Call in de membr'.

> SIR GEORGE-ETIENNE CARTIER, in the Assembly, especially about 1860, in terminating debates on Rep. by Pop.; "The really solid argument was Cartier's contemptuous conclusion to all debate: "Call in de membr" – O.D.Skelton, *Sir A.T. Galt*, 212.

Free and independent men in the Legislature, as in the country, are the best counterpoise to faction and the main-spring of a nation's progress and greatness.

> EGERTON RYERSON, *New Canadian Dominion*, 1867, 25.

Yes, 'tis pleasant to think as I sit in the gallery,
They agree upon one thing, and that is their salary.

> *GRIP* (Toronto), Feb. 15, 1879.

Men who know no more about the geography of their native land than they do of that of Patagonia; who think that the sun rises in Halifax, shines all day straight over Montreal and Ottawa, and sets in Toronto – whose hymn book is the praise of England and whose Bible is the example of the United States.

> EDMONTON *BULLETIN* , Dec. 27, 1880.

Harsh is the cackle of the little turkeycocks of Ottawa, fighting the while as they feather their own nests of sticks and mud, high on their river bluff.

> STEPHEN LEACOCK, "Greater Canada", in *University mag.*, 1907.

A man goes to Ottawa burning with zeal to inaugurate political liberation. Six months or a year produces sleeping-sickness.

> AUGUSTUS BRIDLE ("Domino"), *Masques of Ottawa*, 1921, 279.

Of all careers from which we draw
(Or so M.P.s have found it)
The best is training in the law,
The better to get round it.

> MAVOR MOORE, "The politician", *And what do you do?*, 1960, 35.

It's not Confederation that has betrayed us. We have betrayed ourselves by sending French-Canadian members to Ottawa who didn't know how to stand on their own feet, who didn't know how to fight for the French fact.

> RÉAL CAOUETTE, speech to Le Ralliement des Créditistes annual convention at Granby, Que., Sept. 2, 1963.

If it weren't for the oddballs, the fanatics, the pests, and the cranks, the human race would most surely remain stuck in the mud.

> ELMORE PHILPOTT, former Vancouver MP, commenting on some of the members in the Commons who ask absurd questions, qu. in *Liberty*, Feb. 1964.

Whipped by the discipline of the party machines; starved for information by the mandarin class; dwarfed by the Cabinet and by bigness, generally, in industry, labour, and communications; ignored in an age of summitry and the leadership cult.

> JOHN N. TURNER, *Politics of purpose*, 1968, 18.

These 70, 60-odd men elected by the people of Quebec to go to Ottawa – what are they? Dummies? What are they? Nonentities? Are they unimportant? Are they nothings? Do they not represent the people who elected them? Who elected them? The people of Quebec? Do they not have some standing, some authority in the nation's Parliament?

> JOSEPH SMALLWOOD, Federal-Provincial Conference on the Constitution, Ottawa, Feb. 5-7, 1968.

The best place in which to talk, if they want a forum, is, of course, Parliament. When they get home, when they get out of Parliament, when they are fifty yards from Parliament Hill, they are no longer honourable members, they are just nobodies.

> PIERRE ELLIOTT TRUDEAU, H. of C. *Debates,* July 25, 1969, 11635.

Women who have been successful at the polls confirm that winning the nomination is a more formidable hurdle than winning the election.

> CANADA. ROYAL COMM. ON STATUS OF WOMEN. *Report,* 1970, 349.

There is no system where an MP with reasonable qualifications can play a useful role; the government is a dinosaur and not responsive to the problems of today.

> PHILIP GIVENS, M.P., former mayor of Toronto on resigning in mid-term of Parliament in 1971, qu. in G. Aiken, *Backbencher,* 1974, 179.

What the private Member gets as a law-maker is a fast ride on a square-wheeled chariot.

> DOUGLAS HOGARTH, M.P. for New Westminster, on leaving Parliament in 1972; qu. in G. Aiken, *Backbencher,* 1974, 53.

The truth is, I am engaged is a passionate love affair with people and places in the area I represent in Parliament.

> GORDON FAIRWEATHER, M.P. for Fundy-Royal, N.B., in *Maclean's,* Jan. 1973, 27.

Parliamentary Debates

It happens, unfortunately, to be true, that there is no kind of intelligence about which the public are so indifferent as that which is usually contained in the speeches delivered on the floor of Parliament.

> TORONTO *DAILY LEADER* , May 19, 1855.

That vast repository of talk.

> J.W. DAFOE, *Clifford Sifton,* 1931, 166; ref. to *Hansard.*

Parliamentary Procedure

That is rule by majority, not rule by the rule book.

> STANLEY KNOWLES, H. of C., *Debates,* June 1, 1956, 4551.

Parliamentary Representation

Representation by population. Justice for Upper Canada! While Upper Canada has a larger population by one hundred and fifty thousand than Lower Canada, and contributes more than double the amount of taxation to the general revenue, Lower Canada has an equal number of representatives in Parliament.

> TORONTO *GLOBE,* Oct. 1, 1853, statement of policy.

The Upper Canadians boast of their rapidly increasing population, but wealth ought to be taken into account as well as population, and the codfish of Gaspé Bay ought to be represented as well as the 250,000 Grits of Western Canada.

> SIR GEORGE-ETIENNE CARTIER, H. of Assembly, April 5, 1861. "Codfish" was a word much used thereafter by Upper Canada advocates of Rep. by Pop.

We say we have representation by population, but we have not representation by population unless the population has a representation in the legislature equivalent to its strength at the polls.

> EDWARD BLAKE, speech at Aurora, Oct. 3, 1874.

I do not think a system under which a majority in one constituency elects a member, the minority being hopeless, helpless, without any representation of its own at all, is a good system.

EDWARD BLAKE, speech at Aurora, Oct. 3, 1874.

It is all very well to tell contemporaries that posterity must reap the benefit of the enormous public works undertaken at the consolidation of the Dominion. But posterity has no representative in Parliament.

CANADIAN MONTHLY, Vol. 1, 1878, 239.

Parti Québécois

If you don't want to see a bloody revolution in Quebec within a year, don't vote for the Parti Québécois.

RÉAL CAOUETTE, speech, St. Georges de Beauce, Que., Apr. 5, 1970. (Trans.)

Participation

To participate in anything in human society means entering into a common bond of guilt, of guilt and of inevitable compromise. I am not saying that we accept the evils of what we join: I am saying that whatever we join contains evils, and that what we accept is the guilt of belonging to it.

NORTHROP FRYE, CBC Symposium. "The ethics of change", Queen's University, Nov. 7, 1968.

Parties

You may talk of Clara Nolan's Ball or
    anything you choose,
But it couldn't hold a snuff-box to the
    spree at Kelligrews.
If you want your eyeballs
    straightened, just come out next
    week with me,
And you'll have to wear your glasses at
    the Kelligrews Soirée.

ANON., "The Kelligrews Soiree", New-foundland song.

Partridges

A partridge breaks his buried bed
And hurtles through the solitude
And then the silence of the dead
Is held within the listening wood.

ARTHUR S. BOURINOT, "Winter sketch", 1953.

The Pas, Manitoba

During the day, the people of The Pas bemoan the poverty and debauchery of the Indians while selling them over-priced food and second-rate clothes. At night, they steal the little bit of money and dignity the Indians have left. The Pas lives by scavenging from the Indians. The Pas is a mudlark.

HEATHER ROBERTSON, Reservations are for Indians, 1970, 154.

The Nip House is valuable to the police. The accused return there after a crime. The plan is hatched there. People tell us. It makes it easier for the police.

ANON., R.C.M.P. corporal, qu. in Heather Robertson, Reservations are for Indians, 1970, 156.

Passion

First passion is instantaneous – electrical. It cannot be described, and can only be communicated through the same mysterious medium.

SUSANNA MOODIE, Geoffrey Moncton, 1855, 83.

In a moment it will borrow,
    Flashing in a gusty train,
Laughter and desire and sorrow
    Anger and delight and pain.

ARCHIBALD LAMPMAN, "Passion", 1888.

The natural man has only two primal passions, to get and to beget.

> WILLIAM OSLER, *Science and immortality*, 1904, ch. 2.

Never was she so beguiling, never so merry of speech
(For passion ripens a woman as the sunshine ripens a peach.)

> ROBERT W. SERVICE, "The ballad of the brand", 1907.

What gives keenest joy is the evocation of latent passion.

> ARNOLD HAULTAIN, *Hints for lovers*, 1909, 135.

There is little passion in Canadian life. Suspicion and jealousy of the United States and admiration for England are not passions.

> A.L. PHELPS, in *Univ. of Tor. quart.*, 1939, 87.

Maybe if you keep waiting for the grand passion it will never come and then you'll know that what you had was all there was to have. Then you'll be sorry.

> JANET BONELLIE, "Why are the people staring?", in *Tamarack rev.*, No. 48, 1968, 21.

The Past

Here there are no historical associations, no legendary tales of those that came before us.

> CATHERINE PARR TRAILL, letter, May 9, 1833, in *The backwoods of Canada*.

It is the most unpoetical of all lands, there is no scope for imagination; here all is new – the very soil seems newly formed; there is no hoary ancient grandeur in these woods; no recollections of former deeds connected with the country.

> ANON., in Catherine P. Traill, *Backwoods of Canada*, 1836, 154.

But yet, do not withhold the grateful tear
For those, and for their works, who are not here.
Not here? O yes! our hearts their presence feel,
Viewless, not voiceless; from the deepest shells
On memory's shore harmonious echoes steal,
And names which in the days gone by were spells
Are blent with that soft music.

> JOSEPH HOWE, "Our fathers", ode written for the first Provincial Industrial Exhibition of Nova Scotia, Oct., 1854.

Now is the burden of it all "No more".
No more shall, wandering, we go gather flowers,
Nor tune our voices by the river's brink,
Nor in the grotto-fountain cool our limbs,
Nor walking in the winter woo the sun.

> CHARLES HEAVYSEGE, *Jephthah's daughter*, 1865.

Tho' boasting no baronial halls,
Nor ivy-crested towers,
What past can match thy glorious youth,
Fair Canada of ours?
Fair Canada,
Dear Canada,
This Canada of ours!

> JAMES D. EDGAR, "This Canada of ours", 1870.

Still we hear the tones regretful for the goodly times no more;
Still that sentimental slobbering for the brave old days of yore,
And sometimes we can't help thinking, while folks of the by-gone dream,
Of the comforts we're enjoying in these sneered-at days of steam.

> H.K. COCKIN, in *Canadian birthday book*, 1887.

The dead hand has too long hampered the freedom of the living.

> JAMES ROBERTSON, D.D., *Report to Presbyterian Assembly*, 1895.

May every joy that perished
Be mirrored in our gaze,
And in our speech the beauty
Of all our vanished days.

> ETHELWYN WETHERALD, "A wish", 1907.

Whatever a man has been he continues to be.

> GEORGE ILES, *Canadian stories*, 1918, 178.

We have become so accustomed to saying, and hearing others say, that we have no past, that we forget that what may have been true of a hundred years ago has had time in which to change. It has changed. We have made history. We have acquired customs, legendary lore, relics. Above all, relics.

> HELEN E. WILLIAMS, *Spinning-wheels and homespun*, 1923, 173.

While other animals have memory, man alone builds up a formal story of his life in the past and is governed by its traditions.

> G.M. WRONG, in *Can. hist. rev.*, 1933, 4.

As a matter of truth, health and happiness have been better in adversity and no man need feel he has failed unless, in looking back, the retrospect is blank, or unless time and events have proved that he was wrong. Whether now judged right or wrong, whatever I have said, whatever I have done, is going to remain unrevised and unrepented.

> ARTHUR MEIGHEN, speech in Winnipeg, Conservative Convention, Dec. 9, 1942.

The past must be accepted with birth. It should never be considered as a sacred value. We owe the past nothing.

> PAUL-EMILE BORDUAS, *Refus global*, 1948, 11. (Trans.)

In the past people showed what they thought of themselves much more openly than they do now.

> JAMES REANEY, *Twelve letters to a small town*, 1962, 15.

One day we shall look back
into those staring eyes
and there will be nothing left but
was.

> F.R. SCOTT, "Was", 1964.

The persistence of the dead in the
living,
if recognized, makes us sane.
This park is a wood where brown
men walked. As I walk. Now.

> TOM MARSHALL, "Sequiturs", 1969.

In search of Owen Roblin
I discovered a whole era
that was really a backward extension
of myself
built lines of communication across
two centuries
recovered my own past my own
people
a long misty chain stretched thru time
of which I am the last but not final
link.

> AL PURDY, *In search of Owen Roblin*, 1974, [80].

Patent Medicines

The sciences of Chemistry and Medicine have been taxed to their utmost to produce this best, most perfect purgative which is known to man.

> "AYER'S CATHARTIC PILLS", advertisement in Halifax *British colonist*, Feb. 28, 1857.

So swift is the patient transformed from pain, misery, weakness, and decrepitude, to the delightful enjoyment of health and strength, that patients frequently ascribe its talismanic power to the supernatural influence of enchantment.

> "RADWAY'S READY RELIEF", advertisement in Halifax *Morning chronicle*, July 18, 1863.

Paths

There is no path, there is no path at all
Unless perhaps where abstract things
   have gone
And precepts rise and metaphysics fall
And principles abandoned stumble on.
No path, but as it were a river in spate
Where drowning forms, downswept,
   gesticulate.

> MALCOLM LOWRY, "No still path", 1962.

Patriotism

A patriot is none of your raving, railing, ranting, accusing radicals – nor is he one of your idle, stall-fed, greasy, good for nothing sinecurists or pluralists; he is in deed and in truth a friend to his country.

> WILLIAM LYON MACKENZIE, *Colonial advocate*, May 4, 1826.

O Canada, my country, my love.

> GEORGE-ETIENNE CARTIER, "O Canada, mon pays, mes amours", song, 1834, title and refrain.

He lived a Patriot, and died for popular rights.

> ANON., inscription on monument erected in St. James Cemetery, Toronto, in 1893, in memory of Samuel Lount and Peter Mathews, hanged for treason, Apr. 12, 1838.

He was known and respected as an honest and prosperous farmer, always ready to do his duty to his adopted country, and died as he lived – a Patriot.

> ANON., inscription on monument erected in St. James Cemetery, Toronto in 1893 in memory of Samuel Lount and Peter Mathews, hanged for treason, Apr. 12, 1838.

Patriotism is the trump card of a scoundrel.

> T.C. HALIBURTON, *Sam Slick*, 1840, 28.

Let patriots flourish, other deeds
   displace,
Let adverse men now politics
   embrace;
Yet come it will when wisdom may
   control,
And one sound policy conduct the
   whole.

> STANDISH O'GRADY, "The emigrant", 1841.

I hope to see the day . . . when there will be no other term to our patriotism, but the common name of Canadian, without the prefix of either French or British.

> THOMAS D'ARCY MCGEE, letter to constituents, 1859.

You will believe me, I trust, when I say to you: I love my country. Have I loved her wisely, have I loved her foolishly? . . . On the outside opinions may be divided. Nevertheless, having conscientiously consulted my heart, then my head, I am able to decide that I love her as she ought to be loved. I imbibed this feeling with the milk of my nurse, my beloved mother. It is best expressed MY COUNTRY BEFORE ALL, no doubt I babbled it at my father's knee.

> LOUIS-JOSEPH PAPINEAU, speech to Institut Canadien, Montreal, Dec. 17, 1867. (Trans.)

Love your country, believe in her, honor her, work for her, live for her, die for her. Never has any people been endowed with a nobler birthright, or blessed with prospects of a brighter future.

> LORD DUFFERIN, speech in Toronto, Sept. 24, 1878.

There can be no patriotism without nationality.

> GOLDWIN SMITH, *Political destiny of Canada*, 1878, 61.

The breasts of some of our Canadian birds of song throb with patriotism, but on opening an American magazine you will find them, at least as soon as they are feathered, warbling on a foreign bough.

> GOLDWIN SMITH, *The Week*, Aug. 31, 1894, 950.

For Home and Country.

> ADELAIDE HOODLESS, Motto of Federated Women's Institutes of Canada, founded by Mrs. Hoodless, Stoney Creek, Ont., Feb. 19, 1897.

When we heard that they [the Gordon Highlanders] had justified fully the confidence placed in them, that they had charged like veterans, that their conduct was heroic and had won for them the encomiums of the Commander-in-Chief and the unstinted admiration of their comrades, who had faced death upon a hundred battlefields in all parts of the world, is there a man whose bosom did not swell with pride, that noblest of all pride, that pride of pure patriotism, the pride of the consciousness of our rising strength, the pride of the consciousness that on that day it had been revealed to the world that a new power had arisen in the West?

> SIR WILFRID LAURIER, H. of C., *Debates*, Mar. 13, 1900, 1847.

Some men, and all cattle, lack patriotism.

> GEORGE M. GRANT, qu. in *Principal Grant*, 1904, 396.

Patriotism is not based upon prejudice.

> SIR WILFRID LAURIER speech in Sorel, Sept. 28, 1904.

There is Ontario patriotism, Quebec patriotism, or Western patriotism, each based on the hope that it may swallow up the others, but there is no Canadian patriotism, and we can have no Canadian nation when we have no Canadian patriotism.

> HENRI BOURASSA, address, Canadian Club, Toronto, Jan. 22, 1907.

Our patriotism is of such a pure, ethereal essence, its aims are so wide and so clearly linked with matters of faith that our youth can rightly rely upon this patriotism to promote a more perfect flowering of their Canadian soul and their religious conviction: the chivalric ideal of nationalism will lead us to the devotion of apostles.

> ABBÉ LIONEL GROULX, *La révue de la jeunesse de Paris*, Jan., 1910; repr. in *Le Devoir*, Feb. 12, 1910. (Trans.)

Canadians waved the flag, but Canada buttoned up her pocket.

> ALAN SULLIVAN, *Blantyre – alien*, 1914, 61.

Patriotic sentiments have never in the history of the world stood long against the pocket-book. This is an unhappy truth which cannot be escaped.

> SIR W. VAN HORNE, letter, 1914?;qu. in Vaughan, *Van Horne*, 1920, 345.

Friends have I found in far and alien
places,
Beauty and ardour in unfamiliar faces,
But first in my heart this land I call
my own!
Canadian am I in blood and bone!

> CHARLES G.D. ROBERTS, "These three
> score years", 1927.

True patriotism is as quiet and cheerful as sunlight, as modest as a maid
used to be, as faithful under difficulties as a dog or a good wife, as
solicitous for the national honour as for
the individual's interest and as ready
to die in a fair and honest quarrel as a
man to go to bed after a hard day's
work.

> CECIL F. LLOYD, *Sunlight and shadow*,
> 1928.

Mr. Lower has long been a patriot in
search of a *patria*.

> P.E. CORBETT, in *Can. hist. rev.*, 1941,
> 117, on A.R.M. Lower.

The mainspring of a Canadian's patriotism is not love, but duty.

> ROBERTSON DAVIES, *Fortune, my foe*,
> 1949, 82.

Everybody says Canada is a hard
country to govern, but nobody men-
tions that for some people it is also a
hard country to live in. Still, if we all
run away it will never be any better.
So let the geniuses of easy virtue go
southward; I know what they feel too
well to blame them. But for some of us
there is no choice; let Canada do what
she will with us, we must stay.

> ROBERTSON DAVIES, *Fortune, my foe*,
> 1949, 98.

There is still no proper substitute for
love of one's country, a profound belief in its latent strength and legitimate
destiny.

> LORNE PIERCE, A *Canadian nation*,
> 1960, viii.

I know there are some who feel a sense
of embarrassment in expressing pride
in their nation, perhaps because of the
fear that they might be considered
old-fashioned or parochial. I do not
belong to that group. I realize that a
warped and twisted nationalism is productive of tyranny and war, but that a
healthy loyalty and devotion to one's
country constitutes a most fruitful inspiration in life.

> JOHN G. DIEFENBAKER, H. of C., *Debates*,
> July 1, 1961, 7349.

You said "land" as if
you'd just baked it in the oven,
and "love " as if you had it
cupped in your hand.

> ELDON GRIER, "A north country accent",
> 1963.

True patriotism doesn't exclude an
understanding of the patriotism of
others.

> QUEEN ELIZABETH II, at Quebec City,
> Oct. 10, 1964, speech in Legislative
> Council Chamber following rowdy
> demonstration by students.

I've got a gut feeling for Canada.

> PIERRE E. TRUDEAU, May 21, 1969, qu. in
> *The best of Trudeau*, 1972, 11.

This country is something that must be
chosen — it is so easy to leave — and
if we do choose it we are still choosing
a violent duality.

> MARGARET ATWOOD, *The journals of
> Susanna Moodie*, 1970, 62.

I know a man whose school could
never teach him patriotism but who
acquired that virtue when he felt in
his bones the vastness of his land, and
the greatness of those who founded it.

> PIERRE E. TRUDEAU, qu. by Peter New-
> man in *Saturday rev.*, Mar. 13, 1971, 18.

Patronage

Patronage is power; our men won the victory, and they are entitled to the prize money.

J.H. PRICE, letter to Robert Baldwin, Feb. 6, 1843.

O! patronage! patronage! It is that which constitutes the whole power of the Executive Government of this Province; and when the future historian of New Brunswick records the history of these times, he may sum up the whole duties of the Executive in these few words — The Hon. Mr. Hazen, by command of His Excellency, lays before the House certain Returns from the Crown Land Office!

L.A. WILMOT, in N.B., House of Assembly, Mar. 24, 1847.

If you have any axes to grind, send them down to Toronto by Mr. O'Reilly.

JOHN SANDFIELD MACDONALD, speech in Hamilton, 1867; a reference to O'Reilly, the government candidate in an election; known as the "Axe-grinding speech".

Half my time is taken up with this question of patronage in Nova Scotia and Prince Edward Island. My life has become a torment to me about it.

ALEXANDER MACKENZIE, (Prime Minister), letter to A.G. Jones, Nov. 18, 1874. (Pub. Arch. Can.)

Friends(?) expect to be benefited by offices they are unfit for, by contracts they are not entitled to, by advances not earned. Enemies ally themselves with friends and push the friends to the front. Some dig trenches at a distance and approach in regular siege form. A weak minister here would ruin the party in a month and the country very soon.

ALEXANDER MACKENZIE, letter to Thomas Hodgins, Apr. 27, 1875.

Every government selected for the civil service their own friends, and no one could object to it.

SIR JOHN A. MACDONALD, H. of C., *Debates*, Apr. 27, 1878, 2229.

To think that after naming my only son William Lyon Mackenzie, I am still denied any post by a government that calls itself Liberal!

ANON., letter to Sir Wilfrid Laurier, 1896; qu. Skelton, *Laurier*, II, 273.

I wish to say, in general terms, in reference to the contracts which are made with my departments, that, in every case, wherever I can do it fairly and justly, with due regard to the public exchequer, I am prepared to give the preference to my own political friends. I do not think that anybody expects anything different, and if they do, they will expect something which never happened in Canada before.

SIR FREDERICK BORDEN, H. of C., *Debates*, Apr. 3, 1900, 3103.

He has sent me bishops and archbishops, priests and laymen, until I am absolutely familiar with all his merits, and his one demerit of being over zealous in his own behalf.

SIR WILFRID LAURIER, letter to John Willison, Oct. 12, 1903.

Ever since I have been here I have used whatever influence I possessed against the abominable political 'pull', which nearly everyone in Canada looks to and which is ruining the individuality of the people.

EARL OF MINTO, letter to Goldwin Smith, July 8, 1904, qu. in Elisabeth Wallace, *Goldwin Smith, Victorian liberal*, 1957, 237.

The patronage system is one of Canada's social evils — a canker, a disease more blighting, more demoralizing than any other social disease that infects the body politic today.

> WILLIAM IRVINE, in *Nutcracker*, Feb. 3, 1917, 6.

We farmers work on the principle that the hog that gets fat first will be the one to be killed off first.

> JOHN OLIVER, Premier of British Columbia, about 1920, to his friends, on patronage.

The distribution of patronage was the most important single function of the government.

> O.D. SKELTON, in *Life of Laurier*, 1921, II, 270.

Gratefulness was always regarded as an important factor in dealing with democratic governments.

> R.O. SWEEZEY, quoting John Aird, Canada. H. of C. Spec. comm. on Beauharnois power project, *Proc.*, 1931, Vol. 2, 823, statement regarding his contributions to the Ontario Conservative Party.

Patronage spells the death of efficiency in its largest and broadest sense; it invariably places the emphasis not only on the wrong factors but on the irrelevant ones . . . Party patronage in the civil service is now a sign of political immaturity, a relic of barbaric days, a sure symptom of pettifogging politics.

> R. MACGREGOR DAWSON, in *Can. jour. econ. and pol. sci.*, 1936, 291.

It is our principle — and I am not hiding it — that when there are two school commissions asking for grants and one is friendly, we take care of the friends first; when there is enough to take care of opponents we do so generously without political considerations.

> MAURICE DUPLESSIS, qu. in Montreal *Gazette*, Feb. 24, 1954, 2.

The Canada Council is of course only one partner in the enterprise of patronage.

> CANADA COUNCIL, *Annual report*, 1962-63, 18.

I can buy any government.

> HAL BANKS, infamous former head of Seafarers' International Union, qu. by Peter C. Newman in *Distemper of our times*, 1968, 279.

Payment

So eat, drink and be merry, have a
  good time if you will,
But God help you when the time
  comes, and you
Foot the bill.

> ROBERT SERVICE, "The reckoning", 1907.

All
must be taken into account
sooner or later
later or sooner; eyeglasses
only magnify the mysteries.

> GWENDOLYN MACEWEN, "Poem for G.W.", 1963.

Peace

I knew by the smoke that so peacefully
  curled
  Above the green elms, that a cottage
    was near;
And I said, if there's peace to be found
  in the world,
  A heart that is humble might hope
    for it here.

> THOMAS MOORE, lines inspired by a scene on Burlington Bay, Ontario, 1804.

There is very little peace to be had for you, or for me, or for any animate thing in this world, for perfect peace here means stagnation, and stagnation is death.

> J.J. PROCTER, *The philosopher in the clearing*, 1897, 132.

And still I preached, and wrought, and
    still I bore my message,
  For well I knew that on and upward
    without cease
The spirit works for ever, and by Faith
    and Presage
  That somehow yet the end of
    human life is Peace.

> ARCHIBALD LAMPMAN, "The land of Pallas", 1899.

When the strength of man is shattered,
And the powers of earth are scattered,
  From beneath the ghastly ruin
    Peace shall rise!

> ARCHIBALD LAMPMAN, "War", 1899.

I do not believe that universal peace is
either possible or desirable. If it were
possible and could be brought about, I
feel sure it would result in universal
rottenness.

> SIR W. VAN HORNE, letter to S.S. McClure,
> 1910, in Vaughan, *Van Horne*, 1920,
> 364.

Peace comes by power rather than by
preaching.

> SIR JOHN S. WILLISON, speech, International Polity Club, Toronto, Feb. 12,
> 1914.

When our children's children shall talk
  of War as a madness that may not
  be;
When we thank our God for our grief
  to-day, and blazen from sea to sea
In the name of the dead the banner of
  Peace . . . *that will be Victory.*

> ROBERT W. SERVICE, "The song of the
> pacifist", 1916.

The making of peace is in fact more
difficult than has been the winning of
the war.

> JOHN W. DAFOE, speech, Canadian Club,
> Winnipeg, Apr. 8, 1919.

In civilisation there is no peace. Here,
in the North, in my country, there *is*
peace. No past, no future, no regret,
no anticipation; just doing. That is
peace.

> GEORGE WHALLEY, *The legend of John
> Hornby*, 1962, 325, summation of the
> philosophy of John Hornby, perished,
> Apr., 1927.

I'll stand by those who strive to chart
A world where peace is everyone's,
A peace that does not rot the heart
With hunger, fear, and hopeless hate,
Nor rust the cunning wheels nor still
The subtle fingers, peace that will
Unlock to every man the gate
To all the leaping joys his hand
Creates.

> EARLE BIRNEY, "On going to the wars",
> 1942.

Peace is what is found
When the sailor sets his will
To turn from a rough sea
To a rougher still.

> ELIZABETH BREWSTER, "Peace", 1951.

You never know what peace is until
you walk on the shores or in the fields
or along the winding red roads of
Prince Edward Island in a summer
twilight when the dew is falling and
the old stars are peeping out and the
sea keeps its mighty tryst with the
little land it loves. You find your soul
then. You realize that youth is not a
vanished thing but something that
dwells forever in the heart.

> L.M. MONTGOMERY, qu. in Hilda M. Ridley, *The story of L.M. Montgomery*,
> 1956, 111, a message to her friends.

There is always a period of peace
Between two blows, when a smiling
  landscape
Surrounds with blue light the resting
  warrior.
The raised arm hardly shows among
  the ferns.

GEORGE JONAS, "Peace", 1962.

What is needed, in fact, is an entirely new arrangement by which these nations would establish an international peace force, its contingents trained and equipped for the purpose, and operating under principles agreed in advance.

LESTER B. PEARSON, *Maclean's*, May 2, 1964, 11.

A peace-loving nation is one that has already obtained, by aggression, all the territory it can handle.

RICHARD J. NEEDHAM, *A friend in Needham*, 1969, 41.

we pray for our people, moving
together, to see this is how the Earth is,
Father, you let us walk on, live on,
teach us to grow together in Peace
on your Earth.

BILL BISSETT, "No one owns th earth", 1971.

I sometimes wonder if there is any other sphere of human activity in which so many fine words have been uttered, and so little actually achieved as in the pursuit of disarmament and a stable peace.

GEN. E.L.M. BURNS, *A seat at the table*, 1972, 115.

International co-operation for peace is the most important aspect of national policy.

LESTER B. PEARSON, *Mike*, Vol. 1, 1972, 283.

Peace of Mind

Religion versus Dionysianism: peace of mind is obtained by ignoring the contradictions of existence; ecstasy, by embracing them.

IRVING LAYTON, "Aphs", *The whole bloody bird*, 1969, 89.

Pearson, Lester B.

I don't mind Mike running the whole legation but I wish, sometimes, that he'd tell me what we're doing.

LEIGHTON MCCARTHY, Canadian Minister to Washington, to Bruce Hutchison referring to Lester Pearson's activities as his assistant, 1941-42.

I think I may be the only diplomat here who has ever been paid money for playing baseball.

LESTER B. PEARSON, at San Francisco Conference, 1945, qu. in *Maclean's*, Apr. 15, 1951, 7.

This is one of the dangers of having Pearson take too sudden a lead in any matters of the kind. He can get us much more deeply involved with world situations than we should ever be. He likes keeping Canada at the head of everything, in the forefront in connection with United Nations affairs. He does not see that the Big Powers are using us.

W.L. MACKENZIE KING, Mar., 1948, *The Mackenzie King record*, Vol. 4 , 1970, 177.

Pearson seems to be as active as possible in selling us down the river to the United States.

HAROLD A. INNIS, letter to Gerald Graham, Nov., 1948; qu. in D.G. Creighton, *Harold Adams Innis*, 1957, 133.

He contrived to give the idea that he was less concerned with victory in the election than with the triumph of sound principles of government.

JOHN A. STEVENSON, *Saturday night*, Mar. 15, 1958, 6, referring to election campaign, Mar., 1958.

The Prime Minister has never quite forgiven the Leader of the Opposition for being awarded the Nobel Peace Prize in 1957.

> LUCIEN CARDIN, H. of C., *Debates,* Feb. 22, 1962, 1142, referring to John Diefenbaker.

He'll do.

> JOHN F. KENNEDY, after visit of Pearson to Hyannis Port, May 11, 1963, qu. in D. G. Creighton, *Canada's first century,* 1970, 334.

His mind, constructed layer by layer in a series of Chinese boxes, had never revealed its inner contents to any colleague, perhaps not even to its owner. Usually considered a genial extrovert, Pearson was the most popular and the most solitary public person of his times.

> BRUCE HUTCHISON, *Mr. Prime Minister, 1867-1964,* 1964, 350.

We are so happy to have Mr. Wilson here with us.

> L.B. JOHNSON, U.S. President, Jan. 15, 1965, on welcoming the Canadian Prime Minister to his LBJ Ranch, Texas; an error for Harold Wilson.

I am an unrepentant and insistent internationalist. Any other position seems to me a rejection of reality as absurd as relying on the bayonet for defence.

> LESTER B. PEARSON, speech to Private Planning Assoc., Montebello, Que., Nov. 16, 1966, qu. in P. Newman, *Distemper of our times,* 1968, 226.

My sixty days of decision were too decisive. I failed to get three maple leaves on the flag and I lost the blue border. I failed to get Vancouver into the NHL or Gabon into the Canadian confederation. I failed to realize that unification of the armed forces should have been preceded by unification of the Cabinet. I was wrong in relying entirely on the Sermon on the Mount as the guideline for Cabinet solidarity.

> LESTER B. PEARSON, farewell to the Parliamentary Press Gallery, Mar. 30, 1968.

Pearson did not possess Meighen's towering intellect, nor Mackenzie King's adroit political footwork, nor Bennett's administrative capability, nor St. Laurent's dignified aloofness from the partisan bickering, nor Diefenbaker's gift of compelling oratory. But he perhaps had a more winsome quality: immense personal charm. As a likeable man, warm, witty, and indeed loveable, Lester Pearson towered above those five predecessors.

> PATRICK NICHOLSON, *Vision and indecision,* 1968, 370.

Mike is happiest when he's clinging to a precipice and just about to fall off.

> GRANT DEXTER, qu. in Peter Newman, *Distemper of our times,* 1968, 43.

Well, I am glad you have at last become a Minister, if only a second-class one.

> MRS. ANNIE S. PEARSON, qu. by her son in *Mike,* Vol. 1, 1972, 296, referring to her hope that he would become a minister of the Gospel.

Peasants

While the poor peasant, whose laborious care
Scarce from the soil could wring his scanty fare,
Now in the peaceful arts of culture skilled,
Sees his wide barn with ample treasure filled.

> OLIVER GOLDSMITH, "The rising village", 1825.

Pemmican

Take scrapings from the driest outside corner of a very stale piece of cold roast beef, add to it lumps of tallowy rancid fat, then garnish all with long human hairs (on which string pieces, like beads, upon a necklace), and short hairs of oxen, or dogs, or both, – and you have a fair imitation of common pemmican.

EARL OF SOUTHESK, *Saskatchewan and the Rocky Mountains: Diary*, Nov. 20, 1859.

Penguins

No matter what the hour may be
Penguins are dressed to dine,
And have a gentle dignity,
Stuffy – but yet benign,
As though their minds dwelt much on soup,
On walnuts, and on wine.

VIRNA SHEARD, "Penguins", 1932.

Penguin, penguin! *comme il faut*
Amid Antarctic ice and snow,
Tell us, what divine decree
Ordains thy strict formality?

MICHAEL HORNYANSKY, "The penguin", qu. in R. Charlesworth, *Imagine seeing you here*, 1975, 161.

Pensions

A pensioner in Prince Edward Island doesn't need anything like a pensioner living in Toronto.

JUDY LAMARSH, speech in Preston, Ont., election campaign, Oct., 1965, qu. in P. Newman, *Distemper of our times*, 1968, 358.

People

Some people are too good to be interesting.

ROBERT C. (BOB) EDWARDS, Calgary *Eye Opener*, Oct. 28, 1911.

No nation, however advanced in its industrialism or powerful in its accumulated wealth, can long survive the shock of time except through the strength derived from the character of its people. That strength must assuredly be based upon faith and upon ideals.

ROBERT L. BORDEN, speech, by telephone to Associated Press, New York, Apr. 25, 1912.

All men are essentially noble. Constitutionally, there are no common people.

ALBERT D. WATSON, "The immortals", 1913.

Somehow the people who do as they please seem to get along just about as well as those who are always trying to please others.

ROBERT C. (BOB) EDWARDS, Calgary *Eye Opener*, Mar. 9, 1918.

The salvation of the people must come from the people.

M.J. COLDWELL, speech to Regina People's Forum, Sept. 24, 1922.

When you find a man about whom people speak no evil, it is evidence, not that the man, but that the people are unusual.

PETER MCARTHUR,, d. 1924, qu. in *The best of Peter McArthur*, 1967, 172.

It is the wishes and likings of the mass which largely dictate what the rest of us shall see and hear.

STEPHEN LEACOCK, *Humour, its theory and technique*, 1935, 264.

On you, the founders, faith is laid;
On you, the makers, strength is stayed;
By you, the builders, worlds are made.
Life honours you – "The People".

NORA M. DUNCAN, "The people", 1938.

The people . . . may make mistakes
but they will be their own mistakes
and will be the better for them than if
someone tried to think for them too
much, and probably be just as apt to
be mistaken.

ALEX. J. MCPHAIL, *Diary*, 1940, 93.

I discovered that the way to win the
hearts of the lowly was to tell them
that they were the salt of the earth;
this is a lie, but they love it.

ROBERTSON DAVIES, *The diary of Samuel Marchbanks*, 1947, 144.

I've always found that you can control
people better if you don't see too
much of them.

W.L. MACKENZIE KING, qu., Hardy, *Mackenzie King of Canada*, 1949, 94.

The points of resemblance between
great people and paltry people are
infinitely more numerous than the
points of difference: they all eat, sleep,
fall in love, catch cold, and use handkerchiefs.

ROBERTSON DAVIES, *Table talk of Samuel Marchbanks*, 1949, 31.

I believe people today hear, smell, talk
and swallow too much.

SIDNEY E. SMITH, to a convention of eye,
ear, nose and throat specialists, qu. in
Saturday night, Sept 28, 1957, 47.

You can't change people very quickly.
I don't believe I could save the world.

E.P. TAYLOR, qu. in P. Newman, *Flame of power*, 1959, 228.

My god what an agony to be
    sub-divided like
this and to be continuous and to be
    every-
where like a bunch of children's blocks
disappearing into each other my god.

AL PURDY, "Archaeology of snow", 1962.

We must not fall into the totalitarian
way of thinking of people merely as
instruments, to be developed as the
community needs them; rather, must
we think of the community as an
instrument for developing the talents
of individuals.

ASSOCIATION OF UNIVERSITIES AND COL-
LEGES OF CANADA, *Financing higher education in Canada*, 1965, 1.

People are interesting! They may be
fascinating, loathsome, beautiful, hideous, dull, brilliant, endearing, or repulsive, but all are interesting. None
more so than ourselves. We tick!

WILLIAM E. BLATZ, *Human security*,
1966, 15.

Perfection

There is a passion for perfection which
you will rarely see fully developed;
but you may note this fact, that in
successful lives it is never wholly lacking.

BLISS CARMAN, *The friendship of art*,
1904, 196.

If a man wants to be of the greatest
possible value to his fellow-creatures
let him begin the long, solitary task of
perfecting himself.

ROBERTSON DAVIES, *A jig for the gypsy*,
1954, 85.

The juggler comes closest to our hearts
when he misses the ball.

RICHARD J. NEEDHAM, *A friend in Need-ham*, 1969, 12.

Performance

The thrush on the farthest-out bough sings the best song his heart will allow.

And if we haven't liked what we've heard
there's tomorrow and another bird.

> RAYMOND SOUSTER, "Thrush", 1964.

My performance has not been really first class in any of the things to which I have turned my hand – music, sport, linguistics, translation, original prose and verse, teaching, administration, research, nature study, soldiering, politics, church work or social service.

> WATSON KIRKCONNELL, *A slice of Canada*, 1967, 362.

An ounce of image is worth a pound of performance.

> LAURENCE J. PETER and RAYMOND HULL, *The Peter principle*, 1969, 134.

Periodicals

I do not consider *Time* a Canadian magazine.

> HENRY LUCE, owner of *Time*, to Canada. Royal Commission on publications, 1960; in its *Report*, 1961, 97.

If this house votes for this legislation it will be voting for the proposition that Washington has a right to interfere in a matter of purely Canadian concern, and voting a probable death sentence on Canada's periodical press, with all that this can entail for our future voyage through history.

> GRATTAN O'LEARY, Senate, *Debates*, June 28, 1965, 283; re exemption of *Time* and *Reader's digest* from tax on advertising.

Permafrost

And you know it occurs to me about 2 feet under
these roots must touch permafrost
ice that remains ice forever
and they use it for their nourishment
use death to remain alive

> AL PURDY, "Trees at the Arctic Circle", 1967.

Permission

PLEASE WALK ON THE GRASS

> TOMMY THOMPSON, Parks Commissioner, Toronto, sign erected in Edwards Gardens, 1960. Has since become the motto of the Parks Department.

Personalities

– BARRETT, DAVID

The government fired me and now the people have hired me.

> DAVID BARRETT, on being elected Premier of B.C., Aug. 30, 1972. He had been fired by the Social Credit government in 1959 for making political statements while employed as a social worker.

– DAVIS, HENRY FULLER

H. F. Davis, Born Vermont, 1820, Died, Slave Lake, 1893. Pathfinder, Pioneer, Miner, Trader. He was everyman's friend and never locked his cabin door.

> ANON., friends of "Twelve-Foot" Davis, inscription on his gravestone overlooking town of Peace River, Alta., nickname derived from his twelve-foot-wide mining claim which during the Cariboo gold rush yielded him $15,000.

— JOHNSON, DANIEL

The man we hate to love.

> ANON., a member of the Quebec Legislative Press Gallery, referring to Daniel Johnson, leader of the Union Nationale party, qu. in Thomas Sloan, *Quebec: the not-so-quiet revolution*, 1965, 78.

— PELLETIER, GERARD

Only a country with a death wish would tolerate a man like Pelletier in high public office.

> W.F.W. NEVILLE, *Jour. of Can. stud.*, Nov., 1970, 62; Pelletier was Secretary of State.

— PICKERSGILL, J. W.

Jack Pickersgill knows where all the bodies are buried in Ottawa.

> JOSEPH R. SMALLWOOD, qu. by Hugh Winson, *Globe mag.*, May 30, 1970, 6.

— STRACHAN, JOHN

One insolent 'Bishop of Toronto', triumphant Canadian but Aberdeen by dialect.

> THOMAS CARLYLE, *Reminiscences*, 1881, 241, after meeting John Strachan in London, 1824.

— TARTE, ISRAEL

The mildest mannered man that ever scuttled a ship or cut a throat.

> THE WEEK, Toronto, May 15, 1891, in quotes in "Ottawa Letter" signed by "X".

— TORY, H. M.

He delighted in seeing things grow.

> R. C. WALLACE, in Foreword to E. A. Corbett, *Henry Marshall Tory*, 1954, vii.

— UNDERHILL, FRANK H.

People would say that I was just a natural minoritarian, an individualist who never fitted into institutions very well and who always found his most congenial companions among those who were protesting against something or other. My belief is that they were justly protesting.

> FRANK H. UNDERHILL, *In search of Canadian liberalism*, 1960, ix.

— VANIER, GEORGES P.

It is Vanier's distinction to have been the first Canadian diplomat to tender his resignation on an issue of principle.

> JAMES EAYRS, *In defence of Canada*, Vol. 3, 1972, 39, referring to Vanier's resignation as Minister to France, May 17, 1941, which was never officially acknowledged.

Personalties (Nicknames)

The Abe Lincoln of Canada.

> ANDREW BRODER, M.P. for Dundas, Ont., 1896 to 1917.

The Apostle of the Prairies.

> DR. JAMES ROBERTSON, Superintendent of Presbyterian missions in the West, 1881-1902.

Archibald the Arctic.

> ARCHIBALD FLEMING, Anglican Bishop of the Arctic, 1933 to 1948, official signature.

The Baron of the Kootenays.

> H.W. (BERT) HERRIDGE, M.P. for Kootenay West for 23 years, died 1973, so-called by Ottawa Press Gallery.

The Bear.

> EDWARD ELLICE, (d.1863) usually "Bear" Ellice, English merchant and M.P., long connected with the fur-trading companies in Canada; his son, also named Edward, was sometimes called "Young Bear".

The Belted Knight.

SIR ALLAN MACNAB, knighted in 1838 for his services in leading the loyal forces in the Niagara peninsula during the rebellion of 1837.

Big Thunder.

E.B. WOOD, M.P., so-called by T.D. McGee because of his loud voice; also, WILLIAM PATERSON, so-called by his Indian constituents in South Brant.

Bismarck.

PETER MITCHELL, member of Sir John A. Macdonald's cabinet, 1873.

The Black Tarte and the Yellow Martin.

J. ISRAEL TARTE and JOSEPH MARTIN, Liberal leaders, so-called by Sir John Thompson, speech in Pictou, N.S., 1894.

The Boy Millionaire.

GEORGE MCCULLAGH, Publisher, Globe and Mail, 1930's.

Calamity Cora.

E. CORA HIND, prairie crop inspector, and agricultural expert, Winnipeg Free press, early 1900's. Her forecasts, though accurate, were disturbing to the country.

The Coon.

MALCOLM C. CAMERON, member of the House of Commons, 1867 to 1898.

The Demosthenes of Canada.

LOUIS JOSEPH PAPINEAU, later applied to SIR GEORGE FOSTER.

L'enfant terrible.

J.B.E. DORION, (1826-1866), politician and journalist.

Father of Astronomy.

WILLIAM FREDERICK KING, first Director, Dominion Observatory, d. 1916.

The Father of British Preference.

SIR LOUIS DAVIES, who introduced the preferential policy in 1892.

The Father of Canadian Geology.

ABRAHAM GESNER, of Nova Scotia after publication of his book, Remarks on the geology of Nova Scotia, 1836.

The Father of the Ottawa.

PHILEMON WRIGHT, 1760-1839, first settler in the Hull, Quebec, district, 1800.

Father of the Railway.

SIR ALLAN MACNAB, a term popular in Hamilton where he was instrumental in bringing the Great Western Railway to the city in 1854.

The Father of the Saguenay.

WILLIAM PRICE, English lumber operator, 1789-1867.

The Father of the Yukon.

JACK MCQUESTEN, Yukon trader, 1860's.

Fighting Frank Carvell.

FRANK B. CARVELL, Minister of Public Works in the Union Government, 1917-19.

Fighting Joe.

JOSEPH MARTIN, member of Manitoba Legislature, 1883-92; led the attack on separate schools; Premier of British Columbia, 1900.

The First Great Canadian.

PIERRE LE MOYNE, SIEUR D'IBERVILLE, from title of a biography by Charles B. Reed, 1910.

The Flying Bishop.

ARCHIBALD FLEMING, Bishop of the Arctic, 1933-1948, name given by the newspaper press.

General and Complete [Disarmament] Burns.

GEN. E.L.M. BURNS, nickname, qu. by Richard A. Preston, Univ. of Tor. quart. July, 1967, 492.

The Good Samaritan of Labrador.

SIR WILFRED GRENFELL , early 20th century.

The Governor-General of Durham.

DR. DAVID JAMIESON, member for South-East Grey in Ontario legislature from 1898 and Speaker, 1914-19, applied by Agnes Macphail.

The Grand Old Man of Canada.

SIR CHARLES TUPPER, in his later years; he died Oct. 30, 1915, age 94; also, SIR WILLIAM MULOCK, died 1944, age 100.

The Great White Mother.

QUEEN VICTORIA, so-called by western Indians, middle Nineteenth Century.

The Hanging Judge.

SIR MATTHEW BAILLIE BEGBIE, appointed a judge in British Columbia, 1858, and Chief Justice, 1870.

The Hero of Kars.

SIR WM. FENWICK WILLIAMS, of Nova Scotia, from his defeat of the Russians, Sept. 29, 1855, during his defence of the Fortress of Kars, later surrendered.

Holy Joe.

JOSEPH E. ATKINSON, Publisher, Toronto Star, 1899-1948.

Honest John.

Popular term applied to JOHN CARLING, JOHN COSTIGAN, JOHN OLIVER, and others.

Hug-the-machine Preston.

W.T.R. PRESTON, a civil servant, sent a telegram on Jan. 12, 1899, to Donald McNish, Liberal Party victor in a West Elgin by-election, worded: "Hug the machine for me". The telegram was obtained by the Conservatives and published.

The Hungry Adventurer.

W.R. MEREDITH, Ontario Conservative leader, from a manifesto by Archbishop James V. Cleary read in Kingston churches, May 28, 1894, during an election.

The Hyena.

SIR FRANCIS HINCKS, used about 1850 by George Brown and his supporters; a reference to his ruthlessness in debate.

J. Watson MacZero.

J. WATSON MACNAUGHT, M.P. for Summerside, P.E.I., appointed Chairman, Dominion Coal Board, Mar. 5, 1966, so-called by Liberal Party members.

Janey Canuck.

JUDGE EMILY MURPHY, (d.1933), of Alberta.

King of the Fur-Traders.

SIR GEORGE SIMPSON, (1792-1860), governor of the Hudson's Bay Company.

The King of the Gatineau.

ALONZO WRIGHT, member of the Assembly and House of Commons, 1862-91.

The Laird of Dundurn.

SIR ALLAN MACNAB, who built Dundurn Castle, Hamilton.

Laird of the Arrow Lakes.

HERBERT W. (BERT) HERRIDGE, N.D.P. Member of Parliament, 1945-1965, for constituency of Kootenay West (B.C.). Also known as "Baron of the Kootenays".

The Lion of the Yukon.

SAM STEELE of the North West Mounted Police during the Klondike gold-rush.

The Little Bigot of Little York.

JOHN STRACHAN, 1778-1867.

The Little Corporal of Lower Canadian Politics.

SIR GEORGE-ÉTIENNE CARTIER, (1814-1873).

Little Thunder.

ARTHUR STURGIS HARDY, Premier of Ontario, 1896-99, in his early political days, because of his oratory.

The Master of the Administration.

J. ISRAEL TARTE, member of Laurier's cabinet, so-called by Conservatives, 1902.

The Minister of Elections.

ROBERT ROGERS, Conservative government minister under Borden, so termed by the Liberals, about 1917.

The Mother of the Saskatchewan C.C.F.

LOUISE LUCAS, of Mazenod, Saskatchewan, farmer and political worker, died 1945; J.F.C. Wright, *The Louise Lucas story*, 1965, 12 and 132.

The Nation-maker.

AMOR DE COSMOS, so-called by his political opponents in Victoria, B.C. after his speech of Apr. 2, 1882; (see, TREATIES.)

Old To-morrow. (See, MACDONALD, SIR JOHN A.)

Old Velvet Belly.

JOHN DUNCAN MCLEAN, Premier of B.C. 1927-28; also known as "Velvet Vest".

The Other MacNab.

Sir Allan MacNab's inscription on the reverse of the visiting card of Archibald, Chief of MacNab, known as "The MacNab", and returned to him.

The People's Dick.

RICHARD MCBRIDE, Premier of B.C., 1903-1915, so-called because of his ability to mix easily with all classes of the population. Also known as "Glad-hand Dick".

Peter the Great and Ivan the Terrible.

PETER J. VENIOT, Liberal Premier, and *IVAN T. RAND*, Attorney General, so-called by John B.M. Baxter, N.B. election, 1925.

That picturesque buffalo.

RICHARD MCBRIDE, Premier of B.C., 1903-1915, so-called by Lord Grey in letter to Sir Wilfrid Laurier, Oct. 4, 1906. (Pub. Arch. Can.)

The Pope of Methodism.

EGERTON RYERSON, so-called by John Langton; see, RYERSON, EGERTON – John Langton, 1855. Later applied to *Dr. ALBERT CARMAN*, general supt. Methodist Church, 1883-1915; applied to *REV. S.D. CHOWN*, at formation of United Church in 1925.

The Prince of the Prairies.

GABRIEL DUMONT, a Métis, so-called by his followers, about 1885.

The professional Canadian.

JOHN FISHER, described by Peter Newman in *Renegade in power*, 1963, 84.

Radical Jack.

LORD DURHAM, an English nickname used in Canada after 1837.

The Ram of Cumberland.

SIR CHARLES TUPPER, so-called because of his propensity for handsome women.

Red Michael.

DR. MICHAEL CLARK, Progressive, later Liberal, member of the House of Commons, about 1920.

The Sage of Bothwell.

DAVID MILLS, Member of Parliament and Senator from 1867 to 1902.

Sage of Brewery Bay.

STEPHEN B. LEACOCK.

The Sage of Ekfrid

PETER MCARTHUR, (See McArthur: *Around home*, 1925, Intro. by M. O.Hammond, 9.)

Sailor Jack.

J.W. PICKERSGILL, elected as M.P. for Twillingate, Nfld., 1953.

Sham Shoes.

> COLONEL SAM HUGHES, Minister of Militia and Defence in Canadian Cabinet, 1914, referring to issue of army boots which were agony to march in and quickly rotted in the mud and water.

Smooth William.

> SIR WILLIAM WHYTE, Superintendent, western lines, C.P.R., d.1914.

Spanish John.

> FATHER JOHN MCLACHLAN, priest in Alexandria, Ont., so-called because of his jesuitical tendencies, about 1854.

Steele of the Mounted.

> SAM STEELE, of the North West Mounted Police. James Oliver Curwood, American novelist used the phrase for one of his books about the North.

Sweet William.

> WILLIAM PUGSLEY, also called "Slippery Bill" by his opponents because of his soft voice; also, WILLIAM H. DRAPER, because of his oratorical powers.

The Tiger.

> WILLIAM DUNLOP, or "Tiger" Dunlop, surgeon in the war of 1812, adventurer in India, and later a settler in the Huron district and member of the Legislative Assembly.

"Twelve-Foot" Davis. (See: PERSONALITIES – DAVIS, HENRY F.)

Wandering Willie.

> WILLIAM MCDOUGALL, (1822-1905), a founder of the Clear Grit Party, later joined the Conservatives at Confederation.

Warden of the Plains.

> CUTHBERT GRANT, a Métis who kept the Métis hunters in order, Red River settlements, early nineteenth century.

The Watch-dog of the Treasury.

> J. LORN MCDOUGALL, Auditor-General of Canada who resigned, June 21, 1904.

Personality

The potency of personality exceeds the potency of beauty.

> ARNOLD HAULTAIN, Hints for lovers, 1909, 128.

I have never known an important issue in Canadian politics which has not been deeply influenced and sometimes determined in its result by factors of the most purely personal kind.

> JOHN W. DAFOE, to George V. Ferguson, paraphrased in his Dafoe, 1948, 46.

Personality is largely a matter of social patterns. It is acquired and only incidentally inborn.

> WILLIAM E. BLATZ, Human security, 1966, 8.

Each of us contains multitudes, every one of whose personalities is split.

> ALDEN NOWLAN, "On names and misnomers", 1974.

Persons

The term person means an individual other than an Indian.

> CANADA, Indian Act of 1880, Sect. 12.

[A person is] a male person, including an Indian and excluding a person of Mongolian or Chinese race.

> CANADA, Franchise Act, 1885.

Their Lordships have come to the conclusion that the word persons includes members of the male and female sex, and that therefore the question propounded by the Governor must be answered in the affirmative; and that women are eligible to be summoned and become members of the Senate of Canada.

> PRIVY COUNCIL (London, Eng.), Decision, as reported in Montreal Gazette, Oct. 19, 1929.

Every time I try to define a perfectly stable person, I am appalled by the dullness of that person.

J.D. GRIFFIN, "J.D.G. interviewed", in *Let just praise be given,* 1971.

Perversion

O where is that heaven of the
    imagination,
The first and least accessible of cities,
If not in the impossible kingdom of
    perversion
Its angels have no sexes and no bodies,
Its speech, no words, its instruments,
    no uses.
None enter there but those who know
    their vices.

DARYL HINE, "The destruction of Sodom", 1960.

Pessimism

The torture goes on forever as we in
    perpetual motion
breed and destroy ourselves for any
    reason
even intelligent ones
All of which we have always known in
    despair and amusement at ourselves.

JOHN NEWLOVE, "Notes from and among the wars: 14", 1972.

Petroleum

Oil was always there. It was discovered under Social Credit and there might be a reason for that. Perhaps even Providence might have said "We are not going to place this wealth into the hands of just anybody."

REV. E.G. HANSELL, President, National Social Credit Assoc., at Calgary Bible Institute, about 1951.

The policy of the government of Canada is to refuse permits for moving natural gas by pipe line across an international boundary until such time as we are convinced that there can be no economic use, present or future, for that natural gas within Canada.

C. D. HOWE, H. of C., *Debates,* Mar. 13, 1953, 2929.

I do not believe that the money for the natural gas and oil development program that is underway could be raised if the present stable Government of British Columbia is displaced by a socialistic one, or if it is weakened by a vote which will so divide the Legislature among the various parties that none has the strength to guarantee continuity of policy at Victoria.

FRANK MCMAHON, qu. in Vancouver *Province,* Sept. 10, 1960, 1.

We just don't have the centrality, the force, the direction, or the policy-making overview that is necessary to make or give effect to a national goal. Nowhere is this more apparent than in the inability of Canada to come to grips on an overview basis with the uncontrolled but controllable monster I have chosen to call the Arctic Imperative, which is taking off like a wild rocket going in all directions concurrently. The people who are in control of the Arctic Imperative, if anyone is, are the American oil and natural gas firms to whom we have sold the commodity in the ground for a pittance, and the gigantic American natural gas and oil distribution firms which control the market.

RICHARD ROHMER, *Arctic imperative,* 1973, 217.

That "Eastern Bastard" is My Brother!

ROD SYKES, bumper sticker, to offset effect of earlier sticker, "Let the Eastern Bastards Freeze in the Dark", Nov., 1973, [by reducing the flow of oil].

Pets

Indeed, my friend you bite very hard!

> DUKE OF RICHMOND, Aug., 1819, at Richmond, Ont., to the pet fox from which he contracted hydrophobia.

Always have a pet, Child; a dog can share your dreams, aspirations peculiarly your own; no mortal can comprehend our innermost wants. A pet can save a heart a lot of breaking.

> EMILY CARR, qu. in Carol Pearson, *Emily Carr as I knew her*, 1954, 143.

Philanthropy

There are fifty or sixty people around here who can make or break a campaign. If they don't participate in it one way or another, such as even having their names on the letter-head, the campaign won't go over. When I am asked to give, I look at the names of the people who are organizing the campaign.

> ANON., Vice-pres. of large corporation, qu. by Aileen D. Ross, *Can. journ. econ. and pol. sci.*, XVIII, No. 4, Nov., 1952, 479.

Philanthropy rests squarely on the shoulders of big business. We use that as a weapon to try to force business to give. We tell them if we want the system of free enterprise to continue they *must* continue to give.

> ANON., President of large retail firm, qu. by Aileen D. Ross, *Can. journ. econ. and pol. sci.*, XVIII, No. 4, Nov., 1952, 482.

We realize that it is good public relations to help in this sort of thing, and the high executives in large corporations are all in philanthropy today for that reason.

> ANON., President of large retail firm, qu. by Aileen D. Ross in *Can. journ. econ. and pol. sci.*, XVIII, No. 4, Nov., 1952, 483.

Philanthropic foundations in Canada will come perhaps when our capitalists come to believe that a man who dies rich beyond his family's real needs, dies disgraced.

> DR. WILDER PENFIELD, in Montreal, qu. in *Liberty*, "Cross Canada", July, 1963.

Philosophers

The philosopher is likely to spend much of his time in an attempt to show that the problems of living are much harder even than the "ordinary man" had already supposed.

> F.E. SPARSHOTT, *An enquiry into goodness*, 1958, 3.

Philosophy

The philosophies of one age have become the absurdities of the next, and the foolishness of yesterday has become the wisdom of tomorrow.

> SIR WILLIAM OSLER, *Montreal med. jour.*, 1902, 684.

The modern English-speaking world finds underneath itself an embarrassing amount of Thomist foundation, and woe to it if it ever discards that for sheer expediency, for its liberties will disappear with its absolutes.

> A.R.M. LOWER, *Canadians in the making*, 1958, 59.

Literature itself is not a field of conflicting arguments but of interpenetrating visions. I suspect this is true even of philosophy, where the place of argument seems more functional. The irrefutable philosopher is not the one who cannot be refuted, but the one who is still there after he has been refuted.

> NORTHROP FRYE, letter to the English Institute, 1965.

In moving towards an account of philosophy as having to do with the limits of the knowable and hence of the sayable – an account traditional enough in itself – the argument has in effect moved towards an approximation of philosophy to poetry. This approximation must now be reckoned with and to some extent neutralized.

F.E. SPARSHOTT, *Looking for philosophy*, 1972, 133.

Philosophy in our day has become so caught up in the academic machine that its vital relation to the realities of human intercourse has been obscured.

F. E. SPARSHOTT, *Looking for philosophy*, 1972, 134.

Photography

Photography was the mechanization of the perspective painting and of the arrested eye; it broke the barriers of the nationalist, vernacular space created by printing. Printing upset the balance of oral and written speech; photography upset the balance of ear and eye.

MARSHALL MCLUHAN, *Counterblast*, 1954.

There is a brief moment when all there is in a man's mind and soul and spirit may be reflected through his eyes, his hands, his attitude. This is the moment to record. This is the elusive "moment of truth".

YOUSUF KARSH, *In search of greatness*, 1962, 95.

The trouble with photographing beautiful women is that you never get into the dark room until after they've gone!

YOUSUF KARSH, New York *Mirror*, May 2, 1963.

The camera always lies.

HUGH HOOD, title of novel, 1967.

All I know is that within every man and woman a secret is hidden, and as a photographer it is my task to reveal it if I can.

YOUSUF KARSH, *Faces of our time*, 1971, 10.

Pigs

The silent pig is the best feeder, but it remains a pig still, and hastens its death by growing too fat.

T.C. HALIBURTON, *Nature and human nature*, 1855, I, 201.

Pig had to do some routine work
To make a thousand pounds of pork;
But our stomach it doth not incline,
To eat a hog seven foot-nine.

JAMES MCINTYRE, "Lines on a hog weighing one thousand pounds", 1891, in *Poems*, 1891, 216.

Pine Trees

There were three pines above the
   comb
That, when the sun flared and went
   down,
Grew like three warriors reaving home
The plunder of a burning town.

DUNCAN CAMPBELL SCOTT, "The piper of Arll", Dec. 14, 1895.

A keen, sweet fragrance lies along the
   air,
The odour of the tall Canadian pine:
How soft the sunbeams on his needles
   shine,
And where the snow has left the
   forests bare,
He spreads his russet carpet
   everywhere.

WILLIAM T. ALLISON, "The Canadian pine", 1909.

Pioneers

I have not often in my life met contented and cheerful-minded women, but I never met with so many repining and discontented women as in Canada. I never met with *one* woman recently settled here, who considered herself happy in her new home and country.

> ANNA JAMESON, *Winter studies and summer rambles in Canada*, 1838, Vol. II, 133.

Can you imagine the position of a fretful, frivolous woman, strong neither in mind or frame, abandoned to her own resources in the wilds of Upper Canada? I do not believe you *can* imagine anything so pitiable, so ridiculous, and, to borrow the Canadian word, "so shiftless".

> ANNA JAMESON, *Winter studies and summer rambles in Canada*, 1838, Vol. II, 134.

I hear the tread of pioneers
Of nations yet to be,
The first low wash of waves where soon
Shall roll a human sea.

> JOHN G. WHITTIER, "The seer", written 1846, on receiving an eagle's feather from Lake Superior.

None but those who have experienced it can ever realise the utter weariness and isolation of Bushlife. The daily recurrence of the same laborious tasks, the want of time for mental culture, the absence of congenial intercourse with one's fellow-creatures, the many hours of unavoidable solitude, the dreary unbroken silence of the immense forest which closes round the small clearings like a belt of iron; all these things ere long press down the most buoyant spirit, and superinduce a kind of dull despair.

> MRS. H. B. KING, *Letters from Muskoka*, 1878, 158.

There is a history which, if it were only recorded or capable of being recorded, would be interesting indeed, and would furnish us with a religion of gratitude. It is the history of the pioneer in all his lines. The monument of that history is the fair land in which we live.

> GOLDWIN SMITH, *The Bystander*, Oct., 1883, 329.

Rannie began with just two cows,
Which he in winter fed on brouse,
And now he hath got mighty herds,
Numerous as flock of birds,
May he long live, our hearts to cheer,
This great and useful Pioneer.

> JAMES MCINTYRE, "The cheese pioneer; lines on Rannie, the cheese pioneer, written a quarter of a century ago", 1884.

For here in the latter-day morning,
  Where time to Eternity clings,
Midwife to a breed in the borning,
  I behold the Beginning of Things!

> ROBERT STEAD, "The homesteader", 1911.

No one who has made a study of the pioneers of Ontario can doubt for a moment the inspiration of their toil. They wanted homes.

> PETER MCARTHUR, *In pastures green*, 1915, 43.

Wind-swept and fire-swept and swept
  with bitter rain,
This was the world I came to when I
  came across the sea –
Sun-drenched and panting, a
  pregnant, waiting plain
Calling out to humankind, calling out
  to me!

> ISABEL ECCLESTONE MACKAY, "The homesteader", 1922.

The pioneer's present is always so rough that he quickly learns to live for tomorrow.

GEORGE V. FERGUSON, *John W. Dafoe*, 1948, 25.

Taking possession of a new land psychologically is a far slower process than merely occupying it physically.

R. E. WATTERS, in *Can. lit.* No. 7, 1961, 16.

Pioneers did not produce original works of art, because they were creating original human environments; they did not imagine utopias because they were shaping them.

GEORGE WOODCOCK, "An absence of utopias", in *Can. lit.* No. 42, 1969, 5.

In Roblin's Mills old Owen Roblin
Came almost fully awake in his
    lifetime once
owned 6 houses and built an octagonal
    one he
slept alone with his woman beside him
beard outside the quilts in zero
    weather
breath smelling of snoose and apple
    cider
dreaming not of houris and other
    men's wives
but his potash works and the sawmill
    hearing
only the hard tusked music of wheels
    turning

AL PURDY, "Music on a tombstone", 1970.

but they had their being once
and left a place to stand on.

AL PURDY, "In search of Owen Roblin", 1974, last lines.

Pipeline Debate, 1956

Now, the House is master of its own rules and it is my right to submit a matter to the House. I intend at the moment to submit to the House that, in my view, the House should revert to the position where it was yesterday when I was brought back to the chair to receive the chairman's report at 5:15.

RENÉ BEAUDOIN, Speaker of the House of Commons, June 1, 1956, on reversing a ruling of the previous day which was unfavourable to the Liberal government, H. of C., *Debates*, page 4540.

Mr. Speaker, this is a demonstration on the part of all Liberals in the House which shows a great disrespect for authority. I protest against this. Parliament has ceased to function.

M. J. COLDWELL, H. of C., *Debates*, June 1, 1956, 4552.

This is black Friday, boys.

THOMAS M. BELL, H. of C., *Debates*, June 1, 1956, 4553.

I've been working on the pipeline all
    the day through,
I've been working on the pipeline just
    to make the Tories blue,
Can't you hear the Tories moaning,
    getting up so early in the morn';
Hear the C.C.F.'ers groaning, for the
    pipeline's getting warm.

LIBERAL PARTY, Members of the House of Commons, song based on "I've been working on the railroad", H. of C., *Debates*, June 1, 1956, 4553.

What shall it profit Canada if we gain a pipeline, and lose this nation's soul? What shall it profit the people of Canada if we gain a thousand pipelines, and lose Parliament!

STANLEY KNOWLES, H. of C., *Debates*, June 5, 1956, 4733.

Nearly as long as the pipeline itself, and quite as full of another kind of natural gas.

> LOUIS ST. LAURENT, Winnipeg, Apr. 29, 1957, election campaign speech.

Place Names

The Greeks, with all their wood and river gods, were not so qualified to name the natural features of a country, as the ancestors of these French Canadians; and if any people had a right to substitute their own for the Indian names, it was they.

> HENRY THOREAU, "Excursion to Canada", in *Putnam's monthly mag.*, Vol. 1, Mar., 1853, 327.

Let us sing in a song together:
 Mattawa, Napanee,
Manitowaning, Ottawa,
 Nipissing, Ville Marie.

Missanabie, Manitoulin,
 (Whisper them soft and low)
Espinola, Michipicoten,
 Iroquois, Orono.

> WILSON MACDONALD, "Singing words", 1934.

Stuffy, unimaginative British loyalty triumphed — as it had with the deadly names of Prince Albert, New Westminster, Victoria, and indeed British Columbia and Alberta — in spite of the availability of indigenously beautiful Indian names or unique and traditional fur-trade names.

> DOUGLAS HILL, *The opening of the Canadian west*, 1967, 174.

If I lived in Temagami,
Temiskaming, Kenagami,
Or Lynx, or Michipicoten Sound,
I wouldn't stir the whole year round

Unless I went to spend the day
At Bawk, or Nottawasaga Bay,

Or Missanabi, Moosonee,
Or Kahshe or Chicoutimi.

> DENNIS LEE, "Kahshe or Chicoutimi", 1974.

Places

We shan't be here again. But do not grieve;
This is the place I think we shall not leave.

> ROY DANIELLS, "Col de Tende", 1963.

but in spite of diagrams
at every corner, labelled
in red: YOU ARE HERE
the labyrinth holds me

> MARGARET ATWOOD, "A night in the Royal Ontario Museum", 1968.

The feeling of place is a power within us.

> JAMES REANEY, frequent assertion, qu. by Germaine Warkentin in introd. to his *Poems*, 1972, xiii.

Why, good heavens, man! Pugwash is right there between Shinimicas and Tatamagouche!

> CYRUS EATON, qu. in *Globe and Mail*, July 13, 1972, 7, referring to locale of his international conferences.

Plains of Abraham

I swear to you that a hundred men posted there would stop their whole army.

> MARQUIS DE MONTCALM, letter to the Marquis de Vaudreuil-Cavagnal, July 29, 1759, referring to trail leading up from St. Lawrence river, qu. in F. Parkman, *Montcalm and Wolfe*, 1884, Vol. 2, 276.

Planning

My idealistic schemes and plans of life, like those of other people, are apt to be upset by the small motives – of pique, ill-temper, nervous distaste – with which my everyday decisions are often swayed.

M. ALLERDALE GRAINGER, *Woodsmen of the West*, 1908, 89.

The establishment of a planned, socialized economic order, in order to make possible the most efficient development of the national resources and the most equitable distribution of the national income.

C.C.F., *Regina manifesto*, Regina, 1933.

I know a very tiresome Man
Who keeps on saying, "Social Plan,"
    At every Dinner, every Talk,
    Where Men foregather, eat and
        walk,
No matter where, – this Awful Man
Brings out his goddam Social Plan.

STEPHEN B. LEACOCK, *Hellements of hickonomics*, 1936, 3.

Socialist panegyrics about the mystic beauties of Planning are apt to be just as silly, and sometimes dishonest, as the hymns to Free Enterprise which are intoned by their opponents.

FRANK H. UNDERHILL, *Can. forum*, Vol. 27, Aug., 1947, 110.

I firmly believe that effective economic planning is more likely to be handicapped in the future by deeply ingrained prejudices about what governments should or should not do than by our inability to determine what correct economic policy should be.

CLARENCE L. BARBER, in T.E.H. Reid, ed., *Economic planning in a democratic society?*, 1963, 73.

Plan ahead, not for years but for generations.

DALTON CAMP, in Lewis Hertzman, *Alliances and illusions*, 1969, xviii.

There's nothing the matter with planning, but what counts is flexibility.

ROBERT BALLON, *Financial post*, Aug. 22, 1970.

Plants

Yet love may tell one who grows a
    plant
How a miraculous ignorance
    surrounds
Each living thing – and it still be
Perfect and wise, and beautiful as a
    bud.

LOUIS DUDEK, "Flower bulbs", 1952.

Platforms, Political

'Our platform is our leader, and our leader is our platform' is sometimes openly avowed, and it is a maxim that is almost always accepted in practice. It follows, therefore, that the leader is the master of the platform, and tends to accept it as a general indication of the way in which the party would like him to move when and if he finds it desirable to do so.

R. MACGREGOR DAWSON, *Government of Canada*, 1954, 506.

A political platform is impossible and dishonest. The most a party should do is lay down a set of principles.

GRATTAN O'LEARY, editorial in Ottawa *Journal*, just before the Conservative leadership convention, 1956, qu. in *Maclean's*, June 7, 1958, 23.

Why didn't they do it then? Why didn't they do it when they were in power?

    JOHN DIEFENBAKER, opening election campaign speech in Winnipeg, Feb. 12, 1958, referring to the Liberal Party platform.

Once at an auction sale, my father mounted a large manure pile to speak to the assembled crowd. He apologized with ill-concealed sincerity for speaking from the Tory platform. The effect on the agrarian audience was electric.

    JOHN KENNETH GALBRAITH, *The Scotch*, 1964, 75.

Play

All day I play at Hop-Scotch
And hop and hop and hop
And when I go to bed at night
I dream I cannot stop.

    ISABEL ECCLESTONE MACKAY, "Hop-Scotch", 1918.

A boy alone out in the court
Whacks with his hockey-stick, and whacks
In the wet, and the pigeons flutter, and rise,
And settle back.

    MARGARET AVISON, "Thaw", 1960.

Plays

Every Canadian play should contain a Mountie. The scarlet uniform is so picturesque, and they make everything so Canadian.

    ANON., remark made at session on drama, Annual Meeting, Canadian Authors Assoc., Vancouver, July, 1947, qu. by Lister Sinclair, *Here and now*, June, 1949, 16.

Pleasure

When pleasure is the business of life it ceases to be pleasure.

    T. C. HALIBURTON, *Sam Slick's wise saws*, 1853, I, 205.

This life ain't all beer and skittles.

    T. C. HALIBURTON, *Nature and human nature*, 1855, I, 60.

Oh! in youth I sail'd unusual seas,
And still I recall me lands like these,
Where they do whatever they please,
    dear Lord,
Whatever and ever they please.

    TOM MACINNES, "In amber lands", 1910.

When winter pulls the blind
A bliss as keen —
On native stone of sin
Cold men whet their pleasure
Cussed by the black north wind.

    ANNE WILKINSON, "South, north", 1955.

Gentle and just pleasure
It is, being human, to have won from
    space
This unchill, habitable interior
Which mirrors quietly the light
Of the snow, and the new year.

    MARGARET AVISON, "New Year's poem", 1960.

Such arctic pleasure she enjoys,
So low a temperature of sense,
As only music without noise
Or portrait without line presents.
Such pureness of experience
Which form from matter sets apart
A purpose to her anguish grants.
With privilege the broken heart
Is crowned by the intelligence of art.

    DARYL HINE, "Proserpina", 1960.

I have the Canadian's remorseless conscience, unalloyed by the experience of raw pleasure.

    HUGH HOOD, in *Tamarack rev.*, No. 44, 1967, 73.

The puritan gets his pleasure by denying it to himself and to others.

> IRVING LAYTON, "Aphs", *The whole bloody bird*, 1969, 99.

Pledges

Pledge of the Twenty.

> ANON., a pledge to keep in touch at least once a year made by twenty men encamped high on the Great Divide near Kicking Horse Pass during the search for a route through the Rockies and the Selkirks for the C.P.R., 1881. (See P. Berton, *Last spike*, 1971, 157.)

Plowing

A shining plow makes a full mow.

> ANON., saying of pioneer Ontario farmers.

Put him to the PLOUGH, the most natural, the most happy, the most innocent and the most healthy employment in the world.

> T. C. HALIBURTON, *Sam Slick*, 1836, ch. XXVI.

Kind heaven speed the Plough!
And bless the hands that guide it;
God gives the seed –
The bread we need,
Man's labour must provide it.

> CHARLES SANGSTER, "The happy harvesters", 1860.

Poems

I would rather have written that poem, gentlemen, than take Quebec tomorrow.

> MAJOR-GENERAL JAMES WOLFE, 1759, the night before he was killed on the Plains of Abraham, referring to Gray's "Elegy written in a country church-yard", and its famous line "The paths of glory lead but to the grave"; see Hume, *History of England*, ch. 30.

Now this one – it has some feeling, some sensitivity, some sense of structure. But – well, damn it all, it isn't worth *money*.

> E. J. PRATT, remark to Northrop Frye about 1933, quoted in *Can. lit.*, No. 21, 1964, 7.

A poem is not the conflagration complete, it is the first kindling.

> A. M. KLEIN, *The second scroll*, 1951, 105.

Anyone who reads a good poem with understanding – a poem that bites into the evil, or that retrieves a truth – creates an order in himself.

> LOUIS DUDEK, *Cerberus*, 1952, 13.

A poem is a watch designed
To tick forever in the mind.

> FRED COGSWELL, "Descent from Eden", 1959.

There is no such thing as an isolated image; poetry being sensation, image is omnipresent in a poem.

> FRANK DAVEY, *Tish*, Sept., 1961, 6.

A poem to me is a poem only when it transcends its specific origin, when it leaps out of its time-context, stands up on its own two feet and says: "I am; I was; I will be".

> GWENDOLYN MACEWEN, *Teangadoir*, V, 1961, 60.

My best poems
Don't get written,
Because I'm still scared

> ALDEN NOWLAN, "Explanation", 1962.

To have written even one poem that speaks with rhythmic authority about matters that are enduringly important is something to be immensely, reverently thankful for – and I am intoxicated enough to think I have written more than one.

> IRVING LAYTON, *Collected poems*, 1965, xxii.

To be truthful, I did not write them even for them, but out of compulsion to talk to another man within me, an intermittent madman who finds unpredictable emblems of the Whole in the trivia of my experience, and haunts me with them until I have found a spell of words and rhythms to exorcise them and, for the moment, appease them.

EARLE BIRNEY, *Selected poems*, 1966, xi.

A poem is a poet
who writes poems
for everyone
who is listening

Are you listening?

RED LANE, "What is a poem is a poem is a poem", 1968.

Poems are not "truth" and poets are blessedly not on a *legal* witness stand testifying about themselves. Their witness stand is living – literary, their testament is poems which are truth by being lies or lies by being truth, neither of which is an absolute.

AL PURDY, book rev., in *Can. forum*, March, 1968, 284.

Give the same poem to a model American, a model English and a model Canadian critic: the American will say "This is how it works"; the Englishman "How good, how true to Life" (or, "How boring, tasteless and trite"); the Canadian will say "This is where it fits into the entire universe".

MARGARET ATWOOD, *Can. lit.* No. 49, 1971, 63.

To write you no more poems.
No more, I tell myself, no more.
But still the words come out
as once, as ever, as now.

DAVID HELWIG, "Resolution", 1971.

The poems don't love us anymore
they don't want to love us
they don't want to be poems
Do not summon us, they say
We can't help you any longer

LEONARD COHEN, in *The energy of slaves*, 1972, 117.

When I read your book of poems
I could not fall asleep
When finally I fell asleep
I did not want to wake up.

IRVING LAYTON, "On reading Cohen's *The energy of slaves*", 1973.

Poetry

There is probably no country in the world, making equal pretensions to intelligence and progress, where the claims of native literature are so little felt, and where every effort in poetry has been met with so much coldness and indifference, as in Canada.

EDWARD H. DEWART, *Selections from Canadian poets*, 1864, x.

Poetry in our rude Canada is a field which bears ordinarily more flowers than fruit.

WILLIAM KIRBY, letter to Benjamin Sulte, July 25, 1865, qu. by Lorne Pierce in *William Kirby: the portrait of a Tory loyalist*, 1929, 241.

Poetry in Canada is at a discount. Epic, dramatic, lyric, spasmodic, it is a drug, a very assafetida pill, in the literary market. The publishers keep it at arm's length; the public turns up its nose at it. It has no exchange value at all.

JOHN READE, *Can. illus. news*, Jan. 20, 1872, 42.

Nothing will sustain you more potently than the power to recognize in your humdrum routine, as perhaps it may be thought, the true Poetry of life — the poetry of the commonplace, of the ordinary man, of the plain, toil-worn woman, with their loves and joys, their sorrows and their griefs.

WILLIAM OSLER, "The student life", address, 1905, in *Aequanimitas*.

Canadian poetry is such definitively, not because its authors or its material (subject, theme) or even its form, color and music, are Canadian. It is such only by virtue of some distinctive "note" in it. That note is not Imperialism, as some allege; it is not Individual Nationhood, as others submit; it is not even Confederate Unity, as others say. It is this and this alone, — *an inexpungable Faith in ourselves*.

J. D. LOGAN, *Songs of the makers of Canada*, 1911, 28.

And so if you will examine the best Canadian poetry, whether it be hymns, nature songs, or war lyrics, you will find an undertone of a consciousness of self-controlled destiny, which passes from Cheerful Faith (before Confederation) to Triumphant Exultation (since Confederation).

J. D. LOGAN, *Songs of the makers of Canada*, 1911, 29.

Great deeds are greater than great sonnets, and Canada's call to her sons is a stirring one of action; for the poetry of action exists just as does the poetry of words and the great deed that is accomplished is more glorious than the great sonnet.

SIR ARTHUR C. DOYLE, Canadian Club, Montreal, June 4, 1914.

Sensibility is no longer enough, intelligence is also required. Even in Canada.

A. J. M. SMITH, "Wanted: Canadian criticism", in *Can. forum*, April, 1928, 601, re: poetry criticism.

The bulk of poems written in Canada may be briefly classified under four heads. They are Victorian, Neo-Victorian, Quasi-Victorian, and Pseudo-Victorian. We find the Indians of Canadian poetry represented as one of Nature's Noblemen; the French Canadian virtues are metamorphosed by English hands into qualities characteristically Wordsworthian. Our poets carol (regrettably) in Victorian English.

S. I. HAYAKAWA, on Canadian poetry, qu. in *Can. mercury*, Apr., 1929, 100.

Humanity is the most precious thing about us and the essence of humanity is in poetry.

ALAN CREIGHTON, "Conquest by poetry", in *Can. poetry mag.*, Apr., 1942, 7.

In what Canadian poets have tried to do there is an interest for Canadian readers much deeper than what the achievement in itself justifies.

NORTHROP FRYE, *Can. forum*, Dec., 1943, 207.

A piece of writing is not poetry just because it rhymes. Nor is it poetry just because it doesn't rhyme. Nor again does a thing become poetical because it makes no sense as prose, and is quite intelligible to ordinary common sense. Nor will any amount of disturbance of the ordinary rules of grammar, the freedom called "poetic license", in and of itself make poetry, any more than a liquor license can make liquor.

STEPHEN B. LEACOCK, *How to write*, 1944, 153.

Unschooled, but unspoiled, this simple country girl has captured in her net of poesy the flatness of that great province.

> PAUL HIEBERT, *Sarah Binks*, 1947, xi, referring to Saskatchewan.

A poem is not a destination, it is a point of departure. The destination is determined by the reader. The poet's function is but to point direction.

> A. M. KLEIN, *The second scroll*, 1951, 105.

Poetry as we have presented it is transfigured prose, and it is not the addition of some entirely new ingredient that brings about the transfiguration; rather poetry is a new mixture, a rearrangement of the ingredients shared in common with unpoetic speech.

> REID MACCALLUM, *Imitation and design and other essays*, 1953, 70.

[The] two central themes in Canadian poetry: one a primarily comic theme of satire and exuberance, the other a primarily tragic theme of loneliness and terror.

> NORTHROP FRYE, "Preface to an uncollected anthology", 1956; repr. in his *Bush garden*, 1971, 166.

It is not a nation but an environment that makes an impact on poets, and poetry can deal only with the imaginative aspect of that environment.

> NORTHROP FRYE, Roy. Soc. Can., *Studia varia*, 1957, 21.

All poetry nowadays, anyhow, is someone's effort to save his soul.

> LOUIS DUDEK, editorial, *Delta*, Oct. 1957.

The Canadianism of Canadian poetry is of course not a merit in it, but only a quality in it; it may be revealed as clearly in false notes as in true ones, and may be a source of bad taste as well as of inspiration.

> NORTHROP FRYE, in Malcolm Ross, ed., *The arts in Canada*, 1958, 84-85.

We have often been told of our necessary dullness because we had no Revolutionary War, no French Revolution, no War Between the States. In poetry likewise we had no Renaissance, no Neo-Classicism, no Romanticism. But one of the advantages of a poetry less than a hundred years old is that all the things that couldn't happen when they should have happened keep happening all the time.

> MILTON WILSON, address, Assoc. of Canadian Univ. Teachers of English, Edmonton, June, 1958.

Canada is today the poetry centre of the world. We no longer need look abroad for inspiration. It is right here where we have a ringside seat at the collapse of American superiority. We have the advantage of the CBC, which gives us a national audience, and of critics, who watch and encourage a poet's growth.

> IRVING LAYTON, *The Montrealer*, Aug., 1959, 8.

The critic to whom falls the enviable task of studying Canadian poetry in the sixties will, I trust, be dealing with a fully-matured culture, no longer preoccupied with the empty unpoetics of Canadianism, but with the genuine tasks of creative power.

> NORTHROP FRYE, "Letters in Canada, 1959", repr. in his *Bush garden*, 1971, 127.

Wherefore no person lives
Until he is alive:
No poetry's in the head;
As none is written until read.

> RALPH GUSTAFSON, "The disquisition",
> 1960.

The poem's linguistic function can be called communication, but its musical function is evocation. And this musical-evocative characteristic is most important, because it is *the* distinguishing feature of poetry.

> LIONEL KEARNS, letter in *Tish*, No. 11,
> July, 1962.

Poetry is a voice art. A poem does not exist on the page any more than a song exists on a piece of sheet music. The poem and the song exist in TIME as sound.

> LIONEL KEARNS, "Stacked verse", Preface, dated Aug., 1962.

I have long been impressed in Canadian poetry by a tone of deep terror in regard to nature . . . It is not a terror of the dangers or discomforts or even the mysteries of nature, but a terror of the soul at something that these things manifest.

> NORTHROP FRYE, in C. F. Klinck, ed.,
> *Literary history of Canada*, 1965, 830.

In 1868 it was more important that the verse be written by a Canadian than that it be poetry.

> NORMAN SHRIVE, *Charles Mair, literary nationalist*, 1965, 42.

Whatever else a poem is, it is a word-thing, a thing made out of language. For poetry there is no definable quality: but poetry is a state into which language may fall and into which a person may (by grace) come.

> GEORGE WHALLEY, in John Glassco, ed.,
> *English poetry in Quebec*, 1965, 74.

You have a thought
And you're struck dumb;
put words into that
and it's a poem.

> RENALD SHOOFLER, "Nature abhors a vacuum", 1966.

The oustanding achievement of Canadian poetry is in the evocation of stark terror. Not a coward's terror, of course; but a controlled vision of the causes of cowardice. The immediate source of this is obviously the frightening loneliness of a huge and thinly-settled country.

> NORTHROP FRYE, in L. Dudek and M.
> Gnarowski, eds., *The making of modern poetry in Canada*, 1967, 93.

oh, admit this, man, there is no point
in poetry
if you withhold the truth
once you've come by it

> ALDEN NOWLAN, "And he wept aloud, so that the Egyptians heard it", 1967.

But even though we speak, and think,
in prose
We ought to try to feel and live in
verse,
Else life is not a blessing but a curse.

> DARYL HINE, "Letter from British Columbia", 1970.

I believe that poetry
Is the sound
Of the wound .
With its red mouth
Speaking to itself.

> JAMES REANEY, "A table of contents",
> unpublished, qu. by Germaine Warkentin in introd. to his *Poems*, 1972, x.

It is an art of concentration. Complacency, urbanity, sentimentality, whimsicality — all those qualities that make a pleasant folksy radio talk, a good-humored popular magazine article, or an effective advertisement — these are foreign to the hard, sharp, concentrated intensity of poetry. Poetry is language and feeling purified of the superficial.

A. J. M. SMITH, *Towards a view of Canadian letters*, 1973, 189.

Poets

The truth is, I am addicted both to the Muses, and New-found Land.

SIR WILLIAM VAUGHAN, *The Newlanders cure*, 1630, "The epistle dedicatory".

The poets of 1861.

ANON., a reference to poets born in or near that year: C. G. D. Roberts, Bliss Carman, Archibald Lampman, Duncan Campbell Scott, and Wilfred Campbell.

I do not know whether a Baron or a Poet Laureate gets any wages in England. In Canada there is no pay.

JAMES GAY, letter to Lord Tennyson, 1883, in *Poems*.

Dear Sir: Now Longfellow is gone there are only two of us left. There ought to be no rivalry between us two.

JAMES GAY, Poet Laureate of Canada and Master of All Poets, Letter to Lord Tennyson, 1883, in *Poems*.

We have scarcely time to tell thee
Of that strange and gifted Shelley,
Kind hearted man, but ill-fated,
So youthful drowned and cremated.

JAMES MCINTYRE, "Shelley", 1884.

A gift more perilous than the painter's:
  he
In his divine moments only sees
The inhumanities of color, we
  Feel each and all the inhumanities.

GEORGE F. CAMERON, 1885, foreword to "Lyrics in pleasant places".

You've piped at home, where none
    could pay,
  Till now, I trust your wits are riper,
Make no delay, but come this way,
  And pipe for them that pay the
    piper!

CHARLES G. D. ROBERTS, "The poet bidden to Manhattan Island", 1887.

The Birchbark School.

E. B. OSBORN, London critic, resident in Canada, 1895-1900, referring to Charles G. D. Roberts and Bliss Carman, qu. by J. D. Logan in *Can. mag.*, Vol. 40, Feb. 1913, 343.

The vision of the better and the higher things come to the people not so often through the preacher as through the poet.

SIR WM. OSLER, Canadian Club, Toronto, Dec. 29, 1904.

He was a half-cut schoolmaster and a quarter-cut poet.

ROBERTSON DAVIES, quoting his great-grandmother on J. R. (Andrew John) Ramsay, versifier who died 1907.

The Great Lakes School of Poets.

J. D. LOGAN, *Can. mag.*, Vol. 40, Feb., 1913, 343, referring to Archibald Lampman, Wilfred Campbell and Duncan Campbell Scott.

The Maple Leaf School.

ANON., a term sometimes applied to writers of patriotic verse. See *Dalhousie rev.*, Vol. 52, Winter, 1972/73, 555, where typical Canadian symbols are extolled.

The only poet in Canada was very nice to me in Ottawa. Canada's a bloody place for a sensitive real poet like this to live all his life in.

> RUPERT BROOKE, letter to Wilfred Gibson, from Toronto, 1913, on D. C. Scott.

The first time I ever felt the necessity of inevitableness of verse, was in the desire to reproduce the peculiar quality of feeling which is induced by the flat spaces and wide horizons of the virgin prairie of western Canada.

> T. E. HULME, "A lecture on modern poetry", about 1914, qu. in Michael Roberts, *T. E. Hulme*, 1938, 266.

We require more rage in our poets.

> D. C. SCOTT, "Poetry and progress", 1922.

Rosie wrote some little rhymes
For the *Birdseye Centre Times:*
Gushing friends did then exclaim:
"This will surely bring you fame!
You must join the C.A.A."

> ANON., "God Bless the C.A.A.!", (Canadian Authors Association), 1929.

First Statement Group.

> ANON., a group of young writers and artists in Montreal during the 1940's who produced the first six or seven issues of an eight-paged mimeographed sheet which they named *First Statement*.

Go, find your house and insert the key
and put down the night-lock.
Undress with the blinds down and
touch the pillows, and dream
Of Pickthall walking hand in hand
with her fairies
And Lampman turning his back on
Ottawa.

> RAYMOND SOUSTER, "To the Canadian poets", 1944.

His lines run wherever his pen goes,
Mine grope the miles from heart to
head;
His will tire before he does;
Mine will move when I am dead.

> ROBERT FINCH, "Poet on poet", 1946.

"But, but . . . ", you say, "But,
but . . . " But me no buts.
The one thing that our poets need is
guts.

> L. A. MACKAY, "And spoil the child", 1948.

The poet's daily chore
Is my long duty;
To keep and cherish my good lens
For love and war
And wasps about the lilies
And mutiny within.

> ANNE WILKINSON, "Lens", 1955.

And me happiest when I compose
poems.
Love, power, the huzza of battle
are something, are much;
yet a poem includes them like a pool
water and reflection.

> IRVING LAYTON, "The birth of tragedy", 1956.

Clear away all evil influence
That can hurt me from the States.
Keep me pure among the beaver
With un-Freudian loves and hates,

Where my Conrads are not Aiken
Where John Bishop's Peales don't
sound,
Where the Ransoms are not crowing
And the Ezras do not pound.

> F. R. SCOTT, "The call of the wild", 1957.

I said the moon looks like a lost gull,
Just as the shrapnel pierced my skull;
And as I stumbled I thought how blood
Equally can rhyme and mix with mud.

> IRVING LAYTON, "Epitaphs: Poet killed in action", 1959.

No dead Canadian poet has had any influence at all.

> MILTON WILSON, "Recent Canadian verse", 1959, in Eli Mandel, ed., *Contexts of Canadian criticism*, 1971, 205.

. . . the Canadian poet has one advantage – an advantage that derives from his position of separateness and semi-isolation. He can draw upon French, British, and American sources in language and literary convention; at the same time he enjoys a measure of detachment that enables him to select and adapt what is relevant and useful. This gives to contemporary Canadian poetry in either language a distinctive quality – its eclectic detachment.

> A. J. M. SMITH, ed., *The Oxford book of Canadian verse*, 1960, li.

The poet roams, the professor ruminates. The one experiences; the other expatiates. The one is a peasant, a vulgarian; the other must permit his training and associations to turn him into a gentleman.

> IRVING LAYTON, *The swinging flesh*, Foreword, 1961, xi.

I had three choices: madness, death or
> verse,
each of which asks more questions
> than it settles.

> ALDEN NOWLAN, "Three choices", 1962.

     I run ragged to elude
The Great Iambic Pentameter
who is the Hound of Heaven in our
> stress
because I want to die
writing Haiku
or, better,
long lines, clean and syllabic as
> knotted
>   bamboo. Yes!

> PHYLLIS WEBB, "Poetics against the angel of death", 1962.

With only a few exceptions – the modern poet has been an empty windbag and a chatterer.

> IRVING LAYTON, Foreword to *Balls for a one-armed juggler*, 1963, xix.

You certainly wouldn't turn to contemporary poets for guidance in the twentieth century world.

> NORTHROP FRYE, *The educated imagination*, (CBC Massey Lectures, 1963), 1964, 25.

I watch their faces for the gleam
which tells me that the end begins
that ecstasy in which they burn my lies
and tear from me the poems which I
> cannot write.

> ELI MANDEL, "Orpheus in the underworld", 1964.

O it's not hard to see why these poets
give us little poetry
nourished, sustained by the dried-up
> drugs
of the university.

> RAYMOND SOUSTER, "La belle dame", 1964.

I often wish I had the ability
To recollect my emotions
In tranquility,
But since I don't
And since I understand it's the
> necessary proem
To writing a poem,
I won't.

> COLIN NORMAN, "Manifesto", [1965?].

The poet dies with every poem he writes, with every volume he publishes. That is, if he is *alive*, to put the matter paradoxically.

> IRVING LAYTON, *Collected poems*, 1965, xix.

Personally, I want to be a creative man, not a bee nor a rat nor a grizzly nor a mouse. Which means that I strive, in this herding age, to remain a cayuse, an unbroken horse, who will have to be dragged, or ridden and broken to arrive at the roundup or the horse butcher's.

> EARLE BIRNEY, *The creative writer*, 1966, 69.

Let gentility cry out on me
because I write verses neither
Wordsworth nor Keats might have
   conceived
yet in god's name let's have done with
   lies.

> IRVING LAYTON, *The shattered plinths*, 1968, 14.

I write poems like spiders spin webs, and perhaps for much the same reason: to support my existence.

> ALFRED PURDY, interview, in *Can. lit.*, Summer, 1969, 66.

It's the style for poets to be inspired liars, insane prophets and tormented human beings.

> MIRIAM WADDINGTON, in *Can. lit.* No. 41, 1969, 75.

A Canadian poet is a man who gets snowed on.

> ELIZABETH RODRIGUEZ, *Fiddlehead*, No. 84, Mar., 1970, 125.

It isn't just the euphoric dreams of lovers I want to evoke, it's the ridiculosity inherent in the whole comic disease. And the mordant happiness of despair as well. Pain and its red blot in the brain, sorrow that things end, fade into little rags of memory that haunt us in their absence.

> AL PURDY, *Love in a burning building*, 1970, Preface.

Poets have become unamiable, untamable, innumerable, unnameable.

> LOUIS DUDEK, "Continuation I", in *Collected poems*, 1971, 327.

Our poets must give themselves to a
   kind of unsensible madness;
they must hear music not meaning as
   they write.

> ELDON GRIER, "An ecstasy", 1971.

I scratch the frosted pane
with nails of love and faith
and the crystalled white opens
a tiny eye
reveals
the wide, the shining country.

> F. R. SCOTT, "Signal", 1973.

Why did you flee from me?
John Robert Colombo
With elastic smiles
You encouraged me
with nasty phrases
you discourage me.
I'll see you later
you say fleeing
as if I had the plague.

> IWASUK, "Misunderstanding", 1974.

Poker (Game)

Poker is not a game but an education.

> SIR WILLIAM VAN HORNE, qu., W. Vaughan, *Van Horne*, 1920.

I hold only two pairs of deuces.

> CHARLES J. DOHERTY (d. 1931), in his first poker game.

Police

This whole lousy world *is* a police state.

> HERBERT STEINHOUSE, *Ten years after*, 1958, 146.

>   Is tyrant of cities
rescuer knight errant blue bully you.

> ALFRED PURDY, "Policeman", 1965.

Policy

There developed a danger of assuming that a plausible, lucidly expounded policy must necessarily be the wisest one.

ROBERT A, SPENCER, *Canada in world affairs: From UN to NATO, 1946-1949*, 1959, 406.

Politeness

Canadians, say our American friends, are too polite to argue. Let us be honest. We are not too polite; no one can be too polite. But we may be too lazy or too timid.

VINCENT MASSEY, *Speaking of Canada*, 1959, 40.

Stalemate. Politeness is the only way out. What would we do without these well-thumbed phrases to extricate us?

MARGARET LAURENCE, *The stone angel*, 1964 (1968, 121).

Political Parties

It was not until the Governor committed an indiscretion with the wife of the Chief Justice that political divisions emerged. The electoral system thereupon transformed what was essentially a personal feud into a political feud and imposed this political division right across the Island.

JOHN GARNER, *The franchise and politics in British North America, 1755-1867*, 1969, 42, referring to Governor Walter Patterson and Chief Justice Peter Stewart, election, 1784, P.E.I.

Party is merely a struggle for power.

ANON., attributed incorrectly to Sir John A. Macdonald. At London, Ont., 1860, he said, "There were, unfortunately, no great principles on which parties were divided . . . politics became a mere struggle for office".

We must support our supporters.

JOHN SANDFIELD MACDONALD, Premier of Ontario, 1867-71.

[But in this country] what is there for Conservatives to conserve or for Reformers to reform?

GOLDWIN SMITH, in *Can. monthly*, Apr., 1872, 321.

To divide all the world into two parties by the constitution of their minds is preposterous; you must have parties without number, as many parties in fact, as there are minds. It is the bisection of a rainbow, the demarcation of a wave.

GOLDWIN SMITH, *Can. monthly*, Vol. 3, No. 2, Feb., 1873, 140.

Now, the country has pronounced its condemnation of the Pacific Scandal. If anyone indulged a belief in the existence of hard-and-fast party lines held more sacred than the interests or the honour of the country, he is now undeceived. The country, when there is any adequate occasion for the exertion of its power, is always found an overmatch for party.

CANADIAN MONTHLY AND NATIONAL REVIEW, Mar., 1874, 233; "Current events".

When a matter of great importance is brought home to the minds of the people the withes of party become as tow. This is our encouragement and the source of our hope.

W. A. FOSTER, speech before Canadian National Association, Feb., 1875.

The idolatry of the heathen is not greater than the idolatry of party politics today.

GEORGE M. GRANT, 1884; qu., Can. Hist. Assoc., *Report*, 1942, 6.

It would be simply suicidal to French Canadians to form a party by themselves. Why, so soon as French Canadians, who are in a minority in this House and in the country, were to organise as a political party, they would compel the majority to organise as a political party, and the result must be disastrous to themselves. We have only one way of organising parties. This country must be governed, and can be governed, simply on questions of policy and administration and the French Canadians who have had any part in this movement have never had any other intention but to organise upon those party distinctions and upon no other.

SIR WILFRID LAURIER, H. of C., *Debates*, Mar. 16, 1886, 175.

The ins and outs cannot be segregated under the old names of Reformer and Conservative. Tory and Grit are merely synonomous with cat and dog and convey no notion save that of difference in momentum.

W. A. FOSTER, *Canada first; memorial*, 1890, 55.

You cannot influence a Political Party to do Right, if you stick to it when it does Wrong.

J. W. BENGOUGH, *The prohibition Aesop*, about 1896, 19.

Parties are not made to order. They are born out of great issues. They degenerate into factions.

JOHN WILLISON, speech, Canadian Club, Toronto, Feb. 15, 1904.

The Liberals and Conservatives differ very little really in their opinions upon crucial questions, and their views as to administration are almost identical . . . They have come to regard each other without alarm: they know each other too well and resemble each other too closely.

ANDRÉ SIEGFRIED, *Race question*, 1907, 143.

[Politicians] exert themselves to prevent the formation of homogeneous parties divided according to creed or race or class. The purity of political life suffers from this, but perhaps the very existence of the Federation is the price. The existing parties are thus entirely harmless.

ANDRÉ SIEGFRIED, *Race question*, 1907, 143.

The first duty of a public man is to consider the welfare of the people he represents. If he is a party man his next duty will be to work faithfully in the interests of his party, and in so doing he will be working both in the interests of his party and of the country. But he must never forget that the permanent strength of any party must rest on the firm basis that its policy and administration is superior to that of any other party offering its services.

JOHN OLIVER, Premier of B. C., 1918-27, in J. Morton, *Honest John Oliver*, 1933, 155.

The member for Winnipeg North Centre is the leader of the party and I am the party.

WILLIAM IRVINE, 1920's, qu. by Frank H. Underhill, at dinner to inaugurate Ontario Woodsworth Memorial Foundation, Toronto, Oct. 7, 1944. Ref. is to J. S. Woodsworth.

In Canada ideas are not needed to make parties, for these can live by heredity and, like the Guelfs and Ghibellines of mediaeval Italy, by memories of past combats.

JAMES BRYCE (Viscount), *Canada, an actual democracy*, 1921, 19.

Parties are not, as their philosophers claim, servants of the state cooperating in its service; their real desire is the mastery of the state and the brooking of no opposition or rivalship.

JOHN W. DAFOE, *Laurier*, 1922, 50.

Another stand would be more popular in the West but a great party cannot shuffle and a leader worthy of the name never shuffles.

ARTHUR MEIGHEN, letter to G. H. Hart, Sept. 25, 1924 (Pub. Arch. Can.), commenting on criticism of his rigid tariff policy in the Canadian West.

The day is passing when political parties can get into office and run the country merely because they are political parties.

BROOKE CLAXTON, in *Can. hist. rev.*, 1934, 68.

In Canada more than anywhere else it is possible to define a party as being a body of supporters following a given leader. Parliamentary elections are primarily occasions on which the electors choose between party leaders and prospective prime ministers.

HUGH M. CLOKIE, *Canadian government and politics*, 1944, 91.

The political party is apparently no longer able to provide necessary compromise without the sacrifice of principles. The absence of consistency in the attitude of any English Canadian party or public leader points to the fundamental corruption of Canadian political life.

H. A. INNIS, *Political economy in the modern state*, 1946, xii.

Great, nation-wide, easygoing, omnibus vehicles whose occupants often have difficulty in recognizing their fellow passengers or in understanding why the driver of the vehicle let them in.

GEORGE V. FERGUSON, American Academy of Political and Social Science, *Annals*, CCLIII, 1947, 32.

While it may be advantageous for a Dominion Government to have its own party in power in the provinces, it may well be that a Provincial Government is more secure if it is politically opposed to the party in power in Ottawa.

R. MACGREGOR DAWSON, *Government of Canada*, 1947, 580.

Our Liberal Party
    (after 22 years)
        is our conservative party.
Our Conservative Party
    is a Progressive
        Conservative Party,
Social Credit
    holds no brief
        for social credit,
and the C.C.F.
    is but a leftover
        from "the old Left".

LOUIS DUDEK, "A political breakdown", 1956.

Canadian political parties have no policies at all; they cultivate the art of electioneering.

LOUIS DUDEK, *Delta*, No. 3, Apr., 1958, 1, editorial.

There are less sons of bitches in the Liberal party than in the Tory.

JOHN W. DAFOE, on why he was a Liberal, qu. in R. L. McDougall, ed., *Our living tradition*, 4th ser., 1962, 97.

A leftist party believes that ordinary people should have more power in the society. To the degree that it is liberal it stresses equality of opportunity. To the degree that it is socialist it stresses equality of condition.

> GAD HOROWITZ, in J. McLeod & T. Lloyd, eds., *Agenda 1970: proposals for a creative politics*, 1968, 248.

The Tories and Socreds are as alike as strychnine and arsenic.

> DAVID LEWIS, N.D.P. Leader, re Alberta Premier Peter Lougheed's "Philosphically we're not that far apart"; qu. in *Time*, Sept. 13, 1971, 11.

Rent-a-politician.

> ANON., facetious phrase applied to candidacy of Claude Wagner, federal election, October, 1972.

Political Phrases

Action Canada.

> PAUL HELLYER, movement launched to support his charge that the Liberal government failed to respond to the needs of the people, Press conference, May 25, 1971.

The average Canadian.

> JOHN G. DIEFENBAKER, phrase used frequently during his term as Prime Minister, 1957-1963.

Baldwin Reformers.

> Dissatisfied Reformers who joined with Sir Allan MacNab, 1854; Baldwin, in retirement, gave approval to the combination which came to represent Liberal-Conservatism under Sir John A. Macdonald; also, "Baldwin Liberals".

Ballots Before Bullets.

> Phrase originating in the policy advocated by Arthur Meighen in his speech in Hamilton, Nov. 16, 1925.

The Baneful Domination letter. (See: ENGLAND – letter by Joseph Hume, 1834.)

The Battle of the Maps.

> ANON., The negotiations which led to the fixing of the boundary between Canada and Maine by the Webster-Ashburton Treaty of Aug. 9 1842, during which both parties concealed maps favourable to the other.

Better Red than dead. (See: COMMUNISM, D. Fleming, 1962.)

Better Terms.

> The readjustment of financial relations between the Dominion and Nova Scotia, sanctioned by order-in-council, Jan. 25, 1869, and which led Joseph Howe, who had been demanding better terms, to enter Sir John A. Macdonald's cabinet five days later.

Big Blue Machine.

> Name given to Ontario Conservatives' organization, Provincial election, Oct. 21, 1971.

The Big Push letter.

> See: ELECTION FUNDS – letter by George Brown to John Simpson, 1872.

The Big Seven.

> Phrase sometimes applied to the leaders of Confederation: Macdonald, Galt, Brown, Cartier, McGee, Tupper, and Tilley.

The Blank Cheque. (See: LABOUR UNIONS, E. Forsey, 1957.)

The Blockers' Brigade.

> E. Macdonald, Frank B. Carvell, and A. K. MacLean, followers of Laurier, noted for their ability to prolong debate in the House of Commons.

Blue ruin speeches.

LIBERAL PARTY, reference to speeches made by R. B. Bennett on Canada's economic state under the Liberals; H. of C., *Debates*, 1930, Vol. 1, 36, Vol. 2, 1022.

The Brawling Brood of Bribers.

C. F. FRASER, Commissioner of public works, Ontario, in debate on a bribery case, Mar. 17, 1884. Originally "This prowling brood of bribers, hatched under the eaves of the *Mail* building", a stenographic error resulted in the alliterative phrase.

The Bread and Butter Assembly.

Popular name for Upper Canada Assembly session of 1836-37.

The British Party.

Term used in Lower Canada before 1837; the small but powerful minority among the English-speaking people who exploited English and French alike; *cf.* Durham's, *Report*, 1839.

The Brownites.

Also, "The Brownies"; followers of George Brown in Ontario especially those who opposed Macdonald in the first general election, 1867.

The Bureaucrats.

The English-speaking minority in Lower Canada who held monopoly of administration, before 1841; also called the "Château Clique".

The Cabinet of All the Talents.

The members of Laurier's government formed July 13, 1896, including Fielding, Mowat, Mulock, Sifton, Cartwright, Blair, and others; also, "The Ministry of All the Talents", from the phrase used to describe Pitt's cabinet of 1806.

The Cabinet of Antiques.

NICHOLAS FLOOD DAVIN, M.P. for West Assiniboia, on the Bowell Administration, 1894-96.

The Campaign of Picnics.

The election of 1878, won by the Conservatives, returning Sir John Macdonald to power, after the Pacific Scandal.

Canada First.

The motto, based on a suggestion by J. D. Edgar, of the Toronto nationalist group called after this phrase, sometimes known as The Twelve Apostles; the movement was active, 1868-75; also the title of a pamphlet by a leader, W. A. Foster, pub. in 1871, which served as a guide; used as a slogan by Conservatives, general election, 1930.

Canada for the Canadians.

Used by opponents of Sir John Macdonald's government in 1872, when advocating that the charter for a transcontinental railway be refused Sir Hugh Allen's Canada Pacific company which was claimed to be dominated by Americans. Sir John A. Macdonald used the phrase as an election slogan, 1878. An editorial section in *Canadian magazine* in early 1900's was entitled: "Canada for Canadians. A dept. for business men". Associated with the Canadian Manufacturers' Association, about 1910. Used as election slogan by Arthur Meighen in 1920's; by R. B. Bennett in 1930's.

The Canada question.

Term referring to the grievances of the Canadian colonists which led to the rebellions of Upper and Lower Canada in 1837 and the appointment of Lord Durham to deal with the problem.

Carnarvon Terms of Separation.

British Columbia's union with Canada was dependent on construction of the Canadian Pacific Railway, the completion of which was delayed after 1873; Lord Carnarvon, colonial secretary, in 1874, arranged an adjustment of the terms, including completion by Dec. 31, 1890.

The Castor Party.

Phrase originated in 1885 to designate the Ultramontane element in Quebec.

The Champion of Provincial Rights.

A reference to Sir Oliver Mowat, Liberal Premier of Ontario, 1872-96.

Charter-sellers.

LIBERAL PARTY, term for those who continued to support Sir John A. Macdonald, after the Pacific Scandal, 1873.

The Château Clique.

The English-speaking minority in Lower Canada who held monopoly of administration, before 1841; also called "The Bureaucrats".

The Chicago water steal. (See: WATER)

Clear Grits. (See: CLEAR GRITS)

The Clergy Reserves.

The land set apart by the Constitutional Act of 1791 "for the support and maintenance of a Protestant Clergy" in Upper Canada; in Lower Canada reserves were established in 1796. In Upper Canada the Clergy Reserves were first considered an obstruction to settlement, later, a grievance on religious grounds.

Code of ethics.

A document setting out Lester B. Pearson's Code of Ethics drafted by Tom Kent and Gordon B. Robertson, released November 30, 1964, relating to the conduct of Cabinet ministers.

Commercial Union.

L. S. HUNTINGTON, H. of C., *Debates*, Mar. 21, 1870, in a speech advocating a customs union with the United States. The scheme was first proposed by Ira Gould in a speech to the Montreal Board of Trade (Montreal *Gazette*, Feb. 18, 1852). The term "unrestricted reciprocity" was later adopted as less repugnant to Canadians.

A Contradictory Meeting.

A traditional Quebec oratorical contest between political rivals. Trans. of "une assemblée contradictoire".

Co-operative federalism.

MAURICE LAMONTAGNE, Secretary of State, 1964-65, term invented by him to describe a strictly bilingual and bicultural federal policy.

Corporations and politicians holding hands in your pocket.

DAVID LEWIS, during election campaign, Oct., 1972.

The Country above Party.

CANADA FIRST GROUP, the watchword of the group, 1868-75.

Cross Benchers.

Term used in 1920 to describe dissident Liberals, including T. A. Crerar and Michael Clark, who moved to seats between the right and left of the Speaker in the semi-circular theatre in Victoria Museum where the House of Commons convened after the Parliament Building fire, 1916; the Independent Party.

The Dark Lantern Brigade.

Conservative press term for the Liberal government members of H. of C. Public accounts committee, 1908, investigating sales of timber limits in the North West.

The Devil's Dozen. (See, "The Noble Thirteen".)

Dief's cowboys.

LIBERAL PARTY, phrase used to describe Prairie political supporters of John G. Diefenbaker, during his term of government.

The Double C. B.

In 1867, when Sir John A. Macdonald received the K.C.B., Sir Alexander Galt declined the lesser honour of Commander of the Bath, out of pique; the same year Galt, who had an interest in the Commercial Bank (Ontario), quarrelled with Macdonald over its winding-up, and resigned from the cabinet.

Double Majority.

Political support of English from Upper Canada and French from Lower Canada in Legislature which sustained administrations in power during 1850's, until 1858, when it was condemned. *Cf.*, letter, Réné Caron to William Draper, Sept. 17, 1845, qu., W. Weir, *Sixty years in Canada*, 1903, 23.

The Double Shuffle.

On August 6, 1858, the Macdonald-Cartier government changed the portfolios of all ministers to avoid by-elections ("the shuffle"), and the next day each returned to his original department ("the double shuffle").

Duff'll do what Dief did.

CONSERVATIVE PARTY, Manitoba, slogan 1960's; ref. to Duff Roblin and John Diefenbaker.

The Family Compact.

MARSHALL S. BIDWELL, letter to William W. Baldwin, 1828: "I shall be happy to consult with yourself and Mr. Rolph on the measures to be adopted to relieve this province from the evils which a family compact have brought upon it."

The Family-Company-Compact.

AMOR DE COSMOS, in Victoria, B. C., *British colonist*, 1859, Vol. 1, No. 10; a reference to the policies of the Governor, Sir James Douglas.

The Farmers' Platform.

Demands on tariff reform presented by delegates from the West and Ontario to the Laurier government, Dec., 1910, during "Siege of Ottawa".

The Fathers of Confederation. (See: CONFEDERATION, FATHERS OF)

The Fathers of Responsible Government.

Term applied to *Robert Baldwin* and *Louis Lafontaine*, about 1851.

Fifty-four forty or fight! (See: ANNEXATION — W. Allen, 1844.)

Fight Ottawa.

GEORGE WALKEM, platform on which he was elected Premier in B. C., in 1878.

The five-cent speech. (See: SUBSIDIES, FEDERAL, W. L. M. King, 1930.)

The Fourteenth Colony.

American Revolutionary term for Canada.

French Canadians First!

PARTI ROUGE, plank, withdrawn in 1850.

French domination.

LIBERAL PARTY, slogan under leadership of George Brown prior to Confederation.

The Gagging Bill.

A nickname for "An Act to prevent certain meetings within this Province", passed by the Legislative Assembly, Upper Canada, 1817 (58 Geo. III, ch. 11); Robert Gourlay in the Niagara *Spectator*, Dec. 3, 1817 wrote some doggerel verses titled, "Gagg'd — Gagg'd, by Jingo", in protest.

Gentlemen, I am within the lines of Torres Vedras. I will get out of them when it suits me, and not before.

> SIR WILFRID LAURIER, speech in Morrisburg, Oct. 8, 1895, on Manitoba schools remedial legislation. Laurier told the story of Wellington's campaign in Portugal where he spent a safe summer within the lines of Torres Vedras, watching the enemy, to the frustration of Marshall Massena, commander of the French, who could not assail Wellington 'within the lines'.

The Ginger Group.

> The six, later ten, members of the Progressive Party in the House of Commons who seceded in June, 1924. The phrase was earlier used to denote a group of Conservative members, including W. F. Nickle, during the term of Union Government, 1917-21.

The Great Coalition.

> On June 30, 1864, Sir John A. Macdonald formed a ministry which included Reform Liberals George Brown, Oliver Mowat, and William McDougall.

The Great Ministry.

> The second Lafontaine-Baldwin government, Mar., 1848-Oct., 1851; a popular term; also called, "The Ministry of all the Talents", and, "The Great Administration".

Grosart tactics.

> The public relations approach adopted by Allister Grosart to enhance the appeal of John Diefenbaker to the voter, 1957-58.

Growing to beat 70.

> Slogan of the Manitoba CONSERVATIVE PARTY government, late 1960's.

The Halifax Award.

> In 1877 Canada received $4,420,882 from U.S. as compensation for value of her inshore fisheries.

Hands off Manitoba — No coercion.

> The motto of the EQUAL RIGHTS LEAGUE; on the Manitoba School question; in an address issued by the League, of which D'Alton McCarthy was president, in 1896; used by Liberals in general election of that year.

Has the N. P. made *you* rich?

> WILLIAM PATTERSON, Liberal campaigner, a favorite phrase during 1896 election, ref. to National Policy.

Hepburn's Hussars.

> Popular name for police body organized by Premier Mitchell Hepburn at the time of the Ontario Automobile Workers' strike, Oshawa, Ont., Apr., 1937.

Hiving the Grits.

> SIR JOHN A. MACDONALD, phrase, Apr., 1882, when there was a redistribution of Ontario seats and an alteration of boundaries to the disadvantage of the Liberals.

Hunting in couples.

> A reference to the political campaigning of Sir John A. Macdonald, and John Sandfield Macdonald, first Premier of Ontario, in 1867.

The Just Society.

> PIERRE E. TRUDEAU, phrase used in Mount Royal, federal election campaign, 1965; in speech to Young Liberals, Ottawa, Apr. 5, 1968, and frequently thereafter; it was orig. used by Goldwin Smith in his address to the Mechanics' Institute in 1872; also used by the NDP (C.C.F.) in 1956 Declaration: the promise of a Just Society.

The Khaki Election.

> A popular name for the election of 1917.

The land for the people!

> CONSERVATIVE PARTY, rallying cry, 1904, referring to western lands described by Sifton as suitable only for grazing.

The land for the settler, the price for the public.

EDWARD BLAKE, address to electors of West Durham, May 23, 1882; Liberal party slogan in general election of that year; a reference to railway land-grant policy.

The landswap scandal.

Quebec phrase for an affair which forced the resignation of Gédéon Ouimet, Premier, in 1874.

The last one out, turn out the light.

ANON., usually associated with anti-NDP government in Saskatchewan in the 1960's, presumably directed at those departing the province.

The Liberals give to foreigners and Duplessis gives to his province.

J. P. DESCHATELETS, H. of C., *Debates*, May 23, 1958, 425: "I well remember a slogan which was used against us, perhaps the most pernicious and demagogic ever contrived".

Liberals in a hurry.

A popular phrase for the twelve Liberal-Progressives and Progressives who, under the leadership of Robert Forke, joined the Liberals in H. of C., 1926; also applied by Hon. L. St. Laurent to C. C. F. in 1953.

Maritime Rights.

First mentioned in Editorial, HALIFAX HERALD, July 27, 1922; phrase given publicity by H. J. Congdon, of Dartmouth, N. S., in a series of newspaper articles, late 1924; used in political campaign, 1925, in demands for economic readjustments considered necessary to balance losses since Confederation.

Masters in our own home. (Maîtres chez nous.)

RENÉ LÉVESQUE, campaign slogan for the Quebec Liberal Party for the election of Nov. 14, 1962.

Men in sheep-skin coats. (See: IMMIGRANTS — C. Sifton, 1922.)

The Ministry of All the Talents.

Also, "The Great Ministry", applied to the second Baldwin ministry, 1848-51. (See also, "Cabinet of all the Talents".)

Mr. Speaker, there ain't nothing to it!

JOHN HENRY POPE, Minister of Railways, about 1885; attributed to him by Peter Mitchell (*Debates*, 1888, II, 1689). Some authorities say this was Pope's curt answer to charges made by Edward Blake.

The National Policy.

SIR CHARLES TUPPER, phrase originated in House of Commons, 1870, to describe a policy of economic nationalism and protection. Adopted by Macdonald in the election of 1878. Introduced in the budget speech of Mar. 14, 1879, by Tilley. (See also: NATIONAL POLICY,) 1878.

A Nest of Traitors. (See, "The Seven Bolters".)

A New Deal.

Popular term, from U.S., given to policies proposed by R. B. Bennett in a series of broadcasts, Jan., 1935.

The New National Policy.

Term used for the platform of the National Progressive Party, at Winnipeg convention, Jan. 6, 1920. (See also: NATIONAL POLICY, 1878.)

The New Nationality. (See: NATIONALITY.)

The New Society.

PIERRE E. TRUDEAU, TV interview, Dec. 28, 1975, in ref. to inadequacy of the free-market economy, and a need for some sort of new society.

The Nigger-King hypothesis.

ANDRÉ LAURENDEAU, from an editorial in *Le Devoir*, July 4, 1958, ref. to English newspapers in Quebec and their uncritical attitude towards Maurice Duplessis. (See: NEWSPAPERS, 1958)

The Night of the Long Rubber Knives.

A reference to the night of Feb. 6, 1963. Conservative caucus meeting (actually held in the morning) following the fall of the Diefenbaker government in Parliament at which a rebellion of some cabinet ministers was overcome.

The Nine Martyrs.

The Liberals who supported the Coalition in Ontario's first government, 1867, among them McGill, Lauder, Cockburn, Boyd, and Beatty.

No Pay to Rebels!

Tory denunciation of the Rebellion Losses Bill, 1849.

No Yankee Dictation!

A cry raised, 1872, by opponents of American control of the Canadian Pacific Railway Company.

The Noble Thirteen.

The Conservatives who voted against Macdonald on the Jesuit Estates Act, 1889; so-called by their Ontario supporters; nicknamed the "Devil's Dozen" by Macdonald.

Not party, but the people.

GOLDWIN SMITH, slogan adopted for his publication, *The Bystander*, Feb., 1880.

Nuclear arms, no. Bread and butter, yes.

RÉAL CAOUETTE, at meeting in Montreal, Feb. 24, 1963.

The Old Guard.

The 45 Conservative followers of Macdonald in the House of Commons, 1874 to 1878, after the "Pacific Scandal".

On to Ottawa!

Slogan of the B. C. relief-camp strikers on their march to Ottawa, ended at Regina, July 1, 1935; organized by Communists.

The Pacific Scandal.

On Apr. 2, 1873, Lucius S. Huntington charged in the House of Commons that Sir Hugh Allan and associates of the Canadian Pacific Railway had advanced money to Sir John A. Macdonald and his supporters to aid them in elections; these charges were proved correct and the result led to the election of the Liberals to power. (See also: PACIFIC SCANDAL.)

Le Parti rouge.

The party organized in Lower Canada under the auspices of Louis-Joseph Papineau about 1850; other leading members were A. A. Dorion, J. B. E. Dorion, L. H. Holton, and C. J. Laberge.

Participatory Democracy.

ANON., phrase associated with Trudeau platform, general election, 1968.

The Patent Combination.

Originated by Hincks to describe J. Sandfield Macdonald's alliance with the Tories in his, Ontario's first, provincial government, 1867; also used by Macdonald to describe his cabinet.

The Patriots.

From the French "patriotes", the name assumed by Papineau's followers in Lower Canada who were associated in the rebellion of 1837.

Peasants in sheep-skin coats.

Conservative Party speakers, phrase used in election, Nov. 1900, to describe the immigrants preferred by Clifford Sifton, the responsible Minister. (See: IMMIGRANTS − C. Sifton, 1922.)

Prairie radicals.

Phrase applied to Prime Minister John Diefenbaker and Alvin Hamilton, 1960's.

"Progress" is our watchword, "Principle" our motto.

J. J. MORRISON, Secretary of the United Farmers of Ontario to V. A. Clarke, Nov. 18, 1919.

Put me among the yeas.

SIR FRANCIS HINCKS, in House of Assembly, Sept. 5, 1854, on changing his vote for Speaker in favour of an opponent from Lower Canada, Louis V. Sicotte.

Ready, aye ready! (See: CANADIAN-BRITISH RELATIONS, Arthur Meighen, 1922.)

The Rebellion Losses Bill.

The popular name for the Act of Indemnification, 1849, which provided for a commission to inquire into losses incurred during the rebellion of 1837.

Reciprocity of trade, or reciprocity of tariffs.

CONSERVATIVE PARTY, 1876-78, especially during election of 1878.

The Red Parlour.

LIBERAL PARTY, phrase, 1878, used in denunciation of consultation between the government and the manufacturers in determining amount of protection for various industries as part of the "National Policy".

Regina Manifesto.

CO-OPERATIVE COMMONWEALTH FEDERATION, Programme adopted at first National Convention, Regina, July, 1933.

Rep. by Pop.

An abbreviation of Representation by Population, a Tory Party plank, about 1849 to 1853, later supported by the Clear Grits and the Brown Reformers, in Upper Canada. (See also: PARLIAMENTARY REPRESENTATION.)

Responsible Government.

A phrase first used by the Upper Canada Reformers in 1829, meaning complete departmental responsibility of the Executive. (See also: GOVERNMENT, RESPONSIBLE.)

Responsible Government and the Voluntary Principle.

THE EXAMINER, motto established by Francis Hincks, Toronto, July 3, 1838; also of the Baldwin Reform party.

Revolt of the Eighteen.

Repudiation of Reciprocity in election of 1911, by group of Toronto Liberals, organized by Clifford Sifton and Zebulon Lash.

The Ross Bible.

Readings, omitting parts of the Old Testament, adopted by Sir George W. Ross for Ontario schools; term used in provincial election of 1886.

Rule or ruin.

Phrase used by the Reformers in criticising Sir Francis Hincks when he joined with Sir John A. Macdonald in the first coalition government, 1854, known as the McNab-Morin government.

The Sandfield Macdonald surplus.

The surplus of three million dollars gathered from the small revenues of the province of Ontario during the four years of government under John Sandfield Macdonald, 1867-71.

The Sanhedrin.

HARRY SIFTON, name applied to Winnipeg Liberals dominant in Liberal federal and provincial political circles, 1920's: A.B. Hudson, T.A. Crerar, Frank Fowler, E.J. Tarr, H.J. Symington, J.B. Coyne, J.R. Murray.

The Scandal Session.

House of Commons Session, 1891-2. Conservatives, especially Sir Hector Langevin, were charged with political corruption; in Quebec, similar charges were brought against the Liberals, especially Honoré Mercier.

The Seven Bolters.

The ministers, George E. Foster, Sir Charles H. Tupper, A.R. Dickey, W.H. Montague, J.G. Haggart, W.B. Ives, J.F. Wood, who resigned Jan. 4, 1896 from the cabinet of Sir Mackenzie Bowell, who called them "A Nest of Traitors".

The Shadow Government.

Also called "The Shadow Cabinet"; the ministry of seven members without portfolio who were unable to sit in the House until re-elected after accepting office under the Crown; formed by Arthur Meighen at noon, June 29, it lasted to the morning of July 2, 1926.

The Short Administration.

The Brown-Dorion administration, Aug. 2 to 6, 1858.

The Siege of Ottawa.

Representations made to the Laurier government against the tariff by 811 farmers from the West and Ontario, December, 1910.

Siftonism.

CONSERVATIVE PARTY, Opposition, phrase of 1906, on the extending of the discretionary powers of departmental officials.

The Sixty Days of Decision.

HON. LESTER B. PEARSON, Mar. 25, 1963, Liberal meeting in Hamilton, said "more constructive things will be done in the first sixty days of a new Liberal Government than in any similar period of Canadian history". In Vancouver a week later he said "The first 60 days of a new Liberal administration will be 60 days of decision". The Sixty Days ended June 20, 1963.

The Smuggling Inquiry.

Popular name for the investigation of the Customs and Excise Department by a special committee of the House of Commons beginning Feb.8, 1926.

The Solid Eighteen.

The Liberals who won all seats in Nova Scotia in the election of 1904.

A solid Quebec will vote to rule all Canada. Only a solid Ontario can defeat them.

CITIZENS UNION COMMITTEE, 1917 federal election poster.

The Supergroup.

Term applied to close Cabinet associates of Prime Minister Pierre E. Trudeau, 1968-69.

Truth squad.

LIBERAL PARTY, group of three people including Judy LaMarsh (former M.P. for Niagara Falls) assigned to follow John Diefenbaker to correct statements Liberals considered to be inaccurate; operated Mar. 10 to 16, general election campaign, 1963.

Thicken population!

HERBERT GREENFIELD, Premier of Alberta, slogan originated in 1925.

The thin red line.

CONSERVATIVE PARTY, term, Manitoba, Feb., 1905, when court investigations revealed that R.E.A. Leach, Liberal party organizer, crossed off names of Conservatives from voters' lists with red ink.

This is the vision, Canadians! (See: VISION, John Diefenbaker, 1958.)

Throw the rascals in.

JOHN G. DIEFENBAKER, suggested election slogan for the Liberal Party, late 1964.

The Twelve Apostles. (See, "Canada First".)

The two Johns.

Ref. to Sir John A. Macdonald and Sir John S.D. Thompson, 1880's.

The Uncertain Giant.

MERVYN JONES, British journalist, in Toronto *Star*, Dec. 10, 1965, ref. to Canada.

The Unholy Alliance.

SIR WILFRID LAURIER, term used in speech, St. John, N.B., Aug. 28, 1911, in Reciprocity election, to describe link between Borden and the Quebec Nationalists.

The United Farmers of Alberta, Our Motto Equity.

UNITED FARMERS, the official title, after joining with the Canadian Society of Equity, 1909.

Unrestricted Reciprocity.

Free trade with the U.S., advocated by the Liberals, especially Cartwright, in 1887, and a chief plank in their platform of 1891. (See also, "Commercial union"; RECIPROCITY.)

Political Support

You hear nothin' but politics, politics, politics, one everlastin' give, give, give.

T.C. HALIBURTON, *Sam Slick*, 1836, ch. XXXI.

You may rest assured . . . those who support me, I will support.

SIR CHARLES METCALFE, to Sir Alexander Galt; qu. in letter, Galt to G.R. Robinson, Dec. 7, 1843.

What the hell has Strathroy ever done for me?

JOHN SANDFIELD MACDONALD, Premier of Ontario, to deputation from town of Strathroy asking that it be made a separate county seat, 1868.

Anybody may support me when I am right. What I want is a man that will support me when I am wrong.

SIR JOHN A. MACDONALD, to Senator Dickey, of Nova Scotia, at Confederation, qu., Biggar, *Anecdotal life*, 1891, 117; also applied to Toronto *Mail* when it became independent. L.J. Burpee, *Oxford encyclopedia of Canadian history*, 1926, 248, states Macdonald said it to George M. Grant, of Nova Scotia, later Principal of Queen's University.

If you can't boost, don't knock.

RICHARD MCBRIDE, Conservative Party, speech in Toronto, 1905.

Politicians

As for his Religion, he could mix,
And blend it well with politics,
For 'twas his favourite opinion
In mobs was seated all dominion:
All pow'r and might he understood
Rose from the sov'reign multitude:
That right and wrong, that good and ill,
Were nothing but the rabble's will.

REV. JACOB BAILEY (supported author), "The factious demagogue", Halifax, May 13, 1780.

I have no great faith in him as a politician: he is too honest a man!

WILLIAM DUNLOP, *Recollections of the war of 1812*, 1847, chap. IV; (1908 ed., 89) ref. to Marquis of Tweeddale, brigade Commander at Queenston, Ont.

Send me better men to work with and I will be a better man.

SIR JOHN A. MACDONALD, to a farmer-elector, qu. by Cartwright, *Reminiscences*, 1912, 46; inscription on his statue in Kingston, unveiled Oct. 23, 1895.

There are two classes of politicians: those who sit still, and make all the money; and those who go about the country, and make all the speeches.

> J.J. PROCTER, *The philosopher in the clearing*, 1897, 17.

Why is it that when people have no capacity for private usefulness they should be so anxious to serve the public?

> SARA JEANETTE DUNCAN, *The imperialist*, 1904, 303.

A politician must have a sense of humour.

> MITCHELL HEPBURN, speech, Saints and Sinners Club, New York, Sept., 1941.

George, you know the trouble with you is you don't read any poetry.

> GRATTAN O'LEARY, qu. in *Maclean's*, June 7, 1958, 66, referring to Conservative leader George Drew, early 1950's.

Surely scholars are more worthy than politicians. A scholar meets every problem with an open mind, a politician with an open mouth.

> LOUIS BLAKE DUFF, Oct., 1952, at Univ. of Western Ontario, London.

The ambitions and actions of politicians, if one does not stand too near to them, are powerfully romantic.

> ROBERTSON DAVIES, *A jig for the gypsy*, 1954, vi.

Generally speaking people think all politicians are crooked. But if they were, they wouldn't go into politics. They could make more money as crooks.

> JUDY LAMARSH, speech at Chipman, N.B., election campaign, Oct. 20, 1965.

Are you a politician, or a woman?

> GERALD WARING, to Judy LaMarsh, 1960, qu. in her, *Memoirs of a bird in a gilded cage*, 1968, 303.

Politics

Now with us the country is divided into two parties, of the mammoth breed, the *ins* and the *outs*, the administration and the opposition.

> T.C. HALIBURTON, *Sam Slick*, 1836, ch. XVIII.

Politics is the science which teaches people to care for each other.

> WILLIAM LYON MACKENZIE, *Selected writings 1824-37*, 1960, 171.

Our objects are open and avowed. We seek no concealment, for we have nothing to conceal.

> ROBERT BALDWIN, speech, Mar. 25, 1844, to Reform Association, Toronto.

Here lies the man who denounced party government, that he might form one; and professing justice to all parties, gave every office to his own.

> JOSEPH HOWE, N.S. Assembly, Feb. 24, 1845, a suggested epitaph for James W. Johnston, Premier.

Political life is ruin to men in these Countries & the best will not remain in it a day longer than they can help. Land-jobbers, swindlers, young men who wish to make a name when starting into life, may find in public life here or in the States a compensation for the sacrifices it entails, but with honest men who are doing well in their own line of business, & who have not private fortunes to fall back upon, it is otherwise.

> LORD ELGIN, letter to Earl Grey, Aug. 24, 1848 (private).

If we don't make a disturbance about this, we shall never get in.

> SIR ALLAN MACNAB, remark to John Wilson, on the demonstrations made during the trial of leaders of the rioters who burned down the legislative building, Apr., 1849, in Montreal.

I may say generally, that, if elected, my desire is to perform my duty in Parliament in the spirit and with the views which become a Christian politician.

> SIR OLIVER MOWAT, letter, *To the free and independent electors of South Ontario, Dec. 15, 1857;* the phrase "Christian politician" was frequently used by Mowat's opponents.

Politics is a game requiring great coolness and an utter abnegation of prejudice and personal feeling.

> SIR JOHN A. MACDONALD, letter to Sidney Smith, Oct. 13, 1860. (Pub. Arch. Can.)

If public life is the noblest of all callings, it is the vilest of all trades.

> GOLDWIN SMITH, *Lectures on modern history,* 1861, 19; also: "Politics, the noblest of all callings, but the meanest of all trades", in *Essays on questions of the day,* 1893, 100.

Politically we were a pack of fools, but we were honest in our folly, and no man need blush at forty for the follies of one-and-twenty, unless indeed, he still perseveres in them.

> THOMAS D'ARCY MCGEE, speech in Wexford, Ireland, May, 1865, on the Young Ireland movement.

We are all mere petty provincial politicians at present; perhaps by and by some of us will rise to the level of national statesmen.

> SIR JOHN A. MACDONALD, statement to the Governor-General at time of Confederation.

Poetry was the maiden I loved, but politics was the harridan I married.

> JOSEPH HOWE, in his later years.

The question would be decided at once and forever if decided in a sense of leniency, but not if decided in a harsh sense, in a sense of mistaken justice; for there is no more certain fact, as proved by the most unerring testimony of historical events, than that political offences must sooner or later be forgiven.

> SIR WILFRID LAURIER, H. of C., *Debates,* Feb.12, 1875, 117; Riel debate.

Our religious opinions should be held entirely separate from our political leanings. No greater calamity can befall a community than when the cleavage of political parties is coincident with the cleavage of religious bodies.

> EDWARD BLAKE, H. of C., *Debates,* Mar. 17, 1884, 908.

For us, sons of France, political sentiment is a passion; while, for the Englishmen, politics are a question of business.

> SIR WILFRID LAURIER, speech in Montreal, May 19, 1884. (Trans.).

Great is the mugwump and his mission is to teach the divine right of bolting. May his shadow never grow less.

> JOHN W. DAFOE, Ottawa *Journal,* Jan. 27, 1886, editorial; qu. in R. Cook, *Politics of John W. Dafoe,* 1963, 9.

[The politics of British Columbia are] government appropriations.

> ANON., to Goldwin Smith, qu. in his *Canada and Canadian question,* 1891, 220.

Politics is the one blessed thing on this changing scene in which there is always money: it has various aspects, and appears under various forms; patriotism, public spirit, enterprise, etc., etc., but you can always tell it by that characteristic. If there is no money in it, it's not politics.

> J.J. PROCTER, *The philosopher in the clearing*, 1897, 16.

Ah! Politics, politics, always politics.

> GOLDWIN SMITH, qu. by H. Charlesworth, *Candid chronicles*, 1925, 120.

Politics, even more than misery, makes strange bed-fellows.

> FRANCIS W. GREY, *The curé of St. Philippe*, 1899, ch. 2.

I believe that with a strong following the Ross government will carry out their policy of developing New Ontario. I am chiefly interested in that; for my own constituency must get a big share of the benefit and, in this respect, Manitoulin is my politics.

> ROBERT R. GAMEY, Ontario Legis. member for Manitoulin Island, interview in Toronto *Globe*, Jan. 30, 1903.

Our politics, our public life and thought, rise not to the level of our opportunity. The mud-bespattered politicians of the trade, the party men and party managers, give us in place of patriotic statecraft the sordid traffic of a tolerated jobbery. For bread, a stone. Harsh is the cackle of the little turkey-cocks of Ottawa, fighting the while as they feather their mean nest of sticks and mud, high on their river bluff.

> STEPHEN B. LEACOCK, Empire Club speech, Mar.19, 1907.

Contracting!

> ANON., the laconic answer of a financier, who had contributed to both Liberal and Conservative parties in the election of 1911, on being asked what his politics really were; qu. by Peter McArthur in *The Forum*, Nov., 1911, 539.

Politics has not ceased to make strange bedfellows or, at least, the politicians of both parties continue to share the same bunk. You know the kind of bunk we mean.

> ROBERT C. (BOB) EDWARDS, in 1921, qu. in J.W.G. MacEwan, *Poking into politics*, 1966, 91.

The art of politics, which is the art of free human beings living together, is therefore the most interesting of all arts. It can only seem dull and dry to us if we don't see what it is and how it concerns us.

> HOWARD A. KENNEDY, *The book of the West*, 1925, 153.

If we can find the things which the men of French Canadian descent have in common with the settlers of the plains and base our policy on this common ground, we need have no fear as to what the result will be at the extremities or near the heart, as I assume Ontario would like to consider itself.

> W.L. MACKENZIE KING, letter to I.A. Mackay, Nov. 23, 1925.

Our fight in the West was more *against* Meighen and his policies than *for* King.

> JOHN W. DAFOE, letter to Sir Clifford Sifton, Sept. 27, 1926, referring to federal election, Sept., 1926.

I am not one of those who believe in divorcing federal and provincial politics in their entirety. It cannot be done. One cannot be a political chameleon.

> GORDON S. HARRINGTON, N.S. Minister of Mines, provincial election, Sept., 1928.

Politics is working patriotism.

> CHARLES J. DOHERTY, statesman, d. 1931, qu. in C.G.D. Roberts ed. *Canadian who was who*, I, 154.

The political system, as it exists in all British countries, arose from rivalries which were fought out on battlefields before they were transferred to the civil arena; and in its ethics and its philosophies it reveals its origin. Politics in its more primitive and vigorous manifestations is not a game nor a sport, but a form of civil war, with only lethal weapons barred.

> J.W. DAFOE, in *Clifford Sifton*, 1931, 172.

Politics is not a game. It is a battle. There is the difference between us. You English, you *play* politics. But, we French we *fight* politics.

> ADRIEN ARCAND, in 1935, qu. in *Maclean's*, Apr. 15,1938, 66.

More than any country in the world, Canada is the result of political, not economic forces.

> JOHN W. DAFOE, *Canada: an American nation*, 1935, 119.

No man should ever become a candidate who is not either independently rich or independently poor.

> ANON., qu. by R.J. Manion, *Life is an adventure*, 1936, 226.

In politics one has to do as one at sea with a sailing ship; not try to go straight ahead, but reach one's course having regard to prevailing winds.

> W.L. MACKENZIE KING, *Diary*, Jan. 22, 1938.

From the point of view of democracy the highest value, *the ultimate for politics*, is the liberation of and respect for individual personality.

> J.A. CORRY, *Democratic government and politics*, 1951, 26.

Politics is war.

> W.A.C. BENNETT, aphorism frequently said while Premier of B.C., 1952-1972.

Politics are a jealous mistress. If you aren't careful they .will take more of your time than you bargained for.

> RALPH CAMPNEY, qu. in Ottawa *Journal*, Sept. 30, 1958, 17.

Well now, sir, I look at this from the barber chair at Lindsay.

> LESLIE FROST, Premier of Ontario, 1958-1961, qu. in J. Manthorpe, *The power and the tories*, 1974, 41.

We have our own dread of the world coming to an end, though the nearest thing we have yet produced to compare with a Last Judgment is a series of Summit Meetings.

> ROBERTSON DAVIES, *A voice from the attic*, 1960, 350.

Politics is an art. I have heard it called the adaptation and administration of the unintended. Sometimes it is the art of adjusting to the inevitable with the minimum of disturbance – economic, social or electoral. Nearly always it is the art of using effectively and skilfully, blunt instruments, including especially public opinion.

> LESTER B. PEARSON, address, Study Conference on National Problems, Kingston, Sept. 6, 1960.

It is the most important of all secular callings; yet it is one in which many men and women of integrity and ability scorn to participate actively. It is considered as a rather unworthy pursuit; like running a confidence game or managing a prize fighter in New York.

> LESTER B. PEARSON, address, Study Conference on National Problems, Kingston, Sept. 6, 1960.

A moral view of socialism is contrary to a belief held by certain politicians and political theorists in Canada: that the art of politics is just the balancing and refereeing of the interests of various pressure groups. This is the Mackenzie King theory of politics.

> GEORGE P. GRANT, in M. Oliver, ed., *Social purpose for Canada*, 1961, 17.

The main distinction between the conservative and the progressive mind is that, in seeking the solution to the foregoing problem, the progressive will tend to overestimate the people's desire for justice, freedom, and change, whereas the conservative will tend to err on the side of order, authority, and continuity. The true tactical position of the *democratic* socialist is on the left, *but no further*.

> PIERRE E. TRUDEAU, in Michael Oliver, ed., *Social purpose for Canada*, 1961, 374.

Grosart's a thorn to Diefenbaker; he's a continuing reminder that the man's divinity is limited.

> JOSEPH SMALLWOOD, qu. by P. Newman, *Renegade in power*, 1963, 160, re: Allister Grosart, National Director, Progressive Conservative Party.

I find Canadian politics actually more interesting, more fruitful, and more creative than the politics of almost any country I have studied, because it is so wonderfully varied, because it is plural.

> RICHARD CROSSMAN, M.P., Coventry East, England, in G. Hawkins, ed., *Order and good government*, 1964, 142 (Proc., 33rd Couchiching Conf., July, 1964).

The political game is a great one to play. It is exciting even to watch; it brings with it disappointments and frustrations, but there are compensations in the acquaintances it brings, in the friendships formed, and in the knowledge acquired of humanity, sometimes at its worst, more often at its best.

> CHARLES G. (CHUBBY) POWER, *A party politician*, 1966, 404.

I have no politics, I am a Canadian.

> GEORGE MCCULLAGH, Publisher of the *Globe and Mail*, qu. in *Can. hist. rev.*, 1966, 203.

We got into politics in the first place because we felt that if Quebeckers concerned themselves only with Quebec, and not with Ottawa, then Canada would fall apart by default.

> GÉRARD PELLETIER, qu. in Martin Sullivan, *Mandate '68*, 1968, 285, referring to Jean Marchand and Pierre E. Trudeau.

The circumstances that allowed Jack Pickersgill to flourish were part of a cynical old-style approach to politics in Canada. But even in that context he was one of a kind.

> PETER NEWMAN, *Distemper of our times*, 1968, 240.

You must draw limits in your political commitment otherwise you become uncivilized.

> LESTER B. PEARSON, qu. in P. Newman, *Distemper of our times*, 1968, 82.

If you have too highly developed a sense of the ridiculous you can't get through daily political life in Ottawa without laughing, and that's not allowed.

> WALTER GORDON, qu. in P. Newman, *Distemper of our times*, 1968, 215.

Tell me where the centre is and I'll tell you where I stand.

> ROBERT H. WINTERS, qu. in P. Newman, *Distemper of our times*, 1968, 440.

What strikes me as significant about the Canadian experience, then, is the cultivation of an attitude that constitutes a repudiation of one of the main dogmas of Western culture. The dogma, namely, that politics is the chief goal of men.

> LIONEL RUBINOFF, in Andy Wainwright, ed., *Notes for a native land*, 1969, 47.

The English officials of Lower Canada had a duty to introduce an alien people to the best traditions of representative government; instead they showed the French Canadian people that the franchise was merchandise to be bought and sold, that controverted election laws were to be circumvented, that electoral honesty meant political failure and electoral dishonesty success, public office, and power.

> JOHN GARNER, *The franchise and politics in British North America, 1788-1867*, 1969, 198.

Politics is largely made up of irrelevancies.

> DALTON CAMP, *Gentlemen, players and politicians*, 1970, 284.

A high proportion of the Canadians who have the most to be discontented about do not feel that they are capable of having any influence over political allocations. To some extent, they may be right. Their lack of efficacy combined with a lack of resources leads them to abstain from participating in politics and their abstention makes their low level of efficacy a self-fulfilling prophecy.

> RICK VAN LOON, *Can. jour. of pol. science*, Vol. 3, 1970, 394.

In British Columbia politics is a recreation, on the Prairies it's a protest, in Ontario a business, in Quebec a religion and in the Maritimes a disease.

> ANON., attributed to Paul St. Pierre; also a favourite saying of Angus McInnes.

Politics is best suited for two kinds of people, young, unmarried, intelligent men in their twenties, or men near retirement but still active. In between, it's no good.

> PAUL ST. PIERRE, former M.P. for Coast-Chilcotin, about 1971, qu. in G. Aiken, *Backbencher*, 1974, 92.

If there's one thing I've learned from W.A.C. Bennett, it's how to kill. The time to hit a politician is when he's down.

> DAVE BARRETT, Premier of B.C., in *Maclean's*, June, 1973, 72.

Pollution

Settling here and there in its course down the streams, it forms a compact mass of pollution all along the bottoms and margins of the rivers and inlets, filling up the crevices on the gravel beds, and among stones, where aquatic life is invariably produced and fed. It becomes a fixed, imperishable foreign matter, and adheres to the beds of streams and other waters, and forms a long, continuous mantle of death.

> CANADA. DEPT. OF FISHERIES, *Annual report*, 1889, Part II, 14, referring to sawdust.

Lord, Lord, pollution everywhere
But I breathe still.

> ELI MANDEL, "Woodbine", 1967.

I am also what surrounds you:
my brain
scattered with your
tin cans, bones, empty shells,
the litter of your invasions.

I am the space you desecrate
as you pass through.

MARGARET ATWOOD, "Backdrop addresses cowboy", 1968.

I think there is a very great tendency to be carried away by the territorial imperative here. What can happen? Take some of our ice? Why do we want to own it? What is the danger up there now? Well, it is essentially pollution, I think. This is the latest kick, pollution. Everyone has got the pollution kick. So, we want to make sure that there is no pollution up there.

PIERRE E. TRUDEAU, CBC-TV program, "Under Attack", Feb. 24, 1970, referring to Arctic waters.

It would be a sad day for the town if the pollution stopped because it would signify the closing of the industry, and so, year after year, housewives hang out their laundry in the air filled with black, greasy smuts; mature trees wilt in fluorine fumes; dinners are eaten in the stench of mercaptans and children swim in polluted waters.

REX A. LUCAS, Minetown, milltown, railtown, 1971, 103.

We hope our discussion assists in making realists out of the economists, and economists out of the realists.

R. BIRD and L. WAVERMAN, in D.A.L. Auld, ed., Economic thinking and pollution problems, 1972, 100.

How to solve pollution? Simple. We should just do away with toilets. Every citizen in the country should then deliver human excrement in a box once a day to the president of every offending industry, with a note saying: "Since you're giving us yours, we thought you'd like to have ours".

JERRY GOODIS, in Maclean's, Apr., 1972, 12.

Poor

Well may I love the poor, greatly may I esteem the humble and the lowly, for poverty and adversity were my nurses, and in youth and want and misery my familiar friends; even now it yields a sweet satisfaction to my soul, that I can claim kindred with the obscure cottar, and the humble labourer, of my native, ever honoured, ever loved Scotland.

WILLIAM LYON MACKENZIE, Colonial advocate, June 10, 1824.

The poor are every where more liberal, more obligin' and more hospitable, according to their means, than the rich are.

THOMAS C. HALIBURTON, Sam Slick, 1838, 41.

This country is full of people who are starving up to their positions.

PETER MCARTHUR, To be taken with salt, 1903, 158.

No man is so cruel to the poor as the poor man grown rich.

G. SHELDON WILLIAMS, Westward ho, July, 1907, 39.

That is one consolation when you are poor — there are so many more things you can imagine about.

L.M. MONTGOMERY, Anne of Green Gables, 1908, 325.

Hum a hymn of sixpence,
A tableful of cards
Fingers slowly shuffling
Ambiguous rewards.

When the deck is opened
The pauper once more gave
His foes the kings and aces
And took himself the knave.

> ABRAHAM KLEIN, "Soirée of Velvel Klein-
> berger", 1936.

The sheep graze on a thousand hills,
The cattle roam upon the plains.
The cotton waits upon the mills,
The stores are bursting with their
    grains,
And yet these ragged ones that kneel
To take thy grace before their meal
Are said to be thy chosen ones,
Lord of the planets and the suns!

> E.J. PRATT, "The depression ends", 1937.

I found out the poor have no brains.
They believe whatever they're told so
long as it's easy to remember. But the
main thing is, they're all lazy.

> HUGH MACLENNAN, *Two solitudes*, 1945,
> 140.

A characteristic of poor people in
Canada is the multiplicity of their
possessions. In this, in their need for
and love of possessions, resides much
of their poverty.

> RICHARD J. NEEDHAM, *A friend in Need-
> ham*, 1969, 8.

Poor people are Mr. and Mrs. Welfare.
They're ugly and dirty. We don't want
pictures of women without teeth
depressing our readers.

> ANON., an editor of *Maclean's*, qu. in I.
> Adams, *The poverty wall*, 1970, 12.

Poverty is to be without sufficient
money, but it is also to have little hope
for better things. It is a feeling that
one is unable to control one's destiny,
that one is powerless in a society that
respects power. The poor have very
limited access to means of making
known their situation and their needs.
To be poor is to feel apathy, alienation
from society, entrapment, hopelessness
and to believe that whatever you do
will not turn out successfully.

> CANADA. ROY. COMM. ON THE STATUS OF
> WOMEN, *Report*, 1970, 311.

We're all poor in some way too, each
of us reaching for different riches.

> TERRY CRAWFORD, "Statement", in A.
> Purdy, ed., *Storm warning*, 1971, 45.

Consumers of welfare services.

> JOHN MUNRO, Min. of Nat. Health and
> Welfare, qu. in Vancouver *Sun*, Nov. 6,
> 1971, 16.

To be poor in our society is to suffer
the most outrageous kinds of violence
perpetuated by human beings on other
human beings.

> I. ADAMS, *The real poverty report*,
> 1971, xi.

Popularity

Transitory popularity is not proof of
genius. But permanent popularity is.

> STEPHEN LEACOCK, *Charles Dickens: his
> life and work*, 1934, 307.

Population

The whole interior of the British dominions must ere long, be filled with
an English population, every year increasing its numerical superiority over
the French.

> LORD DURHAM, *Report*, 1839, ed. Lucas,
> Vol.2, 1912, 290.

Get population, and all else shall be
added unto you.

> JOSEPH CHAMBERLAIN, speech, London,
> Eng., Nov. 11, 1895, applied by others
> to Canada. Chamberlain said in Toron-
> to, Dec. 30, 1887, "The first object is to
> get population on the land".

Your first and last need is men — men
of your own stock and ideals to develop and to fill your land that it may
stand erect above the shadow of any
fear from without or within.

> RUDYARD KIPLING, Canadian Club, Otta-
> wa, speech, Oct., 21, 1907.

Aye, such a little people, but growing,
growing, growing, with a march that
shall make us ten millions to-morrow,
twenty millions in our children's time
and a hundred millions yet ere the
century runs out.

> STEPHEN LEACOCK, Empire Club speech,
> Toronto, 1907.

We can never be really prosperous
until we are populous.

> A.C. FLUMERFELT, Canadian Club, Mont-
> real, Jan. 22, 1917.

Canada is one of the very few big free
spaces which are still left on our
planet. Who will take possession of it?
The question seems to be senseless at
first sight. For Canada is already in
somebody's possession. But we have to
become accustomed to the idea that
there is nothing stationary, unshakable
now; neither the inherited habits and
forms of government, nor the existing
rights and possessions. It is very doubtful whether those nations who suffer
from a tremendous surplus population
will allow a few million people to call
a whole continent their own, just because they happened to be the first to
arrive there.

> COLIN ROSS, Canadian Nazi, Hamburg,
> Germany, 1934.

During the last two centuries, world
population has been multiplied by
three, European population by four,
and French-Canadian population by
eighty, in spite of net emigration
which can be estimated roughly at
800,000.

> JACQUES HENRIPIN, to Can. Pol. Science
> Assoc., Montreal, June 6, 1956.

We'll build a nation of fifty million
within the lifetime of many of you
here.

> JOHN G. DIEFENBAKER, election cam-
> paign, Mar., 1958, Grand Falls, Nfld.

You are the last. Explode no more
The ripened seed within the womb.
We must decrease or crowded starve;
Our earth a living tomb.

> VAL HAIGH, "Explosions", 1961.

Canada is horizontal. Only a comparatively narrow strip above the American border is populated. Like a layer
of cream on a jug of milk.

> ANDREI VOSNESENSKY, Russian poet,
> "North country passing", in *Maclean's*,
> Dec. 1971, 44.

Pornography

People who have a taste for bathing in
a cesspool cannot be made much dirtier by being allowed to do it. To
prosecute is to advertise; to advertise is
far the most effectual way of all.

> GOLDWIN SMITH, *The Bystander*, 1880,
> 390, on the proposed banning of Zola's
> works as immoral.

Pornography is another intellectual
mode which serves as a substitute for
feeling.

> MIRIAM WADDINGTON, in *Can. lit.*,
> No.41, 1969, 76.

In 1950 we recall it was Toronto the capital – the Queen City of the province of Ontario. Toronto – the city of churches – Toronto-the-good. Today it is Toronto, the city of Toronto, the pornographic capital of the world, the smut capital of the North American continent.

GORDON CARTON, Ontario, Legislature, *Debates*, Oct. 22, 1969, 7417.

I must learn to
sing the joy of
penises and all
their frequencies;
the gloriousness
of blow jobs and
how avant garde
is everything in
London Ontario.

MIRIAM WADDINGTON, "Sad winter in the land of Can. Lit.", 1972.

Possession

It's not what a man profess;
It's what a man possess.

JAMES GAY, "Barnum and Gay", [1885].

Lest you should lightly prize me, I
  withhold
Myself from you in countless little
  ways.

CLARA BERNHARDT, "Lest you should lightly prize me", 1939.

And never the body is free,
  nor the heart,
  nor the mind,
  until it has mastered the law
  that which we hold, we must lose;
  that willingly given away is our
  own.

IRENE H. MOODY, "Jealousy", 1940.

It is the peculiarly American philosophy of life that to have is more important than to be or to do; in fact, that to be is dependant on to have.

FREDERICK P. GROVE, *In search of myself*, 1946, 452.

Trying to possess another person is like trying to grasp water; you can do it only by turning the water to ice.

RICHARD J. NEEDHAM, *A friend in Needham*, 1969, 3.

Post Office

For the Benefit of the PUBLICK. There is now open'd at the first House without the South Gate, an Intelligence and Outward POST-OFFICE viz . . .

If any Gentlemen, Merchants, or others, wants to send any Letters to any foreign Port, they may depend on having their Letters carefully deliver'd to the Captain of the first Vessel bound for the Place to which their Letters are directed, by paying One Penny per letter to said Office . . . Their humble Servant.

BENJAMIN LEIGH, Halifax, Apr. 23, 1754, qu. in Halifax *Gazette*, Apr. 27, 1754, 2.

Postage Stamps

Three-penny beaver.

ANON., phrase used to describe the first Canadian stamp, designed by Sanford Fleming, 1851.

Posterity

We should try to arrange ourselves so that we will appear as plausible as possible to posterity.

R.D. CUMMING, *Skookum Chuck fables*, 1915, 157.

Posterity pays our debts but repudiates our excuses.

> ROBERT C. (BOB) EDWARDS, Calgary *Eye Opener*, Feb. 8, 1919.

Potatoes

How are your potatoes?
Very Small.
How do you eat them?
Skins and all!

> ANON., New Brunswick folk song, qu. by Lord Beaverbrook in *Courage: the story of Sir James Dunn*, 1961, 34.

It's Bud the Spud, from the bright red mud,
Rollin' down the highway smilin',
The spuds are big, on the back of Bud's rig,
They're from Prince Edward Island.

> STOMPIN' TOM CONNORS, song, "Bud the spud", 1960.

Potlatch

Every Indian or other person who engages in or assists in celebrating the Indian festival known as the "Potlach" or in the Indian dance known as the "Tamanawas" is guilty of a misdemeanor, and shall be liable to imprisonment for a term of not more than six nor less than two months.

> CANADA. LAWS, STATUTES, etc., "Indian Act amendment" 1884, 44 Vic., ch. 27, sec. 3.

Poverty

Poverty is keen enough, without sharpening its edge by poking fun at it.

> T.C. HALIBURTON, *Sam Slick*, 1836, ch. XXI.

Honest poverty is encouraged, not despised, in Canada. Few of her prosperous men have risen from obscurity to affluence without going through the mill, and therefore have a fellow-feeling for those who are struggling to gain the first rung on the ladder.

> SUSANNA MOODIE, *Roughing it in the bush*, 1871, 10.

Thank God for poverty
That makes and keeps us free,
And lets us go our unobtrusive way,
Glad of the sun and rain,
Upright, serene, humane,
Contented with the fortune of a day.

> BLISS CARMAN, "The word at St. Kavin's", 1901.

It is not unreasonable to assume that Canadian literature might have been different if Canada's status and condition among nations had been different. We had a new country but old peoples; wealth collectively and in the future, but individual poverty; a store of tradition and a prevalent illiteracy.

> RAYMOND KNISTER, *Canadian short stories*, 1928, Intro., xii.

The war on poverty.

> LIBERAL PARTY, phrase describing expanded welfare measures, Apr., 1963.

Poverty in Canada is real. Its numbers are not in the thousands, but the millions. There is more of it than our society can tolerate, more than our economy can afford, and far more than existing measures and efforts can cope with. Its persistence, at a time when the bulk of Canadians enjoy one of the highest standards of living in the world, is a disgrace.

> ECONOMIC COUNCIL OF CANADA, *Fifth annual review*, 1968, 103.

The statement that at least one Canadian in every five suffers from poverty does not appear to be a wild exaggeration.

ECONOMIC COUNCIL OF CANADA, *Fifth annual review*, 1968, 110.

Poverty in the worst areas of the city core is abundantly visible in the decrepit structures which form its housing, the cracked pavement of the streets which are its recreational area, and the rodents which are its wild life. This poverty you can see – and hear – and taste – and smell. Its residents are not simply families struggling to catch up to the average national income; too often they are people fighting to retain a vestige of human dignity and self-respect.

CANADA. FEDERAL TASK FORCE ON HOUSING AND URBAN DEVELOPMENT, *Report*, 1969, 11.

The Canadian War on Poverty began and ended at the federal-provincial conference on Poverty and Opportunity in April, 1965.

JOHN ELEEN, Ontario Federation of Labour, qu. in I. Adams, *The poverty wall*, 1970, 26.

Poverty is an unnecessary affliction that begins in the womb and can be solved with a quart of milk a day.

AGNES HIGGINS, Nutritionist, qu. in *Weekend mag.*, Oct. 12, 1973, 2.

Power

Power is of various kinds; there is the power of wealth and the power of office, and when these are combined with executive power and the power of legislation, any one may see that there is a dangerous and unconstitutional combination.

JOTHAM BLANCHARD, election speech, Halifax, Sept. 13, 1830, qu. in *The Novascotian*, Sept. 15, 1830, 290.

Power has a natural tendency to corpulency.

T.C. HALIBURTON, *Sam Slick*, 1836, ch. 18.

Anything that gives power to the masses will please the masses.

T.C. HALIBURTON, *Sam Slick*, 1838, 34.

A power imprudently given to the executive, or to the people, is seldom or never got back.

T.C. HALIBURTON, *Sam Slick*, 1838, 63.

We have founded a great empire which will extend from the Atlantic to the Pacific Ocean; we intend that all that immense territory will be well governed and governed not merely as a selfish principle as applied to us, but in order to add to the power and to the prosperity of the Mother country.

SIR GEORGE-ETIENNE CARTIER, speech in London, Mar. 10, 1869.

No man and no party can be safely entrusted with uncontrolled power.

SIR RICHARD CARTWRIGHT, *Reminiscences*, 1912.

He loved power. He must rule; he could not reign.

F.W. HOWAY, *British Columbia* (Scholefield), 1913, II, 175, on Sir James Douglas.

The final Court of Appeal is military power.

JAMES MAVOR, Canadian Military Inst., Jan. 27, 1914.

Till power is brought to pooling
And masses share in ruling
There will not be an ending
Nor any peace for spending.

F.R. SCOTT, "Dedication", in *Poetry mag.*, Apr., 1941.

For us, how small the power
To build our dreams a tower
Or cast the molten need.
For us, how small the power.

F.R. SCOTT, "Dialogue", 1945.

Power and control are in all cases paid
for by loss of freedom and flexibility.

MARSHALL MCLUHAN, "Culture without
literacy", *Explorations*, Dec., 1953, 118.

I want to touch people like a magician,
to change them or hurt them, leave
my brand, make them beautiful. I
want to be the hypnotist who takes no
chances of falling asleep himself.

LEONARD COHEN, *The favourite game*,
1963, 101.

Men in power resemble men of all
levels of the social structure in believing that their own values are the
superior ones which all others should
share, though experience tells them
that all men are not as wise.

JOHN PORTER, *The vertical mosaic*, 1965,
265.

You should strive for power. Power is
the most important thing in the world.

HARRY C. HINDMARSH, qu. in Roy Greenaway, *The news game*, 1966, 14.

I am not a man: I am a glorious power.
Ignorant men say, "I am a body and I
possess a soul", when in truth it should
be: "I am a soul and I possess a body".
I cannot sin, so any woman joining
with me cannot sin.

EDWARD ARTHUR WILSON, qu. in H.E.
Wilson, *Canada's false prophet*,
1967, 13.

The only real and lasting power in this
world is absolute incorruptibility.

PETER HENDRY, *Epitaph for nostalgia*,
1968, 109.

Power accrues to nations capable of
technological leadership, and technical
change is an important source of economic growth.

CANADA. TASK FORCE ON THE STRUCTURE
OF CANADIAN INDUSTRY, *Report*,
1968, 35.

Men want power over others
– To revenge themselves on their
fathers!

IRVING LAYTON, "Aphs", *The whole
bloody bird*, 1969, 100.

Famous poets know
how power runs.
It ticks in youthful gonads
like a bomb.

PETER THOMAS, "Hearing the famous
poet", 1970.

I sensed that power is a blind and
omnipresent force, that it is indis-
criminate and amoral, and that men
who wield it are also prisoners of it.
The young cannot have power, for if
they possessed it, they would only
despise it.

DALTON CAMP, *Gentlemen, players and
politicians*, 1970, 3.

So long as there is a power in here
which is challenging the elected representatives of the people, I think that
power must be stopped and I think it's
only, I repeat, weak-kneed bleeding
hearts who are afraid to take these
measures.

PIERRE E. TRUDEAU, C.B.C. interview,
qu. in Toronto *Daily star*, Oct. 14, 1970,
9, referring to the Quebec crisis and the
Front de Libération du Québec (FLQ).

Pragmatists

The men who save the world are those who work by rule of thumb; who do the day's work by the day's light and advance on chaos and the painful dark by inches; in other words, the practical men.

> GOLDWIN SMITH, *The onlooker;* attributed.

Prairies

This plain affords nothing but Beast and grass.

> HENRY KELSEY, *Journal of a voyage, 1691,* in the *Kelsey papers,* 1929, 3.

Fertile Belt.

> HENRY YOULE HIND, *Narrative of the Canadian Red River exploring expedition of 1857 and of the Assiniboine and Saskatchewan exploring expedition of 1858,* 1860, 234, referring to the area "from a few miles west of the Lake of the Woods to the passes of the Rocky Mountains".

Palliser's Triangle.

> CAPT. JOHN PALLISER, *Report,* 1863, 7: "This central desert extends, however, but a short way into the British territory, forming a triangle having for its base the 49th parallel from longitude 100° [Boissevain, Man.] to 114° W [Waterton Lakes, Alta.] with its apex reaching to the 52nd parallel of latitude [lat. of Saskatoon, Sask.]" Probably first used in discussion regarding best route for the C.P.R., late 1870's.

The opening of the prairie lands would drain away our youth and strength. I am perfectly willing personally to leave the whole country a wilderness for the next half century, but I fear if the English do not go in, the Yankees will, and with that apprehension, I would gladly see a crown colony established there.

> SIR J. A. MACDONALD, Mar. 27, 1865, letter to E. W. Watkin, *Macdonald papers.* (Pub. Arch. Can.)

There the awful solitude opens upon the sight and swells into an ocean, and the eye wanders over the "silent space" of the West. The man must be corrupt as death who, unaccustomed, can look unmoved upon this august material presence, this calm unutterable vastness. Man is a grasshopper here – a mere insect, making way between the enormous discs of heaven and earth.

> CHARLES MAIR, letter, Apr. 25, 1869, Toronto *Globe* May 28, 1869.

The great ocean itself does not present more infinite variety than does this prairie-ocean of which we speak. In winter, a dazzling surface of purest snow; in early summer, a vast expanse of grass and pale pink roses; in autumn too often a wild sea of raging fire. No ocean of water in the world can vie with its gorgeous sunsets; no solitude can equal the loneliness of a night-shadowed prairie; one feels the stillness and hears the silence, the wail of the prowling wolf makes the voice of solitude audible, the stars look down through infinite silence upon a silence almost as intense.

> WILLIAM F. BUTLER, *The great lone land,* 1872, 199.

Midst the smoke and hum of cities, midst the prayer of churches, in street or *salon,* it needs but little cause to recall again to the wanderer the image of the immense meadows where, far away at the portals of the setting sun, lies the Great Lone Land.

> WILLIAM F. BUTLER, *The great lone land,* 1872, 351.

A view so vast that endless space seems for once to find embodiment, and at a single glance the eye is satiated with immensity. There is no mountain range to come up across the skyline, no river to lay its glistening folds along the middle distance, no dark forest to give shade to foreground or to fringe perspective, no speck of life, no track of man, nothing but the wilderness.

WILLIAM F. BUTLER, *The wild northland*, 1873, 30.

Throughout our prairie lands is found not the illimitable level of treeless prairies which distinguish Illinois, but a charming alternation of woods and prairie, upland and meadow.

THOMAS SPENCE, *The prairie lands of Canada*, 1879, 13.

We believe we have there the garden of the world.

SIR CHARLES TUPPER, H. of C., *Debates*, 1879, 1893.

The greatest country I ever struck. There are hundreds of towns and cities between Winnipeg and Moosejaw, and it takes a rich man to own the ground under his shoes in those places. Wherever there's a siding that's a town; and where there's a siding and a tank, that's a city!

ANON., C.P.R. conductor to E. B. Osborn, on the 1881 landfever in the West.

The Prairie Bubble.

ANON., a term used to describe the inflation of western land values, followed by collapse in 1882.

Great prairies swept beyond our
    aching sight
Into the measureless West; uncharted
    realms,
Voiceless and calm, save when
    tempestuous wind
Rolled the rank herbage into billows
    vast,

And rushing tides which never found a shore.

CHARLES MAIR, *Tecumseh*, 1886.

That great prairie ocean, that sea of green and gold in this month of May.

GEORGE M. GRANT, address to Canadian Club, New York, 1887.

Her Valley of Saskatchewan alone, it has been scientifically computed, will support eight hundred millions.

W. D. LIGHTHALL, *Songs of the great Dominion*, 1889, xxii.

I failed to induce the Canadian Government to adopt this plan because such a thing had never been done before — which, as you know, is a conclusive reason with governments.

SIR WILLIAM VAN HORNE, letter to Rudyard Kipling, about 1892, on his proposal to sub-divide land so as to reduce the isolation of the homesteaders, qu. in W. Vaughan, *Life and work of Sir William Van Horne*, 1920, 202.

The country should have been left the same side up as God A'mighty made it.

ANON., popular local statement regarding the land of south-east Alberta, about 1900.

With the help of the waters of the Bow we will make these prairies stink with flowers.

LORD SHAUGHNESSY, to a friend, 1903, on irrigation.

To me the welfare and interests of this great Western country are more and always have been more important than the success or convenience of any political party.

F.W.G. HAULTAIN, letter to the Editor, Regina *Leader*, Aug. 7, 1905.

Where wide as the plan of creation
   The Prairies stretch ever away,
And beckon a broad invitation
   To fly to their bosom and stay;
The prairie-fire smell in the gloaming
–
The water-wet wind in the spring
–
An empire untrod for the roaming –
   Ah, this is a life for a king!

ROBERT STEAD, "The prairie", 1908.

The Prairie which is the High Veldt,
plus Hope, Activity, and Reward.

RUDYARD KIPLING, Letters to the family, 1908, 47.

A great untimbered, level, dried-up sea of land.

THOMAS WILBY, A motor tour through Canada, 1914, 162.

I'll dream again of fields of grain that
   stretch from sky to sky
And the little prairie hamlets where
   the cars go roaring by,
Wooden hamlets as I saw them –
   noble cities still to be,
To girdle stately Canada with gems
   from sea to sea.

SIR ARTHUR CONAN DOYLE, "The Athabaska Trail", 1919.

No one is born in the prairies who can avoid it, and no one dies there who can get out in time.

ANON., qu. by Ramsay Traquair, Atlantic monthly, June, 1923, 822.

Those of us of the old new West who have been privileged to travel the prairie trails in summer heat and winter cold, in the awakening beauty of the springtime, the promise of summer, and the golden fulfillment of autumn, when we set out alone 'on the longest trail of all', we will 'go west' with great content, if the soft southwest wind brings to us the tang of wild sage and the prairie roses, the beat of a thousand hooves as the herds go down to water, or the sibilant sigh of the wind through miles of ripening wheat.

E. CORA HIND, about 1925, qu. in Kennethe M. Haig, Brave harvest, 1945, 76.

The Dust Bowl.

ANON., the area centered in Southern Saskatchewan, from an American phrase, early 1930's.

Next-year country.

ANON., the Dry Belt, so-called in the 1930's because of the hope that every crop of wheat planted will turn out to be a "million dollar crop" (Jean Burnet, Next year country, 1951, 5).

Without immigration the railways could not function. Empty town-sites with miles of new sidewalks looked out over empty sidings and empty sheds. The frame was too big for the picture. It fell out.

STEPHEN LEACOCK, Fortnightly, Nov., 1936, 526, referring to the "crash" of 1929, and later.

They said, "Sure, it'll rain next year!"
When that was dry, "Well, next year
   anyway."
Then, "Next – "

ANNE MARRIOTT, "The wind our enemy", 1939.

To the native of the prairies Alberta is the far West; British Columbia the near East.

EDWARD A. MCCOURT, Canada West in fiction, 1949, Preface.

You could spend half a lifetime in that rangeland setting without ever seeing a play, hearing a lyric well read, meeting an author, browsing in a bookstore, seeing a publisher, attending a literary society, or talking with a literary critic.

WILFRID EGGLESTON, The frontier and Canadian letters, 1957, 142.

The dust, light brown,
lightens as it sifts thru eyebrows
on the face you see
looking to the prairie wind.

> GEORGE BOWERING, "The dust", 1968.

A few speculative images
shyly define our place
trying to embrace our world
the necessarily outrageous flats
pitted against the huge sky.

> PETER STEVENS, "Prairie: time and place", 1969.

Those who live in the region have usually tended to identify themselves with all of it rather than with a part.

> ANDREW H. CLARK, in D.K. Elton, ed., *One prairie province? A question for Canada*, 1970, 330.

Man, the giant-conqueror, and man, the insignificant dwarf always threatened by defeat, form the two polarities of the state of mind produced by the sheer physical fact of the prairie.

> HENRY KREISEL, in E. Mandel, ed., *Contexts of Canadian criticism*, 1971, 256.

Praise

Praise to the face is open disgrace.

> THOMAS C. HALIBURTON, *Sam Slick's wise saws*, 1853, ch. 26.

Praise is pleasant, but I never seem able to apply it to myself.

> MARJORIE PICKTHALL, letter to Sir Andrew Macphail, 1921.

Praise and appreciation itself, the very soil in which art best flourishes, may prompt too rank a growth.

> STEPHEN LEACOCK, *Charles Dickens*, 1934, 171.

Pratt, E.J.

The greatest poem in Canadian literature.

> NORTHROP FRYE, Roy. Soc. Can., *Studia varia*, 1957, 30, referring to Pratt's "The Truant", (presented June 11, 1956.)

When *Brebeuf and his brethren* [by E.J. Pratt, pub. in 1940] first came out, a friend of mine said that the thing to do now was to write the same story from the Iroquois point of view.

> JAMES REANEY, *Univ. of Tor. quart.*, Apr., 1957, 291.

E.J. Pratt, for all his warmth can't let himself go with mankind the way he can with a whale or a locomotive.

> BARKER FAIRLEY, "F.H. Varley", in R.L. McDougall, ed., *Our living tradition*, ser. 2 & 3, 1959, 164.

Prayer

Saying one's prayers isn't exactly the same thing as praying.

> L.M. MONTGOMERY, *Anne of Green Gables*, 1908, 107.

If I, a mere automaton
In a brief and paltry play,
Am but a group of atoms drawn
Powerless upon my way
To mud again, as savants say
Why then at the heart of me
What is this that needs must pray?
There is no end to mystery.

> TOM MACINNES, "The ballade of the mystic and the mud", 1918.

The shape of prayer is that —
curved and going nowhere, to fall
in pure abstraction saying everything
and saying nothing at all.

> PHYLLIS WEBB, "The shape of prayer", 1956.

The shape of prayer
is like the shape of the small
beach stone, rounded smooth, but
    individual
in its despair.

> PHYLLIS WEBB, "The shape of prayer",
> 1956.

Prayer makes speech a ceremony. To observe this ritual in the absence of arks, altars, a listening sky: this is a rich discipline.

> LEONARD COHEN, "Lines from my grandfather's journal", 1961.

I believe in praying as though God were all and then doing as though man were all.

> RABBI ABRAHAM L. FEINBERG, Storm the gates of Jericho, 1964, 291.

We prayed for miracles, and had no
    wands
Nor wits about us; strained in a
    pointed prayer
We were so many windmills without
    hands
To whirl and drag the water up to air.

> DOROTHY LIVESAY, "The outrider", 1968.

Preachers

Our equipage for the battle field was a portmanteau and valise; in them we stored our wearing apparel, Bible and what other books we were able to get, and but a few dollars in our pockets. Our outward dress and appearance when mounted gave us the name of the Methodist cavalry.

> J. CARROLL, Case and cotemporaries, 1869, II, 319; reference to preachers.

The fault nowadays is not with the preaching so much as with the hearing.

> RALPH CONNOR, The prospector, 1904, 71.

It has been commonly believed, also, that the formal Anglican service had little attraction for backwoodsmen who liked a man to preach as if he were fighting bees.

> GERALD M. CRAIG, Upper Canada: the formative years, 1784-1841, 1963, 169.

Precambrian Shield

The manner in which natural obstacles have isolated the country from all other British possessions in the East is a matter of considerable weight; indeed it is the obstacle of the country, and one, I fear almost beyond the remedies of art.

> CAPT. J. PALLISER, Gt. Brit., Parl. papers, 1860, cd. 2732, 5.

This region of swamps and sterile pinelands has opposed an effectual barrier to communication towards the Canadas, and has forced the traffic of these remote settlements to find an outlet through Minnesota.

> CAPT. W.J. TWINING, Reports upon the boundary, 1878, 48.

The Canadian Shield.

> EDUARD SUESS, Autlitz der erde, 1888, 42. (Trans.)

The Precambrian Shield dominates the history as it dominates the landscape of Canada.

> MARY Q. INNIS, Econ. hist. of Can., 1935, viii.

Precedents

People too often forget that common sense is the basis of all the conventions of the constitution. The precedents arose out of common-sense responses to concrete situations; and, it may be added, if old situations recur, in the same or altered form, even very old precedents may become relevant for precisely this reason.

EUGENE FORSEY, letter, *Globe and Mail*, Mar. 11, 1968, 6.

Prediction

The habits or biases of individuals which permit prediction are reinforced in the cumulative bias of institutions and constitute the chief interest of the social scientist.

HAROLD A. INNIS, *Can. jour. econ. and pol. sci.*, 1935, 1, 283.

Prefaces

I like prefaces. I read them. Sometimes I do not read any further, and it is possible you may do the same.

MALCOLM LOWRY, "Preface to a novel", in *Under the volcano*, 1950, French ed.; in *Can. lit.*, No. 9, 1961, 23. (Trans.)

Pregnancy

Inventor of maternity dress made pregnancy respectable.

EDMONTON *JOURNAL*, Column heading, Mar. 29, 1965, 15.

Prejudice

Whether they come from the Catholics of Quebec or from the Protestants of Ontario, appeals to prejudice are deplorable. For my part, I have as much aversion for the man who appeals to Catholic prejudices in the province of Quebec, as for the man who appeals to Protestant prejudices in the province of Ontario.

SIR WILFRID LAURIER, speech at Somerset, Que., Aug. 2, 1887. (Trans.)

The Present

So all desire and all regret,
  And fear and memory, were
    naught;
One to remember or forget
  The keen desire our hands had
    caught;
  Morrow and yesterday were naught.

BLISS CARMAN, "Low tide on Grand Pré", 1889.

When we are young our time is all present. When we are old there is no present, but our time becomes the aggregate days and years.

R.D. CUMMING, *Skookum Chuck fables*, 1915, 158.

The Is is the same as the Will Be
And both the same as before.

A.J.M. SMITH, "For ever and ever, Amen", 1926.

Ah! how one forgets
All the high moments of love. For the
  living
Present is all.

NORMAN GREGOR GUTHRIE, "Sweetheart Rose", 1928.

And far from pagan thought is this
That out of travail, I can say
I need no future world of bliss —
I have it here to-day.

CHARLES F. BOYLE, "Vita Anabilis", 1942.

I have always found the present sufficiently interesting to occupy most of my thought.

W.L. MACKENZIE KING, qu., Hardy, *Mackenzie King of Canada*, 1949, 367.

Reading a dead poet
Who complained in his time
Against bad laws, bad manners,
And bad weather in bad rhyme,

I thought how glad he'd be
To be living in our time
To damn worse laws, worse matters
And worse weather, in worse rhyme.

> LOUIS DUDEK, "The progress of satire",
> 1958.

Your climate is the mood
Of living, the hinge of now,
In time the present tense.

> ALFRED PURDY, "Where the moment is",
> 1959.

There is no real escape from the present. Here and now is where everyman lives; and his greatest gifts in a world where both faith and justice have perished are his ability to endure and to love.

> HUGO MCPHERSON, in *Can. lit.* No.1,
> 1959, 49.

The present is inescapable; it is now; the past and the future are delusions.

> HUGO MCPHERSON, in *Can. lit.* No.1,
> 1959, 50.

All men are powerless against chance, but the defeated know the secret. They live for the present – the future has already betrayed them. They are the children of reality.

> STEPHEN VIZINCZEY, *The rules of chaos*,
> 1969, 79.

Presents

Let no man imagine that he knows what a present is worth, till he has found what happiness can be produced by a blue bead, a yellow button, a needle, or a piece of an old iron hoop.

> SIR JOHN ROSS, *Narrative of a second voyage in search of a Northwest Passage*, 1835, 180.

The Press

At that time, in the history of the world, it was almost impossible to be an editor without being a politician also.

> GEORGE M. GRANT, *Joseph Howe*, 1904, 2, referring to the early nineteenth century.

The press, more than the pulpit, more even than parliament and the people, is really the guide to the destinies of Canada.

> W.B. LANIGAN, of the C.P.R. in 1917, qu. by M.E. Nichols, *(CP) the story of the Canadian press*, 1948, 139.

The anxious thrill of battle; delight of
    wielding power,
The sturdy joy of labour; bliss of an
    idle hour,
These, and a thousand raptures, are all
    bound up I guess
In the thunder from the basement as
    the paper goes to Press!

> NORMAN MACKINTOSH, Feature Editor, Toronto *Telegram*, 1922. Inscribed in Album of J. Alex. Edmison, qu. in *Queen's quart.*, Vol. 75, 1968, 169.

Printed in the sage brush country of the Lillooet every Thursday, God Willing. Guarantees a chuckle every week and a belly laugh once a month, or your money back. Subscription: $5 in Canada. Furriners: $6. This week's circulation 1796, and every bloody one of them paid for.

> MARGARET (MA) MURRAY, *Bridge River-Lillooet news* (B.C.), editorial page, published by Murrays, 1933-1973.

Freedom of discussion is essential to enlighten public opinion in a democratic state; it cannot be curtailed without affecting the right of the people to be informed through sources independent of the government concerning matters of public interest. There must be an untrammelled publication of the news and political opinions of the political parties contending for ascendancy.

JUDGE LUCIEN CANNON, *Supreme Court reports*, 1938, 145.

Powerful urban newspapers have been concerned with the control of space (i.e. domination of a particular region) and also with domination of time (they can release information when they choose) . . . under the guise of democracy freedom of the press has led to the defence of monopoly.

HAROLD A. INNIS, Values Discussion Group, University of Toronto, 8th meeting, 1949, transcript.

Only a truly Canadian printing press, one with the "feel" of Canada and directly responsible to Canada, can give us the critical analysis, the informed discourse and dialogue which are indispensable in a sovereign society.

CANADA. ROY. COMM. ON PUBLICATIONS, *Report*, 1961, 7.

The press is the greatest instrument for the distribution of filth in the world today. Salacious literature available today is 100-per-cent worse than we had to deal with 10 years ago.

VINCENT KELLY, Ontario provincial state deputy, Knights of Columbus, speech, Columbus Day dinner, Toronto, Oct. 21, 1963.

The Times made more money producing paper without words than paper with words. The Spruce Falls Power & Paper Co. Ltd., of Toronto, which supplied two-thirds of *The Times'* paper, had accounted for fifty-three per cent of the New York Times Company's total profit in recent years.

GAY TALESE, *The kingdom and the power*, 1969, 249.

It doesn't matter whether the North Bay *Nugget* belongs to Roy Thomson, Max Bell, or a local drygoods merchant. They are all, without a single exception, in the same kind of hands. They all belong to the Canadian business community and they do what that community wants. And if Canadian businessmen assume an automatic, infallible identity between their views and those of every right-thinking Canadian, they are hardly unique among the oligarchs of history.

DESMOND MORTON, qu. in Special Senate Comm. on Mass Media, *Report*, Vol. I, 1971, 6.

The Press, Freedom of

While we do not assume too much for the Press, we are fully aware of its influence, and of the benefits which it confers. Among other things which renders an unshackled press so important in a civilized land, is its being the instrument by which legal and legislative occurrences are circulated over a vast extent of country.

PHILIP HOLLAND, in *Acadian recorder*, Feb. 27, 1830.

I conjure you to judge me by the principles of English law, and to leave an unshackled press as a legacy to your children. You remember the press in your hours of conviviality and mirth — Oh, do not desert it in this its day of trial.

JOSEPH HOWE, Halifax, speech at his trial for criminal libel, Mar. 2, 1835.

Let not the sons of the Rebels look across the border to the sons of the Loyalists, and reproach them that their press is not free.

> JOSEPH HOWE, Halifax, speech at his trial for criminal libel, Mar. 2, 1835.

We would wear the coarsest raiment; we would eat the poorest food; and crawl at night into the veriest hovel in the land to rest our weary limbs, but cheerful and undaunted hearts; and these jobbing justices should feel, that one frugal and united family could withstand their persecution, defy their power, and maintain the freedom of the press. Yes, gentlemen, come what will, while I live, Nova Scotia shall have the blessing of an open and unschackled press.

> JOSEPH HOWE, Halifax, speech at his trial for criminal libel, Mar. 2, 1835.

If I can be proscribed to-day for defending myself and my friends in the newspapers, another Nova Scotian may be rejected to-morrow because the Governor likes not the colour of his hair.

> JOSEPH HOWE, speech in Cumberland County, Autumn, 1844.

Suppose we take the rule about the press. Be free, but not personal; free, but decent; free, but not treasonable to each other; free, but not licentious.

> T.C. HALIBURTON, Sam Slick's wise saws, 1853, II, 194.

It is too late in the day to stop men thinking. If allowed to think they will speak. If they speak, they will write, and what they write will be printed and published. A newspaper is only a thought-throwing machine, a reflex of the popular mind.

> AMOR DE COSMOS, in 1859, qu. in R. Wilk, Amor de Cosmos, 1958, 19.

The freedom of the press was not won for the sake of the press. It was won for the sake of the people. And if the time comes when the press ceases to fight for the freedom of the people, then the time will follow, and quickly, when the people will no longer fight for the freedom of the press.

> GRATTAN O'LEARY, address to Canadian Club, in 1953, qu. in J.W.G. MacEwan, Poking into politics, 1966, 183.

Freedom of the press is freedom of the printing press. That is only a freedom of speech and a freedom of assembly, and they are always limited: no freedom is absolute.

> GRATTAN O'LEARY, qu. in Queen's quart., Summer, 1965, 408.

Press Gallery, Ottawa

The eyes and ears of the people are in that Press Gallery.

> GORDON GRAYDON, in the House of Commons, Debates, May 29, 1951, 3535, qu. in Maclean's, April 17, 1965, 9.

Don't quote me, but since the pipeline [debate of 1956] the real party in opposition is always the parliamentary press gallery.

> ANON., civil servant, qu. in Maclean's, Apr. 17, 1965, 11.

The Second Line of Opposition.

> ANON., qu. in J.W.G. MacEwan, Poking into politics, 1966, 180.

Pretence

Candor may be devilish,
    And truth untimely open hell;
Better pretend the thing you wish;
Anon you may, if you wish and wish,
    Achieve a miracle.

> TOM MACINNES, "White magic", 1923.

Prevention

An ounce of prevention is worth a pound of cure.

THOMAS C. HALIBURTON, *Sam Slick's wise saws*, 1853, ch. 15.

I must make increasingly clear to the world that prevention of wrong courses of evil and the like means more than all else that man can accomplish.

W.L.MACKENZIE KING, *The Mackenzie King record*, Vol.2, 272; *Diary*, Dec. 8, 1944.

Prevention is less costly than cure – and not only in money.

WILLIAM E. BLATZ, *Human security*, 1966, 12.

Prices

A cheap article ain't always the best; if you want a real right down first chop, genu*wine* thing, you must pay for it.

T.C. HALIBURTON, *Sam Slick*, 1838, 123.

We hear little at this moment throughout Canada save the talk of prices rising, real estate and rents going up, mechanics and labourers striking for more wages, provisions growing dearer day by day.

TORONTO *GLOBE*, June, 1854.

What do you want, gentlemen? Name your price and you shall have it.

JOHN SANDFIELD MACDONALD, Premier of Ontario, 1867-1871, to a delegation; attributed.

Our regular way in arriving at our prices is to find out the cost of material and labour, and then double, to make sure of the overhead. We then add the telephone number and multiply by two. But in this case we discovered that no one but ourselves has any supply, so the price has rocketed.

ANON., a Toronto manufacturer to a buyer, qu., *Dalhousie rev.*, 1929, 376.

Pride

Pride and temper is almost always at the bottom of schism, you will find.

T.C. HALIBURTON, *Sam Slick*, 1840, 45.

I knew humility was the dress coat of pride.

T.C. HALIBURTON, *Sam Slick*, 1840, 46.

Wounded pride should be touched lightly. The skin is thin and plagy sensative.

T.C. HALIBURTON, *Sam Slick's wise saws*, 1853, I, 294.

I have no fear of present wrong;
I cannot dream of future ill,
Against the demon of regret
My pride must prove an amulet.

GEORGE F. CAMERON, "Ysolte", 1887.

Pride was my wilderness, and the demon that led me there was fear. I was alone, never anything else, and never free, for I carried my chains within me, and they spread out from me and shackled all I touched.

MARGARET LAURENCE, *The stone angel*, 1964, 292.

Pride wears many masks, including that of humility.

RICHARD J. NEEDHAM, *A friend in Needham*, 1969, 16.

When a woman's in love, she throws her pride out the window — meanwhile making a mental note of where it landed.

RICHARD J. NEEDHAM, *A friend in Needham*, 1969, 31.

Prime Minister

I have no sinecure in trying to keep together a crowd of French Liberals Irish Catholics Methodists Free Traders Protectionists Eastern Province men Western Men Central Canada men Columbians Manitobans all jealous of each other and striving to obtain some advantage or concession. I always knew it was very hard to keep liberals together but my experience has been far in excess of my utmost belief.

ALEXANDER MACKENZIE, letter to Charles Mackenzie, Oct. 20, 1876. (Pub. Arch. Can.)

Joe, if you would know the depth of meanness of human nature, you have got to be a Prime Minister running a general election.

SIR JOHN A. MACDONALD, to Joseph Pope in Feb., 1891, during the general election; qu. in Pope, *Public servant*, 1960, 77.

It was said that Sir John could refuse the request of a deputation with better grace than Mackenzie could grant what was asked.

SIR GEORGE W. ROSS, *Getting into parliament and after*, 1913, 132.

A Prime Minister under the party system as we have had it in Canada is of necessity an egotist and autocrat. If he comes to office without these characteristics his environment equips him with them as surely as a diet of royal jelly transforms a worker into a queen bee.

JOHN W. DAFOE, *Laurier*, 1922, 99.

A Prime Minister can be accommodated to any type of colleague, but there is a limit beyond which tolerance can go. Ignorance can be excused, but treachery is an unforgivable sin in the conduct of government.

RICHARD B. BENNETT, letter to Col. C.D.H. McAlpine, July 8, 1935. (Pub. Arch. Can.)

In our Dominion where sections abound, a Dominion of races, of classes and of creeds, of many languages and many origins, there are times when no Prime Minister can be true to his trust to the nation he has sworn to serve, save at the temporary sacrifice of the party he is appointed to lead.

ARTHUR MEIGHEN, tribute to R.B. Bennett, Toronto, Jan. 16, 1939.

I'm going home.

R.B. BENNETT, on leaving Canada, Jan. 28, 1939, to take a seat in the House of Lords, qu. by Thomas Franck, Vancouver *Sun*, July 11, 1964, 3.

He cannot be first among his equals for the very excellent reason that he has no equals.

R. MACGREGOR DAWSON, *The government of Canada*, 1947, 221.

When I saw him bring whole batteries of rhetoric, whole arsenals of guided missiles of vitriol and invective in order to shoot one forlorn sitting-duck – a sitting-duck, indeed, already crippled with a self-inflicted wound – I wondered if the Prime Minister really believes in the humane slaughter of animals.

COLIN CAMERON, H. of C., *Debates*, Jan. 21, 1958, 3572, on John Diefenbaker's treatment of L.B. Pearson's motion to dissolve the government.

I am the first Prime Minister of this country of neither altogether English nor French origin.

> JOHN G. DIEFENBAKER, *Maclean's*, Mar. 29, 1958, 57-8.

I like power; we both enjoy being Prime Minister.

> MRS. JOHN DIEFENBAKER, Feb. 9, 1963, attributed, qu. by P. Nicholson, *Vision and indecision*, 1968, 265.

To be Prime Minister of Canada, you need the hide of a rhinoceros, the morals of St. Francis, the patience of Job, the wisdom of Solomon, the strength of Hercules, the leadership of Napoleon, the magnetism of a Beatle and the subtlety of Machiavelli.

> LESTER B. PEARSON, to a Liberal rally about 1964, qu. in Vancouver *Sun*, Jan. 27, 1965, 4.

Their lives, eight in failure, five in success and one yet to be judged, cannot measure the nation's life; but they have pervaded, articulated, unified or disrupted it from the beginning.

> BRUCE HUTCHISON, *Mr. Prime Minister*, 1964, 2.

Mackenzie King and his generation were not Canadians by instinct; they could never quite take the Canadian nation for granted because they had helped to create it and were deeply conscious of how fragile the creation was, and how divided the loyalties of many Canadians were. For Louis St. Laurent, Canada was the only country he knew.

> J.W. PICKERSGILL, qu. in B. Hutchison, *Mr. Prime Minister*, 1964, 297.

Good Lord, we can't have Prime Ministers investigated when they make a decision on their own. It's a Prime Minister's prerogative to make a wrong decision, and it's not subject to checks. We can't investigate a Prime Minister.

> LESTER B. PEARSON, to a friend, Mar. 13, 1966, regarding J.G. Diefenbaker and the Gerda Munsinger scandal; next day he announced an inquiry.

God save our gracious Prime
Keep him in every clime
B.C. to Maritime
And in between,
Send him victorious
Strong and uxurious
Loud and uproarious
God save our Preem.

> PAUL HIEBERT, *Willows revisited*, 1967, 15; suggested anthem by John Swivel and Osiris Jones-Jones, associates of Sarah Binks.

If you want to see me again, don't bring signs saying 'Trudeau is a pig' and don't bring signs that he hustles women, because I won't talk to you. I didn't get into politics to be insulted. And don't throw wheat at me either!

> PIERRE E. TRUDEAU, July 17, 1969, Saskatoon, qu. in *The best of Trudeau*, 1972, 16.

With Lester's vacuous face
Plastered all over the place
I find it a relief
To watch the demoniac Dief

> W.W.E. ROSS, qu. in *Can. lit*. No. 39, 1969, 59.

Okay, I have no lust for power. I'm not going to die an unhappy man if I don't become Prime Minister of this country.

> ROBERT STANFIELD, May, 1972, qu. in Walter Stewart, *Divide and con*, 1973, 91.

Prince Edward Island

Al the said land is low and plaine and the fairest that may possibly be seene, full of goodly medowes and trees.

> JACQUES CARTIER, *Diary*, June 29, 1534, (Trans.). Inscription on cairn unveiled July 1, 1934, Queen's Square, Charlottetown.

Parva sub ingenti. (The small under [the protection of] the great.)

> P.E.I., provincial coat-of-arms, motto decreed 1769, taken from Virgil's *Georgics*, Book 2, line 19.

Spud Island.

> ANON., popular name in Canada, an association with potato growing from the late 1700's.

Pay Ay.

> ANON., "P.E.", or "Prince Edward Islander", an epithet used by Maine lumberjacks about 1840. Maritime lumberjacks accepted lower wages than the Americans.

. . . send down a little tug boat and draw you up into one of our lakes.

> THOMAS D'ARCY MCGEE, qu. by J.E. Hodgetts, *Can. hist. rev.*, March, 1958, 71.

There is a band within this land
who live in pomp and pride,
To fill their store they rob the poor;
in pleasure will they ride.
With dishes fine their tables shine;
they move in princely style.
Those are the knaves that made us slaves
and sold Prince Edward Isle.

> LARRY GORMAN, song, "The history of Prince Edward Island", 1873.

Long courted; won at last.

> ANON., words on arch of welcome to Lord Dufferin, in Charlottetown, July, 1873; a reference to the entry of the Province into Confederation nine years after the Charlottetown conference.

I found the Island in a high state of jubilation and quite under the impression that it is the Dominion that has been annexed to Prince Edward.

> LORD DUFFERIN, letter to Sir J.A. Macdonald, 1873, qu. in *Can. hist. rev.*, 1933, 160.

The Garden of the Gulf.

> ANON., popular term for the province.

The Million Acre Farm.

> ANON., a popular term.

Prince Edward Isle, to thee
Our hearts shall faithful be,
    Where'er we dwell;
Forever may we stand
As brothers, hand in hand,
And sing God save the land
    We love so well.

> L.M. MONTGOMERY, "Island hymn", 1908.

Diminutive and proud, dour and lovable, Prince Edward Island still remains among the provinces unique and a paradox.

> W.M. WHITELAW, *The Maritimes and Canada before Confederation*, 1934, 28.

Since I'm Island-born home's as precise
as if a mumbly old carpenter,
shoulder-straps crossed wrong,
laid it out,
refigured to the last three-eighths of a shingle.

> MILTON ACORN, "The island", 1963.

Principles

People have great courage when pressing for a principle.

> WILLIAM E. BLATZ, *Human security*, 1966, 9.

Women only admire men of principle.
The principles may be good or bad.

> JOHN GLASSCO, *Tamarack rev.*, No. 58,
> 1971, 61.

Print

Thanks be to God for the heritage
Of a printed word on a plain white
page.

> ROSA MARY CLAUSEN-MOHR, "Print",
> 1953.

The difference between the man of
print and the man of scribal culture is
nearly as great as that between the
non-literate and the literate.

> MARSHALL MCLUHAN, *The Gutenberg
> galaxy*, 1962, 90.

The notion of moving steadily along
on single planes of narrative awareness
is totally alien to the nature of language and of consciousness. But it is
highly consistent with the nature of
the printed word.

> MARSHALL MCLUHAN, *The Gutenberg
> galaxy*, 1962, 244.

Printers

Once a printer, always a printer.

> TORONTO TYPOGRAPHICAL SOCIETY,
> motto, 1845.

Priorities

Second Things First.

> JACK LUDWIG, *Confusions*, 1963, 10.

Prisons

My prison window is not large
Five inches high, six inches wide,
Perhaps seven.
Yet it is large enough to show
The whole unfettered to and fro
Of heaven.

> JOE WALLACE, "How high, how wide",
> written in prison, Petawawa, 1941, in
> *Night is ended*, 1943.

What a miserable conscience we have
towards our custodial institutions!

> C.L. BURTON, *A sense of urgency*, 1952,
> 277.

The test of a prison system is the
number of prisoners who never return.

> JUDGE HELEN GREGORY MACGILL, to Ca-
> nadian Penal Conference, Montreal, qu.
> in E.M.G. MacGill, *My mother, the
> judge*, 1955, 220.

The calculation of the life and occupational hazards for prison staff and
inmates indicates that these hazards
are infinitesimal.

> DOGAN D. AKMAN, *Can. jour. of correc-
> tions*, Oct., 1966, 296.

Privacy

Privacy is a privilege not granted to
the aged or the young.

> MARGARET LAURENCE, *The stone angel*,
> 1964, 6.

It is perhaps the value of privacy and
the capacity to afford it which has
become the dividing line between the
real and the apparent middle class.

> JOHN PORTER, *The vertical mosaic*,
> 1965, 5.

It's easier for single people to find
companionship than for married people to find privacy.

> RICHARD J. NEEDHAM, *A friend in Need-
> ham*, 1969, 5.

A man's right to privacy includes
protection from any type of surveillance without his consent.

> JOHN TURNER, (Justice Minister) qu. in
> *Maclean's*, Mar., 1970, 3.

Private Enterprise

The unwarranted and arbitrary exercise of power by governments, often influenced by collectivist theories, destroys initiative and curtails the dynamic qualities which are essential to the productive operation of private enterprise.

CANADIAN CHAMBER OF COMMERCE, brief to Senate. Special Committee on Manpower and Employment, *Proceedings*, No. 3, Dec. 14, 1960, 167.

It is our responsibility to illustrate to the public at large that there is no alternative to private enterprise.

STEPHEN B. ROMAN, qu. in G. Lonn, *Builders of fortunes*, 1963, 60.

Probabilities

Errors in judgment must occur in the practice of an art which consists largely in balancing probabilities.

SIR WILLIAM OSLER, "Teacher and student", 1897, in *Aequanimitas*.

Problems

Our problems have indeed reached new dimensions. We are in outer space and in inner turmoil; we have both Cobalt bombs and hydrogen bombs. We can communicate with a satellite 25 million miles away, but not with a human across a curtain.

LESTER B. PEARSON, address, Study Coference on National Problems, Kingston, Sept. 6, 1960.

Canada has been called 'America's problem', but the United States has many problems which loom as large or larger; for Canada, the United States is *the* problem.

MASON WADE, The American Assembly, *The U.S. and Canada*, 1964, 30.

Canadians should stop harping about their problems. We have our problems, but they are as nothing compared with those that other nations have to face.

WALTER L. GORDON, *A choice for Canada: independence or colonial status*, 1966, 122.

Canada is a country whose major problems are never solved.

A.R.M. LOWER, *My first seventy-five years*, 1967, 213.

We know we have a very fortunate country, fortunate almost beyond belief. We have problems, but we know that they are not great compared with the problems of other peoples. But we need to solve them before they become great, and before someone comes to solve them for us.

PIERRE E. TRUDEAU, speech, Renfrew, Ont., June 24, 1968.

There are two kinds of problems, those that get better and almost solve themselves and those that get worse. You can afford to let the first type ride, but you better get the second fast.

JOHN TURNER, qu. in *Maclean's*, Aug., 1973, 34.

Professionalism

The price of success must surely be constant vigilance with a steady effort to combine loyalty with independence of mind, discipline with individual responsibility and, in the last analysis, obedience to orders with the strictest professional standards.

VINCENT MASSEY, to the Professional Institute of the Public Service of Canada, Ottawa, Mar. 1, 1958.

Professions

The bankers class me as a lawyer; the lawyers class me as an economist, and I'd hate to think what the economists class me as.

> JAMES E. COYNE, qu. in P. Newman, *Renegade in power*, 1963, 296.

Profits

I have come from the heart of a nation where they are sweating blood to win this war. Profits! I stand before you to say this: in the past we have all had our ideas about profits, but – with men sacrificing their lives for us, to hell with profits.

> SIR JOSEPH FLAVELLE, address to munitions manufacturers, Toronto, Dec., 1916, on return from England.

I claim that we have come to a period in the history of our country when we must decide once and for all which shall prevail, profits or human welfare.

> J.S. WOODSWORTH, H. of C., *Debates*, Mar. 14, 1922, 87.

Capitalism revolves around profit – an ugly word, but if you do away with the profit motive you are acting in a manner totally contrary to the human instinct. There is strength in capitalism. Money in itself doesn't bring happiness, but often the *pursuit* of money does.

> J.V. CLYNE, Chairman of MacMillan Bloedel Co., in *Maclean's*, June, 1973, 41.

Programs

These are not so much programs as slogans directed to troubled people looking for simple answers to complicated problems.

> ANTHONY WESTELL, Toronto *Star*, May 27, 1971, 6.

Progress

Then (in 1868) new blood pulsed in our veins, new hopes fired our hearts, new horizons lifted and widened, new visions came to us in the night watches. We faced geography and distance and fought them to a standstill. We shamed the croaker and the pessimist and the coward into silence, and then re-created him into a good citizen at the glowing fires of optimism and of hope. The plains were belted with steel, the mountains tamed and tunnelled, our national arteries were well filled with the rich blood of commerce, our industries grew, our workmen multiplied, our villages became towns and our towns became cities, with astonishing rapidity. Across the seas we clasped hands with our sister nations within the Empire and surrounded with a cordon of love and defence the old empire that gave birth to us all.

> GEORGE E. FOSTER, H. of C., *Debates*, Feb. 14, 1911, 3562.

True progress can come only as the result of thoughtful, continuous, cooperative effort. This progress will necessarily be slow, but it must be continuous. Nothing can hinder it more than the mistakes of thoughtless impatience.

> HENRY WISE WOOD, *Grain growers' guide*, Jan. 29, 1919, 28.

For it must be remembered that in politics, as in moral character, there is no static condition; and there is just the danger that we may mistake movements for progress, and confuse activity with advance.

> W.P.M. KENNEDY, *Can. hist. rev.*, 1921, 7.

It is not within the power of the properly constructed mind to be satisfied. Progress would cease if this were the case. The greatest joy of life is to accomplish. It is the getting, not the having. It is the giving not the keeping. I am a firm believer in the theory that you can do or be anything that you wish in this world, within reason, if you are prepared to make the sacrifices, think and work hard enough and long enough.

> SIR FREDERICK BANTING, qu., *Univ. of Tor. quart.*, 1940-41, 252.

All the answers face the same dilemma: Those who want to maintain separateness also want the advantages of the age of progress. These two ends are not compatible, for the pursuit of one negates the pursuit of the other.

> GEORGE P. GRANT, *Lament for a nation*, 1965, 76.

To progress is to destroy what one thought had been acquired.

> JEAN-PAUL RIOPELLE, on programme "Telescope", C.B.C.-TV, May 21, 1965; attributed.

For most thoughtful people progress has lost most of its original sense of a favourable value-judgment and has become simply progression, towards a goal more likely to be a disaster than an improvement.

> NORTHROP FRYE, *The modern century*, 1967, 34.

My generation of Canadians grew up believing that, if we were very good or very smart, or both, we would someday *graduate* from Canada.

> ROBERT FULFORD, *Saturday night*, Oct., 1970, 11.

Progressive Party

The record of two ideas warring in the bosom of a single group.

> EUGENE FORSEY, *Can. jour, econ and pol. sci.* Vol. 17, May, 1951, 257, referring to W.L. Morton's *The progressive party in Canada*, 1950.

Prohibition

Experience has convinced me that public sentiment in this country is not ripe for prohibition and never will be in my time. Any attempt to enforce such a law would be a failure and would be injurious to the administration of all laws.

> SIR GEORGE W. ROSS, Premier of Ont., 1899-1905, qu. in H.W. Charlesworth, *More candid chronicles*, 1928, 192.

Committee of One Hundred.

> Leading prohibition organization active in Ontario, 1919.

Promiscuity

A woman will transfer herself bodily over and over again, but only because the previous owner lightly esteemed, or weakly maintained, his ownership.

> ARNOLD HAULTAIN, *Hints for lovers*, 1909, 64.

Promises

Mankind lives on promises.

> THOMAS C. HALIBURTON, *Sam Slick's wise saws*, 1853, ch. 11.

Now a promise is a debt unpaid, and
    the trail has its own stern code.
In the days to come, though my lips
    were dumb, in my heart how I
    cursed that load.

> ROBERT W. SERVICE, "The cremation of Sam McGee", 1907.

It will not be an easy time, but it will, I pledge you, be a time to excite the daring, to test the strong, and to give new promise to the timid.

LESTER B. PEARSON, Apr. 23, 1963, in Ottawa, on being sworn in as head of a minority government.

We will never sacrifice, in the name of progress, a clean and healthy environment to industrial or commercial development. We will never allow, in the name of efficiency or social welfare, an omnipresent government to substitute itself to the right to privacy or to any other individual freedom. We will not allow, in the name of freedom of speech, sectarianism to replace tolerance; violence, dialogue; discrimination, moderation.

PIERRE E. TRUDEAU, H. of C., *Debates*, Oct. 24, 1969, 40; version in *Best of Trudeau*, 1972, 20 and *Conversations with Canadians*, 1972, 13, differ from the Hansard version.

Promises, Political

The next time you see Jesus Christ, ask Him what happened to the just society He promised 2,000 years ago.

PIERRE ELLIOTT TRUDEAU, Regina, Sept. 29, 1972, in reply to a high school student's question about what happened to Trudeau's "Just Society" promises.

Propaganda

The propagandist who operates on human appetites and human emotions leaves us no time for study and reflection. His noisy exhortations drown out the quiet, critical, questioning voices which, exposing error, used to help to open the way to truth.

VINCENT MASSEY, address to the Alumni of the Collège de Montréal, Oct. 27, 1954.

Canadians: Stand Together, Understand Together.

INFORMATION CANADA, poster issued early 1970's.

Learn, Baby, Learn.

INFORMATION CANADA, poster issued early 1970's.

The successor to politics will be propaganda. Propaganda, not in the sense of a message or ideology, but as the impact of the whole technology of the times. So politics will eventually be replaced by imagery. The politician will be only too happy to abdicate in favour of his image, because the image will be so much more powerful than he could ever be.

MARSHALL MCLUHAN, to Peter Newman, qu. in *Maclean's*, June, 1971, 45.

Property

The line of the ruling class everywhere is – Property first, Man afterwards. We say: "Man first, Property afterwards!"

JOHN MCCORMACK, Toronto unionist, 1872, qu. in Charles Lipton, *The trade union movement of Canada: 1827-1959*, 1967, 53.

It is surely an inescapable conclusion that a social structure in which the rights of property are paramount, and an economic order in which the motive power is acquisitiveness and the certain result a division of society into rich and poor, are incompatible with the mind of Christ.

R.B.Y. SCOTT, in R.B.Y. Scott and G. Vlastos eds., *Towards the Christian revolution*, 1937, 104.

The best land is the human mind.

MAURICE L. DUPLESSIS, qu. by Gérard Bergeron in *Univ. of Tor. quart.*, Vol. 27, Apr., 1958, 357.

I only buy, and then rent; I never sell.

> ALEXIS NIHON, Montreal industrialist, qu. in *Can. mag.*, July 29, 1972, 18.

Prophecy

The perjured evidence of W.B. Crew, Thorne and Bridgeford will haunt them in after years. They will never die a natural death; and when you, sir, and the jury, and all those who take part in my sentence, shall have died and perished in hell's flames, John Montgomery will yet be living on Yonge Street.

> JOHN MONTGOMERY, (paraphrased), tavern-keeper, to Judge John Beverley Robinson after sentence of execution, Apr. 10, 1838. He outlived two men who were suicides, and the judge, jurors, witnesses and the prosecutor.

I am not a prophet, but I would predict five great coming events: first, the prevalence of the Anglo-Saxon tongue; secondly, the removal of the tariff; third, political equality; fourth, equal distribution of wealth according to skill and ability; and fifth, restriction of liquor traffic to such an extent as to guarantee absolute sobriety.

> REV. CHARLES W. GORDON, speech at suffragists' meeting, May, 1912; qu. in C.L. Cleverdon, *The woman suffrage movement in Canada*, 1974, xviii.

Prophecy consists of carefully bathing the inevitable in the eerie light of the impossible, and being the first to announce it.

> ROBERTSON DAVIES, *Samuel Marchbanks' almanack*, 1967, 112.

Proselytizing

In the pluralism of modern Christianity, there is no reason why one should try to win over another group to one's own convictions.

> ERNEST HARRISON, *A church without God*, 1966, 80.

Prospecting

There's a saying among prospectors, "Go out looking for one thing, and that's all you'll ever find".

> ROBERT FLAHERTY, qu. in A. Calder-Marshall, *The innocent eye*, 1963, 23.

Prospectors

Nothing to him was lack of company or of newspapers; short days and approach of winter; seas of mountains and grassless valleys, equally inhospitable; risk of sickness and certainty of storms; slow and exhausting travel through marsh and muskeg, across roaring mountain torrents and miles of fallen timber; lonely days and lonely nights; – if he found gold he would be repaid.

> GEORGE M. GRANT, *Ocean to ocean*, 1873, 267.

Prosperity

I, therefore, need scarcely state my firm belief that the prosperity of Canada depends upon its permanent connection with the Mother country, and that I shall resist, to the utmost, any attempt (from whatever quarter it may come) which may tend to weaken that union.

> SIR JOHN A. MACDONALD, letter, "To the Free and Independent Electors of Kingston", Oct. 5, 1844; his first political address.

Love for Canada has to be acquired by the prosperity of the country, and from our children.

> JOHN S. HELMCKEN, B.C., *Debates on Confederation*, 1870, 13.

Prosperity never spoils men that adversity cannot crush.

> ROBERT C. (BOB) EDWARDS, Calgary *Eye Opener*, Nov. 24, 1917.

In time of prosperity prepare for trouble.

> CLIFFORD SIFTON, letter to his son, Harry, Feb. 9, 1929.

There can be no betterment in the standard of living by any distribution of unearned money. Nothing but a distribution of goods needed by humanity can help the standard of living, and these goods must first be brought into being. You cannot Beveridge a country into prosperity any more than a lawyer can make his client rich by drawing up his Will.

> ARTHUR MEIGHEN, speech in Vancouver, Oct. 21, 1943.

I would never wish anyone a life of prosperity and security. These are bound to betray. I would wish instead for adventure, struggle and challenge.

> DR. MARION HILLIARD, *A woman doctor looks at love and life*, 1957, 180.

Prostitutes

You want it or you don't
You got five bucks or no
I'm twenty-one I ain't
Got any time to waste
You want it or you don't
Make up your jesus mind.

> RAYMOND SOUSTER, "Girl at the corner of Elizabeth and Dundas", 1955.

Prostitution

Our painful sacrifice protects
The more fastidious of our sex;
If horizontal trade were halted
Upright girls might be assaulted.

> MAVOR MOORE, "The oldest", *And what do you do?*, 1960, 41.

Important as the economic and sociological explanations were for women's turning to prostitution, the impression will not down that many women were born with a predisposition toward the trade.

> JAMES H. GRAY, *Red lights on the prairies*, 1971, 24.

Protection

Protection.

> SIR ALEXANDER GALT, introduced the protection principle in the Tariff Act of 1858.

The word 'protection' itself must be taboo, but we can ring the changes on National Policy, paying the U.S. in their own coin.

> SIR JOHN A. MACDONALD, letter to D.L. MacPherson, Feb. 20, 1872.

Protection is a monster when you come to look at it. It is the essence of injustice. It is the acme of human selfishness. It is one of the relics of barbarism.

> ALEXANDER MACKENZIE, Prime Minister, letter of 1876.

Those who cared to be protected at all, wanted all the protection they could get. They were like the squaw who said of whisky, that 'a little too much was just enough'.

> SIR JOHN A. MACDONALD, in debate on introduction of National Policy, 1878; qu. in Biggar, *Anecdotal life*, 1891, 137.

Yes, Protection has done so much for me I must do something for Protection!

> SIR JOHN A. MACDONALD, to Goldwin Smith on the eve of 1878 election; qu. by Smith in letter to Toronto *Globe*, Sept. 23, 1895.

I denounce the policy of protection as bondage – yea, bondage; and I refer to bondage in the same manner in which American slavery was bondage.

> SIR WILFRID LAURIER, speech in Winnipeg, Sept. 3, 1894.

When the workers of Canada wake up they will find that Protection is only one among the several economic fangs fastened in their "corpus vile" by the little group of railroad men, bankers, lumber men and manufacturing monopolists who own their country.

> J.A. HOBSON, *Canada today* , 1906, 47.

I have no politics other than Protection, and I hope none of you have. If you have them, I think you should sink them for the good of the Association, for Protection is the only politics the Association should recognize.

> W.H. ROWLEY, 1910, address to Canadian Manufacturers' Assoc., in *Industrial Canada*, Oct., 1910, 322.

I am a Chinese-wall protectionist. I don't mean merely in trade. I mean – everything. I'd keep the American idea out of this country.

> SIR WILLIAM VAN HORNE, qu. in A. Bridle, *Sons of Canada*, 1916, 198.

Protest

These moralists are growing over-nice:
Surely, my friend, some need there is
    for spice!
The salt and pepper of impropriety–
I would not call it vice.

> TOM MACINNES, "Protest", 1918.

The way to get things out of a government is to back them to the wall, put your hands to their throats, and you will get all they have.

> AGNES MACPHAIL, speech to Southern Progressive Assoc., Regina, Sask., 1927.

Protestants

The killing of a Protestant is not murder, and therefore no crime!!!!

> *CHRISTIAN GUARDIAN*, Toronto, Mar. 5, 1856, qu. in John S. Moir, *Church and state in Canada West*, 1959, 19.

Had I but consented to take the popular side in Upper Canada, I could have ridden the Protestant horse much better than George Brown, and could have had an overwhelming majority. But I willingly sacrificed my own popularity for the good of the country, and did equal justice to all men.

> SIR JOHN A. MACDONALD, letter to a friend, Ottawa, Apr. 20, 1869.

He has raised the Protestant flag and sounded the Protestant war cry – Down with the French, if not with the ballot in this generation then with the bayonet in the next.

> *MANITOBA FREE PRESS*, July 26, 1889, on Dalton McCarthy.

It was the so-called genius of Protestantism to invent a form of Christianity without sacrifice.

> REV. BERNARD VAUGHAN, S.J., speech in St. Patrick's church, Montreal, Sept. 7, 1910.

Proverbs

Proverbs are distilled facts steamed down to an essence.

> THOMAS C. HALIBURTON, *Sam Slick*; attributed.

Provinces

Each little Province is a little nation by itself.

> SIR CHARLES TUPPER, Halifax *British colonist*, Nov. 17, 1864, unsigned editorial.

It seems that the smaller the province the more trouble it will be. Columbia, Manitoba, and Prince Edward Island give me more trouble than Ontario and Quebec.

ALEX. MACKENZIE, letter to Lord Dufferin, July 27, 1874.

Confederation, so far, has done nothing to fuse the races, and very little even to unite the provinces . . . From the composition of a cabinet to the composition of a rifle team, sectionalism is the rule.

GOLDWIN SMITH, *Political destiny of Canada*, 1878, 16.

Each Province has attractions for its children.

GEORGE M. GRANT, address to Canadian Club, New York, 1887.

Canadian Provinces they lay
Divided by river and by bay,
Many a separate division
Among them there was not cohesion.

JAMES MCINTYRE, "Canada before the Confederation of the Provinces", 1889.

Our opponents' array, on the other hand, is most literally a thing of shreds and patches, made up of the ragged remnants from half a dozen minor Provinces, the great majority of whom do not even pretend to be actuated by any principle save that of securing a good slice of booty for themsleves.

SIR RICHARD CARTWRIGHT, Toronto *Globe*, Mar. 9, 1891, 6, referring to the Maritimes and B.C. after the election of Mar., 1891, as the source of Sir John A. Macdonald's small majority; sometimes phrased "the shreds and patches of Confederation" from Shakespeare, "A thing of shreds and patches".

Provincial rights are not a species of squatter sovereignty. A province cannot acquire exclusive authority over a subject by usurpation.

DAVID MILLS, H. of C., *Debates*, Mar. 18, 1896, 3835.

I am now simply what I have always been − a Province man.

LEMUEL J. TWEEDIE, speech in New Brunswick Legislature, Mar. 1, 1901.

Provincial rights.

ANON., a term derived from the provincial decisions of the Privy Council.

Each province should be an independent country with power to do whatever it pleases. And I would have a wall between the provinces and the Dominion, and I would have no appeal, no veto, and no remedial appeal, none of all that misery we have had here since Confederation; and each province would have its own courts.

ARTHUR BEAUCHESNE, in House of Commons, *Method of amending B.N.A. Act*, 1935, 134.

The Provincial conception of nationhood.

R.B. BENNETT, a phrase used in a speech in Winnipeg, July 5, 1937.

No Province has the right to reduce in that Province the political rights of its citizens as compared with those enjoyed by the citizens of other Provinces of Canada.

LAWRENCE A.D. CANNON, Supreme Court decision, Mar. 4, 1938, on Alberta newspaper muzzling act.

National unity must be based on provincial autonomy, and provincial autonomy cannot be assured unless a strong feeling of national unity exists throughout Canada.

CANADA. ROY. COMM. ON DOMINION-PROVINCIAL RELATIONS (Sirois), *Report*, Book II, Sect. G, 1940, 269. .

Provincial autonomy will be gone. Provincial independence will vanish. Provincial dignity will disappear. Provincial governments will become mere annuitants of Ottawa.

> ANGUS I. MACDONALD, Premier of Nova Scotia, in Canada. Dominion-Provincial Conference on Reconstruction, Ottawa, Apr. 29, 1946, *Report of proceedings*, 39, re surrendering rights to collect income and corporation tax.

Some of the hallowed nonsense that goes into the theory of Canadian federalism is that each of the provinces constitutes a particular culture which federalism safeguards, but with the exception of Quebec it is never made clear just what these cultural differences are, or if the differences exist why they are more important than the similarities.

> JOHN PORTER, *The vertical mosaic*, 1965, 382.

I believe the time has come to recognize that in the interests of economic realities the boundaries of some of the Provinces will have to be altered and the separate existence of some other Provinces will have to be abolished so as to provide five viable and effective political units consonant and in conformity with the five economic regions of Canada.

> W.A.C. BENNETT, *Proposals of the Province of British Columbia on the Constitution of Canada*, 1968, 13.

One Prairie Province.

> ANON., phrase associated with the feasibility of amalgamating three prairie provinces; also, *One Prairie Province Conference*, May, 1970.

There's a basic difference between power and image. Image is going on television a lot. Power is doing things. Federal politics is image. Provincial politics is power. For the last 10 years we've all been looking in the wrong place. We thought Ottawa ran the country. [The premiers] know better. Ottawa runs itself. *They* run the country.

> *MACLEAN'S,* editorial, Feb. 1973, 19.

Provincial Subsidies

Provincial subsidies are a tangle of opportunism and necessity.

> A.W. BOOS, *Financial arrangements*, 1930.

When a subsidy is increased in order to equalize the treatment among the provinces, further adjustments became immediately necessary in order to overcome the injustices which have been occasioned by the very act of equalization.

> R. MACGREGOR DAWSON, *The government of Canada*, 1947, 123.

Provincialism

Provincialism and nationality are different degrees of the same thing, and both take their rise in the same feeling, love of country.

> T.C. HALIBURTON, *Sam Slick*, 1840, 271.

I am not one of those who thank God I am a Nova Scotian merely, for I am a Canadian as well.

> JOSEPH HOWE, speech in Halifax, Aug. 13, 1864, to leaders of Confederation from the Canadas.

If you just hole up in Canada and refuse to educate yourself you are going to be provincial. But if you flee the country, cut yourself off from your roots, you may end up not even being that.

JAMES REANEY, *Univ. of Tor. quart.*, Apr., 1957, 293.

Prudence

Prudence will get us what nothing else can. Remember prudence means a combination of two important qualities, piety and practical sagacity.

WILLIAM ABERHART, in his later years, qu. in *Maclean's*, Mar. 15, 1953, 59.

Prudery

The colonial position of Canada is therefore a frostbite at the roots of the Canadian imagination, and it produces a disease for which I think the best name is prudery.

NORTHROP FRYE, *Can. forum*, Vol. 23, 1943, 208.

The sort of prudery that once proscribed the discussion of vice now proscribes the discussion of virtue.

ANON., qu. by J.A. Corry in address at Convocation, Queen's University, Oct. 20, 1967.

Psychology

Psychology can make us conscious of our disguises, can make us wrestle with them, despise them, sneer at them, weep over them; but only love can remove the necessity for wearing them.

DONALD PEARCE, *Journal of a war*, 1965, 81.

Ptarmigan

The ptarmigan – a kind of grouse,
Lives in the Arctic with his spouse.
The ptarmigan is smart and perky
And tastes much better than a
    pturkey.

FARLEY MOWAT, "The ptarmigan", 1967.

The Public

Sarve the public nine hundred and ninety-nine times, and the thousandth, if they don't agree with you, they desart and abuse you.

T.C. HALIBURTON, *Sam Slick*, 1836, ch. 15.

There is no gratitude to be expected from the public. I have found that out years ago.

SIR JOHN A. MACDONALD, letter to George Stephen, Aug. 7, 1888. (Pub. Arch. Can.)

The Canadian public is ignorant, cowardly and snobbish; it is mortally afraid of ideas and considers the discussion of first principles as a betrayal of bad manners.

FREDERICK PHILIP GROVE, *Univ. of Tor. quart.*, Vol. VII, No. 4, July, 1938, 459.

Politicians love to refer to the little people, or the common man or the small farmer or businessman. If you listen close enough, you'll soon become aware that Canada is populated by midgets.

J.L. WILD, speaking to London, Ont. Junior Chamber of Commerce, qu. in *Liberty*, Aug., 1963.

Public Life

I hate politics, and what are considered their appropriate methods. I hate notoriety, public meetings, public speeches, caucuses, and everything that I know of that is apparently the necessary incident of politics – except doing public work to the best of my ability. Why should I go where the doing of honest work will only make me hated and my ministry unpopular, and where I can only gain reputation and credit by practising arts which I detest, to acquire popularity?

SIR JOHN J.C. ABBOTT, letter to a friend in Ottawa, June 4, 1891.

A public man should have no resentments.

SIR JOHN A. MACDONALD, to his secretary, Joseph Pope; qu. in Pope, *Sir John A. Macdonald vindicated*, 1912, 19.

Public Opinion

Its [Upper Canada's] inhabitants scattered along an extensive frontier, with very imperfect means of communication, and a limited and partial commerce, have, apparently no unity of interest or opinion.

LORD DURHAM, *Report*, 1839. (Lucas ed. 1912, II, 146.)

Is there no public opinion in that country?

SIR JOSEPH CHAMBERLAIN, to Sir Oliver Mowat, Premier of Ontario, 1872-1896, when he said he had been in office many years.

There is no public opinion in Canada.

PETER MCARTHUR, qu. a friend, in *New era in Canada*, ed. by Miller, 1917, 333.

Quebec does not have opinions, but only sentiments.

SIR WILFRID LAURIER; attributed.

Government, in the last analysis, is organized opinion. Where there is little or no public opinion, there is likely to be bad government, which sooner or later becomes autocratic government.

W.L. MACKENZIE KING, *Message of the carillon*, 1927, 139.

The genius of the British peoples for political association consists perhaps not so much in a power of constructing good institutions as in the invincible habit of worshipping what they have constructed. This makes even a bad organization work well.

P.E. CORBETT, *Can. jour. econ. and pol. sci.*, 1938, 114.

Public opinion nearly always demands the irrational.

FREDERICK P. GROVE, *The master of the mill*, 1944, 299.

Do you wish to know what public opinion is? It is the opinion of those who are against us.

MAURICE DUPLESSIS, qu. in P. Laporte, *The true face of Duplessis*, 1960, 34.

Public Ownership

There is no virtue in "public ownership" outside the wisdom, capacity and integrity of those who direct such enterprises.

SIR JOHN WILLISON, *Willison's monthly*, June, 1925, 9.

Public Relations

No firm today can be without
A P.R. representative:
No football team, no sect devout,
No charity, nor Guide nor Scout
Nor even lords of beer and stout
Can get along without a tout's
Encomiums frequentative.

MAVOR MOORE, "The P.R. representative", *And what do you do?*, 1960, 47.

Public Service

A public servant has no right to an opinion on any subject that's got two sides to it.

ROBERTSON DAVIES, *A voice from the attic*, 1960; attributed.

We're pushing the ministers from behind all the time. And so far, so good.

> ANON., Quebec civil servant, early
> 1960's, qu. in Peter Desbarats, *The state
> of Quebec*, 1965, 106.

Any civil servant above clerical or
stenographic grades who has spent any
substantial time in a job without contributing to some degree to the policy
he administers should be fired, whatever the security of his employment is
supposed to be.

> R.G. ROBERTSON, *Can. public admin.*, XI,
> No. 3, 1968, 272.

You have a system where people who
are neither elected nor appointed, not
accountable to anyone but the Prime
Minister, are making all the decisions.
A policy comes across your desk, and
you are asked to comment on it, but
you know the final say is going to
come from somebody in the Super-
group.

> ANON., senior civil servant, August, 1970,
> qu. in W. Stewart, *Shrug*, 1971, 173.

Publicity

People just read headlines. The secret
of political success is getting the press
— with or against is immaterial as far
as I'm concerned.

> TOM CAMPBELL, Mayor of Vancouver,
> qu., *Maclean's*, June, 1973, 84.

Publishing

I would, perhaps, have attempted to
do more, but while I have published a
volume a year for every year that I
have been in business — by none of
them making much, and by some of
them losing heavily, I trust I have
done something, to point the way
towards a field which will by and by
admit of more brilliant and profitable
cultivation.

> JOSEPH HOWE, *The Novascotian*, Dec.
> 30, 1841, final editorial.

The growth of literature in every
country depends a good deal on the
enterprise and liberality of its publishers. In this branch of my profession I
have endeavoured, I trust, to set a
good example.

> JOSEPH HOWE, *The Novascotian*, Dec.
> 30, 1841, final editorial.

In the articles of paper, ink and type;
and in the whole book trade, the
reciprocity is all on one side. The
Americans have an advantage in this
market, of from fifteen to twenty
percent, over the resident capitalists
who might be disposed to embark or
who are embarked, in their production. The consequence is that Montreal
and Toronto houses are mere agencies
for New York publishers, having no
literary wares to exchange with Harper, or Putnam, or the Sadliers, or
Appleton.

> THOMAS D'ARCY MCGEE, *New era*, July
> 25, 1857, editorial.

Here we are in this business of Canadian literature with writers writing and
publishers publishing and booksellers
bookselling and lending libraries lending and readers reading — all going at
it like the milltail of hell, and all to
please the good doctor, and yet we
can't satisfy him.

> HUGH EAYRS, letter to the editor, *Mail
> and empire*, Nov. 7, 1934, referring to
> W.A. Deacon, book editor, decrying
> dearth of Canadian titles; qu. in On-
> tario. Roy. Comm. on Book Publishing,
> *Background papers*, 1972, 30.

To serve its constituency it must reveal the nation to itself, not only in its parts but as a unity.

> W.A. IRWIN, Editor of *Maclean's*, referring to periodical press, qu. in Periodical Press Assoc., *Brief* to Royal Comm. on Nat. Dev. in the Arts, Letters and Sciences, Oct. 27, 1949, 2.

Never again can the whim of a foreign publisher numb us. Never again can a foreign publisher tyrannize over our policy. Never again will any publisher anywhere tell us what we must or must not do, and when we must or must not do it. We have grown up.

> LORNE PIERCE, *The house of Ryerson*, 1954, 51. Ryerson was sold to McGraw-Hill, U.S. Publisher, Nov., 1970.

Those Canadian writers who derive any important part of their income from their books (apart of course from textbooks) do not earn it in Canada and are not dependent on a Canadian publisher.

> JOHN GRAY, in George Whalley, ed., *Writing in Canada*, 1956, 58.

I have always felt Canadian magazines, like any other Canadian business, should stand on their own two feet or go under.

> STUART KEATE, Publisher of Victoria *Times*, in Toronto *Star*, June 16, 1961, 51.

Canadian editions.

> ANON., phrase referring to editions of American magazines, notably *Time* and *Reader's digest*.

Publication is a self-invasion of privacy.

> MARSHALL MCLUHAN, *Counterblast*, 1969, 103.

I find it ironical that *Made in Canada* is printed in England.

> J.A. HARRIS, review of *Made in Canada: new poems of the seventies*, 1970, ed. by Douglas Lochhead and Raymond Souster, in *Can. forum*, June, 1971, 38.

Those sons of up there will steal anything they can get their hands on . . . possible suits for damages and felony would be no more restraint upon them, I think, than would the presence of a young lady be upon a stud horse who had just found a mare unprotected by international copyright.

> MARK TWAIN, ca. 1880, qu. in Ron Poulton, *The paper tyrant*, 1971, 90.

If Canadians spoke Swahili and dealt in razbuckniks, Canada would have a healthy and vigorous Canadian-owned book publishing industry. But, because we have the misfortune of speaking English and dealing in dollars, our publishing industry is fighting for its survival.

> PETER MARTIN, *Brief* to Ontario Royal Comm. on Book Publishing, Mar., 1971, 8.

Publishing is the interface between a nation's writers and readers.

> ONTARIO. ROY . COMM. ON BOOK PUBLISHING, *Report*, 1973, 10.

Pudenda

It amazes me that organs that piss
Can give human beings such perfect bliss

> IRVING LAYTON, "Aphs", *The whole bloody bird*, 1969, 97.

Punctuality

Punctuality is the soul of business.

> THOMAS C. HALIBURTON, *Sam Slick's wise saws*, 1853, ch. 3.

Pundits

Some holy men so love their cells they
make
Their four gray walls the whole
damned stinking world
And God comes in and fills it easily.

A.J.M. SMITH, "Bird and flower", 1954.

Puritanism

Puritans, whether in or out of church
make more sinners than they save by a
long chalk. They ain't content with
real sin.

THOMAS C. HALIBURTON, *Nature and
human nature*, 1855.

Purpose

Some bond more uniting than a shiftless expediency; some lodestar more
potent than a mere community of
profit.

W.A. FOSTER, *Canada first: or, our new
nationality*, 1871, 29-30, on national
purpose.

This North whose heart of fire
Yet knows not its desire
Clearly, but dreams, and murmurs in
the dream.
The hour of dreams is done. Lo, on the
hills the gleam!

CHARLES G.D. ROBERTS, "Ode for the
Canadian Confederacy", 1880.

A purpose, a determined will,
Can soar above earth's highest hill,
And bid the troubled waves be still.

ALEXANDER MCLACHLAN, *Canadian
birthday book*, 1887, 18.

Many people regard an earnest selfishness as the only earnest purpose.

PETER MCARTHUR, *To be taken with salt*,
1903, 153.

Set the strong shaft of purpose to the
cord
And send it singing to the mark.

ROBERT NORWOOD, *Witch of Endor*,
1916, 28.

If we be true to our just cause, the
upward way will not deter us; the
giants cannot overcome us.

HENRY WISE WOOD, address at U.F.A.
convention, in *U.F.A.*, Feb. 1, 1923, 17.

That puzzled moment when you look
up and ask, 'What is it I was going to
say?' and it won't come. There are
those who to the end of their days are
haunted by the unanswered query,
'What was it I was going to do?'

DONALD PEARCE, *Journal of a war*,
1965, 81.

The void we sense
surrounding us
is only indirection.

RED LANE, "The realization", 1968.

Pursuits

What shadows we are, what shadows
we pursue.

J. HOWE, speech at Ottawa Y.M.C.A.,
Feb. 27, 1872.

Quebec Act, 1774

By being made perpetual, it is evident that this constitution is meant to be both an instrument of tyranny to the Canadians, and an example to others of what they have to expect; at some time or other it will come home to England.

> EDMUND BURKE, Gt. Brit., H. of C., *Debates* (Cavendish), May 31, 1774, 89.

Quebec (City)

Nothing struck me as so beautiful and grand as the location of the town of Quebec, which could not be better situated even were it to become, in some future time, the Capital of a great Empire.

> FRONTENAC, in a letter, Nov. 2, 1672, qu. in *Can. hist. rev.*, 1921, II, 365. (Trans.)

Quebec is impregnable.

> MARQUIS DE VAUDREUIL-CAVAGNAL, in 1759, just before the capture of Quebec, attributed by C. Hibbert, *Wolfe at Quebec*, 1959, 53.

The French thought building a fortress was colonization, and the English that blowing it up was the right way to settle the country.

> T.C. HALIBURTON, *Nature and human nature*, 1855, II, 388.

Such works do not consist with the development of the intellect. Huge stone structures of all kinds, both in their erection and by their influence when erected, rather oppress than liberate the mind.

> HENRY THOREAU, *Yankee in Canada*, 1866, (1961, 99).

Quebec, the grey old city on the hill,
Lies with a golden glory on her head,
Dreaming throughout this hour so fair, so still,
Of other days and her beloved dead.

> JEAN BLEWETT, "At Quebec", 1897.

Like some grey warder who, with
    mien sedate
  And smile of welcome, greets the
    throngs who pour
  Between the portals of a
    wide-thrown door,
Quebec stands guardian at our water
    gate,
And watches from her battlemented
    state
  The great ships passing with their
    living store
  Of human myriads coming to our
    shore,
Expectant, joyous, resolute, elate.

> FREDERICK GEORGE SCOTT, "Quebec", 1928.

Quebec Conference, 1864

We consulted the oracles of history and our race. We strove to build upon an old foundation, not to run up a showy edifice for ourselves, but a

piece of solid British masonry as solid
as the foundation of Eddystone which
would bear the whole force of democratic winds and waves.

THOMAS D'ARCY MCGEE, speech at Montreal, Oct. 29, 1864.

Quebec (Province)

I believe that France can be happy
without Quebec.

VOLTAIRE, letter to Choiseul, Sept. 6,
1762. (Trans.)

Quebec, at least for an American, is
certainly a very peculiar place.

BENJAMIN SILLIMAN, *Tour of Quebec,
1819,* 1822, 110.

My aim was to elevate the Province of
Lower Canada to a thoroughly British
character, to link its people to the
sovereignty of Britain, by making
them all participators in those high
privileges, conducive at once to freedom and order, which have long been
the glory of Englishmen. I hoped to
confer on a united people a more
extensive enjoyment of free and responsible government, and to merge
the petty jealousies of a small community, and the odious animosities of
origin, in the higher feelings of a
nobler and more comprehensive nationality.

LORD DURHAM, Proclamation, issued
Oct. 9, 1838.

Is it just that the prosperity of this
great majority, and of this vast tract of
country, should be for ever, or even
for a while, impeded by the artificial
bar which the backward laws and
civilisation of a part, and a part only,
of Lower Canada, would place between them and the ocean? Was it to
be supposed that such an English population would ever submit to such a
sacrifice of its interests?

LORD DURHAM, *Report,* 1839. (Lucas ed.,
1912, II, 290.)

We will consent to no compromise
whatever on a principle so closely
bound up with the existence of our
nationality, of our religion, of all that
remains of our heritage from our fathers. Either equality of representation
for the two provinces [sic] or the
dissolution of the Union. Such ought to
be, and such without question will be
the program of all Lower Canadians,
to whatever religion, to whatever origin they belong. All those who will
sacrifice one iota of that program will
be traitors to justice, traitors to Lower
Canada, traitors to the fatherland.

LA MINERVE (Montreal), Feb. 2, 1861,
qu. in W.L. Morton, *The critical years,*
1964, 93. (Trans.)

An antediluvian relic of old French
society with its torpor and bigotry,
utterly without value for the purposes
of modern civilization.

GOLDWIN SMITH, *The Empire,* 1863, 5.

My warmest aspiration for this Province has always been to see its French
inhabitants executing for Canada the
functions which France herself performs for Europe.

LORD DUFFERIN, reply to an address
presented by Legis. Assembly of Quebec, June, 1878.

Je me souviens. (I remember.)

EUGÈNE TACHÉ, architect, motto added
to the coat-of-arms of Quebec, Feb. 9,
1883.

Quebec is the most interesting thing
by much that I have seen on this
continent.

MATTHEW ARNOLD, letter to Walter Arnold, Feb. 28, 1884; *Letters,* 1895, II,
308.

That this House is of opinion that the Province of Quebec would be disposed to accept the breaking of the Confederation Pact of 1867 if, in the other provinces, it is believed that she is an obstacle to the union, progress and development of Canada.

> J.N. FRANCOEUR, motion proposed in Legislative Assembly of Quebec, Jan. 17, 1918. (Trans.)

Quebec remained British because it was French.

> GEORGE M. WRONG, *Canada and the American revolution*, 1935, 260.

Can our brothers in the minority groups really believe that they would be worse off for the establishment of an autonomous French State, a true centre of culture which would radiate life and vigour?

> ABBÉ LIONEL GROULX, *Directives*, 1937, 127. (Trans.)

Whether one wishes it or not, we shall have our French State; we shall have it a young, strong, shining and beautiful, spiritual home, dynamic pole for all French America.

> ABBÉ LIONEL GROULX, address, Deuxième Congres de la Langue Française, Quebec, June 29, 1937.

It may take time, as much possibly as 50 years, but Quebec will become English-speaking. And there is great promise for Canada in the greater unity that will bring the nation.

> SIR WILLIAM MULOCK, interview on eve of 97th birthday, Toronto, Jan. 18, 1941.

Two solitudes.

> HUGH MACLENNAN, title of novel published in 1945; from Rainer Maria Rilke, "Love consists in this, that two solitudes protect and touch and greet each other", *Letters to a young poet*, May 14, 1904. (Trans.)

Every inch of it is measured, and brooded over by notaries, and blessed by priests.

> HUGH MACLENNAN, *Two solitudes*, 1945, 4.

The advantages of living with two
　　cultures
Strike one at every turn,
Especially when one finds a notice in
　　an office building:
"This elevator will not run on
　　Ascension Day".
Or reads in the *Montreal Star:*
"Tomorrow being the Feast of the
　　Immaculate Conception,
There will be no collection of garbage
　　in the city";
Or sees on the restaurant menu the
　　bilingual dish:
DEEP APPLE PIE
TARTE AUX POMMES PROFONDES.

> F.R. SCOTT, "Bonne entente", 1954.

Canada is an English country, inside which survives a French Canadian province, which is really an economic and political colony of the English Canadians.

> MICHEL BRUNET, *Canadians et Canadiens*, 1954, 165. (Trans.)

With regard to French-Canadian culture, the Province of Quebec assumes alone the responsibilites which the other provinces jointly assume with regard to Anglo-Canadian culture.

> QUEBEC. ROY. COMM. OF INQUIRY ON CONSTITUTIONAL PROBLEMS, *Report*, Vol. III; 2, 1956, 290.

In the land of the besieged, monolithism is *de rigueur*.

> JEAN-PAUL DESBIENS, *Les insolences du Frère Untel*, 1960, 35. (Trans.)

What does Quebec want?

> ANON., question raised by many Canadians, early 1960's.

To those who keep repeating 'What exactly does Quebec want'. I ask, 'What exactly do you want Quebec *not* to want?'

> JEAN LESAGE, Premier of Quebec, 1960-1966, speech at laying of cornerstone of Champlain College, qu. by D.G. Creighton, *Jour. of Can. stud.*, Vol. 1, May, 1966, 3.

No more than the United States allowed the South to secede would Canada voluntarily allow herself to be split in two. Never yet have we been shown how Quebec could peacefully achieve independence.

> ANDRÉ LAURENDEAU, *Le Devoir*, Feb. 20, 1961, 4. (Trans.)

Whether or not the Conquest was the origin of all evils and whether or not the English have been the most perfidious occupiers in the memory of man, it remains none the less true that the French-Canadian community holds in its hands, *hic et nunc*, the essential instruments for its regeneration.

> PIERRE E. TRUDEAU, *Cité libre*, No. 35 (new ser.), Mar., 1961, 3. (Trans.)

Open the frontiers, this people dies of asphyxiation!

> PIERRE E. TRUDEAU, *Cité libre*, No. 35 (new ser.), Mar., 1961, 5. (Trans.)

During the war, many French Canadians in Quebec felt as if they were living in an occupied country.

> ANDRÉ LAURENDEAU, *La crise de la conscription*, 1962, 156. (Trans.)

Quebec is not a province like the others. She is a little more stupid.

> GÉRARD FILION, in 1962, qu. by Brian Moore, *Canada*, 1963, 88.

Quebec is a State with limited jurisdiction which, designated as a province,

participates in the Canadian Federation. Quebec is also the national State of French Canadians; it governs, within the area of its jurisdiction, the majority of the descendants of the colonists of New France and the territory colonized by the latter.

> QUEBEC, *Quebec yearbook* (Annuaire), 1963, 23. (Trans.)

Once one is convinced that Quebec finds itself, because of its position as a "colony", in a situation of violence forced on it by the English from the time Wolfe defeated Montcalm in however fair a battle according to the monument erected in its memory on the edge of the Plains of Abraham — once one is convinced of that and believes that educating is propagating one's convictions, I declare that at that point there is not only an incitement to violence, but also, by anticipation, a sort of justification for violence.

> LEON DION, *Can. forum*, Aug., 1963, 106. (Trans.)

Where is there a change of borders that has made a single people any happier? Where is the geographic line, a wall or a fence, that can allow anyone to say, "Within this reserve happiness reigns?"

> PREMIER JEAN LESAGE, Christmas Message to the people of Quebec, Dec. 20, 1963.

I have lived for the past month a terrifying life. I have worked for my province as no man has ever worked for it. I have made use of all the means which Providence granted me. I have made use of all my colleagues, of all the experts available to me so that Quebec, finally, could be recognized as a province which has a *statut spécial* in Confederation, and I have succeeded.

> JEAN LESAGE, Québec, Assemblée legis., *Débats*, 1964, 2650. (Trans.)

He wavers between the past and the present, between dependence and independence, between regression and adventure, between his home and the world. If we accuse others of not understanding us, it is because we do not understand ourselves.

> DR. CAMILLE LAURIN, Univ. of Montreal, comparing modern Quebec to an adolescent, qu. in *Liberty*, Feb., 1964.

The malaise in Quebec cannot easily be defined, but it exists, and we know, or should know why; we, all of us, French- and English-speaking, are paying the price now for our attitudes in former years.

> VINCENT MASSEY, address, Assoc. of Canadian Clubs, Charlottetown, June 1, 1964.

There is a Latin beat in the air, the kind of excitement that you find only in countries where the Roman Catholic Church has attempted to inoculate a hot-blooded people with the conflicting serums of chastity and fertility.

> PETER DESBARATS, *The state of Quebec*, 1965, 73.

Quebec is not asking, from now on it is *demanding* respect for its jurisdiction.

> RENÉ LÉVESQUE, discussion period after speech at McGill University, Jan. 25, 1966.

This province is a country within a country. Québec the original heart. The hardest and deepest kernel. The core of first time. All around, nine other provinces form the flesh of this still-bitter fruit called Canada.

> ANNE HÉBERT, *Century 1867-1967*, 1967, 16.

Vive Montréal, vive le Québec, vive le Québec libre, vive le Canada francais, vive la France!

> CHARLES DE GAULLE, speech, Montreal, July 24, 1967, from the balcony of the Montreal City Hall.

I am closing the door to a solution which would destroy the country. I think particular status for Quebec is the biggest intellectual hoax ever foisted on the people of Quebec and the people of Canada.

> PIERRE E. TRUDEAU, press interview, Canadian Bar Association, Quebec City, Sept. 5, 1967.

Let us make every reasonable effort, every reasonable concession, to keep Quebec as part of a single Canadian political nationality: every *reasonable* concession: we cannot provide the dry water, sour sugar, boiling ice, stationary motion, which most of the "special status" proposals demand. But if the effort fails, as I am afraid it well may, let the rest of us, English-speaking and French-speaking, face the future without Quebec, in a Canada truncated, indeed, but viable, united and free:
'One equal temper of heroic hearts,
   To strive, to seek, to find, and not to yield'.

> EUGENE FORSEY, speech, Acadia Univ., Oct. 19, 1967.

Now if Quebec were to become another country, an associate state, or to be given some very special status or to become — well, if she were to become independent — she wouldn't be interested in Canada's Constitution, obviously. But where is the consensus in Canada: where is the consensus in this Conference of ten premiers that Quebec shall have anything that all other provinces haven't got, anything perhaps other than linguistic rights?

> JOSEPH R. SMALLWOOD, Confederation of Tomorrow Conf., Toronto, Nov. 28, 1967; *Proceedings*, 78.

Let us not confuse the rights of French Canadians with the desire of a provincial government to build a little empire for itself.

PIERRE E. TRUDEAU, speech to Quebec Liberal Party convention, Montreal, Jan. 28, 1968, qu. in *Le Devoir* (Montreal), Jan. 29, 1968, 1. (Trans.)

For me, Canada is a homeland, but one which is limited to the Province of Quebec.

ANON., French-Canadian student qu. in A.B. Hodgetts, *What culture? What heritage?*, 1968, 83. (Trans.)

Regardless of the discords among political parties, regardless of the often only half-concealed interests of certain classes of society, regardless of the deep, emotional fear of risk, it appears indisputable that Quebec is heading down a one-way street to sovereignty.

JEAN BLAIN, preface to René Lévesque, *An option for Quebec*, 1968, 9.

Without Quebec, Canada wouldn't have any heart and Canadian life would cease.

PIERRE E. TRUDEAU, speech, Aug. 2, 1969, at St. Georges de Beauce, Que., qu. in *The best of Trudeau*, 1972, 21. (Trans.)

If Quebec were alone, there would be no Quebec as we have known it, but you won't get rid of Quebec by wishing, fearing, hoping, suspecting, picking at sores. Quebec is our conscience.

HUGH HOOD, in Andy Wainwright, ed., *Notes for a native land*, 1969, 31.

In the past the Church had been the major institution of *la survivance:* today it is the state.

RAMSAY COOK, qu. in *Quebec, the threat of separation*, 1969, 13.

we will make you, Land of Quebec
a bed of resurrections
and in the myriad lightnings of our
   transformations
in this leaven of ours from which the
   future is rising
in our uncompromising wills
men will hear your pulse beating in
   history

GASTON MIRON, "L'Octobre", 1970. (Trans.)

There's no question of your obtaining socialist independence gradually in Quebec. So it must of course be through violence. I do not say this lightheartedly, it is the same everywhere.

JEAN-PAUL SARTRE, video-tape interview shown in Montreal, Jan. 16, 1971. (Trans.)

No one in the West any longer asks, "What does Quebec want?" The question has been replaced by a statement: "Let them go".

PETER DESBARATS, Toronto *Star*, Nov. 23, 1971, 9.

Washington has moved into first place in the hierarchy of enemies, Ottawa into second.

MARIO DUMAIS, French-Canadian radical, in *La barre du jour*, Nos. 31-32, Winter, 1972. (Trans.)

The Queen

The Executive Government and authority of and over Canada is hereby declared to continue and be vested in the Queen.

BRITISH NORTH AMERICA ACT, 1867, Sect. 9.

God save the Queen if she ever comes to Quebec.

> MICHAEL BEAULIEU, Editor, Univ. of Montreal student newspaper, speech on Confederation, Feb. 29, 1954, qu. in Vancouver *Sun*, Mar. 2, 1964, 21.

Some of the separatists are resolved to let her know brutally that she is not welcome in Quebec or French Canada.

> MARCEL CHAPUT, Toronto, Feb. 24, 1964, referring to proposed visit of the Queen to Quebec City in October, 1964.

Queen Victoria

Here's to thee, Queen Victoria
In all your bright regalia,
With one foot in Canada
And the other in Australia.

> JAMES GILLIS, also attributed to James Gay, qu. by F.R. Scott, address, Joint Dinner of the Assoc. of Can. Law Teachers and the Can. Pol. Science Assoc., Charlottetown, June 11, 1964.

Queen's University

On the old Ontario strand, my boys,
Where Queen's for evermore shall
    stand,
For has she not stood
Since the time of the flood,
On the old Ontario strand?

> ANON., chorus of students' song (*Songbook*, 1903); originally an America college song, adopted by Victoria College (Cobourg, Ont.), with wording of the last line "On the banks of the old Raritan", later adopted by Queen's.

Oil thigh na Banrighinn gu brath!
Cha Gheill! Cha Gheill! Cha Gheill!

> Queen's University yell adopted 1891; composed by Alfred E. Lavell and Messrs. F.A. McRae, D. Cameron, and McLean; see, *Queen's journal*, Nov. 8, 1946; trans: "The House of Learning of the Queen forever, – Never yield! Never yield! Never yield!"

Questions

The question is, how many pounds of powder put under a bull's tail would blow his horns off?

> SIR JOHN A. MACDONALD, to a Col. Playfair who was laying siege to Sir John A. in order to be made a road superintendent; qu. in Vancouver *Sun*, June 30, 1964.

I came upon a sudden door,
Which gave me no reply;
The more I questioned it, the more
A questioner was I.

> BLISS CARMAN, "Behind the arras", 1895.

A woman asks a woman questions in order to discover something. She asks a man questions in order to discover the man.

> ARNOLD HAULTAIN, *Hints for lovers*, 1909, 31.

Some analytic philosophers have seemed to go on the assumption that "there are no sides to every question".

> F.E. SPARSHOTT, *An enquiry into goodness*, 1958, 118.

It is possible to destroy
me.
One simply asks
the right
question.

> ANDREAS SCHROEDER, *#2*, in *File of uncertainties*, 1971.

Quiet

Most of life and most of art is best enjoyed quietly.

> FRANCIS SPARSHOTT, *Looking for philosophy*, 1972, 10.

Quotations

A wise saw is more valuable than a whole book, and a plain truth is better than an argument.

> T.C. HALIBURTON, *Nature and human nature*, 1855, I, 349.

And speaking of quotation, what is its use? The use is like that of an illustration, to make a point or situation more vivid, more emphatic, by a new light, by a suggestion which may be ridiculous, elevating, degrading, which enables you sometimes to put in the hearer's mind what you hardly dare, and could not, put into your own words.

> NICHOLAS F. DAVIN, in *Canadian monthly*, 1881, 285.

Perhaps the reader may ask, of what consequence is it whether the author's exact language is preserved or not, provided we have his thought. The answer is, that inaccurate quotation is a sin against truth. It may appear in any particular instance to be a trifle, but perfection consists in small things, and perfection is no trifle.

> ROBERT W. SHANNON, *Can. mag.*, Oct. 1898, 474.

Nothing can stand against a really resolute quoter.

> GOLDWIN SMITH, qu., *Empire Club speeches*, Apr. 11, 1911.

The phrase, beating its rhythm,
    preening its crest
against a critical oar, draws at the
    secret
till the day the oar rests as the wave
    sunders
and the fastidious implication emerges
a bloom to pelt, an excalibur to wield.

> ROBERT FINCH, "The reticent phrase", 1946.

To be apt in quotation is a splendid and dangerous gift. Splendid, because it ornaments a man's speech with other men's jewels; dangerous, for the same reason.

> ROBERTSON DAVIES, Toronto *Star*, Oct. 1, 1960, 30.

No great fat thick book of quotations can be called "familiar"; very few people can identify more than a dozen of them. Furthermore there are hundreds of quotations in such books which I solemnly swear are not familiar to anybody. The fake profundities of dead politicians, the treacly outpourings of fifth-rate poets, the moonlit nonsense of minor essayists – this junk makes up the bulk of most quotation books.

> ROBERTSON DAVIES, *Samuel Marchbanks' almanack*, 1967, 121.

Everyone knows that the apparatus of quotations and references needs careful staffwork.

> P.B. WAITE, *Dalhousie rev.*, Vol. 50, Winter, 1970-1971, 565.

R

Race

The idea of unity of races was utopian, it was impossible.

> GEORGE-ÉTIENNE CARTIER, *Confederation debates*, 1865, 60.

We come of a race that never counted the number of its foes, nor the number of its friends when freedom, loyalty, or God was concerned.

> GEORGE M. GRANT, *Ocean to ocean*, 1873, 366.

Race means here this very simple, very objective and independent aspect of our thought: An ethnical type which slowly developed in the course of the eighteenth century, which kept the mark of the old race and of its original civilization, which has never ceased to belong to it, but which, modified by environment and historical circumstances, possesses a distinctive soul and existence in the great French family.

> ABBÉ LIONEL GROULX, *Vers l'emancipation*, 1921, 9. (Trans.)

Canada's cursed heritage of race.

> A.R.M. LOWER, *Colony to nation*, 1947, 460.

To recommend what steps should be taken to develop the Canadian Confederation on the basis of an equal partnership between the two founding races, taking into account the contribution made by the other ethnic groups to the cultural enrichment of Canada and the measures that should be taken to safeguard that contribution.

> CANADA ROY. COMM. ON BILINGUALISM AND BICULTURALISM, *Report*, 1967, App. I, 173, one of the terms of reference.

Radicalism

Canadians can be radical, but they must be radical in their own peculiar way, and that way must be in harmony with our national traditions and ideals.

> AGNES MACPHAIL, speech, Canadian Club, Toronto, Mar.4, 1935.

Andrew would have made a fine radical, if he hadn't hated radicalism.

> STEPHEN LEACOCK, "Andrew Macphail", *Queen's quart.*, Winter, 1938, 452.

If this brain's over-tempered
consider that the fire was want
and the hammers were fists
I've tasted my blood too much
to love what I was born to.

> MILTON ACORN, "I've tasted my blood", 1963.

Radio and Television

We regard the use of radio as a national trust. It is essentially both a national and a local-service institution. As such it adds to the social and economic life of the nation.

> SIR HENRY THORNTON, address, Toronto, Oct. 20, 1929, opening the All-Canada Symphony Concerts.

Service to the listener is the primary consideration. In the final analysis the listener himself makes the program. The future of broadcasting rests with the individual who turns the dial.

SIR HENRY THORNTON, address, Toronto, Oct. 20, 1929, opening the All-Canada Symphony Concerts.

Canadian radio listeners want Canadian broadcasting.

CANADA. ROY. COMM. ON RADIO BROADCASTING, *Report*, 1929, 6.

Canadian radio for Canadians.

CANADIAN RADIO LEAGUE, slogan used in the 1930's.

The State or the United States?

CANADIAN RADIO LEAGUE, Brief to Special Comm. on Radio Broadcasting, Apr. 18, 1932.

We look to you in Canada to lead radio in North America out of the morass in which it is pitiably sunk. May Canada fulfill my early dream!

LEE DE FOREST, Canada. H. of C., Special Committee on Radio Broadcasting, *Minutes of proceedings and evidence*, 1932, 491.

Canadians have the right to a system of broadcasting from Canadian sources equal in all respects to that of any other country.

RICHARD B. BENNETT, H. of C., *Debates*, Feb. 16, 1932, 236.

From the political standpoint, it is most important that we should have this license given to those who are absolutely our friends rather than those who are not.

R.B. HANSON, letter, May 12, 1933, on the granting of a radio broadcasting license to CFNB, Saint John, N.B. (Pub. Arch. Can., Bennett papers).

If Canadian radio makes no lasting contribution to a better understanding between the so-called French-Canadian and the so-called English-Canadian, between the East and the West, between the town and the country, between those of us who are fortunate enough to enjoy the privilege of labor and those of our fellow citizens who through no fault of their own are denied the opportunity, then we shall have faltered our stewardship.

LEONARD W. BROCKINGTON, C.B.C. radio broadcast, Nov. 4, 1936.

Some men among the evangelists get microphonitis – they need publicity. Indeed, they die a slow death if taken off the air.

E.H. MCGUIRE, Manager, Radio station CFCN Calgary, about 1945 qu. by W.E. Mann, *Sect, cult and church in Alberta*, 1955, 129.

The national system with extensive coverage, co-operation of national and local stations, and programmes in both languages emanating from every part of the country, has contributed powerfully, we were told, to a sense of Canadian unity. It does much to promote a knowledge and understanding of Canada as a whole, and of every Canadian region, and therefore aids in the development of a truly Canadian cultural life.

CANADA. ROY. COMM. ON THE NATIONAL DEVELOPMENT IN THE ARTS, LETTERS AND SCIENCES, 1951, *Report*, 28.

Don't worry about diction . . . In fact if your diction is too good louse it up a bit . . . Don't worry if you stumble. An occasional stumble merely proves to the audience that politicians are human, and it will give you a sympathetic response . . .

PROGRESSIVE CONSERVATIVE PARTY, New Brunswick, *Data file*, issue No. 2, 1953: hints to election campaigners; qu. in H.

G. Thorburn, *Politics in New Brunswick*, 1961, 124.

You make your own success.

LESLIE BELL, qu. by June Callwood in *Maclean's*, Feb. 1, 1953, 49.

May I ask how much freer the American air is than our own? It is freer in the sense of there being more mutually interfering stations, as a casual turn of the dial indicates. The American radio has the traditional American form of freedom – anarchy. But is *opinion* there any freer? Is news any more accurately and impartially broadcast? Who dares to contend that such is the case?

A.R.M. LOWER, *Queen's quart.*, Vol. 60, Summer, 1953, 175.

This is a democracy, and one of the principles of democracy is that everybody should be allowed what they want. Not that everybody should have what most people want.

LISTER SINCLAIR, *Maclean's*, Apr. 14, 1956, 118.

As a nation, we cannot accept in these powerful and persuasive media, the natural and complete flow of another nation's culture without danger to our national identity.

CANADA. ROY. COMM. ON BROADCASTING, *Report*, Vol. 1, 1957, 8.

Canadian content.

CANADA. ROY. COMM. ON BROADCASTING, *Report*, 1957, 64; ascribed to Andrew Stewart, Chairman, Board of Broadcast Governors; the Broadcasting Act of 1958 enabled the BBG to rule that all TV stations carry a minimum of 45% Canadian content as of Apr. 1,1961 and 55% a year later.

I will be more interested in seeing people than in talking to cameras.

LOUIS ST. LAURENT, to a T.V. reporter, election campaign, 1957, qu. in P. Newman, *Renegade in power*, 1963, 54.

Owning a television station is as good as a government licence to print money.

ROY H. (LORD) THOMSON OF FLEET, qu. in *Maclean's*, Jan. 1969, 12 about his ownership of Scottish Television and his profit of five million dollars after two years of ownership, 1957 to 1959.

It's hard to remember what we used to do before television.

BERNARD BRADEN, qu. by J. Gray in *Maclean's*, Nov. 7, 1959, 97.

The monumental appetites of the broadcast arts can be sated only by a steady diet of the mediocre; the mediocre served up with great professional skill.

GEORGE ROBERTSON, in *Can. lit*. No. 2, 1959, 65.

In case anyone should accuse newspaper publishers of a shameful lack of enterprise for only controlling 20 per cent of their greatest rival's private outlets, it should be remembered that the Board of Broadcast Governors has seemed to regard giving television franchises to newspaper owners as somewhat akin to "giving an extra tentacle to an octopus in a tankful of goldfish" as one Vancouver columnist put it.

JOHN CARTWRIGHT, *Can. commentator*, Feb., 1962, 2.

I am convinced that our cultural life needs both protection against impoverishment and stimulus to improvement, and that a deliberate effort to these ends, in which government must have a large role, is not only justified but is most urgently required. Government must insure Canadian ownership and control over our means of communication.

MAURICE LAMONTAGNE, speech to Canadian Assoc. of Broadcasters, Quebec City, Apr. 6, 1964.

The only thing that really matters in broadcasting is program content; all the rest is housekeeping.

CANADA. COMMITTEE ON BROADCASTING, *Report*, 1965, 3.

One of the essential tasks of a broadcasting system is to stir up the minds and emotions of the people, and occasionally to make large numbers of them acutely uncomfortable.

CANADA. COMMITTEE ON BROADCASTING, *Report*, 1965, 4.

An adequate Canadian content in television programs is unlikely to be achieved by a *laisser faire* policy of minimum regulations, governing advertising volume, morality and the like. Economic forces in North America are such that any substantial amount of Canadian programs will not appear on television schedules unless room is reserved for them by regulation.

CANADA. COMMITTEE ON BROADCASTING, *Report*, 1965, 63.

The Golden Age of Radio was also the Golden Age of Music.

E. AUSTIN WEIR, *The struggle for national broadcasting in Canada*, 1965, 276.

After all, are we really masters in our own house when Ottawa rules on everything concerning radio and television, media which in our age are perhaps the most effective arms of culture?

DANIEL JOHNSON, *Égalité ou indépendance*, 1965, 120 (trans.) re: Quebec province.

Television has made democracy workable. Gone, or going, are the phony rhetoric, the wheeling and dealing, the rule of the oligarchy. To gain power these days a politician has to present himself to the people through TV, a medium that tears the mask from all who dare appear before it.

ROY SHIELDS, Toronto *Daily star*, about 1966, qu. in P. Newman, *Distemper of our times*, 1968, 69.

The Canadian sound.

ANON., term sometimes applied to popular music by Canadian singers and musicians, late 1960's.

Broadcasting may well be regarded as the central nervous system of Canadian nationhood.

H. OF C. STANDING COMMITTEE ON BROADCASTING, FILMS, AND ASSISTANCE TO THE ARTS, *Proceedings*, No. 42, Mar. 21, 1967, 2088.

T.V. is remaking us in its own image.

MARSHALL MCLUHAN, qu. in *Weekend mag.*, Mar. 18, 1967, 4.

National broadcasting service should (iv) contribute to the development of national unity and provide for a continuing expression of Canadian identity.

CANADA. LAWS, STATUTES, etc., 1967-68, *Broadcasting act*, C. 25, Part I: 2(g).

The Canadian broadcasting system should be effectively owned and controlled by Canadians so as to safeguard, enrich and strengthen the cultural, political, social and economic fabric of Canada.

CANADA. LAWS, STATUTES, etc., 1967-68, *Broadcasting act*, C. 25, Part I: 2(b).

A listener is the most lavish producer there is. He or she can soar on sound much higher than the looker can on pictures.

ESSE W. LJUNGH, qu. in Toronto *Telegram*, May 31, 1968, 48.

Good night Marshall McLuhan, wherever you are.

NORMAN DEPOE, C.B.C. commentator, at close of election night broadcast, June 25, 1968.

National control is not an end in itself, and never has been in Canada. It is the necessary condition for a system designed, in the North American context, to assist Canadians to know the changing society around them and to adapt successfully to it. The framework for such broadcasting was established in Canada forty years ago. The struggle to improve, even to maintain it, is greater today than ever before, and more crucial to our survival as a Nation.

FRANK W. PEERS, *The politics of Canadian broadcasting, 1920-1951*, 1969, 450.

It is destroying our entire political, educational, social, institutional life. TV will dissolve the entire fabric of society in a short time.

MARSHALL MCLUHAN, qu. by J. Harvey Perry, *Can. banker*, Mar./Apr., 1969, 4.

There's nothing decent
to look at on T.V.

I'm going into the bathroom
to cut my wrists.

You can have
the rest of the beer.

JOHN NEWLOVE, "Song of the man who just came in to say that he wouldn't be getting a telegram for money", 1970.

What is at stake is not only the vigor of our democracy. It also involves the survival of our nationhood. A nation is a collection of people who share common images of themselves. Our love of the land and our instinctive yearning for community implant that image in the first place. But it is the media — together with education and the arts — that can make it grow.

SENATE. SPECIAL COMMITTEE ON MASS MEDIA, *Report*, Vol. 1, 1970, 11.

Privately owned radio has often been successful in its own terms: profitability, stability, unflagging mediocrity.

SENATE, SPECIAL COMMITTEE ON MASS MEDIA, *Report*, Vol. 1, 1970, 92.

We're public therapists. We're a public wailing wall, a public listening post, we're — I mean all open-liners — a veritable mine of information.

JACK WEBSTER, radio "hot-liner", Station CJOR, Vancouver, qu. in *Maclean's*, June, 1973, 92.

Radio and Television Commercials

This sweet music that I hear,
Is it Soap, or is it Beer?
Do I owe the string quartet
To Foulness of the Breath, or Sweat?
When the Chopin Prelude comes
Will it help Massage the Gums?

F.R. SCOTT, "Command of the air", 1954.

If it isn't worth saying, sing it.

ANON., qu. by Bruce Legge, Empire Club, Toronto, Mar. 5, 1959.

Assembling words and visualizations for the modulation of memory is, in most instances, more important to product or corporate survival and growth than multiplication of message.

GEORGE ELLIOTT, in John A. Irving, ed., *Mass media in Canada*, 1962, 176.

My favourite music is the sound of the radio commercials at ten bucks a whack!

> ROY THOMSON, when asked what was his favourite music, qu. in Russell Braddon, *Roy Thomson of Fleet Street*, 1965, 138.

Never in the whole history
Of the mass media
Has so much had to be borne
By so many
For so few.

> F. R. SCOTT, "For whom the bell tolls", 1972.

Rage

For growl and cough and snarl are the tokens of spendthrifts who know not the ultimate economy of rage.

> E. J. PRATT, "Silences", 1937.

Railway Trains (Nicknames)

The Confederation Train.

> Train carrying the story of Canada and its people from coast to coast, 1967.

The Moccasin. Newfie Bullet.

> Train which ran from St. John's, Nfld. to Port-aux-Basques, June 29, 1898 to July 2, 1969.

The Rapido.

> C.N.R. train which ran from Montreal to Toronto, 1965-1968, replaced by turbo train.

Works, Clerks and Shirks.

> A nickname given to three suburban local trains that ran into Saint John, N.B., about 1915.

Railways

Far away to the South is heard the daily scream of the steam-whistle — but from Canada there is no escape: blockaded and imprisoned by Ice and Apathy, we have at least ample time for reflection — and if there be comfort in Philosophy may we not profitably consider the *Philosophy of Railroads*.

> THOMAS C. KEEFER, *Philosophy of railroads*, 1850, 3.

Steam has exerted an influence over matter which can only be compared to that which the discovery of Printing has exercised upon the mind. These two great discoveries — pillars of cloud and fire which have brought us out of the mental wilderness of the dark and middle ages — have combined to supply the mind with daily food and to illustrate the value of time.

> THOMAS COLTRIN KEEFER, *Philosophy of railroads*, 1850 (Repr., 1972, 11).

I am neither a prophet, nor the son of a prophet, yet I will venture to predict that in five years we shall make the journey hence to Quebec and Montreal and home through Portland and St. John by rail; and I believe that many in this room will live to hear the whistle of the steam-engine in the passes of the Rocky Mountains and to make the journey from Halifax to the Pacific in five or six days.

> JOSEPH HOWE, speech in Mason's Hall, Halifax, May 15, 1851.

To the advocates of legislative union I say, your scheme is impracticable without the railroads.

> JOSEPH HOWE, speech in Quebec, July 4, 1851.

Railways are my politics.

SIR ALLAN MACNAB, in Legislative Assembly, speech made as leader of the Opposition on granting of a charter to the Grand Trunk Railway, 1853. (See: *Can. hist. rev.*, Vol. 28, 171, for quotation by R.J. Macgeorge from Streetsville *weekly rev.*, Nov. 25, 1854; also, speech by Thomas White, H. of C., *Debates*, Feb. 8, 1884; J.M.S. Careless in *Union of the Canadas*, 1967, 193, states that "my politics now are railroads" was contemporary usage.

I hope to see, or at least that my children will see, a railway wholly on British territory from the Atlantic to the Pacific Oceans.

WILLIAM DRAPER, special commissioner to Gt. Brit., H. of C. Committee on Hudson's Bay Co., 1857.

The years 1852 to 1857 will ever be remembered as those of financial plenty, and the saturnalia of nearly all classes connected with railways.

THOMAS C. KEEFER, *Eighty years' progress of British North America*, 1865, 221.

Great railway corporations are the most dangerous enemies popular government ever had.

DAVID MILLS, in *Can. monthly*, Nov., 1872; see also, H. of C., *Debates*, 1880-81, 274.

I swing to the sunset land –
The world of prairie, the world of
  plain,
The world of promise and hope and
  gain,
The world of gold, and the world of
  grain,
And the world of the willing hand.

E. PAULINE JOHNSON, "Prairie greyhounds – C.P.R. 'No.1' Westbound", 1903.

I swing from the land of morn;
The grey old east with its grey old
  seas,
The land of leisure, the land of ease,
The land of flowers and fruit and
  trees,
And the place where we were born.

E. PAULINE JOHNSON, "Prairie greyhounds – C.P.R. No.2' Eastbound", 1903.

Purgatory for me will be five hundred years of catching trains and two thousand years of remembering names.

FREDERICK GEORGE SCOTT, *Can. mag.*, Mar., 1909, 460.

The railway found Canada scarcely a geographic expression and made it a nation.

O.D. SKELTON, *Railway builders*, 1916, 12.

Consult the annals of Canada for the past fifty years at random and whatever party may be in power, what do you find? The government is building a railway, buying a railway, selling a railway, or blocking a railway.

PAUL LAMARCHE, speech, Bibliothèque Saint Sulpice, Montreal, 1917. (Trans.)

If there is one thing that has bedevilled the public life of this country it has been the influence of railway corporations.

NEWTON W. ROWELL, H. of C., *Debates*, Oct. 21, 1919, 1259.

The illegitimate offspring of two unnatural parents, conceived in political expediency and misshaped in the guise of a half-million dollar campaign fund.

JOHN OLIVER, Premier of B.C., during debate in B.C. Legislature, Feb. 19, 1920, qu. in Vancouver *Daily province*, Feb. 20, 1920, 7, re: Pacific Great Eastern Railway in B.C.

We are at the penalty stage of railway development in this country. A price in some form has to be paid by the people of Canada. We are now at the point when an awakening bitterness follows a night of intoxication: an ebb of retribution now follows in the wake of a flood-tide of railway construction.

ARTHUR MEIGHEN, address, Canadian Club, Montreal, 1920, qu. in G.R. Stevens, *Canadian national railways*, 1960, Vol. 2, 499.

They snared a savage continent in steel.

CHARLES G.D. ROBERTS, "These three score years", read at New Brunswick celebration of Canada's Diamond Jubilee, Fredericton, July 1, 1927.

Railways in Canada are far from being merely an economic problem. They were born of, nourished in, are, and will continue to be, part of Canadian politics.

R. MCQUEEN, in *Can.hist.rev.*, 1936, 334.

The railway line, that tenuous thread which bound Canada to both the great oceans and made her a nation, lay with one end in the darkness of Nova Scotia and the other in the flush of a British Columbia noon.

HUGH MACLENNAN, *Barometer rising*, 1941, 120.

Intercolonial, the Canadian Southern, Dominion-Atlantic, the Great Western
    — names
That caught a continental note and tried
To answer it.

E.J. PRATT, "Towards the last spike", 1952.

The Grand Trunk was a financial failure — but a public asset.

A.W. CURRIE, *The Grand Trunk railway of Canada*, 1957, 481.

Railways (Nicknames)

Alberta Great Eastern (Athabasca Railway).— Always Giving Employment.

Alberta Great Waterways.— Almighty God Wonders.; And God Willing.; Alberta's Greatest Worry.

Algoma Central and Hudson Bay.— All Curves, Hills and Bridges.

Atlantic, Quebec and Western.— The All Queer and Wobbly.

Brockville, Westport and Sault Ste. Marie.— Bad Wages and Seldom See Money.

Canadian National Railways.— Certainly No Rush; Collects No Revenue.

C.N.R. (Component lines and sections).— *Brandon to Portage la Prairie.*— Brandon Short Line. *Campbellford subdivision.*— The Submarine Division. *Charlottetown to Murray Harbour.*— The Gaelic Express. *Edmonton to Blue River.*— The Duck and Dodge. *Irondale, Bancroft and Ottawa.*— In and Back Out.; Italian Bums and Orphans.; The Mary Ann. *London to Clinton.* — The Butter and Egg. *Jasper to Prince Rupert.*— The Burma Road (1939-45).; The Trap Line.; The Turkey Trail. *Point Tupper to Inverness.*— The Juridique Flyer. *Saskatoon to Calgary.*— The Goose Lake Line. *Winnipegosis to Rorketon.*— Coast to Coast. *Vancouver Island Section.*— Route of the Christmas Tree.; Two Streaks of Rust.

Canadian Northern Railway.— Canadian Now and Then.; The Wooden Axle.

Canadian Pacific Railway.– Can't Pay Rent.; Can't Promise Returns.; Chinese Pacific. (Local to Vancouver, because of Oriental labour used on construction.); The Great Octopus.; The Sleepy R.

C.P.R. (Component lines and sections). — *Arrow Lake Subdivision.* — The Bow and Arrow. *Lyndonville Subdiv., Maine.* — Snake Alley. *Montreal to Mattawamkeag sections.* — The M. & M. (From Moosehead, and Mattawamkeag sections.); The Short Line. *Montreal to Boston.* — The Air Line. *Osoyoos subdiv.* — The Cantaloupe Trail. *Temiskaming subdiv.* — The Moccasin Line.

Cumberland Railway and Coal Co.– Can't Run and Can't Crawl.

Dominion Atlantic Railway.– The Blueberry Special.; The Dust and Rust.; The Land of Evangeline Route.; The Midland. (Windsor to Truro to Windsor.)

Duluth, Winnipeg and Pacific.– Derailments, Wrecks, and Profanity.

Edmonton, Dunvegan and British Columbia.– *(Northern Alberta Railways).*– Eat, Drink and be Cheerful.; Endless Ditches and Big Curves ; Enormously Dangerous and Badly Constructed.; Eternally Damned and Badly Constructed.; Evilly Designed and Badly Constructed.

Esquimalt and Nanaimo Railway.– The Easy and Noisy.; The Easy and Nice.

Flin Flon.– The Flim Flam.

Grand Trunk Pacific.– Get There Perhaps.

Grand Trunk Railway.– The Big Suitcase.; The Big Valise.; The Leaky Roof. (From stencilling on many box cars.)

Great Northern.– Grand Nord.; Great Now and Then.

Halifax and South Western.– Hellish Slow and Weary.; The Fish Line. (Lunenburg branch.)

Hudson Bay.– The Highball Railway.; The Muskeg Special.; The Muskeg Unlimited.

Intercolonial.– The Antigogaelicer. (Truro to Mulgrave); The Pawns. (Branches from Halifax to Windsor, and to Pictou.)

Kettle Valley.– Tea Kettle Valley.

Kingston and Pembroke.– Kick and Push.

Lake Erie and Northern.– Late Every Night.

London and Port Stanley.– Late and Poor Service.; Least Possible Service.; Liver and Pork Sausage.

Minneapolis, St.Paul and Sault Ste. Marie.– The Soo Line.

Minnesota and Manitoba.– Murder all Manitobans.

Napanee, Tamworth and Quinte.– None too Quick.

Newfoundland Railway.– The Reid Railway (1898).

Niagara, St. Catharines and Toronto. – Naturally Slow and Tiresome.; Never Starts on Time.

North-Western Coal and Navigation Co.– The Turkey Trail.(Narrow gauge, between Lethbridge and Dunmore Jct.;1885.)

Northern Railway.– Oats, Straw and Hay.

Ontario Northland.– (Formerly, *Temiskaming and Northern Ontario*). – The Clay Belt Airline.; (North Bay to Cochrane.); Hepburn's Folly.; (Cochrane to Moosonee.)

Ottawa, Arnprior and Parry Sound.– Only Abuse and Poor Salary.

Oxford and New Glasgow.– The Short Line.

Pacific Great Eastern. — Pat Gets Everything.; Pat's Greatest Effort.; Please Go Easy.; Prince George Eventually.; Proctor's Great Effort.; The Province's Greatest Expense.; Provincial Government Expense.; Promoters Get Everything.; Past God's Endurance.

Pontiac, Pacific Junction.– Push, Pull and Jerk.; Push, Pull, Jump and Run.

Port Arthur, Duluth and Western.– The P. and D.; Poverty, Agony, Distress and Want.; Poverty, Desperation and Want; Pee Dee.

Quebec, Montreal and Southern.– Quel Maudit Service.

Quebec, Montreal, Ottawa and Occidental.(C.P.R).– The North Shore.

St. John and Quebec.– The Valley Line.

Souris-Reston.– Peanut Line.

Sydney and Louisburg.– Slow and Lazy.

Temiskaming and Northern Ontario. – (Now, Ontario Northland).– Time No Object.

Temiscouata Railway.– The Sportsmen's Route.

Toronto, Hamilton and Buffalo.– To Hell and Back.; Tramp, Hobo and Bum.; Tried Hard and Busted.

Yarmouth and Annapolis.– The Missing Link. (Digby to Annapolis.)

Whitby and Port Perry Extension Railway.– Nip and Tuck.

White Pass and Yukon.– Wait Patiently and You'll Ride.

Rain

All signs of rain fail in a dry spell.

ANON., saying of pioneer Ontario farmers.

When the pigs run and play expect a rainy day.

ANON., saying of pioneer Ontario farmers.

It was a little bit arter daylight down, rainin' cats and dogs.

T.C. HALIBURTON, *Sam Slick*, 1836, ch. XXVIII.

The rain it falls, and the wind it blows,
And the restless ocean ebbs and flows
But the why and the wherefore no one knows.

ALEXANDER MCLACHLAN, "The rain it falls", 1874.

Washboard sky,
Not three days dry.

ANON., weather proverb, Western Ontario.

And ghosts of buried summers
Walk with the lonely rain.

BLISS CARMAN, *Songs of the sea children;* XXVI, 1894.

If a cock crows as he goes to bed,
He will wake up with a wet head.

ANON., Simcoe, Ont., rhyme; qu., *Jour. of Amer. folklore*, 1918, 7.

These comforts only have I for my
    pain –
    The frantic laws of statesmen
    bowed with cares
    To feed me, and the slow,
    pathetic prayers
Of godly men that somehow it shall
    rain.

FREDERICK E. LAIGHT, "Soliloquy", 1937,
on prairie drought.

God, will it never rain again? What
    about
    those clouds out west? No, that's
    just
    dust, as thick and stifling now as
    winter
    underwear.
No rain, no crop, no feed, no faith,
    only wind.

ANNE MARRIOTT, "The wind our
enemy", 1939.

Sometimes, upon a crowded street
I feel the endless rain come down,
And in the old magnetic sound
I hear the opening of a gate
That loosens all the seven seas.

F.R. SCOTT, "Lakeshore", 1950.

Yesterday, and also the day before,
when I was in Brandon several localities received rain for the first time.

JOHN DIEFENBAKER, Prime Minister, during question period, H. of C., *Debates*,
1958, 1827.

The rain is only the river
grown bored, risking everything
on one big splash.

RAYMOND SOUSTER, "The rain is only the
river", 1964.

Rainbows

Of a sudden the Indians gave a loud
shout, and called out "Oh, there is the
mark of life, we shall yet live," On
looking to the eastward there was one
of the widest and most splendid Rainbows I ever beheld; and joy was now
in every face.

DAVID THOMPSON, *Narrative of his explorations in Western America,
1784-1812*, (Champlain Soc., 1916, 89).

Ranchers

With them there had been no feeling
for their farms; no love for the land; no
harmony with the earth or nature.
With them the raw soil and virgin
timber were something to rape and
ruin in their drive for dollars. They
had plundered their portion of the
planet, to leave as evidence of their
passing, derelict spots in which man
and his environment were utterly out
of joint . . . desolate, sad, wretched
wrecks of what had been once a lovely
land.

W. PHILLIP KELLER, *Under wilderness
skies*, 1966, 29.

Rape

Among the porcupines, rape is unknown.

GREGORY CLARK, attributed by Gillis
Purcell (head of Canadian Press) as a
remark to Jimmy Frise, at Lake Scugog,
Ont., 1933.

Ravens

The Raven's house is built with reeds,
    Sing alas and woe is me!
And the Raven's couch is spread with
    weeds
    High on the hollow tree;
And the Raven himself telling his
    beads

In penance for his past misdeeds,
Upon the top I see.

THOMAS D'A. MCGEE, "The penitent
raven, a nursery rhyme", 1858.

Reaction

Always in human history at periods of
great change, when in that change the
most sensitive feel the most deeply
insecure, there has been the tendency
to seek an answer to that insecurity by
turning to the certainties of the past.
Therapies which turn back the wheel
of history are proposed as remedies for
that insecurity. Such reactionary experiments are always vain.

GEORGE P. GRANT, Philosophy in the
mass age, 1966, 7.

Reactionaries

And still in the honest working world
With posture and hint and smirk,
These sons of the devil are standing by
While Man does all the work.
They balk endeavor and baffle
    reform,
In the sacred name of law;
And over the quavering voice of Hem,
Is the droning voice of Haw.

BLISS CARMAN, "Hem and Haw", 1895.

Readers

Reader, in your hand you hold
A silver case, a box of gold.
I have no door, however small,
Unless you pierce my tender wall,
And there's no skill in healing then
Shall ever make me whole again.
Show pity, Reader, for my plight:
Let be, or else consume me quite.

JAY MACPHERSON, "Egg", 1957.

The clerisy are those who read for
pleasure, but not for idleness; who
read for pastime but not to kill time;
who love books, but do not live by
books.

ROBERTSON DAVIES, A voice from the
attic, 1960, 7.

Reading

We have beside us a mountain of
Books, Magazines, Pamphlets and
Newspapers, that have been accumulating for the last two months, uno-
pened and unread. Like a Turk, in the
dim twilight of his Harem, we scarcely
know which to choose . . .

JOSEPH HOWE, in Novascotian, May 2,
1833.

What we hear with pleasure we afterward read with diminished satisfaction.

T.C. HALIBURTON, Sam Slick, 1840, 263.

Never read a book, squire; always
think for yourself.

T.C. HALIBURTON, The attaché, 1843.

Some books are read in the parlour
and some in the kitchen, but the test of
a real genuine book is that it is read in
both.

T.C. HALIBURTON, Sam Slick's wise saws,
1853, ch. 19.

What was good enough for me is good
enough for my boys. They have the
Bible and the Toronto Globe, all that I
had, and that is enough for them.

ANON., a story popular on the hustings in
Ontario after about 1860, always followed by the rejoinder, "Well, at any
rate, you are giving them both sides of
the question".

At present our people are too busy to read, too busy at least to read with discernment, and where there are no discerning readers there will be no writers.

ARCHIBALD LAMPMAN, "Two Canadian poets", speech, Ottawa, Feb. 19, 1891, in *Univ. of Tor. quart.*, XIII, July, 1944, 408.

Spend the last half-hour of the day in communion with the saints of humanity.

SIR WILLIAM OSLER, *Montreal med. jour.*, 1903, 771.

With half an hour's reading in bed every night as a steady practice, the busiest man can get a fair education before the plasma sets in the perigang-lionic spaces of his grey cortex.

SIR WILLIAM OSLER, *Aphorisms*, 1950, 77.

On lit Proust à Rideau Hall. (Proust is read in Rideau Hall)

ANON., French Canadian, qu. in Janet Adam Smith, *John Buchan*, 1965, 388, referring to his term of office as Governor-General, 1935-1940 (with title of Lord Tweedsmuir) terminated with his death.

It is possible that a child may pass from infancy to maturity without encountering one book that will satisfy him in his search for experience and pleasure; that will offer him reality in the place of a shadow of reality.

LILIAN SMITH, *The unreluctant years*, 1953, 190.

All right, all right,
    so I write too much!
But I can't say for you, dear reader,
    that you read too much.

LOUIS DUDEK, "To the reader", 1958.

The reader reads for stimulation, pleasure, and even for information and by that form of osmosis which true readers share with writers, he acquires perhaps discrimination, perhaps a Catholic and an adventurous taste, and the gates of perception are open to him.

ETHEL WILSON, in *Can. lit.* No. 2, 1959, 18.

No writing in Canada carries such influence as journalism. People who seldom or never read a book, read the newspapers.

MAZO DE LA ROCHE, Intro. to G.E.Nelson ed., *Northern lights*, 1960, 9.

Reading is my theme and reading is a private, interpretative art.

ROBERTSON DAVIES, *A voice from the attic*, 1960, 8.

Yet how many people there are who read as though some prize awaited them when they turned the last page! They do not wish to read a book; they want to have read it — no matter how.

ROBERTSON DAVIES, *A voice from the attic*, 1960, 9.

We shall find nothing in books which has no existence in ourselves.

ROBERTSON DAVIES, *A voice from the attic*, 1960, 13.

Good reading is the only test of good writing.

ROBERTSON DAVIES, *A voice from the attic*, 1960, 20.

Reading confers status.

ROBERTSON DAVIES, *A voice from the attic*, 1960, 253.

Those who did not belong did not read.

JOHN KENNETH GALBRAITH, *The Scotch*, 1964, 77.

The lizard rejoices because I read
Pascal and other religious thinkers at
   night
who've much to say about conscience
   and grace;
for the light by which I read them
brings the summer insects to his
   mouth:
gauzy-winged creatures
with wings like small sails.

> IRVING LAYTON, "The lizard", 1964.

I should read all things like braille in
   this season
with my fingers and I should read
   them
lest I go blind in both eyes reading
   with
that other eye the final hieroglyph

> GWENDOLYN MACEWEN, "Poems in
> braille", 1966.

A print addict is a man who reads in
elevators. People occasionally look at
me curiously when they see me standing there, reading a paragraph or two
as the elevator goes up. To me, it's
curious that there are people who do
not read in elevators. What can they
be thinking about?

> ROBERT FULFORD, Crisis at the Victory
> Burlesk, 1968, 141.

She wears glasses
and has a slightly intellectual
   expression
as if she'd intended to read a book
then decided against it.

> AL PURDY, "Poem for Eda", 1968.

He not only doesn't write books and
articles about what he feels, he doesn't
even read them.

> C.G. POWER, qu. by Norman Ward in
> Nelles and Rotstein, eds., Nationalism
> or local control, 1973, 29., referring to
> "the man in the street".

Real Estate

Men no longer regard the place where
they live as a home. It is merely a
speculation in real estate.

> PETER MCARTHUR, Affable stranger,
> 1920, 69.

Blessed the men this day
Whether at death or birth
Who own good sites, for they
Shall inherit the earth.

> A.M. KLEIN, "The diary of Abraham
> Segal, poet", in Can. forum, May, 1932,
> 297.

The basic view of the property industry, that a city is a machine for making
money for the industry, is taken for
granted.

> JAMES LORIMER, A citizen's guide to city
> politics, 1972, 77.

Reality

Who are we? What is the reality in us?
That which we feel ourselves to be? Or
that which others conceive us to be?

> FREDERICK P. GROVE, The master of the
> mill, 1944, 52.

Shall I keep my feet
upon the ground
when the earth itself
is become an ooze
of shit puke quicksand.

> GERALD FULTON, "An answer from Job",
> 1963.

I have always been tethered to reality,
always compelled by an unfortunate
kind of probity in my nature to prefer
a bare-faced disappointment to the
luxury of a future I have no just claims
upon.

> SINCLAIR ROSS, "Cornet at night", 1968.

What is reality and what is fantasy is always determined by those in power.

SATU REPO, *This book is about schools*, 1970, 437.

Everything must learn
How *I* have dreamed it.

SUSAN MUSGRAVE, "Finding love", 1972.

Reason

Only emotion can cope with emotion; reason but beats the air. Wherefore, a wise man will neither oppose nor appeal to a woman through reason.

ARNOLD HAULTAIN, *Hints for lovers*, 1909, 189.

I like to keep my feet on the earth – in good Canadian mud.

PETER MCARTHUR, *In pastures green*, 1915, 71.

Only in terms of a synthesis of philosophy and the social sciences can the rational man wage a successful battle against the forces of unreason in the world.

JOHN A. IRVING, *Science and values*, 1952, 124.

The rise of reason in politics is an advance of law; for is not law an attempt to regulate the conduct of men in society rationally rather than emotionally?

PIERRE E. TRUDEAU, *Federalism and the French Canadians*, 1968, 196.

Reason, when accompanied by superior force, always emerges triumphant.

RICHARD J. NEEDHAM, *A friend in Needham*, 1969, 37.

Rebellion

If you'd done a little rebelling yourself you'd be a happier woman today!

HUGH MACLENNAN, *Two solitudes*, 1945, 313.

Rebellion against the codes of society begin at the top, not at the bottom. Stir the bottom and you get nothing but mud.

ROBERTSON DAVIES, *At the gates of the righteous*, in *Eros at breakfast and other plays*, 1949, 128.

The twentieth century is a bad time for rebels: there are so many of them.

IRVING LAYTON, "Aphs", *The whole bloody bird*, 1969, 104.

Rebellion, 1837

Government is founded on the authority, and is instituted for the benefit, of a people; when, therefore, any Government long and systematically ceases to answer the great ends of its foundation, the people have a natural right given them by their Creator to seek after and establish such institutions as will yield the greatest quantity of happiness to the greatest number.

DECLARATION OF THE REFORMERS OF THE CITY OF TORONTO, July 31, 1837.

As for me, I am of a different opinion from that of M. Papineau. I claim the time has come to melt our spoons to make bullets.

WOLFRED NELSON, at a political meeting, St. Charles, Que., Oct. 23, 1837, qu. in L.O. David, *Les Patriotes de 1837-1838*, 1884, 23. (Trans.)

Be vigilant, patient and active – leave punishment to the Laws – our first object is, to arrest and secure all those who have been guilty of Rebellion, Murder and Robbery. And to aid us in this, a Reward is hereby offered of ONE THOUSAND POUNDS to anyone who will apprehend, and deliver up to Justice, WILLIAM LYON MACKENZIE; and FIVE HUNDRED POUNDS to anyone who will apprehend, and deliver up to Justice, DAVID GIBSON — or SAMUEL LOUNT — or JESSE LLOYD — or SILAS

FLETCHER – and the same reward and a free pardon will be given to any of their accomplices who will render this public service, except he or they shall have committed, in his own person, the crime of Murder or Arson.

SIR FRANCIS BOND HEAD, Proclamation, Toronto, Dec. 7, 1837.

We are wearied of these oppressions, and resolved to throw off the yoke. Rise Canadians! Rise as one man, and the glorious object of our wishes is accomplished.

WILLIAM LYON MACKENZIE, *A Proclamation for a Provisional Government for the State of Upper Canada, to be established on Navy Island*, (Buffalo, N.Y., Dec. 13 (i.e. 12), 1837).

Now good folks all, both great and
    small,
  Your voices raise to Heaven,
With heart felt thanks for health and
    peace,
  At the end of thirty seven.

ANON., (THE PATRIOT BOY), untitled, qu. in *The Patriot*, Jan. 2, 1838, 3.

And now that the rebellion's o'er
  Let each true Briton sing,
Long live the Queen in health and
    peace,
  And may each rebel swing.

ANON. "New words to an old song; or, John Gilpin travestied", Cobourg *Star*, Feb. 7, 1838, qu. Moir, *Rhymes of rebellion*, 1965, 10.

The nights I saw, the griefs I bore,
Shall unto me return no more,
Farewell dark prison, iron bands,
And the sad cords that bound my
    hands!
Farewell to all that round me stood,
To all earth's joys; 'tis blest and good
To give my life, by God's command,
Farewell distressed and troubled land!

SAMUEL LOUNT, "Lount's farewell", patriot blacksmith, hanged Apr. 12, 1838, qu. in John S. Moir, ed., *Rhymes of rebellion*, 1965, 42.

Four rebels captured; shot accordingly.

COL. JOHN PRINCE, in his account of the Battle of Windsor, Dec., 1838; attributed.

When I was a rebel.

SIR GEORGE-ETIENNE CARTIER, a favourite expression of his later years.

I carried my musket in '37.

SIR JOHN A. MACDONALD, in his later years, qu. in Joseph Pope, *Memoirs of Sir John A. Macdonald*, Vol. I, 1894, 9.

The enterprise of a few vain, vicious feather-brained men: it had neither spirit nor substance, deriving what poor strength it had from enemies of England . . . in America.

J.W. FORTESCUE, *History of the British army*, Vol. XI, 1923.

What Canada lost was a small army of so-called renegades, among whom were some thugs, criminals, and a sprinkling of the hare-brained, but the great majority were men with character, ability, and ideals of good citizenship. Canada has been vastly the poorer for their exile.

LOUIS B. DUFF, *Can. hist. rev.*, 1938, 215.

Militarily, both sides behaved in the best traditions of comic opera.

A.R.M. LOWER, *Colony to nation*, 1946, 242.

Since 1837 the word "Quebec" is the name of a sickness.

MICHEL VAN SCHENDEL, *Parti pris*, Mar., 1964, 25. (Trans.)

the loyalists, scared skinny by the
    sound of their own gunfire,
gawked and bolted south to the fort
    like rabbits,
the rebels for their part bolting north
    to the pub: the first
spontaneous mutual retreat in the
    history of warfare.
Canadians, in flight.

DENNIS LEE, "Civil elegies", No.1, 1972.

Rebirth

If necessary, be conceived again.
Swim in the river of the womb
till, cast up fishlike on dry land
you grow a mouth and scream.

ELIZABETH BREWSTER, "Advice to the
fearful self", 1972.

Reciprocity, 1854

It was floated through on champagne.

ANON., a taunt made by those opposed to
the treaty which was signed in Washington; qu. by Laurence Oliphant, Lord
Elgin's private secretary, *Episodes in a
life of adventure*, 1887, 47.

I remember, and you remember also,
that since the abolition of the Reciprocity Treaty in 1866, we have sent
delegation after delegation to Washington to obtain Reciprocity. We are
not sending any more delegations.

SIR WILFRID LAURIER, speech to Can.
Manufacturers' Assoc., Montreal, Nov.
6, 1901; see also his speech in Toronto,
qu., Toronto *Globe*, Apr. 2, 1907, p.2.

Reciprocity, 1911

I am for it [the Reciprocity Agree-
ment] because I hope to see the day
when the American flag will float over
every square foot of the British North
American possessions clear to the
North Pole.

CHAMP. CLARK, Speaker, in House of
Reps., Washington, Feb. 14, 1911;
Cong. record, 61st. Cong., 3rd sess.,
2520.

There are six and one-half per cent of
fools in Canada, of which one per cent
are for Reciprocity.

SIR WILLIAM VAN HORNE, a favourite
saying, 1911.

I am out to do all I can to bust the
damned thing.

SIR WILLIAM VAN HORNE, a remark on the
Reciprocity movement of 1911.

May I congratulate you heartily on the
victory just won in the Senate by your
patient, luminous advocacy of the
plan? It is only most privately and
confidentially I can venture to do this,
lest I be accused in Canada and England of being an accomplice in the
work of Delilah, sweeping up, perhaps, the locks that fall from the head
of the shorn Fielding.

VISCOUNT JAMES BRYCE, Ambassador to
U.S., to President Taft on passage of
Reciprocity Agreement, Apr., 1911, qu.
in H.S. Duffy, *W.H. Taft*, 1930, 265.

President Taft he made a pact
With Laurier and Fielding
And in the trade that Tafty made
He found them very yielding.

CONSERVATIVE PARTY, campaign song,
1911.

We are opposed to this agreement
because its tendency is to disintegrate
this Dominion, to separate the provinces, to check intercourse and commerce between the provinces and between the east and the west. The
Dominion of Canada was conceived in
audacity.

ROBERT L. BORDEN, speech at Winnipeg,
June 19, 1911.

I am absolutely opposed to Reciprocity and if the West were prepared to make me Prime Minister to-morrow, if I would support that policy, I would not do it.

> ROBERT L. BORDEN, speech in Brandon, June 20, 1911.

Our trade is about $97.00 per capita, and their's $33.00 per capita. In other words the water in our mill-pond stands at 97 and their's at 33 — and they want us to take away our dam. Shall we not say: — "Not by a 'dam' site!"

> SIR WILLIAM VAN HORNE, speech at St. Andrews, N.B., Sept. 2, 1911; similar to a press statement made at Montreal, Feb. 22, 1911.

On September 21, 1911, the Canadian people put behind them the temptation to break the economic bonds by which they had been welded as a nation, affirming their determination to remain loyal subjects of St. James and King Streets.

> FRANK H. UNDERHILL, in *Can. hist. rev.*, 1935, 387.

Recognition

Our follies and vices receive an instant recognition that is not accorded to our virtues.

> PETER MCARTHUR, d. 1924, qu. in *The best of Peter McArthur*, 1967, 187.

Records

Man is a recording animal.

> ROBERT F. GOURLAY, 1829; as in:"Often has my declaration of 1829 been repeated, that 'Man is a recording animal', but never before, was there such happy opportunity for putting records to profitable use." in his *The banished Briton and Neptunian*, Apr. 6, 1843, No.2, 1.

No self-respecting society can neglect or wantonly destroy the records of its own development without living to regret it.

> CAN. HIST. REV., editorial, 1934, 247.

Red Cross

I had a spring wagon drawn by two horses in which we carried the stretchers and other medical equipment. To distinguish it from ordinary transport I made a flag of factory cotton and sewed on it a Geneva Red Cross made from pieces of Turkey red which I got from the ammunition column. This was the first Red Cross flown in Canada.

> GEORGE STERLING RYERSON, *Looking backward*, 1924, 81, referring to Northwest Rebellion, 1885.

Red River (Manitoba)

The Red River is an oasis in the midst of a desert, a vast treeless prairie on which scarcely a shrub is to be seen. The climate is unfavourable to the growth of grain; the summer though warm enough is too short in duration, so that even the few fertile spots could with difficulty mature a potato or a cabbage.

> MONTREAL TRANSCRIPT, 1856.

Many wealthy people are married to half-breed women, who, having no coat of arms but a "totem" to look back to, make up for the deficiency by biting at the backs of their "white" sisters. The white sisters fall back upon their whiteness, whilst the husbands meet each other with desperate courtesies and hospitalities, with a view to filthy lucre in the background.

> CHARLES MAIR, letter, Nov. 19, 1868, Toronto *Globe*, Jan. 4, 1869.

Red River Cart

Red River Carts.

> ANON., carts made entirely of wood, used by the Hudson's Bay Co. for freightage in the West, middle and late 19th century.

The North West fiddle.

> ANON., so named by early pioneers because of the screeching sound emitted by dust-caked wheels.

A little axle grease will make the Red River cart go a long way and so will friendship, if applied wisely.

> ARCHBISHOP ALEXANDRE TACHÉ, qu. in Dan Kennedy, *Recollections of an Assiniboine chief*, 1972, 55.

A den of wild beasts cannot be compared with its hideousness. Combine all the discordant sounds ever heard in Ontario and they cannot reproduce anything so horrid as a train of Red River carts. At each turn of the wheel they run up and down all the notes of the scale without sounding distinctly any note or giving one harmonious sound.

> JEAN D'ARTIGUE, *Six years in the Canadian North-West*, 1882, 45.

Scrub-oak shaganappi and squeals.

> JOHN MCDOUGALL, pioneer Fort Edmonton trader, qu. in James G. Macgregor, *Edmonton trader*, 1963, 30.

Red River Expedition

Come, boys, cheer up! We'll have a
   song in spite of our position
To help us in our labors on this
   glorious Expedition!
We'll keep our spirits up, my boys;
   and don't look sad or sober
Nor grumble at our hardships on our
   way to Manitoba!

> ANON., "Jolly boys", sung by members of force under Col. Garnet J. Wolseley, 1870.

Reform

Reforms are not applicable to reformers, for those who liberate others must themselves be free.

> T.C. HALIBURTON, *The old judge*, 1849.

You can't reform 'em, the only way is to chloriform them.

> T.C. HALIBURTON, *Sam Slick's wise saws*, 1853, II, 282.

No great reform can be achieved except at the sacrifice of some opinion, even by those who are the most ardently in favour of it. The true reformer is not he who always adheres stubbornly to his own ideas, but the true reformer is he who, after having earnestly combatted for his opinions then yields in order to attain some greater end, and to facilitate the change from the old to the new order of things.

> SIR WILFRID LAURIER, H. of C., *Debates*, Mar. 25, 1907, 5294.

I have recovered the radicalism of my youth.

> CLIFFORD SIFTON, to his friends, 1919.

I am for reform. And, in my mind, reform means Government intervention. It means government control and regulation. It means the end of *laissez-faire*.

> RICHARD B. BENNETT, radio address, Ottawa, Jan. 2, 1935.

Do not forget that in the history of social reform it is difficult to name a time when reactionary interests have not sought to block progressive measures by the specious argument that, by them, personal liberty was endangered.

> RICHARD B. BENNETT, radio address, Jan. 7, 1935.

The reform of society will come, not through the indoctrination of the young, but from the intellectual conversion and convictions of the adult.

> PETER SANDIFORD, in his *Adult education in Canada*, 1935 (mimeo), qu. in J.R. Kidd, *Adult education in Canada*, 1950, 11.

Why do the proposals for social measures always come from the C.C.F. and never from the Liberals?

> THÉRÈSE F. CASGRAIN, *A woman in a man's world*, 1972, 122, ref. to early 1940's.

We are all here, we of a new generation whose turn has now come to express itself.

> *CITÉ LIBRE*, Editorial, Vol. 1, No. 1, June, 1950, 1. (Trans.)

Reform Party

Up, Brother Reformers! organize committees; appoint canvassers; call meetings; put forth your strength in a good cause, and manifest at the hustings that to you the peace and prosperity of Upper Canada are dear. Be diligent, untiring, faithful and watchful – bring up your brethren who are unable to walk to the polls – cheer the hearts of the downcast – confirm the wavering – and let the frowns of honest men abash every mercenary hireling.

> WILLIAM LYON MACKENZIE, address to the Reformers of Upper Canada, Toronto, Sept., 1834.

It has always been the boast of the Reform party that it was greatly made up of the sturdy yeomanry of the land and by far the most intelligent and incorruptible of that.

> TORONTO *GLOBE*, Aug. 1, 1867.

Refugees

We remind our American exiles that the political life in their own country is the reason most of them left it. And what may seem to them like provincialism in Canadian life is the reason why they have been able to find sanctuary here.

> TORONTO *STAR*, Editorial, Aug. 4, 1970, 6.

Regimentation

left-right one-two Jerusalem
is just left-right around the corner
we are all big brothers, big brothers
serving one-two time in battle dress

> HENRY BEISSEL, *New wings for Icarus*, 1966, 19.

Regiments – Nicknames

Hasty P's.

> ANON., Hastings and Prince Edward Regiment, popular name.

The Little Black Devils.

> ANON., 90th Regiment of Winnipeg (Royal Winnipeg Rifles), name given by the Métis, Northwest Rebellion, 1885.

Regina, Saskatchewan

Success to Regina, queen city of the plains!

> JUDGE F.G. JOHNSON, toast proposed at official christening of the townsite, Aug. 23, 1882.

What mounds are those, carefully
    plowed around?
Some hunters' graves or Indian burial
    ground?
Not so, my friend – some twenty
    years gone by,
A town sprang up right here where
    you and I
Now stand, which first as Pile of Bones
    was known.

FUTURO (pseud.), "Pile of Bones", in Winnipeg *Times*, Jan. 3, 1884.

If you had a lit-tle more wood, and a lit-tle more water, and here and there a hill, I think the prospect would be improved.

SIR JOHN A. MACDONALD, on transcontinental trip via C.P.R., 1886, to a Regina citizen who asked what he thought of the "prospect".

No one lives here who is not obliged to, & its absolutely flat, arid, treeless surroundings do but typify the life of the place.

LADY ABERDEEN, *Journal*, July 13, 1898.

Golden-girdled by the harvest,
Youth triumphant in her eyes,
Starry splendours crown Regina
When the sunset's crimson dies.

A.M. STEPHEN, "Wascana", 1928.

No cities with the possible exception of Sodom and Gomorrah have ever been founded in less congenial physical surroundings than Regina, the Queen City of Saskatchewan.

EDWARD MCCOURT, *Saskatchewan*, 1968, 83.

Regionalism

The trouble with this whole country is that it's divided up into little puddles with big fish in each one of them.

HUGH MACLENNAN, *Two solitudes*, 1945, 28.

Canada is so intransigently regional that few generalizations about its national character are valid.

KILDARE DOBBS, *Canada*, 1964, 18.

The Canadian style, as expressed in regionalism, tends to be suspicious, narrow, nasty, even paranoid.

ROBERT FULFORD, *Saturday night*, July, 1971, 7.

Rehabilitation

The key to successful rehabilitation isn't the doctor's skill but the patient's will.

DR. GUSTAVE GINGRAS, qu. by David MacDonald, in *In search of Canada*, 1971, 237.

Rejuvenation

O engineer of spring!
maple magic me
out of insanity
from scarecrow in girl again
then dance me toss me
catch!

DOROTHY LIVESAY, "Sorcery", 1969, rev. 1971.

Release

the essence is
    to catch the bird in season
hold, hold a snowdrop
    capped and cool
in the cold snow
then let it go.

DOROTHY LIVESAY, "Old song", 1967.

Relief

Soup Is Good But We Want Right To Work.

J.W. BENGOUGH, "Lesson XXIX", *The up-to-date primer*, 1896, 43.

Religion

Every man's religion is his own, and nobody else's business.

T.C. HALIBURTON, *Sam Slick*, 1836, ch.XXIV.

If I had my religion to choose, and warn't able to judge for myself, I'll tell you what I'd do: I'd jist ask myself, Who leads the best lives?

T.C. HALIBURTON, *Sam Slick*, 1836, ch.XXIV.

The mackerel run as freely into a Catholic's or Baptist's net as into any other, and I naturally enough ask myself why as a legislator I should make distinctions which God in His own good providence has not made?

JOSEPH HOWE, letter to his constituents, Oct. 22, 1840.

They are Crees, their language a pretty one; the astonishing thing was to hear them repeat long exercises, such as the creed, sing hymns, read the Testament etc. in English: *not one word of which* any of them understood.

JOHN HENRY LEFROY, letter to Sophia Lefroy, Aug. 8, 1843, Norway House.

By means of Church Endowments, church has been set against church, family against family, sectarian hatred has been fostered, religion has been brought into contempt by the scramble for public plunder, and infidelity has been in no small degree promoted by the sight of men preaching one day the worthlessness of lucre, and battling on the next to clutch a little of that same commodity, though gained by the grossest partiality and injustice – and all this to serve the cause of religion.

GEORGE BROWN, 1851; qu., Buckingham, *Life of Mackenzie*, 12.

They have the ten commandments at their fingers' end.

THOMAS C. HALIBURTON, *Sam Slick's wise saws*, 1853, ch. 15.

Let me know only this – *I was lost and undone*
But am saved by the blood of the Crucified One
And I'm *wise* although knowing no more!

PAMELIA S.V. YULE, "Littlewit and Loftus", 1881.

So long as I have a seat in this House, so long as I occupy the position I do now, whenever it shall become my duty to take a stand upon any question whatever, that stand I will take, not from the point of view of Roman Catholicism, not from the point of view of Protestantism, but from a point of view which can appeal to the consciences of all men, irrespective of their particular faith, upon grounds which can be occupied by all men who love justice, freedom, and toleration.

SIR WILFRID LAURIER, H. of C., *Debates*, Mar. 3, 1896, 2759.

The more I think about such matters, the more the distinction between sacred and secular diminishes. Theoretically, for me, there is no such distinction.

JAMES S. WOODSWORTH, letter to Charles Sissons, Feb. 14, 1901.

The essence of religion is the emotion, not the thought – the sure and certain conviction, not the logical conclusion.

BLISS CARMAN, *The kinship of nature*, 1904, 95.

About the only people who don't quarrel over religion are the people who haven't any.

ROBERT C. (BOB) EDWARDS, Calgary *Eye Opener*, Oct. 15, 1910.

There are dangers: all may become secular; there are wonderful possibilities: all may become sacred. For good or for evil we are out into the new world. Exclusive religion must more and more give way to an all-inclusive religion. Religion in the future will no longer be identified with the Church and Sundays and prayers and priests, it will become the every day life of the common man — that or nothing.

> JAMES S. WOODSWORTH, "Sermons for the unsatisfied", in *Grain growers' guide*, July 7, 1915, 8.

I have no temple and no creed,
I celebrate no mystic rite;
The human heart is all I need
Wherein I worship day and night.

> ROBERT NORWOOD, "After the order of Melchisedec", 1917.

Religion is for me not so much a personal relation between "me" and "God" as rather the identifying of myself with or perhaps the losing of myself in some larger whole.

> J.S. WOODSWORTH, "My religion", scrapbook clipping, 1926, qu. in K. McNaught, *A prophet in politics*, 1959, 159.

We have reluctantly come to the conclusion that the denominational divisions, of which the people are daily reminded, so far from exercising a beneficent influence in the direction of cleaner politics, have failed to check, if indeed they have not contributed to, the general demoralization.

> GREAT BRITAIN. NEWFOUNDLAND ROYAL COMMISSION, *Report*, 1933, 88.

The religion of tomorrow will be less concerned with the dogmas of theology and more concerned with the social welfare of humanity.

> T.C. DOUGLAS, *Research rev.*, Regina, 1934, 2.

The basis of all religious belief is the child's fear of the dark.

> HUGH MACLENNAN, *Two solitudes*, 1945, 74.

My religion and my philosophy of life are founded upon a belief in the scientific development of man, up to an ultimate knowledge of the Truth as taught by Christ; and the development of a social system in perfect harmony with Nature's laws, which are the laws of God.

> HENRY WISE WOOD, "My religion", qu. in Rolph, *Wood*, 1950, 63.

I believe there are more religious floaters in Calgary than in any other city I have ever seen.

> H. FRASER, Calgary businessman to W.E. Mann, qu. in W.E. Mann, *Sect, cult and church in Alberta*, 1955, 135.

Religion was insurance. It meant you got security afterwards. It meant you could always turn over a new leaf. Just as long as you got an act of perfect contrition said before your last end, you'd be all set.

> BRIAN MOORE, *The lonely passion of Judith Hearne*, 1955 (1965, 49).

To the Indian the white man's Christian principles appear as a false front to conceal his real ends: power, prestige and money.

> JOHN ANAQUOD, address, Welfare Council of Regina Conference, Oct. 30-Nov. 1, 1958.

These studies have convinced us that the religious life of man must find embodiment in cultural forms and that cultural forms must be animated by ultimate religious interests. If religion without culture is empty, culture without religion is blind.

> R.C. CHALMERS and J.A. IRVING, eds., *Challenge and response*, 1959, vii.

Big Cyrus in the old religion trod.
He was no reed whom winds of
    pleasure bowed;
With face as stony as the land he
    plowed
He read his Bible and he loved his
    God.

> FRED COGSWELL, "Big Cyrus", 1960.

In few countries in the western world
has religion exerted as great an influence upon the development of the
community as it has in Canada.

> S.D. CLARK, *The developing Canadian
> community*, 1962, 168.

Religion as we know it, as distinct
from Christianity, is, in my opinion,
coming to an end, in spite of the
present evidences of its power.

> PIERRE BERTON, *The comfortable pew*,
> 1965, 139.

Religion and "race" are the two basic
conditioning categories of Canadian
life, for they determine all the others.
They are the dominant factor in education, school attendance, literacy, size
of family, economic status, type of
housing, occupation, in birth rate,
death rate, life-expectancy.

> A.R.M. LOWER, in W.J. Megill, ed., *Pat-
> terns of Canada*, 1966, 149.

In the mathematics of God
there are percentages beyond one
    hundred.

> MARGARET AVISON, "First", 1966.

It is one of the discoveries of the
present age that you can be both a
Christian and an atheist.

> ERNEST HARRISON, *A church without
> God*, 1966, 40.

The most obvious perpetuator of old
traditions and prejudices is the ethnic
church.

> DAVID MILLETT, in D.I. Davies & K.
> Herman, eds., *Social space: Canadian
> perspectives*, 1971, 176.

Remembrance

What Love anticipates may die in
    flower,
What Love possesses may be mine an
    hour,
    But redly gleam in life's unlit
        Decembers
    What Love remembers.

> ETHELWYN WETHERALD, "What love re-
> members", 1907.

Remembrance
is a foolish act, a double-headed snake
striking in both directions.

> JOHN NEWLOVE, "The double-headed
> snake", 1968.

The greatest
beauty is to be alive, forgetting
    nothing,
although remembrance hurts,
like a foolish act, is a foolish act.

> JOHN NEWLOVE, "The double-headed
> snake", 1968.

Renewal

Let me renew myself
in the midst of all the things of the
    world
which cannot be connected.

> LEONARD COHEN, "The glass dog", 1964.

Repression

We have for generation after generation been a repressed people, the repressed civility covering rage. A Canadian has been defined as someone who
says "I'm so sorry" to a fellow who
steps on his toe.

WILLIAM KILBOURN, *Globe and Mail*, Dec. 12, 1970, 7.

Republicanism

Because our monarch is not resident,
Some people want to have a president.
They feel we should be much more
    up-to-date
If we were to elect our Head of State.
Republic's what they want; perhaps
    banana,
Perhaps akin to Kenya or to Ghana?

EUGENE FORSEY, "Something gay from Bali?", qu. in his *Freedom and order*, 1974, 19.

Reputation

What is the boasted bubble,
    reputation?
To-day it is the world's loud cry
Which may to-morrow die,
Or roll from generation unto
    generation
And magnify and grow to fame,
That quenchless glory round a great
    man's name.

CHARLES HEAVYSEGE, "Good deeds", 1865.

Research

It is important to consider how much of the "research" that goes on represents investigations truly rewarding in the intellectual sense. It is also desirable to consider how much teaching is really calculated to nourish and liberate the mind rather than to convey useful facts and techniques. It is a nice question whether the intellectual light of the universities, in becoming diffused over an ever widening area, may not also be growing correspondingly dim.

HILDA NEATBY, in G. P. Gilmour, ed., *Canada's tomorrow*, 1954, 212.

How is it that by now
The shaft of vision falling on obscurity
Illumines nothing, yet discovers
The ways of the obscure?

MARGARET AVISON, "The Agnes Cleves papers", 1960.

If careful, critical inquiry be accepted as the essence of research, and the inquiring mind as the one instrument essential to the carrying on of research, then surely, whether that mind engages in formal and elaborate research projects or whether it ponders over problems of teaching and learning and attempts to work out ways of bringing students to a clearer understanding of a difficult subject, such a mind and its possessor, in either case, are equally worthy of admiration, academic honour, and monetary reward.

KENNETH F. CLUTE, *The general practitioner*, 1963, 372.

The scientist will have to accept the fact that most research activities have become political in the best sense of that word and must be guided by national goals and subjected to systematic review in the light of these objectives.

CANADA. SENATE SPECIAL COMM. ON SCIENCE POLICY, *Report: a science policy for Canada*, 1970, 271.

Resistance

There is no maxim which experience teaches more clearly than this, that you must yield to the times. Resistance may be protracted until it produces revolution. Resistance was protracted in this country until it produced rebellion.

SIR JOHN A. MACDONALD, in H. of C., qu. in *Globe*, Nov. 10, 1854, 2.

Our civilization, it seems to me, runs a risk of making us too effeminate. It admits the right of passive resistance, but it shudders overmuch at any man advocating the right (and sometimes the duty) of armed resistance to grievous wrong.

SIR RICHARD CARTWRIGHT, speech to Young Liberal Club, Seaforth, Ont., Oct., 27, 1886.

There is nothing higher or holier in human nature than the sacred germ of resistance, that leads us to resist oppression and fight for liberty. The spineless worker who wipes his eyes and groans and says, "Thank God it is no worse" is of no more use to the world than a dead rabbit.

HERBERT N. CASSON, *Toronto souvenir Labour day programme*, 1898.

Resistance on the part of a woman is an effort put forth for the purpose of defeating its own object.

ARNOLD HAULTAIN, *Hints for lovers*, 1909, 139.

We must resist. We must refuse to disappear.

MARGARET ATWOOD, "Roominghouse, winter", 1968.

Respect

Some people have so much respect for their superiors they have none left for themselves.

PETER MCARTHUR, d. 1924, qu. in *The best of Peter McArthur*, 1967, 204.

Responsibility

My rule is to let everyone skin his own foxes.

THOMAS C. HALIBURTON, *Sam Slick's wise saws*, 1853, Intro.

Rest

Roughing it is the best form of rest, a lesson which needs to be learned by this work-shunning generation of ours.

GEORGE M. GRANT, letter to his wife, Summer, 1883, qu. in W. L. Grant, *Principal Grant*, 1904, 253.

Rest, with nothing else, results in rust. It corrodes the mechanisms of the brain. The rhubarb that no one picks goes to seed.

WILDER PENFIELD, address, Canadian Club, Montreal, Dec., 1959.

Retaliation

Retaliation always breeds violence.

WILLIAM E. BLATZ, *Human security*, 1966, 6.

Retirement

The child says, "When I am a big boy". But what is that? The big boy says "When I grow up". And then, grown up, he says, "When I get married". But to be married, what is that after all? The thought changes to "When I'm able to retire". And then, when retirement comes, he looks back over the landscape traversed; a cold wind seems to sweep over it; somehow he has missed it all, and it is gone. Life, we learn too late, is in the living, in the tissue of every day and hour.

STEPHEN LEACOCK, "Education eating up life", in *Too much college*, 1939, 19.

Listen, it's like this. Have you ever been out for a late autumn walk in the closing part of the afternoon, and suddenly looked up to realize that the leaves have practically all gone! You hadn't realized it. And you notice that the sun has set already, the day gone before you knew it — and with a cold wind that blows across the landscape. That's retirement.

STEPHEN B. LEACOCK, *Too much college*, 1939, 175.

Don't resign. Wait until you're sacked. Don't retire. Wait until you're dead.

SIR JAMES DUNN, qu. in Lord Beaverbrook, *Courage: the story of Sir James Dunn*, 1961, 30, improving on Tim Healey's advice.

The time for retirement should be reorganized and renamed. It is the time for embarking on a new career.

WILDER PENFIELD, address, Canadian Club, Montreal, Dec., 1959.

I'll continue working as long as I'm able, but now it's a day to day basis. I never look too far ahead. In fact, with the traffic situation the way it is, I only look a few hours ahead.

DR. J. EDGAR DAVEY, 90, of Hamilton, one of Canada's oldest practising physicians, qu. in *Liberty*, Aug., 1963.

Though I am retired, I am now working for a new company, the Honeydo Corporation. My wife now tells me: "Honey, do this. Honey, do that".

MAX MCDONALD, age 62, retired after 37 years with Inco, Sudbury, Ont., qu. in D. J. Baum, *Final plateau*, 1974, 54.

Retreat

It was then that I made myself into an envelope into which I could thrust my work deep, lick the flap, seal it from everybody.

EMILY CARR, *Growing pains*, 1946, 187.

Return

Hurled back, defeated, like a child I sought
The loving shelter of my native fields,
Where Fancy still her magic sceptre wields,
And still the miracles of youth are wrought.

PETER MCARTHUR, "Earth born", 1907.

Reunions

Almost from the moment friends separate, or lovers,
each becomes somebody else, another living on inside the other.
A year passes, five years, ten.
Something always dies when we meet again.

ALDEN NOWLAN, "Reunion", 1971.

Revenge of the Cradle

Revenge of the cradle.

ANON., trans. of "La revanche des berceaux", popular in Quebec; refers to the objective of revenge against the British Conquest of 1759 by means of overwhelming French-Canadian re-population; see Louis Lalande S.J. "La revanche des berceaux" in *L'action francaise*, Vol. 2, No. 3, Mar., 1918, 98-108.

The revenge of the cradles should naturally lead to thinking about the protection of the cradles.

ABBÉ LIONEL GROULX, address, Monument National, Montreal, Apr. 10, 1918. (Trans.)

In the ensuing battle both the British and French generals were mortally wounded, but the British refused to admit that it was a draw. The French therefore went back to their farms swearing that they would have "La revanche du berceau", a French expression meaning the family allowance.

ERIC NICOL, *An uninhibited history of Canada*, 1959, [10].

Reverence

Reverence rather than freedom is the matrix of human nobility.

GEORGE P. GRANT, *Technology and empire*, 1969, 43.

Revolution

No revolution, however justifiable on other grounds, should be attempted without an almost certainty of success.

> CHARLES HINDENLANG, Defendant, *Report of the state trials, Montreal, 1838-9*, 1839, Vol. 2, 27.

The world no longer believes in the divine right of either kings or presidents to govern wrong; but those who seek to change an established government by force of arms assume a fearful responsibility – a responsibility which nothing but the clearest and most intolerable injustice will acquit them for assuming.

> GEORGE BROWN, speech in Toronto, 1863.

Revolt is essential to progress, not necessarily the revolt of violence, but always the revolt that questions the established past and puts it to the proof, that finds the old forms outworn and invents new forms for new matters.

> DUNCAN CAMPBELL SCOTT, Presidential address, Roy. Soc. of Can., May 17, 1922.

Revolution has always brought reaction and this is sadly true even when the revolution has been beneficent in spirit and friendly to liberty.

> GEORGE M. WRONG, paper read at First Annual Conservative Summer School, Newmarket, Ont., Sept., 1933.

Replace the slave state face
With a face of bread:
Each shall choose his place,
Be Dead, or Red.
The cards are no way stacked,
And he may live by grace
Who wills to act.

> A. J. M. SMITH, "The face", 1938.

If we are no longer in a democracy, then let us begin the revolution without delay. The people are being asked to commit suicide. Citizens of Quebec, do not be content to complain. Enough of patchwork solutions, now is the time for cataclysms.

> PIERRE E. TRUDEAU, speech against wartime conscription, Outremont by-election campaign, Nov., 1942; qu. in W. Stewart, *Shrug*, 1971, 8.

In Canada we have no revolutionary tradition; and our historians, political scientists, and philosophers have assiduously tried to educate us to be proud of this fact. How can such a people expect their democracy to be dynamic as the democracies of Britain and France and the United States have been?

> F. H. UNDERHILL, in *Can. hist. assoc.*, 1946, 12.

Quebec's revolution, if it had taken place, would first have consisted in freeing man from collective coercions: freeing the citizens brutalized by reactionary and arbitrary governments; freeing consciences bullied by a clericalized and obscurantist Church; freeing workers exploited by an oligarchic capitalism; freeing men crushed by authoritarian and outdated traditions. Quebec's revolution would have consisted in the triumph of the freedoms of the human being as inalienable rights, over and above capital, the nation, tradition, the Church, and even the State.

> PIERRE E. TRUDEAU, *Cité libre*, May, 1964, 3. (Trans.)

Not dissenters, but those who would diminish or deny the right to dissent are the really dangerous revolutionaries.

> LESTER B. PEARSON, *Queen's quart.*, Vol. 76, Spring, 1969, 20.

It was a case of six kids trying to make a revolution.

> JAMES R. CROSS, after his release from Front du Libération du Québec kidnappers, Dec. 3, 1970.

Rewards

It is human nature to work harder at a price.

> R. O. SWEEZEY, Canada. H. of C. Spec. comm. on Beauharnois power project, *Proc.*, 1931, Vol. 2, 728.

The Rich

What a country! Here all the knaves grow rich, and the honest men are ruined.

> MONTCALM, 1758; qu., Parkman, *Montcalm and Wolfe*, II, ch. 23. (Trans.).

He made himself a great name in his
  day,
A glittering fellow on the world's hard
  way;
He tilled and seeded and reaped
  plentifully
From the black soil of human misery.
He won great riches, and they buried
  him
With splendour that the people's
  wants make grim;
But some day he shall not be called to
  mind
Save as the curse and pestilence of his
  kind.

> ARCHIBALD LAMPMAN, "Epitaph on a rich man", Dec. 18, 1893.

Parvenues are as plentiful as blackberries and the vulgar ostentation of the common rich is not a pleasant sight.

> GEORGE T. DENISON, (Police magistrate of Toronto), letter to Charles Mair, Dec. 31, 1911.

The great way to inspire brotherly love all round is to keep on getting richer and richer till you have so much money that everyone loves you.

> STEPHEN LEACOCK, "Over the grape juice", in *Further foolishness*, 1916, 109.

The rise of the great trusts, the obvious and glaring fact of the money power, the shameless luxury of the rich, the crude, uncultivated and boorish mob of vulgar men and overdressed women that masqueraded as high society – the substitution, shall we say, of the saloon for the salon – all this seemed to many an honest observer of humble place as but the handwriting on the wall that foretold the coming doom.

> STEPHEN LEACOCK, in J.O. Miller, *The new era in Canada*, 1917, 17.

Make money and the whole nation will conspire to call you a gentleman.

> ROBERT C. (BOB) EDWARDS, *Summer annual*, 1920, 69.

Because the fellow thinks me rich
  These days he bows to me:
The beggar bows to dollars;
  He does not bow to me.

> TOM MACINNES, "Just so", 1923.

I don't want my children and sons-in-law to be rich. But I want them to show me to my satisfaction that they can make their daily bread.

> FREDERICK PHILIP GROVE, *Our daily bread*, 1928, 217.

Borne in charioted ease,
Human bodies grow effete;
Sunk in soft prosperities
Fervent spirits lose their heat.
Happier he who tries in vain
Heights no travail can attain.

> WATSON KIRKCONNELL, "Labor salvator", 1930.

Never before in history has the disparity between the rich and the poor, the
comfortable and the starving, been so
extreme; never before have mass communications so vividly informed the
sufferers of the extent of their misery;
never before have the privileged societies possessed weapons so powerful
that their employment in the defence
of privilege would destroy the haves
and the have-nots indiscriminately.

PIERRE E. TRUDEAU, speech, University of
Alberta, Edmonton, May 13, 1968.

Ridicule

I wish nature had not given me such a
quick perception of the ridiculous –
such a perverse inclination to laugh in
the wrong place; for though one cannot help deriving from it a wicked
enjoyment, it is a very troublesome
gift, and very difficult to conceal.

SUSANNA MOODIE, *Life in the clearings*,
1854, 349.

Riding

At 100 Mile House the cowboys ride in
rolling
stagey cigarettes with one hand
reining
restive equine rebels on a morning
grey as stone . . .

ALFRED PURDY, "The Cariboo horses",
1965.

Riel, Louis

Men of Ontario, Shall Scott's Blood
Cry in Vain for Vengeance?

ANON., plea on posters protesting the
execution by Louis Riel of Thomas
Scott, Red River, Mar. 4, 1870.

We must make Canada respect us.

LOUIS RIEL, referring to the execution of
Thomas Scott, Mar. 4, 1870.

This is the most thorny business I ever
have had to deal with, thanks to the
imbecility of almost everyone who has
hitherto meddled with it.

LORD DUFFERIN, letter to Earl of Carnarvon, Dec. 4, 1874, re: Riel rebellion.

I suppose when he dies he will be
canonized.

ALEXANDER MACKENZIE, letter to Lt.-
Gov. A. Morris, Dec. 11, 1874.(Pub.
Arch. Can.)

God, who has always led you and
assisted you until the present hour, will
not abandon you in the dark hours of
your life, for He has given you a
mission which you must fulfil entirely.

BISHOP IGNACE BOURGET of Montreal,
letter to Louis Riel, July 14, 1875.
(Trans.)

I was treated there as charitably as any
lunatic could be.

LOUIS RIEL, letter, 1878, to doctor who
had been attending him during period
of confinement at St. Jean de Dieu
asylum at Longue Pointe and Beauport
asylum, Mar., 1876 to Jan., 1878.

Sir John A. Macdonald doth govern
proudly
The provinces from which his power
flows;
While his bad faith perpetuates my
woes –
And all his countrymen applaud him
loudly.

LOUIS RIEL, "To Sir John A. Macdonald",
1879. (Trans.)

The Prophet of the New World.

LOUIS RIEL, term by which he referred to
himself, ca. 1883.

O my God, do not permit England to
get the better of me, for she would
annihilate me, together with my nation.

LOUIS RIEL, *Diary*, May 8, 1885. (Trans.)

Politics will save me.

> LOUIS RIEL, after battle of Batoche, May 11, 1885, qu. by John S. Thompson, Minister of Justice, H. of C., *Debates*, Mar. 22, 1886, 268.

Strangle Riel with the French flag! That is the only use that rag can have in this country.

> TORONTO *NEWS*, May 18, 1885.

I know that through the grace of God, I am the founder of Manitoba.

> LOUIS RIEL, July, 1885, words sandblasted into concrete shell housing statue of Riel, Provincial Legislature Buildings, Winnipeg.

So I see they have sentenced my poor friend Riel. By heaven they ought to string up a number of the Government officials if they hang him.

> A.G.B. BANNATYNE, in 1885, qu. in H. Bowsfield, *Louis Riel*, 1969, 2.

He shall hang though every dog in Quebec bark in his favour.

> SIR JOHN A. MACDONALD, 1885, to a friend who urged that Riel be shown mercy.

Had there been no neglect there would have been no rebellion. If no rebellion then no arrest. If no arrest, then no trial. If no trial, then no condemnation. If no condemnation, then no execution. They therefore who are responsible for the first are responsible for every link in that fatal chain.

> EDWARD BLAKE, on the execution of Riel, 1885, qu. in George R. Parkin, *Sir John A. Macdonald*, 1910, 280.

The God damned son of a bitch is gone at last.

> ANON., Police officer at hanging of Riel, Regina, Nov. 16, 1885, qu. in Regina *Leader*, Nov. 19, 1885, 4.

Henceforth there are no more conservatives nor liberals nor castors. There are only PATRIOTS AND TRAITORS – THE NATIONAL PARTY AND THE PARTY OF THE ROPE.

> MONTREAL *LA PRESSE*, Nov. 16, 1885, 2. (Trans.)

Riel will leave no trace in the memories of men by the work he has done, the ideas he has given forth, the doctrines he has preached, and yet his name marks a deep furrow in the political soil of our young country. The reason is that the hand that placed the gallows rope about his neck wounded a whole people. It is because the cry of justice, calling for his death in the name of the law, has been drowned by the cry of fanaticism calling for revenge. That is why the death of this criminal takes on the proportions of a national calamity.

> *LA MINERVE*, Montreal, Nov. 17, 1885.

At the dawn of day on the 12th I had decided to give up the seat I had in the Cabinet and follow the current, but suddenly I glanced in front of me, in the distance such a sight, tumult, fighting, bloodshed, misery and prostration; and a madman looking from the window of a prison and laughing, rubbing his hands and shouting incoherent words of malediction.

> J.A. CHAPLEAU, letter to W.W. Lynch, Nov. 21, 1885.(Pub. Arch. Can.)

Riel, our brother, is dead, the victim of his devotion to the cause of the Métis of whom he was the leader, the victim of fanaticism and treason – of the fanaticism of Sir John and some of his friends, of the treason of three of our own, who, to keep their portfolios, have sold their brother.

> HONORÉ MERCIER, speech, Champ de Mars, Montreal, Nov. 22, 1885. (Trans.)

If the French desire to destroy Sir John Macdonald, in God's name let them do it on grounds other than the execution of Riel. The Dominion is not bound up in the fate of any one political leader or party.

TORONTO *DAILY MAIL*, editorial, Nov. 23, 1885, 4.

Riel was fairly tried, honestly convicted, laudably condemned, and justly executed.

WINNIPEG *FREE PRESS*, Dec. 17, 1885.

It cannot be said that Riel was hanged on account of his opinions. It is equally true that he was not executed for anything connected with the late rebellion. He was hanged for Scott's murder; that is the simple truth of it.

SIR WILFRID LAURIER, letter to Edward Blake, Dec. 31, 1885.

I do not propose to construct a political platform out of the Regina scaffold, or to create or cement party ties with the blood of the condemned.

EDWARD BLAKE, speech in London, Jan. 14, 1886.

The Little Napoleon of Red River.

ANON., a nickname quoted in W.J. McRaye, *Town hall tonight*, 1929, 162.

In essence the troubles associated with the name of Louis Riel were the manifestation, not of the traditional rivalries of French Catholic Quebec and English Protestant Ontario, but of the traditional problems of cultural conflict, of the clash between primitive and civilized peoples.

GEORGE F.G. STANLEY, *Louis Riel, patriot or rebel*, 1955, 3.

By the Resistance Riel saved the French element in the North-West from neglect and oblivion. He saved them both from the heedless aggression of Ontario and the parochial indifference of Quebec. By the Resistance Riel challenged Quebec to play a positive part in Confederation, to maintain French institutions throughout Canada and not merely in Quebec.

W. L. MORTON, in W. L. Morton, ed., *Alexander Begg's Red River journal*, 1956, 148.

Riel's criminal conduct in inciting the Indians all over the Northwest territories to go on the warpath itself settles the question of his guilt, and makes simply ludicrous the desire of a certain number of Canadians to have him viewed as a hero and a martyr.

G. H. NEEDLER, *Louis Riel: the rebellion of 1885*, 1957, Preface.

Riel Rebellion

I can remember once at a party somebody sneering at one of the Riel Rebellions: only seven people killed. What on earth would he be satisfied with? Tamburlaine's pyramid of human skulls?

JAMES REANEY, *Edge*, Autumn, 1964, 20.

There on the prairie there were people waiting to stop moving. Somewhere west was too far
and the day eased away into language.

PATRICK LANE, "For Riel in that Gawdam prison", 1973.

Right and Wrong

Right hath the sweeter grace,
But wrong the prettier face.

FREDERICK G. SCOTT, "Wrong and right", 1894.

We come indeed from Hell and climb to Heaven; the Golden Age stands at the never-attainable end of history, not at Man's origins. Every step forward is bound to be a compromise; right and wrong are inseparably mixed; the best we can hope for is to make right prevail more and more; to reduce wrong to a smaller and smaller fraction of the whole till it reaches a vanishing point.

FREDERICK PHILIP GROVE, *A search for America*, 1927, 436.

Righteousness

My countrymen, is it not meet, right and our bounden duty that we who have been helped so much in the past by our parents and neighbours should now, in the young manhood of our national life, go forth into the world and let our light so shine before men that they may see our good works and glorify our Father which is in heaven?

D. W. AMBRIDGE, in *Canada's tomorrow; Quebec City, November, 1953*, 1954, 116.

Rights

What peoples hope for, they think at last they have a right to, and when they are disappointed, they actilly think they are ill-used.

T.C. HALIBURTON, *Sam Slick's wise saws*, 1853, I, 239.

We have no absolute rights among us. The rights of each man, in our state of society, end precisely at the point where they encroach upon the rights of others.

SIR WILFRID LAURIER, speech on political liberalism, Quebec, June 26, 1877.

In any civilized community private rights should cease when they become public wrongs.

W. L. MACKENZIE KING, "Report of the Deputy Minister of Labour, 1906-7", Canada. Parliament. Sessional papers (1907-8), No. 36, 50.

1. It is hereby recognized and declared that in Canada there have existed and shall continue to exist without discrimination by reason of race, national origin, colour, religion or sex, the following human rights and fundamental freedoms, namely (a) the right of the individual to life, liberty, security of the person and enjoyment of property, and the right not to be deprived thereof except by due process of law; (b) the right of the individual to equality before the law and the protection of the law; (c) freedom of religion; (d) freedom of speech; (e) freedom of assembly and association; and (f) freedom of the press.

CANADA. LAWS, STATUTES, etc. *Canadian Bill of Rights*, enacted Aug. 10, 1960, Vol. I, Ch. 44.

The "right" to a minimum wage, for example, or to adequate and inexpensive medical care, or to an education, or to a free and creative use of the intellect, is simply a "right" to behave in a way that is intrinsic to being human; it needs no more justification than the crowing of a cock.

LIONEL TIGER and ROBIN FOX, *The imperial animal*, 1971, 238.

Riots

Shiner Riots.

ANON., outbreaks of violence in Bytown (Ottawa) between 1828 and 1843. "Shiner" was an anglicized version of *cheneur* or oak-cutter.

Any foreigners who make any threats of any kind or in any way intimidate or worry would-be workers in the slightest degree can expect immediate deportation to Russia or wherever they come from. We intend to purge the city of any lawless element and prosecute to the full rigor of the law.

> ANON., form of "Riot Act" read in Winnipeg, June 23, 1919, reproduced in *Manitoba Free press*, June 23, 1919.

Her Majesty the Queen charges and commands all persons meeting assembled immediately to disperse and peaceably to depart to their habitation or their lawful business upon pain of being guilty of an offence for which upon conviction they may be sentenced to imprisonment for life. GOD SAVE THE QUEEN.

> CANADA. LAWS, STATUTES, etc. "The Riot Act", (Criminal Code, 1953-4, c. 51, s. 68).

Rivals

All women are rivals. And this they never forget.

> ARNOLD HAULTAIN, *Hints for lovers*, 1909, 41.

Rivers

Who ever calmly views the admirable formation and distribution of the Rivers so wonderfully conducted to their several seas; must confess the whole to have been traced by the finger of the Great Supreme Artificer for the most benevolent purposes, both to his creature Man, and the numerous Animals he has made, none of whom can exist without water.

> DAVID THOMPSON, *Narrative of his explorations in western America 1784-1812.* (Champlain Soc., 1916, 189).

Out and in the river is winding
The links of its long red chain,
Through belts of dusky pine-land
And gusty leagues of plain.

> JOHN G. WHITTIER, "Red River voyageur", 1854.

He who drinks Red River water once, must drink it again.

> ANON., became a popular saying in the West, about 1880, later applied to other rivers, such as the Peace, etc.; *The Week*, Dec. 4, 1884, 7.

Oh, rivers rolling to the sea
From lands that bear the maple tree.

> CHARLES G.D. ROBERTS, "Canadian streams", 1893.

Wind-silvered willows hedge the
		stream,
And all within is hushed and cool.
The water, in an endless dream,
Goes sliding down from pool to pool.
And every pool a sapphire is
From shadowy deep to sunlit edge,
Ribboned around with irises
And cleft with emerald spears of
		sedge.

> MARJORIE PICKTHALL, "Dream river", 1905.

Peace and Athabasca and Coppermine
		and Slave,
And Yukon and Mackenzie – the
		highroads of the brave.

Saskatchewan, Assiniboine, the Bow
		and the Qu'Appelle,
And many a prairie river whose name
		is like a spell.

> BLISS CARMAN, "Rivers of Canada", Apr. 27, 1922.

A river is never quite silent; it can never, of its very nature, be quite still; it is never quite the same from one day to the next. It has its own life and its own beauty and the creatures it nourishes are alive and beautiful also. Perhaps fishing is, for me, only an excuse to be near rivers.

RODERICK HAIG-BROWN, *A river never sleeps*, 1950, 352.

Roads

The King's Highway.

ANON., from early French-Canadian usage.

It may be said, indeed, that each traveller makes his own road. If he be aware of the direction which he ought to follow, he chooses the part of the prairie where the ground is best fitted for driving. Nothing is easier than to drive over the stoneless and springing turf of the virgin prairie, and if the traffic be not too great, an excellent "trail" is made by the passage of successive vehicles.

W. FRASER RAE, *Newfoundland to Manitoba*, 1881, 249.

From plains that reel to southward, dim,
    The road runs by me white and bare;
Up the steep hill it seems to swim
    Beyond, and melt into the glare.

ARCHIBALD LAMPMAN, "Heat", 1888.

De corduroy road go bompety bomp,
    De corduroy road go jompety jomp,
An' he's takin' beeg chance upset hees load
    De horse dat'll trot on de corduroy road.

WILLIAM H. DRUMMOND, "The corduroy road", 1902.

Half a log, half a log,
    Half a log onward,
Shaken and out of breath,
    Rode we and wondered.
Ours not to reason why,
    Ours but to clutch and cry
While onward we thundered.

CARRIE M. HOOPLE, "The corduroy road", 1909.

From igloo to igloo.

LESTER B. PEARSON, at a rally in Regina, Mar. 1, 1958, during election campaign, referring to Diefenbaker's northern road building program.

Roads to Resources.

ALVIN HAMILTON, Minister of Northern Affairs and National Resources, H. of C., *Debates*, July 7, 1958, 1980. Programme of federal assistance available to all provinces for road-building for northern development.

I think policemen should come out from behind the bushes and travel on the highway like everyone else.

PHILIP GAGLARDI, B. C. Highways Minister and multiple speeding offender, qu. in *Liberty*, Sept., 1963.

There will be four lanes west, four lanes east and four lanes for ambulances.

PAUL HANOVER, announcer, CHML, Toronto, observing Bypass Highway 401 being widened to 12 lanes, qu. in *Liberty*, Nov., 1963.

No doubt we on this continent have always tended to exaggerate the importance of mere size; none the less, it is gratifying to know that the 5,000-mile Trans-Canada Highway is the longest continuous road on earth.

EDWARD MCCOURT, *The road across Canada*, 1965, 2.

I have travelled this road many times
though not in this place . . .

JOHN NEWLOVE, "By the church wall",
1965.

The road curved
down and down.
Footsteps of others in the snow
told me the way I must go on.

RAYMOND SOUSTER, "The walk", 1967.

The mental highways are far more
important than those built of asphalt
and cement.

W. GUNTHER PLAUT, in Canadian Mental
Health Assn., *Probings*, 1968, 64.

And each new curve
moves us further on
both poem and high
way, taking
us out of
ourselves

into what passes.

DOUGLAS BARBOUR, *A poem as long as
the highway*, 1971, [2].

Rocky Mountains

A sea of mountains.

W. B. CHEADLE and VISCOUNT MILTON,
The northwest passage by land, 1865,
366. The phrase was used in the sentence "Cariboo is a sea of mountains and
pine-clad hills, the former rising to a
height of 7,000 or 8,000 feet, surrounded by a confused congeries of the latter". The phrase was much used in the
1870's. See T. Anglin, *Parliamentary
debates*, 1871, II, 718, and G. M. Grant,
From ocean to ocean, 1873, 267 (see
below), 292. It was popularized by Edward Blake in his speech at Aurora,
Ontario, Oct. 3, 1874, and in his *A
national sentiment*, 1874.

Seas of mountains and grassless valleys,
equally inhospitable.

GEORGE M. GRANT, *Ocean to ocean*,
1873, 267.

The Rockies run the length of the
continent, and are in league with
Eternity.

FREDERICK JOHN NIVEN, "The call of the
West", *Can. mag.*, LV, No. 3, July,
1920, 224.

There is told in the Northwest, the
story of an old prospector of whom,
returning home after many years, it
was asked what he had to show as the
equivalent of so much lost time; and
he answered only, "I have seen the
Rocky Mountains".

J. MONROE THORINGTON, *The glittering
mountains of Canada*, 1925, ix.

When we go into the Rockies we may
have the sense that gods are there. But
if so, they cannot manifest themselves
as ours. They are the gods of another
race, and we cannot know them because of what we are and what we did.
There can be nothing immemorial for
us except the environment as object.

GEORGE P. GRANT, *Technology and empire*, 1969, 17.

Roman Catholic Church

I would say this, to their honour and
credit, that, if to-day Canada is a
portion of the British Empire, it is due
to the conservatism of the French
Canadian clergy.

SIR GEORGE-ETIENNE CARTIER, *Confederation debates*, Feb. 7, 1865, 59.

The mission with which Providence
entrusted French Canadians is basically religious in nature: it is, namely, to
convert the unfortunate infidel local
population to Catholicism, and to expand the Kingdom of God by developing a predominantly Catholic nationality.

LOUIS LAFLÈCHE,, Bishop of Three Rivers, *Quelques considérations sur les
rapports de la société civile avec la
religion et la famille*, 1866. (Trans.)

Not only is the Church independent of the Commonwealth – she stands above it . . . It is not the Church that is comprised in the State; it is the State that is comprised in the Church.

> QUEBEC EPISCOPATE, Collective letter, Sept. 22, 1875. (Trans.)

Priests at large do not feel that they must work for truth; they have it, and with their changelessness they do not need a restatement.

> JEAN C. BRACQ, *The evolution of French Canada*, 1924, 263.

You have observed that the Roman Catholic Church never builds a church on a back street?

> DR. T. T. SHIELDS, sermon at Jarvis St. Baptist Church, Toronto, Oct. 11, 1931.

The bishops eat out of my hand.

> MAURICE DUPLESSIS, phrase frequently used in speeches as Premier of Quebec, 1936-39, 1944-59.

As long as I can keep the Jesuits scrapping with the Dominicans, I can get on with the business of the province.

> MAURICE DUPLESSIS, when Premier of Quebec, private remark, qu. in J. Barber, *Good fences make good neighbors*, 1958, 203.

Loyalty was bartered for religious freedom, and the church was as good as her word. During the wars of 1775, 1812, 1914, and 1939 the Catholic hierarchy preached submission to His Majesty's government.

> PIERRE E. TRUDEAU, *Can. journ. econ. and pol. sci.*, Vol. 24, No. 3, Aug., 1958, 300.

When in our society a person can be born, married, have children or adopt them, avail himself of social services and of the law, provide his sons and daughters with schooling and employment, then die, *without the compulsory intervention of the Church*, freedom of conscience for believers as well as non-believers will be respected. Until then, because the presence of the Church is *compulsory* at every level of civil life, the citizen of Quebec is colonized much more deeply by the grip of Rome than by American dollars.

> JACQUES GODBOUT, *Le mouvement du 8 avril*, 1966, 7. (Trans.)

Roman Catholics

The free exercise of the Catholic, Apostolic, and Roman religion, shall subsist entire, in such manner that all the states and the people of the towns and countries, places and distant posts, shall continue to assemble in the churches and to frequent the sacraments as heretofore, without being molested in any manner, directly or indirectly.

> MARQUIS DE VAUDREUIL, a demand incorporated as Article XXVII, in the Capitulation of Montreal, 1760. (Trans.)

I have taken a multitude of notes on Canada. What a frightful country! It is enough to let you know that it is essentially Catholic – Irish and French (what French? Low Normans of the seventeenth century) vying with each other in fervent rage, that is, as to which shall have the most churches, sermons, monks, and of white, black, and gray nuns.

> LOUIS MOREAU GOTTSCHALK, May, 1864, *Notes of a pianist*, 1964, 228.

797

The Martyrs of the North.

> POPE PIUS IX (1846-1878), designating the Oblates of Mary Immaculate.

I will be denounced as Anti-Christ.

> SIR WILFRID LAURIER, letter to James Young, Dec. 1875, qu. in J. Schull, *Laurier*, 1965, 106.

I hear my Curé; my curé hears the Bishop; the Bishop hears the Pope; and the Pope hears our Lord Jesus Christ, who aids with his Holy Spirit to render them infallible on the teaching and government of His Church.

> IGNACE BOURGET, Roman Catholic Bishop of Montreal, Pastoral letter, Feb. 1, 1876. (Trans.)

You wish to organize all the Catholics into one party, without other bond, without other basis, than a common religion; but have you not reflected that, by the very fact, you will organize the Protestant population as a single party and that then, instead of the peace and harmony now prevailing between the different elements of the Canadian population, you throw open the door to war, a religious war, the most terrible of all wars?

> SIR WILFRID LAURIER, speech at Quebec City, June 26, 1877. (Trans.)

I am not here to parade my religious sentiments, but I declare I have too much respect for the faith in which I was born to ever use it as the basis of a political organization.

> SIR WILFRID LAURIER, speech in Quebec, June 26, 1877. (Trans.)

I am afraid I shall have to give you the answer of the Irish servant who got into a place where the food was not as it should be — 'there's too much to swallow and too little to eat'.

> SIR JOHN A. MACDONALD, to Madame D — , wife of Judge D — , on being asked to join her church; qu., E. B. Biggar, *Anecdotal life*, 1891, 230.

I know enough of English literature, to be aware that when Shakespeare put into the mouth of King John the proud words which he made him address to the Pope's legate: —

> No Italian priest
> Shall tithe or toll in our dominion.

he touched the British heart in its most responsive chord.

> SIR WILFRID LAURIER, speech in Toronto, Sept. 30, 1889.

This violent section, you know it — comprises the Pharisee end of Canadian Catholicism; those who have constituted themselves the defenders of a religion which no one attacked; those who handle the holy water sprinkler as though it were a club; those who have arrogated to themselves the monopoly of orthodoxy; those who excommunicate right and left all whose stature is a little greater than theirs; those who seem to have only hatred and envy for motive and instinct; those who insulted Cardinal Taschereau when he was alive and who, now that he is dead, attack his memory; those who made Chapleau's life bitter; those, originally, whom the people with their picturesque language have designated under the name of Castors.

> SIR WILFRID LAURIER, speech in Montreal, Oct. 10, 1910. (Trans.)

The French Canadians are more Catholic than the Pope.

> HUGH MARTIN, *Dalhousie rev.*, 1925, 425.

A Catholic is too rich to go borrowing ideas from socialists or communists.

> ABBÉ LIONEL GROULX, address, Montreal, Nov. 29, 1943, "Why we are divided". (Trans.)

Economic status correlates closely with racial origin and religious denomination. Catholicism is the religion of the relatively poor.

> A. R. M. LOWER, in *Can. hist. rev.*, 1946, 240.

It was only the British Conquest which freed the Canadian church, so much so indeed that ever since the beginning of the English regime, it has found itself freer than under the kings of France.

> GUSTAVE LANCTOT, *Une nouvelle France inconnue*, 1955, 171. (Trans.)

The routine Catholicism of the villages does not resist the corrosion of the towns. In another generation it will perhaps be anti-clerical and anti-religious, in a second generation it will seek an answer to its questions and a hope for its miseries in Marxism.

> *LE DEVOIR*, editorial, Feb. 18, 1956. (Trans.)

Our sole religion is a psychologically contaminated Catholicism.

> JEAN LE MOYNE, *Convergence*, 1966, 44.

Many of those who have experienced French-Canadian Catholicism – it would be nonsensical to say in its fullness, but at least in the multiplicity of its excrescences – find themselves today as poor and backward as the unwashed squatting outside the temple.

> JEAN LE MOYNE, *Convergence*, 1966, 47.

The Québécois owe nothing to the Church, unless it is three centuries of obscurantism.

> PIERRE VALLIÈRES, *White niggers of America*, 1971, 175.

Roosters

O sign and wonder of the barnyard, more
beautiful than the pheasant, more melodious
than nightingale! O creature marvellous!

Prophet of sunrise, and foreteller of times!
Vizier of the constellations! Sage,
red-bearded, scarlet turbaned, in whose brain
the stars lie scattered like well-scattered grain!
Calligraphist upon the barnyard page!
Five-noted balladist! Crower of rhymes!

> A. M. KLEIN, "Psalm XXVII", 1944.

Roses

If folks will let the roses alone, the thorns will let them be.

> THOMAS C. HALIBURTON, *Sam Slick's wise saws*, 1853, ch. 17.

The rose was given to man for this:
He, sudden seeing it in later years,
Should swift remember Love's first lingering kiss
And Grief's last lingering tears.

> ISABELLA VALANCY CRAWFORD, "Rose", 1905.

Royal Canadian Mounted Police

Who are the soldiers at Red River wearing dark clothes? Our old brothers who formerly lived there [the 6th. Regiment at Fort Garry] wore red coats. We know that the soldiers of our great mother wear red coats and are our friends.

> ANON., Indians, 1872, quoted by Col. P. Robertson-Ross, *Sess. papers*, 1873, No. 9, cxi; a reference to army scarlet, and the reason for its adoption by the Police.

They are to be purely a civil, not a military body, with as little gold lace, fuss, and fine feathers as possible, not a crack cavalry regiment, but an efficient police force for the rough and ready — particularly ready — enforcement of law and justice.

SIR JOHN A, MACDONALD, May 3, 1873, in the House of Commons, on introducing the bill establishing the North West Mounted Police.

I solemnly swear that I will perform the duties required of me as a member of the Royal Northwest Mounted Police, without fear, favour or affection of or towards any person.

R.N.W.M.P. oath of office required on enlistment of the original force, estab. 1873.

Maintiens le droit.

R.N.W.M.P., motto of the force; advocated in 1873, in use 1875.

They always get their man.

JOHN J. HEALY, Editor, Fort Benton (Montana) Record, Apr. 13, 1877, as "Fetched their man every time"; R. Atkin, Maintain the right, 1973, 115.

If the Police had not come to the country, where would we be all now? Bad men and whisky were killing us so fast that very few indeed of us would have been left today. The Police have protected us as the feathers of the bird protect it from the frosts of winter. I wish them all good, and trust that all our hearts will increase in goodness from this time forward.

CROWFOOT, Blackfoot chief, on signing Treaty No. 7, at Blackfoot Crossing, Alta., Oct. 20, 1877.

We muster but three hundred
In all this great lone land,

Which stretches o'er this Continent
To where the Rockies stand;
But not one heart doth falter,
No coward lip complains,
That few, too few, in numbers are
The Riders of the Plains."

Our mission is to plant the flag
Of British freedom here:
Restrain the lawless Savage,
And protect the Pioneer;
And 'tis a proud and daring trust
To hold these vast domains,
With but three hundred mounted
men,
The Riders of the Plains.

THOMAS A. BOYS, "The riders of the plains". Authorship so attributed in Calgary Herald, Dec. 11, 1909. The poem appeared in Saskatchewan Herald, Sept. 23, 1878, signed W.S., N.W.M.P., dated "Cobourg, 1878". See also Niagara Hist. Soc. Papers 1911-12, No. 23, p. 50 for text and authorship "T.A. Boys". See also R.C.M.P. [Archives] Old Series, Ottawa, #389 "Thomas A. Boys".

Gophers.

MAJ.-GEN. FREDERICK DOBSON MIDDLETON, term used during Northwest Rebellion, 1885. A gopher was defined as "a prairie animal that retreats into a hole at the first sign of danger".

I regret to hear that such a large proportion of your command are drunkards.

LAWRENCE HERCHMER, Commissioner, R.C.M.P. to Supt. Samuel B. Steele stationed at Fort McLeod, 1892. (Pub. Arch. Can., RG 18B-3, V. 100, p. 740).

Why, these fellows would ride all day for the government, then all night for a bottle of whisky, and spend the whole of their leisure devising devilments, yet by the trickery of an oath and a uniform, Romance has created the frailest of them into perfect constables of the peace.

ROGER POCOCK, A frontiersman, 1903.

These are the men who battle the
  blizzards, the suns, the rains,
These are the famed that the North
  has named the "Riders of the
  Plains,"
And theirs is the might and the
  meaning and the strength of the
  bulldog's jaw,
While they keep the peace of the
  people and the honour of British
  law.

> E. PAULINE JOHNSON, "The riders of the
> plains", 1903.

On the 17th instant, I, Corporal Hogg,
was called to the hotel to quiet a
disturbance. I found the room full of
cowboys, and one Monaghan, or Cowboy Jack, was carrying a gun, and
pointed it at me, against sections 105
and 109 of the Criminal Code. We
struggled. Finally I got him hand-
cuffed.

> CORPORAL HOGG, report on an arrest at
> North Portal, Sask., 1906.

No more wildly impossible undertaking was ever staged than the establishment of Canadian authority and Canadian law throughout the western prairies by a handful of mounted police.

> FRANK OLIVER, Editor, Edmonton *Bulle-
> tin*, qu. in C. E. Denny, *The law
> marches west*, 1939, 4.

You have a splendid example of the
legitimate, the indispensable, the eminently useful police force in Canada
– the Northwest Mounted Police.

> CHARLES W. ELIOT, address in Ottawa, to
> the Canadian Club, Feb. 23, 1907.

In the little Crimson Manual it's
  written plain and clear
Those who wear the scarlet coat shall
  say good-bye to fear.

> ROBERT W. SERVICE, "Clancy of the
> Mounted Police", 1909.

Yellowlegs.

> ANON., from the yellow trouser-stripes of
> the Police uniform; used by malcon-
> tents.

Sergeant Blue of the Mounted Police
  was a so-so kind of guy;
He swore a bit, and he lied a bit, and
  he boozed a bit on the sly;
But he held the post at Snake Creek
  Bend in the good old British way,
And a grateful country paid him about
  sixty cents a day.

> ROBERT STEAD, "A squad of one", 1917.

I should not like to suggest how many
thousands of dollars I have cost Canada in having the police trail me
around. I want to make that very
clear; possibly I was worth watching.

> J. S. WOODSWORTH, H. of C., *Debates*,
> Apr. 4, 1922, 673.

The Silent Force.

> ANON., also a popular name from the
> title of a book by T. Morris Longstreth,
> 1927.

The Royal Canadian Mounted Police
have a well-deserved reputation for
getting their man but the fact remains
that they have to do this too often.

> C. NORTHCOTE PARKINSON, *The law of
> delay*, 1970, 22.

Royal Commissions

The politics of Billy King
  Make honest blood to boil.
His omissions are staggering,
  His Commissions are Royal.

> "CYNIC", *Can. forum*, June, 1938.

The Englishman's creed would be: "As it was in the beginning, is now, and ever shall be, world without end, Amen"; the American creed would be: "As it was in the beginning, is now, and by gosh it's got to stop"; . . . the Canadian creed would go . . . "As it was in the beginning, is now, and ladies and gentlemen, if we are going to make any changes we will appoint a Royal Commission to tell us how it is to be done".

> HENRY M. TORY, address, June 21, 1939, to Conference on Canadian-American affairs, *Proceedings*, 1940, 171.

Royal Commissions are instruments of national conscience or symptoms of national crisis.

> ROBERT WEAVER, in *Tamarack rev.* No. 4, 1957, 37.

This marks somewhat of a red-letter day in the history of economic forecasting; never before, I am sure, in the history of mankind since the time of Joseph has economic prophesying been performed on so exalted a level.

> JACOB VINER, *Queen's quart.*, Autumn, 1957, 306, referring to the Report of the Royal Commission on Canada's economic prospects, 1957.

Paris was worth a mass. Perhaps Canada is worth a royal commission?

> ANDRÉ LAURENDEAU, *Le Devoir*, Jan. 20, 1962, 4 (trans.), proposing an inquiry into bilingualism.

Royal Society of Canada

Whether or not they are men of distinction, they confer distinction upon one another.

> JOHN PORTER, *The vertical mosaic*, 1965, 497.

Upward social mobility is limited, the British charter group dominates, the political system is depoliticized in a crippling federalism. Over all this ruminate the disengaged fellows of the Royal Society of Canada, section II.

> JOHN PORTER, *The vertical mosaic*, 1965, 504.

Royalty

In truth, our boyhood imaginings suggested to us that God was a member of the Royal family or the Queen a member of the Divine family. God and the Queen were equally remote, and as it seemed to us, of about approximate ages.

> J. V. MCAREE, *Cabbagetown store*, 1953, 44, on Queen Victoria.

I think I feel the way most Canadians feel — indifferent.

> JOYCE DAVIDSON, C.B.C. commentator, referring to Royal Tour, on N.B.C. network, June, 1959, a remark which resulted in her dismissal from C.B.C.

Ruins

See that the wreck of all things made
    with hands
Being fixed and certain, as all flesh is
    grass,
    The grandiose design
Must marry the ragged matter, and of
    the vision
Nothing endure that does not gain
    through ruin
    The right, the wavering line.

> JOHN GLASSCO, "Gentleman's farm", 1958.

Some troubled joy that's half despair
    Ascends within me like a breath:
I see these silent ruins wear
The speaking look, the sleeping air
    Of features newly cast in death.

JOHN GLASSCO, "Deserted buildings under Shefford Mountain", 1958.

Rules

Surely we have learned that society and governments must play the game according to the rules of the game. If we do not, then everyone will make up his own rules as he goes along. Some of them may be better rules, but if we have two sets of rules, or eleven sets of rules we will have first suspicion, then friction, then disruption of the social order, and finally anarchy.

PIERRE E. TRUDEAU, H. of C., *Debates*, Apr. 25, 1969, 7981.

Rumour

Rumour, always willing to believe what flatters the interest of the many.

FREDERICK P. GROVE, *Fruits of the earth*, 1933, 168.

Russia

One can only conclude that the human race is hell-bent toward both bankruptcy and suicide. This is incredible folly. I feel we ought to move vigorously and immediately to avert the catastrophe. I believe we can and must reach a workable accommodation with the Russians.

CYRUS EATON, *Saturday night*, Apr. 12, 1958, 10.

Ryerson, Egerton

The Americans had their Arnold and the Canadians have their Ryerson . . . I was the dupe of a Jesuit in the garb of a Methodist Preacher, and believed Egerton that I had been in error in opposing the Union — but he and his new allies, the Church and state gentry, shall now have me on their rear.

WILLIAM LYON MACKENZIE, in *Colonial advocate*, Oct., 1833.

He is the Pope of Methodism in this country, but he mistook his profession. Nature intended him for a Jesuit.

JOHN LANGTON, letter to W. Langton, Dec. 30, 1855.

My Jesuitical friend Ryerson has got the genius of order and system. His accounts and vouchers are a model for all our public departments.

J. LANGTON, Auditor of Public Accounts, in a letter to his brother William, Toronto, Feb. 24, 1856.

The Doctor's ambition has not lain in the direction of coveting office, but (and there was no truly great man without ambition) in the direction of influencing public opinion on those questions and measures the carrying of which he deemed to be for the good of the Church and the country.

JOHN CARROLL, in *Can. Methodist*, Feb., 1874, 103.

Sable Island

The graveyard of the Atlantic.

> ANON., popular term for the Island be-
> cause of the many shipwrecks caused by
> it.

Sacrifice

Men who make the greatest sacrifices
ask nothing in return.

> SIR RICHARD CARTWRIGHT, qu., *Standard
> Dictionary of Canadian biography*,
> 1934, 103.

I think the majority of men would
prefer the spirit of sacrifice to bread.

> W. L. MACKENZIE KING, H. of C., *Debates*,
> May 11, 1923, 2687, re: erection of
> National War Memorial in Confedera-
> tion Square, Ottawa.

Sadness

Let virtue lie in joy and song,
The only sin is sadness.

> ROBERT SERVICE, "The concert singer",
> 1921.

They'll not be green for very long,
Those pastures of my peace, nor will
The heavens be a place for song,
Nor the still waters still.

> A. M. KLEIN, "Psalm IV", 1944.

It's not sad enough.
nor long enough.
Bring me something
sadder than silence,
longer than snow.

> GAIL FOX, in *Royal collector of dreams*,
> 1970, 1.

Sailors

Bridegrooms of the Sea.

> ANON., term applied by Newfoundland-
> ers to men lost at sea.

The blood that flowed from Nelson's
death-wound in the cockpit of the
Victory mingled with that of a Nova
Scotian stripling beside him, struck
down in the same glorious fight.

> JOSEPH HOWE, letter to Lord John Rus-
> sell, Sept. 18, 1839.

Who, in frail barques, the ocean surge
    defied,
    And trained the race that live upon
        the wave?
What shore so distant where they have
        not died?
    In every sea they found a watery
        grave.

> JOSEPH HOWE, "Our fathers", Oct. 5,
> 1854.

I was born for deep-sea faring;
I was bred to put to sea;
Stories of my father's daring
Filled me at my mother's knee.

> BLISS CARMAN, "A son of the sea", 1895.

I cut my teeth on a marlin spike, and I
could box the compass before I could
recite the alphabet.

> LIONEL FORSYTH, business executive, qu.
> in P. Newman, *Flame of power*, 1959,
> 138.

Saint John, N. B.

Loyalists, my fathers, builded
  This gray port by the gray sea,
When the duty to ideals
  Could not let well-being be.

BLISS CARMAN, "The ships of St. John", in
Can. mag., Dec., 1893, 149.

O city
With a Loyalist graveyard
In the centre
Of every brain.

JOHN DREW, "Saint John", 1967.

St. John River (N.B.)

Of all Canadian rivers the St. John is
surely the most feminine – broad-bo-
somed, maternal, life-giving, a veritable madonna. Feminine too in her
contradictions, in her power (familiar
to all married men) to reverse the
course of her progress and flow backwards in defiance of reason and natural law.

EDWARD MCCOURT, *The road across
Canada*, 1965, 64.

St. John's, Nfld.

St. John's has two claims to distinction:
it is the oldest town in North America
and it has been burnt more often than
any capital city in the world.

C. R. FAY, *Life and labour in Newfoundland*, 1956, 163.

I was, before Manhattan Isle changed
  hands,
Traded for beads and buckles;
  middle-aged
When Halifax was pink-cheeked and
  full-breasted;
And when proud Rio was a noisome
  swamp
Commerce was striking bargains on
  my docks.

MICHAEL HARRINGTON, Newfoundland's
unofficial poet laureate, qu. in E.
McCourt, *The road across Canada*,
1965, 14.

St. Laurent, Louis

I know nothing of politics and never
had anything to do with politicians.

LOUIS ST. LAURENT, on entering the King
government, Dec. 10, 1941; in B. Hutchison, *Mr. Prime Minister*, 1964, 287.

I have one word of advice to you. The
good God does not expect you to bear
the whole burden of the world on your
shoulders. He expects you to bear only
your fair share of the burden.

CARDINAL VILLENEUVE, to Louis St. Laurent when he decided to enter government service, December, 1941, qu. by
Escott Reid in *Queen's quart.*, 1967,
592.

I'm afraid Uncle Louis will be a hard
one to beat.

NORMAN CAMPBELL, Toronto *Telegram*
reporter, Field, B.C., train stop, federal
election campaign, June, 1949. First use
of "Uncle Louis".

Through all this hubbub, the most
arresting figure on the Government
side was Prime Minister St. Laurent.
He sat, impassive, expressionless, chin
in hand, an open book on his desk. His
aloofness is almost unbelievable. Especially at a time of high controversy,
Prime Ministers, regardless of who the
House Leader may be, always dominate proceedings and lead their own
party. Mr. St. Laurent does neither.

GRANT DEXTER, Winnipeg *Free press*,
May 28, 1956, 19, referring to pipeline
debate.

He was Canadian, the most truly Canadian of all our Prime Ministers up to his time. He felt no nostalgia for the old lands of Europe nor any sense of isolation from the rest of his country in Quebec.

BRUCE HUTCHISON, *Mr. Prime Minister*, 1964, 287.

It was said when St. Laurent was at the zenith of his power and prestige that if he were ever defeated there might be regret but no tears or sorrow, and so it was.

C. G. POWER, *A party politician: the memoirs of Chubby Power*, 1966, 78.

St. Lawrence River

So long indeed as the St. Lawrence flows into the sea, so long will the tide of commerce fall into and follow its natural declivity.

WILLIAM F. COFFIN, *Canal and the rail*, 1848, 3.

Every life within its broad salt waters was charged with this tension of extremes and so the Gulf was a place of compromise. It resisted equally the fanatic ice and the permeating heat. Its lack of allegiance to north or south or hot or cold made it the most diverse place on earth.

FRANKLIN RUSSELL, *Searchers at the Gulf*, 1970, 13. "If the fictional Gulf resembles any place, it is the Gulf of St. Lawrence". (Intro.)

St. Lawrence Seaway

Mutual over-statements contribute to the dreariness of all discussion about the Seaway. Nothing is so dull as a disputed statistic, and all Seaway statistics are in dispute. That is the other and perhaps the major factor against the Seaway. To most people, the whole project is a stupefying bore.

BLAIR FRASER, *Maclean's*, May 15, 1951, 76.

This stone bears witness to the common purpose of two nations whose frontiers are the frontiers of friendship, whose works are the works of freedom, and whose ways are the ways of peace.

ST. LAWRENCE SEAWAY, International Friendship Monument plaque, Can.-U.S. boundary line centre of Moses-Saunders Dam near Cornwall, dedicated by the Queen and others, June 27, 1959.

Saints

A saint is someone who has achieved a remote human possibility. It is impossible to say what that possibility is. I think it has something to do with the energy of love. Contact with this energy results in the exercise of a kind of balance in the chaos of existence.

LEONARD COHEN, *Beautiful losers*, 1966, 95.

Salesmen

Art and intuition just aren't enough any more. Selling has become a science. We won't be running into many "born salesmen" in future; they will be made.

HERBERT H. LANK, President, Du Pont of Canada, address to Canadian Manufacturers of Chemical Specialties Assoc., October, 1960.

Salvation

Salvation and damnation are habits of the soul, slowly acquired by the inner self, becoming inveterate in the passage of time.

WILLIAM HUME BLAKE, *A fisherman's creed*, 1923, 14.

You were never meant to sit in a corner hatching the addled egg of your personal salvation.

JOHN MACNAUGHTON, sermon in a Kingston, Ont., Presbyterian church; *Queen's quart.*, 1933, 363.

Salvation Army

The repeated attacks of a liberal population upon this body are unworthy of Quebec City; . . . it is necessary that the processions of the Salvation Army, ridiculous as they may appear to some, must have full liberty of progress; and if need be I am prepared to march at their head to protect them.

SIR WILFRID LAURIER, 1887; in, Pacaud, ed., *Laurier letters*, 1935, 28.

Saskatchewan

Alone, the valley of the Saskatchewan, according to scientific computation, is capable of sustaining 800,000,000 souls.

EDMUND COLLINS, address to Canadian Club, New York, "The future of the Dominion of Canada", qu. in *Canadian leaves*, 1887, 16.

Down by the old Saskatchewan
    It's lonely, and wild, and free.
And the old rough range by the
        river-side
Looks best in the world to me.

RHODA SIVELL, "The old Saskatchewan", 1912.

The Lord said 'Let there be wheat', and Saskatchewan was born.

STEPHEN LEACOCK, *My discovery of the west*, 1937, 75.

We have many Saskatchewan people who go to British Columbia because of the climate and a lot of them come back because of the weather.

T. C. DOUGLAS, Premier of Sask., at Dominion-Provincial Tax Conference, Ottawa, July 27, 1960.

Silence and solitude — the finest gifts Saskatchewan has to offer bedevilled modern man.

EDWARD MCCOURT, *Saskatchewan*, 1968, 223.

Saskatoon

Arise, Saskatoon, Queen of the North!

JOHN N. LAKE, Temperance Commissioner, in 1882, qu. in Edward McCourt, *Saskatchewan*, 1968, 126.

Satire

Without faith there can be no satire, and without satire no secure and clarified faith.

F. R. SCOTT, in W. P. Percival, *Leading Canadian poets*, 1948, 243.

Satirists

A satirist is a man who discovers unpleasant things about himself and then says them about other people.

PETER MCARTHUR, d. 1924, qu. in *The best of Peter McArthur*, 1967, 234.

Satisfaction

Repletion seems to cause, in the man, temporary indifference; while Repletion causes, in the woman, enduring content.

ARNOLD HAULTAIN, *Hints for lovers*, 1909, 135.

Any man who doesn't want what he hasn't got has all he wants.

> ROBERT C. (BOB) EDWARDS, Calgary *Eye Opener*, Mar. 9, 1918.

I am not carefree, yet I wish for nothing.

> ALFRED W. PURDY, "Visitors", 1959.

Plenty to drink and to eat
  Is how the country is run;
Hungry and sober is merely confusion
    and defeat
  Besides not being much fun.

> GEORGE JOHNSTON, "The Royal Commission", 1966.

Savage

But half of me is woman grown;
The other half is child.
But half my heart loves quiet ways;
The other half is wild.

> CONSTANCE DAVIES-WOODROW, "To a vagabond", 1926.

Savings

There are more fortins got by savin' than by makin', I guess.

> T. C. HALIBURTON, *Sam Slick*, 1836, ch. XXVI.

Saw Mills

And here at hand an open mill,
Strong clamour at perpetual drive,
With changing chant, now hoarse,
    now shrill
Keeps dinning like a mighty hive.

> ARCHIBALD LAMPMAN, "At the ferry", 1900.

Scandal

I want the Right Hon. gentleman to tell the house about his participation in the Monseignor case when he was Prime Minister of this country.

> LUCIEN CARDIN, Minister of Justice, H. of C., *Debates*, Mar. 4, 1966, 2211, to John G. Diefenbaker, first mention of the Gerda Munsinger case.

Scandal is the first weapon, the most continuous one, and the last weapon used against a woman anywhere, and particularly one of political prominence.

> JUDY LAMARSH, *Memoirs of a bird in a gilded cage*, 1968, 304.

Scenery

The scenery is to be sure divine, but one grows weary of meer scenery.

> FRANCES BROOKE, *The history of Emily Montague*, Vol. 1, 1769, 25.

Scepticism

I am still unreconciled to the kind of world I live in and I view many things with alarm besides myself, including most politicians and a good many voters.

> HUGH MACLENNAN, *Thirty and three*, 1954, Preface, vii.

I believe that all truth is very difficult to come by; therefore I must be sceptical.

> RABBI ABRAHAM L. FEINBERG, *Storm the gates of Jericho*, 1964, 290.

Scholars

A fig for your scholar who puzzles and
    looks,
And sees Nature's ways but in musty
    old books!
Can Greek or can grammar, can
    science or art,

Confer on a fool e'er a head or a
heart?

> ALEXANDER MCLACHLAN, "I long not for
> riches", 1856.

Scholars who love minutiae deny
everything.

> STEPHEN B. LEACOCK, speech to Canadi-
> an Pol. Sci. Assoc., 1933.

Oh you and all the other damn Rhodes
Scholars! Get the hell out of here!

> C. D. HOWE, to Jack Davis, qu. in W.
> Kilbourn, *Pipeline*, 1970, 80.

Scholarship

Observe, record, and publish.

> SIR WILLIAM OSLER, qu., in Cushing,
> *Osler*, 1925.

I have seen a work in which on a single
page there were fifteen notes relating
to the same volume. It is all very
thorough and sound but where does
the public come in?

> G.M. WRONG, in *Can. hist. rev.*, 1933, 7.

Pure scholarship is a growth hormone
of civilization as well as a measure of
its quality. To ensure a Canadian
culture and an enlightened and individual Canadian democracy, the scholar in his library and the man of science
in his laboratory are as important as
the high school teacher in his classroom.

> HAROLD A. INNIS, National Conference of
> Canadian Universities, *Report of the
> Comm. on Post War Problems of Cana-
> dian Universities*, Mar., 1944, 26. (Au-
> thorship ascribed by J. B. Brebner in
> Can. Hist. Assoc., *Report*, 1953, 22).

Scholarship is the frontier of the mind.

> J. B. BREBNER, *Scholarship for Canada*,
> 1945.

In our concern with the problems of
modern scholarship we are faced with
the prospects of a new Dark Ages.

> HAROLD A. INNIS, *Political economy in
> the modern state*, 1946, 138.

There is no substitute for scholarship
in the educated individual.

> WILLIAM HENRY CLARKE, address, Lind-
> say (Ont.) Collegiate, Nov. 28, 1947.

We dismiss with contempt any suggestion that it is just a plain mess; once
scholarship has its grappling hooks on
a writer's work there is no room for
doubt.

> ROBERTSON DAVIES, *Leaven of malice*,
> 1954, 214.

Each discipline seeks its own kind of
pattern, and has its own criteria of
validity.

> F. E. L. PRIESTLEY, Roy. Soc. of Can.,
> *Transactions*, June, 1954, sec. 2, 43.

Get a solid piece of scholarship under
your belt and some diploma-mill will
always want you.

> ROBERTSON DAVIES, *Leaven of malice*,
> 1954, 217.

One precept governs Ph.D.s −
And mere M.A.s must never flout it:
Our responsibility's
To reach not Life but Books about it.

> MAVOR MOORE, "The professor", *And
> what do you do?*, 1960, 37.

If one has a steady nerve, it is useful to
contemplate how much is written
about Beowulf in one year in North
America. One can look at the Shakespeare industry with perhaps less sense
of absurdity; but when it comes to
figures such as Horace Walpole having
their own factory, one must beware
vertigo.

> GEORGE P. GRANT, *Technology and em-
> pire*, 1969, 124.

Schools

No method seems better adapted to making good subjects of them than to instruct them in English, to establish an English school in each parish.

> BISHOP CHARLES INGLIS, letter to Lord Grenville, Sept. 8, 1790 (Pub. Arch. Can., *Inglis Papers*, Vol. 1), referring to French Canadians.

As soon as the young hero has attained his seventh or eighth year, he is provided with an *axe*, instead of a *primer;* and when praised for his expertness in the use of this instrument, he imagines himself deeply read in *the philosophy of human life.*

> EDWARD TALBOT, *Five years residence in the Canadas*, 1824, 96.

Schoolhouses are cheaper than gaols, teachers are cheaper than police officers, the taxpayer must be made to pay for the common morality of the people.

> EGERTON RYERSON, about 1850, qu. in *Queen's quart.*, Summer, 1970, 209.

There is a happy spot of busy life
Where order reigns where hushed the din of strife,
Harmonious brethren neath paternal rule,
Ply their glad tasks in Metlakatla's school,
There Duncan holds supreme his peaceful throne,
His power unquestioned, and their rights his own.

> REV. G. MASON, "Lo! the poor Indian", read before the Mechanics' Literary Institute, Victoria, Oct. 28, 1875.

The public school with English bless,
The public school forever;
God save our country and ever bless,
The public school forever.

> ANON., a parody on "The Maple Leaf", proposed as a "war song" by a member of the Sask. Trustees' Assoc. during Separate School controversy, 1921.

If every day in the life of a school could be the last, there would be little fault to find with it.

> STEPHEN LEACOCK, "My memories and miseries as a schoolmaster", *College days*, 1923, 23.

It would appear, however, in the light of judicial decisions, that the claim of French to preferred recognition in the schools of the provinces, other than Quebec, in comparison with German or any other language, must rest on an historic, and perhaps a moral, rather than on a legal basis.

> GEORGE M. WEIR, *The separate school question in Canada*, 1934, 7.

I went to school, obeying traffic
   orders:
avoid collision.
I learned reading – shut God in a
   book
(Of all places for God).

> R. G. EVERSON, "Squeezed the slave out of himself", 1958.

At the turn of the century the Canadian public school was not making young Canadians but young Englishmen. It is not surprising that fourteen years later, those boys rushed off across the seas to fight for a country they had never seen – to fight as perhaps men never fought before.

> A. R. M. LOWER, *Canadians in the making*, 1958, 352.

Like butterflies but lately come
From long cocoons of summer
These little girls start back to school
To swarm the sidewalks,
    playing-fields,
And litter air with colour.

> D. G. JONES, "Beautiful creature brief as these", 1961.

The school system, custodian of print culture has no place for the rugged individual. It is, indeed, the homogenizing hopper into which we toss our integral tots for processing.

> MARSHALL MCLUHAN, *The Gutenberg galaxy*, 1962, 215.

French schools outside Quebec were guaranteed in 1867.

> EUGENE FORSEY, his paraphrase of a statement widely believed but dismissed by him as one of the seven devils of our pseudo-history in his speech "Our present discontents", Acadia Univ., Oct. 19, 1967.

The authorities prevent Canada's young people from getting an education by keeping them locked up in institutions called schools, where they are bored, bullied, and brainwashed into total apathy.

> RICHARD J. NEEDHAM, *Garden of Needham*, 1968, 105.

Our schools are slaves to the timetable, the teacher-dominated lesson, the control and repression of kids, and the suppression of the excitement, spontaneity and the joy of learning.

> JOHN YOUNG, Principal, Campbell River (B.C.) High School, qu. in *Weekend mag.*, Sept. 12, 1970, 4.

Science

The golden rule of science is: Make sure of your facts and then lie strenuously about your modesty.

> PETER MCARTHUR, *To be taken with salt*, 1903, 150.

The future belongs to science. More and more she will control the destinies of the nations. Already she has them in her crucible and on her balances.

> SIR WILLIAM OSLER, introduction, *Life of Pasteur*, by Vallery-Radot, 1911.

Democracy and science do not go to Canossa.

> GOLDWIN SMITH, *Reminiscences*, 1912, 395; Canossa was a castle in Italy where Emperor Henry IV performed penance before Pope Gregory VII in 1077.

In science the credit goes to the man who convinces the world, not to the man to whom the idea first occurs.

> SIR WILLIAM OSLER, "The first printed documents relating to modern surgical anesthesia", paper read, May 15, 1918, to Hist. Sec., Roy. Soc. of Med., England.

It is almost with a sense of shock that we realize that the essence of physics and chemistry alike lies in the arrangements within the atom.

> R. C. WALLACE, in *Can. hist. rev.*, 1933, 374.

The scientist is in harmony with a religion of man's humanity to man. He has no use for organized religious bodies that have enforced their dogmas at the point of the sword and have sold salvation to their followers for profit, or who have kept their people in ignorance.

> SIR FREDERICK BANTING, in Toronto *Star*, July 6, 1935.

Science has taught us to kill before philosophy has taught us to think.

> LISTER S. SINCLAIR, *No scandal in Spain*, (Radio Drama, C. B. C., June 6, 1945).

Science is the new theology.

> HUGH MACLENNAN, *Two solitudes*, 1945, 274.

A little learning of science often breeds the notion that there are equally assured facts in every area of knowledge . . . But in the humanities there is no final appeal except to humanity itself.

> NORTHROP FRYE, *By liberal things*, 1959, 10.

The notion that science, left to itself, is bound to evolve more and more of the truth about the world is another illusion, for science can never exist outside a society, and that society, whether deliberately or unconsciously, directs its course.

> NORTHROP FRYE, *The modern century*, 1967, 41.

When we think science, we think God.

> STANLEY B. FROST, *Standing and understanding*, 1969, 68.

Students who are at the top of the classes in the sciences have a temptation to remain in the comfortable academic environment and carry out research there. The result of this is an expansion of the post graduate research facilities and an ever increasing demand for more and better research workers and money for their support.

> MAURICE KENYON TAYLOR, Senate, Special Comm. on Science Policy, *Proceedings*, June 13, 1969, 7506.

We have the choice of making this the age of wonder, or a further age of scientific endeavour — and if we do the latter, we will go down to defeat.

> LLOYD DENNIS, qu. in *Maclean's*, Sept., 1970, 30.

Scientists

A scientist, as a biologist friend of mine says, is all the better for being an educated person.

> ROBERTSON DAVIES, *A voice from the attic*, 1960, 48.

Scotland

One may be a little homesick for Oxfordshire here, but not for Scotland, for Canada is simply Scotland on an extended scale.

> LORD TWEEDSMUIR, letter to Stair Gillon, about 1936, qu. in Janet Adam Smith, *John Buchan*, 1965, 430.

Scotsmen

From the lone shieling of the misty island
> Mountains divide us and the waste of seas —
Yet still the blood is strong, the heart is Highland,
And we in dreams behold the Hebrides:
> Fair these broad meads — the hoary woods are grand;
But we are exiles from our fathers' land.

> DAVID MACBETH MOIR, "Canadian boatsong", ("The lone shieling"), in *Blackwood's Edinburgh mag.*, Sept., 1829, 400. A shieling is a hut.

As for Canada, why it's as Scotch as Lochaber — whatever of it is not French, I mean. — Even omitting our friend John Galt, have we not *hodie* our Bishop Macdonell for the Papists — our Archbishop Strachan for the Episcopals — and our Tiger Dunlop for the Presbyterians? and 'tis the same, I believe, all downwards.

> *BLACKWOOD'S EDINBURGH MAG.*, Sept., 1829, 393.

If I were not French I would choose to be − Scotch.

SIR WILFRID LAURIER, speech, Toronto Board of Trade, Jan. 5, 1893.

He builds their commerce, he sings
  their songs,
  He weaves their creeds with an iron
  twist,
And making of laws or righting of
  wrongs,
  He grinds them all as the
  Scotchman's grist.

WILFRED CAMPBELL, "The world-mother", 1899.

They are the backbone of Canada. They are all right in their three vital parts − heads, hearts and haggis.

SIR WILLIAM OSLER, favourite remark, about 1911; qu. H. W. Cushing, *Life*, 1925, 969.

Scotsmen more than others seem to cultivate versatility.

H. H. LANGTON, *Sir Daniel Wilson*, 1929, 232.

Oatmeal was in their blood and in
  their names.
Thrift was the title of their catechism.

E. J. PRATT, *Towards the last spike*, 1952, 3.

Their names were like a battle-muster
  − Angus
(He of the Shops) and Fleming (of the
  Transit),
Hector (of the Kicking Horse),
  Dawson,
"Cromarty" Ross, and Beatty (Ulster
  Scot),
Bruce, Allan, Galt and Douglas, and
  the "twa" −
Stephen (Craigellachie) and Smith
  (Strathcona).

E. J. PRATT, *Towards the last spike*, 1952, 4.

And then the everlasting tread of the
  Macs,
Vanguard, centre and rear, their
  roving eyes
On summits, rivers, contracts, beaver,
  ledgers;
Their ears cocked to the skirl of Sir
  John A.,
The general of the patronymic march.

E. J. PRATT, *Towards the last spike*, 1952, 4.

We referred to ourselves as Scotch and not Scots. When, years later, I learned that the usage in Scotland was different it seemed to me rather an affectation.

JOHN KENNETH GALBRAITH, *The Scotch*, 1964, 12.

It was on Saturday night that the Scotch gathered at the McIntyre House to make merry and seek one another's destruction.

JOHN KENNETH GALBRAITH, *The Scotch*, 1964, 119.

Sculpture

The Eskimo carver is inspired with the coming of each season, and by the migration of game. In some subtle way it is thought good luck to carve the animal one is about to hunt.

JAMES HOUSTON, *Can. art*, Spring, 1952, 102.

Some tensile art, precise with joy
Breaks my lines, keens me
  To a tense and resonant thing,
And the vats of boiling gold in my
  brain
  Harden to shrill and intricate
  shapes.

GWENDOLYN MACEWEN, "The metallic anatomy", 1966.

After 600 years
the ivory thought
is still warm.

> AL PURDY, "Lament for the Dorsets",
> 1972.

Carving, like singing, isn't a thing.
When you feel a song within you, you
sing it; when you sense a form emerging from ivory, you release it.

> EDMUND CARPENTER, paraphrasing an
> Eskimo carver, in *Eskimo realities*,
> 1973, 59.

Sea

If the sea was always calm, it would
pyson the universe.

> T. C. HALIBURTON, *Sam Slick*, 1836.

We have in Canada, it is true, the two
principal elements of nationality —
population and territory — but we
also know what we lack. Great as is
our population and our territory, there
is wanting that other element absolutely necessary to make a powerful nation, the maritime element. What nation has ever been powerful without
the maritime element?

> SIR GEORGE-ETIENNE CARTIER, speech at
> Halifax, Aug. 15, 1864.

I rejoice, moreover, that we men of
insular origin are about to recover one
of our lost senses — the sense that
comprehends the sea — that we are
not now about to subside into a character so foreign to all our antecedents,
that of a mere inland people.

> THOMAS D'A. MCGEE, speech at Cook-
> shire, Que., Dec. 22, 1864, on confeder-
> ation with the maritime provinces.

The night has fallen and the tide
  Now and again comes drifting
    home,
Across these aching barrens wide,
  A sigh like driven wind or foam:
  In grief the flood is bursting home.

> BLISS CARMAN, "Low tide on Grand Pré",
> 1889.

Oh, the shambling sea is a sexton old,
And well his work is done,
With an equal grave for lord and
    knave,
He buries them every one.

> BLISS CARMAN, "The gravedigger", 1893.

No sound nor echo of the sea
But hath tradition of your voice.

> BLISS CARMAN, "The end of the trail",
> 1893.

The glad indomitable sea.

> BLISS CARMAN, "A sea child", 1893.

There was in Arll a little cove
Where the salt wind came cool and
    free:
A foamy beach that one would love
If he were longing for the sea.

> DUNCAN CAMPBELL SCOTT, "The piper of
> Arll", in *Truth*, N. Y., Dec. 14, 1895; on
> reading this, John Masefield resolved to
> become a poet.

I was born in the breezes, and I had
studied the sea as perhaps few men
have studied it, neglecting all else.

> JOSHUA SLOCUM, *Sailing alone around
> the world*, 1900, 4.

Take me out, sink me deep in the
    green profound,
To sway with the long weed, swing
    with the drowned,
Where the change of the soft tide
    makes no sound,
Far below the keels of the outward
    bound.

> CHARLES G. D. ROBERTS, "The stranded
> ship", 1902.

Canadian history is full of sea-power;
but Canadian histories are not.

WILLIAM WOOD, *All afloat*, 1914, 13.

The shore has perils unknown to the
deep.

GEORGE ILES, *Canadian stories*, 1918,
169.

And O, Her skies are bright and blue,
   Her waters bright and pure;
There's balm within Her forest shades
All world-worn men to cure;
The wholesome Sea is at her gates
   Her gates both East and West,
Then is it strange that we should love
   This land, our Land, the best?

J. A. RITCHIE, "There is a land", 1920;
origin of the phrase, "The wholesome
Sea is at her gates, Her gates both East
and West".

It took the sea an hour one night,
An hour of storm to place
The sculpture of these granite seams
Upon a woman's face.

EDWIN J. PRATT, "Erosion", 1932.

Most of those who live on the west
coast probably still think of the sea as
merely a place for bathing in.

A. R. M. LOWER, *Can. defence quart.*, Vol.
16, Oct., 1938, 32.

There is no mountain-top but must
   come home
to taste the salt against her heaving
   side,
no crag but is an exiled reef whose
   foam
flashes a far white longing for her tide.
And with our happy tears and tears of
   woe
we too shall swell her song with what
   we know.

KENNETH LESLIE, "The misty mother",
1938.

Come where the seal in a silver sway
   like the wind through grass
goes blowing balloons behind him.

EARLE BIRNEY, "Gulf of Georgia", 1948.

The sea loves to move
   but it is in no hurry,
flops over languidly like an easy
       animal
   waiting for storms,
     never still.

LOUIS DUDEK, *Europe* (Poem 16), 1954.

In a far-off former time
And a green and gentle clime,
Mamma was a lively lass,
Liked to watch the tall ships pass,
Loved to hear the sailors sing
Of sun and wind and voyaging,
Felt a wild desire to be
On the bleak and unplowed sea.

JAY MACPHERSON, "Mary of Egypt",
1957.

The sea belongs to whoever sits by the
shore.

LOUIS DUDEK, *Atlantis*, 1967, 80.

After we had crossed the long illness
that was the ocean . . .

MARGARET ATWOOD, "Further arrivals",
1970.

Sea Gulls

As the waters grey, grace meets you
but only in gulls that hook on the wind
are shaken easily loose
curve to the curving wave

EARLE BIRNEY, "Maritime faces", 1952.

Sea Serpents

Caddy.

ARCHIE WILLS, news editor, who gave
this name to the Cadboro Bay, B. C. sea
serpent, so claimed, in the Victoria
Times, Oct. 17, 1933; from the invented
species "Cadborosaurus".

Sea Shore

Here clove the keels of centuries ago
Where now unvisited the flats lie bare.
Here seethed the sweep of journeying
    waters, where
No more the tumbling floods of Fundy
    flow.

> CHARLES G. D. ROBERTS, "The salt flats",
> 1893.

A bright hard day over harbour where
    sea
in chips of white and blue speaks and
    toys, while
flurries of gulls spinning in wide
    deploys swoon
in sleigh-rides giddy and cold off
    government wharf.

> DOUGLAS LOCHHEAD, "Winter landscape
> – Halifax", 1960.

The act is the sliding out
to the shifting rotting
folds of the sands that lip
slipping to reefs and sinking cliffs
that ladder down to the ocean's abyss
and farther down through a thousand
    seas
of the mantling rock
to the dense unbeating black
    unapproachable heart of this world.

> EARLE BIRNEY, "November walk near
> False Creek mouth", 1964.

Seamen

Sing on, wild sea, your sad refrain
For all the gallant sons of France,
Whose songs and sufferings enhance
The romance of the western main!

> A. W. EATON, "L'Isle Ste. Croix", 1889.

Searching

I bring you naught of value,
No silver-crusted hat;
I questing come, and shall you
Turn me away for that?

> AL PURDY, "The atavist", 1944.

So that wherever I go,
Wherever I wander
I never find
What I should like to find.

> JAMES REANEY, "Whither do you wan-
> der", 1963.

There is the thought
that what they were looking for
might have been found elsewhere.

> AL PURDY, "The North West Passage",
> 1968, in *North*, Jan.-Feb., 1968, 26.

Secession

I deny that any province has any right
to secede. I think that any such attempt should be resisted by every
means, including force if necessary.

> W. L. MORTON, speech to Progressive
> Conservative Conference on Canadian
> Goals, Fredericton, Sept. 9, 1964.

Secord, Laura

Ah! faithful to death were our women
    of yore.
Have they fled with the past, to be
    heard of no more?
No, no! Though this laurelled one
    sleeps in the grave,
We have maidens as true, we have
    matrons as brave;
And should Canada ever be forced to
    the test –
To spend for our country the blood of
    her best –
When her sons lift the linstock and
    brandish the sword
Her daughters will think of brave
    Laura Secord.

> CHARLES MAIR, "Ballad for brave wom-
> en", 1885.

Braver deeds are not recorded
In historic treasures hoarded

Than this march of Laura Secord
through the forest long ago.

> CHARLES E. JAKEWAY, "Laura Secord",
> 1897.

Call up now that sultry morn —
Call up her who sped forlorn
Through the swales and trackless
    woods,
Wolfish wilds and solitudes,
Till at night, with heart aflame,
To the British camp she came
With her priceless tidings then
For FitzGibbon and his men.

> CHARLES MAIR, "Summer", 1901.

One, two, three a-Laura,
Four, five, six, a-Laura,
Seven, eight, nine, a-Laura,
Ten, a-Laura *Se*cord.

> ANON., qu. in B. Hume, *Laura Secord*,
> 1928, 32. (Ball-bouncing rhyme.)

Secrecy

Write the word down, for partitions
have ears.

> THOMAS C. HALIBURTON, *Sam Slick's wise
> saws*, 1853, ch. 11.

Secretaries

Phipps, if you had a secretary you
could govern the universe.

> NICHOLAS F. DAVIN, to R. W. Phipps,
> Ont. supt. of forestry, on agreeing with
> his statement he could govern Canada as
> well as Sir John Macdonald; qu. Willi-
> son, *Reminiscences*, 1919, 52.

Secrets

Down deep we all hug something. The
great forest hugs its silence. The sea
and the air hug the spilled cries of
sea-birds. The forest hugs only silence;
its birds and even its beasts are mute.

> EMILY CARR, *Klee Wyck*, 1941, 10.

If you gave me your secret I would
give you my silence. Exchanges
change people.

> VERA FRANKEL, *Artscanada*, Dec.-Jan.,
> 1970/71, 16.

Sectionalism

From the composition of a cabinet to
the composition of a rifle-team, sectionalism is the rule.

> GOLDWIN SMITH, *The political destiny of
> Canada*, 1878, 16-17.

Security

To sacrifice freedom and dignity for
so-called security is contrary to the
best in human nature. It is the way of
the improvident. No decent human
being wants to see luxury and privilege existing alongside poverty and
want, but certainly no group of individuals constituting a nation, no matter how small or how large, can succeed with a philosophy of penalizing
the industrious and subsidizing the
lazy.

> GEORGE MCCULLAGH, address to Empire
> Club, Toronto, May 20, 1949.

The first essential interest of Canada
in the world today is the security of
the United States; that takes overwhelming priority over everything
else in Canada's external relations.

> TOM KENT, *Foreign affairs*, Vol. 35, July,
> 1957, 581.

Security theory.

> WILLIAM E. BLATZ, *Human security*,
> 1966, viii; definition of the theory pro-
> posed: Security is the state of mind
> which accompanies the willingness to
> accept the consequences of one's acts
> — without equivocation of any sort.
> The feeling accompanying this state
> may be called serenity. (p. 13)

Sedition

It is not sedition to show His Majesty that he has been mistaken in his measures.

> ABRAHAM A. HEAPS, note written Jan. 29, 1920, while on trial for his part in the Winnipeg General Strike, qu. in Leo Heaps, *The rebel in the House*, 1970, 44.

Seduction

He was, as it turns out,
By recent standards of comparison,
A poor lover;
Yet, if I had it to do all over again,
I'd do it all over again,
Only this time I'd relax and enjoy it.
Because there never comes another
   hunting like the first!

> JOAN FINNIGAN, "Black Bob", 1960.

A woman is much more interested in seducing a first-class man than in being seduced by a second-class one.

> RICHARD J. NEEDHAM, *A friend in Needham*, 1969, 36.

Seeing

Uncage the tiger in your eye
And tawny, night and day,
Stalk the landscape for the contour
Of a fern or arm.

> ANNE WILKINSON, "Letter to my children", in *Contemporary verse*, Fall-Winter, 1952, 6.

O my eyes this morning wide as rivers
O the stream of my eyes ready for
   every reflection
And this freshness under my lids
Beyond belief
Surrounding the images I see

> HECTOR SAINT-DENYS-GARNEAU, "My eyes a river", (trans. by F.R. Scott, 1962).

There is a way of seeing that is not
   seeing
Far from the true dimension of our
   being
Who doubts but there is that we
   cannot see?

> DARYL HINE, "Trompe l'oeil", 1965.

Look here
You've never seen this country
it's not the way you thought it was
Look again.

> AL PURDY, "The country of the young", 1967.

Self

Self-preservation, which, next to self interest — from which it doubtless springs — is the strongest of our instincts, naturally includes the preservation of our business, whatever it may be.

> FRANCIS W. GREY, *The curé of St. Philippe*, 1899, ch. 3.

Only the sick are self-conscious; and the first step on the road to health is forgetfulness of self.

> BLISS CARMAN, *The kinship of nature*, 1903, 111.

There is an element of self-love in the very extreme of love.

> ARNOLD HAULTAIN, *Hints for lovers*, 1909, 107.

Everything, it seems to me, has to be purchased by self-sacrifice. Our race has marked every step of its painful ascent with blood.

> L. M. MONTGOMERY, *Rilla of Ingleside*, 1912, Ch. 5.

Do not rely completely on any other human being, however dear. We meet all life's greatest tests alone.

AGNES MACPHAIL, speech to Ottawa Ladies' College graduates, qu. in M. Stewart & D. French, *Ask no quarter*, 1959, 85.

I have two selves and one lives free in hell,
The other down a well in Paradise
Evil has made the first in evil wise,
The second, baffled, stifled in that well.

MALCOLM LOWRY, "Conversations with Goethe", about 1947.

Self-pity is commonly held to be despicable; it can also be a great comfort if it does not become chronic.

ROBERTSON DAVIES, *Tempest-tost*, 1951, 167.

The myriad ghosts of selves I've killed
That this one self might live instead
Come back through corridors long sealed
To throng around my bed.

FRED COGSWELL, "The myriad ghosts", 1960.

Self is the centre of being, the source of our most vital impulses.

WARREN TALLMAN, in *Can. lit.* No. 5, 1960, 18.

Self-expression

The general principle involved is that there is really no such thing as self-expression in literature.

NORTHROP FRYE, *The educated imagination*, (1962) 1964, 72.

Selfishness

In my judgment there is no more urgent reform than educating public and private opinion to unselfishness, & until that reform is achieved all other reforms are impossible.

SIR WILFRID LAURIER, letter to Blake, Dec. 20, 1882.

Most of the problems and dangers of the world are manifestations in countless forms of the anti-social bias of the human mind which is the product of past experience. That bias is towards selfishness – we are selfish as individuals, as families, as groups, as classes, as nations. And because it is a necessity of man to disguise his nature from himself we make virtues and idols of our exclusiveness, our pride, our acquisitiveness and all the other mental inheritances which create these anti-social feelings and prejudices.

JOHN W. DAFOE, Convocation address, University of Manitoba, May 17, 1923.

Senate

In the Upper House, – the controlling and regulating, but not the initiating, branch (for we know that here as in England, to the Lower House will practically belong the initiation of matters of great public interest), in the House which has the sober second-thought in legislation . . .

SIR JOHN A. MACDONALD, *Confederation debates*, Feb. 6, 1865, 35.

Our Lower Canadian friends have agreed to give us representation by population in the Lower House, on the express condition that they shall have equality in the Upper House. On no other condition could we have advanced a step.

GEORGE BROWN, *Confederation debates*, Feb. 8, 1865, 88.

For every vacancy there is a claimant who has done something, or expended something, for the party, and whose claims cannot be set aside. The Minister may feel as strongly as his critics how much the Senate would be strengthened, and his own reputation enhanced, by the introduction of some of the merit, ability and experience which do not take the stump. But party demands its pound of flesh.

> GOLDWIN SMITH, *Can. monthly*, July, 1872, 67.

I do not believe it is consistent with the true notion of popular Government that we should have a Senate selected by the Administration of the day, and holding their seats for life.

> EDWARD BLAKE, speech at Aurora, Ont., Oct. 3, 1874.

An absurdly effete body.

> LORD DUFFERIN, letter to Carnarvon, Oct. 10, 1874.

The other place.

> ANON., a term used by Commoners to describe the Senate. Senators also use the phrase in referring to the Commons.

It is time that we spoke freely on this subject, because the people could not elect a body such as the members of this House are, for intelligence and experience, and we ought to desire to raise the Senate in the public estimation, so that the people will love and honour this body.

> GEORGE ALEXANDER, Senate, *Debates*, Feb. 10, 1882, 15.

The Senate of Sir John Macdonald is nothing but a political infirmary and a bribery fund, nor is it possible to conceive any case in which a body so destitute of moral weight could render real service to the nation.

> *THE WEEK*, May 1, 1884, 338.

I do not say that I must select but I do say to my Hon. friend that when I have come to the moment of selection, if I have to select between a Tory and a Liberal, I feel I can serve the country better by appointing a Liberal than a Conservative, and I am very much afraid that any man who occupies the position I occupy today will feel the same way, and that so long as the appointing is as it is today in the hands practically of the First Minister, I am afraid we stand little chance of reform.

> SIR WILFRID LAURIER, H. of C., *Debates*, Apr. 30, 1906, 2304.

It is not by any manner of means a trifling thing to say when I say that the value of a Senate is not only in what the Senate does but in what the Senate prevents other people from doing.

> SIR RICHARD CARTWRIGHT, Senate, *Debates*, May 17, 1906, 469.

Whatever be the virtues of an ideal system of appointment, the Canadian Senate is a mere parody of it.

> STEPHEN B. LEACOCK, *National rev.* (London), LXI, July, 1913, 995.

If the Senate of Canada stands for anything it must stand as a bulwark against the clamor and the agitation and the caprice of the public upon all such questions as this.

> SIR JAMES LOUGHEED, Senate *Debates*, Apr. 16, 1918, 160.

As to myself, I have to-day signed my warrant of political death . . . How colourless the Senate – the entering gate to coming extinction. Would it have been better to have gone in the midst of conflict?

> SIR GEORGE E. FOSTER, entry in his diary, Aug. 28, 1920; actually appointed to the Senate, Sept. 23, 1921.

A body which does nothing in particular and does it very well.

> ANON., a popular description of the Senate.

The senators take their seats in the Upper House, not as open and fair-minded men, not as impartial critics, not as legislators whose one object is to produce good statutes; but as violent partisans, men whose minds have become warped and twisted with long party controversy, and whose chief end in life is to promote the interests of those whom they have always supported and to whom they owe their position.

> R. M. DAWSON, *The principle of official independence*, 1922, 247.

House of Refuge.

> AGNES MACPHAIL, name given to Senate, ca. 1923.

Over this chamber there might be inscribed a collective *Requiescat in pace*.

> H. J. PEARCE, in *Can. hist. rev.*, 1925, 108.

For ruining a life, six months with the option of a fine; for stealing an automobile, two years; for criticizing a government, twenty years, a pretty fair indication, let me say, of the relative values according to the standards which now exist. I have given these penalties. What is the penalty for debauching a government department? A senatorship.

> J. S. WOODSWORTH, H. of C., *Debates*, June 23, 1926, 4923, referring to the appointment to the Senate of Jacques Bureau after his dismissal from the Customs Dept. following a scandal in that Dept.

You are going to make me the most hated woman in Canada.

> CAIRINE WILSON, to W. L. Mackenzie King on her appointment to the Senate, Feb., 1930, qu. in J. Bannerman, *Leading ladies*, 1967, 162.

A senatorship isn't a job, it's a title. Also it's a blessing, a stroke of good fate; something like drawing a royal straight flush in the biggest pot of the evening, or winning the Calcutta Sweep. That's why we think it wrong to think of a senatorship as a job; and wrong to think of the Senate as a place where people are supposed to work. Pensions aren't given for work.

> GRATTAN O'LEARY, editorial in Ottawa *Journal*, qu. in *Financial post*, Feb. 28, 1942, 15.

The senate will in all likelihood continue to exist as at present constituted for many years to come, not from any high esteem in which it is held, but largely because of its undoubted convenience to the dominant political party and the general indifference of the Canadian people.

> R. MACGREGOR DAWSON, *Democratic government in Canada*, 1949, 68.

We members of the Senate are the highest class of pensioners in Canada.

> JOHN HAIG, Senate, *Debates*, Mar. 31, 1950, 199.

The chief reason why the Senate has never contributed a single creative idea to the solution of any serious problem in our whole history is that it has failed to organize itself with information, research, study and discussion to arrive at conclusions on complicated problems. That's basically the reason why the Senate does not, in fact, know what's going on in the country, or in the world.

> B. T. RICHARDSON, Empire Club, Toronto, Mar. 12, 1959.

We have one, mind you only one, really well-run home for the aged and infirm (prematurely or otherwise) and it is called the Senate.

> HAROLD TOWN, *Enigmas*, 1964, [2].

The Senate should be reformed so as to consist entirely of the Cabinet.

> ROBERTSON DAVIES, *Samuel Marchbanks' almanack*, 1967, 179.

Isn't it awful about those loafers sitting around and taking handouts and simply sponging off the taxpayer? Let's abolish the Senate immediately.

> RICHARD J. NEEDHAM, *A friend in Needham*, 1969, 39.

Surely, if you're called upon to serve, you have a duty to serve.

> FRANK E. FITZSIMMONS, U. S. head of Teamster's Union, to Ed Lawson, Canadian director, on advising him to accept the offer of a seat in the Senate made by Pierre E. Trudeau; accepted Oct. 7, 1970; qu. in *Maclean's*, Aug., 1972, 52.

Sensationalism

To compete with the sensationalists is a losing game.

> HERBERT STEINHOUSE, *Ten years after*, 1958, 326.

Sense

It must be a great deal better to be sensible; but still, I don't believe I'd really want to be a sensible person, because they are so unromantic.

> L.M. MONTGOMERY, *Anne of Green Gables*, 1908, 286.

Some people might just as well be crazy for all the sense they have.

> ROBERT C. (BOB) EDWARDS, Calgary *Eye Opener*, May 11, 1918.

Senses

Five full and fathomed senses, each
A fine precision instrument
To chart the wayward course
Through rock and moss
And riddles hard, or soft as ether, airy
Airy quite contrary
Where will the next wind blow?

> ANNE WILKINSON, "Letter to my children", in *Contemporary verse*, Fall-Winter, 1952, 4.

Sentiment

I'll be as sentimental
as I want and if you don't like it
then to hell with you.

> ALDEN NOWLAN, "Argument", 1974.

Sentimentality

The sentimentalist belongs to the cat family. He is very imperfectly domesticated, but his habit of locality is phenomenally developed.

> BLISS CARMAN, *The friendship of art*, 1903, 34.

The old eternal frog
In the throat that comes
With the words *Mother, sweetheart, dog,*
Excites, and then numbs.

> A. J. M. SMITH, "On reading an anthology of popular poetry", 1940.

Sentimentality is the philosophy of boobs.

> ROBERTSON DAVIES, *A voice from the attic*, 1960, 344.

Separatism

Canada has a bright future. She lacks nothing. Mines, land, industry, factories, everything is here. But a kind of fatalism seems to bring her to a standstill. Division seems to hound her into inactivity. Instead of uniting internally, Canadians amuse themselves, with fatal complacency, by making up nationalities of every colour and description.

> GONZALVE DOUTRE, lecture, Institut Canadien, Montreal, Dec. 1, 1864. (Trans.)

Concerning ourselves and our destiny, but one duty have we clearly understood: that we should hold fast — should endure. And we have held fast, so that, it may be, many centuries hence the world will look upon us and say: — These people are of a race that knows not how to perish.

> LOUIS HÉMON, *Maria Chapdelaine*, 1921, 260.

Grant that they may no more abandon the development of our life to improvisation and to incoherent action; that for the vanity of a too largely Canadian patriotism they may not sacrifice us to the dream of an impossible unity; that they may know how to reserve the future; that before concluding and deciding our destinies they may take account of the premises of our history; and God will not let perish that which He has conserved by so many miracles.

> ABBÉ LIONEL GROULX, qu. in Olivar Asselin, *L'Oeuvre de L'Abbé Groulx*, 1923, 93. (Trans.)

You will live to see Canada split along the Ottawa River.

> RICHARD B. BENNETT, to Bruce Hutchison, qu. in his *Mr. Prime Minister*, 1964, 241.

In the name of French reason, I ask you where is the illusion? In the achievement of one great bilingual Canada where at best we can run a close second, or in the formation of a sovereign, French Quebec in which we would be able to be the sole masters? In the name of French valor, I ask you which is defeatism? The stubborn battle for crumbs, trinkets and trifles, or the enlightened march toward the free country our ancestors wanted?

> MARCEL CHAPUT, *Why I am a separatist*, 1962, 92.

The separatist thesis rests on an ethnic foundation and, whatever its present political orientation, there is a danger that it will veer further and further to the Right, because racist political parties usually do, until they are captured by ultra-nationalists and turn into overt facism.

> GWETHALYN GRAHAM, *Dear enemies*, 1963, 78.

A national revolution cannot, of its very nature, tolerate any compromise. There is only one way of overcoming colonialism: to be stronger than it is! Only the most far-fetched idealism may mislead one into thinking otherwise. Our period of slavery has ended. QUEBEC PATRIOTS, TO ARMS! THE HOUR OF NATIONAL REVOLUTION HAS STRUCK! INDEPENDENCE OR DEATH!

> FLQ (FRONT DE LIBERATION DU QUEBEC) *Manifesto*, Apr. 16, 1963. (Trans.)

The true separatists in Canada are the English because they deny the very existence of bilingualism, or at least its implications, and by so doing, they are, in fact, rejecting Confederation.

> THOMAS SLOAN, Toronto *Globe magazine*, July 13, 1963, 8.

If Quebec still belonged to France I should preach Separatism just as hard as I do today.

> MARCEL CHAPUT, qu. by Mordecai Richler, *Encounter*, Dec., 1964, 78.

Those who want to maintain separateness also want the advantages of the age of progress. These two ends are not compatible, for the pursuit of one negates the pursuit of the other. Nationalism can only be asserted successfully by an identification with technological advance; but technological advance entails disappearance of those indigenous differences that give substance to nationalism.

GEORGE P. GRANT, *Lament for a nation*, 1965, 76.

These overgrown children, these untrained do-it-yourselfers, these quacks who tamper with our political ideals, these peddlars of panaceas who, as dabblers, have discovered truths which escaped the knowledge of the laboratories, these people adore imitating the gestures of an adult, that is, all the gestures except one: paying the bill.

JEAN LESAGE, Premier of Quebec, to Canadian Women's Press Club, Montreal, June 12, 1965. (Trans.)

Those childish but dangerous dreamers who mistake their withdrawal symptoms for an ideal, their violence for strength and their beards for virility.

JEAN LESAGE, Premier of Quebec, to Canadian Women's Press Club, Montreal, June 12, 1965. (Trans.)

A well-treated minority, the French-Canadians are nonetheless a minority. In order to regain control of their destiny they must decide in favour of the sovereign State of Quebec in which they will at last be a majority.

CANADA. ROY. COMM. ON BILINGUALISM AND BICULTURALISM, *Prelim. Report*, 1965, 116, stating the principal proposal of the separatists.

As for the other Canadian majority, it will also find our solution to its advantage, for it will be set free at once from the constraints imposed on it by our presence; it will be at liberty in its own way to rebuild to its heart's desire the political institutions of English Canada and to prove to itself, whether or not it really wants to maintain and develop on this continent, an English-speaking society distinct from the United States.

RENÉ LÉVESQUE, *An option for Quebec*, 1968, 28.

One way of offsetting the appeal of separatism is by investing tremendous amounts of time, energy, and money in nationalism, *at the federal level.* A national image must be created that will have such an appeal as to make any image of a separatist group unattractive.

PIERRE E. TRUDEAU, *Federalism and the French Canadians*, 1968, 193.

Separatism has become a dirty word, a negative word, to many Québecois. But sovereignty is positive. It allows respectable people to join our party.

RENÉ LÉVESQUE, qu. in Toronto *Star*, May 2, 1969, 4.

Who are these men who are held out as latter-day patriots and martyrs? Let me describe them to you. Three are convicted murderers; five others were jailed for manslaughter; one is serving a life imprisonment after having pleaded guilty to numerous charges related to bombings; another has been convicted of seventeen armed robberies; two were once paroled but are now back in jail awaiting trial on charges of robberies.

PIERRE E. TRUDEAU, national television broadcast, Oct. 16, 1970, referring to those in prison whose freedom was demanded by the FLQ in return for release of hostages.

The FLQ has sown the seeds of its own destruction. It has revealed no mandate but terror, no policies but violence and no solutions but murder. Savagery is alien to Canadians; it always will be for collectively we will not tolerate it.

PIERRE E. TRUDEAU, televised statement on the murder of Pierre Laporte, Oct. 18, 1970.

The idea of separatism, ultra-nationalism, is so much against the gut feeling and the gut interest of the average French Canadian that when the elite is ultra-nationalist as it has been at various times in our history, it is not only wrong for itself but it is leaving the people to wander aimlessly and therefore be led passively by outside events, whether those of English Canada or of the United States.

PIERRE E. TRUDEAU, to James Reston, New York *Times*, Dec. 21, 1971.

Toronto separatists.

PIERRE E. TRUDEAU, to Peter Gzowski, C.B.C. radio interview in Toronto, Feb., 1974, qu. in *Peter Gzowski's book on this country in the morning*, 1974, 49.

September

Wild asters burn in fencerows.
Our garden is hungry for bloom,
cosmos, marigold, zinnias,
chrysanthemums crowd and cluster.
Wild morning-glory chokes them
but they eat earth and set alight
savage fires, red, yellow, purple.

DAVID HELWIG, "September", 1967.

Servants

The great legacy given us by the class society is the institution of the domestic servant class. That has got to go.

STEPHEN LEACOCK, "Woman's level", in *Last leaves*, 1945, 98.

Service

A nation, like an individual, to find itself must lose itself in the service of others.

W. L. MACKENZIE KING, *The message of the carillon*, 1927, 23.

Settlers

Americans from the States set themselves down with very little ceremony upon the various townships bordering on their country, and begin to clear the woods, and cultivate the land, often without the knowledge or consent of its proprietors . . . They are certainly enterprising settlers, and improve the country more in two or three years, than the French Canadians do in a century.

JOHN LAMBERT, *Travels through Lower Canada*, 1810, I, 142.

Now, the class of people to whom this country is so admirably adapted are formed of the unlettered and industrious labourers and artisans. They feel no regret that the land they labour on has not been celebrated by the pen of the historian or the lay of the poet. The earth yields her increase to them as freely as if it had been enriched by the blood of heroes.

CATHERINE P. TRAILL, *Backwoods of Canada*, 1836, 154.

My love for Canada was a feeling very nearly allied to that which the condemned criminal entertains for his cell — his only hope of escape being through the portals of the grave.

SUSANNA MOODIE, *Roughing it in the bush*, 1852, Vol. 1, 138.

The settler is of infinitely more importance to the country than the land.

CANADA. COMM. OF CROWN LANDS, *Report*, 1865, xx.

Bite deep and wide, O Axe, the tree!
What doth thy bold voice promise me?
I promise thee all joyous things,
That furnish forth the lives of kings;

For every silver ringing blow
Cities and palaces shall grow.

ISABELLA VALANCY CRAWFORD, "Malcolm's Katie", 1884.

"My axe and I, we do immortal tasks;
We build up nations — this my axe
    and I."

ISABELLA VALANCY CRAWFORD, "Malcolm's Katie", 1884.

Abraham trekked out of Ur of the Chaldees under Divine guidance. Thousands of settlers in the Canadian West were moved by the same influence, though they didn't recognize it in the lantern lectures of the Dominion Government's agents, or the restrained advertisements of steamship and railway companies.

D. B. HANNA, Empire Club, Toronto, speech, Nov. 28, 1907.

Greater than the measure of the heroes
    of renown,
He is building for the future, and no
    hand can hold him down;
Though they count him but a common
    man, he holds the Outer Gate,
And posterity will own him as the
    father of the State.

R. J. C. STEAD, "The homesteader", 1908.

The American pioneer glories in going ahead penniless to match his wits against fate, risk his years and his health on a chance of making $10,000 out of nothing. The Canadian settler goes in only when he is sure he can make $2 out of $1; but the Englishman, like a wary trout on the bite, will only come in when he is sure of a percentage interest on investment.

AGNES C. LAUT, Saturday night, Dec. 7, 1912, 4.

We came to build, and building, a
    mighty structure grew,
And ever as we builded, builded better
    than we knew;
And through the darkening
    wilderness, lo! we were led in might,
Our log-heaps made a smoke by day, a
    pillared flame by night.
Now, when across the continent we've
    seen our task expand,
To our children's children and their
    children's children we do bequeath
    this land.

ROBERT K. KERNIGHAN, "Pioneer's anthem", 1925.

Life on the homesteads was full of hardships, mingled with mirth.

W. C. POLLARD, Pioneering in the prairie west, 1926.

We broke new trails, wild roses at our
    feet,
And by the banks of the Saskatchewan
We found the thorny brakes as scented
    sweet
As any incense Eden gave to Man.

ANDREW GRAHAM, "To a prairie wife", 1945.

They are often called individualists, and in economic matters they were, but in social matters, the dominating concept was that of good neighborliness, a homespun and practical Christianity.

M. M. FAHRNI, Third crossing, 1946, 73.

In theory the whole country was British. Since the end of the French wars Canada had formed one of the weirder of the Crown's dependencies, peopled, where it was peopled at all, mostly by Frenchmen, American loyalists and dispossessed Highlanders.

JAMES MORRIS, Heaven's command, 1973, 116.

826

Sex

There is a curious antagonism between the sexes. They are in a manner foes, not friends. The successful wooer is the captor, the raptor; the bride is the capture, the rapture.

> ARNOLD HAULTAIN, *Hints for lovers*, 1909, 124.

Tell your child the truth about sex, how babies come to be born, how they are conceived. These facts, like any other facts, should be given to children as soon as they show curiosity about them, which would normally be about the age of three.

> G. BROCK CHISHOLM, speech, Ottawa, Nov. 5, 1945.

A refusal or omission to talk about anything as important as sex will indicate, even to a very young child, that this subject is in a special category, that it's a taboo. Whenever this happens the child's desire for knowledge becomes shameful, becomes a guilt. The desire for knowledge should never be shameful.

> G. BROCK CHISHOLM, speech, Ottawa, Nov. 5, 1945.

She keeps her glory in her soul;
Mine's at midnight between my legs.

> JOAN FINNIGAN, "For Monique at midnight", 1959.

Erotic books feed a part of that fantasy life without which man cannot exist.

> ROBERTSON DAVIES, *A voice from the attic*, 1960, 283.

My daughters are pretty level-headed girls and if, in a moment of madness or by calculated design, they find themselves bedded with a youth (and I trust it will be a bed and not a car seat) I do not really believe the experience will scar their psyche or destroy their future marriages. Indeed I would rather have them indulge in some good, honest, satisfying sex than be condemned to a decade of whimpering frustration brought on by the appalling North American practice called "petting".

> PIERRE BERTON, *Maclean's*, May 18, 1963, 66.

Remorse in women
is a sure-fire aphrodisiac;
they can't bear to be thought less than
perfect
and so their contrition
is actually a variant form of vanity
and vanity is a great quickener
of the sexual appetite.

> IRVING LAYTON, "The seduction", 1964.

Unfortunately, under the social conditions existing in some of the more economically backward areas today, it is sadly true that the only luxury available to the ordinary man is procreation. Whether the ordinary woman also considers it a luxury is perhaps open to question.

> HUGH L. KEENLEYSIDE, address, Third World Conference on Medical Education, New Delhi, Nov. 21, 1966.

Literary sex, unlike literary love, is a poor substitute for the real thing.

> MIRIAM WADDINGTON, in *Tamarack rev.* No.45, 1967, 85.

A woman who is attractive, well-educated, and sensible has only one thing on her mind — to get laid.

> IRVING LAYTON, "Aphs", *The whole bloody bird*, 1969, 102.

The Anglo-Saxon hang-up on sex, which has dominated the North American culture for years, has resulted in a society which has more marriage failure, more adultery, more juvenile promiscuity, more broken homes, more violence, more psychotics and more unhappiness than any other society you could name.

JOHN R. LOOME, letter, Calgary *Herald*, Mar. 26, 1969, 5.

The man who goes out with a woman in order to sleep with her is like the one who goes to Banff in order to buy a postcard.

RICHARD J. NEEDHAM, *A friend in Needham*, 1969, 52.

Who can deny that the problem of coming to terms with the fact of sex has caused Canadians more concern than the activities of all their politicians combined?

MICHAEL BLISS, Canadian Historical Association, *Historical papers*, 1970, 108.

When nothing sexual is regarded as obscene, romantic love will cease to exist.

ALDEN NOWLAN, "Scratchings", 1971.

Twentieth-century man is obsessed with sex like the baboons in a zoo, and for the same reason: it's the only emotional outlet from his captivity.

ALDEN NOWLAN, "Scratchings", 1971.

Dearest girl, my hands are too fond of flesh
For me to speak to you; and you are too tall
For me to think you beautiful, though beautiful
You are.

IRVING LAYTON, "Dans le jardin", *Collected poems*, 1971, 216.

The impression grows that Grove's people might be in paradise on this earth if only nature had not thought up the distasteful device of genitalia.

MARGARET R. STOBIE, *Frederick Philip Grove*, 1973, 109.

The essence of any problem is that it can be solved, so we can now solve even the problems of sex by techniques in mechanical engineering, which we can learn from the manuals available at any drug store.

HUGH MACLENNAN, speech, University of British Columbia, Mar. 3, 1973.

Sexual Union

The more you use the penis muscle, the weaker it becomes; but the less you use the penis muscle, the stronger it becomes.

ARTHUR W. BEALL, *The living temple, a manual on eugenics for parents and teachers*, 1933; qu. by Michael Bliss in Can. Hist. Assoc., *Historical papers*, 1970, 107.

We are not sure yet if flesh
Has merely sprung a trap,
But, between the not-knowing and the knowing,
Bed will span the gap.

JOAN FINNIGAN, "Honeymoon", 1957.

With your body and your speaking
you have spoken for everything,
robbed me of my strangerhood,
made me one
with the root and gull and stone, . . .

LEONARD COHEN, "Owning everything", 1961.

but here, on lovewet
sheets, we play again
the ancient comedy,
your orifice my oracle!

HARRY HOWITH, "Joanne", 1963.

I refuse to believe that the act of procreation, which is at once the most sublime and mysterious and ennobling of all acts, can be designated as sinful.

PIERRE BERTON, *The comfortable pew*, 1965, 24.

Sexual Union

Had I the talent
Of Ovid or Horace
I'd write for Chloris
An extravagant sonnet
Who lives for her belly
And another on it.

> IRVING LAYTON, "Personae: Chloris",
> 1965.

Whoever you love it is me beneath you
over and over.

> GWENDOLYN MACEWEN, "Cartaphilus,"
> 1966.

So far as pleasure is concerned, sexual
intercourse is only ten decibels ahead
of an ice cream cone on a hot day.

> FATHER JOHN H. MCGOEY, of Toronto,
> upholding celibacy requirements for
> priests, qu. in Vancouver Sun, Dec. 30,
> 1967, 6.

I place a metaphor
into your wide-spread groans
do you coast onto the lost shores of
    Lapland
while I speak in your body with my
    verbs' fingering
my tonguing nouns, the closing,
    unclosing
clauses of my limbs?

> ELI MANDEL, "Cosmos, the giant rose
> flower", 1967.

Shame

Abashment intensifies a woman's love
for him so making her abashed. And
there is a shame that is sweeter than
joy.

> ARNOLD HAULTAIN, Hints for lovers,
> 1909, 54.

Sharks

That strange fish,
Tubular, tapered, smoke-blue,
Part vulture, part wolf,
Part neither — for his blood was cold.

> E.J. PRATT, "The shark", 1923.

Ships

Nova Scotian ships, bearing the British
flag into every quarter of the globe,
are some proofs of enterprise.

> JOSEPH HOWE, letter to Lord John Rus-
> sell, Sept. 18, 1839.

To handle a ship you must know all
the ropes.

> THOMAS C. HALIBURTON, Sam Slick's wise
> saws, 1853, ch. 3.

Within Cayuga's forest shade
The stocks were set — the keel was
    laid —
Wet with the nightly forest dew,
The frame of that first vessel grew.

> THOMAS D'A. MCGEE, "The launch of the
> Griffin", 1858. The Griffin was built by
> La Salle and launched in Lake Erie in
> 1679.

    Proud ships rear high
On ancient billows that have torn the
    roots
Of cliffs, and bitten at the golden lips
Of firm, sleek beaches, till they
    conquered all
And sowed the reeling earth with
    salted waves;
Wrecks plunge, prow foremost, down
    still, solemn slopes,
And bring their dead crews to as dead
    a quay.

> ISABELLA VALANCY CRAWFORD, "Mal-
> colm's Katie", 1884.

O ship incoming from the sea
    With all your cloudy tower of sail,
Dashing the water to the lea,
    And leaning grandly to the gale.

> DUNCAN CAMPBELL SCOTT, "Off Rivière
> du Loup", 1893.

The fog still hangs on the long
    tide-rips,
  The gulls go wavering to and fro,
But where are all the beautiful ships
    I knew so long ago?

> BLISS CARMAN, "The ships of Saint John",
> 1921.

The little ship we launched ran swiftly
Into the ruffled waves, and headed
For an unknown shore. We followed
    her
Until our straining eyes could tell no
    longer
The birch bark sails from a drift of
    foam.
All the great ships in the world have
    vanished so
To some last watcher; all the summers
Have ripened and been borne away.
The watchers of ships have turned and
    sighed;
A thousand summers have ended in an
    afternoon.

> LENORE PRATT, "Return", 1956.

Palatia, Quisetta, Companion,
    Vendetta,
Mattawa, Nicola and Jean Madeline,
Sigrid, Amanda, Natanga, Marina,
Montana, Nahada and Princess Arlene.
Clintonia, Mahaska and Caroline Rose,
And queen of them all,
The gallant Bluenose.

> G.J. GILLESPIE, with the information
> branch of the N.S. Dept. of Fisheries,
> 1963, a jingle made up of the names of
> the schooners of yesteryear.

All the fine yachts
Are going out like ships
Deserting a sinking earth.

> STUART MACKINNON, "A new Atlantis",
> 1969.

Shyness

I know a man who's too discreet!
He has apologetic feet,
His nose and mouth and chin retreat—
He seems just leaving when you meet.

> ROBERT FINCH, "A man", *Can. forum*,
> July, 1925, 305.

Sickness

Humanity has but three great enemies: fever, famine and war; of these
by far the greatest, by far the most
terrible, is fever.

> SIR WILLIAM OSLER, address, "Study of
> the fevers of the South", Atlanta, May 6,
> 1896.

Sickness is a crime for habitual
    offenders
The penalty is death.

> ALDEN NOWLAN, "X-ray", 1969.

Sighs

Generally, a woman's sighs are by no
means those of remorse.

> ARNOLD HAULTAIN, *Hints for lovers*,
> 1909, 39.

A woman can say more in a sigh than
a man can say in a sermon.

> ARNOLD HAULTAIN, *Hints for lovers*,
> 1909, 47.

The beginning, middle, and end of
love is — a sigh.

> ARNOLD HAULTAIN, *Hints for lovers*,
> 1909, 71.

Significance

To continually mortify themselves
over insignificant failings is for many
people their only means for feeling
significant.

> IRVING LAYTON, "Aphs", *The whole
> bloody bird*, 1969, 77.

There are brightest apples on those
trees
but until I, fabulist, have spoken
they do not know their significance
or what other legends are hung like
garlands
on their black boughs twisting . . .

IRVING LAYTON, "The fertile muck",
Collected poems, 1971, 28.

Silence

Silence is a powerful weapon.

SIR WILLIAM OSLER, *Johns Hopkins hosp.
bull.*, 1919, 198.

There is no silence upon the earth or
under the earth like the silence under
the sea.

E.J. PRATT, "Silences", 1937.

Silence, if deliberate, is artificial and
irritating; but silence that is unconscious gives human companionship
without human boredom.

STEPHEN LEACOCK, "A lecture on walking", *Last leaves*, 1945, 25.

What Montrealers know best about
each other they never say in public.
Silence, an experienced and at times a
cynical silence, has always been gold-
en here.

HUGH MACLENNAN, *McGill, the story of
a university*, 1959, preface.

Silence is a pocket of possibility. Anything can happen to break it.

R. MURRAY SCHAFER, *Ear cleaning*,
1967, 7.

I prefer the murmur to the shout, for
in silence, there is real presence.

YVES GAUCHER, qu. by Normand The-
riault, *Artscanada*, Feb., 1969, 45.
(Trans.)

Simplicity

It is my misfortune to be a plain man;
and my mistake to have told a plain
story to plain people in plain terms.

THOMAS MCCULLOCH, *The letters of Mephibosheth Stepsure*, 1821, Letter 17.

Man is large in his view; he loves size,
and he likes complexity rather than
simplicity.

J.J. PROCTER, *The philosopher in the
clearing*, 1897, 196.

The only simplicity that is desirable is
simplicity of soul, a certain singleness
of aim and quiet detachment of vision,
a mood of enduring repose not at
variance with constant endeavour, a
habit of content, contemplation and
peace.

BLISS CARMAN, *The friendship of art*,
1904, 223.

Man makes all his first inventions in
the most complex way possible, and it
takes him years before he can hit on
the simple and obvious way of doing
things.

PETER MCARTHUR, "In pastures green",
1915, 87.

Sin

The greater the sinner the greater the
saint.

THOMAS C. HALIBURTON, *Sam Slick's wise
saws*, 1853, ch. 8.

Always sinning and repenting,
    promising to sin no more;
Now resisting, now consenting,
    Human to the very core.

ALEXANDER MCLACHLAN, "David, King
of Israel", 1874.

We are all miserable sinners.

SIR JOHN A. MACDONALD, Summer, 1878; a remark at a political meeting when the Liberal Prime Minister, Alexander Mackenzie, paused in a scathing attack on the "Pacific Scandal". Macdonald emphasized his interjection by drinking the remainder of the water in a glass that Mackenzie had just half-emptied.

The sinner gets many pleasant pickings that never fall in the way of the righteous.

PETER MCARTHUR, *To be taken with salt*, 1903, 154.

The way of the trangresser is very popular.

ROBERT C. (BOB) EDWARDS, Calgary *Eye Opener*, May 8, 1915.

Past sins will take plentiful care of themselves in their consequences; morality would collapse were it otherwise.

WILLIAM HUME BLAKE, *A fisherman's creed*, 1923, 14.

We have bowed our necks to the conception of sin, we have swallowed all manner of poisonous certainties fed us by our parents, our Sunday and day school teachers, our politicians, our priests, our newspapers and all the others with a vested interest in controlling us.

G. BROCK CHISHOLM, speech in Washington, D.C., Oct. 23, 1945.

Only the sinner can become the saint because only the sinner can understand the need and the allness of love.

HUGH MACLENNAN, *Each man's son*, 1951, 66.

Well, boy, life is a kind of stew, and no matter what anybody says it goes better with a pinch of sin. Not too much, mind you. Just a pinch.

HARRY J. BOYLE, *With a pinch of sin*, 1966, 9.

I find depression soon begins
When I start brooding on my sins,
Or view, with even sadder eyes,
My efforts to be good and wise.

GEOFFREY B. RIDDEHOUGH, "Ash Wednesday", 1972.

Singing

The swooning of the golden throat
Drops in the mellow dusk and dies.

DUNCAN CAMPBELL SCOTT, "The voice and the dusk", 1926.

Mount, my soul, and sing at the height
Of thy clear flight in the light and the
   air,
Heard or unheard in the night in the
   light
   Sing there! Sing there!

DUNCAN CAMPBELL SCOTT, "Ecstasy", 1926.

I will sing to the barren rock
Your difficult, lonely music, heart,
Like an old proud king in a parable.

A.J.M. SMITH, "Like an old proud king in a parable", 1936.

Often, we learn our songs when it is too late to sing.

EMILY CARR, qu. in Carol Pearson, *Emily Carr as I knew her*, 1954, 148.

sung as the shrill
bird. the word
offers the ear
cheer, as it be
to be the chor-
us for us, &
by our sense of
hear, as ear, here

VICTOR COLEMAN, "A song", 1966.

The pulse of our flesh
beats at your ear-drums
as we caper ungainly
singing out of tune
but singing
after a lonely and menaced
apprenticeship of silence.

> PETER STEVENS, "After this message",
> 1969.

Dear God, you gave me a voice, I didn't ask for it. So help me.

> LOUIS QUILICO, qu. in Toronto *Globe and Mail*, Feb. 12, 1972, 25.

I'll be happy to sing some of them nice Nashville songs just as soon as them fellers in Nashville start singin' some of my songs about my country.

> STOMPIN' TOM CONNORS, qu. in *Maclean's*, Aug. 1972, 31.

I can sing the morning I'm giving birth, and even during. It doesn't bother me. It's just the conductors who get nervous.

> MAUREEN FORRESTER, singer, qu. in *Herstory* (Sask. Women's Calendar Collective), 1975, (Sept. 22).

Singles

The world is divided into couples, so being single can feel like playing musical chairs and every time they stop the music, you're the one who's out.

> MERLE SHAIN, *Some men are more perfect than others*, 1973, 112.

Size

The superior confidence which people repose in the tall man is well merited. Being tall, he is more visible than other men and being more visible, he is much more closely watched. In consequence, his behavior is far better than that of smaller men.

> JOHN KENNETH GALBRAITH, *The Scotch*, 1964, 54.

Skating

My glad feet shod with the glittering
  steel
I was the god of the winged heel.

> CHARLES G.D. ROBERTS, "The skater",
> 1896.

Skiing

While the crowd, on skiis
  As thick as biis
  Slid down
  To the town
  On their hands and kniis.

> STEPHEN LEACOCK, "The diversions of a professor of history – August 20, 1896", 1923.

The iron hills surround us, solemn in
  their sleep,
The susurrus of swishing skis fills the
  atmosphere,
As rythmically gliding, swift where
  slopes are steep
We rush the narrow speedway,
  dropping sudden, sheer.

> ARTHUR S. BOURINOT, "Canadian ski song", 1923.

Skunks

By'n bye I'm close up by ze skunk.
  I raise my axe on high.
When . . . up, kerplunk . . . zis
    damdam skunk
  He's tro something in my eye . . .

An' so I hunt ze skunk no more
  For ze meat or for ze fur.
For she's smell so damdam bad
  Jez Cris! I can't stan' her.

> ANON., "Ze skunk", French-Canadian verse of lumbering days; from "publishable" version, *Jour. of Amer. folklore*, 1944, 211.

Sky

All one great daffodil, on which do lie
The sun, the moon, the stars, all seen
    at once
And never setting, but all shining
    straight
Into the faces of the trinity —
The one beloved, the lover, and sweet
    love!

> ISABELLA VALANCY CRAWFORD, "Malcolm's Katie", 1884.

For seas are skies and skies are seas,
    where float
Cool swansdown clouds that sundown
    has subdued.

> DOUGLAS LE PAN, "Interval with halcyons", 1953.

Slaves

I'm on my way to Canada,
That cold and dreary land;
The dire effects of slavery
I can no longer stand . . .
Farewell, old master,
Don't come after me,
I'm on my way to Canada
Where coloured men are free.

> ANON., "Away to Canada", American slave song; in *Voice of the fugitive*, Sandwich, Ont.,1851-52.

Far better to breathe Canadian air
Where all are free and well.
Than live in slavery's atmosphere
And wear the chains of hell.

> ANON., runaway slave from U.S., written in 1850's qu. in *Time*, Apr. 6, 1970, 8.

I had rather live in Canada, on one potato a day, than to live in the South with all the wealth they have got.

> MRS. CHRISTOPHER HAMILTON, a Mississippi slave, qu. in Benjamin Drew, *The refuge*, 1856, 177.

O, righteous Father, wilt thou not pity
me.
And help me on to Canada, where all
de slaves are free.

> ANON., fugitive slave song, recorded in S. Bradford, *Harriet Tubman*, in 1869; R. Winks, *Blacks in Canada*, 1971, 243.

Sleep

Here I consider that my Indian travels finish, as the rest of my journey home to Toronto was performed on board steamboats; and the greatest hardship I had to endure, was the difficulty I found in trying to sleep in a civilized bed.

> PAUL KANE, October 1, 1848, in *Wanderings of an artist among the Indians of North America from Canada to Vancouver's Island* . . . , 1859, 455.

To carry care to bed is to sleep with a pack on your back.

> THOMAS C. HALIBURTON, *Sam Slick's wise saws*, 1853, ch. 20.

Sleep on it.

> THOMAS C. HALIBURTON, *Sam Slick's wise saws*, 1853, II, 55.

When the Sleepy Man comes with the
    dust on his eyes
(Oh, weary, my Dearie, so weary!)
He shuts up the earth, and he opens
    the skies.
(So hush-a-by, weary, my Dearie!)

> CHARLES G.D. ROBERTS, "Sleepy man", 1896.

After all, why should I go to bed every night? Sleep is only a habit.

> SIR WILLIAM VAN HORNE, qu., *Can. mag.*, Sept., 1913, 451.

I only wish I knew some great
Exultant vice to stimulate
What spark of Life remains to spend:
But this I feel, as the hour grows late,
Sleep is the best thing in the end.

TOM MACINNES, "Ballade of sleep", 1918.

Turn Thou the key upon our thoughts,
    dear Lord,
And let us sleep;
Give us our portion of forgetfulness,
Silent and deep.

VIRNA SHEARD, "At midnight", 1922.

There is that in sleep which reduces us
all to one common denominator of
helplessness and vulnerable humanity.
The soft rise and fall of the unconscious sleeper's breast is a miracle. It is
a binding symbol of our humanity.
The child in the lost attitude of sleep is
all children, everywhere, in all time. A
sleeping human being is all people,
sleeping, everywhere since time began. There is that in the sleeper that
arrests one, pitying, and that makes us
all the same.

ETHEL WILSON, *Hetty Dorval*, 1947,111.

Lilies and archangels began
The gradual gentling of the lion,
The burred bear fell asleep again —
a snowfall lulled him to a lamb.
Like velvet toys they lie there prone
and dream the cactus plant of pain.

P.K. PAGE, "The event", 1954.

After a while in sleep your fingers
    clutch tightly
and I know that whatever may be
    happening
the fear coiled in dreams or the bright
    trespass of pain
there is nothing at all I can do except
    hold your hand
and not go away

ALFRED PURDY, "Poem", 1970.

Slogans

Always bear in mind that the good old
patriotic slogan of the C.M.A., "Canada for the Canadians", means Canada
for 2,500 Canadians.

GRAIN GROWERS' GUIDE , Feb. 23, 1910;
qu. in G.R. Cook, *Maple leaf forever*,
1971, 211, referring to the Canadian
Manufacturers' Assoc.

The slogans we have are as good as
any we are likely to get; if one is not
satisfied with them it is not because
better slogans are needed but because
slogans by themselves are useless.

F.E. SPARSHOTT, *An enquiry into goodness*, 1958, 3.

Slums

Cabbagetown had one unique feature
which has amazed some people who
haven't given it any thought. It happened to be the largest Anglo-Saxon
slum in North America.

HUGH GARNER, interview with Allan
Anderson, *Tamarack rev.*, No. 52, 1969,
26, referring to Toronto's east end and
his first book, *Cabbagetown*.

Smallness

Smaller than the little end of nothing.

JOHN HENRY POPE, qu. in P.B. Waite,
Canada, 1874-1896, 1971, 96.

Smallwood, Joseph

Who else could have done it but Joe
Smallwood?

R.A. MACKAY, *Dalhousie rev.*, Vol. 50,
Summer, 1970, 232, on Smallwood
bringing Newfoundland into Confederation, 1949.

I love this job. I love it to death. I love every waking minute of it, from the time I get up to the time I go to bed.

> JOSEPH SMALLWOOD, qu. in R. Gwyn, *Smallwood*, 1972, 138, on being Premier.

Smiles

A woman has two smiles that an angel might envy, the smile that accepts the lover afore words are uttered, and the smile that lights on the first-born baby, and assures him of a mother's love.

> T.C. HALIBURTON, *Sam Slick's wise saws*, 1853, II, 52.

A sweet smile from the teeth outwards.

> SIR JOHN A. MACDONALD, to Joseph Pope referring to J.J.C. Abbott, qu. in M. Pope, ed., *Public servant*, 1960, 43.

Does you always run to meet him
    when you see that pleasant smile?
Now does you? Why NO!

> ANON., Queen's University song referring to the custom of Principal George M. Grant to smile broadly when trouble was brewing, about 1880.

Smith, Goldwin

The wild man of the cloister.

> BENJAMIN DISRAELI, referring to Goldwin Smith's association with Oxford University, 1846-1868, qu. in A. Haultain, *Goldwin Smith*, [1913], 205, 231.

The Sage of the Grange.

> ANON., *Goldwin Smith*, from the name of his home in Toronto.

Goldwin Smith was . . . a Little Englander of Little Englanders. He saw nothing in the Empire . . . but a burden on England.

> TIMES WEEKLY, London, June 10, 1910, 420.

Smoking

The moment a man takes to a pipe he becomes a philosopher; — it's the poor man's friend; it calms the mind, soothes the temper, and makes a man patient under trouble.

> T.C. HALIBURTON, *Sam Slick*, 1838, 39.

Don't smoke until you have reached the age of thirty summers, as the nicotine will weaken your sinews, weaken your heart and make you short of breath, and you will be no match for the enemy when you come to grips with him.

> ASSINIBOINE INDIANS, lesson of the tribal sages to young warriors, 1850's.

Oh, it's good is grub when you're
    feeling hollow,
But the best of a meal's the smoke to
    follow.

> ROBERT SERVICE, "The black Dudeen", 1916.

There isn't a woman living so bad in arithmetic that she cannot calculate how much her husband would save if he didn't smoke.

> ROBERT C. (BOB) EDWARDS, in Calgary *Eye Opener*, July 20, 1918, 2.

Sometimes, I think you're an ass, my
    pet,
and sometimes I wonder if that grey
    stuff inside your head
is brain or cigarette ash,
exhaling smoke from your ears, you
    chug along
like a crippled tug.

> DAVE SOLWAY, "Dedication", 1960.

Smugglers

The smuggler is a check upon the extravagance of governments and the increase of taxation. Any government that raises its tariffs too high, or increases its taxation too far, will be kept in check by smugglers.

> JOSEPH HOWE, speech at Detroit, Aug.14, 1865.

Snobbery

A little snobbery, like a little politeness, oils the wheels of daily life.

> ROBERTSON DAVIES, *Tempest-tost*, 1951, 13.

The true snob acknowledges the existence of something greater than himself, and it may, at some time in his life, lead him to commit a selfless act.

> ROBERTSON DAVIES, *Tempest-tost*, 1951, 72.

Snow

A year of snow makes apples grow.

> ANON., saying of pioneer Ontario farmers.

If, Pilgrim, chance thy steps should lead
Where, emblem of our holy creed,
  Canadian crosses glow —
There you may hear what here you read,
And seek in witness of the deed
  Our Ladye of the Snow!

> THOMAS D'A. MCGEE, "Our Ladye of the Snow", 1858; a reference to the original church, Notre Dames des Neiges, which stood on 'the Priests' farm', Montreal.

Snow — snow — fast-falling snow!
Snow on the house-tops — snow in the street
Snow overhead, and snow under feet
Snow in the country — snow in the town,
Silently, silently sinking down;
Everywhere, everywhere fast-falling snow,
Dazzling the eyes with its crystalline glow!

> JENNIE E. HAIGHT, "Snow", in Dewart, *Selections*, 1864, 132.

March is slain; the keen winds fly;
Nothing more is thine to do;
April kisses thee good-bye;
Thou must haste and follow too.

> ARCHIBALD LAMPMAN, "Godspeed to the snow", 1893.

A few bronzed cedars in their fading dress,
Almost asleep for happy weariness,
Lean their blue shadows on the puckered snow.

> ARCHIBALD LAMPMAN, "Before the robin", 1900.

Our lady of the Snows.

> EMILE NELLIGAN, from the title of his poem, "Notre Dame des Neiges", 1903; first used by Thomas D'Arcy McGee, "Our Ladye of the Snow", 1858.

Down drops the snow, the fleecy hooding snow,
  On town and wood and haggard, wind-blown space,
And hushes the storms, and all weird winds that blow
  Upon the world's dead face.

> WILFRED CAMPBELL, "Snowfall", 1905.

Now soon, ah, soon, I know,
The trumpets of the north will blow,
  And the great winds will come to bring
The pale wild riders of the snow.

> BLISS CARMAN, "Before the snow", 1916.

The wind plays strange pranks with snow; snow is the most plastic medium it has to mould into images and symbols of its moods. Here one of these promontories would slope down, and the very next one would slope upward as it advanced across the open space. In every case there had been two walls, as it were, of furious blow, and between the two a lane of comparative calm, caused by the shelter of a clump of brush or weeds, in which the snow had taken refuge from the wind's rough and savage play.

> FREDERICK P. GROVE, *Over prairie trails*, 1922, 115.

The slightest cover of snow will bury the eyesores. Snow is the greatest equalizer in Nature.

> FREDERICK P. GROVE, "Dawn and diamonds", in, *Over prairie trails*, 1922, 94.

If two Canadians understand snow they are then both Canadians.
If one Canadian understands snow and another doesn't understand snow at all, then one is a Canadian and the other is no Canadian at all.

> CARL SANDBURG, "Canadians and Pottawatomies", 1928.

"Snow in April is abominable", said Anne. "Like a slap in the face when you expected a kiss".

> L.M. MONTGOMERY, *Anne of Ingleside*, 1939, 134.

Set your proud mouth
Snowdrift!
Curve the knife-edge
Of your lip
To a thin, imperious smile.
The sun mounts high today.

> F.R. SCOTT, "Snowdrift", 1945.

Exquisite things have been said about snow,
Snow said them first, those exquisite things.

> ROBERT FINCH, "The tribute", 1949.

Snow puts us in a dream on vast plains without track or colour
Beware, my heart, snow puts us in the saddle on steeds of foam
Ring out for a crowned childhood, snow consecrates us on high seas, dreams fulfilled, all sails set
Snow puts us in a trance, a widespread whiteness, flaring plumes pierced by the red eye of this bird
My heart; a point of fire under palms of frost flows the marvelling blood.

> ANNE HÉBERT, "Snow". (Trans. by F.R. Scott, 1962.)

This sudden snow:
    immediately
The prairie is!

> GEORGE BOWERING, "A sudden measure", 1966.

Social Credit

I have all the damn fools on my side and all the clever men against me.

> C.H. DOUGLAS, founder of Social Credit, after he met Aberhart in Alberta, in Apr., 1934, qu. by Alan Anderson in E. Stafford, ed., *Flamboyant Canadians*, 1964, 271.

We have found a scientific way out of our troubles, and if we don't do it, then nobody else will. We have the best brains in the province at our disposal, let us use them and put Social Credit into force. Where does all the money come from? We don't use money. Then where does all the credit come from? Why out of the end of a fountain pen.

> WILLIAM ABERHART, speech, Edmonton, Jan. 15, 1935.

As a matter of fact, I believe I only have four quarts of blood in me, just about four quarts. Will you tell me how a heart can pump 135 gallons an hour with only four quarts of blood? Well, cannot money circulate the same?

> WILLIAM ABERHART, speech at Annual Convention, United Farmers of Alberta, Edmonton, Jan.16, 1935.

Douglas on the one hand and the Holy Ghost on the other.

> WILLIAM IRVINE, qu. by R.B. Hanson, Board of Trade Dinner, Regina, Apr. 30, 1935, referring to Major C.H. Douglas, British Social Credit theorist.

We face a giant today. By ingenuity we can deprive him of his power. The sling of credit-loans-without-interest and the non-negotiable certificated stones will destroy his grip and deliver us from his power.

> WILLIAM ABERHART, speech, Edmonton, July, 1935.

You don't have to know all about Social Credit before you vote for it; you don't have to understand electricity to use it, for you know that experts have put the system in, and all you have to do is push the button and you get the light. So all you have to do about Social Credit is to cast your vote for it, and we will get experts to put the system in.

> WILLIAM ABERHART, qu. in Calgary *Albertan*, Aug. 14, 1935.

Oh Lord, do Thou grant us a foretaste of Thy millennial reign. Organization is not enough, Lord. Our help must come from above.

> WILLIAM ABERHART, Alberta election campaign, 1935.

I trust the Alberta elections have renewed your faith in humanity.

> EZRA POUND, letter to John Buchan (Lord Tweedsmuir), Sept. 1, 1935, after Aberhart's election, qu. in Janet A. Smith, *John Buchan*, 1965, 383.

When we get control of the money and credit we will pay our dividends so fast it will make your head swim.

> ERNEST MANNING, address, Moose Jaw, May 27, 1939.

There is a government more powerful than governments, this great monetary power that knows no international boundaries. That is what we are attacking, and everyone who opposes Social Credit is either ignorant of that power or a party to it.

> REV. ERNEST HANSELL, to political meeting, Oliver, B.C., May 29, 1952.

It is a subject involving the destiny of the human race.

> REV. ERNEST HANSELL, to political meeting, Vernon, B.C., May 30, 1952.

Now where do we Crediters get this holier than thou attitude? We don't only *think* we are right, we *know* we are right. Primarily because our technique is based on a science and in that there are no half measures. You are either right or wrong.

> *CANADIAN SOCIAL CREDITER*, Apr. 8, 1953, 2; qu. by H. J. Schultz, *Can. hist. rev.*, Sept., 1964, 194.

Social Credit is based upon the foundation of eternal principles. These can never be destroyed; they will be true for all men in all places at all times.

> *CANADIAN SOCIAL CREDITER*, "Foreword" in all issues; qu. by H.J. Schultz, *Can. hist. rev.*, Sept., 1964, 194.

You do not have to understand Social Credit to vote for it. You have nothing to lose.

> RÉAL CAOUETTE, leader of the federal Social Credit Party, during election campaign, 1962.

Social Credit is genuine competitive free enterprise in action, aimed at making everybody richer and nobody poorer. We operate in peacetime as other capitalist systems operate in war.

> W.A.C. BENNETT, Premier of B.C., in London, Eng., Aug., 1963, qu. in Vancouver *Sun*, Aug. 14, 1963, 4.

These trusty men labour by day and
   by night,
They work for the people with
   far-reaching sight,
Return Social Credit for all that is
   right,
Roll on, Social Credit, roll on.

> W.A.C. BENNETT, "personal anthem" used in B.C. election, Sept. 30, 1963.

They see in me what Social Credit stands for – it gets things done.

> W.A.C. BENNETT, qu. in Gerald Clark, *Canada: the uneasy neighbor*, 1965, 260.

Social Credit is confessional. Above all we recognize God. Our philosophy is based on this belief. That is why, in speaking of education, we demand confessional schooling.

> CAMIL SAMSON, interview in St. Georges de Beauce, Que., qu. in Montreal *Star*, Apr. 16, 1970, 10.

None of us was born Creditiste, my friends. I, myself, came from a Liberal family. It was so Liberal we had two pictures on the wall in the living room, Sir Wilfrid Laurier and the Sacred Heart and on some nights we didn't know which one to say our prayers to.

> RÉAL CAOUETTE, qu. by Joseph H. Potts when introducing him as guest speaker, Empire Club, Toronto, Nov. 9, 1972.

Social Security

It has yet to be proved that any democracy which underwrites the social minimum for its citizens is any the weaker or less wealthy for doing so.

> H. OF C., SPECIAL COMMITTEE ON SOCIAL SECURITY, *Report on social security for Canada*, 1943, 119.

It has been said that a country's greatness can be measured by what it does for its unfortunates. By that criterion Canada certainly does not stand in the forefront of the nations of the world although there are signs that we are becoming conscious of our deficiencies and are determined to atone for lost time.

> T.C. DOUGLAS, *Sask. Govt. Presentation*, Dominion-Provincial Conference on Reconstruction. Dominion and Provincial Submissions, 1946, 178.

It is for man, within the law, to make his way, to pay the penalty for his failures, to grow strong by his struggles, to give employment by his enterprise, to inspire others by his victories and to help the unfortunate by his success.

> ARTHUR MEIGHEN, address, London (Ont.) Branch, Univ. of Toronto Alumni Assoc., Jan. 27, 1948.

Social Work

This job is just an extension of social work. Social workers have more business in politics than lawyers do.

> DAVE BARRETT, Premier of B.C., qu. in *Maclean's*, June, 1973, 72.

Socialism

Let Socialism tell us plainly what it means to do and how it means to do it. If inequalities of condition could be levelled to-day, the inequalities of capacity, by which they were originally created, would apparently renew them to-morrow.

GOLDWIN SMITH, letter to Provincial Labour candidate, Toronto, Oct. 12, 1908.

In a population of angels a socialistic commonwealth would work to perfection. But until we have the angels we must keep the commonwealth waiting.

STEPHEN LEACOCK, *The unsolved riddle of social justice*, 1920, 113.

I am not afraid of the word "Socialism" which comes from a perfectly good Latin word which means "comradeship", which means that today we as individuals are no longer living isolated lives, that no nation is any longer living an isolated life, but rather that we are living in society in a thousand and one complicated relationships and that we must adapt our political ideals and our political institutions and our political policies to meet the new situation that confronts us.

J.S. WOODSWORTH, in 1924, qu. in Grace MacInnis, *J.S. Woodsworth*, 1953, 218.

True cooperation has its final goal in socialism, which is the continual observance of the Golden Rule.

E.A. PARTRIDGE, at convention, United Farmers of Canada (Sask.), Feb., 1930.

Socialism is only a bright soap bubble, light as ignorance and floating with its own gas. It would only work in a community of impossible people, guided by impossible leaders, and inspired by an inconceivable goodwill. The angels, no doubt, are Socialists.

STEPHEN LEACOCK, *Stephen Leacock's plan to relieve the depression in six days, to remove it in six months, to eradicate it in six years*, 1933, 15.

This is the end of an economic era. Capitalism will never again work in the old way. The only system which can work hereafter is the system controlled and guided by the state.

W.D. HERRIDGE, speech in Sydney, N.S., Sept. 27, 1937.

Let all men be equal in an economic sense and one incitement to live is gone. Man wants to be able to worship power; and power today, means enormous wealth; wealth that gives him all he needs. He does not want to take or to conquer it; he wants to receive it as a free gift.

FREDERICK P. GROVE, *The master of the mill*, 1944, 258.

The seven-day fireworks of the world's creation matter less than the creation of the socialist state; the cure of earthly ills is to be achieved by economics or psychology rather than by divine intervention.

JOHN SUTHERLAND, *Other Canadians*, 1947, 15.

I am purely a trustee for the nation pending the revolution.

HERBERT W. (BERT) HERRIDGE, M.P., 1945-1968, Socialist, qu. as a reply to the question how he can continue to have capitalist land holdings.

The trouble is that socialist parties have gone a-whoring after the Bitch Goddess. They have wanted Success, Victory, Power; forgetting that the main business of socialist parties is not to form governments but to change minds.

CARLYLE KING, in *Can. forum*, Apr., 1952, 3.

That is the advice I have been given by the Secretary of State from Ottawa, that under no circumstances am I to allow you to form a government.

> LIEUT.-GOV. CLARENCE WALLACE, of B.C., to Harold Winch, C.C.F. Leader, March, 1953, qu. in P. Sherman, *Bennett*, 1966, 134.

I hope that those who are trying to safeguard their futures by underwriting stable government in this Province will fully realize the dangers of splitting the anti-socialist vote in a way that will guarantee a socialist victory.

> FRANK MCMAHON, qu. in Vancouver *Province*, Sept. 10, 1960, 1.

In terms of political tactics, the only real question democratic socialists must answer is: "Just how much reform can the majority of the people be brought to desire at the present time?"

> PIERRE E. TRUDEAU, in Michael Oliver, ed., *Social purpose for Canada*, 1961, 374.

A glib-lib is a socialist in a liberal's raiment. He preaches regimentation in the name of freedom, bureaucracy in the name of democracy, and technology in the name of humanity.

> W. L. MORTON, *Jour. of Can. stud.*, Feb., 1967, 28.

For consolation, the socialists need only look southward.

> GAD HOROWITZ, *Canadian labour in politics*, 1968, 263.

There is nothing wrong with socialism except that it doesn't work.

> ROSS THATCHER, qu. in C.H. Higginbotham, *Off the record*, 1968, 140.

A Canadian and Socialist? Philistinism raised to the second power.

> IRVING LAYTON, "Aphs", *The whole bloody bird*, 1969, 103.

I subscribe to the belief that socialism is not about the public ownership of the means of production, but about the public ownership of power. That means democracy.

> STEPHEN LEWIS, address to Canadian Club, Toronto, Dec. 7, 1970.

Socialists

A wild-eyed bunch that were going to reform the world overnight.

> AGNES MACPHAIL, referring to the delegates from British Columbia to the first C.C.F. convention at Regina, July, 1933.

Socialists belong to movements, capitalists support parties.

> WALTER D. YOUNG, *The anatomy of a party: the national C.C.F., 1932-61*, 1969, 3.

As socialists, we will be hard-nosed capitalists in business ventures.

> DAVID BARRETT, Premier of B.C., qu. in *Financial post*, Mar. 17, 1973, 37.

Society

To put the multitude at the top and the few at the bottom is a radical reversion of society which every reflecting man must foresee can end only by its downfall.

> SIR FRANCIS BOND HEAD, *Narrative*, 1839, 464.

The world is made up of madmen and fools. It is better to belong to the first than to the latter class – to rule, than to be ruled.

> SUSANNA MOODIE, *Geoffrey Moncton*, 1855, 260.

The religion of privilege has lost its power to awe or to control; and if society wishes to rest on a safe foundation, it must show that it is at least trying to be just.

> GOLDWIN SMITH, "The labour movement", speech to Mechanics' Inst., Montreal, 1872.

A hollow age, a materialistic age, a vulgar age – an age of breathless competition and over-production in every economic quarter but the soil, an age of socialistic upheaval and dark prediction, of dynamite and demogogue, and the tyranny of the majority – what can we further say to blacken the reputation of this day of ours, in which, despite our maledictions the birds sing and the sun shines, and the clear streams run, and the corn waves golden and abundant!

> SARA JEANETTE DUNCAN, *The Week*, Mar. 3, 1887, 217.

Society is a half-blind mass, living on its traditions, not knowing whither it is going, requiring leadership that will tell it the truth.

> G.M. WRONG, in *Can. hist. rev.*, 1933, 7.

The whole structure of our national life must be built upon the thought that everything that is good we seize upon and everything that is bad must be rejected.

> R.B. BENNETT, speech at Newmarket, Ont., 1933, in *Can. problems*, 1933, 15.

I am still unreconciled to the kind of world I live in and I view many things with alarm besides myself, including most politicians and a good many voters.

> HUGH MACLENNAN, *Thirty and three*, 1954, vii.

It is one of the characteristics of life, for societies as well as for individuals, that the consequence of success in grappling with problems is often the opportunity and the obligation to meet and master greater ones. We are forever climbing the ever mounting slope.

> LESTER B. PEARSON, *Democracy in world politics*, 1955, 4.

Canadians, not without a sense of wonderment, are now becoming aware that they are living in a society which is virtually free from any generally accepted stratification.

> D.J. GOODSPEED, *Queen's quart.*, Vol. 64, 1957, 523.

The basic fact about Canada is that society is not one but two.

> JEAN-C. FALARDEAU, *Roots and values in Canadian lives*, 1961, 15.

The sacred cow under fire is Canadian life itself, with its determined dullness.

> WILLIAM SOLLY, in *Can. lit.*, No.11, 1962, 27.

To seek withdrawal from the tensions of society by a complete abandonment of responsibility for it, is as destructive of life forces as to move selfishly and aimlessly with no honest convictions as to the real meaning of life.

> DOROTHY HENDERSON, *People have power*, 1964, 268.

After three thousand years of explosion, by means of fragmentary and mechanical technologies, the Western world is imploding.

> MARSHALL MCLUHAN, *Understanding media*, 1964, 3.

Democratic society is just as jealous of its privileges as feudal society was. A member of parliament's wife, who is incorrectly seated at table, can give a scowl as black as any duchess who is received in audience by the king and finds no stool placed ready to support her backside.

ROBERT DE ROQUEBRUNE, *A testament of my childhood*, 1964, 144. (Trans.)

The poet, the artist, the sleuth – whoever sharpens our perception tends to be antisocial; rarely "well-adjusted", he cannot go along with currents and trends. A strange bond often exists among anti-social types in their power to see environments as they really are.

MARSHALL MCLUHAN, *The medium is the massage*, 1967, 88.

I am less worried about what is over the Berlin Wall than about Chicago and what might happen in our great cities in Canada.

PIERRE E. TRUDEAU, to students at Queen's University, Nov. 8, 1968; qu. in *Globe and Mail*, Nov. 9, 1968, 1.

Our society is within measurable distance of sliding out of control. Loss of control is by no means inevitable; it is probably not yet an even money risk. All the same, there is a possibility that one day we shall find that the odds have changed, and that only an uphill effort will save us.

TREVOR LLOYD, *Agenda 1970: proposals for a creative politics*, 1968, 281.

Is The Just Society Just For Quebec?

MANITOBA FEDERATION OF LABOUR, newspaper ad, after transfer of Air Canada overhaul base from Winnipeg to Montreal, Dec., 1968.

The drive for radical change in this society tends only to harden the very directions the society is already taking.

GEORGE P. GRANT, *Technology and empire*, 1969, 77.

It is not merely an external environment which we make and choose to use as we want – a playground in which we are able to do more and more, an orchard where we can always pick variegated fruit. It moulds us in what we are, not only at the heart of our animality in the propagation and continuance of our species, but in our actions and thoughts and imaginings. Its pursuit has become our dominant activity and that dominance fashions both the public and private realms.

GEORGE P. GRANT, *Technology and empire*, 1969, 15.

Our greatest danger today is man's inability to understand and therefore to control, what is going on in his society; to adapt his thinking to new conditions.

LESTER B. PEARSON, *Queen's quart.*, Vol. 76, Spring, 1969, 24.

Canada is one of the few places left where the small decencies are observed. If, as a young man, I was scornful of the country because we always seemed so far behind style-setting New York, I now thank God for the cultural lag. Ours, after all, is the good neighbourhood. A society well worth preserving.

MORDECAI RICHLER, *Life mag.*, Apr. 9, 1971, 62.

Society, Polite

It was none of your skim-milk parties, but superfine uppercrust.

THOMAS C. HALIBURTON, *Sam Slick*, 1836, ch. 28.

The average society woman looks younger than she is and acts younger than she looks.

PETER MCARTHUR, *To be taken with salt*, 1903, 146.

There is no man living who can overcome the ingrained prejudice of social disadvantages.

STEPHEN LEACOCK, *Charles Dickens*, 1934, 3.

Sociology

A whole library of sociological inquiry, without the creative imagination behind it, is not worth a single good novel!

A.R.M. LOWER, *Can. hist. rev.*, Vol. 47, 1966, 161.

Soldiers

Cold on Canadian hills, or Minden's plain,
Perhaps that parent mourn'd her soldier slain;
Bent o'er her babe, her eyes dissolved in dew,
The big drops mingled with the milk he drew,
Gave the sad presage of his future years,
The child of misery, baptized in tears.

JOHN LANGHORNE, "The country justice", 1774.

The British soldier who thought himself superior, actually became so.

JOHN GRAVES SIMCOE, *Military journal*, privately printed, 1787, Intro.

Tramp, tramp, tramp, the boys are marching.

LACHLAN MCGOUN, from the poem, later a song, written while the author was serving in the artillery against the Fenians, 1866.

'Twas only as a volunteer that I left my abode,
I never thought of coming here to work upon the road.
We'll keep our spirits up, my boys, and not look sad or sober,
Nor grumble at our hardships on our way to Manitoba.

ANON., "Expedition song", Red River Expedition, 1870.

Why, what would ye have? There is not a lad that treads in the gallant ranks
Who does not already bear on his breast the Rose of a Nation's Thanks!

ISABELLA VALANCY CRAWFORD, "The rose of a nation's thanks", 1884.

I would not hesitate to leave this country of vain, drunken, lying and corrupt men but I cannot afford to "chuck up".

GENERAL F.D. MIDDLETON, letter to Lord Melgund, Feb. 18, 1886. (Minto papers, Pub. Arch. Can.)

Canadians are, for the most part, the descendants of armies, officers and men, and every generation of them has stood up to battle.

WILLIAM D. LIGHTHALL, *Songs of the great Dominion*, 1889, Intro., xxi.

Your bulwark hills, your valleys broad
Streams where de Salaberry trod,
Where Wolfe achieved, where Brock was slain —
Their voices are the voice of God!

CHARLES G.D. ROBERTS, "Canadian streams", 1893.

The Old Eighteen.

ANON., popular term for the first students at Royal Military College, Kingston, opened June 1, 1876. (1900).

The man who can fight to Heaven's
own height
Is the man who can fight when he's
losing.

ROBERT W. SERVICE, "Carry on", 1916.

So give me a strong right arm for a
wrong's swift righting;
Stave of a song on my lips as my sword
is smiting;
Death in my boots, maybe, but
fighting, fighting!

ROBERT W. SERVICE, "Song of the soldier-
born", 1916.

Under the orders of your devoted
officers in the coming battle you will
advance or fall where you stand facing
the enemy. To those who will fall I say
"You will not die, but step into immortality. Your mothers will not lament
your fate, but will be proud to have
borne such sons. Your name will be
revered forever and ever by your
grateful country, and God will take
you unto Himself".

SIR ARTHUR CURRIE, special order to the
Canadian Corps, France, Mar. 27, 1918.

If there is in Canada to-day one portion of its citizenry which more than
any other is entitled to consideration,
it is the men who risked their lives in
battle and those who shared with them
the dangers and privations of war.

W. L. MACKENZIE KING, speech to Liberal
supporters, Aug., 1919.

From the camp behind the hill
He could hear the bugle shrill,
    "We are here! We are here!
        Soldiers all!
    Good cheer! We are near!
        Ontario! Ontario!
        Toronto! Montreal!"

ARTHUR CONAN DOYLE, "Bugles of Canada", 1922.

Zombies.

ANON., term used in 1944 for home-
defence troops conscripted for European service.

For three centuries and a half Canadians have borne arms. Essentially a
civilian people, an unmilitary people,
they have, through historical necessity,
fought to preserve their freedom and
their identity. No men have fought
better: no men have as quickly discarded the skills of war to return to the
farms and factories of peace.

GEORGE F.G. STANLEY, Canada's soldiers
1604-1954, 1954, 375.

Not only must the Canadian service-
man be trained in the offensive and
defensive technique of ultra-modern
warfare and armed with the most
effective military weapons – he must
also be prepared as never before to
parry unrelenting assaults on his mind
and spirit.

HARRY R. LOW, Queen's quart., Vol. 63,
Spring, 1956, 99.

The men who fought at Vimy and
Falaise, who helped to keep the
Atlantic sea lanes open, who flew the
Sopwiths of one war and the Lancast-
ers of another, deserve to be counted
among the founding fathers of modern
Canada.

C.P. STACEY, in D.J. Goodspeed, ed., The
armed forces of Canada, 1867-1967,
1967, xi.

I wasn't exactly a soldier tho
        only a humble airman
who kept getting demoted and
        demoted and demoted
to the point where I finally saluted
        civilians.

AL PURDY, "About being a member of
our armed forces", 1968.

So Johnny joined the martial strife,
  Agreed to everything:
To shoot, to fight, to give his life
  For God and Mackenzie King.

> W.K. THOMAS, *Dalhousie rev.*, Vol. 51,
> Winter, 1971-72, 524, (quoting himself).

Solitude

Nought remains of all I cherished
In the days that now are gone;
Hope has withered, love has perished,
And I feel I am alone.

> JOHN R. NEWELL, "Song – days depart
> in rapid flight", 1881.

I would advise you to write, my dear
friend, because with your active nature, solitude is simply intolerable to
you, and after some time your solitude
would become perhaps attractive if
you were to people it with creatures of
your own fancy.

> SIR WILFRID LAURIER, letter to Mme
> Joseph Lavergne, Mar. 24, 1892.

One measure of a man is his capacity
for enduring solitude.

> BLISS CARMAN, *The kinship of nature*,
> 1904, 185.

For he who once discerns the
  mountain-plain
Of solitude sees all horizons wane.

> ROBERT FINCH, "The mountain-plain",
> 1948.

We all, I'm sure have many hopes for
Canada on this Centennial day – that
she may grow, thrive, prosper in all
things. To these I would add one hope
more: that Canada will not so greatly
grow, and not so grossly thrive, as to
destroy this heritage of solitude which
makes us what we are and which our
children will know perhaps better than
we how to value.

> BLAIR FRASER, "A Centennial sermon",
> Church of the Messiah, Montreal, July 2,
> 1967.

We have accessible to us something
that until the day before yesterday was
accessible to man almost anywhere,
but that now is increasingly rare –
the cleansing experience of solitude.
The temporary disappeareance, or at
any rate the illusion of disappearance,
of those barriers that man has contrived to place between himself and
Reality.

> BLAIR FRASER, "A centennial sermon",
> Church of the Messiah, Montreal, July 2,
> 1967.

Songs

Will nobody write a few songs for
Canada?

> THOMAS MACQUEEN, in *Huron signal*,
> qu., Morgan, *Biblioteca canadensis*,
> 1867, 273.

The great Canadian patriotic songs of
the Second World War were, "There'll
Always Be An England", and "The
White Cliffs of Dover".

> RAYMOND REID, *Canadian style*,
> 1973, 56.

Sons of Freedom

It is estimated that in the last forty
years, a total of 1,112 depredations by
Sons of Freedom have cost Canada's
tax-payers a minimum of $20,124,185
in actual destruction and for police
and court costs. This figure does not
include the thousands of dollars spent
to police, shelter and feed those involved in hundreds of demonstrations,
nude parades and hunger strikes.

> SIMMA HOLT, *Terror in the name of
> God*, 1964, 8.

Sons of Freedom say God tells them to
burn and strip. But rarely do they
receive the alleged divine message in
other than balmy spring or summer
weather. One of their favourite forms
of entertainment has always been to
jeer and attack police as the symbol of

government and law, which they despise. Also police in their midst are useful for their powerful propaganda machine. It gives them the excuse — especially if arrests occur — of crying, "government persecution".

SIMMA HOLT, *Terror in the name of God*, 1964, [vii].

Sorrow

Ah, sorrow, how close you tread on the heels of enjoyment!

THOMAS C. HALIBURTON, *Sam Slick's wise saws*, 1853, ch. 26.

All is a mystery,
   All is a wonder —
The blue vault above,
   And the green world under.
Amid our heaped knowledge
   The silent soul hears
But the rattling of chains
   And the pattering of tears.

ALEXANDER MCLACHLAN, "A dream", 1856.

O foolish ones, put by our cares!
Where wants are many, joys are few;
And at the wilding springs of peace,
God keeps an open house for you.

BLISS CARMAN, "The mendicants", 1894.

Summers and summers have come,
   and gone with the flight of the
   swallow;
Sunshine and thunder have been,
   storm, and winter, and frost;
Many and many a sorrow has all but
   died from remembrance,
Many a dream of joy fall'n in the
   shadow of pain.

CHARLES G.D. ROBERTS, "Tantramar revisited", 1907.

Now he has gone
Take out your sorrow,
Shake it, and iron it,
And put it on tomorrow.

DOROTHY LIVESAY, "A song for Ophelia", 1932.

Sorrow is not a kind sister
trailing dispensation in her wide
   sleeves
sorrow is not benign
bears no blessings.

MIRIAM WADDINGTON, "House of industry", 1941.

Only the light sorrows are clamorous; the deadly griefs are silent. They bleed inwardly.

EMILY MURPHY ("Janey Canuck"), qu. in B.H. Sanders, *Emily Murphy*, 1945, 63, Chap. heading.

I have my own times,
and I keep my sorrows
carefully to myself,
so with the years
they've become an even
more precious treasure.

RAYMOND SOUSTER, "Mourning dove", 1971.

Souls

Earth, heaven, and the mighty whole—
   I scan them and forget the strife;
'Tis when I read the human soul
   A darkness passes upon life.

ARCHIBALD LAMPMAN, Mss. verse of 1892, qu. in *Univ. of Tor. quart.*, Jan., 1958, 184.

Let your soul grow a thing apart
   Untroubled by the restless day,
Sublimed by some unconscious art,
   Controlled by some divine delay.

DUNCAN CAMPBELL SCOTT, "The ideal", 1893.

There is a beauty at the goal of life;
A beauty growing since the world
   began,
Through every age and race, through
   lapse and strife
Till the great human soul complete her
   span.

> ARCHIBALD LAMPMAN, "The largest life",
> *Atlantic monthly*, Mar., 1899.

Mind the senses and the soul
Will take care of itself,
Being five times blessed.

> ANNE WILKINSON, "Letter to my chil-
> dren", 1955.

It is quite right for me to be anxious to
save my never dying soul; but it is of
greater importance to try to serve the
present age.

> JAMES S. WOODSWORTH, qu. in K.
> McNaught, *Prophet in politics*,
> 1959, 26.

The Sovereign

No one can look into futurity and say
what will be the destiny of this country. Changes come over nations and
peoples in the course of ages. But, so
far as we can legislate, we provide
that, for all time to come, the Sovereign of Great Britain shall be the
Sovereign of British North America.

> SIR JOHN A. MACDONALD, *Confederation
> debates*, Feb. 6, 1865, 33.

Most of us are conscious by this time
that in England the Sovereign's name
is William Ewart, and that in Canada
it is John.

> GOLDWIN SMITH, *The Bystander*, Oct.,
> 1883, 260.

The compact which the King makes
with his people when he ascends the
Throne is a compact which he makes
with us as well as with the people of
the Mother Country.

> ROBERT L. BORDEN, H. of C., *Debates*,
> Mar. 1, 1901.

Surpassed was mystic One in Three
and Three in One: God in three persons was outnumbered by the British
King in seven persons, the Septennity.

> A.R.M. LOWER, *Colony to nation*, 1946,
> 486, re: countries in the Empire.

Sovereignty

I claim for Canada this, that in future
Canada shall be at liberty to act or not
act, to interfere or not interfere, to do
just as she pleases, and that she shall
reserve to herself the right to judge
whether or not there is cause for her to
act.

> SIR WILFRID LAURIER, H. of C., *Debates*,
> Feb. 5, 1900, 72.

In Canada there is no sovereignty in
the people. So far as we are concerned
it is in the Parliament at Westminster,
and our powers to legislate are such,
and only such, as that Parliament has
given us.

> A. E. RICHARDS, *Manitoba law repts.*,
> 1916, 13.

She is a sovereign nation and cannot
take her attitude to the world docilely
from Britain, or from the United
States, or from anybody else. A Canadian's first loyalty is not to the British
Commonwealth of Nations, but to
Canada and to Canada's King.

> LORD TWEEDSMUIR, address, Canadian
> Institute of International Affairs, Mont-
> real, Oct. 12, 1937.

Canada has permitted the United States Air Force a degree of interference in our national sovereignty greater than any Canadian Government would have conceded to Great Britain within my lifetime. Yet the American airmen remain unsatisfied.

MAJ. GEN. W.H.S. MACKLIN, address, 25th Annual Couchiching Conference, Aug., 1956.

Canada, that is, has preserved and confirmed the essentials of the greatest of civilizations in the grimmest of environments. It is an accomplishment worthy of a better end than absorption in another and an alien society, however friendly and however strong in its own ideals. In that accomplishment and its continuance lies the relevance of Canadian history.

W.L. MORTON, Presidential address, Canadian Historical Association, annual meeting, Kingston, Ont., June 11, 1960.

It is not the concept of *nation* that is retrograde; it is the idea that the nation must necessarily be sovereign.

PIERRE E. TRUDEAU, *Federalism and the French Canadians*, 1968, 151.

Space

Looking up into the starry space above my head, I am confounded with the unsolved questions that it presents, and the inscrutable enigma that lies behind it, and yet pervades it.

J. J. PROCTER, *The philosopher in the clearing*, 1897, 73.

Beneath the spandrels of the Way
Worlds rolled to night – from night to day;
In Space's ocean suns were spray.

ISABELLA VALANCY CRAWFORD, "Gisli the Chieftain", 1905.

I've topped the wind-swept heights
with easy grace
Where never lark, nor even eagle
flew
And, while with silent, lifting mind
I've trod
The high untrespassed sanctity of
space,
Put out my hand, and touched the
face of God.

JOHN G. MAGEE, American citizen, killed on active service with the R.C.A.F., Dec. 11, 1941; "High flight", written in Sept., 1941.

I have sat by night beside a cold lake
And touched things smoother than
moonlight on still water,
But the moon on this cloud sea is not
human
And here is no shore, no intimacy,
Only the start of space, the road to
suns.

F.R. SCOTT, "Trans Canada", 1945.

Look up at the colourless dark
that may soon become as familiar to us
as the green of grass.

ELDON GRIER, "An ecstasy", 1963.

People say that heaven is up in the great skies beyond the stars. If a rocket ship left the earth today, I understand it would travel for a long time and still not reach anywhere, for space is vast. As for those of my people who claimed to have gone some place after they were dead and then come back in a matter of two to three days, my idea is, where could they have gone? If the rocket ship could travel for ever without finding heaven, then there must be a heaven right here on earth that we pass every day without being able to penetrate its invisible wall.

NORVAL MORRISSEAU, *Legends of my people*, 1965, 120.

Night has fallen and robot chariots
Boom their moon-eyed ways
Through the impalpable obscure,
Humbug stars in a humbug galaxy
Of pride and power, comets on a
    winter
Sky of the mind.

> HENRY BEISSEL, "New wings for Icarus",
> 1966.

Darkness is to space what silence is to
sound, i.e., the interval.

> MARSHALL MCLUHAN, *Through the van-*
> *ishing point*, 1968, 97.

We in our millions cruise along
in the encapsuling blue
not sure why we belong
on earthship's crew,
all at some instant scared
to find ourselves aboard
and not sure what to do
for safety or for rescue

> MARGARET AVISON, "April 17-18, 1970
> (Apollo XIII)".

Space cold and pure
encapsulated me,
a virus in the universe.

> PAT LOWTHER, "Woman", 1971.

Speaker of the House of Commons

My Dear George: I purpose, if you
have no objection, to knock you into a
cocked hat at the opening of Parliament next week. Yours always,

> JOHN A. MACDONALD, letter to George
> Kirkpatrick, chosen Speaker, Feb. 8,
> 1883; ref. to the headgear worn by the
> Speaker.

Our system of government rests upon
the basis of free and untrammelled
discussion, and the duty of presiding
over the deliberations of the House of
Commons, where this free and untrammelled discussion must take
place, is, we must admit, one of the
most difficult and delicate, when we
remember that the object is, as it ought
to be, to maintain absolute impartiality.

> SIR WILFRID LAURIER, H. of C., *Debates*,
> 1899, 9062.

I am afraid when all men speak well
of me.

> J. A. GLEN, Speaker, H. of C., *Debates*,
> June 14, 1941, 4042.

Mr. Speaker, I wish to say that never
in my life, anywhere, at any time, in
any place, have I used those words
["You bloody fool"] to anyone. Earlier
above the din I had sought to be heard
on privilege. I advanced toward the
table and I said: "You are a dictator,
Mr. Speaker," and I repeated "dictator" several times. Again, let me say
that I have never in my life used the
foul language attributed to me.

> M. J. COLDWELL, H. of C., *Debates*, June
> 4, 1956, 4643, ref. to newspaper account
> of the Pipeline debate of June 1.

The most partisan of politicians; the
most impartial of Speakers.

> ARTHUR BEAUCHESNE, to James H. Aitch-
> ison, June, 1958, qu. in R. M. Clark,
> *Canadian issues*, 1961, 35. Refers to
> Pierre Casgrain, Speaker, 1936-40.

He will require a formidable array of
qualities. He must enjoy our respect
without losing our affection. He must
be firm yet sensitive, a master of
language and a good listener, able to
interpret the law and to understand
human nature. He must be prepared
to cite a precedent, and to know when
to distinguish it. It will be helpful if he
has a good sense of humour, and if he
can be equally witty in both languages. He needs the skills of a judge
and a diplomat. He should combine
the talents of a tight-rope walker, a
juggler and, occasionally, a lion tamer.

In short, he must be a born parliamentarian.

SIR PIERRE E. TRUDEAU, H. of C., *Debates*, Sept. 12, 1968, 1.

Speaking

Consciousness of power, my dear.

SIR JOHN A. MACDONALD, in 1887, to his wife referring to the transformation that came over Sir George Foster on his ascent to the rostrum, qu. in Sir Joseph Pope, *Public servant*, 1960, 64.

It is the easiest thing in the world to say it when you have nothing to say, and, very frequently, the hardest thing when you have. That is the reason why the fair sex are so eminently gifted in the oratorical line, and why men are either silent altogether, or make an awful mess of it when they do speak.

J. J. PROCTER, *The philosopher in the clearing*, 1897, 3.

Stand up, speak up, then shut up. The human mind can absorb only what the human seat can endure.

HUGH SHANTZ, Speaker, B. C. legislature, 1959-1963, qu. in *Liberty*, "Cross Canada", Mar., 1963.

Speculation, Financial

Our railway speculations have provided a very efficient issue which will prevent us dying of plethora.

JOHN LANGTON, letter, Apr. 17, 1856.

Destructive as speculation is commonly supposed to be, there is in it little loss of wealth to the community. It is simply passed from one control to another, and, in the long run, it usually reaches the most capable hands.

ADAM SHORTT, *Can. mag.*, Vol. 13, 1899, 495.

Who knows that gambling does not
  pay?
  The speculator!
Who loves to throw his cash away?
  The speculator.
Who never listens to advice
But robs himself to pay our price,
Because he's very, very nice?
  The speculator.

W. A. MACLEOD, "The philanthropist", 1938.

Speech

Our well-known Canadian laconicism is not always concealed wisdom, but a kind of dumbness, a frustration, a between-ness. We are continually on the verge of something but we don't quite get there. We haven't discovered what we are or where we're going and therefore we haven't much to say.

CHESTER DUNCAN, speech to Winnipeg Poetry Soc., qu. in *Time*, Dec. 29, 1947, 28.

Speech structures the abyss of mental and acoustic space, shrouding the race; it is a cosmic, invisible architecture of the human dark. Speak that I may see you.

MARSHALL MCLUHAN, *Counterblast*, 1954.

Until writing was invented, we lived in acoustic space, where the Eskimo now lives: boundless, directionless, horizonless, the dark of the mind, the world of emotion, primordial intuition, terror. Speech is a social chart of this dark bog.

MARSHALL MCLUHAN, *Counterblast*, 1954.

The relationship between the Prime Minister and the cliché is not that between master and servant; it is that of master and slave because he beats these clichés and bruises them, sets them dangling before us, and then having bludgeoned them with such violence, he buries their bleeding bodies in the pages of *Hansard*.

ALISTAIR STEWART, H. of C., *Debates*, Jan. 3, 1958, 2784, referring to John Diefenbaker.

Where Canadians got the monotone that you're listening to now I don't know – probably from the Canada goose.

NORTHROP FRYE, C.B.C. radio address, 1962, in *The educated imagination*, 1964, 121.

Genuine speech is the expression of a genuine personality. Because it takes pains to make itself intelligible, it assumes that the hearer is a genuine personality too – in other words, wherever it is spoken it creates a community. Bastard speech is not the voice of the genuine self: it is more typically the voice of what I shall here call the ego. The ego has no interest in communication, but only in expression.

NORTHROP FRYE, *The well-tempered critic*, 1963, 41.

Do not speak, my son,
unless you can improve on silence.

IRVING LAYTON, "Advice for David", 1971.

Speech from the Throne

Speeches from the Throne come in three categories. Probably the most common is that which says nothing in the loftiest of phrases. The second makes grand pronouncements about great enterprises that are never acted upon. The third, and it is rare, actually portends the shape of things to come.

TORONTO *GLOBE AND MAIL*, Oct. 24, 1969, 6, editorial.

Speeches

All his speeches would read both ways, so that he could interpret them as he liked: so, which ever way things eventuated, he was always right.

T. C. HALIBURTON, *Sam Slick*, 1840, 192.

We, in Canada, have got into the habit of delivering lectures and essays in parliament. Well, these essays we can all find in books, and it is merely lecture and water that we get as a rule, in long speeches.

SIR JOHN A MACDONALD, speech, 1861; qu. in E. B. Biggar, *Anecdotal life*, 1891, 184.

Elegant flummery.

GOLDWIN SMITH, on speeches made by Marquis of Dufferin while Governor-General, 1872-8.

One of those war, famine, and pestilence speeches which have so often carried constituencies for the Government.

SIR JOHN THOMPSON, Prime Minister, H. of C., *Debates*, June 28, 1892, 4370, on a preceding speech made by Sir Richard Cartwright.

Think not, because thine inmost heart
    means well,
Thou hast the freedom of rude speech;
    sweet words
Are like the voices of returning birds
Filling the soul with summer, or a bell
That calls the weary and the sick to
    prayer.
Even as thy thought, so let thy speech
    be fair.

ARCHIBALD LAMPMAN, "Good speech", 1899.

There comes to mind the juggler who, with great dexterity, keeps several balls in the air. The balls are Isolationism, North Americanism, Imperialism and Collectivism. One sees them going up and coming down with rhythmic regularity, and suddenly they are lost in polished phrases of a platitudinous peroration – the magician's handkerchief. And yet it is statesmanship honestly striving for national unity.

E. J. TARR, in *International affairs*, 1937, 685.

I wish my tongue were a quiver the
    size of a cask
Packed and crammed with long
    venomous rankling darts.
I'd fling you more full of them, and
    joy in the task,
Than ever Sebastian was, or Caesar,
    with thirty-three swords in his heart.

L. A. MACKAY, "The ill-tempered lover", 1938.

I had discovered the power of words and gestures over people and I have never forgotten the power of that preacher to dominate those people.

WILLIAM ABERHART, referring to childhood revival meetings, qu. in *Flamboyant Canadians*, 263.

Time is not the same for the speaker as for the audience. To the speaker it is too, too brief for what he has to say. For the audience it is grim foretaste of eternity.

MARSHALL MCLUHAN, "Culture without literacy", *Explorations*, Dec., 1953, 121.

Spiders

I am a spider
spinning bandage
out of my guts.
Some day
the roll will run
empty.

PAT LOWTHER, "Seven purgative poems", 1968.

Spies

The government realized that questions as to the liberty of the subject and of individual freedom were certain to arise in the exploration of the extent and development of this system of espionage, and that it would therefore be most desirable and indeed, absolutely necessary to have as commissioners persons who, above all, would be most anxious to protect the liberty of the subject, and to see that justice was done – and justice only.

W.L. MACKENZIE KING, H. of C., *Debates*, Mar. 18, 1946, 50, re: Gouzenko case.

The quiet Canadian.

HARRY L. HOPKINS, a phrase quoted in Robert Sherwood, *The White House papers of Harry L. Hopkins*, 1948, 270, and used as a title of a book by H.M. Hyde on the secret service exploits of Sir William Stephenson during the war, 1939-1945.

One can only hope that the Russians will not be such cads as to read the *Canada gazette*.

LONDON (Ont.) *FREE PRESS*, Editorial referring to hitherto classified information about location of DEW Line airfields, etc. being published in the *Canada gazette*, qu. in J. Barber, *Good fences make good neighbors*, 1958, 172.

If I were a spy, would I be working for a living?

GERDA MUNSINGER, qu. in Toronto *Star*, Mar. 11, 1966, 8.

The Americans are always giving us less than our due. They only had 50 C.I.A. agents operating in this country. On a population basis, they should have had at least 300.

> JACK MCCLELLAND, in Vancouver, qu. by Jack Wasserman in the Vancouver *Sun*, Feb. 25, 1975, 31.

Spinsters

I do not know at what age one dare call a woman a spinster.

> SIR WILLIAM OSLER, *Nurse and patient*, 1897.

Spiritualism

My nature and reason revolt against "spiritualism" and all that ilk – but not against things of the spirit – belief in spiritual guidance – thro' intuitions. It is the material manifestations I feel charry [sic] about – on the other hand when in faith & prayer I have asked for them, and they come in such an unmistakable manner, are they not to be accepted in all faith and humility – just at this time when guidance from on High is needed.

> W.L. MACKENZIE KING, *Diary*, Oct. 30, 1925; qu. in H. B. Neatby, *Mackenzie King, Vol. 2, 1924-1932*, 1968, 202.

. . . as I came to 'Mackenzie' – dear Mother's spirit seemed to come between me and the paper, to almost illumine it.

> W.L. MACKENZIE KING, note in diary, Aug. 27, 1928, when he signed the Briand-Kellogg Pact.

Sport

The only thing on the level is mountain-climbing.

> EDDIE QUINN, Montreal wrestling promoter, 1930's, qu. in Montreal *Gazette*, Mar. 17, 1973, 29.

Everybody has an incentive, and if you can bring out that incentive you've got a winner.

> CONN SMYTHE, qu. in *Maclean's*, Jan. 15, 1952, 32.

Fish for Fun.

> ANON., motto of Ontario campaign to promote fishing for sport but not for food because of pollution, late 1960's.

A Canadian has been defined as somebody who does not play for keeps.

> WILLIAM KILBOURN, *Canada: a guide to the peaceable kingdom*, 1970, xv.

The profit motive simply should have no place in spectator sport. Since a sport like hockey is so much a part of the national culture and since the community contributes so much to the development of its athletes, the staging of hockey games should properly be a community enterprise.

> BRUCE KIDD, in I. Lumsden, ed., *Close the 49th parallel, etc.*, 1970, 270.

Sport in Canada rarely generates its own change, but tends to be shaped by other forces in the society. Until more Canadians become concerned about the effects of unregulated commercialism upon other aspects of Canadian society, it is unlikely they will ever be concerned about the effects of commercialism in sport.

> BRUCE KIDD, in I. Lumsden, ed., *Close the 49th parallel, etc.*, 1970, 272.

The playpen.

> DICK BEDDOES, sports editor, Toronto *Globe and Mail*, term used to describe the world of professional sport.

It is unfortunately a fact that the quality of performance on Canada's sport pages is too seldom on a par with that in Canada's sport arenas. The profession is still burdened with hacks who make tin-can gods out of cast-iron jerks. I believe there still is a tendency among sports reporters to slant news in favour of the home team, to defer to local sports management for the sake of maintaining cordial working relationships, and to accept publicity handouts in place of digging for their own stories.

DICK BEDDOES, sports columnist, Toronto *Globe and Mail*, in Canada. Senate. Special Comm. on Mass Media, *Proceedings*, Mar. 3, 1970, No. 24, 65.

Sport is as valid as a performance at the O'Keefe Centre, but not as valid as a farmer's crop being destroyed by hail, or somebody going without food, or people getting shot at.

DICK BEDDOES, Toronto *Globe and Mail* sports columnist, qu. in *Weekend mag.*, Aug. 2, 1975, 16.

Sport is all hoke and hype, but I find it outrageous and wonderful.

DICK BEDDOES, Toronto *Globe and Mail* sports columnist, qu. in *Weekend mag.*, Aug. 2, 1975, 16.

Sport, Professional

Imagine being paid to play the game you love!

FRANCIS "KING" CLANCY, qu. by T. Frayne and P. Gzowski, in *Great Canadian sports stories*, 1965, 118.

Spring

Will spring *ever* come?

ANNA JAMESON, Mar. 8, 1837, Toronto, in *Winter studies*, I, 1838, 171.

The sap flies upward. Death is over
and done.
The glad earth wakes; the glad light
breaks; the days
Grow round, grow radiant. Praise for
the new life!
Praise
For bliss of breath and blood beneath
the sun!

CHARLES G.D. ROBERTS, "The awaking earth", 1893.

Make me over, Mother April,
When the sap begins to stir!
Make me man or make me woman,
Make me oaf or ape or human,
Cup of flower or cone of fir;
Make me anything but neuter
When the sap begins to stir!

BLISS CARMAN, "Spring song", 1894.

The long bright icicles in dwindling
ranks
Dripped from the murmuring eaves
till one by one
They fell. As if the spring had now
begun,
The quilted snow, sun-softened to the
core,
Loosened and shunted with a sudden
roar
From downward roofs.

ARCHIBALD LAMPMAN, "Winter-break", 1899.

She comes with gusts of laughter, —
The music as of rills;
With tenderness and sweetness,
The wisdom of the hills.

BLISS CARMAN, "Over the wintry threshold", *Smart set*, Apr., 1913.

Now hath a wonder lit the saddened
eyes
Long misted by a grievous winter
clime;
And now the dull heart leaps with
love's surprise
And sings its joy. For 'tis the happy
time,

And all the brooding earth is full of
   chime,
And all the hosts of sleepers
   underground
Have burst out suddenly in glorious
   prime;
And all the airy spirits now have found
Their wonted shrines with life and
   love entwined 'round.

> WILLIAM E. MARSHALL, "Brookfield",
> 1914.

Here is the land of quintessential
   passion,
Where in a wild throb Spring wells up
   with power.

> DUNCAN CAMPBELL SCOTT, "Spring on
> Mattagami", 1916.

Now great Orion journeys to the West,
The Lord of Winter from the world
   withdraws
And all his glittering house of cold
   dissolves.

> BLISS CARMAN, "A bluebird in March",
> 1929.

Beyond the dripping nose and tear,
Beyond the chilblain and the bite,
Beyond the scratchy underwere,
Beyond the eighty-below at night,
There still must lie — though drifts
   conceal —
Some hidden good for man's descry,
Some secret bounty for his weal,
Which man should shovel out — or
   try.

> PAUL HIEBERT, *Sarah Binks*, 1947.

Fly streamers from the maypole of my
   arms,
From head to toe
My blood sings green,
From every heart a green amnesia
   rings.

> ANNE WILKINSON, "The red and the
> green", 1955.

Spring is distrusted here, for it
   deceives —
snow melts upon the lawns,
   uncovering
last fall's dead leaves.

> ALDEN NOWLAN, "April in New Bruns-
> wick", 1961.

March winds
And April showers
Always a month late
In this dam country of ours.

> ROBERTSON DAVIES, *Samuel March-
> banks' almanack*, 1967, 204.

New peas and beans and baby beets
Must still await July,
But already tiny rhubarb shoots
Give promise of the pie;
And tips of young asparagus
Their joyful message fling,
And hens will once more lay again —
It's spring, it's spring, it's spring!

> PAUL HIEBERT, *Willows revisited*, 1967,
> 78; "Spring", by Bessie Udderton, asso-
> ciate of Sarah Binks.

The month that pocks the earth with
   scabs of snow
With my blood rhymes;
The juice that navigates the veins of
   trees
Tours all my trunk, explores my
   slumbrous limbs
And in my car a hush awaits the crow.

> ANNE WILKINSON, "March, April, June",
> 1968.

Spruce Trees

Peasant of northern forests, humble
   tree,
Kirtled and frocked in all-year
   homespun green.

> THEODORE H. RAND, "An inland spruce",
> 1897.

Spying

I felt it was of great importance that the scientific war effort on the two fronts should be coordinated.

DR. RAYMOND BOYER, sentenced to two years for spying for the Russians in 1946; qu. in P. Berton, ed., *Historic headlines*, 1967, 106.

The less you talk the more they give. You need only to learn to listen when they speak. They will tell you everything.

NICOLAI ZABOTIN, military attaché, Russian Embassy, Ottawa, qu. in Igor Gouzenko, *This was my choice*, 1948, 224.

War has become a thing of instantaneous combustion, engulfing civilian and soldier alike. Surely it is plain that against enemy attack today, the first defence must be information: to find out when and where an aggressor intends to strike. That is the role of Secret Intelligence, and without it all other means of defence could prove to be of sadly limited avail.

SIR WILLIAM STEPHENSON, qu. in H. M. Hyde, *The quiet Canadian*, 1962, 242.

A loyal ally does not spy; he simply exchanges information.

JAMES STEELE, in Stephen Clarkson, *An independent foreign policy for Canada?*, 1968, 72.

Standards

In surveying Canadian poetry and fiction, we feel constantly that all the energy has been absorbed in meeting a standard, a self-defeating enterprise because real standards can only be established, not met.

NORTHROP FRYE, *The bush garden*, 1971, 222.

Stanfield, Robert L.

I don't want to sound presumptuous, but Mackenzie King was dull, too.

ROBERT L. STANFIELD, on his "dullness" after announcing his candidacy for the Conservative Party leadership, July 19, 1967.

Bob's always unable to say what he means because he suffers from a kind of internal stutter.

ANON., qu. in P. Newman, *Distemper of our times*, 1968, 163.

Bob's every inch a political animal and that's why he never gives up. He understands that sucess and failure are equal imposters, that you may win when you should have lost, that you may lose when you should have won.

GERALD REGAN, Premier of Nova Scotia, interview, Dec., 1972.

There's only one me, and I'm stuck with him.

ROBERT L. STANFIELD, "Weekend", C.B.C.-TV, Mar. 18, 1973.

Stars

Alive all heaven seems! with wondrous
    glow
Tenfold refulgent every star appears,
As if some wide, celestial gale did
    blow,
And thrice illume the ever-kindled
    spheres.

CHARLES HEAVYSEGE, poem no. XIV, in *Jephthah's daughter*, 1865.

Canadian stars are remote and virginal.

RUPERT BROOKE, *Letters from America*, 1916, 117.

Now fades the glowing vesper bars
   That gird the pillars of the west,
And all the lustres of the stars .
   Burn in their rooms of rest.

ALBERT D. WATSON, "Evening peace",
1923.

I glance from humble toil and see
The star-gods go in heavenly pride;
Bright Sirius glittering through a tree
Orion with eternal stride.

J. E. H. MACDONALD, (1893-1932) "Kitch-
en window", 1933.

Let me be a watcher of stars
on lonely nights when the thin moon
slides like a scimitar through the
   clouds
and cuts showers of star-fire loose from
   the sky.

VIOLET ULASOVETZ, "A watcher of stars",
1949.

   I know the stars
are wild as dust
     and wait for no man's discipline
     but as they wheel
from sky to sky they rake
   our lives with pins of light.

LEONARD COHEN, "Another night with
telescope", 1964.

Plain stars in an unheated night
beyond this plain slant out
their temporal fartherings, fine farers;
like the summer's yachts
they dot this lined circumference,
each sphering in a crocus light
to balanced towers,
committed to this season's flight
beyond the cyclones of despair
to the eternal circumstance.

M. TRAVIS LANE, "Plain stars", 1973.

There are those burned out stars
who implode into silence
after parading in the sky
after such choreography what would
   they wish to speak of anyway.

MICHAEL ONDAATJE, "White dwarfs",
1973.

The State

How different the story of the world's
relations would be today had the
Brute, in the name of the State, not
been permitted to control the Man.

W. L. MACKENZIE KING, *Industry and
humanity*, 1918, 114.

Historically the state is an organization
of lawyers and priests; it becomes
destructive of the creative powers of
men when the lawyers decide they are
priests or when the priests get control
of the law.

ROBERT WEAVER, in *Tamarack rev.* No.
4, 1957, 35.

Men do not exist for states: states are
created to make it easier for men to
attain some of their common objectives.

PIERRE E. TRUDEAU, *Federalism and the
French Canadians*, 1968, 18.

Without God we have no rights, only
such privileges as may be granted us
by the state.

ALDEN NOWLAN, "Scratchings", 1971.

Statements

I merely make a statement, judicious
   and polite,
that in this poise of crystal space
I balance and I claim the five gods of
   reality
to bless and keep me sane.

PHYLLIS WEBB, "The glass castle", 1962.

You can't cultivate speech, beyond a certain point, unless you have something to say, and the basis of what you have to say is your vision of society.

> NORTHROP FRYE, *The educated imagination*, (1962) 1964, 149.

Statesmen

The life of a statesman is always an arduous one, and very often it is an ungrateful one.

> SIR WILFRID LAURIER, H. of C., *Debates*, June 8, 1891, 886.

This thing they call irresolution is often the very pith and marrow of statesmanship.

> SIR JOHN WILLISON, *Laurier*, 1903, II, 218.

I know what a statesman is. He is a dead politician. We need more statesmen.

> ROBERT C. (BOB) EDWARDS, Calgary *Eye Opener;* attributed.

Yet we know well enough that the gathering to which these statesmen have come from the four corners of the world will end, for the time at least, in little else than smiles and cigar smoke.

> *CANADIAN GAZETTE*, Apr. 18, 1907, 61, on the Colonial Conference, London, Apr., 1907, attended by Sir Wilfrid Laurier and others; qu. in *Dalhousie rev.*, Autumn, 1973, 495.

The more I see of Statesmen, the greater regard have I for plumbers.

> SAMUEL W. JACOBS, letter to Sidney Nyberg, Sept. 4, 1930.

The essential task of Canadian statesmanship is to discover the terms on which as many as possible of the significant interest-groups of our country can be induced to work together in common policy.

> FRANK H. UNDERHILL, *Can. forum*, Vol. 28, Aug., 1948, 1.

A detached mind may keep watch upon itself, but it watches over wasteland. Only a mind ethically anaesthetized, morally lobotomized, remains detached from what statesmen are doing to our world.

> JAMES EAYRS, lecture, Carleton University, Nov. 20, 1965.

Are statesmen to be excused for their follies if they act in good faith? Are we to judge them for effort in a world which usually judges for result? What is so special about statesmen that when their plans miscarry and their statecraft goes awry we are not to call them guilty men?

> JAMES EAYRS, *Right and wrong in foreign policy*, 1966, 36.

Statistics

Figures are the representatives of numbers, and not things.

> T. C. HALIBURTON, *Sam Slick*, 1838, 208.

When I am Premier, you will not have to look up figures to find out whether you are prosperous: you will know by feeling in your pockets.

> SIR WILFRID LAURIER, speeches in early 1890's, on dubious statistics, qu. Skelton, *Day of Laurier*, 327.

If there are politicians, financiers, economists, whose work the Dominion Statistician has not succeeded in enriching, the fault is likely to be theirs.

> G. E. JACKSON, *Can. hist. rev.*, 1922, 256.

The statistician with his plotted graph showing where we will arrive ten years hence is not as convincing as he was of yore. I have seen too many fine ascending projections dip into the cellar these past few years.

> J. W. DAFOE, in *Can. journ. econ. and pol. sci.*, 1938, 287.

When young people being aided in the choice of a career are required to answer yes or no in eight minutes to a series of questions on such matters as the relation of law to liberty or the abolition of war, one must admire a plan which analyzes and determines the personality of a human being in statistical form in so short a time, but I think the secrets of mind and character do not reveal themselves quite so simply.

> VINCENT MASSEY, address to Canadian Manufacturers' Association, June 6, 1956.

Eight statisticians out of ten
Are blue-eyed, thirty-seven, men,
Married, college graduates, called
J. Wilbur, Protestant and bald.

> MAVOR MOORE, "The statistician", *And what do you do?*, 1960, 25.

Status

A colony, yet a nation — words never before in the history of the world associated together.

> SIR WILFRID LAURIER, speech in Liverpool, Eng., June 12, 1897; a reference to Canada.

We are reaching the day when our Canadian Parliament will claim co-equal rights with the British Parliament and when the only ties binding us together will be a common throne and a common crown.

> SIR WILFRID LAURIER, speech at Tercentenary Celebration, Quebec, July 20-31, 1908.

This policy is in the best traditions of the Liberal party. This policy is the latest link in the long chain of events which, following the principles laid down by the Reformers of old times, Baldwin and Lafontaine, step by step, stage by stage, have brought Canada to the position it now occupies, that is to say, the rank, dignity and status of a nation within the British Empire.

> SIR WILFRID LAURIER, H. of C., *Debates*, Feb. 3, 1910, 2953; on the Naval Service Bill.

The highest future for this Dominion lies within this Empire upon conditions of equal status.

> SIR ROBERT BORDEN, *Liberal-Conservative handbook*, 1913; "Equal status", or, "Equality of nationhood" for Canada within the Empire, also associated with Borden's efforts at Paris Peace Conference. See his *Memorandum*, Mar. 12, 1919.

The same indomitable spirit which made [Canada] capable of that effort and sacrifice made her equally incapable of accepting at the Peace Conference, in the League of Nations, or elsewhere, a status inferior to that accorded to nations less advanced in their development, less amply endowed in wealth, resources, and population, no more complete in their sovereignty, and far less conspicuous in their sacrifices.

> SIR ROBERT BORDEN, H. of C., *Debates*, Sept. 2, 1919, 22.

The status of any country is limited by the average status of its inhabitants.

> JOHN OLIVER, speech to students, Vancouver, when Premier, 1918-27, qu. in James Morton, *Honest John Oliver*, 1933, 156.

Equal Status!

W. L. MACKENZIE KING, remark made on throwing a Canadian cent and an English halfpenny into the running metal, at Croydon, of the bells for the Peace Tower Carillon; a Canadian Press despatch, Imperial Conference, 1926.

Statute of Westminster, 1931

In theory we have been free since the Statute of Westminster; in practice, through the will of the Anglo-Canadians, we cease to be free on important occasions.

ANDRÉ LAURENDEAU, *La crise de la conscription 1942*, 1962, 38. (Trans.)

Stenographers

In their eyes I have seen
the pin-men of madness in marathon
    trim
race around the track of the stadium
    pupil.

P. K. PAGE, "The stenographers", *Can. forum*, Sept., 1942.

Stores

Around his store, on spacious shelves
    arrayed
Behold his great and various stock in
    trade.
Here, nails and blankets side by side
    are seen;
There, horses' collars, and a large
    tureen;
Buttons and tumblers, fish-hooks,
    spoons and knives,
Shawls for young damsels, flannel for
    old wives;
Woolcards and stockings, hats for men
    and boys,
Mill-saws and fenders, silks and
    children's toys;
All useful things and, joined with
    many more,

Compose the well-assorted country
    store.

OLIVER GOLDSMITH, "The rising village", 1825.

Goods Satisfactory or Money Refunded.

T. EATON CO., Toronto, since 1870 a guarantee and Company slogan.

The department store is one of the great developments of the age. As such it is worthy of study from the economic stand-point. It is an institution which increases the conveniences of the individual and adds to the sum total of his comforts and his pleasures. Because of this, it is worthy of the highest commendation. So long as it continues to fulfil its mission it will be counted among the great successes achieved in the progress of the world.

NORMAN PATTERSON, *Can. mag.*, Vol. 27, 1906, 438.

Stories

What story do you want?
Tales of young love, or of that horse
    with wings
The pink-striped circus lady rode,
    standing?

MARGARET AVISON, "The Agnes Cleves papers", 1960.

A tale for children untouched by
violence who smile in their
sleep when they dream of war.

ALDEN NOWLAN, "Down shore", 1967.

Stork Derby, 1926

I cannot find that reproduction of the human race is contrary to morals.

JUSTICE W.E. MIDDLETON, Court decision, 1926, Toronto, re: Charles Miller will and "Stork Derby".

Storms

When swallows fly low a storm will
soon blow.

> ANON., saying of pioneer Ontario farm-
> ers.

The abated blue is blotted from the
  sky
From calm comes chaos, and loud
  grows in rage
The rattling thunder, while the
  lightning leaps
And plays before us 'midst the
  firmament.

> CHARLES HEAVYSEGE, "Jezebel", 1867.

Strangers

The dazzle of the strange reminds us
of the disturbing facts of the familiar.

> KENT THOMPSON, in *Fiddlehead*, No. 77,
> 1968, 1.

They don't like strangers,
So be careful how you smile.

> ALDEN NOWLAN, "Stoney Ridge dance
> hall", 1969.

To be a stranger is enough, to be a
stranger in two worlds: that is the
ultimate loneliness.

> ALDEN NOWLAN, qu. by Keath Fraser,
> *Can. lit.*, No. 45, 1970, 48.

Stratford Festival

Canada, therefore, at the present moment is a "sellers' market" for culture:
the demand is greater than the supply.
That is why the Stratford Festival was
hailed with such enthusiasm, why it
has had such striking economic success, why it has become – out of all
proportion to the size of the undertaking, or its quality in relation to similar
Festivals elsewhere (Salzburg, for instance, or Edinburgh) – "important",
a symbol of a new spirit in Canada.

> TYRONE GUTHRIE, *Twice have the trum-
> pets sounded*, 1954, 155.

We had to go to New York or London
to see the best in the arts. Now we can
see the best right here.

> TOM PATTERSON, address to the Empire
> Club, Toronto, Nov. 15, 1956; ref. to
> Stratford Festival.

We need art. Not Canadian art. But
just art. When I think of the last
twenty years here, the thing that happened that made the most difference
to me – was the success of the Stratford Shakespeare Festival.

> JAMES REANEY, *Edge*, Autumn, 1964, 21.

Strathcona, Lord

His Labrador Lordship.

> VICTORIA (QUEEN), on Donald A, Smith,
> created Lord Strathcona in 1897.

Uncle Donald.

> VICTORIA (QUEEN), reference to Donald
> A. Smith (Lord Strathcona).

I could lick that man Smith quicker
than hell could frizzle a feather.

> SIR JOHN A. MACDONALD, Nov. 5, 1873, in
> lobby, H. of C., after Donald A. Smith
> (Lord Strathcona) stated he could no
> longer "conscientiously" support the
> government on the Pacific Railway
> scandal.

That fellow Smith is the biggest liar I
ever met.

> SIR JOHN A. MACDONALD, H. of C., *De-
> bates*, May 10, 1878, 2564; a reference
> to Donald A. Smith (Lord Strathcona).

Streets

The streets in Toronto are framed with wood, or rather planked, as are those of Montreal and Quebec; but they are kept in better order. I should say that the planks are first used at Toronto, then sent down by the lake to Montreal, and when all but rotted out there, are again floated off by the St. Lawrence to be used in the thoroughfares of the old French capital.

ANTHONY TROLLOPE, *North America*, 1862, 74.

Bleury, a street which runs through Montreal like a frontier, dividing the English from the French.

HUGH MACLENNAN, *Two solitudes*, 1945, 104.

Except when the theatre crowds
        engulf the sidewalks
Precisely at nine and at eleven-thirty
This street is lonely, and the thousand
        lights in a thousand shop-windows
Will not break her lips into a smile.

RAYMOND SOUSTER, "Yonge Street Saturday night", 1947.

Beneath the Malebolge lies Hastings
        Street,
The province of the pimp upon his
        beat.
Where each in his little world of drugs
        or crime
Moves helplessly or, hopeful, begs a
        dime.
Wherewith to purchase half a pint of
        piss
Although he will be cheated, even in
        this.

MALCOLM LOWRY, "Christ walks in this infernal district, too", 1962.

Strength

It may be well to have the strength of a giant, but it should not be used like a giant.

ROBERT BALDWIN, letter to Sir Francis Hincks, Jan. 27, 1848.

Where there is much strength, there ain't apt to be much gumption.

THOMAS C. HALIBURTON, *Sam Slick's wise saws*, 1853, ch. 15.

Strong men have an aura of life; powerful men, one of death. That's why most women are looking for strong men; and few, if any, for powerful ones. The strong man helps people up, especially women; the powerful one slaps them down, especially women.

RICHARD J. NEEDHAM, *A friend in Needham*, 1969, 45.

All political and economic systems come out at the same place – the strong doing what they will, the weak suffering what they must.

RICHARD J. NEEDHAM, *A friend in Needham*, 1969, 42.

Stress

Stress is essentially the rate of all the wear and tear caused by life.

DR. HANS SELYE, *The stress of life*, 1956, viii.

Stress is the state manifested by a specific syndrome which consists of all the nonspecifically induced changes within a biologic system.

DR. HANS SELYE, *The stress of life*, 1956, 54.

Don't be afraid to enjoy the stress of a full life nor too naive to think you can do so without some intelligent thinking and planning. Man should not try to avoid stress any more than he would shun food, love or exercise.

DR. HANS SELYE, *Newsweek,* Mar. 31, 1958, 60.

Students

The value of a really great student to the country is equal to half a dozen grain elevators or a new transcontinental railway.

SIR WILLIAM OSLER, "The student life", 1905.

Except it be a lover, no one is more interesting as an object of study than a student.

SIR WILLIAM OSLER, "The student life", 1905.

The true student is a citizen of the world, the allegiance of whose soul, at any rate, is too precious to be restricted to a single country. The great minds, the great works, transcend all limitations of time, of language, and of race, and the scholar can never feel initiated into the problems of the elect until he can approach all of life's problems from the cosmopolitan standpoint.

SIR WILLIAM OSLER, "The student life", 1905.

The meaning of this [Ph.D.] degree is that the recipient of instruction is examined for the last time in his life and is pronounced completely full. After this no new ideas can be imparted to him.

STEPHEN LEACOCK, *Sunshine sketches of a little town,* 1912, Preface.

Whoever ceases to be a student has never been a student.

GEORGE ILES, *Canadian stories,* 1918, 169.

The real thing for the student is the life and environment that surrounds him. All that he really learns he learns, in a sense, by the active operation of his own intellect and not as the passive recipient of lectures.

STEPHEN LEACOCK, *My discovery of England,* 1922, 112.

The long frugal years of study and scholarships, of frayed jackets and hand rolled cigarettes, were behind him. He had consumed the books. But who knows at what cost?

MORDECAI RICHLER, *Son of a smaller hero,* 1955, 52.

The more mature the student, the less the teacher becomes the dispenser of learning, and the more he becomes a transparent medium of it.

NORTHROP FRYE, in G. Stanley and G. Sylvestre, eds., *Canadian universities today,* 1961, 34.

Universities are predominantly composed of young persons, an enormously larger proportion of their age-group than can sanely be expected to be *preoccupied* with intellectual concerns.

F. E. SPARSHOTT, *Can. forum,* July, 1968, 81.

Stupidity

All down the ages, the stupid men have been swatting the clever men on the jaw. It's their only retort.

FRED JACOB, "The clever one", in his *One-third of a bill,* 1925, 41.

We are punished not for our sins but for our stupidity.

> IRVING LAYTON, "Aphs", *The whole bloody bird*, 1969, 92.

Style

Style! I have no style, I merely wait till the mud settles.

> GOLDWIN SMITH, to Arnold Haultain, qu., Haultain, *Goldwin Smith*, [1913], 129.

Perhaps the ultimate temptation of the contemporary imagination is primitivism.

> ELI MANDEL, *Poets of contemporary Canada 1960-1970*, 1972, xvi.

Submarines

No forbear of the whale or shark,
No saurian of the Pleiocene,
Piercing the sub-aquatic dark
Could rival this new submarine.

> E. J. PRATT, "The submarine", 1943.

This is the swollen silence under the
  sea;
The hush and push of pressure
  soundless, sounding,
Drowning the human splash, the
  man-made tear.

> ANNE WILKINSON, "Theme and variation", 1951.

Subsidies, Federal

With respect to giving moneys out of the federal treasury to any Tory government in this country for these alleged unemployment purposes, with these governments situated as they are to-day, with policies diametrically opposed to those of this government, I would not give them a five-cent piece.

> W. L. MACKENZIE KING, H. of C., *Debates*, Unrev., Apr. 3, 1930.

In preparation of the petition to the Government, there was discreet avoidance of the ugly word 'subsidy', or its somewhat less comely next-of-kin 'government grant'.

> M. E. NICHOLS, *(CP) the story of the Canadian press*, 1948, 128.

Look here boys, a subsidy is just giving you back your own money. When governments handle it, a big chunk disappears somewhere. So why don't you just manage among yourselves.

> TOM KENNEDY, Ontario Minister of Agric., to a delegation of farmers about 1948, qu. in G. Aiken, *Backbencher*, 1974, 83.

Suburbs

My pleasures, how discreet they are!
A little booze, a little car,
Two little children and a wife
Living a small suburban life.

> GEORGE JOHNSTON, "War on the periphery", 1951.

The entire country is a suburb.

> ALAN BROWN, *Can. forum*, Jan., 1955, 218.

Success

It is done by a knowledge of soft sawder and human natur'.

> T. C. HALIBURTON, *Sam Slick,* 1836, ch. II.

There's nothin' like leavin' all's well alone.

> T. C. HALIBURTON, *Sam Slick*, 1838, 136.

It's the early bird that gets the worm.

> T. C. HALIBURTON, *Sam Slick's wise saws*, 1853, I, 146.

We know that success depends not upon absolute perfection, but with individuals as with Governments, to make the fewest mistakes is the criterion of success.

> DONALD A. SMITH (Lord Strathcona), election speech, 1878.

Success is the god of politics and expediency is the supreme law of public life in Canada. Statesmen no longer do right because it is right. The justice or the injustice of every act is established by the answer to the question, Will It Pay?

> JOHN R. ROBINSON, Editor, Toronto *Telegram*, about 1880, qu. in R. Poulton, *The paper tyrant*, 1971, 132.

Have little care that Life is brief,
And less that Art is long.
Success is in the silences
Though Fame is in the song.

> BLISS CARMAN, "Envoy", in *Songs from vagabondia*, 1894.

Quite as much "grit" and a much harder climb are needed to reach distinction from the top as from the bottom of the social scale.

> SIR WILLIAM OSLER, *Philadelphia med. jour.*, 1899, 607.

There is an old motto that runs, "If at first you don't succeed, try, try again." This is nonsense. It ought to read — "If at first you don't succeed, quit, quit, at once."

> STEPHEN LEACOCK, "Simple stories of success . . . ", *Frenzied fiction*, 1917, 198.

There is no better training for uncommon opportunities than diligence in common affairs.

> GEORGE ILES, *Canadian stories*, 1918, 173.

To conquer finely, or to sink
  Debonair against defeat,
This is the rarest grace I think —
  This is the fate that I would meet.

> TOM MACINNES, "Ballade of action", 1918.

The path to success is paved with good intentions that were carried out.

> ROBERT C. (BOB) EDWARDS, Calgary *Eye Opener*, Nov. 22, 1919.

"Get on", the world says, "first of all
  get on,
And then get honor if it comes your
  way;
And, last, when life and strength are
  gone,
Get honest also when you've had your
  day".

> MAURICE HUTTON, address to University Women's Club, Ottawa, Nov. 4, 1929, (paraphrasing Horace).

Few people know how to be pleased at the successes of their friends.

> HUGH MACLENNAN, *Barometer rising*, 1941, 26.

Success is a journey, not a destination.

> JACK MINER, d. 1944, in *Jack Miner, his life and religion*, 1969, lx.

Success in anything is ninety percent inspiration and only ten percent brains.

> GARFIELD WESTON, qu. in *Maclean's*, Aug. 15, 1948, 50.

You'll never hit the jack-pot unless you first become a slug for a machine?

> MARSHALL MCLUHAN, *The mechanical bride*, 1951, 126.

Success is like some horrible disaster
Worse than your house burning, the
  sound of ruination.

> MALCOLM LOWRY, in *Can. lit.* No. 8, 1961, 21.

To deserve success rather than to achieve it.

> LESTER B. PEARSON, his formula for life, qu. in *Time*, Apr. 19, 1963, 17.

Out of infirmity, I have built strength.
Out of untruth, truth.
From hypocrisy, I weaved directness.

> IRVING LAYTON, "There were no signs", 1963.

In my early days as a salesman in Canada, I learned that success is just one step ahead of failure.

> ROY THOMSON, addressing the Canadian Club of London, England, qu. in *Liberty*, "Cross Canada", Nov., 1963.

Just once, though, I'd like to learn something from success.

> JEAN TEMPLETON, qu. in Toronto *Telegram*, Aug. 15, 1964, "Telegram showcase", 3.

If something makes me a buck, I do it, if it don't, I don't.

> ROY THOMSON, qu. in R. Braddon, *Roy Thomson of Fleet Street*, 1965, 163.

Do not be discouraged by lack of immediate success. Bernard Shaw flowered at 17, but nobody smelled him until he was 40.

> ROBERTSON DAVIES, *Samuel Marchbanks' almanack*, 1967, 173.

There's no such thing as permanent station or rank, in all life one can achieve success or failure by the same means; only the direction is different, and each of us has as much capacity for good as for wrong, as much energy for success as for failure.

> DALTON CAMP, qu. in P. Newman, *Distemper of our times*, 1968, 127.

One who is determined to succeed will not neglect to use all means open to him — even that of honesty — should it become necessary.

> IRVING LAYTON, "Aphs", *The whole bloody bird*, 1969, 76.

Grab, with decency.
Magnanimity
    is for those who have grabbed
        enough.

> LOUIS DUDEK, "Canada: interim report", 1971.

Suffering

Suffering may ennoble a man, but suffering without prospect or hope of release makes him a devil.

> J. J. PROCTER, *The philosopher in the clearing*, 1897, 49.

Men become great as Nations grow, they are purified through suffering.

> J. W. ROBERTSON, Canadian Club, Toronto, Jan. 24, 1910.

If the people have not suffered enough, it is their God-given right to suffer some more.

> WILLIAM ABERHART, in the 1930's, qu. in J. J. Barr, ed. *The unfinished revolt*, 1971, 64.

Is our capacity for suffering commensurate with our capacity for happiness: *infinite?*

> HECTOR DE SAINT-DENYS-GARNEAU, *Journal*, June, 1937, 1954. (Trans.)

The sufferer deserves his suffering; in truth, wills it.

> IRVING LAYTON, "Aphs", *The whole bloody bird*, 1969, 84.

Human beings are exceedingly tough creatures and almost never find the sufferings of others beyond their endurance.

> IRVING LAYTON, "Aphs", *The whole bloody bird*, 1969, 101.

Suffrage, Women's

The last fifty years, since woman suffrage was introduced, have seen no appreciable change in the political activities of women beyond the exercise of the right to vote. In the decision-making positions, and most conspicuously in the government and Parliament of Canada, the presence of a mere handful of women is no more than a token acknowledgement of their right to be there. The voice of government is still a man's voice.

> CANADA. ROY. COMM. ON THE STATUS OF WOMEN, *Report*, 1970, 355.

Suicide

Hell can't be worse than this trail. I'll chance it.

> ANON., note left by gold seeker on trail from Edmonton to the Yukon, 1897, before shooting himself.

Some people swim lakes, others climb flagpoles,
some join monasteries, but we, my friends,
who have considered suicide take our daily walk
with death and are not lonely.

> PHYLLIS WEBB, "To friends, who have also considered suicide", 1962.

The dream saw the suicide
then, the wrist or the jugular
cut thru with pieces of
the shattered whole image.

> VICTOR COLEMAN, "The lady vanishes", 1967.

I'm gonna lay my head on a lonesome railroad line
gonna lay my head right down on a lonesome railroad line
and let that two-nineteen train pacify my min'

> PHYLLIS GOTLIEB, *Ordinary moving*, 1969, 54.

And behind the mist I see
Black waters with the look
Of invitation to disaster,

Or self-destruction — in our
Days it is all
The same

> R. A. D. FORD, "The soft walls of love", 1969.

To contemplate suicide is surely the best exercise of the imagination.

> PHYLLIS WEBB, qu. in *Chatelaine*, Oct., 1972, 104.

Summer

What wonder we long for a breeze
 from the islands —
The beautiful islands and blest of the
 sea? —
Vine-lands or pine-lands, lowlands or
 highlands,
So they be *summer* lands nought care
 we!

> GEORGE FREDERICK CAMERON, "Insulae fortunatae", 1882.

In intervals of dreams I hear
 The cricket from the droughty
  ground;
The grasshoppers spin into mine ear
 A small innumerable sound.

> ARCHIBALD LAMPMAN, "Heat", 1888.

Was it a year or lives ago
 We took the grasses in our hands,
And caught the summer flying low
 Over the waving meadow lands,
 And held it there between our
  hands?

> BLISS CARMAN, "Low tide on Grand Pré", 1889.

This short Canadian summer,
 Whose every lonesome breath
Holds hint of autumn and winter,
 As life holds hints of death.

> WILFRED W. CAMPBELL, in Campbell and Martin, *Canada*, 1907, 134.

While we welter
In the swelter
Of the Pestilential Heat
Drinking Sodas
In Pagodas
At the Corner of the Street
    It seems to me
    That it would be
    My highest aspiration
    To sail away
    On a holiday
    Of Arctic Exploration.

STEPHEN LEACOCK, *College days*, 1923,
108.

Sun

And all the swarthy afternoon
    We watched the great deliberate
        sun
Walk through the crimsoned hazy
    world,
    Counting his hilltops one by one.

BLISS CARMAN, "The eavesdropper",
1893.

The sun, down the long mountain
    valley rolled,
A sudden swinging avalanche of gold.

ARCHIBALD LAMPMAN, "A dawn on the
Lievre", 1900.

The sun can find no darkness
    anywhere,
Where'er his bright eye turns is
    daylight fair.

ALBERT D. WATSON, "Lux ubique", 1908.

The harvest sun lay hot and strong
    On waving grain and grain in sheaf,
On dusty highway stretched along,
    On hill and vale, on stalk and leaf.

JEAN BLEWETT, "The firstborn", 1922.

The Sun would gain nothing in beauty
by appearing but once a year.

TOM MACINNES, *Complete poems*, 1923,
193.

Sunday

It must give uneasiness to any person
who has any regard for religion to
witness the general inattention to even
the external duties of the Sabbath,
both in the United States and Canada.
Instead of preserving a tolerably decent behaviour on that day, it is commonly spent in drinking, shooting,
fishing, or some such amusement, and
that even by many who consider
themselves to have good moral character.

J. GOLDIE, *Diary, journey through
Upper Canada*, 1819, 55.

Toronto is one of the most unpleasantly righteous cities I was ever caught in
on a Sunday. Tramways do not run,
and the public-houses are closed from
seven on Saturday night till Monday
morning – not that that makes much
difference in Canada, where prohibi-
tionist laws are strict, but not strictly
regarded.

D. SLADEN, *On the cars and off*, 1895,
154.

Sunday in Toronto is as melancholy
and suicidal a sort of day as Puritanical principles can make it.

W. T. CROSWELLER, *Our visit to Toronto,
the Niagara Falls, and the United
States of America*, 1898, 69; qu. in S. D.
Clark, *Urbanism and the changing Canadian society*, 1961, 83.

Why is it a crime to work from
midnight to four o'clock Sunday
morning, when it is not a crime to
work from eight o'clock Sunday evening until midnight. Is that not absurd? Why is it more criminal to work
before going to divine service on Sunday morning than it is to work after
divine service on Sunday evening?

HENRI BOURASSA, H. of C., *Debates*, June
20, 1906, 5630.

Sunflowers

Erect and towering to the skies,
  Shaggy and rough to sense,
He stares with round expanded face
Full on the sun's meridian rays,
  Picture of impudence.

JACOB BAILEY, "A farewell", 1779; a reference to the sun-flower.

Sunshine

Sunshine is brighter
If our windows are clean.

MRS. J. A. SMITH, "Windows", 1935.

The sunbeam, like a wet "flurry" of kisses,
is essentially plural:
the singular is "sunboom" and measureless.

RICHARD SOMMER, "Notes toward a quick vision", 1969.

Superiority

We sneer and we laugh with the lip
  – the most of us do it,
  Whenever a brother goes down like a weed with the tide;
We point with the finger and say –
  Oh, we knew it! We knew it!
But, see! we are better than he was,
  and we will abide.

GEORGE F. CAMERON, "The way of the world", 1887.

God has many bests.

JOHN M. KING, Manitoba College, 1883-1899; frequently quoted by J. S. Woodsworth.

I have, I must say, a great deal of sympathy with superior persons. Their path in life, in this age of the triumph of the inferior, is terribly hard. It is becoming so difficult for them to convince the inferior persons of their inferiority.

B. K. SANDWELL, *The privacity agent and other modest proposals*, 1928, 50.

A superiority complex quite often outlives the condition that brought it into existence.

ARTHUR STRINGER, *The devastator*, 1944, 117.

The trouble is that the idea of Canadian moral superiority is hard to sustain if you take into account the facts of Canadian history and Canadian society. Most of us solve this problem in the most obvious way. We ignore the facts.

ROBERT FULFORD, "Canada's moral pride", Toronto *Daily star*, Dec. 3, 1964, 43.

Superstition

A superstition is a premature explanation that overstays its time.

GEORGE ILES, *Canadian stories*, 1918, 168.

Survival

There are two miracles in Canadian history. The first is the survival of French Canada, and the second is the survival of Canada.

F. R. SCOTT, *Esprit*, Aug.-Sept., 1952, 178. (Trans.)

Survival is what remains to someone who has not enough to live on. Mere survival is an affliction. What is of interest is life, and the directing of that life. There is no question of mere survival, of being a hopeless onlooker, simply because one is unable to disappear completely. But this last is precisely our situation.

GUY FRÉGAULT, Can. Hist. Assoc., *Report*, 1956, 82, annual meeting, June 6-8, 1956, "Symposium on Canadianism". (Trans.)

Nothing survives by right but only by reason. Besides, nothing is static that lives. A divine yeast works in all created things that live and breathe and need the light.

> LORNE PIERCE, *A Canadian nation*, 1960, 3.

The key decisions which could determine our survival are now made outside of Canada – in centres such as Washington, Moscow, New York, Paris and Peking. We want to be able to influence those decisions, and cannot do so effectively unless we are paying, in the form of armed force, our membership fees in a number of international organizations.

> PEYTON V. LYON, H. of C., Special Comm. on Defence, *Special studies*, 1965, 26.

There can be no greatness for Canada, indeed no Canada, unless it is a country somehow set apart from the United States.

> PETER C. NEWMAN, *Distemper of our times*, 1968, 228.

To the warrior, to the politician, to the nationalist – and are we not all something of each? – survival is the sweetest triumph; to outlive the present danger, to quit the battle only to resume the course.

> DALTON CAMP, in *Can. forum*, Feb., 1969, 243.

The mere fact of survival makes gods out of martyrs and transforms defeat into victory.

> MIRIAM WADDINGTON, in *Can. lit.*, No. 41, 1969, 77.

Canada's survival has always required the victory of political courage over immediate and individual economic advantage.

> GEORGE P. GRANT, *Technology and empire*, 1969, 70.

The nation-state remains, in the end, the central focus of power and authority in our society and, until such time as transcending institutions have been created, we may envisage that it will remain to protect its members by moderating the intrusion of such technological forces as the spreading American corporation. For this reason, I remain conservative in regard to Canadian survival and a radical in regard to the emergent institutions necessary to achieve this task.

> ABRAHAM ROTSTEIN, in I. Lumsden, *Close the 49th parallel, etc.*, 1970, 222.

Suspicion

A woman is more influenced by what she suspects than by what she is told.

> ROBERT C. (BOB) EDWARDS, Calgary *Eye Opener*, Nov. 3, 1917.

Swallows

Swallow's nests in the barn keep away lightning.

> ANON., saying of pioneer Ontario farmers.

All evening, the swallows
weave over the lake, swooping &
    swerving, flicking
the blue water, so fast
the eye sees only motion
with no single body to contain it.

> SUNYATA MACLEAN, *Poems to define the corona of silence*, 1970, 48.

Swearing

Hell's Bells Rogers.

> ANON., reference to Major A. B. Rogers, surveyor, who found the route through the Rockies and Selkirks for the C.P.R., applied by his associates in tribute to his powers of blasphemy.

Sweetness

Too sweet Sally sweet
Too sweet since your vision is
Half marred with sweetness
Sweetness is all you can see
you can see only half
only half for at best
this world is
bitter, sweet.

> STEVE SMITH, "Bitter-sweet", 1964.

Swimming

I did it for Canada!

> MARILYN BELL, Sept. 9, 1954, after swimming Lake Ontario, qu. by Ron McAllister, *Swim to glory*, 1954.

Symbols

Save in symbols can the truth be found?

> PETER MCARTHUR, "Courage", in *The prodigal*, 1907, 26.

Our Canada, from sea to sea,
　Four signs of valour knows;
The thistle and the fleur-de-lys,
　The shamrock and the rose.

> ARTHUR STRINGER, "When maple leaves turn red", 1938.

So few, so worn, the symbols.
No line or word resembles
The vision in its womb.
So few, so worn, the symbols.

> F. R. SCOTT, "Dialogue", 1945.

I know that we've been accused and charged in the House with suppressing the Coat of Arms of Canada because we believed that this was a Royal symbol. But the truth is that the Coat of Arms in Canada doesn't mean a thing in the 20th Century. I would challenge you to put on a federal building the Coat of Arms of Shenley's Rye Whisky or of the Duchy of Lancaster, and how many people would notice it, because the Coat of Arms is not a contemporary language.

> GÉRARD PELLETIER, Sec'y of State, interview, C.B.C.-TV, July 18, 1970.

Tact

With women, tact and jealousy rarely go hand in hand; tact and spite never.

> ARNOLD HAULTAIN, *Hints for lovers*, 1909, 37.

Tact is the saving virtue without which no woman can be a success, as a nurse or not. She may have all the others, but without tact she is a failure. With most women it is an instinct, her protective mechanism in life. It is one of the greatest of human blessings that so many women are so full of tact. The calamity happens when a woman who has all the other riches of life just lacks that one thing.

> SIR WILLIAM OSLER, Commencement address to nurses, Johns Hopkins Univ., May 7, 1913.

Talent

There is no field for ambition, no room for the exercise of distinguished talent in the provinces.

> T.C. HALIBURTON, *Sam Slick*, 1840, 265, referring to the Maritimes.

My talent is my union card.

> ROBERTSON DAVIES, *A masque of Mr. Punch*, 1963, 10.

Talk

I was plaguy apt to talk turkey.

> THOMAS C. HALIBURTON, *Traits of American humor*, 1852, Vol. I, 79 (1840).

Fellows who have no tongues are often all eyes and ears.

> THOMAS C. HALIBURTON, *Sam Slick's wise saws*, 1853, II, 281.

Look wise, say nothing, and grunt. Speech was given to conceal thought.

> SIR WILLIAM OSLER, *Oslerisms* (Bean), 1905.

Consider the virtues of taciturnity. Speak only when you have something to say.

> SIR WILLIAM OSLER, *Johns Hopkins hosp. bull.*, 1919, 198.

I would far rather have a young man talk the uttermost nonsense, provided it is his own, than repeat like a gramophone the sagacities of other people. He may be foolish, but it is better to be foolish than to be dead.

> LORD TWEEDSMUIR, address, University of Toronto, Nov. 27, 1935.

Garrulity is an affliction of the soul.

> MARGARET LAURENCE, "The tomorrowtamer", 1961, in the book of the same title, 83.

Only a thin line divides the articulate man of wisdom from the windbag. The Scotch expected a man to prove his wisdom by putting it to useful purpose.

> JOHN KENNETH GALBRAITH, *The Scotch*, 1964, 55.

I talk too much
but the manner
of your listening
calls the words
out of me.
You say almost
nothing. Yet
there would be
only silence
if you were not here.

ALDEN NOWLAN, "Apology", 1969.

Tariff Policy

As a policy designed to increase the economic strength of Canada and to help secure her from the steady threat of American expansionism the policy of protective tariffs inaugurated in 1879 has been the most conspicuous (but least generally recognized) misdirection of national endeavour in Canada's history.

GEORGE W. WILSON et al., *Canada: an appraisal of its needs and resources*, 1965, xxxi.

Tariffs

I do not approve of needless restrictions on our liberty of exchanging what we have for what we want, and do not see that any substantial application of the restrictive principle has been or can be, made in favor of the great interests of the mechanic, the laborer, the farmer, the lumberman, the ship-builder, or the fisherman.

EDWARD BLAKE, address to the electors of West Durham, May 22, 1882.

Tariff for revenue only.

LIBERAL PARTY, platform plank, adopted at Ottawa convention, 1893.

The tariff of abominations.

LIBERAL PARTY, phrase for the protective tariff of Sir John A. Macdonald and his successors, modified by W.S. Fielding, 1897.

Adequate protection is that which would at all times secure the Canadian market to Canadians in respect to all Canadian enterprises.

ROBERT BORDEN, speech in Montreal, Oct. 15, 1904.

The ramparts of gold.

ARTHUR MEIGHEN, phrase used to denounce the protectionist tariff favoured by some Liberals, in H. of C., *Debates*, 1910, 1917.

The only way to settle the tariff right is to cut its head off just in front of its tail.

MICHAEL CLARK, H. of C., *Debates*, May 25, 1920, 2671.

Protection on apples in British Columbia, Free Trade in the Prairie Provinces and rural parts of Ontario, Conscription in Quebec and Humbug in the Maritimes.

ARTHUR MEIGHEN, speech in Montreal, Nov. 14, 1921, on W. L. Mackenzie King's interpretation of the Liberal platform of 1919, in the election campaign of 1921.

Taste

By the time the average man has time and money to gratify his tastes, he hasn't any.

ROBERT C. (BOB) EDWARDS, Calgary *Eye Opener;* attributed.

I have not the slightest desire to improve the taste of the Canadian public.

JAMES W. MORRICE, letter to Edmund Morris, Feb. 12, 1911 (Toronto Art Gallery).

Canadians are the most tasteless people in the world, with an archaic educational system.

> ARTHUR LISMER, Montreal *Gazette*, Jan. 19, 1954.

Well, there's no explaining tastes, and ugliness is pretty nowadays.

> MARGARET LAURENCE, *The stone angel*, 1964, 62.

Someone once said that the two most important things in developing taste were sensitivity and intelligence. I don't think this is so; I'd rather call them curiosity and courage. Curiosity to look for the new and the hidden; courage to develop your own tastes regardless of what others may say or think.

> R. MURRAY SCHAFER, *The composer in the classroom*, 1965, 4.

There is no disputing about tastes, says the old saw. In my experience there is little else.

> ROBERTSON DAVIES, *Samuel Marchbanks' almanack*, 1967, 110.

Taxation

They pay no taxes for perhaps nearly the same reason that you can't talk the breeks off a Hielandman.

> LORD DALHOUSIE, letter, [1824?] quoted, *Can. hist. rev.*, XII, 122.

Do, Canadians, clean your firelocks and fight like game cocks to get yourselves taxed to uphold the tax gatherer at 30 per cent.

> W.L. MACKENZIE, in the *Constitution*, June 7, 1837.

The Government of Canada acting for its Legislature and people cannot, through those feelings of deference which they owe to the Imperial authorities, in any manner waive or diminish the right of the people of Canada to decide for themselves both as to the mode and extent to which taxation shall be imposed.

> A.T. GALT, Canada Exec. minutes, Nov. 12, 1859; Pub. Arch., Can., *Ser. E*, State book U.

Cop With Club Steals For State Tax On Goods.

> J.W. BENGOUGH, "Lesson XXXIV", *The up-to-date primer*, 1896, 38. '

It is a sound principle of finance, and a still sounder principle of government, that those who have the duty of expending the revenue of a country should also be saddled with the responsibility of levying and providing it.

> SIR WILFRID LAURIER, H. of C., *Debates*, Feb. 21, 1905, 1434.

Taxation is the best gauge of civilization.

> J.W. ROBERTSON, speech to Canadian Club, Toronto, Jan.14, 1907.

TEARS AND TAXES ARE THE PRICE OF LIBERTY. The pockets that pay are more blessed than the eyes that weep.

> JOHN ROBINSON, Editor, Toronto *Telegram*, editorial, June 18, 1917, 10.

The promises of yesterday are the taxes of today.

> W.L. MACKENZIE KING, H. of C., *Debates*, June 16, 1931, 2676.

A tax upon international good will.

> W.L. MACKENZIE KING, H. of C., *Debates*, July 17, 1931, 3880; on taxation of magazines entering Canada.

I found the pot of gold at the end of the rainbow and I found it in Canada. But I was paying out 80 per cent of the gold I'd found in taxes. Man don't work for that.

SIR HARRY OAKES, to Gregory Clark of the Toronto *Star*, qu. in P. Newman, *Flame of power*, 1959, 113.

If a man obtains increased command over goods and services for his personal satisfaction we do not believe it matters, from the point of view of taxation, whether he earned it through working, gained it through operating a business, received it because he held property, made it by selling property or was given it by a relative.

CANADA. ROY. COMM. ON TAXATION (CARTER), *Report*, Vol. 1, 1966, 9; later described as " a buck is a buck".

The major practical problem relating to charitable donations is to ensure that the receipts issued by a charitable body are matched by actual contributions to it.

CANADA. ROY. COMM. ON TAXATION, *Report*, 1966, Vol. 3, 222.

The reason we have a united country, the reason why it will stay united, is because the Canadian people everywhere are prepared to pay the price of that in money terms, in tax terms.

PIERRE E. TRUDEAU, speeches in B.C., election campaign, June 17, 1968.

The Minister of Finance has been far more concerned about making the Liberal Party safe in Bay Street, and making Canada safe for tax consultants, than he has been about bringing genuine tax reform or, for that matter, assisting those who need tax relief.

MAX SALTSMAN, H. of C., *Debates*, June 22, 1971, 7230.

The absence of a capital gains tax, and even now the half capital gains tax, makes it more profitable to sell a business and get your money tax-free than to run it and pay taxes.

MAX SALTSMAN, H. of C., *Debates*, June 22, 1971, 7232.

Taylor, E.P.

Taylor is condemned by socialists as "the crushing Croesus of big business", by Communists as "E(xcess) P(rofits) Taylor – the mad miser of millions", and by righteous temperance advocates as the beer baron personally responsible for the plight of every Canadian alcoholic.

PETER C. NEWMAN, *Flame of power*, 1959, 223.

I lose interest in a business situation when it begins to run smoothly.

E.P. TAYLOR, qu. in P. Newman, *Flame of power*, 1959, 226.

I've got the knack of doing absolutely no administrative work whatsoever.

E.P. TAYLOR, qu. in P. Newman, *Flame of power*, 1959, 226.

Eddie can read a balance sheet like a poem, and tell you where it doesn't scan.

ANON., an associate of E.P. Taylor, qu. in P. Newman, *Flame of power*, 1959, 226.

I'm a Bahamian. People come here for the simpler life. I did myself but I was tempted into business and I succumbed. People want to get away from Socialism.

E.P. TAYLOR, *Sunday times* (London), Dec. 22, 1968, 22.

Teachers

The teacher is the key. To what purpose do you build brick school-houses, elect trustees, and send your children to school unless you have an efficient teacher to instruct them? And you cannot get good teachers at the present rate of pay.

EDWARD BLAKE, speech at Aurora, Ont., Oct. 3, 1874.

The teacher's life should have three periods, study until twenty-five, investigation until forty, professional until sixty, at which age I would have him retired on a double allowance.

SIR WILLIAM OSLER, "The fixed period", address, Feb. 22, 1905, at Johns Hopkins Univ. In *Medical record*, Mar. 4, 1905, Osler denied he advocated chloroform after 60.

It is well for young men to remember that no bubble is so iridescent or floats longer than that blown by the successful teacher.

SIR WILLIAM OSLER, address, Royal Infirmary, Glasgow, Oct. 4, 1911.

I owe a lot to my teachers and mean to pay them back some day.

STEPHEN LEACOCK, "The children's corner", in *College days*, 1923, 92.

A dull teacher, with no enthusiasm in his own subject, commits the unpardonable sin.

R.C. WALLACE, A *liberal education*, 1932, 85.

To be allowed to teach children should be the sign of the final approval of society.

G. BROCK CHISHOLM, speech in Washington, D.C., Oct. 23, 1945.

He had the educator's peculiar genius for imparting knowledge without himself assimilating it.

PAUL HIEBERT, *Sarah Binks*, 1947, 57.

He could have been a success at anything he wanted. Instead he's devoted his life to teaching.

MORDECAI RICHLER, *The apprenticeship of Duddy Kravitz*, 1959, chap. 4.

It is not what the teacher says that is important, it is what it inspires his pupils to go ahead and do.

WILLIAM E. BLATZ, *Human security*, 1966, ix.

Even the great teachers, and I have sat in at the classes of some of the few, I think, in the world, are not as good as their books. I don't accept an excuse from students who say they can't learn because they haven't got great teachers and because the teachers don't spend enough time with them. I think the basic fault is that the students don't spend enough time with their books.

PIERRE E. TRUDEAU, University of Manitoba, Winnipeg, Dec. 13, 1968.

Democracy (whisper it not in Gath) has only a limited usefulness in our trade. To believe that the relationship between master and pupil is the same as between master and slave is a mistake made by democrats who cannot think.

MICHAEL HORNYANSKY, address at Brock University, Feb. 24, 1969.

Teaching

My words impressed his dormant
      thought.
    "How wise," he said, "is nature's
      plan!
Henceforth I'll practise what you've
      taught,
    And be a scientific man."

T. PHILLIPS THOMPSON, "The political economist and the tramp", 1887.

I took to school teaching as the only trade I could find that needed neither experience nor intellect.

> STEPHEN LEACOCK, *Sunshine sketches of a little town*, 1912, Preface, viii.

Schoolteaching is properly a profession for old men.

> STEPHEN LEACOCK, "Woman's level", in *Last leaves*, 1945, 100.

The mere act of teaching is rather secondary to what we are teaching for, and what we are teaching *for* is the kind of society we want to create.

> CECIL CRAGG, *Queen's quart.*, Vol. 65, 1958, 285.

I am saying that we need to teach, and to learn: and that rubbing our souls together in a "learning situation" is not good enough.

> MICHAEL HORNYANSKY, address at Brock University, Feb. 24, 1969.

Tears

Tears are the best balm that can be applied to the anguish of the heart.

> SUSANNA MOODIE, *Roughing it in the bush*, 1852, 46.

A woman's tears are a man's terrors.

> ARNOLD HAULTAIN, *Hints for lovers*, 1909, 58.

Technique

Technique comes forth from and is sustained in our vision of ourselves as creative freedom, making ourselves, and conquering the chances of an indifferent world.

> GEORGE P. GRANT, *Technology and empire*, 1969, 137.

Technology

Revolutions are more rapidly effected in the arts than in the mind. A new process, a new discovery in practical science progresses more in a decade than does a new thought in ten.

> SIR WILLIAM OSLER, address to Bibliographical Soc., London, Eng., Jan., 1914.

It may well be that at the end, there will come a state of affairs in which there are two classes, both slaves; one, the larger, subject to the other; the other, insignificant in numbers, subject to the machine.

> FREDERICK P. GROVE, *The master of the mill*, 1944, 284.

The tidal wave of technology can be more damaging to us than to countries with older cultural traditions, possessing firmer bulwarks against these contemporary perils.

> CANADA. ROY. COMM. ON NAT. DEV. IN THE ARTS, LETTERS AND SCIENCES, 1949-1951, *Report*, 1951, 272.

Modern Canadian life has not grown out of us; it has been imposed on us by technology. That may be why the nation seems almost to have outtravelled its own soul. That may be why, for most of us, Canadian history has not so much become a dead thing as an unknown thing.

> HUGH MACLENNAN, *Seven rivers of Canada*, 1961, viii.

Value judgments have long been allowed to create a moral fog around technological change such as renders understanding impossible.

> MARSHALL MCLUHAN, *The Gutenberg galaxy*, 1962, 213.

Creators of the live machine
We quit the lanes of what has been
Forced by the atom and the jet
To cross the gulphs our hatreds set.

F.R. SCOTT, "No curtain", 1964.

Culture is born in leisure and an awareness of standards, and pioneer conditions tend to make energetic and uncritical work an end in itself, to preach a gospel of social unconsciousness, which lingers long after the pioneer conditions have disappeared. The impressive achievements of such a society are likely to be technological. It is in the inarticulate part of communication, railways and bridges and canals and highways, that Canada, one of whose symbols is the taciturn beaver, has shown its real strength.

NORTHROP FRYE, in Carl F. Klinck, ed., *Literary history of Canada*, 1965, 827.

Nationalism can only be asserted successfully by an identification with technological advance; but technological advance entails the disappearance of those indigenous differences that give substance to nationalism.

GEORGE P. GRANT, *Lament for a nation*, 1965, 76.

Outside the borders of royalty
the barbarians wait in fear,
finding it hard to know which prince
to believe; trade-goods comfort them,
gadgets of little worth, cars, television,
refrigerators, for which they give iron,
copper, uranium, gold, trees, and
    water,
worth of all sorts for the things
the citizens of Empire take as their
    due.

JOHN NEWLOVE, "America", 1968.

Technology creates obsolescence faster than politicians can make up their minds. Military technology creates obsolescence faster than any other; politicians make up their minds about military policy more slowly than any other, except when they go to war.

DALTON CAMP, in Lewis Hertzman, *Alliances and illusions*, 1969, xviii.

Any new technology – and especially electronic technology – is not merely an assortment of *things* that can be abolished with an axe. It is a process, a system, a new part of ourselves. You cannot destroy it. You can only learn to use this new technology to live abundantly and wisely and well.

ALEXANDER ROSS, *Financial post*, Aug. 23, 1969, 7.

When one contemplates the conquest of nature by technology one must remember that that conquest had to include our own bodies. Calvinism provided the determined and organized men and women who could rule the mastered world. The punishment they inflicted on non-human nature, they had first inflicted on themselves.

GEORGE P. GRANT, *Technology and empire*, 1969, 24.

We live then in the most realized technological society which has yet been; one which is, moreover, the chief imperial centre from which technique is spread round the world.

GEORGE P. GRANT, *Technology and empire*, 1969, 40.

Technology is becoming ubiquitous. Some 10 years ago, to the indignation of most educators, it invaded teaching, the most empirical, the most slow-moving and perhaps the most sacrosanct of all disciplines. Already, through the need for planetary survival, it is attacking human reproduction and, therefore, love itself, the most hazardous, the least rationalized of all our ways of feeling and acting.

> PIERRE E. TRUDEAU, speech, Harrison Hot Springs, B.C., Nov. 21, 1969.

A branch-plant economy dependent on imported technology is assured of a perpetual technological backwardness vis-a-vis the metropolis. Furthermore, dependence is addictive and the dynamics of dependence are cumulative.

> KARI LEVITT, *Can. forum*, Jul.-Aug., 1970, 161.

You have built a great technological society but in the process you have forgotten what life is.

> TOM BERNES, in Allen M. Linden, ed., *Living in the seventies*, 1970, 26.

The two big tricks of the twentieth century are: technology instead of grace, and information instead of virtue.

> ULYSÉE COMTOIS, qu. in *Artscanada*, Feb.-Mar., 1971, 20.

In the field of new technology Canadians are not inclined to be very venturesome. There's all sorts of money to look for a new mine — it's risk, but within the technology that is known.

> ROBERT KERR, executive, qu. in R.L. Perry, *Galt, U.S.A.*, 1971, 72.

Telephone

Mr. Watson, come here, I want to see you.

> ALEXANDER G. BELL, to his assistant, Mar. 10, 1876; the first intelligible words transmitted by telephone.

It was I who invented the telephone and it was invented wherever I happened to be at the time. Of this you may be sure, the telephone was invented in Canada. It was made in the United States. The first transmission of a human voice over a telephone wire, where the speaker and the listener were miles apart, was in Canada. The first transmission by wire in which the conversation was carried on reciprocally over the same line was in the United States.

> ALEXANDER G. BELL, Canadian Club, Ottawa, speech, Mar. 27, 1909.

The telephone, which the more affluent place beside beds, and even occasionally in the bathroom, allows the invasion at any hour by a casual caller of the private areas that are regularly denied the nearest of kin and the dearest of friends.

> JOHN R. SEELEY et al., *Crestwood heights*, 1956, 55.

The telephone
> hangs on the wall
always available
> for transmitting messages:
Why is it
> to lift the receiver
is to push the weight
> of a mountain?

> DOROTHY LIVESAY, "And give us our trespasses", 1967.

Temperance

Apostle of Temperance.

> ANON., name given to Father Charles Chiniquy, leader of a mass movement in Quebec, about 1850.

Temptation

The cardinal principle of religion is temptation because it involves resistance; without temptation there is no vice, no virtue.

> W.M. KING, Oakville, Ont., "Petition against prohibition", in H. of C., *Journals*, 1874, Apx. 8, dated 5 June 1874.

Temptation is the same as inspiration; it is the tiger's pounce of the imagination.

> CARLYLE KING, in *Tamarack rev.* No. 10, 1959, 43.

Tenderness

Tenderness is extremely difficult of simulation. Or rather, Tenderness is so delicate and deep-seated a feeling, that few care to attempt its simulation.

> ARNOLD HAULTAIN, *Hints for lovers*, 1909, 133.

Terror

Terror is the normal state of any oral society, for in it everything affects everything all the time.

> MARSHALL MCLUHAN, qu. in N. Frye, *The bush garden*, 1971, 250.

Textbooks

In the state of New York, the course of instruction and the books which are used are under the strictest surveillance and direction of the Government, all this in Upper Canada is left to the care of a few illiterate, ignorant and sometimes disloyal local Township trustees.

> R.B. SULLIVAN, Memb. Exec. Council of Upper Canada, report to Sir George Arthur, Lieut.-Gov., June 1, 1838.

After your catechism, your Canadian history textbook should be the most precious of all your books.

> FRÈRES DES ÉCOLES CHRÉTIENNES, *Mon pays*, 1954, 7, textbook for grades seven and eight, qu. in M. Trudel and G. Jain, *Canadian history textbooks*, 1970, 10 (Canada. Roy. Comm. on Bilingualism and Biculturalism, Study No. 5). (Trans.)

A book found in an Ontario school book catalogue, and on display at teachers' conventions across Canada, is called *How People Live in Canada*. On the cover is a picture of Abraham Lincoln.

> MEL HURTIG, address, Institute on Publishing in Canada, Edmonton, June 30, 1971.

Thanks

"Thank you" is excellent, but formal and English in effect. "Thanks a million" is excellent, but it has an American extravagance which is unbecoming in Canadian mouths. What would you think of "Thanks a hundred thousand"? It seems to me to strike the right Canadian note.

> ROBERTSON DAVIES, *Samuel Marchbanks' almanack*, 1967, 23.

Theatre

I find writing about the Canadian theatre or drama depressingly like discussing the art of dinghy sailing among the bedouins. There is so little to be said on the subject save to point why there is none.

> MERRILL DENISON, in B. Brooker, ed., *Yearbook of the arts in Canada*, 1929, 51.

The two or three indubitably Canadian plays that might be written would never find a welcome in a Canadian theatre, even if there was one.

MERRILL DENISON, in B. Brooker, ed., *Yearbook of the arts in Canada*, 1929, 55.

If we are to be an art we must do as the other arts do, retain control of our superb moments.

ROY MITCHELL, *Creative theatre*, 1929, 222.

The spirit of a nation, if it is to find full expression, must include a National Drama.

EARL OF BESSBOROUGH, message on program of the first Dominion Drama Festival, Ottawa, Apr. 24-29, 1933, later to become a slogan for the Dominion Drama Festival.

If this organization becomes a success, it will have been founded on love and whiskey.

COL. HENRY E. OSBORNE, qu. in Betty Lee, *Love and whiskey*, 1973, 251, referring to Dominion Drama Festival sponsored by Calvert Distillers, about 1933.

Praise God for Marc Lescarbot
Who living Hereabouts 1606-07
Wrote and Produced Nearby
America's First Play

CANADIAN AUTHORS' ASSOCIATION, inscription on cairn of stones erected at Annapolis Royal, N.S., 1947, to commemorate production of "Neptunes theatre", Nov. 14, 1606.

While we may agree that it is impossible to define what is, or is not, distinctively Canadian, and while we may hope that the theatre in Canada may not develop in too isolationist a manner, yet we must remember that what a creative artist needs almost more than anything else is an attachment to a particular environment, usually that in which he was brought up as a child.

TYRONE GUTHRIE, letter from Ireland to Dora Mavor Moore, May 11, 1952.

I don't know how far it may be possible to interpret a classical play in a distinctively Canadian way. I am not even quite sure that there is a distinctively Canadian way of doing anything. I am not even sure, despite innumerable legends in support of the idea, that there is a distinctively British, French, Jewish or Chinese way of doing anything.

TYRONE GUTHRIE, *Twice have the trumpets sounded*, 1954, 166.

To have great plays you must also have great audiences. Art has never flourished in a vacuum and it never will.

HUGH MACLENNAN, "The art of city-living", in *Thirty and three*, 1954, 131.

That is the one commodity common to all branches and members of the Canadian theatre today — hope. The dark days of the century can now be seen to have served an important purpose. Canadians were thrown back on their own resources. Canadians are a people trained to think of themselves as sitting atop the greatest natural resources in the world, smugly wearing the label of The Country with the Greatest Future. In the theatre, as in many other fields of development, that future is upon us now.

HERBERT WHITTAKER, in Julian Park, ed., *The culture of contemporary Canada*, 1957, 179.

Theatre as a mirror and critic of the moods, tones, idioms, paradoxes, virtues, and inadequacies of life on a thinly-populated, four-thousand-mile sub-Arctic strip; as a concentrated artistic statement with a persevering dynamic; as a body of imaginative work with themes and standards — in short, theatre as something of value to a discerning public has never counted in the life of English-language Canada.

NATHAN COHEN, in *Tamarack rev.*, No. 13, 1959, 24.

I was astonished at the university. I was astonished to find that there were educated, admirable people who did not really like the theatre; they liked an intellectual distillation from the theatre called the drama.

ROBERTSON DAVIES, *A voice from the attic*, 1960, 157.

Theatre is not realistic in a vulgar, wide-awake fashion: it is realistic as dreams are realistic; it deals in hidden dreads, and it satisfies hidden, primal wishes. And if that is not psychological truth, what is?

ROBERTSON DAVIES, *A voice from the attic*, 1960, 167.

Let me assure the author that we shall not build an indigenous Canadian theatre on plays with happy endings. We are miserable or we are nothing. Hope is out of fashion.

ROBERTSON DAVIES, *A masque of Mr. Punch*, 1963, 36.

1960 was a good year for playwrights from outside Canada.

ANON., Canadian newspaper headline qu. by Mordecai Richler, *Hunting tigers under glass*, 1968, 8.

I say Canadian students want to know about Canadian theatre, how Canadian playwrights think within the Canadian frame of reference, what influences work on them. I say that in this case Americans positively *obstruct!*

ROBIN MATHEWS, *Weekend mag.*, Mar. 22, 1969, 3.

The theatre is like fireworks. Look at it, look at it, it may not come again.

GRATIEN GÉLINAS, qu. in *Globe and Mail*, June 11, 1973, 8.

If the talent in this country can just go to bed with the money in this country, maybe it can all come together. Otherwise we're just going to be left on the sidelines with our dreams.

GORDON PINSENT, qu. Toronto *Globe and Mail*, July 7, 1973, 29.

Theory

One should never spoil a good theory by explaining it.

PETER MCARTHUR, *To be taken with salt*, 1903, 152.

In Canada the theorist is still an object not only of suspicion but of fear.

P.E. CORBETT, in *Can. hist. rev.*, 1941, 118.

Things

the most common things
    clothes hung out to dry
serve as well as kings
    for your imagery.

D.G. JONES, "Clotheslines", 1957.

Every time I look at the hill across the way, I realize that everything I've done is insignificant. Things are so beautiful.

HAROLD TOWN, interview with Elizabeth Kilbourn, *Waterloo rev.*, Summer, 1960, 12.

It was these tiny things that, collectively, taught me how to live. Too insignificant to have been considered individually, but like the Hundreds and Thousands lapped up and sticking to our tongues, the little scraps and nothingnesses of my life have made a definite pattern.

EMILY CARR, *Hundreds and thousands*, 1966, v, referring to tiny candies made in England.

Everything is a part of everything else. Everything *is* everything else. Everything is not only universal, but its own universe.

> SCOTT SYMONS, *Heritage: a romantic look at early Canadian furniture*, 1971, Intro.

Thompson, David

Thus I have fully completed the survey of this part of North America from sea to sea; and by almost innumerable astronomical observations have determined the position of the Mountains, Lakes and Rivers, and other remarkable places on this continent; the maps of all of which have been drawn, and laid down in geographical position, being now the work of twenty-seven years.

> DAVID THOMPSON, on reaching the Pacific, July 15, 1811.

He was the greatest land geographer the British race has produced.

> J.B. TYRRELL, in *Geographical jour.*, Jan., 1911; also, "He was the greatest practical land geographer the world has produced", in Can. Hist. Assoc., *Report*, 1927, 14.

From Churchill to the Assiniboine
And up the Saskatchewan,
Back and forth, through all the North
His purpose drove him on,
Making a white man's trail for those
Who should come when he was gone.

> BLISS CARMAN, "David Thompson, explorer"; recited by the author, Lake Windermere, B.C., Aug. 30, 1922 at Thompson centenary celebration.

Intrepid, strenuous, indomitable, he overcame every obstacle with a concentrated, prudent, and persistent enthusiasm. Confronting all the perils of the Unknown, taking his life in his hand, forcing his way through mountains by untrodden paths, running furious rapids in improvised canoes, des-

erted by followers and guides, threatened by hostile and suspicious tribesmen, by cold and starvation, his energy and courage never failed or faltered.

> SIR F. WILLIAMS-TAYLOR, in Can. Hist. Assoc., *Report*, 1927, 9.

Thompson, Sir John S.D.

My greatest discovery was Thompson.

> SIR JOHN A. MACDONALD, attributed, qu. in *Dictionary of national biography* 1898/9, Vol. 19, 698.

Thompson has just two faults. He is a little too fond of satire, and a little too much of a Nova Scotian.

> SIR JOHN A. MACDONALD, on Sir John Thompson, about 1885-91, qu. in *Cambridge history of the British Empire*, VI, 1930, 506.

Thompson will never make a politician. He won't even consider whether a thing is good for the party until he is first quite sure that it is good for the country.

> ANON., Conservative supporter, to C.R.W. Biggar, about 1892, qu. in his *Sir Oliver Mowat*, I, 1905, 215.

Thomson, Tom

To the Memory of Tom Thomson Artist Woodsman and Guide who was drowned in Canoe Lake, July 8th, 1917. He lived humbly but passionately with the wild. It made him brother to all untamed things of nature. It drew him apart and revealed itself wonderfully to him. It sent him out from the woods only to show these revelations through his art. And it took him to itself at last.

> J.E.H. MACDONALD, Inscription on Thomson's cairn, Canoe Lake, Algonquin Park, Ont., erected Sept. 27, 1917.

Thought

The thoughts despised, as new or
    strange,
    May yet in regal triumph reign;
The form and garb of truth may
    change,
    And yet the inner life remain.

EDWARD H. DEWART, "A plea for liberty", 1869.

His faculty of picking the brains of
other people was but an imperfect
substitute [for the lack of reading and
thought].

GOLDWIN SMITH, *The Bystander*, 1883,
149.

Thank God, the lowliest man can be
An uncrowned monarch in the world
    of thought.

THOMAS B.P. STEWART, "Lines to my
mother", 1887.

Friend, though thy soul should burn
    thee, yet be still
Thoughts were not made for strife, nor
    tongues for swords.
He that sees clear is gentlest of his
    words,
And that's not truth that has the heart
    to kill.
The whole world's thought shall not
    one truth fulfil.
Dull in our age, and passionate in
    youth,
No mind of man hath found the
    perfect truth,
Nor shalt thou find it; therefore,
    friend, be still.

ARCHIBALD LAMPMAN, "The truth",
1888.

Wisest is he, who, never quite secure,
    Changes his thoughts for better
        day by day:
Tomorrow some new light will shine,
    be sure,
    And thou shalt see thy thought
        another way.

ARCHIBALD LAMPMAN, "The truth",
1888.

In the heart of a man
    Is a thought upfurled,
Reached its full span
    It shakes the world,
And to one high thought
Is a whole race wrought.

CHARLES G. D. ROBERTS, "A song of
growth", 1893.

When we think we are simply trying
our wings in the new state into which
we shall yet be born.

PETER MCARTHUR, *To be taken with salt*,
1903, 151.

Men will not take time to get to the
heart of a matter. After all, concentration is the price the modern student
pays for success. Thoroughness is the
most difficult habit to acquire, but it is
the pearl of great price, worth all the
worry and trouble of the search.

SIR WILLIAM OSLER, "The student life",
farewell address to Canadian and American medical students, Montreal, Apr.
14, 1905, on eve of departure for Oxford.

You know, many a man realizes late in
life that if when he was a boy he had
known what he knows now, instead of
being what he is he might be what he
won't; but how few boys stop to think
that they knew what they don't know
instead of being what they will be,
they wouldn't be?

STEPHEN LEACOCK, "How to make a
million dollars", *Literary lapses*, 1910.

Men will bear almost any evil rather
than go through the awful pain of
thinking, of really thinking, and thinking for themselves, and then of following to the end the results of their
thought.

G.M. WRONG, speech to Canadian Club,
Ottawa, Dec. 8, 1916.

By conscientious smoking and
  drinking
They had kept themselves from the
  horror of thinking.

> STEPHEN LEACOCK, "Admiral Albemarle
> took Havana", *College days*, 1923, 145.

What appears to me to be at the
bottom of the matter is that everything
connected with the Dominion is of a
spasmodic, opportunist tentative nature, and there is no line of thought or
action which is permanent and aiming
at fruition.

> LORD BYNG, letter to Col. H. Willis-
> O'Connor, Dec. 16, 1926.

You say it's this or that,
    That nothing lies between:
Here is all black and foul;
    There is all white and clean.

> WILSON MACDONALD, "The fundamen-
> talist", 1937.

No nation can achieve its true destiny
that adopts without profound and courageous reasoning and selection the
thoughts and styles of another.

> LORNE PIERCE, *A Canadian people*,
> 1945, 24.

I think a lot all day. I haven't anything
else to do. Thinking is fun.

> EDWARD MEADE, *Remember me*, 1946,
> 121.

Only individuals think; gangs merely
throb.

> ROBERTSON DAVIES, *Diary of Samuel
> Marchbanks*, 1947, 27.

Thought (and prose, which is its mode
of utterance) is the agent through
which the life of feeling becomes
aware of itself, and passes from a mere
agitation or commotion to the more
human state of emotion. Poetry,
though a cry, is a cry transfigured by
reason and intelligence.

> REID MACCALLUM, *Imitation and design
> and other essays*, 1953, 73.

You would have me deny my
  murderous thoughts.
It is metaphor I distrust.

> ELI MANDEL, "Poem", 1967.

When I start to think, I quit.

> MAURICE RICHARD, qu. in Peter Hendry,
> *Epitaph for nostalgia*, 1968, 102, on his
> success as a hockey player.

Thought may first arise from the ambiguities of personal history but if it is
to stand fairly before the enormous
ambiguities of the dynamo, it must
attempt to transcend the recurring
distortions of personal history.

> GEORGE P. GRANT, *Technology and em-
> pire*, 1969, 140.

One of Canada's greatest tragedies is
that sober second thoughts so often
prevail.

> RICHARD J. NEEDHAM, *A friend in Need-
> ham*, 1969, 44.

In the black absence between
  thoughts,
waves rush my inlets. Coastlines
  dissolve.
I wait in harbour for a crowning sea.

> MARK YOUNG, "Eye of the gull", 1970.

I do not think out what I will do. My
thought comes out while I work. My
work expresses my thought. My work
is what I think. My work is my
thought.

> TIKTAK, Eskimo sculptor, qu. in *Art-
> scanada*, June, 1970, 47.

Thrift

Save half of what you earn; look
ahead; and hang on — never let go!

> LORD STRATHCONA, qu., Macdonald, *Ca-
> nadian portraits*, 1925, 146.

Thrushes

Into the pale depth of noon
A wandering thrush slides leisurely
His thin revolving tune.

ARCHIBALD LAMPMAN, "Heat", 1889.

A thrush is hidden in a maze
Of cedar buds and tamarac bloom,
He throws his rapid flexile phrase,
A flash of emeralds in the gloom.

DUNCAN CAMPBELL SCOTT, "The voice and the dusk", 1926.

Thunder Bay, Ont.

Two towns stand on the shores of the lake less than a mile apart. What Lloyds is to shipping, or the College of Surgeons to medicine, that they are to the Wheat. Its honour and integrity are in their hands; and they hate each other with the pure, poisonous, passionate hatred which makes towns grow.

RUDYARD KIPLING, *Letters to the family*, 1908, 27, on Fort William and Port Arthur, now Thunder Bay.

Tides

Back to the green deeps of the outer
    bay
        The red and amber currents glide
        and cringe,
        Diminishing behind a luminous
        fringe
Of cream-white surf and wandering
        wraiths of spray.
Stealthily, in the old reluctant way,
        The red flats are uncovered, mile
        on mile,
        To glitter in the sun a golden
        while.

CHARLES G.D. ROBERTS "The herring weir", 1893.

Time

We reckon hours and minutes to be dollars and cents.

T.C. HALIBURTON, *Sam Slick*, 1836, chap. II.

Adown the deep where the angels
    sleep
Came drawn the golden chime
Of those great spheres that sound the
    years
For the horologue of time.
Millenniums numberless they told
Millenniums a millionfold
From the ancient hour of prime.

CHARLES HEAVYSEGE, "Twilight", 1865.

And what is time, with all her cares,
Her wrinkles, furrows, and grey hairs,
The hag that swallows all the bears;

The mystic where, the when and how,
The awful, everlasting now,
The funeral wreath upon my brow?

ALEXANDER MCLACHLAN, "Man", 1874.

Standard Time.

SIR SANDFORD FLEMING, originated standard time in 1879.

Time enough to bid the Devil good morning when you meet him.

EDWARD BLAKE, article in London, Eng., *Daily news*, Aug. 5, 1892, 3.

The mount, the star, the germ, the
    deep,
They all shall wake, they all shall
    sleep.
Time, like a flurry of wild rain,
Shall drift across the darkened pane.

CHARLES G.D. ROBERTS, "The unsleeping", 1896.

Time like a Titan bright and strong
        Spreads one enchanted gleam:
Each hour is but a fluted song,
        And life a lofty dream.

ARCHIBALD LAMPMAN, "Amor vitae", 1899.

I saw Time in his workshop carving
    faces;
      Scattered around his tools lay,
        blunting griefs
      Sharp cares that cut out deeply in
        reliefs
Of light and shade: sorrows that
    smooth the traces
Of what were smiles.

    FREDERICK GEORGE SCOTT, "Time",
    1899.

Singing or sad, intent they go;
They do not see the shadows grow;
    'There yet is time,' they lightly
      say,
    'Before our work aside we lay,'
Their task is but half-done, and lo,
    Cometh the night.

    JOHN MCCRAE, "The night cometh",
    1913.

The passing of time so quickly would
not be so regrettable were life not so
short.

    R. D. CUMMING, *Skookum Chuck fables*,
    1915, 160.

The greatest solvent of political problems, if they are to be solved at all
adequately, is time. The greatest danger lies in hastening the harvest of the
years and in attempting to reap in
advance of general political development.

    W.P.M. KENNEDY, *Constitution of Cana-*
    da, 1922, 458.

At the beginning of the long
dash . . .

    DOMINION OBSERVATORY, phrase intro-
    ducing national time signal, since 1941.

I have looked on time, and been
afraid.

    MARY HALL, "Time is the fire", 1948.

Time is tiger
NOW is wooly-witted lamb.

    ANNE WILKINSON, "Time is tiger", 1951.

Time is the game
Of wave and sand
And of the comet's flight.

    ANTHONY FRISCH, "After Yeats X", 1954.

Among the millions of nerve cells that
clothe parts of the brain there runs a
thread. It is the thread of time, the
thread that has run through each succeeding wakeful hour of the individual's past life.

    DR. WILDER PENFIELD, *Reader's digest*,
    July, 1958, 2.

Hark, as your ear contrives to catch
The semblance of a sound long lost,
The gentle warning of your watch
Rides on the tide within your wrist.

    ROBERT FINCH, "Tomorrow's past",
    1959.

That *turn about* is fair I won't agree
Now time I used to waste is wasting
me.

    FRED COGSWELL, "Turn about", 1959.

No question, time is moving faster
And, maybe, space is curling in.

    MARGARET AVISON, "Mordant for a mel-
    ody", 1960.

alone or with another
the body is our brother
and Messiah will not come
though we may wait the time
till kings of good become
the presidents of wrong
there's nothing left but time.

    MIRIAM WADDINGTON, "The field of
    night", 1966.

Time's fire burns away all unities,
Grass grows on gods and queens and
    courtesans.

    DAVID HELWIG, "After watching 'The
    nature of things' ", 1967.

I sit with a malicious grin
For I am Time and I love to sing!

    LEROY JOHNSON, "The worker", 1967.

Time is the small change of eternity.

> IRVING LAYTON, "Some observations and aphorisms", *Tamarack rev.*, Spring, 1968, 6.

Play, children, play
the time for song is short
and age and sorrow come like frost
to wither up the heart.

> PHYLLIS GOTLIEB, *Ordinary moving*, 10, 1969.

Our earth revolves in 4 minutes less
than 24 hours
in a year goes round the sun 600
million miles
Time is an antelope
running on & on out of my mind.

> RONALD EVERSON, "On & beyond white-mud & stone pile post", 1969.

It takes time to move a mountain
It takes time for love to be
You're never really caged in
But you're never really free.
It takes time for all the answers
To be dealt with properly
And everybody knows that it takes
time.

> SHIRLEY EIKHARD, song, qu. in *Maclean's*, June, 1972, 86.

In the last resort, however, it is we who must do our own promptings, who must make our own choices, and define our own paths. We cannot depend on the ripeness of time, for the time is never ripe.

> HANS GEORGE CLASSEN, *The time is never ripe*, 1972, 12.

Titles of Honour

Half a yard of blue ribbon is a plaguy cheap way of rewardin' merit, as the English do; and, although we larf at 'em (for folks always will larf at what they ain't got, and never can get), yet titles ain't bad things as objects of ambition, are they?

> T.C. HALIBURTON, *Sam Slick*, 1836, ch.XXIX.

I hope the practice of conferring honours will not degenerate into a matter of course and a number of honours be bestowed upon each change of Ministers.

> SIR JOHN A. MACDONALD, memorandum to Governor-General, Mar. 6, 1879.

Simply an egotistical, lying old hog, no more worthy to be knighted than I am.

> ANON., a member of R.C.M.P., commenting on Maj. Gen. F.D. Middleton being made a Knight, 1886; qu. in R. Atkin, *Maintain the right*, 1973, 252.

The fountain of honour is merely one of the taps in the party bar.

> GOLDWIN SMITH, *The Bystander*, May, 1890, 255.

Sir John is a K. C. M. G., and you are Casey, N. G.

> NICHOLAS FLOOD DAVIN, 1898, to George Casey, M.P.; answer to the conundrum as to the difference between him and Sir John Bourinot.

It would simplify matters if the king would hit the Canadian census returns with the flat of his sword and make all the adult males knights.

> ROBERT C. (BOB) EDWARDS, Calgary *Eye Opener*, July 29, 1911.

How could I accept a knighthood? Good heavens! I shovel off my own sidewalk and stoke my own furnace.

> JOHN W. DAFOE, qu. in *Can. hist. rev.*, 1929, 240; Dafoe was offered a title by Sir Robert Borden, Prime Minister, 1911-20.

I am quite prepared, if we can do it without any disrespect to the Crown of England, to bring our titles to the marketplace and make a bonfire of them.

> SIR WILFRID LAURIER, H. of C., *Debates*, Apr. 8, 1918, 500.

We, Your Majesty's most dutiful and loyal subjects, the House of Commons of Canada in Parliament assembled, humbly approach Your Majesty, praying that Your Majesty hereafter may be graciously pleased: to refrain hereafter from conferring any title of honour or titular distinction upon any of your subjects domiciled or ordinarily resident in Canada, save such appelations as are of a professional or vocational character or which appertain to an office.

W.F. NICKLE, proposed address to the King, May 14, 1919; adopted May 22, 1919; H. of C., *Debates*, 2395.

If we are to have no titles, titular distinctions or honours in Canada, let us hold to the principle and have none. Let us abolish them altogether. But if the sovereigns or heads of other countries are to be permitted to bestow honours on Canadians, for my part, I think we owe it to our own sovereign to give him that prerogative before all others.

W.L. MACKENZIE KING, H. of C., *Debates*, 1929, Vol. I, 86.

It's the best way I can prove to Canadians that I'm a success.

ROY THOMSON, qu. in R. Braddon, *Roy Thomson of Fleet Street*, 1965, 338, referring to his desire for a title.

I was born a Canadian. I'm going to die a Canadian. If the country doesn't want me, it's going to be stuck with me anyway.

ROY THOMSON, Publisher, Toronto, Jan. 4, 1963, in response to Prime Minister Pearson's reference to him as a "former" Canadian after Thomson became a British citizen and received a baronetcy.

As long as I live there will be only one Lord Beaverbrook.

SIR MAX AITKEN, on the death of his father, June 9, 1964, and renouncing the baronetcy; qu. in A.J.P. Taylor, *Beaverbrook*, 1972, 671.

Tobacco

Tobacco chewing played a great part in the building of the Canadian Pacific Railway.

T.E. WILSON, qu. in Pierre Berton, *The last spike*, 1971, 160.

Tolerance

Deep down in the Anglo-Saxon nature the world over is enshrined the belief that the toleration of differences is the measure of civilization.

VINCENT MASSEY, speech in New York, Dec. 10, 1928.

The consciousness of political fragility and its national diversity have developed among Canadians a great spirit of tolerance.

PHILIPPE AUBERT DE LA RUE, *Canada incertain*, 1962, 127. (Trans.)

We must learn to accept other people as they are – including their inability, or unwillingness, to accept us as we are.

RICHARD J. NEEDHAM, *A friend in Needham*, 1969, 11.

There have been some aspects of Canadian life which we have felt more than seen. Of these, the most evident and undoubtedly the most important, is the spirit of tolerance and goodwill that is an invaluable Canadian characteristic. Canadians take for granted what so many persons elsewhere seek and envy: human relationships that, by and large, accept without question differences in colour or origin or language.

PIERRE E. TRUDEAU, H. of C., *Debates*, Oct. 24, 1969, 36.

Tools

A French Canadian will accomplish as much with an ax as a man of any other race with a full outfit of tools.

HENRY M. AMI, *Canada and Newfoundland*, 1915, 334.

Toronto

I dreamt not then that, ere the rolling year
Had filled its circle, I should wander here
In musing awe; should tread this wondrous world,
See all its store of inland waters hurled
In one vast volume down Niagara's steep;
Or calm behold them, in transparent sleep,
Where the blue hills of old Toronto shed
Their evening shadows o'er Ontario's bed.

THOMAS MOORE, lines written to Lady Charlotte Rawdon, 1804.

The streets of York are regularly laid out, intersecting each other at right angles. Only one of them, however, is yet completely built; and in wet weather the unfinished streets are, if possible, muddier and dirtier than those of Kingston.

EDWARD A. TALBOT, *Five years residence in the Canadas*, 1824, I, 102; possible origin of phrase "Muddy York".

The situation of the town is very unhealthy, for it stands on a piece of low marshy land, which is better calculated for a frog-pond or beaver-meadow than for the residence of human beings.

EDWARD A. TALBOT, *Five years residence in the Canadas*, 1824, I,102.

Dover is one of the vilest blue-devil haunts upon the face of the earth, except Little York in Upper Canada, when one has been there one day.

JOHN GALT, *Autobiography*, 1833,I,334; frequently misquoted as, "York is one of the vilest bluedevil haunts on the face of the earth"; *bluedevil:* very low spirits.

I did not expect to find here in this new capital of a new country, with the boundless forest within half a mile of us on almost every side, —concentrated as it were the worst evils of our old and most artificial social system at home, with none of its *agremens*, and none of its advantages.

ANNA B. JAMESON, *Winter studies and summer rambles*, 1838, Vol. I, 98.

Toronto is like a fourth or fifth-rate provincial town, with the pretensions of a capital city. We have here a petty colonial oligarchy, a self-constituted aristocracy, based upon nothing real nor upon anything imaginary.

ANNA B. JAMESON, *Winter studies and summer rambles*, Vol. I, 1838, 98.

Toronto [is] a foul, loathsome, disgusting capital abounding in filthy lanes and alleys, muddy and unpaved streets and as a whole, presents a dreary and disagreeable aspect, both from its low situation and contemptible appearance of the buildings.

DONALD MCLEOD, *A brief review of the settlement of Upper Canada*, Cleveland, 1841, 10.

I had been accustomed to see hundreds of Indians about my native village, then Little York, muddy and dirty, just struggling into existence, now the City of Toronto, bursting forth in all its energy and commercial strength.

PAUL KANE, *Wanderings of an artist*, 1859, Pref., vii, comparing Toronto between 1844 and 1859.

Toronto is the handsomest town we have yet seen. Wide streets, good shops, lovely gardens, handsome public buildings, churches rich in spires and traceried windows, spacious hotels, and elegant equipages.

CAPTAIN HORTON RHYS, *A theatrical trip for a wager!*, 1861, 70.

In a few years Toronto is bound to outstrip in enterprise, and solid commercial progress, every other city in Canada as a trading centre.

FRANK SMITH, in Montreal *Gazette*, Jan. 26, 1870.

Toronto, soul of Canada, is wealthy, busy, commercial, Scotch, absorbent of whisky.

RUPERT BROOKE, *Letters from America*, 1916, 82.

It is not squalid like Birmingham, or cramped like Canton, or scattered like Edmonton, or sham like Berlin, or hellish like New York, or tiresome like Nice. It is all right. The only depressing thing is that it will always be what it is, only larger, and that no Canadian city can ever be anything better or different. If they are good they may become Toronto.

RUPERT BROOKE, *Letters from America*, 1916, 84.

Toronto as a city carries out the idea of Canada as a country. It is a calculated crime both against the aspirations of the soul and the affection of the heart.

ALEISTER CROWLEY, *Confessions*, 1970, 502, about 1923.

Indeed I have always found that the only thing in regard to Toronto which far-away people know for certain is that McGill University is in it.

STEPHEN B. LEACOCK, *My discovery of the West*, 1937, 38.

A mournful Scottish version of America.

WYNDHAM LEWIS, letter to Geoffrey Stone, December, 1940.

It must be good to die in Toronto. The transition between life and death would be continuous, painless and scarcely noticeable in this silent town. I dreaded the Sundays and prayed to God that if he chose for me to die in Toronto he would let it be on a Saturday afternoon to save me from one more Toronto Sunday.

LEOPOLD INFELD, *Quest, the evolution of a scientist*, 1941, 324.

Yonge Street for business,
Bay Street for class,
College for shopping
And Jarvis for ass.

ANON., Second World War rhyme, qu. by David Helwig in *Saturday night*, Apr., 1973, 35.

In Toronto the Good, it's quite understood
That sin is a thing to beware-i-O!
But if you *are* bad, you've got to look sad,
For nothing is fun in Ontario.

LISTER S. SINCLAIR, *We all hate Toronto*, (Radio Drama, C.B.C., Jan. 17, 1946).

If you stay in Toronto, the longing remains deep in the soul, and since it can't be satisfied you can't be wearied, and your mind and your imagination should become like a caged tiger. O Toronto! O my tiger city!

MORLEY CALLAGHAN, in M. Ross, ed., *Our sense of identity*, 1954, 123.

If you want to be righteous and rich
And to know you have God on your side
You won't find a cosier niche
Than Toronto can always provide.

F.R. SCOTT, "Ode to Confederation", 1957.

All Canadian cities (I mean English-Canadian cities) as they grow older and bigger tend to become more and more like Toronto.

FRANK H. UNDERHILL, Roy. Soc. Can., *Trans.*, Vol. LII, Ser.III, June, 1958, Sect. 2, 15.

Then let us praise Toronto, since few do.

MIRIAM CHAPIN, *Contemporary Canada*, 1959, 51.

If Toronto stinks, as some of our fellow-Canadians aver, then a slight aroma ought certainly to be discernible from me.

GREGORY CLARK, "Mee Hee", in *The best of Gregory Clark*, 1959, 144.

I am living,
As I am reading,
In the most rapidly growing
City in the world.
But do hearts grow here too?

WALTER BAUER, "Toronto", 1961. (Trans. by W. Kirkconnell).

Clearly, if Confederation is to survive another hundred years Canada must find a national *esprit de corps*. Cohesion cannot depend indefinitely on hating Toronto.

ERIC NICOL, *100 years of what?*, 1966, 43.

When I was born here,
eating was done indoors,
and the only Italians
ran a corner grocery
where my mother didn't like to shop.

DAVID HELWIG, "Toronto", 1967.

Metro must expand or be strangled.

TORONTO *STAR*, Oct. 11, 1969, a ref. to metropolitan Toronto.

It's marvellous being a woman in Toronto; you get to meet so many interesting women.

RICHARD J. NEEDHAM, *A friend in Needham*, 1969, 36.

Toronto *Star*

King Street *Pravda*.

ANON., so-called because of its stand on the left, determined by its editor, J.E. Atkinson, 1930's.

Torture

Don't try to love those who torture you, because if you succeed you'll come to love being tortured.

ALDEN NOWLAN, "Commonplace book", Apr. 8, 1964, qu. in *Fiddlehead*, No. 70, 1967, 53.

Totems

Most people when I was young, wanted to have their own totem poles. But when the Rev. Mr. Crosby, the missionary, arrived in his boat in 1884, he stopped the people and threatened them with jail, if they wanted to raise totems.

HENRY YOUNG, Haida carver, qu. in Marius Barbeau, *Totem poles*, II, 1951, 825.

Touch

Once in a timeless interim I touched it,
Alone in a crowd, crowding the other lonely,
Unheard, unseen, with nothing at all that vouched it,
I touched it, it touched me, once, once only.

ROBERT FINCH, "The certainty", 1961.

Tourists

See Canada! What is there to see?

> MRS. HUMPHRY WARD, *Canadian born*, 1908, 63.

A dollar brought into Canada by a tourist from another country and spent is as important to Canadians as a dollar brought into Canada for wheat going out of the country.

> JACK MINER, a favourite statement, 1910 to 1914; some publications refer to him as "The father of tourism".

Canada is clean, healthy, young, polite, unspoiled and, as I say, just upstairs.

> HORACE SUTTON, *Footloose in Canada*, 1950, 11.

Every province in the Dominion puts out such attractive vacation brochures that it's amazing that everybody doesn't just stay home.

> CALGARY *HERALD*, qu. in Vancouver *Sun*, Aug. 5, 1963, 5.

Somnolent through landscapes and by
 trees
nondescript, almost anonymous,
they alter as they enter foreign cities
the terrible tourists with their empty
 eyes
longing to be filled with monuments.

> P.K. PAGE, "The permanent tourists", 1967.

Track Sports

As Pindar long ago in Greece was
 proud to hail
Thessalian Hippokleas, even so
It is meet we praise in our days
 fleet-footed
Bruce Kidd from Toronto.

> W.H. AUDEN, "Runner", 1969, commentary for National Film Board film.

Trade

Situated in a cold climate, she produces no commodity, except furs and skins, which she could exchange for the commodities of Europe; and consequently she could have little returns to make the English merchant.

> ANON., *A letter to a great minister, on the prospect of a peace, wherein . . . the importance of Canada [is] fully refuted*, 1761.

I do not like to see our hatters importing hats, and shoemakers selling foreign shoes, and tanners offering foreign leather as superior articles. The profits on the manufacture of the goods used by us accumulate in Birmingham, Sheffield, Manchester, Glasgow, Boston, and Pittsburg; to all these places we bear the same relation as the negroes at the Bight of Benin.

> ROBERT B. SULLIVAN, *Lecture*, Mechanics' Institute, Hamilton, Nov. 17, 1847.

It is in vain to suppose that a free trade system will be beneficial to a new and struggling colony, which has nothing to export but raw materials; it is rather calculated to enrich an old commonwealth, whose people by their skill and labour make such raw materials valuable, and then return them for consumption. The result of the system alluded to has been that the suppliers of the raw material at last become hewers of wood and drawers of water to the manufacturers.

> ABRAHAM GESNER, *The industrial resources of Nova Scotia*, 1849, 218.

Unless reciprocity of trade with the United States be established these colonies must be lost to England.

> LORD ELGIN, letter to Grey, May 28, 1849, in (Pub. Arch. Can., *Letters of Lord Elgin*, III).

There is roguery in all trades but our own.

T.C. HALIBURTON, *Nature and human nature*, 1855, II, 12.

God and nature never destined that Nova Scotia and Ontario should trade together. We trade with Ontario, to be sure. Their drummers permeate our country and sell $10,000,000 of goods annually. Where do we get the money? We get it from the people of the United States.

J.W. LONGLEY, speech at Merchants' Club, Boston, Mass., Dec. 30, 1886.

With my utmost effort, with my latest breath I will oppose the "veiled treason" which attempts by sordid means and mercenary proffers to lure our people from their allegiance.

SIR JOHN A. MACDONALD, speech, "To the electors of Canada", Feb. 7, 1891, on commercial union with U.S.; the phrase "veiled treason" is from Disraeli.

I prefer the Yankee dollar to the British shilling, especially when the Yankee dollar is near at hand and the British shilling so far away.

SIR WILFRID LAURIER, speech in Boston, Nov. 17, 1891.

Trade follows the advertisement, not the flag.

JOHN A COOPER, Secretary, Canadian Press Assoc., about 1896.

British preference.

W.S. FIELDING, H of C., Budget speech, Apr. 22, 1897; the Canadian preferential treatment of British imports.

Everything from a needle to an anchor.

REVILLON BROTHERS, general wholesalers, Edmonton, advt. in E.J. Chambers, *The Royal Northwest Mounted Police*, 1906, L.

If we were to follow the laws of nature and geography between Canada and the United States, the whole trade would flow from south to north, and from north to south. We have done everything possible by building canals and subsidising railways to bring the trade from west to east and from east to west so as to bring trade into British channels.

SIR WILFRID LAURIER, at Imperial Conference, London, May 7, 1907.

Now is the accepted time. Canada is at the parting of the ways. Shall she be an isolated country, as much separated from us as if she were across the ocean, or shall her people and our people profit by the proximity that our geography furnishes and stimulate the trade across the border that nothing but a useless, illogical and unnecessary tariff wall created?

WILLIAM H. TAFT, U.S. President, address to Illinois State Legis., Springfield, Feb. 11, 1911.

Their habits are the same as ours, and therefore we are induced to trade [with Americans], and cannot help it, by the force of nature.

SIR WILFRID LAURIER, qu., *Contemporary rev.*, 1911, 481.

I am a reasonable, sane and rational free-trader, but I am not such a free-trader as to strike down any legitimate industry, and I have told the manufacturers that if they are fair and reasonable they can count on my support.

W.S. FIELDING, speech at Digby, N.S., Aug. 29, 1911.

From every point of view, trade is and always will be the vital question upon which patriotism, common defence, and everything else will depend; therefore, I trust that you will pardon my inclination to devote my substance and my efforts to the upbuilding of King Trade.

> SIR W. VAN HORNE, letter, 1914?, qu., Vaughan, *Van Horne*, 1920, 345.

It is part of the irony of fate that it should have fallen to the lot of the first Western Minister of Finance to drop the cut flowers of British preference on the mangled corpse of free trade.

> WILLIAM IRVINE, H. of C., *Debates*, May 6, 1930.

You say our tariffs are only for the manufacturers. I will make them fight for you [farmers] as well. I will use them to blast a way into the markets that have been closed to you.

> R.B. BENNETT, election speech, Winnipeg, June 9, 1930.

To bargain and barter and blast with our own kith and kin is unthinkable.

> W.L. MACKENZIE KING, speech at Prince Albert, Sask., July 12, 1930, in response to a statement made by R.B. Bennett, June 9, at Winnipeg.

Unless we can trade with the outside world our condition must be one of stagnation, with the standards of living falling to ever lower levels, and with increasing strains upon the bonds that keep our federation together.

> J.W. DAFOE, *Canada, an American nation*, 1935, 119.

If we put all our eggs in a Yankee basket
We'll all end up in a Yankee casket.

> J.S. WALLACE, "Trade", 1953.

They're wonderful customers. You can't do business with better businessmen anywhere.

> GEORGE HEES, Minister of Trade and Commerce, Ottawa, Dec. 9, 1960, referring to a Cuban Economic Mission, later refuted by Prime Minister Diefenbaker.

Trade Unions

Thanks to our torpor our trade union movement is almost entirely in the hands of the international federations which call themselves neutral, but who are in reality amoral and irreligious and who are waiting for the day, coming very soon, when they will be clearly socialist and anti-christian.

> HENRI BOURASSA, Montreal *Le Devoir*, Aug. 1, 1914, 1. (Trans.)

A trade unionist is a man who hates his job and is terrified someone may take it from him.

> RICHARD J. NEEDHAM,, *A friend in Needham*, 1969, 19.

Tradition

As for us, a large part of our strength comes from our traditions, let us neither stray from them nor change them, except most gradually.

> FRANÇOIS-XAVIER GARNEAU, *Histoire du Canada*, 4th ed., 1882, Vol. 3, 396. (Trans.)

Tradition is the father of persecutions, the uncle of falsehoods, the brother of ignorance, and the grandsire of a thousand hideous sins against sweetness and light.

> BLISS CARMAN, *The friendship of art*, 1903, 177.

My country, last across the world
    To leave tradition's night,
Strong hater of her seers is she,
    And worshipper of might.

> WILSON MACDONALD, "Sea shore and compline", 1935.

Tradition does not come from rocks and trees: it comes from the hearts and minds of men.

> JOHN LYMAN, about 1939, qu. in J. Park, *Culture of contemporary Canada*, 1957, 133.

Any sensible person would say that what you do with a tradition, after picking out the part of it that seems to go well with you, is follow it. That is, do it over again. I don't mean turning out facsimiles but related works.

JAMES REANEY, *Univ. of Tor. quart.*, Apr., 1957, 291.

As we grapple with the troubles of our proud and angry dust, let us concede that our history and our destiny — our living tradition — is revealed to us not only in *Hansard* and in Royal Commission briefs, but also in such wars of the spirit as this — wars which sometimes must be lost before they ever really can be won.

MALCOLM ROSS, in *Our living tradition*, Ser. 1, 1957, 47.

One thing we are good at in Canada: the art of keeping up with yesterday.

DUNCAN MACPHERSON, caption on Toronto *Star* cartoon, 1967, in his *1967 editorial cartoons*, [18].

A thoroughly modern sea-flower,
Antique custom charmed me not:
Rootless, I rode the waves
And for my pains was early tossed
Upon a cold, forbidding shore.

DENNIS GILLILAND, "Odyssey", 1969.

Civilization should tame barbarism,
Decorum should control passion,
The will subdue the act.
Humanity should be a statue
Senatorial, calm, with a Roman smile
Ironic, wise, malicious, and Augustan.
What I want is stone.

ELIZABETH BREWSTER, "What I want is stone", 1969.

Tragedy

We are a people incapable of tragedy.

FRANK H. UNDERHILL, address, Queen's University, Jan. 10, 1955.

Trails

The Trail hath no langorous longing;
    It leads to no Lotus land;
On its way dead Hopes come
        thronging
    To take you by the hand;
He who treads the Trail undaunted,
        thereafter shall command!

CATHERINE SIMPSON HAYES, (Yukon Bill), "The trail", 1910.

Mother of a mighty manhood, land of
    glamour and of hope,
From the eastward sea-swept islands to
    the sunny western slope,
Ever more my heart is with you, ever
    more till life shall fail,
I'll be out with pack and packer on the
    Athabasca Trail.

SIR ARTHUR CONAN DOYLE, "The Athabasca Trail", July 2, 1914, recited to the Canadian Club, Ottawa.

Trails — Alberta

Calgary-Edmonton Trail. The Calgary Trail. (From Fort Macleod to Calgary, 104 miles.) M. McDougall's Trail. (From the Rocky Mountain House Trail to the Calgary Edmonton Trail; also called the Morley Trail.) Montane Fault Trail. (East of Rocky Mountain Trail, ran north and south.) The Old North Trail. (From the Arctic southward along the east slopes of the Rocky Mountains, from pre-historic times.) Pigeon Lake Trail. (From Pigeon Lake to Edmonton.) The Rocky Mountain Corridor Route. (From Alaska to the south — the way to the interior.) Rocky Mountain House Trail. (From half way between Fort Calgary and Morleyville, north to Rocky Mountain House.) The Whoop-up Trail. (From Fort Benton, Montana to Hamilton at Whoop-up, Alta., 210 miles.) Wolf Track. (From Edmonton southward to the Red Deer Forks.)

Trails – B.C.

Brigade Trails. (Several trails — from Dewdney Trail, midway between Hope and Princeton, through Tulameen to Kamloops, B.C., also from Ft. Okanagan on the Columbia to Ft. Alexandria on the north Fraser. (See *Beaver*, Mar. 1953,11, map) Cariboo Trail. (From Fort Hope on the Fraser north to Barkerville, 1860's; also, Cariboo Road.) Dewdney Trail. (From Hope, B.C., through Princeton, Keremeos, to Rock Creek, later to Fort Steele; built by Royal Engineers, 1860-61.) Ghost Pass Trail. (From the Brigade Trail to the Dewdney Trail, using Eighteen Mile Creek.) The Grease Trails. (From Aiyansh, Kitimit, Kinnsquit, Bella Coola, and other points on the coast, into the B.C. interior, over which oolachan fish oil was carried.) Hudsons Bay Company Brigade Trail. (From Hope, B.C. to Fort Kamloops. Also known as the Brigade Trail.) Poor Man's Trail. (From Ashcroft to Hazleton, to the Stikine River heights northward to the Klondike.) Rocky Mountain Trail. (From north of B.C., southward route, partly following Bow River.) Sheep River Hunting Trail. (From the main north-south route in the foothills of Alberta which may have been the most heavily travelled passage of the Rocky Mountain Corridor.) Whatcom Trail. (A variant of the original Dewdney Trail; see above.)

Trails – Manitoba

Boundary Commission Trail. (From Emerson to Southwestern Manitoba and Brandon before the coming of the railway in 1881.) Brandon Trail. (From Brandon southwest to Homestead lands.) Carlton Trail. (From Fort Garry, Manitoba to Fort Carlton on N. Saskatchewan River. Also known as the Saskatchewan Trail, 1840.) Deloraine Trail. (From Brandon to Deloraine then Northwest, about 1886.) Edmonton Trail. (From the Red River to Edmonton, crossing the North Saskatchewan at Fort Pitt.) Melita Trail. (From the town of Melita, Man., westward; also known as the Old Melita Trail and Main Trail.) Red River Trail. (From the Red River on the International boundary north to Hudson Bay.) Southwest Trail. (From the Brandon-Souris Trail through Hartney and Lauder to Melita.) Touchwood Trail. (From Selkirk, Man., following the telegraph line through Sask. westward to Touchwood Hills, Sask.) Yellow Quill Trail. (From Portage to the mouth of the Souris River, then to the Brandon area.)

Trails – Nova Scotia

Cabot Trail. (A loop road in Cape Breton Island, 185 miles.)

Trails – Saskatchewan

The North Trail. (From the Touchwood Trail near Touchwood Hills, to Birch Lake District.)

Trails – Yukon

Dalton Trail. (Toll route to the Klondike gold fields from the Lynn Canal on the Pacific to Fort Selkirk on the Yukon River.) Dead Horse Trail. (From north of Skagway to the White Pass, a part of the trail to the Klondike, 1897 and later.) Klondike Trail. (Term applied to any trail that led to the goldfields.)

Tramps

Riding the boxcars out of Winnipeg in
a morning after rain so close to
the violent sway of fields it's

like running and running
naked with summer in your mouth.

AL PURDY, "Transient", 1965.

Transportation

You have been blessed with an abundant harvest, and soon I trust will a railway come to carry to those who need it the surplus of your produce, now – as my own eyes have witnessed – imprisoned in your storehouses for want of the means of transport.

LORD DUFFERIN, speech at City Hall, Winnipeg, Sept.29, 1877.

Canada is doing business on a back street. We must put her on a thoroughfare.

SIR WILLIAM VAN HORNE, 1886, a ref. to the C.P.R.

The hopper is too big for the spout.

SIR WILLIAM VAN HORNE, about 1902, describing the shortage of railway cars to ship prairie wheat; appears in *Review historical studies relating to Canada*, as: "Canada has been adding sides to her hopper for a long time, but has neglected to enlarge the spout".

The All-Red route.

SIR WILFRID LAURIER, scheme proposed at the Imperial conference, 1907, for a British line of steamships connecting Britain with Australia, via Canada.

Anderson Chariots.

ANON., two-wheel, horse-drawn vehicles made from a dismantled automobile by farmers of the Prairies during the depression of the early 1930's; Dr. J.T.M. Anderson was Premier of Saskatchewan, 1929-34.

Bennett Buggies.

ANON., term used during prime ministership of R.B. Bennett, 1930-35, to describe motorless horse-drawn automobiles in use in Prairie provinces during drought years.

Diaper Specials.

ANON., popular term applied to ships which brought 40,000 English warbrides and children to Canada 1946 and later; system organized by Maj.-Gen. H.A. Young.

Canada in the first half of the century was the child of her waterways, and in the second the child of her railways.

UNIVERSITY OF MANITOBA. DEPT. OF HISTORY, qu. in Chafe and Lower, *Canada*, 1948, 287.

Are transportation services to be regarded as business institutions like department stores, factories, or farms, or are they to be looked upon as almost eleemosynary agencies wherein the cost-revenue relationship is subordinate to the welfare of the public?

A.W. CURRIE, *Economics of Canadian transportation*, 1954, 23.

Fuel, power, capital and men all follow great industries; but industry itself seeks out areas blessed by nature or history with exceptionally good transportation facilities.

ONTARIO GOVERNMENT, *Submission to Roy. Comm. on Canada's Economic Prospects*, Jan. 26, 1956, 2.

Travel

I am a bird of passage – here today and gone tomorrow.

THOMAS C. HALIBURTON, *Sam Slick's wise saws*, 1853, ch. 14.

Travel a thousand miles up a great river; more than another thousand along great lakes and a succession of smaller lakes; a thousand miles across rolling prairies; and another thousand through woods and over three great ranges of mountains, and you have travelled from Ocean to Ocean through Canada.

GEORGE M. GRANT, *Ocean to ocean*, 1873, 1.

You feel the joy of coming home,
  After long leagues to France or
    Spain,
You feel the clear Canadian foam,
  And the gulf water heave again.

DUNCAN CAMPBELL SCOTT, "Off Rivière du Loup", 1893.

Mere progression, mere moving from place to place, continually toward the unknown, even what dull people call "a prosaic railway journey" is the traveller's joy.

ARCHIBALD MACMECHAN, *The life of a little college and other papers*, 1914, 79.

Aimless explorations of foreign thoroughfares, drifting with the tides of life along unfamiliar streets, are long adventures crammed with episodes. The joy of wandering is slow to pall, and it is to be enjoyed at the full when a man shakes himself free of all aids but his native powers and marches forth alone into the world.

ARCHIBALD MACMECHAN, *The life of a little college and other papers*, 1914, 79.

Pleasure is a pure good, say the philosophers, reacting on and heightening the vitality. But, after all, the pleasure of travel is only a pleasure, like any other; and it passes. It perishes in the using.

ARCHIBALD MACMECHAN, *The life of a little college and other papers*, 1914, 80.

There was a young woman named
    Bright
Whose speed was faster than light.
  She set out one day
  In a relative way,
And returned the previous night.

ARTHUR H. BULLER, Univ. of Manitoba botanist, *Punch*, Dec. 19, 1923, 591.

It appears that many people when they travel really see nothing at all except the reflection of their own ideas.

STEPHEN LEACOCK, "Back from Europe", in *Winnowed wisdom*, 1926, 83.

Madam, the most extraordinary thing
    in this town
Is the shape of your legs.
O communication!
O rapid transit!

F.R. SCOTT, "Tourist time", 1945.

The incredible blueness of the sky in the fall coming through the trees, that I don't think can be duplicated. Of course I have done very little travelling, but it impresses me so much that I have nowhere to go, no reason for going.

HAROLD TOWN, *Waterloo rev.*, No. 5, 1960, 9.

I always wanted to make this trip and now I have.

NATHAN T. BOYA, first Black American to shoot Niagara Falls, on completion of his attempt, July 15, 1961.

I know why many men have stopped
    and wept
Half-way between the loves they leave
    and seek,
And wondered if travel leads them
    anywhere —
Horizons keep the soft line of your
    cheek,
The windy sky's a locket for your hair.

LEONARD COHEN, "Travel", 1961.

See Canada First.

> JOHN FISHER, publicist, qu. in Vancouver *Sun*, Dec. 14, 1962, 4.

I've always been going somewhere –
    Vancouver or
old age or somewhere ever since I can
    remember.

> AL PURDY, "The madwoman on the train", 1965.

Do I gain anything by coming by train
    here
To feel engaged, forced to say this is
    only
A little different from the land I
    passed through,
But becoming more and more the
    characteristic
Of my own self that was abroad
    before.

> DOROTHY ROBERTS, "Own country", 1967.

All travel is like fiction,
    visiting foreign lands, antique
        and new,
that the inhabitants call real.

> LOUIS DUDEK, "Atlantis", 1967, 70.

Do you realize in this modern world
the only place left for privacy is in
travelling? Yes, you have privacy
when you're travelling; people leave
you alone.

> MARSHALL MCLUHAN, qu. in *Weekend mag.*, Mar. 18, 1967, 9.

There is no logic in journeys.
They are all allegories.

> NANCY L. BAUER, "A Christmas pilgrimage", 1969.

No traveller comes here from
    innocence
but for that myth the snow cannot
    provide,
and all our histories lie outside.

> GWENDOLYN MACEWEN, "The thin garden", 1969.

I dream of a journey,
    perpetual, or reaching no visible
        end,
in which I search for what is genuinely
    mine: face, country, home, animals,
        town
        folk, temple
or just a particular combination of
        landscape
which will unlock what is already

> SUNYATA MACLEAN, *Poems to define the corona of silence*, 1970, 52.

dream cities
We travel to see them or hear from
    friends
travelling alone or together the long
    roads
of the country
I hardly care now
if I ever see Vancouver

> DAVID HELWIG, "Report from the city of dreams", 1972.

Wherever I travel I'm too late. The
orgy has moved elsewhere.

> MORDECAI RICHLER, *Shovelling trouble*, 1972, 29.

Treaties

I am one of those who believe that this
country should have the right to negotiate its commercial treaties. I go a step
further, I believe this country should
have the right to negotiate every
treaty.

> AMOR DE COSMOS, H. of C., *Debates*, Apr. 21, 1882, 1084.

Treaty of Washington, 1871

The most abominable thing in our
history.

> BENJAMIN DISRAELI, qu. in Alexander Mackenzie, letter to Alexander Galt, July 15, 1875.

Trees

They would not spare the ancient oak from feelings of veneration, nor look upon it with regard for any thing but its use as timber. They have no time, even if they possessed the taste, to gaze abroad on the beauties of Nature, but their ignorance is bliss.

CATHERINE P. TRAILL, *Backwoods of Canada*, 1836, 154.

A Canadian settler hates a tree, regards it as his natural enemy, as something to be destroyed, eradicated, annihilated by all and any means.

ANNA B. JAMESON, *Winter studies and summer rambles*, 1838, Vol. 3, 96.

You Canadians have a prejudice against trees.

SIR EDMUND W. HEAD, Gov.-Gen., about 1855, qu. by John Langton in Wallace, *University of Toronto*, 1927, 75.

Thou hast a secret, old elm, worth the keeping,
  We children knew it not in early days;
But they who far beyond thy shade are sleeping
  Revealed it to us ere they went their ways.

JAMES MCCARROLL, "The elm tree", 1889.

We stand beneath the pines and enter the grand pillared aisles with a feeling of mute reverence; these stately trunks bearing their plumed heads so high above us seem a meet roofing for His temple who reared them to His praise.

CATHERINE PARR TRAILL, *Pearls and pebbles*, 1894, 134.

Those who attacked the virgin forest did their work well, and were no respecters of trees in a vertical position. Prone on the ground, they represented dollars and cents, lumber or cordwood, but standing upright they were mere cumberers of the earth, defrauding man of his natural and inalienable heritage.

J. J. PROCTER, *The philosopher in the clearing*, 1897, 80.

The elm is aspiration, and death is in the yew,
And beauty dwells in every tree from Lapland to Peru;
But there's magic in the poplars when the wind goes through.

BERNARD F. TROTTER, "The poplars", 1916.

People walking amid trees after night always draw closer together instinctively and involuntarily, making an alliance, physical and mental, against certain alien powers around them.

L. M. MONTGOMERY, *Rainbow valley*, 1919, 135.

How many a tree whose lofty dome
Gave magic birds a magic home
Now shelters in its varnished shade
Books, handkerchiefs, and marmalade!

ROBERT FINCH, "Furniture", in *Can. forum*, Apr., 1929, 125.

There are pleasures you cannot buy,
Treasures you cannot sell,
And not the smallest of these
Is the gift and glory of trees.

ROBERT SERVICE, "Trees against the sky", 1940.

I can approach a solitary tree with pleasure, a cluster of trees with joy, and a forest with rapture; I must approach a solitary man with caution, a group of men with trepidation, and a nation of men with terror.

JOHN D. ROBINS, *The incomplete anglers*, 1943, 187.

Is this the tree that saw our first love's plighting,
And those the leaves that heard our first love's vow,
And yonder limb that saw love's first delighting,
Is that the very limb, the self-same bough?

PAUL HIEBERT, "The plight", in *Sarah Binks*, 1947.

Skyward point the cedar billows,
Birches pinken, poplars green,
Magenta runs the sumach tine
Pouring down the hills like wine.
Yellow catkins on the willows,
Yellow calico on line.

EARLE BIRNEY, "Quebec May", 1948.

In almond trees lemon trees
wind and sun do as they please
Butterflies and laundry flutter
My love her hair is blond as butter.

LEONARD COHEN, "In almond trees lemon trees", 1966.

An orphan tree
forks for air
among the knees of
clanking panoplied buildings.

MARGARET AVISON, "Urban tree", 1966.

" . . . But only God can make a tree."
(He'll never try it in Sudbury.)

RAYMOND SOUSTER, "Very short poem", 1969.

This land like a mirror turns you inward
And you become a forest in a furtive lake;
The dark pines of your mind reach downward,
You dream in the green of your time,
Your memory is a row of sinking pines.

GWENDOLYN MACEWEN, "Dark pines under water", 1969.

Trial by Jury

That sheet anchor, that mainstay, that blessed shield, that glorious institution – the rich man's terror, the poor man's hope, the people's pride, the nation's glory – Trial by Jury.

T.C. HALIBURTON, *Sam Slick*, 1838, 109.

Prisoner: it is far from a pleasant duty for me to have to sentence you only to imprisonment for life . . . Your crime was unmitigated, diabolical murder. You deserve to be hanged! Had the jury performed their duty I might now have the painful satisfaction of condemning you to death, and you, gentlemen of the jury, you are a pack of Dalles horse thieves, and permit me to say, it would give me great pleasure to see you hanged, each and every one of you, for declaring a murderer guilty only of manslaughter.

JUDGE MATTHEW BEGBIE, at trial of the gunman, Gilchrist, in B.C., Jan., 1863.

Trials

In the full furnace of this hour
My thoughts grow keen and clear.

ARCHIBALD LAMPMAN, "Heat", 1889.

Law is not justice and a trial is not a scientific inquiry into truth. A trial is the resolution of a dispute.

EDSON HAINES, Judge, Supreme Court of Ont., address to Ontario Psychiatric Assoc., Toronto, Jan. 27, 1973.

Triumph

The triumph is not in
the man himself, nor in the
women among him.
The triumph is the hazard of the man.

SUSAN MUSGRAVE, "The flight", 1970.

Trouble

Don't meet trouble halfway. It is quite capable of making the entire journey.

ROBERT C. (BOB) EDWARDS, Calgary *Eye Opener*, July 17, 1920.

Trouble is good for mankind. When you are in trouble you get an understanding of life and you find the answers to many questions.

F.H. VARLEY, qu. in *Maclean's*, Nov. 7, 1959, 71.

Trudeau, Pierre E.

His political fate will likely be the political fate of Canada.

KENNETH MCNAUGHT, in *Nationalism in Canada*, 1966, 70.

What if I faint when he comes by?

ANON., Delegate's wife, Liberal Leadership Convention, Ottawa, Apr., 1968, qu. in P. Newman, *Distemper of our times*, 1968, 461.

Pierre is better than medicare — the lame have only to touch his garments to walk again.

JOSEPH R. SMALLWOOD, at Chaudiere Golf & Country Club, Ottawa, Apr. 3, 1968, qu. in P. Newman, *Distemper of our times*, 1968, 460.

He is the man for today. He is the man for tomorrow. He is the man, who, if he gets a majority in the House of Commons, will help to hold his country together and help to move it forward in the right direction to a great future.

LESTER B. PEARSON, speech, City Hall, Toronto, June 19, 1968.

Trudeaumania.

ANON., term describing a phenomenon which swept the country in 1968.

The only constant factor to be found in my thinking over the years has been opposition to accepted opinions. Had I applied this principle to the stock market, I might have made a fortune. I chose to apply it to politics and it led me to power — a result I had not really desired, or even expected.

PIERRE E. TRUDEAU, *Federalism and the French Canadians*, 1968, xix.

Pierre Elliott Trudeau, Prime Minister of Canada, anticipated the 20th century by his French-Canadian tradition. French Canada doesn't have an 18th century or a 19th century to obscure its awareness of the 20th. Backward societies always begin with the latest.

MARSHALL MCLUHAN, *N.Y. Times book rev.*, Nov. 17, 1968, 36.

It is the PM's technique of maximizing options: keeping as many open for as long a time as possible, making supporters feel that great studies are in progress while confirming sceptics in their growing doubts.

LEWIS HERTZMAN, *Alliances and illusions*, 1969, 20.

There but for the grace of Pierre Elliott Trudeau sits God.

DAVID LEWIS, H. of C., *Debates*, July 24, 1969, 11576.

Just watch me!

> PIERRE E. TRUDEAU, response to questioner on how far was he prepared to go in retaliating against separatists' terror tactics, Oct. 13, 1970.

The election is about money, efficiency and human rights. Dope and death and public morals. Law and order in our streets. And yet for many Canadians, after all the speeches and razzmatazz, it is about only one thing. Trudeau.

> TORONTO GLOBE AND MAIL, Oct. 28, 1972, 6, editorial.

I don't like my family life mixed up in politics.

> PIERRE E. TRUDEAU, to reporters in an interview, re: changing diapers, etc., 1972.

He functions best when the people are removed. So do his advisers. They're – futurecrats.

> PETER CALAMAI, science writer, on the government during general election, Oct., 1972, qu., Maclean's, Jan., 1973, 56.

I want to speak of him as a person, as a loving human being who has taught me in the three years we have been married and in the few years before that, a lot about loving.

> MARGARET TRUDEAU, to West Vancouver rally, June 4, 1974, during federal election campaign, qu. in Vancouver Sun, 5 June, 1974, 1.

Trust

As a freeborn British subject I feel that to trust any man as an equal, be he a dustman or a dupe, I am paying him the highest compliment in my power.

> PETER MCARTHUR, To be taken with salt, 1903, 149.

Men are able to trust one another, knowing the exact degree of dishonesty they are entitled to expect.

> STEPHEN B. LEACOCK, "The woman question", Maclean's, Oct., 1915.

I would not trust him with a hot stove. He will go out of here wealthier than any of you fellows when you leave the government.

> PETER CASHIN, Legis. Assem., Newfoundland, about Oct., 1950, ref. to Dr. Alfred Valdamis, economist hired by Premier Smallwood in early 1950. Four years later Valdamis pleaded guilty to defrauding the Nfld. govt. of $200,000; qu. in R. Gwyn, Smallwood, 1960, 148.

Truth

Speak the truth and feel it.

> JOSEPH HOWE, address to Halifax Mechanics' Institute, Sept. 11, 1845.

There is no standard for truth. We cannot even agree on the meaning of words.

> GEORGE BROWN, speech in St. Lawrence Hall, Toronto, July, 1851.

The laws of creation insist on respect;
Believe in the virtues of cause and
  effect;
Trust only to truth, and you'll ne'er be
  misled,
If you would be master and sit at the
  head.

> ALEXANDER MCLACHLAN, "If you would be master", 1874.

Standing on tiptoe ever since my
    youth
  Striving to grasp the future just
    above,
I hold at length the only future –
    Truth,
  And Truth is Love.

> GEORGE F. CAMERON, "Standing on tiptoe", 1885.

In seeking absolute truth we aim at the unattainable, and must be content with broken portions.

> SIR WILLIAM OSLER, "Aequanimitas", May 1, 1889.

To define a truth is to limit its scope.

> PETER MCARTHUR, *To be taken with salt*, 1903, 155.

Every clear statement of truth is a blasphemy against error.

> PETER MCARTHUR, *To be taken with salt*, 1903, 156.

The truth is the best you can get with your best endeavour, the best that the best men accept – with this you must learn to be satisfied, retaining at the same time with due humility an earnest desire for an ever larger portion.

> SIR WILLIAM OSLER, "The student life", address, Montreal, Apr. 14, 1905.

He had grasped as but few men have done the great truth that nothing really matters very much.

> STEPHEN LEACOCK, "A rehabilitation of Charles II", in *University mag.*, 1906, 267.

In historical subjects, truth is not only stranger than fiction; it is frequently more artistic.

> C.W. JEFFERYS, *Can. hist. rev.*, Dec., 1941, 367.

We need fear no sacrednesses. Truth has nothing to fear from the earnest and sincere research for the truth.

> G. BROCK CHISHOLM, speech at New York, Oct. 29, 1945.

It matters little whether things happened as they are said to have happened.

> FARLEY MOWAT, *People of the deer*, 1952, 165.

I like to call a spade a spade, especially the one that is going to bury me.

> IRVING LAYTON, *The swinging flesh*, 1961, ix.

My blasphemy's a synonym for truth
in these stifled courtrooms
where God on the witness stand
identifies Himself, hand over mouth,
inaudibly.

> GWENDOLYN MACEWEN, "Child of light", 1962.

One often has to distort a thing to catch its true spirit.

> ROBERT FLAHERTY, qu. in A. Calder-Marshall, *The innocent eye*, 1963, 97.

My friends, you say "Give 'em hell, John!" I never do that. I tell the truth and it sounds like hell. It simply sounds that way to the Grits.

> JOHN G. DIEFENBAKER, speech at Moncton, N.B., Mar. 13, 1963.

The deepest truths
are in their opposites.

> GUSTAV DAVIDSON, "In their opposites", 1966.

No idea is anything more than a half-truth unless it contains its own opposite, and is expanded by its own denial or qualification.

> NORTHROP FRYE, *The modern century*, 1967, 116.

The supply of truth in this world, though sharply limited, is yet more than adequate to meet the demand.

> RICHARD J. NEEDHAM, *A friend in Needham*, 1969, 20.

I'm constantly reminded of what my grandfather told me: the moon shines just as much on a handful of water as on a lake. We may find truth under a pebble. Truth is probably very small.

> RAYMOND MORIYAMA, qu. in *Maclean's*, Mar., 1970, 62.

Trying

I've done my best, and I begin to see
what is meant by the "joy of the
strife". Next to trying and winning,
the best thing is trying and failing.

> L.M. MONTGOMERY, *Anne of Green Gables*, 1908, 398.

Just have one more try – it's dead
easy to die,
It's the keeping-on-living that's hard.

> ROBERT W. SERVICE, "The quitter", 1912.

Tupper, Sir Charles

The Cumberland War-horse.

> ANON., a popular name for Tupper from
> the name of the Nova Scotia constituency which he represented in the legislature and parliament from 1855 to 1884.

I have been defeated by the future
leader of the Conservative party.

> JOSEPH HOWE, 1855, a comment on his
> defeat by Tupper for election to the
> N.S. Assembly as member for Cumberland.

I will not play second fiddle to that
damned Tupper.

> JOSEPH HOWE, 1864, on his refusal to go
> to the confederation conferences at
> Charlottetown and Quebec.

Oratorical and obstetrical.

> LORD ROSEBERY, *Journal*, Oct. 29, 1873.

Pacific in trouble; you should be here.

> SIR JOHN A. MACDONALD, cablegram to
> Sir Charles Tupper in London, Dec.1,
> 1883, a ref. to the Canadian Pacific
> Railway.

I have only to reply that nothing the
hon. gentlemen could say would degrade any member of the House.

> ALEXANDER MACKENZIE, Prime Minister,
> H. of C., *Debates*, Apr. 1, 1876, 1004.

Your presence during election contest
in Maritime Provinces essential to encourage our friends. Please come. Answer.

> SIR JOHN A. MACDONALD, cablegram to
> Sir Charles Tupper in London, Jan. 21,
> 1891.

In my judgment, the chief characteristic of Tupper was courage; courage
which no obstacle could down, which
rushed to the assault, and which, if
repulsed, came back to the combat
again and again; courage which battered and hammered, perhaps not always judiciously, but always effectively; courage which never admitted defeat and which in the midst of overwhelming disaster ever maintained the
proud carriage of unconquerable defiance.

> SIR WILFRID LAURIER, H. of C., *Debates*,
> Feb. 7, 1916, 584.

Twentieth Century

In the next century Canada may be
expected to assume a somewhat similar position to that occupied by the
United States in the last.

> J.B. TYRRELL, in Dawson (Yukon) *Daily
> times*, Jan. 1, 1901.

Last century was the United States'
century. The present is Canada's century.

> GEORGE JOHNSON, in *Commonwealth*
> (Ottawa), Jan., 1901, 4.

The nineteenth century was the century of the United States. The twentieth century is Canada's century.

> JAMES W. LONGLEY, Attorney-General of
> Nova Scotia, speech in Boston, Apr. 8,
> 1902; qu., Toronto *Globe*, Apr. 12, 1902.

As the 19th century was that of the United States, so I think the 20th century shall be filled by Canada.

> SIR WILFRID LAURIER, speech, Canadian Club, Ottawa, Jan. 18, 1904.

The Twentieth Century shall be the century of Canada and of Canadian development.

> SIR WILFRID LAURIER, speech in Toronto, Oct. 14, 1904.

It has been observed on the floor of this House, as well as outside of this House, that as the nineteenth century had been the century of the United States, so the twentieth century would be the century of Canada.

> SIR WILFRID LAURIER, H. of C., *Debates*, Feb. 21, 1905, 1422.

Last century made the world a neighborhood; this century must make it a brotherhood.

> J.S. WOODSWORTH, *University mag.*, Feb., 1917.

The twentieth century is the bathroom's century. True, the bathroom shares that century with the Dominion of Canada; but now that we have experienced nearly thirty years out of the hundred, I feel that Canada can well afford to let the bathroom have what is left.

> B.K. SANDWELL, *The privacity agent*, 1928, 20.

The twentieth century was once supposed to belong to Canada, but it seems more and more likely that only the first quarter of the century was really ours.

> F.W. BURTON, in *Can. journ. econ. and pol. sci.*, 1936, 598.

If this is to be Canada's century it will also be the century of the New Canadians.

> SHEILA PATTERSON, *Queen's quart.*, Vol. 62, 1955, 82.

Some sixty years ago Sir Wilfrid Laurier declared that the twentieth century belongs to Canada. By the middle of the century it had become clear that Canada belongs to the United States.

> KARI LEVITT, *Silent surrender*, 1970, 58.

Twins

There's two of twins — oh, it must be
　　fun
To go double at everything,
To holler by twos, and to run by twos,
　　To whistle by twos and to sing!

> JEAN BLEWETT, "The boy of the house", 1897.

Two Nations Theory

There are in this country two founding peoples. *You put that down.* We might translate it in French "two nations". You will translate it "two founding races of people" if you want. We cannot say "people" because "*people*" in our case doesn't mean nation, the same way as "nation" in English doesn't mean "*nation*". But let us be reasonable and admit that I can tell you this, and you can listen, and hear, and understand.

> MARCEL FARIBAULT, informal statement, Progressive Conservative Party, Montmorency Conference, Courville, Que., Aug. 7-10, 1967.

That Canada is and should be a federal state. That Canada is composed of two founding peoples (deux nations), with historic rights who have been joined by people from many lands. That the constitution should be such as to permit and encourage their full and harmonious growth and development in equality throughout Canada.

PROGRESSIVE CONSERVATIVE PARTY, *Report on the Montmorency conference,* Courville, Que., Aug. 7-10, 1967, 104, report of the Committee on the Constitution.

If Canada cannot become a political community – one community not two – it is not worth preserving.

DONALD V. SMILEY, *The Canadian political nationality,* 1967, 128.

Typewriters

The typewriter fuses composition and publication, causing an entirely new attitude to the written and printed word.

MARSHALL MCLUHAN, *Understanding media,* 1964, 260.

Ugliness

All ugliness is a distortion
of the lovely lines and curves
which sincerity makes out of hands
and bodies moving in air.

    LOUIS DUDEK, *Europe*, 1954, 95.

Ukrainians

Leave them alone and pretty soon the
Ukrainians will think they won the
battle of Trafalgar.

    STEPHEN B. LEACOCK, *My discovery of
the West*, 1937, 159.

The Ukranians cleared more land in
Western Canada than the French did.

    D.A. ZAHARIA, qu. in Creery, *French for
the French*, 1963, 13.

Umpires

I *always* dispute the umpire's verdict.

    LORD BEAVERBROOK, early years as Brit-
ish M.P., about 1910, qu. in Alan Wood,
The true history of Lord Beaverbrook,
1965, 59.

Uncertainty

I try but I cannot confirm or deny it
I can do nothing to prove or justify it
I could apologize but after all
I am not even certain that it is my
    fault.

    GEORGE JONAS, "Conclusion", 1962.

Understanding

There's a wonderful family called
    Stein —
There's Gert, and there's Ep, and
    there's Ein;
    Gert's poems are bunk
    Ep's statues are junk
And no one can understand Ein.

    ARTHUR H.R. BULLER, (University of Ma-
nitoba; d. 1944), "The Steins".

If what we say and do is quick and
    intense,
And if in our minds we see the end
    before starting,
It is not fear, but understanding that
    holds us.

    F.R. SCOTT, "Meeting", 1954.

Who has the cunning to apprehend
Even everyday easy things
Like air and wind and a fool
Or the structure and colour of a simple
    soul?

    ANNE WILKINSON, "One or three or two",
1955.

Undersense the kept webs widen
of spidery light and sudden centres
of comprehension.

    GWENDOLYN MACEWEN, "Poem for
G.W.", 1963.

Our society lives simultaneously on so
many levels of opinion and experience
that mutual understanding requires
the most strenuous effort.

    ROBERT FULFORD, *Saturday night*, May,
1969, 17.

There is a tendency, it is not infrequent in the culture to which I belong and want to belong, to derive a great deal of pleasure out of just understanding things and saying them. I have a great deal of distrust for this tendency to think that you solve problems just by thinking about them.

PIERRE JUNEAU, qu. by Blaik Kirby in Toronto *Globe and Mail*, Mar. 14, 1970, 27.

Undertakers

The all-important facet concerns the allaying of grief. With the recent recognition of this factor, funeral men have characteristically allowed their imaginations to run wild, coining phrases such as "grief therapy" and "memory picture". Some have even gone so far as to suggest that the purchaser of an expensive funeral relieves people of a sense of guilt for having failed the deceased in some manner during his life.

ROBERT FORREST, *Death here is thy sting*, 1967, 118.

Unemployment

Facing that situation he found it necessary, in order to do what he thought would satisfy the unemployed, to ask not for $20,000,000, $40,000,000, $60,000,000, $80,000,000, or $1,000,000,000, but to ask this parliament to give a blank cheque which he might fill in for as much as he wished to draw.

W.L. MACKENZIE KING, H. of C., *Debates*, Feb. 8, 1932, 37, on the policy of R.B. Bennett; origin of the phrase "blank cheque".

The biggest fraud in Canada is a regular annual affair. It is perpetrated by thousands of people (nobody knows how many) and runs to millions of dollars (nobody knows how much). The victim of this continuous con game is the Unemployment Insurance Fund.

BLAIR FRASER, in *Maclean's*, June 1968, 30.

Canadians don't hate unemployment but they hate the unemployed.

REUBEN BAETZ, executive director, Canadian Council on Social Development, qu. in Vancouver *Sun*, Feb. 28, 1972, 5.

Unemployment really is a good wage, people can live on it really well. I didn't find time heavy on my hands. I found life more meaningful. I found I could start doing things. I had time to talk to people, time to read, time to understand myself. I could just relax and go to beaches when I felt like it. I had a wonderful time.

ANON., a young Canadian, qu. in Toronto *Globe and Mail*, May 1, 1972, 1.

We're not going to allow the Prime Minister to descend to the grubby level of discussing unemployment. He's having a dialogue with the people about the Canadian identity.

JIM DAVEY, Pierre E. Trudeau's press secretary, to Liberal Party election campaign organization in Ottawa, early Oct. 1972, qu. in *Maclean's*, Jan., 1973, 67.

Unicorns

On the Canadian border there are sometimes seen animals resembling horses, but with cloven hoofs, rough manes, a long straight horn upon the forehead, a curled tail like that of a wild boar, black eyes, and a neck like that of the stag.

> O. DAPPER, *Die unbekannte neue Welt*, 1673. (Trans.)

Union

The hour is ripe for union,
And spirit takes communion
From every living touch.

> F.R. SCOTT, "Dialogue", 1945.

Union, 1841-1867

I was, and still am, an advocate of the union of the provinces, but an advocate not of a union of parchment, but a union of hearts and of free born men.

> ROBERT BALDWIN, speech in Legis. Assembly, Kingston, qu., Kingston *Chronicle and gazette*, Sept. 17, 1842. Daniel O'Connell, the Irish agitator, first used the phrase, "A union on parchment".

The only hope felt for the British Party in Upper Canada is a dissolution of the Union; and this conviction aided by the exasperation if the Seat of Government should be placed in Lower Canada, will produce a strong desire for that remedy.

> SIR CHARLES METCALFE, letter to Lord Stanley, July 19, 1843. (Pub.Arch.Can.)

A man and his wife might agree to separate, but what were they to do with the children?

> MALCOLM CAMERON, speech at Reform Convention, Toronto, Nov. 9, 1859.

Whatever you do adhere to the Union — we are a great country, and shall become one of the greatest in the universe if we preserve it; we shall sink into insignificance and adversity if we suffer it to be broken.

> SIR JOHN A. MACDONALD, speech, 1861, qu. in E.B. Biggar, *Anecdotal life*, 1891, 182.

The half civilized people of the sterile shores of the Saguenay — the shivering squatters away up by the Temiscouata Lake — had more political power vested in them than the wealthy, and substantial farmers and tradesmen on the shores of Lake Huron, or Lake Erie. The latter *paid* the taxes, the former controlled them.

> HALIFAX *MORNING CHRONICLE*, Sept. 29, 1864, correspondent's report of Sept. 19, 1864, from Niagara.

Union Jack

Upon the Heights of Queenston one
  dark October day,
Invading foes were marshalled in
  battle's dread array.
Brave Brock, looked up the rugged
  steep and planned a bold attack;
"No foreign flag shall float," said he,
  a-bove the Union Jack."

> ANON., "The Battle of Queenston Heights", about 1824.

All hail to the day when the Britons
  came over,
  And planted their standard, with
  sea-foam still wet,
Around and above us their spirits will
  hover,
  Rejoicing to mark how we honor it
  yet.
Beneath it the emblems they cherished
  are waving
  The Rose of Old England the
  roadside perfumes;
The Shamrock and Thistle the north
  winds are braving,
  Securely the Mayflower blushes and
  blooms.

> JOSEPH HOWE, "The flag of old England", ("Song for the centenary"), June 8, 1849. Written for the one hundredth anniversary of the landing of Lord Cornwallis at Halifax. Howe also wrote "Song for the 8th June", with a first verse as follows:

Hail to the day when the Briton came
    o'er
  And planted his flag where the
    Mayflower blows,
And gathered the blossoms, unheeded
    before,
  To entwine with the Shamrock, the
    Thistle, the rose.

A union of hearts, A union of hands,
A union no man can sever,
A union of tongues, A union of lands,
And the flag — British union forever.

> LINDSAY (ONT.) *WARDER*, motto on mast-head; Sam Hughes was owner from 1885.

We were taunted with waving the old flag; and a lot of traitors, a lot of cowards who have not the courage to be traitors, although they have the will, would sneer at the old flag: sneer at the loyalty we inherited from our fathers; sneer at the institutions which our fathers were so proud to leave us.

> SIR JOHN THOMPSON, speech in Toronto Auditorium, Jan. 14, 1893.

It's only a small piece of bunting,
It's only an old coloured rag;
Yet thousands have died for its honour,
And shed their best blood for the flag.

> JAMES C. MORGAN, "The Union Jack" ("For Queen and Country"), in Borth-wick, ed., Poems, *South African War*, 1901, 1. Morgan was inspector of schools, Barrie and North Simcoe; died 1922.

Men of Canada: keep both hands on the Union Jack.

> LORD DUNDONALD, July 26, 1904, speech on leaving Ottawa, after dismissal as General Officer Commanding, Canadian forces. See: Fred Cook, *Fifty years ago – and since*, in Ottawa *Citizen*, July-Oct., 1934, who gives credit to Sam Hughes.

Then may it wave o'er land and sea,
  Through time's eternal space:
Equality and liberty
  Beneath it find their place.
No change of Flag, no change of State
  Do I e'er want to see;
For the flag that's waved a thousand
    years
  Is good enough for me.

> JOHN A. PHILLIPS, "The flag for me", ca.1945; by a member of the Press Gallery, Ottawa.

Newfoundland will continue to fly the Union Jack if we are the last place on earth to do so.

> JOSEPH SMALLWOOD, May, 1964, qu. in R. Gwyn, *Smallwood the unlikely revolutionary*, 1968, 228.

Union Nationale

Help yourself and heaven will help you. Or, help yourself and the Union Nationale will help you. These two expressions are synonymous.

> MAURICE DUPLESSIS, phrases frequently repeated in his speeches as Premier of Quebec, 1936-39, 1944-59. (Trans.)

The Union Nationale is ready to set the table, to prepare the food, to cook it, and to put it in your mouth. But it would like you to do your own chewing.

> MAURICE DUPLESSIS, phrases frequently repeated in his speeches as Premier of Quebec, 1936-39, 1944-59. (Trans.)

Unisex

If women keep on demanding a vote, cropping their hair, opposing us in the professions, wearing our coats, hats and shirts, and if men continue nursing babies, promoting female dress reform, and using curling tongs, first thing we know there will be a blurred line denoting a merging of the sexes. That would be a fine development in human anatomy with which to mark the close of the nineteenth century.

EDMUND E. SHEPPARD, Editor, in *Saturday night*, May 13, 1893, 1.

United Church

A reflection of the growing dominance of secular values associated with politics and big business.

DELBERT CLARK, *Church and sect in Canada*, 1948, 431. Refers to the formation of the United Church in 1925.

United Empire Loyalists

Late Loyalists.

ANON., a term sometimes scornful, applied to immigrants from the United States after 1785.

When great cataclysms occur in human affairs money becomes dross and men victims. So it was with the loyalists of America. They were sacrificed, and between the upper millstone of the colonies and the nether millstone of the British ministry they were ground into powder. So it ever has been, so it is, and so it ever will be in revolutions.

JOHN WATTS DE PEYSTER, address to N.B. Historical Society, St. John, July 4, 1883.

They would not spurn the glorious old
To grasp the gaudy new.
Of yesterday's rebellion born
They held the upstart power in scorn
To Britain they stood true.

REV. LEROY HOOKER, "The United Empire Loyalists", 1885.

What did they then, those loyal men,
When Britain's cause was lost?
Did they consent
And dwell content
Where Crown, and Law, and
Parliament
Were trampled in the dust?

REV. LEROY HOOKER, "The United Empire Loyalists", 1885.

O Ye, who with your blood and sweat
Watered the furrows of this land,
See where upon a nation's brow
In honour's front, ye proudly stand!

SARAH A. CURZON, "Loyal", 1887.

You Canadians should be proud of the founders of your country. The United Empire Loyalists were a grand type of loyal, law-abiding, God-fearing men. No country ever had such founders, no country in the world. No, not since the days of Abraham!

LADY EMILY TENNYSON, about 1895, to George T. Denison, qu. in *Soldiering in Canada*, 1900, 3.

They passed down the silent rivers
which flow to the mighty lake;
They left what they'd made for
England (but those who have made
can make),
And founded a new dominion for God
and their country's sake.

CLIVE PHILLIPPS-WOLLEY, "The United Empire Loyalists", 1917.

In the loyalist migrations at the close of the revolution, the United States had sown the neighbouring provinces with dragon's teeth, and every reformer from Gourlay to Baldwin reaped an ineradicable harvest of prejudice and suspicion.

CHESTER MARTIN, in *Can. hist. rev.*, 1937, 3.

In its new wilderness home and its new aspect of British North Americanism, colonial Toryism made its second attempt to erect on American soil a copy of the English social edifice. From one point of view this is the most significant thing about the Loyalist movement; it withdrew a class concept of life from the south, moved it up north and gave it a second chance.

A.R.M. LOWER, *From colony to nation*, 1946, 114.

On one hand they brought to Canada a conservative outlook, a quick distrust of any new idea that might be called republican, and a readiness to make loyalty the test for almost everything. On the other, they themselves represented a declaration of independence against the United States, a determination to live apart from that country in North America. As a result, they helped to create not only a new province, but a new nation.

J.M.S. CARELESS, *Canada, a story of challenge*, 1953, 113.

Such settlers, accustomed to the schools and books of their native provinces, found it hard to accept prevailing Canadian conditions of ignorance.

A.R.M. LOWER, *Canadians in the making*, 1958, 165.

United Nations

United Nations.

HENRY WENTWORTH MONK, phrase coined in late 19th century; qu. in R.S. Lambert, *For the time is at hand*, 1947, 10; Monk died in 1896.

It is truly appalling how far the Russians have been permitted and have been able to get ahead in the four years since the war. I cannot but have the feeling that the United Nations with its fiddling and fussing and interfering in everything and affording them the platform they have had, has been responsible as was the League of Nations for enabling the situation to develop to the point it has, a perfectly appalling menace.

W.L. MACKENZIE KING, *Diary*, Mar. 19, 1948, qu. in J.W. Pickersgill and D.F. Forster, *The Mackenzie King record*, Vol. 4, 1947-48, 1970, 177.

It is sheer madness and wanton folly the way in which the United Nations have rushed into these commitments in different places of the world, and, worst of all, the way in which Canada has tagged along at their tail, cheering them on the way as though they were a world power which could effect miracles.

W.L. MACKENZIE KING, *Diary*, Mar. 20, 1948, qu. in J.W. Pickersgill and D.F. Forster, *The Mackenzie King record, 1947-48*, Vol. 4, 1970, 178.

I have been scandalized more than once by the attitude of the larger powers, the big powers as we call them, who have all too frequently treated the charter of the United Nations as an instrument with which to regiment smaller nations and as an instrument which did not have to be considered when their own so-called vital interests were at stake.

LOUIS ST. LAURENT, H. of C., *Debates*, Special Session, 1956-57, 20.

When you come right down to it, the Canadian delegation is the best at the United Nations. Can't understand why.

ANON., a British journalist, qu. by Earl Berger, Toronto *Globe and Mail*, Nov. 27, 1962, 6.

The Canadians give the impression of being typical of their country: affable, plainspoken, and "provincial". But, however broad their accents, they lack neither subtlety nor sophistication. Some delegates are political appointments, politicians, and business men, but their calibre is, frankly, surprisingly high.

EARL BERGER, Toronto *Globe and Mail*, Nov. 27, 1962, 6.

There is something extremely humbling to be at an international organization and note on every hand the high respect in which Canadians are held. I think it is humbling because it is quite a challenge to measure up to the tremendous responsibility constantly put upon Canadians, especially in the U.N. context.

HEATH MACQUARRIE, H. of C., *Debates*, Jan. 24, 1963, 3102.

Our position is one of respectable importance, while we are not big enough to alarm anybody or dominate anybody's way of life. We have American plumbing without American power.

LESTER B. PEARSON, address to the Canadian Club of Ottawa, Press Release, Feb. 10, 1965, 2.

United States

The government of Mr. Lincoln is a standing monument of incompetence and wickedness.

TORONTO *LEADER*, Jan. 4, 1862.

In going from the States into Canada an Englishman is struck by the feeling that he is going from a richer country into one that is poorer, and from a greater country into one that is less.

ANTHONY TROLLOPE, *North America*, 1862, 43.

The Monarchical government of England is a truer application of real Republican principles than that of the United States, and I have no hesitation in saying that the government of Canada is far in advance, in the application of real Republican principles, of the Government of either England or the United States.

EDWARD BLAKE, speech at Aurora, Ont., Oct. 3, 1874.

Oh the Dutch may have their Holland,
  the Spaniards have their Spain,
The Yankee to the south of us must
  south of us remain.

PAULINE JOHNSON, "Canadian born", 1903.

We are living beside a great neighbour who, I believe I can say without being deemed unfriendly to them, are very grasping in their national acts, and who are determined upon every occasion to get the best in any agreement which they make.

SIR WILFRID LAURIER, H. of C., *Debates*, Oct. 23, 1903, 14814.

Little Canada.

ANON., a reference to New England, so-called during the nineteenth century because of the influx of French Canadians.

We have one neighbor and one only, and that one an industrial colossus. It lies for four thousand miles along our border, producing what we produce, and doing constant but legitimate battle to forestall us in the world's markets and in our own. There is the dominating fact that meets Canadians every morning.

ARTHUR MEIGHEN, address at Guildhall, London, on receiving the Freedom of the City, July 15, 1921.

Nothing is more conspicuously lacking in Canada than a generous recognition of the greatness of the American people, in the sense in which they are one of the great peoples of the world.

H.F. ANGUS, *Canada and her great neighbor*, 1938, 342.

The perversity and inherent disposition of elected representatives to betray the public interest are indeed almost assumed in the United States as a constitutional principle.

GEORGE W. BROWN, Can. Hist. Assoc., *Report*, 1944, 9.

What Ottawa thinks today Washington will say tomorrow.

> WILLIAM W. WADE, *International jour.*, 1951, 41.

God looks after fools, drunkards and the United States of America.

> STEPHEN LEACOCK, qu. by Hugh MacLennan, in *Holiday*, Nov. 1958, 55.

To think ill of the dominant American tradition must not allow one to forget that which remains straight and clear among Americans themselves. Living next to them, Canadians should know better than most how incomplete are the stereotyped gibes of Europeans. The cranes and the starlings still fly high through their skies; sane and wise families grow up; people strive to be good citizens; some men still think. Above all, many Americans have seen with clarity the nature of that which chokes them and seek for ways to live beyond it.

> GEORGE P. GRANT, in Al Purdy, ed., *The new Romans*, 1968, 41.

I like America and Americans. I admire them. I've always been profoundly grateful that Canada shares this continent with the American people; God bless America, as I think both Frank Underhill and Marshall McLuhan have said, for saving us from the fate of Australia.

> ROBERT FULFORD, in Al Purdy ed., *The new Romans*, 1968, 50.

O say does that star-spangled banner
   yet wave
O'er the land of debris,
And the home of the grave?

> JAMES EAYRS, in Apr., 1970, repr. in *Greenpeace and her enemies*, 1973, 58.

Unity

Union, Peace, Friendship, and Fraternity.

> LOUIS H. LAFONTAINE, words addressed

to Reformers of Upper Canada, 1841; motto used over platform on which Laurier spoke at Toronto, Oct. 16, 1900.

And oh it were a glorious deed
To show before mankind
How every race and every creed
Might be by love combined;
Might be combined yet still would
   show
The sources whence they rose
As filled with many a rivulet
The lordly Shannon flows.

> T. D'A. MCGEE, (age 17), July 4, 1842, Boston, Mass., address to the people.

The blood of no brother, in civil strife
   poured,
In this hour of rejoicing encumbers our
   souls!
The frontier's the field for the patriot's
   sword,
And cursed is the weapon that faction
   controls!

> JOSEPH HOWE, "The flag of old England", 1848.

One voice, one people, one in heart
and soul, and feeling, and desire.

> CHARLES SANGSTER, "Brock", in *Hesperus*, 1864.

I view the diversity of races in British North America in this way: we are of different races, not for the purpose of warring against each other, but in order to compete and emulate for the general good.

> SIR GEORGE-ETIENNE CARTIER, *Confederation debates*, Feb. 7, 1865, 60.

Now, when we were united together, if union were attained, we would form a political nationality with which neither the national origin, nor the religion of any individual would interfere.

> SIR GEORGE-ETIENNE CARTIER, *Confederation debates*, Feb. 7, 1865, 60.

Let but our statesmen do their duty, with the consciousness that all the elements which constitute greatness are now awaiting a closer combination; that all the requirements of a national higher life are here available for use; that nations do not spring Minerva-like into existence; that strength and weakness are relative terms, a few not being necessarily weak because they are few, nor a multitude necessarily strong because they are many; that hesitating, doubting, fearing, whining over supposed or even actual weakness, and conjuring up possible dangers, is not the true way to strengthen the foundations of our Dominion, to give confidence to its continuance.

WILLIAM A. FOSTER, *Canada first*, 1871, 46.

Is there a man amongst us who forgets that when Papineau was struggling for the rights of his race and for the constitutional liberty which we to-day enjoy, his principal coadjutors were John Nelson, the Scotchman, and O'Callaghan, the Irishman?

SIR WILFRID LAURIER, speech in Quebec, 1877.

Shall we not be one race, shaping and
   wielding the nation?
Is not our country too broad for the
   schisms which shake petty lands?
Yea, we shall join in our might, and
   keep sacred our firm federation,
Shoulder to shoulder arrayed, hearts
   open to hearts, hands to hands.

BARRY STRATON, "85", 1884.

Father of Unity, make this people one.

CHARLES G.D. ROBERTS, "A collect for Dominion Day", 1885.

Below the island of Montreal the water that comes from the north from Otta-

wa unites with the waters that come from the western lakes, but uniting they do not mix. There they run parallel, separate, distinguishable, and yet are one stream, flowing within the same banks, the mighty St. Lawrence, and rolling on toward the sea bearing the commerce of a nation upon its bosom – a perfect image of our nation.

SIR WILFRID LAURIER, speech at Toronto, Dec. 10, 1886.

Were those not brave old races?
   Well, here they still abide;
And yours is one or other,
   And the second's at your side.

W.D. LIGHTHALL, "The battle of La Prairie", 1889.

The one calamity above all others which stands before this country is that political division should follow the division of race or the division of religion. The one danger which menaces the future of this country and the union of this country, now so happily being accomplished is that men should stand arrayed against each other on the question of government, because they differ with regard to religion, because they differ with regard to race.

SIR JOHN THOMPSON, Sept., 1892, qu. in J.C. Hopkins, *Life and work of the Rt. Hon. Sir John Thompson*, 1895, 300.

All Canadians ought to recognize that in a community in which three-fifths are English and Protestant, and two-fifths French and Catholic, concessions and accommodations; assurances and performances of them; toleration, friendliness and sympathy must characterize their political and social relations.

JOHN S. EWART, *The Manitoba school question: a reply to Mr. Wade*, 1895, 41.

If there is anything to which I have given my political life, it is to try to promote unity, harmony and amity between the diverse elements of this country. My friends can desert me, they can remove their confidence from me, they can withdraw the trust they have placed in my hands but never shall I deviate from that line of policy. Whatever may be the consequences, whether loss of prestige, loss of popularity, or loss of power, I feel that I am in the right.

SIR WILFRID LAURIER, H. of C., *Debates*, Mar. 13, 1900, 1842.

There is no bond of union so strong as the bond created by common dangers shared in common.

SIR WILFRID LAURIER, H. of C., *Debates*, Mar. 13, 1900, 1847.

Fraternity without absorption, union without fusion.

SIR WILFRID LAURIER, a phrase used in speech to St. Jean Baptiste Soc., Montreal, June 25, 1901. (Trans.)

To search for the union of the two races of Canada beyond the mutual respect that they owe to their respective rights, is to build a nation on a fragile foundation, to give it as cornerstone an element of ruin and destruction.

HENRI BOURASSA, address, National Monument, Montreal, Apr. 17, 1905. (Trans.)

How are we to unify Canada? There is but one possible way: Make her a nation in name as well as in fact. Let her throw off her mean colonial wrappings and let her assume her rightful place among the nations of the world. Give us a common pride.

JOHN S. EWART, *Kingdom papers*, 1911, I, 55.

So long as the majority of Canadians have two countries, one here and one in Europe, national unity will remain a myth and a constant source of internecine quarrels.

HENRI BOURASSA, *Independence or imperial partnership?*, 1916, 54. (Pamphlet)

Let us draw closer in these narrower
 years,
Before us still the eternal visions
 spread;
We, who outmastered death, and all
 its fears,
Are one great army still – living and
 dead.

CANON FREDERICK G. SCOTT, "The unbroken line", 1922.

For all were pledged, with teeth and
 claws
To racial brood and comradeship,
Devoted to the national cause
And loyal to the boundary strip.

EDWIN J. PRATT, "The witches' brew", 1925.

To-day we are a united people, seeking first and foremost an enduring unity; not a unity which aims at uniformity, but a unity which delights in diversity.

W.L. MACKENZIE KING, *Message of the carillon*, 1927, 103.

Ours is a strange fraternity,
Forged by common calumny,
 And unified by slander.

VINCENT MASSEY, "The angler and the diplomat", Jan. 15, 1929.

I believe that Canada's first duty to the League [of Nations] and to the British Empire, with respect to all the great issues that come up, is, if possible, to keep this country united.

W.L. MACKENZIE KING, H. of C., *Debates*, Mar. 23, 1936, 1333.

Canadian national life can almost be said to take its rise in the negative will to resist absorption in the American Republic. It is largely about the United States as an object that the consciousness of Canadian national unity has grown up.

SAMUEL D. CLARK, in H.F. Angus, ed., *Canada and her great neighbor*, 1938, 243.

A strong and dominant national feeling is not a luxury in Canada, it is a necessity. Without it this country could not exist. A divided Canada can be of little help to any country, and least of all to itself.

W.L. MACKENZIE KING, H. of C., *Debates*, Mar. 30, 1939.

National unity and provincial autonomy must not be thought of as competitors for the citizen's allegiance for, in Canada at least, they are but two facets of the same thing – a sane federal system. National unity must be based on provincial autonomy, and provincial autonomy cannot be assured unless a strong feeling of national unity exists throughout Canada.

CANADA. ROY. COMM. ON DOMINION-PROVINCIAL RELATIONS, *Report*, II, 1940, 269.

You know as well as I, with as sharp
  pain –
Though we were never one, we are not
  twain.

AUDREY ALEXANDRA BROWN, "Postscript", 1943.

Two old races and religions meet here and live their separate legends, side by side.

HUGH MACLENNAN, *Two solitudes*, 1945, 4.

I believe in the unity of all life; in the unity of the urge which compels the atoms of quartz to array themselves in the form of a crystal; with the urge which holds the stars in their courses or which made me sit down to write this last will and testament of my life.

FREDERICK PHILIP GROVE, *In search of myself*, 1946, 230.

It is not enough for all to will the good of the nation; it is important to seek unanimously the methods needed to achieve it.

ESDRAS MINVILLE, *Le citoyen canadien-français*, 1946, Vol. 1, 101. (Trans.)

Here Spaniards and Vancouver's
  boatmen scrawled
the problem that is ours and yours,
that there is no clear Strait of Anian
to lead us easy back to Europe,
that men are isled in ocean or in ice
and only joined by long endeavour to
  be joined.

EARLE BIRNEY, "Pacific door", 1948.

Religions build walls round our love,
  and science
Is equal of error and truth. Yet always
  we find
Such ordered purpose in cell and in
  galaxy,
So great a glory in life-thrust and
  mind-range,
Such widening frontiers to draw out
  our longings,
  We grow to one world through
  Enlargement of wonder.

F.R. SCOTT, "A grain of rice", 1954.

Those who pretend to work for the formation of a single nation called "Canada" desire, consciously or unconsciously, the complete assimilation of the weaker nation by the stronger.

SOCIÉTÉ SAINT-JEAN-BAPTISTE DE MONTRÉAL, *Canada français et l'union canadienne*, 1954, 115. (Trans.)

On the day when every French Canadian, wherever he may be in the country, enjoys the same advantages and the same privileges as his English-speaking compatriot, the last obstacle to the unity of the country will have disappeared.

> GÉRARD FILION, Editor of *Le Devoir*, in *Saturday night*, Nov. 20, 1954, 8.

Canada is the heir of the two great formative traditions of Western Europe; it is her pride and her opportunity to develop both.

> DENIS W. BROGAN, in *Canada's tomorrow*, 1954, 284.

Canada has no cultural unity, no linguistic unity, no religious unity, no economic unity, no geographic unity. All it has is unity.

> KENNETH BOULDING, to a group of Toronto high school students, Nov., 1957; attributed.

Not life, liberty, and the pursuit of happiness, but peace, order, and good government are what the national government of Canada guarantees. Under these, it is assumed, life, liberty, and happiness may be achieved, but by each according to his taste. For the society of allegiance admits of a diversity the society of compact does not, and one of the blessings of Canadian life is that there is no Canadian way of life, much less two, but a unity under the Crown admitting of a thousand diversities.

> W.L. MORTON, *The Canadian identity*, 1961, 111.

Canada will achieve sooner and more powerfully the fusion of its dual cultural heritage by intellectual avenues rather than political.

> JEAN-C. FALARDEAU, *Roots and values in Canadian life*, 1961, 39.

We French, we English, never lost our
civil war,
endure it still, a bloodless civil bore;
no wounded lying about, no Whitman
wanted.
It's only by our lack of ghosts we're
haunted.

> EARLE BIRNEY, "Can. lit.", 1962.

The die is cast in Canada: there are two ethnic and linguistic groups; each is too strong and too deeply rooted in the past, too firmly bound to a mother culture, to be able to swamp the other. But if the two will collaborate inside of a truly pluralist state, Canada could become a privileged place where the federalist form of government, which is the government of tomorrow's world, will be perfected.

> PIERRE E. TRUDEAU, *Cité libre*, Apr., 1962, 15. (Trans.)

Most nations have been formed not by people who desired intensely to live together, but rather by people who could not live apart. That was the spirit of 1867: it will perhaps still be that of 1967.

> JEAN-CHARLES BONENFANT, *Rev. d'histoire de l'Amerique française*, June, 1963, 38. (Trans.)

Canada is one nation, or it is none.

> DUFF ROBLIN, Federal-Provincial Conference, Nov. 26-29, 1963, Ottawa, "Opening statement by the Premier of Manitoba".

Canadian unity is now more striking than Canadian duality.

> MORRIS G. BISHOP, *Champlain: the life of fortitude*, 1963, ix.

People coming from other lands have built a nation in which our varied identities are not thrown into a melting-pot but remain to make their own special contributions to the formation and the maturing of a Canadian identity. This is the very essence of the Canadian adventure, this diversity out of which must come unity.

LESTER B. PEARSON, address, Univ. of Western Ontario, May 29, 1964.

I've had a long and public love affair with Canada. It represents something of unique value. It is dedicated to the idea of unity without uniformity.

SAMUEL FREEDMAN, qu. in G. Clark, *Canada; the uneasy neighbour,* 1965, 47.

How can we integrate the new Quebec into present-day Canada, without curbing Quebec's forward drive and, at the same time, without risking the breaking up of the country?

CANADA. ROY. COMM. ON BILINGUALISM AND BICULTURALISM, *Report,* Vol. 1, 1967, xlvii.

The only unity worth having is one which will permit the greatest possible variety of individual and collective differences.

HUGH MACLENNAN, *The colour of Canada,* 1967, 15.

If we demand before this royal view,
What rub or what impediment there
    is,
Why that the naked, poor and
    mangled Peace,
Dear nurse of arts, plenties, and joyful
    births,
Should not in this best garden of the
    world,
Our fertile Canada, put up her lovely
    visage.

ANDREW BRICHANT, *Option Canada,* 1968, I (based on W. Shakespeare, *King Henry V* Act V, Sc. 2, line 33).

All things are plotting to make us
    whole
All things conspire to make us one.

GWENDOLYN MACEWEN, "The name of the place", 1969.

Should we constantly search for a consensus? Or should we open up deeper questions about power and political structures which will polarize our society into left and right?

CHARLES TAYLOR, *The pattern of politics,* 1970, 15.

The essential element in the national sense of unity is the east-west feeling, developed historically along the St. Lawrence-Great Lakes axis, and expressed in the national motto, *a mari usque ad mare.* The tension between this political sense of unity and the imaginative sense of locality is the essence of whatever the word "Canadian" means.

NORTHROP FRYE, *The bush garden,* Preface, 1971, iii.

So far as I am concerned, this is one whole country: and that is the way it is going to be.

NORMAN WARD, qu. in *One country or two?,* ed. by R.M. Burns,1971,14.

You and I are what Canada ought to be. We represent the two cultures but we do not fight.

THÉRÈSE F. CASGRAIN, to Frank R. Scott, qu. in foreword, *A woman in a man's world,* 1972.

Universe

I compassed time, outstripped the
    starry speed,
And in my soul apprehended space,
Till, weighing laws which these but
    blindly heed,
At last I came before Him face to
    face,

And knew the Universe of no such
    span
As the august infinitude of man.

    CHARLES G.D. ROBERTS, "In the wide awe
    and wisdom of the night", 1893.

The pulse of our life is in tune with the
    rhythm of forces that beat
In the surf of the farthest star's sea,
    and are spent and regathered to
    spend.

    FREDERICK GEORGE SCOTT, "A dream of
    the prehistoric", 1910.

Just try to get the Cosmic touch,
The sense that "you" don't matter
    much.
A million stars are in the sky;
A million planets plunge and die.
A million million men are sped;
A million million wait ahead.
Each plays his part and has his day —
What ho! the World's all right, I say.

    ROBERT W. SERVICE, "The world's all
    right", 1912.

Universities

From this college every blessing may
flow over your country. May it continue to dispense them to the latest ages!
Let no jealousy disturb its peace; let no
lukewarm indifference check its
growth!

    EARL OF DALHOUSIE, at laying of corner-
    stone of Dalhousie College, Halifax,
    May 22, 1820.

No undergraduate shall resort to any
Inn or Tavern, or place of public
amusement without special permission
of the Vice-Principal.

    MCGILL UNIVERSITY, rules for students,
    1840, qu. in Lena Newman, *Historical
    almanac of Canada*, May, 1967.

A college education shows a man how
devilish little other people know.

    T.C. HALIBURTON, *Sam Slick's wise saws*,
    1853, I, 53.

Baldwin's bill converted King's College into the University of Toronto, an
absolutely Godless institution according to the pietists.

    JOHN LANGTON, letter, Nov. 12, 1856.

The colleges with us are a hotbed of
conservatism.

    SIR WILFRID LAURIER, letter to Blake,
    July 10, 1882.

If I had had a university education, I
should probably have entered upon
the path of literature and acquired
distinction therein.

    SIR JOHN A. MACDONALD, qu. by Sir
    Joseph Pope, *The day of Sir John A.
    Macdonald*, 1915, 6.

A university has as its main aim to
supplement the weakness of the individual by the strength of the race.

    JOHN WATSON, in 1900, qu. by W.E.
    McNeil in Roy. Soc. Can., *Proceedings*,
    3d. Ser., Vol. 33, 1939, 161.

If I were founding a university I
would found first a smoking room;
then when I had a little more money
in hand I would found a dormitory;
then after that, or more probably with
it, a decent reading room and a library. After that, if I still had more
money that I couldn't use, I would hire
a professor and get some textbooks.

    STEPHEN B. LEACOCK, "Oxford as I see
    it", *Harper's mag.*, May, 1922.

Our boys and girls must be taught
Right ideas from the start.
There is a great danger
In independent thought —
We'll have none of it here.
No fear!

    A.J.M. SMITH, "College spirit", 1925.

Honoris causa — some one said,
    and all the seers and scholars
Rose up in reverent array and bowed
    the knee to dollars.

> WILSON MACDONALD, "Convocation", 1932.

The most important thing you learn at
    college
is how to live your life *selectively*,
to recognize the seal of excellence,
the caste-mark of those people one
    should know,
the hallmark of those books that one
    should read.

> KENNETH LESLIE, "Cobweb college", 1938.

Always the university must foster the
search for truth and in its search must
always question the pretentions of ora-
ganized power in the hands of church
or state. It will always favour the
existence of a number of centralized
powers in the hope that no one of
them will predominate and exert its
will and that individual freedom will
have a greater chance to survive. It
will always insist that any group which
pretends to have found the truth is a
fraud against civilization and that it is
the search for truth and not truth
which keeps civilization alive.

> HAROLD A. INNIS, "The Canadian situa-
> tion", unpublished address, qu. in Robin
> Néill, *A new theory of value*, 1972, 90.

The university must deny the finality
of any of the conclusions of the social
sciences. It must steadfastly resist the
tendency to acclaim any single solution to the world's problem at the risk
of failing to play its role as a balancing
factor in the growth of civilization.
The Marxist solution, the Keynesian
solution, or any solution, cannot be
accepted as final if the universities are
to continue and civilization is to survive.

> HAROLD A. INNIS, *Political economy in
> the modern state*, 1946, 141.

Campus in the clouds.

> DONALD CAMERON, title of book, pub-
> lished in 1956, on Banff School of Fine
> Arts.

Society may need, and certainly wants
prostitutes but I doubt that this is a
valid argument for a university degree
in the subject.

> E.W.R. STEACIE, address, Assoc. of the
> Universities of the British Common-
> wealth, Toronto, Aug. 26, 1956.

There is nothing more antagonistic to
original thought than business efficiency. In fact, as long as the Universities
can remain inefficient there is hope
for the world.

> E.W.R. STEACIE, address, St. Francis Xavi-
> er Univ., Aug. 29, 1957.

A university cannot be first-rate unless
intellect, passion for ideas, long hours
of work and devotion to one's course
are socially acceptable to the student
body. If the vulgar attitudes to the
longhair or the bookworm are repeated there, we have no university but
only a fresh air camp for the over-
privileged.

> NORTHROP FRYE, Installation address as
> Principal, Victoria College, Toronto,
> Oct. 21, 1959.

The tendency to regard manpower as
a commodity bought, sold, produced,
and consumed is objectionable when
applied to the end-product of an institution of higher learning.

> E.W.R. STEACIE, address, Roy. Soc. of
> Canada, Kingston, June, 1960.

How can universities evolve better
things for this world without both
freedom and local independence?

> WILDER PENFIELD, address, Univ. of
> B.C., October, 1960.

The university, by virtue of its emphasis on the cultural environment, the supremacy of mental discipline over personality, and academic freedom, has the resources for forming a bridgehead of flexible and detached minds in a strategic place in society.

NORTHROP FRYE, in G. Stanley and G.S. Sylvestre, eds., *Canadian universities today*, 1961, 37.

In this new age of governmentalization, I think it is important for universities to formulate their own bill of rights: the freedoms that they think are basic to their own health, the violation of which would threaten their very existence. I would suggest that there are three basic freedoms: the freedom to determine who shall be taught, the freedom to determine what shall be taught, and the freedom to determine who shall teach. I shall add a fourth, although it is implied in the first three: the freedom to distribute its financial resources as it sees fit.

CLAUDE BISSELL, President Univ. of Toronto, speech, Buffalo, February, 1963.

All the arguments boil down to one principal one, namely, that the university is not a parochial institution, not even a provincial one; it is a national institution, and is becoming increasingly an international one.

CLAUDE BISSELL, speech to Ottawa branch of Univ. of Toronto Alumni Assoc., March 20, 1963.

Election, consequently, it seems to me, should be the principle that carries throughout our university structure: election of the chairmen of departments, election of deans, election of presidents. Many arguments can be advanced against this: they will nearly all be found to reside in the timidity of the academic, his own self-distrust.

A.R.M. LOWER, *Queen's quart.*, Vol. 71, Summer, 1964, 211.

When new universities appear, their chairman and chancellors are selected from the boardroom of the nearest dominant corporation.

JOHN PORTER, *The vertical mosaic*, 1965, 300.

The progress of human knowledge in this century has achieved such proportions, has expanded so enormously, has moved into such previously unknown and unimagined areas as well as vastly modifying the already substantial burden of human learning received from the past, that it can be continued and stimulated further, absorbed and made intelligible, only if it is organized.

TORONTO. UNIVERSITY. PRESIDENT'S COMM. ON THE SCHOOL OF GRADUATE STUDIES, *Report*, 1965, 14.

If Canada is to be more than a geographical expression, her nationhood will be born in her Universities. And if her Universities are to discover any merit or mission, then students will educate the educators into that discovery – and salvation. May they come to it before it is too late.

JOHN R. SEELEY, Sept., 1967, in H. Adelman et al., *The university game*, 1968, 145.

Universities can function as restricted guilds only where there is a vigorous intellectual life outside the universities; in most of Canada, there is not.

F.E. SPARSHOTT, *Can. forum*, July, 1968, 80.

Many of the assumptions under which protest in the universities appears to be operating seem to me to take the form of a misapplied reformation, based on a view of the ideal university as a bastard church, resembling the Congregationalists in government, the

Catholics in outlook, the Quakers in doctrine, and the Jehovah's Witnesses in tactics

NORTHROP FRYE, "Ethics of change", in *A symposium, ethics of change; Queen's Univ.,* (Nov. 7, 1968), 1969, 54.

For God's sake, can't you find me a suitable Canadian to teach Canadian government?

JOHN HOLMES, Director, Canadian Institute of International Affairs, citing the plea of almost every chairman of Political Science Depts. in Canada, qu. in *Time,* Dec. 13, 1968, 13.

Because the universities are consumers of their own products, there is the possibility that they can become the centre of a self-sustaining supply and demand cycle. The "ivory tower syndrome" may manifest itself in out-dated courses providing training which finds little application outside the university and represents, potentially, a severe wastage of human and material resources.

JOHN J. CARSON, Public Service Commissioner, *Brief* to Senate, Spec. Committee on Science Policy, Feb. 12, 1969.

Wherever you have a preponderance of Americans the problems and issues will be American.

LOUIS DUDEK, qu. in *Weekend mag.,* Mar. 22, 1969, 4.

Are we losing our faculties?

LOUIS DUDEK, quip made May 17, 1969, at Symposium on the De-Canadianization of Canadian Universities, Sir George Williams Univ., Montreal.

Our Universities are in the process of serious disruption as a result of our local variant of the "Black Power" movement; the proponents of Canadian Power, the academic nationalists. At a time when faculties should be uniting to perform and understand the proper functions of the university, a few second-raters have been able to create dissension and distrust.

RAMSAY COOK, *Can. forum,* July, 1969, 80.

I'm very suspicious of this narrow kind of nationalism. It can only lead to House of Commons committees on Canadian activities.

ALWYN BERLAND, address, Canadian Union of Students, Annual Congress, Port Arthur, Aug. 28, 1969, on criticism of foreigners on university faculties.

We are presently conferring degrees upon Canadian students who are often so ignorant of their own country that they are a disgrace to it, and an indictment of the degree granting institutions from which they come.

J. STEELE and ROBIN MATHEWS, in I. Lumsden, ed., *Close the 49th parallel, etc.,* 1970, 174.

Instead of welcoming the democratizing influence and attempting to remove or mitigate the socially undesirable side-effects, they seek to resist the forces of modernization and democratization by cultivating hatred of Americans, by seeking to "close the 49th parallel", and by seeking to establish in Canada monopoly privileges for the Canadian-born over everyone else. They have been remarkably successful in disguising petit-bourgeois capitalism as idealistic socialism, and white Canadian Anglo-Saxon supremacy as national independence.

HARRY G. JOHNSON, Convocation address, Carleton Univ., May 22, 1970, on critics of large number of foreigners on faculties, qu. in J.H. Redekop, *Star-spangled beaver,* 1971, 57.

Some day soon, one of the Canadian universities will set up a course on the care and feeding of camels. And will the people who graduate in it go to the Middle East? Don't be silly; they'll just go to other Canadian universities and set up courses there on the care and feeding of camels. Graduates from these courses will go to teach the subject in high schools and community colleges. Eventually, Canada will have 10,000 accredited camelologists, none of whom has ever seen a camel.

> RICHARD J. NEEDHAM, Toronto *Globe and Mail*, Nov. 17, 1970, 6.

Since 1961, Canadian citizen participation in Canadian university faculty life has plunged downward, from something like seventy-five per cent to something around fifty per cent in the arts and sciences. In 1968-69, hirings were overwhelmingly non-Canadian; 1,013 positions were filled from the U.S., 545 from Great Britain, 722 from elsewhere, and the remainder, probably only about 360, were filled by Canadians.

> ROBIN MATHEWS, *Saturday night*, May, 1971, 21.

University of Toronto

The University is the glory of Toronto. This is a Gothic building and will take rank after, but next to, the buildings at Ottawa. It will be the second piece of noble architecture in Canada, and as far as I know on the American continent.

> ANTHONY TROLLOPE, *North America*, 1862, 73-74.

Our history is not a progression of acts and amendments but a procession of individuals.

> CLAUDE T. BISSELL, address on being installed President, Univ. of Toronto, Oct. 24, 1958.

The Unknown

We grasp at loved shadows –
  While grasping, they're gone;

The fruit of our knowledge
  Is still the *unknown*.
We scale the blue summits,
  For which we have longed
To sit down and sigh for
  The regions beyond.

> ALEXANDER MCLACHLAN, "A dream", 1856.

Unwanted

When I was warm-hearted
impulsive;
and would've given the skin
off my back
and gone to hell
for any one of them,
people ran from me
as from a leper.

> IRVING LAYTON, "Who's crazy", 1963.

Uranium

A uranium-producing country cannot be neutral.

> DENIS BROGAN, in G.P. Gilmour, ed., *Canada's tomorrow*, 1954, 275; proceedings of a conference held on Canada's future, Nov., 1953, Quebec City.

Urban Renewal

To exempt improvements and at the same time to tax land more heavily would provide a double incentive to the owners of derelict buildings to demolish them and to use the land more intensively. Here surely is a golden key to urban renewal, to the automatic regeneration of the city – and not at the public expense.

> MARY RAWSON, *Property taxation and urban development*, 1961, 28.

Urbanization

Lurid and lofty and vast it seems;
It hath no rounded name that rings
But I have heard it called in dreams
The City of the End of Things.

ARCHIBALD LAMPMAN, "The city of the end of things", *Atlantic monthly*, Mar., 1894.

Our country will grow and prosper only if the clamour of the great cities does not dominate the traditional voice that rises from the fields, only if the plough continues to be recognized as the most essential and the most fruitful instrument of production.

GEORGE BOUCHARD, *Other days, other ways*, 1928, 149.

Value

It's not worth a sou marquee.

> ANON., phrase once common in the Maritime provinces meaning, of trifling value; a reference to French Guiana sous which, counterstamped by other West Indian colonies, were sometimes carried north to Canada.

We always undervalue what we have never been without.

> ROBERTSON DAVIES, *Tempest-tost*, 1951, 164.

Paternal British-type colonialism, exemplified by Canada's treatment of its native populations, is dead. Unfettered free enterprise, U.S.-style, has proved a dismal failure. Canadians young and old want a life of quality not quantity; true Canadian values, not tarnished second-hand imports.

> O. M. SOLANDT, Mid-Canada Development Corridor Conference, Lakehead Univ., Aug. 1969, qu. in R. Rohmer, *Green north*, 1970, 7.

The sense of value is an individual, unpredictable, variable, incommunicable, undemonstrable, and mainly intuitive reaction to knowledge.

> NORTHROP FRYE, qu. by Frank Davey in *From there to here*, 1974, 107.

Vancouver, B.C.

The seaport of the twentieth century! the Constantinople of the West!

> DOUGLAS SLADEN, *On the cars and off*, 1895, 360.

A great sleepiness lies on Vancouver as compared with an American town; men don't fly up and down the streets telling lies, and the spittoons in the delightfully comfortable hotels are unused; the baths are free and their doors are unlocked.

> RUDYARD KIPLING, *From sea to sea*, Vol. II, 1900, 54.

With a hand on my hip and the cup
    at my lip,
And a love in my life for you.
    For you are a jolly good fellow, with
      a great big heart, I know:
So I drink this toast
To the "Queen of the Coast".
    Vancouver, here's a Ho!

> E. PAULINE JOHNSON, "A toast", 1903.

In nineteen-ten
Vancouver then
Will have one hundred thousand men.
Move her! Move her!
Who? – Vancouver!

> ANON., chant of Vancouver citizens, ca. 1905.

Squared it lay, squamous with shingle
    and cement,
Straitly ruled by steel, by stark wire
    and stucco.
South walked a hoary wood-waste of
    houses
Massing to the river like lemmings on
    the march,
Jerry-new cottages jostling jowl by
    jowl
(Except to skirt green fields golfers
    locked away)

Down to the fouled and profit-clogged Fraser,
The pile-impaled river plotting its flood.

EARLE BIRNEY, "Trial of a city", 1952.

O Vancouver, I was a swimmer out of sight
Of land in your backyard ocean, fighting the grey ways,
The driftwood turnings and foam roads going nowhere.

AL PURDY, "Towns", 1964.

It is a city that should have grown straight up, like Manhattan, instead of despoiling great mountainsides and blotching fair valleys.

EDWARD MCCOURT, *The road across Canada*, 1965, 191.

Where else could a loudmouth like me win an election except in a crazy city like this?

TOM CAMPBELL, Mayor, qu. in *Maclean's*, Aug., 1967, 20.

Vancouver Island

When an American dies he goes to Paris, but when the fell hand of the iniquitous income-tax strikes down an Englishman in his prime he passes to his reward in V.I. and lives happy ever after, sharing with the simple-hearted Siwash the innocent pleasures of the chase.

W. E. WALSH, in M. Ross, ed., *Our sense of identity*, 1954, 30.

Van Horne, Sir William

The ablest railroad general in the world, all that Grant was to the U.S.A.

JASON EASTON, qu. in Walter Vaughan, *The life and work of Sir William Van Horne*, 1920, 148.

A dynamo run by dynamite.

D. B. HANNA, *Trains of recollection*, 1924, 40, on Sir William Van Horne.

A Dinner Horne, Pendant, upon a Kitchen Door.

SIR WILLIAM VAN HORNE'S whimsical coat of arms.

Vanity

What a slovenly old world this would be if all the vanity were eliminated.

ROBERT C. (BOB) EDWARDS, Calgary *Eye Opener*, Aug. 28, 1920.

If there is a single quality that is shared by all great men it is vanity. But I mean by "vanity" only that they appreciate their own worth. Without this kind of vanity they would not be great. And with vanity alone, of course, a man is nothing.

YOUSUF KARSH, qu. in J. B. Simpson, *Contemporary quotes*, 1964, 312.

Venereal Disease

Know syphilis in all its manifestations and relations, and all other things clinical will be added unto you.

SIR WILLIAM OSLER, *Aphorisms*, 1950, 129.

Victims

Perhaps one is only a victim when one wants to be a victim.

BRIAN MOORE, in *Tamarack rev.* No. 46, 1968, 18.

Basic Victim Positions: Position One: To deny the fact that you are a victim. Position Two: To acknowledge the fact that you are a victim, but to explain this as an act of Fate, the Will of God, the dictates of Biology (in the case of women, for instance), the necessity decreed by History, or Economics, or the Unconscious, or any other large general powerful idea. Position Three: To acknowledge the fact that you are a victim but to refuse to accept the assumption that the role is inevitable. Position Four: To be a creative non-victim.

> MARGARET ATWOOD, *Survival*, 1972, 36-38; basic victim positions of Canadians relative to their country.

This above all, to refuse to be a victim.

> MARGARET ATWOOD, *Surfacing*, 1972, 191.

Victoria, B.C.

The place itself appears a perfect Eden, in the midst of the dreary wilderness of the North West Coast, and so different is its general aspect, from the wooded, rugged regions around, that one might be pardoned for supposing it had dropped from the clouds into its present position.

> JAMES DOUGLAS, letter to James Hargrave, Feb. 5, 1843, in *Hargrave correspondence 1821-1843*, Champlain Soc., 1938, 420, referring to the future site of Victoria.

To realize Victoria you must take all that the eye admires most in Bournemouth, Torquay, the Isle of Wight, the Happy Valley at Hong Kong, the Doon, Sorrento, and Camps Bay; add reminiscences of the Thousand Islands, and arrange the whole round the Bay of Naples, with some Himalayas for the background.

> RUDYARD KIPLING, *Letters to the family*, 1907, 66.

In Victoria the people turn over in the morning to read the daily obituary column. Those who do not find their names there, fall back and go to sleep again.

> STEPHEN LEACOCK, address, Vancouver, probably 1936, qu. in *Queen's quart.*, Spring, 1961, 145.

I am convinced that had the ancients who dreamed of the Blessed Isles lying far to the west − and in some instances spent their lives searching for them − ever reached Victoria and the islands of the gulf they would have been content to search no farther.

> EDWARD MCCOURT, *The road across Canada*, 1965, 195.

Victoria is God's waiting room. It is the only cemetery in the entire world with street lighting.

> ANON., qu. in S. W. Jackman, *Vancouver Island*, 1972, 154.

Victors

History tends to be partial to the victor.

> GEORGE M. WRONG, *Can. hist. rev.*, Mar., 1933, 4.

Victor Victim.

> MICHAEL CHARTERS, title of novel, 1970.

Victory

Man the afraid, infirm, impure!
Yet how he can love and how endure,−
Endure to the end and rise again,
Victorious victim of passion and pain.

> GEORGE H. CLARKE, "Halt and parley", 1934.

Then, dear God,
Make us worthy of Victory.
Give us the strength
To keep our pledges
To make a better world.

> DICK DIESPECKER, "Prayer for victory",
> 1944.

Be most alert when most victorious,
for though you may not hit your
adversary when he is down, it is
considered plucky in him to kick *you*.

> ROBERTSON DAVIES, *Samuel March-*
> *banks' almanack*, 1967, 191.

Violence

Violence, upheld by authority, decides
everything.

> JACQUES DUCHESNEAU, Intendant of New
> France, 1675-82, qu. in G. Myers, *A*
> *history of Canadian wealth*, 1914, 10.

All violence streamlined into zeal
For one colossal commonweal.

> F. R. SCOTT, "Mural", 1945.

Then come the bold extremities
The justified enormities,
The unrestrained ferocities.

> F. R. SCOTT, "Degeneration", 1964.

Violence is often the only means of
emotional release from a sense of
unreality, in which even wantonly
destructive or sadistic acts help to
create a sense of identity in their
perpetrators.

> NORTHROP FRYE, C.B.C. Symposium,
> Queen's University, Kingston, Ont.,
> Nov. 7, 1968.

I am an optimist for I believe that
humans will be as bored by killing in
the next century as they are by sex in
this one.

> IRVING LAYTON, "Aphs", *The whole*
> *bloody bird*, 1969, 91.

Here violence is accepted as a philosophical base. The danger is that it will
turn totalitarian.

> PHILIPPE GARIGUE, referring to political
> situation in Quebec, qu. in *Saturday*
> *night*, July, 1969, 20.

Violence is the quest for identity . . . When identity disappears
with technological innovation, *vio-*
lence is the natural recourse.

> MARSHALL MCLUHAN, *Culture is our*
> *business*, 1970, 63.

Virginity

She treasured her virginity with all the
tenacity of a poor girl who knows it is
her only asset and never forgets that it
can be lost only once.

> HUGH MACLENNAN, *Two solitudes*,
> 1945, 47.

They called her "virgin", didn't they?
  Oh, the poor dear,
Stigmatised, in this modern day,
  With such a smear!
Surely a little tolerance may
  Be granted here:
She's not in any other way
  The least bit queer.

> GEOFFREY B. RIDDEHOUGH, "Defence of
> a deviant", 1972.

The end of virginity as a value is part
of the demise of the view of women as
possessions instead of people – like
pots fresh from the factory in which
no one's yet baked.

> MERLE SHAIN, *Some men are more per-*
> *fect than others*, 1973, 62.

Virtue

Vice makes virtue look well to its
anchors.

> THOMAS C. HALIBURTON, *Sam Slick's wise*
> *saws*, 1853, ch. 17.

There is no station in this life
  That is from ills exempted;
Virtue would be an easy thing
  If we were never tempted.

> ALEXANDER MCLACHLAN, "Poverty's compensations", 1856.

All the virtue he could boast
Was not found in any creed.

> BLISS CARMAN, "Saint Kavin", 1894.

No special virtues are needed, but the circumstances demand the exercise of them in a special way. They are seven, the mystic seven, your lamps to lighten at . . . tact, tidiness, taciturnity, sympathy, gentleness, cheerfulness, all linked together by charity.

> SIR WILLIAM OSLER, Commencement address, Johns Hopkins Univ. nurses, May 7, 1913.

Some people make their virtues more unendurable than vices.

> PETER MCARTHUR, d. 1924, qu. in *The best of Peter McArthur*, 1967, 111.

We grist our grain with bloody hands,
  We turn our mill with sweat and
    breath:
We are the men that Virtue brands;
  In youth we build the house of
    Death.

> NEIL TRACY, "Penitentes", 1938.

All his virtues have the same pretence:
Amalgamating vice with innocence.

> ROBERT FINCH, "The collective portrait", 1946.

The virtues of those we dislike irritate us even more than their vices.

> IRVING LAYTON, "Aphs", *The whole bloody bird*, 1969, 81.

Virtue is for the pulpit but depravity is for the bed. Ask any woman.

> IRVING LAYTON, "Aphs", *The whole bloody bird*, 1969, 94.

Vision

This is the vision, Canadians, realize your opportunities!

> JOHN DIEFENBAKER, Winnipeg, Feb. 12, 1958. Phrase which was to become the rallying cry of the 1958 election campaign.

From this turret, vision is vast,
all heaviness lifts at the last
and certainty, as an aerial thing,
takes wing.

> PETER MILLER, "Murder jury 3", 1959.

Visitors

If you have come this far
you might as well stay,
you might as well be me
for a day.

> GEORGE BOWERING, "You too", 1969.

Voice

The voice gives the keynote of the soul.

> RALPH CONNOR, *The major*, 1917, 77.

The cadence of the typical Canadian voice is different from the American; it is half nasal twang, quarter Scots, quarter Irish, and has a rather sad tone, as if something once dear and now lost and forgotten is still being endlessly regretted.

> J. B. PRIESTLEY, *The Listener*, June 7, 1956, 744.

I would rather hear an Irish girl say something nasty to me, than hear most Canadian girls say "Take me, Mr. Marchbanks, I am yours".

> ROBERTSON DAVIES, *Samuel Marchbanks' almanack*, 1967, 50.

Voters, Votes and Voting

The viva voce system was more in accordance with the institution of the empire to which we belonged and more congenial to the manly spirit of the British people; and he would not therefore consent to abandon it in favour of the underhand and sneaking system of vote by ballot.

> C. A. HAGERMAN, Solicitor General, Kingston *Chronicle*, Feb. 12, 1831.

Vote for no man whose conduct in private and public life is not above suspicion, and inquire with due diligence before you give your suffrages.

> WILLIAM LYON MACKENZIE, address to the Reformers of Upper Canada, Toronto, Sept., 1834.

Nobody would ask for the vote by ballot but from gross ignorance: it is the most corrupt way of using the franchise.

> JOHN STRACHAN, Upper Canada. House of Assembly, Select Comm. on Grievances, *7th Report*, W. L. Mackenzie, chairman, 1835, 86.

Sir, I will oppose the bill *in toto* — I think it is an endeavour of the friends of the United States government to put our institutions on the same footing as theirs, to destroy our principles of government, for I say, the ballot system is hostile to the principles of the British Constitution — it destroys British freedom.

> OGLE GOWAN, Upper Canada, House of Assembly, Apr. 1, 1835, on secret ballot.

I would be most willing to vote confidence in the Government [loud cheers from the Government side], if I could do so conscientiously [loud cheers from the Opposition].

> DONALD A. SMITH, (Lord Strathcona), H. of C., *Debates*, Nov. 5, 1873, on the "Pacific Scandal".

Elections cannot be carried without money. Under an open system of voting, you can readily ascertain whether the voter has deceived you. Under vote by ballot, an elector may take your money and vote as he likes, without detection.

> JOHN H. CAMERON, speech in H. of C., Apr. 21, 1874.

Religion and race are, of course, observable forces within our body politic; but as far as I have remarked the divisions of party are perpendicular rather than horizontal, and in a country or borough election, as often as not, Catholic will be found voting against Catholic, Orangeman against Orangeman, Frenchman against Frenchman, and, what will perhaps cause less surprise, Irishman against Irishman.

> LORD DUFFERIN, speech in London, England, July 8, 1875.

I cannot vote for Mr. Laurier, for you tell me that if I vote for a Liberal, I shall be damned; I cannot vote for Mr. Bourbeau, for you tell me that if I do not follow my conscience, I shall be damned; I cannot vote for neither, for you tell me that if I do not vote at all I shall be damned. Since I must be damned anyway, I'll be damned for doing what I like. I am going to vote for Mr. Laurier.

> ANON., to his curé, by-election campaign, Oct., 1877, qu. by Mason Wade in C. T. Bissell, ed., *Our living tradition*, 1957, 96.

The great mass of the electors are ignorant, and a great majority of them never read, and remain as much in the dark as to what is going on in this country as if they were residing in Europe.

> SIR WILFRID LAURIER, letter, July 10, 1882, to Edward Blake. (Pub. Arch. Ont.)

There he lies, the noble son of Ontario, perchance in some foreign land where instead of the butternut of his native homestead, the gloomy cypress guards his lonely grave, but though the dread trumpet remain unblown, yet one blast of the old familiar party horn summons him to the same old polling booth.

> WILLIAM H. DRUMMOND, speech, Canadian Club, Toronto, Nov. 21, 1905.

A vote for the Government means that another man will take your place. A vote for the Opposition means that you stay here for the rest of your life.

> ANON., wording of placards displayed at Vimy Ridge, 1917, at time of soldiers' voting, general election.

There's more votes in a bottle of rum than a road grant.

> MICHAEL CASHIN, Newfoundland Prime Minister, 1919, qu. by his son Peter Cashin in *Regionalism in the Canadian community, 1867-1967*, 1969, 244.

There is no real power in money, power is in the vote.

> HENRY WISE WOOD, *Grain growers' guide*, Aug. 4, 1920, 10.

The citizens go on voting Liberal because they are conservative.

> RAMSAY TRAQUAIR, *Atlantic monthly*, June, 1923, 822.

Quebec's women may agitate as they please for better laws; but having no ballot either to tempt or to threaten unheeding representatives they plead in vain. They have not the one thing the politician values – the ballot. They are not the one person he respects – the voter.

> JUDGE HELEN GREGORY MACGILL, in 1936, qu. in E.M.G. MacGill, *My mother, the judge*, 1955, 218.

What the use of giving us the right of vote if we starve to death, or do not know what it is all about. First give us the means of learning how to make a living, and understanding what the vote is about.

> HARRY CHONKALEY, and others, Indians of the Hay Lakes Band, Ft. Vermilion, Alta., to the Jt. Comm. Senate and House of Commons on the Indian Act, Feb. 24, 1947.

The winning of votes, particularly the decisive marginal votes of the middle class, calls for a policy of ideological opportunism and gradualism.

> SEYMOUR M. LIPSET, *Agrarian socialism*, 1950, 157.

At times I have to hold my nose while marking the ballot.

> FRANK H. UNDERHILL, about 1957, after breaking with the C.C.F. party, qu. in P. Newman, *Home country*, 1973, 216.

Let's not worry about whether the man in the street will vote for a woman, will *you* vote for *me?*

> JUDY LAMARSH, question frequently asked of delegates in her campaign for Liberal nomination, Niagara Falls by-election, Summer, 1960.

If you have to trek five miles through snow with a dog team to vote, you will. If you have to walk around the block to the polling station, you'll think about it.

> TERRY CORBETT, Magistrate, who delivered ballot boxes for the Grand Falls – White Bay – Labrador federal riding, commenting in Goose Bay, on the 90% turn-out of electors in Labrador outposts, qu. in *Liberty*, June, 1963.

There are more votes on Main Street than on Bay Street.

JOHN G. DIEFENBAKER, paraphrasing F. D. Roosevelt, qu. in P. Newman, *Renegade in power*, 1963, 193.

We have seen that almost any statement made about Canadian voting behaviour as a whole can be shown to be strongly contradicted in some region or among some section of the population.

JOHN MEISEL, *Papers on the 1962 election*, 1964, 286.

In a democracy the ballot box, not the filibuster, is the ultimate and appropriate technique of assessment.

PIERRE E. TRUDEAU, H. of C., *Debates*, July 24, 1969, 11572.

I vote with the Tories but dine with the Grits.

GRATTAN O'LEARY, d. 1976, favourite saying, qu. in Vancouver *Sun*, Apr. 10, 1976, 39.

You are representing others, by default, as well as yourself. You will be casting more votes than your own. And so the key question is: "Whose proxy are you?"

J. F. LEDDY, President, Univ. of Windsor, Convocation address, Waterloo Lutheran Univ., Nov. 5, 1972.

Voyageurs

What a fairer bastion than a good tongue, especially when one sees his own chimney smoke, or when we can kiss our own wives, or kiss our neighbor's wife with ease and delight? It is a strange thing when victuals are wanting, work whole nights and days, lie down on the bare ground, and not always that happy — the breech in the water, the fear in the buttocks, to have the belly empty, the weariness in the bones, and drowsiness of the body by the bad weather that you are to suffer, having nothing to keep you from such calamity.

PIERRE RADISSON, about 1658, *The explorations of Pierre-Esprit Radisson*, 1961, 80. (Trans.)

We were Caesars, being nobody to contradict us.

PIERRE-ESPRIT RADISSON, "Lake Superior voyage", 1661. (Trans.)

The French and Canadians have always been remarkable for roving in the Desarts and seating themselves amongst the Indians.

GEN. THOMAS GAGE, 1770, in C. E. Carter, *Correspondence of Gage*, 1931, 212.

No portage was too long for me; all portages were alike. My end of the canoe never touched the ground till I saw the end of it. Fifty songs a day were nothing to me. I could carry, paddle, walk, and sing with any man I ever saw.

ANON., old voyageur to Alexander Ross, at Red River, 1825, qu. in his *The fur hunters of the far west*, 1855, II, 236.

No water, no weather, ever stopped the paddle or the song. I have had twelve wives in the country; and was once possessed of fifty horses, and six running dogs, trimmed in the first style. I was then like a Bourgeois, rich and happy: no Bourgeois had better dressed wives than I; no Indian chief finer horses; no white man better-harnessed or swifter dogs. I beat all Indians at the race, and no white man ever passed me in the chase.

ANON., old voyageur to Alexander Ross, at Red River, 1825, qu. in his *The fur hunters of the far west*, 1855, II, 236.

We shun the noise of the busy world,
For there's crime and misery there,
    And the happiest life
    In this world of strife
Is that of the Voyageur.

JOHN F. MCDONNELL, "The voyageur's song", 1864.

The Canadian voyageurs will become a forgotten race, or remembered, like their associates, the Indians, among the poetical images of past times, and as themes for local and romantic associations.

WASHINGTON IRVING, *Astoria*, 1886, 25.

Change was his mistress, Chance his councillor!
Love could not keep him; Duty forged no chain.
The wide seas and the mountains called to him,
And grey dawns saw his campfires in the rain.

THEODORE G. ROBERTS, "Epitaph for a voyageur", 1913.

Waiting

The things that come to the man who waits are seldom the things he waited for.

ROBERT C. (BOB) EDWARDS, Calgary *Eye Opener*, Jan. 27, 1912.

It's very hard to stand and wait
When those we go to
meet − are late.

ANAHID HAGOPIAN, "Waiting", 1960.

Wanderlust

There's a race of men that don't fit in,
A race that can't stay still;
So they break the hearts of kith and
kin,
And they roam the world at will.

ROBERT W. SERVICE, "The men that don't fit in", 1907.

Let us probe the silent places, let us
seek what luck betide us;
Let us journey to a lonely land I know.

ROBERT W. SERVICE, "Call of the wild", 1907.

I cannot stay, I cannot stay!
I must take my canoe and fight the
waves,
For the Wanderer spirit is seeking me.

ANON., "Song to the wanderer", Haida song, trans. by Hermia Fraser, 1945.

Want

(I want all the world's food in my belly
I want all the things I can see
I want all the toys in the world in my
arms
and I want all the arms around ME)

PHYLLIS GOTLIEB, "Ordinary, moving", 1969.

War

The Aristook War.

ANON., the dispute over the boundary between New Brunswick and Maine which led to a settlement in the Ashburton Treaty of 1842; also called, "The Lumbermen's War".

Hurrah! Ye sons of Canada, for that
brave and gallant band,
Who brothers are, and children of, the
same old fatherland
Fear not the din of war, not battle's
fierce alarms,
The red cross flag, and tri-color, defy
the world in arms!

ANON., Crimean War song, qu. in *Pilot*, Jan. 12, 1855, 2.

In some development of Socialism, something that will widen patriotism beyond the bounds of nationalism, may rest the desire of the race in this matter; but the evil is rooted and grounded in the abyss of human passion, and war with all its horrors is likely long to burden the earth.

SIR WILLIAM OSLER, address, "Study of the fevers of the South", Atlanta, May 6, 1896.

Whilst I cannot admit that Canada should take part in all the wars of Great Britain, neither am I prepared to say that she should not take part in any war at all.

> SIR WILFRID LAURIER, H. of C., *Debates*, Feb. 5, 1900, 68.

War everywhere. When Britain is at war, Canada is at war; there is no distinction. If Great Britain, to which we are subject, is at war with any nation Canada becomes liable to invasion, and so Canada is at war.

> SIR WILFRID LAURIER, H. of C., *Debates*, Jan. 12, 1910, 1735; also, speech in Montreal, Dec. 12, 1914.

If England is at war we are at war and liable to attack. I do not say that we shall always be attacked, neither do I say that we would take part in all the wars of England. That is a matter that must be guided by circumstances upon which the Canadian Parliament will have to pronounce, and will have to decide in its own best judgment.

> SIR WILFRID LAURIER, H. of C., *Debates*, Feb. 3, 1910, 2965.

We have taken the position in Canada that we do not think we are bound to take part in every war, and that our fleet may not be bound in all cases, and, therefore, for my part I think it is better under such circumstances to leave the negotiations of these regulations as to the way in which the war is to be carried on to the chief partner of the family, the one who has to bear the burden in part on some occasions, and the whole burden perhaps on other occasions.

> SIR WILFRID LAURIER, Imperial Conference, 1911, *Proc.*, 117.

Let the government try to hold the people of Canada from a British war and the streets would run with blood of civil conflict, and the Confederation of Canada break instantly asunder.

> STEPHEN LEACOCK, *University mag.* X, Dec. 4, 1911, 546.

All the manliness of the civilized world is due to wars or to the need of being prepared for wars. All the highest qualities of mankind have been developed by wars or the dangers of wars. Our whole civilization is the outgrowth of wars. Without wars, religion would disappear. All the enterprise of the world has grown out of the aggressive, adventurous, and warlike spirit engendered by centuries of wars.

> SIR WILLIAM VAN HORNE, letter to S.S. McClure, 1912; qu. in Vaughan, *Van Horne*, 1920, 364.

When England is at war we are at war.

> SIR WILFRID LAURIER, H. of C., *Debates*, Jan. 12, 1912, 1064.

We have long said that when Great Britain is at war, we are at war; to-day we realize that Great Britain is at war and that Canada is at war also.

> SIR WILFRID LAURIER, H. of C., *Debates*, Aug. 9, 1914, 9.

When the call comes our answer goes at once, and it goes in the classical language of the British answer to the call of duty: 'Ready, aye, ready'.

> SIR WILFRID LAURIER, H. of C., *Debates*, Aug. 19, 1914, 10.

I heard the rumble of distant guns,
 And I saw mad, marching men.
Each man was flinging his life away
 For a God he'd found again;
   An old God laughing at war and
     might.
   But Christ I saw not marching
     that night.

ARTHUR R. PHELPS, "What of the Christ", in *Christian guardian*, May 5, 1915, 11.

Now war is a funny thing, ain't it?
  It's the rummiest sort of a go,
For when it's most real,
It's then that you feel
You're a-watchin' a cinema show.

ROBERT W. SERVICE, "The odyssey of 'Erbert 'Iggins", 1916.

The root of strife is not that final force
  That bends the bow to breaking;
Give but one unkind thought free
    course
And war is in the making.

ALBERT D. WATSON, "Making war", 1917.

I know how selfish and individualistic and sordid and money-grabbing we have been; how slothful and incompetent and self-satisfied we have been, and I fear it will take a long war and sacrifices and tragedies altogether beyond our present imagination to make us unselfish and public-spirited and clean and generous; it will take the strain and emergency of war to make us vigorous and efficient; it will take the sting of many defeats to impose that humility which will be the beginning of our regeneration.

R.J. STEAD, *The cowpuncher*, 1918, 318.

Most of the wars and afflictions that have come on the world are due to attempts made by incompetent people to be their brothers' keepers.

PETER MCARTHUR, *The affable stranger*, 1920, Preface, xii.

When women have a voice in national and international affairs, *wars will cease forever*.

AUGUSTA STOWE-GULLEN, 1920's qu. in Jean Bannerman, *Leading ladies*, 1967, 182.

When we, the Workers, all demand:
  "What are we fighting for?" . . .
Then, then we'll end that stupid
  crime, that devil's madness – War.

ROBERT W. SERVICE, "Michael", 1921.

If ever the time should come when the spectre of 1914 should again appear I believe it would be best, not only that Parliament should be called, but that the decision of the Government, which, of course, would have to be given promptly should be submitted to the judgement of the people at a general election before troops should leave our shores. This would contribute to the unity of our country in the months to come and would enable us best to do our duty.

ARTHUR MEIGHEN, speech at Hamilton, Nov. 16, 1925.

In the sweet by-and-by imperialistic ambitions and international fears may possibly give place to the reign of the golden rule; but until that time arrives clashing interests will yield their natural fruits – dislike, fear, hostility, hatred, preparation for war, and war.

JOHN S. EWART, *Roots and causes of wars*, 1925.

The French Canadians, who are of the same race with us only in the sense that we all belong to the human race, cling to us just as hard. They all follow us to war so boldly that we begin to have misgivings as to whether someday they may not make us follow them to war.

GEORGE BERNARD SHAW, *The intelligent woman's guide to socialism and capitalism*, 1928, 159.

There never has been a war of Canadian origin, nor for a Canadian cause.

WILLIAM ARTHUR DEACON, *My vision of Canada*, 1933, 145.

Man must know, if he has any capacity for reason, that modern war doesn't come to an end, that you can't bring it to an end in an honourable peace and make a new start. It sets going a process of destruction that goes on year after year in widening circles of damage and violence.

> J. W. DAFOE, Empire Club speech, Jan. 30, 1936.

It is sometimes well to allow sleeping dogs to lie. This, I believe is especially true where they happen to be the dogs of war.

> W.L. MACKENZIE KING, letter to Thomas Vien, Apr. 11, 1936.

The Church's one foundation
  Is now the Moslem sword,
In meek collaboration
  With flame and axe and chord;
While overhead are floating
Deep-winged with holy love
The battle-planes of Wotan,
The bombing planes of Jove.

> L.A. MCKAY, "Battle hymn for the Spanish rebellion", *Can. forum*, Sept. 1936.

The Canadian parliament reserves to itself the right to declare, in the light of the circumstances existing at the time, to what extent, if at all, Canada will participate in conflicts in which other members of the Commonwealth may be engaged.

> W.L. MACKENZIE KING, League of Nations Assembly, Sept., 1936; H. of C., *Debates*, 1938, 3183.

I do not think I can accept a code of morals that affirms that we shall not do anything until somebody else does it. I submit that we are guilty — I use the word advisedly — of assisting an aggressor nation to kill men, women, and children in China.

> J. S. WOODSWORTH, H. of C., *Debates*, Feb. 11, 1938, 381.

If Canada is faced by the necessity of making a decision on the most serious and momentous issue that can face a nation, whether or not to take part in war, the principle of responsible government which has been our guide and our goal for a century past, demands that that decision be made by the parliament of Canada.

> W. L. MACKENZIE KING, H. of C., *Debates*, Mar. 30, 1939, 2418.

The idea that every twenty years this country should automatically and as a matter of course take part in a war overseas for democracy or self-determination of other small nations, that a country which has all it can do to run itself should feel called upon to save, periodically, a continent that cannot save itself, and to these ends risk the lives of its people, risk bankruptcy and political disunion, seems to many a nightmare and sheer madness.

> W. L. MACKENZIE KING, H. of C., *Debates*, Mar. 30, 1939, 2419.

Calmly, therefore, he begins to speak
    of war,
praises the virtue of being *Canadien*,
of being at peace, of faith, of family,
and suddenly his other voice: *Where
    are your sons?*
He is tearful, choking tears; but not he
would blame the clever English; in
    their place
he'd do the same; maybe.
Where *are* your sons? The whole street
    wears one face,
shadowed and grim; and in the
    darkness rises
the body-odor of race.

> A. M. KLEIN, "Political meeting", 1946.

If there is a Third World War, its strategic centre will be the North Pole.

> GEN. HENRY H. ARNOLD, qu. by James Reston, New York *Times*, Feb. 13, 1947, 17.

In the future no one wins a war. It is true, there are degrees of loss, but no one wins.

> BROCK CHISHOLM, address, Empire Club, Toronto, Apr. 5, 1951.

The grim fact, however, is that we prepare for war like precocious giants and for peace like retarded pygmies.

> LESTER B. PEARSON, acceptance speech, Nobel Prize for Peace, Oslo, Dec. 11, 1957.

Many a brave Canadian youth
Will shed his blood on foreign shores,
And die for Democracy, Freedom, Truth,
With his body full of Canadian ores.

> F.R. SCOTT, "Lest we forget", 1957.

We need no more that light of day,
No need of faces to be seen;
The squadrons in the skies we slay
Through moving shadows on a screen:
By nailing echoes under sea
We kill with like geometry.

> E.J. PRATT, "Cycles", 1958.

War is so small, so sad, so inexcusable.

> GREGORY CLARK, "La mer", in *The best of Gregory Clark*, 1959, 16.

Perhaps it's time the nations of the world forgot about the whole tenuous idea of a lasting peace and just settled down to making some rules for a nice, safe war.

> JACK SCOTT, *From our town*, 1959, 165.

We men like war. We like the excitement of it, its thrill and glamor, its freedom from restraint. We like its opportunities for socially approved violence. We like its economic security and its relief from the monotony of civilian toil. We like its reward for bravery, its opportunities for travel, its companionship of men in a man's world, its intoxicating novelty. And we like taking chances with death.

> DR. G. H. STEVENSON, qu. in L.B. Pearson, *Diplomacy in the nuclear age*, 1959, 109.

When the Jerries come in with their hands up, shouting, "Kamerad", we just bowl them over with bursts of Sten fire.

> ANON., Canadian infantryman, qu. in Alexander McKee, *Caen: Anvil of victory*, 1964, 201.

In those old wars
where generals wore yellow ringlets
and sucked lemons at their prayers,
other things being equal
the lost causes were the best.

> ALDEN NOWLAN, "In those old wars", 1967.

The truth about the war comes out twenty years after you died in it.

> RICHARD J. NEEDHAM, *A friend in Needham*, 1969, 43.

War Dead

Growing to full manhood now,
With the care-lines on our brow,
We, the youngest of the nations,
With no childish lamentations,
Weep as only strong men weep,
For the noble hearts that sleep,
Pillowed where they fought and bled,
The loved and lost, our glorious dead!

> FREDERICK G. SCOTT, "In Memoriam; Those killed in the Canadian North West, 1885".

In Flanders Fields the poppies grow
Between the crosses, row on row,
That mark our place, and in the sky
The larks, still bravely singing, fly,
Scarce heard amidst the guns below.
We are the dead. Short days ago
We lived, felt dawn, saw sunset glow,
Loved and were loved; and now we lie
    In Flanders Fields.

> JOHN MCCRAE, "In Flanders Fields"; originally pub. in *Punch*, Dec. 8, 1915.

Not we the conquered. Not to us the
blame
Of them that flee, of them that basely
yield;
Nor ours the shout of victory, the fame
Of them that vanquish in a stricken
field.

JOHN MCCRAE, "The unconquered
dead", 1919.

If the dead gave their lives without
bitterness and the living are consoled,
Canada, the common mother of both,
is richer for all time for their sacrifice.
In the life of the race a single generation passes like a heart-beat; but the
chosen few from this generation,
whose names are in the lists of the lost,
are secure in their fame and in their
power.

JOHN W. DAFOE, Over the Canadian
battlefields, 1919, 89.

Fifty thousand Canadian soldiers
under the sod in Europe is the price
Canada has paid for the European
statesmanship which drenched the
continent in blood.

NEWTON W. ROWELL, speech, League of
Nations, Geneva, Dec. 8, 1920.

Not since her birth has our earth seen
such worth loosed upon her.

RUDYARD KIPLING, "The children,
1914-18", verse three; inscription in Memorial Chamber, Peace Tower, Ottawa,
about 1920.

Nor was their agony brief, or once
only imposed on them.
The wounded, the war-spent, the sick
received no exemptions:
Being cured they returned and
endured and achieved our
redemption.

RUDYARD KIPLING, "The children,
1914-18", verse four; inscribed in Memorial Chamber, Peace Tower, Ottawa,
about 1920.

That flesh we had nursed from the
first in all cleanness was given
To corruption unveiled and assailed by
the malice of Heaven –

RUDYARD KIPLING, "The children,
1914-18", verse five, inscribed in Memorial Chamber, Peace Tower, Ottawa,
about 1920.

Down the old road, alone he reappears
His promised word he keeps;
All's well, for over there among his
peers
A happy warrior sleeps.

JOHN CEREDIGION JONES, "The returning
soldier"; the last two lines are inscribed
in the Memorial Chamber, Peace
Tower, Ottawa; Jones was born in Wales
in 1883 and died in Chapleau, Ont.,
Aug. 19, 1947. (See, J. Hughes, Ottawa
Journal, Nov. 11, 1948.)

Here in the heart of Europe we meet
to unveil a memorial to our country's
dead. In earth which has resounded to
the drums and tramplings of many
conquests, they rest in the quiet of
God's acre with the brave of all the
world. At death they sheathed in their
hearts the sword of devotion, and now
from the oft-stricken fields they hold
aloft its cross of sacrifice, mutely beck-
oning those who would share their
immortality. No words can add to
their fame, nor so long as gratitude
holds a place in men's hearts can our
forgetfulness be suffered to detract
from their renown. For as the war
dwarfed by its magnitude all contests
of the past, so the wonder of human
resource, the splendour of human heroism, reached a height never witnessed before.

ARTHUR MEIGHEN, address at Thelus Military Cemetery, Vimy Ridge, at unveil-
ing of Cross of Sacrifice, July 3, 1921.

From little towns in a far land we
    came,
To save our honour and a world
    aflame;
By little towns, in a far land, we sleep,
And trust those things we won to you
    to keep.

> RUDYARD KIPLING, lines inscribed on war
> memorial at Sault Ste. Marie, Ont.,
> unveiled Sept. 2, 1924. (See, Ottawa
> *Journal*, Jan. 22, 1936, 6, corresp.)

Take these men for your ensamples
Like them remember that prosperity
    can be only for the free
That freedom is the sure possession of
    those alone
Who have the courage to defend it.

> ANON., inscription on Soldiers' Tower,
> University of Toronto campus, erected
> 1924.

They braced their belts about them
They crossed, in ships, the sea.
They fought, and found six feet of
    ground
And died for you and me.

> DR. R. H. ARTHUR, inscription supplied for
> Sudbury War Memorial, 1928; taken
> from A. E. Housman's poem XXXII,
> *Last poems:* "They braced their belts
> about them, They crossed in ships the
> sea, They sought and found six feet of
> ground And there they died for me."
> The following lines, written by RUD-
> YARD KIPLING in response to a local
> request were rejected at first: "We,
> giving all, gained all; Neither lament us
> nor praise; Only, in all things recall, It is
> fear, not death, that slays." In Nov.,
> 1957, they were added to the Memorial.

Oh! Time shall wait on time in vain,
And Envy die of self-accord
Before a stouter deed shall claim
A prouder laurel for the sword.

> RAYMOND CARD, "Vesper at Vimy",
> 1936; qu. in L. B. Pearson, *Words and
> occasions*, 1970, 266.

We ask but this: that in your brave
    tomorrows
You keep our faith, who, rich in
    youth and pride,
Gave up our lives to quell old fears
    and sorrows
Till you forget, we shall not twice
    have died.

> JOHN E. NIXON, "The unreturning",
> March, 1946.

War, European (1914-1918)

But to-day, while the clouds are heavy
and we hear the booming of the
distant thunder, and see the lightning
flashes above the horizon, we cannot,
and we will not, wait and deliberate
until any impending storm shall have
burst upon us in fury and with disaster.

> SIR ROBERT L. BORDEN, H. of C., *Debates*,
> Dec. 5, 1912, 694.

Because it is the world's fight for
freedom Britain, reluctantly but resolutely, speaks the word, and Canada
also answers Ay!

> TORONTO *GLOBE*, Aug. 4, 1914.

The time of trial is upon this country
and the Empire. It will do us good in
the end. God and the right will finally
triumph.

> SIR GEORGE E. FOSTER, H. of C., *Debates*,
> Aug. 22, 1914, 98.

There is a feeling growing very strongly everywhere that the British generals
one and all are the most incompetent
lot of bloody fools that have ever been
collected together for the purpose of
sacrificing armies in historic times.

> WILLIAM E. OLIVER, letter to Frederick S.
> Oliver, Victoria, B.C., Nov. 24, 1915.

We may be in it for months and we may be in it for years. It is a time for toil and bloody sweat, for courage and good cheer.

ARTHUR MEIGHEN, Empire Club, Toronto, speech, Dec. 17, 1914.

Canada, not forced by any law or rule has voluntarily taken part in this war, placing herself in opposition to great powers. Canada has stepped into nationhood. No longer can we play the part of minors, who cannot transact our own business. Hereafter we shall not be allowed by the great nations of the world to put ourselves in that position. They will say that if we can make war we can do our own business and give our own answers to their questions.

CLIFFORD SIFTON, speech in Montreal, Jan. 25, 1915.

Have you seen the badge of courage on the soldiers who march by?
The deathless name of Canada — the name for which they die?
Does it wake no martial ardour — is your soul put on a shelf?
Can you still go back to nothing — to nothing but yourself?

W. A. FRASER, in Toronto *News*, Nov. 6, 1915.

Are we fighting the English or the Germans?

RICHARD B. BENNETT, letter to Sir Robert Borden, Dec. 7, 1915, referring to problems of British command of Canadian troops.

It can hardly be expected that we shall put 400,000 or 500,000 men in the field and willingly accept the position of having no more voice and receiving no more consideration than if we were toy automata.

SIR ROBERT BORDEN, letter to Sir George Perley, Jan. 4, 1916.

I am not afraid to become a German subject. I ask myself if the German régime might be favourably compared with that of the Boches of Ontario.

ARMAND LAVERGNE, speech in Legislature, Quebec, Jan. 13, 1916.

For the first contingent, our recruiting plans were, I think, different from anything that had ever occurred before. There was really a call to arms, like the fiery cross passing through the Highlands of Scotland or the mountains of Ireland in former days.

SIR SAM HUGHES, H. of C., *Debates*, Jan. 26, 1916, 292.

In conjunction with the Third Army, the Canadian Corps will take Vimy Ridge.

ARMY, British Command, Operation Order, Apr., 1917, qu. in R.C. Fetherstonhaugh, *Royal Montreal regiment*, 1927, 141. Vimy Ridge was taken Apr. 9 in one day.

Remember the *Llandovery Castle!*

CANADIAN ARMY CORPS, cry on going into action, Aug. 8, 1918, east of Amiens; a reference to the hospital ship sunk by Germans with Canadian doctors and nurses aboard.

Canada's Hundred Days.

ANON., the victorious drive of the Canadian Corps, Aug. 4 to Nov. 11, 1918.

Ah! the battlefield is wider than the cannon's sullen roar;
And the women weep o'er battles lost or won.
For the man a cross of honour; but the crepe upon the door
For the girl behind the man behind the gun.

WILSON MACDONALD, "The girl behind the man behind the gun", 1918.

The Great War is past; the war that tried through and through every quality and mystery of the human mind and the might of human spirit.

ARTHUR MEIGHEN, speech at Vimy Ridge, July 3, 1921.

At this time the proper occupation of the living, is first, to honour our heroic dead; next, to repair the havoc, human and material, that surrounds us; and, lastly, to learn aright and apply with courage the lessons of the war.

ARTHUR MEIGHEN, speech at Vimy Ridge, July 3, 1921.

Canada entered the war a colony, she emerged from it close to an independent state.

ARTHUR R. M. LOWER, *Colony to nation*, 1946, 470.

The capture of the Ridge marked a point in Canada's progress towards nationhood.

HERBERT FAIRLIE WOOD, *Vimy!*, 1967, 169, often stated as "Canada became a nation at Vimy" or "Canada's coming of age".

War of 1812

Mr. Madison's War.

ANON., a popular reference; James Madison was President of the U.S., 1809-17.

We are engaged in an awful and eventful contest. By unanimity and despatch in our councils and by vigour in our operations, we will teach the enemy this lesson: that a country defended by free men, enthusiastically devoted to the cause of their King and constitution, can never be conquered.

GENERAL ISAAC BROCK, speech to Upper Canada legislature, July 27, 1812.

The war might be called Madison's Patent-Nostrum. For to our House of Assembly it has been a timely emetic, to our Country, a gently sweating cathartic — one threw up two traitors, the other threw off some, and by the way of appendix, hung up some. A sedative will be prescribed should further symptoms require it.

UPPER CANADA ALMANACK, FOR THE YEAR 1815, printed by John Cameron.

The War of 1812 was not a war engaged in by Canadians for Canada, it was a war to maintain British connection.

GEORGE W. ROSS, Empire Club speech, 1905.

The War of 1812 is to Canadians, a war on land; to Americans, a war at sea; and to Englishmen, a completely forgotten episode of history.

GEORGE F. G. STANLEY, phrase "sometimes said", *Can. hist. rev.*, Vol. 38, 1957, 248.

Very little is known about the War of 1812 because the Americans lost it.

ERIC NICOL, *Say Uncle*, 1961, 37.

War, World (1939-45)

And down the road, not faraway in point of time, will be the world's greatest war, the hyperbolic war, the war that will never stop until the structure of society, as we know it, will sink into the slime.

JOHN W. DAFOE, Winnipeg *Free press*, June 30, 1936, editorial.

I thought the news would knock me out. Instead it was such a relief that the sword had at last come out of its scabbard in a good cause.

JOHN W. DAFOE, letter to George Ferguson, Sept., 1939, qu. by him in *Can. reader*, Vol. 10, No. 6,6.

Let us remember that if the democracies fail, Canada is the richest prize among the nations of the world.

> R. J. MANION, speech, Ottawa, 1939.

The Canadian Corps is a dagger pointed at the heart of Berlin.

> GEN. A. G. L. MCNAUGHTON, speeches in England, 1941, qu. in P. Simonds, *Maple leaf up, maple leaf down*, 1946, 20.

Germany and Japan don't want swamps and jungles. They want you – great, rich, sprawling Canada, rich with her endless wheat-bearing acres where a *Herrenvolk* could lord it over a slave population.

> ERIC KNIGHT, C.B.C. broadcast, Mar. 1, 1942.

We didn't cross the Channel to fight for England, but felt rather that we were going forth to fight, along with England, for Canada.

> ABBÉ J.-ARMAND SABOURIN, on the Dieppe Raid, in *Le Jour*, Dec., 1942. (Trans.)

Not that the war was funny
I took it and myself quite seriously
the way a squirrel in a treadmill does
too close to tears for tragedy
too far from the banana peel for
    laughter
and I didn't blame anyone for being
    there
that wars happened wasn't anybody's
    fault then
now I think it is.

> AL PURDY, "About being a member of our armed forces", 1968.

Water

Man Owns Spring Folks Want Drink Have To Pay.

> J. W. BENGOUGH, "Lesson XXVII", *The up-to-date primer*, 1896, 31.

The Chicago water steal.

> ANON., ref. to the diversion of water illegally from the Great Lakes by way of the Chicago Drainage Canal from 1900 to about 1925.

Sometimes, upon a crowded street,
I feel the sudden rain come down
And in the old, magnetic sound
I hear the opening of a gate
That loosens all the seven seas.
Watching the whole creation drown
I muse, alone, on Ararat.

> F. R. SCOTT, "Lakeshore", 1954.

And if I ask, you shall bring me water.
It will be cold, first, as it comes clear
Out of a granite pool in the northland,
Single as metal, and as metal, clean.

> F. R. SCOTT, "Water", 1954.

Only flush for No. 2, curtail bathing to the Saturday-night tub, go back to the old washrag, which could always move a lot of B.O. if applied often enough.

> MARGARET (MA) MURRAY, *The Alaska Highway news*, advice to readers during water shortage at Fort St. John, B.C., 1958, qu. in Georgina Keddell, *The newspapering Murrays*, 1974, 290.

Diversion of Canadian water to the U.S. is not negotiable. There is no such thing as a continental resource. We own it.

> ARTHUR LAING, Oct. 18, 1965, qu. by H. W. Herridge, H. of C., *Debates*, Jan. 31, 1966, 464.

I have said that of all the resources of Canada, fresh water is the greatest. We have in this nation over 30 per cent of the fresh water on the face of the earth. Now, with exploding population, with declining resources of other kinds in other countries, it seems to me that if we are not hasty, if we reserve as long as we possibly can a final commitment of them, then this nation is going to experience a tremendous national capital gain in the improved value of these resources.

ARTHUR LAING, H. of C., *Debates*, Jan. 31, 1966, 484.

This is a monstrous concept, not only in terms of physical magnitude, but also in another and more sinister sense, in that the promoters would displace Canadian sovereignty over the national waters of Canada, and substitute therefore a diabolic thesis that *all* waters of North America become a shared resource, of which most will be drawn off for the benefit of the midwest and southwest regions of the United States, where existing desert areas will be made to bloom at the expense of development in Canada.

A. G. L. MCNAUGHTON, address to Roy. Soc. Can., June 8, 1966, Sherbrooke, Que., referring to North American Water and Power Alliance.

Even to talk about selling it is ridiculous. You do not sell your heritage.

W. A. C. BENNETT, Premier of B.C., qu. by A. G. L. McNaughton in address to Roy. Soc. Can., Sherbrooke, Que., June 8, 1966.

Canadian water is not now negotiable, and I am not certain that it ever will be.

ARTHUR LAING, Minister of Northern Affairs, speech, American Bar Assoc., qu. in Ottawa *Journal*, Aug. 22, 1966, 6.

Of all the abundance of an abundant land, no statistic is more startling than the fact that Canada has 35 percent of all the fresh water in the world. And of all the domestic problems in the United States, none is becoming more severe than the shortage of "cool, clear water".

S. R. TUPPER and D. L. BAILEY, *Canada and the United States – the second hundred years*, 1967, 113.

Waves

but note, remember, how boxer waves
bully our shores, battling and
   billowing
into the stone's weakness, bellowing
down the deepening caverns
smashing the slate with unappeasable
   fists.

EARLE BIRNEY, "Maritime faces", 1952.

The commotion of these waves,
   however strong
      cannot disturb the
   compass line of the horizon
nor the plumbline of gravity

LOUIS DUDEK, *Europe* (Poem 19), 1954.

Wealth

For the Anglo-Saxon the possession of gold is the supreme means of domination. It is an instrument of action and power. His faculties lead him naturally to financial operations, wealth does not halt his activity or taste for work.

HENRI BOURASSA, address, National Monument, Montreal, Apr. 27, 1902. (Trans.)

The rapid concentration of wealth in Canada is no mere fancy. Already, it is estimated, less than fifty men control $4,000,000,000, or more than one-third of Canada's material wealth as expressed in railways, banks, factories, mines, land and other properties and resources.

GUSTAVUS MYERS, *A history of Canadian wealth*, 1914, i.

As has been said, and not improperly said, I am a man of some wealth. It is true. It is absolutely true, but I got it by my own untiring efforts in this great Western land to which I owe so much; and, what is more, I look upon it as a solemn trust in my hands to enable me to serve my country without fear or regard for the future so far as that is concerned; and I thought myself most fortunate that the good Lord had been good enough to permit me to be in that happy state, for no man may serve you as he should if he has over his shoulder always the shadow of pecuniary obligations and liabilities. Therefore, you may meet that story by saying that such as I have I consecrate with myself to this service in which I am.

> RICHARD B. BENNETT, speech when accepting the leadership of Conservative Party, Winnipeg, Oct. 13, 1927.

Only when I am penniless do I believe that wealth brings unhappiness.

> MARTIN ROHER, *Days of living*, 1959, 55.

The only real wealth is what you have in your mind, and in your heart, and in the hearts of others.

> RICHARD J. NEEDHAM, *A friend in Needham*, 1969, 8.

Weather

There is a rapture in tempestuous
    weather,
    A sympathy with suffering, which
        thrills
When midnight mists around the
        mountains gather,
    And hoarse winds howl among the
        moaning hills.

> ANDREW J. RAMSAY, "Win-on-ah", 1869.

Canada has a climate nine months winter and three months late in the fall.

> ANON., popular American saying, late 19th century; also applied by residents of Ontario and Quebec to Nova Scotia.

Man wants but little here below zero.

> ROBERT C. (BOB) EDWARDS, Calgary *Eye Opener*, Feb. 4, 1905.

There is no such thing as bad weather; only our lack of appreciation of it.

> WILLIAM E. SAUNDERS, remark to P. A. Taverner, May, 1905.

I know of nothing so absolutely pitiless as weather.

> JOHN MCCRAE, letter from the trenches, Jan. 25, 1917.

Were I not cold how should I come to
        know
    One potent pleasure of the sun's
        sweet rays?
Or did I never breast the driving snow
    What bliss were sweetest kernel of
        June days?

> WILSON MACDONALD, "A poet stood forlorn", 1918.

Evening red and morning gray
Is the sure sign of a fair day.
Evening gray and morning red
Sends the shepherd wet to bed.

> ANON., Brantford, Ont. rhyme; qu., *Jour. of Amer. folklore*, 1918, 6.

A fine Christmas, a fat Churchyard.
Winter thunder means Summer's
        hunger.
A year of snow a year of plenty.
A warm Christmas, a cold Easter.
A red sun got water in his eye.

Evening red and morning grey,
Double signs of one fine day.

> ANON., Newfoundland weather proverbs; qu., Devine, *Folk lore of Nfld.*, 1937.

Anyone who foretells Alberta weather is either a newcomer or a fool.

> FRANK OLIVER, qu., *Can. hist. rev.*, 1946, 143.

Mild, isn't it?

> SID BARRON, cartoonist, Toronto *Star*, a phrase found in all his cartoons from early 1960's.

The weather belongs to us all, it doesn't cost us anything, and it's about one of the few possessions we can afford.

MARGARET (MA) MURRAY, Editor of the *Bridge River (B.C.)-Lillooet news*, qu. in Vancouver *Sun*, Aug. 2, 1962, 5.

I want to thank God personally for the beautiful weather He has given us.

P. A. GAGLARDI, Minister of Highways, B.C., speech at opening of Trans-Canada Highway, Rogers Pass, B.C., Sept. 3, 1962.

Weddings

If it is a wedding let it be a wedding.

ANON., Newfoundland outport saying; qu., Devine, *Folk lore of Nfld.*, 1937.

Until I attended my friend's
wedding reception I was unaware
of the progress of barbarism.

JOHN NEWLOVE, "Admiral Hotel", 1968.

Welfare

I have no confidence whatever in any of the schemes propounded for relief. I never accomplished anything myself except by hard work, frugality and self-denial, and I don't believe anybody else ever did. This is the road that Western Canada, in common with the rest of humanity, has to travel.

SIR CLIFFORD SIFTON, letter to John W. Dafoe, Jan. 5, 1923, referring to financial plight of prairie farmers. (Pub. Arch. Can.)

It is one thing to pronounce far-reaching objectives, it is quite another to attain them. In this respect the civil service is the indispensable instrument. Without a competent, honest, and efficient civil service, the welfare state is an empty slogan.

JOHN J. DEUTSCH, *Queen's quart.*, Vol. 63, 1956, 566.

Within relatively few years, welfarism has changed our ideas of how to get ahead in life. In place of hard work and the seeking of opportunity we now look for security and leisure without wanting to earn them. And leisure today is seldom put to use; often it means nothing better than squatting over television's endless stupefaction.

PAUL M. FOX, address, annual meeting, St. Lawrence Corp. Ltd., Apr., 1959.

I hate our growing Welfare State because it will give full play to the very clever people who would reform and remake us.

THOMAS BOYLE, *Justice through power*, 1961, 195.

After medicare, what is next on the womb-to-tomb welfare list? Well, there are legalcare, morticare, carcare, housecare, leisurecare, and endless other possibilities.

LUBOR ZINK, Toronto *Telegram*, July 26, 1965.

It is hard to make an empty bag stand upright; even the most complete Social Security scheme can scarcely achieve it.

ROBERTSON DAVIES, *Samuel Marchbanks' almanack*, 1967, 127.

All man's community life impinges on what we do in the name of welfare, and man's community life, as we know, is in a state of acute disturbance, bordering on chaos.

DORIS FRENCH, *Can. welfare*, Vol. 44, May-June, 1968, 3.

By itself all that money for the poor would do would be to increase the price of pot.

DR. DANIEL CAPPON, referring to welfare payment proposals put forward at Conservative policy conference, Niagara Falls, Oct. 9-13, 1969.

Welfare is for the needy, not big and wealthy multinational corporations.

> DAVID LEWIS, *Louder voices: the corporate welfare bums*, 1972, 37.

The West

Civilization will no doubt extend over these low hills.

> DAVID THOMPSON, *Narrative, 1784-1812.* (Champlain Soc.) 1916, 186.

The temptation to go West where the climate is milder and the land unencumbered with timber – is much greater than is generally supposed. It has existed to such an extent as to be familiarly known as the 'Prairy Fever'.

> A. G. HAWKE, 1840, *Rept., chief emigration agent,* (Pub. Arch., Can., *Upper Can. sundries.*)

The great point is, how govern the territory.

> EDWARD ELLICE, letter to John Rose, Oct. 6, 1856 (Nat. Lib. Scotland).

So long as the present *regime* exists, so long as Lower Canada has reason to fear the growth of the population of the West, so long will there be vacillation and weakness in our annexation policy. At this moment, Lower Canada, aided by the agents of the fur-trading monopoly, prevents our onward march to the West; and it will be so till we have either swept away the French power altogether or have given Lower Canada a position of comparative independence.

> TORONTO *GLOBE*, May 24, 1859, 2.

The Fertile Belt.

> JOHN PALLISER, *Report*, 1863, 18; used in immigration literature, 1880-90; now known as the Park Belt.

Have you heard anything lately as to what is to be done with this country?

> NOR'WESTER (Red River Settlement), editorial, Feb. 6, 1865, 2.

If Canada is to remain a country separate from the United States it is of great importance to her that they (the United States) should not get behind us by right or by force, and intercept the route to the Pacific . . . But in any other point of view, it seems to me that the country is of no present value to Canada. We have unoccupied land enough to absorb immigration for many years, and the opening up of the Saskatchewan would do to Canada what the Prairie lands of Illinois are doing now – drain away our youth and our strength.

> SIR JOHN A. MACDONALD, letter to Sir Edward W. Watkin, Mar. 27, 1865. (Pub. Arch. Can.)

I would be quite willing, personally, to leave that whole country a wilderness for the next half-century but I fear if Englishmen do not go there, Yankees will.

> SIR JOHN A. MACDONALD, letter to Sir Edward Watkin, Mar. 27, 1865. (Pub. Arch. Can.)

Canada is bound to the North-West by the ties of discovery, possession and interest. The country is ours by right of inheritance.

> ALEXANDER MORRIS, speech in House of Commons, Dec. 5, 1867. (Paraphrased)

We hope to see a new Upper Canada in the North-West Territory – in its well-regulated society and government, in its education, morality and religion.

> TORONTO *GLOBE*, June 2, 1869.

I have always feared the entrance of the North-West into Confederation, because I have always believed that the French-Canadian element would be sacrificed; but I tell you frankly it had never occurred to me that our rights would be so quickly and so completely forgotten.

ARCHBISHOP ALEXANDRE TACHÉ, letter to G. Cartier, 1869; qu. in Benoit, *Taché*, II, 7. (Trans.)

Say to England that she does not want these sour grapes which hang so far beyond her reach . . . a country whose destinies God has indissolubly wedded to ours by geographical affinities which no human power can sunder, as He has divorced it from Canada by physical barriers which no human power can overcome.

ST. PAUL [Minn.] *DAILY PRESS*, Dec. 23, 1869.

This was the time of day for quiet in nature, but in fancy we caught the rumble of wagons on well-travelled roads, the shriek of the locomotive, the hum of machinery, the lowing and bleating of herds and flocks, the tinkle of the cow-bell, the ringing of the church and school bells − I could hear all these in anticipation, for verily the land before me was worthy, and in good time it would come to its inheritance.

JOHN MCDOUGALL, *Life in the far west*, 1868-72, (1903), 99.

The Great Lone Land.

WILLIAM BUTLER, *The great lone land*, 1872.

All aboard for the West!

SIR GEORGE-ETIENNE CARTIER, H. of C., *Debates*, June 1, 1872, 938, on the passing of the Pacific Railway Act.

My terms I am going to lay down before you; the decision of our Chiefs; ever since we came to a decision you push it back. The sound of the rustling of the gold is under my feet where I stand; we have a rich country; it is the Great Spirit who gave us this; where we stand upon is the Indians' property, and belongs to them.

MAWEDOPENAIS, Salteaux chief, at treaty parley, North-West Angle, Lake of the Woods, Oct. 3, 1873.

God's country.

ANON., the half-breeds' term for the valley of the Saskatchewan in their trek from Manitoba during 1870's.

I'll sing you a song of that plaguey pest,
It goes by the name of the Great North-West,
I cannot have a beau at all,
They all skip out there in the fall.
One by one they all clear out
Thinking to better themselves, no doubt,
Caring little how far they go
From the poor little girls of Ontario.

ANON., "The poor little girls of Ontario", about 1880.

The average eastern Canadian looks upon the North-West provinces and territories as a foreign land, a land which the rays of civilization are only just beginning to penetrate, and in which it is a hardship to live.

MACLEOD *GAZETTE*, July 21, 1885, 2.

All for the West. All aboard; if you can't get a board get a slab; but go anyway and anyhow, ready or not ready! Everyone must go to the Promised Land!

ANON., slogan qu. by W. C. Pollard, *Life on the frontier*, [n.d.], 17.

It has left us with a small population, a scanty immigration and a Northwest empty still.

> EDWARD BLAKE, to the Members of the West Durham Reform Convention, Feb. 6, 1891; a reference to the Conservative Party; sometimes misquoted: "An empty west, empty still".

The world is fair in this new land, and
yet I envy you,
For we have not the primrose pale,
and though 'tis just as blue,
The violet in exile here throws out a
scentless bloom,
The rose is fair as England's rose, but
has not its perfume.

> BERTRAM TENNYSON, "Broncho days", 1896.

One of the principal ideas western men have is that it is right to take anything in sight provided nobody else is ahead of them. As a rule it is sound policy for the government to fall in with this idea and encourage the people to go ahead.

> CLIFFORD SIFTON, letter to a western Liberal M.P., Aug., 1897.

The American invasion.

> ANON., the settlers from Kansas and other states who moved into the west after 1900.

Barr, Barr, wily old Barr,
He'll do you as much as he can;
You bet he will collar
Your very last dollar
In the valley of the Saskatchewan.

> ANON., jingle sung in Barr colony camp, 1903. Reference is to Isaac Moses Barr, promoter of land settlement scheme.

The winds which blow from the northwest are violent, and sometimes they bring storms which more than once have shaken the foundations of confederation.

> SENATOR L. O. DAVID, in Senate, *Debates*, Jan. 17, 1905, 9.

A new nation will be born in the West, formed of the very flesh and blood of the United States.

> J. OLIVER CURWOOD, *Worlds work*, X, Sept., 1905, 6608.

The Banana Belt.

> ANON., derisive term used by newspapers, especially in Winnipeg, in reference to north-west Saskatchewan, which was depicted in immigration literature as having a mild climate; F. M. Sclanders of Saskatoon Board of Trade, 1908-16, was owner of a carefully nurtured banana tree; also, the name of a school district in north-western Saskatchewan.

The Last Best West.

> CANADA. DEPT. OF THE INTERIOR, title of a pamphlet published about 1905 and distributed in Europe and the U.S. to attract settlers. (Defined by Sandilands, *Western Canadian dictionary*, 1912, as "A favourite term for describing a new district beyond which one must not dream of anything better".)

I shall be content, when the history of this country shall be written, to have the history of the last eight or nine years, so far as Western administration is concerned, entered in my name.

> SIR CLIFFORD SIFTON, H. of C., *Debates*, May 31, 1906.

What care I here for all Earth's creeds
outworn,
The dreams outlived, the hopes to
ashes turned,
In that old East so dark with rain and
doubt?
Here life swings glad and free and
rude, and I
Shall drink it to the full, and go
content.

> ARTHUR STRINGER, "Morning in the Northwest", 1907.

The North-West will be American.

> GOLDWIN SMITH, *Reminiscences*, 1910, 417.

The West is not the whole of Canada, but the potentiality of Canada's destiny is wrapped in it.

> R. B. BENNETT, Canadian Club, Montreal, Mar. 11, 1912.

Had it not been for the mysterious potency of the West, awaiting the day when it should be incorporated in the Union, it is doubtful whether any Dominion would have been called into being.

> SIR ROBERT FALCONER, speech, "The quality of Canadian life", 1917.

Our West never went through a riotous youth; it has few memories to be forgotten.

> SIR ROBERT FALCONER, speech, "The quality of Canadian life", 1917.

Western Canada has paid for the development of Canadian nationality, and it would appear that it must continue to pay. The acquisitiveness of eastern Canada shows little sign of abatement.

> H.A. INNIS, History of the C.P.R., 1923, 294.

I have an idea that the West understands the East far better than the East understands the West, for the simple reason that most of the Westerners were born in the East, and have kept in touch with conditions there.

> T. DUFF PATTULLO, Premier of B.C., letter to R. B. Bennett, about Nov., 1933, qu. in P. Sherman, Bennett, 1966, 25.

The west is not thinking, the west is drinking.

> RICHARD B. BENNETT, election campaign, 1935, when asked "What is the west thinking?".

To the western eye, looking angrily over the rim of the prairies, the banks and the manufacturers and the protective tariff and the railroad and the Ottawa government all merged into one distorted image – the East.

> STEPHEN LEACOCK, The fortnightly, CXL, 1936, 527.

You may trace to its lair the soft
  Chinook,
And the North Wind trail to the
  Barrens' floor;
But you'll always find, or I'm much
  mistook,
That some old Frenchman's done it
  before.

> LORD TWEEDSMUIR, "The forerunners", 1941.

To the native of the prairies Alberta is the far West; British Columbia the near East.

> EDWARD A. MCCOURT, The Canadian West in fiction, 1949, Preface.

Here on sudden shores
slow lines of covered wagons
lines of laboring steam engines
have ended
Ended in rows and rows
of sprawling ranch houses.

> FRANK DAVEY, "West coast", 1965.

The farmer is the guardian of the western dream; without him the West is just the East.

> HEATHER ROBERTSON, Grass roots, 1973, 34.

Whales

Out on the ocean tracts, his mama
Had, in a North Saghalien gale,
Launched him, a four-ton healthy
  male,
Between Hong Kong and Yokahama.

> E. J. PRATT, "The Cachelot", 1945.

Wheat

Ontario cannot compete
With the Northwest in raising wheat,
For cheaper there they it can grow
So price in future may be low.

> JAMES MCINTYRE, "Dairy cheese odes;
> dairy odes", 1889.

It almost now seems all in vain
For to expect high price for grain.

> JAMES MCINTYRE, "Lines read at a dairy-
> men's supper", 1889.

Give us a good harvest and a bloody
war in Europe.

> ANON., a prayer attributed to the Cana-
> dian pioneer in the West, about 1890.

It is pretty certain, in the light of
present knowledge, that the country
cannot be built up on wheat for export.

> ADAM SHORTT, Queen's quart., Vol. III,
> July, 1895, 20.

Our wheat is king.

> MANITOBA FREE PRESS , column headline,
> Oct. 19, 1896, 1.

The Granary of the Empire.

> JAMES A. SMART, Deputy Minister, legend
> on the arch at the Diamond Jubilee,
> London, 1897, worded: "The granary of
> the Empire, Free homes for millions,
> God bless the Royal Family"; in 1902 at
> the Coronation ceremonies London, an
> arch of wheat in the Strand carried the
> motto "Canada the granary of the Em-
> pire".

The world's bread basket is western
Canada.

> CANADA. DEPT. OF INTERIOR, Western
> Canada, 1899 (pamphlet issued under
> authority of Clifford Sifton).

Number One, Manitoba Hard.

> ANON., rating for Canadian wheat from
> about 1899 and much in demand on
> world markets from 1920 to the early
> 1930's.

Travel from Winnipeg westward, and
it is all the same story; nothing between your eye and the skyline but
wheat, wheat.

> CANADA. DEPT. OF THE INTERIOR, Evolu-
> tion of the prairie by the plow, 1903, 3.
> (Pamphlet.)

The Granary of the World.

> CANADA. DEPT. OF THE INTERIOR, Cana-
> da, a pamphlet issued Dec., 1903, subti-
> tled, The granary of the world.

All the speculation in the world never
raised a bushel of wheat.

> ROBERT C. (BOB) EDWARDS, Calgary Eye
> Opener, Feb. 10, 1912.

Raise less hell and more wheat.

> SIR WILLIAM VAN HORNE, qu. in Nichols,
> Canadian Press, 1948, 17; advice given
> to Manitoba farmers, about 1912.

And when the last sheaf has been cut
and the binders are silent, how splendid is the view across the gently rolling
stubble fields: stook beyond stook,
stook beyond stook, for a quarter of a
mile, for half a mile, and still more
stooks as far as the eye can see, stooks
cresting the distant horizon, ten thousand stooks all waiting to be threshed
and each with its promise of bread, the
gift of the New World to the Old.

> A.H. REGINALD BULLER, Handbook of
> Canada, British Assoc. for the Advance-
> ment of Science, 1924, 317.

This country is the granary of the
world. To put it to that use for which
it was meant is serving God; not to do
so is defying God.

> FREDERICK P. GROVE, "The sower", in
> The turn of the year, 1929, 64.

Wheat does not have to be milked in
the winter.

> E. CORA HIND, 1929, referring to the
> introduction of herds of cattle in the
> Peace River district, qu. in Kennethe M.
> Haig, Brave harvest, 1945, 226.

What's our ambition? Why, we aim to
  be
The Empire's, nay, the whole world's
  granary.
A lofty mark, i' faith, to find our place
Just in the belly of the human race.

> L. A. MCKAY, "Fidelia vulnera amici",
> 1931.

The girls in spring call: 'Sweet, Sweet
  Sweet,'
The tree-top birds sing: 'Tweet, Tweet
  Tweet,'
The little lambs go: 'Bleat, Bleat
  Bleat,'
But the damndest word I ever heard
Is: 'Wheat, Wheat Wheat'.

> IAN MACKENZIE, M.P., 1930-1948, on
> House of Commons debates about
> wheat, qu. in G. MacEwan, *Harvest of
> bread*, 1969, 4.

The Wheat Pool was as much a religious institution as the church.

> HENRY WISE WOOD, (d. 1941), in his later
> years.

Too much wheat, they say. Too much
wheat, say the sleek, well-fed men in
the Chateau Laurier. Too much
wheat, say the clever men in the East
Block. Too much wheat, say the frant-
ic men in Parliament. Too much good
food here on our rich prairie earth.

> BRUCE HUTCHISON, *The unknown coun-
> try*, 1942, 289.

It's Northern wheat, our emblem high
Oh, Northern wheat forever
God bless our soil, and Chou En-lai
And Mitchell Sharp forever.

> GEORGE BAIN, parody on "Maple leaf
> forever", entered in a contest. Mitchell
> Sharp had announced large wheat sale
> to mainland China, 1963.

And even wheat, hard won from
  stubborn soil·
Is not secure against time's certain
  chase,
For what the Wheat Board cannot sell
  will spoil,
And what is left the field-mice will
  erase.

> PAUL HIEBERT, "Behold these monu-
> ments", 1967.

Well, why should I sell the Canadian
farmers' wheat? You know, the way I
understand the system, the Canadian
farmer has been very productive, very
progressive, and very aggressive. He
has increased his productivity enormously. He has founded co-operatives,
he has organized the Wheat Board —
which is not a political instrument
once again, it is something which I
think belongs as much to the farmers
as to the Canadian government — and
he has chosen to operate in a free
market economy.

> PIERRE E. TRUDEAU, speech to Liberal
> Party of Manitoba, Winnipeg, Dec. 13,
> 1968.

Global Crop Disaster Seen Only Relief
Hope.

> SASKATOON *STAR-PHOENIX*, Nov. 4, 1969,
> headline referring to glut of wheat in
> Saskatchewan.

Whereabouts

Where are we?

> LESTER B. PEARSON, Winnipeg, Nov. 26,
> 1964, quip on his uncertainty whether
> to stay in Winnipeg or return to Ottawa.

Whip-poor-wills

the whip-poor-will in the blue
evening
drops wavering notes upon the
  harboured air.

> SUNYATA MACLEAN, *Poems to define the
> corona of silence*, 1970, 44.

Whiskey

Canadian nectar.

> CATHERINE PARR TRAILL, Letter IX, Apr. 18, 1833; *The backwoods of Canada*, 1836, 135.

Widows

An Iroquois arrow made many a widow.

> ISABEL FOULCHÉ-DELBOSC, (1650-65), qu. in *Can. hist. rev.*, 1940, 141.

Widows rarely choose unwisely!

> ARNOLD HAULTAIN, *Hints for lovers*, 1909, 164.

She volunteered that she was a widow, and that forty was only her professional age.

> JOHN MURRAY GIBBON, *Pagan love*, 1922.

Wilderness

Lands that loom like spectres, whited
   regions of winter,
   Wastes of desolate woods, deserts of
     water and shore;
A world of winter and death, within
   these regions who enter,
   Lost to summer and life, go to enter
     no more.

> WILFRED CAMPBELL, "The winter lakes", 1889.

I am the land that listens, I am the
   land that broods;
Steeped in eternal beauty, crystalline
   waters and woods.
Long have I waited lonely, shunned as
   a thing accurst,
Monstrous, moody, pathetic, the last of
   the lands and the first.

> ROBERT W. SERVICE, "The law of the Yukon", 1907.

The mighty voice of Canada will ever
   call to me.
I shall hear the roar of rivers where the
   rapids foam and tear,
I shall smell the virgin upland with its
   balsam-laden air,
And shall dream that I am riding
   down the winding woody vale
With the packer and the packhorse on
   the Athabaska Trail.

> ARTHUR CONAN DOYLE, "The Athabaska Trail", 1919.

Give me a good canoe, a pair of Jibway snowshoes, my beaver, my family and ten thousand square miles of wilderness and I am happy.

> GREY OWL, qu. by Hugh Eayrs, Foreword to *Pilgrims of the wild*, 1935, xi.

I tell you the wilderness we fell
is nothing to the one we breed.

> EARLE BIRNEY, "Man is a snow", 1946.

Let whoever comes to tame this land,
   beware!
Can you put a bit to the lunging wind?
Can you hold wild horses by the hair?

> DOUGLAS LE PAN, "Canoe-trip", 1948.

A large and lonely land
Under a lonely sky
Save for the friendly stars;
A land not to be wooed in a day
But by long courting.

> THOMAS SAUNDERS, "Beyond the lakes", 1949.

The wilderness remains a partner in the venture.

> CANADA. ROY. COMM. ON CANADA'S ECONOMIC PROSPECTS, *Final report*, 1957, 6.

Great stretches of wilderness, so that its frontier is a circumference rather than a boundary; a country with huge rivers and islands that most of its natives have never seen; a country that has made a nation out of the stops on two of the world's longest railway lines.

NORTHROP FRYE, in *Studia varia*, Roy. Soc. Can., 1957, 21.

Those old men, my ancestors
perhaps so long in the wilderness
their souls grew gnarled
and like the bush
the roots of their being
bore a home in the desert.

STEVE SMITH, "Wilderness", 1964.

Canoeists and other primitive-trippers are not delighted to encounter others intent on the same private experience. How many visitors constitute the end of wilderness?

JOHN A. LIVINGSTON, in Borden Spears, ed., *Wilderness Canada*, 1970, 118.

Wildlife

The young man looks at our abounding Canadian wildlife, and thinks that we have a precious heritage; the old man looks back at his youth and mourns for the vast numbers of wild things that now exist in a mere shadow of their former abundance; and whether young or old, we need to keep this matter constantly in mind, and be prepared to do our bit to hand on to our successors as full a measure as possible of the wildlife that we have enjoyed.

WILLIAM E. SAUNDERS, *Can. science digest*, Dec., 1937.

Will

For stormy times and ruined plans
Make keener the determined will,
And Fate with all its gloomy bans
Is but the spirit's vassal still:
And that deep force, that made aspire
Man from dull matter and the beast,
Burns sleeplessly a spreading fire,
By every thrust and wind increased.

ARCHIBALD LAMPMAN, "Phokaia", 1900.

The compassed mind must quiver
    north
    though every chart defective;
there is no fog but in the will,
    the iceberg is elective.

EARLE BIRNEY, "World conference", 1945.

The will of man is unconquerable. Even God cannot conquer it.

MALCOLM LOWRY, *Under the volcano*, 1947, 93.

Williams, Percy

Well, well, well. So I'm supposed to be the World's 100M. Champion. (Crushed apples). No more fun in running now.

PERCY WILLIAMS, Diary, July 30, 1928, qu. by Ray Gardner in *Maclean's Canada*, 1960, 130.

The Canadian, Percy Williams, is the greatest sprinter the world has ever seen and he will be even greater before his career is ended.

GENERAL DOUGLAS MACARTHUR, President, U.S. Olympic Committee, after Williams' victories, Olympic Games, Amsterdam, July, 1928.

I was just like any kid of twenty. I was simply bewildered by it all. I didn't like running. Oh, I was so glad to get out of it all.

PERCY WILLIAMS, qu. in *Maclean's*, Nov. 24, 1956, 46.

Wind

Cease, Wind, to blow
And drive the peopled snow,
And move the haunted arras to and
    fro,
And moan of things I fear to know
Yet would rend from thee, Wind,
    before I go
On the blind pilgrimage.
Cease, Wind, to blow.

> BLISS CARMAN, "The red wolf", 1892.

The wind changed every way and fled
    Across the meadows and the wheat;
It whirled the swallows overhead,
    And swung the daisies at my
        feet . . .

Took all the maples by surprise,
    And made the poplars clash and
        shiver,
And flung my hair about my eyes,
    And sprang and blackened on the
        river.

> ARCHIBALD LAMPMAN, "The wind's
> word", *Independent*, July 26, 1894.

There paused to shut the door
    A fellow called the Wind,
With mystery before,·
    And reticence behind.

> BLISS CARMAN, "At the granite gate",
> 1895.

On wan dark night on Lac St. Pierre,
    De win' she blow, blow, blow,
An' de crew of de woodscow "Julie
        Plante"
    Got scar't an' run below –
For de win' she blow like hurricane
    Bimeby she blow some more,
An' de scow bus' up on Lac St. Pierre
    Wan arpent from de shore.

> WILLIAM H. DRUMMOND, "The wreck of
> the *Julie Plante*", 1897.

To know the laws that govern the
winds, and to know that you know
them, will give you an easy mind on
your voyage around the world; otherwise you may tremble at the appearance of every cloud.

> JOSHUA SLOCUM, Nova Scotia seafarer,
> *Sailing alone around the world*, 1900,
> (1949, 143).

Beneath her sloping neck
Her bosom-gourds swelled chastely,
    white as spray,
Wind-tost – without a fleck –
The air which heaved them was less
    pure than they.

> CHARLES MAIR, "Innocence", 1901.

I am Wind, the Deathless Dreamer
    Of the summer world;
Tranced in snows of shade and
        shimmer,
    On a cloud scarp curled.

> WILFRED CAMPBELL, "The wind", 1905.

The Canada wind is the keen north
    wind,
The wind of the secret sea,
And quickens the soul of me.

> HELEN MERRILL, "The Canada wind",
> ca.1912.

The wind upon the hill has sweetest
    hush,
The day is melting into tenderest
    flame,
And from the valley, where the waters
    rush,
Comes up the even song of the lone
    hermit-thrush.

> WILLIAM E. MARSHALL, "Brookfield",
> 1914.

And I have heard the wind awake at nights
Like some poor mother left with empty hands,
Go whimpering in the silent stubble fields
And creeping through bare houses without lights.

FREDERICK LAIGHT, "Soliloquy", 1937.

The wind turns in silent frenzy upon itself, whirling into a smoking funnel, breathing up topsoil and tumbleweed skeletons to carry them on its spinning way over the prairie, out and out to the far line of the sky.

W.O. MITCHELL, *Who has seen the wind*, 1947, last line.

How many leaves have to scrape together to record the rustle of the wind? He tried to distinguish the sound of acacia from the sound of maple.

LEONARD COHEN, *The favourite game*, 1963 (1970, 66).

Wine

The wine we drink is bitter
Compounded of the blood
Of not one Christ but many
Who gained no holihood.

MIRIAM WADDINGTON, "The bread we eat", 1955.

I am thinking what the grapes are thinking
become part of their purple mentality that is
    I am satisfied with the sun and eventual fermenting bubble-talk together.

AL PURDY, "The winemaker's beat-étude", 1968.

Winning

If thou wouldst truly win
The race thou art pursuing.
Heed well the voice within.

CHARLES SANGSTER, "The dreamer", 1860.

I only like winners.

E.P. TAYLOR, qu. in *Holiday*, Apr., 1964, 62.

Winners who win and become heroes make everyone uncomfortable. But winners who chose to be losers allow us all to dream that we, too, have made that choice.

ROBERT HARLOW, *Scann*, 1972, 242.

Winnipeg

The city wants lifting into the air ten or fifteen feet.

GOLDWIN SMITH, *The Week*, Sept. 18, 1884, 659.

So far as Winnipeg is concerned it is a discouraging place and always was, but I would not fret about it. I think it will come around all right. If it does not we can always have the satisfaction of consigning it to a warmer place.

CLIFFORD SIFTON, letter to J. S. Willison, on the election, Dec., 1899.

We're a hundred dollars from anywhere.

ANON., popular saying, Winnipeg, late 19th century.

Winnipeg is the West.

RUPERT BROOKE, *Letters from America*, 1916, 102.

The manners of Winnipeg, of the West, impress the stranger as better than those of the East, more friendly, more hearty, more certain to achieve graciousness, if not grace.

RUPERT BROOKE, *Letters from America*, 1916, 103.

The doors of vast opportunity lay wide open and Canada's adventurous sons flocked to Winnipeg to have a part in the great expansion – the building of a newer and greater Canadian West. They were big men, come together with big purpose. Their ideas were big, and they fought for the realization of them.

GEORGE H. HAM, *Reminiscences of a raconteur*, 1921, 30.

If there ever was a fool's paradise, it sure was located in Winnipeg. Men made fortunes – mostly on paper – and life was one continuous joy-ride.

GEORGE H. HAM, *Reminiscences of a raconteur*, 1921, 51.

The stone-cold hotbed of Canadian radicalism.

JAMES H. GRAY, *The winter years*, 1966, 86.

A sprawling, gap-toothed collection of ghettos.

JAMES H. GRAY, *The boy from Winnipeg*, 1970, 4.

Winnipeg should be the new capital for Canada's second century. Never mind about Ottawa, they've had the good life long enough.

W.A.C. BENNETT, qu. in Toronto *Star*, Aug. 11, 1970, 6.

Winter

I no longer wonder the elegant arts are unknown here; the rigour of the climate suspends the very powers of the understanding; what then must become of those of the imagination? Those who expect to see "A new Athens rising near the pole," will find themselves extremely disappointed. Genius will never mount high, where the faculties of the mind are benumbed half the year.

FRANCES BROOKE, *The history of Emily Montague*, 1769, Vol. 1, 216.

Here the rough Bear subsists his winter year,
And licks his paw and finds no better fare.

STANDISH O'GRADY, "The emigrant", 1841.

When muskrats build their houses high look for a hard winter.

ANON., saying of pioneer Ontario farmers, early 19th century.

A hard winter brings a hot summer.

ANON., saying of pioneer Ontario farmers, early 19th century.

Cold enough to freeze the hair off a dog's back.

THOMAS C. HALIBURTON, *Sam Slick's wise saws*, 1853, ch. 11.

Here winter's breath is rude,
    His fingers cold and wan;
But what's his wildest mood
    To the tyranny of man?

ALEXANDER MCLACHLAN, "The emigrant", 1861.

A constitution nursed upon the oxygen of our bright winter atmosphere makes its owner feel as though he could toss about the pine trees in his glee.

LORD DUFFERIN, address, Gimli, Manitoba, Sept. 15, 1877.

The summers, the winters – I have sometimes doubted whether there could be a great race without the hardy influence of winters in due proportion.

WALT WHITMAN, *Diary in Canada*, [1880], 1904.

Those frozen to death display on their visages a look of contentment achieved only by successful religious mystics.

WILLIAM HALES HINGSTON, *The climate of Canada and its relation to life and health*, 1884; paraphrased in P. Russell, ed., *Nationalism in Canada*, 1966, 11.

Canadian climate must have been
    changeable
  ever since the world begun,
One hour snowing, and the next
    raining like fun,
Our blood sometimes thick, other
    times thin,
This is the time colds begin.

JAMES GAY, "Canadian climate", [1885?].

Sharp is the frost, the Northern Light
Flickers and shoots his streamers
    bright;

Snow-drifts cumber the untracked
    road;
Bends the pine with its heavy load;

Each small star, though it shines so
    bright,
Looks half pinched with the cold
    to-night.

FRANCIS RYE, in *Canadian birthday book*, 1887, 384.

The Winter speeds his fairies forth and
    mocks
  Poor bitten men with laughter icy
    cold,
  Turning the brown of youth to
    white and old
    With hoary-woven locks,

And gray men young with roses in
    their cheeks.

ARCHIBALD LAMPMAN, "Winter", 1888.

The winter comes one month before the autumn.

ABBÉ GEORGES DUGAS, *Un voyageur*, 1890, 97, (trans.), on winter at Hudson's Bay.

The frost that stings like fire upon my
    cheek,
  The loneliness of this forsaken
    ground,
The long, white drift upon whose
    powdered peak
  I sit in the great silence as one
    bound.

ARCHIBALD LAMPMAN, "Winter uplands", 1900.

There was an old man of Quebec,
Who was buried in snow to his neck.
When asked, "Are you friz?"
He replied, "Yes, I is,
But we don't call this cold in Quebec."

RUDYARD KIPLING, (early 20th century), qu. in *Maclean's*, July 1, 1950.

Barley in the heater, salt pork in the
    pantry
How nice that you never feel cold in
    this country.

PAUL HIEBERT, "Song to the four seasons", 1947.

Beyond the dripping nose and tear,
Beyond the chilblain and the bite,
Beyond the scratchy underwere,
Beyond the eighty-below at night,
There still must lie – though drifts
    conceal –
Some hidden good for man's descry,
Some secret bounty for his weal,
Which man should shovel out – or
    try.

PAUL G. HIEBERT, *Sarah Binks*, 1947.

Cold pastoral: the shepherd under the
  snow
Sleeps circled with his sheep.
Above them, though successive winters
  heap
Rigours, and wailing weathers go
Like beasts about, time only rocks
  their sleep

> JAY MACPHERSON, "The faithful shep-
> herd", 1957.

Our winter, though, has paid us back
in kind. It has readily accepted its
double role of judge and justifier.
Before its tribunal, our fear of living,
our inability to exist, our lack of
substance on this earth, all receive
their absolution and condemnation:
absolution for all our failings of the
past, and simultaneous condemnation
for those of the future. Peace be with
you, my son, and sin again! Our winter
whitewashes us, without ever giving us
a taste for true colour, but only for
that of the colour print.

> PIERRE TROTTIER, Mon Babel, 1963, 140.
> (Trans.)

Mon pays, ce n'est pas un pays
C'est l'hiver.

> GILLES VIGNEAULT, "Mon pays", song
> from NFB film, "La neige a fondu sur
> la Manicouagan", 1965; "My country is
> not a country it's the winter".

there is the wind
and the numbing snow five months
  long
at best, blowing endurance
and stupidity into the people

> JOHN NEWLOVE, "Seeing me dazed",
> 1965.

Soon, all too soon
winter will storm in
fall heavily upon us.

> RAYMOND SOUSTER, "Pact", 1968.

We have used winter to create a
beautiful myth with which to apologize for our tardiness in regard to
history, progress, civilization, culture,
art.

> PIERRE TROTTIER, in W. Kilbourn, ed.,
> Canada: a guide to the peaceable king-
> dom, 1970, 83. (Trans.)

winter makes us
know
new negatives: white
darkness.

> DOUGLAS BARBOUR, in White, 1972, 22.

Wisdom

Why should the wisdom of this world
still continue to prevail, to the total
exclusion of any higher wisdom? Why
shouldn't the higher wisdom begin
now to take precedence of mere
worldly wisdom?

> HENRY WENTWORTH MONK, d.1896, in R.
> S. Lambert, For the time is at hand,
> 1947, 162.

The idea that a wise man must be
solemn is bred and preserved among
people who have no idea what wisdom
is, and can only respect whatever
makes them feel inferior.

> ROBERTSON DAVIES, A voice from the
> attic, 1960, 221.

Wisdom is a variable possession. Every
man is wise when pursued by a mad
dog; fewer when pursued by a mad
woman; only the wisest survive when
attacked by a mad notion.

> ROBERTSON DAVIES, Samuel March-
> banks' almanack, 1967, 82.

Here you receive another kind of
  wisdom,
Bitter and icy and not to everybody's
  taste.

> WALTER BAUER, "Canada", 1968.

It isn't the function of the wise to guide the world, or of the good to improve it. The only function of the wise and the good is to pick up the pieces, to keep picking up the pieces.

> RICHARD J. NEEDHAM, *A friend in Needham*, 1969, 38.

Were we wise, we would make less effort to understand other people, and make more effort – through our clarity, through our honesty – to help them understand us.

> RICHARD J. NEEDHAM, *A friend in Needham*, 1969, 11.

Wit

Grip still has a Sir John
But the Grand Old Face has gone.

> GRIP, June 20, 1891, on the death of Sir J. A. Macdonald, who was often caricatured in its pages.

Many a great man's reputation for wit is due to his having been interviewed by a bright reporter.

> ROBERT C. (BOB) EDWARDS, Calgary *Eye Opener*, Feb. 22, 1919.

Witches

The witch of Plum Hollow.

> ANON., a reference to Mrs. Elizabeth Barnes, 1800-1892?, so-called because of her uncanny gift for telling fortunes; lived near Plum Hollow, Leeds and Grenville Counties, Ontario.

Wives

Don't expect a wife to help or hinder you. Don't expect anything. That is the golden rule of marriage.

> ROBERTSON DAVIES, *A jig for the gypsy*, 1954, 55.

Many a promising career has been wrecked by marrying the wrong sort of woman. The right sort of woman can distinguish between Creative Lassitude and plain shiftlessness.

> ROBERTSON DAVIES, *A voice from the attic*, 1960, last page.

Your children grow up, they leave
  you.
They have become soldiers and riders.
Your mate dies after a life of service.
Who knows you? Who remembers
  you?

> LEONARD COHEN, "You have the lovers", 1961.

Honey you're awful lucky
I ever came home you're so bloody
  homely
and the girls out there so beautiful so
hell it must be love I guess.

> AL PURDY, "Engraved on a tomb", 1965.

What can all the men in the world be to a right minded married woman in comparison to her husband, and even if should that husband be a brute her duty remains the same. She has in the sight of God promised to love honour and obey and cleave unto him until death. The lot of some women is very hard but there is another and better world where those who do right receive their reward.

> AMELIA HARRIS, *Diary*, (unpublished), qu. in L. Creighton, *The elegant Canadians*, 1967, 115.

it's a point of honour
with them to treat their wives
like whores, they talk about bedding
them as they talk
about going to the privy.

> ALDEN NOWLAN, "Cousins", 1973.

Wolfe, James

Mat is he? Well, by Gott, I wish he would bite some of my other cheners-als.

> GEORGE III, 1758, answer to a remark made on the appointment of Wolfe by Pitt to command the expedition against Quebec.

He asks no one's opinion and wants no advice.

> JAMES GIBSON, letter to Gov. Lawrence, Quebec, Aug. 1, 1759.

There is such a choice of difficulties that I am at a loss how to determine.

> JAMES WOLFE, despatch to Pitt, Sept. 2, 1759.

Tell me, tell me how goes the battle there?

> JAMES WOLFE, statement ascribed to him before his death, Sept. 13, 1759, by James Henderson, letter, in *Can. hist. rev.*, 1923, 54.

He raiséd up his head
Where the guns did rattle
And to his aide he said
"How goes the battle?"

"Quebec is all our own,
They can't prevent it."
He said without a groan,
"I die contented."

> ANON., colonist's song, 1760's, also known as "Bold Wolfe" or "The death of General Wolfe".

The world could not expect more from him than he thought himself capable of performing. He looked on danger as the favourable moment that would call forth his talents.

> HORACE WALPOLE, 1763, *Memoirs of George III*, 1845, 239.

England, with all thy faults I love thee still.
Time was when it was praise and boast enough
In every clime, and travel where we might,
That we were born her children. Praise enough
To fill the ambition of a private man
That Chatham's language was his mother's tongue.
And Wolfe's great name compatriot with his own.

> WILLIAM COWPER, *The task*, Book II 1785.

Valour gave them a common death, history a common fame, posterity a common monument.

> JAMES C. FISHER, Quebec, trans. of his Latin inscription on the Wolfe-Mont-calm monument, Plains of Abraham, erected 1828. (Mortem virtus com-munem, famam historia, monumentum posteritas dedit.)

Here died Wolfe, Victorious, September 13th, 1759.

> WOLFE MONUMENT, Plains of Abraham, Quebec City, erected 1849, inscription. In July 1965 the monument was restored after being pulled down by separatists in Mar., 1963. A new bilingual inscription was used, omitting the word Victorious.

"They run! they run!" – "Who run?" he cried,
As swiftly to his pallid brow,
Like crimson sunlight upon snow,
The anxious blood returned;
"The French! the French!" a voice replied,
When quickly paled life's ebbing tide,
And though his words were weak and low,
His eye with valour burned.
"Thank God! I die in peace," he said.

> CHARLES SANGSTER, "Death of Wolfe", 1860.

In days of yore, from Britain's shore
Wolfe, the dauntless hero came,
And planted firm Britannia's flag
On Canada's fair domain.
Here may it wave — our boast and
    pride,
And join in love together,
The Thistle, Shamrock, Rose entwine
The Maple Leaf forever!

> ALEXANDER MUIR, "The maple leaf for-
> ever", 1867, popular version. Muir
> wrote in a letter, Toronto *Empire*, Sept.
> 8, 1894, that the first two lines should
> be: "In days of yore the hero Wolfe/
> Britain's glory did maintain".

Wolves

Wolves are scarce in Canada, but they
afford the finest furs in all the country.
Their flesh is white, and good to eat;
they pursue their prey to the tops of
the tallest trees.

> WILLIAM GUTHRIE, *Guthrie's geographi-
> cal grammar*, 1807.

Any man that says he's been et by a
wolf is a liar.

> SAM MARTIN, of Algoma, attributed about
> 1910 by J. W. Curran in his *Wolves
> don't bite*, 1940, 212.

The story of Little Red Riding Hood
has laid an unreasoning fear on countless millions of human beings.

> J. W. CURRAN, *Wolves don't bite*, 1940, 4.

There is no authentic report of wolves
ever having killed a human being in
the Canadian North; although there
must have been times when the temptation was well-nigh irresistible.

> FARLEY MOWAT, *Never cry wolf*, 1963,
> 228.

The Canadian wolf
with flailing
double jointed legs
is to my mind
awesome on this continent.

> MICHAEL ONDAATJE, "Over the garden
> wall", 1967.

Woman

I always feel safe with these women
folk, for I have always found that the
road to a woman's heart lies through
her child.

> THOMAS C. HALIBURTON, *Sam Slick*, 1836,
> chap. X.

No woman wants to be loved; she only
wants to love.

> JAMES DE MILLE, *A strange manuscript*,
> 1888, ch. 20.

Woman is a species of which every
woman is a variety.

> ARNOLD HAULTAIN, *Hints for lovers*,
> 1909, 29.

Amorous creature of exquisite aura —
    Marvel of dark glamorie.

> TOM MACINNES, "Zalinka", 1923.

A woman wants to be taken, not
adored.

> FREDERICK P. GROVE, *Settlers of the
> marsh*, 1925, 130.

In neurasthenia or insanity, "*cherchez
la femme*" — woman is at the bottom
of most troubles.

> SIR WILLIAM OSLER, *Aphorisms*, 1950,
> 136.

For all mankind is matted so within
    me
    Despair can find no earthroom tall
      to grow;
My veins run warm however veers
    time's weather;
    I breathe Perhaps and May and
      never No.
Under the cool geyser of the dogwood
    Time lets me open books and live;
Under the glittering comment of the
    planets
    Life asks, and I am made to give.

    EARLE BIRNEY, *Trial of a city*, 1952, 43.

What she collects is men
as a bee honey, leaving out
the subtlety of that swift winger.
    There's little
in the way her eyes look into theirs (O
    take me),
her body arches forward (possess me
    now).

    RAYMOND SOUSTER, "The collector",
    1955.

A woman sharpens herself to endure.
Since she can be trod on like an egg,
she grows herself to stone.

    SHEILA WATSON, *The double hook*, 1959,
    117.

She must do twice as well as a man to
be thought half as good. But it's not
too hard for a woman to be twice as
good as a man.

    CHARLOTTE WHITTON, Mayor of Ottawa,
    speaking of women in public life, qu. in
    Liberty, Nov., 1962.

I had learned that there were more
important obstacles to overcome in
this world than a difficult woman.

    STEPHEN VIZINCZEY, *In praise of older
    women*, 1965, 189.

The woman I am
is not what you see
move over love
make room for me

    DOROTHY LIVESAY, "The unquiet bed",
    1967.

The only person who can cure you of a
woman is that woman herself; and
given time enough, she usually does.

    RICHARD J. NEEDHAM, *A friend in Need-
    ham*, 1969, 6.

Women

Canadian women are witty, courteous
and pious, at Quebec gamesters, at
Montreal more devoted to conversation and the dance.

    MONTCALM, letter to his wife, Apr. 16,
    1757.

There is not perhaps on earth a race of
females, who talk so much, or feel so
little, of love as the French; the very
reverse is in general true of the English.

    FRANCES BROOKE, *The history of Emily
    Montague*, Vol. 1, 1769, 23.

Women forgive injuries, but never
forget slights.

    T. C. HALIBURTON, *The old judge*, 1849,
    ch.15.

The crass ingratitude of haughty man,
Vested in all the pride of place and
    power,
Brooks not the aspirations of my sex,
However just.

    SARAH ANNE CURZON, *The sweet girl
    graduate*, 1887 (Comedy in four acts),
    Act 1.

If we are ever to be freed from the demon rum in Canada, if we are ever to secure social purity, if we are ever to occupy the position we should occupy as a Christian country in working out the country's true destiny, and elevating the moral tone of Eastern immigrants who are to throng to our coasts, the rights of citizenship must be given to our women.

THOMAS WEBSTER, *The Methodist mag.*, Feb., 1894, 157; qu. in C. L. Cleverdon, *The woman suffrage movement in Canada*, 1974, xix.

ANNIE EDSON TAYLOR
First To Go Over The Horseshoe Falls In A Barrel And Live
October 24, 1901

ANON., inscription on tombstone, Oakwood Cemetery, Niagara Falls, New York; she died in 1921.

In matters amatory and maternal, woman is the truly combative animal.

ARNOLD HAULTAIN, *Hints for lovers*, 1909, 182.

Even when our Mother Eve (the fairest of her daughters) was given the best man ever made, she chose a devil for her confidant and treated the salvation of her race as a matter for a bargain counter, vainly deciding that she could get something better than Paradise from the advance agent of the other shop.

THOMAS C. ROBSON, *Grain growers' guide*, Dec. 11, 1912; qu. in Ward & Spafford, eds., *Politics in Saskatchewan*, 1968, 79.

Women will continue to be wives, mothers, homemakers, but they will no longer be content with the dull routine of homes from which nearly all productive employments have been removed to shop or factory.

CARRIE M. DERICK, Montreal *Daily herald*, Nov. 26, 1913, 4.

People still speak of womanhood as if it were a disease.

NELLIE MCCLUNG, in 1916, qu. in M. Anderson, *Mother was not a person*, 1972, 23.

I say that the Holy Scriptures, theology, ancient philosophy, Christian philosophy, history, anatomy, physiology, political economy, and feminine psychology, all seem to indicate that the place of women in this world is not amid the strife of the political arena, but in her home.

JEAN JOSEPH DENIS, H. of C., *Debates*, 1918, 638.

Few women are enrolled among the Makers of Canada. Yet in all save the earliest years they have formed nearly half the population and done almost half the work. But historians and businessmen tell us little of the part they have played. The women's stage was set not in the limelight but in the firelight.

ISABEL SKELTON, *The backwoodswoman*, 1924, 7.

Her thoughts were as pure as the dawn upon the sea,
But through those ugly eyes and mouth they couldn't get free –
And no one had a kinder heart anywhere about:
O, if God had only made her inside out!

WILSON MACDONALD, "Maggie Swartz", 1926.

How can she be herself without you there to badger and to hector and harass? God help her, she is like a waterfall with nothing to fall over!

MAZO DE LA ROCHE, *Building of Jalna*, 1927 (1945, 168).

There's still a strain of barbarism dormant in every woman.

ARTHUR STRINGER, *Christina and I*, 1929.

Faced with the creator's problem, most women take one of two courses: either they are completely and enchantingly feminine, or else a valiant, impersonal, cold fury masks their feminity, which nevertheless comes through, as a sort of re-agent, suffusing everything they do.

GRAHAM MCINNES, *Can. forum*, Nov., 1937, 274.

A Lady, in Canada, is a dowdy and unappetizing mammal, who is much given to Culture and Good Works, but derives no sinful satisfaction from either; a Lady is without discernible sex, but can reproduce its kind by a system resembling radar; a Lady does not have to be attractive, because it is sufficient in this wicked world to be Good.

ROBERTSON DAVIES, *Table talk*, 1949,15.

There is nothing men like so much as generalizing about women; all women are alike, except the one they love.

ROBERTSON DAVIES, *Tempest-tost*, 1951, 234.

Modern women I see cast in the role of furies striving to castrate the male; their efforts aided by all the malignant forces of a technological civilization that has rendered the male's creative role of revelation superfluous — if not an industrial hazard and a nuisance.

IRVING LAYTON, Foreword, *A red carpet for the sun*, 1959, 4.

This is the inglorious age of the mass-woman. Her tastes are dominant everywhere — in theatres, stores, art, fiction, houses, furniture — and these tastes are dainty and trivial.

IRVING LAYTON, *A red carpet for the sun*, 1959, Foreword.

Oh what a female Jesus. Always suffering for others.

JAMES REANEY, *The killdeer*, 1962, 60.

Look like a girl, think like a man, act like a lady, and work like a dog.

MRS. ADELE GHANADY, National Employment Service, Nanaimo, B. C., advice to career-minded women, qu. in *Liberty*, Feb., 1963.

Up to the age of 18 a woman needs good parents; from 18 to 35 she needs good looks, from 35 to 55 she needs personality, and from 55 on, she needs money.

HOLLY ARMSTRONG, Toronto Dominion Bank public relations consultant, speaking to Leamington Ont., Kiwanis Club, qu. in *Liberty*, Sept., 1963.

who would erase the scribbled slate
of gone years, their jumbled algebra,
their rude designs
junked under a rainbow, all blood and
    bone
that links the mother and the morning
    daughter —
and acknowledge now, armed and still
    insolent
that what is housed in the fragile skull
    — light or learning or verbal
    innocence —
grows from the woman somehow who
    housed the whole body,
who first fed the vessels, the flesh and
    the sense.

GWENDOLYN MACEWEN, "Morning laughter", 1963.

Most women don't even live lives of quiet desperation. (Quiet desperation is far too dramatic.) Most women live lives doing the dishes, finishing one day's dishes and facing the next, until one day the rectal polyp is found or the heart stops and it's over. And all that's left of them is a name on a gravestone.

> BRIAN MOORE, *I am Mary Dunne*, 1966, 156.

It is easy and partly right to blame men and their vested interests for making women's path difficult. But only partly right – many barriers are built and kept in repair by women themselves, tradition-bound, envious or timid.

> MARY QUAYLE INNIS, *The clear spirit*, 1966, xii.

Every woman wants a man who is wicked enough for her to respect and trust.

> RICHARD J. NEEDHAM, *A friend in Needham*, 1969, 28.

In the world of women, it's the man with the past who has the future.

> RICHARD J. NEEDHAM, *A friend in Needham*, 1969, 29.

Regarding women, it might be said that if you're close enough to smell the rose, you're close enough to feel the thorns.

> RICHARD J. NEEDHAM, *A friend in Needham*, 1969, 33.

The formulation of policies affecting the lives of all Canadians is still the prerogative of men. The absurdity of this situation was illustrated when debate in the House of Commons on a change in abortion law was conducted by 263 men and one woman. Nowhere else in Canadian life is the persistent distinction between male and female roles of more consequence. No country can make a claim to having equal status for its women so long as its government lies entirely in the hands of men.

> CANADA. ROY. COMM. ON THE STATUS OF WOMEN, *Report*, 1970, 355.

She makes every boy feel a man and every man feel a boy.

> ANON., about Thérèse F. Casgrain, qu. by F. R. Scott in Casgrain, *A woman in a man's world*, 1972, 10.

The true liberation of women cannot take place without the liberation of men.

> THÉRÈSE CASGRAIN, *A woman in a man's world*, 1972, 190.

We should accept that fact that we are becoming 'the people our parents warned us against'.

> SARAH SPINKS, in *Women unite!*, 1972, 86.

Do You realize, I wonder, what submerged identities women like me can have? How repressed and suppressed we are by a life that can give us no kind of self-expression? Unless You really are female after all, as the Women's Lib girls insist, even You can't know what it's like to be invisible for years on end. To live locked up. Never spontaneous. Never independent.

> CONSTANCE BERESFORD-HOWE, *The book of Eve*, 1973, 9 (a letter addressed to God).

Women in Politics

Women have cleaned up things since time began, and if women get into politics there will be a cleaning up of pigeon-holes and forgotten corners in which the dust of years have fallen.

> NELLIE L. MCCLUNG, speech in Minneapolis, May 7, 1916.

Women understand that men must often be kept from soiling themselves with the dirty details of life in order to accomplish the big shiny jobs unimpeded. And women in politics have generally accepted this role — to do all the hum-drum, tedious, must-be-done jobs.

> JUDY LAMARSH, *Memoirs of a bird in a gilded cage*, 1969, 36.

You can't fight, fight, fight all the time without becoming less feminine. In politics, you have to.

> JUDY LAMARSH, address, Women's Canadian Club of Toronto, Jan. 15, 1969.

Women's Employment

The Canadian government has in the last few years adopted a passive approach with respect to equal employment opportunities for women. For several years before that, there was no approach. And before that, the approach was on the negative side of passive — it was one of promoting unequal opportunities for women.

> KATHLEEN ARCHIBALD, *Sex and the Public Service*, 1970, 127.

Women's Liberation

The phrase the "New Woman" is not unlike the phrase the "New Chemistry": the materials are the same; what is new is the nomenclature.

> ARNOLD HAULTAIN, *Hints for lovers*, 1909, 53.

We may as well admit that there is discontent among women. We cannot drive them back to the spinning wheel and the mathook, for they will not go. But there is really no cause for alarm, for discontent is not necessarily wicked. There is such a thing as divine discontent just as there is criminal contentment.

NELLIE MCCLUNG, *In times like these*, 1915, 58.

OFF THE COCK OFF THE CUNT OFF THE WATER OFF THE SKY OFF BOOKS OFF HISTORY

OFF BOOKS OF RELIGION OFF VISION OFF SMELL OFF KNOWLEDGE OFF
>   FEELING OFF K

>   OFF K
>   OFF K

> MAXINE GADD, "OFF", 1973.

Why are you angry woman? Why do you rise?
You say these walls a prison make,
And you're confined in so many ways.
There's a very good chance you'll learn to survive
If you close the door on your searching mind.

> RITA MACNEIL, song, qu. in *Herstory* (Sask. Women's Calendar Collective), 1975, "Dec. 22-28".

Why not?

> CANADA. DEPT. OF HEALTH AND WELFARE, phrase used in support of International Women's Year, 1975. (See H. of C., *Debates*, Apr. 17, 1975, 4945.)

Women's Rights

Woman's rights movements make small progress in Canada, because the Canadian woman gets what she wants without let or hindrance: because she has so many privileges, the right to vote on a subject in which she takes little or no interest seems not worth striving for. Canadian legislators are quicker to grant privileges to women than Canadian women are to demand them.

> HECTOR CHARLESWORTH, *Can. mag.*, Vol. 1, 1893, 188.

For generations women have been thinking, and thought without expression is dynamic and gathers volume by repression. Evolution when blocked and suppressed becomes revolution.

> NELLIE MCCLUNG, *In times like these*, 1915, 58.

When I hear men talk about women being the angel of the home I always, mentally at least, shrug my shoulders in doubt. I do not want to be the angel of any home; I want for myself what I want for other women, absolute equality. After that is secured then men and women can take turns at being angels.

> AGNES MACPHAIL, H. of C., *Debates*, Feb. 26, 1925, 570.

All I have to say is this. I'm sick and tired of all this 'woman' business. In all the time I've been in the House of Commons I've never asked for anything on the ground that I was a woman. If I didn't deserve it on my own merit I didn't want it! That's all I have to say.

> AGNES MACPHAIL, speech at women's luncheon during first C.C.F. convention, Regina, July, 1933.

The iron dropped into the souls of women in Canada, when we heard that it took a man to decree that his mother was not a person.

> MARY ELLEN SMITH, M.L.A. (B.C.). Reference is to ruling of the Supreme Court of Canada, Apr., 1928, that under the terms of the B.N.A. Act the word "person" referred to men only.

Women should have both – equal rights because they are human beings, special privileges because they are women.

> RICHARD J. NEEDHAM, *A friend in Needham*, 1969, 34.

Women's Suffrage

All social evils will not be voted down, nor the offices all filled with saints at the next election thereafter. It will not be found the panacea for all human, or all womanly, ills. It will scarcely be the *cure* of any. It will be simply the opening of another door – the passage into a larger freedom.

> ANON., "M", *Can. monthly and nat. rev.*, II, May, 1879, 579.

This is a matter of evolution and evolution is only a working out of God's laws. For this reason we must not attempt to hurry it on.

> JAMES P. WHITNEY, on woman suffrage, Toronto *Mail and empire*, Mar. 21, 1911.

You may be our close companion
  Share our troubles, ease our pain,
You may bear the servant's burden
  (But without the servant's gain);
You may scrub and cook and iron
  Sew the buttons on our coat,
But as men we must protect you –
  You are far to frail to vote.

> L. CASE RUSSELL, "You mustn't ask to vote", 1912.

I am opposed by all the short-haired women and the long-haired men in the Province.

> SIR RODMOND ROBLIN, on the women's suffrage agitation, Manitoba, 1912.

I believe woman suffrage would be a retrograde movement, that it will break up the home, that it will throw the children into the arms of the servant girls.

> SIR RODMOND ROBLIN, Winnipeg, Jan. 27, 1914, speaking to delegation from the Political Equality League.

We wish to compliment this delegation on their splendid and gentlemanly appearance. If without exercising the vote, such splendid specimens of manhood can be produced, such a system of affairs should not be interfered with. Any system of civilization that can produce such splendid specimens . . . is good enough for me, and if it's good enough for me it's good enough for anyone. Another trouble is that if men start to vote they will vote too much. Politics unsettles men, and unsettled men mean unsettled bills – broken furniture, broken vows and divorce.

> NELLIE MCCLUNG, meeting of the Manitoba Suffrage League, Winnipeg, Jan. 28, 1914, in the role of premier in a Women's Parliament, paraphrase of the words of Sir Rodmond Roblin, Premier of Manitoba, the previous day but with sex roles reversed.

The idea that women voters would be less influenced by prejudice and partisanship and personal interest than are men is mere sex pride, which experience has not justified. The women whom we see going about the streets hobbled by skirts which will not permit them to take more than half their natural stride, are not likely to be governed by reason and common sense in the casting of their ballots.

> ORILLIA PACKET, Mar. 19, 1917.

Canadian women got the vote as a gift rather than as a reward.

> CHARLOTTE WHITTON, Saturday night, Jan. 26, 1946, 7.

Wood, Henry Wise

The Uncrowned King of Alberta.

> ANON., a reference to Henry Wise Wood, a term popular in the mid-1920's.

He is an American wolf in the Canadian sheep-fold in the skin of a Missouri mule.

> CAN. MILLING AND GRAIN JOUR. , May 15, 1926, 5, on Henry Wise Wood.

Woodpeckers

What cries the difference between
Myself and insect on the tree?
The woodpecker taps on the wrinkled bark
A paradigm of sophistry.

> MYRTLE REYNOLDS ADAMS, "Bird tap", 1960.

Woodsworth, James S.

Now my case has been tried by a larger jury and the verdict is one I may feel proud of. In fact, when Meighen arrested me, it nominated me for Ottawa.

> JAMES S. WOODSWORTH, on election to House of Commons, 1921, referring to arrest for his part in Winnipeg General Strike, 1919.

True to the principles he has so consistently advocated, this kindly, courageous man nailed his colours to the mast and sailed off on the lonely route where conscience is the only compass.

> TORCHY ANDERSON, Vancouver Daily province, Sept. 9, 1939, 8.

The untypical Canadian.

> F. H. UNDERHILL, from title of his book, James Shaver Woodsworth, untypical Canadian, 1944.

He was a kind of political saint.

> A.R.M. LOWER, Colony to nation, 1946, 513.

Woodsworth's work had been in this world, his whole life of labour, poverty, and daily suffering had been devoted to the salvation of human beings here and now, and it had all been in vain.

BRUCE HUTCHISON, *The incredible Canadian*, 1953, 255, referring to Canadian declaration of war, Sept. 8, 1939.

With him, to outgrow an idea was to outgrow at the same time the mode of living based on that idea. He had the courage, always, to leave the old familiar environment for the new, untried adventure.

GRACE MACINNIS, *J. S. Woodsworth, a man to remember*, 1953, 60.

More than any other Canadian public man, he helped transform Canadian politics from the politics of special and sectional interests to the politics of collective concern for the welfare of the individual in a society collectively organized.

W.L. MORTON, *The Kingdom of Canada*, 1963, 443.

He was the saint in our politics. Our politics and all men who knew him, gained a certain purity from his presence and lost a vehement flame in his passing.

BRUCE HUTCHISON, qu. in Walter Young, *Anatomy of a party*, 1969, 157.

Words

Thunderin' long words ain't wisdom.

T.C. HALIBURTON, *Sam Slick's wise saws*, 1853, I, 199.

I like those words that carry in their
   veins
  The blood of lions. "Liberty" is one,

And "Justice", and the heart leaps to
   the sun
When the thrilled note of "Courage!
   Courage!" rains
Upon the sorely stricken will.

ETHELWYN WETHERALD, "Words", 1907.

The phrase is the motive-power of the world. Corporeal man, armed with battle-ax or maxim, is but the vehicle of the phrase; the armature, the dynamo through which that subtle electric fluid which we call Thought is collected, directed, and flies through space, working wonders.

ARNOLD HAULTAIN, *University mag.*, Feb., 1908, 111.

It's as easy to recall an unkind word as it is to draw back the bullet after firing a gun.

ROBERT C. (BOB) EDWARDS, Calgary *Eye Opener*, Nov. 11, 1916.

Give me the words of a thinker,
  When beauty has touched his pen,
That burn with the simple fervor,
  That reaches the soul of men.

JAMES C. SINGER, "Foreword" to *Poems*, 1929.

Take the words, nor seek to find
What, if anything, lies behind.
Damn the meaning! Take the sound!
It's words that make the world go
  round.

L.A. MCKAY (John Smalacombe, pseud.), *Viper's bugloss*, 1938, 5.

There are words that can only be said
  once
And have all been said before that fact
  is plain.
In a sense no word can ever be said
  again
And none can be said again in the
  same sense.

ROBERT FINCH, "Words", 1946.

the torso verb, the beautiful face of the
  noun,
and all those shaped and warm
  auxiliaries!
A first love it was, the recognition of
  his own.
Dear limbs adverbial, complexion of
  adjective,
dimple and dip of conjugation!

> A.M. KLEIN, "Portrait of the poet as
> landscape", 1948.

Words are the real trouble-makers. I
was never any good at using them.

> HUGH MACLENNAN, *Each man's son*,
> 1951, 61.

The words are inadequate and the
exposition probably defective but the
point is clear.

> A.R.M. LOWER, *This most famous stream*,
> 1954, 27.

I would take words
As crisp and as white
As our snow; as our birds
Swift and sure in their flight;

> A.J.M. SMITH, "To hold in a poem", 1954.

        the word said
Which means all that I am:
Not quite meaningless,
Nor easily understood,
The choking sound of a man
In a locked Rosetta stone.

> ALFRED PURDY, "Decree nisi", 1962.

The worth of life being not necessarily
  noise
we kept unusual silence, and then
  cried out
one word which has never yet been
  said —

> ALFRED PURDY, "On Canadian identity",
> 1962.

Words here are simpering imbeciles
and dare not hope to break this silence.

> AL PURDY, "Indian summer", 1962.

Words must be clear bells,
or sound gravely along like horns.
They should detonate, explode like
  lightning
under the sea.

> ELDON GRIER "An ecstasy" Stanza XIV,
> 1963.

I've always had a lot of trouble with
my dangling participle and misplaced
metaphors; but hell, when you have
something to say, just go ahead and
say it.

> MARGARET "MA" MURRAY, Saskatoon *Star-*
> *phoenix*, Nov. 13, 1964, qu. in *Herstory*,
> 1975, Mar. 10-16.

And something I've thought of every
  now and then:
how everything we do or say has an
  effect somewhere,
passes outward from itself in widening
  circles,
a sort of human magic by which
a word moves outside the nature of a
  word
as side effect of itself
        the nature of a word being
that when it's said it will always be
  said
  — a recording exists in the main deep
  of sound.

> AL PURDY, "Method for calling up
> ghosts", 1965.

I have lived here nine months
and in all that time
have never once heard
a gentle word spoken.

I like to tell myself
that is only because
gentle words are whispered
and harsh words shouted.

> ALDEN NOWLAN, "Britain Street", 1967.

Aren't there enough words
flowing in your veins
to keep you going.

> MARGARET ATWOOD, "The shadow voice", 1968.

I care more about this
arrangement of words than about you.

> TOM MARSHALL, "Astrology", 1969.

In Newfoundland, a gulch is what mainlanders call a gully. A gully is what mainlanders call a pond. A pond is what mainlanders call a lake. Fun, isn't it? These verbal musical chairs could go on almost all day.

> HAROLD HORWOOD, *Newfoundland*, 1969, 84.

There are certain three-letter words which it is obscene today to utter in civilized company, notably God and Sin.

> IRVING LAYTON, "Aphs", *The whole bloody bird*, 1969, 87.

In some families, *please* is described as the magic word. In our house, however, it was *sorry*.

> MARGARET LAURENCE, *A bird in the house*, 1970, 92.

I tried to explain about the odd Canadians
Who hide their excretions beneath layers of strange sayings
And had no bread and butter words
To describe these ordinary things.

> JOY KOGAWA, "On meeting the clergy of the Holy Catholic Church in Osaka", 1971.

There are words that are the incomparable beasts of our imagination

> ELDON GRIER, "An ecstasy", 1971.

The words we do not speak
can never make a sound.
The voice the story makes
can only tell itself.

> DAVID HELWIG, "The best name of silence", 1972.

Work

The joy of the hand that hews for
    beauty
Is the dearest solace beneath the sun.

> BLISS CARMAN, "Wanderer", 1893.

Hem and Haw were the sons of sin,
Created to shally and shirk;
Hem lay 'round and Haw looked on
While God did all the work.

> BLISS CARMAN, "Hem and Haw", 1895.

The faltering restless hand of Hack,
And the tireless hand of Hew.

> BLISS CARMAN, "Hack and Hew", 1896.

Work is only toil when it is the performance of duties for which nature did not fit us, and a congenial occupation is only serious play.

> ARCHIBALD LAMPMAN, "Happiness; a preachment", in *Harper's mag.* July, 1896, 310.

The effective, moving, vitalizing work of the world is done between the ages of twenty-five and forty — these fifteen golden years of plenty, the anabolic or constructive period, in which there is always a balance in the mental bank and the credit is good.

> SIR WILLIAM OSLER, "The fixed period", address, Feb. 22, 1905, at Johns Hopkins Univ.

Few are the women who can understand a man's work.

> ARNOLD HAULTAIN, *Hints for lovers*, 1909, 89.

I soon discovered that if I ever accomplished anything in life, it would be by pursuing my object with a persistent determination to attain it. I had neither the training nor the talents to accomplish anything without hard work, and fortunately I knew it.

> GEORGE STEPHEN, (LORD MOUNT STEPHEN), on receiving the freedom of the city of Aberdeen, Scotland, 1911.

No man does as much to-day as he is going to do to-morrow.

> ROBERT C. (BOB) EDWARDS, Calgary *Eye Opener*, Mar. 23, 1912.

If you want work well done, select a busy man – the other kind has no time.

> ROBERT C. (BOB) EDWARDS, in his *Annual*, 1922, 63.

I've done no work. Work consists of doin' somethin' you don't want to do – yet I've always been as busy as a cow's tail in fly-time.

> JACK MINER, from his "Philosophy", qu. in *Canadian mag.*, Oct., 1922, 479.

Work is a great thing to make you forget who you are entirely.

> NATHANIEL A. BENSON, *The patriot*, 1930, in *Three plays for patriots*, 65.

Pray sing at your work. Draw joy from your occupation, however lowly the world may deem it, and give joy to its performances; and thus you will find the truest happiness.

> ROBERTSON DAVIES, *A jig for the gypsy*, 1954, 4.

I never did anything from which I didn't get sixty minutes of pleasure for every hour of work.

> LIONEL FORSYTH, to a friend shortly before his death, Jan. 1, 1957.

I don't work at high pressure and I don't work for money. Maybe I did initially, but certainly not now.

> E. P. TAYLOR, qu. in P. Newman, *Flame of power*, 1959, 222.

Work today and be happy tomorrow – that's the physician's rule of life.

> WILDER PENFIELD, *The torch*, 1960, 136.

Why should I work to support a bum like me?

> L. W. ELLIS, "E. J.", 1964.

Work is for money, not for penance, the glory of God, the exaltation of the nation, or for any reason but an improved standard of living.

> RICHARD E. DUWORS, in C. Zimmerman & S. Russell, eds., *Symposium on the great plains of North America*, 1965, 72.

Good work creates an audience.

> KENT THOMPSON, *The Fiddlehead*, No. 76, 1968, 2.

The reward of work well done is more work.

> COL. JOHN B. MACLEAN, favourite saying, qu. by F. S. Chalmers, *A gentleman of the press*, 1969, 175.

Work is accomplished by those employees who have not yet reached their level of incompetence.

> LAURENCE J. PETER and RAYMOND HULL, *The Peter principle*, 1969, 27.

If you enjoy your work, you don't mind other people not working; in fact, you are happy to support them. But if, like most Canadians, you hate your work, you resent seeing anybody idle. You want everyone to be as miserable as you are.

> RICHARD J. NEEDHAM, *A friend in Needham*, 1969, 9.

Work is what we have to do; play is what we like to do.

> HANS SELYE, address, National Conference on Fitness and Health, Ottawa, Dec. 5, 1972.

"Work"
Keeps us
From ourselves.

> D. B. STEVENSON, untitled poem, 1974.

Work Ethic

The great secret of life is to learn to earn one's bread.

> THOMAS C. HALIBURTON, *Sam Slick's wise saws*, 1853, ch. 6.

Work, for the night is coming!
    Work through the sunny noon;
Fill the bright hours with labor;
    Rest comes sure and soon.
Give every flying minute
    Something to keep in store;
Work, for the night is coming,
    When man works no more.

> ANNA L. WALKER (COGHILL), "Work for the night is coming", hymn, in *Leaves from the backwoods*, Montreal, 1861.

Work! Honest work for and with God in Christ! This is the Gospel that is preached unto us. No form, new or old, no pet doctrine or panacea, no institution or catechism can take the place of that.

> G. M. GRANT, to the Synod of the Presbyterian Church in Nova Scotia, 1866.

Where shall I find a hired man
With a single passion for his job,
With thoughts of work,
And nothing else
Within his knob.

> PAUL HIEBERT, *Sarah Binks*, "Where shall I find?", 1947, 23.

Perhaps, the only end in life is to be functional: to do one's job is as much as a man can ever do.

> COLIN MCDOUGALL, *Execution*, 1958, 129.

Canadians work hard all their lives so that they can finally purchase things which they are too old to enjoy.

> RICHARD J. NEEDHAM, *A friend in Needham*, 1969, 20.

I say that the most sacred law is that a man who lives in society should be able to enjoy his own possibilities to the maximum, but work is not perhaps the way to do it.

> PIERRE E. TRUDEAU, qu. in Toronto *Star*, Mar. 14, 1972, 9.

Workers

I'm a sort of Jack of all trades and master of none.

> THOMAS C. HALIBURTON, *Sam Slick's wise saws*, 1853, ch. 7.

There must be always workingmen, men to work with their hands, to be poor, to be industrious, to be unfortunate, to suffer; it is the will of God and the destiny of the race. That will and that destiny are not to be counteracted by public meetings, by agitations, by the speeches of demagogues, by public orations or other foolish means.

> HALIFAX *EVENING EXPRESS*, Feb. 5, 1874, 2.

I call every honest workman brother, but you are neither honest nor a workman.

> ROBERTSON DAVIES, *A jig for the gypsy*, 1954, 5.

Workmanship

Any short-comings that may be noticed by our friends, must by excused on the score of the work being wholly Canadian in its execution.

> CATHERINE PARR TRAILL, *Canadian wild flowers*, 1868, Preface.

World

The world is wiser than its wisest men,
And shall outlive the wisdom of the
    gods,
Made after man's own liking.

> CHARLES MAIR, *Tecumseh*, 1886.

Harden thy heart to look on cruelties,
To look on truth, to look on life, and
    see
That the world is what it must ever be
    —
An evolution of alternate tyrannies.

> FRANCIS POLLOCK, "Sonnet I", 1937.

When Earth was mostly vapour
It was a dizzy spot;
Small comets cut a caper,
And everything was hot.

> JOHN C. MURRAY, "History", qu. in E. L. Chicanot, ed., *Rhymes of the miner*, 1937, 14.

One reason why I never become completely pessimistic about the long-run future of the world is that I cannot believe that the good God in his infinite wisdom and mercy would permit his work of creation to perish until the resources which he has placed at the disposal of his children are fully exploited.

> LOUIS ST. LAURENT, Ottawa, Dec., 1948, words spoken to emissary from South Africa at dinner, qu. by Escott Reid in N. Penlington, *On Canada*, 1971, 81.

The world was first a private park
Until the angel, after dark,
Scattered afar to wests and easts
The lovers and the friendly beasts.

> JAY MACPHERSON, "The fisherman", 1957.

Sometimes I wish
for a world no bigger than the
    coupling bodies
of two clockless strangers.

> ALDEN NOWLAN, "Sometimes", [1962].

Global village.

> MARSHALL MCLUHAN, *Gutenberg galaxy*, 1962, 21.

I seek this world to its end. This world
Owns me and all I have — and yet
This world is mine.

> EDWARD HUNT, "Untitled", 1966.

One should never be angry or disappointed with the world. Its only function is to be interesting and it does that magnificently.

> RICHARD J. NEEDHAM, *A friend in Needham*, 1969, 17.

This is the world as we have made it,
As you and I together made it.
Do not speak to me of evil,
We know all the secret names of evil.
Do not speak to me of sorrow,
We invented all the shades of sorrow.

> GWENDOLYN MACEWEN, "The name of the place", 1969.

The world is getting
dark but I carry
icons I remember
the summer
I will never forget
the light.

> MIRIAM WADDINGTON, "Icons", 1969.

Worry

Worrying helps you some – it seems as if you were doing something when you're worrying.

> L. M. MONTGOMERY, *Anne of Green Gables*, 1908, 298.

Taking things philosophically is easy if they don't concern you.

> ROBERT C. (BOB) EDWARDS, Calgary *Eye Opener*, Apr. 3, 1915.

Worry is a circle of futile thought, revolving on a pivot of fear.

> PETER MCARTHUR, (d. 1924), a favorite saying.

Writers

If these sketches should prove the means of deterring one family from sinking their property, and shipwrecking all their hopes, by going to reside in the backwoods of Canada, I shall consider myself amply repaid for revealing the secrets of the prison-house, and feel that I have not toiled and suffered in the wilderness in vain.

> SUSANNA H. MOODIE, *Roughing it in the bush*, 1852, Vol. 2, 291.

The less there is happening the more a truly great writer finds to write about.

> PETER MCARTHUR, *To be taken with salt*, 1903, 154.

Personally, I would sooner have written *Alice in Wonderland* than the whole *Encyclopaedia Britannica*.

> STEPHEN LEACOCK, *Sunshine sketches of a little town*, 1912, Preface, xi.

What is not disclosed by contemporary writers will never be disclosed. Hence history can never be a true record, and the exact relation of public men to the causes in which they are concerned never can be determined. If there is reticence in the present and ignorance in the future, at best we can have only light in the darkness.

> SIR JOHN WILLISON, *Reminiscences political and personal*, 1919, 12.

So exquisite was his appreciation of word values that, though others might embody an intention in a series of paragraphs apparently beyond criticism, his mastery of precision and shade was such that he could clothe it in language that had the exactitude of a multiplication table and the clarity of a mirror.

> DAVID BLYTHE HANNA, *Trains of recollection*, 1924, 172, referring to Zebulon Aiton Lash.

The writers of Canada are its first line of patriots, and the fact is established by the mortality tables. If it is true that the righteous are never forsaken there must be few of the righteous among Canadian authors.

> SIR JOHN WILLISON, in *Willison's monthly*, Mar., 1927, 369.

A book arises as much in the mind of the reader as in that of the writer; and the writer's art consists above all in creating response; the effect of a book is the result of a collaboration between writer and audience.

> FREDERICK P. GROVE, *Univ. of Tor. quart.*, Oct., 1940, 63.

Writing is no trouble: you just jot down ideas as they occur to you. The jotting is simplicity itself – it is the occurring which is difficult.

> STEPHEN LEACOCK, qu. in C. T. Bissell, ed., *Our living tradition*, Ser. 1, 1957, 141.

It's not blood the Buchans have in their veins, it is ink.

> ANNA BUCHAN (sister of Lord Tweed-smuir), qu. by J. Cowan, *Canada's Governors general*, 1952, 151.

What does he know? What he suspects is that he's not so much a writer as being *written* – this is where the terror comes in.

> MALCOLM LOWRY, letter to Albert Erskine, Spring, 1953. (*Selected letters*, 332).

A writer is no longer a man but an environment.

> JOHN SUTHERLAND, *Northern review*, Vol. 6, Oct.-Nov., 1953, 26.

There is only one trait that marks the writer. He is always watching. It's a trick of mind and he is born with it.

> MORLEY CALLAGHAN, paper read at Canadian Writer's Conference, Queen's Univ., July 28-31, 1955.

The discursive writer writes as an act of conscious will, and that conscious will, along with the symbolic system he employs for it, is set over against the body of things he is describing. But the poet, who writes creatively rather than deliberately, is not the father of his poem; he is at best a mid-wife, or, more accurately still, the womb of Mother Nature herself: her privates he, so to speak.

> NORTHROP FRYE, *Anatomy of criticism*, 1957, 98.

A writer's mind seems to be situated partly in the solar plexus and partly in the head.

> ETHEL WILSON, *Can. lit.*, Autumn, 1959, 16.

"Write as you fight" is a fine old motto.

> LESLIE MORRIS, intro. to Tim Buck, *Our fight for Canada*, 1959, 15.

The vice of the literary mind is excessive subtlety, just as that of the theatrical mind is trivial profusion.

> ROBERTSON DAVIES, *A voice from the attic*, 1960, 198.

I work with an axe.

> JEAN-PAUL DESBIENS, *Les insolences du frère Untel*, 1960, 17. (Trans.)

Late at night when I look out at the
  buildings
I swear I see a face in every window
looking back at me,
and when I turn away
I wonder how many go back to their
  desks
and write this down.

> LEONARD COHEN, "I wonder how many people in this city", 1961.

They are not required to debate, as their predecessors were, whether or not they are or in what ways they should be Canadian. The lengthy argument over nationality has been talked out. However he is defined, the Canadian exists, and the writer can concentrate on what interests him, in the calm assurance that by being himself he best expresses the nation.

> TIMES LITERARY SUPPLEMENT, editorial, May 18, 1962, 357.

Why have I told you all this? *To make you change your life!* Rilke was right. Every other reason for writing is insignificant.

> JACK LUDWIG, *Confusions*, 1963, 271.

If we try to envisage an "average Canadian writer" we can see him living near a campus, teaching at least part time at university level, mingling too much for his work's good with academics, doing as much writing as he can for the CBC, and always hoping for a Canada Council Fellowship that will take him away for a year.

GEORGE WOODCOCK, "Away from lost worlds", in R. Kostelanetz, ed., *On contemporary literature*, 1964, 99.

Instead of trying to refine the singularity of being Canadian, they may want to dive so deeply that what they have to say can be expressed in terms of what happens in an anonymous setting to an anonymous, or virtually anonymous, hero.

DOUGLAS LE PAN, *Atlantic monthly*, Nov., 1964, 164.

It seems to me that the effective writer is one who is inwardly sure of the entire naturalness of his creative act. For instance, he must be aware that he is writing not merely because he is a neurotic. Everybody's a bit queer and slightly mad, but I'm sure that my compulsion to construct more and more unprofitable verses isn't anywhere near as screwball as the compulsion of businessmen to make more and more money.

EARLE BIRNEY, *The creative writer*, 1966, 64.

Support your fellow Canadians. We should buy lousy Canadian novels instead of importing lousy American novels.

JOHNNY WAYNE, Toronto *Star week*, Apr. 20, 1968, 33.

All writers are derivative; all good writers plagiarize; theft is a literary virtue.

GEORGE WOODCOCK, "The absorption of echoes", in *Can. lit.*, No. 44, 1970, 3.

Welcome to all young writers, but prepare yourselves for the cold climate here.

ROBERT WEAVER, editorial, in *Tamarack rev.*, No. 58, 1970, 6.

What I care about is trying to express something that in fact everybody knows, but doesn't say or can't express.

MARGARET LAURENCE, qu. in *Chatelaine*, Feb., 1971, 28.

Fundamentally, all writing is about the same thing: it's about dying, about the brief flicker of time we have here, and the frustrations that it creates.

MORDECAI RICHLER, *Time*, May 31, 1971, 8.

Dear Nelly Sachs,
dear Nathalie Sarraute,
isn't there anything
you can teach me
about how to write
better in Canada?

MIRIAM WADDINGTON, "Sad winter in the land of Can. lit.", 1972.

What a life! – rolling thin cancerous cigarettes, using a plastic kitchen plate and a knife to slop up flaccid child feces from the floor, washing glass ashtrays bought in supermarkets, reading books, making notes, notes, writing words, words – words, for God's sake! Why can't I draw?

JOHN NEWLOVE, "Or alternately", 1972.

To me the writer is the guy who pays attention to how you get through the twenty-four hour day, on a second-to-second, minute-to-minute basis.

JACK LUDWIG, interview, in Donald Cameron, *Conversations with Canadian novelists*, 1973, 124.

I would say that any serious writer is a moralist and only incidentally an entertainer.

MORDECAI RICHLER, *Notes on an endangered species*, 1974, 46.

all the things I write about I've done
   myself
if not with hands, but with my mind
I am a screen thru which the world
   passes
a thermometer registering pain and
   sorrow
and laughter sometimes at being
   ridiculous.

> AL PURDY, *In search of Owen Roblin*,
> 1974 [81].

Writing

Writin' only aggravates your opponents, and never convinces them.

> T. C. HALIBURTON, *Sam Slick*, 1836, ch.
> XXIV.

The writing of solid, instructive stuff,
fortified by facts and figures, is easy
enough . . . But to write something
out of one's own mind, worth reading
for its own sake, is an arduous contriv-
ance, only to be achieved in fortunate
moments, few and far between.

> STEPHEN LEACOCK, *Sunshine sketches of
> a little town*, 1912, Preface.

That classic that the world has lost,
The Little Book I Never Wrote.

> ROBERT W. SERVICE, *"My masterpiece"*,
> 1921.

I utter the senseless squawks of a
feathered fowl. Often I wonder at the
desire in me being so strong and
driveling out in such feeble words and
badly constructed sentences.

> EMILY CARR, *Hundreds and thousands;
> the journals*, Dec. 11, 1934.

Under the avalanche of manuscripts
the sorrowful conviction was forced
upon me, that in my youthful innocence – I was not yet sixty – I had
been mistaken all the while: the chief
industry of Canada was not agriculture; it was writing; six out of its eight
million English-speaking citizens

dreamed of literary fame.

> FREDERICK PHILIP GROVE, *Univ. of Tor.
> quart.*, July, 1938, 454.

Get to the point as directly as you can;
never use a big word if a little one will
do.

> EMILY CARR, *Growing pains*, 1946, 360.

After a while it began to make a noise
like music; when it made the wrong
noise I altered it – when it seemed to
make thè right one finally, I kept it.

> MALCOLM LOWRY, letter to Derek Pe-
> thick, Mar. 6, 1950.

It is this hunger for words
That makes writing pain!

> IRENE G. DAYTON, "Poem", 1953.

A goose's quill put an end to talk,
abolished mystery, gave architecture
and towns, brought roads and armies,
bureaucracies. It was the basic metaphor with which the cycle of civilization began, the step from the dark into
the light of the mind. The hand that
filled a paper built a city.

> MARSHALL McLUHAN, *Counterblast*,
> 1954.

First know what you want to say, then
sit on it for a long-long time, even a
year at least before you even start
writing, while you think it through.
It's how long you live with the idea
that shows you whether it's worthwhile to write it.

> MALCOLM LOWRY, to Norman Levi, in
> 1954, qu. in T. Kilgallin, *Lowry*,
> 1973, 69.

Remorselessly, my tiger ravages
Fat flocks of metaphor:
Scents the inconstant image to its lair,
And, marrow-hungry, cracks the bones
   of syntax.

> GOODRIDGE MACDONALD, "Tiger", 1958.

In the end, all writing is isolation.

> RODERICK HAIG-BROWN, "The writer in isolation", in *Can. lit.*, No. 1, 1959, 11.

There is nothing that cannot be written. A maxim, told to myself, in the morning.

> FRANK DAVEY, "The reading", 1970.

Children's stories are something you make up one night when you're baby-sitting and the kids all laugh and say, "Tell it again" (so they can stay up longer). Then you put it down on paper, have it published and make a million.

> ANON., publisher, qu. by Sheila Egoff in Ont. Roy. Comm. on Book Publishing, *Background papers*, 1972, 258.

You

You breathe. You be.
Bare, stripped light
Time's fragment flagged
Against the dark.

> DOROTHY LIVESAY, "Lorca", 1939.

Everything I didn't want to know
about you
you told me in the first five minutes
we were alone.
After that
there was nothing more
worth mentioning.

> SUSAN MUSGRAVE, "Once more", 1970.

there are delicacies in you
    like the hearts of watches
there are wheels that turn
    on the tips of rubies
& tiny intricate locks

> EARLE BIRNEY, "There are delicacies in
> you", 1971.

I know less
and less of you
as each day
you confess more . . .

> DON BAILEY, "Saint-Anne on the autopsy
> table . . . ", 1971.

Be my malediction
    That you lust, as you do,
For the loathsome affliction
    Of just being you!

> GEOFFREY B. RIDDEHOUGH, "Contact
> broken", 1972.

Youth

Somewhere he failed me, somewhere
    he slipped away –
Youth, in his ignorant faith and his
    bright array.
The tides go out; the tides come
    flooding in;
Still the old years die and the new
    begin;
But Youth? –
Somewhere we lost each other, last
    year or yesterday.

> THEODORE G. ROBERTS, "The lost ship-
> mate", *Can. mag.*, Apr., 1913.

Fellows, come and ride with me
    Swiftly now to the edge of the end!
Holding the Stars of Joy in fee! –
    Youth is a splendid thing to spend!

> TOM MACINNES, "Ballade of youth re-
> maining", 1918.

The good don't die young; they simply
outgrow it.

> ROBERT C. (BOB) EDWARDS, Calgary *Eye
> Opener;* attributed.

The youngest thing in a youthful
    world
Is a young soul in an old heart;
Full statured at the ending.

> WILSON MACDONALD, "The last portage",
> 1926.

I have lived only nineteen years and
all of them more or less badly.

> MALCOLM LOWRY, letter to Conrad Aik-
> en, 1928.

Still as the land, without a sigh,
Dark images, uncouth,
We stand against a light May sky —
The living-dead of youth.

ALAN CREIGHTON, "Unemployed", 1936.

Is there a sorrow on us, who are young,
And have no grief.

AUDREY ALEXANDRA BROWN, "Lammas-tide", 1937.

My brothers and my sisters, two by
  two,
Sit sipping succulence and sighing sex.
Each tiny adolescent universe
A world the vested interests annex.

F. R. SCOTT, "Saturday sundae", 1944.

The whole world is burdened with young fogies. Old men with ossified minds are easily dealt with. But men who look young, act young and everlastingly harp on the fact that they are young but who nevertheless think and act with a degree of caution which would be excessive in their grandfathers, are the curse of the world.

ROBERTSON DAVIES, The table talk of Samuel Marchbanks, 1949, 118.

One of the really notable achievements of the twentieth century has been to make the young old before their time.

ROBERTSON DAVIES, Tempest-tost, 1951, 84.

In youth we ask for bonfires,
Fed by the fuel of ecstasy, passion,
To light our way.

HILDA RIDLEY, "Little fires", 1951.

The new generations notice that the lives that they are called to live do not correspond to the pastoral idyll that preceding generations have lived. They search in vain to explain to themselves this solution to the continuity between the idealized past and the severely realistic present.

MICHEL BRUNET, Canadians et Canadiens, 1954, 39. (Trans.)

The worst thing that could happen to you is to be a brain.

ANON., a popular adolescent statement, qu. by Hilda Neatby, A temperate dispute, 1954, 18.

    My lettuce life
Was sunny as the leaf is green.
I linger still in daymares of my
  flowering era —
If I blazed no light, I caught and held
  its sheen.

ANNE WILKINSON, "I was born a boy . . . ", 1955.

The affairs of the young are the envies of the middle-aged.

HUGH GARNER, "Hunky", 1961.

It is a pity that we ourselves can never see the promise that others see in us when we are young. Or is it perhaps better that we should not know?

LOVAT DICKSON, The house of words, 1963, 298.

Young people have been lured into the great North American rat race, lured on by the Puritan ethic that to stand still is to go backward.

W. J. REDDIN, addressing senior class banquet, Mount Allison Univ., Sackville, N. B., qu. in Liberty, Sept. 1963.

In saving these arrested young people, it is not them that we save, it is everyone.

> PIERRE BOURGAULT, a Quebec Separatist leader, speech in Montreal, June 12, 1963, on the trial of FLQ members for acts of sabotage and murder. (Trans.)

The young of North America have never been so fascinated and pleased with themselves as they are today. They gaze lovingly into the pool of the mass media, and what looks back at them is a countenance infinitely beautiful, infinitely promising, infinitely idealistic.

> ROBERT FULFORD, *Crisis at the Victory Burlesk*, 1968, 99.

Young people can't possibly be any more wicked than their elders. They don't have the time, the money, or the experience.

> RICHARD J. NEEDHAM, *A friend in Needham*, 1969, 22.

It's easier to have the vigour of youth when you're old than the wisdom of age when you're young.

> RICHARD J. NEEDHAM, *A friend in Needham*, 1969, 23.

The Company of Young Canadians never was a company of young Canadians.

> IAN HAMILTON, *The children's crusade*, 1970, 309.

In the TV age is a generation of children that feels completely at home anywhere in the world – except in their own home.

> MARSHALL MCLUHAN, *Culture is our business*, 1970, 230.

Play, children, play
the time for song is short
and age and sorrow come like frost
to wither up the heart.

> PHYLLIS GOTLIEB, untitled poem, in *Ordinary moving*, 1970, 10.

Yukon

This is the law of the Yukon, that only
  the Strong shall thrive;
That surely the Weak shall perish, and
  only the fit survive.
Dissolute, damned and despairful,
  crippled and palsied and slain,
This is the Will of the Yukon, – Lo,
  how she makes it plain!

> ROBERT W. SERVICE, "The law of the Yukon", 1907.

This is the law of the Yukon, and ever
  she makes it plain:
"Send not your foolish and feeble;
  send me your strong and your sane.
Strong for the red rage of battle; sane,
  for I harry them sore;
Send me men girt for the combat, men
  who are grit to the core".

> ROBERT W. SERVICE, "The law of the Yukon", 1907.

There's a land where the mountains
    are nameless
And the rivers all run God knows
    where;
There are lives that are erring and
    aimless,
And death that just hangs by a hair;
There are hardships that nobody
    reckons;
  There are valleys unpeopled and
    still;
There's a land – oh, it beckons and
    beckons,
And I want to go back and I will.

> ROBERT W. SERVICE, "The spell of the Yukon", 1907.

A bunch of the boys were whooping it
up in the Malemute saloon;
The kid that handles the juke-box was
hitting a jag-time tune;
Back of the bar, in a solo game, sat
Dangerous Dan McGrew,
And watching his luck was his
light-o'-love, the lady that's known
as Lou.

ROBERT W. SERVICE, "The shooting of
Dan McGrew", 1907.

The Yukon is a wonderful country for
men and dogs but it kills women and
horses.

ANON., old-timer, qu. in Amy V. Wilson,
No man stands alone, 1969, 106.

AUTHOR INDEX

NOTE: This Index is arranged by author, or source, subject-heading, and date. Under the subject-heading in the main text the arrangement is chronological. Duplication of a date in the Index means more than one quotation with the same date.

ANDERSON, PATRICK (Poet) Canada
1945; Cities and towns 1945; Cold
1953; Land 1957
ANDERSON, "TORCHY" (Newspaper
correspondent) Woodsworth, J.S. 1939
ANDERSON, VIOLET (Poet) Committees
1957; Housewives 1957
ANGELL, NORMAN (English economist)
Canada 1913
ANGLIN, MARGARET (Actress) Husbands
1971
ANGUS, HENRY F. (Political scientist)
United States 1938
ANKA, PAUL (Singer) Emigrants 1972
ANONYMOUS Aberhart, William 1973;
Ability 19th C.; Abortion 1970;
Advertising 1927; Advice 1963; Alberta
1900, 1970; Alcoholism 1969;
Americanization 1958; Americans
1938, 1941; Arctic 1860's; Art 1931,
1961, 1968; Artists 1972; Automobiles
1962; Banks and banking 1935, 1974;
Beaverbrook, *Lord* 1964; Bees, quilting
1930; Bible 1886; Bilingualism 1964;
Biography 1904; Birth control 1871;
Blessings 1965; Books 1897, 1930's,
1954; Boundary, Canada-U.S. 1877;
British Columbia 1860's, 19th C.;
Budgets 1963; Buffalo 1865; Business
1943; Business men 1963; Cabinet
ministers 1940's, 1968; Calgary 1915,
1950's; Canada 1900, 1916, 1964;
Canadian-American relations 1938,
1946, 1959, 1971; Canadian Pacific
Railway 1885; Canadianism 20th C.;
Canadians pre-1867, 1964; Cartwright,
Sir Richard 1880's;
Children's rhymes (var.); Church
1930's; Cities and towns —nicknames
(var.); Coal 1900; Communism 1935,
1937; Confederation 1965;
Confederation, Fathers of 1950's;
Conformity 1962; Conscription,
military 1870; Conservative Party
1967; Consistency 1968; Constitution
1967, 1971; Courts 1969; Creativity
1967; Crows 1967, 1969; Culture 1965;
Curling 1876; Currie, *Gen. Sir* Arthur
1917; Dance 1791; Davin, N.F. 1887;
The Dead pre-1933; Death 1914, 1959,
1963; Debt 1867; Defeat (no date);
Defence 1867, 1957, 1957; The
Depression (1930-37) 1930's, 1930's;
Disease 1930's; Diversity 1965; Doctors
1938; pre-1942; Dogs 1877;

Doukhobors 1920's; Draft dodgers,
American 1967; Dress 1965; Drinking
19th C., 1870's, 1905; Drugs 1968;
Edmonton, Alta. 1910; Education 1964;
Election slogans 1960; Elections 1878;
Engineering 1920; Equality 1965;
Executives 1971; Factories 1970;
Family allowances 1949; Farmers
1912; Fenians 1866; Fish 1930's;
Fisheries 1886; French language 1886;
Gardens 1940; *The Globe*, Toronto
1863; Government 1971; Government
House 1965; Graveyards 1869; Halifax
1940; Happiness 1965; Hees, George
1950's; Historians 1940's, 1958;
Holidays 1896; Home 1841; Homeless
1930's; Horses 1890's, 1916; Howe,
C.D. 1940's; Howe, Joseph 19th C.,
19th C.; Hudson's Bay Co. 19th C.,
19th C., 1951; Iceworms (no date);
Identity 1943; Immigrants 1896, 1900;
Immigration 1930's; Indians 1800's,
1912, 1960, 1965, 1967, 1970's;
Intellectuals 1956; Investment 1957;
Investment, American 1972; Isolation
1958, 1958; Judges 1926, 1945; King,
W.L.M. 1921, 1967; Labour 1870,
1873, 1886, 1900's, 1900's; Labour
strikes 1919; Labour unions 1885, 1961;
Lacrosse 1860's; Land 1960's;
Languages 1940's, 1955; Laurier, *Sir*
Wilfrid 1884, 1911, 1919; Law and
lawyers 1875, 1961; Leaders 1966;
Liberal Party 1855, 1958; Life 1963;
Liquor 1760, 1880's, 1923; Lobbying
1964; Macdonald, *Sir* John A. 1863,
1873, 1884, 1886; McGill University
1884; Mackenzie, William Lyon 1826;
McLuhan, Marshall 1971;
McNaughton, *Gen.* A.G.L. 1937;
Majorities 1864; Mind 1925; Morals
1971; Montreal 1920; Mothers 1971;
Names 1973; National Policy (1878)
1878; Nationality 1890; Natural
resources 1970; Newfoundland 1948;
North 1973; Novelists 1824; Painting
1966; Parties; The Pas, Man. 1970; Past
1836; Patronage 1896; Personalities;
Personalities (nicknames) (var.);
Philanthropy 1952, 1952, 1952; Plays
1947; Pledges 1881; Poets 1929, 1940;
Political parties 1860; Political phrases
(var.); Politics 1891, 1911, 1936, 1970;
Poor 1970; Prairies 1881, 1923; Press

Gallery, Ottawa 1965, 1966; Prices 1929; Prince Edward Island 1873; Prudery 1967; Public service 1965, 1970; Quebec (Prov.) 1960; 1968; Queen's University 1903; Radio and TV commercials 1959; Railway trains (var.); Railways (nicknames) (var.); Reading 1860, 1935; Reciprocity (1854) 1887; Red River cart 19th C.; Regiments (nicknames) 1885; Revenge of the cradle 1800's; Riel, Louis 1870, 1885, 1929; Riots 1919; R.C.M.P. 1872, 1909; Senate 1921; Skunks 1944; Slaves 1850's; Stanfield, Robert L. 1968; Suicide 1897; Taylor, E.P. 1959; Theatre 1968; Thompson, *Sir* John S.D. 1892; Titles of honour 1886; Toronto 1943; Toronto *Globe* 1863; Toronto *Star* 1930's; Trade 1761; Trails (var.); Transportation 1929, 1930, 1946; Trudeau, Pierre E. 1968, 1968; Tupper, *Sir* Charles 1870; Unemployment 1972; Union Jack 1824; United Empire Loyalists after 1785; United Nations 1962; United States 19th C.; Value 19th C.; Vancouver, 1905; Victoria, B.C. 1972; Voters 1877, 1917; Voyageurs 1825, 1825; War 1842, 1964; War dead 1924; War, European (1914-18) 1918; War of 1812, 1812; Water 1900; Weather 19th C., 1919, 1937; Weddings 1937; The West 1870's, 1880, 1880, 1900, 1905; Wheat 1890, 1899; Winnipeg late 19th C.; Winter early 19th C., early 19th C.; Witches 1892; Wolfe, James 1760's; Women, early 1900's, 1972; Women's suffrage 1879; Wood, H.W. 1920's; Writing 1972; Youth 1954; Yukon 1969

ANON. INSCRIPTIONS Canadian Pacific Railway 1885; Patriotism 1893, 1893

ANON. LOCAL PROVERBS Ability 1800's; Acadia 1800's

ANON. NICKNAMES Army 1914; Swearing (no date); Temperance 1850

ANON. POEMS Forests 1831; Niagara Falls 1853

ANON. POPULAR PHRASES Ethnic groups 1971; Federalism 1966; French Canadians, survival (no date); Political parties 1972; Postage stamps 1851; Provinces 1970; Publishing 1961

ANON. POPULAR SAYINGS Diamonds 1542; Emigration 1880's, 1882; Fishing 1914; Friends (no date); Gold 1880; Halifax 1783; Indian summer 1800's; Maple trees 1800's; Métis 1960; Mining 1898, 1900; Music 1967; Natural resources 1930; Ontario 1879; Plowing (no date); Prairies 1900; Rain (no date); Rivers 1880; Snow (no date); Storms (no date); Swallows (no date)

ANON. POPULAR TERMS Automobiles 1920; Aviation 1909, 1920; Babies 1926, 1944; Beaverbrook, *Lord* 1900; Bible 1886; British Columbia 1860, 1871, 1920, 1966; Buffalo 1850, 1860, 1850; Business 1971; Canadian Pacific Railway 1898; Children 1934; Confederation, Fathers of 1864; Farmers 1915, 1921, 1952; Fishermen 1895; French Canadians 1960's; Gardens 1845; Geography 1900; Gold 1850, 1858; Government 1919; Liquor 1600's, 1880's, 1923; Lumbering 1800's; Macdonald, *Sir* John A. 1880's, 1880's; Manitoba 1879, 1879; Maritimes 1875; Merchants 1875, 1947; Militia 1837; Mining 1900; Money 1750, 1800's, 1800's, 1850, 1870, 1870, 1880, 1880's; National Policy (1878) 1878; New Brunswick 1800's, 1965; Newfoundland 1700's, 1800's, 1890's, 1894, 1915, 1949; Newspapers 1849, 1880's, 1923; Niagara Falls 1830's, 1830's; Nova Scotia 1783, 1787, 1923, 1956; Novels 1824; Ogopogo 1926; Ontario 1824, 1910, 1941, 1972; Ottawa 1858; Parliament 1833, 1836; Poets 1861, 1913; Prairies 1882, 1930, 1930; Prince Edward Island 1769, 1840, 1873, 1873; Provinces 1901; Radio and TV 1960's; Red River cart (no date); Riots 1828; Roads (no date); R.C.M.P. 1927; Sable Island (no date); Sailors (no date); Senate 1874; Smith, Goldwin (no date); Soldiers 1900, 1944

ANON. PROVERBS Love 1917; Rain 1874

ANON. RHYMES Orangemen 1830, 1830, 1830; Rain 1918; Secord, Laura 1928

ANON. SIGNS Automobiles 1962; Cities and towns 1962

ANON. SLOGANS Abortion 1970; Canadian Pacific Railway 1890, 1908, 1908; Drinking 1905; Fruit 1930's; Manufacturing 1911; Pacific Great Eastern Railway 1956; Sport 1960's

ANON. SONGS Annexation 1849; Army 1885; Brock, *Sir* Isaac 1812; Canadian-American relations 1869; Drinking 1911, 1917; Elections 1841; Farmers 1920, 1920; Fishermen (no date); Food 1918; Hunting 1959; Life (no date); Loneliness (no date); Love (no date); Lumbering 1800's, 1800's, 1800's; Macphail, Agnes 1929; Newfoundland 1865, 1869; Nova Scotia 1770; Parties (no date); Potatoes 1961; Queen's University 1903; Rebellion (1837) 1838, 1838; Red River expedition 1870; Schools 1921; Slaves 1851, 1869; Smiles 1880; Soldiers 1870; Wanderlust 1945; War 1855; West 1903

ARCAND, ADRIEN (Quebec fascist) Politics 1935

ARCHIBALD, KATHLEEN (Public servant) Women's employment 1970

ARMOUR, JOHN D. (Judge) Bribery 1884

ARMOUR, LESLIE (Professor) Canada 1971; Ideas 1971

ARMSTRONG, HOLLY (P.R. consultant) Women 1963

ARMSTRONG, WARREN (Publicist) Elections 1962

ARNOLD, *GEN.* HENRY M. (U.S. Army General) War 1947

ARNOLD, MATTHEW (British author) Quebec (Prov.) 1884

ARTHUR, ERIC (Writer on architecture) Architecture 1928

ARTHUR, *DR.* R. H. (Inscriptionist) War dead 1928

ARTIGUE, JEAN D' (French writer on N.W.M.P.) Red River cart 1882

ASHBURTON, *LORD* (Boundary adjuster) See also BARING, ALEX Boundaries 1843; Canada 1816

ASSELIN, OLIVAR (Quebec journalist) Laurier, *Sir* Wilfrid 1909; Lies and liars 1910

ASSINIBOINE INDIANS Smoking 1850's

ASSOCIATION OF UNIVERSITIES AND COLLEGES OF CANADA People 1965

ATLANTIC PROVINCES ECONOMIC COUNCIL Finance 1972

ATKINS, NORMAN (Advertising executive) Organisation 1974

ATKINSON, JOSEPH E. (Newspaper publisher) Conscription, military 1917; Management 1963; Newspapers 1936; Old age 1947

ATWOOD, MARGARET (Poet) Answers 1966; Argument 1971; Art 1970; Authors 1970; Automobiles 1970; Behaviour 1971; Bodies 1971; Canada 1972; Canadians 1970; Clothes 1968; Creativity 1968; Deceit 1971; Divorce 1972; Dreams 1968; Families 1972; Fear 1970; Flowers 1970; Freedom 1968; Friends 1970; Gratitude 1966; Help 1970; Heroes 1974; Heroines 1972; History 1971; Honesty 1972; Humanity 1972; Identity 1971; Immigrants 1970; Isolation 1968; Literature, Canadian 1972, 1972, 1972, 1972; Love 1971, 1972; Painting 1970; Patriotism 1970; Places 1968; Poems 1971; Pollution 1968; Resistance 1968; Victims 1972, 1972; Words 1968

AUBERT DE LA RUE, PHILIPPE (French writer) Moderation 1962

AUDEN, W. H. (English poet) Track sports 1969

AUF DER MAUR, NICK (Political writer) Hockey 1971

AVISON, MARGARET (Poet) Change 1960; Escape 1962; Fear 1960; God 1966; Imagination 1960; Knowledge 1956; Libraries 1959; Lost 1960; Man 1960; New Year 1960; Play 1960; Pleasure 1960; Religion 1966; Research 1960; Space 1970; Stories 1960; Time 1960; Trees 1966

AYER'S CATHARTIC PILLS Patent medicines 1857

AYLESWORTH, ALLAN (M.P.) Deafness 1917

AYRE, ROBERT (Writer) Critics 1958

B

BACON, *LORD* (British writer) Fisheries 1608

BACQUE, JAMES (Novelist) Foreign control 1969

BAETZ, REUBEN (Social scientist) Unemployment 1972

BAFFIN, WILLIAM (Navigator) Northwest
Passage 1615
BAGOT, *SIR* CHARLES (Diplomat) Defence
1817
BAILEY, ALFRED (Poet) Animals 1973
BAILEY, ALFRED G. (Poet and scholar)
Dignity 1973
BAILEY, DON (Poet) Action 1971; Mistakes
1973; You 1971
BAILEY, DOUGLAS L. (American writer)
Finance 1967; Water 1967
BAILEY, JACOB (Poet) Politicians 1780;
Sunflowers 1779
BAIN, GEORGE (Journalist) Birth control
1964; Closure 1956; Investment,
American 1969; Wheat 1963
BAIRD, DONALD (Librarian) Male
chauvinism 1974
BAKER, JOHN (Traitor) Madawaska, N.B.
1827
BALDWIN, ROBERT (Reformer)
Constitution 1844, 1844; Government
1854; Govt., responsible 1838; Politics
1844; Strength 1848; Union
(1841-1867) 1842
BALFOUR, GRANT (Poet) Canada 1910;
Fathers 1910
BALKIND, ALVIN (Art curator) Art 1975
BALL, GEORGE (U.S. representative to
U.N.) Americanization 1968;
Commerce 1968
BALLON, ROBERT J. (American writer)
Planning 1970
BANCROFT, GEORGE (U.S. historian)
Jesuits 1834
BANKS, HAL (Head, Seafarers'
International Union) Patronage 1968
BANNANTYNE, A.G.B. (Councillor of
Assiniboia) Riel, Louis 1885
BANTING, *SIR* FREDERICK G. (Discoverer
of insulin) Affluence 1946; Information
1924; Progress 1940; Science 1935
BARANYAI, TIBOR (Poet) Liberty 1962
BARBEAU, MARIUS (Anthropologist)
Identity 1928; Invasion 1932
BARBER, CLARENCE L. (Economist)
Planning 1963
BARBER, JOSEPH (U.S. politician)
Americanization 1958
BARBOUR, DOUGLAS (Poet) Roads 1971;
Winter 1972
BARING, ALEXANDER (Boundary adjustor)
See also *LORD* ASHBURTON Canada
1816

BARKER, EDWARD JOHN (Newspaper
editor) Enemies 1884
BARKER, LEWELLYS F. (Physician) Age
1942
BARR, ISAAC M. (Colonist) British 1903;
Can.-British relations 1902
BARR, ROBERT (Novelist) Authors 1899;
Books 1899
BARRETT, DAVID (Premier of B.C.)
Personalities; Politics 1973; Social work
1973; Socialists 1973
BARRON, SID (Cartoonist) Weather 1960's
BASSETT, JOHN (Publisher) Bishop,
William 1956; Duplessis, M. 1958
BASSETT, III, JOHN (Film-maker) Luck
1973
BATES, RONALD (Poet) Change 1968, 1968
BATES, STEWART (Public servant) Cities
and towns 1956
BATHURST *COURIER* (Newspaper)
Conservative Party 1836
BATSHAW, *JUDGE* HARRY Competition
1961
BAUER, NANCY L. (Poet) Travel 1969
BAUER, WALTER (Poet) Arctic 1968;
Awakening 1968; Canada 1968;
Communication 1968; Compatibility
1968; Money 1975; Toronto 1961;
Wisdom 1968
BAXTER, BEVERLEY (Journalist) Age 1935
BAYLEY, CORNWALL (English poet)
Canada 1806
BEACH, REX (U.S. novelist) Doctors 1932
BEALL, ARTHUR W. (Sex educationist)
Sexual union 1933
BEATTIE, JESSIE L. (Poet) Motherhood
1940
BEAUCHESNE, ARTHUR (Clerk of the
House of Commons) Provinces 1935;
Speaker of the House of Commons 1958
BEAUDOIN, RENE (Speaker of the House
of Commons) Pipeline debate (1956)
1956
BEAULIEU, MICHAEL (Student newspaper
editor) Queen 1954
BEAVER CLUB, MONTREAL Fur trade
1775
BEAVERBROOK, *LORD* Beaverbrook,
Lord 1949; Canadians 1917;
Consistency 1965; Education 1921,
1921; Hell 1964; Me 1963; Newspapers
1961; Umpires 1910
BECK, J. MURRAY (Historian) Conservative
Party 1957; Leadership 1957

BEDDOES, DICK (Sports columnist) Sport 1970, 1970, 1975, 1975

BEERS, *DR.* W. GEORGE (Writer on lacrosse) Annexation 1888; Lacrosse 1867

BEGBIE, *SIR* MATTHEW BAILLIE (Judge) Funerals 1894; Justice 1870's; Land 1860; Law and lawyers 1882; Trial by jury 1863

BEISSEL, HENRY (Poet) Demography 1966; Regimentation 1966; Space 1966

BELL, ALEXANDER GRAHAM (Inventor) Journalism 1917; Telephone 1876, 1909

BELL, *DR.* LESLIE (Conductor) Radio and TV 1953

BELL, MARILYN (Swimmer) Swimming 1954

BELL, THOMAS M. (M.P.) Pipeline debate (1956) 1956

BELMONT, FRANCOIS (Historian) Montreal 1732

BENCHLEY, ROBERT (American humorist) Boundary, Canada-U.S. 1939

BENGOUGH, JOHN W. (Cartoonist) Brown, George 1880; Crime 1896; Enemies 1896; Flying 1896; Gerrymandering 1882; Land 1896; Landlords 1896; Leadership 1896; Monopoly 1896; Ownership 1896; Political parties 1896; Relief 1896; Taxation 1896; Water 1896

BENGOUGH, PERCY (Labour leader) Labour unions 1949

BENNET, W. S. (U.S. Congressman) Annexation 1911

BENNETT, RICHARD B. (Prime Minister) Bennett, R.B. 1927, 1930, 1935; Cabinet 1930; Can.-British relations 1930; C.N.R. 1930; Conservatism 1933; Credos 1931; Economics 1935; Election slogans 1930; Foreign policy 1937; Happiness 1935; Ideals 1935; Judges 1937; Labour 1930; Majorities 1933; Meighen, Arthur 1914; Political phrases; Prime Minister 1935, 1939; Provinces 1937; Radio and TV 1932; Reform 1935, 1935; Separatism 1923; Society 1933; Trade 1930; War, European (1914-18) 1915; Wealth 1927; The West 1912, 1935

BENNETT, W.A.C. (Premier of B.C.) Bennett, W.A.C. 1965, 1966, 1969; British Columbia 1973; Democracy 1966; Finance 1966; Government 1966; Ideas 1966; Meetings 1966; News 1965; Politics 1952; Provinces 1968; Social Credit 1963, 1963, 1965; Water 1966; Winnipeg 1970

BENOIT, JEHANE (Cooking authority) Cooking 1963

BENSON, NATHANIEL A. (Author) Work 1930

BERENS, HENRY H. (British governor of the Hudson's Bay Co.) Hudson's Bay Co. 1863

BERESFORD-HOWE, CONSTANCE (Novelist) Women 1973

BERGER, CARL (Historian) Imperialism 1970

BERGER, EARL (Newspaper correspondent) United Nations 1962

BERGERON, JOSEPH (Politician and M.P.) Conservative Party 1905

BERLAND, ALWYN (Association executive) Universities 1969

BERNARD, FRANK (Hotelman) Election slogans 1957

BERNES, TOM (Student writer) Technology 1970

BERNHARDT, CLARA MAE (Poet) Grief 1942; Possession 1939

BERNIER, *CAPT.* JOSEPH E. (Explorer) Arctic 1909, 1910; Eskimos 1926

BERRILL, NEWMAN J. (Nature writer) Civilization 1955; Insects 1953; Life 1960

BERTON, PIERRE (Writer and broadcaster) British Columbia ca. 1885; C.P.R. 1971; Canoeing 1973; Christianity 1965; Church 1965; Frontiers 1970; Klondike 1958; Minorities 1968; Modern times 1965; North 1956; Religion 1965; Sex 1963; Sexual union 1965

BESSBOROUGH, *EARL OF* (Governor General) Theatre 1933

BETHUNE, NORMAN (Physician) Artists 1952, 1952; Books 1930's; Doctors 1930's, 1935; Gentlemen 1952; Health 1952; Medicine 1927

BEWLEY, LES (Judge) Judges 1972

BIBLE. Economics, 19th C.

BIBLE. Psalms Dominion 1867

BIBLE. Zechariah Dominion 1867

BIDWELL, MARSHALL S. (Politician)
Political phrases
BIGELOW, CHARLES (Biochemist)
Education 1968
BILKEY, PAUL (Editor) Laurier 1940
BILSFORD, GUY W. (Poet) Boundary,
Canada-U.S. 1939
BIRD, ROBERT A. (Construction engineer)
Pollution 1972
BIRDSALL, L. B. (Poet) Middle age 1936
BIRGE, CYRUS A. (Executive)
Manufacturing 1903
BIRNBAUM, *DR.* JACK (Psychiatrist) Anger
1973
BIRNEY, EARLE (Poet) Bears 1962; Boys
1962; British Columbia 1952; Cities
and towns 1952, 1952; Clouds 1952;
Criticism 1974; Discovery 1952;
Evolution 1945; Fishermen 1952;
Flying 1952; Freedom 1945, 1952;
Future 1973; Ghosts 1962; Glaciers
1949; Humanity 1945; Identity 1939;
Immaturity 1945; Life 1952, 1957;
Loneliness 1947; Love 1952, 1973; Man
1959, 1962; Mind 1944; Mountain
climbing 1942; Mythology 1973; North
1965; Nothing 1961; Ontario 1941;
Peace 1942; Poems 1966; Poets 1966;
Sea 1948; Sea gulls 1952; Seashore
1964; Trees 1948; Unity 1948, 1962;
Vancouver, B.C. 1952; Waves 1952;
Wilderness 1946; Will 1945; Woman
1952; You 1971; Writers 1966
BISHOP, MORRIS G. (American biographer)
Unity 1963
BISHOP, W. A. (BILLY) (R.C.A.F.) Air age
1944
BISSELL, CLAUDE T. (President, U. of
Toronto) Canadians 1966; North 1963;
Universities 1963, 1963; University of
Toronto 1958
BISSETT, BILL (Poet) Canada Council
1971; Earth 1971; Innocence 1971;
Normality 1971; Peace 1971
BLACK, GEORGE (M.P.) Bennett, R.B.
1940; Meighen, Arthur 1940
BLACKBURN, GRACE (Poet) Attraction
1926
BLACKMORE, JOHN H. (M.P.) Collective
security 1938
BLACKWOOD'S EDINBURGH MAGAZINE
Scotsmen 1829
BLAIN, JEAN (Separatist) Que. (Province)
1968

BLAINE, JAMES G. (U.S. politician)
Canadian-American relations 1889
BLAKE, EDWARD (Politician) Annexation
1891; Aristocracy 1880's; British 1874;
British Columbia 1874; B.N.A. Act
(1867) 1880; Cabinet ministers 1874;
Canada 1891; C.P.R. 1870's, 1874,
1880; Church 1874; Deeds and doing
1874; Diplomacy 1882; Elections 1874;
Foreign policy 1874; Free speech 1874,
1891; Free trade 1882, 1887, 1891;
Independence 1892; Justice 1885;
Mountains 1874; Nationalism 1874;
Nationality 1874, 1874; Parliament
1873; Parliamentary representation
1874, 1874; Political phrases; Politics
1884; Riel, Louis 1885, 1886; Rocky
Mountains 1874; Senate 1874; Tariffs
1882; Teachers 1874; Time 1892;
United States 1874; The West 1891
BLAKE, SAMUEL H. (Lawyer) Mackenzie,
Alex. (P.M.) 1892
BLAKE, WILLIAM HUME (Writer)
Disappointment 1915; Fishing 1915,
1915; Salvation 1923; Sin 1923
BLANCHARD, JOTHAM (Politician) Power
1830
BLANCHARD, *MRS.* VITAL (B.C. citizen)
Living 1963
BLAND, SALEM G. (Preacher) Church
1920; Divinity 1920
BLATZ, WILLIAM E. (Educator)
Adolescents 1966; Boredom 1966; Care
1966; Children 1966; Consistency
1966; Delinquents 1966; Friends 1966;
Ideas 1966; Imagination 1966;
Intelligence 1966; Knowledge 1966;
Mistakes 1966; People 1966;
Personality 1966; Prevention 1966;
Principles 1966; Retaliation 1966;
Security 1966; Teachers 1966
BLEWETT, JEAN (Poet) Mothers 1897;
Quebec (City) 1897; Sun 1922; Twins
1897
BLISS, MICHAEL (Historian) Sex 1970
BOCK, W.G. (Billy) (Essayist) Cities and
towns 1958
BOCKING, RICHARD C. (Economist)
Columbia River 1972
BODSWORTH, FRED (Writer)
Conservation 1967
BOIVIN, GEORGE H. (Politician)
Mackenzie, Mann and Co. 1914

BOMPAS, WILLIAM C. (Bishop)
Missionaries 1878
BONELLIE, JANET (Writer) Adults 1968;
Age 1967; Passion 1968
BONENFANT, JEAN-CHARLES (Librarian)
Nation 1963; Unity 1963
BONNER, ROBERT W. (Politician and
lawyer) Capital 1970
BOOS, ARTHUR W. (Economist) Prov.
subsidies 1930
BOOTH, LUELLA (Poet) Flowers 1965
BORDEN, *SIR* ROBERT (Prime Minister)
Army 1933; Brains 1906; Can.-British
relations 1908, 1917; Change 1929;
Conservative Party 1901;
Continentalism 1911; The Crown 1919;
Defence 1912; Governor General 1916;
Modern times 1918; Patronage 1903;
People 1912; Reciprocity (1911) 1911;
Sovereign 1901; Status 1913, 1919;
Tariffs 1904; War, European (1914-18)
1912, 1916
BORDUAS, PAUL-EMILE (Painter) Action
1948; Change 1948; Future 1948; New
France 1948; Past 1948
BOUCHARD, GEORGE (Writer)
Urbanization 1928
BOUCHARD, TELESPHORE-DAMIEN
(Senator) Duplessis, M. 1936
BOUCHER, PIERRE (Historian) New
France 1664
BOUCHETTE, ERROL (Economic
nationalist) Industrialization 1901;
Natural resources 1901
BOUDIN, JEAN (Poet) Grief 1967
BOULDING, KENNETH (U.S. economist)
Unity 1957
BOURASSA, HENRI (Nationalist)
Americanization 1912; Bilingualism
1916; Boer War (1899) 1899, 1900;
Bourassa, Henri 1902, 1907; British
Empire 1901; Canada 1904;
Can.-British relations 1910;
Compromise 1899; Conscription,
military 1917, 1917; Constitution 1913;
Defence 1901, 1911; Democracy 1943;
Disunity 1917; Englishmen 1956;
French Canadians 1905; French
Canadians, destiny 1923; French
Canadians, survival 1918; French
language 1913, 1915; Government
1899; Independence 1911; Law and
lawyers 1935; Liberalism 1900; Me
1900; Mothers 1911; Nationalism 1902,

1902, 1904, 1911, 1914; Patriotism
1907; Sunday 1906; Trade unions 1914;
Unity 1905, 1916; Wealth 1902
BOURGAULT, PIERRE (Quebec separatist
leader) Youth 1963
BOURGET, IGNACE (Bishop of Montreal)
Liberalism 1876; Riel, Louis 1875;
Roman Catholics 1876
BOURINOT, ARTHUR S. (Poet) Death 1955;
Maple trees 1951; Partridges 1953;
Skiing 1923
BOURINOT, *SIR* JOHN G. (Historian)
Literature, Canadian 1881
BOURKE, WILLIAM (Executive) English
language 1963
BOVEY, WILFRID (Educator) French
Canadians 1938
BOWERING, GEORGE (Author) Baseball
1967; Belonging 1968; Consistency
1966; Death 1969; Masterpieces 1971;
Prairies 1968; Snow 1966; Visitors 1969
BOXER, AVI (Poet) Evening 1971
BOYA, NATHAN T. (Black American)
Travel 1961
BOYCHUCK, JOHN (Communist)
Communism 1972
BOYER, *DR.* RAYMOND (Traitor) Spying
1946
BOYLE, *SIR* CAVENDISH (Governor of
Newfoundland) Newfoundland 1901
BOYLE, CHARLES F. (Poet) The Present
1942
BOYLE, HARRY J. (Author and
broadcasting executive) Obsolescence
1963; Sin 1966
BOYLE, THOMAS (Author) Welfare 1961
BOYS, THOMAS A. (Poet) R.C.M.P. 1878
BRACQ, JEAN C. (Historian) Roman
Catholic Church 1924
BRADEN, BERNARD (Radio performer)
Radio and TV 1959
BRADY, ALEXANDER (Historian)
Federalism 1958; Materialism 1953
BRALEY, EPHRAIM (Maine lumberjack)
Canada 1850's
BRANT, JOSEPH (Indian Chief)
Imperialism 1803
BREBNER, JOHN B. (Historian)
Canadian-American relations 1945,
1960; Caution 1960; Emigration 1945;
Nationalism 1940; Scholarship 1945
BRENN, BRIAN (Writer) Emigration 1971
BRETT, GEORGE SIDNEY (Philosopher)
History 1921

BREWIN, ANDREW (Politician)
Canadian-American relations 1971;
C.C.F. 1943

BREWSTER, ELIZABETH (Poet) Cities and
towns 1972; Dreams 1969; History
1969; Identity 1971; Illusions 1972;
Peace 1951; Rebirth 1972; Tradition
1969

BRIAND, JEAN-OLIVIER (Bishop of
Quebec) Obedience 1767

BRICHANT, ANDREW (Political writer)
Federalism 1968; Unity 1968

BRIDLE, AUGUSTUS (Author) Borden, Sir
Robert 1921; Music 1929; Parliament,
Members of 1921

BRIGHT, JOHN (English orator)
Annexation 1861, 1867; Canada 1862;
Continentalism 1861, 1862

BRITISH AMERICAN LEAGUE
Confederation 1849

BRITISH ARMY COMMAND War,
European (1914-18) 1917

BRITISH COLONIST, Victoria (Newspaper)
Chinese 1878

BRITISH COLUMBIA British Columbia
1871

BRITISH COLUMBIA LIBERAL PARTY
Election slogans 1933

BRITISH COLUMBIAN (Newspaper) British
Columbia 1870

BRITISH NORTH AMERICA ACT
Government 1867; Monarchy 1867;
Queen 1867

BROADBENT, ED (New Democratic Party
leader) N.D.P. 1969

BROADFOOT, DAVE (Comedian)
Federalism 1965

BROCK, *SIR* ISAAC (General) Army 1812;
Brock, *Sir* Isaac 1812; War of 1812,
1812

BROCKINGTON, LEONARD (Orator)
Bennett, R.B. 1935; Radio & TV 1936

BRODEUR, LOUIS P. (Politician) Hudson
Bay 1906

BROGAN, *SIR* DENIS (British political
scientist) Culture 1954; Unity 1954;
Uranium 1954

BROOKE, FRANCES (Novelist) Climate
1769; Genius 1769; Scenery 1769;
Winter 1769; Women 1769

BROOKE, RUPERT (British poet) British
Columbia 1919; Canada 1916; Church
1916; Cities and towns 1913, 1916;
Ghosts 1916; Individuality 1913; Poets
1913; Stars 1916; Toronto 1916, 1916;
Winnipeg 1916, 1916

BROOM, LEONARD (American sociologist)
Disunity 1960

BROSNAN, JIM (U.S. writer) Hockey, 1963

BROWN, *DR.* ALAN (Paediatrician)
Experience 1956; Milk 1952, 1952

BROWN, AUDREY ALEXANDRA (Poet)
Beauty 1948; England 1937;
Immortality 1931; Music 1943; Suburbs
1955; Unity 1943; Youth 1937

BROWN, EDWARD KILLORAN (Critic) Art
1944; Colonialism 1944; Disunity 1944;
Literature 1944; Literature, Canadian
1944; Orthodoxy 1961

BROWN, GEORGE (Father of
Confederation) Annexation 1859;
British Columbia 1865; Confederation
1859, 1864, 1865; Disunity 1864;
Education 1850; Election funds 1872;
Election slogans 1857; Fathers 1858;
French Canadians 1865; Government
House 1864; Governor General 1864;
Mackenzie, W. L. 1850's; Newspapers
1867; Parliament bldgs. 1864; Religion
1851; Revolution 1863; Senate 1865;
Truth 1851

BROWN, GEORGE W. (Historian)
Nationalism 1944; United States 1944

BROWN, *COL.* J. SUTHERLAND (Strategist)
Defence 1921; Japanese 1942

BROWN, ROBERT D. (University professor)
Manufacturing 1965

BROWN, ROSEMARY (British Columbia
M.L.A.) Blacks 1975; Feminists 1975

BROWNE, GERALD PETER (Political
scientist) Law and lawyers 1967

BRUCE, CHARLES T. (Poet) Autumn 1951;
Beauty 1932

BRUCE, JOHN (Riel's associate)
Government 1869

BRUNET, MICHEL (Historian) Corruption
1973; Disunity 1954; Durham, *Lord*
1956; French Canadians 1958; French
Canadians, survival 1966; Heroes 1973;
Majorities 1958; Minorities 1954;
Quebec (Province) 1954; Youth 1954

BRYCE, JAMES, *Viscount* (British
diplomat) Political parties 1921;
Reciprocity (1911) 1911

C

CAMPBELL, WILLIAM WILFRED (Poet)
Autumn 1889, 1889, 1893; Climate
1907; Conduct of life 1899; Dreams
1889; England 1899; Ethnic groups
1892; Evening 1893; Forests 1899,
1922; Funerals 1918; Government
1907; Lake Huron 1889; Lakes 1889,
1889, 1889; Man 1905; Music 1886;
National heritage 1905; Night 1889;
North 1905; Obligations 1923;
Parliament Buildings 1907; Scotsmen
1899; Snow 1905; Summer 1907;
Wilderness 1889; Wind 1905
CAMPNEY, RALPH (Politician and lawyer)
Politics 1958
CANADA British Columbia 1871;
Citizenship 1970; Indians 1871, 1873;
Land 1878
CANADA. ARMY War, European (1914-18)
1918
CANADA. CENSUS. 1961 Ethnic groups
1961
CANADA. COMMISSIONERS OF CROWN
LANDS Settlers 1865
CANADA. COMMISSIONERS APPOINTED
TO ENQUIRE INTO THE WORKING OF
MILLS AND FACTORIES Children 1882
CANADA. COMMITTEE ON
BROADCASTING Radio and TV 1965,
1965, 1965
CANADA. CONSTITUTIONAL
CONFERENCE SECRETARIAT B.N.A.
Act (1867) 1971
CANADA. CRIMINAL CODE Associations
1919
CANADA. DEPT. OF ENERGY, MINES AND
RESOURCES Energy 1976
CANADA. DEPT. OF FISHERIES Pollution
1889
CANADA. DEPT. OF HEALTH Women's
liberation 1975
CANADA. DEPT. OF INDIAN AFFAIRS AND
NORTHERN DEVELOPMENT Indians
1967
CANADA. DEPT. OF INTERIOR The West
1905; Wheat 1899, 1903, 1903
CANADA. DEPT. OF MILITIA AND
DEFENCE Death 1914
CANADA. DEPT. OF NATIONAL DEFENCE
Defence 1964
CANADA. EMERGENCY MEASURES
ORGANIZATION Atomic bombs 1961

CANADA. FEDERAL TASK FORCE ON
HOUSING AND URBAN
DEVELOPMENT Housing 1969;
Poverty 1969
CANADA. FRANCHISE ACT Persons 1885
CANADA. GOVERNMENT Federalism
1968; Bethune, Dr. Norman H. 1972;
Conscription, military 1942; Identity
1971
CANADA. HOUSE OF COMMONS. SPECIAL
COMMITTEE ON SOCIAL SECURITY
Social security 1943
CANADA. HOUSE OF COMMONS.
STANDING COMMITTEE ON
BROADCASTING Radio and TV 1967
CANADA. INFORMATION CANADA
Propaganda 1970
CANADA. LAWS, STATUTES Censorship
1859; Defence 1904; Discrimination
1960; Hutterites 1899; Indians 1951;
Languages 1968; Naturalization 1886;
Obscenity 1953, 1959; Potlatch 1884;
Radio and TV 1967, 1967; Rights 1960;
Riots 1953
CANADA. PRIVY COUNCIL Doukhobors
1898; Investment, foreign 1972;
Monarchy 1953
CANADA. ROYAL COMMISSION ON
BILINGUALISM AND BICULTURALISM
Canada 1967; Crises 1965; Disunity
1965; Ethnic groups 1967; Majorities
1965; Race 1967; Separatism 1965;
Unity 1967
CANADA. ROY. COMM. ON
BROADCASTING Radio and TV 1957,
1957.
CANADA. ROY. COMM. ON CANADA'S
ECONOMIC PROSPECTS Economy
1956; Fortune telling 1957; Geography
1957; Wilderness 1957
CANADA. ROY. COMM. ON DISRUPTION
OF SHIPPING ON THE GREAT LAKES
Banks, Harold C. 1963
CANADA. ROY. COMM. ON
DOMINION-PROVINCIAL RELATIONS
Maritimes 1940; Provinces 1940; Unity
1940
CANADA. ROY. COMM. ON HEALTH
SERVICES Health 1964; Medical care
1964
CANADA. ROY. COMM. ON INDUSTRIAL
TRAINING Farming 1913

CARTWRIGHT, JOHN (University professor) Radio and T.V. 1962

CARTWRIGHT, JOHN ROBERT (Judge) Judges 1967

CARTWRIGHT, *SIR* RICHARD (Politician) Associations 1886; Blake, Edward 1912; Canada as intermediary 1911; Canadian-American relations 1874; Corruption 1912; Diplomacy 1888; Emigration 1912; Enemies 1934; *The Globe* Toronto 1912; Power 1912; Lies and liars 1886; Loyalty 1911; Macdonald, *Sir* John A. 1883, 1912, 1915; Provinces 1891; Resistance 1886; Sacrifice 1934; Senate 1906

CARVELL, FRANK B. (Politician) Cabinet ministers 1916

CARVER, HUMPHREY S.M. (Writer and planner) Cities and towns 1962

CASGRAIN, THERESE-FORGET (Politician) Reform 1972; Unity 1972; Women 1972

CASHIN, MICHAEL (Newfoundland Prime Minister) Voters 1919

CASHIN, PETER (M.L.A., Newfoundland) Trust 1950

CASSIDY, CAROL COATES (Poet) April 1939; Flowers 1939; New Year 1941

CASSON, HERBERT N. (American writer) Resistance 1898

CATMUR, DANIEL (Officer of Canadian University Service Overseas) Foreign relations 1971

CECIL, *LORD* ROBERT (British diplomat) Natural resources 1905

CHALMERS, RANDOLPH C. (University professor) Religion 1959

CHAMBERLAIN, JOSEPH (British politician) Laurier, *Sir* Wilfrid 1904; Population 1895; Public opinion 1872

CHAMBERLAND, PAUL (Separatist) Communication 1972; Disunity 1964

CHAMBERS, JACK (Painter) Painting 1972

CHAPAIS, THOMAS (Historian) France 1897

CHAPIN, MIRIAM (Writer) Books 1959; Foreign aid 1959; Health 1959; Investment, American 1959; Labour unions 1959; Maritimes 1959; Nova Scotia 1956; Toronto 1959

CHAPLEAU, *SIR* JOSEPH A. (Politician) C.P.R. 1885; Chinese 1885; Riel, Louis 1885

CHAPMAN, CHRISTOPHER (Poet) Canada 1969

CHAPUT, MARCEL (Separatist) Confederation 1962, 1962; French Canadians 1962; Queen 1964; Separatism 1962, 1964

CHARBONNEL, ANDRE DE (Bishop of Toronto) Education 1856

CHARLES I (King of England) Beavers 1632

CHARLESWORTH, HECTOR (Journalist) Macdonald, *Sir* John A. 1927; Women's rights 1893

CHARLEVOIX, PIERRE F.X. DE (Explorer) Canada (Name) 1744

CHARLOTTETOWN *GUARDIAN* (Newspaper) Newspapers 1891

CHARPENTIER, ALFRED (Labour unionist) French Canadians, survival 1946

CHARTERS, MICHAEL (Novelist) Victors 1970

CHASE, *DR.* A. W. (Writer of medical recipes) Drinking 1868

CHAUVEAU, PIERRE-JOSEPH-OLIVER (Premier of Quebec) Disunity 1876; Education 1843

CHEADLE, WALTER B. (British traveller) Food 1863; Mountains 1865; Rocky Mountains 1865

CHERNIACK, SAUL (M.L.A., Manitoba) Investment, foreign 1967

CHILD, PHILIP (Novelist) Freedom 1945

CHINIQUY, *FATHER* CHARLES (Clergyman) Temperance 1850

CHIPMAN, WARWICK (Poet) Conduct of life 1930; Faith 1930; Future 1930

CHISHOLM, G. BROCK (Director general, World Health Org.) Children 1945; Christmas 1945; Conscience 1946; Democracy 1956, 1956; Innocence 1945; Sex 1945, 1945; Sin 1945; Teachers 1945; Truth 1945; War 1951

CHONKALEY, HARRY (Indian leader) Voters, Votes and Voting 1947

CHOQUETTE, JEROME (Quebec politician) Minorities 1970

CHRISTIAN EXAMINER (Newspaper) Novels 1840

CHRISTIAN GUARDIAN (Newspaper) Protestants 1856

CHRISTIE, DAVID (Clear Grit) Clear Grits 1849, 1849

CHURCHILL, GORDON (Politician) Economics 1957

COLEMAN, VICTOR (Poet) Singing 1966; Suicide 1967

COLLEGE MILITAIRE ROYALE. ST. JEAN, QUE. Bilingualism 1950

COLLIER, JOHN (U.S. Indian commissioner) Indians 1947

COLLINS, JOSEPH EDMUND (Journalist) Civil service 1884; Saskatchewan 1887

COLMAN, MARY ELIZABETH (Poet) Faith 1942

COLOMBO, JOHN ROBERT (Writer) Canada 1968

COLONIAL PATRIOT (Newspaper) Nova Scotia 1829

COMMITTEE FOR POLITICAL REALISM Individuality 1964

COMPTON, NEIL (University professor) Communication 1961

COMTOIS, ULYSEE (Artist) Technology 1971

CONKEY, R.B. (American railroader) C.P.R. 1882

CONNOR, RALPH (pseud. of *Rev.* C.W. Gordon) (Novelist) Emotions 1917; Forests 1901; Ideas 1904; Laughter 1904; Loyalty 1900; Preachers 1904; Voice 1917

CONNORS, STOMPIN' TOM (Folk singer) Hitch-hiking 1972; Potatoes 1960; Singing 1972

CONSERVATIVE AND UNIONIST PARTY Election slogans 1917

CONSERVATIVE PARTY (Federal) Election slogans 1856, 1861, 1867, 1868, 1875, 1882, 1883, 1890, 1891, 1891, 1894, 1894, 1900, 1911, 1911, 1911, 1911, 1911, 1911, 1917, 1921, 1952, 1957, 1957; Macdonald, *Sir* John A. 1882; Political phrases; Reciprocity (1911) 1911; Two nations theory 1967

CONSERVATIVE PARTY (New Brunswick) Radio and TV 1953

CONSERVATIVE PARTY (Nova Scotia) Election slogans 1925

"CONSTANT READER" (pseud.) Corruption 1882

CONWAY, JOHN (University of Toronto historian) The crown 1969

COOK, GREGORY M. (Poet) Life 1970

COOK, HUGH (Poet) Indians 1968

COOK, RAMSAY (Historian) Boundaries 1971; The Conquest (1759) 1966; Dafoe, John W. 1963; Diefenbaker, J.G. 1971; Identity 1967; Nationalism 1971; Quebec (Prov.) 1969; Universities 1969

COONEY, ROBERT (Historian) Isolation 1832

COOPER, JOHN A. (Journalist) Trade 1896

CO-OPERATIVE COMMONWEALTH FEDERATION (Political party) Conscription, military 1942; C.C.F. 1933, 1933; Depression (1930-37) 1933; Planning 1933; Political phrases

COPP, J. TERRY (Historian) Montreal 1890

CORBETT, DAVID C. (Economist) Immigration 1957, 1957

CORBETT, PERCY E. (Lawyer) Patriotism 1941; Public opinion 1938; Theory 1941

CORBETT, TERRY (Labrador magistrate) Voters 1963

CORNING, HOWARD W. (Nova Scotia M.L.A.) Nova Scotia 1923

CORNWALL *OBSERVER* (Newspaper) Newspapers 1835

CORPORATION DES ENSEIGNANTS DU QUEBEC Labour 1971

CORRY, JAMES A. (Political scientist) Democracy 1951; Justice 1968; Law and lawyers 1971; Order 1951; Politics 1951

COUGHTRY, GRAHAM (Painter) Painting 1955

COUNCIL ON FRENCH LIFE IN AMERICA French Canadians, survival 1967

COURCHENE, *CHIEF* DAVE Indians 1973

COWIE, ISAAC (Author) Farming 1903

COWPER, WILLIAM (British poet) Wolfe, James 1785

COX, LEO (Poet) April 1933

COYNE, JAMES E. (Banker) Professions 1963

CRAGG, R. CECIL (University professor) Teaching 1958

CRAIG, GERALD M. (Historian) Canadian-American relations 1954; Preachers 1963

CRAIG, JOHN (Novelist) Olympic games (1976) 1973

CRAN, MARION (English author) Housewives 1910

CRANBORNE, *LORD* (Politician) Massey, Vincent 1951

CRAWFORD, ISABELLA VALANCY (Poet)
Autumn 1884; Burials 1884; Deeds and
doing 1905; Good and evil 1905;
Harvest 1884; Kisses 1905; Love 1884,
1905; March 1884; Roses 1905; Settlers
1884, 1884; Ships 1884; Sky 1884;
Soldiers 1884; Space 1905
CRAWFORD, TERRY (Poet) Poor 1971
CREIGHTON, ALAN (Poet) Clothes 1939;
Cows 1936; Materialism 1942; Poetry
1942; Youth 1936
CREIGHTON, DONALD (Historian)
Americanization 1972; Autonomy
1970; Bilingualism 1972; Biography
1948; Blake, E. 1955; B.N.A. Act (1867)
1945; Canadian-American relations
1945, 1972, 1972; Confederation 1970;
Continentalism 1970, 1970; Dance
1860's; Durham, *Lord* 1959; French
language 1972; Government 1954;
Heroism 1973; Hincks, *Sir* Francis
1952; Historians 1948, 1968, 1972;
History 1972; Horses 1959; Imperialism
1960; Innis, Harold 1957, 1957;
Investment, foreign 1970; Irrelevance
1957; King, W.L.M. 1954, 1957, 1959,
1970, 1970; Liberal Party 1972;
Literature 1968; Macdonald, *Sir* John
A. 1955
CREMAZIE, OCTAVE (Poet) Age 1866
CRERAR, *GEN.* HENRY D.G. (Army leader)
Army command 1944
CROFT, DON (Computer expert)
Computers 1970
CROLL, DAVID (Senator) Labour strikes
1937
CROSBY, JOHN (Columnist) Fashions 1963
CROSS, AUSTIN F. (Journalist) Civil service
1951
CROSS, JAMES R. (Kidnapped trade
commissioner) Revolution 1970
CROSSMAN, RICHARD (British editor)
Politics 1964
CROSWELLER, WILLIAM T. (British
traveller) Sunday 1898
CROWFOOT (Blackfoot chief) Indians
1877; Life 1890; R.C.M.P. 1877
CROWLEY, ALEISTER (British writer)
Canada 1923; Toronto, about 1923
CRUIKSHANK, WILLIAM (Painter)
Painting 1893
CULLEN, THOMAS S. (Surgeon) Doctors
1900's

CUMBERLAND, FREDERIC B. (Historian)
British 1904
CUMMING, ROBERT D. (Writer) Books
1915; Dogs 1915; Posterity 1915; The
Present 1915; Time 1915
CURRAN, JAMES W. (Editor) Wolves 1940
CURRIE, ARCHIBALD W. (Economist)
Transportation 1954
CURRIE, *GEN.* ARTHUR W. (Great War
leader) Railways 1957; Soldiers 1918
CURWOOD, J. OLIVER (American novelist)
The West 1905
CURZON, SARAH A. (Journalist) United
Empire Loyalists 1887; Women 1887
"CYNIC" (Pseud.) Royal commissions 1938

D

DAFOE, CAL (Brother of J.W. Dafoe)
Dafoe, John W. 1962; Journalism 1962
DAFOE, JOHN W. (Newspaper editor) Age
1943; Argument 1948; Books 1923;
Borden, *Sir* Robert 1943; Bourassa,
Henri 1916; British Empire 1920;
Can.-Brit. relations 1922; Canadianism
1925; Confederation, Fathers of 1932;
Dafoe, John W. 1926; Death 1944;
Elections 1931; Future 1936;
Government 1927, 1928, 1948;
Governor General 1927; Heroes 1922;
Immigrants 1913; Jews 1933;
Journalism 1923, 1924; Laurier, *Sir*
Wilfrid 1922; League of Nations 1936,
1936, 1937; Liberal Party 1919;
Meighen, Arthur 1926; Memory 1931;
Newspapers 1936, 1936; No 1922;
Parliamentary debates 1931; Peace
1919; Personality 1948; Political parties
1922, 1962; Politics 1886, 1926, 1931,
1935; Prime Minister 1922; Selfishness
1923; Statistics 1938; Titles of honour
1911; Trade 1935; War 1936; War
dead 1919; War, World (1939-45) 1936,
1939
DAGANOWIDA (Iroquois prophet and
statesman) Law and lawyers ca. 1570
DAILY MAIL (London, Eng.) (Newspaper)
Foreign relations 1903
DALES, JOHN H. (Economist)
Americanization 1967; Economy 1966;
National Policy (1878) 1964, 1964

DE COSMOS, AMOR (B.C. Premier) British Columbia 1870; Political phrases; The Press, freedom of, 1859; Treaties 1882

DE GAULLE, CHARLES (President of France) History 1965; Quebec (Province) 1967

DE LA ROCHE, MAZO (Author) Malice 1927; Manners 1927; Ownership 1926; Reading 1960; Women 1927

DE LA RUE, PHILIPPE A. (Writer) Tolerance 1962

DEMILLE, JAMES (Novelist) Education 1878; Evil 1888; Mountains 1893; New Brunswick 1870; Woman 1888

DENECHOAN, WILLIE (Medicine Man) Indians 1970

DENIS, JEAN J. (Member of Parliament) Women 1918

DENISON, GEORGE TAYLOR (Police magistrate) Courts 1905; Force 1880; North 1869; Rich 1911

DENISON, MERRILL (Writer) Americanism, anti-1952; Boundary, Canada-U.S. 1952; Theatre 1929, 1929

DENNIS, LLOYD (Educator) Children 1969; Science 1970

DENONVILLE, JACQUES-RENE, MARQUIS DE (Governor of New France) Indians 1685

DENT, JOHN C. (Historian) Blake, Edward 1882; Literature, Canadian 1881

DE PEYSTER, JOHN WATTS (American general) United Empire Loyalists 1883

DE POE, NORMAN (CBC Commentator) Radio and TV 1968

DERBISHIRE, STEWART (Public official) Farmers 1838

DERBY, ELIAS H. (U.S. annexationist) Annexation 1866

DERICK, CARRIE M. (Botanist) Women 1913

DESBARATS, PETER (Journalist) Disunity 1965; Giving 1965; Illusions 1972; Quebec (Prov.) 1965, 1971

DESBIENS, JEAN-PAUL ("Frère Untel") (Author) Authority 1962; Conformity 1960; Dignity 1965; Freedom 1965; French Canadians 1962, 1965; French Canadians, destiny 1962; French language 1962; Intelligence 1965; Quebec (Prov.) 1960; Writers 1960

DESCHATELETS, JEAN-PAUL (Member of Parliament) Political phrases

DEUTSCH, JOHN J. (Educator and public servant) Welfare 1956

DEWART, EDWARD H. (Anthologist) Emigrants 1869; Literature, Canadian 1864, 1864; Poetry 1864; Thought 1869

DEWART, LESLIE (Writer) Love 1963

DEWEY, ALEXANDER G. (Historian) Laurier, Sir Wilfrid 1927

DEXTER, GRANT (Press Gallery correspondent) Pearson, L.B. 1968; St. Laurent, Louis 1956

DIABO, ORVIS (Caughnawaga Indian) Hell 1949

DICKENS, CHARLES (British novelist) Canada 1842; Kingston, Ont. 1842

DICKSON, LOVAT (Editor and writer) Youth 1963

DIEFENBAKER, JOHN G. (Prime Minister) Age 1970; British 1926; Americans 1963; Cabinet ministers 1958; Canadian-American relations 1958; Conservatives 1966; Diefenbaker, J.G. 1956, 1963, 1963, 1963, 1963, 1966, 1975; Diplomacy 1962; Discards 1968; Economy 1963; Election slogans 1958, 1965; Elections 1958, 1958; Foreign relations 1961; Freedom 1960; Futility 1958; Gifts 1965; Gordon, Walter 1962; Government 1957, 1958; House of Commons 1964; Liberal Party 1958; Names 1962; North 1958; Nuclear weapons 1963, 1963, 1963; Obsolescence 1968; Opposition 1964; Patriotism 1961; Platforms, political 1958; Political phrases; Population 1958; Prime Minister 1958; Rain 1958; Truth 1963; Vision 1958; Voters 1963

DIEFENBAKER, OLIVE (Wife of Prime Minister) Prime Minister 1963

DIEREVILLE, N. SIEUR DE (Historian of Acadia) Halifax 1699

DIESPECKER, DICK (Poet) Victory 1944

DILKE, SIR CHARLES W. (British parliamentarian) Boundary, Canada-U.S. 1899; Diplomacy 1890; Opposition 1890

DINGMAN, HAROLD (Journalist) Babies 1947

DION, FERNAND (Broadcaster) Liberty 1970

DION, LEON (Political writer) Quebec (Province) 1963

DISRAELI, BENJAMIN (British Prime
Minister) Colonies 1852; Smith,
Goldwin 1846; Treaty of Washington
(1871) 1875
DIXON, FREDERICK A. (Poet) Age 1884;
Defence 1917
DIXON, FREDERICK J. (Political reformer)
Free trade 1915; Liberty 1920
DOBBS, KILDARE (Writer) Canadian
Shield 1970; Failure 1962; Identity
1968; Literature, Canadian 1958, 1958;
Regionalism 1964
DOHERTY, CHARLES J. (Minister of
justice) Democracy 1931; Poker (game)
1931; Politics 1931
"DOMINO" See BRIDLE, AUGUSTUS
DOMINION OBSERVATORY Time 1941
DONNELLY, JOHN F. (Poet) The dead
1967
DONNELLY, MURRAY S. (Educator)
Academics 1964; Government 1963
DOONE, J. J. HAYES (Senator) Maritimes
1952
DORCHESTER, LORD, See CARLETON,
SIR GUY
DORION, ANTOINE-AIME (Politician)
Confederation 1865
DORION, JEAN BAPTISTE E. (Journalist)
Geography 1865
DOUGHTY, ARTHUR G. (Archivist)
Archives 1924; Nationality 1913
DOUGLAS, MAJOR CLIFFORD H. (British
social credit theorist) Social Credit 1934
DOUGLAS JR., JAMES (Metallurgist) Books
1875
DOUGLAS, SIR JAMES Douglas, Sir James
1843, 1877; Duty 1864; Victoria, B.C.
1843
DOUGLAS, THOMAS C. (Leader of New
Democratic Party) Constitution 1966;
Cooperative Commonwealth
Federation 1950; Economics 1971;
Liberal Party 1965; Medical care 1951,
1954; Religion 1934; Saskatchewan
1960; Social security 1946
DOUTRE, GONZALVE (Law reformer)
French Canadians, destiny 1864;
Separatism 1864
DOYLE, SIR ARTHUR CONAN (British
author) Poetry 1914; Prairies 1919;
Trails 1914; Soldiers 1922; Wilderness
1919
DRAPEAU, JEAN (Montreal mayor)
Olympic games (1976) 1975

DRAPER, WILLIAM H. (Chief justice)
Can.-British relations 1841; Railways
1857
DREW, GEORGE (Conservative leader)
Conservative Party 1940
DREW, JOHN (Poet) Saint John, N.B. 1967
DRUMMOND, GEORGE E. (Executive)
Manufacturing 1904
DRUMMOND, LEWIS T. (Politician)
Disloyalty 1844
DRUMMOND, WILLIAM H. (Dialect poet)
Boys 1900; Canadians 1905; Girls 1908;
Old age 1898; Roads 1902; Voters
1905; Wind 1897
DRURY, CHARLES (Politician) Auditor
General 1969
DUCHESNEAU, JACQUES (Intendant)
Violence 1675
DUDEK, LOUIS (Poet) Art 1954; Beauty
1954; Birds 1971; Business men 1963;
Critics 1958; Gardens 1971; Life 1956;
Literature 1963; Media 1969; Moon
1946; Nature 1966; Plants 1952; Poems
1952; Poetry 1957; Poets 1971; Political
parties 1956, 1958; The Present 1958;
Reading 1958; Sea 1954, 1967; Success
1971; Travel 1967; Ugliness 1954;
Universities 1969, 1969; Waves 1954
DUFF, SIR LYMAN P. (Supreme Court chief
justice) B.N.A. Act (1867) 1910
DUFF, LOUIS B. (Historian) History 1957;
Politicians 1952; Rebellion (1837) 1938
DUFFERIN, LORD (Governor General)
Arches 1874; British Columbia 1876;
Civil Service 1878; Duty 1873; Forests
1872; Future 1872, 1877; Governor
General 1873, 1874, 1874, 1877;
Mackenzie, Alexander (P.M.) 1874;
Manitoba 1877; Parliament 1873;
Patriotism 1878; Prince Edward Island
1873; Quebec (Prov.) 1878; Riel, Louis
1874; Senate 1874; Transportation 1877;
Voters 1875; Winter 1877
DUFFY, DENIS (University professor)
Nationalism 1970
DUGAS, ABBE GEORGES (Curé of St.
Boniface) Winter 1890
DUMAIS, MARIO (French Canadian
radical) Quebec (Prov.) 1972
DUMONT, GABRIEL (Riel's adjutant) Fear
1885; Northwest Rebellion (1885) 1888
DUNBAR, MAXWELL J. (Zoologist) Arctic
1968

DUNCAN, CHESTER (Writer) Identity
1947; Speech 1947

DUNCAN, DOROTHY (Writer) Ontario
1941

DUNCAN, NORA M. (Poet) People 1938

DUNCAN, SARA JEANETTE (Author)
Americanization 1904; British Empire
1904; Clothes 1891; Investment,
American 1904; Lovers 1888; News
1904; Newspapers 1886; Politicians
1904; Society 1887

DUNDONALD, *LORD* (Soldier) Union Jack
1904

DUNKIN, CHRISTOPHER (Politician) The
Crown 1865; Nationality 1865

DUNLOP, WILLIAM (Physician and writer)
Authors 1832; Children 1832;
Navigation 1832; Politicians 1847

DUNN, *SIR* JAMES (Executive) Retirement
1961

DUPLESSIS, MAURICE (Premier of
Quebec) Budgets 1949; Cooperation
1936; Diefenbaker, John G. 1957;
Duplessis, M. 1939, 1940's, 1960;
Health 1960; Insurance 1958;
Intellectuals 1960; Labour 1948; Noses
1950; Opposition 1968; Patronage
1954; Property 1958; Public opinion
1960; Roman Catholic Church 1936,
1936; Union Nationale 1936, 1936

DURHAM, *LORD* (Governor-in-chief) The
Crown 1839; Disunity 1839, 1839;
Durham, *Lord* 1840; French Canadians
1839; French Canadians, destiny 1839,
1839; Government 1838; Government,
responsible 1839; Independence 1839;
Land 1839; Languages 1839;
Population 1839; Public opinion 1839;
Quebec (Prov.) 1838, 1839

DUVERNET, FREDERICK H. (Writer) God
1927

DU WORS, RICHARD E. (Poet) Work 1965

E

EADIE, TOM (Poet) Love 1965

EASTMAN, HARRY C. (Economist) Bank of
Canada 1960

EASTON, JASON C. (American railroader)
Van Horne, *Sir* W. 1920

EATON, ARTHUR W. H. (Clergyman and
writer) Acadia 1889; Seamen 1889

EATON, CYRUS (Executive) Places 1972;
Russia 1958

EATON, TIMOTHY (Dept. store owner)
Stores 1870

EAYRS, JAMES (Political scientist) Civil
service 1966; Diplomacy 1967, 1967,
1967, 1970; External Affairs, Dept. of
1969; Foreign policy 1971; Investment,
American 1970; Neutrality 1974;
Personalities 1972; Statesmen 1965,
1966; Publishing 1934; United States
1970

ECONOMIC COUNCIL OF CANADA
Economics 1968; Education 1965;
Poverty 1968, 1968

EDGAR, JAMES D. (Speaker of the House of
Commons) Confederation 1890;
Defence 1870; Outdoors 1893; Past
1870; Political phrases

EDINBOROUGH, ARNOLD (Editor)
Annexation 1962

EDINBURGH REVIEW (Periodical)
Annexation 1825

EDMONDS, ALAN (Writer) Automobiles
1970

EDMONTON *BULLETIN* (Newspaper)
Parliament, Members of 1880

EDMONTON *JOURNAL* (Newspaper)
Pregnancy 1965

EDWARD VII (King of England) Kingston,
Ont. 1860

EDWARDS, MARY F. (Poet) Music 1942

EDWARDS, ROBERT C. (Bob) (Sage) Ability
1912; Agreement 1912; Appearances
1918; Authors 1920; Bats 1920;
Bankruptcy 1910; Beer 1916;
Behaviour 1912; Bennett, R. B. 1912;
Borden, *Sir* Robert 1920; C.P.R. 1906,
1912; Ceremony 1916; Cheating 1973;
Children 1919; Church 1918; Clothes
1918; Complaints 1917; Compromise
1921; Contentment 1913; Corruption
1906; Deeds and doing 1920; Defeat
1912; Dogs 1910; Drinking 1906, 1910,
1910, 1915; Efficiency 1916; Elections
1912; Enemies 1918, 1922; Errors
1917; Facts 1919; Failure 1920;
Farmers 1912, 1919; Fatness 1915;
Faults 1921; Fools 1919, 1920, 1920;
Friends 1915, 1920, 1921; Funerals
1905; Gentlemen (no date); Good and
evil 1917; Graft 1910; History 1916,
1919; Holidays 1913; Honesty 1906;
Ideas 1902; Knowledge 1912, 1918;

Laughter 1918, 1918; Law and lawyers 1909, 1921; Lies and liars 1903, 1903; Life 1916; Liquor 1915, 1918; Love 1915, 1917; Luck 1912; Marriage 1906, 1913; Memory 1917; Men and women 1910, 1912, 1920; Misfortunes 1910; Money 1917, 1920; Neighbours 1917; Night 1921; People 1911, 1918; Politics 1921; Posterity 1919; Prosperity 1917; Religion 1910; Rich 1920; Satisfaction 1918; Sense 1918; Sin 1915; Smoking 1918; Statesmen 1903; Success 1919; Suspicion 1917; Taste 1900; Titles of honour 1911; Trouble 1920; Vanity 1920; Waiting 1912; Weather 1905; Wheat 1912; Wit 1919; Words 1916; Work 1912, 1922; Worry 1915; Youth ca. 1918

EGGLESTON, WILFRID (Journalist) Prairies 1957

EIKHARD, SHIRLEY (Singer) Time 1972

EISENDRATH, MAURICE N. (Rabbi) Canada 1939

EISENHOWER, DWIGHT D. (U.S. president) Canadian-American relations 1956

ELEEN, JOHN (Labour union official) Poverty 1970

ELGIN, LORD (Governor General) Annexation 1849; Baldwin, Robert 1850; Commerce 1848; England 1852; French Canadians, survival 1848; Politics 1848; Trade 1849

ELIOT, CHARLES W. (President of Harvard University) R.C.M.P. 1907

ELIZABETH II (Queen of England) Monarchy 1973; Patriotism 1964

ELLICE, EDWARD (Merchant and politician) The West 1856

ELLIOTT, GEORGE (Advertising executive) Radio and TV commercials 1962

ELLIOTT, WILLIAM E. (Journalist) Oratory 1952

ELLIS, ARTHUR (Hangman) Imagination 1964

ELLIS, L.W. (Poet) Advertising 1964; Laurier, Sir Wilfrid 1939; Work 1964

ELLIS, WILLIAM H. (Poet) Fishing 1914

EMERSON, RALPH W. (American author) Annexation 1872

ENCYCLOPEDIA OF CANADA Civil service 1935

ENGELS, FRIEDRICH (German communist theorist) Annexation 1888

ENGLISH, ARTHUR BARTHOLOMEW (Hangman) Capital punishment 1970; Hangman 1970

ENGLISH, H. EDWARD (Editor) Business 1964; Criticism 1961

EQUAL RIGHTS LEAGUE Political phrases

ERICKSON, ARTHUR (Architect) Architecture 1972

ESPOSITO, PHIL (Hockey player) Hockey 1972

ESTABROOK, ROBERT (American editor) Diefenbaker, J.G. 1963

ESTAING, COMTE D' (French admiral) French Canadians, survival 1778

ETHIER-BLAIS, JEAN (Critic) Geography 1966

EVANS, JAMES (Missionary) Languages 1838; Mystery 1846

EVERSON, RONALD G. (Poet) Creativity 1963; Dreams 1966; Leaders 1963; Schools 1958; Time 1969

EWART, JOHN S. (Political writer) British Commonwealth 1921, 1933; British Empire 1930; Can.-British relations 1904; Colonialism 1911; The Crown 1930; Dates 1932; Definition 1904; Dominion 1933; Geography 1930; Independence 1923; Meaning 1933; Unity 1895, 1911; War 1925

EXAMINER (Toronto) (Newspaper) Political phrases

EXPO 1967 Expo (1967) 1967

F

FAHRNI, MARGARET (Local historian) Settlers 1946

FAIRLEY, BARKER (University professor) Pratt, E.J. 1959

FAIRWEATHER, GORDON (Member of Parliament) Parliament, Members of 1973

FALARDEAU, JEAN-C. (Social scientist) Automation 1961; Canadians 1961; Ethics 1961; Minorities 1961; Society 1961; Unity 1961

FALCONER, SIR ROBERT (Educator) Academics 1922; Climate 1917; The West 1917, 1917

"FAMILY COMPACT" Election slogans 1836

FARIBAULT, MARCEL (Company president) Two nations theory 1967

FARRAR, F. S. (R.C.M.P. officer and writer) Exploration 1960

FARRER, EDWARD (Newspaperman) Old age 1884

FARRIS, JOHN W. DE B. (Senator) Chinese 1958

FARTHING, JOHN COLBORNE (Political scientist) Freedom 1957; History 1957

FAUCHER DE SAINT-MAURICE, NARCISSE H. E. (Author) French Canadians, survival 1890

FAVREAU, GUY (Minister of justice) Friends 1965; Leadership 1965; Monarchy 1965

FAY, CHARLES R. (British economist) Banks and banking 1923; Cooperatives 1924; St. John's, Nfld. 1956

FEINBERG, ABRAHAM L. (Rabbi) Heaven 1964; Life 1964; Prayer 1964; Scepticism 1964

FEINDEL, WILLIAM H. (Neurologist) Brains 1960

FELLOWS, GEOFFREY (Management consultant) Americans in Canada 1971

FENTON, F. W. (Montreal chief of police) Drinking 1874

FENTON, WALTER (Writer) Business 1932

FERGUSON, GEORGE V. (Newspaper editor) Canadian-American relations 1956; Pioneers 1948; Political parties 1947

FERGUSON, JOSEPH D. (Manufacturer) Discovery 1954

FERNS, HENRY S. (Biographer) Conciliation 1955

FERRON, J.-EMILE (Member of Parliament and judge) Destiny 1970

FETHERLING, DOUG (Poet) Absence 1971

FIDELIS See MACHAR, AGNES M.

FIELDING, WILLIAM STEVENS (Liberal Party leader) Independence 1921; Nation 1919; Trade 1897, 1911

FILION, GERARD (Editor of Le Devoir) Corporations 1971; Freedom 1958; Newspapers 1954; Quebec (Province) 1962; Unity 1954

FINANCIAL POST (Newspaper) Conservative Party 1954

FINCH, ROBERT (Poet) Absence 1961; Birds 1961; Blue Jays 1948; Cities and towns 1961; Contrariness 1946; Failure 1943; Flowers 1966; Grief 1946; Incompatibility 1943; Lakes 1946; Love 1961; Middle age 1946; Mountains 1948; Painting 1949; Poets 1946; Quotations 1946; Shyness 1925; Snow 1949; Solitude 1948; Time 1959; Touch 1961; Trees 1929; Virtue 1946; Words 1946

FINLAY, HUGH (Deputy postmaster general) Education 1784

FINNIGAN, JOAN (Poet) Love 1970; November 1965; Seduction 1960; Sex 1959; Sexual union 1957

FISCHER, GERHARD (History teacher) Economics 1971

FISHER, DOUGLAS M. (Columnist) Budget speeches 1963; Civil service 1975

FISHER, JAMES C. (Inscriptionist) Wolfe, James 1828

FISHER, JOHN CHARLTON (Journalist) Travel 1962

FITZSIMMONS, FRANK E. (Union official) Senate 1970

FLAHERTY, DOUGLAS (Poet) Death 1969

FLAHERTY, ROBERT (Film maker) Prospecting 1963; Truth 1963

FLAVELLE, SIR JOSEPH (Executive) Business 1917; Profits 1916

FLEET, BRENDA (Poet) Birds 1971

FLEMING, ALAN (Artist) C.N.R. 1960

FLEMING, DONALD (Politician) Bank of Canada 1960; Communism 1962

FLEMING, SIR SANDFORD (Engineer) Fleming, Sir S. 1879; Time 1879

FLEMING, WILLIAM G. (Educator) Academics 1957

FLETCHER, PEGGY (Poet) Marriage 1971

FLUMERFELT, ALFRED C. (Capitalist) Population 1917

FOIKIS, JOACHIM (Vancouver "town fool") Fools 1968

FORAN, JOSEPH K. (Poet) Northern lights 1895

FORD, ROBERT A. D. (Poet) Suicide 1969

FORD, STEPHEN (Limerick contest winner) Munsinger, Gerda 1966

FOREST, LEE DE (Radio pioneer) Radio and TV 1932

FORKE, ROBERT (Minister of immigration) Land 1926

FORREST, ROBERT (Writer) Coffins 1967;
Funerals 1967, 1967; Undertakers 1967
FORRESTER, MAUREEN (Singer) Singing
1975
FORSEY, EUGENE (Political scientist)
B.N.A. Act (1867) 1967, 1967;
Confederation 1967; Confederation,
Fathers of 1936; Economy 1962;
Future 1970; King, W.L.M. 1951;
Labour unions 1957; Languages 1967;
Marxism 1937; Monarchy 1967;
Precedents 1968; Progressive Party
1951; Quebec (Province) 1967;
Republicanism 1974; Schools 1967
FORSYTH, LIONEL (Business executive)
Cape Breton 1957; Christmas 1957;
Credos 1936; Honesty 1960; Labour
1950's; Medicine 1935; Sailors 1959;
Work 1957
FORT MACLEOD *GAZETTE* (Newspaper)
Floods 1882
FORTESCUE, *SIR* JOHN W. (British writer)
Mackenzie, W. L. 1923; Rebellion
(1837) 1923
FOSTER, *SIR* GEORGE E. (Politician)
Business 1908; Geography 1911;
Isolation 1896; Lotteries 1931; New
Year 1930; Progress 1911; Senate 1920;
War, European (1914-18) 1914
FOSTER, WILLIAM A. (Nationalist)
Identity 1871; Independence 1875;
McGee, T.D. 1871; Political parties
1875, 1890; Purpose 1871; Unity 1871
FOULCHE-DELBOSC, ISABEL (Historian)
Widows 1666
FOULKES, CHARLES (Army general)
Defence 1961
FOURNIER, MICHEL (M.L.A., New
Brunswick) Facts 1953
FOWKE, VERNON C. (Agricultural
economist) Agriculture 1946, 1957;
Confederation 1946; Government 1968
FOWLER, GEORGE W. (Member of
Parliament) Corruption 1907
FOX, GAIL (Poet) Loneliness 1969; Sadness
1970
FOX, PAUL (Political writer) Welfare 1959
FOX, ROBIN (Anthropologist) Automobiles
1971; Hunting 1971; Rights 1971
FRANCA, CELIA (Ballet dancer)
Forgetfulness 1968
FRANCOEUR, JOSEPH N. (M.L.A., Quebec)
Quebec (Province) 1918

FRANKEL, VERA (Writer and artist)
Secrets 1970
FRANKFURTER, FELIX (U.S. judge)
Opposition 1930
FRANKFURTER, GLEN (Writer)
Canadian-American relations 1971
FRANTZ, CHARLES (U.S. anthropologist)
Doukhobors 1963
FRASER, BLAIR (Newspaperman) News
1967; North 1967; St. Lawrence
Seaway 1951; Solitude 1967, 1967;
Unemployment 1968
FRASER, CHRISTOPHER F. (Minister of
public works, Ontario) Political phrases
FRASER, DONALD A. (Poet) Architecture
1930
FRASER, H. (Calgary businessman)
Religion 1955
FRASER, JOHN ARTHUR (Painter) Painting
1943
FRASER, *SIR* JOHN FOSTER (British
traveller) Labour unions 1909
FRASER, RAYMOND (Poet) Behaviour
1969; Children 1971
FRASER, SIMON (Explorer) Fraser Canyon
1808
FRASER, WILLIAM A. (Novelist) War,
European (1914-18) 1915
FRECHETTE, LOUIS (Poet) Future 1887
"FRED" (Pseud.) (Poet) Confederation
1867; McGee, T.D. 1868; Nova Scotia
1868
FREDERICTON *HEADQUARTERS*
(Newspaper) Intercolonial Railway
1865; New Brunswick 1864
FREEDMAN, SAMUEL (Judge) Unity 1965
FREGAULT, GUY (Historian) History 1955;
Survival 1956
FRENCH, DORIS (Writer) Welfare 1968
FRERES DES ECOLES CHRETIENNES
Textbooks 1954
FRISCH, ANTHONY (Poet) Time 1954
FRONT DE LIBERATION QUÉBÉCOIS
(F.L.Q.) Independence 1963;
Languages 1963; Separatism 1963
FRONTENAC, *COMTE* DE (Governor of
New France) Defence 1690; Quebec
(City) 1672
FROST, LESLIE (Premier of Ontario)
Agitation 1965; Culture 1960; Politics
1958
FROST, STANLEY B. (University professor)
Faith 1969; Science 1969

FRYE, NORTHROP (Critic) American revolution 1957; Americanization 1965; Annexation 1971; Anxiety 1967; Art 1962, 1967; Authors 1965, 1965; *Bible* 1964; Boundaries 1967; Canadians 1953; Colonialism 1943; Communication 1967; Compromise 1971; Criticism 1957, 1957, 1957, 1957, 1957, 1957, 1971; Culture 1961; Environment 1971; Experience 1961; Form 1957; Freedom 1962; Garrison mentality 1965; Historians 1953; Identity 1962, 1967, 1971; Imagination 1964, 1964, 1970; Improvement 1967; Leaders 1964; Leisure 1967; Literature 1957, 1957, 1962, 1962, 1962, 1962, 1963; Literature, Canadian 1965, 1967; Mob 1963; Mythology 1957, 1963, 1965; Nation 1967; Nature 1965, 1967; News 1967; Participation 1968; Philosophy 1965; Poetry 1943, 1956, 1957, 1958, 1959, 1965, 1967; Poets 1963; Pratt, E.J. 1957; Progress 1967; Prudery 1943; Science 1959, 1967; Self-expression 1962; Speech 1963, 1964; Standards 1971; Statements 1962; Students 1961; Technology 1965; Truth 1967; Unity 1971; Universities 1959, 1961, 1968; Value 1974; Violence 1968; Wilderness 1957; Writers 1957

FULFORD, ROBERT (Editor) Americanism, anti- 1968; Appeasement 1964; Audacity 1959; Citizenship 1970; Culture 1958, 1961, 1961; Land 1967; Movies 1974; Progress 1970; Reading 1968; Regionalism 1971; Superiority 1964; Understanding 1969; United States 1968; Youth 1968

FULTON, E. DAVIE (Minister of justice) Conservatism 1960

FULTON, GERALD (Poet) Reality 1963

"FUTURO" (Pseud.) Regina, Sask. 1884

G

GADD, MAXINE (Poet) Women's liberation 1973

GADSBY, HENRY F. (Journalist) Painting 1913, 1913

GAETZ, ADOLPHUS (Diarist) Dominion Day 1867

GAGE, THOMAS (Military governor) Indians 1772; Voyageurs 1770

GAGLARDI, PHILLIP A. (B.C. politician) Automobiles 1955; Highways 1955; Lies and liars 1969; Roads 1963; Weather 1962

GALBRAITH, JOHN KENNETH (Can.-Amer. economist) Culture 1967; Drinking 1964; Economics 1972; Marriage 1964; Money 1964, 1964; Platforms, political 1964; Reading 1964; Scotsmen 1964, 1964; Size 1964; Talk 1964

GALINEE, *FATHER* RENE DE BREHANT DE (Sulpician priest and explorer) Ontario 1669

GALT, *SIR* ALEXANDER T. (Father of Confederation) Can.-British relations 1865; Confederation 1858, 1858, 1865; Defence 1866, 1867; Fenians 1866; Government 1860; Independence 1870; Protection 1858; Taxation 1859

GALT, JOHN (British novelist) Toronto 1833

GAMEY, ROBERT R. (Politician) Politics 1903

GARIGUE, PHILIPPE (University dean) The Conquest (1759) 1963; Violence 1969

GARNEAU, FRANCOIS-XAVIER (Historian) The Conquest (1759) 1826; French Canadians 1852; Tradition 1882

GARNEAU, HECTOR DE SAINT-DENYS (Writer) Flowers 1962; French Canadians 1970 See SAINT-DENYS-GARNEAU, HECTOR DE

GARNER, HUGH (Novelist) Slums 1969; Youth 1961

GARNER, JOHN (Political scientist) Political parties 1969; Politics 1969

GARSTIN, C. (British poet) Horses 1916

GASPARINI, LEN (Poet) Me 1967

GAUCHER, YVES (Painter) Silence 1969

GAY, JAMES (Poet laureate) Man 1885; October 1885; Poets 1883, 1883; Winter 1885; Possession 1885

GEDDES, ALVIN (Salesman) Hockey 1967

GEIGER-TOREL, HERMAN (Stage director) Opera 1973

GELINAS, GRATIEN (Actor) Theatre 1973

GEORGE, DAN (Indian chief and actor) Indians 1967; Land 1971

GEORGE III (King of England) Wolfe, James 1758

GEORGE V (King of England) National colours 1921; National emblems 1921

GESNER, ABRAHAM (Geologist) Free trade 1849; Trade 1849

GHANADY, ADELE (Public servant) Women 1963

GIBBON, JOHN MURRAY (Publicist) Artists 1922; Widows 1922

GIBSON, ARTHUR (Writer) Listening 1968

GIBSON, JAMES (British navy officer) Wolfe, James 1759

GILL, M. LAKSHMI (Poet) Canada 1972; Men and women 1972

GILLESPIE, GERALD J. (Public servant) Ships 1963

GILLETT, MARGARET (University professor) Education 1966, 1966

GILLILAND, DENNIS (Poet) Tradition 1969

GILLIS, ANNE (Poet) Ontario 1803

GILLIS, CLARIE (M.P. for Cape Breton) Industry 1971

GILLIS, JAMES D. (Poet) Queen Victoria 1964, Languages 1925

GILLMOR, ARTHUR H. (Member of Parliament) British Columbia 1879; Noses 1879

GILMOUR, CLYDE (Music critic) Agreement 1972

GIMBY, BOBBY (Musician) Confederation centennial (1967) 1967

GINGRAS, GUSTAVE (Physician) Rehabilitation 1971

GIVENS, PHILIP (Mayor of Toronto) Football 1965; Parliament, Members of 1971

GLADESTONE, W. S. (H.B.C. employee) Commerce 1910

GLADSTONE, JAMES (First Indian senator) Indians 1958, 1960

GLASSCO, JOHN (Poet) Buildings 1958; End 1964; Farmers 1958; Individualism 1974; Me 1964; Principles 1971; Ruins 1958, 1958

GLAZEBROOK, G. DE T. (Historian) Isolation 1938

GLEN, JAMES ALLISON (Speaker, House of Commons) Government 1936; Liberal Party 1936; Speaker of the House of Commons 1941

GLOBE See TORONTO GLOBE

GLOOSCAP (Algonkian hero) Children (legend)

GLOVER, GUY (Poet) Geography 1947

GLOVER, TERROT R. (Historian) Canada 1926

GODBOUT, JACQUES (Novelist) Roman Catholic Church 1966

GOLDENBERG, H. CARL (Labour mediator) Labour relations 1962

GOLDFARB, MARTIN (Writer) Affluence 1970

GOLDIE, JOHN (Naturalist) Sunday 1819

GOLDSMITH, OLIVER (Canadian poet) Acadia 1825; Immigrants 1825; Loneliness 1825; Peasants 1825; Stores 1825

GONICK, CY W. (Political writer) Finance (Public) 1970

GOODIS, JERRY (Advertising executive) Advertising 1970, 1972; Me 1972; Pollution 1972

GOODMAN, EDWIN A. (Company executive) Investment, American 1971

GOODSPEED, DONALD J. (Military historian) Coup d'état 1962; Democracy 1962; Society 1957

GORDON, ALEXANDER M. ROSE (Journalist) Germans 1897

GORDON, REV. CHARLES W. (Pseud. "Ralph Connor", novelist) Prophecy 1912

GORDON, DONALD (Transportation executive) Canada 1960's; Caution 1959; Cows 1959; Deeds and doing 1959; Ingenuity 1959; Names 1959; Newspapers 1964

GORDON, JOHN (Commander, Royal Navy) Mountains 1844

GORDON, PAMELA ANNE (Nude) Nudity 1962

GORDON, ROBERT K. (Poet) Parliament 1931

GORDON, WALTER L. (Minister of finance) Cabinet 1973; Canadian-American relations 1966, 1972; Colonialism 1970; Economy 1966; Elections 1965; Independence 1966, 1966, 1966; Investment, foreign 1966; Majorities 1965; Politics 1968; Problems 1966

GORDONSMITH, CHARLES R. W. (Editor) Liberalism 1913

GORMAN, LARRY (Poet) Prince Edward Island 1873

GORMAN, TOMMY (Sports promoter) Hockey 1917

GOTLIEB, PHYLLIS (Poet) Change 1969; Love 1969; Suicide 1969; Time 1969; Want 1969; Youth 1970

GOTLIEB, SONDRA (Cooking expert) Food 1972

GOTTSCHALK, LOUIS (American pianist) Roman Catholics 1864

GOUIN, *SIR* LOMER (Premier of Quebec) Confederation 1918; Federalism 1918

GOULD, GLENN (Pianist) Music 1964, 1967

GOURLAY, ROBERT FLEMING (Agitator) Criticism 1822; Government 1822; Records 1829

GOWAN, OGLE ROBERT (Orange Assoc. leader) Orangemen 1830; Voters 1835

GOWANS, ALAN (Architect) Architecture 1958, 1966, 1966; Art 1971

GRAHAM, ANDREW (Poet) Settlers 1945

GRAHAM, GERALD S. (Historian) Education 1969

GRAHAM, GWETHALYN (Novelist) Education 1963; Imagination 1963; Separatism 1963

GRAHAM, H. ISABEL (Poet) God 1935

GRAHAM, *SIR* HUGH (Newspaper publisher) News 1883

GRAHAM, ROGER (Historian) Aberhart, W. 1970

GRAIN GROWERS GUIDE (Periodical) Slogans 1910

GRAINGER, M. ALLERDALE (Writer) Buying and selling 1908; Honesty 1908; Planning 1908

GRAND TRUNK RAILWAY Business 1922

GRANT, GEORGE MONRO (Principal of Queen's Univ., Kingston) Canada 1873; Climate 1887; Communication 1899; Defence 1887; Destiny 1873; Geography 1887; Ignorance 1900; Patriotism 1904; Political parties 1884; Prairies 1887; The Press 1904; Prospectors 1873; Provinces 1887; Race 1873; Rest 1883; Rocky Mountains 1873; Travel 1873; Work ethic 1866

GRANT, GEORGE P. (Writer) Americanization 1968; Canadians 1965; Communication 1969; Conservatism 1965, 1966; Corporations 1965; Costs 1970; Courage 1971; Culture 1965, 1965; Diefenbaker, J.G. 1965; Education 1965; Freedom 1955; French Canadians 1965, 1969; Future 1965; Institutions 1966; Losers 1969; Modern times 1969; Morality 1966; Nationalism 1969; Politics 1961; Progress 1965; Reaction 1966;

Reverence 1969; Rocky Mountains 1969; Scholarship 1969; Separatism 1965; Society 1969, 1969; Survival 1969; Technique 1969; Technology 1965, 1969, 1969; Thought 1969; United States 1968

GRANT, *REV.* JOHN W. (Editor) Destiny 1972

GRANT, WILLIAM L. (Biographer) Business men 1927; Civil service 1934; Geography 1911; Nationalism 1923

GRAY, FRANCIS W. (Poet) Custom 1899

GRAY, JAMES H. (Newspaperman) Drinking 1972; Palliser Triangle 1967; Prostitution 1971; Winnipeg 1966, 1970

GRAY, JOHN (Playwright) Danger 1957; Publishing 1956

GRAYDON, GORDON (Member of Parliament) Press Gallery, Ottawa 1951

GREAT BRITAIN Canadian-American relations 1794

GREAT BRITAIN. NEWFOUNDLAND ROYAL COMMISSION Newfoundland 1933; Religion 1933

GREAT BRITAIN. PRIVY COUNCIL Monarchy 1791

GREAT BRITAIN. PROCLAMATION Indians 1763

GREELEY, HORACE (U.S. politician) Annexation 1860's

GREEN, H. GORDON (Author) Argument 1967

GREEN, HOWARD (Politician) Diplomacy 1960; External relations 1956

GREEN, JOSEPH (Prince Edward Island pioneer) Marriage proposals 1830

GREENAWAY, ROY (Journalist) Newspapers 1966

GREENFIELD, HERBERT (Premier of Alberta) Political phrases

GRENFELL, *SIR* WILFRED (Missionary) Life 1939

GREY, *EARL* (Governor General) British Empire 1908; Confederation 1909; Governor General 1909; Hudson Bay 1910

GREY, FRANCIS W. (Writer) Politics 1899; Self 1899

GREY OWL (Archibald Belaney, Nature writer) Education 1930's; Wilderness 1935

GRIER, ELDON (Poet) Patriotism 1963; Poets 1971; Space 1963; Words 1963, 1971

GRIERSON, JOHN (Film maker)
Consciousness 1946
GRIFFIN, GERALD (Irish poet) McGee,
T.D. 1840
GRIFFIN, JOHN D. M. (Psychiatrist) Persons
1971
GRIFFIN, MARTIN (Newspaper editor)
Librarians 1882
GRIFFITHS, NAOMI (Historian) Acadians
1973
GRIP (Toronto) (Periodical) Drinking 1874,
1883; Gravity 1873; Mackenzie,
Alexander (P.M.) 1880; Parliament,
Members of 1879; Wit 1891
GROSART, ALLISTER (Publicist)
Diefenbaker, J.G. 1957; Political
phrases
GROSSKURTH, PHYLLIS (Literary critic)
Critics 1970
GROULX, *ABBE* LIONEL The Conquest
(1759) 1922, 1944; Dollard des
Ormeaux 1919, 1919; Economics 1936;
Ethnic groups 1924; French Canadians
1936; French Canadians, survival 1943;
History 1924, 1924; Leaders 1934;
Patriotism 1910; Quebec (Prov.) 1937,
1937; Race 1921; Revenge of the cradle
1918; Roman Catholics 1943;
Separatism 1923
GROVE, FREDERICK PHILIP (Novelist)
Attainment 1927; Audiences 1946;
Blessings 1933; Books 1938, 1938;
Canadians 1938; Civilization 1946;
Clothes 1933, 1944; Colours 1922;
Defeat 1933; Divorce 1927; Dreamers
1929; Dreams 1927, 1933; Faith 1933;
Fate 1933; Graveyards 1927; Greatness
1929; Ideas 1938; Identity 1929; Law
and lawyers 1927; Literature 1939;
Materialism 1933; Nature 1922; Novels
1929; Possession 1946; The Public
1938; Public opinion 1944; Reality
1944; Rich 1928; Right and wrong
1927; Rumour 1933; Snow 1922, 1922;
Socialism 1944; Technology 1944;
Unity 1946; Wheat 1929; Woman
1925; Writers 1940; Writing 1938
GUAY, JOSEPH ALBERT (Bomber)
Hanging 1960
GUERNSEY, GEORGE F. (Politician)
Elections 1894
GUEST, EDGAR A. (American versifier)
Miner, Jack 1969

GULLETT, H. S. (Australian traveller)
Americanization 1911
GUNTHER, JOHN (American writer) King,
W.L.M. 1955
GUSTAFSON, RALPH (Poet) Canada 1969;
Coca-cola 1966; Contentment 1960;
Death 1972; Grief 1972; Poetry 1960
GUTHRIE, HUGH (Politician) King,
W.L.M. 1925
GUTHRIE, NORMAN G. (Poet) The Present
1928
GUTHRIE, TYRONE (Theatre director)
Culture 1954; Stratford Festival 1954;
Theatre 1952, 1954
GUTHRIE, WILLIAM (British geographer)
Wolves 1807
GUTHRIE, WOODY (American musician)
Land 1956
GWYN, RICHARD (Journalist) Cabinet
Ministers 1965

H

HAGERMAN, CHRISTOPHER A. (Judge)
Voters 1831
HAGOPIAN, ANAHID (Poet) Waiting 1960
HAIG, JOHN (Senator) Senate 1950
HAIG-BROWN, RODERICK (Writer) British
Columbia 1959, 1961, 1965; Rivers
1950; Writing 1959
HAIGH, VAL (Poet) Population 1961
HAIGHT, JENNIE E. (Poet) Snow 1864
HAILEY, ARTHUR (Novelist) Invention
1960
HAINES, EDSON (Judge) Trials 1973
HAINES, LLOYD (Poet) Death 1942
HALDANE, *LORD* (British politician)
Constitution 1927; Drinking 1925
HALE, KATHERINE (Poet) Graveyards
1923
HALIBURTON, THOMAS CHANDLER
(Humorist) Ability 1855; Affection
1853; Agitation 1857; Americanism,
anti-1853; Americans 1838;
Appearances 1840; Argument 1853;
Artists 1853; Authority 1853; Belief
1853; Books 1836; British Empire 1840;
Canada 1836; Cant 1853; Care 1853;
Change 1840; Character 1855; Charity
1853; Children 1855; Circumstances
1849; Civility 1853; Classes 1838; Coal
1838; Common sense 1840; Conduct of
life 1838, 1853, 1853; Confederation

1855, 1866; Constitution 1838;
Conversation 1853; Converts 1855;
Courage 1853; Dance 1855; Death
1853; Deeds and doing 1853; Dismissals
1836; Doctors 1853; Dogs 1844;
Drinking 1849, 1853; Elections 1836;
Escape 1843; Expenditures 1855;
Experience 1836, 1836; Eyes 1853;
Facts 1853; Failure 1853; Farmers
1836; Farming 1836; Fear 1853;
Fences 1836; Fiction 1853; Fools 1843,
1853, 1853; French Canadians, survival
1838; Friends 1836; Future 1855; Girls
1844; God 1840; Government 1838;
Halifax 1853; Happiness 1849; Heart
1855; Heat 1838; Home 1838; Honesty
1838; Hope 1853, 1853; Houses 1853;
Humour 1853; Hypocrisy 1853; Ideas
1853; Importance 1853; Individuality
1853; Innocence 1853; Insects 1853;
Irishmen 1836; Jokes 1844; Judges
1835; Justice 1838; Laziness 1853; Lies
and liars 1853; Luxuries 1836;
Majorities 1838; Manners 1838, 1855;
Marriage 1853, 1855; Maxims 1855;
Memory 1853; Men and women 1844;
Misses 1853; Mistakes 1853, 1855;
Modesty 1853; Money 1838, 1853;
Names 1853; Nature 1836; Necessity
1853; Northern lights 1849; Nova
Scotia 1836, 1849; Patriotism 1840; Pigs
1855; Pleasure 1853, 1855; Plowing
1836; Political support 1836; Politics
1836; Poor 1838; Poverty 1836; Power
1836, 1838, 1838; Praise 1853; The
Press, freedom of 1853; Prevention
1853; Prices 1838; Pride 1840, 1840,
1853; Promises 1853; Proverbs;
Provincialism 1840; The Public 1836;
Punctuality 1853; Puritanism 1855;
Quebec (City) 1855; Quotations 1855;
Rain 1836; Reading 1840, 1843, 1853;
Reform 1849, 1853; Religion 1836,
1836, 1853; Responsibility 1853; Rights
1853; Roses 1853; Savings 1836; Sea
1836; Secrecy 1853; Ships 1853; Sin
1853; Sleep 1853, 1853; Smiles 1853;
Smoking 1838; Society, polite 1836;
Sorrow 1853; Speeches 1840; Statistics
1838; Strength 1853; Success 1836,
1838, 1853; Talent 1840; Talk 1852,
1853; Time 1836; Titles of honour
1836; Trade 1855; Travel 1853; Trial
by jury 1838; Universities 1853; Virtue

1853; Winter 1853; Woman 1836;
Women 1849; Words 1853; Work ethic
1853; Workers 1853; Writing 1836
HALIFAX *ACADIAN RECORDER*
(Newspaper) Maritimes 1866
HALIFAX *BRITISH COLONIST*
(Newspaper) Confederation 1867
HALIFAX *EVENING EXPRESS* (Newspaper)
Workers 1874
HALIFAX *HERALD* (Newspaper) Political
phrases
HALIFAX *MORNING CHRONICLE*
(Newspaper) Nova Scotia 1867; Union
1841, 1864, 1867
HALIFAX *MORNING POST* (Newspaper)
Newspapers 1847
HALL, MARY (Poet) Time 1948
HALSBURY, *LORD* (British judge) Meaning
1895
HAM, GEORGE H. (Journalist) Winnipeg
1921, 1921
HAMILTON, ALVIN (Politician) Diplomacy
1963; Roads 1958
HAMILTON, *MRS.* CHRISTOPHER (U.S.
slave) Slaves 1856
HAMILTON, EDWARD P. (American
historian) Drinking 1962
HAMILTON, IAN (Writer) Youth 1970
HAMILTON, JAMES C. (Writer) Manitoba
1876
HAMILTON *TIMES* (Newspaper) Banks
and banking 1867
HAMMOND, MEL (Reporter) *The Globe*,
Toronto 1906
HANLY, CHARLES M. (University
professor) Families 1966; Nation 1966
HANNA, DAVID B. (President of C.N.R.)
Settlers 1907; Van Horne, *Sir* W. 1924;
Writers 1924
HANNA, WILLIAM J. (Ontario politician)
Individuality 1916
HANNON, P.J.H. (British Member of
Parliament) Government 1933
HANOVER, PAUL (Radio announcer)
Roads 1963
HANSELL, *REV.* ERNEST (Member of
Parliament) Petroleum 1951; Social
Credit 1952, 1952
HANSON, R. B. (Politician) Radio and TV
1933
HARDING, JIM (Writer) Indians 1971
HARDING, WARREN G. (U.S. President)
Annexation 1923

HARE, KENNETH (Educator) Academics
1968
HARLOW, ROBERT (Novelist) Immigrants
1972; Winning 1972
HARMON, DANIEL W. (Fur trader)
Drinking 1802; Food 1804; Friendship
1802
HARPER, J. RUSSELL (Art historian)
Painting 1968
HARRINGTON, DAN (Whiskey peddlar)
Fines 1880
HARRINGTON, GORDON S. (Premier of
Nova Scotia) Politics 1928
HARRINGTON, MICHAEL (Poet) St. John's,
Nfld. 1965
HARRIS, AMELIA (Diarist) Wives 1967
HARRIS, J. A. (Book reviewer) Publishing
1970
HARRIS, LAWREN (Painter) Art 1969;
Creativity 1969; North 1969; Painting
1969
HARRIS, WALTER E. (Politician)
Immigrants 1952; Magazines 1956
HARRISON, ERNEST (Theologian) Living
1965; Proselytizing 1966; Religion 1966
HARRISON, LUKE (Fur trader) Mosquitoes
1774
HARRISON, ROBERT (Financial consultant)
Eggs 1974
HARRISON, STANLEY (Versifier) Horses
1968
HARRON, DON (Wit) Englishmen 1972
HARROP, G. GERALD (University
professor) King, W.L.M. 1964
HARTWELL, MARTIN (Air crash survivor)
Food 1973
HARVEY, DANIEL C. (Historian) Dalhousie
University 1938
HARVEY, RUPERT (Drama critic) London,
Ont. 1934
HATHAWAY, ERNEST JACKSON
(Historian) Books 1930
HAULTAIN, T. ARNOLD (Writer) Ardour
1909; Associations 1909; Audacity
1909; Beards 1909; Beauty 1909;
Blushing 1909; Character 1909;
Computers 1909; Conquest 1909;
Courtship 1909, 1909, 1909; Defence
1903; Dependence 1909; Eyes 1909,
1909; Faces 1909; Failure 1909;
Fashion 1909; Females 1909; Flattery
1909; Friends 1909, 1909; Girls 1909,
1909; Goals 1909; Goodness 1909;
Husbands 1909; Indecision 1909;

Individuality 1909; Initiative 1909;
Jealousy 1909, 1909; Kisses 1909;
Knowledge 1909; Law and lawyers
1909; Letters 1909; Loneliness 1909;
Love 1909, 1909, 1909, 1909; Marriage
1909, 1909; Marriage proposals 1909;
Men and women 1909, 1909, 1909;
Modesty 1909; Motherhood 1909;
Nurses 1909; Parents 1909; Passion
1909; Personality 1909; Promiscuity
1909; Questions 1909; Reason 1909;
Resistance 1909; Rivals 1909;
Satisfaction 1909; Self 1909; Sex 1909;
Shame 1909; Sighs 1909, 1909, 1909;
Tact 1909; Tears 1909; Tenderness
1909; Widows 1909; Woman 1909;
Women 1909; Women's liberation
1909; Words 1908; Work 1909
HAULTAIN, *SIR* FREDERICK W. G.
(Politician and judge) Prairies 1905
HAVILAND, WILLIAM E. (Planner)
Farmers 1957
HAWKE, A. G. (Immigration agent) The
West 1840
HAWKES, ARTHUR (Writer) Children
1919; Ideals 1925
HAWTHORN, HARRY B. (Anthropologist)
Indians 1966
HAY, JOHN (U.S. ambassador to London)
Canadian-American relations 1897
HAYAKAWA, SAMUEL I. (American scholar
and politician) Poetry 1929
HAYES, CATHERINE SIMPSON (Poet)
Trails 1910
HAYMAN, ROBERT (Poet) Newfoundland
1628, 1628, 1628
HAYWARD, VICTORIA (U.S. travel writer)
Mosaic 1922
HEAD, *SIR* EDMUND (Governor General)
Confederation 1856; Dominion 1858;
Flag 1851; Geography 1857; Trees
1855
HEAD, *SIR* FRANCIS BOND (Lieutenant
Governor) Family Compact 1839;
Indians 1839; Ottawa 1857, 1857;
Rebellion (1837) 1837; Society 1839
HEALY, JOHN J. (American editor)
R.C.M.P. 1877
HEAPS, ABRAHAM A. (Member of
Parliament) B.N.A. Act (1867) 1928;
Economics 1932; Health 1930; Labour
1929; Natural resources 1928; Sedition
1920

HILLIER, WINNIFRED A. (Poet) Faith 1941

HINCKS, *SIR* FRANCIS (Politician) Political phrases

HIND, E. CORA (Agriculturist) Prairies 1925; Wheat 1929

HIND, HENRY YOULE (Explorer) Prairies 1860

HINDENLANG, CHARLES (Defendant) Revolution 1839

HINDMARSH, HARRY COMFORT (Newspaper editor) News 1930's; Power 1966

HINE, DARYL (Poet) Birth 1970; Dance 1961; Earth 1968; Escape 1960; Independence 1959; Instruction 1970; Lakes 1954; Love 1960; Lovers 1965; Perversion 1960; Pleasure 1960; Poetry 1970; Seeing 1965

HINGSTON, *SIR* WILLIAM H. (Surgeon) Winter 1884

HOAR, VICTOR (Biographer) Callaghan, Morley 1969

HOBSON, JOHN (British economist) Protection 1906

HODGETTS, CHARLES A. (M.D., Health officer) Cities and towns 1915

HODGSON, JOHN E. (British artist) Art 1886

HOGARTH, DOUGLAS (Member of Parliament) Parliament, Members of 1972

HOGG, C. (Corporal, R.C.M.P.) R.C.M.P. 1906

HOLGATE, D. C. (Industrialist) Businessmen 1963

HOLLAND, NORAH M. (Poet) Age 1924; Life 1924, 1924; Love 1924

HOLLAND, PHILIP (Newspaper editor) The Press, freedom of 1830

HOLMES, JOHN (Dir. gen., Can. Inst. International Affairs) Americans 1969; Canadian-American relations 1961, 1969; Defence 1971; Delusions 1970; Diplomacy 1970; Greatness 1961; Identity 1963; Nationalism 1966; Universities 1968

HOLMES, OLIVER WENDELL (American author) The Conquest (1759) 1893

HOLT, *SIR* HERBERT (Financier) Craigellachie, B.C., 1885; The Depression (1930-37) 1931

HOLT, SIMMA (Journalist and Member of Parliament) Doukhobors 1965; Sons of Freedom 1964, 1964

HOLTON, LUTHER H. (Politician) Macdonald, Sir John A., 1878

HONDERICH, BELAND H. (Editor) Americanization 1965

HOOD, HUGH (Novelist) Canadians 1967; Money 1970; Photography 1967; Pleasure 1967; Quebec (Prov.) 1969

HOODLESS, ADELAIDE (Women's leader) Patriotism 1897

HOOKER, *REV.* LEROY United Empire Loyalists 1885, 1885

HOOPLE, CARRIE M. (Poet) Roads 1909

HOPEWELL, CHARLES (Mayor of Ottawa) Boundary, Canada-U.S. 1911

HOPKINS, HARRY L. (U.S. politician) Spies 1948

HOPKINS, J. CASTELL (Statistician) Can.-British relations 1893

HORNBY, *SIR* EDMUND (Railroader) Bribery 1928; Confederation, Fathers of 1854

HORNYANSKY, MICHAEL (Poet) Penguins 1975; Teachers 1969; Teaching 1969

HOROWITZ, GAD (Political scientist) Classes 1966; Decisions 1966; Leadership 1965; Moderation 1970; Nationalism 1967, 1968; Political parties 1968; Socialism 1968

HORWOOD, HAROLD (Novelist) Words 1969

HOUDE, CAMILLIEN (Mayor of Montreal) Conscription, military 1940

HOUSE, ERIC (Actor) Actors 1972

HOUSMAN, ALFRED E. (British poet) War dead 1928

HOUSTON, JAMES (Eskimo art supporter) Eskimos 1967; Sculpture 1952

HOWAY, FREDERIC W. (Judge) Bibliographies 1929; Power 1913

HOWE, CLARENCE D. (Politician) Administration 1950's; Atomic energy 1942; Closure 1956; Elections 1957, 1957; Government 1955; Howe, C.D. 1951, 1950's, 1953, 1955, 1957, 1957; Liberal Party 1957; Manufacturing 1943; Million dollars 1945; Petroleum 1953; Scholars 1970

HOWE, JOSEPH (Nova Scotia leader) Books
1824; Canadian-American relations
1865; Can.-British relations 1846;
Conduct of life 1872; Confederation
1849, 1864, 1865, 1865; Constitution
1828; Duels 1840; Education 1850's;
Fathers 1835; Governor General 1839,
1845, 1846; Heroes 1835; Howe, Joseph
1837; Loyalty 1839, 1865; Memory
1827; National heritage 1871;
Newspapers 1834; Nova Scotia 1834,
1834, 1848, 1866, 1869, 1870, 1870;
Ottawa 1867; Parliament, Members of
1841; Past 1854; Politics 1845, 1870;
The Press, freedom of 1835, 1835,
1835, 1844; Provincialism 1864;
Publishing 1841, 1841; Pursuits 1872;
Railways 1851, 1851; Reading 1833;
Religion 1840; Sailors 1839, 1854; Ships
1839; Smugglers 1865; Truth 1845;
Tupper, *Sir* Charles 1855, 1864; Union
Jack 1849; Unity 1848
HOWELL, BILL (Poet) Dreams 1971
HOWISON, JOHN (Traveller) Forests 1821
HOWITH, HARRY (Poet) Lung cancer
1969; Sexual union 1963
HUBBARD, ROBERT H. (Art historian)
Modesty 1957
HUDSON'S BAY COMPANY Boundary,
Canada-U.S. 1714; Hudson's Bay Co.
1670, 1752
HUGHES, CAMPBELL (Publisher)
Canadians 1971
HUGHES, HELEN (Medium) King, W.L.M.
1930's
HUGHES, *SIR* SAMUEL (Politician) War,
European (1914-18) 1916
HUGHES, SAMUEL H. S. (Judge)
Corruption 1969
HUGILL, JOHN (Writer) Aberhart, William
1937
HULL, RAYMOND (Writer) Change 1953;
Employees 1969, 1969; Incompetence
1969, 1969; Performance 1969; Work
1969
HULME, THOMAS E. (British poet) Poets
1914
HUME, JOSEPH (British politician)
England 1834
HUNT, EDWARD (Poet) World 1966
HUNTINGTON, LUCIUS S. (Politician)
Political phrases
HUNTINGTON, RICHARD (Poet) Indians
1875

HURST, WILLIAM (Winnipeg city
engineer) Floods 1950
HURTIG, MEL (Publisher) Textbooks 1971
HUTCHISON, BRUCE (Writer) Boundary,
Can.-U.S. 1955, 1966; British
Commonwealth 1943; Business men
1967; Canada 1942;
Canadian-American relations 1958;
Canadians 1942, 1955, 1957;
Diefenbaker, J.G. 1964; Fredericton,
N.B. 1942; Future 1972; Gross National
Product 1970; Hockey 1972; Humility
1954; Identity 1957; King, W.L.M.
1938, 1942, 1953, 1953; Loneliness
1943; Pearson, L.B. 1964; Prime
Minister 1964; St. Laurent, Louis 1964;
Wheat 1942; Woodsworth, J.S. 1953,
1969
HUTTON, MAURICE (Educator) History
1935; Success 1929
HYDE, H. MONTGOMERY (British author)
Spies 1948

I

IKTUKUSUK (Baffin Island Eskimo) Food
1970
ILES, GEORGE (Aphorist) Books 1918;
Bragging 1918; Change 1918; Courage
1918; Discovery 1918; Doubts 1918;
Errors 1918; Fathers 1918; Form 1918;
Growth 1918; Hope 1918; Ignorance
1918; Leadership 1918; Memory 1918;
Men 1918; Past 1918; Sea 1918;
Students 1918; Success 1918;
Superstition 1918
ILSLEY, JAMES L. (Politician) The Crown
1945
IMPERIAL CONFERENCE (1926) Dominion
1926; Governor General 1926
INDIAN CHIEFS OF ALBERTA Indians
1970
INFELD, LEOPOLD (University professor)
Toronto 1941
INGLIS, *BISHOP* JOHN Schools 1790
INNIS, HAROLD ADAMS (Political scientist)
Advertising 1952; Advice 1923; Arctic
1935, 1936; Canadian-American
relations 1952; Civilization 1950, 1951;
Colonialism 1956; Communication
1950; Culture 1951; The Depression
(1930-37) 1933; Economics 1923, 1936;
Finance 1956; Foreign relations 1939.

1949; Fur trade 1930; Geography 1930,
1937; Humour 1944; Indians 1930;
Intellectuals 1935; Investment,
American 1952; Klondike 1936; Maple
trees 1930; Mechanization 1934;
Nationalism 1933; Obscenity 1944;
Ottawa 1949; Pearson, L.B. 1948;
Political parties 1946; Prediction 1935;
The Press 1949; Scholarship 1944,
1946; Universities 1938, 1946; The
West 1923

INNIS, MARY QUAYLE (Writer) Faces
1939; Precambrian shield 1935;
Women 1966

IRVINE, A.G. (Police officer) Macdonald,
Sir J.A. 1881

IRVINE, WILLIAM (Member of
Parliament) Classes 1920; Montreal
1924; Patronage 1917; Political parties
1920; Publishing 1949; Social Credit
1935; Trade 1930

IRVING, JOHN A. (University professor and
philosopher) Humanity 1952; Reason
1952; Religion 1959

IRVING, KENNETH C. (N.B. industrialist)
Maritimes 1961

IRVING, WASHINGTON (U.S. author)
Nor'westers 1836; Voyageurs 1886

IRWIN, W. ARTHUR (Editor) Journalism
1970

IWANIUK, WACLAW (Poet) Death 1973

IWASUK (Poet) Poets 1974

J

JACKSON, ALEXANDER Y. (Painter) Arctic
1958; Art 1958; Mountains 1958;
Painting 1958

JACKSON, BARRY (Theatre director)
Buildings 1929

JACKSON, GILBERT E. (Economist)
Statistics 1922

JACKSON, ROBERT W. B. (Educator)
Academics 1957

JACOB, E. FRED (Journalist and author)
Education 1925; Husbands 1925;
Intellectuals 1925; Stupidity 1925

JACOBI, OTTO R. (Landscape painter)
Painting 1875

JACOBS, SAMUEL W. (Member of
Parliament) Canadian-American
relations 1921; Dictionaries 1959;
Emigration 1925; Grand Trunk Ry.
1920; House of Commons 1937;
Immigration 1927, 1927; Jews 1915;
Statesmen 1930

"JACQUES" (Pseud.) Newspapers 1812

JAIN, GENEVIEVE (Author) Disunity 1970

JAKEWAY, CHARLES E. (Poet) Secord,
Laura 1897

JAMES, THOMAS (Navigator) Mosquitoes
1631

JAMESON, ANNA B. (Author) Canada 1838;
Children 1837; Culture 1837;
Education 1838; Marriage 1852;
Niagara Falls 1838; Pioneers 1838;
Spring 1837; Toronto 1838, 1838; Trees
1838; Women 1838

JAMESON, DR. S. (Administrator of
Rhodesia) Laurier, Sir Wilfrid 1902

JAQUES, EDNA (Poet) Drought 1934;
Farms 1953; Kitchens 1939

JEANNERET, MARSH (Publisher)
Journalism 1961

JEFFERSON, THOMAS (U.S. President)
Annexation 1812

JEFFERY, JOHN (British Member of
Parliament) Fisheries 1793

JEFFERYS, CHARLES W. (Artist)
Haliburton, T.C. 1956; Truth 1941

JEHOVAH'S WITNESSES Jehovah's
Witnesses 1946

JELLICOE, LORD (British navy
commander) Isolation 1910

JENKINS, MARIEL (Poet) Genius 1953

JENKINS, W. A. (Public servant) Credit
1962

JENNESS, DIAMOND (Anthropologist)
Eskimos 1959; Indians 1932, 1932, 1954

JENOFF, MARVYNE (Poet) Fathers 1972

JODOIN, CLAUDE (Labour leader) Labour
unions 1961

JOHNSON, DANIEL (Quebec Premier)
Liberty 1965; Personalities; Radio and
TV 1965

JOHNSON, SIR FRANCIS G. (Governor of
Assiniboia) Regina, Sask., 1882

JOHNSON, GEORGE (Statistician)
Twentieth century 1901

JOHNSON, GEORGE W. (poet) Age 1864

JOHNSON, HARRY G. (Economist)
Americanization 1962; Economy 1962;
Identity 1963; Nationalism 1961, 1961;
Universities 1970
JOHNSON, LEROY (Poet) Time 1967
JOHNSON, LYNDON B. (U.S. President)
Pearson, L.B. 1965
JOHNSON, PAULINE (Poet) Canadians
1903; Canoeing 1893; Capitulation
1913; Flag 1912; Halifax 1903; Ideals
1895; Indians 1912; Jews 1894;
Railways 1903, 1903; R.C.M.P. 1903;
Vancouver, B.C. 1903; United States
1903
JOHNSON, R. BYRON (English traveller)
Drinking 1872
JOHNSON, SAMUEL (British writer)
Colonialism 1756
JOHNSTON, GEORGE (Poet) Agreement
1959, Armistice Day 1966; Army 1951;
Betrayal 1966; Dogs 1959; Drunkards
1959; Families 1959; Flight 1959;
Flying 1959, 1959; Friends 1959;
Ghosts 1966; Hanging 1966, 1966;
Home 1959; Judges 1966; Life 1959,
1966; Me 1959, 1966; Morning 1959;
Satisfaction 1966; Suburbs 1951
JOHNSTONE, JAMES W. (Premier of Nova
Scotia) Confederation 1854
JOHNSTONE, JOHN C. (Writer on
bilingualism) Disunity 1969
JOLY, HENRI G. (Member of Parliament)
Confederation 1865
JONAS, GEORGE (Poet) Belief 1970;
Conflict 1962; Credos 1967;
Disappointment 1971; Experience
1969; Girls 1962; God 1970; Humanity
1962; Me 1970; Peace 1962;
Uncertainty 1962
JONES, ALFRED G. (Lieutenant-governor
of Nova Scotia) Citizenship 1888
JONES, DOUGLAS G. (Poet and critic)
Acceptance 1958; Bodies 1961; Chaos
1961; Culture 1970; Decisions 1957;
Hunting 1968; Identity 1970; Land
1970; Mythology 1970; Ospreys 1967;
Schools 1961; Things 1957
JONES, JOHN CEREDIGION (Poet) War
dead 1920's
JONES, MERVYN (British journalist)
Political phrases
JOSIE, EDITH (Newspaperwoman) Cities
and towns 1966; News 1966

JOY, RICHARD J. (Linguist) Languages
1967
JUNEAU, PIERRE (Public servant)
Understanding 1970
JURY, ALFRED F. (Labour leader) Labour
1889

K

KAHN, HERMAN (U.S. defence analyst)
Americanization 1972
KALLMANN, HELMUT (Music librarian)
Music 1960
KALM, PETER (Swedish botanist) Dress
1749
KANE, PAUL (Painter) Sleep 1848; Toronto
1859
KARSH, YOUSUF (Photographer)
Photography 1962, 1963, 1971; Vanity
1964
KATTAN, NAIM (Writer) Americanization
1968
KAVANAGH, JACK (Labour leader) Classes
1919
KEARNS, LIONEL (Poet) Dance 1967; Jesus
Christ 1967; Poetry 1962, 1962
KEATE, STUART (Newspaper editor)
Publishing 1961
KEEFER, THOMAS C. (Civil engineer)
Enterprise 1850; Railways 1850, 1850,
1865
KEENLEYSIDE, HUGH L. (Diplomat)
Arctic 1949; Sex 1966
KEIRSTEAD, BURTON S. (Economist)
Canadian-American relations 1953;
Communism 1956
KEITH, WILLIAM J. (Poet) Literature 1964
KELLER, WELDON PHILLIP (Writer)
Ranchers 1966
KELLY, REV. PETER Indians 1912
KELLY, VINCENT (Knights of Columbus
officer) The Press 1963
KELSEY, HENRY (Explorer) Buffalo 1690;
Canoeing 1691; Mosquitoes 1691;
Prairies 1691
KELSO, JOHN J. (Children's Aid founder)
Charity 1891, 1905
KEMBLE, FANNY (British actress) Montreal
1834
KENNEDY, BETTY (Radio broadcaster)
Fashion 1972

KENNEDY, HOWARD A. (Journalist) British
    Empire 1907; Immigrants 1907;
    Labour 1907; Politics 1925
KENNEDY, JOHN F. (U.S. President)
    Canadian-American relations 1961;
    Diefenbaker, J.G. 1961, 1964;
    Organization of American States 1961;
    Pearson, L.B. 1963
KENNEDY, LEO (Poet) Jesus Christ 1936
KENNEDY, TOM (Politician) Subsidies,
    federal 1948
KENNEDY, WILLIAM P.M. (Legal
    historian) Confederation 1925; England
    1935; Progress 1921; Time 1922
KENNER, HUGH (Literary critic) Identity
    1954
KENT, TOM (Editor and politician)
    Economy 1958; Security 1957
KERMODE, JOHN FRANK (English literary
    critic) McLuhan, M. 1967
KERNIGHAN, ROBERT K. (Poet)
    Columnists 1882; Hay 1925; Liquor
    1882; North 1896; Settlers 1925
KERR, ROBERT (Executive) Technology
    1971
KETCHUM, JOHN D. (Psychologist)
    Monopoly 1944
KETTLE, JOHN (Writer) Guilt 1968
KEY, DR. JAMES Health 1963
KIBSEY, ADAM (Credit manager) Debt
    1964
KIDD, BRUCE (Athlete) Hockey 1972;
    Sport 1970, 1970
KIDD, J. ROBY (Educator) Education 1959,
    1968
KIERANS, ERIC (Politician) Budgets 1963;
    Investment, foreign 1963; Natural
    resources 1973
KILBER, SANDRA (Poet) Future 1969
KILBOURN, ELIZABETH (Critic) Art 1968
KILBOURN, WILLIAM (Writer) Authority
    1960; Buildings 1968; Canada 1970;
    Corporations 1960; History 1956;
    Mackenzie, W.L. 1956; Repression
    1970; Sport 1970
KING, CARLYLE (University professor)
    Socialism 1952; Temptation 1959
KING, MRS. H.B. (Pioneer) Pioneers 1878
KING, JOHN MARK (Moderator,
    Presbyterian Church) Superiority 1887

KING, W.L. MACKENZIE (Prime Minister)
    Academics 1938; Appearances 1927;
    Bennett, R.B. 1935; British
    Commonwealth 1944;
    Canadian-American relations 1948;
    Collective security 1936; Communism
    1948; Conscription, military 1942;
    Constitution, British 1926;
    Continentalism 1948; Culture 1914;
    The Dead 1933; Defence 1938;
    Diplomacy 1947, 1948; Drugs 1908;
    External relations 1943; Family
    allowances 1944; Finance 1935, 1939;
    Foreign policy 1936; Foreign relations
    1921, 1936; Future 1939; Geography
    1936; Government 1931; Hepburn,
    Mitchell 1940; Immigration 1947,
    1947; Industry 1919, 1919, 1933;
    Isolation 1936; King, W.L.M. 1897,
    1911, 1919, 1919, 1925, 1933, 1935,
    1944, 1945, 1964; Leadership 1939,
    1945; Liberal Party 1919, 1931, 1933,
    1948; Mackenzie, W.L. 1898; Marriage
    1912; Meighen, Arthur 1920, 1942;
    Nation 1941; Newspapers 1949;
    Parliament 1926, 1939; Pearson, L.B.
    1948; People 1949; Politics 1925, 1938;
    The Present 1949; Prevention 1944;
    Public opinion 1927; Rights 1907;
    Sacrifice 1923; Service 1927; Soldiers
    1919; Spies 1946; Spiritualism 1925,
    1928; State 1918; Status 1926;
    Subsidies, federal 1930; Taxation 1931,
    1931; Titles of honour 1929; Trade
    1930; Unemployment 1932; United
    Nations 1948, 1948; Unity 1927, 1936,
    1939; War 1936, 1936, 1939, 1939
KING, W. M. (Petitioner) Temptation 1874
KINGSTON, REBA (Autobiographer)
    Fatness 1965
KINGSTON UPPER CANADA HERALD
    (Newspaper) Durham's Report 1839
KINGSTON WHIG-STANDARD
    (Newspaper) National anthem 1956
KIPLING, RUDYARD (British author)
    Canada 1908; Canadian-American
    relations 1911; Can.-British relations
    1897; C.P.R. 1920; Clubs 1907;
    Enemies 1908; Flowers 1895; Halifax
    1896; Labour 1907; Lake Superior
    1908; Law and lawyers 1908; Medicine
    Hat, Alta. 1892, 1907; Population 1907;
    Prairies 1908; Thunder Bay, Ont. 1908;
    Vancouver, B.C. 1900; Victoria, B.C.

L

Loneliness 1894; Memory 1888; Men
1899; Night 1888, 1899; November
1888; October 1893; Old age 1884;
Ottawa River 1900; Parliament
buildings 1888; Passion 1888; Peace
1899, 1899; Reading 1891; Rich 1893;
Roads 1888; Saw mills 1900; Snow
1893, 1900; Souls 1892, 1899; Speeches
1899; Spring 1899; Summer 1888; Sun
1900; Thought 1888, 1888; Thrushes
1889; Time 1899; Trials 1889;
Urbanization 1894; Will 1900; Wind
1894; Winter 1888, 1900; Work 1896

LANCTOT, GUSTAVE (Historian) Roman
Catholics 1955

LANDON, FRED (Historian) Citizenship
1937

LANE, GARY (Hairdresser) Crime 1968

LANE, M. TRAVIS (Poet) Stars 1973

LANE, PATRICK (Poet) Riel Rebellion 1973

LANE, RED (Poet) Answers 1968; Children
1968; Destination 1968; Fate 1968;
Hunting 1968; Me 1968; Poems 1968;
Purpose 1968

LANGEVIN, SIR HECTOR L. (Politician)
Macdonald, Sir John A. 1867

LANGHORNE, JOHN (Missionary) Soldiers
1774

LANGTON, HUGH H. (Historian) Scotsmen
1929

LANGTON, JOHN (Auditor general)
Business 1844; Macdonald, Sir John A.
1856; Mackenzie, W.L. 1834; Ryerson,
Egerton 1855, 1856; Speculation,
financial 1856; Universities 1856

LANIGAN, GEORGE T. (Journalist) Music
1886; News 1878

LANIGAN, W. B. (Traffic manager) The
Press 1917

LANK, HERBERT H. (Executive) Salesmen
1960

LAPALME, GEORGES (Politician)
Duplessis, M. 1950

LA PATRIE (Montreal newspaper) Foreign
relations 1899

LAPOINTE, ERNEST (Politician) French
language 1916; Nationality 1920;
Parliament 1932

LASKI, HAROLD J. (British writer) Labour
unions 1916

LASKIN, BORA (Supreme Court chief
justice) Creativity 1966; Obscenity
1966

LATERRIERE, PIERRE DE SALES
(Physician and author) French
Canadians 1830

LAURENCE, MARGARET (Novelist) Age
1964; Appearances 1962; Emotions
1956; Forgetfulness 1962; Freedom
1969; Greed 1963; Home 1969; Men
and women 1968; Novelists 1974;
Opinion 1968; Politeness 1968; Pride
1964; Privacy 1964; Talk 1961; Taste
1964; Words 1970; Writers 1971

LAURENCE, WILLIAM L. (U.S. editor)
Nuclear weapons 1959

LAURENDEAU, ANDRE (Politician) Death
1973; Newspapers 1958; Quebec
(Province) 1961, 1962; Royal
commissions 1962; Statute of
Westminster (1931) 1962

LAURIER, SIR WILFRID (Prime Minister)
Animosity 1900's; Annexation 1910;
Army 1916; Attack 1899; Bilingualism
1877, 1890; Blake, Edward 1891, 1921;
Boundary, Canada-U.S. 1911; Bourassa,
Henri 1899; Bribery 1882; British
1901; British Empire 1902; Cabinet
ministers 1878; Canada 1908;
Canadian-American relations 1891,
1903, 1907; Can.-British relations 1888,
1900, 1902; Canadians 1900; Closure
1913; Conduct of life 1916;
Confederation 1889, 1896, 1907, 1918;
Conscription, military 1917;
Conservatism 1877; Constitution,
British 1908; Conviction 1896;
Corruption 1881; Crowds 1890; The
Crown 1907; Death 1891; Demands
1918; Diplomacy 1907; Disunity 1891;
Economics 1888; Education 1882;
Elections 1882, 1906, 1908, 1910;
England 1897; Englishmen 1877, 1884,
1884, 1904; Ethnic groups 1889;
Fighting 1916; Freedom 1896, 1897,
1908; French Canadians 1889, 1897,
1899, 1912; French Canadians, destiny
1896; French language 1886, 1913;
Future 1903; Geography 1887; Grand
Trunk Pacific Ry. 1903, 1904, 1904;
Ideals 1904, 1904; Ignorance 1891;
Independence 1892, 1897; Interviews
1909; Isolation 1896; Judges 1884;
King, W.L.M. 1909; Laurier, Sir W.
1864, 1895, 1896, 1904, 1908, 1910,
1911, 1911, 1916, 1917, 1918; Liberal
Party 1877; Liberalism 1877, 1877,

1884, 1896; Liberty 1886, 1889;
Macdonald, *Sir* John A. 1887, 1891,
1891, 1891; Mackenzie, Alexander
(Prime Minister) 1906; Manufacturing
1911; Militia 1902; Monarchy 1877;
Navy 1910; North West Rebellion
(1885) 1885; Old age 1901; Ontario
1911; Opposition 1913; Organization
1893; Ottawa 1884, 1893; Parliament
1913; Patriotism 1900, 1904; Patronage
1903; Political parties 1886; Political
phrases; Politics 1875, 1884; Prejudice
1887; Protection 1894; Public opinion
1917; Reciprocity (1854) 1901; Reform
1907; Religion 1896; Riel, Louis 1885;
Rights 1877; Roman Catholics 1875,
1877, 1877, 1889, 1910; Salvation Army
1887; Scotsmen 1893; Selfishness 1882;
Senate 1906; Solitude 1892;
Sovereignty 1900; Speaker of the House
of Commons 1899; Statesmen 1891;
Statistics 1890's; Status 1897, 1908,
1910; Taxation 1905; Titles of honour
1918; Trade 1891, 1907, 1911;
Transportation 1907; Tupper, *Sir*
Charles 1916; Twentieth century 1904,
1904, 1905; United States 1903; Unity
1877, 1886, 1900, 1900, 1901;
Universities 1882; Voters 1882; War
1900, 1910, 1910, 1911, 1912, 1914,
1914
LAURIN, CAMILLE (University professor)
Quebec (Province) 1964
LAUT, AGNES C. (Novelist and historian)
Bravery 1904; Settlers 1912
LAVALLY, JOE (Indian guide) Fishing
1947
LAVELL, ALFRED E. (Composer) Queen's
University 1891
LAVERGNE, ARMAND (Politician) War,
European (1914-18) 1916
LAWRENCE, ALBERT B. R. (Politician)
Medical care 1971
LAWSON, ED (Labour leader and Senator)
Labour 1972; Labour strikes 1972
LAWSON, MARY JANE (Poet) New Year
1882
LAXER, JAMES (Writer) Calgary 1970;
Natural resources 1970
LAYBOURNE, LAWRENCE E. (American
journalist) News 1960

LAYTON, IRVING (Poet) Academics 1961;
Action 1963, 1963; Adults 1968;
Affirmation 1961; Aggression 1969;
Agreement 1969; Anger 1969; Animals
1969; Aphorisms 1969; Appearances
1961; Artists 1963; Assassination 1969;
Autumn 1955; Beards 1954;
Benefactors 1969; Birds 1971;
Canadians 1956, 1969; Charity 1969;
Christianity 1971; Church 1959;
Communism 1961, 1969; Compassion
1969; Conscience 1969; Culture 1964;
Dance 1959; Death 1956, 1963;
Dentists 1969; Destination 1963;
Egotism 1967; Envy 1969; Existence
1969; Faith 1969; Freedom 1968, 1969;
Genius 1969; God 1969; Golfers 1955;
Good and evil 1971; Goodness 1969;
Graveyards 1968; Happiness 1969;
Hate 1964; History 1971;
Homosexuality 1969; Hypocrisy 1969;
Idealists 1968; Information 1955;
Invention 1969; Jews 1956; Law and
lawyers 1969; Learning 1969; Life
1955, 1961; Love 1962, 1964, 1968,
1969; Malice 1959; Man 1958, 1968;
Manners 1965; Marriage 1969, 1969;
Mediocrity 1962; Mothers 1961;
Nationalism 1969, 1969; Neighbours
1969; Old age 1964, 1968; Opinion
1969; Originality 1969; Peace of mind
1969; Pleasure 1969; Poems 1965,
1973; Poetry 1959; Poets 1956, 1959,
1961, 1963, 1965, 1968; Power 1969;
Pudenda 1969; Reading 1964;
Rebellion 1969; Sex 1964, 1969, 1971;
Sexual union 1965; Significance 1969,
1971; Socialism 1969; Speech 1971;
Stupidity 1969; Success 1963, 1969;
Suffering 1969, 1969; Time 1968;
Truth 1961; Unwanted 1963; Violence
1969; Virtue 1969, 1969; Women 1959,
1959; Words 1969
LEACOCK, STEPHEN (Humourist) Actors
1921; Advertising 1924; Age 1940;
Agitation 1926; Annexation 1907;
Apartments 1945; Artists 1934; Assault
1911; Beds 1910; Birth 1911; Boarding
houses 1914; Books 1913; Boys 1915,
1918; British 1922; British Columbia
1937; Citizens 1920; Cold 1937;
Colonies 1907; Conservative Party
1909; Conversation 1945; Crime 1912;
Death 1912, 1940; Deeds and doing

1923, 1944; Devil 1916; Drinking 1917; Education 1922, 1939, 1939; Egotism 1935; Elections 1912; Electric power 1907; English language 1943; Exaggeration 1924; Faces 1945; Fighting 1942; Flowers 1909; Footnotes 1937; Future 1907; Girls 1912; Golf 1923; Government 1934; Greed 1922; Hanging 1931; Happiness 1945; History 1925; Home 1915; Horses 1911; Humour 1916, 1916, 1916, 1922, 1935; Idleness 1923; Imperialism 1907; Intellectuals 1912; Jokes 1935; Knowledge 1906; Landladies 1910; Languages 1944; Leacock, Stephen 1919; Love 1935; Luck 1930; McGill University 1937; Marriage 1943, 1945; Meals 1910; Millionaires 1910; Missionaries 1923; Morality 1915; National anthem 1912, 1912; North 1936; Old age 1940; Opportunity 1920; Parliament, Members of 1907; People 1935; Planning 1936; Poetry 1944; Politics 1907; Popularity 1934; Population 1907; Prairies 1936; Praise 1934; Radicalism 1938; Retirement 1939, 1939; Rich 1916, 1917; Saskatchewan 1937; Scholars 1933; Schools 1923; Senate 1913; Servants 1945; Silence 1945; Skiing 1923; Socialism 1920, 1933; Society, polite 1934; Students 1912, 1922; Success 1917; Summer 1955; Teachers 1923; Teaching 1912, 1945; Thought 1910, 1923; Toronto 1937; Travel 1926; Trust 1915; Truth 1906; Ukrainians 1937; United States 1958; Universities 1922; Victoria, B.C. 1936; War 1911; The West 1936; Writers 1912, 1957; Writing 1912

LEAGUE FOR SOCIAL RECONSTRUCTION Capitalism 1935, 1935

LECKIE, JOHN E. (Song composer) Mining 1910

LEDDY, J. FRANCIS (President,University of Waterloo) Voters 1972

LEE, DENNIS (Poet) Canadianism 1972; Citizens 1972; Diplomacy 1972; King, W.L.M. 1974; Mackenzie, W.L. 1970; Ookpik 1974; Place names 1974; Rebellion (1837) 1972

LEFOLII, KEN (Writer) Indians 1965

LEFROY, JOHN HENRY (Surveyor) Discontent 1844; Religion 1843

LEGGO, WILLIAM (Historian) Languages 1878

LEIGH, BENJAMIN (Public servant) Post Office 1754

LE MESSURIER, HENRY W. (Writer) Newfoundland 1880

LEMIEUX, RODOLPHE (Speaker of the House of Commons) England 1905; French Canadians 1914; Parliament 1925

LE MOYNE, JEAN (Author) Death 1968; French Canadians, destiny 1966; Heritage 1966; History 1966; Journalism 1966; Nationalism 1966; Roman Catholics 1966, 1966

LE PAN, DOUGLAS (Poet) Boyhood 1953; Grief 1953; Nationalism 1964; North 1948; Sky 1953; Wilderness 1948; Writers 1964

LESAGE, JEAN (Quebec Premier) Autonomy 1963; Quebec (Province) 1960, 1963, 1964; Separatism 1965, 1965

LESCARBOT, MARC (Historian) Farming 1606

LESLIE, KENNETH (Poet) Beauty 1934; Sea 1938; Universities 1938

LESPERANCE, JEAN (JOHN) T. (Novelist and editor) Loyalty 1877, 1889

LETT, WILLIAM P. (Historian of Ottawa) Fairs 1829

LEVERIDGE, LILIAN (Poet) Boys 1918

LEVESQUE, RENE (Quebec Premier) Economics 1962; Finance (Public) 1963; Laurier Sir W. 1965; Mining 1961; Quebec (Province) 1966; Political phrases; Separatism 1968, 1969

LEVEY, GERALD (Vancouver magistrate) Hair 1966

LEVINE, NORMAN (Novelist) Failure 1958

LEVITT, KARI (Economist) Canadian-American relations 1968; Culture 1970; Investment, American 1968; Investment, foreign 1970; Technology 1970; 20th C. 1970

LEWIS, DAVID (N.D.P. leader) Corporations 1972; N.D.P. 1972; Parliament 1970; Political parties 1971; Political phrases; Trudeau, P.E. 1969; Welfare 1972

LEWIS, GLENN (Potter and artist) British Columbia 1973

LEWIS, JOHN (Biographer) Modesty 1900

LOUGHEED, *SIR* JAMES (Politician)
Adultery 1920; Conscription, military
1917; Law and lawyers 1920; Senate
1918
LOUGHEED, PETER (Alberta Premier)
Energy 1973
LOUNT, SAMUEL (1837 patriot) Rebellion
(1837) 1838
LOW, HARRY R. (Public servant) Soldiers
1956
LOWER, ARTHUR R. M. (Historian)
Anglicans 1958; Automobiles 1958;
Banks and banking 1938; Canada 1941;
Canadian-American relations 1938;
Canadians 1941, 1946; Canoeing 1959;
Cartoons 1940; Cities and towns 1965;
Constitution 1942; Death 1967; Debt,
national 1946; Democracy 1930;
Education 1966; Englishmen 1931;
Flag 1967; Future 1961; God 1967;
Government 1946, 1973; Historians
1967; History 1958; King, W.L.M.
1946; Land 1946; Majorities 1967; Man
1954; Modern times 1954; Monarchy
1930; Money 1958; Montreal 1945;
National Policy (1878) 1946;
Nationalism 1958, 1967; Philosophy
1958; Problems 1967; Race 1947;
Radio and TV 1953; Rebellion (1837)
1946; Religion 1966; Roman Catholics
1946; Schools 1958; Sea 1938; Sociology
1966; The Sovereign 1946; United
Empire Loyalists 1946, 1958;
Universities 1964; War, European
(1914-18) 1946; Woodsworth, J.S. 1946;
Words 1954
LOWRY, MALCOLM (Novelist) Anguish
1962; Artists 1968; Chance 1962;
Civilization 1947, 1961; Coca-Cola
1950; Conduct of life 1947; Death
1962; Despair 1961; Doomed 1962;
Drinking 1947; Drunkards 1961; Fame
1962; Fate 1970; Gardens 1947;
Goodness 1962; Literature, Canadian
1950, 1957; Lowry, M. 1962; Man
1947; Movies 1968; Paths 1962;
Prefaces 1950; Self 1947; Streets 1962;
Success 1961; Youth 1928; Will 1947;
Writers 1953; Writing 1950, 1954
LOWTHER, PAT (Poet) Food 1968; Space
1971; Spiders 1968
LUCAS, CHARLES P. (British historian)
C.P.R. 1912
LUCAS, REX A. (Sociologist) Pollution 1971

LUCE, HENRY (U.S. publisher) Periodicals
1960
LUDWIG, JACK (Novelist) Automobiles
1963; Confusion 1963; Existence 1960;
Priorities 1963; Writers 1963, 1973
LYMAN, JOHN (Painter) Tradition 1939
LYMBURNER, ADAM (Merchant) Ontario
1791
LYNCH, CHARLES (Newspaperman)
Culture 1969
LYON, PEYTON V. (Political scientist)
Survival 1965

Mc/Mac

McAREE, JOHN V. (Columnist) McCullagh,
George 1952; Royalty 1953
McARTHUR, *GENERAL* DOUGLAS (U.S.
military leader) Williams, P. 1928
McARTHUR, PETER (Essayist) Ability
1920's; Appreciation 1903; Argument
1903; Art 1903; Artists 1903;
Autobiography 1924; Autumn 1907;
Beavers 1915; Birds 1907; British
Empire 1903; Business 1904; Charity
1903; Clubs 1903; Colonies 1903;
Conscience 1924; Culture 1903; Death
1924; Deeds and doing 1907; Disaster
1900; Englishmen 1903, 1903; Equality
1903; Etiquette 1903; Farming 1915;
Fools 1903; Forgiveness 1924; Genius
1903; Greatness 1903; Growth 1923;
Heaven 1924; Home 1907; Ignorance
1924, 1924; Ingratitude 1924; Jokes
1903; Knowledge 1903; Land 1915;
Life 1915; Loyalty 1923; Money 1903;
People 1924; Pioneers 1915; Poor 1903;
Public opinion 1917; Purpose 1903;
Real estate 1920; Reason 1915;
Recognition 1924; Respect 1924;
Return 1907; Satirists 1924; Science
1903; Simplicity 1915; Sin 1903;
Society, polite 1903; Symbols 1907;
Theory 1903; Thought 1903; Trust
1903; Truth 1903, 1903; Virtue, about
1920; War 1920; Worry 1924; Writers
1903
McBRIDE, *SIR* RICHARD (Premier of B.C.)
Political support 1905
MacCALLUM, REID (Essayist) Poetry 1953;
Art 1953, 1953; Thought 1953
McCARROLL, JAMES (Poet and writer) Old
age 1889; Trees 1889

McCARTHY, D'ALTON (Politician) French
Canadians 1889, 1894; Languages 1889
McCARTHY, LEIGHTON (Diplomat)
Pearson, L.B. 1941
McCLELLAND, JACK (Publisher)
Americanization 1971, 1972; Books
1971; Modern times 1974; Spies 1975
McCLUNG, NELLIE L. (Suffragette and
author) Children 1928; Farms 1908;
Friends 1908; Good and evil 1908;
Horizons 1910; Justice 1915; Love
1915; Marriage 1915, 1915; Women
1916; Women in politics 1916;
Women's liberation 1915; Women's
rights 1915; Women's suffrage 1914
MacCOLL, EVAN (Poet) Ottawa River 1859
MacCORMAC, JOHN (Journalist)
Geography 1940; Isolation 1940;
Loyalty 1940; Monarchy 1942
McCORMACK, JOHN (Labour militant)
Property 1872
McCOURT, EDWARD A. (Novelist) Banff,
Alta. 1965; Books 1951; British
Columbia 1965; Failure 1965; Fame
1965; Forests 1965; Islands 1965; King,
W.L.M. 1965; Prairies 1949; Regina,
Sask. 1968; Roads 1965; St. John River
(N.B.) 1965; Saskatchewan 1968;
Vancouver, B.C. 1965; Victoria, B.C.
1965; The West 1949
McCRAE, JOHN (Poet) Charity 1919;
Enemies 1915; Graveyards 1913; Life
1919; Time 1913; War dead 1915,
1919; Weather 1917
McCULLAGH, GEORGE C. (Publisher)
Hepburn, M. 1937; Politics 1966;
Security 1949
McCULLOCH, THOMAS (Writer) Activity
1821; Bodies 1821; Censorship 1823;
Debt 1821; Discontent 1821; Farming
1821; Fences 1822; Fools 1821;
Idleness 1821; Marriage 1821;
Merchants 1821; Old age 1821;
Simplicity 1821
McCULLY, JONATHAN (Politician)
Confederation 1864; Parliament
buildings 1866
McCURDY, JOHN A. D. (Aviation pioneer)
Aviation 1909
McCUTCHEON, M. WALLACE (Politician)
Management 1967
MacDONALD, ANGUS L. (Premier of Nova
Scotia) Provinces 1946

MACDONALD, GEORGE SANDFIELD
(Politician) Historians 1884
MacDONALD, GOODRIDGE (Poet) Writing
1958
MacDONALD, JAMES A. (Editor)
Canadian-American relations 1914
MacDONALD, JAMES E. H. (Painter)
Hanging 1933; Law and lawyers 1933;
Stars 1933; Thomson, Tom 1917
MacDONALD, J.W.G. ("JOCK") (Painter) Art
1954
MACDONALD, SIR JOHN A. (Prime
Minister) Americanism, anti-1867;
Argument 1857; Behaviour 1870;
Bilingualism 1890; Boundaries 1882;
Brown, George 1865, 1872; Cabinet
1860; Cabinet ministers 1870, 1888;
Canadian-American relations 1891;
Can.-British relations 1861, 1865, 1872,
1875, 1885; C.P.R. 1878, 1878, 1880;
Canals 1891; Cartier, Sir George E.
1885; Common sense 1855;
Confederation 1861, 1864, 1865, 1872,
1889; The Conquest (1759) 1890;
Conservatism 1860; Conservative Party
1854, 1854, 1857, 1885; Constitution
1864, 1864; Corruption 1854; The
Crown 1873; Defence 1886; Deserts
1960; Diplomacy 1871; Dominion
1889; Drunkards 1891; Economics
1878; Election funds 1872; Elections
1877, 1882, 1882; Englishmen 1870;
Fate 1878; Fisheries 1871; Flattery
1880; Foreign relations 1885, 1891;
Foresight (no date); Formalities 1960;
Franchise 1865; Free trade 1870, 1878;
Freedom 1865; French Canadians
1856, 1856; French Canadians, survival
1884; Galt, Alexander 1870;
Government 1861, 1873, 1881;
Governor General 1878; Honesty 1882;
Howe, Joseph 1867, 1886;
Independence 1885; Labour 1872;
Languages 1890; Laurier, Sir W. 1891,
1891; Law and lawyers 1860; Letters
1872; Libraries 1883; Macdonald, Sir
J.A. 1859, 1864, 1865, 1868, 1873, 1873,
1878, 1880's, 1880's, 1880's, 1891, 1891;
McGee, T.D. 1886; Majorities 1869;
Minorities 1865; Missionaries 1861;
Mountains 1886; Mowat, Sir Oliver
1861, 1882; Names 1960; National
Policy (1878) 1878; Negotiators 1873;
Northwest Rebellion (1885) 1885;

Obligations 1880's; Ontario 1856;
Pacific Scandal 1873; Parliament 1861,
1869; Parliament, Members of 1855;
Patronage 1878; Political phrases;
Political support 1867; Politicians 1895;
Politics 1860, 1867; Prairies 1865;
Prime Minister 1891; Prosperity 1844;
Protection 1872, 1878, 1878;
Protestants 1869; The Public 1888;
Public life 1912; Questions (no date);
Rebellion (1837) 1894; Regina, Sask.
1886; Resistance 1854; Riel, Louis
1885; Roman Catholics 1877; R.C.M.P.
1873; Senate 1865; Sin 1878; Smiles
1853; The Sovereign 1865; Speaker of
the House of Commons 1883; Speaking
1887; Speeches 1861; Strathcona, *Lord*
1873, 1878; Thompson, *Sir* John S.D.
1891, 1898; Titles of honour 1879;
Trade 1891; Tupper, *Sir* Charles 1883,
1891; Union (1841-1867) 1861;
Universities 1882; The West 1865, 1865

MacDONALD, JOHN B. (University
president) Books 1964

MacDONALD, JOHN SANDFIELD (Premier
of United Canada) Cabinet Ministers
1870, 1888; Church 1870; Patronage
1867; Political parties 1867; Political
support 1868; Prices 1867

MacDONALD, *Mrs.* JOHN SANDFIELD
(Premier's wife) MacDonald, J.S. 1864

McDONALD, LYNN (Criminologist) Crime
1969

McDONALD, MAX (Retired Inco employee)
Retirement 1974

MACDONALD, WILSON (Poet) Canada
1927; Critics 1931; Funerals 1926;
Future 1926; Humility 1931; Ideals
1931; Niagara Falls 1926; Place names
1934; Thought 1937; Tradition 1935;
Universities 1932; War, European
(1914-18) 1918; Weather 1918; Women
1926; Youth 1926

McDONNELL, JOHN F. (Poet) Voyageurs
1864

McDOUGALL, ALEXANDER (Poet)
Parliament, Members of 1843

MacDOUGALL, COLIN (Novelist)
Execution 1958; Men 1958; Work ethic
1958

McDOUGALL, JOHN (Pioneer Fort
Edmonton trader) Red River cart 1885

McDOUGALL, JOHN (Missionary) Defence
1896; Indians 1874; The West 1868

MacDOUGALL, PATRICK (Writer) Fenians
1866

McDOUGALL, ROBERT L. (University
professor) Literature, Canadian 1963

McDOUGALL, WILLIAM (Politician) Fur
trade 1869

McELCHERAN, WILLIAM (Sculptor) Artists
1971

McELMAN, CHARLES (Senator)
Newspapers 1971

MacEWEN, GWENDOLYN (Poet) Belief
1966; Creativity 1963; Exploration
1969; Growth 1969, 1970; Human
nature 1972; Imagination 1966;
Landscape 1966; Literature 1963;
Music 1963, 1963; Payment 1963;
Poems 1961; Reading 1966; Sculpture
1966; Sexual union 1966; Travel 1969;
Trees 1969; Truth 1962; Understanding
1963; Unity 1969; Women 1963;
World 1969

McGAFFEY, ERNEST (Poet) Outdoors 1861

McGEACHY, JAMES B. (Journalist)
Nationality 1962

McGEE, THOMAS D'ARCY (Father of
Confederation) Americanism,
anti-1861; Annexation 1862;
Aristocracy 1865; Assassination 1865;
Atlantic Ocean 1864; Boundaries 1865;
Canada (name) 1865; Cartier, Jacques
1858; Citizenship 1862; Classes 1865;
Confederation 1864, 1865, 1865, 1865,
1868, 1868; Continentalism 1861;
Debate 1862; Defence 1862, 1862,
1863, 1865; Emigrants 1862; Fame
1869; Fenians 1858, 1865; French
Canadians 1865; Future 1863;
Geography 1863; God 1858;
Government 1861; Hudson Bay 1858;
Immigrants 1862; Immigration 1866;
Independence 1858; Irishmen 1857,
1858, 1862; LaSalle, *Sieur de* 1858;
Literature, Canadian 1867; Maritimes
1863; Marriage 1862; Nationality 1857,
1860, 1862, 1867; Patriotism 1859;
Politics 1865; Prince Edward Island
1840; Publishing 1857; Quebec
Conference (1864) 1864; Ravens 1858;
Sea 1864; Ships 1858; Snow 1858;
Unity 1842

McGEER, PATRICK (Politician) Investment,
foreign 1966

MacGEORGE, *REV*. ROBERT J. (Clergyman and author) Doctors 1854; Parliament, Members of 1853

MacGILL, HELEN GREGORY (Judge) Courts 1920's; Juveniles 1943; Prisons 1955; Voters, Votes and Voting 1936

MacGILL, JAMES (Husband of Judge Helen MacGill) Judges 1955

McGILL UNIVERSITY Universities 1840

McGILLIVRAY, DUNCAN (Fur trader) Drinking 1794; Fur trade 1809; Indians 1794

McGILP, JOHN (Indian agent) Indians 1963

McGOEY, *REV*. JOHN H. (Roman Catholic priest) Sexual union 1967

McGOUN, A.F. (Economist) Happiness 1936

McGOUN, LACHLAN (Song writer) Soldiers 1866

McGUIRE, E. H. (Radio station manager) Radio and TV 1945

McINNES, GRAHAM C. (Writer on art) Women 1937

MacINNES, TOM (Poet) Aviation 1918; British Columbia 1927; Conduct of life 1918; Courage 1918; Death 1918; Desire 1918; Fate 1918; Food 1918; Fools 1918; Friends 1918; Frogs 1923; Girls 1918, 1923; God 1923; Good and evil 1918; Indians 1908; Individuality 1918; Justice 1918; Klondike 1908; Lies and liars 1918; Life 1927; Love 1918; Man 1918; Old age 1947; Pleasure 1910; Prayer 1918; Pretence 1923; Protest 1918; Rich 1923; Sleep 1918; Success 1918; Sun 1923; Woman 1923; Youth 1918

McINNIS, EDGAR (Historian) Canada as intermediary 1961

MACINNIS, GRACE (Politician and daughter of J. S. Woodsworth) Woodsworth, J.S. 1953

McINTYRE, JAMES (Rhymester) Cheese 1884, 1889, 1889; Cows 1884; Dairying 1889; Farming 1891; Gourlay, Robert F. 1860; Nova Scotia 1870; Pigs 1891; Pioneers 1884; Poets 1884; Provinces 1889; Wheat 1889, 1889

MACIVER, ROBERT M. (American political scientist) Americanism, anti-1938

McIVOR, R. CRAIG (Economist) Banks and banking 1958; Inflation 1958

McKAY, ARTHUR (Artist) Art 1964

MACKAY, ISABEL ECCLESTONE (Poet) Immigrants 1922; Pioneers 1922; Play 1918

McKAY, JAMES (Governor) Indians 1876

MACKAY, LOUIS A. (JOHN SMALACOMBE, pseud.) (Poet) Critics 1931; Drinking 1948; Hate 1938; Old age 1946; Poets 1948; Speeches 1938; War 1936; Wheat 1931; Words 1938

McKAY, MOSES (Labour leader) The old 1973

McKAY, ROBERT A. (Political scientist) British Commonwealth 1931; Parliament 1926; Smallwood, Joseph 1970

McKAY, SARA JEAN (Poet) News 1938

MACKENZIE, ALEXANDER (Explorer) Mackenzie, A. 1793, 1793

MACKENZIE, ALEXANDER (Prime Minister) Can.-British relations 1875, 1882; Clear Grits 1867; Conservative Party 1878; Diplomacy 1875; Flag 1876; Governor General 1877; Law and lawyers 1877; Loyalty 1867; Mackenzie, W. L. 1835, 1840, 1846 New Brunswick 1878; Patronage 1874, 1875; Prime Minister 1876; Protection 1876; Provinces 1874; Riel, Louis 1874; Tupper, *Sir* Charles 1876

MACKENZIE, IAN (Politician) British Empire 1936; Wheat 1930

MACKENZIE, NORMAN A. M. (University president) Canadian-American relations 1971

MACKENZIE, WILLIAM LYON (Rebel) Economics 1836; Education 1829, 1830; Family Compact 1833, 1833; Government 1834; Independence 1834; Labour 1837; Patriotism 1826; Politics 1837; Poor 1824; Rebellion (1837) 1837; Reform Party 1834; Ryerson, Egerton 1833; Taxation 1837; Voters 1834

MacKERACHER, WILLIAM M. (Poet) Hockey 1908

MacKINNON, STUART (Poet) Furs 1969; Ships 1969

MACKINTOSH, NORMAN (Editor) The Press 1922

MACKINTOSH, WILLIAM A. (University president) Capital 1959; Individuality 1935; Maturity 1960

MacMURCHY, *DR.* HELEN (Medical writer)
Parents 1920

MacNAB, *SIR* ALLAN (Politician)
Leadership 1856; Politics 1849;
Railways 1853

McNAMARA, ROBERT S. (U.S. secretary of
defence) Nuclear weapons 1963, 1963

McNAUGHT, CARLTON (Historian)
Advertising 1940

McNAUGHT, KENNETH (Historian)
Canadians 1966; Trudeau, P.E. 1966

McNAUGHTON, *GEN.* A.G.L. Agreement
1944; McNaughton, A.G.L. 1939; War,
World (1939-45) 1941; Water 1966

MacNAUGHTON, JOHN (Essayist) Artists
1946; Automobiles 1933; Criticism
1946; Doubts 1946; Heart 1946;
Salvation 1933

MACNEILL, RITA (Writer) Women's
liberation 1975

MACPHAIL, AGNES (Member of
Parliament) Cabinet 1929;
Conservative Party 1935; High
Commissioner to London 1931; House
of Commons 1922, 1923; Judges 1943;
Macphail, Agnes 1940, 1940; Marriage
1925, 1966; Protest 1927; Radicalism
1935; Self 1912; Senate 1923; Socialists
1933; Women's rights 1925, 1933

McPHAIL, ALEXANDER JAMES (Executive)
Democracy 1940; Farmers 1931;
People 1940

MacPHAIL, *SIR* ANDREW (Author)
Democracy 1924; Farmers 1920; Ideas
1925; Imagination 1939; Literature,
Canadian 1939; Loyalty 1909

McPHEE, NEIL (Magistrate, The Pas, Man.)
Judges 1970

MACPHERSON, CRAWFORD B. (University
professor) Historians 1957

MACPHERSON, DUNCAN (Cartoonist)
Election campaigns 1959; Tradition
1967

McPHERSON, HUGO (University professor)
The Present 1959, 1959

MACPHERSON, JAY (Poet) Adoration 1957;
Bodies 1957; Gardens 1957; God 1957;
Love 1957; Man 1957; Me 1957;
Readers 1957; Sea 1957; Winter 1957;
World 1957

McPHILLIPS, ALBERT P. (Member of
Parliament) Metaphors, mixed 1958,
1958

MACQUARRIE, HEATH (Politician) United
Nations 1963

McQUEEN, ROBERT (Historian) Railways
1936

MacQUEEN, THOMAS (Editor) Songs 1867

McRUER, JAMES C. (Judge) Order 1966

McTAGGART, JOHN (British traveller)
Architecture 1829; Lakes 1829; Ottawa
1829

MacTAVISH, NEWTON M. (Journalist)
Painting 1912

M

MACHAR, AGNES M. (Poet) Canada 1879,
1899

MACKLIN, *MAJ.-GEN.* WILFRED H. S.
(Army leader) Sovereignty 1956

MAGEE, JOHN G. (American poet, served
in RCAF) Flying 1941; Space 1941

MAGEE, WILLIAM H. (Literary critic)
Humour 1969

MAHEUX, *ABBE* ARTHUR Bilingualism
1944

MAIR, CHARLES (Poet) Buffalo 1886,
1890; Culture 1891; Destiny 1925;
Hudson Bay 1901; Independence 1888;
Indians 1886; Literature, Canadian
1891; McGee, T.D. 1868; Métis 1868,
1868; Nationality 1888; Prairies 1869,
1886; Red River (Man.) 1868; Secord,
Laura 1885, 1901; Wind 1901; World
1886

MALCOLM, ANDREW I. (Writer) Drugs
1973

MALRAUX, ANDRE (French author)
French Canadians, destiny 1963

MANDEL, ELI (Poet) Criticism 1971;
Dance 1967; Individuality 1963;
Literature 1963; Poets 1964; Pollution
1967; Sexual union 1967; Style 1972;
Thought 1967

MANION, *DR.* ROBERT JAMES (Politician)
Flattery 1936; Government 1936; War,
World (1939-45) 1939

MANITOBA FEDERATION OF LABOUR
Society 1968

MANITOBA FIRST PARTY Manitoba 1884

MANITOBA *FREE PRESS* (Newspaper)
Bicycle 1899; Clericalism 1916; Gas
1881; Government 1914; Immigration
1914; Protestants 1889; Wheat 1896

MANITOBAN (Newspaper) Elections 1887

MANN, LARRY (Actor) Actors 1964

MANNING, ERNEST (Premier of Alberta) Aberhart, William 1943; Medical care 1965; Social Credit 1939

MAO TSE-TUNG (Chinese leader) Bethune, Dr. N.H. 1939

MARCHAND, JEAN (Politician) Newfoundland 1973

"MARIA" (Pseud.) Computers 1972

MARIE DE L'INCARNATION (Quebec religious) Flowers 1653

MARLYN, JOHN (Novelist) Foreigners 1957; Learning 1957; Millionaires 1957; Nationality 1957

MARRIOTT, ANNE (Poet) Belonging 1971; Prairies 1939; Rain 1939

MARSDEN, JOSHUA (British traveller) Forests 1816

MARSDEN, MICHAEL (Writer) Arctic 1966

MARSHALL, TOM (Poet) The Past 1969; Words 1969

MARSHALL, WILLIAM E. (Poet) Death 1907; Failure 1894; Graveyards 1914; Spring 1914; Wind 1914

MARTIN, CHESTER (Historian) Canadian-American relations 1937; Confederation 1937; Dates 1937; Durham's *Report* 1939; History 1955; United Empire Loyalists 1937

MARTIN, GEORGE (Poet) Hope 1887; Life 1887

MARTIN, HUGH (Religious writer) Roman Catholics 1925

MARTIN, PAUL (Politician) Communism 1963; Housing 1968

MARTIN, PETER (Publisher) Publishing 1971

MARTIN, SAM (Native of Algoma) Wolves 1910

MARTYN, HOWE (Economist) Business 1961

MASON, *REV.* GEORGE (Writer) Schools 1875

MASON, JAMES (Soldier) Army 1900

MASSEY, VINCENT (Governor General) Americanization 1964; Boundary, Canada-U.S. 1948; Buildings 1890's; Canada 1924; Canadian-American relations 1955; Canadianism 1957; Credos 1948; Deeds and doing 1965; Economics 1924; Geography 1962; Governor General 1956, 1956; History 1958; Moderation 1948; Monarchy 1963; Nationalism 1963; Politeness

1959; Professionalism 1958; Propaganda 1954; Quebec (Prov.) 1964; Statistics 1956; Tolerance 1928; Unity 1929

MATHER, BARRY (Columnist) British Columbia 1958; Columbia River 1963

MATHEWS, ROBIN D. (University professor) Americanization 1970; Books 1969; Identity 1965; Theatre 1969; Universities 1970, 1971

MATTHEWS, ROY A. (Economist) Canadian-American relations 1969; Future 1970

MAUREPAS, JEAN-FREDERIC-PHELYPEAUX (French minister of state) Beavers 1720

MAVOR, JAMES (Political economist) Culture 1892; Power 1914

MAWEDOPENAIS (Salteaux chief) The West 1873

MAYNE, SEYMOUR (Poet) Lovers 1966

MEADE, EDWARD F. (Novelist) Living 1946; Thought 1946

MEADOWBROOK, ANGUS (Rhymer) Food 1951

MEIGHEN, ARTHUR (Prime Minister) Bennett, R. B. 1930; Borden, *Sir* Robert 1960; Can.-British relations 1922; Capitalism 1941; Classes 1938; Competition 1949; Conscription, military 1942; Conservative Party 1927; Constitution 1926; Credos 1942; Debate 1943; Defence 1937; Democracy 1939; Difficulties 1942; Economics 1935; Heroes 1925; House of Commons 1932; Inflation 1943; Majorities 1939; Facts 1932; Fame 1923; France 1921; Laurier, *Sir* W. 1957; Leadership 1939; Maple trees 1921; Meighen, Arthur 1952; The Past 1942; Political parties 1924; Political phrases; Prime Minister 1939; Prosperity 1943; Railways 1920; Social security 1948; Tariff 1910, 1921; United States 1921; War 1925; War dead 1921; War, European (1914-18) 1914, 1921, 1921

MEISEL, JOHN (Political scientist) Voters 1964

MELLICHAMP, LESLIE (Poet) Death 1952

MENZIES, MERRIL (Economist) National policy (general) 1963

MERCHANT, LIVINGSTON T. (U.S. diplomat) Canada 1964; Canadian-American relations 1965, 1966; Diplomacy 1965

MERCIER, HONORE (Premier of Quebec) Disunity 1885; French Canadians, survival 1890, 1893; Riel, Louis 1885

MERCURE, GILLES (Economist) Constitution 1956

MEREDITH, JOHN (Artist) Art 1972

MERRILEES, HAROLD (Tourist executive) Architecture 1964

MERRILL, HELEN (Poet) Wind 1912

MERRITT, HAMILTON (Soldier) Militia 1923

METCALFE, *SIR* CHARLES (Governor General) French Canadians, survival 1843; Political support 1843; Union (1841-67) 1843

METHODIST CHURCH North 1854

METHODIST MAGAZINE (Periodical) Fishing 1828

MICHELL, HUMFREY (Economist) Co-operatives 1937

MICHENER, ROLAND (Governor General) Governor General 1971

MIDDLETON, *JUSTICE* WILLIAM EDWARD Stork Derby (1926) 1926

MIDDLETON, *SIR* FREDERICK D. (Soldier) R.C.M.P. 1885; Soldiers 1886

MILL, JOHN S. (British thinker) Durham (*Lord*) 1840

MILLAIS, J. G. (British writer) Fresh air 1907

MILLER, E. F. (Poet) Americans 1911

MILLER, MALCOLM (Poet) Exaggeration 1962

MILLER, PETER (Poet) Vision 1959

MILLER-BARSTOW, DONALD H. (Biographer) Business 1951

MILLETT, DAVID (University professor) Religion 1971

MILLIGAN, F. A. (Local historian) Manitoba 1950

MILLS, DAVID (Judge) Provinces 1896; Railways 1872

MILNE, DAVID (Painter) Feeling 1948

MILTON, JOHN (British poet) Confederation 1927

MILTON, *VISCOUNT* (British traveller) Mountains 1865; Rocky Mountains 1865

MINAUDO, ONOFRIO (Sicilian Mafia member) Corruption 1964

MINER, JACK (Bird conservationist) Belief 1944; Laziness 1944; Success 1944; Tourists 1910; Work 1922

MINNEAPOLIS *JOURNAL* (Newspaper) Conservation 1906

MINTO, *LORD* (Governor General) Dance 1924; Patronage 1904

MINVILLE, ESDRAS (Social scientist) French Canadians 1939; Labour unions 1939; Unity 1946

MIRON, GASTON (Poet) Quebec (Province) 1970

MITCHELL, ROY (Theatre director) Theatre 1929

MITCHELL, WEIR (American author) Fishing 1923

MITCHELL, WILLIAM O. (Novelist) Wind 1947

MOFFETT, SAMUEL E. (Scholar) Americanization 1907

MOIR, DAVID MACBETH (Song writer) Scotsmen 1829

MOLSON, *SENATOR* HARTLAND Hockey 1957

MOLSON, JOHN (Brewer) Beer 1786

MONCK, *LORD* (Governor General) Confederation 1867; Nationality 1867

MONCK, FRANCES (Author) Fresh air 1891; Macdonald, *Sir* John A. 1864

MONK, FREDERICK D. (Politician) Navy 1910

MONK, HENRY WENTWORTH (Visionary) United Nations, 19th C.; Wisdom 1896

MONROE, JAMES (U.S. President) Annexation 1784

MONSARRAT, NICHOLAS (British novelist) Americans in Canada 1967

MONTCALM, *MARQUIS DE* (French general) Drunkards 1757; Manufacturing 1759; Montcalm, *Marquis de* 1758; Plains of Abraham 1759; Rich 1758; Women 1757

MONTGOMERY, JOHN (Rebel) Prophecy 1838

MONTGOMERY, LUCY MAUDE (Novelist) Adventures 1909; Children 1908; Discipline 1912; Dreams 1912; Duty 1909; Friends 1936; Hands 1909; Night 1921; Novels 1907; Optimism 1909; Peace 1956; Poor 1908; Prayer 1908; Prince Edward Island 1908; Self 1912; Sense 1908; Snow 1939; Trees 1919; Trying 1908; Worry 1908

MONTGOMERY, RICHARD (U.S. army
general) Invaders 1775, 1775
MONTGOMERY, *FIELD MARSHAL*
BERNARD Canada as intermediary
1946
MONTREAL *LE CANADIEN* (Newspaper)
French Canadians, destiny 1806
MONTREAL *LE DEVOIR* (Newspaper)
Roman Catholics 1956
MONTREAL *GAZETTE* (Newspaper)
Montreal 1870
MONTREAL *LA MINERVE* (Newspaper)
Quebec (Province) 1861; Riel, Louis
1885
MONTREAL *LA PRESSE* (Newspaper) Riel,
Louis 1885
MONTREAL *SEPT-JOURS* (Newspaper)
Confederation 1966
MONTREAL *STAR* (Newspaper) Grand
Trunk Pacific Ry. 1904; Income tax
1917
MONTREAL *TRANSCRIPT* (Newspaper)
Red River (Man.) 1856
MOODIE, SUSANNA (Author) Appearances
1852; Artists 1853; Canada 1852, 1852;
Canadians 1853; Children 1852;
Confidence 1855; Crime 1855; Danger
1852; Debt 1852; Despair 1852;
Dreams 1855; Drinking 1853;
Education 1853; Egotism 1852; Future
1852; Ghosts 1852; Hate 1855;
Immigration 1852, 1852; Indian
summer 1864; Labour 1853; Maple
trees 1852; Nature 1852; Newspapers
1853, 1853; Old age 1853; Passion
1855; Poverty 1871; Ridicule 1854;
Settlers 1852; Society 1855; Tears 1852;
Writers 1852
MOODY, IRENE H. (Poet) Possession 1940
MOODY, *DR.* T. GLENDON (Dentist)
Dentists 1915
MOORE, BRIAN (Novelist) Canadianism
1963; Eskimos 1963; Exaggeration
1960; Failure 1968; Faith 1968; Jesus
Christ 1955; North 1963; Religion
1955; Victims 1968; Women 1966
MOORE, JOHN H. (Company executive)
Business 1971
MOORE, MAVOR (Stage director)
Accountants 1960; Canadians 1956;
Critics 1960; Doctors 1960; Insurance
1960; Janitors 1960; Law and lawyers
1960; Librarians 1960; Parliament,
Members of 1960; Prostitution 1960;

Public relations 1960; Scholarship 1960;
Statistics 1960
MOORE, THOMAS (British poet) Boating
1804; Peace 1804; Toronto 1804
MOORE, WILLIAM H. (Member of
Parliament) French Canadians 1918
MOORHOUSE, HERBERT JOSEPH
(Agriculturist) Farmers 1918
MOORSOM, WILLIAM S. (British soldier)
Music 1830
MORGAN, HENRY J. (Biographer)
Literature, Canadian 1867
MORGAN, JAMES C. (School inspector)
Union Jack 1901
MORGAN, MARY (Poet) Charity 1887
MORISON, JOHN L. (Historian) British
Empire 1921
MORISON, SAMUEL ELIOT (U.S. historian)
Apples 1971; Champlain, *Sieur de* 1972
MORIYAMA, RAYMOND (Architect)
Architecture 1973; Truth 1970
MORRICE, JAMES WILSON (Painter)
Painting 1936; Taste 1911
MORRIER, BERNARD (Critic) Books 1970
MORRIS, ALEXANDER (Lieutenant
governor of Manitoba) Future 1858;
Indians 1873; The West 1867
MORRIS, JAMES (British writer) Canada
1968; Montreal 1960; Settlers 1973
MORRIS, JERROLD (Critic) Painting 1972
MORRIS, LESLIE (Writer) Change 1964;
Writers 1959
MORRIS, *SIR* LEWIS (British song writer)
British Empire 1887
MORRIS, RICHARD (Songwriter) Ontario
1967
MORRISSEAU, NORVAL (Painter) Space
1965
MORRISON, J.J. (Farmer) Democracy
1919; Political phrases
MORSE, ERIC W. (Canoeist) Conservation
1970
MORSE, *COL.* ROBERT (Loyalist)
Maritimes 1784
MORTON, ARTHUR S. (Historian) Fame
1937
MORTON, DESMOND (Law professor)
Classes 1970; The Press 1971
MORTON, WILLIAM L. (Historian)
Americanism, anti- 1964;
Canadian-American relations 1961;
Compromise 1950; Confederation
1946; Culture 1961; Destiny 1961,
1965; Diversity 1960; Franchise 1943;

Frontiers 1961; Government 1961;
Independence 1961; Majorities 1961;
Manitoba 1957, 1957; Monarchy 1961;
Nationalism 1946; Riel, Louis 1956;
Secession 1964; Socialism 1967;
Sovereignty 1960; Unity 1961;
Woodsworth, J.S. 1963
MOTHERWELL, WILLIAM R. (Politician)
Age 1940
MOWAT, FARLEY (Author) Americanism,
anti- 1968; Canadian-American
relations 1968, 1968; North 1967; Owls
1967; Ptarmigan 1967; Truth 1952;
Wolves 1963
MOWAT, SIR OLIVER (Premier of Ontario)
British Empire 1891; Canadian-British
relations 1891; Future 1892; Politics
1857
MOYER, REVEREND KENNETH
Confederation centennial (1967) 1967
MUGGERIDGE, JOHN (Historian) Identity
1971
MUIR, ALEXANDER (Schoolmaster) Maple
leaf 1867; Wolfe, James 1867
MULHOLLAND, WILLIAM (Banker)
Citizenship 1974
MULOCK, SIR WILLIAM (Chief justice of
Ontario) Communism 1931; Credos
1936; Quebec (Province) 1941
MULVANY, CHARLES P. (Poet) Dogs 1887
MUNRO, ALICE (Novelist) Age 1968;
Homes 1972; Men 1968; Miracles 1968;
Nature 1971
MUNRO, JOHN (Politician) Poor 1971
MUNRO, KATHRYN (Poet) Eskimos 1956
MUNRO, WILLIAM B. (Historian)
Confederation, Fathers of 1929
MUNSINGER, GERDA (Associate of
politicians) Munsinger, Gerda 1966;
Spies 1966
MURDOCH, ROBERT (Poet) Men 1890
MURPHY, CHARLES (Politician) Egotism
1918; Laurier, Sir W. 1919
MURPHY, EMILY G. ("Janey Canuck";
Writer and Women's leader)
Acquiescence 1925; Chance 1945;
Conversation 1920's; Courts 1920's;
Experience 1945; Families 1920;
Fighting 1945; Independence 1920's;
Loss 1945; Mothers 1945; National
anthem 1945; Neighbours 1912; Sorrow
1945
MURPHY, OWEN E. (Executive) Bribery
1891

MURRAY, AMELIA (Maid of honour to
Queen Victoria) Mackenzie, W.L. 1853
MURRAY, GEORGE (Poet) Dollard Des
Ormeaux, A. 1874
MURRAY, JAMES (Governor of Quebec)
French Canadians 1764, 1766
MURRAY, JOHN C. (Poet) World 1937
MURRAY, MARGARET "MA" (Editor)
Certainty 1933; The Press 1933; Water
1958; Weather 1962; Words 1964
MURRAY, MARGARET P. (Women's leader)
Imperialism 1900
MURRAY, R.H. (Nova-Scotian) Elections
1933
MURRAY, REVEREND ROBERT Abstinence
1835
MURRAY, RONA (Poet) Birds 1968
MUSGRAVE, SUSAN (Poet) Boredom 1970;
Failure 1970; North 1970; Reality
1972; Triumph 1970; You 1970
MYERS, GUSTAVUS (American writer)
Wealth 1914
MYRDAL, GUNNAR (Swedish social
scientist) French Canadians, survival
1973; Labour unions 1973

N

NADER, RALPH (U.S. investigator)
Canadian-American relations 1971
NAEGELE, KASPAR D. (Sociologist) Canada
1964; Caution 1961, 1964
NAKANO, TAKEO (Poet) Citizenship 1971;
Japanese 1964
NAPOLEON I (Emperor of France)
England 1817
NATIONAL FARMERS' UNION Food 1970
NATIONAL TRADES AND LABOUR
CONGRESS Canada 1904
NAUKATJIK (Eskimo) Marriage 1929
NEATBY, HILDA (Historian) Academics
1953; Education 1953, 1954;
Mediocrity 1953; Research 1954
NEEDHAM, RICHARD J. (Columnist)
Acting 1969; Automobiles 1969;
Behaviour 1969; Books 1966; Caution
1969; Children 1969, 1969; Confidence
1969; Contact 1969; Conversation
1969; Courage 1969; Decisions 1969;
Disaster 1969; Disease 1966; Drugs
1969; Escape 1969; Families 1969;
Farms 1965; Fear 1969; Freedom 1969,
1969; Friends 1969; Happiness 1969,

1969; Help 1969; Homes 1972;
Honesty 1969; Humour 1969;
Husbands 1969, 1971; Journalism 1969;
Killing 1969; Law and Lawyers 1969;
Leaders 1969; Life 1969, 1969; Life
and death 1969; Love 1969, 1969,
1969; Love affairs 1969, 1969;
Marriage 1969, 1969; Meals 1969; Men
1969, 1969; Men and women 1969,
1969, 1969, 1969, 1969, 1969; Mistakes
1969; Modesty 1969; Newspapers 1969;
Nurses 1969; Ownership 1969; Peace
1969; Perfection 1969; Poor 1969;
Possession 1969; Pride 1969, 1969;
Privacy 1969; Reason 1969; Schools
1968; Seduction 1969; Senate 1969; Sex
1969; Strength 1969, 1969; Thought
1969; Tolerance 1969; Toronto 1969;
Trade unions 1969; Truth 1969;
Universities 1970; War 1969; Wealth
1969; Wisdom 1969, 1969; Woman
1969; Women 1969, 1969, 1969;
Women's rights 1969; Work 1969;
Work ethic 1969; World 1969; Youth
1969, 1969

NEEDLER, GEORGE H. (Writer and
historian) Riel, Louis 1957

NEEL, BOYD (Musician) Music 1958

NEILL, ALLAN W. (M.P.) Orientals 1942

NELLIGAN, EMILE (Poet) Snow 1903

NELSON, ROBERT (Rebel) Oppression
1838

NELSON, WOLFRED (Rebel leader)
Rebellion (1837) 1837

NELSOVA, ZARA (Musician) Music 1966

NESTERENKO, ERIC (Hockey player)
Hockey 1972

NEVERS, EDMOND DE (Writer) Land 1896

NEVILLE, WILLIAM F.W. (Political
scientist) Personalities—Pelletier, Gerard

NEW BRUNSWICK GOVERNMENT Forests
1924; New Brunswick (no date)

NEW DEMOCRATIC PARTY N.D.P. 1969

NEW DEMOCRATIC PARTY,
SASKATCHEWAN Election Slogans 1971

NEW YORK WORLD (Newspaper)
Annexation 1890

NEWBOLT, SIR HENRY (British poet)
Literature, Canadian 1923

NEWCASTLE, DUKE OF (1693-1768)
Annapolis (Fort) N.S. 1758; Canada
1760; Cape Breton 1771

NEWCASTLE, DUKE OF (1811-1864)
Intercolonial Railway 1863

NEWELL, JOHN R. (Poet) Friendship 1881;
Solitude 1881

NEWFOUNDLAND Newfoundland 1637

NEWFOUNDLAND. HOUSE OF ASSEMBLY
Newfoundland 1870

NEWLOVE, JOHN (Poet) Beauty 1968;
Frustration 1965; Future 1969; Ghosts
1965; Identity 1968; Innocence 1968;
Justification 1968; Loneliness 1968; Lost
1965; Me 1965; Meaning
1965; Pessimism 1972; Radio and TV
1970; Remembrance 1968, 1968; Roads
1965; Technology 1968; Weddings
1968; Winter 1965; Writers 1972

NEWMAN, COLEMAN J. (Poet and novelist)
Age 1967; Legends 1967

NEWMAN, PETER C. (Editor and writer)
Business 1959; Canadian-American
relations 1971; Change 1973;
Conservative Party 1963; Diefenbaker,
J.G. 1963, 1963; Expo 1967; Foreign
relations 1968; Government 1968;
House of Commons 1966; Identity
1971, 1972, Leadership 1972; Politics
1968; Survival 1968; Taylor, E.P. 1959

NEWTON-WHITE, MURIEL E. (Ecological
writer) Natural Resources 1958

NICHOL, b.p. (Poet) Canadian-American
relations 1969; Morning 1970

NICHOLS, MARK E. (Journalist) Subsidies,
Federal 1948

NICHOLSON, PATRICK (Journalist and
biographer) Pearson, L.B. 1968

NICKLE, WILLIAM F. (M.P.) Titles of
honour 1919

NICOL, ERIC (Humourist) British
Columbia 1958; Canadians 1966;
Confederation 1966; Critics 1968;
Failure 1968; History 1968;
Investment, American 1968; King,
W.L.M. 1966; Revenge of the cradle
1959; Toronto 1966; War of 1812, 1961

NIHON, ALEXIS (Industrialist) Property
1972

NIVEN, FREDERICK JOHN (Novelist)
Rocky Mountains 1920

NIXON, JOHN E. (Poet) War dead 1946

NORMAN, COLIN (Poet) Poets 1965

NORQUAY, JOHN (Premier of Manitoba)
Manitoba 1884

NORTH, LORD (British politician)
Constitution 1774

NORTHCLIFFE, *LORD* (British newspaper proprietor) Canadian-British relations 1908

NORTHCOTE, *SIR* STAFFORD (British politician) Macdonald, *Sir* John A. 1870

NORTHERN PACIFIC RAILWAY, CO. Climate 1882

NOR'WESTER (Red River Settlement newspaper) The West 1865

NORWOOD, GILBERT (Writer) Boundaries 1938; Envy 1938

NORWOOD, ROBERT (Poet) Friends 1917; Purpose 1916; Religion 1917

NOVA SCOTIA Nova Scotia 1867

NOVA SCOTIA PHILANTHROPIC SOCIETY Coal 1836; Fisheries 1836; Nova Scotia 1834

NOVICK, JULIUS (American critic) Americans 1973

NOWLAN, ALDEN (Poet) Argument 1974; Automobiles 1961; Blushing 1967; Bodies 1961; Canada 1971; Causes 1967; Chickens 1958; Children 1971; Communications 1973; Computers 1971; Criticism 1960, 1967; Death 1969; Dreams 1962; Drinking 1974; Emasculation 1970; Farms 1958; Fear 1969; Flowers 1974; Friendship 1969; Generosity 1964; Girls 1961; History 1971; Humility 1968; Hunting 1961; Hypocrites 1971; Intellectuals 1971; Loneliness 1967, 1971; Love 1974; Lumberjacks 1961; Madness 1968; Marriage 1971; Men and women 1971; Modern times 1971; Moon 1971; Morality 1959; New Brunswick 1969; Ottawa 1967, 1967; Parliament 1974; Personality 1974; Poems 1962; Poetry 1967; Poets 1962; Reunions 1971; Sentiment 1974; Sex 1971, 1971; Sickness 1969; Spring 1961; State 1971; Stories 1967; Strangers 1969, 1970; Talk 1969; Torture 1964; War 1967; Wives 1973; Words 1967; World 1962

NULIGAK (Eskimo) Hudson's Bay Co. 1966

NYNYCH, STEPHANIE (Poet) Beauty 1972

O

OAKES, *SIR* HARRY (Executive) Ownership 1959; Taxation 1959

O'BROIN, PADRAIG (Poet) Lovelorn 1963

O'CALLAGHAN, EDMUND BAILEY (Rebel) Agitation 1837

ODAM, JOYCE (Poet) Love 1969

O'GRADY, STANDISH (Poet) Cold 1842; Home 1841; Patriotism 1841; Winter 1841

O'HAGEN, THOMAS (Writer) Criticism 1927; Irishmen 1909

O'LEARY, GRATTAN (Editor and senator) Bennett, R.B. 1940; Conservative Party 1958; Diefenbaker, J. 1956; Drew, George 1958; Freedom 1960; Periodicals 1965; Platforms, political 1956; Politicians 1950; The Press, freedom of 1953, 1965; Senate 1942; Voters, Votes and Voting 1970

OLESON, HELMER O. (Poet) Immortality 1952

OLIVER, FRANK (Journalist) R.C.M.P. 1906; Weather 1946

OLIVER, JOHN (Premier of B.C.) Courage 1918; Government 1927; Ideals 1927, 1927; Patronage 1920; Political parties 1918; Railways 1920; Status 1919

OLIVER, WILLIAM E. (Letter writer) War, European (1914-18) 1915

ONDAATJE, MICHAEL (Poet) Daughters 1967; Stars 1973; Wolves 1967

ONTARIO Ontario 1879

ONTARIO GOVERNMENT Transportation 1956

ONTARIO MAGISTRATES' QUARTERLY (Periodical) Hair 1967

ONTARIO. ROYAL COMMISSION ON BOOK PUBLISHING Publishing 1973

ON-TO-THE-BAY-ASSOCIATION Hudson Bay 1924

ORANGE ASSOCIATION OF BRITISH AMERICA Orangemen 1830

O'REILLY, PETER (Judge) Law and lawyers 1864

ORILLIA *PACKET* (Newspaper) Women's suffrage 1917

O'ROURKE, MICKEY (Soldier) Beer 1956

ORR, BOBBY (Hockey player) Hockey 1971

ORR, OSCAR (Vancouver magistrate) Judges 1962

OSBORN, EDWARD B. (British critic) Poets 1895

OSBORNE, *COL.* HENRY E. (Drama director) Theatre 1973

OSBORNE, WILLIAM F. (Writer) Greatness 1919

OSLER, *SIR* WILLIAM (Physician) Advice
1926; Age 1900; Ambition 1894;
Apathy 1905; Authors 1901; Books
1905; Brains 1904; Change 1918;
Charity 1903; Circumstances 1897;
Conduct of Life 1903; Conservatism
1900; Credulity 1891; Death 1917;
Dictionaries 1914; Doctors 1900's;
Dress 1913; Eating 1905; Education
1894; Errors 1913; Experience 1905;
Faith 1910; Fame 1926; Happiness
1891; Heart 1905; Heaven 1904;
Humbug 1897; Humility 1911; Ideals
1896; Ignorance 1902; Intellect 1892;
Intolerance 1902; Knowledge 1914;
Laughter 1912; Libraries 1920's;
Marriage 1897; Medicine 1891, 1895,
1897; Mind 1913; Old age 1905;
Organization 1897, 1897; Passion 1904;
Philosophy 1902; Poetry 1905; Poets
1904; Probabilities 1897; Reading 1903,
1950; Scholarship 1925; Science 1911,
1918; Scotsmen 1911; Sickness 1896;
Silence 1919; Spinsters 1897; Students
1905, 1905, 1905; Success 1899; Tact
1913; Talk 1905, 1919; Teachers 1905,
1911; Technology 1914; Thought 1905;
Truth 1889, 1905; Venereal disease
1950; Virtue 1913; War 1896; Woman
1950; Work 1905
OSTRY, BERNARD (Public servant)
Conciliation 1955
OUELETTE, DAVID (M.P.) Allegiance 1962
OUELLETTE, FERNAND (Historian)
Confederation 1962; French Canadians
1964; French language 1964
OUGHTON, LIBBY (Poet) Lesbianism 1973
OWER, JOHN B. (Critic) Canadian Legion
1967

P

PACEY, DESMOND (Critic) Americans
1968; Cruelty 1958; Future 1961;
Geography 1952; Libraries 1968;
Literature 1947; Literature, Canadian
1961
PAGE, P. K. (Poet) Art 1967; Death 1947;
Dreams 1967; Egotism 1954; Failure
1947; Headaches 1954; Leaves 1967;
Love 1946; Sleep 1954; Stenographers
1942; Tourists 1967

PALESHNUIK, EDDIE (Song writer) Floods
1950
PALLISER, *CAPTAIN* JOHN (British
explorer) Prairies 1863; Precambrian
Shield 1860; The West 1863
PAPINEAU, LOUIS-JOSEPH (Patriot)
Ambition 1838; Banks and banking
1834; Government 1827; Patriotism
1867
PAQUET, *MONSEIGNOR* LOUIS-ADOLPHE
French Canadians 1902; French
Canadians, survival 1902
PARÉ, LORENZO (Journalist) Nationalism
1958
PARK, LIBBIE C. (Business writer) Capital
1962
PARKER, DOROTHY (American wit)
French Language 1931
PARKER, *SIR* GILBERT (Novelist) Custom
1927; Death 1892; Dreams 1897; Law
and lawyers 1892
PARKER, HEADLEY (Song writer)
Maritimes 1899
PARKER, JOHN (Judge) Indians 1965
PARKES, JOSEPH (British politician)
Canadian-American relations 1861
PARKIN, JOHN C. (Architect) Ethics 1961;
Identity 1971
PARKINSON, C. NORTHCOTE (British
humourist) R.C.M.P. 1970
PARKMAN, FRANCIS (American historian)
The Conquest (1759), 1884, 1884;
Frontenac, *Count* 1877; Indians 1865;
La Salle, *Sieur de* 1869, 1869;
Monarchy 1884; Montcalm, *Marquis de*
1884
PARTI ROUGE (QUEBEC) Political
phrases
PARTRIDGE, E.A. (Farmer) Business 1925;
English language 1951; Lies and liars
1905; Socialism 1930
PATERSON, NORMAN M. (Senator) Stores
1906
PATTERSON, GERRY (Advertising
executive) Achievement 1973;
Advertising 1973
PATTERSON, SHEILA (British sociologist)
20th C. 1955
PATTERSON, TOM (Theatre promoter)
Stratford Festival 1956
PATTERSON, WILLIAM A. (M.P.) Political
phrases

PATTULO, THOMAS D. (Premier of B.C.)
British Columbia 1933; Fish 1924; The
West 1933

PAUL, CHARLES F. (Editor) Modesty 1914

PEACE TOWER, OTTAWA, See: Jones, John
C., and Kipling, R.

PEARCE, DONALD (Canadian-American
university professor) Psychology 1965;
Purpose 1965

PEARCE, HAYWOOD J., Jr. (Writer) Senate
1925

PEARSE, PETER H. (Canadian-American
consultant) Natural resources 1966

PEARSON, ANNIE S. (Mother of
L.B.Pearson) Pearson, L.B. 1972

PEARSON, LESTER B. (Prime Minister)
Agitation 1966; Cabinet ministers 1964;
Canadian-American relations 1951,
1953, 1956, 1964; Canadians 1941;
Confederation 1962; Credos 1972;
Democracy 1955; Diplomacy 1959,
1965; Disarmament 1972; Economy
1963; Elections 1955, 1963, 1965;
Failure 1963; Flag 1964, 1964; Foreign
policy 1960; French Canadians 1965;
Future 1963; Hockey 1939; Identity
1964; Journalism 1959; Languages
1967; Law courts 1960; Leadership
1958; Liberal Party 1948, 1958;
Nationalism 1967; North 1946; Nuclear
warfare 1957; Nuclear weapons 1963,
1970; Opposition 1960; Peace 1964,
1972; Pearson, L.B. 1945, 1966, 1968;
Political phrases; Politics 1960, 1960,
1968; Prime Minister 1964, 1966;
Problems 1960; Promises 1963;
Revolution 1969; Roads 1958; Society
1955, 1969; Success 1963; Trudeau,
P.E. 1968; United Nations 1965; Unity
1964; War 1957; Whereabouts 1964

PEARSON, MARYON (Wife of L.B.Pearson)
Elections 1958; Men and Women 1972

PEERS, FRANK W. (Writer on
broadcasting) Radio and TV 1969

PEGUIS (Ojibwa chief) Indians 1815

PELLETIER, GERARD (Cabinet minister)
Art 1968; Music 1972; Politics 1968;
Symbols 1970

PEMBERTON, JOSEPH D. (Surveyor)
British Columbia 1870; Loyalty 1870

PENFIELD, WILDER (Neurosurgeon)
Achievement 1962; Careers 1959;
Death 1957; Languages 1958, 1970;
Materialism 1958; Mind 1969;
Philanthropy 1963; Rest 1959;
Retirement 1959; Time 1958;
Universities 1960; Work 1960

PENTLAND, BARBARA (Musician) Music
1969

PEOPLE'S ALMANAC (Newspaper) Liberal
Party 1891

PERLIN, ALBERT (Poet) Newfoundland
1949

PERREAULT, JOSEPH FRANÇOIS
(1753-1844) (Writer) The Conquest
(1759) 1763; French Canadians,
survival 1865

PERRY, M. EUGENIE (Poet) Archives 1955

PERRY, ROBERT L. (Journalist) Coca-cola
1971; Dissent 1971; Identity 1971

PERUGINI, PETER (Vancouver
restaurateur) Dominion Day 1963

PETER, LAURENCE J. (Management
consultant) Employees 1969, 1969;
Incompetence 1969, 1969; Performance
1969; Work 1969

PETERSON, SIR WILLIAM (University
president) Industry 1911

PETROWSKY, CHRISTINA (Poet) Autumn
1967

PHARIS, GWEN (Writer; see also
Ringwood, G.P.) Canadians 1940

PHELPS, ARTHUR L. (Writer and speaker)
Americanization 1941; Continentalism
1947; Passion 1939; War 1915

PHILIP, PRINCE Buildings 1969; Hats
1969; Monarchy 1967, 1969, 1969

PHILIP, PERCY J. (Journalist) Defence 1945

PHILLIPPS-WOLLEY, CLIVE (Poet)
Boundary, Canada-U.S. 1917; United
Empire Loyalists, 1917

PHILLIPS, COL. ERIC (Industrialist)
Executives 1964

PHILLIPS, JOHN A. (Journalist) Union Jack
1945

PHILPOT, ELMORE (M.P.) Parliament,
Members of 1964

PICKERSGILL, JOHN W. (Cabinet minister)
Babies 1955; Debate 1956; King,
W.L.M. 1968; Leadership 1960;
Newfoundland 1972; Prime Minister
1964

PUGSLEY, WILLIAM (M.P.) Minorities 1913

PUNCH (LONDON) (Periodical) Macdonald, *Sir* J.A. 1891

PUNSHON, PERCY H. (Poet) Automobiles 1911

PURCHAS, SAMUEL (British compiler of works on travel) Forests 1606

PURDY, ALFRED (Poet) Automobiles 1968; Beauty 1958; Canada 1968; Canadian-American relations 1968; Carving 1968; Change 1961; Church 1968; Complacency 1962; Contentment 1944; Cows 1968; Credos 1966; Death 1965, 1970, 1973; Editors 1969; Farms 1965; Fences 1967; Genealogy 1974; God 1967; Good and evil 1962; Heritage 1974; Hockey 1965, 1969; Identity 1962, 1966, 1968; Illusions 1965; Intellectuals 1960; Intentions 1962; Life 1965, 1970; Listening 1967; Loons 1968; Losers 1965; Love 1958, 1973; Lumberjacks 1968; Me 1944, 1968; Montreal 1962; Moon 1969; Muse 1970; Noses 1970; Ocean 1957; Past 1974; People 1962; Permafrost 1967; Pioneers 1970, 1974; Poems 1968; Poets 1969, 1970; Police 1965; The Present 1959; Reading 1968; Riding 1965; Satisfaction 1959; Sculpture 1972; Searching 1944, 1968; Seeing 1967; Sleep 1970; Soldiers 1968; Tramps 1965; Travel 1965; Vancouver B.C. 1964; War, World (1939-45) 1968; Wine 1968; Wives 1965; Words 1962, 1962, 1962, 1965; Writers 1974

Q

QUARTERLY REVIEW (Edinburgh periodical) Durham's *Report* 1839

QUEBEC ACT 1774 Law and lawyers 1774

QUEBEC. EPISCOPATE Roman Catholic Church 1875

QUEBEC. COMMISSION DES DROITS CIVILS DE LA FEMME Adultery 1930

QUEBEC. LAWS, STATUTES, ETC., French language 1974; Languages 1937

QUEBEC. *QUEBEC YEARBOOK* Quebec (Province) 1963

QUEBEC. ROYAL COMMISSION OF INQUIRY ON CONSTITUTIONAL PROBLEMS Federalism 1956; Quebec (Province) 1956

QUILICO, LOUIS (Singer) Singing 1972

QUINN, EDDIE (Sports promoter) Sport 1930's

QUINN, HERBERT F. (Historian) Government 1963

R

RABELAIS, FRANÇOIS (French author) Canada 1548

RADDALL, THOMAS H. (Novelist) Argument 1945; Courage 1954; Halifax 1967

RADFORD, J. A. (Architect) Art 1893

RADISSON, PIERRE E. (Explorer) Voyageurs 1658, 1661

RADWAY'S READY RELIEF (Commercial product) Patent medicines 1863

RAE, WILLIAM FRASER (British journalist) Roads 1881

RALSTON, JAMES L. (Politician) Letters 1934

RAMSAY, ANDREW J. (J.R.) (Poet) Weather 1869

RAMSAY, J. R. (Poet, as above) Clothes 1869; Grief 1886; Mills 1880

RAND, THEODORE H. (Poet) Birds 1900; Spruce trees 1897

RANDOLPH, JOHN (U.S. congressman) Americanization 1857

RAWSON, MARY (Economist) Urban renewal 1961

READE, JOHN (Journalist) Heart 1870; Poetry 1872

READE, WILLIAM W. (British writer) Arctic 1872

REANEY, JAMES (Poet) Art 1972; Automobiles 1962; Bats 1958; Captives 1949; Childhood 1946; Drama 1966; Education 1962; Eggs 1958; Evil 1959; Fate 1949; Form 1960; Guilt 1949; Hands 1958; Lake Erie 1949; Lake Superior 1949; Lies and liars 1962; Life 1949; Love 1949; Men and women 1949; Paradise 1959; Past 1962; Places 1972; Pratt, E.J. 1957; Poetry 1972; Provincialism 1957; Riel Rebellion 1964; Searching 1963; Stratford Festival 1964; Tradition 1957; Women

1962
REDDIN, WILLIAM J. (University
professor) Youth 1963
REDMOND, MICKEY (Hockey player)
Hockey 1972
REGAN, GERALD (Premier of N.S.)
Stanfield, R. 1972
REGINA *LEADER* (Newspaper) Opposition
1902
REID, ESCOTT (Diplomat) King, W.L.M.
1971; NATO 1967
REID, KATE (Actress) Acting 1967, 1973
REID, RAYMOND (Anthologist) Songs 1973
REPO, SATU (Educator) Reality 1970
RESPONSIBLE GOVERNMENT LEAGUE
Newfoundland 1948
REVILLON BROTHERS (General
wholesalers) Trade 1906
REVELL, VILJO (Finnish architect)
Buildings 1959
REYNALL, W. H. (British poet) The
Conquest (1759) 1761
RHODENIZER, VERNON B. (Poet)
Canadians 1958
RHODES, EDGAR N. (Premier of N.S.)
Nova Scotia 1930
RHYS, HORTON (British traveller) Actors
1861; Brown, G. 1861; Hamilton, Ont.
1861; Montreal 1861; Toronto 1861
RICARD, L. N. (Anti-conscriptionist)
England 1917
RICE, INGRAM (GITZ) (Song writer) Girls
1915
RICH, JOHN (University professor)
Establishment 1968
RICHARD, HENRI (Hockey player) Hockey
1969
RICHARD, MAURICE (Hockey player)
Thought 1968
RICHARDS, ALBERT E. (Judge)
Sovereignty 1916
RICHARDSON, BURTON T. (Newspaper
editor) Senate 1959
RICHARDSON, JAMES H. (Nationalist)
Maple leaf 1860
RICHARDSON, JOAN (Poet) Discontent
1962
RICHLER, MORDECAI (Novelist)
Annexation 1964; Argument 1955;
Beauty 1955; Belief 1955; Culture
1968; Freedom 1955; God 1955;
Identity 1968; Jews 1959, 1968; Land
1959; Society 1971; Students 1955;
Teachers 1959; Travel 1972; Writers

1971, 1974
RICHMOND, *DUKE OF* (Governor-in-chief)
Pets 1819
RICKARD, THOMAS A. (Mining historian)
Dawson, Yukon 1909
RIDDEHOUGH, GEOFFREY (University
professor) Baldness 1972; Birds 1972;
Brides 1972; Cats 1972; Chastity 1972;
Enemies 1972; Funerals 1972; Gossip
1972; Hair 1972, 1972; Lectures 1972;
Sin 1972; Virginity 1972; You 1972
RIDDELL, ROBERT G. (Diplomat)
Confederation 1940
RIDDELL, WILLIAM R. (Judge) British
Empire 1929; Judges 1924; Legislatures
1909
RIDLEY, HILDA M. (Anthologist and
writer) Youth 1951
RIEL, LOUIS (Rebel) Death 1885; Disunity
1870; Government, 1869; Manitoba
1885; Métis 1884; Riel, Louis 1870,
1878, 1879, 1883, 1885, 1885, 1885
RIOPELLE, JEAN-PAUL (Painter) Painting
1972; Progress 1965
RIOUX, MARCEL (Political writer)
Experience 1965
RITCHIE, J. ALMON (Inscriptionist) May
1885; Sea 1920
RITCHIE, JOHN W. (Judge) Judges 1912
RIVARD, ADJUTOR (Author) Children
1914; Cradles 1914
RIVARD, ANTOINE (Lawyer) Law and
lawyers 1960
RIVARD, LUCIEN (Prison escapee) Escape
1965
ROBB, WALLACE H. (Poet) Memory 1966
ROBERTON, THOMAS B. (Journalist) Books
1929; Insects 1936
ROBERTS, CHARLES G. D. (*Sir*) (Author)
Ambition 1903; April 1896; Art 1901;
Authors 1943; Beauty 1893; Belief
1934; Birds 1893; Canada 1885;
Change 1886; Confederation 1880;
Confederation, Fathers of 1927; Cows
1893; Desire 1903; Doubts 1880; Effort
1893; England 1940; Evening 1896;
Fate 1896; Fishing 1893; Freedom
1893; Frogs 1893; Future 1887;
Growth 1893; Happiness 1896; Houses
1886; Immortality 1896; Insight 1893;
Loyalty 1880; Memory 1887;
Montcalm, *Marquis de* 1887;
Mountains 1892; Mysticism 1934;
Nature 1896; Night 1893; Ottawa

1910; Patriotism 1927; Poets 1887;
Purpose 1880; Railways 1927; Rivers
1893; Sea 1902; Sea shore 1893; Skating
1896; Sleep 1896; Soldiers 1893; Sorrow
1907; Spring 1893; Thought 1893;
Tides 1893; Time 1896; Universe 1893;
Unity 1885

ROBERTS, DOROTHY (Poet) Travel 1967

ROBERTS, KENNETH (American novelist)
Northwest Passage 1937

ROBERTS, LESLIE (Writer) Canadians
1952

ROBERTS, LLOYD (Writer) Heart 1937;
Land 1916

ROBERTS, MORLEY (British writer)
Canadian Pacific Railway 1887

ROBERTS, THEODORE G. (Poet) Herons
1923; Voyageurs 1913; Youth 1913

ROBERTSON, FRASER (Financial editor)
Business 1961

ROBERTSON, GEORGE (Writer) Radio and
TV 1959

ROBERTSON, HEATHER (Writer) Drinking
1970; The Pas, Man. 1970; The West
1973

ROBERTSON, JAMES (Clergyman)
Languages 1800's; Past 1895

ROBERTSON, JAMES W. (Agriculturist)
Suffering 1910; Taxation 1907

ROBERTSON, NORMAN (Public servant)
Newfoundland 1946

ROBERTSON, ROBERT GORDON (Public
servant) Public service 1968

ROBICHAUD, LOUIS J. (Premier of N.B.)
New Brunswick 1965

ROBIN, MARTIN (Historian) British
Columbia 1972

ROBINETTE, JOHN J. (Lawyer) Libel 1962

ROBINS, JOHN D. (Humourist) Trees 1943

ROBINS, TOBY (Actress) Actresses 1968

ROBINSON, D. M. (Poet) Consumers 1938

ROBINSON, *SIR* JOHN B. (Chief justice of
Upper Canada) Monarchy 1822

ROBINSON, JOHN R. (Editor) Success 1880;
Taxation 1917

ROBITAILLE, GERALD (Poet) Colours 1969

ROBLIN, DUFF (Premier of Manitoba)
Unity 1963

ROBLIN, *SIR* RODMOND P. (Premier of
Manitoba) Economics 1906; Navy
1909; Women's suffrage 1912, 1914

ROBSON, JOSEPH (Fur trader) Hudson's
Bay Co. 1752

ROBSON, THOMAS C. (Letter writer)
Women 1912

ROCHER, GUY (Sociologist) Classes 1964

RODRIGUEZ, ELIZABETH (Literary critic)
Poets 1970

ROGATNICK, ABRAHAM (Art curator) Art
1975

ROGERS, *MAJOR* A. B. (Discoverer of
Rogers Pass) Swearing (no date)

ROHER, MARTIN (Diarist) Disease 1959;
Fulfilment 1959; Learning 1959;
Living 1959; Lost 1959; Pain 1959;
Wealth 1959

ROHMER, RICHARD (Planner) Geography
1967; Natural resources 1973;
Petroleum 1973

ROLLAND, SOLANGE CHAPUT (Writer)
Disunity 1963, 1970; French
Canadians, survival 1963

ROMAN, STEPHEN B. (Executive) Ethnic
groups 1970; Private enterprise 1963

ROOKE, JOHN K. (Poet) Force 1940

ROOSEVELT, FRANKLIN D. (President of
the U.S.) Defence 1938

ROOSEVELT, THEODORE (President of
the U.S.) Annexation 1895

ROQUEBRUNE, ROBERT DE (ROBERT
LAROQUE) (Writer) Society 1964

ROSE, ALEXANDER MACGREGOR *See*
GORDON, ALEXANDER M.R.

ROSE, GEORGE MACLEAN (Publisher)
Governor general 1868

ROSEBERY, *LORD* (Prime Minister of
Great Britain) Tupper, *Sir* C. 1873

ROSENBLUTH, GIDEON (Economist)
Business 1963

ROSENTHAL, JOE (Artist) Indians 1971

ROSS, ALEXANDER (Fur trader) Métis
1856

ROSS, ALEXANDER (Writer) Technology
1969

ROSS, COLIN (Nazi) Population 1934

ROSS, GEORGE W. (Premier of Ontario)
Canadian-British relations 1901;
Constitution 1905; Election slogans
1902; Foreign relations 1905; Loyalty
1905; Prime Ministers 1913; Prohibition
1899; War of 1812, 1905

ROSS, *SIR* JOHN (Explorer) Presents 1835

ROSS, MALCOLM (University professor)
Canadians 1954; Ghosts 1954; Irony
1954, North America 1954, Tradition
1957

ROSS, PHILIP D. (Editor) Laurier, *Sir* W. 1886

ROSS, SINCLAIR (Novelist) Art 1941; Cities and towns 1941; Harvest 1968; Reality 1968

ROSS, WILLIAM W. E. (Poet) Art 1930; Cities and towns 1930; Depth 1935; Dreams 1945; Fear 1969; Fish 1928; Lakes 1930; Machinery 1930; Mystery 1934; Prime ministers 1969

ROTSTEIN, ABRAHAM (Economist) Americanization 1970; Change 1965; DEW Line 1968; Survival 1970

ROULEAU, CHARLES B. (Judge) Justice 1910

ROVERE, RICHARD H. (American journalist) Advertising 1960; Culture 1960

ROWELL, NEWTON W. (Politician) Citizens 1922; Europe 1920; Railways 1919; War dead 1920

ROWLEY, WILLIAM H. (Manufacturer) Protection 1910

ROYAL COMMISSION See CANADA. ROYAL COMMISSION

ROYAL EMIGRANT'S ALMANAC Liquor 1853

ROYAL LETTER Beavers 1632

ROYAL NORTHWEST MOUNTED POLICE R.C.M.P. 1873, 1875

RUBINOFF, LIONEL (Philosopher) Intellectuals 1968; Politics 1969

RULE, JANE (Novelist) Convention 1964

RUSSELL, FRANKLIN (Nature writer) St.Lawrence River 1970

RUSSELL, L. CASE (Poet) Women's suffrage 1912

RUSSELL, WILLIAM H. (English journalist) Caution 1865; Customs 1865

RUTHERFORD, ALEXANDER C. (Premier of Alberta) Graft 1909

RUTHERFORD, ERNEST (Scientist) Atomic energy 1904

RYAN, ED (Sergeant-at-arms, P.E.I.) Parliament 1773

RYE, FRANCIS (Poet) Winter 1887

RYERSON, EGERTON (Editor and educationist) Christianity 1826; Circumstances 1883; Destiny 1849, 1865; Education 1847, 1849; Growth 1865; Honesty 1873; Parliament, Members of 1867; Schools 1850

RYERSON, GEORGE STERLING (Physician and author) Red Cross 1924

RYERSON, WILLIAM (Brother of Egerton Ryerson) Emigration 1838

RYGA, GEORGE (Dramatist) Clay 1966

S

SABOURIN, *ABBE* ARMAND (Army Padre) War, World (1939-45) 1942

SACHLA, MARY (Poet) Mothers 1972

SAFARIAN, ALBERT E. (Economist) Nationalism 1965

SAFDIE, MOSHE (Architect) Buildings 1970

SAINT-DENIS-GARNEAU, HECTOR DE (Writer) Art 1935; Culture 1954, 1962; Death 1956; Seeing 1962; Suffering 1937 See GARNEAU, HECTOR DE SAINT-DENYS

SAINT JOHN, N.B. *TELEGRAPH JOURNAL* (Newspaper) Economics 1968

ST.LAURENT, LOUIS (Prime Minister) Business 1953; Collective security 1946; Communism 1948; Economics 1953; Governor general 1952; Languages 1967; North 1953; Pipeline debate (1956) 1957; Political phrases; Radio and TV 1957; St.Laurent, Louis 1941; United Nations 1956; World 1948

ST.LAWRENCE SEAWAY St.Lawrence Seaway 1959

ST.LEONARD, QUE., SCHOOL BOARD French language 1968

ST.PAUL, MINN., *DAILY PRESS* (Newspaper) The West 1869

ST.PAUL'S CHURCH, HALIFAX Music 1770

ST.PIERRE, PAUL (Writer) Politics 1971

SALTSMAN, MAX (M.P.) Americanism, anti-1971; Taxation 1971, 1971

SAMPSON, *DR.* JAMES (Mayor of Kingston, Ont.) Housing 1839

SAMSON, CAMIL (Politician) Social Credit 1970

SANDBURG, CARL (American poet) Snow 1928

SANDERSON, DEREK (Hockey player) Fashion 1970

SANDIFORD, PETER (Educator) Reform 1935

SANDWELL, BERNARD K. (Editor) Bosses 1935; Bourassa, Henri 1969; Frogs 1920; Lakes 1928; Languages 1920; Leaders 1928; Libraries 1928, 1928; Massey, Vincent 1952; Superiority 1928; 20th C. 1928

SANGSTER, CHARLES (Poet) Autumn 1860; Brock, Sir Isaac 1859; Civil service 1888; Destiny 1856; Failure 1860; God 1860; Invasion 1860; Love 1860; Night 1856; Plowing 1860; Unity 1864; Winning 1860; Wolfe, James 1860

SANKEY, *LORD* (British judge) B.N.A.Act (1867) 1930

SARTRE, JEAN-PAUL (French philosopher) Quebec (Province) 1971

SASKATCHEWAN COLLEGE OF PHYSICIANS AND SURGEONS Medical care 1962

SASKATOON *STAR-PHOENIX* (Newspaper) Wheat 1969

SATURDAY NIGHT (Periodical) Governor general 1898

SAUNDERS, MARSHALL (Author) Dogs 1894; Obedience 1893

SAUNDERS, RICHARD M. (Historian) Farmers 1935

SAUNDERS, THOMAS (Poet) Wilderness 1949

SAUNDERS, WILLIAM E. (Naturalist) Birds 1943; Hunting 1949; Larks 1939; Weather 1905; Wildlife 1937

SCADDING, *REVEREND* HENRY Beavers 1876

SCAMMELL, ARTHUR R. (Song writer) Fishermen 1895

SCHAFER, R. MURRAY (Composer) Music 1969, 1970; Silence 1967; Taste 1965

SCHENDEL, MICHEL VAN (Marxist writer) Rebellion (1837) 1964

SCHERMANN, KATHERINE (Nature writer) Lemmings 1956

SCHMEISER, DOUGLAS A. (Writer on law) Bill of Rights 1964

SCHROEDER, ANDREAS (Poet) Anger 1969; Questions 1971

SCOTT, DUNCAN CAMPBELL (Poet) Cemeteries 1893; Day 1935; Effort 1916; Faith 1906; Graveyards 1893; Grief 1921; Indians 1931; Kingfishers 1926; Kisses 1893; Lakes 1916; Larks 1926; Loons 1906; Modern times 1922; Parliament buildings 1926; Pine trees 1895; Poets 1922; Revolution 1922; Sea 1895; Ships 1893; Singing 1926, 1926; Souls 1893; Spring 1916; Thrushes 1926; Travel 1893

SCOTT, FRANK R. (Poet and lawyer) Advertising 1954; Art 1936; Atomic bombs 1969; Audacity 1964; Authors 1935; Biology 1945; Bombing 1945, 1945; B.N.A.Act (1867) 1964; Canadian Pacific Railway 1957; Canadian Shield 1954; Canadians 1938; Capitalism 1935; Children 1945; Coca-cola 1963; Colonialism 1942; Conduct of life 1945, 1946; Credos 1964; Dance 1973; Differences 1941; Drug stores 1945; Economics 1950; Emergencies 1950; Eyes 1964; Faith 1945; Fidelity 1954; Financiers 1957; Flowers 1973; Flying 1945, 1945, 1954, 1964; Form 1945; Government 1961; History 1952, 1964; Hope 1945; Icebergs 1973; Judges 1932; King, W.L.M. 1957, 1957, 1957, 1957, 1957; Knowledge 1954; Labour 1941; Lakes 1954; Legs 1954; Life 1945; Living 1954; Lovers 1945; Manners 1964; Me 1964; Mediocrity 1957; Metric measurement 1973; Mining 1932; Mothers 1945; Music 1945; Necessity 1945; Parachutists 1972; Past 1964; Poets 1957, 1973; Power 1941, 1945; Quebec (City) 1928; Quebec (Province) 1954; Radio and TV commercials 1954, 1972; Rain 1950; Satire 1948; Snow 1945; Space 1945; Survival 1952; Symbols 1945; Technology 1964; Toronto 1957; Travel 1945; Understanding 1954; Union 1945; Unity 1954; Violence 1945, 1964; War 1957; Water 1954, 1954; Youth 1944

SCOTT, *CANON* FREDERICK G. (Poet) Courage 1922; Death 1899; Desertion 1934; England 1926; God 1909; Immortality 1899; Lakes 1897; Mountains 1910; Nature 1910; Railways 1909; Right and wrong 1894; Time 1899; Unity 1922; Universe 1910; War dead 1885

SCOTT, JACK (Columnist) War 1959

SCOTT, *REVEREND* R.B.Y. (University professor) Confederation 1967; Property 1937

SCOTT, S. MORLEY (Historian) Canadian-American relations 1938

SCOTT, THOMAS (Executed by Riel) Métis 1870; Murder 1870

SCRIVEN, JOSEPH (Hymn writer) Jesus Christ 1884

SECORD, DONALD N. (Labour leader)
Labour unions 1960
SEELEY, JOHN R. (Social scientist) Business
1956; Church 1956; Clubs 1956; Home
1956; Telephone 1956; Universities
1967
SEGAL, JACOB I. (Poet) Jews 1950
SELBY, JOAN (Librarian) Books 1960;
Childhood 1960
SELYE, HANS (Scientist) Adaptation 1956;
Aging 1959; Causes 1963; Diseases
1951; Facts 1964; Stress 1956, 1956,
1958; Work 1972
SENATE. SPECIAL COMMITTEE ON MASS
MEDIA Communication 1970;
Corporations 1970; Journalism 1970;
Newspapers 1970; Radio and TV 1970,
1970
SENATE. SPECIAL COMMITTEE ON
POVERTY Disabilities 1970
SERVICE, ROBERT W. (Poet) Acceptance
1921; Adversity 1916; Age 1912;
Autobiography 1945; Compulsion
1907; Contentment 1921; Courage
1907; Death 1907; Despair 1907;
Failure 1907; Friends 1921; God 1907;
Gold 1907; Graveyards 1912; Heart
1912; Imagination 1921; Imperialism
1916; Lateness 1921; Life 1907, 1912,
1921; Millionaires 1910; Mothers 1912;
Mountains 1907, 1907; Nature 1907;
North 1907; Northern lights 1909;
Passion 1907; Payment 1907; Peace
1916; Promises 1907; R.C.M.P. 1909;
Sadness 1921; Smoking 1916; Soldiers
1916, 1916; Trees 1940; Trying 1912;
Universe 1912; Wanderlust 1907, 1907;
War 1916, 1921; Wilderness 1907;
Writing 1921; Yukon 1907, 1907, 1907,
1907
SETON, ERNEST THOMPSON (Naturalist)
Animals 1900; Caribou 1911; Fear
1940
SEWARD, WILLIAM H. (U.S. politician)
Annexation 1867; Canadian-American
relations 1857; Independence 1857
SEWELL, JONATHAN (Chief justice)
Immigration 1810
SHADBOLT, JACK (Painter) Me 1973
SHAIN, MERLE (Writer and broadcaster)
Alone 1973; Divorce 1973; Ethics 1973;
Fidelity 1973; Fulfilment 1973; Love
1973, 1973; Marriage 1973; Mistresses
1973; Singles 1973; Virginity 1973

SHANLEY, CHARLES DAWSON (Poet)
Ghosts 1889
SHANNON, ROBERT W. (Writer)
Quotations 1898
SHANTZ, HUGH (Politician) Speaking 1963
SHARP, MITCHELL (Politician) Canadians
1964; Cities and towns 1963; Civil
service 1958; Economy 1971; Foreign
aid 1964; Inflation 1967
SHAUGHNESSY, LORD (President
Canadian Pacific Ry.) Prairies 1903
SHAW, GEORGE BERNARD (British
dramatist) War 1928
SHAW, H.W. (Josh Billings, American
writer) Dogs 1885
SHAW, JOHN (Mayor of Toronto) Buildings
1899
SHEARD, VIRNA (Poet) Penguins 1932;
Sleep 1922
SHEPHERD, GEORGE (Writer on
Saskatchewan) Homesteads 1965
SHEPPARD, EDMUND E. (Editor) Unisex
1893
SHEPPARD, GEORGE (Reformer)
Confederation 1859, 1859;
Government, Responsible 1859
SHERMAN, FRANCIS (Poet) Death 1899
SHIELDS, ROY (Television critic) Radio
and TV 1966
SHIELDS, DR. THOMAS T. (Baptist
preacher) Roman Catholic Church 1931
SHIPWARD, MRS. SPELL (Hamilton, Ont.
tourist) Juveniles 1963
SHIRLEY, WILLIAM (Governor of
Massachusetts) Annexation 1746
SHIRREFF, PATRICK (Traveller) Manners
1835
SHOOFLER, RENALD (Poet) Affluence
1966; Poetry 1966
SHORTT, ADAM (Economist) Competition
1899; Death 1967; Speculation,
financial 1899; Wheat 1895
SHOTWELL, JAMES T.
(Canadian-American historian)
Academics 1947
SHRIVE, NORMAN (Literary historian)
Poetry 1965
SHULMAN, MORTON (Ontario M.L.A.)
Millionaires 1966
SHUMIATCHER, MORRIS C. (Lawyer)
Indians 1959
SIEBRASSE, GLEN (Poet) Grief 1965

SIEGFRIED, ANDRE (French political
scientist) Biculturalism 1937; Canada
1937; Foreign policy 1937; North 1937;
Political parties 1907, 1907

SIFTON, SIR CLIFFORD (Minister of
immigration) Capitalism 1925;
Compromise 1905; Conservation 1910;
Constitution 1922; Corporations 1900;
Election funds 1917; Electric power
1914; Foreign relations 1922; Free
trade 1897; Future 1904; Government
departments 1906, 1906; Immigrants
1922; Independence 1921; Land 1906;
Liberty 1917; Prosperity 1929; Reform
1919; War, European (1914-18) 1915;
Welfare 1923; The West 1897, 1906;
Winnipeg 1899

SILCOX, DAVID (Educator) Canada
Council 1972

SILLIMAN, BENJAMIN (American
traveller) Quebec (Province) 1822

SIMCOE, JOHN GRAVES
(Lieutenant-governor of Upper
Canada) Constitution 1792; Details
1796; Ontario 1791; Soldiers 1787

SIMEON, RICHARD (Political scientist)
Elites 1972

SIMMS, JAMES (Attorney general of
Newfoundland) Debate 1833

SIMON, RENÉ F. (Swiss lawyer) Canada
1963

SIMPSON, SIR GEORGE (Governor of
H.B.C.) Fur trade 1821; Hudson's Bay
Co. 1821

SIMPSON, JIMMY (Mayor of Toronto)
Communism 1934

SIMPSON, THOMAS (Explorer) Fame 1840

SINCLAIR, DONALD (Medical director)
Mental illness 1963

SINCLAIR, GORDON (Author) Journalism
1944

SINCLAIR, LISTER (Writer and
broadcaster) Canadians 1949; English
language 1949; Foreign relations 1949;
Languages 1944; Radio and TV 1956;
Science 1945; Toronto 1946

SINGER, JAMES C. (Poet) Mothers 1929;
Words 1929

SIROIS, DR. JEAN (Neurologist) Medicine
1956

SISSONS, JACK H. (Judge) Civil service
1968; Conviction 1957; Drunk 1968;
Eskimos 1963; Justice 1968

SITTING BULL (Sioux Indian chief)
Boundary, Canada-U.S. 1877; Indians
1877

SIVELL, RHODA (Poet) Saskatchewan 1912

SKALA, DIANA (Poet) Change 1952

SKELTON, ISABEL (Writer) Women 1924

SKELTON, OSCAR D. (Civil servant) British
Empire 1922; Foreign policy 1922;
Geography 1916; Patronage 1921;
Railways 1916

SKELTON, ROBIN (Poet) Love 1968; Music
1955

SLADEN, DOUGLAS (British traveller)
Sunday 1895; Vancouver, B.C. 1895

SLEIGH, BURROWS W.A. (Pioneer and
soldier) Law and lawyers 1853

SLOAN, THOMAS (Journalist) Separatism
1963

SLOCUM, JOSHUA (Nova Scotia seafarer)
Navigation 1899; Sea 1900; Wind 1900

SMALLWOOD, JOSEPH R. (Premier of
Nfld.) Achievement 1972; Ambition
1972; Confederation 1960; Dreams
1950; Economics 1949, 1967;
Federalism 1968, 1968; Fishermen
1954; Invective 1972; Labour unions
1959; Maritimes 1973; Mistakes 1951;
Newfoundland 1948, 1948, 1959, 1967,
1969, 1972, 1972; Ontario 1968;
Parliament, Members of 1968;
Personalities 1970; Politics 1963;
Quebec (Province) 1967; Smallwood,
J.R. 1972; Trudeau, P.E. 1968; Union
Jack 1964

SMART, JAMES A. (Civil servant) Wheat
1897

SMILEY, DONALD V. (Political scientist)
Two nations theory 1967

SMILEY, ROBERT (Editor) Newspapers
1854

SMITH, ALLAN C.L. (University professor)
Continentalism 1970; Culture 1970

SMITH, ARTHUR J.M. (Poet) Art 1928;
Beauty 1943; The Dead 1967; Death
1938, 1959; Intellectuals 1928;
McLuhan, M. 1967; North 1954; Poetry
1928, 1973; Poets 1960; The Present
1926; Pundits 1954; Revolution 1938;
Sentimentality 1940; Singing 1936;
Universities 1925; Words 1954

SMITH, DONALD A. (Lord Strathcona)
Defence 1907; Government 1873;
Judgment 1878; North 1915;
Opportunity 1915; Success 1878; Thrift
1925; Voters, 1873
SMITH, FRANK (Politician) Toronto 1870
SMITH, GOLDWIN (Editor and author)
Annexation 1866, 1910; Atheism 1897;
Bigotry 1880; British Empire 1906;
B.N.A.Act (1867) 1867; Buildings 1880;
Canada 1878; Colonialism 1881;
Colonies 1863; Communism 1872;
Confederation 1872; Continentalism
1890, 1891; Death 1894; Democracy
1887; Disunity 1889; Emigration 1880,
1891; Evolution 1906; Farmers 1910;
Freedom 1890; French Canadians
1878, 1900; Funerals 1910; Geology
1904; The Globe; Toronto 1833, 1833;
Government 1861, 1878; Governor
General 1891; History 1861; Honesty
1906; Humanities 1893; Humanity
1870; Imagination 1879; Industry
1891; Injustice 1883; Journalism 1881;
Liberalism 1891; Liberty 1863;
Literature 1885; Literature, Canadian
1890; 1891; Macdonald, Sir J.A. 1882,
1884, 1884; Mackenzie, Alexander
(Prime Minister) 1910; Markets 1891;
Marriage 1880; Nation 1889; Natural
Resources 1891; Newspapers 1903; Old
Age 1903; Ontario 1889; Opposition
1905; Orthodoxy 1879; Ottawa 1884;
Patriotism 1878, 1894; Pioneers 1883;
Political parties 1872, 1873; Political
phrases; Politics 1861, 1925;
Pornography 1880; Pragmatists (no
date); Provinces 1878; Quebec
(Province) 1863; Quotations 1911;
Science 1912; Sectionalism 1878;
Senate 1872; Socialism 1908; Society
1872; The Sovereign 1883; Speeches
1872; Style (no date); Thought 1883;
Titles of honour 1890; The West 1910;
Winnipeg 1884
SMITH, MRS. J.A. (Poet) Sunshine 1935
SMITH, JOE P. (Historian) Boundary,
Canada-U.S. 1940
SMITH, LEO (Musician) Music 1924
SMITH, LILIAN (Children's librarian)
Reading 1953
SMITH, MARY ELLEN (Member of Legis.
Assembly, B.C.) Women's rights 1928

SMITH, SIR MONTAGUE (British judge)
Law and lawyers 1882
SMITH, OLIVIA (Suffragette) Justice 1910
SMITH, RAY (Writer) Cape Breton 1967;
Confederation centennial (1967), 1967;
Nova Scotia 1967
SMITH, SIDNEY (President, University of
Toronto) Conservative Party 1942;
Education 1934; Intellectuals 1961;
People 1957
SMITH, STEVE (Poet) Cancer 1964; Fate
1964; Gardens 1964; God 1964;
Sweetness 1964; Wilderness 1964
SMITH, WILLIAM (Chief Justice of
Quebec) Constitution, British 1788
SMITH, WILLIAM W. (Poet) Houses 1888;
Northern lights 1888
SMYTH, SIR DAVID W. (Surveyor-general)
Elections 1792
SMYTHE, CONN (Hockey promoter)
Confidence 1967; Hockey 1940's; Sport
1952
SNIDER, CHARLES H.J. (Journalist) Arctic
1928
SNOWBALL, JENNIE (Eskimo) Ookpik
1963
SNOWDEN, VISCOUNT (British politician)
Bennett, R.B. 1934
SOCIAL CREDIT PARTY (CREDITISTE)
Election slogans 1962
LA SOCIETE DES ECRIVAINS CANADIENS
Culture 1949
LA SOCIETE SAINT-JEAN-BAPTISTE DE
MONTREAL Unity 1954
SOLANDT, OMOND M. (Public servant)
Value 1969
SOLLY, WILLIAM (Literary historian)
Society 1962
SOLURSH, DR. LIONEL Behaviour 1969
SOLWAY, ADAM (Indian chief) Indians
1970
SOLWAY, DAVE (Poet) Smoking 1960
SOMERS, HARRY (Composer) Music 1969
SOMMER, RICHARD (Poet) Sunshine 1969
SONS OF FREEDOM SECT Doukhobors
1960's
SOUSTER, RAYMOND (Poet) Academics
1958; Artists 1944; Autumn 1961; Beds
1955; Birds 1969; Blacks 1967; Death
1954, 1961; Emptiness 1968; Falling
1958; Flowers 1972; Identity 1958;
Institutions 1962; Loneliness 1951;
Nature 1965; New Year 1971; Nothing
1949; Performance 1964; Poets 1944,

1964; Prostitutes 1955; Rain 1964;
Roads 1967; Sorrows 1971; Streets
1947; Trees 1969; Winter 1968;
Woman 1955

SOUTHESK, *EARL* OF (British traveller)
Buffalo 1860, 1860; Endurance 1859;
Flies 1859; Meals 1859; Missionaries
1860; Northern lights 1860; Pemmican
1859

SPARSHOTT, FRANCIS (Philosopher)
Academics 1972; Argument 1972;
Criticism 1967; The Dead 1958;
Discussion 1972; Dumb 1958; Love
1960, 1969; Philosophers 1958;
Philosophy 1972, 1972; Questions 1958;
Quiet 1972; Slogans 1958; Students
1968; Universities 1968

SPEARS, HEATHER (Poet) Eyes 1967;
Hospitals 1958

SPECTATOR (LONDON) (Newspaper)
Durham's *Report* 1839

SPENCE, THOMAS (Writer) Prairies 1879

SPENCE, WISHART (Judge) Accusation
1966

SPENCER, ROBERT A. (Historian) Policy
1959

SPENCER, THEODORE (Harvard Univ.
professor) Canada 1949

SPERL, ALLEN (Poet) Noses 1970

SPICER, KEITH (Public servant) Foreign
aid 1966

SPINKS, SARAH (Writer) Women 1972

STACEY, *COL.* CHARLES P. (Army
historian) Army 1955; Soldiers 1967

STANFIELD, ROBERT L. (Politician)
Elections 1972; Prime Ministers 1972;
Stanfield, R.L. 1967, 1973

STANLEY, *LORD* (1799-1886) (Colonial
secretary) Church 1841

STANLEY, *LORD* (1841-1908) (Governor
General) External relations 1891

STANLEY, CARLETON W. (Educator)
Money 1922

STANLEY, GEORGE F.G. (Historian) Flag
1965; French Canadians 1968; Riel,
Louis 1955; Independence 1970;
Soldiers 1954; War of 1812, 1957

STARNES, RICHARD (American columnist)
Canadians 1965

STAUFFER, *REVEREND* B.H. Macdonald,
Sir J.A. 1915

STEACIE, EDGAR W.R. (Scientist)
Universities 1956, 1957, 1960

STEAD, ROBERT J.C. (Novelist) Authors
1943; Canada 1908; Englishmen 1917;
Immigrants 1908; Law and lawyers
1917; Pioneers 1911; Prairies 1908;
R.C.M.P. 1917; Settlers 1908; War 1918

STEDINGH, WAYNE (Poet) Fathers 1970

STEELE, JAMES S. (Educator) Academics
1969; Spying 1968; Universities 1970

STEELE, *SIR* SAMUEL B. (R.C.M.P. officer)
Lynching 1915

STEENMAN, LEONARD F. (Song writer)
Cobalt, Ont. 1910; Ontario 1910

STEFANSSON, VILHJALMUR (Explorer)
Eskimos 1908, 1933; North 1922

STEIN, DAVID LEWIS (Poet) Future 1972

STEIN, HARRY L. (Educationist) Education
1956

STEINBERG, NATHAN (Grocer) Food 1959

STEINHAUR, HENRY B. (Methodist
missionary to the Ojibway) Indians
1898

STEINHOUSE, HERBERT (Author and
broadcaster) Police 1958;
Sensationalism 1958

STEPHEN, ALEXANDER M. (Writer) Man
1963; Maple trees 1923; Regina, Sask.
1928

STEPHEN, GEORGE (President, Canadian
Pacific Railway) Canadian Pacific Ry.
1884; Work 1911

STEPHENSON, HARRY E. (Historian)
Advertising 1940

STEPHENSON, *SIR* WILLIAM (British spy
chief) Spying 1962

STERN, KARL (Religious writer)
Knowledge 1951

STERNE, LAURENCE (British novelist)
Northwest Passage 1759

STEUART, DAVID (Sask. Liberal leader)
Liberal Party 1975

STEVENS, HOMER (Labour leader) Labour
unions 1973

STEVENS, JOHN (Writer) Killing 1963

STEVENS, PETER (Poet) Prairies 1969;
Singing 1969

STEVENSON, D.B. (Poet) Work 1974

STEVENSON, *DR.* GEORGE H.
(Psychiatrist) War 1959

STEVENSON, JOHN A. (Journalist) Pearson,
L.B. 1958

STEVENSON, WARREN (Poet) Museums
1963

STEWART, ALEXANDER C. (Poet) Authors
1896; Critics 1896; Lakes 1896

STEWART, ALISTAIR (M.P.) Norman,
    Herbert 1957; Speech 1958
STEWART, ELIHU (Forester) Forests 1908
STEWART, GEORGE (JR.) (Writer)
    Magazines 1887
STEWART, THOMAS B.P. (Poet) Freedom
    1887; Thought 1887
STEWART, WALTER (Journalist)
    International joint boards 1971;
    Journalism 1971
STINGLE, RICHARD (Writer) Mythology
    1960
STOBIE, MARGARET R. (Literary historian)
    Sex 1973
STOCK, BRIAN (Critic) Expatriates 1964;
    Identity 1964
STONE, LEROY O. (Statistician)
    Immigration 1961
STOWE-GULLEN, DR. AUGUSTA (Women's
    leader) War 1920's
STRACHAN, BISHOP JOHN Confederation
    1839; English language 1851;
    Parliament, Members of 1821; Voters,
    Votes and Voting 1835
STRATFORD, REGINALD K. (Research
    chemist) Industry 1953
STRATHCONA, LORD See SMITH,
    DONALD A.
STRATON, BARRY (Poet) Charity 1884;
    Ducks 1884; Unity 1884
STRICKLAND, MAJOR SAMUEL (Pioneer
    settler) Ghosts 1853; Ontario 1853
STRINGER, ARTHUR (Novelist) Beavers
    1949; Character 1920; Dreams 1929;
    Failure 1929; Freedom 1896; Home
    1907; Housewives 1929; Ideals 1944;
    Love 1907; Marriages 1929; Men and
    women 1944; Superiority 1944;
    Symbols 1938; The West 1907; Women
    1929
STYKOLT, STEFAN (Economist) Bank of
    Canada 1960
SUCH, PETER (Poet) Archery 1973
SUESS, EDUARD (German geologist)
    Precambrian Shield 1888
SULLIVAN, ALAN (Novelist) Patriotism
    1914
SULLIVAN, ROBERT B. (Politician and
    judge) Ontario 1838; Text books 1838;
    Trade 1847
SUNDAY, JOHN (Indian missionary)
    Families 1875
SURPLIS, HERB (Journalist) Business 1964

SUTHERLAND, REVEREND ALEXANDER
    (Writer) Farming 1881; Mosquitoes
    1881
SUTHERLAND, DONALD (M.P.) Civil
    service 1918
SUTHERLAND, JOHN (Critic) Socialism
    1947; Writers 1953
SUTHERLAND, RONALD (University
    professor) Bilingualism 1970;
    Literature 1971
SUTHERLAND, R.J. (Defence research
    writer) Defence 1962
SUTTON, HORACE (American travel
    writer) Tourists 1950
SWAN, SGT. JOE (Vancouver policeman)
    Law and lawyers 1975, 1975
SWAYZE, WALTER E. (University
    professor) Americanism, anti-1957
SWEEZEY, ROBERT O. (Company
    president) Patronage 1931; Rewards
    1931
SWETTENHAM, JOHN (Biographer)
    Currie, General Sir A. 1917
SWINTON, GEORGE (Art critic) Eskimos
    1965
SYKES, ROD (Mayor of Calgary) Petroleum
    1973
SYMONS, SCOTT (Writer) Things 1971

T

"T.D." Mackenzie, A. (Prime Minister) 1892
TACHE, ARCHBISHOP
    ALEXANDRE-ANTONIN Friendship
    1880's; Minorities 1872; Red River Cart
    1882; The West 1869
TACHE, ETIENNE-PASCAL (Premier of
    United Canada) French Canadians
    1846
TACHE, EUGENE Quebec (Province) 1883
TACHEREAU, LOUIS A. (Premier of
    Quebec) Bennett, R.B. 1930
TAFT, WILLIAM H. (U.S. President) Trade
    1911
TALBOT, EDWARD ALLEN (Pioneer
    settler) Montreal 1824; Schools 1824;
    Toronto 1824, 1824
TALESE, GAY (American journalist) The
    Press 1969
TALLMAN, WARREN (Literary critic) Self
    1960

TALON, JEAN (Intendant of New France)
Girls 1670

TARASOV, ANATOLY (Russian hockey
player) Hockey 1969

TARD, LOUIS-MARTIN Medicine 1968

TARDIVEL, JULES-PAUL (Nationalist)
French Canadians, survival 1895, 1902,
1904; Nationalism 1904

TARR, E.J. (Lawyer) Oratory 1937;
Speeches 1937

TARTE, JOSEPH I. (Politician) Cabinet
1896; Elections 1896; French
Canadians 1900

TAYLOR, ANNIE EDSON (American; first
person to go over Niagara Falls)
Niagara Falls 1901

TAYLOR, CHARLES (Writer on politics)
Unity 1970

TAYLOR, EDWARD P. (Financier) Beer
1941; Business men 1959; Management
1957, Nationalism 1963; People 1959;
Taylor, E.P. 1959, 1959, 1968; Winning
1964; Work 1959

TAYLOR, J.W. (U.S. consul) Geography
1862; Manitoba 1861

TAYLOR, MAURICE K. (Company director)
Science 1969

TAYLOR, *SIR* THOMAS W. (Chief Justice)
Justice 1887

TAYLOR, WILLIAM HENRY (Poet) North
1913

TELESCOPE (Kingston Penitentiary
newspaper) Macphail, Agnes 1954

TEMPLETON, JEAN (Actress) Success 1964

TENNANT, VERONICA (Dancer) Dance
1971

TENNYSON, BERTRAM (Poet) The West
1896

TENNYSON, *LORD* ALFRED (British poet)
Canadian-British relations 1872;
Franklin, *Sir* John 1875

TENNYSON, *LADY* EMILY (British poet's
wife) United Empire Loyalists 1895

THATCHER, ROSS (Premier of Sask.)
Constitution 1967; Elections 1971;
Electoral ridings 1971; Socialism 1968

THOMAS, AUDREY (Novelist) Me 1970

THOMAS, JAMES H. (British politician)
Humbug 1930

THOMAS, PETER (Poet) Power 1970

THOMAS, WALTER K. (University
professor) Soldiers 1971

THOMPSON, DAVID (Geographer) Beavers
1784, 1784; Hudson Bay 1784;
Hudson's Bay Co. 1850; Instinct 1784;
Pacific Coast 1811; Rainbows 1784;
Rivers 1784; Thompson, D. 1811; The
West 1784

THOMPSON, *SIR* JOHN S.D. (Prime
Minister) Cartwright, *Sir* R. 1892, 1892;
History 1890; Law and lawyers 1892;
Loyalty 1886; Mosquitoes 1893;
Speeches 1892; Union Jack 1893; Unity
1892

THOMPSON, KENT (Author) Strangers
1968; Work 1968

THOMPSON, ROBERT (Social Credit Party
leader) Canadian-American relations
1963; Flag 1964; House of Commons
1962, 1966

THOMPSON, T. PHILLIPS (Poet)
Economics 1887; Teaching 1887

THOMPSON, TOMMY (Toronto parks
commissioner) Permission 1960

THOMPSON, WILLIAM IRWIN (Professor
of English) Future 1971

THOMSON, DALE C. (Biographer)
Mackenzie, Alexander (Prime Minister)
1960

THOMSON, DON W. (Poet) Computers
1961

THOMSON, *VERY REVEREND* JAMES S.
(Moderator of United Church) Morals
1958

THOMSON, ROY (Publisher) Advertising
1965; Business 1965; Colours 1965;
Convention 1949; Credit 1965;
Frankness 1965; Money 1965;
Newspapers 1960, 1968; Radio and TV
1959; Radio and TV commercials 1965;
Success 1963, 1965; Titles of honour
1963, 1963

THOMSON, TOM (Painter) Painters 1935

THOMSON, WILLIAM A. (Railroader and
M.P.) Economics 1863

THORBURN, HUGH G. (Political scientist)
Business 1963; Cabinet 1961

THOREAU, HENRY DAVID (American
author) Canada 1851; Canadians 1850;
Climate 1850; Government 1866; Place
names 1853; Quebec (City) 1866

THORINGTON, JAMES MONROE
(Mountaineer) Rocky Mountains 1925

THORNTON, SIR HENRY (C.N.R.
Executive) Advertising 1926; Radio and
TV 1929, 1929

THURSTON, HERBERT (Toronto
policeman) Morality 1964
TIGER, LIONEL (Sociologist) Automobiles
1971; Friendship 1969; Hunting 1971;
Rights 1971
TIKTAK (Eskimo) Thought 1970
TOCQUEVILLE, ALEXIS DE (French
political writer) French Canadians,
survival 1838; Happiness 1838
TODGHAM, RON (President, Chrysler
Canada) Automobiles 1965
TOLMIE, SIMON F. (Premier of B.C.)
British Columbia 1930; Election slogans
1933
TOQUE, P. (Writer) Fisheries 1878
TORONTO DAILY LEADER (Newspaper)
Parliamentary debates 1855
TORONTO, DAILY MAIL (Newspaper) Riel,
Louis 1885
TORONTO, GLOBE (Newspaper)
Annexation 1874; Associations 1871;
Banks and banking 1860; British
Columbia 1884; Canada 1861;
Canadian Pacific Ry. 1870, 1891; Cities
and towns 1882; Citizenship 1865;
Clear Grits 1850; Climate 1869;
Confederation 1863; Corruption 1851;
Diplomacy 1858; Dominion Day 1867;
Education 1853, 1853; Egotism 1865;
Elections 1882; Foreign policy 1874;
Galt, Sir A. 1858; Governor General
1860; Grand Trunk Ry. 1857; Holidays
1924; Howe, Joseph 1872; Hudson's
Bay Co. 1852; Labour strikes 1872;
Labour unions 1872; Macdonald, Sir
J.A. 1858, 1870; Macdonald J.S. 1870;
National Policy (1878) 1880;
Nationality 1847; Pacific scandal 1874;
Parades 1872; Parliamentary
representation 1853; Prices 1854;
Reform Party 1867; The West 1859,
1869; War, European (1914-18) 1914
TORONTO, GLOBE AND MAIL
(Newspaper) Canadian-American
relations 1957; Doctors 1962; Housing
1967; Ontario 1960; Speech from the
throne 1969; Trudeau, P.E. 1972
TORONTO, LEADER (Newspaper) Canada
1870; United States 1862
TORONTO, MAIL (Newspaper) Emigration
1887
TORONTO, NEWS (Newspaper) Riel, Louis
1885

TORONTO, REFORMERS Government
1837
TORONTO, STAR (Newspaper) Governor
General 1905; Refugees 1970; Toronto
1969
TORONTO, TYPOGRAPHICAL SOCIETY
Labour unions 1844; Printers 1845
TORONTO, UNIVERSITY. PRESIDENT'S
COMMITTEE Universities 1965
TORY, HENRY MARSHALL (Educator)
Royal commissions 1939
TOWN, HAROLD (Painter) Art 1975,
Artists 1964; Canada Council 1964;
Crime 1964; Gardens 1964; Horses
1964; Painting 1960, 1961, 1965;
Senate 1964; Things 1960; Travel 1960
TOYE, WILLIAM (Editor) Disunity 1962
TOYNBEE, ARNOLD (British historian)
French Canadians, destiny 1949;
French Canadians, survival 1948
TRACY, NEIL (Poet) Virtue 1938
TRAILL, CATHERINE PARR (Author)
Clothes 1855; Duty 1855; Fashion
1855; Ghosts 1833; Hope 1834; Land
1833; Laziness 1855; Necessity 1836;
Past 1833; Settlers 1836; Trees 1836,
1894; Whiskey 1833; Workmanship
1868
TRAQUAIR, RAMSAY (Architect)
Canadians 1923; Voters 1923
TREATY OF PARIS Canada 1763
TREMLETT, THOMAS (Judge) Lies and
liars 1811
TRIQUET, PAUL (Army leader) Enemies
1943
TROLLOPE, ANTHONY (British novelist)
Canadian-American relations 1862;
Insolence 1862; Parliament Buildings
1862; Streets 1862; United States 1862;
University of Toronto 1862
TROTTER, BEECHAM (Autobiographer)
Canadian-American relations 1925
TROTTER, BERNARD F. (Poet) Death
1912; Trees 1916
TROTTER, REGINALD G. (Historian)
Colonialism 1940; Confederation 1930;
History 1924; Nationality 1945
TROTTIER, PIERRE (Poet) Winter 1963,
1970
TROW, JAMES (Traveller) Grasshoppers
1875
TRUDEAU, MARGARET (Wife of the
Prime Minister) Trudeau, P.E. 1974

TRUDEAU, PIERRE ELLIOTT (Prime
  Minister) Abortion 1971; Arctic 1969;
  Atomic missiles 1969; Auditor General
  1972; Authority 1968; Bennett, W.A.C.
  1972; Bilingualism 1968; Bravery 1968;
  British Commonwealth 1969; Cabinet
  1968; Canadian-American relations
  1963, 1969, 1969, 1969, 1971;
  Canadian-French relations 1969;
  Canadians 1968, 1971; Change 1970,
  1970; Civil service 1973; Climate 1972;
  Communism 1968; Compromise 1969;
  Conduct of life 1969; Confederation
  1965; Constitution 1971; Defence 1968,
  1969; Democracy 1957, 1958, 1958,
  1968; Diplomacy 1969; Discipline
  1968; Ecology 1970, 1970; Economics
  1968; Elections 1972; Experience 1968;
  Federalism 1962, 1969; Finance 1961;
  Flowers 1973; Foreign relations 1968;
  Freedom 1968; French Canadians
  1962, 1962, 1968, 1968; French
  Canadians, destiny 1968; French
  language 1968; Future 1971; God
  1972; Government 1968, 1972; Gross
  National Product 1971, 1971; Hecklers
  1969; Identity 1970, 1972; Indians
  1969, 1969; Individuality 1964, 1968,
  1968; Inflation 1970; Insurrection
  1970; Intentions 1974; Invective 1971,
  1971; Justice 1970, 1972; Kisses 1969;
  Labour unions 1975; Languages 1968;
  Liberalism 1968; Memory 1976;
  Minorities 1970; Monarchy 1967, 1970;
  Morality 1971; Morals 1967; Nation
  1968; Nationalism 1962, 1962, 1964,
  1969, 1971; Natural resources 1970;
  NATO 1969; Olympic games 1972,
  1976; Opposition 1968, 1968, 1969,
  1972; Ottawa 1970; Parliament,
  Members of 1969; Patriotism 1969,
  1971; Political phrases; Politics 1961;
  Pollution 1970; Power 1970; Prime
  Minister 1969; Problems 1968;
  Promises 1969; Promises, political 1972;
  Quebec (Province) 1961, 1961, 1967,
  1968, 1969; Reason 1968; Revolution
  1942, 1964; Rich 1968; Roman Catholic
  Church 1958; Rules 1969; Separatism
  1968, 1970, 1970, 1971, 1974; Socialism
  1961; Society 1968; Sovereignty 1968;
  Speaker of the House of Commons
  1968; State 1968; Taxation 1968;
  Teachers 1968; Technology 1969;

Tolerance 1969; Trudeau, P.E. 1968,
  1970, 1972; Unity 1962; Voters 1969;
  Wheat 1968; Work ethic 1972
TRUDEL, MARCEL (Historian) Disunity
  1970
TUCKER, ALBERT (Principal, Glendon
  College) Identity 1972
TUPPER, SIR CHARLES H. (Prime
  Minister) Animosity 1880's; Canadian
  Pacific Ry. 1880; Laurier, Sir W. 1900;
  Mind 1860; National Policy (1878)
  1876; Pacific Scandal 1873; Political
  phrases; Prairies 1879; Provinces 1864
TUPPER, STANLEY R. (American
  politician) Finance 1967; Water 1967
TURNER, JOHN N. (Politician) Crises 1967;
  House of Commons 1968; Parliament,
  Members of 1968; Privacy 1970;
  Problems 1973
TWAIN, MARK (American author) Girls
  1881; Montreal 1881; Publishing 1971
TWEEDIE, LEMUEL J. (Premier of N.B.)
  Provinces 1901
TWEEDSMUIR, LORD (John Buchan;
  Governor General) Bridges 1937;
  British Empire 1936; Canada 1901;
  Doctors 1936; Durham's Report 1939;
  Ethnic groups 1936; Foreign relations
  1937; Genius 1937; Governor General
  1937, 1937, 1956; Loyalty 1937; North
  1937; Scotland 1936; Sovereignty 1937;
  Talk 1935; The West 1941
TWINING, W.J. (Soldier) Precambrian
  Shield 1878
TYRRELL, JOSEPH B. (Explorer) Living
  1965; Thompson, David 1911; 20th C.
  1901
TYSON, THOMAS F. (Accountant) Civil
  service 1963

U

ULASOVETZ, VIOLET (Poet) Stars 1949
UNDERHILL, FRANK H. (Historian)
  Americanism, anti- 1954; Annexation
  1951; Biography 1945; Blake, E. 1957;
  Books 1946; Business 1931;
  Canadian-American relations 1957;
  Caution 1951; Classes 1935;
  Confederation centennial (1967) 1966;
  Conservatives 1954; Culture 1959;
  Definition 1944; Diplomacy 1953;
  Economics 1944; Economists 1933;

Freedom 1947; Ideas 1946; Identity 1964; Irony 1945; King, W.L.M. 1944, 1944, 1948, 1948, 1950; Leaders 1939; Liberalism 1946; Nation 1964; Neighbours 1959; No 1962; Personalities 1960; Planning 1947; Reciprocity (1911) 1935; Revolution 1946; Statesmen 1948; Toronto 1958; Tragedy 1955; Voters 1957; Woodsworth, J.S. 1944

UNITED CHURCH OF CANADA Capitalism 1933; Christianity 1932; Church 1932

UNITED FARMERS Political phrases

UNITED STATES. ARTICLES OF CONFEDERATION Annexation 1777

UNITED STATES, CONGRESS Annexation 1886

UNITED STATES, CONTINENTAL CONGRESS Dominion 1774

UNITED STATES, DEPT. OF STATE Defence 1963

UNITED STATES, SENATE Annexation 1869

UNIVERSITY OF MANITOBA. DEPT. OF HISTORY Transportation 1948

UNTEL, *FRÈRE See* DESBIENS, JEAN-PAUL

UNWIN, J.L. (Writer on social credit) Bankers 1938

UPPER CANADA ALMANAC War of 1812 1815

V

VALLIERES, PIERRE (Radical) French Canadians 1971; Roman Catholics 1971

VANCOUVER *PROVINCE* (Newspaper) Boundaries 1903

VANCOUVER, *SUN* (Newspaper) Bennett, W.A.C. 1959

VANDRY, *MONSEIGNEUR* FERDINAND (University rector) Duplessis, M. 1952

VAN HORNE, *SIR* WILLIAM C. (Railway builder) Books 1920; Canadian-American relations 1891; Canadian Pacific Ry. 1880's, 1880's, 1884, 1885, 1890, 1890, 1895; Collections 1920; Competition 1920; Conduct of life 1920; Conservative Party 1884; Discipline 1920; Enterprise 1920; Families 1909; Fools 1891, 1895; Genealogy (no date); Hudson's Bay Co. 1891; Humbug 1909; Independence

1920; Industry 1890's; Labour strikes 1912; Laziness 1920; Motives 1959; Painting 1920; Patriotism 1920; Peace 1910; Poker (game) 1920; Prairies 1892; Protection 1916; Reciprocity (1911) 1911, 1911; Sleep 1913; Trade 1914; Transportation 1886, about 1902; Van Horne, *Sir* W. (no date); War 1912; Wheat, about 1912

VANIER, GEORGES (Governor General) Aging 1967

VAN LOON, RICK (University professor) Politics 1970

VAN STOLK, MARY (Writer on social problems) Children 1972

VARLEY, FREDERICK H. (Painter) God 1959; Trouble 1959

VARSITY (TORONTO) (Newspaper) Editors 1886

VAUDREUIL-CAVAGNAL, *MARQUIS DE* (Governor of New France) Quebec (City) 1759; Roman Catholics 1760

VAUGHAN, BERNARD (Jesuit) Protestants 1910

VAUGHAN, *SIR* WILLIAM (British poet) Poets 1630

VERCHERES, MADELEINE DE (Heroine) Fame 1699

VERIGIN, JOHN J. (Doukhobor leader) Doukhobors 1947

VERIGIN, MICHAEL (Doukhobor leader) Doukhobors 1950

VICTORIA *(QUEEN)* Smith, Donald A. (*Lord* Strathcona) (no date)

VICTORIA *BRITISH COLONIST* (Newspaper) Airplanes 1911; National Anthem 1926

VICTORIA, *DAILY BRITISH COLONIST* (Newspaper) Chinese 1878; Confederation 1871; Mountains 1871

VIGER, DENIS B. (Politician) Maple trees 1836

VIGNEAULT, GILLES (Singer) Nationality 1972; Winter 1965

VILLENEUVE, *CARDINAL* JEAN M.R. St. Laurent, L. 1941

VILLENEUVE, ARTHUR (Painter) Painting 1972

VINCENT, HENRY (English writer) Canadian-British relations 1838

VINER, JACOB (Economist) Royal commissions 1957

VIZINCZEY, STEPHEN (Novelist) Freedom
1969; Love 1965; The Present 1969;
Woman 1965
VOLKOFF, BORIS (Dancer) Dance 1974
VOLTAIRE (French author) Canada 1759,
1760; Quebec (Province) 1762
VOZNESENSKY, ANDREI (Russian poet)
Population 1971

W

"W. TORONTO" (Pseud.) Curling 1877
WADDINGTON, ALFRED (Pioneer and
author) Gold rushes 1858
WADDINGTON, MIRIAM (Poet) Canadians
1967; Children 1967; Conduct of life
1972; Death 1957; Dreams 1955; Fear
1972; Forests 1958; Home 1966; Hope
1969; Identity 1966; Jews 1967; Life
1955; Me 1966; Modern times 1955;
Nationalism 1969; Negation 1958;
Poets 1969; Pornography 1969, 1972;
Sex 1967; Sorrow 1941; Survival 1969;
Time 1966; Wine 1955; World 1969;
Writers 1972
WADE, MASON (American writer on
Quebec) Culture 1957; Problems 1964
WADE, WILLIAM W. (American editor)
United States 1951
WAITE, PETER B. (Historian) Blake,
Edward 1971; Media 1970; Quotations
1970
WALKEM, GEORGE (Premier of B.C.)
Political phrases
WALKER, ANNA L. (Hymn writer) Work
ethic 1861
WALKER, DEAN (Writer) Guilt 1968
WALKER, SIR EDMUND (Banker)
Institutions 1918
WALLACE, CLARENCE (Lieutenant
Governor of B.C.) Socialism 1953
WALLACE, JOE (Poet) Age 1956; Freedom
1956; Prisons 1941
WALLACE, JOSEPH S. (Poet)
Canadian-American relations 1953;
Trade 1953
WALLACE, ROBERT C. (University
president) Education 1932;
Improvement 1954; Personalities-Tory,
H.M. 1954; Science 1933; Teachers
1932
WALLACE, W. STEWART (Librarian)
Geography 1920; McGee, T.D. 1920

WALPOLE, HORACE (British writer)
Wolfe, James 1763
WALSH, JAMES M. (Inspector, R.C.M.P.)
Métis 1885
WALSH, W.E. (Writer) Vancouver Island
1954
WALTERS, ANGUS J. (Skipper of the
Bluenose) *Bluenose* 1921
WALTERS, HAROLD (Writer) Emigration
1971
WARD, *MRS.* HUMPHRY (British novelist)
Tourists 1908
WARD, NORMAN (University professor)
Canadianism 1973; Unity 1971
WARDELL, MICHAEL (Publisher) New
Brunswick 1973
WARING, GERALD (Journalist) Politicians
1960
WARKENTIN, GERMAINE (Editor) Identity
1964
WARMAN, CY (Poet) Indians 1908
WARNER, CHARLES DUDLEY (American
writer) Halifax 1899
WARNOCK, JOHN W. (Political scientist)
Americanism, anti- 1967;
Canadian-American relations 1970;
Defence 1969
WARWICK, JACK (University professor)
North 1968
WASHINGTON, GEORGE (President of
U.S.) Canadian-American relations
1775
WASSERMAN, JACK (Columnist) Middle
age 1963
WATKIN, *SIR* EDWARD W. (President,
Grand Trunk Ry.) Grand Trunk Ry.
1861
WATKINS, MELVILLE H. (Economist)
Economics 1969; Future 1966; Natural
resources 1970
WATSON, ALBERT D. (Poet) Beauty 1917;
Christmas 1914; Crows 1921; Deeds
and doing 1913; Duty 1908; Freedom
1920; Heroes 1917; Immortality 1923;
July 1917; Justice 1913; Love 1913,
1917; Music 1923; People 1913; Stars
1923; Sun 1908; War 1917
WATSON, HOMER (Painter) Painting 1936
WATSON, JAMES W. (Geographer and
poet) Agriculture 1969; Labour 1942
WATSON, JOHN (Philosopher) Universities
1900
WATSON, SHEILA (Author) Glory 1959;
Woman 1959

WATSON, WILFRED (Poet) Carr, Emily 1955

WATSON, *LORD* (British justice) B.N.A. Act (1867) 1892

WATTERS, REGINALD E. (Bibliographer and university professor) Pioneers 1961

WAVERMAN, LEONARD (Political scientist) Pollution 1972

WAYNE, JOHNNY (Comedian) Writers 1968

WEAVER, ROBERT (Editor) Artists 1957; Callaghan, Morley 1968; Royal commissions 1957; State 1957; Writers 1970

WEBB, BERNICE L. (Poet) Loneliness 1967

WEBB, PHYLLIS (Poet) Affirmation 1962; Age 1962; Beauty 1965; Bodies 1962; Creativity 1962; Destruction 1962; Incest 1965; Intelligence 1965; Life 1962; Love 1954; Prayer 1956, 1956; Poets 1962; Statements 1962; Suicide 1962, 1972

WEBSTER, JACK (Radio commentator) Radio and TV 1973

WEBSTER, *REVEREND* THOMAS (Methodist biographer) Women 1894

WEEK (THE) (TORONTO) (Newspaper) Personalities–Tarte, J.I. 1891; Senate 1884

WEES, FRANCES SHELLEY (Writer) Boundaries 1937; Children 1947

WEIR, E. AUSTIN (Broadcasting executive) Radio and TV 1965

WEIR, GEORGE M. (Educator) Schools 1934

WEIR, R. STANLEY (Judge and author) National anthem 1908, 1974

WELD, ISAAC (JR.) (Irish traveller) Indians 1799

WELLINGTON, *DUKE OF* (British army leader) Ontario 1837

WERRUN, EDDIE (Song writer) Floods 1950

WEST, BENJAMIN (Painter) Painting 1770

WEST, PAUL (Literary critic) Humanity 1963; Intellectuals 1963; Landscape 1962; Legends 1962

WEST RIVER, N.S. FARMING SOCIETY Farmers 1817

WESTALL, STANLEY (Journalist) Foreign aid 1963

WESTELL, ANTHONY (Journalist) Programs 1971

WESTERN CANADIAN-AMERICAN ASSEMBLY Energy 1964

WESTERN LABOUR NEWS (Newspaper) Labour strikes 1919

WESTON, GARFIELD (Industrialist) Business 1948; Success 1948

WETHERALD, ETHELWYN (Poet) Absence 1907; Bluebirds 1907; Death 1896; Fighting 1907; Life 1907; Past 1907; Remembrance 1907; Words 1907

WETMORE, ANDREW R. (Premier of N.B.) Confederation 1865

WHALLEY, GEORGE (University professor) Discussion 1956; Disunity 1961; Experience 1958; Peace 1927; Poetry 1965

WHELAN, EDWARD (Author) Constitution 1864; Dance 1864

WHELAN, PATRICK J. (Convicted murderer) Drinking 1868

WHITBOURNE, *SIR* RICHARD (English writer on Newfoundland) Mosquitoes 1622

WHITE, *SIR* THOMAS (Politician) Immigration 1884; Industry 1917

WHITELAW, WILLIAM M. (Historian) Confederation 1938; Prince Edward Island 1934

WHITEWAY, *SIR* WILLIAM (Prime Minister of Newfoundland) Newfoundland 1897

WHITMAN, JEAN (Poet) Nature 1938

WHITMAN, WALT (American poet) Canada 1855; Winter 1880

WHITNEY, *SIR* JAMES P. (Premier of Ontario) Honesty 1908; Women's suffrage 1911

WHITTAKER, HERBERT (Critic) Theatre 1957

WHITTIER, JOHN G. (American poet) Evening 1854; Manitoba 1854, 1860; Pioneers 1846; Rivers 1854

WHITTON, CHARLOTTE (Mayor of Ottawa) Conduct of life 1961; Mayors 1951; Woman 1962; Women's suffrage 1946

WIELAND, JOYCE (Painter) Art 1971, 1972

WIGGINS, T. (Letter writer) Land 1851

WIGHTMAN, *REVEREND* FREDERICK A. Defence 1905

WILBY, THOMAS (Traveller) Mud 1914; Prairies 1914

WILD, J.L. (Speaker) The Public 1963

WILDE, OSCAR (British author) Niagara
Falls 1882
WILGAR, W.P. (Professor of English)
Literature 1944
WILKES, HARRY (Executive) Business 1971
WILKINS, MARTIN (Politician)
Confederation 1867
WILKINSON, ANNE (Poet) Belief 1955;
Bodies 1955; Change 1955; Children
1955; Death 1957; Forests 1951; June
1955, 1968; Love 1957; Lovers 1955,
1955; Mothers 1955; Night 1955;
Pleasure 1955; Poets 1955; Seeing
1952; Senses 1952; Souls 1955; Spring
1955, 1968; Submarines 1951; Time
1951; Understanding 1955; Youth 1955
WILLAN, HEALEY (Composer) Music 1972
WILLIAM IV (King of Great Britain)
Canada 1816
WILLIAMS, G. SHELDON (B.C. writer)
Poor 1907
WILLIAMS, HELEN E. (Writer) Past 1923
WILLIAMS, NORMAN (Playwright) Money
1956
WILLIAMS, PERCY (Olympics sprinter)
Williams, P. 1928, 1960
WILLIAMS-TAYLOR, *SIR* FREDERICK
(Banker) Thompson, David 1927
WILLISON, *SIR* JOHN S. (Editor) Blake, E.
1892, 1919; Canadian-American
relations 1888; Confederation 1917;
Elections 1927; Geography 1900;
Government 1919, 1919; Independence
1908; Journalism 1917; Laurier, *Sir* W.
1913; Liberal Party 1919;
Manufacturing 1919; Men and Women
1919; Newspapers 1919; Peace 1914;
Political parties 1904; Public ownership
1925; Statesmen 1903; Writers 1919,
1927
WILLS, ARCHIE (News editor) Sea serpents
1933
WILMOT, LEMUEL A. (Politician)
Patronage 1847
WILSON, *SENATOR* CAIRINE Senate 1930
WILSON, *SIR* DANIEL (Writer and
educator) Brown, G. 1880; Knowledge
1887
WILSON, EDMUND (American critic)
Callaghan, M. 1960, 1960; Identity
1965; Reading 1959
WILSON, EDWARD ARTHUR (Cult leader)
Power 1967

WILSON, ETHEL (Novelist) Coincidence
1954; Memory 1956; Sleep 1947;
Writers 1959
WILSON, GEORGE E. (Historian) History
1951
WILSON, GEORGE W. (Economist) Tariff
policy 1965
WILSON, HAROLD (Prime Minister, Great
Britain) Help 1953
WILSON, JOHN (Scottish writer) Dunlop,
W. 1832
WILSON, MILTON (Critic) Dullness 1958;
Poetry 1958; Poets 1959
WILSON, THOMAS (Song writer) Fenians
1866
WILSON, TOM E. (C.P.R. packer, 1880's)
Tobacco (1971)
WILTON, MARGARET HARVEY (Poet)
Love 1956
WINCH, ERNEST (Politician) Old age 1973
WINKS, ROBIN (American historian)
Canadians, black 1968; Continentalism
1960
WINNIPEG *FREE PRESS* (Newspaper)
(Manitoba *Free Press*) Appeasement
1938; Riel, Louis 1885
WINNIPEG GENERAL STRIKE Labour
strikes 1919
WINNIPEG *TRIBUNE* (Newspaper)
Governor General 1905
WINTEMBERG, WILLIAM J.
(Archaeologist) Archaeology 1960
WINTERS, ROBERT H. (Politician) Politics
1968
WISEMAN, ADELE (Novelist) Change
1956; Dreams 1956; Families 1956;
Jews 1956
WITHROW, WILLIAM H. (Historian)
Lumbering 1889
WITHROW, WILLIAM J. (Art gallery
director) Artists 1972
WOLFE, JAMES (British general) Poems
1759; Wolfe, J. 1759, 1759
WOLFE MONUMENT, QUEBEC CITY
Wolfe, J. 1849
WOOD, HENRY WISE (Alberta leader)
Classes 1919; Democracy 1918, 1919;
Mistakes 1941; Progress 1919; Purpose
1923; Religion 1950; Voters 1920;
Wheat, about 1935
WOOD, HERBERT FAIRLIE (Author) War,
European (1914-18) 1967
WOOD, WILLIAM (Historian) Canoeing
1921; Sea 1914

WOODCOCK, GEORGE (Author) Agitation
1947; Birthdays 1969;
Canadian-American relations 1968,
1970; Change 1947; Censorship 1959;
Creativity 1970; Criticism 1966; Critics
1955; Folly 1967; Geography 1970;
Life 1970; Literature 1959; Pioneers
1969; Writers 1964, 1970
WOODFORD, JAMES (Writer) North 1972
WOODHOUSE, ARTHUR S.P. (Educator)
Culture 1941
WOODS, N.A. (Journalist) Ottawa 1861;
Parliament Buildings 1860
WOODSWORTH, JAMES SHAVER (C.C.F.
leader) Cities and towns 1911; C.C.F.
1934; Divorce 1921; Economy 1922;
Force 1916; Grace before meals 1920;
Monarchy 1937, 1937; Neighbours
1911; Northwest Rebellion (1885) 1917;
Profits 1922; Religion 1901, 1915,
1926; R.C.M.P. 1922; Senate 1926;
Socialism 1924; Souls 1959; 20th C.
1917; War 1938; Woodsworth, J.S.
1921
WORDSWORTH, WILLIAM (British poet)
Forests 1820
WRATHELL, MALCOLM (Poet) Escape
1956
WREFORD, JAMES Pseud. of J.W. Watson
WRIGHT, FRANK LLOYD (American
architect) Buildings 1958
WRONG, DENNIS H. (Diplomat) Law and
lawyers 1955
WRONG, GEORGE M. (Historian)
Canadian-American relations 1909;
Change 1921; Democracy 1916, 1917,
1933; Fear 1933; French Canadians
1922; History 1927, 1932, 1936;
Liberty 1938; Literature 1929;
Nationalism 1916; Newspapers 1921;
Past 1933; Quebec (Province) 1935;
Revolution 1933; Scholarship 1933;
Society 1933; Thought 1916; Victors
1933
WRONG, HUMPHREY HUME (Diplomat)
Diplomacy 1927

Y

YATES, J. MICHAEL (Writer) Fishing 1970;
Machinery 1973; North 1970
YEVTUSHENKO, YEVGENY (Russian poet)
Hockey 1973
YOUNG, ARCHIBALD H. (Historian)
Church 1932
YOUNG, EGERTON RYERSON (Missionary)
Dogs 1893
YOUNG, HENRY (Haida Indian carver)
Totems 1951
YOUNG, JOHN (School principal) Schools
1970
YOUNG, SIR JOHN (Lord Lisgar) Fisheries
1870
YOUNG, MARK (Poet) Thought 1970
YOUNG, SCOTT (Columnist) Hockey 1966
YOUNG, WALTER D. (Political scientist)
Socialists 1969
YUILL, MARY (Poet) Motherhood 1972
YULE, PAMELIA V. (Poet) Charity 1881;
Religion 1881

Z

ZABOTIN, NICOLAI (Russian spy) Spying
1948
ZACHARIA, D.A. (Realtor) Ukrainians 1963
ZIMMERMAN, WILLIAM (Planner) Old
Age 1974
ZINK, LUBOR (Journalist) Welfare 1965
ZOLF, LARRY (Commentator)
Americanism, anti- 1968
ZUBICK, J.J. (Newspaper editor) Aberhart,
W. 1937